SERTA TURYNIANA

Alexander Turyn

SERTA TURYNIANA

Studies in
Greek Literature and Palaeography
in honor of
ALEXANDER TURYN

Edited by
JOHN L. HELLER

with the assistance of
J. K. NEWMAN

UNIVERSITY OF ILLINOIS PRESS
Urbana Chicago London
1974

Printed in Great Britain
by William Clowes & Sons, Limited, London, Beccles and Colchester
Library of Congress Catalog Card No. 73–81567
ISBN 0–252–00405–1

FOREWORD

To Alexander Turyn, Professor Emeritus of the Classics at the University of Illinois in Urbana-Champaign, formerly Professor Extraordinary of Classical Philology at the University of Warsaw in his native Poland and now distinguished among classicists throughout the world, his admirers present this volume of studies. Written in one or another of five languages by men and women from twelve different countries, the studies represent international classical scholarship in its best effort to honor an international scholar and leader in the study of Greek literature and palaeography. They are arranged in four categories (Lyric Poetry, Drama, Later Prose and Poetry, Palaeography and Codicology) which compose four garlands of praise. In all these areas, moreover, he has himself made notable and lasting contributions—as attested by the *vita* and bibliography with which the volume opens.

The project to honor Professor Turyn was conceived in the fall of 1969 by a committee of his colleagues in the Department of the Classics: J. J. Bateman, M. Marcovich, M. Naoumides, J. K. Newman, R. P. Oliver, and L. Wallach; the present editor was not in residence at the time. It was their hope that a suitable volume could be solicited and presented to Professor Turyn on his seventieth birthday, which he would celebrate on the day after Christmas, 1970. So generous was the response to their invitations, however, that severe limitations had to be placed on the number and content of the articles accepted for publication. Moreover, once a selection of 38 papers (out of some 60 that had been promised) had been made and a sampling of pages had in fact been presented to Professor Turyn shortly before his birthday, so many obstacles developed in the way of the proper editing of the papers and in the securing of the necessary funds that the date of publication had to be postponed again and again. As a consequence, a number of papers have been withdrawn because our delay made them out-of-date with respect to their authors' other publications and the progress of scholarship generally. For these disappointments to various people, the committee apologizes. We also note below the names of all those scholars who in 1970 actively desired to honor Professor Turyn, though their contributions could not be included in the present volume.

John J. Bateman, Champaign, Ill.
Aristide Colonna, Roma, Italy
R. D. Dawe, Cambridge, England
Marlene Demarque, Hamden, Conn.
Hans Dietz, Spokane, Wash.
Max H. Fisch, Urbana, Ill.
D. J. Geanakoplos, New Haven, Conn.
Marcello Gigante, Napoli, Italy
John L. Heller, Urbana, Ill.
C. J. Herington, Stanford, Calif.
Howard Jacobson, Champaign, Ill.
Henry and Renée Kahane, Urbana, Ill.
S. G. Kapsomenos, Thessaloniki, Greece

Hugh Lloyd-Jones, Oxford, England
Cyril Mango, Washington, D.C.
Benedetto Marzullo, Bologna, Italy
H. J. Mette, Hamburg, Germany
R. E. A. Palmer, Philadelphia, Pa.
Hans A. Pohlsander, Albany, N.Y.
T. G. Rosenmeyer, Berkeley, Calif.
C. F. Russo, Bari, Italy
Stephen C. Shucard, Eugene, Ore.
Jerry Stannard, Lawrence, Kans.
Franz Stoessl, Graz, Austria
J. B. Van Sickle, Philadelphia, Pa.
Luitpold Wallach, Urbana, Ill.
Günther Zuntz, Manchester, England

Finally, we acknowledge with gratitude the very substantial help of the University of Illinois Foundation and Mr. Joseph W. Skehen, its Executive Director; the Graduate College of the University of Illinois in Urbana-Champaign and its former Dean and Chairman of the Research Board, Daniel Alpert; and the College of Liberal Arts and Sciences and its Dean, Robert W. Rogers.

For the Committee,   J. L. H.
Urbana, 10 January 1973

CONTENTS

PLATES

following p. 566

A NOTE ON ABBREVIATIONS

Abbreviated references to the titles of journals and collections generally follow the system of Liddell-Scott-Jones-McKenzie (herein abbreviated as *LSJ*), *A Greek-English Lexicon* (Oxford 1940), except that acronyms for the titles of journals have been avoided. For collections, the following acronyms are used throughout the volume, in addition to those listed in *LSJ*, pp. xlvi–xlviii:

PG = Patrologiae Graecae cursus completus, ed. Migne
PMG = Poetae Melici Graeci, ed. Page
RE = Real-Encyclopädie der classischen Altertumswissenschaft
SVF = Stoicorum Veterum Fragmenta, ed. Arnim

A very few others are explained in early footnotes of the articles in which they occur.

Our *Index auctorum* (609 ff.) collects all references, as made on the pages indicated, to modern editors or critics (but not scribes or owners of manuscripts). Here will be found the last names of editors (e.g. Diels and Kranz) who are cited in the volume only by the initial letter (e.g. as D.-K.).

Other abbreviations are those which are ordinary and usual in the writing of the several languages. Capitalization and the spelling of proper names are likewise subject to the writing-conventions of the particular language.

ALEXANDER TURYN:
PUBLICATIONS AND VITA

Born in Warsaw, Poland, 26 December 1900, and at an early age showing proficiency in languages both modern and ancient, Alexander Turyn was trained in classical philology at the University of Warsaw, receiving the degree of Doctor of Philosophy in 1923. After a year of further study at the University of Berlin he returned to Warsaw as Instructor in 1925 and became successively Docent (1929) and Professor Extraordinary (1935) of Classical Philology.

Leaving his storm-tossed homeland in the fall of 1939, Turyn made his way to Rome, where he worked at research in the Vatican Library for six months, and then to Athens. Early in 1941 he came to the United States on a fellowship granted by the Rockefeller Foundation and the University of Michigan. He remained at Michigan as Research Fellow and Lecturer through the year 1941 and then served for three years (1942–45) as Associate Professor at the New School for Social Research in New York. In 1945 he was called to the University of Illinois as Visiting Professor and in 1947 was appointed Professor of the Classics on indefinite tenure. He retired in 1969, for the last seven years holding full membership in the Center for Advanced Study, the highest academic distinction the University could confer. He and his wife Felicia, who became naturalized citizens in 1946, continue to reside in Urbana. They visit Europe from time to time and maintain a steady correspondence with scholars and friends all over the world.

Among Turyn's other honors may be mentioned the Golden Cross of the Greek Order of Phoenix (1934), corresponding membership in the former Polish Academy in Cracow (1946) and in the Academy of Athens (1954), honorary membership in the Epistê-monikê Hetaireia of Athens (1957), a Guggenheim fellowship in 1959, an honorary doctorate from the University of Athens in 1965, membership on the Board of Scholars of the Dumbarton Oaks

Center for Byzantine Studies (1956–62) and (currently) on the United States National Committee for Byzantine Studies. His appointment as research collaborator (1960) of the Vatican Library was followed in 1964 by the Library's publication of his *Codices Graeci Vaticani* (see below), while his publication (1957) of *The Byzantine Manuscript Tradition of the Tragedies of Euripides* was graced in 1960 by the American Philological Association's Award of Merit.

A complete list of his publications to date now follows.

1922 "Observationes metricae," *Eos* 25 (1921/22), 91–104.

1924 "Lyrica graeca," *Eos* 27 (1924), 110–12.

1925 "Kazimerz Morawski †25.VIII.1925," *Nowiny Naukowe* (Warszawa), I (1925), no. 3, p. 1.

Rev. of P. Maas, *Die neuen Responsionsfreiheiten bei Bakchylides und Pindar, I–II* (1914–21), and *Griechische Metrik* (1923), in *Eos* 28 (1925), 184–90.

1926 "Casimir Morawski," *Bull. Ass. Budé* 10 (janvier 1926), 4–7.

1927 "Abermals zu Pindar *Pyth.* I 42 ff." *Philol. Woch.* 47 (1927), 138.

"ἐπισκοτεῖν und ἐπισκιάζειν," *Hermes* 62 (1927), 371–72.

"Zu Valerius Aedituus," *Hermes* 62, 494.

1928 "Sapphicum," *Eos* 31 (1928), 236.

"Tantum sui similis (Tac. *Germ.* 4)," *Eos* 31, 236.

"De epistularum loco quodam proverbiali," *Eos* 31, 262.

"Studia byzantina. I. De Homeri et Ioannis Actuarii codicibus Varsoviensibus. II. De Theodosio Zygomala observationes," *Eos* 31, 505–18.

"Aeschyli Prometh. λυόμ. fgm. 199, 6," *Eos* 31, 518.

"De Meletii Pigae patriarchae *Dialogo*," *Eos* 31, 518.

"Edward Norden," *Kurjer Polski* (Warszawa), XXXI no. 266 (Sept. 25, 1928), 3.

1929 *De Aelii Aristidis codice Varsoviensi atque de Andrea Taranowski et Theodosio Zygomala* (Polska Akademja Umiejętności, Archiwum Filologiczne, nr. 9), Cracoviae, Academia Polona Litterarum, 1929. 78 pp., 5 plates.

Studia Sapphica (Eos, Supplem. vol. 6), Leopoli, Societas Philologa Polonorum, 1929. 108 pp.

"Wiktor Porzeziński," *Kwartalnik Klasyczny* 3 (1929), 250–51.

"Niektóre kwestje prozodyczne liryki greckiej," *Comptes Rendus des Séances de la Société des Sciences et des Lettres de Varsovie*, Classe I, 22 (1929), 1–22.

"Laberianum," *Eos* 32 (1929), 17.

1930 "Charakter sztuki Sapphony," *Kwart. Klas.* 4 (1930), 97–98.
"Stan badań i zagadnienia metryki greckiej," *Kwart. Klas.* 4, 387–98.
"Infandum regina," *Eos* 33 (1930/31), 39–41.

1931 Rev. of O. Schroeder, *Grundriss der griechischen Versgeschichte* (1930), in *Gnomon* 7 (1931), 513–20.

1932 *De codicibus Pindaricis* (Polska Akad. Um., Arch. Filol., nr. 11), Cracoviae, Academia Polona Litterarum, 1932, 88 pp.
Rev. of T. Fitzhugh, *Triumpus-Θρίαμβος. Pyrrhichia Indoeuropaeorum anima vocis, ῥυθμός-μέτρον-προσῳδία* (1930), in *Deutsche Literaturzeitung*, 53 (1932), 596–97.
Rev. of W. Weinberger, *Wegweiser durch die Sammlungen altphilologischer Handschriften* (1930), in *Gnomon* 8 (1932), 331–33.
Rev. of T. Sinko, *Literatura grecka I, 1* (1931), in *Gnomon* 8, 548–49.

1933 Rev. of J. Parandowski, *Dysk olimpijski* (1933), in *Wiadomości Literackie*, X (1933), nr. 21 (492), 3.
Rev. of T. Sinko, *Literatura grecka I, 1–2* (1931–32), in *Pamiętnik Literacki*, 30 (1933), 146–51.

1934 "Sylwety greckie," *Wiedza i Życie* 9 (1934), 623–41.
"Symbolae ad recensionem Pindaricam pertinentes," *Charisteria Gustavo Przychocki a discipulis oblata* (Varsoviae, Gebethner et Wolff, 1934), 210–19.
[A speech to honor Gustaw Przychocki], in *W 25-lecie pracy naukowej Dr. Gustawa Przychockiego, profesora Uniwersytetu Warszawskiego. Przemówienia...* (Warszawa, Komitet obchodu, 1934), 12–16.

1935 "Zur Geschichte der griechischen Abstrakta in den europäischen Sprachen," *Actes du IVe Congrès International des Études Byzantines*, I (Bulletin de l'Institut archéologique bulgare, tom. 9, 1935), 151–60.
"Zur Pindar-Überlieferung," *Philologus* 90 (1935), 115–19.

1936 "Anecdoton Ianicianum," *Munera philologica Ludovico Ćwikliński... oblata* (Posnaniae, Libraria Universitatis, 1936), 375–80.
"Bieńkowski, Bronisław (1848–1903)," *Polski Słownik Biograficzny*, 2 (Kraków, Polska Akademja Umiejętności, 1936), 72.
Rev. of C. M. Bowra, *Pindari carmina cum fragmentis* (1935), in *Gnomon* 12 (1936), 360–67.

1937 "*Σαπφώ-Σόλων-Πίνδαρος*" (translated by I. A. Thomopoulos from "Sylwety greckie" above), *Νέα Ἑστία* XI (1937) tom. 21, 247–52, 365–68, 436–41.

1942 "The Sapphic Ostracon," *Trans. Am. Philol. Ass.* 73 (1942), 308–18.

1943 *The Manuscript Tradition of the Tragedies of Aeschylus* (Polish Institute Series, no. 2), New York City, Polish Institute of Arts and Sciences in America, 1943. v, 141 pp. Repr. Hildesheim, Georg Olms, 1967.

1944 *Pindari Epinicia* edidit A. T. (Polish Institute Series, no. 5), Novi Eboraci, Institutum Polonicum Artium et Scientiarum in America, 1944. XVI, 224 pp.

"The Manuscripts of Sophocles," *Traditio* 2 (1944), 1–41.

1946 "Tadeusz Zieliński," *Tygodnik Polski* (New York, N.Y.), vol. 4 nr. 5 (162) (Febr. 3, 1946), 4–5.

1948 *Pindari Carmina cum Fragmentis* edidit A. T., Cracoviae, Academia Polona Litterarum et Scientiarum, 1948. XVI, 403 pp. Repr. Oxford, B. Blackwell; Cambridge, Harvard Un. Pr.; München, R. Oldenbourg, 1952.

1949 "The Sophocles Recension of Manuel Moschopulus," *Trans. Am. Philol. Ass.* 80 (1949), 94–173.

1950 Rev. of T. Sinko, *Literatura grecka II, 1–2* (1947–48), in *Books Abroad* 24 (1950), 312–13.

1952 *Studies in the Manuscript Tradition of the Tragedies of Sophocles* (Ill. Stud. Lang. & Lit. 36, nos. 1–2), Urbana, Un. Illinois Pr., 1952. XI, 217 pp., 18 plates. Repr. Roma (Studia philologica, 15), "L'Erma" di Bretschneider, 1970.

1957 *The Byzantine Manuscript Tradition of the Tragedies of Euripides* (Ill. Stud. Lang. & Lit. 43), Urbana, Un. Illinois Pr., 1957. x, 415 pp., 24 plates. Repr. Roma (Studia philologica, 16), "L'Erma" di Bretschneider, 1970.

1958 "On the Sophoclean Scholia in the Manuscript Paris 2712," *Harvard Stud. Class. Philol.* 63 (honoring Werner Jaeger, 1958), 161–70.

1960 "Miscellanea," *Studi in onore di Luigi Castiglioni* (Firenze, G. C. Sansoni [1960]), II, 1011–23.

1964 *Codices Graeci Vaticani saeculis XIII et XIV scripti annorumque notis instructi.* Congessit, enarravit eorumque specimina protulit . . . A. T. (Codices e Vaticanis selecti quam simillime expressi, vol. 28), in Civitate Vaticana, Bybliotheca Apostolica Vaticana, 1964. XVI, 206 pp., 205 plates.

1972 *Dated Greek Manuscripts of the Thirteenth and Fourteenth Centuries in the Libraries of Italy*, Urbana, Chicago, London, Un. Illinois Pr., 1972. Vol. I: LIV, 294 pp.; vol. II: XXXII pp., 265 plates.

Urbana, Ill.
1 December 1972

ORNEMENTS ÉROTIQUES
DANS LA POÉSIE LYRIQUE ARCHAÏQUE

FRANÇOIS LASSERRE

Bien que la philologie achoppe constamment au délicat problème d'interprétation que pose la poésie amoureuse, voire érotique, de Sappho, rares sont encore les études où l'on ait tenté de circonscrire dans toute son étendue l'usage poétique du langage de l'amour à l'époque archaïque. De fait, il n'en existe à ce jour qu'une seule, bien oubliée, qui est le long développement suggéré à F. G. Welcker par la publication des *Ibyci carminum reliquiae* de F. W. Schneidewin (Goettingae 1833) et paru dans le compte-rendu qu'il en fit dans le *Rheinisches Museum*.[1] Sur l'ensemble de la question, on ne rencontre plus ensuite que des allusions ou de brèves prises de position, dont les plus circonstanciées sont, dans l'ordre chronologique, une ré-flexion de P. Von der Mühll sur le thème "Persönliche Verliebtheit des Dichters," à propos de la 8ᵉ Néméenne,[2] une réplique de B. Gentili dans les *Studi Urbinati*[3] et quelques observations sagaces, mais marginales, de P. Janni touchant les parthénées d'Alcman dans son excellente monographie *La cultura di Sparta arcaica*.[4] D'autres philologues en plus grand nombre, à la vérité, n'ont pas manqué de soulever quelques doutes sur la sincérité des poèmes les plus ardents de Sappho, mais toujours à partir de considérations morales ou en référence à l'histoire des moeurs.[5] Et pourtant le simple fait

---

[1] *Rh. Mus.* 2 (1834), 211–44, réimprimé dans une version revue et complétée dans les *Kleine Schriften*, I (Bonn 1844), 220–50, d'après laquelle je cite.

[2] *Mus. Helv.* 21 (1964), 168–72. On trouvera dans cet article et dans ses notes les éléments bibliographiques permettant de remonter l'histoire du sujet, principalement à travers les interprétations de la 8ᵉ *Néméenne*, jusqu'à Welcker.

[3] "Aspetti del rapporto poeta, committente, uditorio nella lirica corale greca," *Studi Urbinati* 39 (1965), 78 sq., note 18.

[4] *La cultura di Sparta arcaica, Ricerche I* (Roma 1965), 107–109.

[5] Personne n'est allé plus loin dans ce sens, à ma connaissance, que R. Merkelbach, "Sappho und ihr Kreis," *Philol.* 101, 1957, 1–29. Mais il faut citer aussi l'étude de M. F.

d'une formulation poétique liée aux circonstances précises dans lesquelles s'effectue la publication d'un poème pendant le VIIe et le VIe siècles commande d'approcher la question d'abord sous son angle littéraire. Ce sera ici mon propos.

Revendiquer pour les critères littéraires un droit de priorité présuppose qu'on définisse littérature la poésie archaïque. À ce terme, les objections surgissent en nombre, car il est évident que l'oeuvre orale ou écrite, en tant précisément qu'on la qualifie de littéraire, remplit aujourd'hui une fonction toute différente de celle qu'on doit imaginer dans la Grèce archaïque. On peut même se demander si le mot, en son sens premier, est applicable à des poèmes dont l'existence commence dans une récitation. Il conviendrait donc de le définir d'abord en termes appropriés à ce cadre historique. Je ne m'y arrêterai cependant pas, ou qu'à peine un instant, estimant suffisant, en l'occurrence, l'usage courant. Ainsi, j'entends par littéraire et par littérature ce qui caractérise communément les oeuvres justiciables de cette qualification dans tous les temps et dans toutes les civilisations héritières de l'antiquité classique, à savoir le supplément d'art, ou d'artifice, qui les différencie au sein de la catégorie plus large des productions verbales, soit orales, soit écrites.

Cela posé, commençons par les deux parthénées d'Alcman où se rencontrent pour la première fois, à notre connaissance, des propos érotiques ambigus et formulons d'emblée le plus généralement possible, mais sans dépasser le cadre de la poésie chorale, la question qui se pose nécessairement au sujet de ceux-ci: quelle part de vérité comporte une déclaration d'amour exprimée par un choeur, publiquement, dans le moment unique de la récitation et à la première personne du singulier, à l'adresse d'une personne nommément désignée? Restreignons-en d'ailleurs aussitôt l'amplitude en ajoutant par anticipation: par un choeur de jeunes filles à l'adresse d'une jeune fille dans le cas des parthénées, par un choeur de jeunes garçons à l'adresse d'un adolescent ou d'un éphèbe dans le cas des poèmes d'Ibycos et de Pindare étudiés plus loin, car on ne connaît pas de circonstance où un sexe s'adresse à l'autre, sinon lors des

---

Galiano, *Safo* (Cuadernos de la Fundacion Pastor, 1, 1958 [= M. F. Galiano, J. S. Lasso de la Vega, F. R. Adrados, *El descubrimiento del amor en Grecia* (Madrid 1959), 9-54]), qui insiste davantage sur les critères moraux et psycho-physiologiques.

épithalames, genre qui n'entrera pas dans cette étude.[6] On a répondu le plus souvent, non sans arbitraire, que les poètes les plus anciens décrivaient sincèrement leurs sentiments, tandis que les plus récents le font par convention et trahissent l'inauthenticité de leurs prétendus aveux dans l'excès des procédés littéraires qu'ils mettent alors en oeuvre. Outre le fait que la limite entre la normale et l'abus en matière de préciosité se laisse difficilement tracer, ce type de réponse procède d'une conception romantique singulièrement contestable, selon laquelle la poésie serait en principe un cri du coeur. Or les conditions dans lesquelles s'effectuent la composition d'une ode lyrique chorale et sa représentation publique, si je puis dire, ainsi que les raisons qui poussent le choeur à la chanter et les auditeurs à se déplacer pour l'entendre créent un ensemble de servitudes directement contraires à l'éclosion d'oeuvres spontanées. Aussi partirons-nous ici de positions toutes différentes: acceptation du poème comme un événement public et non d'abord comme une confidence, interprétation de la poésie par rapport à sa fonction initiale et non par rapport aux valeurs intemporelles d'un musée—imaginaire—des littératures.

Dans le fameux parthénée auquel les éditeurs assignent à tort le numéro 1 depuis Diehl—les attestations des métriciens imposent à sa place le numéro 1 de Bergk, devenu 7 chez Diehl et 14 chez Page, ou à la rigueur 67 Diehl (= 27 Page)[7]—le moment amoureux intervient en fin de strophe, au point culminant de l'éloge d'Hagésichora. L'ayant proclamée de diverses manières plus belle que ses

---

[6] Archiloque, Mimnerme, Anacréon en sont également exclus, non pas parce qu'ils sont auteurs de monodies—Sappho appartient à la même catégorie—mais parce que le lieu de récitation ou le public de leurs poèmes, la fonction assumée par ceux-ci et, en dernière analyse, les mobiles de leur activité poétique forment un ensemble de circonstances très différent. Quant à Alcée, arbitrairement peut-être, je le range aux côtés d'Anacréon en matière de poésie érotique, posant comme critère de différenciation la présomption suivante: dans la poésie chorodique et dans celle de Sappho, la déclaration d'amour oriente l'intérêt d'un des auditeurs sur la personne visée par elle, tandis que les poèmes d'Archiloque et des poètes nommés à sa suite veulent plaire ou divertir, ou captiver, par le tableau de la situation amoureuse du poète lui-même. On voit que le classement de Sappho hors de sa catégorie naturelle constitue une anomalie: il s'agira précisément ici de le justifier.

[7] Je cite dorénavant les *Poetae melici* uniquement d'après l'édition de D. L. Page (Oxford 1962), les *Poetae Lesbii* d'après celle de E. Lobel et D. L. Page (Oxford 1955). Les restitutions évidentes admises par les éditeurs ne seront pas signalées.

compagnes, le choeur évoque à leur tour ses rivales et s'écrie (vv. 73-77):

> οὐδ' ἐς Αἰνησιμβρότας ἐνθοῖσα φασεῖς·
> Ἀσταφίς τέ μοι γένοιτο
> καὶ ποτιγλέποι Φίλυλλα
> Δαμαρέτα τ' ἐρατά τε Fιανθεμίς·
> ἀλλ' Ἀγησιχόρα με τείρει.[8]

Qui hésiterait à lever les réserves émises notamment par A. Garzya et, avec plus de circonspection, par Page sur l'interprétation érotique des expressions μοι γένοιτο, ποτιγλέποι et τείρει?[9] Non seulement leurs significations amoureuses s'imposent à l'exclusion de toute autre en raison de leur voisinage réciproque, mais encore la vraisemblance d'une telle interprétation dans le cadre d'un parthénée a trouvé confirmation dans le parthénée de découverte plus récente dont seront analysés plus loin des passages de même contenu beaucoup plus explicites (frg. 3). Comme le montrent les citations produites en note, ποτιγλέποι et τείρει impliquent très précisément la notion d' ἔρως, qui est attestée d'autre part pour εἴ μοι γένοιτο par l'inscription de cette locution sur le pied d'une coupe attique du Ve siècle, présent d'amant à son καλός.[10] Dans ce contexte, même

---

[8] Sans vouloir rouvrir ici le débat relatif aux situations d'Hagésichora et d'Aenésimbrota l'une par rapport à l'autre, je précise cependant que je crois qu'il s'agit des monitrices de deux ἀγέλαι rivales. Ἐς Αἰνησιμβρότας (73) me paraît compatible avec cette interprétation dans la mesure où l'agélé féminine, citée par Pindare, frg. 123 Turyn, implique comme la masculine un logement séparé. Surtout, toutes les caractéristiques qu'A. Brelich, *Paides e Parthenoi*, I (Roma 1969), 157–66, attribue avec la plus grande prudence à l'agélé féminine me paraissent applicables aux compagnes d'Hagésichora, en particulier la participation probable de l'agélé comme choeur aux fêtes d'Artémis Orthia.

[9] Comparer pour la première Hippon. frg. 124 Sousa Medeiros (= 119 Masson) εἴ μοι γένοιτο παρθένος, pour la deuxième Ibyc. frg. 6 Ἔρος αὖτέ με κυανέοισιν ὑπὸ βλεφάροις τακέρ' ὄμμασι δερκόμενος et le beau chapitre d'A. Turyn, "De momenti optici usu lyrico tragico comico," dans ses *Studia Sapphica* (Lwow 1929), 31–41, enfin pour τείρει (littéralement "c'est Hagésichora qui me fait souffrir," tandis que τηρεῖ préféré en dernier lieu par J. A. Davison, *Proc. of the IXth Intern. Congress of Papyrology, Oslo 1958* [1961], 44 [= *From Archilochus to Pindar* (London 1968), 189], n'offre guère de sens) Hes. frg. 298 Merkelbach-West δεινὸς γάρ μιν ἔτειρεν ἔρως Πανοπηΐδος Αἴγλης. Je ne retiens pas ici l'interprétation de κλεννά (44) dans un sens érotique analogue à καλός proposée par H. Diels, *Hermes*, 31 (1896), 353, qui allègue que les Crétois appelaient κλεινοί les éromènes (Strab. X, 4, 21, et Ath. XI 782ᶜ): l'adjectif est ici épithète de χοραγός et non substantif.

[10] Berliner Museum für Völkerkunde, Inv. 10984, publiée par J. Boehlau, *Philol.* 60 (1901), 329 (avec planche hors-texte).

le banal ἐρατά (76) récupère le sens fort propre à son étymologie et contribue par là de manière non négligeable au dessein du poète.

Quels sentiments véritables ces accents passionnés entendent-ils manifester à cet endroit de l'ode? Nous connaissons et comprenons aujourd'hui suffisamment l'argument de celle-ci pour oser affirmer que toute sa seconde partie, celle qui occupe les vers 36 à 105, commençant après l'exposé du mythe des Hippocoontides et s'achevant avec la dernière strophe, a pour sujet l'éloge d'Hagésichora. Elle comprend successivement une comparaison de sa beauté avec celle d'Agido, traitée en plusieurs images (39–59),[11] une comparaison en deux temps entre le choeur rival [12] et celui du parthénée, destinée à montrer que celui-ci triomphe grâce à l'attrait insurpassable de sa coryphée, Hagésichora (60–77), une comparaison entre les mérites respectifs d'Artémis et d'Hagésichora (78–91), enfin une comparaison, malheureusement défigurée par les mutilations du papyrus, entre le chant des Sirènes, celui du choeur et celui d'Hagésichora (92–101). Dans cet enchaînement de louanges, le passage érotique ne saurait avoir pour objet de faire connaître l'amour des jeunes filles pour celle qui les conduit et de la rendre sensible à leurs appels, mais il doit certainement aussi contribuer à l'éloge et il le fait en liant sa beauté à la séduction qu'elle exerce. Qu'Alcman se réfère en cela à de réelles relations amoureuses, à des liens d'amitié stylisés dans le langage de l'amour charnel ou au seul langage de l'amour sans support sentimental concret, il importe moins d'en décider que d'identifier dans son procédé un moyen et non une fin. En d'autres termes, il ne s'est pas soucié de savoir si les jeunes filles pour lesquelles il compose et qu'il prépare à chanter son ode à la fête d'Artémis ressentent les élans amoureux qu'il leur prête, même s'il n'est pas niable qu'ils appartinssent à l'éthique de la cellule féminine spartiate comme de la cellule masculine, circon-

---

[11] J'interprète la dernière (58–59), qui a fait couler beaucoup d'encre, en opposant ἁ δὲ δευτέρα...Ἀγιδώ (au nominatif!) à Ἁγησιχόρα μὲν αὖτα, avec πεδ(ὰ)...δράμηται en tmèse: "Mais Agido, qui vient en second pour sa beauté, la talonne comme un cheval de Colaxa le coursier ibénien." C'est la solution proposée pour la première fois par A. Garzya dans son édition d'Alcman de 1954 et reprise par lui avec l'appui du commentaire du *P. Oxy.* 2389 (p. 7 Page) dans ses *Studi sulla lirica greca* (Messina-Firenze 1963), 32–34.

[12] Selon l'interprétation de Page, *Alcman, the Partheneion* (Oxford 1951), 52–57.

stance sur laquelle j'aurai à revenir[13] : il les évoque seulement en
hommage à Hagésichora et les convertit ainsi en motif littéraire. À
plus forte raison n'imaginera-t-on pas qu'il exprime à travers la
voix des choristes sa propre passion pour elle.

Il en va de même des propos érotiques plus développés du fragment 3 déjà mentionné. On lit en effet à partir du vers 61, après une
grande lacune, λυσιμελεῖ τε πόσῳ, expression qui décrit les sentiments
du choeur à la vue d'Astymélousa, puis τακερώτερα δ' ὕπνω καὶ
σανάτω ποτιδέρκεται, évocation du désir qu'éveille son regard.[14]
La phrase qui suit, οὐδέ τι μαψιδίως γλυκ . . ήνα, est moins claire à
cause de la mutilation du texte, mais γλυκ( ) y rappelle à nouveau
l'un des pouvoirs d'Eros, mentionné par Alcman dans le fragment
59ᵃ Ἔρως με . . . γλυκὺς κατείβων καρδίαν ἰαίνει. Indifférente à cet
appel—Ἀστυμέλουσα δέ μ' οὐδὲν ἀμείβεται—Astymélousa n'en reçoit
pas moins l'hommage d'une louange qui se développe jusqu'au
vers 75 en plusieurs comparaisons relatives à l'éclat de sa beauté
(65–68), à sa démarche (69–70), à l'apprêt de ses cheveux (71–72),
à l'impression qu'elle produit sur le peuple qui la regarde passer
(73–75), pour se muer ensuite, dès le vers 76 (λέγω), en un voeu.
Passablement mutilés, ses deux premiers vers n'offrent aucun sens
certain, mais la suite suffit à peu près à rétablir la signification
générale :

>]α ἴδοι μ', αἴ πως μεσιο . φιλοι
> 80 ἀσ]σον [ἰο]ῖσ' ἀπαλᾶς χηρὸς λάβοι,
> αἶψά κ' [ἐγὼν .]κέτις κήνας γενοίμαν·
> νῦν δ' [   ]δα παίδα βα[θ]ύφρονα . . .

Les sérieuses difficultés de ce passage demanderaient à elles seules
un long examen. Comme ce n'est pas le lieu d'y procéder, je me
contenterai de relever ici les indices qui m'engagent à lui prêter une
intention amoureuse au moins en apparence. Ils sont au nombre
de trois : le geste de prendre la main, la formulation d'un souhait,
le génitif possessif κήνας.

[13] Brelich, op. cit. 158, tend à l'admettre sur la foi de Plutarque, Vit. Lycurg. 18, 4,
tout en insistant sur la possibilité que les rapports sexuels attestés ne fussent que des
simulacres rituels. Il en existe une confirmation absolue dans le fait qu'Alcman appelait
ἀΐτις le pendant féminin de l' ἀΐτας (frg. 34), nom laconien de l'éromène dans la relation
pédérastique guerrière.

[14] Comparer Ibyc. frg. 6 Ἔρος αὖτέ με . . . τακέρ' ὄμμασι δερκόμενος et Anacr. frg. 114
(= 139 Gentili) τακερὸς δ' Ἔρως.

Premièrement, qu'on écrive ἴδοιμ᾽, αἴ ou ἴδοι μ᾽, αἴ et qu'on accentue selon le système du papyrus φίλοι (d'où σιοὶ φίλοι chez Peek[15]) ou φιλοῖ, la présence d'un "je" oblige à rapporter ἀπαλᾶς χηρός à la personne qui parle, c'est-à-dire au choeur: chacune des choristes souhaite pour elle qu'Astymélousa la prenne par la main. Or si le geste désiré n'a rien de spécifiquement érotique, l'emploi de l'adjectif ἀπαλός, "haptisches Empfindungswort" selon la définition de M. Treu,[16] implique par contraste la fermeté de la main d'Astymélousa et suggère ainsi une relation de dominé à dominant comparable au premier chef, mais non exlusivement, cela va sans dire, à celle d'éromène à éraste.

En second lieu, de quelque manière qu'on rattache l'un à l'autre les trois optatifs, ils expriment nécessairement un ou plusieurs voeux dont νῦν δ(ὲ), au vers 82, confirme le caractère irréalisable. Lobel, qui a le premier défini les termes de ce problème dans son commentaire de l'édition princeps du papyrus, a sans doute eu raison d'identifier dans αἶψά κ(ε) le commencement de l'apodose. Quant à la protase, dont l'extension demeure incertaine, elle comprend au minimum la proposition αἴ πως...λάβοι, qu'on ne peut ni scinder, ni subordonner à une autre proposition et qui pose par conséquent la condition immédiatement nécessaire à l'hypothèse αἶψά κ(ε)...γενοίμαν: il faut qu'Astymélousa me prenne par la main pour que je devienne.... Reste l'optatif ἴδοιμ(ι) ou ἴδοι μ(ε), dont je ne vois pas qu'on puisse le rattacher à autre chose qu'à αἰ γὰρ ἄργυριν du vers 77, les lacunes du vers 78 et du commencement du vers 79 n'étant pas assez grandes pour recéler un autre optatif, protase d'une apodose s'achevant sur ἴδοιμ(ι) ou ἴδοι μ(ε). Il y aura donc deux protases en asyndète, puis l'apodose: αἰ γὰρ...αἴ πως...αἶψά κ(ε). À cause de l'asyndète et comme pour la compenser, attribuer un même sujet aux deux optatifs paraît souhaitable; on écrira donc: αἰ γὰρ...ἴδοι μ᾽, αἴ πώς με... λάβοι. Ainsi, sans souscrire à toutes les conjectures de Peek, je rétablirais volontiers à sa suite un texte tel que αἰ γὰρ ἄργυριν [....].[.]ία [θεῖσ]α <F>ίδοι μ᾽, αἴ πώς με, σιοὶ φίλοι, ἆσσον ἰοῖσ᾽ ἀπαλᾶς χηρὸς λάβοι, αἶψά κ(ε)...γενοίμαν. Me voir, s'approcher de moi, me prendre

[15] "Das neue Alkman-Partheneion," *Philol.* 104 (1960), 175 sq. J'emprunte au même article les citations subséquentes de Peek.

[16] *Von Homer zur Lyrik*[2] (München 1968), 178–83, avec le supplément relatif à notre passage, 322 sq. Qu'on interprète encore ἀπαλός dans son sens homérique de *faible*, *délicat*, *vulnérable* avec Treu, ou qu'on lui prête déjà le sens affectif de *tendre*, ou *raffiné*, que lui connaîtra Sappho, ici moins probable puisque la jeune fille n'a pas à s'émouvoir de l'apparence de sa propre main, l'adjectif insiste sur la faiblesse de celle-ci.

par la main, ces gestes souhaités ne sont-ils pas les signes naturels ou rituels propres à l'élection d'une amie? À tout le moins ils peuvent l'être et le tour hypothétique favorise une telle interprétation en ce qu'il les affecte d'une tension sentimentale.

Troisièmement enfin, même si l'on accepte, faute de mieux, la conjecture αἶψά κ' [ἐγὼν ἱ]κέτις κήνας γενοίμαν, le génitif κήνας—le papyrus donne κηνᾶς—établit inéluctablement une relation de possession entre celle qui parle et Astymélousa. J'avoue d'ailleurs n'être pas convaincu que le mot à restaurer comme attribut de γενοίμαν soit ἱκέτις, tout au moins si l'on doit comprendre ἱκέτις κήνας comme ἱκετεύω αὐτήν. D'une part le trait oblique qu'on attribue à un κ dont ce serait la branche supérieure me semble légèrement incurvé vers la droite alors qu'il s'incurve vers le haut dans les autres κ du texte (mais je conviens que l'épaississement du trait à l'extrémité peut fausser l'appréciation et qu'il se retrouve dans tous les κ). D'autre part ἱκέτις est difficile à comprendre. Prend-on par la main celui ou celle qu'on veut amener à la posture de la supplication? Le terme ἱκέτις n'évoque-t-il pas la supplication d'une divinité s'il n'est pas précisé d'autre manière? Peek l'a bien senti qui écarte la traduction "ich würde sie bitten" et voit dans ἱκέτις le titre d'une fonction quelconque au sein du chœur. Je préférerais, pour ma part, renoncer au κ et conjecturer à partir de]χετις ou]υετις, voire]τετις, également admissibles. Si l'on admet possible une locution αἶψα πάγχυ sur le modèle de l'homérisme αἶψα μάλα, on se risquera à proposer αἶψά κ[ε πάγχυ] Fέτις κήνας γενοίμαν. Mais l'expression serait lourde et ne le serait pas moins si l'on faisait porter πάγχυ sur γενοίμαν plutôt que sur αἶψα. Tout en pensant que ἔτις, ou Fέτις, comme féminin de ἔτας pris dans le sens de ἑταῖρος, offrirait une bonne solution, je crois encore plus sage de constater ici la présence d'un mot inconnu désignant la titulaire d'une relation de faveur dans le cadre de l'*agélé* féminine ou de quelque autre institution spartiate.[17] En tout état de cause, ce terme implique un lien sentimental exclusif entre deux amies puisque, par νῦν δ[ὲ .....]δα παῖδα βαθύφρονα, le chœur exprime dès le début de la strophe suivante son dépit de ce qu'Astymélousa entretient déjà cette relation "de couleur amoureuse," comme le note Peek, avec une autre adolescente. J'ajoute, pour la même raison, qu'il faut chercher hors du chœur la relation en question s'il s'agit d'une coutume instituée et non d'une liaison spontanée.

---

[17] On peut penser à la rigueur à un composé de ἔχετις analogue à ὁμωχέτας, qui désignait au pluriel en Béotie, selon Thuc. IV 97, 4, des dieux associés.

Ajoutés les uns aux autres, les trois indices que l'analyse de ce texte permet de cerner produisent une certitude: au terme d'une série de comparaisons louangeuses, le poète a placé une déclaration d'amour. Elle ne peut avoir d'autre rôle à jouer, dans ce contexte, que celui de l'éloge. De même, comme l'a déjà relevé Peek, évoquer avec jalousie la favorite d'Astymélousa, c'est encore faire à cette dernière un compliment sur ses mérites. Davantage, du fait même que la déclaration est avouée illusoire, inutile, par les choristes, elle fait figure de pur ornement poétique, elle sert par son prestige littéraire la gloire de la jeune fille. On retrouve donc dans ce parthénée les artifices mis en oeuvre dans le précédent. Il en confirme le caractère conventionnel. Il assure une base stable à leur interprétation dans les autres oeuvres de même type où nous allons à nouveau les rencontrer.

* * *

S'interrogeant sur la sincérité des poèmes amoureux d'Ibycos, Welcker fondait ses doutes à juste titre sur l'idée que l'amour ne naît pas sur commande comme la poésie. Quand il avait à composer des odes en l'honneur de personnages qu'il ne choisissait pas et dans des circonstances généralement imposées, le poète n'était pas censé s'éprendre à chaque nouvelle occasion de celui qu'on lui demandait de chanter. Les historiens de la littérature ont aisément vérifié cette présomption dans le style des fragments érotiques les plus typiques, dont Wilamowitz a le premier démonté les mécanismes.[18] Bowra, qui leur a consacré les meilleures pages de son chapitre sur Ibycos, s'est montré plus habile encore à faire le départ, dans l'oeuvre d'art, entre symboles traditionnels, exaltation verbale et réelle émotion.[19] Mais il s'est abusé sur la signification de ce type de poésie quand il imagine qu'elle est vraie dans la mesure où le poète s'est pris à son jeu: "No doubt Ibycus felt the emotions of which he sang, but he was encouraged to feel them and to sing of them" (256). Il faut d'ailleurs reconnaître que s'il pose mal le problème en se demandant si la passion décrite est feinte ou non. Welcker ne l'a ni mieux posé en se demandant qui l'éprouvait réellement ni mieux résolu en la supposant véritable chez les clients du poète, c'est-à-dire chez ceux

[18] *Sappho und Simonides* (Berlin 1913), 121–27.
[19] *Greek Lyric Poetry from Alcman to Simonides*[2] (Oxford 1961), 256–64.

qui lui commandaient une ode. Si l'on se demande plutôt dans quel contexte et à quelle fin s'exprime l'aveu d'amour, si l'on se dégage du carcan de l'interprétation biographique et qu'on s'interroge sur la fonction du poème au lieu de conjecturer sur la personne du poète, alors la vérité des sentiments sort du champ de la critique tandis que s'inscrit à sa place l'appareil poétique de l'ἐγκώμιον avec ses significations propres et son objet précis.

L'évocation érotique à but laudatif occupe peu de place dans le poème à Polycrate (frg. 1), encore que tout repose sur elle puisque Ibycos, après avoir écarté toute autre comparaison possible dans un développement rhétorique fort ample, choisit finalement de comparer le jeune prince à Troïlos à cause de "sa beauté désirable" (44): ἐρόεσσαν μορφάν. Mais elle constitue le brillant exorde et sans doute une bonne partie de la louange d'Euryalos, favori des Grâces, des Muses, de Cypris et de Péitho (frg. 7), de même qu'elle fait le sujet de l'ode à Gorgias par l'entremise du mythe du rapt de Ganymède (frg. 8).[20] Enfin les deux fameux fragments sur la puissance d'Eros qui ont provoqué les réflexions de Welcker, tous deux, semble-t-il, préambules d'un ἐγκώμιον, rapportent à un "je" les supplices du désir amoureux, exactement comme le second parthénée d'Alcman, mais ne visent pas d'autre objet, comme celui-ci, que l'éloge de l'homme que le poète feint d'aimer (frg. 5 et 6). Que le public, lors de l'exécution de l'ode, ait ressenti ce "je" comme la déclaration du poète—l'exemple de Pindare dans l'ἐγκώμιον de Théoxénos de Ténédos (frg. 131 Turyn) m'incite à le croire—ou comme celle des choreutes à l'instar des auditeurs des parthénées d'Alcman, voire comme son aveu à lui, public, exprimé en une sorte de sentiment collectif, l'intention des paroles prononcées ne le trompait pas et comptait seule pour lui: louer la beauté du destinataire. La description de la passion amoureuse guidait son attention non pas vers celui qui disait la subir mais vers celui qui était dit l'inspirer. Le "je" n'est qu'un mode de présentation ou, si l'on veut, une figure de style à valeur affective apte à affirmer une vérité reçue comme telle indépendamment de qui l'énonce.

---

[20] À la fin de l'ode, l'allusion à l'enlèvement de Tithon par Aurore répète le motif, pour montrer sans doute que la beauté de Gorgias lui vaut aussi l'hommage du sexe féminin. En insistant uniquement sur le fait qu'il s'agit dans les deux cas de divinités enlevant un mortel, Bowra, *op. cit.* 259, réduit par trop la portée du second mythe.

Ces poèmes, en particulier les deux derniers, cités par eux à titre de preuves, n'en ont pas moins abusé les biographes antiques, qui ont qualifié Ibycos—la formule remonte probablement à Chaméléon—de poète ἐρωτομανέστατος περὶ μειράκια (*Sud.*).[21] Mais Bowra—nous l'avons vu—se montre aussi peu clairvoyant à son sujet et G. Perrotta encore moins que lui quand il imagine, pour innocenter Ibycos, un thiase d'éromènes dans le cadre duquel l'ἐγκώμιον érotique aurait été l'expression naturelle d'un sentiment amoureux collectif, étonnante résurgence de la théorie romantique sur l'origine de la poésie![22] Dans le catalogue des poètes érotiques dressé par Chaméléon auquel Athénée doit une partie importante de son treizième livre (voir la note 21), avant Ibycos figure Alcman, donné comme l'initiateur du genre. Nous savons ce qu'il faut en penser. Puis vient Stésichore, pour lequel nous ne disposons pas de moyens de vérification, faute de fragments adéquats. On ne se trompera pas, cependant, en supposant que Chaméléon a aussi mal compris que ceux d'Alcman les poèmes sur lesquels il fondait son jugement.[23] Selon lui, donc: Στησίχορος οὐ μετρίως ἐρωτικὸς γενόμενος συνέστησε καὶ τοῦτον τὸν τρόπον τῶν ᾀσμάτων, ἃ δὴ καὶ

---

[21] Diogène de Babylone tire déjà argument de cette réputation quand il écrit τοὺς νέους τοῖς μέλεσι διέφθειρον Ἴβυκος καὶ Ἀνακρέων καὶ οἱ ὅμοιοι (frg. 76 Arnim, rétabli ici en discours direct). Elle date au moins de deux siècles plus tôt puisque Chaméléon, qui lui a fait naturellement une large publicité, en rend responsable Archytas de Tarente (frg. 25 Wehrli, à prolonger jusqu'aux citations de Pindare chez Athénée, XIII 601e, avec Wilamowitz, *op. cit.* 122, note 1). En fait, comme d'ordinaire en pareil cas, la comédie attique en est l'origine: Aristophane, *Thesm.* 161, l'atteste à propos d'Alcée et d'Anacréon usant du mode iastien relâché. Mais Archytas, qui semble s'être prononcé seulement sur les modes musicaux propres aux poèmes érotiques et n'avoir rien dit des moeurs de leurs auteurs—on observera que son opinion nous est connue seulement à travers Chaméléon—, reste probablement étranger à cette influence. Quant aux deux fragments les plus typiques de la poésie dite érotique d'Ibycos, les fragments 5 et 6, il est frappant qu'on les trouve cités précisément à l'appui de l'assertion de Chaméléon, le premier chez Athénée, le second chez Proclus, *In Plat. Parmen.* 5, 316 Cousin: peut-être n'existait-il pas d'exemple plus probant et l'accusation repose-t-elle toute entière sur eux seuls.

[22] *Polinnia*² (Messina-Firenze 1965), 298.

[23] Puisqu'il nomme Stésichore entre Alcman et Ibycos, dans l'extrait conservé par Athénée, et que de toute manière il ne s'intéresse qu'aux poètes archaïques, Chaméléon n'a pu le confondre avec Stésichore le Jeune, poète dithyrambique de la première moitié du IVe siècle, ainsi que le déclare encore Bowra, *op. cit.* 87: il sait de quoi et de qui il parle. G. E. Rizzo, "Questione Stesicoree," *Rivista di Storia antica* 1 (1895), 2, 26, qu'on cite rituellement sur ce point, se contentait de suggérer l'existence de poèmes apocryphes dans l'oeuvre de Stésichore d'Himère, ce qui est bien différent.

τὸ παλαιὸν ἐκαλεῖτο παίδεια[24] καὶ παιδικά. En plus de ce qu'il en-
seigne sur l'oeuvre de Stésichore, ce témoignage présente le grand
intérêt de transmettre une terminologie classique, voire archaïque,
sur le genre qui nous occupe. Les deux adjectifs que cite Chaméléon,
apparemment synonymes et d'ailleurs attestés séparément avec le
même sens, comme on le verra plus loin, le premier chez Pindare et le
second chez Bacchylide, autorisent à affirmer que Stésichore avait
composé des odes chorales célébrant en termes d'amour la beauté
d'un jouvenceau. Quel que soit l'espace qu'y occupait réellement le
propos amoureux—il pouvait avoir été limité à l'exorde ou à la conclusion—ces poèmes constituent une sorte de chaînon entre Alcman
et Ibycos. Plus exactement, ils attestent l'existence d'ἐγκώμια à
ornements érotiques sous d'autres climats que celui de Sparte et
dans d'autres circonstances que celles des parthénées d'Alcman
sans que s'impose en aucune façon l'idée d'une imitation.

Est-ce à dire que Chaméléon et avant lui Archytas, sa source,
trompés par les apparences en ce qui concerne les sentiments des
poètes qu'ils appellent érotiques, méritent plus de crédit sur l'élaboration du "genre érotique" au sein du lyrisme choral? En réalité, s'il
n'y a rien à leur objecter sur ce qu'ils disent d'Ibycos, comme on va
le voir, leur opinion sur Alcman paraît téméraire. Se référant à
Archytas, Chaméléon allègue après lui deux fragments dont le
premier doit attester non pas l'intensité du désir amoureux qu'il
décrit, mais la fréquence des ἐρωτικὰ μέλη dans sa poésie, διὸ καὶ
λέγειν ἔν τινι τῶν μελῶν (frg. 59ᵃ):

> Ἔρως με δηῦτε Κύπριδος Ϝέκατι
> γλυκὺς κατείβων καρδίαν ἰαίνει.

En tenant compte scrupuleusement des deux καὶ qui suivent la
lacune reconnue par Garzya dans l'introduction de la citation, on
peut reconstituer ce texte à peu près comme suit: Ἀλκμᾶνα γεγονέναι
τῶν ἐρωτικῶν μελῶν ἡγεμόνα καὶ ἐκδοῦναι πρῶτον μέλος < . . . καὶ
εἰσαγαγεῖν ἐρωτικὰ ᾄσματα, περὶ τὰς παρθένους > ἀκόλαστον ὄντα καὶ
περὶ τὰς γυναῖκας, καὶ τὴν τοιαύτην Μοῦσαν εἰς τὰς διατριβάς. Ce
qu'il faut souligner, c'est que le pluriel εἰς τὰς διατριβάς et le tour
διὸ καὶ λέγειν au lieu de λέγειν γὰρ attirent l'attention sur le sens
itératif de la formule Ἔρως με δηῦτε plutôt que sur la licence de ces

---

[24] Correction de Welcker, op. cit. 242, pour παιδιά.

vers, en somme anodins : Alcman aurait introduit dans *les* divertisse-
ments, tant pour les paroles que pour le mode musical, le chant
érotique. Quant au second fragment, il atteste indirectement que
Mégalostrata, "bienheureuse entre les jeunes filles," exécutait dans
le parthénée un chant—Μωσᾶν δῶρον—évoquant les hommages
amoureux suscités par elle (frg. 59ᵇ) :[25]

> τοῦτο Ϝαδειᾶν ἔδειξε Μωσᾶν
> δῶρον μάκαιρα παρσένων
> ἁ ξανθὰ Μεγαλοστράτα.

Les deux citations servaient donc très précisément à prouver l'existence de poèmes érotiques dans l'oeuvre d'Alcman, les observations de
Chaméléon sur ses penchants libertins (ἀκόλαστον ὄντα, τῆς Μεγαλοστράτης οὐ μετρίως ἐρασθείς) demeurant marginales et n'ayant
d'autre utilité que de lier biographiquement l'invention de ce
nouveau genre à sa manière d'être. Mais ces preuves sont faibles :
ni δηὖτε, ni Μωσᾶν δῶρον ne circonscrivent les caractères distinctifs
d'un ἐρωτικὸν μέλος au point qu'on puisse affirmer que le poète
les avait ressentis comme spécifiques d'un genre au même titre, par
exemple, qu'un thrène ou qu'un épithalame. Il n'est pas niable, en
revanche, que le retour de la formule Ἔρως με δηὖτε chez Sappho
(frg. 130), chez Ibycos (frg. 6), chez Anacréon (frg. 68) fait référence
à une tradition et équivaut par là-même à la reconnaissance d'un
type de poème dûment individualisé.

* * *

Pindare et Bacchylide apportent une dernière et double confirmation aux vues développées jusque ici. Au commencement de la 2ᵉ
Isthmique, qui fête à titre posthume une victoire de Xénocrate
d'Agrigente et s'adresse pour cette raison à son fils Thrasyboulos,
Pindare évoque la liberté d'un temps révolu où les poètes improvi-
saient des chants pour dire la beauté des jeunes gens et leur pouvoir
séducteur (3–5) :

---

[25] Athénée écrit λέγει δὲ καὶ ὡς τῆς Μεγαλοστράτης οὐ μετρίως ἐρασθείς, ποιητρίας μὲν
οὔσης, δυναμένης δὲ καὶ διὰ τὴν ὁμιλίαν τοὺς ἐραστὰς προσελκύσασθαι. Chaméléon a tiré ποιητρίας
μὲν οὔσης de ἔδειξε Μωσᾶν δῶρον (mais ἔδειξε désigne l'exécution du chant, selon B.
Marzullo, *Helikon* 4 [1964], 4 sqq.) et δυναμένης . . . τοὺς ἐραστὰς προσελκύσασθαι du chant
lui-même.

ρίμφα παιδείους ἐτόξευον μελιγάρυας ὕμνους,
ὅστις ἐὼν καλὸς εἶχεν Ἀφροδίτας
εὐθρόνου μνάστειραν ἁδίσταν ὀπώραν.

Ces vers ont suscité d'abondants commentaires, du fait qu'ils
semblent révéler un penchant amoureux que le poète aurait
éprouvé à l'égard du prince sicilien. C'est bien ce sentiment, en effet,
que Pindare feint de n'oser dire aussi franchement que ses devanciers.
Mais on reconnaît sans peine dans les termes qu'il emploie à propos
de leurs poèmes, καλός et Ἀφροδίτας ὀπώρα, le dessein encomiastique
de ceux-ci. Loin de commettre l'erreur de Chaméléon, il interprète
leurs déclarations amoureuses comme des compliments. Aussi,
venant à poser ensuite la question de leur sincérité, pense-t-il
uniquement à la sincérité de l'éloge, que ne dictait pas encore,
dira-t-il, une Muse mercenaire: l'image ne saurait s'appliquer à un
aveu d'amour.[26] L'emploi de ὕμνος, terme que Pindare reprendra
dans la dernière strophe pour désigner sa propre ode (45 τούσδ'
ὕμνους), confirme qu'il assimilait à des ἐγκώμια les poèmes qu'il
rappelle à la mémoire de ses auditeurs. Ὕμνος, en effet, n'a pas
d'autre sens: sur les soixante-trois exemples de son Lexicon to Pindar
(Berlin 1969) aux mots ὕμνος, ὑμνέω, ὕμνησις et ὑμνητός, W. J.
Slater en range soixante sous la traduction "song of praise" et deux
sous celle de "dirge," qui s'explique par l'assimilation du thrène à
un éloge funèbre; et seul ferait exception notre passage avec le sens
malencontreusement proposé de "love song," si l'unanimité des
soixante-deux autres n'obligeait à lui assigner la même signification
contrairement à l'interprétation traditionnelle. Par παίδειοι ὕμνοι,
donc, Pindare entend ici l'éloge d'un παῖς en forme de déclaration
d'amour tel qu'Ibycos, notamment, nous l'avons vu, le concevait.
Il en a, comme on sait, composé lui-même: sans parler d'une autre
épinicie en l'honneur de Thrasyboulos écrite quelque vingt ans plus
tôt, la 6ᵉ Pythique, qui ne contient qu'une allusion liminaire aux
thèmes érotiques—v.1 Ἀφροδίτας ἄρουραν... ἀναπολίζομεν—citons

---

[26] Sur le sens de tout ce passage, voir en dernier lieu l'excellente analyse de E.
Thummer, Pindar. Die Isthmischen Gedichte, 2 (Heidelberg 1969), 39 sq., qui non seulement
explique enfin de façon satisfaisante comment Pindare évoque sa situation de poète
mercenaire pour rendre plus difficile et partant plus méritoire sa protestation de sincérité,
mais aussi reconnaît à l'éloge de la beauté de Thrasyboulos sa juste fonction de motif
littéraire contribuant à l'ἐγκώμιον.

la 8ᵉ Néméenne en l'honneur de Déinis d'Égine et surtout les deux
ἐγκώμια dont les fragments 127 et 131 conservent les exordes, celui
du même Thrasyboulos d'Agrigente et celui de Théoxénos de
Ténédos![27]

Témoin irrécusable sur la fonction des παίδειοι ὕμνοι archaïques,
qu'il s'agisse des siens propres ou de ceux de ses devanciers et de
poésie rémunérée ou de poésie en apparence désintéressée, Pindare
l'est aussi sur leur existence en tant que genre poétique distinct. Il
confirme en cela le témoignage plus vulnérable d'Archytas. Moins
explicite en ce qui concerne le premier point, Bacchylide aide à
mieux imaginer le second en évoquant de plus près l'une des occasions
d'ἐγκώμια érotiques, le banquet public (Péan 4, 79):

συμποσίων δ' ἐρατῶν βρίθοντ' ἀγυιαί,
παιδικοί θ' ὕμνοι φλέγονται.

Ces deux vers s'inscrivent dans une énumération des activités que
procure la paix après la dureté du temps de guerre: la joie des
banquets règne à nouveau sur la voie publique et avec elle "les
chants de louange en l'honneur des adolescents." Subordonnant
pour le sens, par l'hendiadys, le second vers au premier, Bacchylide
fait allusion uniquement à des poèmes chantés dans le cadre
symposiaque, scolies ou ἐγκώμια. Qu'il les appelle παιδικοί plutôt
que παίδειοι à l'instar de Pindare tient apparemment à ce qu'il
désire insister sur la tournure érotique—on comparera les Παιδικά
de Théocrite—plutôt que sur l'intention de louange, volonté
qu'implique aussi le verbe φλέγονται. Mais ὕμνοι préserve la notion
d'éloge, qui reste première même si les protestations d'amour et la
peinture de la passion, de l'avis de Bacchylide, captent davantage
l'intérêt des auditeurs. Bref, l'allusion embrasserait-elle aussi des
poèmes tels que les élégies ῏Ω παῖ du second livre de Théognis,
passant alors du banquet public au banquet privé, dans lesquels
l'anonymat du destinataire abolit parfois la notion d'éloge, qu'on
ne devrait pas moins admettre, à cause du mot ὕμνος précisément,

---

[27] Rappelons pour mémoire que B. A. van Groningen, *Pindare au banquet* (Leyde
1960), assimile ces poèmes à des scolies, et pour mémoire aussi qu'il a proposé du premier
l'interprétation biographique la plus romanesque qui soit, après celles de Chaméléon
(cf. Ath. XIII 601ᶜ καὶ Πίνδαρος δ' οὐ μετρίως ὢν ἐρωτικός ... suivent les citations des
fragments 134 et 131) et des biographes antiques à sa suite (*op. cit.* 76–81).

que Bacchylide leur prête en tant que poèmes érotiques, par une
sorte d'association d'idées, un dessein louangeur.

* * *

Relativement sûre dans la poésie chorale parce que l'inter-
position nécessaire d'un choeur, le faste de l'exécution musicale et
le caractère largement public des cérémonies composent une situation peu favorable à l'expression de sentiments intimes, fussent-ils
fictifs, la démonstration poursuivie jusqu'ici n'a théoriquement pas
de prise sur la poésie monodique de parénèse ou de divertissement.
Tandis que d'Alcman à Pindare l'auteur de chorodies joue à certains
égards le rôle d'animateur d'un festival musical, un Mimnerme, un
Alcée, un Anacréon récréent leurs auditeurs en payant, si je puis
dire, de leur personne, ne serait-ce que parce qu'ils ajoutent à leur
qualité de poète la fonction de récitant ou de chanteur, comme les
chansonniers d'aujourd'hui. Dans la chanson à boire comme dans
la chanson d'amour, leur "je" les représente vraiment, sinon toujours
véridiquement, et ce qu'ils ont à dire les engage personnellement. Il
n'en résulte pas nécessairement dans la pratique que leur poésie
ne se prête pas à l'ἐγκώμιον. Au contraire, à en croire Strabon, XIV,
1, 16, l'oeuvre d'Anacréon, par exemple, "était pleine du nom de
Polycrate." Mais il n'existe aucun indice sûr qu'elle ait usé à cet
effet de prétextes amoureux. Aussi doit-elle demeurer hors du champ
de notre étude.

Il en va tout autrement de Sappho, qui occupe une place à part
dans le lyrisme monodique. En effet, bien que la tradition soit
muette à cet égard, tout porte à croire qu'elle n'a pas composé ses
chants, sauf exception, pour les produire dans le cadre habituel de
la monodie, le banquet: sa condition de femme, sa fonction de
prêtresse [28] et surtout le fait que nombre de ses poèmes, autant qu'on
en peut juger par ce qu'il en subsiste et par le témoignage de plusieurs auteurs antiques, avaient pour destinataires des jeunes filles.
Dans cette situation particulière, sa poésie assumait évidemment une
fonction différente de celle que détermine le cadre symposiaque.
Ses épithalames, par exemple, qu'on connaît un peu par les quelque
trente vers lisibles de celui qui achevait le livre II (frg. 44), les dix

---

[28] Démontrée en dernier lieu par B. Gentili, *Quaderni Urbinati* 2 (1966), 37–62, à
partir d'Alcée, frg. 384 ἰόπλοκ' ἄγνα μελλιχόμειδε Σάπφοι.

incipit du livre intitulé Ἐπιθαλάμια (frg. 103)[29] et des fragments isolés, s'apparentent aux productions chorales, ayant comme elles pour objet de rehausser le lustre d'une cérémonie. Quant aux autres poèmes, notamment ceux-là mêmes qui font problème à cause de leur contenu érotique, je pose ici par hypothèse qu'ils sont pour la plupart des poèmes de circonstance et qu'ils sont soumis de ce fait aux mêmes servitudes que les productions du lyrisme choral, à cela près que Sappho y tient le rôle normalement dévolu au choeur. Je crois pouvoir le démontrer au moins de tous les poèmes exprimant des sentiments amoureux en les interprétant comme des ἐγκώμια, sans nier pour autant une certaine ambiguïté tenant au "je" de Sappho, qui n'est pas superposable au "je" d'un choeur.

Il faut donc rouvrir une fois de plus le dossier du fastidieux, mais inévitable problème saphique. Si l'on rejette comme mésinterprétations de son oeuvre les jugements que l'antiquité a portés sur la personne de la poétesse et à leur tour comme mésinterprétations de ces jugements quantité de jugements modernes, il reste que quelques poèmes et fragments de poèmes formulent à l'endroit de jeunes filles, à la première personne du singulier, des sentiments d'amour ou de désir amoureux et qu'on ne peut esquiver les questions qui se posent nécessairement à leur sujet sous peine de superficialité. À les considérer selon l'intensité de la passion décrite, ou, plus justement, selon l'abondance et la force des moyens stylistiques mis au service de la description, nous trouvons en tête deux fragments qui font penser aux citations d'Ibycos les plus colorées, le fragment 47:

> Ἔρος δ' ἐτίναξέ μοι
> φρένας, ὡς ἄνεμος κὰτ ὄρος δρύσιν ἐμπέτων,

---

[29] Sa première ode, cependant, n'était pas un épithalame et le titre vaut seulement pour les neuf autres, si l'on en croit le commentaire des *incipit*. On doit restituer, en effet, aux lignes 14 et 15, autrement que ne l'ont fait Lobel et Page: [ᾠδὴ] ᾱ στίχοι ρλ[.], puis...αἱ δὲ] μετὰ τὴν πρώτην κτλ. Sur ᾱ au lieu de ῆ, voir *Ant. class.* 24 (1955), 470: non seulement le *ductus* légèrement incurvé de la verticale s'accorde mieux avec α qu'avec η, mais encore le trait horizontal qui surmonte le chiffre est centré sur elle, ce qui ne serait pas le cas si l'on avait affaire à la haste de droite d'un η. Au surplus, le nombre des vers indiqué est évidemment celui d'un poème, non du livre entier comme on doit l'admettre si on lit ῆ. Quant au frg. 44, j'en admets l'interprétation classique et ne puis suivre l'hypothèse qu'il n'appartiendrait pas à un épithalame proposée par A. Lesky, *Gesch. d. gr. Lit.*[2] (Bern 1963), 165, et développée par J. Th. Kakridis, *Wien. Stud.* 79 (1966), 21–26.

et le fragment 130, un début de poème:

"Ερος δηὖτέ μ' ὁ λυσιμέλης δόνει,
γλυκύπικρον ἀμάχανον ὄρπετον.

À cause d'Ibycos et à cause de la formule *"Ερος δηὖτέ με*, le moins qu'on puisse dire de ces deux déclarations, c'est qu'elles pourraient provenir d'un *ἐγκώμιον*. On ne saurait cependant affirmer quoi que ce soit de certain en l'absence d'indices plus tangibles. On ne préférera donc pas cette interprétation à d'autres plus obvies avant de disposer d'analogies livrées par Sappho elle-même dans d'autres poèmes de son oeuvre.

Il s'en présente une très probante dans le célèbre poème représenté par les dix-sept vers du fragment 31, *Φαίνεταί μοι κτλ.*,[30] qui vient en troisième rang selon le critère adopté. Depuis que L. Rysbeck a montré que *κῆνος...ὄττις* (1–2) équivaut hors d'Attique à *ἐκεῖνος ὅς* du dialecte attique et ne comporte donc pas la signification *quiconque*, contrairement à l'opinion de Page,[31] le texte contraint à revenir à la traduction "l'homme qui est assis en face de toi" adoptée déjà par Catulle dans son *Ille mi ...* (51, 1). On doit dès lors regarder à nouveau comme la plus vraisemblable, à l'instar de Welcker,[32] une situation de fête nuptiale. Je l'estime même, pour ma part, seule concevable, et cela pour la raison que voici. Compo-

[30] Je conserve *μοι* à cause de Catulle 51, 1 *Ille mi*. Si *φαίνεταί ϝοι* repris du frg. 165 peut à la rigueur signifier *sibi videtur* comme *φαίνομ' ἔμ' αὔτᾳ* du v. 16 *mihi videor*, Gallavotti, *Riv. Fil.* 94 (1966), 257–67, ne m'a pas convaincu que le contraste s'établit entre la satisfaction ressentie par l'homme (*ϝοι*) et la souffrance de Sappho (*ἔμ' αὔτᾳ*). *Φαίνομ' ἔμ' αὔτᾳ* est grammaticalement inséparable de *τεθνάκην δ' ὀλίγω ἐπιδεύης*, ce qui limite à cette seule dernière image sa portée réelle de signification. Mais si l'on veut que cette image, elle, polarise un contraste entre deux situations, on peut juger suffisante une opposition entre le bonheur de l'homme "comblé autant qu'un dieu" et la douleur mortelle de Sappho sans y ajouter le sentiment qu'en éprouve celui-là, ce qui rend inutile la substitution de *ϝοι* à *μοι*. Qu'on adopte d'ailleurs l'une ou l'autre leçon, l'interprétation du poème comme *ἐγκώμιον* n'en est pas sérieusement modifiée. Tout au plus l'éloge de l'homme s'alourdirait-il, avec *ϝοι*, d'un soupçon de jalousie, nuance peu heureuse en pareille conjoncture. Est-il nécessaire d'ajouter après cette observation que je ne partage en aucune manière le sentiment de G. Broccia, *Tradizione ed esegesi* (Brescia 1969), 108, qui qualifie après quelques autres auteurs de "fondamentale e vessatissima" la question de savoir si l'ode dépeint l'amour ou la jalousie?

[31] *Hermes* 97 (1969), 161–66, contre Page, *Sappho and Alcaeus* (Oxford 1955), 20 sq.

[32] *Kleine Schriften* II, 99, et IV, 89. On trouvera chez G. Broccia, *op. cit.* 122 sq., lui-même opposé à la thèse épithalamique, la dernière bibliographie du sujet, à compléter par H. Rüdiger, *Griechische Lyriker*[2] (Zürich 1968), 308 sq.

sant son ode avant le jour où elle la chantera publiquement, comment Sappho peut-elle savoir que la jeune fille à laquelle elle l'adresse sera alors assise vis-à-vis de l'homme qui l'aime? Il faut non seulement qu'elle ait pu prévoir cette circonstance précise, mais encore que celle-ci se soit prêtée par avance, du consentement de tous les intéressés, à un tel intermède musical. Il s'agit donc d'un rite et je n'en vois qu'un seul qui corresponde aux divers éléments de la donnée: le premier face à face de l'époux et de l'épouse sur les sièges conjugaux, si je puis dire, cérémonie dont N. Condoléon a récapitulé récemment l'abondante iconographie archaïque [33] et à laquelle Homère semble déjà faire indirectement allusion quand il décrit les retrouvailles d'Hélène et de Pâris (Γ 425 sq.) et celles de Pénélope et d'Ulysse (ψ 164 sq.). Le même livre d'odes qui contenait ce poème s'achève, on le sait, sur une pièce destinée à introduire une παννυχις nuptiale (frg. 30) et a laissé d'autre part un fragment adressé à la fiancée qui quitte la maison de ses parents (frg. 27). Cette constatation accessoire apporte le *nihil obstat* à la thèse proposée: le fragment 31 est un poème de mariage. Or quel sens donner à la "pathographie" amoureuse des quatre premières strophes dont A. Turyn, je me plais à le rappeler ici, a si brillamment démontré jadis le caractère entièrement littéraire,[34] sinon celui de célébrer implicitement la beauté de la jeune épouse? Soupçonner dans cette conjoncture la moindre intention amoureuse et admettre par conséquent que les auditeurs de Sappho devaient concevoir le même soupçon serait illogique: sollicitée d'embellir par son chant le moment peut-être le plus solennel de la fête, il est inconcevable non seulement que la poétesse ait choisi cette occasion de déclarer sa passion déçue, mais même qu'elle ait pu pressentir le risque d'une équivoque dans l'esprit de ses auditeurs. Elle savait d'avance, bien au contraire, qu'ils ne prendraient pas ses paroles à la lettre et que leur intérêt se porterait seulement sur le traitement d'un thème ressenti par eux comme conventionnel. De là l'extrême recherche du langage, l'audace des hyperboles, l'accumulation insolite des effets de pure littérature.

Que l'on confronte maintenant à ce poème nuptial les deux fragments 47 et 130 précédemment cités, on se rendra compte que

[33] Χαριστήριον εἰς Ἀναστάσιον κ. Ὀρλάνδον, 1 (Athènes 1965), 352-413.
[34] *Studia Sapphica*, passim, en particulier 69-82.

l'analogie autorise pleinement à leur dénier tout mobile amoureux, en dépit des apparences. Comme le fragment 31, ils esquissent une "pathographie" érotique, et ils usent comme lui à cet effet des artifices les plus tapageurs du style lyrique, renforcés dans le second par leur position au commencement de l'ode. Quelque circonstance qu'on imagine, célébration nuptiale ou toute autre cérémonie en l'honneur de quelqu'un, ils annoncent une louange.

Avec ces trois textes, comme on sait, la liste des témoignages de première main sur ce qu'on est convenu d'appeler le problème saphique est presque épuisée. Page a fait justice de quelques fragments moins expressifs, mais souvent allégués, auxquels leur brièveté et l'absence d'un contexte explicite ôtent toute valeur de preuves.[35] Il reste encore à montrer comment tous ceux qui évoquent avec l'accent d'une indéniable tendresse et sans ornements littéraires la grâce des jeunes compagnes de la poétesse relèvent eux aussi de l'éloge et répondent à des circonstances déterminées, car ils sont sans nul doute à l'origine de la plupart des accusations portées par les auteurs antiques et conservent une dangereuse vigueur tant qu'on n'a pas pris conscience que celles-ci procèdent de leur ignorance ou de leur indifférence à l'égard de la raison d'être de chaque poème incriminé. Malheureusement, le hasard des citations ou les mutilations des documents papyrologiques font que nous connaissons rarement les contextes aptes à nous renseigner sur l'occasion d'une ode de cette catégorie, et les connaîtrions-nous que nous risquerions encore, faute de les trouver assez éclairants, de nous ranger par résignation à l'avis naïf d'Aristoxène, typique de l'incuriosité antique dans ce domaine (frg. 71[b] Wehrli): *Sapphonem et Alcaeum volumina sua loco sodalium habuisse.* Dans ces conditions, il faut se contenter à nouveau d'analogies, et nous en avons par chance une fort instructive à disposition, le fragment 96.

[35] *Sappho and Alcaeus*, 144 sq., note 1 (frg. 46, 126, 94). En ce qui concerne le fragment 94, où le contexte est relativement bien conservé et suffisamment clair, la possibilité évoquée par Page d'une interprétation *in malam partem* résiste mal à l'examen: ἐξίης πόθο[ν . . .].νίδων à l'imparfait, a pour sujet la femme à qui Sappho rappelle les joies du passé et évoque ses relations avec ses compagnes; il ne s'agit pas d'un amour de Sappho. Quant au mystérieux distique χόρδαισι διακρέκην (ou χόρδαισ' ἴδια—ἰδίᾳ?—κρέκην) | ὀλισβοδόκοισ<ι> περκαθ....ενος en 99, col. I, 4–5, il suit à un vers d'intervalle la mention d'un nom détesté de Sappho, Πωλυανακτ[ίδ]αις, et peut être attribué à une invective. Il n'implique donc pas un contexte érotique.

Dans le poème auquel il appartient, Sappho évoque pour Atthis le souvenir récent d'une compagne aujourd'hui mariée en Lydie. Dès les premiers vers intelligibles, elle lui rappelle les compliments qu'elles échangeaient entre elles lorsqu'elles étaient ensemble (2–5) :

πόλ]λακι τυίδε [ν]ῶν ἔχοισα
ὤσπ.[. . .].ώομεν, .[. . .]..χ'[ἔτι-]
σε θέαι σ' ἰκέλαν ἀρι-
γνώται, σᾶι δὲ μάλιστ' ἔχαιρε μόλπαι.

L'absente comparait Atthis à une déesse, Atthis chantait pour lui plaire. Ce qu'exprimait le chant d'Atthis, Sappho ne le dit pas et peut-être devons-nous simplement comprendre que sa compagne aimait le son de sa voix. Mais après avoir évoqué la beauté de l'absente au moyen de quelques comparaisons (6–14), elle imagine que celle-ci, de son côté, ne cesse de penser à son amie et qu'un sentiment d'amour se mêle à ses souvenirs (15–17) :

πόλλα δὲ ζαφοίταισ', ἀγάνας ἐπιμνάσθεισ' Ἄτθιδος ἰμέρωι
λέπταν Ϝοι φρένα κ[α]ρδίαι βόρηται.[36]

Par le rapprochement des paroles de naguère, ἔτισε θέαι σ' ἰκέλαν, et des pensées d'aujourd'hui, ἐπιμνάσθεισ' Ἄτθιδος ἰμέρωι, Sappho reconstitue la trame d'une louange amoureuse, telle qu'on pourrait se la représenter sortant non pas de sa propre bouche, mais de celle de l'absente. Et de fait, après trois vers incertains où l'on discerne seulement, grâce au verbe γαρύει (20), que cette dernière, du lieu de sa résidence lydienne, fait monter un chant pour Atthis, ses premières paroles reprennent l'éloge au point même où elle l'avait laissé, c'est-à-dire à la comparaison de sa compagne avec une déesse (21–23)[37] :

[36] Sur ϝοι et sur la restitution admise ici, voir C. Calame, *Quaderni Urbinati* 4 (1967), 101–106.

[37] Au vers 18, τόδ' ou τάδ' fait attendre une explication qu'il semble impossible de situer avant le vers 21, ce qui empêche de fixer la fin du poème au vers 20, comme on l'a souvent voulu. Je lie donc ainsi : τόδ' οὐ †νῶντ' ἄ[κο]υστον . . . γαρύει . . . ε]ῦμαρ[ες μ]έν. Mais outre l'insoluble νωντ, le nominatif masculin πόλυς fait difficulté et d'autres graves obscurités subsistent.

ϵ]ὔμαρ[ϵς μ]ὲν οὐκ ἄμ[μ]ι θέαισι μόρ-
φαν ἐπή[ρατ]ον ἐξίσω-
σθαι, σὺ [δ' ἦ]ρος ἔχησθ' α[. .].νίδηον.

"For us, it is not easy to rival goddesses for beauty of form; but
you..." traduit Page. Écho d'un chant plus ancien, le nouveau
chant en reprend le thème dans une sorte de variation où l'on ne
s'étonne pas de voir bientôt des ornements érotiques renforcer les
sentiments d'admiration. Malgré les mutilations du papyrus, en
effet, on les reconnaît sans peine aux noms d'Aphrodite dispen-
satrice des attraits de l'amour—26-27 Ἀφροδίτα. . .νέκταρ ἔχευ(ϵ)—
et de Péitho.

Du fait que ce chant imaginaire rappelle à l'intention d'Atthis
un poème réel de contenu analogue, il atteste de toute première
main l'existence d'ἐγκώμια érotiques dans l'entourage immédiat de
la poétesse. N'y parle-t-elle pas elle-même de sa poésie ou de celle
de ses émules? En outre, il constitue en soi un nouvel ἐγκώμιον
d'Atthis, dans lequel l'habile fiction élaborée par Sappho aboutit à
diminuer le rôle du "je" au profit de celui du "tu," car il importe
moins de savoir si la louange émane de l'amie absente ou de la
poétesse que d'entendre proclamer une louange. Quant à la circonstance qui la provoque, sans la désigner expressément, le poème
en indique au moins le cadre: les relations d'amitié entre les jeunes
filles qui se réunissaient chez Sappho pour s'initier aux arts des
Muses. Fallait-il même une circonstance? On peut penser dans le
cas présent au récent départ de l'amie, par exemple, ou à la nouvelle
de son mariage. Mais je serais aussi disposé à croire que l'ἐγκώμιον
était l'un des sujets de poésie exercés par ses élèves et j'en vois la
preuve ici-même, puisque l'absente, nous l'apprenons de la bouche
de Sappho, en avait composé un pour Atthis. Quoi qu'il en soit de
ce point secondaire, les sentiments de la poétesse sont d'autant moins
engagés dans les poèmes de ce genre qu'il s'agit d'oeuvres destinées
souvent à être chantées par d'autres ou à servir de modèles, le je
perdant alors son identité. Outre plusieurs fragments traditionnellement allégués à l'appui de cet emploi scolaire des chants composés
par elle, notamment le fragment 150 à cause de l'expression ἐν
μοισοπόλων †οἰκίᾳ et ceux qui mentionnent ses concurrentes Andro-
mède et Gorgo, je vois la meilleure illustration de son rôle d'éduca-

trice dans l'inoubliable hydrie polygnotéenne qui montre, groupées autour d'elle, trois élèves attentives aux vers qu'elle lit et que l'une d'elles, Kallis, la lyre à la main, s'apprête sans doute à chanter ou à imiter après elle.[38]

Faut-il d'autres preuves du sens encomiastique des poèmes produits dans ce cadre? Il en reste une que je crois aussi forte que la démonstration de Welcker sur le caractère contradictoire de sentiments authentiques à l'égard d'amants constamment nouveaux dans la poésie d'Ibycos: le témoignage direct d'Ovide. Citant quelques uns des nombreux noms de jeunes filles qu'il s'émerveillait de rencontrer dans ses vers, l'auteur des *Héroïdes* a justement noté que Sappho exprimait à leur endroit des sentiments amoureux. Mais il n'a pas compris la véritable intention de ce langage et ne nous rend service, d'abord, que comme garant de son fréquent usage (*Her.* 15, 15–19):

> Nec me Pyrrhiades Methymniadesve puellae,
> Nec me Lesbiadum cetera turba iuvant;
> Vilis Anactorie, vilis mihi candida Cydro,
> Non oculis gratast Atthis, ut ante, meis
> Atque aliae centum, quas non sine crimine amavi.

Ensuite et surtout ces vers, en particulier le dernier,[38a] éveillent le soupçon confirmé par le fragment 96 que l'amour dont il s'agit, suscité successivement par une multitude de jeunes filles, n'est pas un ἔρως au sens propre du terme, mais un ornement poétique contribuant à leur louange. Le fragment 96 nous apprend en plus que ces jeunes filles usaient entre elles du même procédé littéraire, probablement dans les poèmes qu'elles s'adressaient l'une à l'autre. Nouons le raisonnement: si le fragment 96 démontre qu'elles associaient les ornements érotiques à l'éloge dans leurs propres compositions lyriques, n'est-il pas évident qu'elles devaient prêter sans hésitation la même signification à ceux qu'elles rencontraient dans les poèmes composés pour elles par Sappho?

Je me crois donc fondé à dire que la poésie réputée érotique de la poétesse de Lesbos admet, *mutatis mutandis*, la même explication que celle d'Alcman, d'Ibycos et de Pindare. Existe-t-il une preuve

[38] Voir K. Schefold, *Die Bildnisse der antiken Dichter, Redner und Denker* (Basel 1943), 57, 3.
[38a] J'y souligne seulement *atque aliae centum*.

contraire? Je ne sache pas qu'on puisse en avancer d'autre que celle
de la première ode du livre I, dans laquelle Sappho fait état de
l'appui accordé par Aphrodite à ses entreprises amoureuses (18–20):

$$\tau\acute{\iota}\nu\alpha \ \delta\eta\hat{\upsilon}\tau\epsilon \ \Pi\epsilon\acute{\iota}\theta\omega$$
$$\lambda\hat{\alpha}\iota\sigma' \ \check{\alpha}\gamma\eta\nu \ \grave{\epsilon}s \ \sigma\grave{\alpha}\nu \ \varphi\iota\lambda\acute{o}\tau\alpha\tau\alpha; \ T\acute{\iota}s \ \sigma', \ \hat{\omega}$$
$$\Psi\acute{\alpha}\pi\varphi', \ \grave{\alpha}\delta\iota\kappa\acute{\eta}\epsilon\iota;[39]$$

Wilamowitz s'est tiré de l'embarras dans lequel, avocat de la chasteté
de Sappho, ne manquait pas de le jeter l'expression $\grave{\epsilon}s \ \sigma\grave{\alpha}\nu \ \varphi\iota\lambda\acute{o}\tau\alpha$
en assimilant $\varphi\iota\lambda\acute{o}\tau\alpha s$ à $\varphi\iota\lambda\acute{\iota}\alpha$. Dans la bouche d'Aphrodite, à vrai
dire, on attend plutôt le sens fort propre à l'homérisme $\varphi\iota\lambda\acute{o}\tau\eta\tau\iota \ \kappa\alpha\grave{\iota}$
$\epsilon\grave{\upsilon}\nu\hat{\eta}$, surtout s'il faut entendre avec A. Privitera $\grave{\epsilon}s \ \varphi\iota\lambda\acute{o}\tau\acute{\alpha} \ \sigma\upsilon$,[40]
bien qu'Homère connaisse aussi le sens faible et que les autres
exemples de $\varphi\iota\lambda\acute{o}\tau\alpha s$ et de $\varphi\acute{\iota}\lambda\eta\mu\mu\iota$ chez Sappho permettent les deux
interprétations, comme l'a montré Page dans le commentaire de ce
passage. La question qui se pose est cependant moins celle du sens
précis de l'expression que de savoir si elle est compatible avec une

[39] J'ai introduit une conjecture nouvelle (sauf erreur) au vers 19, $\lambda\hat{\alpha}\iota\sigma(\iota)$ (= $\theta\acute{\epsilon}\lambda\epsilon\iota s$)
$\check{\alpha}\gamma\eta\nu \ \grave{\epsilon}s \ \sigma\acute{\alpha}\nu$, qu'il faut brièvement justifier. Les manuscrits de Denys d'Halicarnasse
hésitent entre $\mu\alpha\iota \ \sigma\alpha\gamma\eta\nu\epsilon\sigma\sigma\alpha\nu$ (avec une correction $\beta\alpha\iota$ pour $\mu\alpha\iota$) et $\kappa\alpha\iota$ (ou $\kappa\alpha\grave{\iota}$)
$\sigma\alpha\gamma\eta\nu\epsilon\sigma\sigma\alpha\nu$. Le papyrus, affirment ses éditeurs, présenterait $.]\psi\sigma\check{\alpha}\gamma\eta\nu[$, avec l'alternative
d'un φ au lieu d'un ψ, ce qui conduit à $\check{\alpha}]\psi \ \sigma' \ \check{\alpha}\gamma\eta\nu[$, leçon évidemment corrompue. En
réalité, comme je l'ai déjà indiqué dans un compte-rendu des *Poetarum Lesbiorum
Fragmenta* paru dans *L'Antiquité classique* 24 (1955), 468, la photographie comporte sans
doute possible l'éventualité d'un α, peut-être surmonté d'un trait horizontal. On s'en
convaincra en constatant que l'oblique de cette lettre a la même hauteur que celle de
l'α de $\alpha\gamma\eta\nu$, qu'elle lui est rigoureusement parallèle et qu'elle accuse la même légère
incurvation. Le trait horizontal, dont les éditeurs omettent de faire mention et qui n'est
effectivement pas certain, marquerait la longueur de la voyelle; il ne peut convenir à une
consonne. Je lis donc $.]\bar{\alpha}c$. De leur côté, les variations du texte de Denys procèdent de la
confusion classique entre les signes de la série $\beta\kappa\mu$, qui embrasse encore, comme on sait,
les lettres λ et ν. On dispose donc à chances rigoureusement égales des cinq possibilités
$\beta\alpha, \ \kappa\alpha, \ \lambda\alpha, \ \mu\alpha, \ \nu\alpha$, toutes compatibles avec le témoignage du papyrus. J'ai écarté $\mu\hat{\alpha}\iota\sigma'$,
avec Lobel et Page, parce que $\mu\alpha\hat{\iota}\mu\iota$ n'est pas attesté à côté de $\mu\acute{\alpha}o\mu\alpha\iota$ et n'ai pas retenu
$\check{\alpha}\psi$ parce qu'il ne fait pas sens et diffère trop des leçons de Denys. $\Lambda\hat{\alpha}\iota\sigma'$, forme d'un $\lambda\alpha\hat{\iota}\mu\iota$
non attesté, est à $\lambda\hat{\omega} \ \lambda\hat{\eta}s$ (voir *LSJ* sous $\lambda\hat{\omega}$) comme $\gamma\acute{\epsilon}\lambda\alpha\iota\sigma'$ (de $\gamma\acute{\epsilon}\lambda\alpha\iota\mu\iota$) à $\gamma\epsilon\lambda\hat{\omega} \ \gamma\epsilon\lambda\hat{\alpha}s$, mais
$\lambda\hat{\alpha}s$ éolien à partir de *$\lambda\acute{\alpha}\omega$ paraît également recevable. $\Lambda\alpha\iota\delta\rho\acute{o}s$ atteste le thème $\lambda\alpha$- malgré
d'autres explications possibles (*LSJ* signale $\lambda\epsilon\iota$-, stade antérieur de $\lambda\eta$- dorien selon E.
Schwyzer, *Gr. Grammatik* 1, 676; M. Lejeune, *Traité de phonétique grecque*, (Paris 1947),
136, et P. Chantraine, *Morphologie historique du grec*² (Paris 1961), 11, s'en tiennent à
wlē-, proposé par W. Prellwitz, *Etymologisches Wörterbuch der gr. Sprache*² (Göttingen 1905),
268). Outre Hesych. †$\lambda\acute{\alpha}\eta\tau\alpha\iota\cdot \ \beta\omicron\acute{\upsilon}\lambda\eta\tau\alpha\iota$, ambigu, et $\lambda\hat{\omega}\sigma\alpha\cdot \ \theta\acute{\epsilon}\lambda\omicron\upsilon\sigma\alpha$, Philoxène d'Alexandrie
atteste $\lambda\hat{\omega} \ \lambda\acute{\alpha}\sigma\omega$ (Orion, *Etym.* 95, 12; cf. H. Kleist, *De Philoxeni Grammatici Alexandrini
studiis etymologicis* (Greifswald 1865), 54 sq.).

[40] *Quaderni Urbinati* 4 (1967), 39.

signification encomiastique des poèmes érotiques. Car si l'on doit admettre qu'ils ne veulent exprimer que des sentiments d'admiration, sincères ou conventionnels, dans les relations qui unissent Sappho à ses élèves, comment faire place à des sentiments d'amour au sein des mêmes relations et comprendre que la poétesse puisse demander ici à Aphrodite de "livrer à son amour" une jeune fille qui la fuit?

La difficulté se résout, à mon sens, quand on considère que Sappho parle ici en prêtresse d'Aphrodite. En effet, cette qualité lui donne le droit de demander à cette déesse plutôt qu'à toute autre l'aide désirée et déjà plus d'une fois requise (5 αἴ ποτα κἀτέρωτα), à savoir de lui assurer l'attachement d'une élève. À son tour, l'évocation d'Aphrodite, puis de Péitho, appelle l'usage de termes appropriés, et c'est ainsi qu'il n'y a pas à s'étonner de voir appeler amour et même ressentir sous forme d'amour la fidélité de l'une d'elles. Les lois ordinaires de l'amour, feint ou réel, sentimental ou charnel, régissant en principe les rapports des jeunes filles qui fréquentaient sa maison, les sentiments amoureux nourrissent une part importante du vocabulaire de Sappho, ainsi que l'a montré G. Lanata dans un article récent qui en augmente considérablement le lexique jusqu'alors reconnu.[41] Mais il n'en résulte pas nécessairement que le langage emprunté à cette source conserve en toute occasion sa destination première. De même que le vocabulaire religieux a fourni de tout temps au style élevé des termes choisis pour leur noblesse ou leur gravité et non pour leur signification propre, de même il faut admettre que le langage de l'amour se prêtait à la louange poétique en raison de son pouvoir affectif et non à cause de ce qu'il exprimait. La transposition, au reste, ne s'est pas opérée au seul niveau du langage: elle est impliquée par nature dans le processus psychologique qui lie la beauté au désir, l'admiration à l'amour, l'éloge aux assiduités. Loin donc de contredire l'intention encomiastique des propos amoureux, le contexte sentimental la rattache, dans

[41] "Sul linguaggio amoroso di Saffo," *Quaderni Urbinati* 2 (1966), 63–79. Précisons qu'en concluant à l'existence d'un διδασκαλεῖον de Sappho je rejette autant l'idée du *Mädchenbund* défendue avec enthousiasme par R. Merkelbach, *Philol.* 101 (1957), 1–29, que le scepticisme radical de Page, *Sappho and Alcaeus*, 139: "We have found, and shall find, no trace of any formal or official or professional relationship between them: no trace of Sappho the priestess, Sappho the president of a cult-association, Sappho the principal of an academy...."

le cas de Sappho, à un ensemble d'émotions qui en accroissent la ferveur par une sorte d'ambivalence. La louange n'en demeure pas moins l'unique raison de ces propos dans les poèmes réputés érotiques, tandis que le sentiment se situe, si je puis dire, à l'échelon des épiphénomènes. Dans ces conditions, le lien que les philologues ont toujours établi entre les moeurs de Sappho et sa poésie, sans se rendre compte qu'ils n'en pouvaient faire qu'un postulat, s'atténue au point de disparaître : ce n'est plus dans les fragments érotiques de son oeuvre qu'il faudra désormais chercher la solution du problème saphique, à supposer même que ce problème subsiste en dehors d'eux.

* * *

Comparés aux poèmes similaires d'Ibycos et de Pindare, les ἐγκώμια de Sappho, ou plutôt les parties encomiastiques de ses odes, n'accusent de différence marquante que sur le point que je viens de mettre en évidence : un certain accent de tendresse. L'exception est-elle unique et découle-t-elle seulement d'une activité poétique et musicale accomplie sous les auspices d'Aphrodite ? On est d'abord tenté de répondre affirmativement, car l'antiquité ne fournit pas d'exemple analogue et n'atteste pas non plus que se soient trouvées réunies en une autre occasion les conditions qui l'ont permise à Mitylène. Je me risque pourtant après mûre réflexion à supposer une légère ambivalence du même genre dans les parthénées d'Alcman, due pour une part à la sentimentalité inhérente à toute collectivité de jeunes filles—cet argument de psychologie élémentaire vaut naturellement aussi pour Sappho et son entourage—et pour le reste à un climat érotique inséparable de l'éducation spartiate, donc imposé dans une certaine mesure au poète comme un élément des chants qu'il avait à composer. C'est sur cette hypothèse, à peine vérifiée par les textes actuellement connus, que je voudrais conclure la partie descriptive de cette étude, parce qu'elle est susceptible d'éclairer l'origine du motif littéraire dont j'ai cherché à cerner l'existence.

Me permettra-t-on, à partir de ce résultat, une conjecture sur les modèles éventuels d'Alcman ? L'éducation spartiate, on le sait, incluait les rapports charnels dans son système. Ce que les historiens antiques unanimes rapportent de l'homosexualité masculine, Plutarque l'affirme formellement des relations des matrones avec

les adolescentes.[42] Vestiges de rites d'initiation sexuelle, habitudes
liées à la cohabitation, effets naturels d'une stricte séparation des
sexes, ou tout cela cumulé, ces pratiques apparemment courantes et
nullement secrètes puisqu'on les avait plus ou moins codifiées
devaient entretenir en permanence ou à tout le moins développer
dans certaines occasions une ambiance d'érotisme qui suffit largement à expliquer l'audace verbale des parthénées analysés au commencement de notre recherche. Y a-t-il lieu de remonter au delà
de ce stade, où l'amour ne fournit plus à la louange que son langage
et à travers ce langage sa chaleur, jusqu'à une époque primitive dans
laquelle on devrait imaginer au contraire une poésie érotique par
intention et louangeuse par corollaire? Soucieux de trouver des
précurseurs à Ibycos, Welcker avait suivi ce chemin et proposait à
pareille fin les poètes de Chalcis d'Eubée, métropole de Rhégion, sa
ville natale, en alléguant un chant choral contemporain de la guerre
de Lélante en l'honneur de Cléomaque, tombé sous les coups des
Erétriens pour avoir voulu prouver sa bravoure à son éromène.[43]
Comme il désirait surtout démontrer l'ancienneté de la poésie à
sujet amoureux, cette preuve suffisait à la rigueur à son dessein. Mais
elle ne saurait servir ici, car les vers que cite Aristote, version
approximative d'un scolie archaïque de facture savante, s'ils sont en
effet une invite à l'amour et s'ils font mention de traditions pédéras-
tiques d'une haute antiquité, célèbrent les plaisirs d'Eros comme les
chansons à boire célèbrent ceux du vin et ne préfigurent ni l'éloge à
prétexte érotique, ni la déclaration amoureuse (*carm. pop.* 27):

ὦ παῖδες ὅσοι Χαρίτων τε καὶ πατέρων λάχετ' ἐσθλῶν
μὴ φθονεῖθ' ὥρας ἀγαθοῖσιν ὁμιλεῖν·
σὺν γὰρ ἀνδρείᾳ καὶ ὁ λυσιμελὴς
Ἔρως ἐνὶ Χαλκιδέων θάλλει πόλεσιν.

L'origine de l'ἐγκώμιον érotique échappe donc à notre connaissance. À cause du rôle qu'il joue dans la poésie d'Alcman, cependant,

---

[42] Voir la note 13.

[43] Plut. *amat.* 17, probablement d'après Ephore, qui démontrait par cette anecdote et
le témoignage du chant cité l'origine de la pédérastie chevaleresque à Chalcis. Aristote,
l'autre témoin, sans récuser cette interprétation, écarte le nom de Cléomaque et renchérit
sur le motif amoureux en relatant que l'éromène avait lui-même envoyé son amant au
combat (frg. 98 Rose).

il ne sera pas téméraire d'émettre l'hypothèse qu'il est apparu dans le lyrisme choral spartiate à l'occasion des grandes fêtes d'initiation éphébique. Muette sur ce sujet en ce qui concerne Terpandre, "fondateur" des Carnéennes en 676 ou plutôt premier vainqueur attesté du concours musical qui s'y déroulait, la tradition livre de frêles indices touchant Thalétas de Gortyne et Polymnestos de Colophon, tous deux associés à l'institution plus récente des Gymno-pédies en 665.[44] De Thalétas, en effet, d'une part Ephore relate sur la foi d'une légende crétoise qu'il avait enseigné à Lycurgue les lois de Sparte, après quoi il cite comme particulièrement remarquables le régime des ἀγέλαι et les épreuves initiatiques, d'autre part l'historien laconien Sosibios atteste qu'on chantait ses poèmes avec ceux d'Alcman aux Gymnopédies: ajoutés l'un à l'autre, ces deux témoignages recréent les conditions d'érotisme juvénile dans lequel a pu—ce n'est qu'un possible!—s'élaborer la poésie dont Alcman s'inspire.[45] De Polymnestos, dont Alcman, frg. 145, évoquait le nom quelque part, on sait par Cratinos, frg. 305 Kock, et par Aristophane, *Eq.* 1287, que ses poèmes les plus connus, les Πολυμνήστεια, étaient des poèmes érotiques et que Pindare les citait élogieusement (frg.

---

[44] Contrairement à Brelich, *op. cit.* 186 sq., qui attribue à ces deux poètes la réglementa-tion de ces fêtes, je tiens que les historiens antiques n'ont connu que leur qualité de musiciens vainqueurs de concours par les documents à leur disposition, témoignages de poètes archaïques et listes de vainqueurs, et qu'ils en ont imprudemment conclu à leur participation dans l'organisation des jeux. Sur Terpandre, les deux témoignages à juxtaposer sont Hellanic. 4 F 85ᵃ Jacoby Τὰ Κάρνεια πρῶτος πάντων Τέρπανδρος νικᾷ (tiré des Καρνεονῖκαι οἱ καταλογάδην), et Ps. Plut., *de mus.* 9 Ἡ μὲν οὖν πρώτη κατάστασις τῶν περὶ τὴν μουσικὴν ἐν τῇ Σπάρτῃ Τερπάνδρου καταστήσαντος γεγένηται (tiré de Glaucos de Rhégion ou d'Héraclide de Pont). Sur Thalétas et Polymnestos, on n'a que la suite du second témoignage: Τῆς δὲ δευτέρας Θαλήτας τε ὁ Γορτύνιος καὶ Ξενόδαμος ὁ Κυθήριος καὶ Ξενόκριτος ὁ Λοκρὸς καὶ Πολύμνηστος ὁ Κολοφώνιος καὶ Σακάδας ὁ Ἀργεῖος μάλιστα αἰτίαν ἔχουσιν ἡγεμόνες γενέσθαι· τούτων γὰρ εἰσηγησαμένων τὰ περὶ τὰς Γυμνοπαιδίας τὰς ἐν Λακεδαίμονι λέγεται κατασταθῆναι, τὰ περὶ τὰς Ἀποδείξεις τὰς ἐν Ἀρκαδίᾳ, τῶν τε ἐν Ἄργει τὰ Ἐνδυμάτια καλούμενα, et Paus. I 14, 4 Θάλητα δὲ εἶναί φησι Γορτύνιον Πολύμναστος Κολο-φώνιος ἔπη Λακεδαιμονίοις ἐς αὐτὸν ποιήσας. Le mot κατάστασις, que Brelich traduit abusive-ment par *riforma*, désigne l'institution de la fête, sans plus, la première étant celle des Carnéennes, la seconde celle des Gymnopédies. Il est impensable, dans le second cas, que la tradition ait retenu les noms de plusieurs musiciens ayant élaboré ensemble le rè-glement: ou ils figuraient sur des listes de vainqueurs, ce que j'hésite à croire en l'absence de témoignages sur des listes propres aux concours énumérés, ou plutôt ce qu'on savait de leur oeuvre s'accordait avec telle ou telle fête, probablement mentionnée dans leur texte même.

[45] Ephore 70 F 149 §§ 19-21 (cf. Arstt. *pol.* 2, 1274 a 29), Sosibios 595 F 5 Jacoby.

218 Turyn = frg. 188 Snell). Si ces échos extrêmement vagues n'apportent aucune confirmation à la thèse que j'ai tenté de démontrer au cours de cette étude, ils aident du moins à la replacer dans un cadre historique adéquat et permettent ainsi d'en achever l'exposé sur une incertitude limitée.

Lausanne, 2 juillet 1970

ΔΙΟΡΘΩΣΑΙ ΛΟΓΟΝ:

LA SEPTIÈME OLYMPIQUE

JEAN DEFRADAS

Quand on relit les travaux des philologues qui, depuis un siècle et demi, se sont efforcés d'éclairer le sens des Odes pindariques, on reste étonné souvent de la manière fausse dont certains problèmes ont été posés. Que Boeckh et ses disciples aient cherché à y trouver une unité de composition à tout prix ne pouvait manquer de susciter la contradiction de ceux qui, comme Drachmann, en soulignaient au contraire le caractère désordonné.[1] Assurément, les uns comme les autres se représentent mal la réalité de la création poétique qui est sans doute inconcevable sans la liberté de l'inspiration, mais où ne peut pas ne pas s'imposer la personnalité d'un poète dont l'idéal religieux, moral et esthétique est partout présent. Que la Septième Olympique, ode adressée à Diagoras de Rhodes, ait pu être prise comme modèle d'un poème où il serait vain de chercher une quelconque unité[2] montre bien la fausseté du problème que se posaient alors les philologues: il n'est peut-être pas d'ode qui comporte une plus nette unité objective:[3] d'un bout à l'autre, elle est exclusivement rhodienne puisque, pour célébrer un vainqueur rhodien, le poète ne chante que des mythes rhodiens. Mais cette unité objective indéniable recouvre une "unité subjective" qui n'a peut-être pas toujours été reconnue: faut-il admettre, avec H. Jurenka, qu'il n'y a, entre les épisodes de ce mythe rhodien, aucune unité possible, ou ne faut-il pas se demander si une critique qui aboutit à cette conclusion ne repose pas sur une interprétation défectueuse?

[1] Cf. W. Schadewaldt, *Der Aufbau des pindarischen Epinikion* (Halle 1928), et le compte-rendu de H. Fraenkel, dans *Wege und Formen frühgriechischen Denkens* (2e éd., München 1960), 350–69.

[2] Par H. Jurenka, "Pindars Diagoras-Lied und seine Erklärer," *Wiener Studien* 17 (1899), 180–96.

[3] Pour reprendre une expression de G. Hermann, citée par H. Fraenkel, *op. cit.* 351.

Il va de soi que, si nous cherchons le sens d'un poème de Pindare, c'est que nous y voyons autre chose qu'une oeuvre de circonstance, adressée à un boxeur que nous imaginerions comme un être brutal et inculte, incapable de comprendre une poésie savante et élevée. Il est bien difficile d'admettre que les Anciens et les Modernes se soient aussi profondément trompés en y trouvant tant de beauté et de profondeur, si, comme l'affirme l'auteur d'un livre récent,[4] les milieux athlétiques de l'antiquité étaient vraiment aussi impénétrables à ce genre de poésie que le seraient les milieux sportifs d'aujourd' hui. Une telle vision des choses mérite à peine d'être signalée: les essais d'interprétation de l'oeuvre de Pindare ont abouti à des résultats assez cohérents pour lui apporter une réfutation définitive et la reléguer au niveau du paradoxe. Si la majorité des interprètes cherchent un sens profond dans les Odes, certains, trop fidèles peut-être à la lettre d'une des expressions (*Olymp.* 2, 84) du poète, y voient une poésie ésotérique, qui s'adresserait à des initiés, et à des initiés au sens religieux du terme, qu'ils aient participé aux céré-monies éleusiniennes ou qu'ils soient affiliés à des sectes orphico-pythagoriciennes. J'ai dit ailleurs[5] pourquoi il me paraissait inutile et dangereux de chercher dans la poésie pindarique ce sens caché et l'explication de la Septième Olympique que je propose ici s'insère dans une recherche qui s'efforce de rattacher avec précision le poète thébain à la religion d'Apollon Pythien et aux doctrines qui s'éla-boraient dans l'entourage de l'oracle de Delphes.[6]

* * *

La belle image de la phiale, cette coupe d'apparat que les con-vives se passent de l'un à l'autre dans le banquet de fiançailles, et à laquelle le poète compare l'ode dans laquelle il verse le nectar de son éloge, a été remarquablement commentée par C. M. Bowra[7] qui en a bien débrouillé l'admirable richesse. Soulignant le caractère somptueux de cet objet d'or, il évoque à son propos une offrande des

[4] Elroy L. Bundy, *Studia Pindarica, I* (Berkeley and Los Angeles 1962). Voir mon compte-rendu, *Rev. Ét. Grecques,* 76 (1963), 197 sqq.

[5] *Rev. Ét. Grecques,* 70 (1957), 224–34, et, dans un article sur la II° Olympique, *ibid.* 84 (1971), 131–43.

[6] *Les thèmes de la propagande delphique* (Paris 1954), 176–81, et "Pindare, poète delphique," *L'Information littéraire* 21 (1969), 127–34.

[7] *Pindar* (Oxford 1964), 24 sqq.

Cypsélides. Je pense que ce mot φιάλαν, chargé de sens, mis à la place d'honneur, au début de l'ode,—et l'on sait l'importance de ce coup d'archet initial—, a peut-être, dans le cérémonie rhodienne en l'honneur de Diagoras, une résonance particulière. Une inscription célèbre[8] nous a conservé un inventaire des offrandes déposées dans le sanctuaire d'Athéna à Lindos, ville dont Diagoras était citoyen et où se célébrait la fête en l'honneur de sa victoire. Or une des premières et des plus vénérables de ces offrandes était justement une phiale d'or offerte par Tlépolème, le héros fondateur auquel Pindare va consacrer la première partie de son mythe: Τλαπολεμος φιαλαν εφ ας επεγεγραπτο Τλαπολεμος Αθαναι Πολιαδι και Δι Πολιει.

Trois autres passages de Pindare citent des phiales d'or, et chaque fois une valeur exceptionnelle leur est conférée. Dans la 4ᵉ Pythique (193), le devin Mopsos prend en mains une phiale d'or pour invoquer Zeus; dans la Première Isthmique (20) des phiales d'or sont comptées, avec des chaudrons et des trépieds, au nombre des trésors accumulés par des athlètes victorieux; dans la 6ᵉ Isthmique (40) une phiale d'or est offerte à Héraclès par le héros Télamon. Ces rapprochements soulignent combien la phiale d'or est un objet particulièrement précieux, et l'on comprendra mieux sa présence au début de l'ode rhodienne si l'on se souvient de la phiale d'or offerte par Tlépolème à Athéna Lindia.

La correspondance entre les deux termes de la comparaison permet encore de préciser le sens d'une expression qui me paraît avoir été mal comprise. Il est remarquable, dans cette ode, que le troisième vers du système strophique soit d'une brièveté assez rare, composé d'un seul élément rhythmique, qu'on l'appelle un épitrite ou une dipodie iambique. Il semble que l'on puisse affirmer que le poète a utilisé de façon intentionnelle, pour mettre en valeur chaque fois un mot essentiel, ce vers court et détaché: d'un bout à l'autre de l'ode, on constatera que ce troisième vers n'est jamais indifférent. Entre la 1ᵉ strophe et la 1ᵉ antistrophe, la correspondance entre δωρήσεται et ἱλάσκομαι ne saurait être due au hasard et l'équivalence sémantique s'ajoute à un écho phonétique. Au présent solennel que développe la strophe répond l'offrande de gloire accordée au vain-

---

[8] Voir Ch. Blinkenberg, *Lindos, Fouilles de l'acropole, Inscriptions*, t. I (Berlin et Copenhague 1941), 148-99.

queur par le poète. Il est donc inutile de supposer, avec H. Fraenkel,[9] un complément sous-entendu à ἱλάσκομαι, et de comprendre:
"demander aux dieux leur faveur pour les vainqueurs." Il n'est pas
moins faux d'admettre, avec les scholiastes, une confusion entre
ἵλαος et ἱλαρός, pour interpréter ἱλαροὺς ποιῶ, c'est-à-dire "ré-
jouir." Le mieux est de conserver à ἱλάσκομαι la valeur religieuse
qu'il a, lorsqu'il a pour complément le nom d'une divinité: "chercher à se rendre favorable," mais d'admettre qu'il a ici pour complément les vainqueurs des grands jeux, auxquels le poète confère une
part d'immortalité en leur offrant le nectar de ses vers.

Ces deux remarques liminaires sur le prélude de l'ode soulignent
suffisamment l'élévation du ton, l'ambiance religieuse dont Pindare
enveloppe l'hommage qu'il va rendre au boxeur Diagoras, et, à
travers lui, à la cité rhodienne dont il est l'une des gloires les plus
brillantes. La récitation de l'ode se présente comme la célébration
d'un rite et le poète est comme le prêtre de cette χάρις Ζωθάλμιος qui
accorde aux vainqueurs une récompense d'où leur vitalité sort
réchauffée et accrue.[10]

* * *

La mention de l'île de Rhodes, "l'île aux trois villes, proche de
l'éperon formé par l'Asie aux vastes territoires" (18 sq.), permet au
poète, selon un procédé qui lui est habituel, d'introduire, grâce à
une transition fournie par un simple complément, Ἀργείᾳ σὺν
αἰχμᾷ, le mythe qui occupe le centre de l'ode et qui rappelle l'histoire mythique de l'île du Soleil. Cet hymne s'articule en trois
épisodes, qui remontent le cours du temps: après le rappel de
l'installation à Rhodes des colons conduits par Tlépolème, vient le
récit de la fondation du culte d'Athéna Lindienne, suivi de l'attribution de Rhodes au Soleil, à l'origine du partage du monde. Ce
serait peut-être déjà un principe suffisant d'unité que Pindare ait
choisi trois moments de l'histoire légendaire de Rhodes pour composer son mythe. Les commentateurs ont cherché des raisons plus
profondes pour justifier cette unité et ils ont constaté que tous les

[9] *Op. cit.* 359. Sens adopté par W. J. Slater, *Lexicon to Pindar* (Berlin 1969), s.v.
ἱλάσκομαι.

[10] Tel paraît, d'après l'étymologie, le sens de cet adjectif, à rapprocher, peut-être, de
φυτάλμιος.

épisodes "ont ce caractère commun qu'ils ont pour matière une faute—grave ou légère—qui amène des conséquences heureuses." [11] H. Jurenka n'a peut-être pas tort (voir note 2) de souligner ce qu'il y a de superficiel dans cet essai d'unification, les fautes et leurs résultats étant chaque fois très différents.

À ce rapprochement extérieur et formel, il faut s'efforcer de substituer une interprétation plus attentive de l'ensemble qui permette de déceler des correspondances plus profondes entre les épisodes du mythe et l'on peut y parvenir en examinant de plus près sa structure d'ensemble qui est extrêmement soignée: on s'apercevra que les parties ne sont pas liées cette fois, selon le procédé cher à Pindare, par de simples associations verbales, mais que chaque scène est encadrée de maximes qui en marquent les limites et aident à en saisir la signification. Une analyse minutieuse de ces formules d'introduction et de conclusion, jointe à l'étude de chaque épisode, permettra d'éclairer le sens du mythe.

Mais une remarque préalable s'impose et il ne semble pas qu'on lui ait accordé une attention suffisante. Quand il aborde le récit mythique, Pindare affirme son intention de raconter l'histoire de Rhodes en la "redressant." Car c'est bien le sens du verbe διορθῶσαι (21), rendu de façon insuffisante par A. Puech, "expliquer exactement." C. M. Bowra va jusqu'à dire (voir note 7) que Pindare ne cherche pas à déguiser les faits ni à altérer le récit, négligeant ainsi complètement l'expression διορθῶσαι λόγον. [12] On est en droit de s'étonner que les dictionnaires offrent, du mot διορθῶσαι, un sens valable seulement pour ce passage: "diriger dans la droite voie" (Bailly); "*tell* my tale *aright*" (*LSJ*), alors que tous les autres exemples du verbe et des mots de la même famille expriment l'idée de "remettre droit," "remettre dans le droit chemin," "redresser," "set right," "restore to order."

Les interprétations des scholiastes manquent de netteté, et l'un d'eux a dû orienter les interprétations des modernes, en donnant comme équivalente la paraphrase suivante: διορθῶσαι λόγον, τουτέστιν ἀκριβῶσαι καὶ διασημῆναι. Mais un autre était peut-être plus près du sens en ajoutant: βούλεται δὲ τῆς τοῦ Τληπολέμου φυγῆς ὑπεραπολογήσασθαι. J'ajouterai seulement que Pindare n'a pas seulement "re-

---

[11] A. Puech, éd. des Olympiques (Paris 1922), 90. Cf. Bowra, *op. cit.*, 301 sq.
[12] C'est le seul exemple du mot chez Pindare.

dressé" son récit pour "défendre" Tlépolème: le "redressement"
opéré par Pindare s'applique aux trois épisodes du mythe et nous
devons en chercher le sens chaque fois.

Il n'y a pas lieu de s'étonner que Pindare se propose de "redresser" un mythe: les exemples abondent, dans son oeuvre, de ces
interprétations personnelles, qu'il substitue aux versions tradition-
nelles, pour donner une idée plus morale du comportement des dieux
et des héros. L'une de ces prises de position les plus nettes et dont il
se justifie de la manière la plus explicite est celle qu'il adopte dans
la Première Olympique, quand il substitue à la légende courante
de Pélops, offert en festin par son père Tantale aux dieux qu'il
recevait, une explication nouvelle qui lui permet d'absoudre les
dieux de l'accusation de gloutonnerie. La 6e Olympique montre
aussi, dans la légende de la naissance et de l'investiture du devin
Iamos, la combinaison de deux versions surajoutées l'une à l'autre
qui justifie l'attribution à l'Apollon de Delphes d'un patronage sur
l'oracle institué à Olympie.[13] J'ai relevé ailleurs [14] d'autres exemples
de ce souci réformateur de Pindare: quand une légende présente les
dieux sous un mauvais jour, il n'hésite pas à la modifier; quand il a
le choix entre plusieurs versions d'une légende, comme dans le récit
de l'expédition des Argonautes, il choisit celle qui a dû être influen-
cée par les milieux delphiques, et qui attribue à Apollon Pythien un
rôle prépondérant.

S'il a dans cet esprit modifié et "redressé" les légendes rhodiennes,
il nous reste à chercher de quelle manière il l'a fait et quelle intention
le guidait. Les indications qu'il nous donne nous permettent de
saisir les points sur lesquels il a modifié la tradition et il nous est
possible, parfois, de le vérifier par d'autres témoignages. L'esprit
dans lequel il a introduit ces modifications pourra peut-être se révéler
dans les maximes qui ponctuent son récit comme un véritable
commentaire moral.

* * *

Dans un premier épisode, Pindare rappelle comment Tlépolème,
le héros fondateur de Rhodes, à la suite d'un crime commis contre
son oncle Licymnios, s'est exilé du pays d'Argos pour fonder une

---

[13] Cf. H. W. Parke, *The Oracles of Zeus, Dodona, Olympia, Ammon* (Oxford 1967).
[14] Art. cité (*supra* n. 6), 130 sqq.

colonie à Rhodes. Le récit est introduit par les considérations morales suivantes:

$$\dot{a}\mu\phi\grave{\iota}\ \delta'\ \dot{a}\nu\theta\rho\acute{\omega}\pi\omega\nu\ \phi\rho\alpha\sigma\grave{\iota}\nu\ \dot{a}\mu\pi\lambda\alpha\kappa\acute{\iota}\alpha\iota$$
$$\dot{a}\nu\alpha\rho\acute{\iota}\theta\mu\eta\tau\omega\iota\ \kappa\rho\acute{\epsilon}\mu\alpha\nu\tau\alpha\iota\cdot\ \tauο\tildeυτο\ \delta'\ \dot{a}\mu\acute{a}\chi\alpha\nu\omega\nu\ \epsilon\dot{\upsilon}\rho\epsilon\tilde{\iota}\nu,$$
$$\dot{o}\tau\iota\ \nu\tilde{\upsilon}\nu\ \dot{\epsilon}\nu\ \kappa\alpha\grave{\iota}\ \tau\epsilon\lambda\epsilon\upsilon\tilde{\alpha}\ \phi\acute{\epsilon}\rho\tau\alpha\tau\omega\nu\ \dot{a}\nu\delta\rho\grave{\iota}\ \tau\upsilon\chi\epsilon\tilde{\iota}\nu\ (24\text{–}26).$$

Le premier de ces vers contient le mot $\dot{a}\mu\pi\lambda\alpha\kappa\acute{\iota}\alpha\iota$ qui désigne "une faute, un péché." Il désigne ailleurs les fautes d'Ixion, coupable d'avoir versé le sang d'un membre de sa race et d'avoir convoité l'épouse de Zeus (*Pyth.* 2, 30), la faute de Coronis qui trompe l'amour d'Apollon (*Pyth.* 3, 13), les fautes de Laomèdon que punit Héraclès (*Isthm.* 6, 29). C'est donc chaque fois une faute grave qui frappe un homme comme un coup de folie. Après le récit du meurtre commis par Tlépolème, une nouvelle formule fera écho à celle-ci:

$$\alpha\dot{\iota}\ \delta\grave{\epsilon}\ \phi\rho\epsilon\nu\tilde{\omega}\nu\ \tau\alpha\rho\alpha\chi\alpha\acute{\iota}$$
$$\pi\alpha\rho\acute{\epsilon}\pi\lambda\alpha\gamma\xi\alpha\nu\ \kappa\alpha\grave{\iota}\ \sigma\omega\phi\acute{o}\nu\ (31\text{–}32).$$

Le "trouble de l'esprit" répond à la faute commise sur un coup de folie: c'est assez dire que ces deux formules qui se complètent donnent une interprétation du crime de Tlépolème.

La formule d'introduction contient une autre idée: "Il est impossible de dire ce qui est le meilleur pour un homme, à la fois sur le moment et à la fin." On reconnaîtra, dans cette formule un peu énigmatique, une idée bien connue, dont la meilleure illustration se trouve dans l'entretien de Crésus et de Solon: tant qu'un homme n'a pas achevé sa vie, il est impossible d'affirmer qu'il est heureux. Cet apologue et sa moralité semblent bien avoir été élaborés sous l'influence des milieux delphiques.[15] Pindare en fera dans cette ode une application nouvelle en montrant que ce qui avait pu sembler mauvais peut, à l'occasion, se révéler bon dans ses conséquences.

L'épisode de Tlépolème assassin de Licymnios est déjà raconté par Homère dans le Catalogue des Vaisseaux (B, 658–670). "Tlépolème," raconte le poète, "l'illustre guerrier, qu' Astyochè a mis au monde pour le puissant Héraclès... n'était pas plus tôt devenu un homme, qu'il tuait l'oncle de son père, Licymnios, le rejeton d'Arès, déjà vieillissant. Bien vite alors il construisait des nefs, puis, rassemblant un fort parti, prenait le large et s'exilait, sous les

---

[15] Voir J. Defradas, *Les thèmes* (*supra*, n. 6), 208–28.

menaces des fils et des petits-fils du puissant Héraclès. Sa course errante ainsi le mène à Rhodes, à travers bien des peines" (trad. P. Mazon).

On voit que, dans le récit d'Homère, rien ne précise la manière dont Tlépolème a tué son oncle: mais le poète nous apprend que ses frères et ses neveux l'ont jugé coupable et contraint à l'exil. Aucune excuse n'est en effet donnée à son crime, et le grand âge de sa victime est sans doute une circonstance aggravante.

Si nous passons au récit de Pindare, nous voyons au contraire s'accumuler les circonstances atténuantes. D'abord Licymnios était peut-être bien le frère d'Alcmène, mais c'était un bâtard, νόθον, c'est-à-dire, sans doute, un fils d'esclave. Il l'a frappé de son bâton de bois d'olivier dur, σκληρᾶς ἐλαίας: si le bois avait été moins dur, l'accident ne se serait pas produit. L'expression suivante reste obscure: ἐλθόντα ἐκ θαλάμων Μιδεάς. Midéa désigne-t-elle la bourgade de Midéa, voisine de Tirynthe, ou une femme qu' aurait fréquentée Licymnios? Le pluriel θαλάμων désigne-t-il une maison ou une chambre à coucher? Les textes parallèles permettent ces diverses interprétations et rien ne nous permet de choisir.[16] Si le contexte, qui accumule les circonstances atténuantes en faveur de Tlépolème, devait nous guider, on pourrait faire l'hypothèse d'un crime provoqué par la jalousie, Tlépolème ayant surpris son oncle alors qu'il sortait de la chambre d'une femme nommée Midéa.[17] Mais aucune preuve certaine ne confirme cet essai d'interprétation romanesque.

La structure de la phrase semble conduire l'auditeur, de détail en détail, vers le plus important et il faut en souligner tout particulièrement la chute: τᾶσδέ ποτε χθονὸς οἰκιστὴρ χολωθείς. Après ce récit où chaque mot est lourd de sens, le titre de Tlépolème, le Fondateur de Rhodes, évoque tous les honneurs dont il est entouré et un dernier mot, isolé, dans une sécheresse dépouillée, vient expliquer la faute, l'égarement qui a frappé le criminel. Pour en apprécier la valeur, il faut savoir que la colère était, en cas de crime,

---

[16] Θάλαμοι au pluriel au sens de 'maison': *Olymp.* 5, 13; *Pyth.* 4, 160; frg. 221, 3 (Sn.³). Au sens de 'chambre à coucher', les exemples relevés par Slater sont tous au singulier; mais il y rattache celui-ci et *Pyth.* 2, 33, en précisant que le pluriel est mis pour le singulier.

[17] Dans la 10ᵉ *Ol.*, 66 Μιδέαθεν désigne évidemment la ville.—Mais les scholiastes, glosant sur le texte, hésitent et l'un d'eux prétend que Licymnios était fils d'Electryon et de Midéa, femme de race phrygienne.

considérée comme une circonstance atténuante parce qu'elle privait l'acte criminel de son caractère volontaire. Je n'en donnerai pour preuve qu'un texte des *Lois* de Platon (IX 866 d) sur les meurtres par colère, où une analyse subtile est faite de différents cas, montrant que certains meurtres non prémédités, commis par suite d'un accès subit de colère, sont assimilables à un meurtre involontaire. On sait que la législation des *Lois* de Platon n'est pas un système utopique, mais qu'il s'inspire de réalités contemporaines. On sait aussi quel rôle l'oracle de Delphes a pu jouer dans la distinction entre meurtre volontaire et meurtre involontaire; [18] on sait enfin quel respect montrait Platon à l'égard de la religion delphique et la place que tenait dans sa législation l'autorité de l'oracle. [19] On pourra en conclure que la place accordée ici par Pindare à la colère comme circonstance atténuante répond bien à ce que l'on peut attendre d'une interprétation delphique de la légende de Tlépolème.

Cette conclusion est immédiatement confirmée par la suite du récit. Victime d'un égarement momentané, le héros reste un σοφός. Et ce mot doit ici recouvrir deux de ses sens habituels, celui de l'"habileté," signifiant que Tlépolème sait ce qu'il faut faire en toute circonstance, et celui de "sagesse morale," puisqu'il prend l'attitude convenable à celui qui veut réparer une faute. Il va donc consulter l'oracle de Delphes. Inutile de rappeler que les héros de l'*Iliade* ne consultaient pas l'oracle de Delphes et que les consultations qu'on leur prête, à commencer par celle d'Agamemnon, sont des inventions tardives. [20] Celle de Tlépolème s'insère dans une série bien connue, celle des consultations préalables à la fondation d'une colonie, [21] qu'il est difficile de faire remonter au delà du VIIe siècle, mais qui révèle une des manifestations les mieux attestées et les plus constantes de l'oracle. Substituer à la version homérique, dans laquelle Tlépolème était contraint à l'exil par les parents de sa victime, une version d'après laquelle il est chargé par le dieu de Delphes d'une mission colonisatrice; substituer au coupable qui s'enfuit un fondateur glorieux que le dieu a su absoudre et purifier d'une faute

---

[18] Voir mon interprétation de l'*Orestie* dans *Les thèmes* (*supra*, n. 6), 160–204.

[19] En particulier, *Rép.* 427 b-c.

[20] Defradas, *Les thèmes*, 28–45.

[21] *Ibid.* 233–57. Ajouter H. W. Parke et D. E. W. Wormell, *The Delphic Oracle*, I (Oxford 1956), 49–81.

involontaire, c'était bien "redresser" le récit traditionnel, le moraliser aussi, puisque le héros fondateur n'était plus désormais considéré comme un coupable. Telle est l'interprétation nouvelle donnée par Pindare de ce premier épisode des légendes rhodiennes et cette innovation semble bien avoir été élaborée sous une influence delphique.

* * *

Le deuxième épisode du mythe est d'une structure complexe. Il se place au moment de la naissance d'Athéna, scène brièvement évoquée, pour situer dans un passé lointain l'événement qui prélude à la gloire et à la richesse de Rhodes. Le Soleil a ordonné à ses fils d'offrir les premiers un sacrifice à Zeus et à Athéna dès sa naissance, pour qu'elle accorde à leur île sa prédilection et y installe son premier sanctuaire. Ils montent bien à temps sur l'acropole pour fonder un autel, mais oublient le feu et doivent offrir un sacrifice sans feu, τεῦξαν δ' ἀπύροις ἱεροῖς (48). Le père et la fille ne leur ont pas tenu rigueur de leur oubli: Zeus fait tomber sur eux une abondante pluie d'or et Athéna leur donne une supériorité sur tous les autres hommes dans les arts.

Le sens de ce récit est en partie clair: c'est d'abord un mythe étiologique, destiné à expliquer la pratique de sacrifices sans feu dans le culte d'Athéna à Lindos. Ces offrandes qui n'étaient pas brûlées étaient sans doute aussi des offrandes non sanglantes, consistant en fruits et en gâteaux ou en graines de toute sorte, comme celles que l'on destinait aux divinités chtoniennes.[22] L'existence de tels rites permet de supposer sans doute qu'Athéna Lindienne a pris la succession d'une déesse primitive de la fécondité, divinité d'une religion agraire.

Mais ce qu'il importe de se demander, c'est si, sur ce point aussi, Pindare a cru devoir redresser un récit légendaire traditionnel. Or nous savons que l'oubli du feu, attribué aux Héliades par la légende, était destiné à expliquer la priorité obtenue par Athènes sur Rhodes: les Rhodiens, n'ayant pu offrir les premiers le sacrifice rituel à Athéna, avaient été devancés par les Athéniens, et c'est à Athènes que résidait effectivement la déesse.[23] L'interprétation de Pindare

[22] Cf. l'article ἄπυρα ἱερά (Stengel) dans la *RE*, 2¹, 292–93 (1895).
[23] Diodore V 56, 5.

est soulignée par la façon même dont il introduit l'épisode: il annonce dès le début la pluie d'or envoyée par Zeus (34), et après avoir raconté la naissance d'Athéna et l'institution du sacrifice sans feu, il y revient de façon plus explicite (49 sq.) et, ajoutant les privilèges accordés par Athéna, montre que cet oubli n'a pas eu de conséquences mauvaises.

Pourquoi Zeus et Athéna ont-ils, malgré leur oubli, comblé les Rhodiens de richesse et de gloire? C'est un fait auquel Pindare ne semble pas répondre clairement. C'est dans la maxime du vers 44 qu'il exprime le sens du mythe:

$$\grave{\epsilon}\nu \; \delta' \; \grave{\alpha}\rho\epsilon\tau\grave{\alpha}\nu \; \breve{\epsilon}\beta\alpha\lambda\epsilon\nu \; \kappa\alpha\grave{\iota} \; \chi\acute{\alpha}\rho\mu\alpha\tau' \; \grave{\alpha}\nu\theta\rho\acute{\omega}\pi o\iota\sigma\iota \; \pi\rho o\mu\alpha\theta\acute{\epsilon} o\varsigma \; \alpha\grave{\iota}\delta\acute{\omega}\varsigma.$$

Mais l'interprétation de cette maxime est discutée. Je pense qu'il faut d'abord écarter une explication qui remonte à Hermann et qui est admise par A. Puech, celle qui consiste à voir dans προμαθέος un nom propre désignant Prométhée. La note de Puech, fondant cette lecture sur une comparaison avec la 5ᵉ Pythique où est cité le nom d'Epiméthée, apporte, quoi qu'il en dise, une raison bien insuffisante. Si l'on pensait ici à Prométhée parce qu'il a donné le feu aux hommes, on comprendrait mal le mot αἰδώς et l'on croirait lire une énigme plutôt qu'une maxime morale. Il vaut mieux voir dans προμαθέος un adjectif substantivé au sens de προμήθεια, comme le suggèrent les scholiastes:[24] on comprendra alors προμαθέος αἰδώς comme "le respect de la prévoyance," dans lequel on verra la source de la vertu qui entraîne des joies pour les hommes. En donnant à ses fils le conseil qu'il vient de leur donner, le Soleil les engage à être prévoyants et cette prévoyance qui a été en fait la leur, leur a mérité joie et vertu.

On pourrait rapprocher la formule προμαθέος αἰδώς d'une maxime dont l'origine est inconnue, mais qui peut s'apparenter aux maximes delphiques. Sur une liste de cinquante-six maximes conservées par une inscription du IIIᵉ siècle av. J.-C., découverte dans le gymnase de Milétopolis,[25] on lit, à la 7ᵉ ligne de la 1ᵉ colonne: π]ρόνοιαν τ[ί]μ[α] qui correspond précisément à l'expression de

---

[24] On lit dans l'apparat critique d'A. Puech: "Sch. alia Promethea, alia τὸ προμαθές interpretantur." En fait on ne voit rien de tel dans les scholies qui, unanimement, parlent de προμήθεια ou de προμηθεῖσθαι.

[25] Dittenberger, *Sylloge³*, no. 1268. Cf. G. Mendel, *Bull. Corr. Hell.* 33 (1909), 402 sqq.

Pindare. Ces listes de maximes, dont on connaît d'autres exemples, contiennent souvent, parmi de nombreuses formules nouvelles, les trois célèbres maximes delphiques, et l'on a pu se demander si d'autres n'avaient pas été élaborées à Delphes, où l'on avait ajouté, à l'expression condensée d'une sagesse des nations, une signification plus profonde.

Si les fils du Soleil ont été récompensés par Zeus et Athéna, c'est donc sans doute qu'ils avaient satisfait en intention à cette maxime et qu'ils avaient tout préparé pour la fondation du culte de la déesse. C'est au dernier moment qu'un égarement de leur esprit leur a fait oublier le feu. Cet égarement, qui avait servi de circonstance atténuante au crime de Tlépolème, leur permet de recevoir les bienfaits des dieux. Que cet égarement soit souligné par le poète, il suffit, pour le prouver, de noter que le 3ᵉ vers de l'antistrophe 3, ἔξω φρενῶν, met en valeur un thème qui rappelle les ἀμπλακίαι et les φρενῶν ταραχαί. Ce rapprochement permet d'approfondir la parenté entre les deux épisodes du mythe : en modifiant comme il l'a fait ce second épisode, Pindare a tenu à montrer que les dieux n'étaient ni mesquins ni vindicatifs, que, à leurs yeux, tout résidait dans l'intention et qu'ils pardonnaient aisément un moment de distraction, comme ils pardonnaient l'égarement de la colère, même si elle était cause d'un crime.

* * *

Un dernier exemple d'une erreur, ou d'un oubli que l'on a d'abord pu considérer comme un dommage et qui aboutit en réalité à d'heureuses conséquences, constitue le troisième épisode du mythe rhodien. Remontant aux origines, le poète évoque le moment où les dieux se partagèrent le monde. Le Soleil, qui se trouvait absent, n'avait pas reçu de lot. Mais Rhodes n'avait pas encore surgi des profondeurs de la mer. Seul le Soleil avait pu l'apercevoir et, sans demander que l'on refît le tirage au sort, il l'avait revendiquée. Ainsi, avec l'agrément de Zeus il obtint comme épouse la nymphe Rhodes et leurs enfants devinrent les maîtres de l'île.

Quelles innovations Pindare a-t-il apportées à cette partie du mythe ? Il est bien difficile de la dire, puisque aucune autre version n'en est connue. Il faut donc le lire attentivement pour en déceler le sens exact. Le mythe peut comporter des éléments que l'on pourrait interpréter au désavantage des dieux: qu'ils aient pu oublier l'un d'entre eux dans le partage du monde; ou au désavantage de Rhodes, attribuée après coup, comme un lot qui aurait été laissé pour compte. Une dispute aurait pu surgir entre les dieux, exigeant une redistribution et un nouveau tirage au sort. En fait tout se règle à l'amiable, parce que le Soleil a vu de ses propres yeux l'île de Rhodes, encore attachée au fond de la mer et qui ne se montrait pas à la surface: εἶπέ τιν' αὐτὸς ὁρᾶν.... Mieux informé que tous les autres dieux, celui dont Homère disait qu'il voit tout et qu'il entend tout, n'a donc pas subi de dommage et il a obtenu le lot qu'il désirait en connaissance de cause.

Il y aurait lieu de s'étonner que ce dernier épisode ne soit pas, comme les deux autres, éclairé par des maximes qui en apporteraient le commentaire. D'après les interprétations courantes, le récit commence brusquement: φαντὶ δ'ἀνθρώπων παλαιαὶ ῥήσιες... (54 sq.). Mais on n'a pas suffisamment remarqué que le vers précédent,

$$\text{δαέντι δὲ καὶ σοφία}$$
$$\text{μείζων ἄδολος τελέθει,}$$

présente des difficultés insurmontables, si on le rattache, comme on le fait habituellement, à l'épisode précédent. A. Puech traduit: "L'art qu'engendre la science sait grandir, toujours plus beau, sans recourir à la fraude." Une note précise: "Le poète oppose cet art *innocent* à la magie suspecte que la légende attribuait aux Telchines." [26] On reste étonné de cette explication que rien ne vient appuyer dans le texte de Pindare. Dans les vers précédents le poète célèbre le talent des sculpteurs rhodiens dans des termes traditionnels, quand il dit de leurs statues qu'elles ressemblent non seulement à des êtres vivants, ζωοῖσιν, mais à des êtres qui marchent, ἑρπόντεσσί τε: il n'y a pas là d'allusion à une magie maléfique. La vraie conclusion était donnée dans la formule: ἦν δὲ κλέος βαθύ.

Les scholiastes, insistant sur le mot δαέντι, voient dans cette formule une opposition entre le don inspiré par la divinité et la science, qui augmente l'art des Rhodiens. Mais un mot manifestement les embarrasse, ἄδολος, qu'ils expliquent de façon diverse: ἄδολον, ὅ ἐστιν ἁπλῆν (BEQ), ἄδολος: ἡ φυσική (B^s1). Un autre

---

[26] Voir, dans le même sens, Bowra, *op. cit.* 339, qui rassemble les témoignages antiques sur l'activité des Telchines.

écrit: τῷ δὲ μετ' εὐφυίας μεμαθηκότι ἡ σοφία καὶ ἐπὶ τὸ μεῖζον ἀδόλως καὶ ἀνεμποδίστως ἐπαίρεται (BCDEQ). La juxtaposition de ἀδόλως et de ἀνεμποδίστως suggère pour ἄδολος une interprétation différente de celle qui est adoptée traditionnellement. On lui donne toujours un sens actif et l'on est bien embarrassé de l'expliquer. Mais on le comprendrait peut-être mieux si on lui donnait un sens passif, que la formation du mot n'interdit nullement. Tous les adjectifs de même structure—ἄλυπος par exemple—ont tantôt le sens actif, tantôt le sens passif. Si ἄδολος, qui ne se rencontre nulle part ailleurs chez Pindare, est toujours attesté au sens actif, rien n'empêche qu'il puisse avoir aussi le sens passif. Au lieu de "qui ne trompe pas," il peut très bien signifier : "qui ne se laisse pas tromper." Je suggère donc de traduire : "Pour celui qui connaît, sa sagesse plus grande ne se laisse pas tromper." Dès lors, au lieu d'une formule énigmatique et, de toute façon, inattendue, ce vers devient une introduction naturelle à l'épisode où nous voyons le Soleil, qui a failli être privé de son lot, obtenir l'un des plus beaux, parce que la connaissance qu'il en avait personnellement acquise lui a permis de faire réparer l'oubli dont il avait été victime. On comprend alors que le verbe δαέντι soit placé en tête d'un récit qui célèbre le triomphe de la connaissance.

Peut-être n'est-il pas indifférent de trouver cet éloge de la connaissance chez un poète qui est un fervent d'Apollon, le dieu omniscient de l'oracle, que personne ne peut tromper (*Pyth.* 3, 29 sq.) : "Il n'a aucun contact avec le mensonge et aucun dieu, aucun mortel ne peut lui dérober la vérité, ni en acte, ni en intention." C'est le même dieu qui, d'après Plutarque (*Moral.* 384 e), soumettait aux philosophes le célèbre E inscrit sur son temple, pour les inviter à la réflexion intellectuelle. Affirmer que celui qui sait verra grandir sa σοφία, que l'on prenne ce dernier mot au sens de l'habileté pratique ou de la sagesse sous toutes ses formes, n'est-ce pas une doctrine que l'on peut mettre en rapport avec celle de Socrate, celui que le dieu de Delphes considérait comme le plus sage de tous les hommes et d'après qui l'on ne faisait le mal que par ignorance ?

* * *

Les derniers mots du mythe, en revenant à Tlépolème, ramènent le poète à son sujet actuel, la glorification de la victoire de Diagoras, qui, parmi ses victoires, compte celles qu'il a remportées dans les jeux de Tlépolème, à Rhodes. Le début de la strophe 5 est le couronnement du mythe : Pindare, rappelant à la fois le crime commis par Tlépolème et son oeuvre de fondateur, proclame qu'il a reçu "une compensation[27] de son épreuve, instituée à Rhodes pour l'archégète des Tirynthiens, comme pour un dieu" et il désigne ainsi la procession et les jeux organisés en son honneur.

C'est bien à tort que les scholiastes, rejetant le témoignage de Pindare, prétendent que les jeux de Rhodes étaient organisés en l'honneur du Soleil et non de Tlépolème. Il est bien connu que, partout où il existait des jeux, ils remontaient à un rituel funéraire en l'honneur d'un héros, rituel dont le 23e chant de l'*Iliade* contient le prototype et qui était célébré à Olympie en l'honneur de Pélops et à Delphes peut-être en l'honneur de Python. Mais on peut encore citer le témoignage irréfutable de l'épigraphie : dans des inscriptions agonistiques qui, par leur forme ressemblent exactement à la dernière triade de cette ode, avec l'énumération des victoires obtenues aux différents jeux, on relève à plusieurs reprises la mention des Τλαπολέμεια parmi ceux que l'on célébrait à Rhodes.[28]

L'importance de ces honneurs attribués à Tlépolème est bien marquée par la formule qui le compare à un dieu, ὥσπερ θεῷ, formule qui emplit le 3e vers de la 5e strophe, à la place d'honneur. Le rôle de l'oracle de Delphes dans le développement des cultes héroïques est bien connu.[29] La colonie, conduite par un οἰκιστής ou un ἀρχηγέτης, accordait à l'homme qui l'avait conduite, investi par l'oracle, des honneurs héroïques et la cité nouvelle lui vouait désormais un culte dont l'organisation était décidée par le dieu de Delphes.[30]

* * *

On voit à quel point l'unité objective de la 7e Olympique est stricte. Non seulement tous les éléments du mythe sont empruntés

---

[27] Il faut noter ce mot λύτρον qui désigne habituellement la compensation payée par le criminel à la famille de sa victime. Ici c'est le criminel, définitivement absous, qui reçoit la compensation.

[28] P. ex. Dittenberger, *Syll.*[3], 1067. On relève aussi une allusion aux honneurs accordés aux ἀρχαγέταις et aux ἥρωσι, donc, entre autres, à Tlépolème, dans un traité entre Rhodes et Hiérapytna (*ibid.* 581).

[29] Cf. Parke et Wormell, *op. cit.* 340–61.

[30] Cf. Aristotélès-Battos à Cyrène : *Pyth.* 5, 95.

aux légendes rhodiennes, mais le vainqueur a autrefois remporté la couronne dans les jeux rhodiens; l'image initiale évoque peut-être une offrande célèbre du temple d'Athêna Lindienne, où devait être exposée plus tard, si nous en croyons les scholiastes, une copie de l'ode elle-même, inscrite en lettres d'or,[31] confirmation de son caractère essentiellement rhodien et hautement religieux.

La dernière triade confirme ce lien étroit avec Rhodes que Pindare a tenu à établir strictement: l'énumération des victoires de Diagoras, je l'ai dit, rappelle les inscriptions agonistiques; elle a la sécheresse dépouillée d'une nomenclature officielle et le poète a dû s'inspirer directement du texte d'une de ces inscriptions en l'honneur de Diagoras, qu'elle ait été exposée dans le sanctuaire d'Olympie ou dans celui de Lindos. Une inscription de ce genre, relatant les victoires de Dorieus, le propre fils de Diagoras de Rhodes, sur la base d'une statue d'Olympie, est connue grâce à Pausanias (VI 7, 1–4) et l'on a tenté de l'identifier avec une inscription retrouvée dans les fouilles du sanctuaire, en y introduisant des compléments fournis par le Périégète.[32] Les inscriptions agonistiques associaient habituellement la famille du vainqueur à sa gloire[33] et, sur ce point encore, Pindare peut s'inspirer d'une inscription réelle, d'une de ces stèles où étaient consignés les honneurs attribués aux vainqueurs et que l'on trouve citées au vers 86, sous le nom de λιθίνα ψῆφος.[34]

Mais cette unité objective se double d'une unité plus essentielle, unité d'inspiration qui résulte des profondes convictions morales et religieuses de Pindare. Fidèle à l'esprit du dieu qui règne à Delphes, il n'hésite pas, quand il emprunte des récits légendaires, à en modifier l'interprétation, afin de donner toujours, des dieux et des héros qu'il met en scène, l'image la plus haute. Il ne saurait prêter à un personnage divin une pensée indigne de sa sublime condition. La Septième Olympique est un exemple très représentatif de cette

---

[31] Voir Ch. Graux, "Notes épigraphiques, 1, Une Olympique de Pindare écrite à l'encre d'or," *Rev. Phil.* 5 (1881), 117–21, qui croit à un rouleau de cuir ou de parchemin plutôt qu'à une stèle de marbre.

[32] *Syll.*[3] 82: en vérité les arguments mis en avant par Pomtow pour cette identification n'emportent pas absolument la conviction.

[33] Cf. L. Robert, "Les épigrammes satiriques de Lucillius sur les athlètes. Parodie et réalité," dans *L'Épigramme grecque* (Entretiens Hardt, 14, Vandoeuvres et Genève), 193 sqq.

[34] Οὐχ ἕτερον . . . ἔχει λόγον signifie évidemment: "ne contient pas un *nombre* différent."

doctrine si souvent mise en œuvre par le poète qui, pour ses actes et ses poèmes, avait mérité du clergé delphique les plus hautes récompenses.[35]

Lille, 7 juillet 1970

---

[35] Depuis la rédaction de cet article, j'ai rassemblé, dans une "Postface" à la 2ᵉ édition des *Thèmes de la propagande delphique* (Les Belles-Lettres, Paris 1972), des témoignages sur les rapports de Pindare et de Delphes, et, à la suite d'une importante étude de L. Robert, des éléments nouveaux sur les maximes delphiques.

BOEOTIAN
AND OTHER LINGUISTIC INFLUENCES
ON PINDAR

ANTONIO TOVAR

For the relationship of Pindar to his native dialect we have to refer the reader to the few pages which Wilamowitz devoted to the question.[1] A grammatical classification of Pindaric forms would permit a detailed picture of the poet's position within the history of the Greek language, but lacking such an inventorial instrument,[2] we can only try to make a few points.

When placing the Theban poet in relation to the dialects, we meet with several difficulties. Boeotia was not a unified country. Although Thebes struggled to impose her supremacy, some Boeotian towns seem to have retained a linguistic personality until a late date, as we can judge from inscriptions. Such is clearly the case with Tanagra.[3] The linguistic composition of the different

---

[1] U. von Wilamowitz-Moellendorff, *Pindaros* (Berlin 1922), 97 ff., 466 ff. He begins by pointing out, rightly, "man ist nicht gewohnt, die nötigen Vorfragen zu stellen, hier also, wie sprach Pindar und welche Kultursprache musste er lernen."

For all quotations from Pindar I use *Pindari carmina cum fragmentis*, edidit Alexander Turyn (Oxford 1952), except that for more recent fragments I refer to the edition of Snell. See also the *Lexicon to Pindar* by W. J. Slater (Berlin 1969).

[2] See the bibliography on the linguistic study of Pindar in A. Thumb, *Handbuch der gr. Dialekte*, 2nd ed. by A. Scherer (Heidelberg 1959), 2, 16. There are not many publications to add to those quoted there: the Soviet scholar N. S. Grinbaum has written several papers, among which I have seen "Mikenskaja koine i problema obrazovanija jazyka drevno-grečeskoj khorovoj liriki" (with Italian transl.), *Atti Congr. Internaz. di Micenologia* (Roma 1968), 869–74 and 875–79, and "Jazyk Pindara i nadpisi Kreta," *Studii Clasice*, Acad. România, 11 (1969), 31–38. His method in this last paper is that of mechanically comparing similarities without any historical or genetical consideration, which does not help much to solve the question of the formation of our poet's literary language. Other references in María Rico, *Ensayo de bibliografía pindárica* (Madrid 1969), 263 ff.

[3] Thumb-Scherer 16. For the history of Boeotia in the dark ages see the works of P. Guillon, *La Béotie antique* (Paris 1948) and *Le Bouclier d'Héraclès* (Publications des Annales de la Faculté des Lettres, Aix en Provence 1963).

Boeotian subdialects was still far from uniform in the fifth century
B.C.[4]

Accordingly the dialect which Pindar supposedly learned as a
child was not exactly the "Boeotian" of our manuals, but its
Theban variety, of whose peculiarities we are ignorant. The older
inscriptions of Boeotia are all short, containing scarcely more than
proper names. No poetical epigrams, no extensive legal codes have
been preserved. One fact alone, that it resisted for a long time
without yielding to the pressure of the koinê, gives the dialect its
marked personality.

We might look for the relationship of Pindar to local literature, but
besides the fact that our knowledge is limited, the literary positions
of the Ascrean Hesiod and the Theban poetess Corinna are different.

Corinna, who traditionally appears as a teacher or rival of Pindar,
in any case as a contemporary, writes a different sort of poetry.[5]
She could therefore write in a more thoroughly Boeotian idiom than
Pindar.[6] The literary problem of the transcription of her works,
preserved for us in papyri, into the later Boeotian spelling strengthens
the impression of her Boeotianism. There is not much in her dialect
to compare with that of Pindar.

Hesiod, the old Boeotian master, had used the epic dialect and
linguistically could not have given any guidance to the choral poet
Pindar. Like Hesiod,[7] Pindar had to avoid the less literary features
of his native dialect, for instance such crude dialectal forms as ἰράνα
or Ἰστίη. It was only occasionally and for metrical convenience that
he used acc. pl. in -ός like Hesiod, but in such a restricted way that

---

[4] Even if we accept the idea of R. J. Buck, "The Aeolic dialect in Boeotia," *Class.
Philol.* 63 (1968), 268 ff., concerning the conquest of Boeotia by invaders coming from
Thessaly and already speaking a mixture of Aeolic and North-Western Greek, local
differences are not excluded. In the light of Archaeology—says Buck 280—Aeolic must
not be regarded as "the speech of Bronze Age inhabitants of Boeotia"; at that time, he
thinks, "the ancestral form of Ionic was the speech of central Greece."

[5] The thesis of D. L. Page, *Corinna* (London 1953), who like E. Lobel puts the poetess
in Hellenistic times, has not met with general approval: see for instance P. Maas, *Gnomon*
26 (1954), 426, and A. Lesky, *Anz. f. die Altertumswiss.* 11 (1958), 6–8.

[6] On the language of Corinna see the important paper of K. Latte, *Eranos* 54 (1956),
57 ff. For an analysis of the literary differences between Pindar and Corinna, see C. M.
Bowra, *Pindar* (Oxford 1964), 279 ff.

[7] F. Schwenn, *RE* 20, 1615, gives a list of Hesiodic literary motives and influences on
Pindar. See also W. Schmid, *Gesch. der gr. Lit.*, I 1, 547.

he never used the corresponding feminine in -ᾰς.[8] Pindar could address himself to a Theban lady Ἀνδαισιστρότα by name (*Parth.* 2, 39 = frg. 106) although he never employed the form στροτός of his dialect, only the literary στρατός.

We find traces of Pindar's familiarity with Hesiod and also with the Hesiodic school which for centuries flourished in Boeotia and in other north-eastern regions of Greece in the composition of genealogies and catalogues.[9] For example, a quotation from Hesiod appears in the middle of a poem, *Is.* 6, 62 f.:

$$Λάμπων\ δὲ\ μ ε λ έ τ α ν$$
$$ἔ ρ γ ο ι ς\ ὀπάζων\ ʽΗσιόδου\ μάλα\ τιμᾷ\ τοῦτ'\ ἔπος.$$

The gnome which Lampon, the father of the boy whom the poet praises, is supposed to follow is this: μελέτη δὲ τὸ ἔργον ὀφέλλει (*Opera* 412).

Wilamowitz goes so far as to affirm[10] that the "gewaltsame Sprünge" in the composition and the lack of a "ruhiger Fluss der Gedanken" which characterize the literary expression of both poets, Pindar and Hesiod, is a common Boeotian feature.

In the sphere of vocabulary we find both poets using a specific Boeotian term: ἀγών meaning ἀγορά appears precisely in the oldest of our Pindaric poems (*Py.* 10, 30), just as in Hes. *Theog.* 91. An inscription from the region of Thespiae has τὺ ἀγώναρχυ, i.e. οἱ ἀγορανόμοι (*IG* 7, 1817). Eustathius (ad *Il.* Ω 1335, vol. IV p. 332 ed. Leipzig 1830) already knew that this was a Boeotianism.

In the word ἀπάλαμον (*Ol.* 1, 59) Pindar coincides precisely with Hesiod *Opera* 20, where the metrical lengthening and the ending[11] testify to direct imitation. Pindar also used βαρυπάλαμος (*Py.* 11, 23) and πυρπάλαμος (*Ol.* 10, 84), taking metrical advantage of the double form -μος/-μνος.[12]

The favorite word προμάθεια, an abstract term, appears in Pindar for the first time in literature (*Ne.* 11, 46, one of his latest poems;

[8] Cf. H. Troxler, *Sprache und Wortschatz Hesiods* (Zürich 1964), 75.

[9] Cf. J. Schwarz, *Pseudo-Hesiodea, Recherches sur la composition, la diffusion et la disposition ancienne d'oeuvres attribuées à Hésiode* (Leiden 1960), 565 ff.

[10] *Pindaros*, 56.

[11] The word appears as ἀπάλαμνος in Homer, Alcaeus, Simonides etc., and also i Pindar, *Ol.* 2, 63.

[12] And so does Aeschylus with δυσ- and εὐπάλαμος.

Is. 1, 40 and *Pai.* VIII b = frg. 50, 25, also the adjective προμαθής, *Ol.* 7, 44). Besides the importance of Prometheus in the Hesiodic poems, where he appears for the first time, we must remember the existence of an old cult of the hero at the Theban Kabirion.[13]

Pindar's education in Athens, which is well attested in the ancient tradition,[14] must have consisted, in large part, of learning the poetical language. The choruses of Attic tragedy at the time when Pindar was an apprentice in Athens attained their peak in Choirilos and Pratinas.

What was the curriculum of a young poet-apprentice in Athens shortly before 500 B.C.? This of course is a difficult question. What centuries later appears in grammars and lexica had not yet been collected. And although the memorization of poems and songs must have been the principal exercise,[15] to decide in practice whether a form or a word was literary and preferable to another must often have been a difficult personal choice. It is in this way that some forms belonging to the native dialect could have entered into his compositions.[16] Literary standards, in a language which we know was highly artificial, were by that time not easy to control. Furthermore, as B. Forssman[17] has proved, the imitation of chosen poets led Pindar to use their dialectal forms, even against his own normal usage. Forssman has shown[18] that our manuscripts, notwithstanding the secular normalizing activity of the grammarians, keep some irregularities which are based on quotations or direct imitations.

[13] We cannot resolve the question of the priority of προμήθεια, προμηθής (for which see Frisk, *Gr. etym. Wörterb.* 2, 599) relative to the proper name of the hero, with his deep religious roots in Thebes.

[14] Wilamowitz, *Pindaros* 88 ff.; W. Schmid I 1, 551 f., 559; A. Lesky, *Gesch. der gr. Lit.²*, 217 ff.

[15] W. Schmid, I 1, 547, presents a vivid picture of the literary perspectives and models for Pindar. Since books did not exist, a professional poet had to make copies for himself, as we know the rhapsodists did. See also, for literary influences on Pindar, the book of Bowra, 192 ff.

[16] Here may be cited some of the poet's known Boeotianisms: τά (like Megar. σά) 'what for' (*Ol.* 1, 82), cf. Wilamowitz, *Pindaros* 99; on δίδοι (4 times) as an Aeolic imperative see K. Strunk, *Glotta* 39 (1961), 114 ff. Of ἐν with accus. Slater gives 8 examples, not all of them certain. Other peculiarities are collected in Hoffmann-Debrunner *Gesch. der gr. Sprache*, 99 ff., Meillet, *Aperçu d'une histoire de la langue grecque³*, 199 ff. Thumb-Scherer 12 f.

[17] *Untersuchungen zur Sprache Pindars* (Wiesbaden 1966).

[18] *Op. cit.* 13 ff., 18, 22 ff., 32 ff., 163.

Thus some Attic influences can be discovered in the text of Pindar, and this at a time when Attic was still far from winning literary dignity. In his Hymn to Persephone (frg. 30) Pindar calls the goddess πότνια θεσμοφόρε. It is the only time that he uses the form θεσμο- instead of Doric τεθμός. Perhaps it was clear to Pindar that the Demeter Thesmophoros who had a temple in the Cadmeia, the fortress of his native Thebes (RE VI A 24 f.), was a pre-Dorian relic, preserving the tradition of the Thesmophoria, a feast that was brilliantly celebrated in Athens.[19]

It was probably in Athens that Pindar learned the logical term συμβάλλειν with the meaning "conclude, infer, conjecture, interpret." The dictionaries cite the first examples of the verb with this meaning in Attic tragedy and comedy, and of course in Plato, but the passage of Pindar Ne. 11, 23 (one of his latest poems, to be sure) is by far the oldest.

B. Forssman[20] has convincingly shown that an Attic τέμνων (Py. 3, 68) comes directly from an Atticism of the Odyssey (γ 175).

It is interesting to discover that when Greek poetry flourished but books did not exist, a strong literary movement carried words and thoughts across the whole area of Greek. This language grew as an instrument of rich poetical expression as well as of advanced thinking in this kind of non-literate literature. But the poets were professionals in the art of reading, and that reading was beginning to be practiced unofficially is said by our poet as he begins his Ol. 10:

> Τὸν ᾿Ολυμπιονίκαν ἀνάγνωτέ μοι
> Ἀρχεστράτου παῖδα, πόθι φρενός
> ἐμᾶς γέγραπται.

"Read ye where in my heart is written the name of the son of Archestratos..." (transl. L. R. Farnell).

Let us consider, as an example of grammatical development

---

[19] Cf. Schwenn, RE 20, 1616, for the attractions that Athens could exert on the young poet. For the Attic use of θεσμός (by Solon, for instance), see F. R. Adrados, Emerita 21 (1953), 131.

[20] Glotta 44 (1967), 5 ff.: τέμνων is the only form given by the manuscripts. See Turyn's critical apparatus: τάμνων is a correction by Tycho Mommsen of a form which had long resisted regularizing grammarians.

within a language which was becoming ever more abstract, the verbal adjectives with the meaning of obligation. We do not intend to say that their development is the exclusive property of a specific dialect. As an isolated type we find in Hesiod what is given [21] as the oldest example of tempus obligationis: οὔ τι φατειὸν Κέρβερον (*Theog.* 310, with imitations in the pseudo-Hesiodic *Scut.* 144 Φόβος οὔ τι φατειός and 161 ὀφίων δεινῶν, οὔ τι φατειῶν). Similar but independent of the Hesiodic example is Pindar's (*Ol.* 2, 5) Θήρωνα δὲ τετραορίας ἕνεκα νικαφόρου γεγωνητέον. This is not the same form (-τειός) as in Hesiod,[22] but it is oriented in a significant way towards the coming era: it is in Attic poetry and prose that the tempus obligationis in -τέον was going to be used.

The results of an examination of the development of verbal adjectives in -τος are somehow comparable. In this case the origin is also Indo-European,[23] but it is Greek which developed the possibility of contrast by means of accent: a passive meaning (e.g. διάλυτος "dissolved") and a potential use (διαλυτός "soluble").[24]

We may assume that this fact helped to advance the development of the type -τέον,[25] and that ultimately, in the need for a logically developed language capable of expressing antitheses, it also created numerous -τος forms which were sometimes used as tempus obligationis.

Take for instance ἄπιστος, a non-Homeric word. We find it with the meaning "*infidus*" in frg. 280: πιστὸν δ'ἀπίστοις οὐδέν; but the newer signification "*incredibilis*" is found in other passages: *Ne.* 9, 33, *Py.* 10, 50, and above all, with the antithesis which clearly developed the type, *Ol.* 1, 31 ἄπιστον ἐμήσατο πιστὸν ἔμμεναι τὸ πολλάκις. Hesiod did not use this form, but the abstract ἀπιστίαι

---

[21] E. Schwyzer, *Gr. Gramm.* 1, 811.

[22] On the distinction of -τέον and -τειός see J. Wackernagel, *Kuhn's Zeitschr.* 25 (1877), 274; for the relationship of the Greek to Skr. -*tavya*- see Wackernagel—Debrunner, *Altind. Gramm.* II 2, 615; J. W. Poultney, *Language* 43 (1967), 872, 875 f. Ernst Fraenkel, *Lexis* 2 (1949), 175 f., made a very plausible proposal, that of interpreting the Hesiodic form as a metrical adaptation of the normal φατεός.

[23] Brugmann, *Grundr.* II 1², 394 ff., Schwyzer 1, 810.

[24] J. Kuryłowicz, *Indogerm. Gramm.* 2 §§ 35, 114; Schwyzer 1, 501 ff., 810 f.

[25] Except for the Pindaric example, we find only Attic use, with very few examples older than the last decades of the fifth century: cf. Kühner–Gerth, *Gr. Gramm.*, *Satzlehre* 1, 447; Schwyzer–Debrunner, *Gr. Gramm.*, *Syntax* 409; P. Chantraine, *La formation des noms en grec ancien* (Paris 1933), 308 f.

"disbelief" occurs in *Opera* 372 as the opposite of πίστιες, in a characteristic antithetical development.

Διδακτός (*Ol.* 9, 107/8, *Ne.* 3, 39, in both passages with overtones of contempt for instruction as incapable of competing with noble nature) is a word which Pindar must have learned in his apprentice years in Athens: neither Homer nor Hesiod, neither lyric poets nor pre-Socratics used it. Its early use by Pindar preludes that of Sophocles and Euripides, and of course that of Plato.[26]

Θαητός "*admirandus,*" often used by Pindar, is non-Homeric, but appears in Hesiod *Theog.* 31 and then in Tyrtaeus and Simonides.

Θαυμαστός is used by Pindar no less than 9 times; to confirm the post-Homeric development of this type we find it in the Hymn to Demeter, 10, and θαυματός in the pseudo-Hesiodic *Scut.* 165.

Θεμιτός "permitted" (*Py.* 9, 42 καὶ γὰρ σέ, τὸν οὐ θεμιτὸν ψεύδει θιγεῖν) is only found in older times in the same Hymn to Demeter.

Ἰατός "curable" (*Is.* 8, 15) is a very rare word. It appears only in Plato and later writers (Stephanus, *Thes. Gr. Linguae,* 4, 496). But the opposite ἀνίατος appears in medical literature and is much more used. Pindar frg. 211 (= 260 Snell) has ἀνίατον.

Μεμπτός "contemptible" had been used by Alcaeus (A 1, 8) and later by the tragic poets; we find it with a less frequent word, μεταλλακτός, frg. 259:

> τῶν οὔτε τι μεμπτόν
> οὔτ' ὢν μεταλλακτόν, ὅσσ' ἀγλαὰ χθών
> πόντου τε ῥιπαὶ φέροισιν

("nothing is to be disparaged, nothing to be made different, of all the boons of the glorious earth, and of the rushing sea," transl. Sandys).

Ὀνοτός "to be blamed, scorned" (*Is.* 3/4, 68) is unique, and equally unique is Homeric ὀνοστός (I 164);[27] Hesiod uses (once) the verb ὀνοτάζω, and ὀνοταστός (as Clarke corrected the ὀνότατον of the mss) appears in the Homeric Hymn to Aphrodite, 254.

Παρφυκτός (*Py.* 12, 30 τὸ δὲ μόρσιμον οὐ παρφυκτόν) is an example

---

[26] A comparison with διδασκαλία (*Py.* 4, 102) is interesting. The word emerges again in Anaxagoras and Protagoras. In poetry it appears just once in an epigram of Simonides (77, 5 D.) which has an Attic theme.

[27] The Homeric form is of a more recent type than that of Pindar without *s*; cf. Schwyzer 1, 503.

of how an adjective in -τος comes to be a *tempus obligationis*. The verb παρφυγέειν appears in Homer, μ 99.

'Ρητ[ό]ν (*Pai.* 17 a 4 Snell) appears once in Homer (Φ 455) and also in Hesiod, *Opera* 4 ῥητοί τ' ἄρρητοί τε, where the antithesis illustrates the formation of the type.

'Υμνητός "*celebrandus*" is very characteristically used twice, *Py.* 10, 22; 11, 61; the precedent is, as often, the compound πολύμνητος, found in *Ne.* 2, 5; cf. the Muse Πολύμνια Hes. *Theog.* 78.

Οὐ φατός (*Ol.* 6, 37, *Is.* 7, 37) recalls Hes. *Opera* 3 f. ἄφατοί τε φατοί τε, ῥητοί τ' ἄρρητοί τε, cf. *Scut.* 230.

Φορητός (frg. 156, 5, cf. *Pai.* 7 B 43 = frg. 48) is used once as applied to the travelling island of Delos. The origin of this formation in an older compound is to be seen in Homer Θ 527 in an insult to the menacing Trojans, regarded as κύνας κηρεσσιφορήτους.

All these examples confirm the development of a *tempus obligationis*, beginning with compounds and simple forms attaining later autonomy. Of course -τός formations are much more frequent and developed in Hesiod, but this is in accordance with the Ionic language. It is, however, interesting to see the conservative spirit of Pindar adopting the new abstract formation.

"We do not think of him as a poet of ideas" says C. M. Bowra in his book on Pindar (p. 392). Pindar did not study books, the treatises of Ionian philosophers, which were to him dangerous novelties. In a famous fragment (248) he says of the φυσιολογοῦντες that

ἀτελῆ σοφίας δρέπειν καρπόν,

"they reap the immature fruit of *sophia*." But let us take as a test the word σοφία: only recorded once in Homer (Ο 412), applied, as the scholia say, οὐ τὴν λογικὴν ἀλλὰ τὴν τεκτονικὴν τέχνην,[28] then used in the Hymn to Hermes (483, 511), it appears in Pindar, meaning either "wisdom, art" (8 examples) or specifically "poetic art, skill" (11 examples, see Slater). In the older lyric poets we find the forerunners of Pindar: Theognis, Anacreon, Solon.[29]

Also σόφισμα (which will appear frequently in Attic tragedy and comedy) is used by our poet as a non-derogatory term (*Ol.* 13, 17). Hesiod (*Opera* 649) had used σεσοφι(σ)μένος.

[28] On σοφία see the doctoral thesis of B. Snell, *Ausdrücke für den Begriff des Wissens in der vorplatonischen Philosophie* (Philologische Untersuchungen, 29; Berlin 1924), p. 5 ff.

[29] See G. Fatouros, *Index verborum zur frühgriechischen Lyrik* (Heidelberg 1966), p. 349.

Similarly Pindar uses σοφισταί, speaking of poets:

μελέταν³⁰ δὲ σοφισταῖς
Διὸς ἕκατι πρόσβαλον (Is. 5, 31)

("through God's benison these have thrown down a theme to the craftsmen of song," transl. Farnell).

Pindar was familiar with this group of words and it was only when the word σοφία began to be used by the new professionals in the art of thinking that he found premature the fruit which they pretended to pick.

But, it is interesting to discover how new philosophical words were also used by the poet. Αἰτία, a legal term meaning "guilt, accusation" (thus Ol. 1, 35), appears with the meaning "motive" in Ne. 7, 11:

εἰ δὲ τύχῃ τις ἔρδων, μελίφρον᾽ αἰτίαν
ῥοαῖσι Μοισᾶν ἐνέβαλε

("but, if a man prospereth in his doings, he supplieth a sweet source for the Muses' rills," Sandys). This word with the meaning "cause" appears clearly in Aesch. Prom. 226, with possible precedents in Thales and Anaximander, and sure examples from the Corpus Hippocraticum and Herodotus.

Ἀπορία is one of those prosaic words which are not to be expected in Pindar. Neither Homer nor Hesiod nor any of the lyric poets used it. Only after Diogenes of Apollonia and Democritus, will Euripides and Aristophanes employ it. But Pindar anticipated them all in the last line of the same Ne. 7:

ταὐτὰ δὲ τρὶς τετράκι τ᾽ ἀμπολεῖν
ἀπορία τελέθει, τέκνοισιν ἅτε μαψυλάκας 'Διὸς Κόρινθος'

("but to say the same thing three or four times again is poverty of wit, like the senseless-whining refrain in the children's game, 'Korinthos, son of God'," transl. Farnell).³¹

---

³⁰ The word μελέτη does not appear in Homer, but it is used 3 times by Hesiod and 4 times by Pindar, one of them in the above-mentioned quotation from the Ascraean poet.

³¹ The philosophical word ἄπειρος with the meaning 'boundless, infinite' was believed to appear in one fragment: Thr. 135, 9, as in Ibycus and in Xenophanes, but Turyn's reading makes of this case another example of the adjective ἀπείρων (Py. 2, 64, Pai. 6 = frg. 46, 131):

ἔνθεν τὸν ἀπείρον᾽ ἐρεύγονται σκότον

(instead of the ἄπειρον of other editors: Bergk, Christ, Schroeder, Puech, Bowra, Snell).

For the history of the word ἀλήθεια, whose oldest known examples
are Alcaeus Z 43, Mimn. 8, 1 Diehl, and Simonides 541, 5 and 598
Page, it is important to count the 9 cases in Pindar, and the 8 of
ἀληθής, which is not known to the lyric poets.

In the same sphere belongs κατελέγχω, a word much liked by
Pindar (5 cases) and which also comes from Hesiod (*Opera* 714). In
the lyric poets it is only recorded in Tyrt. 6, 9 Diehl.

Political words were new in the period of transition from archaic
to classical times. A few examples: νόμος, a non-Homeric word, as
is well known, which appears in Hesiod (5 examples), and then in
Alcaeus and in Theognis, is very frequent in Pindar, who personifies
it in the famous Platonic quotation of Νόμος βασιλεύς (frg. 187, 1,
cf. 169 Snell).

Στάσις, with similar distribution: Theognis, Alcaeus, Solon, the
scolia.... Six or seven examples in Pindar prove its vitality in the
era of the tyrants, democrats, and resisting aristocrats. Its absence
in Hesiod shows when the word came to be used in the meaning
"faction, party, sedition."

In one case the text as it is given by our honorand confirms how
open Pindar was, even against his wishes, to the new developments
of thought. In *Ol.* 2, 57 many editors (Bergk, Christ, Schroeder,
Puech, Snell) read δυσφρονᾶν (MSS δυσφροσυνᾶν), a correction of
W. Dindorf, who in that passage was faced with metrical difficulties
and preferred a less Ionic form. The development of the abstract
terms in -σύνη is an Ionic feature:[32] δυσφροσύνη is found in Hes.
Theog. 102, 1189 and in Simon. 73 Diehl. Turyn reads ἀφροσυνᾶν
with P. Oxy. 2092 and Bowra. This reading, of which there are
traces in the scholia, resolves the metrical difficulties and confirms
for Pindar the use of a typically Ionic form. We also find 7 cases of
εὐφροσύνη in Pindar, a word not found in the Iliad, but 5 times in
the Odyssey.

Μανία, an Ionic word, coming perhaps from popular medicine,[33]
used by Hippocrates and Herodotus, has its first recorded examples
in Theogn. 1231, Solon, Anacreon and in our poet: *Ol.* 9, 42, *Ne.*
11, 48, *Dith.* 2, 13 Snell.

---

[32] B. Snell in the monograph cited above (note 28), 31 Anm. 2, points out rightly that
γνωμοσύνη for instance appears (Solon frg. 16 D.) earlier than γνώμη.

[33] Cf. Luis Gil, *Therapeia, La medicina popular en el mundo clásico* (Madrid 1969), 264.

Thus we see that Pindar was not interested in contemporary philosophical novelties, and did not appreciate the advancement of science but found the ambitions of thinkers suspect. But though he read not prose but poetry, still, at the banquets of tyrants and aristocrats and in conversations with contemporaries and rivals like Simonides,[34] he met the new world of reason, which thus enters the archaic soul of the poet.

In this way he has also acquired a place in the history of the Greek language: a transitional one. He felt himself bound to the past. But circumstances brought him to the places where the new world of classicism and rationalism was coming to life. With respect to language we can also recall the words with which one scholar[35] has characterized the transitional place of Pindar in the history of the Greek mind: "Begriffsfülle und vorlogisches, das heisst nicht struktives Denken, gehören zu- und ineinander als gegenseitig sich bedingende Korrelate." In the archaic world of the aristocrats, honoring the gods or competing for victory in sports and games, the poet remained (perhaps unwillingly) open to the intellectual development which was going to transform it.

Tübingen, 25 June 1970

---

[34] Very revealing is the list of words common to Pindar and Simonides, in Bowra, *Pindar* 197 f.

[35] W. Schadewaldt, "Der Aufbau des pindarischen Epinikion," in *Schriften der Königsberger Gelehrten Gesellschaft*, Geisteswiss. Kl. 5.3 (1928), 308.

THEONS PINDARKOMMENTAR
(PAP. OXY. 2536)

MAX TREU

"Much has been written about Theon (see, for example, C. Wendel, *RE* s.v. Theon (9); H. T. Deas, *Harvard Studies in Cl. Philology* XLII (1931), pp. 31 seqq.)."—Diese summarischen, jedes qualifizierende Urteil vermeidenden Sätze von E. G. Turner (*Pap. Oxy.* vol. XXXI [1966], p. 17) seien als neutraler Ausgangspunkt gewählt für vorliegende Studie, die ein ehemaliger Rigenser dem polnischen Gelehrten zu seinem 70. Geburtstag widmen möchte, dem unser Jahrhundert wohl die gründlichsten Untersuchungen zur Tragikerüberlieferung verdankt und der zuvor, nach eingehender Prüfung der Pindar-Hss. (*De Codicibus Pindaricis*, 1932), uns mit einer wertvollen Pindarausgabe (1948, Neudruck 1952) beschenkt hat. Auszugehen hat zunächst auch unser Streifzug von den bisherigen Versuchen, einen möglichst vollständigen Überblick zu gewinnen von der vielseitigen philologischen Tätigkeit des Theon, Sohnes des Artemidoros. C. Wendel, als Herausgeber der Scholien zu Theokrit und zu Apollonios von Rhodos wie kaum ein anderer dazu legitimiert, von Theon als—unseres Wissens[1]—erstem Kommentator der alexandrinischen Dichter zu handeln, hat in seinem bereits erwähnten, 1934 erschienenen *RE*-Artikel einen gut brauchbaren, vom Gesicherten ausgehenden Überblick gegeben. H. T. Deas konnte ihn noch nicht verwerten; allerdings ist auch umgekehrt festzustellen, daß der Aufsatz des genannten amerikanischen Gelehrten, "The Scholia Vetera to Pindar," von Wendel nicht mit herangezogen worden ist.

Will man nun aus Wendels Überblick kurz das Fazit ziehen, so läßt sich zusammenfassend sagen:

---

[1] "Nullus commentarius (sc. in Callimachum) notus est ante illum Θέωνος τοῦ Ἀρτεμιδώρου (v. ad frg. 274) Augusti aetate scriptum" (R. Pfeiffer, *Callim.* II, p. XXVII).

I. Hypomnemata Theons waren belegt für Homers Odyssee, für Kallimachos (s. jetzt Pfeiffer in den Prolegomena seiner Ausgabe, vol. II, p. XXVII), ferner zu Apollonios Rhodios, Theokrit, Nikander, Lykophron.

II. Angenommen hat Wendel auch ein Hypomnema zur Ilias, mindestens zum Schiffskatalog, sowie

III. ein Hypomnema zu Pindar, worin Wendel sich der Ansicht von Ahrens anschließt, gegen Giese u.a. Hier ist nun auch die konziliatorische Ansicht von H. T. Deas zu nennen, der (a.O. 31) argumentiert: "So long as this note [sc. schol. Pind. Ol. v 42 a Drachmann mit 'so sagt Theon'] was the only evidence for Theon's work on Pindar, it used to be doubted whether it was legitimate to infer a commentary, but Theon now appears as responsible for a reading in the papyrus of the Paeans (*Pap. Oxy.* 841; Pa. II 37) and it must be assumed that he did edit Pindar." Wie wenig zwingend dieses Muß—d.h., nach Deas (a.O. 34 ff.), die Annahme einer Pindaredition Theons und eines Pindarkommentars von ihm—ist, mag allein schon aus der Tatsache abgelesen werden, daß Wendel, unter Verweis auf die gleichen Theonzitate zu zwei Pindarstellen, nur ein Hypomnema des Grammatikers zu Pindar annahm.

IV. Weniger präzise drückt sich Wendel zunächst aus, wenn er "textkritische Arbeit" Theons an Sophokles bezeugt findet durch das Faktum, daß im Ichneutai-Papyrus, *Pap. Oxy.* 1174, am Rande des Textes zu nicht weniger als 15 Stellen Textvarianten Theons angeführt sind: meist übrigens mit bloßer Namensnennung Theons, einige Male jedoch mit der Anspielung auf den Buchtitel (im Neutrum oder Masculinum), was m.E. nicht unwichtig ist: οὕτως ἦν ἐν τῷ Θέωνος, οὕτως ἦν μόνον ἐν τῷ Θέωνος, οὕτως τὸ πρῶτον (τοᾶ pap.) ἀπεγέγραπτο ἐν τῷ Θέωνος. Einige Spalten weiter (a.O. S. 2058) hat Wendel dann seine Ansicht von der "textkritischen Arbeit" Theons dahingehend präzisiert, daß er vor allem eine Sophokles-Ausgabe annimmt, wie Pearson (*The Fragments of Sophocles*, I, p. 224 [1917]: "particularly from the edition of Theon") und andere vor ihm getan hatten. Dazu bemerkt Wendel: "Gab die Sophokles-Ausgabe sicher den vollen Text und dann nur Randbemerkungen (falls sie überhaupt mit Erklärungen ausgestattet war),..." Mit "falls überhaupt" hat sich der Zweifel m.E. gerade noch rechtzeitig bei Wendel zu Worte gemeldet, da für das Altertum

bis ins 6. Jhdt.[2] zwar Textausgaben und, gesondert, Hypomnemata
(= Kommentare) nachweisbar sind, der Nachweis von Textausgaben, die der Diorthot selbst mit ausführlichen Randbemerkungen kommentiert hätte, jedoch schwer fallen dürfte, mindestens
für die Zeit der Papyrusrollen. Aber auch der einleitende Satz
Wendels über Theons Sophokles-Ausgabe basiert auf purer Konjektur, die alles andere als sicher ist, so sicher diese Hypothese sich
auch gibt mit der Konstatierung: "Theon, whose edition is mentioned a dozen times in the papyrus of the Ichneutae" (Deas
a.O. 31). Solche Behauptungen gehen an der Tatsache vorüber,
daß, in Gegensatz etwa zu ἄμεινον προκρίνειν τὴν Ἀριστάρχου, in
unserem Fall der Artikel ἐν τῷ sich keinesfalls auf eine Ekdosis oder
Diorthosis beziehen läßt, allenfalls auf ein Antigraphon, vielleicht
auf ein Hypomnema. Unanfechtbar bleibt im Gegensatz zu Wendel
u.a., die vorsichtiger formulierte Konstatierung, die Hunt 1912 in
der Praefatio zu seiner Ausgabe der Ichneutae (*Fragmenta Tragica
Papyracea*, p. VI) gegeben hatte: "...manus altera, quae non
solum textum correxit sed lectiones non nullas varias e diversis
exemplaribus praesertim Theonis grammatici exscripsit." Hiermit
vergleichen mag man heute die Erwähnung verschiedener Anti-
grapha im schol. *Pap. Oxy.* 2387 zu Alkman (jetzt = 3 frg. 3 Page,
PMG): ein solches (sc. Antigraphon) des Aristonikos, ein weiteres
des Ptolemaios sind da besonders erwähnt bei der Diskussion der
Frage, in welches Liederbuch Alkmans das folgende Tanzlied ein-
zuordnen sei. Auch auf die terminologischen Untersuchungen von
H. Erbse im Hinblick auf Aristarch (*Hermes* 87 [1952], 275 ff.) können wir uns berufen und *last not least* auf Rudolf Pfeiffers Urteil
über Didymos, in dessen Nähe wir ja mit Theon, Artemidoros'
Sohn, kommen. Pfeiffer stellt fest (*Hist. of Cl. Scholarship*, p. 277):
"The διάφορα ἀντίγραφα cited in the subscription of the Scholia on
Medea included a copy of Didymus from which extracts were made.
These ἀντίγραφα were, of course, ὑπομνήματα; no clear reference
has yet been found to an ἔκδοσις or διόρθωσις by Didymus of any
lyric or dramatic poet."

[2] Im wesentlichen richtig über Hypomnemata als "separate rolls" urteilt Deas a.O.
78. Vor dem anderen Extrem warnt Pfeiffer (*History of Classical Scholarship* [1968], 270
note 3): "A unique papyrus-codex of the sixth century A.D. published in 1952 refuted the
assumption that large marginal commentaries around the text could not have been
written before the time of Photius, see Call. II, p. XXVII 3."

Vom Grammatiker Theon, der gemeinhin als Nachfolger des Didymos gilt, ist ehrlicherweise das Gleiche zu sagen, vor allem wegen des Artikelgebrauchs ἐν τῷ (nicht ἐν τῇ) bei Hinweisen auf seine Buchtitel. Auch für Theon ist bisher nirgends klar bezeugt, daß er eine kritische Textausgabe gemacht hätte. Mit "exemplar Theonis" kann, wie bei der Ilias des Apellikon, primär lediglich der Besitzer einer HS gemeint[3] sein.

Zwei Theonzitate in literarischen Papyri, die erst 1957 bzw. 1959 veröffentlicht wurden, stehen einem solchen skeptischen Urteil nicht nur nicht im Wege, sondern verstärken noch die Bedenken gegen eine editorische Tätigkeit Theons. Im *Pap. Oxy.* 2390, einem Kommentar zu Alkman (jetzt = Alcm. 5 frg. 2 col. I 4-5, Page, *PMG*), werden Theon und Tyrannion[4] zitiert als Gewährsmänner für die Lesung χρυσῶ als Genitivform: in einem Lobpreis Alkmans auf die Schönheit eines Mädchens, das, sogar neben Gold sich stellend, von ihm nicht übertroffen würde. Daß Theon zu allem übrigen sich auch noch mit dem Lyriker Alkman beschäftigt hat, war bisher nicht bekannt. Ein eigenes Hypomnema Theons über diesen hocharchaischen Lyriker ist damit zwar noch lange nicht gesichert, da Alkman ja auch in irgendeinem anderen Zusammenhang zitiert worden sein kann: vgl. Alcm. frg. 79 und frg. 125 Page, beide aus den Pindarscholien. Daß der kompilierende anonyme Alkmankommentator sich aber Theons Äußerung zu Alkman, sagen wir, aus Theons Pindarkommentar hervorgesucht hätte, scheint allerdings noch unwahrscheinlicher. Bis auf weiteres bleibt hier die neu aufgetauchte Frage nach einem weiteren Buchtitel Theons offen.

Das zweite neuere Theonzitat bringt eine Randnotiz zu einem stark zerstörten Epicharmtext im *Pap. Oxy.* 2427 frg. 53 a col. I οὐκ ἦν τὸ χ̄ ἐν τοῖς Θέ(ωνος). Schon bisher war Theons Interesse für λέξεις κωμικαί (und τραγικαί) bekannt (s. Wendel a.O. S. 2057). Ein Theonzitat zu einer Epicharmstelle bedeutet daher keine thematische Überraschung wie Theons Alkmanerklärung. Sachlich

---

[3] "Ed. Apelliconis" (Allen zum Iliasproöm) ist mißverständlich. Daß es sich um einen Bibliophilen handelt, geht daraus nicht hervor. Daß es zum guten Ton gehörte, sich mehrere Homerausgaben zu kaufen, hält Lukian einem ungebildeten vor (*Πρὸς ἀπαίδευτον* cap. 7): καὶ τὸν Ὅμηρον ἐπρίω πολλάκις.

[4] Θέων [καὶ Τ]υραννίων pap. "The first may be supposed the Augustan grammarian, son of Artemidoros" Lobel z. St.

scheinen wir, da der zugehörige Dichtertext so gut wie völlig zerstört ist, vor einem unlösbaren Rätsel zu stehen, da wir nicht wissen, ob ein strittiges Chei am Wortanfang, in der Wortmitte oder am (evtl. elidierten?) Wortende gemeint war. Voraussetzung für eine *varia lectio* im Dichtertext muß aber, streng genommen, in jedem Fall die metrische Gleichwertigkeit oder Indifferenz, annähernde inhaltliche Synonymität und syntaktische Konstruierbarkeit des Satzes sein, womit die theoretischen Möglichkeiten immerhin etwas eingeschränkt würden. Zugegeben, daß die Praxis der Grammatiker von solchen theoretischen Postulaten abweichen kann: schol. Pind. Ol. II 42 e Dr. "wenn man ohne Sigma schreibt" (πρό: πρός), ib. Ol. VIII 10 e "Asklepiades schreibt ohne Sigma" (λιταί: λιταῖς), ib. Ol. II 177 d "Aristarch schreibt ohne Iota" (κρύφον: κρύφιον). Bei einem X, das ja nicht zu den regulären Schlußkonsonanten des Griechischen gehört, scheint Wortanfang das Wahrscheinlichste (Wortmitte möglich, Wortende unwahrscheinlich), und mit λιαρός kann hier dann auch ein annäherndes Synonym zu χλιαρός (vgl. Ps.-Epicharm Ep. 290 Kaibel) offeriert werden. Eben diese beiden Adjektiva machen sich, in der Wortverbindung ὕδατί τε λιαρῷ, auch in den Ilias-HSS gegenseitig den Rang streitig (Ilias XI 829; 845; XXII 149),[5] während die Komödie die Form ohne Chei sonst zu meiden schien. Theon hier auf den Spuren guter Homerphilologie wandeln zu sehen wäre nicht verwunderlich. Die Buchangabe im Papyrus ist hier erstmals eine pluralische, ἐν τοῖς Θέωνος, im grammatischen Genus weder mit "Glossai" noch mit "Lexeis" vereinbar. Sie muß wohl als recht allgemein (sc. συγγράμμασιν?) hingenommen werden.

So bleibt, aufs Ganze gesehen, schon beim bloßen Versuch einer Bestandsaufnahme der Werke Theons eine ganze Reihe von Einzelfragen offen. Wenigstens in einer bislang strittigen Frage hat jedoch unlängst der bedeutendste Papyrusfund zu Theon, der von E. G. Turner 1966 im XXXI. Band der Oxyrhynchos-Papyri veröffentlichte Papyrus nr. 2536, durch die erhaltene *subscriptio* ein für alle Mal Klarheit gebracht. Diese *subscriptio* lautet: Θέω[νος] τοῦ Ἀρτεμιδώρου Πινδάρου Πυθιονικῶν Ὑπόμνημα. Gegen alle Zweifel gesichert sind damit Pindarkommentare Theons, und da der

---

[5] Für die Wortverbindung ἀπήμονά τε λιαρόν τε in der Odyssee (V 268, VII 266) wäre das Gleiche zu erwarten, um auch hier Iktusdehnung zu vermeiden.

erhaltene Textteil des Hypomnemas zu Py. XII u.a. zwei Textvarianten bringt (mit ἔνιοι δέ bzw. γράφεται καί), verliert die marginale Textvariante im *Pap. Oxy.* 841 (zu Paean II 37 ἀλκᾶ Θέων,
ἀλκαῖ pap.) jede Beweiskraft für eine Pindaredition durch Theon.
Ob hinfort noch Grund besteht, der antiken HS der Paeane einen
Sondercharakter zuzusprechen, wie es Wilamowitz nachdrücklich
tat,[6] wird jetzt zum mindesten fraglich. Wir brauchen uns aber
wohl nun auch nicht mehr so vorsichtig auszudrücken, wie es J.
Irigoin tat (*Histoire du Texte de Pindare* (1952), p. 65), der von Theons
Interesse für Pindar, von seinen Pindarstudien sprach ("Théon
avait étudié les Péans") und von einer "leçon qu'il avait adoptée."
Bei der Alternativfrage, Editor oder Kommentator Pindars, hatte
Wendel sich richtig für Theon als Hypomnematisten entschieden.

Die Freude über diesen neuen Theon-Papyrus wird allerdings
in manch anderer Hinsicht beeinträchtigt.[7] Nicht weniger als 3
Schreiberhände sind da am Werk gewesen, die zweite hat zwei
Marginalnoten hinzugefügt, "the surviving parts are in some
disorder" (Turner), 4 Textzeilen von dritter Hand, heute kaum
mehr lesbar, waren durchgestrichen. So ist das Ganze, trotz der
subscriptio, nicht gegen den Verdacht gefeit, nur Excerpte aus
Theons Hypomnema zu bieten. "The disorder of the entries
suggests that the writers may have been selecting as they copied:
they took only what they wanted from Theon's work and felt no
obligation to copy it as a whole. It seems that right from the outset
learned commentaries such as Theon's were subjected to a process
of epitomizing and abstracting" (Turner). Immerhin sind sämtliche
im neuen Text angeführten Lemmata auch sonst in den Pindarscholien vertreten,[8] wörtliche Anklänge der Erklärungen Theons
hat Turner in den Scholien ebenfalls schon festgestellt. Nur auf
eine auffällige Eigenart werden wir in der *princeps editio* nicht

---

[6] U. v. Wilamowitz-Moellendorff, *Pindaros* (1922), 2 f.: "Denn so steht es: die
Varianten unserer Handschriften sind fast alle durch Schreibfehler der Byzantiner
entstanden, nur bei ganz wenigen muß man auf eine Doppellesart in der Urhandschrift
schließen, deren Text sich gerade darin von vielen anderen unterschied, dass er keine
Varianten bot; die antike Handschrift der Paeane ist darin anders."

[7] Vgl. meine Rezension im *Gnomon* 40 (1968), 346 ff., bes. 350.

[8] "It is worth noting that all the lemmata of the extant scholia are represented,
except apparently at the very end of the poem," meint Turner. Aber schon für Z. 4–5
trifft das nicht zu, s.u.

hingeweisen: der Kommentar bringt auch einiges, was der Dichter
in diesem Epinikion, Py. XII, überhaupt nicht berührt hat. Nicht
zuletzt unter diesem Gesichtspunkt sei hier der Text von Pap. Oxy.
2536 betrachtet, und zwar in drei Abschnitten. Über Theons
Mythenerzählung und seine Stellung zu gnomischen Sätzen des
Dichters mögen sich dabei einige merkenswerte Folgerungen ergeben, auch wenn solche Beobachtungen nicht ausreichen können,
als persönliche Eigenart dieses Grammatikers im Unterschied zu
seinen Vorgängern gewertet zu werden.

Die Anfangspartie des neuen Papyrus nr. 2536, col. I, Z. 1–12
lautet:

$$]Πολυδέκτηι.\ \mathbf{λυγρόν\ τ'}\ [ἔρανον$$
[**θῆκε**· Σεριφίοις· εὖ]ωχουμένοις γ(ὰρ) αὐτοῖς τούτοις
[ἔδειξεν ὁ Περσεὺς τὴ]ν κεφαλὴν κ(αὶ) οὕ(τως) ἀπελιθώθησαν
[   ]οσ^ε ε[.]ωθεσωθεν ἵν' ἦ<ι> καὶ τὴν
5 [   ]σ.. [ ]βιαζομένης γ(ὰρ) τῆς Δα-
[νάης ὑπὸ τοῦ Πολυδ]έκτου συνέβη αὐτὴν κατα-
[φυγεῖν πρὸ]ς τὸν βωμὸν τοῦ   τὸν δὲ
[Πολυδέκτην] εὐλαβούμενον τὸν Περσέα πέμψαι
[ἐπὶ Μεδούσης] καρατομίαν ὡς ἀπολούμενον καὶ
10 [μηκέτι ἀνιόντα.] τὸν μ(ὲν) Πολυδέκτην θεωρήσαντα
[τὴν τῆς Γοργόνο]ς κεφαλὴν ἀπολιθωθῆναι καὶ σωθῆ-
[ναι τὴν Δανάη]ν.

Die Ergänzungen stammen zumeist von Turner, die nur *exempli
gratia* gemeinten Vorschläge für Z. 2 und 10 von mir, vgl. Py. x
74 m. Schol. νασιώταις· τοῖς Σεριφίοις. Z. 4 ἵν' ἦ<ι> verteidigt
M. Maehler (*Zeitschrift für Papyrologie und Epigraphik*, 3 [1968],
100) unter Verweis auf schol. Pind. Isthm. 1 60 (Didymos) βέλτιον
...ἵν' ἦ<ι> (vor Paraphrase). Am Rande von Z. 4–6 hat eine
zweite Hand die Notiz hinzugefügt ἢ ἀπὸ κοινοῦ τὸ ἀμαύρωσε.
Inhaltlich ist das = schol. Py. XII 25 b Drachmann κοινῶς δὲ
ληπτέον τὸ ἡμαύρωσε. τὰς Γοργόνας δηλονότι, inhaltlich gleichwertig
auch mit schol. 24 a Dr. τοῦτο ἐπὶ τῶν τριῶν ἀκουστέον, ὅτι τὴν μὲν
μίαν ἐκαρατόμησε, τὰς δὲ δύο ἐτύφλωσε (durch Wegnahme des einen,
allen drei Gorgonen gemeinsamen Auges). Eine andere, unserem
Grammatiker nicht unbekannte (s.u.) Erklärung bringt dagegen
schol. 35 b Dr. ἄλλως· ἀπὸ μιᾶς ἤρκεσε καὶ τὸ περὶ τὴν ἑτέραν τὴν Σθενὼ
πάθος παραστῆσαι. In Z. 7 hatte der Schreiber für den Namen eines

Gottes freien Raum gelassen. "A blank space in col. I, 7 suggests a place where the copyist could not read his exemplar" (Turner) ist wohl die einzige Erklärung, die sich anbietet. Uns dürfte es nicht schwer fallen, hier den Namen des Zeus, des göttlichen Verführers der Danae, zu ergänzen, dessen Mitschuld dadurch gemindert würde, daß sein Altar für die bedrohte Danae doch zu etwas nütze gewesen ist.

Aufs Ganze gesehen gibt sich die ausgeschriebene Partie des Theon-Kommentares als Mythenparaphrase. Ausschließlich vom erwachsenen Perseus scheint sie zu handeln. "The marginal addition to the end of l. 4 should belong to the previous lemma" (Turner). Stimmt letztere Annahme, so ist hier die Mythener-zählung von Perseus—anders als bei Pindar selbst—nicht durch den Bericht von der Tötung der Gorgo 'belastet' bzw. unterbrochen: auch nicht in den Zeilen 4–6, die in ihrem fragmentarischen Zustand zugegebenermaßen "a puzzle" enthalten (das in den Scholien behandelte Lemma τό τ' ἀναγκαῖον λέχος hier unter-zubringen gestatten sie jedenfalls m.E. nicht). Vielleicht wird das Rätsel etwas geringer, wenn man in der Wortgruppe ε[.]ωθεσωθεν, die durch *spatium* vom vorhergehenden und folgenden Text abgesetzt ist, wie üblich in derlei Fällen ein Dichterzitat anerkennt, d.h. aber nicht unbedingt ein Lemma aus Pindar, woran Turner gedacht hat. *Prima facie* mag hier die ganze Mythenerzählung Theons "clumsily told" erscheinen. Und in der Tat: so hübsch der Reihe nach erzählt wie im schol. zu Py. x 72 Dr. lesen wir hier die Geschichte nicht. Dort hören wir, nach der Einleitung ἡ ἱστορία ἐστὶ τοιαύτη, von der Aussetzung von Mutter und Kind durch Akrisios und davon, daß die Lade in Seriphos an Land getrieben wird, wo Polydektes König ist. Dann wird allerdings eine große Zeitspanne stillschweigend übersprungen, ehe die Erzählung mit καί ποτε weitergeht. Da heißt es dann: "Und einst, als er zum Mann herangewachsen war und bei Polydektes bewirtet wurde und ein jeglicher zum Freundschaftsmahl (εἰς τὸν ἔρανον) seinen Beitrag beisteuerte, versprach er, das Haupt der Gorgo zu bringen. Poly-dektes nahm das als willkommenen Anlaß, verlangte von ihm die Erfüllung des Versprechens und trieb ihn fort von der Insel, daß er das Haupt der Gorgo bringe. Polydektes begehrte nämlich seine Mutter. Und er ging fort, schnitt der Gorgo den Kopf ab, brachte

ihn als Beitrag zum Freundschaftsmahl (εἰς τὸν ἔρανον) und verwandelte alle, die beim Symposion waren (πάντας ... τοὺς ἐν τῷ
συμποσίῳ), in Steine, auch Polydektes selbst." Zu dieser Erzählung
braucht der Leser kaum etwas inhaltlich zu ergänzen: gerade nur
so viel, daß der erwachsene Perseus einem Liebesabenteuer des
Königs mit Danae im Wege gestanden haben muß, was andernorts
denn auch *expressis verbis* gesagt wird: Apollod. Bibl. II 4, 2, 1 ἠνδρω-
μένου Περσέως μὴ δυνάμενος αὐτῇ συνελθεῖν, wozu Maehler a.O. mit
Recht Schol. Apoll. Rhod. I 515 (= Pherekydes 3 F 11) und Tzetzes
zu Lykophron, Alexandra II 269.10 Scheer gestellt hat. Hinnehmen
als echtes Märchenmotiv muß der Leser das zweimalige Freundschaftsmahl (εἰς τὸν ἔρανον). Wie in der Gyges-Geschichte die
entehrende Bloßstellung der Frau und ihre Rache nur am gleichen
Ort[9] stattfinden kann, so auch hier im Perseusmythos die Provoka-
tion und die strafende Erfüllung des Auftrags. Dabei scheint der
zeitliche Abstand zwischen dem einen und dem anderen Eranos,
zwischen Aufbruch und Rückkehr des Perseus, keine Rolle zu
spielen oder doch nur eine sekundäre, vielleicht durch die vom
Gott Hermes beschafften Flügelschuhe[10] bagatellisierte, wenn nicht
gar fast ganz aufgehobene. Ohne hieran etwas zu ändern,[11] hat nun
Theon ein rational begreifliches, auch dramatisch verwertbares
Motiv in die Mythenerzählung von Perseus aufgenommen, ein
Motiv, von dem sonst nur bei Ps.-Apollodor ein Schimmer übrig-
geblieben war. "Sich selbst abwendend,"[12] heißt es da (Bibl.
II 4, 3, 6), habe Perseus den Zechern das Medusenhaupt gezeigt
(ἀπεστραμμένος ... ἔδειξε) und Diktys und Danae hätten sich an
Altäre[13] geflüchtet und seien (*scilicet*) so gerettet worden: καταλα-

---

[9] Vgl. K. Reinhardt, "Herodots Persergeschichten" in *Von Werken und Formen* (1947),
175 = *Vermächtnis der Antike* (1960), 141.

[10] Hermes ist neben Athena schon bei Pindar Dith. IV 37 in die Perseusgeschichte
einbezogen.

[11] Danaes Lage—z.B. in all den Jahren, bis ihr Sohn heranwuchs—wird nicht in
allem klar. Von Diktys als ihrem bisherigen Beschützer spricht Theon nicht.

[12] Das Nichthinblickendürfen ist aus Leukotheas Weisung an Odysseus (Hom. Od.
V 350 αὐτὸς δ' ἀπονόσφι τραπέσθαι), vor allem aber aus dem Orpheus-Mythos
hinlänglich bekannt. Unterwegs mag den Perseus sein Schnappsack immunisiert haben
gegen den Medusenblick, wenn man so vorwitzig ist, hiernach zu fragen. Apoll. Bibl. II
4, 2, 8 sagt immerhin auch noch, daß Perseus beim Enthaupten nur ihr Spiegelbild in
seinem ehernen Schild angeblickt habe.

[13] Den Götternamen erfahren wir auch hier nicht; doch s.o.

βῶν προσπεφευγυῖαν τοῖς βωμοῖς μετὰ τοῦ Δίκτυος τὴν μητέρα διὰ τὴν
Πολυδέκτου βίαν. Bei der Erfindung dieses Motivs dürfte die rationale
Überlegung mitgespielt haben, wie es denn bei der allgemeinen
Wirksamkeit des bösen Zaubers überhaupt Ausnahmen hat geben
können und Überlebende unter lauter Versteinerten: ein Problem,
das für frühe Fassungen des Mythos wohl gar nicht existierte, da
ein Überleben guter Menschen für das Märchen eine Selbstverständ-
lichkeit ist. Für Theon ist dieses Motiv jedoch so wichtig, daß er mit
σωθῆ[ναι τὴν Δανάη]ν als Höhepunkt seinen Mythenbericht schließt.
Das dramatische Motiv der Altarflucht mag letztlich einem Tragiker verdankt werden:[14] Turner dachte an die Danae des Euripides—auch der euripideische Diktys sei genannt—, doch eher noch
mag man an den aischyleischen Polydektes aus seiner Perseus-
Trilogie denken. Zwar ist uns nur der Titel bezeugt (frg. 462 Mette)
und nichts erhalten, doch trat da, ebenso wie in den Phorkides,
sicher der erwachsene Perseus auf; seine Kindheit, beginnend mit
der Landung der Lade mit Mutter und Kind in Seriphos, hat
Aischylos bekanntlich im Satyrspiel Diktyulkoi behandelt. Aber
wie dem auch sei: pindarisch ist dieses aus einem rationalen
Denkanstoß ableitbare, dramatisch überaus dankbare Motiv keineswegs. Dem thebanischen Lyriker genügt es vollauf, einmal, Py.
x, summarisch vom steinernen Tod zu sprechen, den Perseus bei
seiner Ankunft "den Nesioten" (= den Seriphiern, schol.) brachte.
Ein andermal, im *Pap. Oxy.* 2445 (= Dith. IV Snell), in dessen
fragmentarischen Resten Edgar Lobel scharfsichtig den Perseus-
Mythos erwähnt fand, sind sowohl die Seriphier als auch ihr
"Heerführer" als die Opfer genannt, und auch in unserem xii.
Pythischen Epinikion büßen "die Mannen" (λαοί) und Polydektes.
Letzterer ist allemal als der Schuldige gekennzeichnet: nach einer
Mitschuld oder Teilschuld der λαοί fragt Pindar nicht nur nicht:
in einem vergleichbaren Fall, bei der Koronisgeschichte Py. iii,
läßt er mit dem schuldigen Mädchen auch "viele Nachbarn" mit
in das Verderben gerissen werden: unschuldige, wie das schol. Py.
iii 64 b Dr. mit Recht bemerkt. Dort wie hier hat Pindar nach den
Überlebenden, von der Bestrafung Ausgenommenen nicht gefragt.

[14] Was bei Ps.-Apollodor nicht erstaunen würde. Über des Altarmotiv bei Euripides
(und Aischylos) s. H. Strohm, *Euripides* (Zetemata 15; 1957), 18 ff. Vgl. auch Aischylos,
Isthmiastai.

Derlei Genauigkeit braucht das Mythenmärchen nicht in seiner "einsträngigen"[15] Erzählweise. "Omnesque ab humana specie sunt informati in saxum" (Hygin. fab. LXIV 4) genügt vollauf; πάντας τοὺς ἐν τῷ συμποσίῳ ist da schon genauer.

Sehr anders und, wie gesagt, von einer andersartigen, vielleicht dramatischen Quelle letztlich nicht unbeeinflußt erzählt Theon den Mythos hier gerade unter dem zweifachen Aspekt "wurden versteinert" / "wurden gerettet." Zweimal hören wir ersteres: am Anfang, in der Paraphrase eines Lemmas aus Pindar, und am Schluß der zusammenhängend erzählten ἱστορία: dort ἀπελιθώθησαν, hier ἀπολιθωθῆναι. Am Schluß ist in σωθῆ[ναι auch die Rettung Danaes erwähnt, womit der zweite Aspekt des zwiefachen Themas zu seinem Recht kommt. Müßte nicht—so wird man fragen dürfen— die ganze Mythenerzählung weit weniger ungeschickt erscheinen als man bisher argwöhnte, wenn auch diese Seite des Doppelthemas, das σωθῆναι, bereits am Anfang ein erstes Mal berührt war (und zwar ebenfalls in einer Paraphrase eines Zitates, das allerdings unserem Pindartext von Py. XII nicht zu entnehmen war)? Vor dem γάρ-Satz und den genaueren Aussagen, die er—rückver- weisend—einleitet und in der Rettung Danaes gipfeln läßt? Wenn ja, dann kommt nur die "rätselhafte" Partie, Zeile 4–5, hierfür, d.h. für ein erstes Erwähnen des σωθῆναι, in Frage. Was steht nun aber dem Versuch entgegen, in eben jener Zeile 4 das sicher lesbare ECⲰⲐⲈⲚ als Nebenform für ἐσώθησαν (in einem Dichterzitat, einem jambischen vielleicht?) zu verstehen? Nur der Gleichklang mit dem Ortsadverb "von innen her," der gewiß keine Empfehlung andersartiger Auslegungen ist, wie immer sie lauten mögen?

Lassen wir es uns trotzdem nicht verdrießen, das Für und Wider eines solchen hypothetischen Erklärungsversuches gegeneinander abzuwägen! Einwände gibt es noch viele andere, z.T. sehr schwer- wiegende. Unerklärt bleibt die erste Hälfte der Wortgruppe, und eine halbe Erklärung ist nun einmal keine überzeugende Erklärung. In der betreffenden ersten Buchstabengruppe ϲ[.]ωθ scheint aller-

---

[15] Noch von Euripides kann man sagen: "Jede doppelsträngige Handlung lag ihm fern. Schon aus diesem Grunde kam für unser Iphigeniendrama eine innere Einbeziehung der Thoaswelt in die Tantalidensphäre, eine Verschränkung mit dem Rettungswerk so wenig in Frage wie eine innere Genesung des Orestes, eine Verschränkung mit der äußeren Befreiung. Umso fester geht der Weg des einfachen Geschehens" (Ernst Buschor in seiner Übersetzung von Euripides, *Iphigenie im Taurerlande* (1946), 99).

dings nach der Photographie zu urteilen, nur das Ѳ sicher, ѡ gut möglich, der Anfangsbuchstabe jedoch sehr unsicher. Wohl findet sich das Adv. ἔξωθεν geradezu als *terminus technicus* im Scholiastengriechisch,[16] in Wendungen wie ἔξωθεν ἀκουστέον, ἔξωθεν...προσληπτέον, ἔξωθεν ληπτέον τὸ ὥς, ἵνα ᾖ...u.dgl. Wohl scheint die Theon-Ꜧꜱ, die den Kopisten vorlag, unleserliche Stellen enthalten zu haben (s.o.): aber mit Schreibversehen[17] (etwa teilweiser Haplographie oder Dittographie) rechnen, ohne eine überzeugende Lösung anbieten zu können, hieße eine faule Ausrede suchen, zumal zwei Adverbien auf -θεν nebeneinander absurd wären,[18] bzw. zwei verschiedene Wörter auf -θεν sehr unschön und mißverständlich: und da eine Änderung von Ѳ in Т oder ⅄ doch recht gewaltsam wäre, die Wendung "von oben wurden sie gerettet" inhaltlich zwar vielleicht akzeptabel scheinen könnte, sich jedoch im fragmentarischen Text dieser Zeile nicht glatt wiederfinden läßt, so muß, nicht viel anders als Turner und Maehler, auch der Schreiber dieser Zeilen hier resignieren. Auch das "Wortende"]ocε (mit hoch gestelltem ε, also wohl -ε(ν)) vor dem angenommenen "Fremdzitat" lasse ich lieber unerklärt, als allen möglichen Spekulationen nachzugehen.

Andererseits wäre gegen die Verwendung der kurzen Endung in der 3. p. plur. im Aorist des Passivs, -θεν statt jüngerem -θησαν, nichts einzuwenden. Bei Homer weit überwiegend, im Dorischen durchaus gebräuchlich (bei Pindar, oft bei Epicharm, ἐφίλαθεν gelegentlich bei Theokrit), ist die kürzere Form auch für das attische Drama belegt: Eur. Hipp. 1247 ἔκρυφθεν (Trim.), Aristophanes, Vesp. 662 κατένασθεν (Anap.), s. Kühner-Blaß, *Ausführliche Grammatik der griechischen Sprache*, I 2, S. 54 f. Auch der Plural "sie wurden gerettet" würde, vom Inhalt her gesehen, keineswegs stören. Das kann dann zwar keine Aussage über Danae allein sein, doch hatten ja, laut Ps.-Apollodor, Diktys und Danae an Altären Zuflucht gesucht und gefunden. Der Plural im—sagen wir—"Fremdzitat" wäre aber nicht nur inhaltlich gut möglich,

[16] Die Stellen führt Drachmanns Index des *sermo technicus* an (Bd. III S. 384 seiner Ausgabe der Pindarscholien).

[17] Eine amüsante Verschreibung brachte der neue Pap. Bodmer XXVI (edd. Kasser-Austin, 1969) in Menanders Aspis v. 31: ΚΑΤΑΧΑΡΑΣ für χάρακα, τάς. Alle Buchstaben sind richtig, nur sind die Silben völlig durcheinandergeraten.

[18] Wenn auch Pindar οἴκοθεν οἴκαδε pointiert nebeneinander gebraucht, Ol. VI 99 und sich in den Scholien οὐκ ἐγγύθεν, ἀλλὰ μακρόθεν dicht beieinander findet.

sondern geradezu erforderlich im Hinblick auf die anschließende, mit ἵν' ᾖ καὶ τὴν beginnende Kommentierung. An ἵν' ᾖ<ι> ist dabei mit Maehler unbedingt festzuhalten. Zu dem einen, von ihm angeführten Beleg (schol. Isthm. I 60) lassen sich viele hinzufügen: allein in den Scholien zu Ol. I zählte ich 7 Beispiele. Diese Wendung gehört durchaus zum *sermo technicus*, wenn sie auch in Drachmanns Indices nicht aufgenommen ist. Richtig ist auch, daß nach ἵν' ᾖ meistens unmittelbar (sc. nach leichter Interpunktion) die Paraphrase zu kommen pflegt. Maehlers Satz "...is apparently the phrase used in the scholia to introduce a paraphrase of the poet's text" kann jedoch nicht ganz ohne Widerspruch hingenommen werden. Einen grammatisch nicht ungewöhnlichen Finalsatz auf einen einzigen Anwendungsbereich festlegen hieße eine unnötige Einengung postulieren. Aber nicht auf solche allgemeine Erwägungen allein stützt sich der Einwand gegen Maehler: Gegenbeispiele wie die folgenden sind anzuführen: [19] πρόσθες σύνδεσμον γάρ, ἵν' ᾖ συναρμοστέος ὁ λόγος τοῖς ἄνωθεν, καὶ εἰπέ κτλ., ἵν' ᾖ οὖν ὁ νοῦς οὕτως, ἵν' ᾖ ἡ ἀρχὴ οἷον κτλ., ἵν' ᾖ τὸ κρύβδαν ἐπὶ τοῦ δευτέρου γάμου (vgl. ἵνα καὶ τὸ ἑξῆς τοῦ λόγου οὕτως ἔχῃ κτλ., ἵνα πάσας τὰς βιωτικὰς ἀρετὰς εἴπῃ). Maehlers Behauptung trifft also doch nicht für sämtliche Einzelfälle zu, wohl für die meisten. Auch an unserer Textstelle im Theonpapyrus ἵν' ᾖ καὶ τήν kann (leichte) Interpunktion in Frage kommen und der begonnene Aussagesatz ähnlich wie im schol. Ol. VIII 37 b Dr. zu Ende geführt worden sein, wo es heißt: ἵν' ᾖ· τὴν Αἴγιναν...ἡ κρίσις τῶν θεῶν ὑπέστησε. Aber auch eine (interpunktionslose) Weiterführung im AcI ist denkbar.[20] Im einen wie im anderen Fall muß ein Akkusativ das Nomen zum weiblichen Artikel τήν gebracht haben. Bleibt man bei der Voraussetzung, daß hier in Z. 4 trotz der Marginalnote nicht von den Gorgonen (Σθενώ z.B.) die Rede war, so stehen für jenes weibliche Objekt (bzw. logische Subjekt im AcI) wohl nur zwei Möglichkeiten zur Wahl: "die Danae" oder "die Rettung (Danaes)," und das "auch" (das, nach Turner, vielleicht durchgestrichen war) ginge auf implizit mit Einbegriffenes bzw. "Hörbares" (ἀκουστέον, συνυπακουστέον, auch δεῖ νοεῖσθαι sind hierfür die gebräuchlichen

---

[19] Schol. Pind. Ol. IX 85 a; Ol. I 97 g; Ol. VI 4 b; Py. III 25 b; Ol. VI 23 c; Ol. I 20 g Dr.

[20] Eher sogar, da man das Verbum im Passiv erwarten möchte wie Z. 11.

Termini). Beide Möglichkeiten führen jedoch auf das Gleiche hinaus: auf eine erste Erwähnung Danaes im nicht erhaltenen Text von Z. 5. Und noch ein weiteres Ergebnis darf festgehalten werden. Die stereotype Wendung ἵν' ᾖ ist aufschlußreich nicht nur für den folgenden Kontext, sondern auch für den vorhergehenden. Sie knüpft, meist unmittelbar und sofort, seltener mittelbar (τοῦτο εἶπεν, ἵνα...), an ein Dichterzitat an. Nicht paläographische Gründe allein (das *spatium*) sprechen dafür, daß in ϵ[.]ωθεϲωθεn ein Zitat zu erblicken ist: das anschließende ἵν' ᾖ läßt hieran kaum einen Zweifel.

Eine Beobachtung, die an Grundsätzliches rührt, an Methoden-fragen der philologischen Interpretation, sei hier angeschlossen, zumal diese Beobachtung dazu angetan ist, einen möglicherweise auftauchenden Einwand gegen den hier zur Diskussion gestellten Interpretationsversuch unserer Textstelle zu widerlegen. Eher ak-zeptabel als ein Finalsatz könnte uns nämlich eine Formulierung mit einem Konsekutivsatz erscheinen, etwa: "XY hat gesagt, 'sie wurden gerettet,' so daß die Danae da mit einbegriffen ist." Antike Kommentatoren sind jedoch selbstsicher genug, sich nicht von Einzelbeobachtungen zu einer Folgerung (= Konsekutivsatz) leiten zu lassen, sondern von der Absicht des Dichters auszugehen, so als ob diese ohne weiteres zu erkennen wäre. Sätze wie βούλεται δὲ λέγειν, θέλει δὲ εἰπεῖν "er will sagen" (schol. Pind. Ol. ΙΙ 19 b; 62 b) sind hierfür typisch. Sie dominieren bei weitem. Unklarheiten (ἀδήλως ... εἶπεν, ὁ δὲ νοῦς ἐπαμφοτερίζει schol. Ol. VII 151; Py. I 121 c) werden nur ganz selten zugegeben. So können denn auch Unarten der Philologie, die wir uns und anderen Adepten dieser Kunst abzugewöhnen suchen, wie sich zeigt, recht alt sein. Vergessen scheint die platonische Skepsis, die bedauern muß, daß man die alten Dichter nicht nach ihrer Absicht befragen kann,[21] und die den Sokrates einmal sagen läßt:[22] dies scheine ihm der Dichter sich gedacht zu haben bei der Abfassung des Gedichtes. Unter den Erben alexandrinischer Philologen ist Theon mit seiner Selbst-sicherheit keine Ausnahme, wenn er in Finalsätzen argumentiert.

Ein Übersetzungsversuch der bisher betrachteten elfeinhalb

---

[21] Plat. Hipp. min. 365 c 8 f.; Prot. 347 e 3 ff.

[22] Plat. Prot. 347 a 3: ταῦτά μοι δοκεῖ...Σιμωνίδης διανοούμενος πεποιηκέναι τοῦτο τὸ ᾆσμα.

Zeilen des Theonkommentares mag weniger die beseitigten als die immer noch verbleibenden Schwierigkeiten deutlich machen. Er könnte so lauten: "...(nicht nur) dem Polydektes. Zu einem leidigen Mahl machte er es: (den Seriphiern), denn als eben diese fröhlich zechten, (zeigte ihnen Perseus) das (Medusen-) Haupt und so wurden sie versteinert. (XY hat gesagt) '...sie wurden gerettet,' damit sich ergibt, daß auch die (Danae gerettet wurde). Denn es geschah, daß Danae, als Polydektes sie zu vergewaltigen versuchte, Zuflucht gesucht hatte am Altar des (Zeus), daß Polydektes aber, sich vor Perseus in acht nehmend, ihn ausgeschickt hatte zur Enthauptung der Medusa, damit er umkäme und (nicht wieder zurückkäme), (und) daß Polydektes (sc. nun) durch den Anblick des Gorgonenhauptes versteinert wurde und daß errettet wurde die Danae."

Die ganze, mit γάρ beginnende Mythenerzählung ist, abhängig von συνέβη, im AcI gegeben. Daß die beiden ersten der insgesamt vier Infinitive (καταφυγεῖν, πέμψαι) Vorvergangenes meinen, ist sprachlich nicht zu beanstanden. Eher ist zu bemängeln, daß für das in Z. 2–3 (mit αὐτοῖς τούτοις) so energisch hervorgehobene Thema "die übrigen Seriphier" in der auf die Hauptpersonen beschränkten Mythenerzählung kein Platz bleibt. Aber das reicht doch wohl nicht aus, um den Vorwurf aufrecht zu halten, die Geschichte sei "clumsily told."

Der weitere Text von col. I, d.h. Z. 12–30, lautet:

ἔνιοι δ(έ) φα(σιν) οὐ ταύτην (εἶναι) τὴν Γορ-
[γόνα ἀλλὰ τὴν] γηγενῆ ἦν ἡ γῆ ἀνέδωκεν ἐν τῶι πολέ-
[μωι τῶι τῶν γι]γάντων πρὸς τοὺς θεούς. τὸν ἀπὸ
15 [χρυσοῦ φαμεν αὐ]τορύτου τὸν Περσέα· ὁ γ(ὰρ) Ζεὺς χρυ-
[σὸς γενόμενος] συνῆ[λ]θε τῆι Δανάηι· ἀλλ' ἐπεὶ ἐκ
[τούτων   ] ἀλλ' ἐπεὶ ἡ Παρθένος φ(ησ)ὶ ἤγ(ουν) Ἀθηνᾶ
[ἐρρύσατο τὸν φί]λον ἄνδρα τότε κατεσκεύαζε τὸ μέ-
[λος· οὕτω γ(ὰρ) φ(ησ)ι σ]υνεργῆσαι τὴν Ἀθηνᾶν τῶι Περσεῖ
20 [   ]εοι.ς τῆς Γοργόνος. ὄφρα τὸν Εὐρυάλας ἐκ καρπαλιμ.]ᾶν γεν[ύων] ἕως τοῦ εὖρεν θεός
[εὖρεν γ(ὰρ) ἡ θεὸς ἤγ(ουν)] Ἀθηνᾶ τὴν αὐλητικὴν ὅπως μι-
[μήσαιτο σὺν ἔν]τεσι τῶν αὐλῶν τουτέστιν τοῖς
[ὀργάνοις θρῆνον] τῶν καρπαλίμων γενύων τῆς
25 [Γοργόνος Εὐρυά]λας ἱστᾶσ[α] γόον· ἀπὸ δὲ τῆς μιᾶς
[καὶ τὴν ἑτέραν τ]ὴν Σθεννὼ παρίστησι· ἀλλά μιν

[λεπτοῦ διανι]σόμενον χαλκοῦ θ᾿ ἄμα ἔνιοι θαμά.
[καὶ δονάκων] τοὶ παρὰ καλλίχορον νάοισι ἄκυρον τὸ
[ναίοισιν· Εὐριπί]δης δ᾿ ἐν Οἰδίποδι· τόν θ᾿ ὑμνοποιὸν δόνα-
30 *[κα ὂν ἐκφύει (?) Μέ]λας ποταμὸς ἀηδόν᾿ εὐπνόων αὐλῶν σοφήν*

Auch zu diesem Textabschnitt stammen die Ergänzungen zumeist vom Erstherausgeber, E. G. Turner. In Z. 16 und 18 hat
er Vorschläge von H. Erbse aufgenommen; zu Z. 20 s.u. Zu einem
nicht geringen Teil sind die Ergänzungen durch den pindarischen
Wortlaut in den Lemmata gesichert, zumal ja auch die Paraphrase
gern auf den Originaltext zurückgreift, sofern es sich nicht um
seltene Wörter handelt. Dabei fällt auf, daß in Z. 15 das bei Theon
ausgeschriebene Lemma um ein Wort (*αὐτορύτου*) länger ist als im
schol. Py. xii 29 Dr. Ähnlich ist es in Z. 21 (und in Z. 27 f. und 35 f.):
das gleiche Lemma in den Scholien endet mit *Εὐρυάλας*. In Z. 17
könnte es ebenso sein: wenn man sich den verbleibenden Raum
von 5–6 Buchstaben mit dem pindarischen Wort *πόνων* ausgefüllt
denkt, das allerdings im Liedtext erst nach 2 weiteren Wörtern
folgt: andernfalls und eher noch wäre nach dem mit *ἐκ τούτων*
endenden Lemma, vor dem mit *ἀλλ᾿ ἐπεί* beginnenden Erläuter-
ungssatz, die Ergänzung *ὁ (δὲ) νοῦς* vorzuschlagen. Diese einleitende Wendung wird (mit oder ohne *δέ*) von Kommentatoren
gerade dann gern gebraucht,[23] wenn eine zusammenhängende, all-
gemeinverständliche Wiedererzählung eines umfangreicheren Text-
abschnittes geboten wird, nicht die Erklärung der im Lemma
ausgeschriebenen Ausdrücke. Abweichend von Turner lese ich den
zweiten Buchstaben in Z. 20. Turner las hier *]εσι.ς τῆς Γοργόνος*
und vermerkte: "a high dot of ink before *σ*; hardly room for *ω*."
Nach der Photographie zu urteilen ist das erste Sigma in Wahrheit
jedoch ein Omikron (zustimmend Pfeiffer): *]ε οῖος τῆς Γοργόνος*
wird damit zu einer sehr wahrscheinlichen und e.gr. *[ὥστε ἐκράτησ]ε*
οῖος τῆς Γοργόνος zu einer möglichen Ergänzung. Zwar finden sich
bei Ps.-Apollodor über die tätige Mithilfe Athenas bei der Enthauptung der Medusa andere und genauere Angaben: Athena
habe dem Perseus die Hand beim Zuschlagen geführt (a.O. II 4,
2, 8 *κατευθυνούσης τὴν χεῖρα Ἀθηνᾶς*): das aber kann hier in
der Lücke im Papyrustext nicht gestanden haben und ein Vorlieb-

---

[23] Vgl. z.B. schol. Ol. VII 19 g; 71 a; 164 Dr.

nehmen mit einer summarischen Aussage erscheint durchaus glaubhaft. Man wende nun nicht ein, göttliche Hilfe (συνεργῆσαι) schließe ein Alleinvollbringen (οἷος) aus. Nur für Gleichgestellte würde das zutreffen, nicht für die Vereinigung von göttlicher und menschlicher Motivierung.—Zu Z. 21–22 bringt eine Marginalnotiz im Papyrus (von zweiter Hand) die Worterklärung ἐρικλάγκταν· μεγαλοκλάγκταν. In Z. 29 schließe ich mich Maehler an: ἄκυρον τὸ [ναίοισι scheint eher möglich als ἄκυρον τὸ [δονάκων (Turner), da nicht leicht einzusehen ist, inwiefern hierbei etwas "improprie dictum"[24] sein sollte. Daß dagegen Schilf nur in uneigentlichem Sinn irgendwo 'wohnen' kann, ist nur zu wahr: eine "Binsenwahrheit" allerdings, wie man im Deutschen sagt, aber an banalen Erklärungen fehlt es bei Theon auch sonst nicht. Strenger als er urteilen hier die Scholien (45 b Dr.): σκληρῶς und διθυραμβωδῶς sei das Verbum gebraucht: ἔδει γὰρ εἰπεῖν φύονται. Das neue Euripidesfragment aus dem Oidipus, das diesem Theonkommentar verdankt wird, hat C. Austin bereits 1968 in *Nova fragmenta Euripidea in papyris reperta* (Kleine Texte, 187) als frg. 100 abdrucken können.[25] Z. 27–30, letztere übrigens die Schlußzeile in dieser Kolumne, sind von dritter Hand geschrieben. Sie hat Raum für mindestens 1 Zeile zwischen Z. 26–27 freigelassen. Tatsächlich ist hier eine Textlücke festzustellen, eine Lücke geringeren Umfangs m.E., in der das mit ἀλλά μιν begonnene Lemma mit εὑροῖσα zu Ende geführt war und die Paraphrase vielleicht mit der aitiologischen Benennung des Nomos Polykephalos schloß. Der freigelassene Abstand kann als Andeutung der Textlücke gedeutet werden und die Lücke selbst vielleicht auch hier mit der Unleserlichkeit des Exemplares, das den Kopisten vorlag, entschuldigt werden. Z. 27–30 sind jedenfalls kein Nachtrag, sondern stehen, wenn auch von anderer Hand geschrieben, am richtigen Platz. Für die Beurteilung ähnlich gelagerter Fälle[26] kann das von Interesse sein.

Eigenheiten des Theon-Kommentares sind in dieser Textpartie weniger auffällig als im Vorhergehenden: nicht zuletzt deshalb,

---

[24] Vgl. Drachmann a.O. Indices (III p. 362).

[25] Die Ergänzung ὃν ἐκφύει überzeugt mich nicht: eine "uneigentliche," metaphorische Wendung wäre m.E. eher zu erwarten, da nur dann das Euripideszitat eine Parallelstelle zu Pindar ergäbe.

[26] Vgl. z.B. die merkwürdige anapästische "Visit to the Underworld" nr. 94 Page, *Select Papyri* = E. Heitsch, *Die griech. Dichterfragmente der röm. Kaiserzeit* (1961), nr. LVIII.

weil hier eine Vielzahl von Lemmata behandelt wird: davon das eine über die Vaterschaft des Zeus in auffälliger Kürze und eines in der bekannten summarischen Weise, die den Text von... bis... zitiert und dabei einiges überspringen kann. Aber auch in dieser mehrteiligen Partie fällt manches auf. Reichlich primitiv mutet da z.B. die Worterklärung an "Parthenos d.h. Athena," "die Göttin d.h. Athena" (das zweite Beispiel ist allerdings ergänzt). Ganz banale Erklärungen fehlen zwar auch sonst in den Scholien nicht: daß z.B. mit "Kastalische Quelle" Delphi gemeint ist, daß an dem Ufer des Alpheios Olympia liegt u.a.m. So schlimm wie die Behauptung, Pindar müsse das Geschichtswerk des Ephoros gekannt haben,[27] ist das alles nicht, doch so banal wie Theon mit seinem ἤγουν Ἀθηνᾶ sind wenige antike Erklärer. Mit der Rücksicht auf Schulzwecke mag dieser Hang zum Banalen sich erklären, und er würde sich wohl teilweise entschuldigen lassen, wenn andererseits auch die seltenen und schwierigen Wörter erklärt wären. Einiges Interesse hierfür verraten die Marginalnotizen von zweiter Hand. Da auch sie doch wohl Auszüge aus dem Theon-Kommentar bringen, wird man mit Theon diesbezüglich nicht zu hart ins Gericht gehen dürfen. Die Lexika verdanken ihm viel glossematisches Material. Nicht unbedingt zu Theons Lasten, vielleicht ebenfalls nur auf das Konto des Abschreibers geht die Tatsache, daß die Mythenvariante (ἔνιοι δέ φασιν) über die Genealogie der Gorgo nicht an ein inhaltlich entsprechendes Lemma anknüpft. Aber das diesbezügliche, eben die Genealogie berührende Lemma Φόρκοι᾽ ἀμαύρωσεν γένος, auf das sich auch die Marginalnote Z. 4–6 (über ἀμαύρωσε) bezieht, wird vorher, im nicht erhaltenen Teil von Theons Kommentar gestanden haben. Dann bliebe nicht Wegfall eines Lemmas zu konstatieren, nur Einordnung einer Texterklärung an falscher Stelle. Dieser Vorwurf wiegt nicht schwer, zumal im Pindartext die in Seriphos spielende Geschichte nicht nur umrahmt ist vom Gorgonenthema, sondern immer wieder mit ihm verflochten und verwoben. Das mythische Hauptthema von Athenas Liederfindung (Παλλὰς ἐφεῦρε... τεῦχε μέλος... εὗρεν θεός) umrahmt dann noch in der bekannten Art der Ringkomposition die gesamte Mythenerzählung dieses Liedes. Schwerer als eine Störung

---

[27] Schol. Pind. Py. I 146 b Dr. Vgl., über Absurditäten (auch geographische) in den Pindarscholien, Deas a.O. 55 f.

in der Reihenfolge der Erklärungen wiegt jedoch die kritiklose
Übernahme der Mythenvariante: "Manche meinen, nicht diese
Gorgo sei gemeint, sondern die erdgeborene, von der Ge im Kriege
der Giganten gegen die Götter hervorgebrachte." Gewiß steht auch
hinter dieser Variante einige Gelehrsamkeit, die sich mindestens
auf Euripides, Ion 988 f. berufen könnte und die Bescheid weiß in
den Mythen von der Herkunft der Aigis mit Medusenhaupt, wie
Athena sie zu tragen pflegt. Aber eine Variante anführen, die am
pindarischen Wortlaut "Geschlecht des Phorkos" scheitern muß,
heißt mit Gelehrsamkeit am unrechten Ort prunken. Ein positives,
nicht unkritisches Gegenstück präsentiert sich uns im schol. Ol.
VII 24 c οὐχ ὥς τινες..., ἐναντίον γὰρ τὸ ἐπαγόμενον; vgl. στασιάζεται
ἡ ἱστορία schol. Py. 1 31 c Dr. Man wende nun nicht ein, der
von Theon nicht vermerkte Widerspruch sei nicht so eklatant, da bei
Pindar nur der Vater, in der Mythenvariante nur die Mutter der Gorgo
genannt wird. Dieser Einwand gilt nicht, denn auf konziliatorische
Vereinigung beider Zeugnisse kommt es dem, der die Mythenvariante
über "die andere Gorgo" offerierte, ganz und gar nicht an. Doch
gehen wir weiter. In Z. 17–20, der ersten etwas ausführlicheren Paraphrase dieses Abschnitts, bedient sich Theon weitgehend des pindarischen Vokabulars, bis auf τότε κατεσκεύαζε (für τεῦχε, ebenso schol. 31
Dr.) und συνεργῆσαι κτλ., wozu es im Pindartext keine Entsprechung
gibt. Wäre die Ergänzung [οὕτω γάρ φησι σ]υνεργῆσαι richtig, so
ergäbe dieser Satz mit "er sagt" eine unwahre oder mindestens
nicht belegbare Behauptung, sofern der Kommentator nicht an ein
anderes Lied Pindars gedacht hat. Vielleicht ist daher die Ergänzung
φασί = "man sagt" vorzuziehen. Auch dann bleibt unbestreitbar,
daß hier die Mythenerzählung über eine Paraphrase des Pindartextes
hinausgeht. Das Mehr, das der Kommentator hier anbringt, besteht—sagen wir—aus erfreulichen, ohne blutige Details erwähnten
Tatsachen: Athena half mit, so daß Perseus allein (s.o.) die Medusa
bezwang. Der nächste Abschnitt (Z. 20–26) gibt sich schon durch
das einleitende Lemma mit von...bis...als summarisch. Die
Paraphrase beginnt mit dem Schluß, der Erfindung der Auletik,
berührt dann manche Aussagen aus dem vorhergehenden Text, ohne
sich um deren Erklärung zu bemühen, um, nach der Erwähnung der
Euryala, auch ihre Schwester Stheno "dazuzustellen," wie es, fast
gleichlautend, das schol. 35 b Dr. tut (o.S. 68).

Daß der dritte Schreiber (Z. 27 ff.) zu einem reichlich langen Lemma gerade nur eine *varia lectio* zu bringen hat (ἔνιοι θαμά) und, vor dem Euripideszitat, die Mitteilung über "uneigentlichen" Wortsinn des Wortes "wohnen," finde ich recht knapp und dürftig. Von seinen Ausführungen in col. II, die es nun noch zu betrachten gilt, wird man gerade das nicht sagen können. Allerdings wird jedes Urteil über den Text in col. II aus mehreren äußeren Gründen ungemein erschwert. Niemand kann ahnen, wie viele Zeilen am Kolumnenanfang voraufgegangen[28] und uns völlig verloren sind. Warum die vier Zeilen 31–34 durchgestrichen wurden, bleibt ungeklärt, ist jedoch vielleicht nicht so wichtig für den, der keine Bedenken hat, auch diesen Text dem Theon zuzuweisen. Leider ist nur der Text selbst hier so stark zerstört, daß er erst ab Z. 35 verständlich wird. Col. II:

ε.ọ[.].εχọυ,[.......]ε.τọ..[....]νọν[....]...[
δαι.[.]νιανοθ.[...]φ......[.]παρεχεταιητοι
[.].[....]τον.ον.[.....].[......]ηνημε.....στα
ω.[...]ουδειπρ[.].[...]νειν..ασ..θουσα...ρας
35 τοῦ[τ]ο δὲ ὥσπ(ερ) ἐπισφραγίζων [π]ọεῖ. τὸ γὰρ μόρσιμο(ν)
οὐ πᾶ φυκτόν. [τ]ὸ γ(ὰρ) μοιρίδι[ο]ν οὐκ (ἔστι) παραφυγεῖν
ἀλλ' ὅ[σ]α ἡ μοῖρα β[ού]λεται τᾳ̈δε δεῖ εὐτυχῆσαι
γ[ράφετ(αι)] κ(αὶ) οὐ παρφ[υ]κτόν

Deutlich wird wenigstens, daß hier durchweg, auch in Z. 31–34, der gnomische Schlußteil von Py. XII paraphrasiert war: nicht unähnlich, möchte man vermuten, den Scholienerklärungen, die diese zu den Lemmata εἰ δέ τις ὄλβος, ἐκ δὲ τελευτάσει νιν ἤ τοι σάμερον bringen. Aber weder läßt sich eines dieser Lemmata in Z. 31–34 wiederfinden noch lassen sich sonst pindarische Wörter in der Paraphrase nachweisen noch auch gleicher Wortlaut wie in den Scholien. Alle diese eventuellen Hilfen versagen hier. Wenn man z.B. Z. 32 ergänzt zu δαιμ[ο]νίαν ὁ θε[ὸς.]φ......[.] παρέχεται ἤτοι, so bleibt das vom pindarischen δαίμων τὸ μόρσιμον gleich weit entfernt wie von θεὸς τὸ εἱμαρμένον in den Scholien, und weder das pindarische ἐκ δὲ τελευτάσει vermag ich wiederzufinden noch das τελέσει bzw. ἐπὶ τέλος ἄξει der Scholien. Nur

---

[28] "The lemma from l. 22...seems unfinished...; probably it was continued at the top of col. III, where the interpretation of an important action was given" (Turner), bleibt mir auch dann z.T. unverständlich, wenn ich col. II statt col. III lese.

aus der Tatsache, daß bei Pindar auf ἤτοι das Wort σάμερον
folgt und in den Scholien ἤτοι σήμερον ἢ ὕστερον steht, ergibt
sich ein Anhaltspunkt für die Ergänzung des zerstörten Textes,
nach ἤτοι, am Beginn von Z. 33 (vielleicht [σ]ή[μερον] τὸν πόνο[ν].
Vom Inhalt her gesehen scheint es wahrscheinlich, daß auch bei
Theon der Hinweis nicht gefehlt hat, etwas Unausgesprochenes
müsse mitverstanden, "mitgehört" werden (συνυπακουστέον schol.
49 Dr.). Für Z. 34 ließe sich dann die Ergänzung δειπρ[ο]σ
[ακο]νειν in Erwägung ziehen, obwohl dieses Kompositum weder
zum *sermo technicus* gehört noch auch sonst häufig gebraucht worden
zu sein scheint. Mit alledem ist nicht gerade viel geholfen, und weiter
bin ich nicht gekommen.

Halten wir uns an die verständlichen Zeilen 35 ff.: ein allgemeines,
"aesthetisches" Urteil über Pindars Gnome: das Lemma das (in
kürzerer Form) in den Scholien das vorletzte ist: seine Paraphrase
und, zuletzt, eine *varia lectio* (mit γράφεται καί eingeleitet) vor der
subscriptio. Das Urteil, gleichsam "besiegelnd" dichte Pindar [29]
diese Gnome, hat in den Pindarscholien nicht seinesgleichen.
Wohl begegnet da das Verbum ἐπισφραγίζω noch einmal (schol.
Isthm. 1 90 b Dr.): dort aber (ῥητῶς ἐπεσφράγισται) als Bestätigung
für die Wahrheit einer einzelnen Aussage (daß dieser Herodotos
tatsächlich Thebaner war). So eng dürfte sich der Sinn an unserer
Theonstelle kaum fassen lassen. Stereotyp und damit entwertet
(wie γνωμικῶς) ist der Ausdruck nicht. Gern wüßte man, ob bei
Theon auch schon zu Py. 1 gesagt war, was im schol. Py. 1 17 b Dr.
steht: γραφικώτατα...τὸν ἀετὸν ὑπετύπωσεν: auch das ein keineswegs schulmäßiges Urteil. So hübsch aber nun auch durch den
Vergleich mit einem aufgedrückten Siegel Pindars Gnome gekennzeichnet ist: daß Theons Paraphrase ihrem—vorwiegend skeptischen
—Inhalt gerecht wird, finde ich nicht. Bei Pindar ist hier eine
zweimalige Scheidung durchgeführt: einmal scheidet er die heu-
tige Erfüllung von der künftigen Zeit, zum anderen in der künftigen
Zeit eine teilweise Erfüllung der Erwartung von einem "Noch
nicht." Das schol. 51 Dr. reduziert das auf die einfache Alternative: es wird erfüllt werden heute oder später, und bemängelt
ausdrücklich: das sei nachzutragen, da Pindar es unterlassen habe:

[29] Turners Zweifel "...of the poet or...of δαίμων or χρόνος" teile ich nicht.

ἐπὶ τέλος ἄξει, ἤτοι σήμερον ἢ ὕστερον· τοῦτο γὰρ ἔδει ἐπενεγκεῖν, ὃ δὴ παρέλιπεν. Theon folgert in ähnlicher Weise, nur noch entschiedener: wenn das Schicksal es will, muß es gelingen (δεῖ εὐτυχῆσαι), was Pindar nie gesagt hat. Das Erfreuliche darf bei Theon nicht zu kurz kommen, sei es auch um den Preis, daß der "polare Gegensatz" hinzuerfunden wird. Solche "Polarisierung" der Aussagen in paraphrasierenden Scholien war schon K. Lehrs aufgefallen:[30] vgl. schol. Ol. IX 54 a (zu ἐχθρὰ σοφία) ἀλλότριον τοῖς σοφοῖς, ἀνοήτοις δὲ οἰκεῖον, schol. Py. IV 7 a (zu οὐκ ἀποδάμου Ἀπόλλωνος τυχόντος) οὐκ ἀποδημοῦντος τοῦ θεοῦ ἀλλὰ παρόντος. Sie ist verständlich und mag im Bereich der Mythenparaphrase harmlos sein: bei der Paraphrase gnomischer Aussagen ist sie nicht ungefährlich, da sie eine Verschiebung des Sinnes zur Folge hat. Theon ist hierin sehr weit gegangen: δεῖ und εὐτυχῆσαι, "Muß" und "Glückhaben," spannt er in den gleichen Satz, was andere—auch dem logischen Gegensatz des Kontextes zuliebe—nicht täten.

Ein abschließendes—natürlich nur vorläufig[31] abschließendes—Gesamturteil über Theons Hypomnemata zu Pindar wird, wie die Marginalnoten nahelegen, mit einem vollständigeren Exemplar rechnen müssen, das uns im Pap. Oxy. 2536 an manchen Stellen nur exzerpiert vorliegt. Größer als hier scheint ursprünglich, in der Vorlage, der Anteil gewesen zu sein, den die Worterklärung einnahm (für die sich der zweite Schreiber interessiert hat). Trotzdem bleibt bestehen, daß bei Theon καρπαλιμῶν nicht, wie in den Scholien, mit ἰσχυρῶν übersetzt war. In den Paraphrasen scheint Theons Stärke zu liegen. In ihnen löste sich, wie mindestens zu 3 Stellen zu bemerken war, die Paraphrase vom Pindartext und ging eigene Wege. Die Richtung dieser eigenen Wege zu bestimmen soll nicht unversucht bleiben. Das Eingehen auf Danaes Rettung, das erste dieser Beispiele, schien ableitbar von einem rationalen Denkanstoß. Man kann ihn sich konkret in Form von Fragen vorstellen: "Doch nicht alle?" etwa oder "Und die übrigen?" Fragen dieser Art haben Theon und andere Erklärer auch dazu geführt, nach der Erwähnung der Medusa und ihrer Schwester Euryala auch

---

[30] K. Lehrs, *Die Pindarscholien* (1873), 27 m. Anm. (mit weiteren Beispielen); Deas a.O. 67. Über einige Schrullen in Pindarscholien vgl. H. Fränkel, *Hermes* 89 (1961), 385 ff.

[31] Auf die Apollonios- und Theokritscholien wurde hier nicht Bezug genommen.

noch die dritte Schwester, Stheno, in ihre Aussagen einzubeziehen,
über die Pindar kein Wort verloren hatte, obwohl er die Dreizahl
der Gorgonen erwähnt hat. Fragen solcher Art können sich ergeben,
wenn Bildungswissen und Information durch den Dichter diver-
gieren. Sie haben etwas Vorwitziges in der Bereitschaft, dem Dichter
etwas "am Zeug zu flicken" und das Bildungswissen—es gab doch
3 Gorgonen: was tat die dritte?—in jedem Fall anzubringen, und
Vorwitz ist ein Vorrecht der Jugend. Eine wahre, nun schon 50
Jahre zurückliegende Begebenheit aus dem Schülerleben kann das
illustrieren. Während Oberlehrer XY seinen Sekundanern etwas
von Goethe und Frau v. Stein vorschwärmt, meldet sich einer der
Schüler zu Wort mit der Frage: "Und Herr v. Stein?" Die Frage
kam für den Lehrer völlig unerwartet: dementsprechend hilflos war
auch seine Antwort. Den möglichen Fragen "Und Danae?" "Und
die dritte Gorgone?" hat Theon vorgebaut, die Form des Frage-
und Antwortspiels, das einige Scholien zeigen, hat er verschmäht.
Aber wie seine Trivialerklärungen "die Göttin, d.h. Athena" auf
das geistige Niveau von Lernenden zugeschnitten sind, so paßt auch
der—"didaktische"—Optimismus von $\delta\epsilon\hat{\iota}$ $\epsilon\dot{\upsilon}\tau\upsilon\chi\hat{\eta}\sigma\alpha\iota$ (in der Paraphrase der Gnome) und die erfreuliche Mitteilung: Athena half,
so daß Perseus allein die Gorgo bezwang—*sit venia verbo*—, zu
einem Schulmeister: obwohl H. T. Deas zu zeigen versucht hatte,
daß Theon kein "educationist" sei (a.O. 38). In jenem Aufsatz
wird aber auch sonst die Bedeutung Theons für die Pindarphilologie
doch wohl überschätzt. Kritische Stellungnahme Theons zu den von
ihm (ohne Namensnennung) zitierten Text- und Mythenvarianten
vermißt man, daß er keine Vorwürfe gegen Pindar erhebt, ist
anzuerkennen, und sein ästhetisches Urteil über Pindars Gnome
kann mit manchem Manko aussöhnen. Anerkennend muß das
Urteil über den Pindartext ausfallen, den Theons Pythien-Kom-
mentar voraussetzt, zitiert und erklärt. Mit dem Akkusativ $\pi\alpha\rho\grave{\alpha}$
$\kappa\alpha\lambda\lambda\acute{\iota}\chi\upsilon\rho\upsilon\nu$ bestätigt er eine—von Turyn akzeptierte—Konjektur
Gottfried Hermanns; in zwei Einzelheiten, in der von Turyn
aufgenommenen Lesung $\chi\alpha\lambda\kappa\upsilon\hat{\upsilon}$ θ' $\ddot{\alpha}\mu\alpha$ (v.l. $\theta\alpha\mu\acute{\alpha}$) und in $\upsilon\dot{\upsilon}$ $\pi\hat{\alpha}$
$\varphi\upsilon\kappa\tau\acute{\upsilon}\nu$ (v.l. $\upsilon\dot{\upsilon}$ $\pi\alpha\rho\varphi\upsilon\kappa\tau\acute{\upsilon}\nu$) stimmt er mit dem cod. V überein,
dem Parisinus graecus 2403, der hierin jedenfalls nicht byzantinische
Konjekturen enthält. Eine Einzelheit bei Theon, $\nu\acute{\alpha}\upsilon\iota\sigma\iota$ für $\nu\alpha\acute{\iota}\upsilon\iota\sigma\iota$,
hat sich begreiflicherweise nicht hinüberretten können in unsere

mittelalterlichen Handschriften. ἀλλά μιν hat an unserer Stelle cod. B, τό γε alle HSS bis auf Triclinius (τὸ δέ).

München, 5. Mai 1970

[Korrekturzusatz: Eine briefliche Auskunft, für die ich Professor Turner auch hier herzlich Dank sage, bestätigt meine Lesung (Z. 20) nicht. "I do not think it would be easy to read οιος ... I should in any case feel rather doubtful whether a commentator would use this rare word in explaining a passage."]

PROBLEMI DI METRICA, II:
IL CARME 17 SNELL DI BACCHILIDE*

BRUNO GENTILI

Il problema metrico e testuale degli 'Ηίθεοι di Bacchilide dopo le edizioni di B. Snell sembra non destare più alcun interesse. L'energica e autorevole presa di posizione dell'editore in difesa della colometria serbataci dai due importanti testimoni, i papiri A e O, e, suo grande merito, il cauto conservatorismo nella giusta valutazione di alcune presunte licenze metriche,[1] non del tutto coerenti con le rigide norme enucleate da P. Maas,[2] hanno rappresentato una svolta decisiva nella critica testuale del carme. Altre soluzioni non sembrerebbero ormai possibili soprattutto dopo le obiezioni mosse dallo stesso Snell[3] alla sistemazione del testo e del metro operata dal Wilamowitz:[4] "Ex iambis ortum est metrum carminis 17, et Wilamowitz...operam dat, ut omne carmen in iambos dissolvat, sed facere non potest non modo quin textum nonnullis locis commutet, sed etiam quin alia metra inducat, sc. dochmios (⏑⏔ _ ⏑ _) et trochaeos; at quae cum concedas nulla lege statui potest qui versus sint iambi, qui trochaei, qui dochmii et omnia libidini tradita sunt."

A queste critiche precisazioni è possibile opporre un'obiezione di fondo che riguarda la natura stessa del metro, genericamente definito "metra ex iambis orta"; di qui l'altra generica designazione

---

* La prima parte di queste ricerche ("Problemi di metrica I") fu pubblicata in *Maia* 15 (1963), p. 314 sgg. (*Studi in onore di Gennaro Perrotta*).

[1] *Bacchyl.*[8] p. 34*: "Sunt autem ancipitia etiam in media periodo (102 nom. prop.), duo brevia in str. 10. 11, tria longa (v. 94?), quattuor brevia ep. 4 (v. 116), quattuor longa (v. 102?)."

[2] *Greek Metre*, transl. by H. Lloyd-Jones (Oxford 1962), par. 56 (cfr. *Responsionsfreiheiten bei Bacchyl. u. Pind.* 2 [Berlin 1921], par. 16): "The basic principle of this (sc. il metro di Pind. *Ol.* 2, Bacchyl. 17) seems to be that longa occur together in ones and twos, brevia in ones and threes, ancipitia only at the beginning of the period."

[3] *Loc. cit.*

[4] *Griech. Versk.* (Berlin 1921), p. 299 sgg.

di "freie Iamben."[5] Ancor più generica e puramente indicativa
la denominazione maasiana (*loc. cit.*: "ritmo Ἀναξιφόρμιγγες")
desunta dal primo verso dell' *Ol.* 2 di Pindaro composta nello stesso
metro. Sequenze metriche quali ad es.:

Pind. *Ol.* 2	str.	1	⏑‿⏑__‿_⏑⌣‖	ia tr
		2	⏑⏜⏜_‿__⏑⏑⏑‿⏑⏑⏑‿⏑⏑⌣‖	
				do cr cr cr
	ep.	1	__‿__‿⏜⏜‿⏑⌣‖	ia cr cr
		4	__‿__‿⏑⏝⏝‿⏑⏑⏑‿⌣‖	
				ia cr reiz
Bacch. 17 (ed. Sn.)	str.	4	_‿__‿⏑⏑⌣‖	lecyth
		15	__‿__‿⏑⌣‖	ia cr
		16	_‿⏑⏑‿_‿__	cr tr
		20	⌣_‿⏜⏜⏑⏑⏑‿_‿_‖	ia do
	ep.	4	_‿⏑⏝⏝‿_‿__‿_‿_⌣|	
				lecyth ithyph
		7	_‿⏑⏑‿_‿__‿___‖	cr cr tr
		18/19	_‿⏑⏝⏝‿_‿_‿_|‿⏑⏑⏑__|	
				tr ia tr

come potrebbero ritenersi derivate dai giambi o anche giambi liberi
se ai giambi si associano palesemente cretici, trochei, lecizi, itifallici,
reiziani e alcune varietà del docmio, almeno tre nell' *Ol.* 2, come
emerge dall'analisi del Turyn,[6] e in numero ancora maggiore,
come si vedrà in seguito, nel nostro carme? Sarebbe allora altrettanto
legittimo definirli "ex trochaeis orta" o "trochei liberi", data
l'ambivalenza dei cretici rispetto ai trochei oltre che ai giambi.

 In realtà gli elementi di base che operano in queste polivalenti
associazioni ritmiche, solo apparentemente indistinte, sono i cretici,
i giambi e i trochei, metri strettamente affini, come è provato non
solo dalla possibilità dell'anaclasi ditrocheo = digiambo, ma anche
dalla valenza cr-ia (∧ _ ⏑ _), cr-tr (_ ⏑ _ ∧). Due esempi imme-
diati proprio in Bacchilide, in questo stesso carme, str. 21 (ed.
Sn.), dove cr cr (⏑⏑⏑_⏑⏑⏑_) è in responsione con ia cr
(⌣_⏑_⏑⏑⏑_, 87, 110 ed. Sn.) e nell' epinicio 5, str. 8, dove
_⏑__⏑_ (δεῦρ' ἄθρησον νόῳ) equivale a _⏑_⌣_⏑_ nel
verso corrispondente delle altre strofe. Responsioni che lo Snell

---

[5] D. Korzeniewski, *Griech. Metrik* (Darmstadt 1968), p. 158.
[6] *Pindari carmina cum fragmentis* (Oxonii 1952), p. 9.

ha con ragione difese soprattutto per l'epinicio 5.[7] Non desterà mera-
viglia dunque trovare, in un contesto cretico-trocaico-giambico, il
docmio, il reiziano, il lecizio, l'itifallico, ritmi chiaramente giambici
e trocaici, e tanto meno alcune forme anaclastiche del dimetro
coriambico. Non aveva torto il Wilamowitz a ravvisare il docmio
nel carme 17 e neppure lo Schroeder[8] a individuare il lecizio e
l'itifallico nell'epodo di questo stesso carme. Del resto strutture
ritmiche di questo tipo non sono così rare, come riteneva P. Maas
(*loc. cit.*). Sono ben documentate non solo in Simonide[9] e di nuovo
in Pindaro, fr. 108 Sn. (117 Turyn), ma anche nella tragedia.
L'*Agamennone* di Eschilo ha due interi amebei (1072–1177; 1407–
1430) costruiti sul filo di questo sussultante ritmo cretico-giambico-
trocaico, anche se un maggiore spazio è dato al movimento
docmiaco. S'intende che pur nell'ambito delle strutture dello
stesso genere ritmico emergono le variazioni o le innovazioni di
stile di ciascun autore in rapporto al contenuto specifico del
carme e a tutte le sue implicazioni espressive. Se in Pindaro i
gruppi di brevi e di lunghe non vanno mai oltre il limite di
tre e di due, in Bacchilide al contrario compaiono sequenze di
quattro brevi e di tre e quattro lunghe (cfr. *infra*, p. 98) e in
Eschilo persino di cinque (*Ag.* 1142) e sei brevi (*Ag.* 1091). Come
si vede, l'osservazione di P. Maas[10] sul limite numerico dei gruppi
di brevi e di lunghe vale per Pindaro, ma non per Bacchilide ed
Eschilo. Le affinità e le consonanze di stile tra Bacchilide e Pindaro
traspaiono invece nell' uso di due elementi ritmici, il dimetro
coriambico anaclastico e il reiziano (‿ ∪ ∪ ∪ ‿ ‿) che, come si è

---

[7] Da ultimo W. Steffen (*Eos* 51 [1961], p. 14) ha proposto per str. 8 la correzione δεῦρ'
⟨ἄρ'⟩ ἄθρησον νόῳ che ha più o meno il valore di molte altre escogitate dal Kenyon in
poi (cfr. B. Gentili, *Bacchilide. Studi* [Urbino 1958], p. 18 sg.); ἄρ(α) ha tutta l'evidenza di
una inutile zeppa, cfr. Eur. *Hipp.* 300 φθέγξαι τι, δεῦρ' ἄθρησον. Ancor meno felice il
tentativo di correggere nella stessa strofa per motivi metrici i vv. 11–12 dove egli propone
πέμπεῖ ἐς κλεινὰν πόλιν. Il solo esempio che si conosca di abbreviamento in iato in una
siffatta sequenza, ma con nome proprio, ricorre forse in un'iscrizione del 500 a.C.
(*I. G. A.* 32; *Inschr. v. Olympia* 250; 174 Friedl.-Hoffl.) τἀργ[εῖ]οῖ ἀνέθεν τῷ ΔιϜὶ τῶν
Ϙορινθόθεν, cfr. Fr. D. Allen, "Greek Versification in Inscriptions," *Papers Am. School
Class. Stud. Athens* 4 (1888), p. 124. Ma l'interpretazione giambica non è affatto sicura, cfr.
Wilamowitz, *Griech. Versk.* p. 108.

[8] *Grundriss d. griech. Versgesch.* (Heidelberg 1930), p. 60.

[9] Fr. 541 P.; cfr. B. Gentili, *Gnomon* 33 (1961), p. 339; *Maia* 16 (1964), p. 302 sgg.;
C. M. Bowra, *Hermes* 91 (1963), p. 17 sgg.

[10] Cfr. *supra*, n. 2.

detto, non sono dissonanti fra metri cretico-giambico-trocaici. Nel fr. 108 Sn. (117 Turyn) di Pindaro il dimetro ⏑ _ _ ⏑ _ ⏑ ⏑ _ è clausola di periodo dopo ia tr, ia cr cr, ia cr; nell' *Ol.* 2 lo stesso dimetro leggermente variato chiude la strofa dopo ia cr;[11] nell'epodo 4 il reiziano _ ⏑ ⏑ ⏑ _ _ è clausola di periodo dopo ia cr.[12] Analogamente in Bacchilide: il primo nella forma cho ia all'inizio di verso, il secondo alla fine di verso dopo digiambo (cfr. *infra*, p. 92). Da rilevare infine la presenza di questa stessa forma di reiziano nel carme 16, 9 di Bacchilide, sempre alla fine di periodo.[13] In una posizione assolutamente autonoma si colloca il fr. 541 Page di Simonide, nonostante alcune coincidenze di struttura soprattutto con il carme 17 di Bacchilide.[14] Un dato stilistico rilevante, la presenza, unica fra ritmi di questo tipo, di una cadenza metrica, l'encomiologico (v. 7 ἐς τ]έλος· οὐ γὰρ ἐλαφ|ρὸν ἐσθλ[ὸν ἔμμεν _ ⏑ ⏑ _ ⏑ ⏑ _ ⏑ _ ⏑ _ _ |) che, come altrove in Simonide,[15] assolve una precisa funzione espressiva come veicolo dell'idea personale dell'autore, come punto limite nell'antitesi, a livello linguistico e concettuale, tra le paratattiche formulazioni sui sommi valori (vv. 1–5) e le articolate movenze del discorso sui valori relativi (v. 8 sgg.). L'enfatico encomiologico, che nella clausola sottolinea la sua consonanza con metri trocaico-giambici, collabora qui con il senso, ed è il segno paralinguistico del messaggio del poeta.

L'altro aspetto del problema che si dovrà considerare è la presentazione del testo del carme 17. Diversamente che per il testo di Pindaro, per il quale egli ha seguito la divisione boeckhiana in versi lunghi o periodi, lo Snell ha vigorosamente difeso per il testo di Bacchilide la colometria del papiro: "Quae divisio versuum non modo magna cum diligentia sed etiam cum consilio et ratione a grammaticis antiquis confecta optime papyris nostris servata est"

[11] Turyn, *loc. cit.*

[12] Turyn, *loc. cit.*

[13] Cfr. Snell, *op. cit.* pp. 33* e 55.

[14] V. 4 χρυ]σὸς οὐ μαίνετ[α]ι _ ⏑ _ ⏑ _ ⏑ _ ‖ᴴ lecyth, cfr. *infra* Bacchyl. ep. 10; v. 5 ἁ δ'] Ἀλάθε[ι]α παγκρατής _ ⏑ _ _ ⏑ _ ⏑ _ | tr ia, cfr. Bacchyl. ep. 15; v. 9 κέρ]δος ἀμάχητον ἢ δολοπλ[όκου _ ⏑ ⏑ ⏑ _ ⏑ _ ⏑ _ ⏑ _ | cr lecyth, cfr. Bacchyl. ep. 12. Almeno tre docmi sicuri nella forma ⏑ ⏑ ⏑ _ ⏑ _ ai vv. 2, 3, 11 (cfr. i miei studi cit. a n. 9). I gruppi di brevi e di lunghe non superano il limite numerico di tre (tre lunghe al v. 1).

[15] Fr. 542, 1, 11, 21 P.; cfr. i miei articoli cit. a n. 9 e il mio commento al fr. 541 P. in *Polinnia, Poesia greca arcaica* (Messina-Firenze 1965²), p. 313 sgg.

(p. 31*). Ma, come è stato più di una volta rilevato da J. Irigoin,[16] la colometria adottata dagli editori alessandrini per il testo di Pindaro e di Bacchilide[17] non è esente da errori e incoerenze, non si fonda cioè sull'univoco e solo criterio obiettivo della ricorrente dieresi o fine di parola come elemento discriminante del verso.[18] I criteri che troviamo applicati nel nostro carme sono i seguenti:[19]

 1. il *colon* contiene da uno a tre elementi ritmici;

 2. dei 23 *cola* che compongono la strofa, 9 terminano sempre con fine di parola;

 3. dei 20 *cola* che compongono l'epodo, 15 terminano sempre con fine di parola; da rilevare che nell'edizione di Snell non è indicata la fine di parola alla l. 18;

 4. variazioni da una strofa all'altra o da un epodo all'altro, consistenti in *cola* più lunghi e più corti di una o due sillabe, compaiono sicuramente in un caso nel papiro A[20] e in due casi nel papiro O[21];

 5. dei 13 *cola* della strofa che non terminano con fine di parola, 6 sono metricamente corretti, coincidendo con gli elementi costitutivi del verso: 1 e 2 (str. 1), 8 (str. 5), 14 (str. 7, secondo elemento), 16 (str. 8, primo elemento), 21 (str. 11, primo elemento);

 6. dei 4 *cola* dell'epodo che non terminano con fine di parola, due sono metricamente corretti: 11 (ep. 11, prim. elem.); 15 (ep. 13, prim. elem.).

I fatti qui enucleati provano con chiarezza l'incoerenza del sistema colometrico degli alessandrini nell'incostante attenzione da

---

[16] *Histoire du texte de Pindare* (Paris 1952), pp. 44-47; *Les scholies métriques de Pindare* (Paris 1958), pp. 17-34; "Prolégomènes à une édition de Bacchylide," *Rev. ét. gr.* 75 (1962), p. 61 sgg.

[17] È molto probabile che la colometria di Bacchilide risalga allo stesso Aristofane di Bisanzio, l'autore della colometria di Pindaro (cfr. Irigoin, *Histoire*, p. 45 sg.).

[18] Cfr. Irigoin, *art. cit.* p. 62: "Son auteur (sc. della colometria di Bacchilide), ignorant l'existence du vers lyrique, n'a pas marqué de difference entre le *côlon* initial ou intérieur de vers, et le *côlon* dont la fin coïncide avec une fin de vers; plus sensible aux coupes partielles, qui facilitaient la mise en page, qu'à la rareté des diérèses, il a déterminé des *côla* souvent plus longs ou plus courts d'une syllabe que les éléments métriques constitutifs du vers, allant même jusqu'à admettre des variations d'une strophe à l'autre, par exemple aux deux premiers *côla* de la strophe de la première *Épinicie*, ou aux *côla* 5 et 6 de l'épode de l'*Épinicie* V."

[19] I numeri in parentesi rinviano alla numerazione di sinistra nel nostro testo. Quando è preceduto da str. ed ep., il numero rinvia alla numerazione sticometrica della strofa e dell'epodo.

[20] δάκρυ ascritto interamente al *colon* 95 (55).

[21] μῆτιν posto erroneamente alla fine del v. 51 (29) invece che all'inizio del v. 52 (30); Ποσειδᾶνι ascritto interamente al *colon* 59 (36).

essi prestata alla fine di parola, ma provano anche con altrettanta chiarezza che circa nella metà dei casi la divisione per *cola* è metricamente corretta. Comunque debbano interpretarsi i sette casi della strofa e i due dell'epodo, nei quali la divisione colometrica non è corretta, e le rare variazioni da una strofa all'altra e da un epodo all'altro nella lunghezza dei *cola*, sia che debbano attribuirsi ad una necessità "editoriale", come ha supposto l'Irigoin (cfr. *supra*, n. 18), o, come è anche probabile, a negligenze o errori dei copisti, un dato certo è che il sistema colometrico non appare così casuale, arbitrario e senza valore, come sembrò al Wilamowitz.[22] Certo la divisione per versi lunghi coincidenti sempre con la fine di parola, inaugurata dal Boeckh per Pindaro, s'impone per la sua maggiore coerenza, ma questo non deve significare rifiuto totale della colometria alessandrina che, debitamente corretta, può orientarci sulla struttura interna del verso e, come ha notato lo Snell,[23] per alcune libertà ammesse dai grammatici alessandrini all'inizio o alla fine (e, potremmo aggiungere, all'interno) del *colon*, permetterci di reperire uno stato prealessandrino del testo. Procedimento, s'intende, legittimo quando lo stato del testo papiraceo ci consente di verificare la coerenza della colometria antica. Per questo motivo ho difeso[24] per i nuovi testi di Anacreonte[25] la colometria del papiro, proprio perché nelle otto strofe superstiti la fine di linea coincide con la fine di parola. Né d'altra parte è lecito presumere che nelle parti perdute del testo il criterio fosse diverso; allo stato attuale sarebbe imprudente intervenire introducendo una diversa sticometria.

Queste considerazioni giustificano la diversa sticometria qui presentata del carme 17, nel modo che segue:

(Per alcune forme ricorrenti del docmio e dell' ipodocmio sono adottate le seguenti sigle: do ($\cup$ _ _ $\cup$ _); do¹ (_ $\cup$ _ $\cup$ _); do² (_ $\cup\cup$ _ $\cup$ _); do³ ($\cup\cup\cup$ _ $\cup$ _); doᵏ ($\underset{\cup\cup}{\cup}$ _ $\cup$ _ $\cup$ _ docmio kaibeliano). Nel seguito della trattazione i numeri in parentesi rinviano all' edizione dello Snell).

---

[22] *Textgesch. d. griech. Lyriker* (Berlin 1900), p. 42. Alcune mie ricerche in corso sulla versificazione delle iscrizioni arcaiche in metro lirico lasciano fin d'ora presumere che il *colon* non fu una pura astrazione grammaticale e, di conseguenza, il tanto discusso sistema colometrico degli alessandrini una loro invenzione.

[23] *Op. cit.* p. 35* sg.

[24] "Problemi di metrica I", *Maia* 15 (1963), p. 318.

[25] Frr. 60, 71, 72 Gent. = 346, 347 P.

STROFA

1. [53] ⏑⏑—⏑——⏑—⏑— —⏑⏑⏑—⏑⏑⏑⏑—⏑ [53] [41] [53]
do³ do¹ ∼ do² do¹   cr tr tr ∼ cr tr ion

—⏑—⏑—|
doᵏ

2. —⏑———⏑⏑⏑⏑ ‖ᴴ [54]
lecyth

3. —⏑⏑⏑⏑——⏑⏑⏑ —⏑—(—)—⏑——⏑—| [55] [43]
ia ia   cr cr cr ∼ cr ia cr

4. ⏑—⏑⏑⏑—⏑⏑⏑——|
ia reiz

5. ⏑—⏑———⏑⏑⏑ —⏑—⏑—⏑—| [45]
ia cr   lecyth

6. —⏑⏑—⏑—⏑— ⏑—⏑⏑—⏑⏑— ⏑—⏑—⏑—| [18]
cho ia (dim)   prosod   doᵏ [58]

7. ⏑—⏑——⏑—⏑— ⏑—⏑⏑⏑⏑⏑⏑⏑—⏑ [59] [59]
ia do¹   ia tr
∧ [19]
——⏑——⏑⏑ ‖
ia cr ∼ cr cr

8. —⏑⏑⏑—⏑—— ⏑—⏑—⏑⏑ ‖ [48]
⏑⏑
[20]
cr tr   doᵏ

9. [21] ⏑—⏑—⏑—⏑— ⏑——⏑⏑⏑—⏑—⏑|
ia ia   ba cr ba

10. [22, 50] ⏑—⏑⏑⏑⏑⏑⏑⏑—⏑— ‖ᴴ [62] [10]
ia do¹ ∼ ia do³

11. [51, 63] x— ⏑⏑⏑—⏑⏑⏑— ⏑—⏑——⏑—|
cr cr ∼ ia cr   ia cr

12. —⏑—⏑⏑⏑— ⏑⏑⏑—⏑⏑ ‖‖‖ [64]
cr cr   do ∼ do³

EPODO

1. ∪ _ ∪ ∪ ∪ _ ∪ _ _ |
    ia tr

2. ∪ _ ∪ _ ∪ _ |
    do^k

3. _ ∪ ∪ ∪ _ ∪ _ |
    cr cr

4. _ ∪ ∪∪∪ _ ∪ _   _ ∪ _ ∪ _ ∪ |
    lecyth   ithyph
    (68)

5. ∪ _ ∪ ∪ ∪ _ ∪ _ |
    ia cr

6. (∪) _ ∪ _ _ ∪ ∪ ∪ _ ∪ _ |
    cr cr cr ∼ ia cr cr
    (70)

7. _ ∪ ∪ ∪ _ ∪ _ _ ∪ _ _ ‖^H
    cr cr tr
    (71)

8. _ _ ∪ _ _ ∪ _ _ ∪∪ ‖
    ia cr cr

9. _ ∪ _ ∪ _ ∪ _ ∪ _ |
    cr do^k vel do^I ia

10. ∪ ∪ ∪ _ ∪ _ ∪ _ |
    lecyth

11. _ ∪ _ _ ∪ _   ∪ _ ∪ _ _ ∪ _ |
    cr cr   ia cr

12. _ _ ∪ ∪ ∪ _ ∪ _ _ ∪ _   _ ∪ _ ∪ _ ∪ _ ‖^H
    ia cr cr   lecyth
    (76)

13. _ ∪ _ ∪ ∪ ∪ _   ∪ _ ∪ _ ∪ _ _ ∪ _ |
    cr cr   do^k cr

14. ∪ _ ∪ _ _ ∪ ∪ ∪ _ ∪∪ ‖
    ia cr cr

15. _ ∪ ∪∪ _ ∪ _ ∪ _ | ∪ ∪ ∪ _ _ |
    tr ia   tr
    (79)

16. ∪ _ ∪ ∪∪ _ ∪ _ _ ∪ _ ⫴
    ia cr cr
    (80)

   1   Κυανόπρωιρα μὲν ναῦς μενέκτυ[πον]
       Θησέα δὶς ἑπτά τ᾽ἀγ^ιλαοὺς ἄγουσα κούρους Ἰαόνων   στρ. α′

   2   Κρητικὸν τάμνε{ν} πέλαγος·

   3   τηλαυγέϊ γὰρ ἐν φάρεϊ βορήϊαι πίτ^ινον αὖραι κλυτᾶς   5

   4   ἕκατι π[ε]λεμαίγιδος Ἀθάνας·

5 5   κνίσεν τε Μίνωϊ κέαρ ἱμεράμπυκος θεᾶς

   6   Κύπ^ιριδος [ἀ]χ^ινὰ δῶρα· χεῖρα δ᾽ οὐ[κέτι] παρθενικᾶς
       ἄτερθ᾽ ἐράτῳεν,   10

   7   θίγεν δὲ λευκᾶν παρηΐδων· βόασέ τ᾽ Ἐρίβοια χαλκο-
       θώρακα Πανδίονος   15

   8   ἔκγονον· ἴδεν δὲ Θησεύς, μέλαν δ᾽ ὑπ᾽ ὀφ^ιρύων

   9   δίνασεν ὄμμα, καρδίαν τέ οἱ σχέτ^ιλιον ἄμυξεν ἄλγος,

10 10   εἶρέν τε· "Διὸς υἱὲ φερτάτου,   20

  11   ὅσιον οὐκέτι τεᾶν ἔσω κυβερνᾷς φρενῶν

  12   θυμ[όν]· ἴσχε μεγαλοῦχον ἥρως βίαν.   23a/23b

   1   ὅ, τι μὲν ἐκ θεῶν μοῖρα παγκρατὴς
       ἄμμι κατένευσε καὶ Δίκας ῥέπει τάλαντον, πεπρωμέναν 25 ἀντ. α′

   2   αἶσαν ἐκπλήσομεν, ὅταν

15 3   ἔλθῃ· [σ]ὺ δὲ βαρεῖαν κάτεχε μῆτιν. εἰ καί σε κεδ^ινὰ τέκεν

   4   λέχει Διὸς ὑπὸ κ^ιρόταφον Ἴδας   30

   5   μιγεῖσα Φοίνικος ἐρατώνυμος κόρα βροτῶν

   6   φέρτατον, ἀλλὰ κἀμὲ Πιτθέος θυγάτηρ ἀφνεοῦ
       πλαθεῖσα ποντίωι   35

   7   τέκεν Ποσειδᾶνι, χρύσεόν τέ οἱ δόσαν ἰόπ^ιλοκοι κά-
       λυμμα Νηρηΐδες.

20 8   τῶ σε, πολέμαρχε Κνωσίων, κέλομαι πολύστονον   40

   9   ἐρύκεν ὕβ^ιριν· οὐ γὰρ ἂν θέλοιμ᾽ ἄμβροτον ἐραννὸν Ἀο[ῦς

  10   ἰδεῖν φάος, ἐπεί τιν᾽ ἠϊθέ[ων

  11   σὺ δαμάσειας ἀέκοντα· πρόσθε χειρῶν βίαν   45

  12   δείξομεν· τὰ δ᾽ἐπιόντα δα[ίμω]ν κρινεῖ."   46a/46b

25 1   τόσ᾽ εἶπεν ἀρέταιχμος ἥρως·   ἐπ. α′

   2   τάφον δὲ ναυβάται

   3   φωτὸς ὑπεράφανον

   4   θάρσος· Ἀλίου τε γαμβρῶι χόλωσεν ἦτορ,   50a/50b

   5   ὕφαινέ τε ποταινίαν

30 6   μῆτιν, εἶπέν τε· "μεγαλοσθενές

   7   Ζεῦ πάτερ, ἄκουσον· εἴπέρ με νύμ[φ]α

   8   Φοίνισσα λευκώλενος σοὶ τέκεν,

   9   νῦν πρόπεμπ᾽ ἀπ᾽ οὐρανοῦ θοάν   55

  10   πυριέθειραν ἀστραπάν

35   11   σᾶμ᾽ ἀρίγ⌐νωτον· εἰ δὲ καὶ σὲ Τροιζηνία

      12   σεισίχθονι φύτευσεν Αἴθρα Ποσειδᾶνι, τόνδε χρύσεον   60

      13   χειρὸς ἀγ⌐λαὸν ἔνεγκε κόσμον ἐκ βαθείας ἁλός,

      14   δικὼν θράσει σῶμα πατρὸς ἐς δόμους.

      15   εἴσεαι δ᾽ αἴκ᾽ ἐμᾶς κλύηι Κρόνιος εὐχᾶς   65

40   16   ἀναξιβρέντας ὁ πάντω[ν με]ᾳ̑[έω]ν."

      1   κλύε δ᾽ ἄμεμπτον εὐχὰν μεγασθενὴς

          Ζεύς, ὑπέροχόν τε Μίνωι φύτευσε τιμὰν φίλωι θέλων   στρ. β′

      2   παιδὶ πανδερκέα θέμεν,   70

      3   ἄστραψέ θ᾽· ὁ δὲ θυμάρμενον ἰδὼν τέρας χεῖρας πέτασσε κ⌐λυτάν

      4   ἐς αἰθέρα μενεπτόλεμος ἥρως

45   5   εἶρέν τε· "Θησεῦ τάδ᾽ ἐ<μὰ> μὲν βλέπεις σαφῆ Διὸς   75

      6   δῶρα· σὺ δ᾽ ὄρνυ᾽ ἐς βαρύβ⌐ρομον πέλαγος· Κρονίδας

          δέ τοι πατὴρ ἄναξ

      7   τελεῖ Ποσειδᾶν ὑπέρτατον κλέος χθόνα κατ᾽ ἠΰδενδρον."

          ὣς εἶπε, τῶι δ᾽ οὐ πάλιν   80

      8   θυμὸς ἀνεκάμπτετ᾽, ἀλλ᾽ εὐπάκτων ἐπ᾽ ἰκ⌐ρίων

      9   σταθεὶς ὄρουσε, πόντιόν τέ νιν δέξατο θελημὸν ἄλσος.   85

50   10   τάφεν δὲ Διὸς υἱὸς ἔνδοθεν

      11   κέαρ, κέλευσέ τε κατ᾽ οὖρον ἴσχεν εὐδαίδαλον

      12   νᾶα· μοῖρα δ᾽ ἑτέραν ἐπόρσυν᾽ ὁδόν.   89a/89b

      1   ἵετο δ᾽ ὠκύπομπον δόρυ· σόει

          νιν βορεὰς ἐξόπιθε{ν} πνέουσ᾽ ἀήτᾱ· τρέσσαν δ᾽ Ἀθαναίων   ἀντ. β′

      2   ἠΐθέων <–> γένος, ἐπεί

55   3   ἥρως θόρεν πόντονδε, κατὰ λειρίων τ᾽ ὀμμάτων δάκ⌐ρυ χέον,

      4   βαρεῖαν ἐπιδέγ⌐μενοι ἀνάγκαν.   96

      5   φέρον δὲ δελφῖνες {ἐν} ἁλιναιέται μέγαν θοῶς

      6   Θησέα πατ⌐ρὸς ἱππίου δόμοῦ· ἔμολέν τε θεῶν

          μέγαρον. τόθι κ⌐λυτάς   100

      7   ἰδὼν ἔδεισε<ν> Νηρῆος ὀλβίου κόρας· ἀπὸ γὰρ ἀγ⌐λα-

          ῶν λάμπε γυίων σέλας

60   8   ὧτε πυρός, ἀμφὶ χαίταις δὲ χρυσεόπ⌐λοκοι   105

      9   δίνηντο ταινίαι· χορῶι δ᾽ ἔτερπον κέαρ ὑγροῖσι ποσσίν.

      10   εἶδέν τε πατ⌐ρὸς ἄλοχον φίλαν

      11   σεμνὰν βοῶπιν ἐρατοῖσιν Ἀμφιτρίταν δόμοις·   110

      12   ἅ νιν ἀμφέβαλεν ἀϊόνα πορφυρέαν,   112a/112b

65   1   κόμαισί τ᾽ ἐπέθηκεν οὔλαις   ἐπ. β′

      2   ἀμεμφέα π⌐λόκον,

      3   τόν ποτέ οἱ ἐν γάμωι   115

    4 δῶκε δόλιος Ἀφ|ροδίτα ῥόδοις ἐρεμνόν.   116a/116b

    5 ἄπιστον ὅ, τι δαίμονες

70 6 θέλωσιν οὐδὲν φρενοάραις βροτοῖς·

    7 νᾶα πάρα λεπτόπρυμνον φάνη· φεῦ,

    8 οἵαισιν ἐν φροντίσι Κ|νώσιον   120

    9 ἔσχασεν στραταγέταν, ἐπεί

  10 μόλ' ἀδίαντος ἐξ ἁλός

75 11 θαῦμα πάντεσσι, λάμπε δ' ἀμφὶ γυίοις θεῶν

  12 δῶρ', ἀγ|λαόθρονοί τε κοῦραι σὺν εὐθυμίαι νεοκτίτωι   125

  13 ὠλόλυξαν, ἔκλαγεν δὲ πόντος· ἤϊθεοι δ' ἐγγύθεν

  14 νέοι παιάνιξαν ἐρατᾶι ὀπί.

  15 Δάλιε, χοροῖσι Κηΐων φρένα ἰανθείς   130

80 16 ὄπαζε θεόπομπον ἐσθλῶν τύχαν.

Da questa diversa disposizione sticometrica risulta che la formulazione categorica del Maas (cfr. *supra*, n. 2) sulla ricorrenza degli "ancipitia" (cioè delle sillabe indifferenti) soltanto all'inizio di periodo non è una norma valida per Bacchilide, ma solo per l'*Olimpica* 2 di Pindaro.

La sillaba indifferente ricorre:

a. cinque volte all'inizio del verso o del periodo: str. 1 (1); 5 (8); 9 (18); 10 (20); 11 (21).

b. cinque volte all'interno del verso o del periodo: str. 1 (2); 6 (12); 7 (13); 8 (17). Di questi casi converrà prendere in esame soltanto i due casi di str. 1, vv. 41 (68), 53 (91). Per i rimanenti basterà limitarci ad alcuni confronti esemplificativi; essi non pongono problemi. Lo Snell li ha ammessi giustificandoli con la loro ricorrenza all'inizio del "verso" coerentemente con la divisione colometrica del papiro;[26] il solo che egli ammette all'interno di periodo e che giustifica col nome proprio è str. 7, v. 59 (102) ἔδεισε⟨ν⟩ Νηρῆος (-σε Νηρέος pap.: Kenyon). Per la str. 1 (2) lo Snell (p. 57) dà il seguente

schema: $\_ \cup \cup \cup \_ \cup \_ \cup \underset{=}{\cup} \mid \cup \_ \cup$; al v. 41 (68) Ζεύς, ὑπέροχόν τε Μίνωϊ φύτευσε, seguendo il Wilamowitz[27] egli scandisce Μινώϊ e nota in apparato: "colometriam papyri…non mutavi (exceptis v. 37 et v. 95) quamquam finem periodi esse suspicor str. 2 post elementum nonum(?)." A questa interpretazione molto dubbia, come

---

[26] Cfr. *Bacchyl.*[8] p. 35*.
[27] *Op. cit.* p. 300.

ammette lo stesso Snell, può obiettarsi che l'elisione dopo la nona sillaba al v. 53 (91) πνέουσ' ἀήτα sembra escludere la dieresi e di conseguenza la fine di periodo, sebbene quest'ultima compaia, eccezionalmente, in Bacchilide, una volta fra la preposizione e il verbo (5, 74 sg. e un'altra dopo τε καί 7, 1).[28] Ma alla str. 5, v. 5 (8) Μίνωϊ = _ _ ∪. Sempre alla str. 1 (2), v. 53 (91) in A e in O si legge: νιν βορεὰς ἐξόπιθεν πνέουσ' ἀήτα. Il Kenyon corresse ἐξόπιν (correzione comunemente accolta tranne che dal Blass il quale si limitò al lievissimo emendamento ἐξόπιθε{ν} [cfr. 23 πρόσθε]), e il Wilamowitz propose ἄητᾰ giustificando la sua proposta con la suggestiva invenzione: "Das ist so zugegangen, dass sie ein normales lesbisches Maskulinum ἄητα = ἀήτης als Femininum fassten, was der Deutsche, der "Hymne" und "Mythe" aus dem Französischen nahm und zu einem Femininum machte, den Ioniern nicht übel nehmen darf" (loc. cit.). Un maschile ἄητα, si può con tutta tranquillità affermare che non è mai esistito in eolico: l'ode dell'ostrakon fiorentino di Saffo (2 Lobel-Page) ci attesta chiaramente il femminile ἀήτα: v. 10 αἰ δ' ἄηται μέλλιχα πνέοισιν.[29] Due violenti interventi sul testo per evitare all'interno del verso responsioni non eccezionali (imposte in un caso dalla presenza del nome proprio) che i grammatici alessandrini, come è provato dalla concordanza dei due papiri A e O, avevano ammesse.[30] Rispetto ai versi corrispondenti 1 (2) e 13 (25) _ ∪ ∪ ∪ _ ∪ _ ∪ _ ∪ _ ∪ cr tr tr, i vv. 41 (68) e 53 (91) presentano le seguenti variazioni:

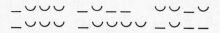

Il primo ha lunga la sillaba indifferente del primo tr e l'anaclasi tr ⌣ ion; il secondo il biceps in luogo del longum nel primo tr e lunga la sillaba indifferente del secondo tr: variazioni che non hanno bisogno di essere documentate. L'anaclasi tr⌣ion ha il suo antece-

[28] Cfr. Snell, Bacchyl.[8] p. 22*.

[29] Cfr. anche Hesiod. Op. 675 δεινὰς ἀήτας e Simon. fr. 595 P. οὐδὲ γὰρ ἐννοσίφυλλος ἀήτᾱ, un perfetto alcmanio. Quanto all' isolato e falso (e tale apparve agli antichi grammatici) δεινὸς ἀήτης Il. 15, 626, cfr. Ernst Fraenkel, Gesch. d. griech. Nomina agentis II (Strassburg 1912), p. 134.

[30] Per ἀήτα lo riconosce anche Snell, p. 63 app.: "in versibus respondentibus ultima syll. brevis, sed grammatici hic anceps admiserunt."

dente immediato nell'anaclomeno anacreontico[31] e il *biceps* in luogo del *longum* ha una cospicua frequenza in questo stesso carme. Per il gruppo di quattro brevi (ἐξόπιθε πνέουσ') e quattro lunghe (ἀῆτα τρέσσαν δ' Ἀ.) al v. 53 (91–92) basterà confrontare ep. 4, v. 68 (116) e str. 7, v. 59 (102).

Per le forme del docmio kaibeliano con sillaba iniziale indifferente abbiamo a confronto sicuri esempi in Pindaro, in una contestualità ritmica equivalente:

Ol. 13, str. 3   ∪ _ ∪ ∪ ∪ ∪ _ _ _ ∪ ⌣ ‖   ia do^k

          4   _ _ _ ∪ ⌣⌣ ∪ _ ⌣ _ ∪ ⌣ ‖   ia do^k

Pyth. 8, str. 6   ⌣ _ ∪ _ ∪ ∪ _ _ ⌣ _ ∪ _ ∪ ⌣ ‖   enopl do^k

          7   ⌣ _ ∪ _ ⌣ _ ⌣ _ ∪ ⌣ ‖‖   ia do^k [32]

Pyth. 8, str. 6 ha una struttura analoga alla sequenza prosod (∪ _ ∪ ∪ _ ∪ ∪ _) do^k di str. 6 (11 e 12).

Restano le quattro responsioni cr cr ∼ ia cr di str. 11, vv. 51, 63 (87, 110); ep. 6, v. 70 (118); str. 3, v. 43 (72) e ia cr ∼ cr cr di str. 7, v. 19 (37), delle quali le prime due sono state accolte anche dallo Snell; converrà perciò esaminare soltanto le ultime due. Str. 3, v. 43 (72): χεῖρας πέτασσε κλυτὰν ἐς αἰθέρα è il testo in A e in O; χεῖρα corregge O¹. Conservando χεῖρας si avrà ia _ _ ∪ _ (χεῖρας πέτασ-σε) in responsione al cretico delle altre strofe come negli altri due casi sopra citati. Il rimedio che sino all'edizione di Snell ha avuto più credito è stato quello del Ludwich: πέτασε χεῖρας. Un rimedio troppo facile, tanto è vero che lo Snell non lo ha preso in considerazione, proponendo la correzione del Richards χέρα (*biceps* in luogo del *longum* nel cr ∪∪∪ ∪ _). Ma anche questa soluzione non convince. Il gesto del sollevare o del tendere le mani al cielo o verso gli dei ricorre con frequenza in Bacchilide, in una formulazione pressoché identica e sempre con l'oggetto al plurale,

---

[31] Cfr. Anacr. fr. 28 Gent., 408 P.:

       ∪∪ _ _ / ∪∪ _ _ / ∪∪ _ _ |

       ∪∪ _ ∪ / _ ∪ _ _ / ∪∪ _ _ |

       ∪∪ _ _ / ∪∪ _ ∪ / _ ∪ _ _ |

dove risulta chiara, come nel nostro caso, l'equivalenza _ ∪ _ _ ∼ ∪∪ _ ∪.

[32] Cfr. Turyn, *op. cit.* pp. 63, 122.

χεῖρας o χέρας.³³ Di questo si rese conto il Blass che si limitò a correggere lievemente χεῖρας in χέρας.³⁴ Il testo appare dunque corretto e tale esso era nell'archetipo di A e di O. Per str. 7, v. 19 (37) trovare un rimedio è molto difficile; se escludiamo la brutta congettura del Ludwich (ἰόπλοκοι κά-λυμμ' ‹ἁδὺ› Νηρηΐδες), non resterebbe che limitarsi a ritenere corrotto con lo Snell per motivi metrici il testo in κάλυμμα Νηρ.: un' ipotesi poco persuasiva se si considerano i casi sicuri di responsione cr ∼ ia sopra esaminati.

Le conclusioni che scaturiscono da questa sistemazione del carme non sono certo confortanti per le tendenze attuali, nel campo dell'interpretazione metrica dei testi, a normalizzare, entro un rigido sistema di norme, fatti che spesso le smentiscono o sembrano rifiutarle. Queste tendenze, se hanno il merito di aver reagito a un certo ottimismo del passato nel convalidare libertà metriche facilmente eliminabili, rischiano ora di cadere nella reazione opposta di presumere guasti e corruttele in tutti quei luoghi nei quali il fatto metrico smentisce la norma, cioè non s'inquadra nel sistema costruito sui casi non abnormi: un sistema che nella sincronia rifiuta i diversi livelli della diacronia. In sostanza non si può, né si deve analizzare il metro del carme 17 tenendo d'occhio la struttura dell'*Ol.* 2, meno varia, meno libera, più normativa. Ma il carme di Bacchilide ha resistito agli attacchi della critica congetturale, e lo dimostra proprio l'edizione dello Snell. Se si esaminano i luoghi nei quali egli è intervenuto per motivi metrici (p. 58), il numero è esiguo e le correzioni lievissime; se ad essi togliamo i tre casi che, come ho cercato di mostrare, sono corretti, il numero è persino irrisorio. Possiamo tranquillamente affermare che i papiri ci hanno restituito un testo sicuro e corretto.

Di là dalle analogie di struttura con Simonide e con Pindaro, il carme 17 si distingue per una maggiore varietà nelle libere associazioni dei cretici, dei trochei e dei giambi e per l'assidua presenza del docmio in forme prevalentemente di valenza giambica. Alla maggiore complessità della strofa dominata dall'inquieto ritmo dei docmi e dei giambi fanno riscontro nell'epodo le movenze più

---

³³ Cfr. 3,35 χέρας δ' [ἐς αἰ]πὺν αἰθέρα σφετέρας ἀείρας; 11,100 χεῖρας ἀντείνων πρὸς αὐγάς; 13,138 θεοῖσιν ἄντειναν χέρας; 15,45 θεοῖς δ' ἀνίσχοντες χέρας.

³⁴ La responsione ia ∼ cr, come è ovvio, rimane; egli evidentemente preferiva la breve nella sillaba indifferente del digiambo.

semplici e più agili dei ritmi cretico-giambici e cretico-trocaici.[35] Ma per le libere responsioni il carme non è un *unicum* in Bacchilide: esse ricompaiono nel proemio dell'epinicio 5 che è del 476, cioè più o meno coevo del carme 17, che fu composto negli anni della lega delia, fra il 478 e il 470.[36]

Urbino, 3 agosto 1970

Addendum, 1 settembre 1973.

La nuova edizione di H. Maehler (*Bacchylidis carmina cum fragmentis* [Leipzig 1970]) non apporta novità di rilievo per il c. 17 rispetto all'edizione di B. Snell, tranne qualche parentesi quadra in più nel testo e qualche lieve emendamento nell'apparato (cfr. v. 83 della sua edizione) resosi indispensabile dalla revisione del papiro Kenyon. Egli ha giustamente corretto l'impossibile ἄητα difeso dallo Snell senza tuttavia modificare l'apparato *ad loc*. Coerentemente con il metodo da lui seguito, sarebbe stato più corretto scrivere soltanto: "ἄητα Housm." e non "AΗΤΑ: ἄητα Housm.", poiché egli appunto accoglie nel testo ἀήτα del papiro. Nello schema metrico a p. 58 sg. sarebbe stato opportuno ovviare a una lieve inesattezza, indicando la fine di parola alla l. 18 dell'epodo (15 nella mia divisione sticometrica). Per la responsione impura nel c. 5, 8 rinvio alla n. 7 e alle conclusioni del saggio. Basterà solo aggiungere che nella sistemazione testuale e metrica del proemio del c. 5 questa nuova edizione rappresenta un regresso rispetto alla precedente dello Snell.

Ringrazio il dr. M. Haslam dell'Institute of Classical Studies di Londra per alcune utili osservazioni su particolari tecnici della mia ricerca e per la proficua collaborazione alle ricerche metriche sui lirici (cfr. *Quad. Urb.* 17, 1974) presso l'Istituto di Filologia Classica di Urbino nell'anno accademico 1972–73.

---

[35] Da notare che la sequenza ritmica str. 6: prosod (∪ _ ∪∪ _ ∪∪ _) do[k], ricompare pressoché identica nel ditirambo 19, str. 5–7:

∪ _ ∪∪ _ ∪∪ _	prosod
∪ _ ∪∪ _ ∪∪ _ |	prosod
∪ _ ∪ _ ∪ _ _ |	ia ba

[36] A. Severyns, *Bacchylide, essai biographique* (Liège 1933), p. 59.

DITHYRAMB, TRAGEDY, AND COMEDY

T. B. L. WEBSTER

In the many discussions of the origins of tragedy not very much heed has been paid to the unique structure of tragic choral lyric as a sequence of metrically unlike pairs of strophe and antistrophe. Yet this shape is only found in tragedy and comedy; the rest of Greek choral lyric is either monostrophic (with identical strophes repeating through the whole poem) or triadic (with identical triads repeating through the whole poem) or astrophic. And the form would seem to have originated in tragedy rather than comedy or satyr play since they both still use monostrophic form on occasions, and the early form of tragic chorus with more than three pairs of strophe-anti-strophe, which is not found in tragedy after Aeschylus, is not found in comedy or satyr-play (but here it is of course right to remember how little of early comedy and early satyr-play survives).

Wilamowitz[1] noted the phenomenon and explained it by the definitive influence of the dance, whereas in Pindar the music was much more important. This is no explanation. Dance must have been as important in the monostrophic partheneia of Alkman as in the choruses of tragedy, and on the other hand the long periods of some Aeschylean choruses must have been danced in the same stately fashion as the long periods of other choral lyric. Kraus[2] also notes the phenomenon but has a quite different explanation: lyric poetry is the unfolding of a moment, but drama is a representation of time, which is stylized in dramatic lyric as an advance from step to step. This again is unsatisfactory: there is plenty of straightforward narrative in non-dramatic lyric and plenty of reflection in dramatic lyric so that the difference of matter will not account for the difference of form.

[1] *Griechische Verskunst* (Berlin 1921), 464 f.
[2] *Sitzungsb. Wien* 231, 4 (1957), 21.

Kranz[3] however does give a genetic explanation. He finds the origin of the tragic stasimon in the epirrhematic form. The epirrhematic form gives a speech or song A followed by a strophe a, then a corresponding speech or song A' followed by an antistrophe a', then a variant $B\ b$ followed by a corresponding $B'\ b'$, and so on. Leave out the speeches or songs, and you get a stasimon $a\ a'\ b\ b'$. There are at least two difficulties here. It is true that in our earliest Greek tragedy, the *Persae*, we have two examples of the developed epirrhematic form as described by Kranz: the lyric dialogue between the messenger and the chorus (249 ff.) and the lyric dialogue with Xerxes (931 ff.). But we have no evidence for this developed form earlier. It is a very long way from "the women groaned thereto" after the solo laments in the *Iliad* or from the *tênella kallinike* of Archilochos' hymn to Herakles to the more complicated choral responses in the lyric dialogues of the *Persae*. The second difficulty is the more fundamental one: is it reasonable to derive the form of a choral performance from a non-choral performance, particularly when the traditional view is that the decisive act in the creation of tragedy was the addition of non-choral elements to existing choral elements?

Let us look for a moment at the choruses of the *Persae*. After the long opening in recitative anapaests the parodos consists of three pairs of strophe-antistrophe and a mesode in ionics and then two pairs in iambo-trochaics. The first stasimon (532) again has an anapaestic introduction and then one pair in iambo-trochaic and two pairs in double-short. The second stasimon (628) has three pairs and an epode after the anapaestic introduction. The first pair starts choriambic; the second goes into ionic, the third mixes iambic, choriambic, and ionic. So far the individual elements can be parallelled in Anakreon and the Lesbian poets, and there is surely a considerable influence also from wild laments, which however we cannot control.

The third stasimon is quite different (852), three pairs of strophe-antistrophe and an epode, describing the glories of Dareios' empire and only returning to the present disaster at the very end. This great enkomion is in long dactylic lines running out into single-short at the ends of the periods. It is extremely interesting that in

[3] *Stasimon* (Berlin 1933), 21.

472 when the periodic style of Pindar, both in its aeolic and in its dactylo-epitrite form, had been established as the obvious form for such stately choral lyric for twenty years and more, Aeschylus does not use it (and there is no sign of its influence on tragedy until the *Prometheus Vinctus*) but harks back to what we can now with the recent papyrus finds of the *Geryoneis, Eriphyle,* and *Iliou Persis,* recognise as the metrical style of Stesichoros.[4] The vase evidence shows that Stesichoros was well-known in Athens in the second half of the sixth century, and it is at least possible that Thespis had already adopted his metrical forms for solemn choruses of this kind. Certainly Aeschylus is writing in an old metrical tradition, possibly in an old tragic metrical tradition.

But none of this helps us with our problem because we know that Stesichoros wrote in triads and that the triads were metrically identical through the whole of his very long poems. Nor is any help to be found in the kind of lyric where we should naturally seek it, the dithyramb.[5] Archilochos' dithyramb may have been a solo with an ejaculatory chorus like his hymn to Herakles. At least there seems to have been a distinction between his dithyramb and Arion's dithyramb at the beginning of the sixth century. Arion's dithyramb seems to have been purely choral and to have been performed on a dancing-floor instead of being processional. The natural conjecture is that it was monostrophic like Alkman's partheneia. This is supported by Pindar's reference to Lasos of Hermione who was writing dithyrambs at the end of the sixth century. Pindar himself wrote dithyrambs in triads, and he clearly regards himself as developing a tradition which started with Lasos of Hermione. He describes the dithyramb before Lasos as a "rope-stretched song" which, if one remembers Aristotle's description of pre-periodic prose as *lexis eiromenê*, seems a perfectly apt name for a monostrophic dithyramb.

I want to suggest that we should look for the origin of the sequence of metrically unlike pairs of strophe-antistrophe which characterizes

---

[4] *Geryoneis*: P. Oxy. 2617 (vol. 32); Page, *Lyrica Graeca Selecta* (Oxonii 1968), p. 263; *Eriphyle* and *Iliou Persis*: P. Oxy. 2618–19 (32); Page, *Proc. Cambr. Philol. Soc.* 1969, 69. Cf. also Fuehrer, *Hermes* 97 (1969), 115 on *Poetae Melici Graeci* (Oxford 1962, hereafter *PMG*), 222.

[5] On this sequence cf. my *Greek Chorus* (London 1970), 68, 91.

tragic choral lyric in quite a different direction. Among the many
lyrics of Aristophanes, comic, satiric, and paratragic, there is one
class which seems to be serious, appeals to the gods to appear and
sometimes "to join our chorus." We have too little of earlier comedy
to know whether they are traditional, but it is reasonable to suppose
that they are, and that it was the custom of comic poets to appeal for
the participation of the gods. The songs generally invoke more than
one god, and the metre generally changes from god to god. In the
Clouds (563) the strophe invokes Zeus in choriambic dimeters,
Poseidon in a choriambic trimeter followed by dimeters, Aither in
dactyls, and Helios in aeolo-choriambic. The antistrophe is divided
in exactly the same places for Apollo, Artemis, Athena, and Dionysos.
The *Thesmophoriazusae* (311) has an astrophic kletic hymn; the
opening general invocation is iambic, then Zeus and Apollo are
invoked in a dactylic tetrameter A followed by a lekythion,[6] Athena
in trochaic, Artemis in dactylic, Poseidon in iambo-anapaests, the
Nereids in dactylic, and the Nymphs in syncopated iambics; the
conclusion follows in dactylo-epitrites. In the parodos of the *Frogs*
(323) the form is different and even more relevant to our purpose.
The chorus first invokes Iakchos in a strophe-antistrophe of ionics.
This is followed by recitative anapaestic tetrameters by the leader
inviting the uninitiated to stand aside and calling on the mystics to
sing. They sing a strophe-antistrophe in melic anapaests and in the
antistrophe invoke Soteira. The leader then calls on them to summon
Demeter (two recitative anapaestic tetrameters). They invoke her
in a strophe-antistrophe of iambic dimeters. Then the leader tells
them in two syncopated catalectic iambic tetrameters to summon
Iakchos, and they invoke him in three identical stanzas consisting
of two catalectic iambic trimeters, an iambic metron, an iambic
tetrameter catalectic, and an iambic trimeter. The repeated invocation to Iakchos gives the whole series of invocations a ring form,
and the rest of the parodos does not concern us.

I should like to argue that the *Frogs* preserves an original ritual
form in which each god has a complete pair of metrically unique
strophe-antistrophe, and that the restriction of the single gods to a
period within the strophe-antistrophe (*Clouds*) or astrophic song

---

6 Following Wilamowitz' transposition in 316.

(*Thesmophoriazusae*) is an adaptation of the original form to the needs of the particular comedy. Even the kletic hymn of the Elian women, as emended by Page,[7] is six lines long, the length of a short strophe; and Alkaios' kletic hymn to the Dioskouroi had originally six Alcaic stanzas.[8]

It is easier to derive the tragic chorus with its series of metrically different pairs of strophe-antistrophe from a series of short kletic hymns, like the parodos of the *Frogs*, than from the epirrhematic form postulated by Kranz. The brief injunctions to the chorus could easily be omitted, whereas in the original postulated by Kranz the solo part is more important than the chorus.

It might be wiser to leave the case here as an intriguing hypothesis. But it is tempting to suggest that we may have Aristotle's authority for it. Themistios (*Orat.* 26, 316 D) asks: "Did solemn Tragedy with all its trappings and chorus and actors come before the audience at a single moment? Do we not believe Aristotle that first the chorus came in and sang to the gods, then Thespis invented prologue and speech, then Aeschylus the third actor and *okribantes*, while we owe the rest to Sophocles and Euripides?" There is no reason to doubt that Themistios is reproducing what Aristotle said; the minor contradiction with the view expressed in the *Poetics* that Sophocles invented the third actor is unimportant since Aeschylus certainly used the third actor in the *Oresteia* and Aristotle may have noted this fact. It is curious that in a rather similar account Diogenes Laertius, (3. 56) who does not refer to Aristotle, attributes the second actor to Aeschylus and the third to Sophocles. But Diogenes Laertius differs from Themistios also in his formulation of the two first stages. He says: "Formerly the chorus by itself performed the whole drama, and later Thespis invented a single actor to give the chorus a rest." If he did form any clear picture of the development, he must have thought of something like e.g. Stesichoros' *Oresteia* as the original tragedy, purely choral, and then this choral continuum interrupted by speeches from Thespis' actor "to give the chorus a rest." Themistios' account, for which he claims the authority of Aristotle, is entirely different. He must have had some such development as this in mind. Thespis found an existing ceremony in which the

---

[7] *PMG* 871, *Lyrica Graeca Selecta*, 437.

[8] Lobel–Page (Oxon. 1955), 34; *Lyrica Graeca Selecta*, 109.

chorus came in and sang to the gods; he took the form but not
necessarily the subject-matter for his tragic choruses from this
ceremony. He started his play with a prologue speech, then the
chorus sang in reaction to it, then there was another speech, perhaps
followed by another song. We do not know, unfortunately, whether
Themistios' speech (*rhêsis*) is a technical term meaning messenger-
speech or even whether we should be justified in taking it as singular
for plural. But it certainly looks as if he (and Aristotle) thought that
Thespis made a change in kind by the invention of prologue and
speech, not a change from choral drama to actor drama, but a
change from choral hymns to drama.

In the original ceremony, as described by Themistios, the chorus
"came in and sang to the gods," or if we may stress the present
tense of the participle and the imperfect tense of the main verb,
"were singing to the gods on their way in." Certainly the songs were
to a plurality of gods. If we may accept the second rendering, the
passage naturally recalls Xenophon's remark[9] that at the Dionysia
the choruses do honour in addition (to Dionysos) to other gods and to
the Twelve by their dances. He clearly thinks of a progress through the
Agora with stops at various altars to sing hymns to the gods of the
altars. This is exactly the kind of ceremony that is needed to explain
Themistios and the kletic hymns of Aristophanes. Opinion[10] has
been divided as to whether Xenophon means the Anthesteria or the
City Dionysia. At Xenophon's date the City Dionysia is the more
likely reference, and if the equation with Themistios is right, the
occasion must be the City Dionysia since Thespis produced tragedy
at that festival. Xenophon's choruses have also been equated with
the choruses which Kallimachos (Frg. 305 Pf.) says were sung to
Dionysos Limnaios: even if the equation is accepted, Kallimachos
uses the imperfect tense, and in a fragmentary scholiast of Thucydides[11] the line follows a mention of Eleuther. Kallimachos may
therefore have spoken of a transference of these choruses from the
Anthesteria to the City Dionysia.

---

[9] *Hipparchicus* 3. 2.

[10] See K. Friis Johansen, *Arkaeol. Kunsthist. Medd. Dan. Vid. Selsk.* 4, 2 (1959), 41;
Pickard-Cambridge, *Dramatic Festivals at Athens*[2] (Oxford 1968), 16 f.

[11] P. Oxy. 853 (6), col. x, discussed by Pfeiffer *ad loc.* Cf. also Wycherley, *Am. J.
Archaeol.* 67 (1963), 78.

There is, of course, one last question. Can Themistios' account be reconciled with the statement in the *Poetics* that tragedy was an improvisation by the leaders of the dithyramb?[12] It is perfectly possible that these are two different points: that in the *Poetics* Aristotle found an analogy for the actor in the kind of leader that Archilochos claimed to be, but that in the passage referred to by Themistios he was asking what choral performance at the City Dionysia could Thespis have developed. But dithyramb need not be either Archilochos' dithyramb or the tribal competition at the City Dionysia. It is perfectly possible that the song which Xenophon's choruses sang to Dionysos was called a dithyramb and that the name of their chief performance (chief, because they performed at the Dionysia) could be used as a cover-name for their whole performance. In that case the leader is the man who tells them to sing at each altar, just as the leader instructs the chorus of mystics in the parodos of the *Frogs*. Much of this is speculation; what I am chiefly concerned to establish is that a possible origin for the unique form of tragic choruses is given by the ceremony of songs to the gods which, according to Themistios, Aristotle saw as already existing in the time of Thespis.

Stanford, 6 January 1970

[12] 1449 a 9. Gudeman interprets "leaders" quite generally; Else sees a specific reference to Archilochos.

THE *AGÔN*
AND THE ORIGIN OF THE
TRAGIC CHORUS

FRANCISCO R. ADRADOS

In his recently published book on the *Supplices* of Aeschylus,[1] A. F. Garvie discards previous opinions as to the date of this play which are based on the characteristics of the chorus. As is well known, the fact that the Danaides who make up the chorus of the *Supplices* are the real protagonist had been considered by many to indicate an early date. No less well known is it that since the publication in 1952 of the Oxyrh. Pap. 2256, frg. 3, a new phase in the problem of the dating of the *Supplices* has opened up. Numerous philologists claim to find support in the papyrus for a later date for this play, which previously had been reckoned as the earliest of all Aeschylean plays and thus of all extant Greek drama. Garvie's book, which deals thoroughly with the problem of the dating of the *Supplices* and discusses its archaic features, comes to the conclusion that its chorus, rather than being archaic, is of an unusual character within the Greek theatre. A chorus like that of the *Persae* where a messenger brings news to a chorus of anonymous citizens would come, according to Garvie, much closer to what is considered normal in the tragic chorus.

The opinion which one might hold on the primitive function of the chorus in Tragedy is intimately bound up with that which one might form on the origins of Tragedy. From this point of view we now make some remarks on the function of the chorus, at the same time presenting some of the results of a book we are preparing on the origins of the Athenian drama.

Garvie, like several authors among whom one must mention

[1] *Aeschylus'* Supplices: *Play and Trilogy* (Cambridge 1969). See now the review by M. McCall, *Am. J. Philol.* 91 (1970), 352–57.

Kranz in the first place, rightly sees that the true dramatic nucleus of Tragedy is made up of the scenes in which the chorus and an actor take part simultaneously. However, as with other authors, he tends to see in this confrontation of chorus and actor something secondary: the actor would merely have been brought in from outside and the coryphaeus would also have been introduced subordinately in order to isolate within the chorus one of its members, so that he could engage in dialogue with the actor. This theory is based fundamentally on the scarcity of dramatic and mimetic elements in the Greek Lyrics that we know, that is, the literary Lyrics, and on our scanty knowledge of the preliterary ritual Lyrics of dramatic or mimetic nature. We know, Garvie says, the masked *kômoi* which represent satyrs, animals, etc., but there are no corresponding ones in relation to the heroic myth. Therefore a chorus like that of the *Supplices*, which is the real protagonist of the dramatic action, is a more recent literary product, a creation of Aeschylus and not a remnant of the ancient dramatic choruses.

Garvie's ideas in this book follow a line of thought whose most qualified representative is probably Else. In his book, *The Origin and Early Form of Greek Tragedy*,[2] he makes Tragedy out to be an artificial synthesis of epic narration and nondramatic, choral Lyrics performed in Athens. I think, putting it briefly, that there is much to be said against this position. It breaks all the existing connections between Greek Tragedy and the more or less closely related genres which exist in various cultures and which spring from mimetic dances. It breaks the connections that exist within Greece between Tragedy, Comedy, Satyr Play, and various rituals. It leaves no room for explanations of such essential facts as, for example, the existence of the mask. In short, Tragedy springs from the medium to which it belongs, the mimetic rituals organized around the mimic dance of a chorus.

But one thing is certain and that is that evaluation of mixed scenes where chorus and actor speak to each other, in keeping with the origins of Tragedy, does pose difficulties. Kranz, who follows the ideas of Wilamowitz when the latter—at the same time basing his opinion on Aristotle—sees the origin of Tragedy in the dialogue between the chorus and the coryphaeus, certainly faces up to these

[2] Cambridge, Mass., 1966.

difficulties. In his *Stasimon*,[3] he firmly sets the origin of Tragedy in the *epirrhêma* between chorus and coryphaeus and then between chorus and actor; but he persists in considering this phase as derived from an ancient confrontation of two choruses,[4] and he finds himself contradicting the theory he had shared of the origin of Tragedy in the Dithyramb of satyrs; for neither the *epirrhêma* nor the remaining mixed scenes of chorus and actor contain anything satyr-like. On the other hand, Peretti,[5] who acknowledges this fact, separates these mixed scenes from the origin of Tragedy. They would be elements proceeding from the severer Lyrics, mainly those that are threnodic, which would have been incorporated secondarily into Tragedy.

We believe that the best method of approaching the origins of Tragedy is to analyze the tragedies that we possess, above all the earliest ones, with the object of picking out in them elementary unities of form and content, of discovering those nuclei of dramatic action which have been preserved in them, trying to establish the earliest form of the same. This task has been performed only in part and has been disturbed by the perpetual search for affinities between the results thus obtained and the ideas of Aristotle— interpreted in various ways—and those of Wilamowitz, which are in turn an attempt to reconcile elements from the *Poetica* which are in themselves irreconcilable: the two theories that Tragedy derives from the Dithyramb, a serious genre by definition, and that it derives from the *Satyrikon*, a festive genre.

We concede—and here we agree with Else—that Aristotle proceeds from philosophic propositions rather than from historical facts and that it is preferable to proceed independently by way of analyzing our material. And we find that one can push forward even further in this analysis, without of course contemning the achievements of Kranz, Peretti, Schadewaldt, Nestle, Duchemin and so many other scholars. In an article published recently we have set out the fundamental principles of the method which in our opinion must be followed.[6] Basically it deals with this isolating of elementary unities,

---

[3] Berlin 1933.

[4] Cf. also J. Lammers, *Die Doppel- und Halbchöre in der antiken Tragödie* (Paderborn 1931).

[5] *Epirrema e tragedia* (Firenze 1939).

[6] "Ideas metodologicas para el estudio de la evolución y estructura del teatro griego," *Revista de la Universidad de Madrid*, 18 (1969), 299–319.

restoring to them the earliest possible form and content. A subsequent study shows how these unities have influenced each other along with the widening and evolution of theatrical action. A new phase of the research consists in finding parallels to these elementary unities of Tragedy in various rituals—and yet another that of discovering outside Greece more or less parallel facts, where theatrical genres are created from mimetic rituals in which the dance and frequently the mask play a part.

Naturally we are not going to attempt this study here. We merely note down a few things about one of these elementary unities which is found in Tragedy and which is known to us in various rituals not always strictly theatrical: the *agôn* in which the chorus takes part. For as we have seen, the question arises whether the ancient chorus of Tragedy has a central role in the action of Tragedy or whether the action involves the actors only, the chorus being a simple witness. Of course the chorus has evolved greatly throughout the history of Tragedy and has tended to acquire a more or less sub-ordinate role. But there do exist remains of an ancient type of action in which a chorus confronts an actor in what we call an *agôn*. Naturally, this does not mean that the chorus has the most important part in the action. The chorus can have at its side an actor who is usually its commander, such as Danaus is with respect to the Danaides in the *Supplices*. In fact it is perfectly normal that the chorus be made up of the subjects or servants or friends of the protagonist; and Garvie is right in pointing out that the centering of the *Supplices* on the Danaides rather than on Danaus is an innova-tion of Aeschylus. But the confrontation of the chorus and the Egyptian herald who threatens and pursues them, that is to say, the *agôn*: chorus/actor, has further parallels; it is not an isolated scene. On the other hand one must point out that the *agôn*: chorus/actor is nothing more than one of the elementary unities to which we have referred, although we believe that it could be the one around which the whole Tragedy is organized. Another very important elementary unity in which chorus and actor take part is the dirge or *thrênos*, several of which, for example, are to be found in the *Persae*. However, in the dirge the chorus can address its commander while in the *agôn* the existence of an adversary is essential; this is the most dramatic element of all. Perhaps one could say there is no Greek Tragedy without an *agôn*—with the exception of the *Persae*.

Having come to this point we must stop a moment to take note of the fact that usually the typical *agôn* of Tragedy is considered to be that which takes place between two actors, the chorus playing a subordinate role. Really this is the more frequent; in this direction Tragedy has evolved. In the typical *agônes* of Euripides the two *rhêseis* of the two actors who confront each other are each followed by two lines of the coryphaeus who comments briefly on their words, sometimes however siding with one against the other as in the *Bacchae*. But if this is the more usual type of tragic *agôn*, it does not follow that it is the only one or the earliest. This, it seems to me, is the mistake of a book, otherwise excellent, *L'agon dans la Tragédie grecque* by J. Duchemin.[7] Here only those structures of the latter type are called *agôn*; when in Aeschylus or in Sophocles there are confrontations which are formally different, Mme Duchemin says that it is a question of situations of *agôn* without the form of *agôn*. And yet while the author tentatively proposes to attribute the origin of the *agôn* consisting of countervailing speeches to Euripides, she recognizes the archaism of some types of confrontation different from this one, above all the confrontation of chorus and actor.

If then we recognize the fact that various *agônes* of Tragedy in which actor and chorus confront each other (the latter sometimes accompanied by the actor) are archaic, we now find ourselves in a position to compare them, on the one hand, with *agônes* of Comedy in which the same occurs, and on the other with various archaic rituals to be found in Greece and outside Greece, rituals where an individual is pursued by a chorus or vice versa. To quote some Greek examples, we refer to the ritual of the Agrioniae of Orchomenus in which the priest pursues the Maenades with his sword, or to several involving the expulsion of the *pharmakos* to the sound of a mourning dirge accompanied by the flute. It is to those rituals, including those in which speech plays a subordinate role, that the drama is related, and also to others whose reflections we find in the analysis of Greek dramas. All this shows us that chorus and actor form a unit and that they belong to the same unit from the earliest times. Without doubt, the actor is one of the choral dancers who,

[7] Paris 1945.

when the action becomes mimetic (in the *agôn* it is always so, in the dirge it may or it may not be), represents or personifies a mythical character. But this, of course, must be proved by way of a thorough analysis of the relationship of actor and chorus in Tragedy. Sometimes it is all too clear that the actor performs some of the functions which are more appropriate for the coryphaeus; so in *Eumenides* 117 ff. the function of Clytaemestra is the same as that of the coryphaeus in 140 ff.—this confirms the theory that the actor originates in the coryphaeus; or to put it better, that both derive from the exarchon. The tragic *agôn*, founded on the confrontation of chorus and actor and of which we are going to offer some examples, is comparable, as will now be seen, to the comic *agôn*; and this deserves some explanation. We believe that this can only be understood in the context of the theory we have set out in detail in a recent article in the journal *Emerita*.[8] In it we have shown that the term *kômos* refers to any chorus which exists in order to perform a ritual action, including for example the intoning of a dirge before a hero's grave or the singing of the epinikion in honour of the victor in the athletic games. This is to say that not only Comedy but all drama originates in the *kômos*, the usage of the word being, in words like κωμῳδία, κωμικός, the result of a restriction in meaning so that it contrasts precisely with the word τραγῳδία. At the beginning of the didascaliae contained in *IG* II 971 the term κῶμοι still refers to the theatrical genres as a whole and at the same time to the Dithyramb. According to my theory, Tragedy would be no more than a specialization within the multiform genus of *kômoi*. The *kômoi* which gave birth to Tragedy would be those of a heroic nature, and the name would come from those performed by the τράγοι, that is to say, the antecedent of Satyr Play. From the remaining *kômoi* would have emerged Comedy whose nature became specialized in a definite way, in opposition to Tragedy. For if it is true that the τραγῳδοί performed within their mythical themes both the serious and festive genre (Tragedy and Satyr Play respectively), no less certain is it that with the passing of time, it was Tragedy which was considered as essential and against which the term that contrasted most was Comedy, rather than Satyr Play.

[8] "*Komos, Komoidía, Tragoidía.* Sobre los orígenes del teatro," *Emerita* 35 (1967), 249–94.

Thus we consider the theatrical genres as the result of specializations starting from a multiform genus, the *kômoi* taking part in quite diverse rituals. Even when both in Tragedy and Comedy common elementary unities are found such as the *agôn* of chorus and actor which we are now studying, these *agônes* may have and doubtless did have different intentions and evolved in opposite directions on being enclosed in different genres. However, we do not wish to go into the general problem about which I have already presented items in the above-mentioned article and which I must study in greater detail in the book of which the present article is a foretaste. Here I am referring rather to the *agôn*. And it is easy to reach the conclusion that this elementary unity, which is the *agôn* of chorus and actor in Tragedy, finds its parallel in Comedy, as I have already pointed out. It is easy to see that beneath the great differences between comic and tragic *agôn* there do exist, both in form and content, elements in common.

In the examination of the comic *agôn* something similar to what happens in the examination of tragic *agôn* occurs: its most common and typical features, which really proceed from a development which moved in the opposite direction to that experienced by the tragic *agôn*, have been continually pointed out. Gelzer's book on the *agôn*[9] is symptomatic in this respect. He attains a greater coherence than is apparent in the material, thanks to two methods: one, he distinguishes between the struggle (*Streit*) and the *agôn* or discussion, a much more formalised part; and the other, he denies the name *agôn* to passages which do not possess a regular structure. Inversely, Gelzer calls *agôn* those passages in which there is no true confrontation and in which, however, the structure is that of a typical *agôn*. This, as we know, is a double structure. The first semichorus sings the ode and its coryphaeus incites the actor to expose his reasons (*katakeleusmos*). There ensues the discussion between the two actors in the *epirrhêma*, ending in the *pnigos*: and everything is repeated in a symmetrical counterpart.

However, even within the canonical form there are variations. One of the characters can simply be the coryphaeus (as in the *Aves*) as a result of which there is confrontation of chorus and actor, not of two actors. But there also exist simple and not double *agônes*.

---

[9] *Der epirrhematische Agon bei Aristophanes* (München 1960).

And as for content it is of a most varied nature, ranging from a violent confrontation through all kinds of verbal threats to a peaceful discussion. The chorus pursues or is in turn pursued, persuades or allows itself to be persuaded. At other times there is a proposal which is either accepted or denied, or the problem remains unsolved and the play consists of a series of *agônes* until a solution is reached, at times by deceit or violence.

All this shows that the form of the *agôn* is highly variable, as is its content. In form there is a constant element which is the epirrhematic structure, which in Comedy tends to be double. In content the only constant feature is the confrontation either violent or dialectical. In this confrontation is included the persuasion, either successful or unsuccessful, of a chorus by an actor or vice versa. With successful persuasion the actor ends up by being converted from antagonist into the commander of the chorus as in the *Acharnenses* (chorus convinced by actor).

We would like to point out briefly that in Tragedy, as we have anticipated, there are scenes which as regards both form and content are comparable to the scenes from Comedy already referred to; that is to say there are *agônes* of chorus and actor which vary as regards form and content but which have essential features in common with the *agônes* of Comedy. Among them the *epirrhêma* predominates. (An *agôn* in the form of a *kommos* or lyrical dialogue, such as that of the *Supplices*, is an exception.) And there are examples in which this *epirrhêma* tends to adopt a double structure, as in Comedy. As for the content there is again a very varied range of motives—from hostile confrontation to friendly persuasion. In the latter case the actor who addresses the chorus can be considered as its superior from the very beginning: as with Clytaemestra, Eteocles, or Prometheus before their respective choruses. It is obvious that the actor originates in the chorus whether he figures as its commander or antagonist. And when the *agôn* takes place between two actors, with the role of the chorus thus fading into the background or even entirely disappearing, we must consider this as secondary, however frequent it later becomes. What happens in this respect in the *Agamemnon* is interesting. Here Agamemnon and Clytaemestra confront each other though not in a formal *agôn*, since she proceeds to dissemble and not to reveal her true thoughts until Agamemnon is dead. Neither is there, properly speaking, an *agôn* between the chorus and Agamemnon although there is a concealed confrontation, criticism voiced by the former against the latter. But once Agamemnon dies, leaving on stage only the actors from one of the confronting parties, that is Clytaemestra and then Aegisthus, the chorus recovers the central role. And there is a true *agôn*: chorus/Clytaemestra; a complex *agôn* with epirrhematic elements and others from the *kommos*, since threnodic motives are blended in. There then ensues a second *agôn*, this in trimeters and tetrameters, between the coryphaeus (who represents the chorus) and Aegisthus.

Let us now look at some of the *agônes* of chorus and actor in Tragedy, without by any means intending to exhaust the subject. We attempt simply to note the fact of their existence and the importance that these *agônes* have for the investigation of the origins of Greek drama. One might say that the task of the tragic author consists essentially in organizing together the mythical material into a series of *agônes* (to which certainly other elements were added): *agônes* some of which were performed on stage and others off stage, being reported by the messenger. Mythical material did not always lend itself to expression in *agônes* of chorus and actor—for this reason the type of *agôn* between actor and actor tended to predominate. But nevertheless there do exist examples of this type.

In the *Eumenides* Aeschylus discovered the possibility of dramatizing the happy ending of the *Oresteia* with the help of a *kômos* of deities who intervene in a series of *agônes*. The persecution of a character by these terrible deities and the persuasion achieved by them look back to possible archaic rituals: numerous parallels could be cited. Throughout the play there is a series of confrontations of the chorus (85 ff., 235 ff., 778 ff.) or the coryphaeus (397 ff., 566 ff.) and Orestes' party: either Orestes himself or his defenders Athena and Apollo. The themes are common to those of Comedy—persecution, abuse, threats, acceptance of judgment, judgment, persuasion.

Without doubt the *Eumenides* is the play in which the chorus most clearly takes part in agonistic action. However, it is by no means the only one. The *Philoctetes* by Sophocles is another good example. Although Neoptolemus and Odysseus are those who, in fact, attempt to carry off Philoctetes, either by deceit or violence, the chorus also has an agonistic role. Thus in 135–219 (*parodos*) we have a chorus in the act of search; it is an *epirrhêma*: chorus/Neoptolemus (the latter recites anapaests) who are searching for Philoctetes and end up discovering him. In 826 ff. there is another *epirrhêma* in which Neoptolemus again acts as chief of the chorus. Even in 974 ff., during an *agôn* between Odysseus and Philoctetes, the chorus binds the latter upon the orders of the former and in a lyrical dialogue 1081–1217 the chorus attempts, in vain, to convince the hero that he must follow it to Troy.

The *parodos* of the *Oedipus Coloneus* (117–257) presents us with the chorus of inhabitants of Colonos in the act of expelling Oedipus, first from the sanctuary of the Eumenides and then from the entire territory. The chorus then takes part in two *agônes* of actors which follow—between Oedipus and Creon and between Theseus and Creon. The latter is a different action—not a continuation of the preceding.

We also find a chorus in action, prevailing throughout the play, in the *Rhesus* by Euripides, which as is known has an archaic structure. The tragedy begins immediately with the *parodos*—as in the *Persae* and the *Supplices*—in which a chorus of action is presented, the guards of the Trojan camp who follow up their chief Hector. But most significant is the choral *agôn* of 674–727 in which the chorus attacks Odysseus and Diomedes, the two Greek spies who have just killed Rhesus, and they escape.

In plays like these the chorus intervenes in the action throughout and at times this action bears the characteristics of an *agôn*. It is the type which comes nearest to that of Comedy and also to that of Satyr Play, such as the *Dictyoulkoi* or the *Theoroi* by Aeschylus or the *Cyclops* by Euripides. In other tragedies the agonistic performance of the chorus is less important but it is still noteworthy. Let us look at some examples.

The *Supplices* by Aeschylus, towards which we first turn our attention, presents a chorus which, apart from its role as protagonist, follows in line with the preceding, if one adds passages of persuasion to those of confrontation. We think that both fall within the meaning of *agôn*. Here we have a chorus which flees and which has sought refuge at an altar. The chorus then proceeds to persuade king Pelasgus in *rhêsis* and *stichomythia*: chorus/king, in *epirrhêma*: chorus/king, in a *stasimon* of the chorus, in a new dialogue in iambic trimeters with *rhêsis* and *stichomythia*. Only from here on does the chorus take part in a confrontation, that is, with the Egyptian herald. In 825 ff., an *agôn* develops in which a lyrical dialogue and an epirrhematic dialogue follow an initial *astrophon* of the Danaides. Afterwards there is a new *agôn*, this time between two choruses, the Danaides and the serving women.

In the *Septem* there is an initial *agôn* of persuasion between the coryphaeus and Eteocles (181 ff.) but then there is another between the chorus and Eteocles (677 ff., *epirrhêma*). At the end there is an *agôn* of actors (Herald and Antigone). We have already commented on the *Agamemnon*: here the choral *agôn* combines with the dirge. On the other hand in the *Choephoroi* there is no choral *agôn* and yet there are signs of it in the repeated *agônes* in which the chorus takes part. In 84 ff. Electra persuades the chorus (although the dialogue is only with the coryphaeus) to implore Agamemnon to help Orestes kill Clytaemestra; in 164 ff. Electra convinces the coryphaeus of Orestes' presence, upon which the chorus implores Agamemnon to take vengeance. In 510 ff. the coryphaeus incites Orestes to action. In 770 ff., the same coryphaeus persuades the wet nurse to tell Aegisthus to come alone so that his death will be easier. In 1059 ff. the coryphaeus again tries to persuade Orestes, after the crime, not to be afraid and to cleanse himself. The *Prometheus* on the other hand presents true choral *agônes*—all of persuasion.

As can be seen, the differences are noteworthy: sometimes there is violent action, sometimes only persuasion; sometimes only the chorus intervenes, at other times only the coryphaeus. Sometimes the form of the *epirrhêma* is kept, sometimes it is not. And this occurs not only in Aeschylus. We saw that the *Philoctetes*, *Oedipus Coloneus*, and *Rhesus* have choruses which take part in *agônes* practically throughout the whole play. However, there are isolated, partial *agônes* in other plays with the participation of the chorus. Thus in the *Oedipus Rex* where the basic *agônes* are of actors, the chorus is present in some. In 634 ff. Jocasta appears, playing the part of a peacemaker, upon hearing the dispute between Oedipus and Creon. When these quarrel in front of her the chorus takes a hand in the persuading of Oedipus. In the *Heraclidae* by Euripides, on the other hand, we find an *agôn* of confrontation. The chorus comes on stage calling for Jocasta to prevent Euristheus' herald from pulling the suppliants

off the altar (73 ff.); then there is an epirrhematic *agôn*: chorus/
herald, followed by a stichomythic one, coryphaeus/herald.

We could give more examples but we believe that the above
are sufficient to enable us to see that *agônes* with chorus are not
lacking in Tragedy and that sometimes they are in the very centre
of its argument. The tragic choral *agônes* have the most varied
tones and intentions, moving between the two extremes of violent
attack and persuasion, and forming an alliance sometimes with
other diverse forms or tending to be replaced by the *agônes* of the
actors.

The formal study of the *agônes* is too complex to be undertaken
here. One must proceed from the fact that the *agôn* is an open form
subject to multiple variations. When the chorus takes part in it, it
may end with the latter singing a *stasimon* just as the actor may
recite a *rhêsis*. But there is a clear tendency toward the epirrhematic
structure, which gave place to the *stichomythia* when the chorus was
replaced by the coryphaeus. But one must not think that all the
epirrhêmata are agonistic.

The agonistic *epirrhêmata* of Aeschylus tend to adopt a symmetric
structure in which the chorus sings strophes and antistrophes and
the actor recites iambic trimeters or anapaestic dimeters; in Sophocles
there are comparable forms, as in *Philoctetes* 135 ff., *Ajax* 866 ff.
But we must not fail to note the appearance of certain double
structures, also present in Euripides, which remind us of the *agônes*
of Comedy. The earliest types are those in which after the strophe
and the antistrophe there are stichic dialogues of coryphaeus and
actor. Already in Aeschylus there exist some signs of these double
structures. Compare the *Agamemnon*, 1407 ff. (combination of
dirge and *agôn*), where the chorus sings the strophe and the antistrophe, and each is followed by the trimeters of Clytaemestra;
but in Sophocles and Euripides they appear even more clearly,
without this meaning that we are dealing with later creations
(although in details they do, undoubtedly, contain some later
elements).

Let us look at some examples, without trying to systematize them.
In the *Philoctetes* 391 ff., 827 ff.; *Oedipus Coloneus* 116 ff., 833 ff.,
1447 ff.; *Oedipus Rex* 634 ff.; *Ion* 1229 ff., we find various types of
choral *agônes* with double structure. The oldest are without doubt

those in which after the strophe and the antistrophe there occur stichic dialogues between coryphaeus and actor. It can happen that the stichic dialogue no longer represents a confrontation but takes place between two actors on the same side; and that the choral parts may be attributed to the actors. However in Comedy too there are diverse innovations.

What we really want to show, even though superficially, is that the participation of the chorus in the action, confronting an actor or persuading him, is not anomalous in Tragedy: it is a phenomenon that exists here as well as in Comedy. Even in the actor-*agônes* there are signs of some participation by the chorus in the conflict.

To sum up, we believe that it can no longer be maintained that the elements of the drama in which a chorus takes part are a secondary addition, nor can it be maintained that the drama itself (or Tragedy) is a creation from nondramatic lyrical elements and narrative elements. On the contrary, the drama springs from mimetic rituals in which there is a confrontation; also from other rituals, the dirge for example, which may or may not be mimetic. The *agôn* is in its very centre—as in that of so many predramatic rituals. Without doubt it was used in the celebration of heroic rituals and not only those in which satyrs, nymphs, and the like take part. In the history of rites we are familiar with the process of historization by which omnipresent archaic rituals are interpreted as referring to myths or changing historical facts. But even if this were not the case, it is clear that when the tragic poets wanted to represent the heroic myth with the help of a chorus, they were forced to have this chorus take part in the action in the same way as was usual in the *kômos* of so many religious celebrations, in keeping with the traditional patterns of the dirge, the *agôn*, the entreaty, the hymn, etc. The hero's army and his servants or subjects could easily be made into scenic reality by *kômoi* like these. And so too Eumenides or Bacchae. At other times the tragic poets got into difficulty and tended logically to make the role of actors more and more important while diminishing that of the chorus. Hence the differences with respect to Comedy. The latter, not being subject to the narration of fixed myths, continued to use the traditional *kômoi* which were adaptable to all kinds of actions—such as are usual in Comedy. Those *kômoi*, essentially the same, might incorporate all kinds of animals, fantastic beings, dead people. They could be modified in any detail according to the poet's wish. In Tragedy the *kômoi* were open to much greater alterations; but it is easy to see that they were present at its origin just as they were in that of all Greek drama.*

Madrid, 10 September 1970

---

* [For further details, see now (1973) my book, *Fiesta, Comedia y Tragedia. Sobre los orígenes griegos del Teatro* (Barcelona, Planeta 1972). An English translation will be issued by Brill at Leiden.]

DU LYRISME À LA TRAGÉDIE:
RÉFLEXIONS SUR L'*AGAMEMNON*
ET LES *PERSES* D'ESCHYLE

Au cours de ces dernières années, nous nous sommes trouvée amenée à plusieurs reprises à réfléchir sur la conception eschyléenne du temps. Une première fois, nous avions choisi l'exemple d'Eschyle pour nous faire une idée du rapport Espace-Temps dans la Grèce archaïque.[1] Une deuxième fois, invitée à présenter une communication au Congrès international du Drame antique à Syracuse, il nous avait paru intéressant d'étudier à nouveau ce rapport, mais en nous attachant davantage cette fois à l'élément Temps. Nous avions choisi de l'étudier de façon plus précise dans une oeuvre particulière du dramaturge, dans l'*Agamemnon*, qui permet de poser dans toute son ampleur le problème.[2] Une troisième fois enfin, nous reprenions notre réflexion sur l'*Agamemnon*, en étendant notre examen à la composition d'ensemble de la pièce, envisagée à la fois dans son aspect dramatique et dans la chronologie des événements.[3] Cette triple étude devait nous amener, touchant plus particulièrement l'*Agamemnon* et peut-être touchant l'ensemble de la dramaturgie d'Eschyle, à un éclairage qui nous a paru suggestif sur les rapports de la tragédie la plus ancienne à nos yeux—puisque nous ignorons à peu près tout des devanciers d'Eschyle—avec le lyrisme dont elle est issue.

[1] "L'Espace et le Temps dans le théâtre d'Eschyle," participation au Colloque organisé par le Centre international de Synthèse sur l'Espace et le Temps dans l'Antiquité grecque, Paris, Avril 1967; publication dans la *Revue de Synthèse* (Paris, A. Michel, Janvier-Juin 1970), 80–95.

[2] Voir les *Actes du Deuxième Congrès international du Drame antique* (*SIRACUSA*, Mai 1967), publiés par les soins de l'Istituto nazionale del Dramma antico (Roma-Siracusa, s.d. 1969), 197–218.

[3] "Le déroulement du temps et la composition de l'Agamemnon d'Eschyle," dans *Information Littéraire* (Octobre 1967), 165–172.

Nous avions d'abord, en étudiant la composition du premier drame de l'*Orestie*, vu notre attention appelée avec insistance sur le caractère régressif de la chronologie des événements dramatiques. Nous assistions d'une part, dans ce drame, à une succession étonnante d'étirements et de resserrements du temps dans lequel s'inséraient les événements vécus par les personnages au cours de la pièce, succession plus étonnante encore à propos des événements antérieurs, notamment ceux rapportés par le Choeur. De l'autre, nous ne pouvions manquer de remarquer la façon dont le Choeur, en rappelant ses souvenirs, procédait par larges ondes, dont les remous nous entraînaient chaque fois davantage dans la profondeur des temps antérieurs. Succédant au prologue où l'apparition du signal de feu, dans une transmission quasi instantanée, apprend à tous que Troie est prise, les longs systèmes anapestiques nous reportent d'abord dix années en arrière, au moment où la flotte grecque, cinglant vers la Troade, quittait le mouillage d'Aulis. Puis le chant lyrique rappelle le fameux présage de l'aigle dévorant la hase pleine et la colère d'Artémis exigeant d'Agamemnon, en rançon, le sacrifice d'Iphigénie.[4] Le premier *stasimon* remonte encore plus haut dans le cours du temps en évoquant le rapt d'Hélène, cause originelle des événements racontés dans la *parodos*. Si donc nous considérons en eux-mêmes les chants du Choeur, la composition, de l'un à l'autre ou d'une partie à l'autre de la *parodos*, est indéniablement régressive. Si par ailleurs nous considérons de plus près le détail, nous nous apercevons que, par un art très savant, le poète fait osciller sans cesse du présent au passé le parcours sinueux de sa méditation. Entre temps les retours au présent s'entrecroisent, soit lorsque les Vieillards argiens, entre deux évocations du passé, s'adressent à la Reine absente[5] pour savoir d'elle ce qu'elle attend d'eux, soit lorsque Clytemnestre, au cours du premier épisode, nous ramène à l'instant du prologue, à l'instant aigu où les signaux de feu, traversant l'espace, atteignent le palais des Atrides. Nous sommes ainsi, à chaque moment, transportés comme d'un bord à l'autre du

---

[4] En réalité, on le sait, la déesse entend ainsi interdire au roi de Mycènes d'emmener à l'assaut de Troie l'armée grecque. Agamemnon, en persistant dans son dessein et dans ses ambitions, devra choisir d'immoler sa fille, et sera ainsi coupable des événements qui suivront.

[5] Certains, contre toute vraisemblance, ont voulu qu'elle fût présente. Voir, dans l'édition commentée de Fraenkel, la discussion sur ce passage.

temps, prêts à en franchir les limites et à passer du temps des hommes dans le temps des dieux. Celui-ci nous reçoit, c'est à dire que nous plongeons dans l'immobile éternité, lorsque, au cours du second développement lyrique de la *parodos*,[6] vient s'insérer cet Hymne à Zeus (160–83) parfaitement intemporel, immuable comme la divinité elle-même. Oscillation du présent au passé et *vice-versa*, réversibilité continuelle des successions normales nous projettent de façon très sûre hors du temps.

L'examen de la composition d'ensemble et celui de la structure des parties lyriques nous permettait en même temps de prendre conscience de la parenté profonde de la tragédie, prise globalement ou en détail, avec les oeuvres proprement lyriques, nommément avec celles que nous connaissons le mieux, les *Odes triomphales* de Pindare. Les deux poètes étaient à peu de chose près contemporains.[7] Leur art à tous deux, leur tempérament même, et peut-être aussi leur formation personnelle, présentent de remarquables points de concordance.[8] Le poète lyrique est plus tourné vers une tradition religieuse et mythique archaïque, qu'il plie néanmoins d'une main vigoureuse aux exigences d'une morale très critique. Le poète tragique, lui, plus douloureusement frappé par certaines cruautés inhérentes aux vieilles croyances, opère sur elles tout un travail d'épuration et de libération qui l'oriente plus résolument vers l'avenir. Le premier se situe vers la fin d'une lignée poétique consacrée encore uniquement au chant, à la musique, et, par-delà celle-ci, à la danse originelle. Le second n'abandonne certes pas ce lien qui unit encore son art et son oeuvre à la χορεία antique; mais il invente des formes nouvelles, ou, à tout le moins, fait progresser dans leur direction propre les formes nouvelles qui se font jour. Délaissant même progressivement le rythme trochaïque—celui des plus anciennes parties parlées—au profit de l'iambique, il

---

[6] Celle-ci se compose en effet de trois éléments successifs: les systèmes anapestiques (40–103), un premier chant lyrique, véritable chant de deuil (104–59), puis un second chant antistrophique (160–257), au rythme différent, plus proche d'un récit lyrique.

[7] La naissance d'Eschyle, combattant de Marathon, est généralement placée, d'après la *Vie*, aux environs de 525. Celle de Pindare doit être placée (malgré Boeckh, qui la faisait remonter quatre ans plus haut) entre 520/19 et 517/16. Eschyle mourut à Géla en 456/55; Pindare, lui, vécut plus âgé: il mourut en Argos, sans doute peu après 446.

[8] Le livre de J. H. Finley Jr, *Pindar and Aeschylus* (Cambridge, Mass. 1955), laisse un peu dans l'ombre ce qui nous paraît ici l'essentiel. Il se place surtout au point de vue de la cité, et voit surtout des différences.

insère au sein du lyrisme les scènes parlées dont le mouvement pousse l'oeuvre aux échanges et aux dialogues qui sont des actes.[9] D'où le mot de δρᾶμα et toute sa postérité. Gilbert Murray mettait avec raison l'accent sur le rôle de *créateur* joué dans l'histoire de la tragédie par Eschyle.[10] Nous irions nous-même jusqu'à dire le poète athénien, de façon globale, créateur du *drame*.[11] On voit dès lors l'intérêt d'une comparaison entre les formes d'art personnelles aux deux poètes. Cette comparaison s'est imposée à nous en étudiant le déroulement du temps dans l'*Agamemnon* d'Eschyle, c'est à dire à la fois la conception abstraite du temps et sa mise en oeuvre dramatique.

Les larges ondes selon lesquelles Eschyle organise, dans une structure globalement régressive, ses éléments lyriques et leurs entours, nous font invinciblement songer aux innombrables exemples de composition régressive offerts par l'oeuvre conservé de Pindare: cela ne se limite pas à la IVème *Pythique*. Celle-ci, nous devons toutefois le dire, présente peut-être le cas le plus caractéristique de cette forme de composition chère à l'auteur des *Épinicies*. D'apparence complexe et touffue, l'*Ode* monumentale écrite pour Arcésilas de Cyrène[12] est en réalité bâtie selon des lignes simples, celles même qui président à l'architecture et à la décoration des frontons doriques. Au centre Pélias et Jason face à face. L'auditeur y admire le calme souverain du jeune héros devant l'usurpateur, le calme même et le détachement que le poète suggère au roi de Cyrène, duquel il voudrait obtenir le pardon de l'exilé Damophile. La partie ascendante développe bien à loisir certains épisodes du mythe groupés autour des préliminaires à la quête de la Toison d'or et des préparatifs de Jason. La partie descendante, elle, brûle les étapes, expédiant entre le v. 189 et le v. 246 tout le récit de l'expédition. Mais là n'est pas le plus remarquable. Le fulgurant éclair de la

[9] Nous avons en cours une étude qui, de ce point de vue entre autres, essaye de faire remonter la tragédie à ses structures de départ.

[10] *Aeschylus Creator of Tragedy* est, on s'en souvient, le titre de son livre.

[11] On sait qu'Eschyle fut aussi un auteur fécond et très prisé de drames satyriques: il ne faut donc pas oublier qu'il ne s'est pas limité au genre tragique, et cela peut aider à éclairer les rapports des deux genres.

[12] Sur cette *Ode* et les différents problèmes qu'elle soulève, complexes à la vérité, voir dans notre édition commentée (Pindare, *Choix de Pythiques*, coll. Erasme, Paris 1967) les notices et les notes qui s'y rapportent.

poésie pindarique illumine, aux tout premiers vers du poème, l'oracle d'Apollon rendu à Battos, lui ordonnant la fondation de Cyrène. Puis, sans désemparer, le poète remonte le cours du temps jusqu'à dix-sept générations en arrière, lors du mouillage à l'île de Théra et à la prédiction de Médée sur cet épisode de la colonisation dorienne. Mais il faut, pour comprendre la perte de la motte de terre libyenne, remonter encore au temps de l'escale au bord du lac Triton, là où le dieu du lac remit à Euphamos, compagnon de Jason et ancêtre des Battiades, la motte, symbole de sa souveraineté future. La troisième triade ménage un repos, au cours duquel l'oracle de Médée se développe en détails explicatifs. Puis c'est un nouveau bond dans les profondeurs des temps mythiques: quelle fut l'origine de l'expédition? demande le poète au seuil de la strophe IV. D'où le récit de la venue de Jason à Iolcos, sa ville natale, récit dans lequel s'insère, sur les lèvres de Jason lui-même, le rappel de l'usurpation ancienne, puis, sur celles de Pélias, celui du fabuleux voyage des enfants d'Athamas portés par le bélier à la toison d'or. Ainsi se déroule le fil du poème, capricieux en apparence, mais en apparence seulement, car les auditeurs ont déjà entendu bien des fois l'histoire et reconnaissent au passage les épisodes, dont les variantes ne leur échappent pas. Cette forme de composition relève de façon évidente des formes de la poésie orale et met en oeuvre, en des siècles encore relativement archaïques de la littérature écrite, les plus purs procédés de l'improvisation (vraie ou simulée) familière aux poètes et aux conteurs populaires. Nul n'en saurait éprouver la moindre gêne, ni le poète ni son auditoire, car la pensée va librement, par les sentiers ou par les raccourcis ($o\hat{\iota}\mu os$ $\beta\rho\alpha\chi\acute{\upsilon}s$, dit Pindare lui-même au v. 248) de la mémoire, et le sentier peut aussi bien être la voie large des chars ($\kappa\alpha\tau$' $\dot{\alpha}\mu\alpha\xi\iota\tau\acute{o}\nu$, *ibid.*). Partout au long de cette route, le faisceau du projecteur se pose ici ou là, plus ou moins longuement selon la fantaisie ou les intentions du poète. Nous n'apprendrons à personne rien de nouveau si nous considérons comme une évidence le caractère purement intemporel d'une semblable poésie, libre de faire se succéder les épisodes dans l'ordre qui, au moment considéré, lui convient le mieux, sans référence rigoureuse et obligatoire à ce que nous appelons, nous, la chronologie, et croyons être plus raisonnable.

Prenons un autre exemple. La VIIème *Olympique*, d'un mouvement grandiose en sa simplicité, du Rhodien Diagoras et de sa victoire présente, remonte, dans une série majestueuse d'impressionnants coups d'aile, jusqu'à l'aube des temps mythiques. Annonçant au passage l'éloge qu'il va faire de la fille marine d'Aphrodite, Rhodes, la nymphe éponyme de l'île et l'épouse d'Hélios, le poète part, tout naturellement, des exploits et de la lignée, célèbre depuis des générations, de l'illustre pugiliste. Mais, dès la strophe II, il prend son vol pour remonter, dit-il, à l'origine, c'est à dire à la colonisation des temps héroïques, conduite par le fils d'Héraclès, le héros Tlépolème, selon l'ordre reçu de Delphes après le meurtre de Licymnios. De là le poète remonte à la naissance d'Athéna et à la neige d'or que Zeus, à cette occasion, fit pleuvoir sur l'île merveilleuse. De là les prescriptions sacrificielles en l'honneur de la déesse et l'oubli (malheureux, mais finalement heureux) de Tlépolème omettant d'emporter avec lui la semence du feu ardent (αἰθοίσας σπέρμα φλογός) pour la célébration du premier sacrifice offert sur l'Acropole. D'où, de façon à la vérité peu claire à nos yeux, les dons et les faveurs de la déesse de Lindos à son peuple. C'est de là qu'enfin, par un dernier bond dans la claire nuit des temps bienheureux, Pindare, ayant nommé les fils d'Hélios, s'explique en remontant au premier matin du monde, à celui du moins où les dieux en firent le partage, oubliant d'attribuer son lot à l'un des plus grands d'entre eux, au dieu Soleil, qui se trouvait justement absent. Hélios revenant se plaignit à Zeus, mais refusa l'offre d'un nouveau tirage au sort, car juste à ce moment, du haut des cieux, on pouvait voir naître et grandir, du fond de la mer jusqu'à la surface des eaux, la Rose divine, la fleur merveilleuse, Rhodes elle-même, la nymphe de beauté dont il allait faire son épouse et dont un fils (ils en eurent sept) devait être le père des trois éponymes rhodiens, Camiros, Ialysos, et Lindos. Ainsi vient se boucler, au début de la Vème triade, la chaîne mythique aux maillons inversés lancée par le poète, dès la Ière épode, à travers le temps. Il ne lui reste plus ensuite qu'à célébrer l'athlète aux victoires innombrables. Bel exemple de composition régressive, dont le principe—toujours le même—est, comme dans les chants des improvisateurs populaires ou dans les récits oraux des conteurs, d'expliquer, à chaque étape, ce que l'on vient de dire par les événements antérieurs. On saisit ainsi, derrière une poésie aussi complexe, aussi élaborée que celle de Pindare, la permanence des procédés issus des origines lointaines, venus en droite ligne des techniques de la littérature telle qu'elle était chantée ou récitée avant l'avènement de la littérature écrite.

Partie de l'examen de la première pièce de l'*Orestie* d'Eschyle, il est normal que nous prenions aussi chez Pindare l'exemple de l'*Ode* appelée parfois, elle aussi, *Orestie*, de cette XIème *Pythique* où le poète thébain a introduit comme mythe l'histoire d'Oreste. Ici Pindare semble adopter un cadre d'ensemble conforme à la chronologie, puisqu'il part du moment où, pendant que son père était assassiné, Oreste fut sauvé[13] et envoyé en Phocide, au pays de Pylade (17 sqq.), pour aboutir au dénouement sanglant, à l'assassinat par Oreste d'Égisthe et de Clytemnestre (37). Mais, à l'intérieur de ce cadre, la composition régressive reprend ses droits. La mention du double crime de Clytemnestre tuant Agamemnon et Cassandre est en effet immédiatement suivie du rappel du sacrifice d'Iphigénie, à propos duquel le poète se demande s'il fut la cause d'une horrible vengeance, ou si c'est l'amour d'Égisthe qui poussa au meurtre l'épouse adultère. Un nouveau regard sur le retour fatal du roi, immolé avec la fille de Priam, est suivi cette fois d'un retour plus loin en arrière et traité, de façon d'ailleurs rapide et presque allusive, selon une double ligne, celle qui unit la mort d'Agamemnon d'abord à l'enlèvement d'Hélène, ensuite à l'incendie des palais troyens:

"Il mourut, lui, le héros fils d'Atrée, dès son retour—après longtemps—dans l'illustre Amyclées. Il entraîna dans la mort la vierge prophétesse, après qu'à cause d'Hélène les Troyens eurent disparu dans les flammes avec la mollesse de leurs palais,"

> ...ἐπεὶ ἀμφ' Ἑλένᾳ πυρωθέντων
> Τρώων ἔλυσε δόμους
> ἁβρότατος   (33-34 b).

On remarquera aisément qu'il y a, dans ce mythe assez court, aux allusions toujours rapides, car les faits sont bien connus, à peu près toute la matière de la tragédie d'*Agamemnon*.[14] Même, bien qu'il soit

---

[13] D'après Pindare, qui suivait en cela, semble-t-il, l'*Orestie* de Stésichore, il fut sauvé par sa nourrice. On sait qu'Eschyle, imité par Sophocle et Euripide, attribue à Électre le salut d'Oreste. Chez Stésichore (voir *scholie* à *Pyth.* 25 a, d'après Phérécyde), la nourrice s'appelle Laodamie, chez Pindare Arsinoé.

[14] Celle des *Choéphores* est réduite à sa plus simple expression. Celle des *Euménides* en est entièrement absente, à moins qu'il n'en faille rapprocher la mention de Θέμις ἱερά au v. 9 du prologue, rappelant la succession à Delphes des divinités oraculaires.

malaisé d'affirmer, nous ne pouvons nous empêcher de voir la similitude de lignes entre le mythe pindarique et l'architecture du drame eschyléen, si nous ramenons celui-ci à son schéma le plus simple, le dépouillant par la pensée de ses plus riches et plus luxuriants ornements. Il y a, de la composition eschyléenne à la composition pindarique, plus d'une analogie, puisque les deux thèmes régressifs, le rapt d'Hélène et le sacrifice d'Iphigénie, se retrouvent de part et d'autre, l'un précédant l'autre chez Eschyle, le suivant chez Pindare. Le rapport semble évident entre les deux textes. Le plus récent a suivi, en l'adaptant à son dessein, le schéma du plus ancien. Mais lequel est le plus ancien? Si la date de l'*Orestie* d'Eschyle (458) est bien connue, celle de la XIème *Pythique* est sujette à discussion, et les savants hésitent, car les *scholies* font état de deux victoires pythiques du jeune Thrasydée, l'une en 474, l'autre en 454.[15] L'argument littéraire peut être, comme dans de nombreux cas, retourné dans un sens ou dans l'autre. Toutefois, certains détails de fait sur lesquels Pindare diffère d'Eschyle nous paraissent plaider en faveur de l'antériorité de l'*Épinicie*. On conçoit mal en effet que Pindare ait, après l'*Agamemnon*, encore pu désigner le fils d'Atrée comme souverain d'Amyclées, non d'Argos ou de Mycènes. On voit bien, par contre, pourquoi l'Athénien Eschyle en est resté à la tradition homérique et a placé en Argos le lieu de la célèbre trilogie.

Si nous insistons particulièrement sur le rapprochement entre Eschyle et Pindare, c'est, bien entendu, parce qu'il s'agit ici d'un mythe qui fut porté au théâtre—avec quel éclat, et combien de fois! —après avoir été familier au lyrisme.[16] Puisque nous avons la chance de posséder à la fois la trilogie d'Eschyle et le poème de Pindare (à défaut de celui de Stésichore), nous pouvons, à l'aide du moins d'un exemple de choix, nous faire une idée de la façon dont la mise en oeuvre d'un mythe variait en passant de la poésie

[15] On penche en général pour la première de ces deux dates. L'*Orestie* du poète d'Himère était, elle, de toute façon antérieure à l'une et à l'autre des deux oeuvres dont il s'agit. Elle avait évidemment été utilisée par Eschyle, mais ne semble pas avoir été prépondérante, pour autant que nous en ayons une idée, dans l'inspiration de Pindare. Voir là-dessus la notice de l'édition P. Mazon, ainsi que le commentaire de l'édition Fraenkel.

[16] Il fut aussi familier aux peintres de vases, et ceci dès la première partie du Vème siècle.

lyrique à la poésie dramatique. Certes l'*Agamemnon* appartient à la fin de la carrière d'Eschyle. Les ressemblances, à tout prendre, n'en seront que plus probantes, et peut-être trouverons-nous ensuite des indications concordantes dans telle ou telle pièce plus ancienne. La tragédie, au moins pour une part importante, est sortie du lyrisme choral. Nous aurons à nous demander plus loin si ce lyrisme se réduit ou non au *dithyrambe*, et dans quel sens, restreint ou moins restreint, il convient d'entendre le terme διθύραμβος. Le problème, pour les premiers poètes qui présentèrent le mythe sous la forme nouvelle du drame, fut évidemment de l'organiser selon une action à déroulement chronologique. Plus tard, lorsque la δύναμις du genre dramatique, selon l'expression bien connue d'Aristote, eut atteint le terme de son développement et donné naissance à une forme définitive, l'action se présenta sous la forme de parties successives parfaitement distinctes et séparées par des chants lyriques de plus en plus extérieurs au mythe lui-même. Mais, avec Eschyle, la tragédie ne fait encore que s'orienter vers ce devenir somme toute assez éloigné.

L'*Agamemnon*, ainsi que nous le remarquions en commençant, présente, du point de vue du déroulement chronologique de l'action, un caractère très particulier, puisque, selon la partie de la pièce où l'on se trouve, le temps s'étire ou se resserre à l'excès. Il est temps de revenir sur ce point et de nous expliquer, même brièvement, de façon plus précise. Le thème de l'attente est, on le sait, familier à Eschyle: attente du Veilleur, attente des Vieillards argiens se prolongent jusqu'à l'entrée de Clytemnestre au v. 264. Puis c'est la rapidité incroyable de l'irruption des signaux de feu propageant la nouvelle, et telle que l'arrivée du fanal en Argos semble coïncider, à travers l'espace et le temps, avec l'incendie même de Troie. Suivent de larges développements du Choeur, selon lesquels se déploient les souvenirs anciens dans la *parodos* et le premier *stasimon*, prolongés, après le récit du Héraut, au long du second *stasimon*. Après l'entrée (782) d'Agamemnon et de Cassandre, qui marque d'une façon extraordinairement tardive le début de l'action proprement dite, le temps s'allonge encore selon deux lignes parallèles et successives dans la scène Agamemnon-Clytemnestre (782–974) et dans l'épisode de Cassandre (1035–1326), séparés par le troisième *stasimon*. Le double meurtre, au contraire, est condensé dans les v. 1342–71, c'est à dire dans un très court passage d'une étonnante densité dramatique. Mais à quoi se ramène, en fait, l'action, dans l'*Agamemnon*? En quels endroits de la pièce se déroule-t-elle? Énumérons l'irruption du signal de feu au v. 21, l'arrivée de l'Atride au v. 782, puis la scène du meurtre en 1342–71. En celle-ci se condense tout le contenu dramatique de la tragédie. Nous pouvons vraiment dire qu'Eschyle a ici atteint, et peut-être dépassé le record fulgurant de la rapidité pindarique, saisissante, nous l'avons vu, dans la IVème *Pythique*. Dans celle-ci les préparatifs et les épisodes choisis pour être enchâssés en forme de prophétie, tableaux descriptifs, discours, énumération d'Argonautes, etc., occupaient les v. 1–246, cependant qu'à la fin de l'*Ode* l'énigme et la supplique concernant Damophile allaient de 263 à 299. Restent les v. 247 à 262 pour le fameux "raccourci" résumant le plus clair de la fameuse navigation héroïque. L'*Agamemnon* fait s'accomplir le double meurtre de l'Atride et de la princesse troyenne en moins de trente vers sur les mille six cent soixante treize du drame. C'est qu'en réalité la pièce est, pour l'essentiel, un long et somptueux poème lyrique, au long duquel se développe la méditation du poète, parfaitement intemporelle. Cette méditation procède par bonds et survols, nous reportant le plus souvent en arrière, dans les temps proches ou lointains dont s'est nourrie la sanglante action d'aujourd' hui. Et de même que le poète lyrique, tout comme s'il pressentait l'éclosion du futur genre dramatique, présente par exemple Jason et Pélias affrontés en une scène préfigurant d'une certaine manière l'ἀγών tragique (IVème *Pythique*), ou projette le faisceau lumineux sur la mort et le rappel à la vie de Castor (Xème *Néméenne*), Eschyle a concentré son éclairage sur la présentation solennelle des deux victimes promises au couteau meurtrier. Ce n'est nullement ainsi que ses suc- cesseurs athéniens, Sophocle et Euripide, et plus tard les auteurs de tragédies classiques, concevront le déroulement d'un drame. En vérité, la tragédie eschyléenne est encore très près de ses origines lyriques, et l'on pourrait, à propos de chacune des pièces conservées, effectuer une analyse analogue à celle que nous venons d'esquisser.

Nous aimerions, après avoir réfléchi sur l'un des drames les plus tardifs du poète athénien, examiner d'un même point de vue non l'une de ses pièces les plus anciennes—nous n'en possédons pas, et c'est dommage—du moins la plus ancienne des pièces conservées, la tragédie des *Perses*, jouée, comme on sait, dans Athènes en 472, c'est à dire à une époque où le grand lyrisme choral, celui de Pindare et de Bacchylide, était encore en pleine floraison. Si l'action proprement dite de l'*Agamemnon* est en fait limitée à un très court passage de la pièce, que dirons-nous des *Perses*? Il y a encore moins d'action dans les *Perses*. Mieux: aucune action directe n'est présentée au cours de ce drame. On ne peut en effet appeler action ni le récit du songe de la Reine, ni l'évocation de Darios. Procédé traditionnel à l'épopée, le songe se transporte aisément au théâtre, cela sans changer de forme, en demeurant à l'état de récit. Si certains songes, comme celui de Clytemnestre dans l'*Électre* de Sophocle, ont une influence sur l'action, l'on ne saurait en dire autant de celui d'Atossa. Acte rituel, l'évocation de l'ombre de Darios, roi et mort illustre, ne fait en rien progresser le drame. Elle en éclaire certains aspects. Surtout elle rend plus poignante l'angoisse. À ce titre elle approfondit la méditation du poète. Elle amplifie les échos du malheur et nos propres sentiments de pitié. Elle incite, comme toute la pièce, le public athénien à ne pas s'abandonner à l'enivrement d'une victoire, exaltante certes sur le plan national, mais, sur le plan humain, lourde de tant de peine, de larmes et de sang. L'épisode constitue surtout une méditation sur les événements, une méditation à l'état pur. Le récit—les récits plutôt—de la bataille de Salamine ne sont pas davantage une action. Ils renouvellent la présence de l'événement familier à tous, mais seulement par la mémoire et l'imagination, nullement en le présentant—ce serait chose difficile!—aux yeux des spectateurs. Seul nous est présenté Xerxès, fugitif lamentable, clamant son malheur et chantant sa plainte, accompagné des gémissements et des cris aigus des Choreutes, les Vieillards perses, ses conseillers et son soutien. Est-ce là une action? Nullement. Ainsi que l'a remarqué la Reine elle-même dès le début de la pièce (211 sqq.), un roi de Perse, lorsqu'il échoue, n'a de comptes à rendre à personne. Certes la Reine, au v. 531, prévoyait, dans son angoisse, la possibilité d'un suicide.[17] Mais celui-là ne se produit pas. Il n'y a pas, dans les *Perses*, de dénouement en action. Le compte est donc fait, pour ce drame encore, plus rapidement et plus radicalement que pour l'*Agamemnon*.

Mais qu'est-ce alors que le drame des *Perses*? Comme l'*Agamemnon*,

[17] La chose était fréquente en cas de catastrophe nationale. On se souvient qu'un descendant de Darios, portant son nom, se tua lorsqu'il eut été battu par Alexandre.

la pièce est, elle aussi, dans ses profondeurs, une méditation, une méditation sur la mort et sur le destin. Toute tragédie, on le sait, est ordonnée à la mort. Dans le premier drame de l'*Orestie*, l'enjeu était le destin et la mort d'un homme—un roi victorieux—et d'une femme—une prophétesse de sang royal, la propre fille du roi vaincu.[18] Dans les *Perses*, il s'agit du destin et de la vie ou de la mort d'un peuple. L'acte mis au théâtre offre même de saisissantes analogies avec le sacrifice aux dieux, avec la mise à mort d'une victime.[19] Sans doute n'est-ce point par hasard. Dans les deux drames symétriques de l'*Orestie*, les victimes sont d'une part Agamemnon et Cassandre, de l'autre Égisthe et Clytemnestre. Même, afin que nul n'en ignore, les cadavres sont présentés, amenés devant le public par les portes ouvertes du palais au moyen de l'*eccyclème* ou de toute autre manière que l'on voudra,[20] offrandes au regard des dieux, pièces à conviction mises sous les yeux des hommes. Dans les *Perses*, c'est un peuple entier qui tombe aux pieds des dieux, frappé à mort, victime de sa démesure et de l'orgueil aveugle de son chef. L'accent, qui pourrait être mis sur le triomphe grec et la gloire d'Athènes, comme dans une *Épinicie*, ne l'est en aucune manière, à part peut-être quelques allusions fugitives à des thèmes familiers à la propagande athénienne.[21] Il est mis bien plutôt sur la démesure et le châtiment. Il est mis plus encore sur le deuil d'un peuple entier. Les *Perses* ne s'apparentent nullement à un chant triomphal, sinon, ainsi que le remarquait P. Mazon,[22] par antiphrase en quelque sorte, gravure en creux d'un relief inverse. La pièce s'apparente encore moins, sans doute, à un *dithyrambe*. C'est à un *thrène* qu'elle nous fait penser.[23] L'analyse de détail va nous permettre de préciser davantage notre pensée.

[18] On saisit ici l'un des aspects de la pensée profonde d'Eschyle: la guerre et la prise de Troie unissent finalement les vainqueurs et les vaincus dans une même catastrophe.

[19] Voir notre article "Reflexions sur la tragédie des Perses," dans *Information Littéraire* (1956), 15 sqq.

[20] L'ἐγκύκλημα dont nous parle Pollux est assez vraisemblablement une invention tardive.

[21] Nous songeons surtout au court dialogue d'Atossa et du Coryphée après le récit du songe (230–45), ainsi qu'à certains passages du récit de la bataille navale.

[22] Voir sa notice, à la p. 59 de son édition.

[23] En était-il de même des *Phéniciennes* de Phrynichos, jouées en 476? Nous l'ignorons. L'argument des *Perses* indique que les premiers vers du prologue de Phrynichos étaient placés dans la bouche d'un eunuque perse annonçant la défaite de Xerxès.

S'il n'y a, dans les *Perses*, comme nous l'avons noté, aucune action véritable (δρᾶμα), quel en est le principe de progression? On pourrait dire que tout s'organise en *crescendo*, depuis l'angoisse sourde des Fidèles (*parodos*) et le récit du songe de la Reine, suivi des récits successifs du Messager relatant les épisodes de la bataille (premier *épisode*) jusqu'à l'évocation de Darios (préparée au deuxième *épisode*, opérée au troisième) et à l'*exodos* où Xerxès misérable apparaît lui-même pour disparaître à la fin, suivi des Fidèles, dans son palais. Le *crescendo* toutefois est-il vraiment si régulier? Se décompose-t-il bien ainsi? L'évocation de Darios, en fait, interromprait plutôt la progression. Ininterrompue, celle-ci, ayant suivi la ligne de crête du songe aux récits, devrait nous amener directement à l'apparition de Xerxès. Il en est autrement. La remontée au jour du "roi défunt égal aux dieux" (642) constitue en elle-même un sommet, du haut duquel la majesté tragique ne peut plus que redescendre. Du point de vue scénique comme du point de vue religieux, la cérémonie incantatoire fait appel à toutes les ressources d'un rituel haletant, tel que les Grecs apparemment n'en pouvaient concevoir qu'en pays barbare. Si la scène de Xerxès est, de son côté et à sa manière, elle aussi un sommet, ce ne peut être que par le pathétique. Cette scène, entrée et sortie (l'*exodos* proprement dite) est, au sens le plus précis du terme, un *thrène* chanté sur les morts de la Perse. Cette partie pourrait sembler la moins originale, puisqu'on la retrouve en fait dans toutes les tragédies grecques connues, et l'on peut ajouter hardiment "et inconnues." À tort. Elle est en réalité l'un des noyaux du genre qui, ayant pour centre une mort accomplie ou quelquefois manquée,[24] est là dans son indubitable élément. Le *thrène* est donc partie intégrante, sauf exception, de la tragédie. Pourquoi, dans ces conditions, le poète a-t-il interrompu le mouvement qui nous mène jusqu'au *thrène* final, à seule fin d'y introduire l'évocation de l'ombre de Darios? C'est évidemment que celle-ci était à ses yeux d'une capitale importance. De ceci nous pouvons entrevoir deux raisons. L'une est la même qui le portera, dans les *Choéphores*, à montrer les enfants d'Agamemnon l'invoquant longuement sur son tombeau et

---

[24] C'est le cas des *Euménides* ou d'*Alceste* entre autres. Bien entendu, il n'y a plus alors de *thrène*—sauf dans *Alceste* toutefois. Il peut être remplacé, par exemple dans les *Euménides*, par une πομπή solennelle.

procédant en somme à la déploration cérémonielle, partie obligatoire des funérailles d'un mort illustre, mais dont le roi d'Argos avait été frustré par ses meurtriers. Il y a là un aspect chthonien de la tragédie dont on ne peut faire abstraction et dont la signification est pour nous amplifiée du fait que nous la retrouvons dans deux drames aussi différents. L'autre raison, au moins aussi importante, est que l'épisode de Darios formule et résume l'enseignement de la pièce. Condamnation de l'ὕβρις des Perses, célébration de la valeur athénienne, conseils de modération morale aux vainqueurs, tous les thèmes de la méditation eschyléenne y sont traités et mis, les uns par les autres, en valeur. On se croirait en présence d'un poème pindarique où le mythe propose à nos regards un enseignement, pour le méditer et pour l'imiter. Voilà, nous semble-t-il, ce qu'une première vue, superficielle encore, des *Perses* pourrait nous apprendre.

Il est une autre architecture, plus subtile, du drame—nous allions dire du poème, puisque la tragédie naissante est encore, par bien des traits, un poème lyrique. L'*Agamemnon*, nous l'avons vu, présentait encore en 458 cet aspect, d'une façon très prononcée, et nous avons pu en esquisser une analyse, en mettant l'accent sur son caractère intemporel. Ferons-nous les mêmes constatations sur la pièce qui est pour nous la plus ancienne d'Eschyle, les *Perses*, antérieure de quatorze ans à l'*Orestie*? La *parodos*, très développée, commence par de longs systèmes anapestiques (1–64), exactement comme celle de l'*Agamemnon* (40–102). Suit le chant lyrique (65–139), qui s'achève sur quelques anapestes de transition (140–54). Les anapestes, orientés vers le passé, nous reportent au moment où l'armée perse, en marche vers l'Hellade, a quitté le pays. Les Vieillards, "avec les yeux de l'âme," la revoient dans sa splendeur, puis, en deux mouvements lyriques, essaient d'imaginer le présent et le futur immédiat. Le premier, sur le rythme plus large des groupes antistrophiques I à IV (65–113), évoque l'arrivée en Grèce de l'armée royale; le second, sur un rythme plus âpre (groupes antistrophiques I et II, 114–39), esquisse déjà le chant de deuil sur les guerriers dont on est sans nouvelles. Ainsi, à l'intérieur d'une méditation rétrospective qui sert en même temps d'exposition, le Choeur reprend la progression normale du temps. La scène d'Atossa ensuite, avec le récit du songe suivi de la description d'un effrayant présage, laisse encore nos coeurs en suspens. Le passé immédiat de la nuit qui précède, entièrement orientée vers un avenir qui peut-être est déjà présent, est une sorte de pause angoissée hors du temps, une de ces attentes lourdes de crainte familières à l'oeuvre d'Eschyle.

L'arrivée du Messager et sa longue succession de récits font de cette attente angoissée une douleur effroyablement présente. Cependant, si présente soit-elle, elle nous fait retourner à nouveau vers le passé, un passé que le sceau de la mort a rendu définitif, ainsi qu'en témoigne l'usage du parfait: στρατὸς γὰρ πᾶς ὄλωλε βαρβάρων (255), suivant le κατέφθαρται du v. 251 et précédant le διαπεπραγμένα du v. 260. Si l'on réfléchit à la succession réelle des événements, il est clair que le désastre de Salamine est antérieur au début de la pièce. Mais y songe-t-on? Le spectateur est transporté dans un temps fictif, ou plus exactement un "temps-hors-du-temps," bien plus réel en fait que le temps vécu, le même temps que celui des oeuvres lyriques ou de la musique. Il ne s'agit pas d'un temps proprement dramatique tel que le poseront les successeurs d'Eschyle. Nous en sommes encore ici au temps intérieur, celui d'un Pindare. La pièce, psalmodiée, chantée ou parlée tour à tour, se déroule à la façon intemporelle d'un poème lyrique, d'un poème dans lequel seraient insérés de place en place, pour la clarté des choses, des dialogues, et des tirades tantôt trochaïques et tantôt iambiques.[25] Le premier *stasimon*, chant lyrique (548–97) précédé de quelques systèmes anapestiques, donne carrière à la lamentation des Fidèles: sur une catastrophe sur laquelle il n'y a pas à revenir, enracinée dans un passé proche encore et déjà lointain parce qu'irréversible, se greffe le deuil présent qui commande un sombre avenir. Les événements ici sont davantage ressentis dans leur réalité historique, ainsi qu'en témoigne l'emploi du présent et de l'aoriste:

> Νῦν δὲ πρόπασα μὲν στένει
> γαῖ' Ἀσὶς ἐκκενουμένα.
> Ξέρξης μὲν ἄγαγεν, ποποῖ,
> Ξέρξης δ' ἀπώλεσεν, τοτοῖ,
> Ξέρξης δὲ πάντ' ἐπέσπε δυσφρόνως κτλ.

---

[25] On sait, d'après Aristote dans la *Poétique* (1449 a 21–27), que les parties parlées étaient anciennement écrites en tétramètres trochaïques catalectiques, auxquels se substituèrent plus tard les trimètres iambiques. Nous avons des deux dans les *Perses*: la scène du songe les fait alterner, ainsi que le dialogue d'Atossa et de Darios.

Les derniers vers du chant découvrent un présent dépourvu de gloire et sans joie. Le très court deuxième *épisode* (598–622), uniquement et parfaitement présent, celui-ci, est employé au déroulement des préparatifs d'Atossa en vue de l'évocation de Darios. Celle-ci est, sur un mode aigu et sauvage, le lancinant et pathétique appel des vivants aux puissances d'outre-tombe. Elle est d'une toute autre qualité de présent, l'infini présent immobile de l'éternité, à laquelle, pour un bref instant, les vieux compagnons de Darios vont arracher leur roi, dans une intrusion fulgurante et sans lendemain du temps des dieux au coeur du temps des hommes provisoirement suspendu. Le troisième *épisode* lui-même (681–851) est une continuelle oscillation entre le déroulement ici-bas de l'histoire humaine et la contemplation *sub specie aeternitatis* de cette histoire passagère par le regard d'un homme au destin héroïque, transporté personnellement de l'autre côté des choses, puis, pour un bref instant, ramené sous le ciel des apparences. Le mort d'ailleurs, par des lois mystérieuses, est à la fois le royal héros révéré par les Perses et un pauvre mortel soumis aux règles de fer et aux servitudes du royaume des trépassés. Darios, dans l'immédiat, ignore encore le désastre des siens, et il faut que son épouse le lui apprenne. Mais, d'un regard plus élevé, plus lointain, se souvenant d'antiques oracles (739 sqq.), le roi défunt comprend, sait et juge. Tel un prophète, il voit les causes et les effets, il connaît même les événements futurs. Il conseille les Perses, selon la réflexion sage et profonde d'un esprit qui embrasse à la fois le passé, le présent, l'avenir. Il domine, et voit le temps comme une carte déroulée, depuis ses ancêtres glorieux dont il rappelle la succession (765 sqq.) et qui firent l'empire perse; il le voit sans doute comme le verraient les dieux, comme en tout cas le voit le poète inspiré, dont le roi mort est, à vrai dire, le porte-parole. Rien d'étonnant si, renversant le temps historique, le quatrième *stasimon* est, dans son développement lyrique, l'exaltation de la puissance perse, telle qu'elle était sous Darios, telle que Xerxès et les siens, par leur faute, ne la reverront plus. C'est ici, au cours de la tragédie des *Perses*, le saut le plus profond dans le passé, le passé glorieux d'avant la démesure et d'avant le malheur. Nous avons là l'effet le plus marqué, s'il en fut, de composition régressive. Après cela se manifeste, avec le retour de Xerxès, le présent le plus proche, celui où la ligne des événements se déroulant à Suse rejoint celle du déroulement des catastrophes morale et militaire subies au loin: Xerxès et ce qui reste de son armée se retrouvent à leur point de départ. La lamentation du roi et des siens, après avoir exploré le passé, va durant l'*exodos* s'épanouir dans un présent unique et définitif. Ainsi se clôt la méditation du poète, intemporelle ici aussi comme un chant lyrique, se développant au rythme de la musique.

Au rythme de la musique, disons-nous: il faudrait y ajouter la danse ou, plus précisément, les évolutions chorales. Nous y reviendrons après avoir essayé de mieux préciser à quel ordre de poème lyrique il convient de rattacher la tragédie des *Perses*. Le drame, auquel nous assistons du côté des victimes, ne saurait, de ce fait, revêtir la nature d'un chant triomphal, et les quelques passages—indispensables pour une représentation athénienne—où la victoire grecque est caractérisée comme telle[26] ne peuvent y changer grand chose. Les Perses de Suse et d'Ecbatane pleurent leurs morts et la défaite de leur peuple. D'un bout à l'autre de la pièce, les morts sont constamment présents, et c'est autour de leur pensée que gravitent les actions et les sentiments des vivants. Bien plutôt que la foule des morts anonymes, portant sur eux leurs espoirs perdus et toutes leurs souffrances, le poète évoque les chefs aux noms prestigieux, à la bravoure insigne. Ces noms aux consonnances exotiques, dont Eschyle aime parer la somptuosité de sa poésie, défilent aux regards de l'imagination—celle des Fidèles et la nôtre—dès le début des anapestes de la *parodos*. C'est bien un défilé, en effet, derrière le seigneur Xerxès, le roi fils de Darios, dont le nom reviendra paré de la même titulature à la fin de la *parodos* (144–45). Le défilé est d'une grandiose majesté, l'appel des capitales—ces joyaux de la couronne perse—et celui des régions doublant celui des hommes:

"Quittant Suse et Ecbatane et les vieux remparts kissiens, ils sont partis, les uns à cheval, d'autres sur des vaisseaux, les fantassins à pied, formant le gros de la masse guerrière."[27]

D'autres ont quitté le Nil nourricier, le Tmôlos sacré. D'autres encore sont venus de Babylonie et de l'Asie entière. Ainsi sont partis "Amistrès et Artaphrénès, Mégabatès et Astaspès, rois vassaux du Grand Roi (βασιλῆς βασιλέως)" avec tous leurs

---

[26] Ainsi l'évocation du fameux *péan* des Grecs à Salamine, pendant que défile la flotte allant à la bataille.

[27] Nos citations sont faites d'après la traduction P. Mazon.

soldats, archers et cavaliers. Puis ce sont "Artembarès sur son destrier et Masistrès, et Ismaios le brave, archer triomphant, et Pharandakès, et Sosthanès qui presse ses coursiers." Ce cortège qui part en grande pompe pour le triomphe et qui va rencontrer le désastre et la mort, évoque pour nous les reliefs de Persépolis, et probablement bien d'autres, inconnus à nos yeux. On ne peut pas ne pas les voir, des yeux de l'esprit, cependant qu'au rythme des anapestes les Vieillards perses se déplacent eux-mêmes dans l'*orchestra*, frappant le sol de leurs bâtons. Et tandis que se déroule le double chant de la *parodos* lyrique, le roi Xerxès, fils de Darios, semblable non à ce qu'il fut vraiment, mais tel que les sculptures de son palais le présentaient à l'adoration des peuples prosternés, "press(e) du haut de son char son attelage syrien," dominant de sa haute stature et du "regard bleu sombre du dragon sanglant" la foule de ceux que, dans son aveuglement volontaire, il conduit à la mort. Leur cortège, la πομπή de ce sacrifice innombrable, est parti sans retour vers son destin.

En écho, après l'événement, le récit du Messager fait entendre à nouveau l'appel funèbre des mêmes noms ou d'autres tout pareils:

"En foule," s'écrie le Messager, "les cadavres de nos malheureux morts couvrent à cette heure le rivage de Salamine et tous ses alentours" (272–73).

Et nous les imaginons en effet, comme l'aurait dit Victor Hugo, "heurtant de leurs fronts morts des écueils inconnus." Puis la Reine et les Fidèles veulent en savoir davantage. Une fois rassurés sur le sort de Xerxès lui-même, c'est à un véritable appel des morts que se livre le Messager pour répondre à l'angoisse des Vieillards. Des anapestes de la *parodos*, les noms passent en écho dans les trimètres du récit. Certes beaucoup de ces noms varient, mais des rappels précis prolongent l'effet sonore:

"Mais Artembarès,[28] naguère chef de dix mille cavaliers, à cette heure va se heurtant à chaque roc de la côte de Silénies! Et Dadakès le chiliarque, sous le choc d'une javeline, n'a fait qu'un léger bond du haut de sa galère!...Lilaios, Arsamès, Arghestès tournaient, eux, autour de l'île des colombes, chargeant le dur rivage de leurs fronts vaincus!...Et les riverains du Nil égyptien...." L'énuméra-

---

[28] Le nom d'Artembarès martèle, à lui tout seul, toute la pièce, comme ferait un gong funèbre. D'autres noms se répètent un petit nombre de fois.

tion sans fin continue. Les sonorités exotiques, renouvelées de la *parodos*, sonnent maintenant comme un glas funèbre. Que reste-t-il du triomphant cortège, parti de Perse par un éclatant matin, revêtu de sa gloire neuve? Le mouvement est intense et irréversible: le douloureux cortège à présent ne trouve plus que deux issues, la fuite sur la terre ou la mort dans les flots. Xerxès qui, de son trône dérisoire, a suivi le déroulement de la catastrophe, donne le signal de la déroute; "Il déchire ses vêtements, lance un sanglot aigu, puis soudain donne un ordre à son armée de terre et se précipite dans une fuite éperdue" (468 sqq.). Une brève tirade (480–514) résume, resserrant l'espace et le temps, l'immense parcours de Salamine en Perse et des mois de souffrance. Le public ne sera pas surpris de voir, aussitôt après l'évocation de l'ombre de Darios, arriver Xerxès devant son palais, l'espace et le temps étant abolis par le mouvement poétique, lancé à la vitesse de la pensée. La marche ainsi accélérée du temps suit le rythme intérieur du poète et commande les pulsations de l'oeuvre dramatique. Le mouvement se précipite encore dans le chant du Choeur:

"Fantassins et marins, tel un grand vol d'oiseaux vêtus de sombre azur, les nefs les ont emmenés, hélas! les nefs les ont perdus, hélas! les nefs aux abordages de désastre! les nefs et les bras des Ioniens!" (558 sqq.). Mais le sommet du pathétique est atteint lorsqu'apparaît un Xerxès lamentable, avec sa maigre suite et ses vêtements déchirés. À part les anapestes de son entrée, le rôle de ce personnage est entièrement lyrique. Sa lamentation sur son propre sort, rencontrant les questions haletantes du Choeur, se résout au *thrène* final, aboutissement logique et point culminant d'une oeuvre qui en réalité est tout entière un *thrène*, chant de deuil sur les guerriers perses. "Cette terre gémit sur la jeunesse sortie d'elle," commence le Choeur (922 sqq.), qui très vite précise en propres termes la nature de son chant:

> Πρόσφθογγόν σοι νόστου τάν
> κακοφάτιδα βοάν, κακομέλετον ἰάν
> Μαριανδυνοῦ θρηνητῆρος
> πέμψω, πολύδακρυν ἰαχάν (935 sqq.).

Et les questions pressées du Choeur reprennent une fois de plus l'appel des morts, face à Xerxès le responsable:

"Où sont tes lieutenants, Pharandakès, Sousas, Pélagôn, Dotamas
et Agdabatas, Psammis, Sousiskanès, qui naguère quittait Ecbatane?"
Puis:

"Las! Hélas! Où est ton Pharnoukos? et le preux Ariomardos?
Où donc sire Seualkès? Lilaios aux nobles aïeux, Memphis, Tharybis?
Et Masistras, Artembarès, Hystaichmas?"

Deux autres répliques semblables de ce dialogue lyrique prolongent l'énumération de deuil. On a discuté, dès l'Antiquité,[29] sur
l'exactitude des noms, moins inexacts apparemment que certains ne
l'ont cru,[30] vrais en tout cas d'une sauvage et douloureuse vérité
poétique. Il vient même s'y greffer toute la densité de la pitié
humaine, car ceux d'entre les noms qui reviennent finissent par
sembler familiers, et chacun croit connaître ceux qui les ont portés,
et qui, vraisemblablement, au cours de la guerre, avaient été déjà
connus des Grecs.

Et, comme tous les *thrènes* accompagnant la dépouille des morts,
celui-ci, même si les morts sont restés sur la terre étrangère,
s'organise en un réel cortège, celui de Xerxès et des Fidèles pénétrant
dans le palais sans interrompre leurs manifestations de deuil et
leurs lamentations rituelles:

$$\Delta \acute{\iota}\alpha\iota\nu\varepsilon \ \delta\iota\alpha\hat{\iota}\nu\varepsilon \ \pi\hat{\eta}\mu\alpha\cdot \ \pi\rho\grave{o}\varsigma \ \delta\acute{o}\mu\sigma\upsilon\varsigma \ \delta' \ \check{\iota}\theta\iota,$$

chante le Roi qui, au v. 1038 (début de la *str.* VI), prend la tête du
cortège, comme dans la réalité le ferait un chef de Choeur.

$$A\check{\iota}\alpha\kappa\tau\grave{o}\varsigma \ \grave{\varepsilon}\varsigma \ \delta\acute{o}\mu\sigma\upsilon\varsigma \ \kappa\acute{\iota}\varepsilon \ (1068),$$

chante encore Xerxès dans l'*épode* finale, avant que la πομπή
douloureuse ne pénètre dans le palais des Achéménides, la πομπή de
ceux qui se frappent la poitrine en poussant des cris aigus et, comme
le Roi lui-même, s'arrachent les cheveux et déchirent leurs vêtements.

Ce *thrène* final des *Perses* est le prototype de tous les *thrènes* qui
orneront l'*exodos* des tragédies aussi longtemps que les Tragiques
grecs écriront des tragédies. Mais son trait distinctif est d'être pour
nous le premier, le modèle de tous les autres. Là n'est cependant
pas l'essentiel. En fait, c'est toute la tragédie des *Perses* qui est un

---

[29] Cf. *scholie* au v. 35.
[30] Voir éd. P. Mazon et éd. E. Fraenkel, *ad locum*.

immense *thrène*. Le *thrène* ici n'est pas une partie de la tragédie. Sans doute en est-il le noyau. Mais il serait plus vrai de dire que cette tragédie—et d'autres avec elle—est elle-même un *thrène*. Nous n'irons pas jusqu'à dire que toute tragédie est un *thrène*. L'examen de cette proposition demanderait une étude plus approfondie et plus étendue que nos quelques pages d'aujourd'hui. Nous avons pu du moins nous rendre compte comment la tragédie est bien, au moins pour l'un de ses principaux éléments constitutifs, issue en droite ligne du lyrisme choral. Un second point nous semble acquis: c'est que l'oeuvre lyrique dont elle est sortie n'est pas forcément, loin de là, le seul *dithyrambe*, à moins de donner à ce mot un sens beaucoup plus vague et plus large, ainsi que, dans un ouvrage récent, le propose Gerald Else.[31] Il est en tout cas évident que la forme lyrique dont est parti Eschyle quand il a écrit les *Perses* est celle du *thrène* et nulle autre. Qui s'en étonnerait, sachant la place de la mort dans cette tragédie en particulier? Et le fait que ce drame, poème lyrique encore autant que tragédie archaïque, soit pour nous la plus ancienne des tragédies connues, ne peut que nous inciter à la réflexion. Cette réflexion s'alimente aujourd'hui des traits convergents relevés au cours d'une étude de l'*Agamemnon*, tragédie qui n'est pas un *thrène*, mais la mise en oeuvre en partie lyrique d'un mythe immense préparant le *thrène* des *Choéphores*. Nous espérons un jour, si les dieux le veulent, en étudiant les autres tragédies d'Eschyle, élargir dans une même perspective le champ de nos investigations sur les rapports étroits de la tragédie, rameau récent encore, avec le tronc puissant de la grande lyrique chorale.

Paris, 24 juillet 1970

---

[31] *The Origin and Early Form of Greek Tragedy* (Cambridge, Mass. 1965), *passim*.

AESCHYLUS' *PERSAE*:
A LITERARY COMMENTARY

D. J. CONACHER

The *Persae* of Aeschylus, a fine play which has been much misunderstood and undervalued, is of great interest to us for many reasons.
Not the least of these is the fact that it is the only extant Greek
tragedy based not on ancient myth but on nearly contemporary
history and so the first historical play in extant western literature.
More important still, perhaps, is the point that it shows us, even at
this early period in the history of Greek Drama (the *Persae*, at
472 B.C., is now generally admitted to be the earliest Greek play that
we possess) [1] just how historical material should be approached, if it
be approached at all, by the writer of imaginative literature. The
tragic poet, if he follows Aeschylus' example, will select only
historical events of sufficient grandeur to have seized the popular
imagination in such a way that they have already acquired something
of a mythic quality, that is, events which seem to all to imply causes
or meanings (however defined) belonging to a higher order of
reality than the particular events themselves. Secondly, (and this is,
perhaps, merely the subjective side of the same observation) our
tragic poet will choose only such historical events as provide, in his
own poetic or imaginative reaction to them, a striking example,
almost as good as myth itself, of some great truth or insight about
life which he finds fundamental to his own view of tragic experience.
This implies, of course, that the element of choice on the poet's part
does not end with the choice of an historical subject that suits his
theme. However, before exercising the necessary freedom of the
artist, the poet of contemporary history has also to recognize a certain

---

[1] The earlier date of Aeschylus' *Supplices* is now, in the view of most scholars, discredited;
see *Ox. Pap.* xx (1952), 2256, frg. 3 and (for the most recent and lucid discussion of its
significance in dating the *Supplices*) A. F. Garvie, *Aeschylus' Supplices: Play and Trilogy*
(Cambridge 1969), Chap. I.

responsibility: he must present events in such a way that they are
acceptable to those familiar with the actual happenings. Herein lies
the limiting or restrictive element in composing historical drama
but it is, in a sense, the debt which the poet owes to the great events
he has borrowed in order to exploit them for his own (quite
legitimate) purposes, for, as I have indicated, much of the play's
authority, of its grip on the popular imagination, depends initially
on the impact which these events have made upon it. Moreover, if
the reader or member of the audience is so irritated by a distortion
of events with which he is familiar that he cannot attend to the new
event (what the poet makes of his historical material), then the poet
has lost credibility in more senses than one.[2] Still more important,
perhaps, for the student of the *Persae* is the consideration of the
freedom with which a poet may be expected to approach his
historical material. Once the minimum of historical responsibility
(of the kind suggested above) has been met, the poet of an historical
tragedy must continue to exercise his privilege of choice by selecting
and emphasizing, or even by distorting and repressing, various
aspects of the events, which belong to history, in the interest of the
theme, which belongs to the poet alone. More, he must invent qualities in his "historical" characters and supporting details in his "historical" events to suit his theme and the dramatic personalities which
he has created to express it.

This sort of adaptation, transformation rather, of particular
events and their circumstances is what the critics have in mind when

[2] "The willing suspension of disbelief" cannot be expected to extend indefinitely in
the treatment of events which have radically affected the lives of the audience. Among
contemporary historical plays, Hochhuth's "Soldiers" is, perhaps, a good example of a
border-line case. This play undoubtedly owed much of its initial excitement to the
presentation, in a realistic and recognizable form, of certain famous near-contemporary
national figures in historic situations and dilemmas more or less (sometimes less) familiar
to the audience. Some viewers were so incensed with what they believed to be the
distortion of the character and the decisions of these figures that they could not attend
to the fascinating poetic truth which the playwright was attempting to express through
his use of an historical situation.

With regard to the situation in the *Persae*, Professor Lattimore's comments on the
responsibility of the poet to the historical actualities should also be considered, particularly
his conclusion: "... we have no right to assume that the Athenians would award first
prize to a tragic poet for dealing wildly with known facts in a contemporary theme." See
R. Lattimore, "Aeschylus on the Defeat of Xerxes," in *Classical Studies in Honor of William
Abbott Oldfather* (Urbana 1943), 87.

they speak of Aeschylus' "mythologizing" history for his purposes. In this way he so converts particular events as to make them express, more powerfully than they would in their original form, the general pattern or idea about human experience, or about the ways of Zeus with man, which he wishes to express.[3]

Whether history unadapted can ever provide the stuff of tragedy is debatable;[4] certainly it could never produce a tragedy as powerful as the *Persae*. Nevertheless, the simple historical facts of Xerxes' Greek experience, viewed in the light of Greek ethical thought, clearly suggest the theme of divine nemesis. On the one hand we have the Solonian doctrine[5] concerning the dangerously changeable quality of great good fortune and particularly of fortunes unjustly acquired beyond one's right or *moira*; on the other hand, we have the extraordinary fact of the Persian defeat by the Greeks, which must have seemed (to victors and vanquished alike) impossible without the hand of God—and the combination, in the tragic sufferer, of Persian despotism and over-reaching ambition made Xerxes a perfect subject for the Solonian lesson. Possibly it is the very simplicity of the *koros-hybris-atê* theme (great wealth, feeding on pride and greed, tempted by the gods to the fateful and ruinous overstepping of the *moira* which the gods have themselves set down) which leads some critics to replace it with other themes (the celebration of Athenian triumph, for example, or the vindication of the

---

[3] This familiar distinction between "poetry" and "history" (cf. Aristotle, *Poetics* 1451 b 5–7) should, perhaps, need no comment except that the numerous comparisons made between the poetic and the historical treatments of Xerxes' enterprise have tended to muddy the distinction. Compare, for example, Bruno Snell's suggestion, in *Aischylos und das Handeln im Drama* (Leipzig 1928), 66, that in Aeschylus' time there was no clear-cut distinction between myth and history, with Karl Deichgräber's refutation of this view in "Die Persae des Aischylos," *Nachrichten d. Akad. d. Wiss. in Göttingen*, Phil.-Hist. Kl. (1941), 200–201. Compare also A. W. Gomme's interesting comparison of Herodotus and Aeschylus in *Greek Attitudes to Poetry and History* (Berkeley 1954), 98 with Gilbert Murray's similar comparison in *Aeschylus, the Creator of Tragedy* (Oxford Paperbacks 1962) 125: Gomme's comparison of two isolated passages in Herodotus and Aeschylus tends to confound the Aristotelian distinction but Murray's significant *addendum*, "The first secret of the *Persae* is that Aeschylus preserves [the exaltation of the contemporary to the legendary] from beginning to end," reinstates it.

[4] Cf. Murray's comment (126) "If one Greek general had been named the play would have become modern and been exposed to all the small temporary emotions of the immediate present, the gratified vanity, the annoyance, the inevitable criticism."

[5] See Solon, frg. 1 (Diehl); cf. frg. 3.

policies and cunning of Themistocles) which are, at best, peripheral
to the tragic meaning of the play. There is, in any case, a tendency
in recent Aeschylean criticism generally to reject such simple ethical formulations of Aeschylean themes as that suggested above.[6]
Sometimes it is argued that Aeschylus had little idea of any element
of human responsibility in his depiction of the ruin of tragic heroes;
sometimes, that the Greek audience would already be thoroughly
familiar with this view of Xerxes' defeat. It is possible that behind
these recent rejections lies a certain boredom with the constant
re-statement of what is, after all, a very simple theme (the divine
nemesis which overtakes the hybristic man) and a certain irritation
with scholars who feel that that is really all that need be said about
much Aeschylean tragedy. This irritation is understandable but the
point which needs making is not that the traditional critics have got
the theme wrong but that it is not so much the theme as the way in
which the poet converts it into a dramatic reality that marks the
real achievement. The themes of great tragedies must always be
profound and important statements about life but they need not be
particularly subtle, complex, or original. It is the way in which a
dramatist makes his audience experience his theme which determines
the greatness of a play. Thus, though the theme of the *Persae* can be
quickly understood or at least mentally pigeon-holed by any school-
boy who can read a handbook, it cannot be experienced as
Aeschylus meant us to experience it in this instance, until every
fibre of its simple but powerful structure has been grasped as
bearing, each time from some new direction, on the same central
pathos which we are asked to share with Xerxes. It is this intensive,
centripetal character of the play which is completely missed by those

[6] The ethical, "*hybris—atê*" formulations of Aeschylean themes [such as one finds,
for example, in H. D. F. Kitto, *Greek Tragedy* (London 1950), Albin Lesky, *Die Griechische
Tragoedie* (Leipzig 1938), Gilbert Murray, *Aeschylus* (Oxford 1940)] have been questioned,
from one aspect or another, by several scholars in recent years: cf., for example, D. L.
Page's edition of Aeschylus, *Agamemnon* (Oxford 1957), especially Introduction, xx-xxix;
H. Lloyd-Jones, "Zeus in Aeschylus," *J. Hellenic Stud.* 76 (1956), 55–67 and "The Guilt
of Agamemnon," *Class. Qt.* n.s. 12 (1962), 187–99; R. D. Dawe, "Inconsistency of Plot
and Character in Aeschylus," *Pr. Cambr. Philol. Assn.*, n.s. no. 9 (1963), 47 ff., 61; and
"Some Reflections on *Atê* and *Hamartia*," *Harv. Stud. Class. Philol.* 72 (1967), 108–11;
see also below, note 32 of the present paper. Rebuttal of some of these criticisms has been
offered (occasionally in somewhat rhetorical terms!) in Kitto's most recent work, *Poiesis*
(Berkeley and Los Angeles 1966), Chap. II, especially pp. 38 ff.

critics who, feeling that the play needs some apology for the simplicity of its theme and its lack of complication, developing action, and the like, praise its vivid passages of descriptive narrative, its moving and theatrical incidents (such as the evocation of Darius) as if these were bonuses by which the play is made acceptable even though they do little to advance the action.[7]

Both the setting of the play and the most obvious adaptations which Aeschylus makes in historical events and personages serve as a preliminary indication of the centre of dramatic interest. The scene is set in Susa in the Persian court for the obvious purpose that we may experience the action and share the sufferings of Xerxes as much as possible through Persian eyes and ears and minds and hearts. Tragic experience must always be vicarious, but clearly, to reach a tragic sufferer as distant as Xerxes, we shall need such intermediaries as these. Further advantages of this setting, quite necessary to the play's effect, appear as the structure of the play unfolds.

The three or four most obvious liberties with history which the dramatist has taken all clearly point in the same direction. The depiction of Xerxes as the only Persian King who has sought to cross from Asia to Europe to extend Persian rule; the contrast with his father, the wise restrained ruler who understood the *moira* which the gods allowed him—these two features, however unhistorical, mark the Xerxes of this play as the egregiously hybristic one who alone has put himself and his people in such awful jeopardy. The incontinent flight of Xerxes immediately after the defeat at Salamis; the playing-down (though not the omission) of the battle at Plataea— these distortions render the central dramatic catastrophe at Salamis more simple, swift, and absolute; finally, the freezing, then melting of the River Strymon to drown the remnants of Xerxes' army limping home—this invention (or partial invention)[8] of the poet's serves to isolate the god-inflicted aspect of the ruin in a way which

[7] See, for example, Herbert Weir Smyth, *Aeschylean Tragedy*, 82 and Chap. III, *passim*. Cf. Dawe, "Inconsistency etc." (above, note 6), 30-31, who seems to regard the Darius scene, in part at least, as "a skilful way of making a limited amount of material stretch a long way without tedium."

[8] There seems little doubt that the disaster at the River Strymon as related at *Persae* 495 ff. is an Aeschylean invention. It does not appear in Herodotus' account of the return of Xerxes and his army (Herod. VIII 115-20) and it is particularly well suited to Aeschylus' tragic treatment of his theme. See also Broadhead's note to *Persae* 495-97

was impossible at Salamis, where Greek and particularly Athenian *aretê* joins with the *daimôn* in bringing catastrophe upon the King.

The theme of the *Persians*, then, is simply the demonstration of divine nemesis answering the overreaching ambition of human greed and puffed-up confidence in power and wealth, the old sequence of *koros-hybris-atê* familiar to the Athenian audience since Solon's day. Even Aeschylus' recurrent paradoxes—divine temptation to abet human transgression, doom pre-ordained to balance human choice—succeed (more clearly than elsewhere in Aeschylus) in complementing the ethical theme. Both the basic idea and the action (the defeat of Xerxes) by which it is to be demonstrated, are known to the audience and in any case the movements of ships and troops can never be confused with the movements of a drama. Thus in a play such as the *Persians*, there will be little occasion for forward-moving or linear action and none at all for a complex development of plot. (Among Greek Tragedies, the *Persians* stands at the exact opposite pole to, say, the *Philoctetes* of Sophocles.) What we must look for, rather, are the ways by which Aeschylus, starting from the Persian position of, it would seem, absolute power and confidence, imposes his theme dramatically with ever-increasing power and fullness of meaning on the consciousness of his audience. While there is little linear plot development (historically, the defeat of Xerxes must already have happened before the initial pondering of the Chorus in the parodos), the theme is developed, as if in a symphonic tone-poem, from premonitory hints of disaster in the parodos (soon to be lost in a rush of triumphant brass), through the central portions of the play where every instrument is tuned to the disaster, to the final lament of the King himself as he sings his grief and guilt antiphonally with the Chorus' questioning. In this progression, the theme is viewed from four different aspects, each view adding something which could not be achieved before. In the first, the anticipatory, movement of the play, the *hybris-atê* theme can only

---

(which agrees with this conclusion) and references to supporting views there given. On the other hand, that *something* untoward happened to Xerxes' force, or part of it, at or near the River Strymon, seems probable when we consider, in addition to the episode narrated in the *Persae*, the account of a storm assailing Xerxes' ship at the mouth of the Strymon, in a tale told to Herodotus (VIII 18), though Herodotus has his own reasons for not believing fully in that account (VIII 119–120).

be hinted at by the waiting Persian court, and the most sinister
motives are introduced almost unconsciously, with only the audience
aware of their dread significance. The second movement presents
the fulfilment of these dramatic expectations, news of the actual
disaster itself in the Messenger's eye-witness report of Salamis and
further Persian woes. Next, the Ghost of Darius looks back upon his
son's exploit and now for the first time the premonitions of the Queen
and the Chorus and the hints of the Messenger about the hand of
God are fully realized in these ghostly revelations. Anticipation,
fulfilment, retrospection, and finally, with the long-awaited appearance of Xerxes himself, the awful evidence, in the person of the
ruined King, of the operation of justice from the gods.

* * *

We are called the trusted ones, the guardians of the Persians whose
warriors have gone forth against the land of Greece; guardians of
Persia's rich and gold-encrusted royal seat, chosen, for our years, by
Xerxes himself, King and son of a King, Darius, to keep watch over
this land.

But about the King's return and the return of his army rich in gold
even now my evilly prophetic heart is troubled (for the whole strength
of the Asian people has fared forth with him) and mutters ($\beta\alpha\ddot{v}\zeta\epsilon\iota$)
against my youthful King. For no messenger and no horseman has
reached the city of the Persians. (*Persae*, 1–15)

An opening heavy with foreboding. Even before the prophetic
spirit of the Chorus voices its fears for the absent host, Persian
riches and gold (Aeschylean danger-signs)[9] have been mentioned
thrice. "Xerxes, King and son of a King, Darius" is soon to become
a sinister contrast and already in $\beta\alpha\ddot{v}\zeta\epsilon\iota$, a complaining word, the
Chorus of Elders anticipates its final role as the Great King's
inquisitors.[10]

[9] Cf. J. H. Finley, *Pindar and Aeschylus* (Cambridge, Mass. 1955), 210 ff.

[10] $\beta\alpha\ddot{v}\zeta\epsilon\iota$, v. 13, is admittedly difficult. I follow J. T. Sheppard in taking $\theta\upsilon\mu\acute{o}\varsigma$ (the
Chorus' troubled spirit) in v. 11, as subject. Certainly the word has a hostile overtone, as
the parallel in a similar context at *Ag.* 449 (cf. Sidgwick's note, *ad loc.*) indicates. I can
see little in support of Gilbert Murray's translation "baying" (like dogs), agreeing with
$\iota\sigma\chi\grave{v}\varsigma$ $\mathit{Å}\sigma\iota\alpha\tau\sigma\gamma\epsilon\nu\acute{\eta}\varsigma$ as subject. The only alleged parallel quoted (Heracl., frg. 97 D.-K.)
has dogs barking in a *hostile* way—and that is precisely the sense which must be avoided
if the glorious, departing army (and not the worrying Chorus, which has long awaited
news) is to be the subject. See Broadhead's Notes and Supplementary Notes, *ad loc.*,
citing various editors' views.

A glorious roster of the Persian army, its leaders and allies ("men like Amistres or Artaphernes, Megabates or Astaspes, fearful to look upon, terrible in battle") sweeps away the Chorus' worries for fifty marching, anapaestic lines. Splendid processional to match the final grim recessional. Even so, sinister words keep creeping in: πολύχρυσος again (45), ἁβροδίαιτοι (41) of the Lydians (some compound of ἁβρός—a soft word for fighting men—is to be used no less than five times of the Persian host),[11] φοβερός (48) and δεινός (40; 58), both used "bravely" here, have uncomfortably ambiguous overtones (Xerxes' summons will turn out "dread" indeed). Words for the army too are unfortunate, to say the least: ὄχλος (42) is meant to emphasize the number of the Lydians but anticipates the disordered rabble (see 422, 470) which the whole host is to become; τοιόνδ' ἄνθος Περσίδος αἴας / οἴχεται ἀνδρῶν (59–60) is a pretty phrase for the departed youth of Persia but bloom suggests fading, blossoms suggest picking, and οἴχεται can be used of one who makes the last departure. (τὸ Περσῶν δ' ἄνθος οἴχεται πεσόν: these words of the Messenger at 252 soon fulfill the ironic meanings latent here.)

The Chorus, as if depressed by its own overtones, shifts to full mourning in the closing lines of these "triumphant" anapaests:

> Such is the power of the Persian land which has left us, warriors whom all the land of Asia, their nurse, now bemoans with violent longing; parents and wives alike tremble with fear at the ever-lengthening stretch of days (59–64).

In the lyric part of the parodos, the variations in mood follow a similar decline from martial confidence through uncertainty to outright fear, for now the fear becomes specific as some hint of danger from the gods makes its first appearance. The first two strophic pairs give stirring pictures of Xerxes (θούριος ἄρχων, 73)[12]

---

[11] Cf. W. B. Stanford, *Aeschylus in his Style* (Dublin 1942), 113. Cf. fn. 29 below.

[12] Both this expression, θούριος ἄρχων and διχόθεν, used of Xerxes and his double thrust will remind readers of the *Agamemnon* of the θούριος ὄρνις of Agamemnon's eagle portent and of the twin-throned power of the Atreidae (*Ag.* 112 and 108, respectively). Indeed many anticipations of the *Agamemnon* are to be noted in the *Persae* not only in the recurrent use of significant and sinister images (for "yoke" and "net" images so used, compare *Persae* 50, 72, 107–14, with *Ag.* 44, 218, 358–61, 866–68, 1116, 1382) but also in the use of certain dramatic and, in particular, lyric sequences to reflect the tragic rhythm of the action and in the use of a prophetically endowed character (Darius may be compared with Cassandra in the *Agamemnon*) to concentrate in a single scene the dramatic meaning o the whole piece.

crossing the Hellespont on his bridge of boats and of the whole host sweeping into Greece: irresistible army under a King who

> glaring about him with a dragon's murderous glare, 'mid myriad ships and myriad arms, on Syrian chariot onward speeds, bringing war of bowmen against famed warriors of the spear (81–86).

But again dangerous ambiguities gleam through the shining facade. Xerxes is περσέπτολις (65), but *whose* city will he destroy? He is ἰσόθεος (80), innocent in epic but not in tragic imitation of epic, and sprung, through Danaë, from Zeus' golden seed (79–80: more dangerous gold). More sinister (if unconsciously so) is the Chorus' first reference to Xerxes' bridging of the Hellespont: "casting a yoke on the sea's neck" picks up the expression used a moment before of the planned enslaving of Greece (ζυγὸν ἀμφιβαλεῖν δούλιον Ἑλλάδι, 50; ζυγός is another of the thematic "danger-words" in this play) [13] and the careful reminder "Helle, child of Athamas" (for the Hellespont) underlines the personal aspect of the sea's enslavement. Finally, at the end of this triumphant passage, Xerxes' "invincible" host is called a flood (ῥεῦμα) which no man can withstand, "an irresistible wave of the sea" (87–90). All these unconscious anticipations are later to be grimly and fully realized. [14]

Suddenly, with one of those exciting leaps in which Aeschylean lyrics excel (often to the despair of textual critics), [15] the suppressed fears of the Chorus rise to the surface:

[13] Cf. Stanford's list, with line references, of dominant images and image-sequences in various Aeschylean plays, *op. cit.*, 96 ff, and his comment, "In varying degrees, each dominant image has some literal reference to an important aspect of the action in five of the plays." (His examples have been drawn from *Suppl.*, *Pers.*, *Sept.*, *P.V.*, *Ag.*); this indicates, Stanford argues, "a close interplay between the world of symbol and the world of fact."

[14] Cf. A. E. Wardman's observation (*Historia* 8 [1959], 53) that it is proper and just that Xerxes' defeat should actually occur on the insulted element.

Bengt Alexanderson (*Eranos* 65 [1967], 4) is, I think, wrong in suggesting that the first suggestion of danger in Xerxes' bridge comes with Darius' pronouncements. This may be the first clear and overt statement of that danger but the sinister aspect of Xerxes' yoking of the Hellespont is certainly hinted at (with increasing awareness on the part of the Chorus) in the passages just cited and in the complementary one at 93–114 (in the original line sequence of the mss).

[15] Müller, Murray, and others would have vv. 93–100 follow 101–14. Both sequences make sense, though the sequence of the mss gives a more striking example of Aeschylus' technique. There is certainly no compelling reason for accepting Müller's transposition. See also Sidgwick's defence of the original line sequence in his notes on 91 and 101 ff., with which I agree except for his exaggerated suggestion about "the whole play being the glorification of Salamis."

Guileful deception of god, what man can avoid it? What man, be he
ever so nimble, can leap such a leap to escape it? For Atê, false-smiling,
gulls man into nets of destruction, whence no one unscathed can escape
(93–100).

Whence this sudden panic? The Chorus has remembered that land,
not sea, is the god-given Persian element (πολέμους πυργοδαΐκτους . . .
ἱππιοχάρμας τε κλόνους: marvellous, untranslatable Aeschylus for
"rampart-smashing wars" and "the uproar of cavalry battle"); the
strophe ends with a final terrified glance at swirling waves beneath
the slender fastenings of Xerxes' fatal bridge (108–14). This, then,
is the net of destruction, as the sequel and later the ghostly Darius
are to show us; already the god-fearing language of the Chorus
hints at more flagrant ways in which the Persian *moira* (101) has been
trangressed.

The Chorus now gives itself over to unrelieved foreboding ("now
shudders my black-robed heart. . .", 115 ff.), to pictures of the city
greeting the dreadful news (no hint of which has yet reached them),
with tears and lamentation. The confident and powerful water-
images (μεγάλῳ ῥεύματι φωτῶν, 88; ἄμαχον κῦμα θαλάσσας, 90,
for the Persian army) now give way to a terrestrial image ("like a
swarm of bees," 128) but this *land* army (as the image impresses on
us) has now irrevocably crossed the sea (130–32). And so the lyric
ends in deeper gloom than did the anapaests, as the Chorus now
sings of Persian wives softly grieving (ἀβροπενθεῖς) in their lonely
beds (133 ff.), a poignant contrast to the martial vigour of its
opening.

It is the Queen's role to repeat in dramatic terms the apprehensions
which the Chorus has expressed in lyrics. A neat transitional passage
(much belaboured by the critics) precedes her entry: the Chorus
begins to debate, in solemn conclave, whether Persian arrows or
Greek spears will prevail, only to be interrupted by the Queen who
with her premonitions, dreams, and omens, provides the only sort of
answer which the Chorus' questions can, at this stage, receive.[16]

---

[16] Critics worried about what they regard as the quite abortive nature (at least from a
dramatic point of view) of the Chorus' proposed session of deep thought on Xerxes'
prospects have sought to explain it in terms removed, to a greater or lesser degree, from
its dramatic context. Stoessl (*Mus. Helv.* 2 [1945], 150), followed by Lesky (*Die Tragische
Dichtung* [Göttingen 1956], 62), thinks that the proposed pondering of the Chorus of

The Queen travels in a few lines the same distance which it has taken the Chorus a full lyric to traverse. Leaving "her gold-decked chambers," she trembles, "lest Wealth [retaining πλοῦτος, as in the MSS] rushing headlong, may trip and overthrow, mid clouds of dust, the prosperity which Darius reaped with some god's help" (163–64). Wealth is at the heart of the Queen's fear: her thought is Solonian in its ambiguity—a good reason for retaining πλοῦτος at v. 163, for in Solon Wealth can lead to the overthrow of the very prosperity which it brings; it is left to the play to add the Aeschylean emphasis that not without some deed of *hybris* will Wealth bring ruin.[17]

The Persian catastrophe (as we know) has already happened. The dramatic action cannot affect it; prophetic dreams and visions must replace action in the opening episodes of plays like this. The ominous import of Atossa's visions (the Greek woman, yoked to the Persian one, who overthrows her would-be master; the eagle fleeing for safety before the little falcon) is clear enough but the language and details of the Queen's narration heighten their significance. Xerxes' yoking of the mares (ζεύγνυσιν αὐτῷ καὶ λέπαδν' ἐπ' αὐχένων / τίθησι 191–92) echoes the King's yoking of the Hellespont (ζυγὸν ἀμφιβαλὼν αὐχένι πόντου, 72) as well as his intention of yoking Greece in slavery (ζυγὸν ἀμφιβαλεῖν δούλιον Ἑλλάδι, 50)—and both ζυγόν and λέπαδνον are words which Aeschylus uses elsewhere with sinister overtones.[18] In the telling of the same dream-omen, two telling cameos appear with the instant

---

Elders is introduced merely in slavish imitation of the *Phoenissae* of Phrynichus: the Alexandrian Hypothesis to the *Persae* quotes one Glaucus as saying that Aeschylus imitated Phrynichus in this play and we learn from the same Hypothesis that a eunuch tells of the defeat of Xerxes as he prepares the seats for a Council of Elders meeting, presumably, to discuss this crisis. Wilamowitz' explanation (*Hermes* 32 [1897], 382–83) that the passage is simply a flaw, a sign of a developing poet, is still less convincing.

[17] Cf. Solon Frg. 1 (Diehl), esp. 7–32, 71 ff., *Ag.*, 750 ff. In the present passage the Queen goes on to express two supplementary fears suggestive of the whole Persian dilemma: the fear that wealth without manpower is not to be honoured (this will be Xerxes' position, after his defeat) and the fear that without wealth a man's true strength cannot shine forth (165–67). However, the whole passage is fraught with difficulties; see Sidgwick's helpful note on 163–64 and Broadhead's discussion of the entire passage (163–67) and of other views upon it.

[18] Cf., for example, *Ag.* 218, ἐπεὶ δ'ἀνάγκας ἔδυ λέπαδνον (of Agamemnon's fatal decision to sacrifice Iphigenia) and *Ag.* 1071, εἴκουσ' ἀνάγκῃ τῇδε καίνισον ζυγόν (the Chorus' advice to Cassandra to yield to the inevitable).

completeness of dream-imagery: one is the image of the Persian mare preening herself (ἐπυργοῦτο, 192, is the untranslatable word) in the luxury of her enslavement; the other is the image of Xerxes' despair, "rending his robes" (199) when the Greek mare overthrows him, while father Darius looks down in pity. This emphasis on the relation of raiment to Persian pride and Persian ruin is to recur (832-36, 846 ff., 1030, 1060) at the climactic moments of the play.

Before the arrival of Xerxes' Messenger, another brief transition (230-45) prepares us for the switch from the Persian court to the battle in Greece. Three points in the Chorus' answers about the distant enemy heighten the tragic expectation: Greece's distance ("by the setting of the sun's decline," 232) plays up the overreaching quality of Asiatic Xerxes; Greece's wealth, *thêsauros chthonos*, "the land's own treasure house" (238), contrasts with the Persian ruler's individual magnificence;[19] Greek freedom opposes Persian despotism —and yet its army "subject to no man" has once before prevailed (241-44, 236).[20]

* * *

[19] Cf. Finley, *op. cit.* (above, note 9), 210, who comments on the contrast between Persian gold and Greek silver as paralleling the contrast between Persian *hybris* and Greek piety. But the contrast is rather between the use of Persian gold for ostentatious adornment and the use of Athens' natural treasure-house of the land for the defence of the realm. On this latter point, cf. A. J. Podlecki, *The Political Background of Aeschylean Tragedy* (Ann Arbor 1966), 15; he reminds us that this use of the wealth from the Laureion silver mines was an important part of Themistocles' policy (Herodotus VII 144) and so uses this reference in the *Persae* (238) in support of his thesis that much of the play's motivation lies in Aeschylus' desire to vindicate Themistocles and his policies. On this view, see below, note 25.

[20] The Queen has asked (235) whether the Athenians have a large army. The Chorus replies "καὶ στρατὸς τοιοῦτος, / ἔρξας πολλὰ δὴ Μήδους κακά": "such an army indeed, as has (already) wrought many woes on the Persians" (236). The Chorus is referring to the defeat inflicted on the Persians at Marathon, ten years earlier, but there is perhaps an ironic ambiguity in the explanatory participial expression, for the audience knows that even as the Chorus speaks the Athenians have already inflicted another far greater defeat upon the Persians. (The syntactical difficulty of v. 236 has, however, led to various different interpretations of this exchange. See Sidgwick's note defending the explanatory participle ἔρξας in place of the consecutive infinitive which we might expect. Cf. also Broadhead's longer but inconclusive note; I think he reads more than is necessary into the Queen's question, viz., "Have the Athenians such a large army that their subjugation would bring the rest of Greece into subjection?" Nor do I see the necessity for such elaborate justifications of τοιοῦτος followed by an explanatory participle as Page and others, cited by Broadhead, have suggested, e.g., the loss of another question and answer before v. 236.)

O Persian land...at one stroke our great fortune is destroyed, the bloom of Persian manhood turned to dust (250–52).

This "final" announcement of the Messenger's, at the very moment of his entry, epitomizes the nature and effect of the *Persae*'s special structure: the four discrete but related aspects of Xerxes' fall so placed that we may grasp them, *in toto et in partibus*, in a single dramatic experience. During the Messenger Scene we are as close to the actual catastrophe as the dramatic scope (let alone the dramatic convention) of the play can tolerate. Once again (as in the preparatory movement) lyric precedes dramatic treatment, though now, for obvious reasons, the proportions are reversed: after a series of brief laments interrupting the initial headlines of the bitter news (the disaster at Salamis, the uselessness of Persian bows, the hated name of the Athenians), the rest of this movement is taken up with the vivid and detailed narration of the events themselves. It has been suggested that this initial prominence of the Chorus in the Messenger Scene shows that Aeschylus has not yet shaken himself free of the conventions of one-actor tragedy.[21] But surely it is appropriate that, at the first bleak announcement of the disaster, the emotional effect upon the Persian people should be expressed at once—and this only the Chorus can do. When the Queen Mother speaks, *her* concern must be personal ("Who is *not* dead?" she asks at 296—and the Messenger, whose tactful understanding at this juncture has been praised *ad nauseam* by the critics, assures her that Xerxes lives), and such personal concern for the life of Xerxes must lead away from the central issue of the play, had not the Chorus already sounded the

[21] "The play retains some of the archaic features of early tragedy, and the handling of the second actor is awkward." Broadhead (xxxii) admits some truth in this traditional charge concerning the prominence of the Chorus in certain episodes of the *Persae*. Later (xli–ii), he explains the emphasis on the Chorus rather than the Queen as recipients of the Messenger's disastrous news partly in terms of archaism, partly in terms of the appropriate dramatic effect. Kitto, too, admits "traces of its [the Chorus'] ancient supremacy" (44) in this and other episodes of the *Persae* but goes on to give a perceptive account of the interesting and important characterization of Atossa whose prominence is due, he believes, to the dramatist's desire to show the personal as well as the political side of Xerxes' *hybris*: if the downfall of Persia and not the *hybris* of Xerxes had been the central theme of the play, then we might well have expected the Chorus to dominate it. A wise judgment—and one which well illustrates this critic's constant awareness that, when due consideration has been given to the historical position of a given play in the development of drama, it is usually the dramatic requirements of the precise theme which the poet has chosen which answer more questions about its structure.

note of national mourning. Once again, the dramatic priorities and not the dramatist's fumbling with unfamiliar counters provide the sounder explanations of procedures which strike the modern reader as unusual.

The Messenger Speeches have a formal structure of their own. First, as introduction, the stark and vivid roll-call of dead heroes, drowned or slain ("The noble Tenagon now comes and goes [πολεῖ: a terrible word in the context!] along the sea-washed shores of Ajax' isle" 306–307; "Metallus in death has changed to red the colour of his thick and shaggy beard" 314 ff.); [22] then the trilogy of disaster (Salamis, Psyttalea, and the River Strymon), each incident complete with its divine temptation, tragic overreaching, and catastrophe. [23] "Guileful deception of god" the Chorus has warned (93 ff.); so, too, the Messenger explains the whole incredible defeat at Salamis ("Were we outnumbered? No, some god (δαίμων τις) destroyed our host" 337–38, 345) and, in particular, the fatal deception which lured Xerxes to block the straits (φανεὶς ἀλάστωρ ἢ κακὸς δαίμων ποθέν 354). [24] A series of brilliant pictures (364 ff.) suggestive at once of lively action and of divine design describes the fatal sequence at Salamis. Night ("aithêr's darkened grove") deceives King Xerxes; day, returning, reveals the scope of that deception; then night again, at the end of the day's battle, quenches forever the false hopes of the night before.

> Groans swept the deep with lamentation,
> Till night's dark face erased the scene from view (426–28).

Earlier in the play, Atossa has wondered how a people "subject to

[22] Cf. Lattimore's comment "What would it (the Persae) be without the poetry?" (Richmond Lattimore, The Poetry of Greek Tragedy, Baltimore 1958). In particular, Lattimore speaks (35) of the great series of catalogues in the Persae as opening "splendors to ear and eye," and (38) of the "eye-witness report of battle and retreat where Aeschylus, using the language of poetry, is still as tough and bitter as the best prose writer could be."

[23] Cf. M. Croiset, Eschyle (Paris 1928), 90, who speaks of these three Messenger Speeches as providing "presqu'une tragédie en soi, avec son commencement, son milieu, son dénouement," and of the three successive phases of the Persian disaster as joined together by a common bond.

[24] Of the many tactical and technical studies of the Battle of Salamis and its treatment in the Persae, see in particular N. G. L. Hammond, "The Battle of Salamis," J. Hell. Stud. 76 (1956), 32–54, and bibliography there given, and Podlecki, op. cit. (above, note 19), Appendix A, 131–41. The subject is beyond the scope of the present study of the Persae. On the celebrated reference to the ruse of Themistocles at 355 ff., see the following note.

no man" could ever stand firm against the Persian host. In the event, it is the democratic Greeks from their first cry, "Now is the struggle on behalf of all" (405) who act as a single man throughout.[25] The descriptions of Persians in battle (the babble of Persian tongues, 406; the flight in mad disorder, "φυγῇ δ' ἀκόσμως" 422; the "mob" [πλῆθος, 432] of Persians likened in defeat to "a haul of fish" 424) all contrast grimly with the earlier descriptions of one splendid, ordered army under one great King.

"There is an island fronting Salamis..." (447 ff.). Again, the false hope born of over-confidence begets the action of this second catastrophe, at Psyttalea.[26] Xerxes, κακῶς τὸ μέλλον ἱστορῶν, dis-

[25] The marked anonymity of the Greek host in Aeschylus' treatment of Salamis has often been observed. Cf. M. Patin, Études sur les Tragiques Grecs. Eschyle. (Paris 1865), 214, who thinks that this feature puts the emphasis on national rather than personal and individualized pride in accomplishment on the part of the Athenians. To this explanation we might add the more pedestrian but perhaps more cogent dramatic point that, since the whole tragedy is presented as a Persian tragedy, seen through Persian eyes, it is natural enough that the Persians should be named and given individual identities and that the Greeks should remain as the anonymous agents of divine nemesis. It may be true that, as Professor Lattimore has observed ("Aeschylus on the Defeat of Xerxes" [above, note 2], 90 ff.), Aeschylus' treatment of Persian defeat does concentrate attention on the Athenians more than on the other Greeks but this (as Lattimore notes) also suited the unity of the piece which chose to concentrate the Persian catastrophe principally on Salamis. Even when (as at 355 ff.) the exploit of some individual Greek (or, as *we* know, Athenian) is referred to, there is no dramatic reason why the Messenger should mention his name, nor, indeed, any reason, historical or dramatic, why he should even know it.

This is not to say that the Athenian audience would not thrill with pride at this treatment of their exploits or that the supporters of Themistocles would not be justifiably gratified at the clear reference to Themistocles' successful ruse (if ruse it was) in persuading Xerxes that the Greek fleet was about to flee (see *Persae* 355 ff.; cf. Herod. VIII 75). Against the suggestion that Aeschylus' emphasis on the *daimôn* would somehow diminish, in the Greek mind, the credit due to Themistocles, see Podlecki's arguments, *op. cit.*, 22–23. However, it should be clear from the present treatment of the play as the tragedy of Xerxes' *hybris* that I would not go as far as this critic when he suggests (12–15) that the vindication of Themistocles and his policies was one of the main motivating forces in the composition of the play. I would prefer to view such vindication (which, as Podlecki shows, appears in several places) as a *parergon* (perhaps an important one: Greek dramatists were capable of doing several things successfully at once) rather than as a central issue of the play.

[26] Aeschylus develops the Psyttalea incident rather more than Herodotus does at VIII 76 and 95. Some commentators think that his particular purpose is to honour Aristeides (cf. Herod. VIII 95) and champions of Aeschylus as the champion of Themistocles are at pains to play down the alleged significance of *this* particular historical reference. (See Podlecki, *op. cit.*, 23–25, and references there given.) But surely one cannot have it both ways: here we see, perhaps, some of the dangers surrounding "historical critics" who burden the playwright with specific political causes.

patches a picked band to slaughter "those Greeks, an easy prey," who might take refuge there after defeat at Salamis, and again, with the god's help (454–55), the move results in fresh disaster for the Persians. Apparently incidental touches in the dramatic narrative heighten the tragic effect by ironic anticipations and contrasts: the lovely strand "where Pan is wont to walk" is the one which bodies of shipwrecked Persian sailors soon will nudge; the single shout (ἐξ ἑνὸς ῥόθου, 462) of the Greeks echoes their triumphant cry (κέλαδος...μολπηδόν 388–89) before Salamis, and contrasts with the babble of Persian fear (406); and again the action ends with the same disordered flight of the Persians (ἤϊξ᾽ ἀκόσμῳ ξὺν φυγῇ, 470) as did the larger engagement (φυγῇ δ᾽ ἀκόσμως πᾶσα ναῦς ἠρέσσετο, 422).

It is in the third and final episode of our little trilogy that we have the clearest demonstration of divine temptation and human over-stepping. The scene is laid at the penultimate stage of the long march of Persian survivors back to Asia and this time no human power shares with the gods the agency of retribution.

> That very night, θεός raised a wintry storm all out of season and froze the whole stream of sacred Strymon. Any man who had thought before that the gods were nowhere then assailed them with their prayers worshipping earth and heaven... And whoever of us set off to cross before the sun's bright rays (θεοῦ ἀκτῖνας) were sent abroad hit upon lucky safety. For soon the orb of the sun with blazing countenance melted the middle passage. In a heap men fell and lucky then was he who quickly breathed his last (495–507).

With the word θεός Aeschylus exploits the traditionally "religious" weather language of the Greeks[27] to express in a single description the idea of Persian destruction by natural phenomena and by divine nemesis. Nor should we miss the overtone in "sacred Strymon" (ἁγνοῦ Στρυμόνος, 497); the Bosporos which Xerxes yoked is also sacred (Βόσπορον ῥόον θεοῦ, 746): Xerxes' crime against the sea (like Agamemnon's treading on the purple) may be merely symbolic of his hybristic ambition but it is fitting that the sufferings of his host should begin in a battle at sea (where, as bowmen, 147, Persians are out of their element) and end in other sacred waters

[27] See *LSJ*, θεός, s.v., I.1.d.

which freeze and melt with a very special vindictiveness.[28] The ambiguities of "god" and "weather" (or "the skies", "the sun") are finally resolved (if they need resolving) in the lines with which the Messenger concludes his tale of Persian woe.

> All this is true. Yet many things have I left out of my account in telling of the evils descending on the Persians from the hand of god (θεός, 514: the Messenger ends his account as he began it, 353 ff., with the god).

The second stasimon (532–97) provides a splendid transition between the actual and retrospective views of Xerxes' catastrophe. Three major themes stand out: Zeus the avenger ("King Zeus, now you have destroyed..." 532 ff.); Xerxes the guilty leader ("Xerxes led them, alas; Xerxes ruined them, o woe! For Xerxes ordered all unwisely..." 550 ff.); and the deathknell of Persian power ("No longer will there be Persian-ruling [περσονομοῦνται is the verb in the original] throughout Asia..." 584 ff.). Interwoven with these themes are the chants of suffering and lamentation as the Chorus reflects the grief of Persian wives, "rending their clothes with their soft hands" (537–38), of brides, "abandoning the soft, rich beds of young delight" (543–44), and of the old, parents now childless, bewailing total woe (580 ff.).

The language and imagery of the mourning brides passage (541–47) in this Chorus remind us that Aeschylus, far from being merely the poet of "chariots heaped on chariots and corpses piled pell mell" (as Aristophanes, *Frogs*, 403, would have him), could, when he wished, be as effective in a soft, feminine, even sensual mode. Once, in anticipation, this softly mourning note (ἀβροπενθεῖς, 135; ἀβρόγοοι, 541) has already been sounded at the end of the parodos. In both instances, the contrast provided by the confident and strongly masculine descriptions of the glorious army departing for the war makes the soft passages the more beguiling and the grief they express more poignant. It may be that such passages are indicative

---

[28] Cf. Wardman, *op. cit.* (above, note 14), 52–53, who notes the first but not the second of these ironically apt reversals. With regard to "sacred Strymon," 297, it is not enough to note, as Broadhead does in his note *ad loc.*, that "the Persians regarded rivers as sacred and that the Greeks too applied the epithet to rivers, water and other elements"; the point is, rather, Aeschylus' exploitation of such epithets to underline the ironic justice of Xerxes' fate.

of Aeschylus' attitude to the Persians and of the light in which he
wished to cast them; one critic, for example, has noted the unusual
number of *habro-* compounds in the play.[29] Nevertheless, effects and
contrasts of this kind are not limited to the *Persae*; one thinks, for
example, of the second stasimon of the *Agamemnon* with the sensuous
description of fatal Helen slipping out of "her softly-woven
(ἁβροπήνων) curtained bower" (*Ag.* 690–91) to sail with Paris, "a
gentle adornment of wealth, a soft weapon of loving-glance, a
heart-piercing flower of passion" (*Ag.* 741–43) by which Priam and
the seed of Priam would be destroyed. And here too we have an
ironic contrast with the martial vigour of the parados, for the
confident Greeks and their King are also to suffer in the end, in
this war waged "for another man's wife" (*Ag.* 447–48).

The contrast provided by the last strophic pair (584–597), with its
muted note of triumph, is truly remarkable. For the first time the
Chorus deserts its role as loyal guardians of the Persian court: it
hints at the good which is to come of all this suffering but the good
no longer concerns the glory of Xerxes and Persia but the freedom
of Asia now saved from despotism.

> Now Persian sway through Asia's lands exists no longer...
> No longer will men grovel on the ground in worship,
>   for the power of the King is destroyed.
> No longer will the tongues of men be held in bitter constraint,
>   for the people are freed and free will be their speech,
> since the yoke of armed might has been destroyed (584–94, in part).

...λέλυται γὰρ / λαὸς ἐλεύθερα βάζειν, / ὡς ἐλύθη ζυγὸν ἀλκᾶς (592–94):
a nice play (and a neat Aeschylean jingle: λέλυται...ἐλεύθερα...
ἐλύθη) on λύω in its positive and negative senses of "free" and
"destroy": still more significant is ζυγόν, for here we celebrate the
final destruction of that Persian yoke which has already appeared in
various ambiguous and sinister contexts throughout the play.

* * *

Tragic expectation and tragic fulfilment have now been expressed.
The third movement of the play is retrospective: through the
wisdom of the ghostly Darius the full significance of the catastrophe

---

[29] Stanford, *op. cit.*, 113, counts five *habro-* compounds in the *Persae*: at 41, 135, 541,
543, 1073 (which should read "1072").

will be revealed. The summoning of Darius' ghost by ritual and by choral incantation (609 ff., 628 ff.) anticipates the less literal evocation of Agamemnon's spirit in the *Choephoroe* (315 ff.). In the present instance, the poet's purpose is more complex and it is this complexity which accounts for certain mild inconsistencies in the presentation of Darius. Darius' utterances have two functions: first (and most important) to make explicit the tragic meaning of Xerxes' fall; second, to warn the Persians against the folly of further attacks on mainland Greece—and in so doing to complete the play's debt to history by prophecies of what will happen at Plataea.[30] Both these functions require of Darius a special degree of knowledge, as well as of wisdom, beyond that of all living Persians and no one would balk at such attributes of a ghostly King who, even in life, was regarded almost as a god (...Πέρσαις ὡς θεός, 711). Why, then, does the poet limit Darius to the somewhat piecemeal and even inconsistent knowledge provided by certain convenient oracles? Darius knows, for example, that Persia was doomed to defeat at the hands of the Greeks (739, 787–93, 796–97, 800 ff.) but not that this fate would fall on Xerxes; he is unaware, until he is told, of Xerxes' expedition against Greece, yet later (800 ff.) his oracles appear to have supplied him with detailed information about the Persian land army and its final discomfiture at Plataea. The advantages of thus circumscribing Darius' knowledge are twofold and outweigh the inconsistencies.[31] In the first place, the device allows Darius to

---

[30] Cf. *supra*, pp. 143 f. and note 2.

[31] Editors and critics from Blomfield (1814) on have worried about the inconsistencies and *lacunae* in Darius' knowledge in the *Persae*. It is, I think, misguided to try to explain them away as do, for example, M. Patin, *op. cit.*, 214, and Broadhead in his note to vv. 739 ff., by pontificating on the sort of knowledge that Darius may, and may not, be expected to have. True, Aeschylus makes a gesture at explaining the inconsistency in his two references to oracles at 739 and at 800 ff., for oracles are notoriously incomplete in their information. But the real reason for Darius' piecemeal knowledge is, of course, that the poet wants him to have just as much and as little as is convenient (as we shall see) for his (the poet's) dramatic purposes.

More recent critics have accepted this inconsistency. Cf. Dawe's comment on Darius "whose omniscience has certain *lacunae* very convenient for the poet's exposition." See R. D. Dawe, "Inconsistency of Plot and Character in Aeschylus" (above, note 6), 30–31. See also B. Alexanderson's sensible discussion of the problem, especially his conclusion, "the poet endows him (Darius) with knowledge and deprives him of it as suits him best when creating an effective scene and stressing what he wants to stress" ("Darius in The Persians," *Eranos* 65 [1967], 1–11).

ask the right questions, that is, the questions whose answers will provide the cues for the sort of comment here required of him. Secondly, the oracle about the Persian defeat, combined with the uncertainty as to the time and circumstance of that defeat, provide, as we shall see, just the right proportions of freedom and necessity that Xerxes' tragedy requires. Even so, it should be admitted that for once the requirements of history, of the poet's need to mention at least the major events which actually happened, tend slightly to exacerbate the sensitive areas of Darius' piecemeal knowledge. Salamis, in the poet's presentation, is the central catastrophe for Xerxes and nothing must be allowed to distract from that. Yet in the picture, however exaggerated, of total Persian ruin, someone must be made to mention Plataea. Darius is the obvious one to do so: obviously it cannot be the Messenger and Darius can place Plataea in the future, outside of Xerxes' personal tragedy and yet a part of the total picture of Persian *hybris* (808 ff.) and Persian ruin.

Darius' questions, once he has heard of Xerxes' defeat, go right to the crucial point: "The reckless one, was it by land or sea he made his mad attempt?" (719) and then: "How did so great a *land army* succeed in crossing over?" (721). And so we come to the symbolic nub of the matter. The poet chooses the Queen's words with care: "By man-made contrivances (μηχαναῖς) he yoked the strait of Hellê" (722). Even before Darius pounces, the Queen is aware of the sinister aspect of her revelation. "Surely (she hazards) some god settled himself (ξυνήψατο) upon his mind" (724). "Alas, some mighty god," (the Ghost assures her) "and so he lost all judgement" (725).

In expounding the necessary fulfilment of the oracle, Darius makes the personal guilt of Xerxes crystal clear:

I for my part prayed that only after much time would the gods bring these things to pass. But when a man himself is eager, then the god fastens on him (740–42).

Nowhere do we have a clearer statement of Aeschylus' tragic theology—of the double motivation of the hybristic transgressor and of the god who leads him on, once he has shown his hand; of the doom or the curse which hangs over a royal house and of the tragic hero who reaches up, as it were, and pulls the cloud down on himself.

Thus (as in the celebrated "yoke of necessity" passage at *Ag.* 218 ff.) does Aeschylus provide both for "dooms," oracle-or-curse-fulfilments, and for the free (if any man is free) and fatal decisions of the tragic hero.[32]

The egregious quality of Xerxes' mad career stands out, in the speeches of Darius, against the whole tapestry of wise and prosperous Persian rule. Here at last the symbol, the yoking of the Hellespont,

---

[32] It is fashionable in current Aeschylean criticism to reduce, sometimes almost to the vanishing point, the element of human responsibility, of fault (however qualified) in Aeschylus' tragic sufferers. This tendency has, of course, gone hand in hand with the tendency to question the justice of Zeus in Aeschylus, at least in any sense which might provide some measure of meaning, some hint of an ethical pattern in human suffering, from which man might be said to learn, and to find some consolation in the tragic catastrophes presented by the poet. The best that can be said for the new doctrine is that it has pretty well overthrown the over-simplified, pietistic interpretations of Aeschylus which presented him more as a theologian, particularly a theological champion of Zeus, and a moral philosopher than as a tragic poet. It is curious that two of the most eloquent and learned spokesmen for the god-doomed tragic hero in Aeschylus (viz., D. L. Page in his Introduction to the *Agamemnon* [Denniston and Page, *Aeschylus, Agamemnon,* Oxford 1957], esp. pp. xxii–xxix, and H. Lloyd-Jones in his two important articles, "Zeus in Aeschylus," *J. Hell. Stud.* 76 [1956], 55–67 and "The Guilt of Agamemnon," *Class. Quart.* 12 n.s. [1962], 187–99) make no use at all of this passage in the *Persae* (739 ff.) in their estimate of Aeschylus' treatment of the role of Zeus and of human guilt in tragic suffering. And yet this passage, in my opinion, sheds great light on the subtler and more vexed problem of the guilt of Agamemnon in the sacrifice of Iphigenia. I am not ignoring the greater complexity—and the greater element of ambiguity and doubt— in the question of Agamemnon's moral responsibility but at least the present passage does succeed in showing, in the simpler and more clear-cut situation of the *Persae,* how a tragic king can labour under a divinely ordained doom and yet have a measure of freedom and responsibility in the choice which activates that doom. It should perhaps be admitted that in the second of the two articles by Professor Lloyd-Jones, above, the author does, to be sure, allow some responsibility to Agamemnon but it is the responsibility of a man already driven mad by Zeus (see p. 193)! R. D. Dawe, *Harv. Stud. Class. Phil.* 72, 109–10, cf. *Eranos,* 64 (1966), 1–21, supports a very similar interpretation of *Ag.* 218 ff. by a most ingenious argument and this author does, in alluding to other Zeus-driven tragic heroes in Aeschylus, refer to at least part of the passage in the *Persae* to which I am here drawing attention. But he omits that part of the passage, 742, which stresses the prior responsibility of Xerxes before the god fastens on him, although elsewhere in this article, e.g. *Harv. Stud.* 94, 97 and note 16, 100, he clearly shows his awareness of multiple causation and "over-determination" (including divine and human "responsibility") of various catastrophic events in Greek Tragedy and in Greek literature in general. There is not space here to discuss in detail the complex arguments in the articles of Lloyd-Jones and Dawe in the articles here cited and perhaps I do them an injustice in thus isolating what I regard as their over-emphasis on the "Zeus-control," through the "maddening process," over the Aeschylean tragic hero at the crucial moment of decision or of decisive action.

is allowed to dissolve into the real hybris for which it stands. The former is treated briefly, in the first of the two speeches on Xerxes (739–52), and is surrounded by all the characteristics (lack of judgement, 725, boldness of ignorance, 744, delusive hope, 745–46, sickness of mind, 750) associated with major affronts against the divine scheme of things. But the real significance of what Xerxes has done is reserved for the second and longer of the two speeches (759–86). Here the disaster which Xerxes has brought to his people is contrasted with the ever-increasing prosperity of Persia "from that time when Zeus laid it down that one man was to rule all Asia, nurse of sheep" (763–64). Xerxes alone "being young, thought fresh young thoughts" (782); disobeying his father's injunctions to him, he sought to go beyond the *moira* of Zeus and to attack mainland Greece as well. (The lesson is brought home still more explicitly at the end of Darius' next speech, with its summary of Xerxes' career,

$$\ddot{v}\beta\rho\iota\varsigma \ \gamma\grave{\alpha}\rho \ \grave{\epsilon}\xi\alpha\nu\theta o\hat{v}\sigma' \ \grave{\epsilon}\kappa\acute{\alpha}\rho\pi\omega\sigma\epsilon\nu \ \sigma\tau\acute{\alpha}\chi\upsilon\nu$$
$$\ddot{\alpha}\tau\eta\varsigma, \ \ddot{o}\theta\epsilon\nu \ \pi\acute{\alpha}\gamma\kappa\lambda\alpha\upsilon\tau o\nu \ \grave{\epsilon}\xi\alpha\mu\hat{q} \ \theta\acute{\epsilon}\rho o\varsigma \ [821–22],$$

and the warning that $Z\epsilon\grave{v}\varsigma \ \kappa o\lambda\alpha\sigma\tau\acute{\eta}\varsigma$ is the harsh corrector of the man who, despising $\tau\grave{o}\nu \ \pi\alpha\rho\acute{o}\nu\tau\alpha \ \delta\alpha\acute{\iota}\mu o\nu\alpha$, lusts after other things). This then, is the real offence of Xerxes: the crossing from Asia to Greece against the ordinance of Zeus. No Greek (as Professor Kitto has pointed out) [33] would normally regard a bridge of ships as an impiety but Aeschylus has managed to play it up as such to secure a powerful visual symbol (comparable to Agamemnon's walking on the purple) to convey with the immediacy of drama the essential nature of Xerxes' overreaching hybris.

Like the Messenger's account, the utterances of Darius fall into three parts (Aeschylus' fondness for sets of three is well attested).[34] The third speech prophesies the fate at Plataea of the picked band

[33] *Greek Tragedy*, 38.

[34] Three murders and their resolutions form the core of the *Oresteia* and it is to "Zeus, the triple-thrower" that the Chorus of the *Agamemnon* looks to bring wisdom, however harshly, in the end (*Ag.* 168 ff.); Darius, in the *Persae*, 818–20, warns that even to the third generation the heaps of dead at Plataea will warn man as silent witnesses against thoughts beyond mortality. F. Solmsen in an interesting study suggests that Aeschylus' development of the trilogy as the most suitable form for tragic expression is all a part of the Greek and particularly the Aeschylean fascination with triplicity; see F. Solmsen, *Hesiod and Aeschylus* (Ithaca N.Y. 1949), Chap. II, esp. 127 ff., and 157 ff.

of the Persian army left to fight on in Greece. Once again, as in each of Darius' speeches and in the Messenger's accounts of disasters at Salamis, Psyttalea, and the Strymon, the tale begins with references to delusive hope (κεναῖσιν ἐλπίσιν πεπεισμένος, 804) and to violence and outrage (the ravaging of Greek temples, 807–12),[35] on the part of Xerxes and his army:

> Here (in Boeotia) there awaits them to suffer the last and greatest of their woes, in payment for their outrage (ὕβρεως ἄποινα, 808) and their impious designs (807–808).

> Wherefore, for evil deeds, they suffer evils no less themselves, and will suffer (813–14).

The heaps of Persian dead at Plataea will make known even to the third generation the lesson "that man, being mortal, must not think more than mortal thoughts" (818–20).

Just before his return to the nether world, Darius adds a minor, but thematically significant, instruction to Atossa: she is to go to meet Xerxes with "whatever raiment is suitable," for all his rich clothing is torn to tatters in his grief at his disasters (832–36). The Queen, as she sets about fulfilling this command, observes (846 ff.) that, of all their woes, the dishonour attached to Xerxes' ragged attire is the one which most oppresses her. This brilliant oriental touch (which has been misunderstood by some editors)[36] reminds us to what degree the *Persae* is concerned with symbols, with appearances, and, in the last tragic analysis, with loss of face. In the anticipatory movement of the play, we have noted numerous references, some proud, some fearful, to Persian wealth, Persian magnificence, and Persian gold. After the first wave of bad news, the Queen, perhaps unconsciously, symbolizes the coming decline in Persian magnificence

---

[35] The whole passage in which Darius, with his special knowledge, describes the Persian outrage to the temples of the gods and the sure reprisal it will bring provides another clear anticipation of a passage in the *Agamemnon*: Clytemnestra's almost psychic fears (at *Ag.* 338 ff.) lest the Greek army desecrate Trojan temples and bring ruin on themselves are also disastrously fulfilled in the Herald's speeches at 527 and 634 ff.

[36] See, for example, Broadhead's approval (in his note to 847–48) of Schütz's comment, "in his verbis et matrem et mulierem facile agnoscas etc." But this concern for proper regal appearance and shame at the loss of it is not limited to the Queen Mother. It is a *Persian* characteristic as Darius' instructions at 832–36 and the numerous references earlier in the play to Persian magnificence attest. See Sidgwick's more sensible note *ad loc.*

by her appearance (as she goes to make her tomb-offerings) "without my chariot, without my former luxury" (607–608) and Darius ends his tale of woe with the sardonic *carpe diem* observation, "Take pleasure while you can: wealth profits not the dead!" (841–42). Thus the reminder concerning Xerxes' physical appearance, and so of the whole theme of magnificence and its decline, of gold and tarnish, as it were, comes most appropriately at the end of this last episode before the arrival of the King himself. The two abortive attempts to meet and, in some sense, to escort and protect Xerxes (viz., the Queen's instruction to the Chorus at 527–31 and her own preparations at 849–51) come to nothing: R. D. Dawe is no doubt correct in asserting against critics who would meddle with these unfulfilled passages that their purpose is to whet our expectation of Xerxes' arrival on stage.[37] But an important part of this expectation is the emphasis which it throws on the riches-to-rags theme and on the futile attempts to avert its climax. When Xerxes does appear in this "waiting-for-Xerxes" play, he appears in all his rags, surely the crowning catastrophe of a Persian tragedy.

In his own character (apart from his hierophantic, didactic role), the function of Darius is to provide contrast with the ruinous Xerxes, as the wise and temperate Persian King who waged successful wars but knew his *moira* (Asia, not Greece) and sought without success to impose these wise restraints upon his son. Darius himself has already established this position (779–86); it is now the function of the Chorus (as so often in this play) to expound it with the greater expansiveness available to lyric treatment. The first strophic pair (852–64) gives a litany of Darius' kingly virtues and of the prosperous attributes of the state he ruled; the remaining three strophic sets provide, in the sweepingly vague style of Aeschylean geography, a panorama of Darius' exploits and of the mighty empire which he ruled. (Poetry, as opposed to history, dictates, of course, the suppression of all mention of the first Persian expedition, in Darius' reign, on mainland Greece, though Darius' conquest of the Ionian cities of Asia Minor and the islands [879–900] is accepted without demur. Conquests clearly beyond Asia, specifically of Thracian cities from the Bosporos to the River Strymon, are

[37] See Dawe, "Inconsistency etc." (above, note 6), 27 ff., especially his conclusion on p. 30.

dealt with tactfully: first of all they are achieved, in the Chorus' version, without Darius himself having to leave even Persian territory [864–66]; second, the cities chosen for particular emphasis, "the Acheloian cities of the Strymonic Lake" [867], are in all probability those which were actually removed, under Darius' orders, to Asia.[38] Thus does the poet reduce to the minimum any suggestion of Darius himself committing the extra-Asiatic follies of his son.) Not till the last few verses of this ode is the contrast with Xerxes' exploits—the purpose of this whole paean of praise of Darius—made explicit:

> But now, sorely defeated by dreadful blows at sea,
> we suffer all too surely a change of fortune from the gods (904–7).

* * *

Unlike most tragedies (and unlike all Sophoclean tragedies), the *Persae* does not present its catastrophe as evolving from the action presented on the stage. Rather we have viewed the inevitable fall of the hybristic Xerxes from three aspects: through the foreboding of the Chorus, through the eye-witness account of the Messenger and through the wise retrospection of the Ghost of King Darius.[39] Now at last we see the thing in itself in the ragged and moaning person of King Xerxes whose power and magnificence have been so firmly established in the opening passages of the play. The effect is all the more powerful for its long postponement; indeed, after all that has gone before, the mere presentation of the King, ragged and lamenting with the Persian Elders, is sufficient to effect the tragic catharsis. This effect is further enriched, and the various strands of the action drawn together, by the fulfilment, in this final *kommos*, of various tragic expectations previously provided.

First must come the shock of Xerxes' physical appearance. Despite the battle horrors and the political ruin, Darius and Atossa have

[38] See Herod. V 14–16; cf. Broadhead's note to *Persae* 867–70.

[39] The role of Darius provides us with one of the *Persae*'s most striking anticipations of the *Agamemnon*'s dramaturgy in the use of a prophetic character to relate, in a single scene, the significant moments in the past, present, and future of the tragic themes. Cassandra in the *Agamemnon* is by far the more brilliant example of this device, which could not indeed be fully exploited till its use in a trilogy like the *Oresteia*, where the past and future, both immediate and remote, are so fully, and dreadfully, furnished. But the ghost of Darius is, dramatically speaking, Cassandra's ancestor.

still retained the Persian emphasis on appearance, on the regal
trappings proper to the King. Thus in this instance, Spectacle, the
rags of Xerxes, must contribute powerfully to the tragic effect, and
the King himself adds to it by his directives ("Tear your hair and
rend your robes!" 1056 ff.) to his grieving Elders.

To the earlier description of Xerxes' mighty armament, the "re-
sistless wave" of men with their chariots, lances, javelins, and bows
(especially bows), this brief exchange provides a grim antithesis:

> *Xerxes:* You see this arrow-bearing —
> *Chorus:* What's this you say you've saved?
> *Xerxes:* this treasury for shafts?
> *Chorus:* Slim saving from such might![40] (1020–23)

So, too, the fearsome list of chieftains is answered by a dread roll-call
of the drowned, now nosing the shores of Salamis, as Xerxes, once
the King of Kings, is forced, like a criminal at the bar of justice, to
answer the relentless questions of the Chorus (956–1001).

But of all the fulfilments of this dreadful scene, the final emphasis
lies on the unnamed *daimôn* who, throughout, has hovered over the
spectacle of Xerxes' *hybris*:

> Woe for my fate which without warning fell,
> How savagely the god (δαίμων) has fallen on the Persian race!
>
> (909–12).

> ...and alas for that proud array of men (κόσμου τ' ἀνδρῶν) [41]
> whom the god (δαίμων) has now shorn (920–21).

> Alas, you gods (δαίμονες) you have set on us
> a woe unlooked-for and far-shining, like to the glance of *Atê*!
>
> (1005–1007).

Toronto, 17 June 1970

---

[40] Wardman, *op. cit.*, 49–52, observes the sequence of references in the play to Persian
arrow-power (86, 147, 556, 926); the present passage completes the *motif* with nice irony.

[41] κόσμου τ' ἀνδρῶν (920): an ironic term for the Persian host, for the Messenger has
described the Persians as fleeing in wild disorder (ἀκόσμως, 422) in contrast to the
surprising discipline (οἱ δ' οὐκ ἀκόσμως ἀλλὰ πειθάρχῳ φρενί, 374) of the democratic
Athenians and their allies (cf. vv. 241–43).

ZUR EXODOS DER *SIEBEN*:
(AISCH. *SEPT*. 1005–78)

HARTMUT ERBSE

Wenn es zukünftig möglich sein wird, aus der grossen Anzahl mittelalterlicher Handschriften der drei klassischen griechischen Tragiker die wirklich wichtigen auszuwählen und auf ihren Angaben einen zuverlässigen Text aufzubauen, so ist das nicht zuletzt das Verdienst Alexander Turyns. Er hat nicht nur Versuche seiner Vorgänger fortgesetzt, verbessert und vervollständigt, sondern hat sich als erster die Aufgabe gestellt, Eigenart und Bedeutung der zuvor nur wenig beachteten byzantinischen Editionen gründlich zu untersuchen. Die Ergebnisse vor allem dieser Leistung wird in Zukunft jeder berücksichtigen müssen, der sich um die Echtheit des Tragikertextes und um die Geschichte seiner Überlieferung bemüht. Als bescheidenes Zeichen des Dankes und der aufrichtigen Bewunderung für das Lebenswerk des Jubilars möchten auch die nachfolgenden Seiten, ein Beitrag zum Verständnis eines umstrittenen Tragödientextes, angesehen werden.

I

Zunächst sollen einige sprachliche Einzelprobleme der Exodos (1005–78) behandelt werden. Mit den beiden ersten Versen (1005–6)

$$\delta o\kappa o\hat{v}\nu\tau\alpha \; \kappa\alpha\grave{\iota} \; \delta\acute{o}\xi\alpha\nu\tau' \; \dot{\alpha}\pi\alpha\gamma\gamma\acute{\epsilon}\lambda\lambda\epsilon\iota\nu \; \mu\epsilon \; \chi\rho\acute{\eta}$$
$$\delta\acute{\eta}\mu o\upsilon \; \pi\rho o\beta o\acute{\upsilon}\lambda o\iota\varsigma \; \tau\hat{\eta}\sigma\delta\epsilon \; K\alpha\delta\mu\epsilon\acute{\iota}\alpha\varsigma \; \pi\acute{o}\lambda\epsilon\omega\varsigma$$

hat sich zuletzt P. Nicolaus[1] befasst. Er bemerkt (a.O. 59): "$\delta o\kappa o\hat{v}\nu\tau\alpha$ $\kappa\alpha\grave{\iota} \; \delta\acute{o}\xi\alpha\nu\tau'$ bedeutet kaum Verschiedenes, sondern ist als Abundanz zu erklären. Sie soll der Amtssprache die nötige Feierlichkeit verleihen. Dazu trägt auch die Mittelzäsur bei." Offenbar bezieht sich Nicolaus auf Verralls Kommentar (London 1887), wo S. 117

---

[1] *Die Frage nach der Echtheit der Schlussszene von Aischvlos' Sieben gegen Theben* (Diss. Tübingen 1967).

gesagt wird, δοκοῦντα sei Partizip des Imperfekts. Die Formel des Dekretes, das der Dichter im Auge habe, laute: ἐδόκει καὶ ἔδοξε Ersteres bezeichne die Ansicht, letzteres die Resolution der Behörde. Trifft diese Deutung Verralls zu, dann darf man nicht von stilistischer Abundanz sprechen, sondern muss anerkennen, dass der Autor bereits in den ersten Worten der Szene die steife Korrektheit dieses Heroldes zum Ausdruck bringen möchte. Offenbar bemüht sich dieser Abgesandte seiner Behörde um genaue Berichterstattung. Er wird auch später die Grenzen seiner Instruktion nicht über- schreiten. Für die Beurteilung unserer Szene ist das nicht ohne Bedeutung. Auch auf die Wirkung der Mittelzäsur hat Verrall hingewiesen: "The effect...is happily aided by the stiff and peculiar rhythm of the verse (with only the quasi-caesura after the preposition ἀπ-αγγέλλειν), in this place artistic and quite justifiable." Man sollte nie versäumen, in dieser Weise nach dem Sinn des Aussergewöhnlichen (freilich nicht des Falschen) zu fragen, um voreilige Schlüsse aus Statistiken zu vermeiden.[1a]

Nicolaus fährt (nach einigen Bemerkungen über die exponierende Funktion der Verse) fort (a.O. 60): "Der Dativ προβούλοις kann von δοκοῦντα καὶ δόξαντ' abhängen oder sich auf ἀπαγγέλλειν beziehen. Die Wortstellung spricht für eine Verbindung von προβούλοις mit ἀπαγγέλλειν, doch das ist in diesem Zusammenhang sinnlos." Da Nicolaus auf *Ag.* 604 (ταῦτ' ἀπάγγειλον πόσει) verweist, scheint er dem Verfasser der Verse *Sept.* 1005–6 auch in diesem Punkt Ungeschicklichkeit vorzuwerfen. Nun kann man sich zwar darauf versteifen, dass die überlieferte Wortstellung neben δοκεῖν und einem weiteren den Dativ regierenden Verb nicht nachweisbar ist. Nicolaus hätte sich sogar auf inschriftlich erhaltene Wendungen berufen können, die seine Skepsis zu rechtfertigen scheinen; man vergleiche z.B. Dittenberger, *Sylloge*[3] 181, 10 (Symmachievertrag Athens mit peloponnesischen Staaten aus dem Jahre 362/1):[2]...ἐὰν συνενείγκῃ Ἀθηναίων τῷ δήμῳ τὰ δόξαντα περὶ τῆς συμμαχίας und ebend. 581, 4 (Vertrag zwischen Rhodos und Hierapytna, etwa 201/200):[3] εὔξασθαι...τοῖς θεοῖς...

[1a] Vgl. auch Aisch. *Hik.* 931: καὶ γὰρ πρέπει κήρυκ' ἀπαγγέλλειν τορῶς und J. Descroix, *Le trimètre iambique* (Mâcon 1931), 257 (freundlicher Hinweis von J. K. Newman).

[2] H. Bengtson, *Die Staatsverträge des Altertums, II* (München 1962), Nr. 290.

[3] Bengtson a.O., III, bearbeitet von H. H. Schmitt (München 1969), Nr. 551, 4.

συνενεγκεῖν 'Ροδίοις καὶ 'Ιεραπυτνίοις τὰ δόξαντα περὶ τὰς συμμαχίας. Immerhin besteht ein erheblicher Unterschied: In beiden Fällen folgt das Partizip dem durch ein intransitives Verb bereits bestimmten Dativ, so dass eine Doppeldeutigkeit kaum eintritt. In unseren Versen aber ist das Verb (ἀπαγγέλλειν με χρή) zwischen die Partizipen und den von ihnen abhängigen Dativ gestellt; ein Missverständnis ist also nicht ausgeschlossen. Jedoch könnte man ähnliche Vorwürfe mancher aeschyleischen Konstruktion machen, die auf den ersten Blick schwerfällig wirkt und ihren Sinn erst bei genauer Betrachtung der Verschränkungen freigibt, dann allerdings mit besonderer Eindringlichkeit. Man vergleiche etwa *Ag.* 545: ποθεῖν ποθοῦντα τήνδε γῆν στρατὸν λέγεις; *Ag.* 635: (πῶς γὰρ λέγεις χειμῶνα...|) ἐλθεῖν τελευτῆσαί τε δαιμόνων κότῳ;—*Ag.* 1349: (λέγω|) πρὸς δῶμα δεῦρ' ἀστοῖσι κηρύσσειν βοήν, u.a.[4] Auch im vorliegenden Fall ist es möglich, die nicht alltägliche Wortstellung zu rechtfertigen: Wir dürfen sie als wirkungsvolle Sperrung bezeichnen, ohne befürchten zu müssen, dass der intendierte Sinn verkannt wird; denn der mit seiner Amtssprache vertraute Zuhörer wird den Dativ des Verses 1006 (δήμου προβούλοις) sofort mit den Verbalformen verbunden haben, von denen er auch sonst abzuhängen pflegte (also mit den Partizipien δοκοῦντα καὶ δόξαντ'), nicht mit dem Infinitiv ἀπαγγέλλειν.[5] Er mag augenblicklich empfunden haben, dass der Dichter eine andere Konstruktion gewählt haben würde, wenn er einen dem jetzigen Zusammenhang widerstrebenden Sinn gewünscht hätte, vgl. *Cho.* 264–67: ὦ παῖδες... | σιγᾶθ' ὅπως μὴ πεύσεταί τις, ὦ τέκνα, | γλώσσης χάριν δὲ πάντ' ἀπαγγελεῖ τάδε | π ρ ὸ ς τ ο ὺ ς κ ρ α - τ ο ῦ ν τ α ς. Wir werden also gut daran tun, die wirkungsvolle Sperrung zu billigen.

Über die Junktur δήμου προβούλοις hat Lloyd-Jones in einem grundlegenden Aufsatz[6] alles Erforderliche gesagt (a.O. 94). Auch Nicolaus kann sich den von Lloyd-Jones vorgetragenen Argumenten nicht entziehen, hält es jedoch für seltsam, "dass am Schluss des Stückes plötzlich noch eine neue Regierung eingeführt wird, deren

---

[4] Vgl. noch Soph. *Ant.* 904 mit der zugehörigen Literatur.

[5] Vgl. das Schol. zu 1005: δ ο κ ο ῦ ν τ α κ α ὶ δ ό ξ α ν τ'· τὰ δόξαντα τοῖς προβούλοις ἀπαγγεῖλαί με χρή.

[6] *Class. Quart.* 53 (1959), 80–115.

einzige Tat, der Erlass des Bestattungsverbots, ohne jeden Erfolg, ohne Folgen für das Stück bleibt" (a.O. 49). Sehen wir von der Vergeblichkeit des Verbotes vorerst ab, so dürfen wir vermuten, dass vor allem das Auftauchen einer "demokratischen" Behörde (Robert[7] sprach sogar von einer "radikalen Demokratie") Überraschung und Befremden ausgelöst hat: Nicolaus betont (im Anschluss an Robert), dass Aischylos im vorangehenden (echten) Teil des Stückes nur einmal vom Demos spricht (199: λευστῆρα δήμου δ' οὔ τι μὴ φύγῃ μόρον), während er sonst stets das Wort πόλις gebraucht (a.O. 48). Snells glücklichem Hinweis[8] auf die verwandte Sachlage in den Hiketiden legt er kein Gewicht bei. Trotzdem wird man, ausgehend von Snells Beobachtung, grundsätzlich feststellen dürfen, dass es bei Aischylos nur eine einzige absolute Monarchie gibt, die des Xerxes, während überall sonst eine Volksversammlung oder (den Belangen des Spieles entsprechend) ein Kronrat der Alten als Vertreter des Volkes neben dem Herrscher stehen: auch im Agamemnon (844–46: τὰ δ' ἄλλα πρὸς πόλιν τε καὶ θεούς / κοινοὺς ἀγῶνας θέντες ἐν πανηγύρει / βουλευσόμεσθα)[9] und in den Eumeniden (vgl. 290: αὐτόν τε καὶ γῆν καὶ τὸν Ἀργεῖον λεών). Die Frage, ob sich der Dichter bei Konzeption dieser Staatsform von den argivischen Verhältnissen seiner Zeit hat anregen lassen, möglicherweise mit dem unausgesprochenen Ziel, zur athenischen Politik der 60er Jahre Stellung zu nehmen,[10] braucht uns hier nicht aufzuhalten. Wir können uns bei der Feststellung beruhigen, dass er ein mythisches Exempel geschaffen hat, welches als Urbild und Ausgangspunkt einer zeitgenössischen Staatsform gelten sollte.[11] Für unsere augenblicklichen Zwecke sind einige Verse des Agamemnon aufschlussreich, an denen die Stellung des Chores (d.h. des Rates der Alten) zum König sichtbar wird. Man denke an die dem Tod

[7] C. Robert, Oidipus, I (Berlin 1915), 376.

[8] B. Snell, Aischylos und das Handeln (Philol. Suppl. 28 [1928]), 90: "Ähnliche Widersprüche zwischen dem im Mythos gegebenen König und der dem Aischylos lebendigen Polis finden sich auch in den Hiketiden."

[9] Zu diesen Versen bemerkt E. Fraenkel, Kleine Beiträge zur Klass. Philologie, I (Rom 1964), 342, "der König wolle die notwendigen Staatsgeschäfte in verfassungsmässiger Versammlung der Bürger" verhandeln lassen.

[10] Vgl. A. J. Podlecki, The Political Background of Aeschylean Tragedy (Ann Arbor 1966), 42 ff.

[11] Siehe besonders E. R. Dodds, "Morals and Politics in the 'Oresteia'," Proc. Cambr. Philol. Soc. 186 (1960), 19–31, bes. 25 u. 31.

Agamemnons unmittelbar folgende Szene! Ein Choreut möchte das Volk (die Bürger) zu Hilfe rufen, zwei andere fürchten, dass man eine Tyrannis errichten wird, vgl. 1354–55 (φροιμιάζονται γὰρ ὥς | τυραννίδος σημεῖα πράσσοντες πόλει und 1364–65 (ἀλλ᾽ οὐκ ἀνεκτόν, ἀλλὰ κατθανεῖν κρατεῖ· | πεπαιτέρα γὰρ μοῖρα τῆς τυραννίδος). Lloyd-Jones (a.O. 94) hat mit Recht auch auf *Ag.* 883-84 und auf die Erläuterung im Kommentar von Denniston – Page hingewiesen: Die Worte εἴ τε δημόθρους ἀναρχία | βουλὴν καταρρίψειεν beziehen sich vermutlich ebenfalls auf den Kronrat der Alten ("Council"). Die Annahme liegt also nahe, dass auch in der Exodos der *Septem* ein solcher in Angelegenheiten (also im Namen) des Demos sprechender Rat[12] gemeint ist: Eteokles war sein König, der Mann, mit dem er bisher (vor allem in der Notzeit der Belagerung) zusammengearbeitet hatte. Nach seinem Tod treten diese königlichen Räte für die Bestattung ihres Herrn ein, während sie die Leiche des Hochverräters von jeder Totenehrung auszuschliessen wünschen. Das ist für den, der nicht sachfremde Vorstellungen in den Text legt, folgerichtig gedacht und deutlich gesagt.

Mit dem Hinweis auf die staatsrechtlichen Verhältnisse der *Orestie* hoffen wir auch Dawes Behandlung der Wendung δήμου προβούλοις[13] entkräftet zu haben. Dawe versucht, Lloyd-Jones' zutreffende Bemerkung über die *Hiketiden* ("the δῆμος figures in it as a political entity," a.O. 94) mit dem Einfall abzutun, dieses Drama sei in einer Zeit entstanden, in der das demokratische Bewusstsein ("democratic feelings") schon weiter ausgebildet war als im Jahre 467. Ausserdem seien Anspielungen auf den Demos lediglich "nominis causa" (a.O. 22). Das erste ist unkontrollierbar, das zweite nachweislich falsch. Also kann auch Dawes Schlussfolgerung nicht richtig sein (a.O. 22): "This preoccupation with the πόλις as a political entity (sc. in der Exodos der *Septem*) is strangely at variance with the rest of the play. Therefore the scene is not by Aeschylus."

Die Formulierungen der beiden folgenden Verse (1007–8)

> Ἐτεοκλέα μὲν τόνδ᾽ ἐπ᾽ εὐνοίᾳ χθονός
> θάπτειν ἔδοξε γῆς φίλαις κατασκαφαῖς

---

[12] Vgl. Schol. B (rec.) 1006: τοῖς βουλευομένοις ὑπὲρ τοῦ δήμου. Ähnlich Lloyd-Jones a.O. 94: "...men who take counsel on behalf of the people."

[13] R. D. Dawe in *Class. Quart.* 59 (1967), 21.

hat Ed. Fraenkel (*Mus. Helv.* 21 [1964], 62) beanstandet. Der Ausdruck ἐπ' εὐνοίᾳ pflege üblicherweise nur so gebraucht zu werden, "dass die εὔνοια dem eignet, der das Subjekt des dabeistehenden Verbums ist." Das Substantiv κατασκαφαί aber sei in ungewöhnlicher Weise für den Begriff "Begräbnis" gesetzt, obwohl es doch sonst "Zerstörung" bedeute. Der erste Vorwurf wiegt nicht schwer: Fraenkel selbst verweist auf eine bemerkenswerte Ausnahme, auf die Junktur ἐπαινέσαι ἐπὶ τῇ εὐνοίᾳ (*Syll.*³ 443, 20; 548, 6), wodurch der Ausdruck des Verses 1007 aus seiner scheinbaren Isolierung schon erlöst ist. Schwerlich lässt sich ja erwarten, dass zu dieser singulären Situation eine exakte Parallele gefunden werden könne. Obendrein ist aber nachweisbar, dass der neben ἐπί stehende Dativ durchaus nicht immer den Grund für das Handeln des grammatischen Subjekts enthält. Man vergleiche Xen. *mem.* 2, 6, 12 (τοῖς ἐπ' ἀρετῇ φιλοτιμουμένοις οὕτως ἐπῇδον, sc. αἱ Σειρῆνες) oder *Syll.*³ 352, 6 (aus dem Jahre 311; die Ephesier beschliessen, Demetrios Poliorketes zu bekränzen): καὶ στεφανηφορεῖν Ἐφεσίους...ἐπὶ τοῖς εὐτυχήμασιν τοῖς ἐξηγγελμένοις (natürlich sind das glückliche Erfolge des Demetrios).—Aufregender ist der zweite Fall: κατασκαφαί bedeutet tatsächlich nur einmal (Soph. *Ant.* 920: ζῶσ' εἰς θανόντων ἔρχομαι κατασκαφάς) soviel wie Grab, sonst (auch bei Aischylos, sc. *Sept.* 46 und *Cho.* 50) "Zerstörung". Jedoch lasse man sich durch die Verteilung der Belege nicht beirren! Die Grundbedeutung des zugehörigen Verbums ist ja *fodere*, und erst in einem engeren Anwendungsbereich wird daraus *suffodiendo evertere*, vgl. Hesych κ 1411 κ α τ α σ κ ά ψ α ι · κατορύξαι. Mit Recht zitieren unsere Lexika an erster Stelle, als Beleg für diesen ursprünglichen Sinn, Theophr. *H. plant.* 4, 13, 5:...μετὰ δὲ ταῦτα κατασκάψαντα ἐπὶ θάτερα τῆς ἀμπέλου περικαθᾶραι πάσας τὰς ῥίζας (siehe auch ebend. § 6: θάτερον μέρος παρασκάπτειν). Man sollte sich also nicht darüber wundern, dass der Dichter der Exodos das deverbale Nomen in der Bedeutung "Aufgraben, Begräbnis" verwendet. Italie gibt den Text treffend wieder: "met een liefderijke begrafenis."¹⁴

---

¹⁴ Nicolaus (a.O. 60) merkt zu 1008 an, dass die Verse "eine typische Unbestimmtheit" aufweisen, weil kein Dativ neben ἔδοξε stehe. Er übersieht hierbei, dass ἔδοξε die Partizipien des Verses 1005 wieder aufnimmt, die mit dem Dativ (δήμου) προβούλοις eng verbunden sind. Jeder bereitwillige Hörer ergänzt diesen auch zu dem Impersonale des Verses 1008.

Auf die Schwierigkeiten der Verse 1009–11 hat—von den englischen Kommentatoren abgesehen—in neuerer Zeit nur Nicolaus (a.O. 61 ff.) aufmerksam gemacht, sie jedoch wohl zu rasch im Sinne seiner These behoben. Die Verse lauten:

στυγῶν γὰρ ἐχθροὺς θάνατον εἵλετ' ἐν πόλει,
ἱερῶν πατρῴων δ'(δ' om. M¹) ὅσιος ὢν μομφῆς ἄτερ
τέθνηκεν οὗπερ τοῖς νέοις θνῄσκειν καλόν.

Nicolaus meint, das Motiv des freiwilligen Heldentodes, das im Verbum εἵλετο anklinge, sei Aischylos, der sich dem Ehrencodex des Epos verpflichtet fühle, fremd. Vor allem aber vertrage es sich nicht mit dem bisherigen Verlauf der dramatischen Handlung; denn Eteokles habe den Entschluss zum tödlichen Bruderkampf unter dem Zwange des Daimons gefasst. Die Bezeichnung "Opfertod" passe also nur in sehr eingeschränktem Sinne auf seinen Untergang.

Der erste Einwand soll uns nicht aufhalten: Nicolaus selbst weist anhand sehr interessanten Materiales nach, dass die Vorstellung vom freiwillig gewählten Schlachtentod zur Zeit der Perserkriege lebendig, also auch Aischylos verfügbar war. Gegen den zweiten hilft bereits das alte Mittel der λύσις ἐκ προσώπου. Der Sprecher fasst nicht die aeschyleische Darstellung der Entscheidung des Eteokles zusammen, sondern gibt die behördliche Interpretation des Ereignisses wieder. Nach ihr, die das Wirken des Fluchdaimons nicht kennt oder geflissentlich ignoriert, hat Eteokles den Tod gewählt, um die Stadt zu retten. Sehr richtig sagt Italie zu unserer Stelle: "θάνατον κτλ. met deze uitdrukking is hetzelfe bedoeld als met πόλεως ὑπερμαχῶν ὄλωλε τῆσδε in Soph. Ant. 194." Es erhebt sich freilich sofort die Frage, ob die überlieferten Worte des Verses 1009 diesen Sinn überhaupt hergeben; denn ἐν πόλει kann weder "vor der Stadt" heissen[15] noch "zum Heile der Stadt." Herausgeber, die den Verfasser der Exodosverse als Dichter ernst nahmen, haben deshalb eine Verderbnis angezeigt. Verrall schlug vor θάνατον ἰλητὸν πόλει (...τέθνηκεν), belegte jedoch die Wendung θάνατον τέθνηκεν aus der Sprache der Tragödie nicht.[16] Noch weiter entfernte sich Weil mit seinen Vorschlägen von der Über

---

[15] Vgl. J. Geffcken, *Griech. Epigramme* (Heidelberg 1916), Nr. 65 b 2: στεσαμ πρόσθε πυλῶν (nach 480).

[16] Ausserdem muss er das von zweiter Hand in M nachgetragene δ' im Vers 1010 (also eine Berichtigung der ersten Abschrift) weglassen.

lieferung; er konjizierte ὄλεθρον εἶργε τῇ πόλει und στέφανον εἷλε τῇ πόλει. Andere Kritiker haben sich auf Berichtigung der beanstandeten präpositionalen Wendung konzentriert: Jacobs befürwortete θάνατον εἷλετ᾽ ἐν τέλει, Francken θάνατον εἷλετ᾽ ἐν πύλαις. Tucker druckte θάνατον εἷλετ᾽ εὖ πόλει ("he chose death for the country's good") und betonte mit Recht, dass so die beiden offiziellen Gründe für den Tod des Königs klarer hervortreten: Eteokles starb im Dienst des Staates; er fiel ohne eine Gottheit zu beleidigen. Sprachlich besonders elegant ist Broadheads Vorschlag,[17] σχεθὼν γὰρ ἐχθροὺς θάνατον εἴληχεν πόλει zu schreiben. Broadhead musste allerdings in Kauf nehmen, dass dann die Aussagen der Verse 1009 und 1011 (τέθνηκεν οὗπερ τοῖς νέοις θνῄσκειν καλόν) inhaltlich einander sehr nahe kommen: Jeweils drückt ein präsentisches Perfekt den augenblicklichen Zustand des Königs aus. Hierbei passt σχεθών nicht besser als στυγῶν. Vermutlich haben Jacobs, Francken, und Tucker die Korruptel an der richtigen Stelle gesucht; denn die Form εἷλετο und das in ihr enthaltene Lob wird man nur ungern aufgeben. Hinzu kommt aber nun, dass sich der nüchterne Dativ (πόλει) in ähnlichen Zusammenhängen nicht nachweisen lässt, offenbar auch nicht auf attischen Grabinschriften.[18] Der Gedanke an den Vorteil des Staates pflegt dort umschrieben zu werden. An unserer Stelle ist er bereits in der ersten Hälfte des Verses 1009 angedeutet. Unter diesen Voraussetzungen verliert auch Tuckers Vorschlag an Glaubwürdigkeit. Da Francken mit εἷλετ᾽ ἐν πύλαις eine in der jetzigen Situation nicht mehr relevante Einzelheit (ἐν πύλαις) zu stark unterstreicht, bleibt als besonders treffende Konjektur nur die von Jacobs gewählte Wendung (εἷλετ᾽ ἐν τέλει) übrig, es sei denn, man bevorzuge am betonten Versende einen allgemeinen Begriff, etwa ein Adverb (denkbar ist z.B. θάνατον εἷλετ᾽ εὐκλεῶς, vgl. *Ag.* 1304 und ähnliche Stellen).[19] Sichere Ergebnisse sind freilich auch mit diesen Über-

---

[17] *Class. Quart.* 44 (1950), 121.

[18] Die üblichen Wendungen der Prosa sind ὀλέσθαι πρὸ πόλεως oder μάχεσθαι ὑπέρ τινος, vgl. Isokr. *or.* 4, 77: καλῶς ὑπὲρ τῆς πόλεως ἀποθνῄσκειν.

[19] In Vers 1011 möchte Broadhead ὥσπερ statt οὗπερ lesen. Aber der Vergleich eines Zustandes mit dem ihm vorangehenden Vorgang ist abwegig. Eteokles liegt dort, wo es sich für junge Leute zu sterben ziemt, d.h. auf dem Schlachtfeld (zu dem in unserem Fall die Stadtbefestigung gehört).—Den Vers 1010, dessen Schwierigkeiten Nicolaus (a.O. 69) unnötig übertreibt, hat in neuerer Zeit Italie hinreichend erklärt.

legungen nicht gewonnen; denn wenn, wie soeben festgestellt, die Stadtbefestigung ein Teil des Schlachtfeldes ist, lässt sich die Überlieferung halten.

> 1020 οὕτω πετηνῶν τόνδ' ὑπ' οἰωνῶν δοκεῖ
> ταφέντ' ἀτίμως τοὐπιτίμιον λαβεῖν.

"So, das heisst von den geflügelten Vögeln bestattet, soll er in ehrloser Weise seinen Lohn empfangen." Die Kommentatoren fühlen sich an Gorgias erinnert. Nicolaus (a.O. 70 f.) formuliert: "…ὑπ' οἰωνῶν…ταφέντ' ist die bekannte gorgianische Vorstellung γῦπες ἔμψυχοι τάφοι" (vgl. Vors.⁶ 82 B 5a). Aber der von Nicolaus wenig später gezogene Schluss, der Dichter unserer Verse habe ein von Gorgias geprägtes Bild aufgenommen, überzeugt nicht; denn im Text des Dramas handelt es sich um die besondere Art der Bestattung, die der ehrenvollen Behandlung des Eteokles betont gegenübergestellt wird (vgl. unsere Verse mit 1008 θάπτειν ἔδοξε γῆς φίλαις κατασκαφαῖς).²⁰ Dieser Gedanke wächst aus dem Zusammenhang ungezwungen hervor; um ihn formulieren zu können, brauchte der Dichter nicht auf vorgeprägte Wendungen zurückzugreifen. Berücksichtigt man, dass der Begriff des Begrabens durch den Gegensatz zu den Anordnungen über die Behandlung des Eteokles hervorgerufen ist, also eine entsprechende Formulierung nahelegte (vgl. 1008 θάπτειν, 1021 ταφέντ'), so kann man alle in 1020–21 vereinigten Vorstellungen schon bei Homer finden. Man vergleiche besonders X 335–6 (σὲ μὲν κύνες ἠδ' οἰωνοί / ἑλκήσουσ' ἀϊκῶς, τὸν δὲ κτεριοῦσιν Ἀχαιοί) und Λ 453–4 (ἀλλ' οἰωνοί / ὠμησταὶ ἐρύουσι, περὶ πτερὰ πυκνὰ βαλόντες). Der Verfasser des beanstandeten Textes ist ein Schüler Homers gewesen und sicherlich kein schlechter. Das zeigt schon der ausgewogene Bau beider Verse: Im ersten gruppieren sich die einzelnen Begriffe systematisch um das Demonstrativpronomen, in der Mitte des zweiten steht, eingerahmt von zwei Verbalformen, die Vorstellung einer unehrenhaften Belohnung, also ein grimmiges Oxymoron. Wenn bei den modernen Interpreten in diesem Zusammenhang, nicht selten in verächtlichem Ton, von rhetorischen Figuren die Rede ist (vgl. Nicolaus a.O. 71),²¹ so sollten sie uns wissen lassen, weshalb gerade

---

²⁰ Mit vollem Recht bemerkt Tucker (zu 1020 f., d.i. 1011 f. seiner Zählung): "But here it is ταφή and not τάφος which is in point."

²¹ "Daher begnügt man sich am besten mit der Feststellung der rhetorischen Figur."

Nachdichter (Interpolatoren) diese Kunst eindringlicher Wort-
fügung beherrschen dürfen, Aischylos aber nicht.

> 1022 καὶ μήθ' ὁμαρτεῖν τυμβοχόα χειρώματα
> μήτ' ὀξυμόλποις προσσέβειν οἰμώγμασιν,
> ἄτιμον εἶναι δ' ἐκφορᾶς φίλων ὕπο.

Alle Erklärer sind sich darüber einig, dass Polyneikes hier von den
beiden wesentlichen Teilen der Totenehrung ausgeschlossen wird,
vgl. z.B. X 386 (κεῖται πὰρ νήεσσι νέκυς ἄκλαυτος ἄθαπτος /
Πάτροκλος). Das anderenorts nicht belegte Verb προσσέβειν wird
deshalb die Bedeutung "ausserdem ehren" haben (vgl. LSJ),
nicht aber "weiterhin ehren," wie Verrall wollte ("honour him
further than they have already done in the foregoing θρῆνος").[22] So
weit bestehen keine ernsthaften Schwierigkeiten. Trotzdem ist das
Verständnis der ausgeschriebenen Verse für den heutigen Leser
erschwert. Der Grund hierfür ist nicht auf den ersten Blick ersicht-
lich, ergibt sich aber aus folgenden Feststellungen: Χείρωμα ist ein
nomen rei actae, abgeleitet von χειροῦσθαι, das seinerseits von
χείρων deriviert ist. Es bedeutet "Unterwerfung" als Ergebnis des
Unterwerfens.[23] Nun hat Wackernagel im Jahre 1890 behauptet,[24]
vermittels einer "durch assoziation bewirkten bedeutungsverschiebung" sei die Bildung χείρωμα mit χείρ in Verbindung
gebracht worden. Wackernagels Formulierung ist sehr vorsichtig,
sie lässt die formale Regelwidrigkeit seiner Annahme absichtlich
deutlich werden: "Nehmen wir dagegen χειρόω als derivat von
χείρων, so ist formell alles in ordnung, und die entwicklung der
bedeutung 'inferiorem reddo' zu der bedeutung 'opprimo' erklärt
sich durch die assoziation mit χείρ. Am stärksten tritt der einfluss
des letzteren wortes in Aeschylus' τυμβοχόα χειρώματα (Sept. 1022)
hervor." Zuversichtlicher spricht Ernst Fraenkel:[25] "Erst durch
Volksetymologie wurde es (sc. das Verbum χειροῦν) mehr und
mehr mit χείρ verknüpft, was in dem äschyl. τυμβοχόα χειρώματα

---

[22] Für bedeutungslos hält das Präverb Italie. Er verweist auf Ag. 317 (θεοῖς μὲν
αὖθις...προσεύξομαι) und auf Prom. 937 (σέβου, προσεύχου). Indessen überzeugt keine
der beiden Parallelstellen.

[23] Vgl. Soph. O.T. 560: ἄφαντος ἔρρει θανασίμῳ χειρώματι. Ferner Debrunner, Griech.
Wortbildungslehre (Heidelberg 1917), § 309–311; Schwyzer, Griech. Grammatik, I (München
1939), 523.

[24] Kuhns Ztschr. 30, 300 = Kleine Schriften, I (Göttingen 1953), 663.

[25] Griech. Denominativa (Göttingen 1906), 89.

(τὰ διὰ χειρῶν ἐργαζόμενα schol. rec.) seinen stärksten Ausdruck gefunden hat." Als erwiesene Tatsache sieht das Ed. Fraenkel (zu Aesch. *Ag.* 1326, Kommentar III 619) an. Lloyd-Jones folgt ihm (a.O. 109: "the *abusio* is a notable one"), versucht indessen, die vermeintliche Katachrese durch Hinweis auf Soph. *O.K.* 698 (ἀχείρωτον φύτευμα "nicht von Menschenhand gepflanzt") zu rechtfertigen. So hat sich denn Weckleins Übertragung "Hantierungen" (kommentierte Ausgabe Leipzig 1903) fast ausnahmslos durchgesetzt, ungeachtet der Tatsache, dass der Satz nun kaum noch konstruiert werden kann (vgl. Nicolaus a.O. 71). Die skizzierte Geschichte des Problems ist in der Tat sehr merkwürdig: Aus einer vagen, keineswegs befriedigenden Übersetzung (etwa "Tätigkeit der Hände beim Aufwerfen des Grabhügels") schloss man auf eine für dieses Nomen unbelegbare, angeblich volksetymologisch bedingte Bedeutungsverschiebung und leitete aus ihr das Recht ab, die Sprache des Verfassers zu tadeln. Es fragt sich, ob diese Rüge nicht doch voreilig erteilt worden ist.

Die Nomina auf -μα bezeichnen in klassischer Zeit fast ausschliesslich das Ergebnis der Handlung, worunter eine Abstraktion (z.B. παίδευμα, ἅρπαγμα, δόγμα), häufig aber eine Sache vorgestellt wird (bei Aischylos z.B. βόσκημα, δώρημα, πύργωμα u.a.). Daneben stehen Fälle, in denen unter der *res acta* eine Person verstanden ist. Berücksichtigt man nur die Nomina auf -ημα und -ωμα, so kann man folgende aeschyleische Beispiele namhaft machen (die meisten sind Deverbalia): ἀπαιόλημα (*Cho.* 1002) = *fraudator*,[26] μέλημα (*Cho.* 235) = *deliciae* (als Bezeichnung Orests), μίσημα (*Eum.* 73) = *persona odiosa*, φρούρημα (*Sept.* 449, 537) = *custos*, ὠφέλημα (*Prom.* 613) = *adiutor*, auch πίστωμα (*Pers.* 171: γηραλέα πιστώματα = πιστοὶ γέροντες) und τέκνωμα (Frg. 315, 2 N.² = 625, 2 M.). Vergleiche ferner Χρυσηΐδων μείλιγμα (*Ag.* 1439) = *deliciae* und Ἑλλάδος λωτίσματα (Frg. 99, 17 N.² = 145, 18 M.). Unter den neueren Kommentatoren hat es nur Tucker gewagt, diesen Befund für das Verständnis der oben ausgeschriebenen Verse auszunutzen. Er versteht unter χειρώματα (dem Ergebnis des Unterwerfens) Sklaven (σώματα κεχειρωμένα), von denen Bestattung und Totenklage ausgeführt wird. Damit entfallen die schwersten Anstösse an der Konstruktion; das jeweilige Objekt in Vers 1022 und in Vers

---

[26] Vgl. Groeneboom z.St. (Kommentar S. 268) mit weiteren Belegen.

1023 (αὐτῷ bzw. αὐτόν) ergänzt sich ebenso leicht wie der Subjekts-akkusativ in Vers 1024 (αὐτόν). Der Inhalt der Verse befremdet nicht: Auch in den *Choephoren* werden die Klagegesänge von einem Sklavenchor vorgetragen. Die Vorstellung, dass Unfreie die mit der Anlage des Grabes verbundenen Erdarbeiten verrichten, war für den Griechen des 5. Jahrhunderts selbstverständlich. Wir werden in Kürze sehen, dass sich ein wirkungsvoller Kontrast ergibt, wenn Antigone, die Königstochter, sich bereit erklärt, eine Tätigkeit auf sich zu nehmen, die üblicherweise Sklaven oblag.

Zu Vers 1024 zitiert Nicolaus (a.O. 71) eine längere Aussage P. Corssens,[27] der behauptet hat, die ἐκφορά setze voraus, "dass der Tote im Hause vorher aufgebahrt und dann vom Haus aus bestattet wurde." Corssen meinte, der freiere Gebrauch an unserer Stelle gestatte den Schluss auf Abhängigkeit von Eur. *Phoin.* 1627–28, wo gesagt ist, man solle die Leiche des Eteokles in den Palast tragen, natürlich um sie dort vor der Bestattung auszustellen. Nicolaus zweifelt die Richtigkeit dieser Folgerung an, weil "beim Pathos des Siebenschlusses die Logik vernachlässigt" worden sein könne, was dann Euripides auf seine Weise kritisiert haben mochte. Wir indessen meinen, auf diese subtilen Überlegungen verzichten zu dürfen; denn Corssen's Folgerung ist zwar für die von Solon geregelten Gebräuche des attischen Bürgers verbindlich (vgl. Dem. *or.* 43, 62: τὸν ἀποθανόντα προτίθεσθαι ἔνδον), schwerlich aber für die Situation der *Septem*. Die beiden Threnoi (875–1004), vorgetragen vom weiblichen Chor und von den beiden nächsten Angehörigen, den Schwestern, sind vor den auf der Bühne auf-gebahrten Toten erklungen, und diesen Hergang musste jeder athenische Zuschauer als heroische Form der Prothesis ansehen; denn die rituelle Totenklage war ja gerade in Athen mit der Prothesis fest verbunden.[28] Trifft diese unsere Überlegung zu, dann darf auch der Ausdruck ἐκφορά in V. 1024 nicht beanstandet werden.

1025   τοιαῦτ' ἔδοξε τῷδε Καδμείων τέλει.

[27] P. Corssen, *Die Antigone des Sophokles, ihre theatralische und sittliche Wirkung* (Berlin 1968), 34.

[28] Vgl. Mau, *RE* 3 (1897), 335, 20 s.v. Bestattung; E. Reiner, *Die rituelle Totenklage der Griechen* (Tübinger Beiträge 30, Stuttgart 1938) 41; ferner Plat. *Leg.* 960 a 1.

Deiktische Verwendung des Demonstrativpronomens ist nicht zwingend; denn Aischylos hat es an zahlreichen Stellen anaphorisch gebraucht (vgl. z.B. *Cho.* 510, 765; *Eum.* 438). Es ist also von dem oben (sc. V. 1006) genannten τέλος die Rede. Zwar ist Lloyd-Jones' Vorschlag eleganter (a.O. 95): "τῷδε...τέλει might mean 'the government which I represent'." Ich habe jedoch keinen Beleg für diesen speziellen Gebrauch des Pronomens finden können.—Der Singular τέλος als Bezeichnung einer Behörde ist in der Tat einzigartig, aber nicht unverständlich. *Τέλος* ist die Autorität (vgl. Hes. *Op.* 669), auch die der Behörde. Die Möglichkeit, darunter nicht nur das autorisierte (staatliche) Amt zu verstehen, sondern auch dessen jeweiligen Inhaber, lag nicht fern. Der Verfasser unseres Verses mag von Wendungen wie Pind. *N.* 11, 9 ausgegangen sein: ἀλλὰ σὺν δόξᾳ τέλος / δωδεκάμηνον περᾶσαί νιν ἀτρώτῳ καρδίᾳ, d.h. "das zwölfmonatige Amt" ("peragat magistratum duodecim mensuum" Dissen). Der Vers 1025 besagt also: "Solches hat die oben bezeichnete Autorität (Behörde) der Kadmeer beschlossen."

Ihren Entschluss, Polyneikes ungeachtet des öffentlichen Verbotes zu bestatten, begründet Antigone mit folgenden Worten (1031–32):

> δεινὸν τὸ κοινὸν σπλάγχνον, οὗ πεφύκαμεν
> μητρὸς ταλαίνης κἀπὸ δυστήνου πατρός. [29]

Gegen diese Verse erhebt Nicolaus (a.O. 75) folgenden Vorwurf: "Die Schwester beruft sich nicht auf die Religion, sondern allein auf die Blutsverwandtschaft. Der Horizont des Göttlichen, innerhalb dessen das tragische Geschehen sonst bei Aischylos stattfindet, fehlt hier." Zunächst muss man jedoch, so wenden wir ein, feststellen, dass Antigone auf das Ansinnen des Heroldes reagiert. In ihrer Antwort an den Überbringer des staatlichen Bestattungsverbotes hat sie keine Veranlassung, die Bedeutung blutsverwandtschaftlicher Bande metaphysisch zu begründen. Hephaistos tut derartiges auch nicht, wenn er dem drängenden Schergen Kratos zu verstehen gibt, wie schwer es ihm fällt, die Strafe an Prometheus zu vollziehen (*Prom.* 39): τὸ συγγενές τοι δεινὸν ἥ θ' ὁμιλία. In beiden Fällen genügt der Hinweis auf die Kraft dieser Beziehung. Der Unterschied besteht lediglich darin, dass Hephaistos gegen sein besseres Wissen,

---

[29] Zur Konstruktion des Satzes vgl. die sorgfältige Erläuterung Tuckers (1022–23 seiner Zählung). Tucker übersetzt: "Mighty the bond of the common loins whence we are sprung—from unhappy mother and from ill-starred sire."

nur aus Furcht vor Zeus, sofort nachgibt, während Antigone
entschlossen ist, ihre Worte durch die Tat zu bekräftigen. Sie ist
zwar von desselben Überzeugung beseelt wie die Heldin des
sophokleischen Dramas (d.h. in dieser besonderen Situation vom
Vorrang geschwisterlicher Liebe vor der Zuständigkeit staatlicher
Behörden und vor der Berechtigung öffentlicher Vergeltung),[30]
begnügt sich aber ganz naiv mit dem Vorhandensein dieses sittlichen
Gebotes. Sie hört die Stimme ihres Innern und gehorcht ihr. Erst
Sophokles lässt seine Heldin über Wert und Herkunft beider Aspekte
reflektieren, er füllt also etwas aus, was in unserer Szene fehlt, bzw.
nicht ohne Berechtigung ausgelassen worden ist. Wir werden unten
sehen, dass sich dieses Ergebnis auch von anderer Seite her
bestätigt.[31]

Wir übergehen die Verse 1233–34, zu denen Lloyd-Jones (a.O.
109 f.) Entscheidendes gesagt hat, und wenden uns der schwierigen
Partie 1035–41 zu:

$$
\begin{aligned}
1035 \quad & \text{τούτου δὲ σάρκας οὐδὲ κοιλογάστορες} \\
& \text{λύκοι πάσονται· μὴ δοκησάτω τινί·} \\
& \text{τάφον γὰρ αὐτὴ καὶ κατασκαφὰς ἐγώ,} \\
& \text{γυνή περ οὖσα, τῷδε μηχανήσομαι,} \\
& \text{κόλπῳ φέρουσα βυσσίνου πεπλώματος,} \\
1040 \quad & \text{καὐτὴ καλύψω· μηδέ τῳ δόξῃ πάλιν.} \\
& \text{θάρσει παρέσται μηχανὴ δραστήριος.}
\end{aligned}
$$

Antigones feurige, fast wilde Entschlossenheit spiegelt sich in der
Emphase ihrer Beteuerungen. "Dessen Fleisch werden nicht einmal
heisshungrige Wölfe fressen können. Keiner soll derartiges beschliessen!"[32] Wenn die Art des Grabes selbst Wölfen den Zutritt
verwehrt, sind Hunde und Vögel erst recht ausgeschlossen. Diese
harmloseren Tiere brauchen nicht genannt zu werden, Priens

---

[30] Vgl. Groeneboom z.St. (Kommentar S. 252): "In de eerste beide versen (sc. in
1031–32) ligt de grondgedachte van Sophocles' Antigone: het geslacht zegeviert oven
den staat."

[31] Wir werden also Nicolaus nicht folgen können wenn er (im Anschluss an die oben
zitierten Sätze) meint, der Zusammenstoss zwischen Staat und Familie sei nur vorder-
gründig, eine "Podiumsdiskussion des Begriffspaares φύσει δίκαιον—νόμῳ (θέσει) δίκαιον"
werde in dramatische Handlung umgesetzt. Diese Unterstellung ist deshalb unstatthaft,
weil Antigone instinktiv handelt. Der Dichter gibt nirgends zu erkennen, dass er die
sophistische Antithese gekannt habe.

[32] Vgl. Tucker z.St.: "'Let none resolve it' is more pointed than 'let none think it'."

Vermutung (nach σάρκας 1035 fehle die zweite und vor οὐδέ 1036 die erste Hälfte je eines Verses) ist also nicht berechtigt.— Das Verständnis des folgenden Begründungssatzes ist durch das Fehlen eines Objektes beim Partizip φέρουσα etwas erschwert. Indessen sollte über die Art der erforderlichen Ergänzung kein Zweifel bestehen. Die Konstruktion legt es nahe, die als Objekte zu μηχανήσομαι genannten Nomina (τάφον und κατασκαφάς) zu supplieren. Ersteres tat Verrall ("'carrying a grave', i.e. carrying the sufficient means of burial"), letzteres Blomfield ("sinu autem latura erat τὰς κατασκαφάς, i.e. satis pulveris ad inspargendum cadaver"). Groeneboom lehnte das ab (Komment. S. 253: "alles geforceerd; men verwacht bij φέρουσα een object als κόνιν"), kaum mit Recht; denn Antigones Trumpf besteht ja gerade darin, dass sie das "Grab" mit ihren bescheidenen Mitteln herbeischaffen kann. Dass sie mit ihrer Formulierung Erde (bzw. Staub) bezeichnet, sollte sich von selbst verstehen (vgl. 1040: καὐτὴ καλύψω).[33] Man ist indessen nicht berechtigt, unter dem Eindruck des sophokleischen Dramas an eine symbolische Bestattung zu denken, als ob eine Hand voll Staub genügt hätte, ohne dass Antigone ihr Gewand zu beschmutzen brauchte (so Nicolaus a.O. 77). Nein, die Sprecherin betont ja nachdrücklich, dass auch heisshungrige Wölfe dem Toten nichts anhaben werden. Sie beabsichtigt also, mit eigener Kraft Erde für einen ganzen Grabhügel herbeizuschaffen. Das Pathos ihrer Worte hat nicht zuletzt den Zweck, unüberhörbar darzutun, dass sie zu dieser schweren Arbeit fest entschlossen ist.—Nur beiläufig sei bemerkt, dass Lloyd-Jones (a.O. 97–99) versucht hat, die von Schütz und Stanley vertretene Auffassung wieder zu Ehren zu bringen und den Leichnam selbst als Objekt zu φέρουσα zu ergänzen. Dawe[34] hat ihm erfolgreich widersprochen. Der spottende Ton freilich, in dem er sich mit der mutigen, anregenden Arbeit des Oxforder Gräzisten auseinandersetzt, dient der Sache wenig, da der Leser allzu oft vom eigentlichen Problem abgelenkt wird. Ausserdem ist es untunlich, von der falschen Voraussetzung auszugehen (a.O. 24 oben), der Dichter habe ἐν κόλπῳ geschrieben;

---

[33] Vgl. auch Tucker z.St. (1028 f. seiner Zählung): "With φέρουσα we must supply some word naturally suggested by the context, e.g. γῆν or κόνιν ... or perhaps more strictly a vague τὸ δέον."

[34] *Class. Quart.* 59 (1967), 23–25.

denn damit wird eine wesentliche Pointe verdeckt, nämlich die, dass Antigone im Gewandbausch ihr einziges Hilfsmittel erblickt. Durch Hervorhebung dieser ihrer armseligen Ausrüstung gewinnt auch die Kühnheit ihres Entschlusses an Gewicht.

Zu unserer Versgruppe noch folgende Bemerkungen! Nicolaus (a.O. 71) lehnt Piersons Konjektur in V. 1037 (τάφον γὰρ αὐτὴ καὶ κατασκαφάς ἐγώ...für überliefertes αὐτῷ) ab. Er meint, die Änderung nehme dem Vers die gesamte, auf das in Endposition stehende Pronomen (ἐγώ) hin angelegte Spannung. Dagegen lässt sich folgendes vorbringen: Eine so weite Sperrung wie αὐτῷ...τῷδε lässt sich beim deiktischen Pronomen schwerlich finden,[35] hingegen ist die Trennung αὐτὴ...ἔγωγε, wie sie durch Piersons Konjektur entsteht, durchaus harmlos, da nur das zweite Objekt (κατασκαφάς) zwischen beide Nomina tritt. Es liegt also einfache Verschränkung vor.[36]—Der Ausdruck μηδέ τῳ δόξῃ πάλιν (1040) bietet keine unüberwindlichen Schwierigkeiten. Zwar hat πάλιν die Bedeutung 'contra' an den übrigen Belegen bei Aischylos nicht. Wohl aber ist diese Verwendung bereits Homer vertraut (vgl. I 55–56: οὔ τίς τοι τὸν μῦθον ὀνόσσεται.../οὐδὲ πάλιν ἐρέει). Der Sinn ist also: "Niemand möge einen gegenteiligen Beschluss fassen!" Mit Recht weist Tucker darauf hin, dass Antigone mit diesen Worten ihre Wendung aus 1036 wiederaufnimmt (μὴ δοκησάτω τινί, "let no man resolve it"). Derartige Wiederholungen gehören zur Kraft der Sprache, die das mutige Mädchen hier führt, um die Unumstösslichkeit ihres Entschlusses zu bekräftigen.

Den beiden Reden folgt eine Stichomythie von 12 Versen. Zunächst warnt der Herold seinem Auftrag getreu vor Ungehorsam, worauf Antigone diese Äusserung als verfehlt bezeichnet. Dann erinnert der Herold an den Zorn des Volkes, die Oidipustochter aber bleibt trotzdem bei ihrer Absicht:

[35] Vgl. Cho. 904: ἕπου, πρὸς αὐτὸν τόνδε σε σφάξαι θέλω, auch Cho. 208: αὐτοῦ τ' ἐκείνου καὶ συνεμπόρου τινός.

[36] Auch Nicolaus' Hinweis auf ein Satzform αὐτῷ...ἐγώ.../γυνή περ οὖσα, τῷδε (Chiasmus) kann die Überlieferung nicht rechtfertigen; denn es besteht von der erwähnten Singularität des Ausdrucks abgesehen, kein Grund, Polyneikes so kräftig hervorzuheben.—Übrigens verstehe ich Nicolaus' anderen Einwand gegen Pierson nicht. Er schreibt: "Dagegen ist einzuwenden dass αὐτή an keiner betonten Stelle des Verses, nicht am Anfang und nicht nach der Zäsur steht." Es steht freilich vor der Zäsur, ist aber doch ähnlich hervorgehoben wie in Hik. 939: εἴσῃ σύ τ' αὐτὸς χοἰ ξυνέμποροι σέθεν.

Κη. αὐδῶ πόλιν σε μὴ βιάζεσθαι τάδε.
Αν. αὐδῶ σε μὴ περισσὰ κηρύσσειν ἐμοί.
Κη. τραχύς γε μέντοι δῆμος ἐκφυγὼν κακά.
Αν. τράχυν᾽· ἄθαπτος οὗτος οὐ γενήσεται (1042–45).

Auffällig ist die schroffe Entschiedenheit, mit der jeder Sprecher seinen Standpunkt verteidigt, ohne einen gedanklichen Fortschritt zuzulassen. Sinn der vier Verse kann es nur sein, die Unvereinbarkeit der Meinungen nochmals zu verdeutlichen: Antigones Worte sind die Negation dessen, was der Herold sagt, und umgekehrt. Durch diese einzigartige scharfe Grenzziehung wird also auch die singuläre formale Parallelität der Ausdrucks bedingt: Diese ist situations-gebunden und sollte nicht als Kennzeichen nachäschyleischer Dialogführung bezeichnet werden.[37] Erst ab 1046 versucht der Herold (bezeichnenderweise in einer Frage), auf Antigones Vor-stellungen einzuwirken:

ἀλλ᾽ ὃν πόλις στυγεῖ, σὺ τιμήσεις τάφῳ;

Wirklich nimmt Antigone seinen Gedanken auf. Aber sie begnügt sich nicht damit, ihr Vorhaben zu rechtfertigen (vgl. 1046 τιμήσεις: 1047 διατετίμηται), sondern versucht gleichzeitig, in ihrer Antwort den Hass des Staates zu entkräften:

ἤδη τὰ τοῦδ᾽ οὐ διατετίμηται θεοῖς;

"Have not the questions of his honour or dishonour been already settled by a higher power—the Gods?" So Tucker, dessen vor-züglicher Erklärung ich folge.[38] Die Auffassung des Satzes als einer Frage gestattet es, die Überlieferung beizubehalten. Fast denselben Sinn erhält Lloyd-Jones durch Übernahme von Paley's Konjektur τοῦδε (statt τοῦδ᾽ οὐ): "Already the Gods have dealt him his full punishment" (a.O. 110 f.).[39] Schlagartig lösen diese Verse eine lebhafte Debatte aus, durch

---

[37] So W. Jens, *Die Stichomythie in der frühen griech. Tragödie* (Zetemata 11, München 1955), 10. Gerade ein Nachahmer hätte sich vermutlich an übliche Formen des Streit-gespräches gehalten.

[38] Vgl. auch Italie: "Is dan de zaak van zijn τιμή niet reeds door de goden uitgemaakt?"

[39] Paley selbst verstand den Satz so: "Since the gods have ceased to honour him I must honour him"—grammatisch unbefriedigend (vgl. Verrall z.St.). Fehlerhaft auch Groeneboom: "Nog niet is door de goden een beslissend oordeel uitgesproken over Polynices' zaak."

die es auf kürzestem Raum möglich wird, nun auch die Motive
beider Partner sichtbar zu machen:

> Κη. οὐ πρίν γε χώραν τήνδε κινδύνῳ βαλεῖν.
> Αν. παθὼν κακῶς κακοῖσιν ἀντημείβετο.
> Κη. ἀλλ᾽ εἰς ἅπαντας ἀνθ᾽ ἑνὸς τόδ᾽ ἔργον ἦν.
> Αν. Ἔρις περαίνει μῦθον ὑστάτη θεῶν.
> ἐγὼ δὲ θάψω...

Die Vergeltung (sc. im Bruderkampf) so betont der Herold, ist
Polyneikes erst durch den Zug gegen die Heimat möglich geworden.
—Er hat Gleiches mit Gleichem vergolten, antwortet Antigone,
einem anerkannten hellenischen Grundsatz folgend.[40]—Der Herold
hält ihrer Ansicht entgegen, dass eine solche Rache den ganzen Staat
in Mitleidenschaft gezogen habe. Daraufhin bricht Antigone das
Gespräch ab.

Die Argumentation des Streitgespräches setzt, wie Kaufmann-
Bühler[41] gezeigt hat, folgendes voraus: Polyneikes ist nach der
Ansicht beider Parteien gewaltsam vertrieben worden und hatte ein
Recht auf Rückkehr. Er setzte sich jedoch ins Unrecht, als er diese
persönliche Fehde auf den Staat ausdehnte. Kaufmann-Bühler hat
ausserdem nachgewiesen, dass die Gedankenschritte der Verse
1048–50 mitsamt den oben genannten Voraussetzungen nur aus
dem aeschyleischen Drama, nicht aber aus Sophokles oder Euripides
hergeleitet werden können. Daran zu erinnern, scheint für das
Verständnis unserer Stichomythie wichtig zu sein; denn Antigone
bricht das Gespräch eben deshalb ab, weil sie an ihrer kurz zuvor
erwähnten Ansicht (die göttliche Strafe sei an Polyneikes bereits
vollzogen worden, sie bedürfe also menschlicher Ergänzung nicht)
unbedingt festhält. Sie weiss zwar, dass auch der Herold ein
unantastbares (göttliches) Recht vertritt, glaubt jedoch, diesem
einen noch höheren Anspruch entgegenstellen zu müssen. Da sie
spürt, dass der Staatsvertreter den Kreis seiner Instruktionen nicht
verlassen kann, hält sie eine weitere Diskussion nicht für möglich.
In der kurzen Stichomythie sind also die beiden Ansichten durch-
sichtiger geworden, sie stehen jedoch am Ende einander genauso

---

[40] Vgl. Archil. Frg. 66 D.² = 126 West: Ἕν δ᾽ ἐπίσταμαι μέγα / τὸν κακῶς μ᾽ ἔρδοντα
(μ᾽ ἔρδ.Turyn, δρῶντα Theophil.) δέννοισ᾽ (Herzog, δεινοῖς Theophil.) ἀνταμείβεσθαι κακοῖς.

[41] D. Kaufmann-Bühler, *Begriff und Funktion der Dike in den Tragödien des Aischylos*
(Diss. Heidelberg 1951), 55.

unvereinbar gegenüber wie zuvor. Wahrscheinlich würde der moderne Betrachter der Gedankenführung leichter folgen können, wenn Antigone ihren wichtigsten Gedanken (1047: ἤδη τὰ τοῦδ' οὐ διατετίμηται θεοῖς;) nach Vers 1050 (Κη. ἀλλ' εἰς ἅπαντας ἀνθ' ἑνὸς τόδ' ἔργον ἦν) in einprägsamer Verallgemeinerung wiederholt hätte. Dann läge ein äusserlich abgerundetes Gespräch vor. Das geschieht jedoch nicht. Statt eine Grundsatzerklärung zuzulassen, leitet der Dichter rasch zur Tat über, die der Herold nicht verhindern kann, weil die Wiederholung des Verbotes sein einziges Machtmittel ist (1051–53):

> Αν. Ἔρις περαίνει μῦθον ὑστάτη θεῶν.
> ἐγὼ δὲ θάψω τόνδε· μὴ μακρηγόρει.
> Κη. ἀλλ' αὐτόβουλος ἴσθ', ἀπεννέπω δ' ἐγώ.

Über den Sinn dieses auf den ersten Blick befremdenden Ausgangs des Gespräches soll später noch gesprochen werden. Vorerst halten wir nur so viel fest: Für den Handlungsablauf ist es nicht ohne Bedeutung, dass Antigone lediglich mit einem Überbringer staatlicher Befehle konfrontiert wird, nicht aber mit einer Person, die befugt wäre, Gegenmassnahmen zu ergreifen. Schon deshalb ist es ausgeschlossen, dass die Probulen auf der Bühne erscheinen, wie man aus τῷδε...τέλει (1025) geschlossen hat.[42] Vielmehr lautet die Voraussetzung unserer Szene: Die Probulen hielten ihren Beschluss für so selbstverständlich, seine Ausführung für so sicher, dass sie nicht einmal eine Strafe für den Fall der Übertretung festgesetzt haben. Das hat zur Folge, dass der Herold, der Repräsentant der neuen Regierung in der Öffentlichkeit, am Ende des mit Antigone geführten Gespräches keine wirksamen Drohungen aussprechen kann. Seine Hilflosigkeit wird kurz darauf noch sinnfälliger, wenn die Hälfte des Chores, der bislang den weiblichen Teil der Bevölkerung Thebens darstellte, für Antigone Partei ergreift und sich am Begräbnis des Polyneikes beteiligt. Es ist undenkbar, dass ein Dichter, mag er auch noch so schlecht gewesen sein, diese etwas komplizierten Voraussetzungen für eine Szene schuf, ohne bestimmte dramatische Aufgaben damit zu verbinden.

---

[42] Vgl. Wilamowitz, *Aischylos-Interpretationen* (Berlin 1914), 89, 1; richtig Lloyd-Jones a.O. 94. Auch Italie geht also zu weit, wenn er (zu 1025) annimmt, es sei nicht ganz sicher, ob die Probulen anwesend sind. Man darf wohl zuversichtlich behaupten: Ihre Anwesenheit würde den Sinn der Szene zerstören.

Der Interpret muss also versuchen, diese zu finden, was unten geschehen soll. Eines aber dürfen wir schon jetzt behaupten: Die erwähnten Besonderheiten sprechen eindeutig gegen die Vermutung, der Verfasser unserer Szene könne von Sophokles (*Antigone*) oder Euripides (*Phoinissen*) abhängen. Hätte er sich nämlich die Aufgabe gestellt, die Ansichten seiner Antigone durch ihren Gesprächspartner in Frage stellen zu lassen und ihr eine Begründung ihres Vorhaben zuzumuten, dann hätte er ihr einen verantwortlichen Staatsbeamten zum Mitunterredner geben müssen, einen Mann, der seinen Anspruch auch unter Androhung schwerster Strafen durchzusetzen versucht. Obwohl das so nahelag, hat es der Dichter unterlassen. Handelte er wirklich nur aus Unverstand?

II

Ehe wir diese Frage beantworten können, müssen zwei weitere Voraussetzungen geklärt werden, die Frage nach dem Verhältnis der *Septem* zu den sogenannten *Epigonoi* und die nach der Herkunft des Bestattungsverbotes im thebanischen Sagenkreis.

1. Den ersten Punkt können wir in aller Kürze erledigen. Lloyd-Jones (a.O. 87–92) hat geglaubt, Erwähnungen der Oidipusenkel im aeschyleischen Drama nachweisen zu können. Wie jedoch Dawe's Widerlegung (a.O. 19–21) dartut, ist dieser Versuch nicht gelungen. Die Entscheidung der Frage hängt vom richtigen Verständnis dreier Stellen ab:

(a) 827–28: ἢ τοὺς μογεροὺς καὶ δυσδαίμονας / ἀτέκνους κλαύσω πολεμάρχους; "Soll ich das grausame und unglückliche Schicksal der kinderlosen Feldherren beweinen?" Es geht nicht an, ἀτέκνους als "unglücklich in ihrer Sohnesschaft" zu verstehen; denn ein Beleg für diese Bedeutung existiert nicht.

(b) 902–903: μένει / κτέανά τ' ἐπιγόνοις. Die Beziehung auf die eigentlichen *Epigonoi* ist möglich, aber nicht zwingend. Aischylos kann die junge Generation meinen ("die Nachgeborenen") oder (mit Schneidewin, *Philol.* 3 [1848], 360, Anm. 14 a.E.), nicht ohne grimmigen Humor, "die Nachkommen, die nicht vorhanden sind."[43]

---

[43] Schadewaldt (*Griechisches Theater* [Frankfurt 1964], 83) übersetzt schlicht: "Nun bleibt den Nachgeborenen / Der Besitz..."

(c) 843–44: μέριμνα δ' ἀμφὶ πτόλιν· / θέσφατ' οὐκ ἀμβλύνεται. Diese Verse brauchen nicht zu besagen, dass der Chor sich *um* die Stadt *sorge*, etwa weil er ungeachtet des gegenwärtigen Sieges neue Gefahren (den Sieg der Epigonen) befürchte. Abgesehen davon, dass diese Anspielung kaum verständlich wäre,[44] würde sie sich auch dem Gedankengang des 3. Stasimons nicht recht einfügen; denn der Chor befasst sich in diesem Lied nur mit dem Familienfluch, nicht mit dessen Folgen für das Schicksal des Staates. Es empfiehlt sich deshalb, Klotz' Auffassung der Stelle gutzuheissen. Klotz lehnt Wilamowitz' Wiedergabe der ausgeschriebenen Worte[45] ab, da μέριμνα auch die *Klage um* einen Toten bedeuten kann. Die Worte des Textes besagen also: "Und Sorge herrscht rings in der Stadt. / Göttersprüche stumpfen nicht ab" (Schadewaldt).

Damit ist klar erwiesen, dass unser Drama keine Anspielung auf eine Fortsetzung des Konfliktes enthält. Der die Handlung bestimmende Fluch muss sich im Tode der Brüder vollenden. Diese Feststellung sollte bei Betrachtung der Exodos berücksichtigt werden.[46]

2. Wichtiger als das eben behandelte Problem ist die Frage, ob das Bestattungsverbot und eine entsprechende Reaktion Antigones in der mythischen Tradition vorgegeben waren. Meist pflegt man den Sachverhalt folgendermassen zu rekonstruieren:[47] Sophokles habe—ein fast beispielloser Fall in der Geschichte der griechischen Tragödie—das dramatische Hauptmotiv seiner *Antigone* erfunden. Beeindruckt durch seine wirkungsvolle Schöpfung habe ein Unbekannter das aeschyleische Drama um die berüchtigte Schlussszene erweitert.[48] Die neueste Konfrontierung dieser These mit den

---

[44] Vgl. Tucker z.St. (S. 171 seines Kommentares zu Vers 828 f. seiner Zählung).

[45] Wilamowitz, *Aischylos-Interpretationen* 83: "Nun sorge ich um die Stadt, Orakelsprüche werden nicht stumpf." Dagegen Klotz, *Rhein. Mus.* 72 [1917/18], 619.

[46] Vgl. die zutreffenden Bemerkungen von R. D. Dawe, "Inconsistency of Plot and Character in Aeschylus," in: *Proc. Cambr. Philol. Soc.* 189 (1963), 421.

[47] Vgl. bes. Corssen a.O. 28 ff.

[48] Von den überlieferungsgeschichtlichen Schwierigkeiten dieser These sehen wir hier ab: Wer die Exodos athetiert, muss bekanntlich auch die Anapäste 861–74 für interpoliert halten und mit kleineren Eingriffen in den folgenden lyrischer Partien (875–960 und 961–1004) rechnen (vgl. Nicolaus a.O. 19). Da nun Lykurg bei seiner Revision der Tragikertexte nur einwandfreie Exemplare verwendet, also auf die im Besitz der Nachkommen des Dichter befindlichen Originale zurückgegriffen haben dürfte, ist die These eigentlich nur in Bergks Fassung denkbar: Man ist zur Annahme gezwungen, dass die angebliche Überarbeitung auf einen Erben des Aischylos zurückgeht, der gleichzeitig die Möglichkeit hatte, die aeschyleische Urfassung zu vernichten.

mythologischen Zeugnissen findet sich in G. Müllers *Antigone*-Kommentar (Heidelberg 1967), 21–24. Müller meint, mit Sicherheit dartun zu können, dass die Bestattung des Polyneikes in der kyklischen *Thebais* nicht erwähnt war.[49] Gewiss werden wir dem Bericht des Ps.-Apollodor (*Bibl.* 3, 78), in dem Wilamowitz eine vorsophokleische Sage hat finden wollen, skeptisch gegenüberstehen. Er lässt sich mit demselben Recht als wenig exakte Zusammenfassung des sophokleischen Stückes oder vielleicht noch eher als Kompilation aus mehreren dramatischen Handlungen ansehen (vgl. Müller a.O. 22). Noch weniger Anspruch auf Ursprünglichkeit haben die Fassungen, in denen Antigone zusammen mit der Gemahlin des Polyneikes gegen Kreons ausdrückliches Verbot den Leichnam bestattet (vgl. Hyg. *fab.* 72; Stat. *Theb.* 12, 340 ff.; Liban. *Διηγ.* VIII 40 Först.; vgl. auch Philostr. *Imag.* 2, 39, p. 121, 8 ed. Vind.).—Anders steht es mit den zwei restlichen Zeugnissen, mit Pindars 6. Olympischer Ode und mit einer Bemerkung des Pausanias (9, 25, 2). Die Ode Pindars liefert zwar nach Müllers Auffassung "einen sicheren Beleg dafür, dass in der Thebais Polyneikes' Leiche mit denen von fünf anderen Angreifern Thebens verbrannt wurde." Denn, so hören wir, in den Versen 12 ff. vermisse Adrast angesichts der sieben Scheiterhaufen den Amphiaraos, nicht aber den Polyneikes. Und da Asklepiades von Tragilos (4. Jh.), der Angabe des Scholions zufolge, die *Thebais* als Pindars Quelle bezeichnet, sei der erwünschte Beweis erbracht.[50] Schwerlich aber lässt sich ein solches Argumentum e silentio auf den Text Pindars anwenden. Der Dichter möchte dem Syrakusaner Hagesias, einem Angehörigen des Priestergeschlechtes der Iamiden, jenes bekannte Wort Adrasts zurufen; denn es lässt besser als jedes andere die beiden Vorzüge des Gepriesenen erkennen: Hagesias ist,

---

[49] Vgl. auch E. Wüst, *RE* 21, 12 (1952), 1785, 42: "Das Epos wusste wohl weder von der Verbrennung der Leichen der Gefallenen noch von einem Verbot ihrer Bestattung etwas." Wüst beruft sich auf Bethe, *Thebanische Heldenlieder* (Leipzig 1891), 97 und C. Robert, *Oidipus* I (Berlin 1915), 251, 342, 360. Er hätte auch Corssen a.O. 21 ff. nennen sollen.

[50] Müller sagt es sei "von der Klage des Adrast die Rede, der angesichts von sieben errichteten Scheiterhaufen (ἑπτὰ...πυρᾶν νεκροῖς τελεσθέντων, νεκροῖς Wilamowitz statt νεκρῶν) einen der sieben Helden, dem die letzte Ehre zu erweisen war, schmerzlich vermisste, d.h. also den Polyneikes nicht." —Das Zeugnis des Scholions betrifft übrigens nur die Worte des Adrast (Sch. Pind. *Ol.* 6, 26): ποθέω· ὁ Ἀσκληπιάδης φησὶ ταῦτα εἰληφέναι ἐκ τῆς κυκλικῆς Θηβαΐδος (vgl. die folgende Anmerkung).

ebenso wie einst Amphiaraos, Priester und Krieger zugleich. Weil Adrast beeindruckt war von der einzigartigen Kombination dieser Tugenden, konnte er angesichts der lodernden Scheiterhaufen sagen: "Ich vermisse das Auge meines Heeres, ihn, der beides war, trefflicher Seher und bewährter Kämpfer."[51] Da Pindar indessen keine Veranlassung hatte, auf die Frage einzugehen, wen Adrastos ausser Amphiaraos noch vermisste, ist die Folgerung unstatthaft, die Leichen der übrigen sechs Helden seien vollständig zur Stelle gewesen. Adrast konnte ja in dem von Pindar geschaffenen Zusammenhang seine Klage auch dann nicht anders formulieren, wenn sich der tote Polyneikes in Feindeshand befand. Müllers Irrtum scheint nicht zuletzt darauf zurückzugehen, dass er in V. 15 Wilamowitz' bedenkliche Konjektur einsetzt, ohne sich an der entstehenden Katachrese zu stossen: ἑπτὰ δ' ἔπειτα πυρᾶν νεκρῶν ⟨νεκροῖς Wil.⟩ τελεσθέντων. Das kann nicht heissen "als die sieben Scheiterhaufen...vollendet waren"; denn es gibt bei Pindar keinen Beleg für die Verbindung πυρᾶν...τελεσθέντων (statt τελεσθεισῶν). Vielmehr wird man Thummer[52] folgen und übersetzen müssen: "Als die Toten der sieben Scheiterhaufen als Schuld entrichtet waren," d.h. als die zu den sieben Scheiterhaufen gehörenden Toten vom Sieger ausgeliefert waren. Vermutlich handelt es sich um die Leichen und um die Scheiterhaufen der sieben Heeresabteilungen, nicht um diejenigen allein der Feldherren.[53]

Unter den genannten Voraussetzungen verliert Müllers Interpretation an Wahrscheinlichkeit.[54] Schwerer fällt es, der anderen Stelle gerecht zu werden (Paus. 9, 25, 2). Pausanias berichtet: καλεῖται δὲ ὁ σύμπας οὗτος ⟨τόπος⟩ (add. Barth) Σύρμα Ἀντιγόνης· ὡς γὰρ τὸν τοῦ Πολυνείκους ἄρασθαί οἱ προθυμουμένη νεκρὸν οὐδεμία ἐφαίνετο ῥᾳστώνη, δεύτερα ἐπενόησεν ἕλκειν αὐτόν, ἐς ὃ εἵλκυσέ τε καὶ ἐπέβαλεν ἐπὶ τοῦ Ἐτεοκλέους ἐξημμένην τὴν πυράν. Müller

---

[51] A.O. 16–17: Ποθέω στρατιᾶς ὀφθαλμὸν ἐμᾶς / ἀμφότερον μάντιν τ' ἀγαθὸν καὶ δουρὶ μάρνασθαι. Über den epischen Charakter des Zitates vgl. Corssen a.O. 24.

[52] E. Thummer, *Die Religiosität Pindars* (Innsbruck 1957), 17, 2. Thummer vergleicht *I.* 1, 68: ψυχὰν Ἀΐδᾳ τελέων.

[53] Weshalb sollte man denn auch sieben errichtet haben, obwohl doch Amphiaraos schon während der letzten Schlacht im Erdboden versunken war? Wo die Beisetzung zu denken ist (in Attika?), lässt der pindarische Text nicht erkennen.

[54] Vermutlich vermöchte auch die Parallelstelle Pind. *N.* 9, 24 f. seinen Schluss nicht verbindlicher zu machen.

meint (a.O. 23), es sei erlaubt, den Namen der thebanischen Lokalität auf den Einfluss einer Tragödie zurückzuführen. Indessen sehe ich nicht, wie man diese Vermutung empfehlen könnte. Gerade Orts- und Flurnamen pflegen alte Traditionen zu bewahren, aber sie sträuben sich gegen neue Bezeichnungen literarischer Herkunft. Hinzu kommt, dass Pausanias von der *Verbrennung* der toten Brüder spricht, während die uns hier interessierenden klassischen Tragödien ihre *Bestattung* meinen.[55] Vielleicht ist es also doch richtiger, der Ortssage ihr Recht zu belassen. Das schlägt auch Lloyd-Jones vor (a.O. 98): "Local tradition may well have corresponded with the local epic, and there is some ground for believing that this story may have come from the *Thebais*."

Aber selbst dann, wenn man Müller und seinen Vorgängern folgt, d.h. das Vorhandensein einer mythischen Tradition, die in der Schlussszene der *Septem* aufgegriffen worden sein könnte, leugnet, hat man schwerlich ein Recht, aus dem Schweigen der Sagengeschichte ein Argument für die Unechtheit der Exodos herzuleiten. Dürfte man nicht dem Aischylos dasselbe zutrauen wie auch Sophokles, nämlich die mutige Tat Antigones samt ihren Voraussetzungen erfunden zu haben, falls er eine solche Wendung des Geschehens zur Abrundung seiner dramatischen Konzeption benötigte? Letzteres nun ist in der Tat der springende Punkt: Nicht quellenkritische Überlegungen helfen weiter, sondern allein eine Antwort auf die Frage nach der Funktion der inkriminierten Schlussszene im Rahmen der ganzen Tragödie. Zur Klärung dieses Problemes mögen die folgenden Überlegungen beitragen, die bei Beurteilung des Textes nicht selten vergessen werden. Über dem anerkannt echten Teil des Dramas steht unbeantwortet die Frage nach dem Schicksal der Leiche des Landesverräters. M. Wundt[56] hat sie klar formuliert: "Wie konnten die toten Brüder jetzt so friedlich nebeneinander liegen? Wie konnten sie beide mit den gleichen Ehren

---

[55] Müller nennt neben Pausanias Stat. *Theb.* 12, 411–46, wo die Schleifung der Leiche und das Wunder der sich spaltenden Flamme verbunden sind. Beide Dinge vereinigte auch Kallimachos (vgl. Frg. 105 Pf.), von dem Ovid (*Trist.* 5, 5, 33) abhängt. Haben wir jedoch ein Recht zur Behauptung, Kallimachos folge einer Tragödie (wie Müller anzunehmen scheint)? Und dürfen wir, falls er das wirklich getan haben sollte, folgern der Verfasser dieses verlorenen Dramas habe Antigones Tat (das Schleifen des Leichnams) erfunden?

[56] *Philol.* 55 (1906), 377.

in der Gruft des Vaters bestattet werden?" Gleichzeitig hat Wundt gezeigt, dass dieses Problem für die Zeitgenossen des Aischylos besondere Aktualität besass. Er erinnerte an die heimliche Bestattung des Themistokles in attischem Boden.[57] Damit soll nicht gesagt sein, Aischylos habe seinen Zuschauern eine zeitgemässe Fragestellung gewissermassen an den Augen abgelesen, um sie auf der Bühne zu beantworten, also in seinem Metier eine lautstarke Konfession abzulegen. Ein solcher Rekurs auf die Bekennerfreude des angeblich politisch engagierten Dichters hilft uns nicht, da er die Forderung nach gedanklicher Einheit des Dramas[58] missachtet. Er liesse sich sogar gegen die Echtheit der Exodos ausspielen. Wohl aber wäre es denkbar, dass der Dichter (falls man ihn nicht frei erfinden lassen will) Andeutungen jener sein Publikum bewegenden Frage in einer epischen Vorlage gefunden und mit dem Grundgedanken seiner dramatischen Konstruktion verbunden habe, und zwar so, dass die im Spiel gebotene Lösung als ein mythisches Modell der gegenwärtigen Problematik gelten durfte. Diese Möglichkeit der Deutung wäre gegeben, wenn sich dartun liesse, dass die sog. Bestattungsfrage nicht erst in der Schlussszene gestellt, sondern in den vorangehenden Teilen des Stückes wenigstens so vorbereitet wäre, dass sie ungezwungen aus ihm hervorwächst.

Unseren Überlegungen steht indessen die übliche Deutung entgegen: Durch den Wechselmord, so meint man, sei das Fluchgeschehen beendet, eine Versöhnung ($\delta\iota\alpha\lambda\lambda\alpha\gamma\acute{\eta}$), wenn auch besonderer Art, vollzogen, der Einfluss des Daimon endlich erloschen (vgl. 960: $\check{\epsilon}\lambda\eta\xi\epsilon\ \delta\alpha\acute{\iota}\mu\omega\nu$). Diese Feststellungen stehen im Text, und eine Verbindung mit der Problematik der Schlussszene scheint tatsächlich nicht möglich zu sein. Ein sinnvoll planender Geist wie der des Aischylos könnte sie, so glaubt man schliessen zu dürfen, ohne nähere Andeutungen nicht gewünscht haben.

Dieser Einwand hat beachtliches Gewicht. Trotzdem schlägt er nicht durch, und zwar aus zwei Gründen nicht.

1) In den dem Botenbericht folgenden lyrischen Teilen wendet sich

---

[57] Vgl. Thuk. 1, 138, 6, auch B. Knox, *Gnomon* 40 (1968), 748: "...if the Athenians refused the body of Themistocles burial in home soil because of suspected collaboration with Pausanias, what would they have thought proper treatment for the body of a man who led a foreign army in an assault on his own city?"

[58] Das heisst nicht nach "consistency" in Dawe's Sinn.

der Chor sofort dem Schicksal des Königshauses zu: Er singt im kurzen 3. Stasimon von der unentrinnbaren Wirksamkeit der Erbsünde des Laios, als deren Fortsetzung der Fluch des Oidipus zu gelten hat.[59] Die Folgerichtigkeit des von der Gottheit gelenkten Geschehens ist bewiesen, und sie wird anschliessend durch die Schaustellung der beiden Leichen sichtbar gemacht. Im 1. Threnos, einem Wechselgesang der Halbchöre,[60] läuft der Gedanke, ausgehend vom Tod der königlichen Brüder, zum Anlass des gegenwärtigen Unglücks und klingt dann in die Feststellung aus, die Feindschaft habe ein Ende, der Sieg aber gehöre der Fluchgottheit (vgl. 937: πέπαυται δ' ἔχθος..., 953: τελευταῖαι δ' ἐπηλάλαξαν | Ἀραὶ τὸν ὀξὺν νόμον..., 956: ἔστακε δ' Ἄτας τροπαῖον ἐν πύλαις, | ... καὶ δυοῖν κρατήσας ἔληξε δαίμων). Welche Trostlosigkeit, aber auch welche Einseitigkeit! Die vorgetragenen Gedanken entsprechen der Einstellung des Chores, die er seit dem Auszug des Eteokles (seit dem Amoibaion 683 ff.) bekundet. Auf diesen Kontrast zum anfänglichen Verhalten der Choreutinnen hat man oft hingewiesen:[61] Im Eingang des Dramas eine bis zur Hysterie gesteigerte Angst um das Schicksal der Stadt, sogar dieser Verzweiflung entspringende Visionen von den grauenhaften Einzelheiten der Eroberung—jetzt Warnung vor Übereilung, Mahnung zur Besonnenheit und wenig später eine gerade in ihrer schlichten Nüchternheit und Geradlinigkeit ergreifende Analyse des Labdakidenschicksals. Das Interesse der Frauen gilt nur noch diesem Unglück, dessen letzten Akt sie soeben miterlebt haben. Auch das Ergehen der Stadt wird nur im Verhältnis zum Ende des bisherigen Königshauses gesehen, vgl. 900–902: διήκει δὲ καὶ πόλιν στόνος, | στένουσι πύργοι, στένει | πέδον φίλανδρον. Kein Wort davon, dass die Stadt im Kampf auf Leben und Tod soeben einen entscheidenden Sieg errungen und neben der Trauer um das Herrscherhaus auch Grund zur Freude hat![62] Man vergleiche mit diesen düsteren Tönen des Threnos die Parodos der sophokleischen *Antigone*! Dabei vergessen wir nicht, dass die Gedanken des äschyleischen Chores durch den Ablauf der

[59] Vgl. 832 (ὦ μέλαινα καὶ τελεία | γένεος Οἰδίπου τ' Ἀρά) und 842 (βουλαὶ δ' ἄπιστοι Λαΐου διήρκεσαν).

[60] Vgl. H. Patzer, *Die Anfänge der griech. Tragödie* (Wiesbaden 1962), 3.

[61] Vgl. neuerdings Dawe, "Inconsistency" (s. Anm. 46), 31 f.

[62] Anders der Bote 792 ff.

Handlung provoziert, also mit vollem Recht nur auf die Schattenseite der Ereignisse gerichtet sind. Es ist jedoch recht zweifelhaft, ob der Dichter sich auf den einseitigen Aspekt der klagenden Frauen beschränken, also die Anteilnahme der Polis am Untergang der Fürstensöhne ganz ignorieren wollte, obwohl er doch im ersten Teil des Dramas die Abhängigkeit der Bürger vom Ausgang des Bruderzwistes kräftig hervorgehoben hatte. Darf schliesslich der Zuschauer erwarten, dass der mit Hingabe klagende Chor, vor allem bei der Einseitigkeit seiner Gesichtspunkte, eine erschöpfende, auch den unbeteiligten Betrachter befriedigende Deutung des Wechselmordes gibt? Diese Frage muss man entschieden verneinen; denn

2) die Versöhnung (διαλλαγή), von welcher der Chor mehrmals spricht, ist kein echter, Frieden stiftender Ausgleich. Schon in der ersten Strophe des 2. Stasimon, unmittelbar nach dem Auszug des Eteokles, äussert der Chor die zunächst rätselhaften Worte, ein Schiedsrichter aus der Fremde verteile den Besitz zwischen den beiden streitenden Brüdern: Der fremde Richter ist nicht etwa der angesehene Bürger einer Nachbarstadt, wie man erwarten müsste, sondern ein Barbar aus dem Chalyberland, das unbarmherzige Eisen (730: ὠμόφρων σίδαρος).[63] Den beiden Gegnern teilt dieser Richter so viel Boden zu, wie viel ihre Leichen als Grab benötigen.[63a] Er wird im Threnos (sc. 941) als "bitterer Friedensstifter" (πικρὸς λυτὴρ νεικέων) bezeichnet, und kurz vor dieser Stelle muss er sich bescheinigen lassen, dass er keinen Dank verdiene (vgl. 908–10: διαλλακτῆρι δ' οὐκ ἀμεμφεία φίλοις, οὐδ' ἐπίχαρις Ἄρης). Das ist, wie Engelmann gezeigt hat, eine Umkehrung der Wendungen, in denen man üblicherweise einem staatlichen Schiedsrichter öffentlich Dank abzustatten pflegte. Trotzdem heisst das Eisen διαλλακτήρ, und 884 wird obendrein versichert, dass der Erfolg seiner Tätigkeit "Versöhnung" sei (ἤδη διήλλαχθε σὺν σιδάρῳ). Das alles kann nur besagen, dass Aischylos in grimmigem Hohne

---

[63] Vgl. die Ausführungen von H. Engelmann, *Rhein. Mus.* 110 (1967), 97–102.

[63a] Der Aussage des Chores, jeder der beiden Brüder werde nur so viel Land erhalten, wie viel sein Grab beansprucht, lässt sich kaum ein Argument gegen die Echtheit der Exodos entnehmen, in der ja einem Bruder die Beerdigung verweigert werden soll; denn der Chor bezeichnet (sc. 731–3) den Begräbnisplatz als Maximum dessen, was jedem zufallen werde; theoretisch könnte es sogar noch weniger sein. In Wahrheit sichert gerade die Exodos *beiden* Toten eine gleichermassen angemessene Bestattung.

spricht, wenn er den vom Hass gelenkten Wechselmord als Versöhnungsakt bezeichnet. Beide Brüder sterben als bittere Feinde. Mit ihrem Tod endet wohl das Wirken des Daimon (vgl. 959–60), aber das Siegesbanner der Ate steht auf den Toren, und die Fluchgottheiten (Ἀραί) stossen ein Triumpfgeschrei aus (vgl. 953–54). Statt echter Versöhnung also grauenhafte Vernichtung! Gewiss ist der Daimon nun beruhigt (er hat sich im echten Sinne des Wortes ausgetobt), aber nur Hass und Mord haben seinem Wirken ein Ende setzen können.

Wir halten es für unwahrscheinlich, dass eine aeschyleische Trilogie mit diesem Missklang enden könne. Die einzige Person nun, die einen Ausweg aus dieser Situation der Verzweiflung kennt, ist die Antigone der inkriminierten Schlussszene. Der Dichter provoziert sie zu ihrem erlösenden Vorschlag dadurch, dass er, sobald die Totenklage verklungen ist, den bislang zurückgehaltenen politischen Massstab an das Geschehen anlegt. Die Verordnung der Probulen zeigt nämlich in voller Klarheit, dass die Brüder nicht als Privatleute um ihr Erbe stritten, sondern als Königssöhne um den ganzen Staat. Diese Betrachtungsweise rückt Eteokles, den Verteidiger der Heimat, augenblicklich in ein vorteilhaftes Licht, mochte er im Nachfolgestreit auch Unrecht haben. Polyneikes aber gilt nun als Hochverräter, auch wenn er gewaltsam vertrieben worden war und das bessere Recht auf die Krone hatte. Dementsprechend möchte die Behörde die Toten verschieden behandelt wissen, und es sieht am Anfang der Exodos so aus, als ob die Unzulässigkeit der Versöhnung (der διαλλαγής) offenkundigt gemacht und verewigt werden solle. Es ist jedoch unverkennbar, dass die Anordnung der neuen thebanischen Regierung nur als Mittel zu einem höheren Zweck konzipiert worden ist, keineswegs als gleichberechtigter Gegensatz zu den Idealen einer Antigone sophokleischen Gepräges. Die in der Exodos erwähnte Behörde besteht aus gewählten Volksvertretern (δήμου πρόβουλοι), sie spricht nicht etwa im Auftrag eines zielbewussten Tyrannen. Während der sophokleische Kreon selbst vor die Öffentlichkeit tritt, um sein Verbot mit allen bei einer möglichen Übertretung zu erwartenden Folgen zu verkünden, bleiben die Probulen, wie wir oben sahen, im Hintergrund. Sie entsenden einen Herold, der die eng gezogenen Grenzen seines Auftrages nicht überschreitet. Wie die Stichomythie 1042–53 zeigt, ist er ungeachtet seiner dialektischen Fähigkeiten nicht in der Lage, Antigones Standpunkt zu verstehen. Antigone lehnt es deshalb ab, die unfruchtbare Diskussion fortzusetzen. Noch bezeichnender ist die Tatsache, dass der Herold seiner Gesprächspartnerin, die ja öffentlich ankündigt, die Anordnung der Behörde zu übertreten, keine Strafe anzudrohen vermag. Er muss Antigone und die ihr folgenden Choreutinnen gewähren lassen.

Der Sinn dieser auf den ersten Blick befremdenden behördlichen Massnahmen lässt sich nicht verkennen: Sie zwingen Antigone zum Widerspruch und geben ihr die Möglichkeit zu handeln. Letzteres ist in doppelter Hinsicht bedeutsam: (1) Antigone ist nicht allein, sondern die Hälfte des Chores schliesst sich ihr an. Die Frauen tun das aus freien Stücken und sie dokumentieren damit ihre Ablehnung der staatlichen Anordnung. Das von den Volksvertretern ausgegangene Bestattungsverbot kann also nicht mehr als Ausdruck des gesamten Volkswillens angesehen werden.[64] Nun zeigt sich, dass die neue Regierung auch bei den Bürgern Thebens kein rechtes Ansehen geniesst. Man ahnt, dass sie, sofern sie nur bereit ist, den Willen des Demos zu achten, kaum noch das Recht hat, Antigone nach der Bestattung des Polyneikes zur Rechenschaft zu ziehen. Diese Sachlage ist Antigones Begleiterinnen keineswegs verborgen; sie fühlen, dass sie nicht viel riskieren, vgl. 1070–71: καὶ πόλις ἄλλως / ἄλλοτ' ἐπαινεῖ τὰ δίκαια. (2) Folgender Gesichtspunkt ist noch wichtiger. Der Threnos galt zwei Toten, die sich in gegenseitigem Hass getötet hatten. Der Jammer über die Gründe dieses Verhängnisses bestimmte in der Tat den Gedankenablauf beider Klagegesänge, vornehmlich den des ersten. Das Entsetzen über das Zustandekommen des Wechselmordes ist fast grösser als der Schmerz über den menschlichen Verlust. Dieser Missklang wird erst durch die Auseinandersetzung der Exodos beseitigt. Sobald sich Antigone entschlossen hat, ihr Vorhaben auch gegen den Willen der augenblicklichen Regierung in die Tat umzusetzen (vgl. 1052), schickt sich der Chor an, beide Königssöhne in derselben Weise zu bestatten, beide nebeneinander in derselben Familiengruft. Beim Abzug teilt er sich in zwei gleiche Hälften, deren jede einem Toten folgt. Damit ist die Gleichstellung der Brüder auch äusserlich demonstriert: Der

---

[64] Damit ist auch die Warnung des Heroldes vor dem Zorn des Volkes (1044: τραχύς γε μέντοι δῆμος ἐκφυγὼν κακά) entkräftet.

Zuschauer soll verstehen, dass Antigones Argumente durchgedrungen sind. Erst jetzt weicht die Bitterkeit, die man noch während der Totengesänge über den Ausgang des Labdakidengeschlechtes empfand, einer wohltuenden Stimmung der Versöhnlichkeit. Wie mehrmals am Ende äschyleischer Trilogien ist göttliche Gnade (*Charis*) auch hier der köstliche Lohn schwerer Leiden.

In obigen Ausführungen wollten wir nicht versuchen, die Bedenken, die der moderne Betrachter bei Lektüre des überlieferten Tragödienschlusses empfindet, zu verringern oder gar zu zerstreuen; denn es lässt sich keineswegs verheimlichen, dass Sprache und Gedankenführung der Exodos ungewöhnlich sind. Jedoch ist unser Befremden kein zuverlässiges Kriterium, jedenfalls nicht, solange wir aufgrund der Überlieferungslage nur einen Bruchteil des aeschyleischen Werkes besitzen, die ganze Kunst des Dichters und ihre Möglichkeiten also nur unvollständig kennen. Vorstehende Blätter verfolgen ein bescheideneres Ziel: Sie möchten alle diejenigen, die das Wirken eines Nachdichters zu verspüren glauben, dazu anregen, ihre Bedenken in stringente Argumente zu fassen. Allerdings sollten sie Rückgriffe auf ihr persönliches Stilgefühl tunlichst aus dem Spiele lassen, da in dieser Kontroverse nur dasjenige Gewicht besitzt, was sich demonstrieren lässt. Wenn sich die Gegner des überlieferten Textes entschlössen, ihr Unbehagen zu präzisieren, könnte es gelingen, die Frage nach der Echtheit der Exodos endlich zu beantworten.

Bonn, 26. Februar 1970

LES STASIMA DU *PROMÉTHÉE ENCHAÎNÉ*

JEAN IRIGOIN

Avec trois *stasima*, le *Prométhée enchaîné* offre le type de composition le plus fréquent chez Eschyle; seules les *Euménides*, avec deux *stasima*, s'en écartent. En revanche, par la longueur réduite de ces éléments comme par leur structure métrique, le *Prométhée* diffère grandement des autres tragédies d'Eschyle. On en a même tiré argument contre l'authenticité de la pièce, en considérant que les parties lyriques y rappelaient plus les odes pindariques que les choeurs tragiques.[1] Sans chercher à prendre parti sur cet aspect du débat, il m'a paru qu'une étude métrique détaillée des trois *stasima* du *Prométhée* serait un hommage adapté à l'auteur de *The Manuscript Tradition of the Tragedies of Aeschylus* comme à l'éditeur des *Pindari carmina cum fragmentis*.

* * *

Les trois *stasima* du *Prométhée*, dont on trouvera l'édition plus loin, en appendice, offrent la composition strophique suivante:

$$
\begin{array}{llll}
\text{I} & \text{A A'} & \text{B B'} & \text{C} \\
\text{II} & \text{A A'} & \text{B B'} & \\
\text{III} & \text{A A'} & \text{B} &
\end{array}
$$

qui est sans parallèle exact chez Eschyle et chez Sophocle, alors qu'Euripide l'adopte telle quelle dans son *Électre*.[2] Chaque *stasimon* comporte une strophe de moins que le précédent: le second n'a pas l'épode C du premier;[3] le troisième, perdant l'antistrophe B' du

---

[1] Voir par exemple W. Kranz, *Stasimon* (Berlin 1933), 226, pour les IIe et IIIe *stasima*.

[2] L'ensemble de la composition est identique dans *Hécube*, mais suivant l'ordre II, III, I. Dans les *Phéniciennes*, chaque *stasimon* comporte un élément strophique de moins que dans le *Prométhée*.

[3] Voir plus bas, p. 207, pour la composition du Ier *stasimon*.

second, fait de la strophe restante une épode. En raison des problèmes d'ordre textuel que pose le premier *stasimon*, il semble préférable de traiter d'abord des deux autres parties chorales, avec l'espoir d'y trouver quelque aide pour l'interprétation de la première.

Après un court dialogue entre Prométhée et le coryphée, le choeur des Océanides chante en deux couples de strophes la faiblesse des hommes et la volonté souveraine de Zeus. Tel est le contenu du IIe *stasimon*.

Strophe et antistrophe 1 (526–35 et 536–44) [4]

_ ⏑⏑ _ ⏑⏑ _	D
_ ⏑ _ | _ _ | ⏑⏑ _ ⏑⏑ _ _	e _ D _
_ ⏑ _ _ _ ⏑⏑ _ ⏑⏑ _	e _ D
_ _ ⏑⏑ _ ⏑⏑ _	_ D
5 _ ⏑ _ | ⏑̄ _ ⏑⏑ _ ⏑⏑ _ _ _ ⏑ _	e ⏑̄ D _ e
_ ⏑⏑ _ ⏑⏑ _	D
⏑̆⏑ _ | ⏑̄ _ ⏑ _ | _ _ ⏑ _ ⏑ _ _	e ⏑̄ e _ e ⏑ _ _

Strophe et antistrophe 2 (545–52 et 553–60)

{ ⏑⏑ _ ⏑⏑ _ ⏑⏑ _ ⏑⏑ _
{ ⏑ _ ⏑ _ _
{ ⏑⏑ _ ⏑⏑ _
{ ⏑ _ ⏑ _ ⏑ _ _
{ ⏑ ⏑ _ ⏑ ⏑ _
{ ⏑ _ ⏑ _ ⏑ _ ⏑ \| _ ⏑ _ _
  ⏑⏑ _ ⏑⏑ _ ⏑⏑ _ ⏑⏑ _ ⏑⏑ _ _

5 { _ ⏑⏑ _ ⏑⏑ _ | _	D _
{ _ | ⏑ _ ⏑ _ ⏑ _ _	e ⏑ e _

La première strophe du IIe *stasimon* est formée de séries dactylo-trochaïques (ou anapesto-iambiques) identiques à celles qui constituent une bonne part des odes de Pindare et de Bacchylide, de sorte qu'il est possible de les décrire, comme on l'a fait ci-dessus, avec les sigles proposés par Maas.

Dans la suite des trois premiers vers, tous de rythme descendant, les éléments dactyliques (mesures à quatre temps) [5] et les éléments

---

[4] Dans le schéma métrique, le trait vertical indique une fin de mot commune à la strophe et à l'antistrophe.

[5] On se gardera de confondre les temps des mesures et les temps marqués, dont il sera parlé plus loin à propos de la périodologie.

trochaïques (mesures à trois temps) alternent régulièrement. Une double rupture se produit entre les vers 3 et 4: l'alternance des éléments est suspendue (un élément anapestique fait suite à un élément dactylique) et l'attaque du vers 4, de rythme ascendant, fait contraste avec l'attaque descendante des trois premiers vers. À cette réserve près—fondamentale, il est vrai—les vers 4 à 6 présentent la même suite alternante de mesures à trois temps et à quatre temps que les vers 1 à 3. De plus, tout se passe comme si le vers 4 reprenait en écho la seconde partie du vers 3 (_D), alors que les vers 5 et 6 reproduisent symétriquement, dans une véritable rétrogradation, le début du vers 3(e), le vers 2 et le vers 1 (e ᴗ D _ e D ⟩ ⟨ D e _ D _ e). La différence porte sur l'attaque du vers 4 et la répartition des éléments entre les deux derniers vers (2–3 et 5–6) de chaque groupe.

Le vers 7, final de la strophe, tout entier trochaïque et soumis à une double catalexe (c'est, dans la terminologie antique, un tétramètre trochaïque brachycatalectique), faisant ainsi contraste avec les vers précédents, constitue la clausule attendue à cette place. Seule la double catalexe la distingue des clausules les plus courantes chez Pindare et Bacchylide.

La seconde strophe comporte un mélange d'éléments anapestiques et d'éléments iambiques, les premiers sous forme de monomètre (vv. 2, 3), de dimètre (v. 1) ou de trimètre (catalectique, v. 4), les autres sous forme de tripodie (catalectique, v. 1), de dimètre (catalectique, v. 2) ou de trimètre (catalectique, v. 3). Dans les trois premiers vers, les deux types métriques sont associés. Le vers 4 est entièrement anapestique. Avec le vers 5, des éléments de rythme descendant, identiques à ceux de la première strophe, apparaissent: une tripodie dactylique (ou hémiépès féminin) y est suivie d'un dimètre trochaïque. Dans les vers formés de mètres anapestiques et de mètres iambiques, l'élément final est toujours catalectique (vv. 1, 2, 3, 4), alors que la clausule dactylo-trochaïque est acatalecte (v. 5).

La comparaison des deux strophes met en lumière leurs principes de composition respectifs. La première, dans un ensemble de rythme descendant, présente un seul vers, le vers médian (v. 4), de rythme ascendant. La seconde, dans un ensemble de rythme ascendant, offre un seul vers de rythme descendant, le dernier (v. 5). L'association, dans un même vers, de deux types métriques différents paraît soumise à des règles. Dans la première strophe, l'élément trochaïque précède l'élément dactylique (vv. 2, 3) ou l'encadre (v. 5). Dans la seconde, l'élément iambique suit régulièrement l'élément anapestique (vv. 1, 2, 3). Au renversement du rythme d'une strophe à l'autre répond l'interversion des éléments métriques. Le vers final de cette seconde strophe, de type dactylo-trochaïque après un ensemble de mètres iambiques et anapestiques associés, présente ses éléments dans le même ordre que l'ensemble: les mesures à quatre temps précèdent les mesures à trois temps.

La synaphie verbale est de règle entre les éléments métriques constitutifs du vers. Elle n'admet aucune exception dans la première strophe, où des coupes, décalées d'une syllabe en avant ou en arrière de la suture des éléments, sont généralisées aux vers 2 (*bis*), 5 et 7 (*bis*). Dans la seconde strophe, deux infractions se manifestent, l'une entre le monomètre anapestique et le trimètre iambique du vers 3 (strophe), l'autre entre les deux mètres trochaïques du vers final (antistrophe); des coupes généralisées, décalées d'une syllabe en avant ou en arrière de la suture des éléments, apparaissent aux vers 3 (avant la suture des deux derniers mètres iambiques) et 5 (de part et d'autre de la suture de la tripodie dactylique et du dimètre trochaïque).

Le décompte des temps marqués, vers par vers, est le suivant:

	Première strophe	Seconde strophe
v. 1	*3*	*7*
v. 2	*5*	*6*
v. 3	*5*	*8*
v. 4	*3*	*6*
v. 5	*7*	*7*
v. 6	*3*	
v. 7	*8*	

Pour la première strophe, le renversement du rythme avec le vers 4 laisse attendre un début de période, que confirme une ponctuation forte, dans l'antistrophe, à la fin du vers 3, final de la première période; celle-ci compte donc *13* temps marqués (*3 + 5 + 5*). La composition toute trochaïque du vers 7 l'isole de ce qui précède; une ponctuation forte, dans la strophe, à la fin du vers 6, confirme qu'une période s'achève avec lui: elle compte, comme la première, *13* temps marqués (*3* + *7* + *3*). Le dernier vers constitue à lui seul une période de *8* temps marqués. Au total, la première strophe compte *34* temps marqués (*13* + *13* + *8*).

La seconde strophe présente une symétrie interne, de part et d'autre du vers 3: le vers 5 répond au vers 1, le vers 4 au vers 2. Ni la composition métrique, qui détacherait le vers 5 du reste, ni la ponctuation, qui, dans l'antistrophe, sépare le vers 1 du vers 2, ne fournissent d'indication décisive (on pourrait penser à une division en trois périodes: vers 1, avec *7* temps marqués, vers 2 à 4, avec *20* temps marqués, vers 5, avec *7* temps marqués). Le plus simple est sans aucun doute de retrouver des périodes identiques à celles de la première strophe, mais disposées autrement: une première période de *13* temps marqués (*7* + *6*), avec les vers 1 et 2, une seconde période constituée par le seul vers 3, avec *8* temps marqués, une troisième période égale à la première, avec les *13* temps marqués des vers 4 et 5 (*6* + *7*). Comme la première strophe, la seconde compte au total *34* temps marqués, disposés en trois périodes (*13* + *8* + *13*). À l'ordre A A B de la première correspond, dans la seconde, la variation A B A.

* * *

Le triste exemple d'Io fait chanter au choeur, dans le IIIe *stasimon*, les avantages d'un mariage bien assorti; mais il reste que nul n'échappe à la volonté de Zeus.

Strophe et antistrophe (887–93 et 894–900) [6]

⌠ ‗ ∪ ∪ ‗ ∪ ∪ ‗ ‗	D ‗
⎨ ‗ ∪ ‗ ‗ ‗¦∪ ∪ ‗ ∪ ∪ ‗ ‗	e ‗ D ‗
⌡ ‗ ∪ ∪ ‗ ∪ ∪ ‗ ‗	D ‗
‗ ∪ ‗ ‗ ‗|∪ ∪ ‗ ∪ ∪ ‗ ‗ ‗ ∪ ‗	e ‗ D ‗ e
‗ ‗ ∪¦‗ ‗ ‗ ∪ ∪ ‗ ∪ ∪ ‗	‗ e ‗ D
‗ ∪ ‗ ‗ ‗|∪ ∪ ‗ ∪ ∪ ‗	e ‗ D
5 ‗ ∪ ‗ ‗ ‗|∪ ‗ ‗ ‗|∪ ‗	e ‗ e ‗ e

[6] Le trait vertical a la même valeur que dans le schéma métrique du IIe *stasimon*. Le trait vertical pointillé indique qu'une des fins de mot est discutable, dans la strophe ou dans l'antistrophe.

Épode (901–906) [7]

∪ _ ∪∪ ∪ ∪ ∪∪ ∪ ∪ ∪∪ ∪ ∪∪ _
_ ∪ _ ∪ _ ∪ _
∪ _ ∪ _ ∪ _ ∪ _ ∪ _ ∪̆
{ ∪ ∪ ∪∪ ∪ ∪ ∪∪ ∪ ∪∪ ∪ ∪ ∪ ∪∪ ∪ _
{ ∪ _ ∪ _ ∪ _
5   _ ∪ _ ∪ _ ∪ _
     _ ∪ ∪∪ ∪ _ _

La première strophe du IIIe *stasimon* est du même type que la strophe correspondante du IIe *stasimon*. Les vers dactylo-trochaïques dont elle est faite pourraient avoir été composés tels quels par Pindare ou Bacchylide.

Le premier vers, disposé sur trois lignes dans les éditions, est de rythme descendant tout comme le second. Un renversement du rythme se produit avec le vers 3, mais les deux derniers vers reviennent au rythme descendant du début. La partie centrale du vers 1 (e _ D _) est encadrée de deux éléments dactyliques identiques (D _). Le vers 2, fait d'un élément dactylique (D _) encadré de deux éléments trochaïques dont le second est catalectique, se présente comme une interversion du vers 1, avec simplification de la partie médiane. Cette même partie du vers 1, reprise avec renversement du rythme, constitue le vers 3 (_ e _ D). Reprise une troisième fois, sous forme catalectique (e _ D), elle forme le vers 4. La strophe s'achève par un vers trochaïque, comme la première strophe du IIe *stasimon*; c'est un trimètre catalectique. Mesures à trois temps et mesures à quatre temps alternent régulièrement dans chaque vers, à l'exception du premier et du dernier, les mesures à trois temps précédant les mesures à quatre temps (vv. 3 et 4), à moins qu'elles ne les encadrent (v. 2), tout comme dans le IIe *stasimon*.

Les séries iambiques syncopées dont est formée l'épode sont aussi étrangères aux dactylo-trochaïques (ou anapesto-iambiques) que l'étaient les séries anapestiques et iambiques mêlées de la seconde strophe du IIe *stasimon*. Les vers 1 et 3, identiques malgré les résolutions nombreuses dans le premier, sont des trimètres iambiques

---

[7] Faute de *responsio*, aucune fin de mot n'est indiquée dans le schéma de l'épode.

lyriques, dont le dernier mètre prend la forme d'un bacchée. Le vers 4, disposé sur deux lignes par commodité est un pentamètre iambique du même type. Les vers 2, 5 et 6 (ce dernier avec résolution et catalexe) sont identiques : à première vue, on y reconnaîtrait des dimètres trochaïques catalectiques, le dernier étant même brachy-catalectique ; mais il est plus probable qu'on a affaire à des dimètres iambiques lyriques dont le premier élément est acéphale (crétique plus iambe, et dans le vers final, avec catalexe, crétique plus bacchée). Les trois premiers vers présentent une composition embrassée qui rappelle celle du premier vers de la strophe et aussi celle du vers 2. Le vers 4 est quasi identique, aux résolutions près, à l'ensemble des vers 1 et 2. Les vers 5 et 6 ne font que reprendre, avec une catalexe dans le vers final de l'épode, le schéma du vers 2.

Au delà des différences formelles, la comparaison de la strophe et de l'épode permet des observations instructives. Chacune comporte un long vers mêlé à des vers plus courts. La strophe, de rythme descendant dans l'ensemble, présente un vers de rythme ascendant qui, tout comme dans le IIe *stasimon*, occupe une position centrale (c'est le troisième vers, sur cinq). Dans l'épode, le rythme est ascendant, avec trois attaques d'apparence descendante aux vv. 2, 5 et 6. Comme dans le IIe *stasimon*, les éléments iambiques purs de l'épode s'opposent aux éléments trochaïques ou iambiques de la strophe, qui ne sont jamais purs (les prétendus épitrites). Dans la strophe, les éléments trochaïques ou iambiques précèdent les éléments dactyliques ou anapestiques (vv. 3, 4), à moins qu'ils ne les encadrent (v. 2). Seul le vers initial de la strophe fait exception à cette règle, déjà signalée à propos du IIe *stasimon*. Dans l'épode, selon l'analyse adoptée plus haut, tous les vers iambiques sont catalectiques (vv. 1, 3, 4) ou acéphales (vv. 2, 5), le dernier (v. 6) étant à la fois l'un et l'autre.

La synaphie verbale est respectée sans exception dans la strophe dactylo-trochaïque ; des coupes généralisées, décalées d'une syllabe en avant ou en arrière de la suture des éléments, apparaissent aux vers 2, 4 et 5 (*bis*), peut-être aussi aux vers 1 et 3. Faute de *responsio*, l'épode ne permet pas d'observations décisives à cet égard ; toutefois, jamais une fin de mot ne coïncide avec une fin d'élément iambique pur, qu'il y ait ou non résolution.

Voici, vers par vers, le décompte des temps marqués :

	Strophe	Épode
v. 1	*11*	*6*
v. 2	*7*	*4*
v. 3	*5*	*6*
v. 4	*5*	*10*
v. 5	*6*	*4*
v. 6		*4*

Dans la strophe, le renversement du rythme au vers 3 indique un début de période, ce que confirme la rupture de l'alternance entre les éléments métriques, d'un vers à l'autre (l'initiale iambique du vers 3 faisant suite à la finale trochaïque du vers 2), ainsi que la ponctuation forte à la fin du vers 2 dans l'antistrophe, et la composition de la strophe, où la partie négative (καὶ μήτε...μήτε...) commence avec la seconde période. Chacune des périodes se termine par un élément trochaïque catalectique, alors que les autres vers ont une finale dactylique ou anapestique. La première période compte *18* temps marqués (*11* + *7*), la seconde *16* (*5* + *5* + *6*). Le total de la strophe est de *34* temps marqués (*18* + *16*).

La première partie de l'épode présente une symétrie interne autour du vers 2, comme on l'a vu plus haut; de plus, le vers 3 s'achève avec une ponctuation forte. La fin de la première période peut donc être fixée là, ce qui lui donne *16* temps marqués (*6* + *4* + *6*). Les trois autres vers forment une seconde période, avec *18* temps marqués (*10* + *4* + *4*). Les vers initiaux de période et le vers final de l'épode, c'est-à-dire du *stasimon* entier, sont les seuls à présenter des résolutions; le vers médian des deux périodes (vv. 2 et 5) est identique. Le total des temps marqués de l'épode est de *34*, les deux périodes, *16* et *18*, répondant symétriquement aux deux périodes, *18* et *16*, de la strophe; dans les deux éléments, le vers long (v. 1 de la strophe, v. 4 de l'épode) se trouve à l'initiale de la période la plus longue. À l'ordre A B de la strophe correspond dans l'épode l'ordre B A.

Les éléments strophiques des IIe et IIIe *stasima* ont donc tous les quatre la même ampleur—*34* temps marqués—, c'est-à-dire le même nombre de mesures, mais la composition périodologique varie d'un *stasimon* à l'autre: trois périodes respectivement égales, disposées dans l'ordre A A B ou A B A, dans le IIe *stasimon*; deux périodes, elles aussi respectivement égales, disposées dans l'ordre

A B ou B A, dans le IIIe. Cette uniformité dans la diversité nous permettra peut-être d'apporter quelque lumière sur la composition du Ier *stasimon*, où les difficultés de texte sont grandes.

* * *

Dans le Ier *stasimon*, le chœur des Océanides, comme le pays tout entier, comme les peuples voisins, gémit sur le destin de Prométhée; à leurs lamentations répond en écho la plainte de la mer, de l'Hadès et des fleuves.

Strophe et antistrophe 1 (397–405 et 406–14) [8]

⏑ _ ⏑ _ _ ⏑ ⏑ _ | ⏑ _ ⏑ _ _

{
⏑ ⏑ _ _ ⏑ ⏑ _ _

⏑ ⏑ _ | _ ⏑ ⏑ _ ⏑ _ ⏑ _ _

⏑ ⏑ _ ⏑ _ ⏑ | _ _

⏑ ⏑ _ ⏑ _ ⏑ _ _

5   ⏑ ⏑ _ | ⏑ _ | ⏑ _ _

{
⏑ ⏑ _ ⏑ _ ⏑ _ | _

⏑ ⏑ | _ _ _ ⏑ | _ _

Strophe et antistrophe 2 (415–19 et 420–24)

⏑ ⏑ ⏑ _ ⏑ _ ⏑ _ _

_ ⏑ _ ⏑ _ | ⏑ _ _

_ ⏑ _ | ⏑ _ ⏑ _ _

{
_ ⏑ _ | ⏑ ⏑ | _ ⏑ _

_ ⏑ | ⏑ _ ⏑ _ _

Épode (431–35)

⏑ _ ⏑ _ ⏑ _ ⏑ _

_ ⏑ _ ⏑ _ ⏑ _

⏑ _ ⏑ ⏑⏑ ⏑ ⏑⏑ ⏑ _ ⏑ _ _

{
_ _ _ ⏑ ⏑ _ ⏑ ⏑ _ ⏑ _

⏑ _ ⏑ _ _

Le Ier *stasimon* est composé de deux couples de strophes suivies d'un élément peu clair, sur la nature duquel—troisième couple de strophes? épode?—les avis des éditeurs varient fortement.

Les difficultés commencent, en fait, avec la première couple de strophes, dont la scansion a donné lieu à des interprétations métriques toutes différentes. Les uns, comme Studemund,

[8] Le schéma métrique a été disposé de façon que les éléments identiques soient superposés.

Wilamowitz, Schroeder, B. Gentili, W. Theiler et W. Kraus, y voient des épichoriambiques (un mètre iambique pur suivi d'un choriambe). Les autres, avec Mazon et Murray, Dale, Dain et Korzeniewski, les considèrent comme des vers ioniques mineurs, purs ou sous la forme anaclastique de l'anacréontique ($\cup\cup\_\cup\_$ $\cup\_\_$). Ce qui est fin de vers pour les uns est césure pour les autres, et vice versa. Il faut donner raison à ceux qui soutiennent la seconde interprétation, d'abord parce que les prétendus épichoriambiques ne présentent jamais, dans le mètre qui précède le choriambe, l'habituelle liberté des quatre syllabes, ensuite parce que cette interprétation s'accorde mieux avec le mouvement de la phrase dans la strophe et dans l'antistrophe correspondante.

Le premier vers est formellement identique[9] au premier vers de la *parodos*:

$$\text{Μηδὲν φοβηθῇς· φιλία γὰρ ἅδε τάξις (128).}$$

À première vue, il est fait d'un anacréontique précédé d'un *rufulianum* ou penthémimère iambique. Cette tripodie syncopée, qui recouvre exactement, quand son initiale est brève, la suite des cinq dernières syllabes de l'anacréontique, sert d'introduction à la strophe, avec une ambiguïté voulue. En effet, il est plus probable que le premier vers est formé d'un mètre iambique suivi d'un ennéasyllabe choriambique,[10] le tout équivalent à un hendécasyllabe sapphique prolongé d'un iambe. La finale bivalente de l'ennéa-syllabe entraîne une véritable ἐπιπλοκή et le passage au type anacréontique, mais l'équivoque reste entretenue jusqu'à la fin de la strophe par une série de coupes généralisées au même point du vers.

La suite est claire. Le long vers 2 est un véritable pentamètre, formé d'un mètre ionique mineur, d'un mètre trochaïque (auquel correspond dans l'antistrophe un mètre ionique), d'un mètre ionique et d'un dimètre anacréontique. Les vers 3, 4 et 5 sont des

[9] À l'exception de la syllabe initiale qui est un *anceps*, long dans la *parodos*, bref dans le Ier *stasimon*.

[10] On trouve d'autres emplois de cet ennéasyllabe choriambique, ou dimètre choriambique hypercatalectique, par exemple dans *Oedipe à Colone*, 129: καὶ παραμειβόμεσθ' ἀδέρκτως, ou dans *Iphigénie à Aulis*, 761: μαντόσυνοι πνεύσωσ' ἀνάγκαι (ces deux vers sont cités par W. J. W. Koster, *Traité de métrique grecque*[3] [Leyde 1963], 218, à qui je les emprunte).

anacréontiques. Le vers 6 est fait d'un anacréontique et d'un dimètre ionique (un ionique mineur suivi d'un mètre trochaïque).

Dans la strophe et dans l'antistrophe, le mouvement de la phrase s'accorde mieux avec l'interprétation ionique qu'avec la choriambique, car pauses du sens et fins de vers coïncident dans la première, alors que dans l'autre les enjambements sont continuels (par exemple 398: οὐλομένας | τύχας, et 407: στονόεν | λέλακε χώρα) et que l'on aboutit à un vers démesuré (400–404 et 409–13) qui disloque la phrase.

Quelle que soit l'interprétation adoptée, le nombre total des temps marqués de la strophe reste le même: *37*, mais leur répartition semble être en faveur de l'interprétation ionique. En effet, la périodologie adoptée par Schroeder entraîne la répartition suivante des temps marqués: *14 (4 + 10)*, *18*, *5*. Il est préférable, comme l'a fait Dain avec une répartition en vers un peu différente de celle que j'ai adoptée, de distinguer trois périodes, d'ampleur croissante par le nombre des vers comme par celui des temps marqués:

I (v. 1):   7 temps marqués;
II (vv. 2–3):   *14* temps marqués (le double de I);
III (vv. 4–6):   *16* temps marqués.

La première période, grâce à l'ἐπιπλοκή, se termine par un anacréontique, tout comme la seconde, où il est précédé d'un autre anacréontique et d'un trimètre ionique; la troisième période est comme un renversement amplifié de la seconde; trois anacréontiques y sont suivis d'un dimètre ionique.

Avec la seconde strophe apparaissent des séries trochaïques continues, dont il n'est pas d'autre exemple chez Eschyle. Trois dimètres trochaïques, formant chacun un vers, sont suivis d'un tétramètre choriambique, variante du priapéen: un glyconien et un dimètre choriambique catalectique (au lieu de l'usuel phérécratien), qui rappelle le vers initial de la première strophe. La synaphie est de règle entre les deux mètres des vers trochaïques, avec une seule exception, au vers 1 de la strophe.

La répartition en périodes n'est pas nette. À en juger par le texte de la strophe, il y aurait une division entre les vers 2 et 3. Mais le texte de l'antistrophe indiquerait plutôt une coupure entre les vers 3 et 4, ce qui s'accorde mieux avec la composition du passage: les

trois vers trochaïques formeraient une période de *12* temps marqués
(*4 + 4 + 4*), le tétramètre choriambique une période de *8* temps
marqués. Quoi qu'il en soit du détail de la périodologie, le total des
temps marqués est de *20*.

Les vers 425–30, comme l'a montré Wilamowitz[11] après Badham,
sont une interpolation qui s'inspire très précisément d'un passage
de la *parodos* (v. 148) et de la tirade de Prométhée dans le premier
épisode (vv. 347–50). Outre les difficultés textuelles et métriques
qu'ils présentent, ils rompent le développement de l'ensemble du
stasimon: le chœur gémit sur le sort de Prométhée, condamné par
Zeus (str. 1); le pays tout entier et l'Asie gémissent aussi (ant. 1),
de même que les peuples voisins: Amazones et Scythes (str. 2),
Arabes et habitants du Caucase[12] (ant. 2); à ces plaintes terrestres
s'unissent celles de la mer, de l'Hadès et des fleuves (épode). La
remarque sur Atlas, son sort et ses gémissements, n'a que faire à
cette place, semble-t-il.

Les cinq derniers vers (431–35) constituent à eux seuls l'épode,
d'une ampleur comparable à celle de la seconde couple de strophes.
En gardant en tête le βοᾷ de la tradition manuscrite, au lieu d'y
substituer, avec Wilamowitz, ὑποστενάζει, mot final du passage
interpolé, on obtient une composition très claire. Le premier vers
est un dimètre iambique. Le second, un dimètre aussi, semble être
trochaïque et catalectique, mais il faut plutôt le considérer comme
iambique et acéphale, tout comme nous l'avons vu dans l'épode
du IIIe *stasimon*. Le vers 3 est un trimètre iambique catalectique avec
deux résolutions. Plutôt que de reconnaître dans les deux dernières
lignes deux vers, un dimètre dactylique catalectique *in syllabam*
(*alcmanicum*), avec un spondée au lieu du dactyle initial, suivi d'un
dimètre iambique catalectique, il vaut mieux, comme on l'a fait
plus haut dans le schéma métrique, considérer ces deux lignes
comme un seul vers, formé d'un glyconien à redoublement dactylique
(‒ ‒ ‒ ∪ ∪ ‒ ∪ ∪ ‒ ∪ ‒) et d'une tripodie iambique cata-

[11] U. von Wilamowitz-Moellendorff, *Aischylos. Interpretationen* (Berlin 1914), p. 161.

[12] En gardant ici le texte de la tradition manuscrite unanime, on évite, au prix d'une
liberté banale dans la *responsio* (‒ ∪ ‒ ‒ ‒ répondant à ‒ ∪ ‒ ∪), de faire placer
par Eschyle les Arabes dans le Caucase et l'on retrouve en même temps la quadruple
expression spatiale, chère aux poètes grecs, qui correspond peu ou prou aux quatre
points cardinaux. L'épode présente de même une division en quatre, un peu artificielle,
avec κλύδων, βυθός, μυχός et παγαί.

lectique ($\cup \_ \cup \_ \_$), rappel très net, dans son équivoque voulue, du vers initial de la première strophe et, dans une moindre mesure, du vers final de la seconde strophe.

Quelle que soit l'interprétation métrique du vers 2 et des deux dernières lignes, le décompte des temps marqués reste le même: *4* pour chacun des deux premiers vers, *6* pour le troisième, *4 + 4* ou *8* selon qu'on distingue ou non deux vers dans les deux dernières lignes. Une division en trois périodes—deux périodes égales encadrant une période plus courte—est possible:

I (vv. 1–2)	*8* temps marqués
II (v. 3)	*6* temps marqués
III (vv. 4–5 ou v. 4)	*8* temps marqués

mais une division en deux périodes inégales:

I (vv. 1–3)	*14* temps marqués
II (vv. 4–5 ou v. 4)	*8* temps marqués

s'accorde peut-être mieux avec l'opposition métrique des trois premiers vers et des deux lignes finales, ainsi qu'avec le jeu stylistique des propositions en asyndète dans ceux-là et reliées par *θ'* dans celles-ci. Les deux périodes ainsi déterminées correspondent respectivement, par leur longueur, à la période médiane de la première strophe et à la période initiale ou finale, selon l'interprétation choisie, de la seconde.[13]

Le total des temps marqués dans le premier *stasimon* est de: *37 × 2 + 20 × 2 + 22*, soit *136*, c'est-à-dire le même que dans le second *stasimon* (*34 × 2 + 34 × 2*), alors que le troisième en compte *102* (*34 × 2 + 34*). Tout se passe comme si les trois *stasima* étaient bâtis sur une unité de *34* temps marqués, de façon voilée dans le premier, d'une manière visible dans les deux autres. Cette rencontre, qui ne saurait être fortuite, confirme l'athétèse des vers 425–30.

Paris, 28 mai 1970

[13] Des rappels du même genre relient le Ier *stasimon* à la *parodos*. La strophe initiale du *stasimon*, avec *37* temps marqués, est égale à la seconde strophe de la *parodos*, alors que l'épode du même *stasimon*, avec *22* temps marqués, est la moitié de la première strophe de la *parodos* (*44* temps marqués). De telles correspondances contribuent à assurer l'unité et le rythme de la tragédie.

APPENDICE

On trouvera ci-après le texte des trois *stasima* du *Prométhée enchaîné*, disposé selon l'analyse métrique qui a été présentée et discutée dans le corps de l'article. Quand un vers, en raison de sa longueur ou de sa composition, est réparti sur deux ou plusieurs lignes, un retrait signale leur unité. Les périodes déterminées à l'intérieur des éléments strophiques sont séparées par un interligne plus fort.

L'apparat critique, fondé pour une large part sur le travail de R. D. Dawe (*The Collation and Investigation of Manuscripts of Aeschylus* [Cambridge 1964], pp. 198–246 pour le *Prométhée*), vise à fournir au lecteur les données essentielles de la tradition; il n'a pas paru possible, dans le cadre de cet article et du sujet qu'il traite, de justifier le choix des variantes ou des corrections.

Stasimon I

$$\Sigma\tau\acute{\epsilon}\nu\omega\ \sigma\epsilon\ \tau\hat{a}\varsigma\ o\dot{v}\lambda o\mu\acute{\epsilon}\nu a\varsigma\ \tau\acute{v}\chi a\varsigma,\ \Pi\rho o\mu\eta\theta\epsilon\hat{v},\qquad\text{Str. 1}\qquad 397$$

$$\delta a\kappa\rho v\sigma\acute{\iota}\sigma\tau a\kappa\tau o\nu\ \delta'\ \dot{a}\pi'\ \ddot{o}\sigma\sigma\omega\nu$$
$$\qquad\dot{\rho}a\delta\iota\nu\hat{\omega}\nu\ \lambda\epsilon\iota\beta o\mu\acute{\epsilon}\nu a\ \dot{\rho}\acute{\epsilon}o\varsigma\ \pi a\rho\epsilon\iota\grave{a}\nu\qquad\qquad 400$$
$$\nu o\tau\acute{\iota}o\iota\varsigma\ \ddot{\epsilon}\tau\epsilon\gamma\xi a\ \pi a\gamma a\hat{\iota}\varsigma\cdot$$

$$\qquad\dot{a}\mu\acute{\epsilon}\gamma a\rho\tau a\ \gamma\grave{a}\rho\ \tau\acute{a}\delta\epsilon\ Z\epsilon\grave{v}\varsigma$$
$$5\qquad i\delta\acute{\iota}o\iota\varsigma\ \nu\acute{o}\mu o\iota\varsigma\ \kappa\rho a\tau\acute{v}\nu\omega\nu$$
$$\qquad\dot{v}\pi\epsilon\rho\acute{\eta}\phi a\nu o\nu\ \theta\epsilon o\hat{\iota}\varsigma\ \tau o\hat{\iota}\varsigma$$
$$\qquad\pi\acute{a}\rho o\varsigma\ \dot{\epsilon}\nu\delta\epsilon\acute{\iota}\kappa\nu v\sigma\iota\nu\ a\dot{\iota}\chi\mu\acute{a}\nu.\qquad\qquad 405$$

$$\Pi\rho\acute{o}\pi a\sigma a\ \delta'\ \ddot{\eta}\delta\eta\ \sigma\tau o\nu\acute{o}\epsilon\nu\ \lambda\acute{\epsilon}\lambda a\kappa\epsilon\ \chi\acute{\omega}\rho a,\qquad\text{Ant. 1}$$

$$\mu\epsilon\gamma a\lambda o\sigma\chi\acute{\eta}\mu o\nu\acute{a}\ \tau'\ \dot{a}\rho\chi a\iota\text{-}$$
$$\qquad o\pi\rho\epsilon\pi\hat{\eta}\ \langle\_\ \cup\ \cup\ \_\rangle\ \sigma\tau\acute{\epsilon}\nu o v\sigma\iota\ \tau\grave{a}\nu\ \sigma\grave{a}\nu$$
$$\xi v\nu o\mu a\iota\mu\acute{o}\nu\omega\nu\ \tau\epsilon\ \tau\iota\mu\acute{a}\nu\cdot\qquad\qquad 410$$

$$\qquad\dot{o}\pi\acute{o}\sigma o\iota\ \tau'\ \ddot{\epsilon}\pi o\iota\kappa o\nu\ \dot{a}\gamma\nu\hat{a}\varsigma$$
$$5\qquad\dot{A}\sigma\acute{\iota}a\varsigma\ \ddot{\epsilon}\delta o\varsigma\ \nu\acute{\epsilon}\mu o\nu\tau a\iota$$
$$\qquad\mu\epsilon\gamma a\lambda o\sigma\tau\acute{o}\nu o\iota\sigma\iota\ \sigma o\hat{\iota}\varsigma\ \pi\acute{\eta}\text{-}$$
$$\qquad\mu a\sigma\iota\ \sigma v\gamma\kappa\acute{a}\mu\nu o v\sigma\iota\ \theta\nu a\tau o\acute{\iota}\cdot$$

399 δ' om. BO (del. Tricl.)
400 ῥαδινῶν MPCBI: ῥαδινὸν rell. codd.
405 ἐνδείκνυσιν Tricl.: ἐνδεικνύειν M ἐνδεικνύει IOᶜ δείκνυσι(ν) QKVPNBY δεικνύει CH
409 τ' ἐσχατιαὶ suppl. Weil θ' ἑσπέριοι Wecklein τ' οἰχομέναν Mazon.

Κολχίδος τε γᾶς ἔνοικοι   Str. 2   415
παρθένοι, μάχας ἄτρεστοι,
καὶ Σκύθης ὅμιλος, οἳ γᾶς

ἔσχατον τόπον ἀμφὶ Μαι-
ῶτιν ἔχουσι λίμναν,

Ἀραβίας τ' ἄρειον ἄνθος,   Ant. 2   420
ὑψίκρημνόν θ' οἳ πόλισμα
Καυκάσου πέλας νέμονται,

δάϊος στρατὸς ὀξυπρώ-
ροισι βρέμων ἐν αἰχμαῖς.   424

Βοᾷ δὲ πόντιος κλύδων   Ep.   431
ξυμπίτνων, στένει βυθός,
κελαινὸς Ἄϊδος ὑποβρέμει μυχὸς γᾶς,

παγαί θ' ἁγνορύτων ποταμῶν στένου-
σιν ἄλγος οἰκτρόν.   435

Stasimon II

Μηδάμ' ὁ πάντα νέμων   Str. 1   526
θεῖτ' ἐμᾷ γνώμᾳ κράτος ἀντίπαλον Ζεύς,
μηδ' ἐλινύσαιμι θεοὺς ὁσίαις

θοίναις ποτινισσομένα   530
5 βουφόνοις παρ' Ὠκεανοῦ πατρὸς ἄσβεστον πόρον,
μηδ' ἀλίτοιμι λόγοις·

ἀλλά μοι τόδ' ἐμμένοι καὶ μήποτ' ἐκτακείη.   535

Ἀδύ τι θαρσαλέαις   Ant. 1
τὸν μακρὸν τείνειν βίον ἐλπίσι, φαναῖς
θυμὸν ἀλδαίνουσαν ἐν εὐφροσύναις·

416 μάχας M Iᵃᶜ Oᵃᶜ Y: μάχαις rell. codd.
421 θ' del. Tricl. (unde 420 Ἀβαρίας Boissonade Ἀβασίας Freshfield Καλυβίας Schütz
alii alia)
422 νέμονται QKVPNYIO: νέμουσι MCHB
425–30 μόνον—ὑποστενάζει secl. Badham
432 βυθός: βοθύς V βαθύς MH]
433 κελαινὸς Lachmann: κελαινὸς δ' codd.
435 οἰκτρόν: πικρόν CHB
535 ἀλλά codd.: βάλε Maas μάλα Hermann (cf. 543 ἰδίᾳ)
536 ἀδύ: ἡδύ codd.

φρίσσω δέ σε δερκομένα   540
5 μυρίοις μόχθοις διακναιόμενον ⟨_ _ ◡ _⟩
Ζῆνα γὰρ οὐ τρομέων

ἰδίᾳ γνώμᾳ σέβῃ θνατοὺς ἄγαν, Προμηθεῦ.

Φέρ' ὅπως ἄχαρις χάρις, ὦ φίλος, εἰ-   Str. 2
πέ, ποῦ τίς ἀλκά,   545
τίς ἐφαμερίων
ἄρηξις; οὐδ' ἐδέρχθης

ὀλιγοδρανίαν
ἄκικυν ἰσόνειρον ᾆ τὸ φωτῶν

ἀλαὸν γένος ἐμπεποδισμένον; οὔποτε ⟨_ _⟩   550
5 τὰν Διὸς ἁρμονίαν θνα-
τῶν παρεξίασι βουλαί.

Ἔμαθον τάδε σὰς προσιδοῦσ' ὀλοὰς   Ant. 2
τύχας, Προμηθεῦ·
τὸ διαμφίδιον
δέ μοι μέλος προσέπτα   555

τόδ' ἐκεῖνό θ' ὅ τ' ἀμ-
φὶ λουτρὰ καὶ λέχος σὸν ὑμεναίουν

ἰότατι γάμων, ὅτε τὰν ὁμοπάτριον ἔδνοις
5 ἄγαγες Ἡσιόναν πεί-
θων δάμαρτα κοινόλεκτρον.   560

Stasimon III

Ἦ σοφός, ἦ σοφὸς ἦν ὃς   Str. 887
πρῶτος ἐν γνώμᾳ τόδ' ἐβάστασε καὶ γλώσ-
σᾳ διεμυθολόγησεν,
ὡς τὸ κηδεῦσαι καθ' ἑαυτὸν ἀριστεύει μακρῷ,   890

---

541 χαλκευμάτων suppl. Fritzsche θνατῶν χάριν Murray Ζηνὸς κότῳ Dodds alii alia.
544 ἄχαρις χάρις Tricl.: χάρις ἄχαρις codd. χάρις ἁ χάρις Headlam
550 γάρ τοι suppl. Bergk alii alia
556 ἐκεῖνό θ' ὅ τ' Tricl.: ἐκεῖν' ὅτε τότ' M ἐκεῖνό τε ὅτ' QKVNOP ἐκεῖν' ὅτ' HBI ἐκεῖνο ὅτ'
Υ ἐκεῖν' ὅτε τ' C
557 λουτρὰ MQKCHO: λοετρὰ PVNBY λουτρὸν I
560 πείθων M: πιθὼν QKPVNCOΥI ποθῶν BH.

καὶ μήτε τῶν πλούτῳ διαθρυπτομένων
μήτε τῶν γέννα μεγαλυνομένων
5   ὄντα χερνήταν ἐραστεῦσαι γάμων.

Μήποτε μήποτέ μ᾽, ὦ Μοῖ-   Ant.
    ραι <∪ _ _ _>, λεχέων Διὸς εὐνά-   895
    τειραν ἴδοισθε πέλουσαν·
μηδὲ πλαθείην γαμέτᾳ τινὶ τῶν ἐξ οὐρανοῦ.

Ταρβῶ γὰρ ἀστεργάνορα παρθενίαν
εἰσορῶσ᾽ Ἰοῦς ἀμαλαπτομέναν
5   δυσπλάνοις Ἥρας ἀλατείαις πόνων.   900

Ἐμοὶ δ᾽ ὅτε μὲν ὁμαλὸς ὁ γάμος, ἄφοβος·   Ep.
μηδὲ κρεισσόνων θεῶν
ἔρως ἄφυκτον ὄμμα προσδράκοι με.

Ἀπόλεμος ὅδε γ᾽ ὁ πόλεμος, ἄπορα πόριμος, οὐδ᾽
    ἔχω τίς ἂν γενοίμαν·   905
5   τὰν Διὸς γὰρ οὐχ ὁρῶ
    μῆτιν ὅπᾳ φύγοιμ᾽ ἄν.

---

895 μακραίωνες suppl. Hermann τελέστειραι Headlam alii alia
897 πλαθείην Tricl.: πλαθείη ἐν M πλαθείην ἐν OI πλασθείην ἐν M²QKVYBCHPᶜ
899 ἀμαλαπτομέναν Dindorf (γ᾽ ἀμαλαπτομέναν Weil): γάμῳ δαπτομέναν (-μένην) codd.
900 δυσπλάνοις Tricl.: δυσπλάγχνοις (-νων BH -νας K) codd.; ἀλατείαις Tricl.: ἀλατείαισι codd.
901 ὅτε Arnaud: ὅτι codd.; ἄφοβος Bothe: ἄφοβος οὐ δέδια codd.
903 προσδράκοι Salvini: -δάρκοι M -δέρκοι rell. codd.

CONJECTURES AND INTERPRETATIONS IN AESCHYLUS' *SUPPLICES*

DOUGLAS YOUNG

†24 October 1973

It is with the heartiest goodwill and gratitude that I offer a small contribution to the volume honouring Professor Alexander Turyn, for I have, over many years, greatly benefited from the insights to be found abundantly in his works on the text transmissions of the Attic tragedians. In a humble way I have been developing part of his field, by collating and investigating in full all the extant manuscripts of the *Septem*, with a view to isolating and evaluating the independent witnesses. My study, not yet quite completed, has reinforced my impression that M is by far the most reliable witness to the text of Aeschylus. Applying this conviction to the *Supplices*, I note that earlier scholars have defended readings of M at nearly 90 places where the currently most used edition, that of Murray (2 ed. 1955), departs from the paradosis. But I find almost a score further places where the reading of M seems to be defensible, and an additional two score where the letters of M appear to need little emendation to yield something fairly plausible. Taking them in their order, the places where I would defend or emend are these:

44. M's readings are acceptable with barytone accentuation of the preposition appropriate to its postposition. Thus 40–45 would run:

νῦν δ' ἐπικεκλομένα
Δῖον πόρτιν ὑπερ-
πόντιον τιμάορ' ἶνίν τ'
ἀνθονομούσας (Porson) προγόνου
βοὸς ἐξ ἐπιπνοίαις
Ζηνός·...

"And now calling upon the heifer of Zeus overseas as helper, and the son from our flower-browsing ancestress cow by the onbreathings of Zeus:..."

51–55 I would read thus:

...τῶν
πρόσθε πόνων μνασαμένα
τά τε νῦν, ἐπιδείξω
πιστὰ τεκμήρια γαιονόμοις,
ἴδ' (= ἰδὲ) ἄελπτά περ ὄντα φανεῖται. (οἶδ' M)

"...after making mention of the former troubles and the present matters, I will display trustworthy proofs to the dwellers in the land, and, un-expected though they be, they shall be manifested." M's οἶδ' would be an itacist corruption of ἰδέ 'and', which is restored by conjecture in Soph. *Ant.* 969.

59 and 64 present problems of responsion, for which the *lenissima medicina* might be as follows:

58 εἰ δὲ κυρεῖ τις πέλας οἰωνοπόλων
59 ἐγγάϊος οἶκτον οἴκτρ' ἀίων,...
~64 πενθεῖ νέον οἶκτον ἠϊθέων,

"But if any expert in birds, dwelling in the land, hearing (our) lament lamentfully,..." The only change is from M's οἰκτρὸν to my οἴκτρ' (for adverbial neuter plural οἰκτρά). In 64 I write quadrisyllabically ἠϊθέων. The metre of 59 ~ 64 consists of a reizianum and a choriamb:
_ _ ∪ ∪ _ ∪ + _ ∪ ∪ _.

60 δοξάσει τις ἀκούων...(M) "someone will think himself hearing ..." It is a participial construction after a verb of thinking, of the type μέμνημαι ἀκούσας. Wellauer keeps, but interprets otherwise.

86–87 might be best punctuated thus:
εἴθ' εἴη Διὸς εὖ παναληθῶς.
Διὸς ἵμερος οὐκ εὐθήρατος ἐτύχθη.

"Would that the weal of Zeus might exist in full reality! The desire of Zeus is fashioned in ways not easy to grasp." Compare *Agam.* 217, εὖ γὰρ εἴη, and, with the article, *Agam.* 121, τὸ δ' εὖ νικάτω. 87 is taken as a single sentence by Wellauer, Hermann, Paley, Tucker, Smyth, and Mazon. It means that the will of Zeus is inscrutable.

100–103 I would read

πᾶν ἄπονον δαιμόνιον. (τὰν ἄποινον M, corr. Wellauer, δαιμονίων
                                              M, corr. Bothe)
ἤμενον ἂν φρόνημά πως (ἤμενονᾶν M fere)
αὐτόθεν ἐξέπραξεν ἔμ-
         πας ἑδράνων ἐφ' ἁγνῶν.

"All divinity is effortless. Sitting still, it continually accomplishes its intent on the spot, nonetheless, on its divine seats." *LSJ*, s.v. ἄν, III, C, state that iterative ἄν with aorist is not in Pindar or Aeschylus; but this seems an instance. Without the modal particle the aorist would be called 'gnomic'.

121, 132. Why not M's σινδονίᾳ, made of σινδών? Cf. Aesch. frg. 240 Mette (153 Nauck).

146–47 ἔχουσα σέμν' ἐνώπι' ἀ- / σφαλής,... (for M's ἀσφαλές) would be an easy re-interpretation, meaning "possessing in security august façades."

165. M's ἄταν γαμετουρανόνεικον could be a brachylogical way of saying "an infatuation causing strife of spouses in heaven."

176. M's ἵκετε can scan with a long iota, as in Homer and Pindar.

186–87. M's τεθειμένος / ὠμῇ ξὺν ὀργῇ can be equivalent, by anastrophic tmesis, to συντεθειμένος ὀργῇ, "having made with anger a compact, συνθήκη." ὄχλος (182) is suppliable as subject, with the retention at 187 of M's τόνδ'...στόλον, as in many editions from Wellauer to Smyth.

254. For M's διάλγος Murray accepts Wordsworth's δι' ἁγνός. But one may consider whether ἄλπος is a possible form of the adjective *ἄλπνος, in the sense of Latin 'almus'. Compare *LSJ* s.vv. ἄλπνιστος, ἀλπαλέον; ἔπαλπνος is Pindaric. If so, the verse might run: καὶ πᾶσαν αἶαν, ἧς δι' ἄλπος ἔρχεται / Στρυμών,... The corruption of uncial *pi* to *gamma* is easier than that implied by Wordsworth's suggestion.

306. M's text is intelligible with re-punctuation thus: τί οὖν; ἔτευξε δ' ἄλλο δυσπότμῳ βοΐ; "How then? And did she cause something else for the ill-fated heifer?"

339. M's collocation of particles καὶ δυστυχούντων τ' can be paralleled by *Eum.* 713. Cf. Italie's Index s.v. τε, V, 5.

362–64 might be restored with some plausibility thus:

ποτιτρόπαιον αἰδόμενος οὐρανοῦ (Young, ex οὖν M)
⟨δώρων οὐ πένῃ.⟩ πάτερ, ἱεροδόκα (πάτερ Young, ex περ M)
θεῶν λήματ' ἀπ' ἀνδρὸς ἁγνοῦ.

"Respecting (if you respect) a suppliant, you do not lack the gifts of heaven. Father, the gods' tempers are receptive of sacred gifts from a holy man." In 363 Hermann supplied οὐ πένῃ from the scholiast's οὐ πτωχεύσεις, and I suggest supplying δώρων. My conjectures at 362–63 assume corruption by misreading of *nomina sacra*, which is fairly frequent, though I know of no double occurrence in successive lines. In dochmii there is no need for exact responsion syllable by syllable. As restored 363 constitutes two dochmii, as does the corresponding verse 352.

430. A capital initial should be given to Δίκας.

443–48 may be most conservatively interpreted thus, with nominative absolutes at 444 and 446 (or an anacoluthon at 444):

443   καὶ χρήμασιν μὲν ἐκ δόμων πορθουμένων (M)
444   Ἄτην γεμίζων καὶ μέγ' ἐμπλήσας γόμου (γε μείζω M, corr. Scaliger)
445   γένοιτ' ἂν ἄλλα Κτησίου Διὸς χάριν.
446   καὶ γλῶσσα τοξεύσασα μὴ τὰ καίρια
447   γένοιτο μύθου μῦθος ἂν θελκτήριος.
448   ἀλγεινὰ θυμοῦ κάρτα κινητήρια.

"On the one hand, with wealth from pillaged homes if I glut Ate, filling her up greatly with the cargo,—other (wealth) could accrue, thanks to Zeus of possessions. On the other hand, if a tongue fires shafts not on the mark, one word might be assuaging of another word. Painful (words are) very apt to move wrath." For Aeschylus' use of the nominative absolute cf. Fraenkel on *Agam.* 980.

458 †τύχαν† γυναικῶν ταῦτα συμπρεπῆ πέλοι. (M) Recalling Aristophanes' τύχἀγαθῇ for τύχη ἀγαθῇ at *Av.* 675, one may be tempted to interpret M's τύχαν as τύχη ἄν. "These would be appropriate to the condition (status) of women," taking the sense of *LSJ*, s.v. τύχη, IV, 3. Or else simply render τύχη ἄν "perchance", like Marckscheffel's τάχ' ἄν.

468. M has καὶ μὴν πολλαχῇ γε δυσπάλαιστα πράγματα,... I propose καὶ πολλαχῇ μὴν δυσπάλαιστα πράγματα,...
This assumes corruption by approximation of μὴν to καὶ, followed by insertion of a stopgap γε.

514. ἀνάκτων of M merely needs re-accenting to make the verse ἀεὶ δ' ἀνακτῶν ἐστι δεῖμ' ἐξαίσιον. Cf. *Agam.* 1211. "The fear of persons liable to be brought back from flight (ἀνάγω) is always extraordinary." The king almost implies that the Chorus are runaway slaves; and they react by saying "Give us comfort by speaking and acting *wisely*, with (good) wit," where M's φρενί should be retained.

556. M has the word εἰσικνουμένου with the two last letters in erasure and a chi over the kappa. Allowing for scribal interpretation of Aeschylus'

original omicron as either omega or omicron-upsilon, one may wonder whether the poet meant what he wrote to be interpreted as εἰσιχνωμένου, in the sense ἰχνεύοντος. *LSJ* cite the simple verb ἰχνάομαι from Hesychios and the Souda.

584. M's τὸ δὴ could be re-divided to give acceptable sense:

φυσιζόου γένος τόδ᾽ ἦ
Ζηνός ἐστιν ἀληθῶς·

"This progeny truly belongs to life-creating Zeus, in reality."

595–97 can be interpreted with this punctuation and accenting:

ὑπ᾽ ἀρχὰς δ᾽ οὔτινος θοάζων
τὸ μεῖον κρεισσόνων κρατύνει. (κρεῖσσον ὢν M, corr. Turnebus)
οὔτινος ἄνωθεν ἡμένου σέβει κάτω. (M)

"Not under anyone's orders hurrying does he have his sway as the lesser (sway) than (that of) greater (gods). He does not pay reverence below while someone sits above."

633–34 μήποτε πυρέφατον
       [τὰν] Πελασγίαν πόλιν . . .

M's πυρέφατον, from πυρή, πυρά 'pyre', gives good sense, 'pyre-slain', 'slain as on a pyre', appropriate to a burned out city. Wellauer deleted the article as an intruded gloss. There is synizesis of iota in Πελασγίαν.

659–60 μήποτε λοιμὸς ἀνδρῶν
       τῶνδε πόλιν κενῶσαι. (M)

"Never may pestilence empty *these* men's city!" Surely a better emphasis than Hermann's τάνδε, accepted by Murray: "Never may pestilence empty this city of *men*!" (but only of women and children, or of gods?).

667–9 M's text could be acceptably punctuated thus:

καὶ γεραροῖσι πρε- /
σβυτοδόκοι γεμόν- /
των. θυμέλαι φλεγόντων.

"And may the elder-receiving (seats) be full of venerable men. May altars flame."

680. M's δαίξων makes good sense as a future participle of purpose. The unnecessary alteration of the Aldina has persisted by that *vis inertiae* of the existing printed text which seems to clog all editorial efforts even now.

698. M offers φυλάσσοι τ᾽ ἀτιμίας τιμάς..., with a marginal ἀσφαλίας.

Wilamowitz saw that there had been misreading of a delta as a lambda, and proposed ἀσφάδαστα. I assume also haplography of τι, and believe Aeschylus may have written: φυλάσσοι τ' ἀσφαδαιστὶ τιμὰς...ΑΣΦΑΔΑΙΣ gave rise to ΑΣΦΑΛΙΑΣ by 'Verbesserungsversuch'. ἀτιμίας τιμάς might be the error of M's copyist, or have been taken over from the antigraph, along with an interlinear or marginal ἀσφαλίας there.

711. †μῆτρες ἀεὶ† of M is usually emended to μὴ τρέσητε, with Turnebus. But at v. 729 M originally wrote μὴ τρέσαιτέ νιν. The optative makes the phrase a negative wish, "May you not be afraid," where the subjunctive makes it a prohibition, "Do not be afraid." Perhaps we should read the optative at both 711 and 729.

716–18 would run, with a small change of M in 718, thus:

καὶ πρῷρα πρόσθεν ὄμμασιν βλέπουσ' ὁδόν,
οἴακος εὐθυντῆρος ὑστάτου νεὼς
ἄγαν καλῶς κλύουσ', ἅτ' οὖσ' ἂν οὐ φίλη. (Μ κλύουσα τῶσ* ἂν...)

718 means: "...as capable of being unfriendly."

740. One might well punctuate: ...θάρσει μαχοῦνται... "They will fight with courage."

740. M's form ἐγών is supported by Pers. 931.

744. M's † ἐπεὶ τάχει † (κότῳ) suggests a possible hapax ἐπιταχεῖ, "with hasty anger." A verb ἐπιταχύνω exists from Thucydides on.

748. M's aorist suggests the reading, with a supplement lost by haplography: μόνην δὲ μή <με> πρόλιπε.

751. M's δυσάγνοις φρεσσίν should be kept, with double sigma, for we do not know how much sibilance Aeschylus intended in the passage. It is quite wrong to try and force dochmiac passages into exact syllabic correspondence: for the metre, like syncopated iambics, is normally used to express agitation, where a less strict responsion is appropriate.

766–69. M's division at 768 is quite correct, with ὥστε in the sense ὥσπερ:

...οὐδ' ἐν ἀγκυρουχίαις
θαρσοῦσι ναῶν ποιμένες παραυτίκα,
ἀλλ' ὥστε καὶ μολόντες ἀλίμενον χθόνα
ἐς νύκτ' ἀποστείχοντος ἡλίου.

"...nor are the shepherds of ships straightway confident in their anchor-holdings, but just like (shipmasters) arriving at a harbourless land while the sun is departing into night."

774. With the Escorialensis (E) and Robortello, read

πράξασ' ἀρωγὴν ἄγγελον δ' οὐ μέμψεται / πόλις γέρονθ',...

(δ' in fourth place: cf. Italie p. 64, IX 2, c). "And the city, when it effects succour, will not blame an old man messenger..."

782. M's αισδός, as an epithet of dust, may be ἄισδος (=*ἄιζος), 'not settling down.'

784. M's ἄφυκτον needs division, not emendation, to yield ἆ, φυκτὸν δ' οὐκέτ' ἂν πέλοι, κέαρ.
"Alas! escape would no longer be possible, my heart."

792–93. M's readings at 793 do make good enough sense:

πόθεν δέ μοι γένοιτ' ἂν αἰθέρος θρόνος,
πρὸς ὃν νέφη δ' ὑδρηλὰ γείνεται χιών,...

"Whence might I get a throne of ether, against which and the wet clouds snow is produced?" For δέ connecting single words there is some doubt: cf. Denniston, *Greek Particles*, p. 162, note 3. But here it connects a two-word phrase to the foregoing. If δ' be rejected the easier solution is Bothe's τ'.

806–807. The smallest change from M is to read

τίν' ἀμφυγᾶς ἔτι πόρον (ἀμφ' αὐτᾶς M, corr. Weil)
τέμνω γάμου λυτῆρα;

"What path of refuge am I to cut (= traverse), liberating from marriage?" 806 is a syncopated iambic dimeter, with the syncopation falling in a different half of the dimeter from the antistrophic 798. There are several parallels in Aeschylus, on which I hope to publish soon elsewhere.

842. M offers σοῦσθε σοῦσθ'† ὀλύμεναι ὀλόμεν' ἐπαμίδα†. Cf. 836, σοῦσθε σοῦσθ' ἐπὶ βᾶριν ὅπως ποδῶν. I rather fancy

842A   σοῦσθε σοῦσθ', ὀλούμεναι. (trochaic dimeter catalectic)
842B   ὀλοῦμεν. ἐπ' ἀμάδα. (dochmius) [ἐπ' ἀμάδα Schütz]

"Hurry! Hurry! Wretches due to perish!
We will destroy you. To the ship!"

847. M offers αἵμονες ὡς, which Paley re-divided. I would then punctuate 847 thus: αἷμον' ἔσω σ'. ἐπ' ἀμάδα (ἐπαμίδα M). If from ἕννυμι, the verb gives the literal sense, taking the adjective as proleptic, "I will clothe you bloody." Compare the "stony tunic" at *Iliad* 3. 57. The sense is: "I will thrash you till you are covered with blood." Then follows the refrain, "To the ship!"

848. M offers ἦ σύ † δουπια τάπιτα †. Recalling the chorus's reference immediately before, 845, to the 'outrage of a boss', δεσποσίῳ ξὺν ὕβρει, and looking forward to the Aegyptid comment at 853, ἀτίετον ἄπολιν οὐ σέβω, I suspect a reference to the chorus's servile and exiled status, as the Aegyptids would have it; and find the letters of M derivable from mis-readings of an original ἦ σὺ δουλὶς ἀπατρία. "Truly, you are a slavegirl in exile."

849–51 only need some re-punctuation and accenting to make sense:

κελεύω βίᾳ μεθέσθαι
ἵχαρ φρενί τ'ἄταν.
ἰῶ ἰόν;

"I command you under compulsion to give up the passion and infatuation in your heart. Am I to shoot an arrow (at you)?"

859. M's † ἄγειος ἐγὼ βαθυχαῖος might be slightly revised to ἁγνὸς (Burges) ἐγὼ βαθυχάϊος, which makes a glyconic. "I am ritually pure (and so able to enter this sanctuary) and of ancient nobility."

860. From M's βαθρείας βαθρείας, γέρον, accepting Murray's idea βᾶθ' ἕκας, I would form another glyconic colon, βᾶθ' ἕκας βᾶθρείας, γέρον. Here there is internal correption of the ει in βαθρείας. The sense is: "Come away from the pedestal (with the statues on it), old man." This assumes some actors' business, in which an Aegyptid confronts an old man defending the Danaids, perhaps a member of their escort, or some priest emerging from a shrine abutting on the sanctuary. Also possible would be a bacchius and hypodochmius scheme: βᾰθρείας βᾶθ' ἕκας, γέρον.

861–63 might be best colometrized thus:

σὺ δ' ἐν ναΐ ναΐ βάσῃ τάχα, (two dochmii)
θέλεος ἀθέλεος βίᾳ, (trochaic dimeter catalectic)
βίᾳ τε πολλᾷ φροῦδᾱ. (syncopated iambic dimeter)

"But you [addressed to a Danaid] shall go on board, on board, quickly by force, and by great force, clean away [ruined]."

864–5. M has † βάτεαι βαθυμιτροκακὰ παθῶν †
Murray emends to βᾶτ' ἀεί. βᾶθ'. ὑμῖν ‹ἔτι κακὰ› πρόκακα παθεῖν.
Even closer to the paradosis might be this:

864A βᾶτ' ἀεί, βᾶθ'. ὑμῖν (two cretics, with short upsilon)
864B ‹ἔνι› πρόκακα παθῶν (dochmius)
865   ὀλομέναις παλάμαις. (dochmius)

"Keep going. Go. For you there remain extremely evil ones among sufferings, through the ruin of your devices." 865 shows both the dative of cause and the "Ab Vrbe Condita" construction, which is commoner in Greek than many readers realise.

874–75 perhaps need merely punctuation, and deletion of M's final *nu* in 875, to be acceptable thus:

> ἴυζε καὶ βόα πικρότερ' ἀχέων.
> Οἰζύος ὄνομ' ἔχω.

"Yell and shout more bitterly than your hurts. My name is Misery." [= I personify or incarnate Misery.] The Danaids cry more than they are hurt. The metre, iambic dimeter plus dochmius, is transitional from the broken lyric metres of 826 on, largely dochmiac, to the settled trimeters of the Herald later, from 882 on.

876–81 seem to call the Herald a crocodile and stress his Egyptian origin. In this context a new approach may be made to the difficult line 877, which in M runs, according to Wecklein - Vitelli:

>   οι
> λυμασισ ὑπρογασυλασκει.

Σ M: εἰς ὑπὲρ τῶν Αἰγυπτίων πρεσβεύοι. The antistrophe could have originally been:

> 876–77   οἰοῖ, οἰοῖ, / λῦμ', ἄσει σὺ πρὸ γᾶς ὑλάσκεις.
> 878   περί, χάμψα, βρυάζεις (περιχαμπτὰ M, corr. R. Ellis)
> 879   ὅσ' ἐρωτᾷς. ὁ μέγας
> 880–81   Νεῖλος ὑβρίζοντά σ' ἀποτρέ-/ψειεν ἄιστον ὕβριν.

"Oh, you offscouring! On mud in front of the land you bark (or grunt). [= You are a crocodile.] You wax wanton to excess, you crocodile, in all your demands..."

909. M's ἀποσπάσας should be re-divided thus:

> ἕλξειν ἔοιχ' ὑμᾶς ἄπο, σπάσας κόμης.

It is an anastrophic tmesis for ἀφέλξειν. "He seems likely to drag you off, pulling you by your hair."

950. M offers ἴσθι μὲν τάδ' ἤδη..., where the initial iota sigma may derive from an uncial kappa. There occurs to me the repunctuated arrangement:

> κεἰ μὲν τάδ' ἤδη, πόλεμον ἀρεῖσθαι νέον,—
> εἴη δὲ νίκη καὶ κράτη τοῖς ἄρσεσιν.

"Even if this is your pleasure, to start a new war,—then may victory and mastery be with the males!" Either one has an aposiopesis of threat after 950, or the δέ at 951 is apodotic.

959. For M's ἐντυχούσῃ ναίειν δόμοις I would read εὐτυχέσι ναίειν δόμοις, confining the assumed corruption to a single word in the phrase, whereas Murray's text assumes corruption of two separate words. "To dwell in wealthy, or fortunate, houses" is opposed to living in monorrhythmic seclusion, 961.

989–90 could be economically restored thus:

τοιῶνδε τυγχάνοντας εὖ πρύμνῃ φρενός (εὐπρυμνῇ M, corr. Sidgwick)

χάριν σέβεσθαι τιμιωτέραν νέμω. (ἐμοῦ M, corr. Young)

"I appoint that those who are fortunate enough to meet with such treatment should reverence gratitude more honourably with the stern of their mind" [= the governing, steering, part of it].

1001–2 might yield suitable meanings in this form:

καρπώματα στάζοντα κηρύσσει Κύπρις,

$$\overset{\epsilon\iota\nu}{}$$

κάλωρα, κωλύουσ' ἀθῷα μένειν ἔρῳ. (κωλύουσαν θωσμένην M, θωσαμένην E, corr. Young)

"Kypris proclaims juicy fruits, in the beauty of maturity, preventing them from remaining untouched by passion." There is internal correption of the ῷ in ἀθῷα. The manuscript paradosis has been affected by some scribe's thinking of ἄνθος in connection with fruits, by a natural association of ideas. The marginal independent value of E, in the Escorial, proved by Professor K. Friis Johansen, appears again here, in its preservation of an important alpha lost in M.

1009. οἰκήσεις M in its plurality recalls the multiplicity of housing mentioned at 957–61, and perhaps calls for the change of M's διπλῆ to the plural διπλαῖ, to make the verse οἰκήσεις δὲ καὶ διπλαῖ πάρα. "For there are two sets of dwellings available."

1043. Noting M's ἐπιπνοίαι, Murray comments: "fortasse recte." With a full stop at the end of the verse I would read φυγάδεσσιν δ' ἐπιπνοῖαι κακά τ' ἄλγη. "Fugitives have contrary winds and evil pains."

For helpful comments on my suggestions about many of the above passages I am indebted to Professor Friis Johansen, of Aarhus, Dr A. F.

Garvie, of Glasgow, and Professor C. W. Whittle, of the University of Birmingham.

Tayport (Fife), 14 May 1970

[Additional note, August 27, 1973. Since submitting the above suggestions, I have found that I had been anticipated in some of them: at 86 by Arsenios of Monemvasia in *Paris. gr.* 2886, at 306 by Wellauer, at 468 by H. L. Ahrens, at 584 by Headlam, at 744 by Boissonade.]

NOTES ON MANUSCRIPTS OF
AESCHYLUS

DENYS PAGE

My own interest in the MSS of Aeschylus was first thoroughly aroused
by Professor Turyn's book, *The Manuscript Tradition of the Tragedies
of Aeschylus* (1943). This book convinced me immediately that the
foundations of all modern texts of Aeschylus were unstable, and that
they would remain so until a considerable number of MSS, hitherto
imperfectly or not at all collated, had been collated in full. The
years went by, and nobody took much notice. Then Roger Dawe
undertook the huge task, and published in 1964 a book which will
remain the foundation for all further work in this field, *The Collation
and Investigation of Manuscripts of Aeschylus*. The future editor has now
at his disposal collations (the most detailed and accurate ever made
for any Greek author, so far as I know) of sixteen MSS and selections
from a couple more. Having undertaken to produce a new text of
Aeschylus for the Oxford Classical Texts series, I have added to
Dawe's assembly full collations of six other MSS; of the two from
which he gave selections (W and D); and of F and Triclinius. Thus
I have full collations of twenty-six MSS at my disposal for the Triad;
and there (for the time being) I draw the line. The object of the
present paper is to show cause (however briefly) why the MSS which
I have added to Dawe's assembly—three of them hitherto uncollated,
three generally neglected—should be included among the sources
for the Triad.[1]

I. The codex G.

G = Ven. Marc. gr. 616 (now 663), saec. xiv; Turyn 69, 102.
There are few places in the Triad where the truth (not counting

[1] I am deeply indebted to Dr Dawe, who scrutinized my notes with close attention;
I have profited greatly from his acute observations.

very minor and purely orthographical points) is preserved in only one MS. The Medicean tops the list with about a dozen such places. G is alone in what I take to be the truth in the following places:

PV 465 γένοινθ᾽ G: γένωνθ᾽ rell. This is surely not conjectural; it may be accidental, or it may be an unique preservation of the truth.

PV 1060 ποι Gsscr: που G rell.[2] Obviously not accidental, and surely not conjectural; που was good enough for most editors up to and even including Hermann. ποι in G comes from collation with a source unknown to us.

ScT 270 πολεμίων φόβον G: πολέμιον φόβον rell. Perhaps due to the common interchange of ο and ω, but it may be an ancient reading uniquely preserved in G.

ScT 1047 τὰ τοῦδε διατετίμηται G: τὰ τοῦδ᾽ οὐ διατετ. rell. (τὰ τοῦδ᾽ ἐκτετ. Nd). This is the only reading which gives the sense required by the schol. in M, τὰ περὶ τῆς τιμῆς τούτου ὑπὸ θεῶν κέκριται; it is surely neither conjectural nor accidental, and it may be the truth.

In two other places G is the only MS[3] which has the truth *in linea*:

Pe 22 Μεγαβάτης G: Μεγαβάζης vel Μεταβάτης rell. A clear example of an old and true reading being preserved in G only (elsewhere only Pγρ).

ScT 616 ἄθυμον G Psscr: ἄθυμος rell. Turnebus wrote ἄθυμον by conjecture, rightly, I believe. In G it may be due to assimilation to σφε, or it may be a true reading uniquely preserved.

G is one of a small minority of MSS which have preserved the truth in the following places:

Pe 22 Ἀστάσπης GMIAD; G is the only MS which has both the Persian names correctly in this line.

Pe 1025 Ἰάνων GI (Dawe 120).

PV 100 τέρματα GMPΔpc

PV 838 παλιμπλάγκτοισι G (παλιπλ-G)HaPpc

ScT 753 ματρός GM (μητρός XOacIγρ, μητρός πρός Y, μὴ πρός rell.) Equally significant are the following places, where G coincides with Triclinius:

Pe 556 πολιήταις GFTr: πολήταις Ms, πολίταις rell. In G, whose lyrics are unemended (see below), πολιήταις can only be a unique

---

[2] "ποι F²(?)," Wilamowitz: there is no trace of ποι in F.

[3] Throughout this paper, "only MS" = the only MS among those for which full collations are available.

preservation of the truth; it is certain that this reading is not owed by G to Triclinius.

Pe 687 ὀρθρίζοντες G: ὀρθιάζοντες FTr, ῥοθιάζοντες rell. In F and Tr ὀρθ- is an emendation; in G ὀρθ- comes from a source unknown to us which had preserved this part of the truth.

Pe 1056 πέρθε GLcKFTr and schol. A: ὕπερθε(ν) rell. The truth here (surely not restored by conjecture; see Dawe 137) survived in very few mss.

The virtues of G include some very uncommon orthographical niceties: *PV* 319 and 330 γίγν-, 369 γύας, 585 ἄδην; *Pe* 306 ἰθαιγενής, 417 ἀφρασμόνως, 700–701 δίομαι.

The relation between G and Triclinius:

Substantial differences between G and Tr in *PV* and *ScT* are to be counted in the hundreds; the following are a small selection from *PV*: 21 θεῶν G, βροτῶν Tr; 87 τύχης G, τέχνης Tr; 100 χρὴ τέρματα G, τέρμα χρὴ Tr; 111 πέφηνε G, πέφυκε Tr; 185 ἀπαράμυθον G, οὐ παράμ. Tr; 186 θρασύς τε καὶ G, τραχὺς καὶ Tr; 204 τἄριστα G, τὰ λῶιστα Tr; 223 ἐξημείψατο G, ἀντημείψατο Tr; 257 ἄθλου G, ἄθλων Tr; 296 ποτέ φης G, ποτ' ἐρεῖς Tr; 328 ἢ οὐκ G, οὐκ Tr; 357 θέλων G, βίαι Tr; 386 δοκήσει G, δοκεῖ σοι Tr; 394 λευρῶν... οἴμων...ψαύει G, λευρὸν...οἶμον...ψαίρει Tr; 419 πόρον G, τόπον Tr; 422 νέμονται G, νέμουσι Tr; 449 χρόνον G, βίον Tr; 477 δόλους G, πόρους Tr; 525 βίας G, δύας Tr; and so forth. I doubt if any two other mss in our collection are more unlike each other. It will be noticed that in numerous places G is right, Tr wrong.

The same discord prevails in *ScT*, most evidently in the lyrics, where G (like the other mss) presents a text abounding in inherited errors, immune from Triclinius' interference. There are many notable differences in the dialogue also: e.g. 12 βλάστημον G, βλαστὴν μὲν Tr; 254 κἀμὲ καὶ σὲ καὶ πόλιν G, κἀμὲ καὶ πᾶσαν πόλιν Tr; 257 ἄνδρες G, ἄνδρας Tr; 268 παιάνισον G, παιώνισον Tr; 372 τέκος G, τόκος Tr; 392 ὄχθας ποταμίας G, -αις -αις Tr; 415 ὁμαίμων G, ὁ δαίμων Tr; 426 κραίνοι G, κράνοι Tr; 462 πύλαις G, πύλας Tr; 513 φέρων G, φλέγων Tr; 549 δεῖν'...κραίνοι G, τοῖσδ'...κράνοι Tr; 603 ἐν πανουργίαι G, καὶ παν. Tr; 607 ἐνδίκως G, ἐκδίκως Tr; 622 φέρει G, φύσει Tr; 648 πατρῴαν G, πατρῴων Tr; 658 Πολυνείκη G, -κει Tr; 710 φασμάτων ἐνυπνίων G, ἐνυπνίων φαντασμάτων Tr; 803 παρὸν G, πλέον Tr; etc.

The relation is different in The Persians. Concord between the two texts and the presence of a Triclinian metrical scholion in G indicate that Triclinius' final edition of this play was at least partly based on a source which had much in common with G, although Tr is in numerous points inferior to G.

In the dialogue, where mss differ Tr and G usually coincide except where Tr thinks that the reading which he adopts (whether by conjecture or by selection) improves the metre or sense: e.g. 194 δίφρου G, -ρον Tr; 216 θρασ- G, θαρσ- Tr; 223 κάτοχος G, κάτοχ' Tr; 228 δὲ...τάδ' ὡς G, δὴ...ταῦτα δ' ὡς Tr; 248 καὶ G, εἰ Tr; 255 γε G, γὰρ Tr; 372 ὑπερθύμου G, ὑπ' ἐκθύμου Tr; 375 τ' om. G, add. ‚Tr; 470 ἴησ' G, ἤιξ' Tr; etc. etc. There remain, however, some striking discords, e.g. 22 Μεγαβάτης...Ἀστάσπης G, Μεγαβάζης...Ἀστάπης Tr; 28 ἐν τλήμονι G, εὐτλήμονι Tr; 94 θνατὸς G, θνητὸς Tr; 157 εὐνάτειρα G, εὐνήτ- Tr; 845 ἐσέρχεται G, ἐπέρχεται Tr (as if he knew no alternative to the otherwise standard reading εἰσέρχεται).

It is to be noticed that G has half a dozen of the conjectures in iambics (or apparent iambics) which re-appear in Tr: 326 σύνεσίς τε πρῶτος ⟨αὐτὸς⟩ εἰς εὐψυχίαν GNdQᵖᶜKLcFTr; 329 τοιῶνδέ γ' ἀρχόντων GFTr; 761 ἐξεκείνωσ' εἰσπεσὸν GFTr; 796 νῦν τόποις τῆς Ἑλλάδος GYaPʸᵖFTr; 850 παιδί γ' ἐμῶ GPLh²FTr; 1030 πέπλον δ' ἐπέρρηξά γ' ἐπὶ GFTr.

In the anapaests and lyrics G is much like the other mss, reproducing the large number of inherited errors common to the general tradition; Tr alters freely. The following selection suffices to show the difference: 3 ἀφνειῶν G, ἀφνεῶν Tr; 35 Αἰγυπτιογενὴς G, Αἰγυπτογενὴς Tr; 44 βασιλεῖς δίοπτοι G, βασιλεὺς διέπει Tr; 82 φοινίου G, φον- Tr; 84 ἀσσύριον G, σύριον Tr; 112 πίσσυνοι G, πίσυνοι Tr; 128 μελισσάων G, μελισσῶν Tr; 152 προσπίτνω G, προσπίτνω δὴ Tr; 286 στύγν' Ἀθᾶναι G, στυγναὶ δ' Ἀθ. Tr; 532 νῦν Περσῶν G, νῦν Περσῶν μὲν Tr; 553 βαρίδες τε πόντιαι G, βαρίδεσίν γε ποντίαις Tr; 554 τίποτε G, τίπτε Tr; 558 γὰρ καὶ G, γάρ τε καὶ Tr; 571 στένε G, πένθει Tr; 579 στερηθεὶς G, om. Tr (who writes δῶμα for δόμος, which G accidentally omits); 580 τοκῆες G, τοκέες Tr; 582 ὀδυρόμενοι G, δυρόμενοι Tr; 588 προσπίτν- G, προπίτν- Tr; 637 παντάλαινά τ' ἄχη G, παντάλαν' ἄχη Tr; 643 αἰνέσατε G, αἰνέσατ' ἐκ Tr; 644 πέμπετ' ἄνω G, πέμπετε δ' ἄνω Tr; 665 καινά G, καινά τε Tr; 854 γεραιὸς G, γηρ- Tr; 860 ἐπέθυνον G, ἐπεύθυνον Tr; 863 ἐς οἴκους G, om. Tr; 864 ὅσας G, ὅσσας Tr; 896 στεναγμάτων G, στεναγμῶν Tr; 906 δαμασθέντες G, δμαθέντες Tr; 914 ἐσιδόντες G, ἐσιδόντ' Tr; 932 πατρίαι G, πατρώαι Tr; 933 ἄρ' ἐγενόμαν G, ἆρα γενοίμαν Tr; 955 βόα G, λέγε Tr; 956 ποῦ δέ σοι G, οἲ οἲ ποῦ δέ σοι Tr; 959 sq. καὶ Πελάγων καὶ Δοτάμας ἠδ' Ἀγδαβάτας G, ἠδὲ Πελάγων καὶ Δοτάμας ἠδ' Ἀγδαβάτας γε Tr; 962 sq. ὀλοοὺς ἔλιπον ναὸς G, οἲ οἲ ὀλοοὺς ἔλιπον ἐκ ναὸς Tr; 965 σαλαμίνισι G, σαλαμινίτισι Tr; 967 τ' ἀγαθὸς G, ὠγαθὸς Tr; 979 σὸν G, τὸν σὸν Tr; 993 μυριόνταρχον G, μυριόναρχον Tr; 1001 σκηναῖσιν οὐκ ἀμφὶ G, οὐκ ἀμφὶ ταῖς σκηναῖς Tr; 1014 στρατὸν G, στρατὸν μὲν Tr; 1017 τόδε G, τάσδε Tr; 1025 Ἰάνων δὲ λαὸς οὐκ ἐκφυγαιχμίας G, Ἰαόνων δὲ λαὸς οὐ φυγαιχμίας Tr.

These examples suffice to prove that G represents a text un-affected by Triclinius' textual criticism in anapaests and lyrics. If there happen nevertheless to be a few apparent conjectures in lyrics in G, their source is probably other than Triclinius (even though they re-appear in Triclinius). There are, I think, three such places (not counting 556 πολιήταις, which I take to be an ancient reading uniquely preserved by G):

287 πάρεισ' GFTr (πάρα rell.); 986 κακὰ πρὸς κακοῖς GFTr (κακὰ πρόκακα vel κακὰ πρὸς κακὰ rell.; see Dawe 57); 992 ἄλλο γέ τι GFTr (ἄλλον γε Iᵖᶜ, ἄλλο γε rell.)

II. The codices Nc X Ha.

Among the relatively early codices of Aeschylus hitherto un-collated are:

Nc = Laur. 28.25, saec. xiii exeuntis; Turyn 40.

X = Laur. 31.2, saec. xiv ineuntis; Turyn 30 f.

Ha = Matrit. 4617, saec. xiv ineuntis; Turyn 62.

Of these I now possess complete collations made for me (from photographs at present in my possession) by N. G. Wilson, who willingly placed his immense experience and learning at my disposal; I gratefully acknowledge that almost all the work on these mss is his.

These three mss are very like most of the others in Dawe's assembly, inasmuch as they are "veteres" in his sense. There are few signs of emendation in the dialogue and none (I believe) in the lyrics. They are "typically eclectic manuscripts with every imaginable kind of affiliation" (Dawe 39); they "bear the same despondent message as the other sixteen manuscripts,—that the recension is entirely open" (Dawe 42, with reference to codd. W and D). They have much the same degree of individuality, and as much right to a place in the Apparatus Criticus, as most of the other mss in Dawe's list. At present I confine myself to a brief note of their small but not inconsiderable virtues, i.e. to a selection of places where their evidence is valuable as corroboration of true readings which are corrupt in the great majority of the mss.

(a) The codex Nc.

The positive contribution of Nc is small but respectable. It is the only ms (except Tr) which has δυσπλάνοις *in linea* in *ScT* 900 (also P^{γρ}; see Dawe 147 f.), and the only ms (except perhaps Δ) which has ἀγγέλου *in linea* in *ScT* 285 (also Q^{spc} P^{γρ}). In a number of places it has a true reading rarely preserved elsewhere, e.g. *PV* 156 μήτε NcLhTr, 371 θερμοῖς NcXVFP^{sscr}, 762 πρὸς αὐτὸς αὐτοῦ NcMILcLhTr, 835 προσσαίνει NcXOPVTrI^{sscr}, *Pe* 194 δίφρου NcMXIYaG (sscr. plerique), 372 ὑπ' ἐκθύμου NcMIACHaF^{sscr}, 685 πρευμενὴς NcXMLhPKQ. It has some moments of uncommon virtue in orthographical points: *ScT* 129 ῥυσίπολις NcΔYO^{ac}, 86 ὀροτύπου NcMI^{γρ}, 87 ὀρόμενον NcMΔIBC, *Pe* 817 Δωρίδος NcIBDΔ. It has two unique features, τῆσδε πημονῆς in *PV* 745 and ἠινιγμένους in *PV* 662 (a more exquisite word than the otherwise universal εἰρημένους; but probably a gloss). It is the only ms which has βλάβην *in linea* in *PV* 784 (a gloss recorded as a variant in P and Ya). In *Pe* 79 the reading ἀφέταις, hitherto attested only in CK^{γρ}, recurs in Nc^{γρ}.

(b) The codex X.

X is the only ms which has *in linea* what I take to be the correct reading in *ScT* 355, λελιμμένος (also V^{isscr}); perhaps accidentally. There is nothing to be said for two other unique readings, αὐτοφόνων in *ScT* 893 and μετακλυσθῆναι in *ScT* 1078. διοδότων in *ScT* 948 may be right.

X is one of few sources for the truth in e.g. *PV* 191 ἀρθμὸν (*in linea*, XVW only; also M^{2pc}P^{γρ} and perhaps I^{ac}O^{pc}); 371 θερμοῖς

XNcVFP^{sscr}; 770 πλὴν...λυθεὶς *in linea* XMBHW, also F^{sscr} and
I^{ac}; 835 προσσαίνει XNcPOVTrI^{sscr}; 864 ἐπ' XHaVWDYP^{γρ}, *ScT* 12
βλάστημον XMOLcGI^{ac}P^{sscr}, πολὺν XMODNd^{ac}P^{γρ} (any MS which
has this line correct at both beginning and end deserves some respect;
M and O are the only others); 194 ὑπ' αὐτῶν XQ^{2γρ}; 236 οὗτοι
XMBQTr; 318 ῥήτορες XMIGFQ² or Q^{ac}; 918 οὐ (for δ' οὐ) XNdP^{pc};
Pe 194 δίφρου XNcMIYaG (sscr. plerique).

(c) The codex Ha.

Ha has the truth in company with a small minority of MSS more
frequently than is usual in such comparisons: *PV* 138 θ' εἰλ-
HaΔPLhGFTr; 219 μελαμβ- HaMI^{sscr}; 236 τὸ μὴ HaMI^Σ; 384
τήνδε τὴν νόσον (probably true; Dawe 146 f.) HaLcLhG^{sscr}
P^{γρ} Tr; 543 γνώμα HaMI and perhaps C^{ac}; 838 παλιμπλάγκτοισι
HaP^{pc}, παλιπλ- G; 858 θηρεύοντες HaCHFΔ^{sscr}; 864 ἐπ'
HaXVYWDP^{γρ}; 945 ἐφημέρους (*sine* τὸν) HaLhYaΔ; 969 φῦναι
HaLcLhΔF; *ScT* 205 ὅτε Ha only, but as Ha omits the following τε
this is probably a mere slip; 382 θείνει HaCQ^{ac}LcLhDFTr; 466
προσαμβάσεις (as one word) HaLcLh²; 613 πάλιν HaMIAB^{s γρ}; 734
αὐτοκτόνως HaΔQKLcLhGFTr; 751 ἐγείνατο HaΔF^{ac}Tr and
perhaps Q^{ac}; 784 ἀπ' om. HaTr; *Pe* 82 φονίου HaNOQ^{ac}W^{ac}FTr;
218 τὰ δ' ἀγαθ(ὰ) HaOGFTr; 372 ὑπ' εὐθύμου HaMIANcCF^{sscr};
375 ναυβάτης HaMKYaTr; 431 μηδάμ' HaLcQKP^{γρ}; 582 δυρ- Ha(ut
vid.)MQFTr; 642 μεγαυχῆ HaQ; 714 εἰπεῖν ἔπος HaPQKLcLhGTr;
1011 ναυβατᾶν HaGF.

Ha has some uncommon orthographical virtues (e.g. *PV* 935
ποείτω, *ScT* 6 Ἐτεοκλέης, 129 ῥυσίπολις, *Pe* 417 ἀφρασμόνως) and
is much more punctilious about moveable *nu* than most MSS. It has
one unique (and wrong) variant, *ScT* 1040 καὐτόν. In *Pe* 855 it is
the only MS which has *in linea* the variant παντάρχης (A^{γρ}). In *Pe* 152
it has the reading προσπίτνω προσκυνῶ in common with MICW.

III. *The codices Lc, Lh.*

Lc = Cambridge Univ. Library Nn III 17 A, saec. xiv; Turyn 75.
Lh = Cambridge Univ. Library Nn III 17 B, saec. xiv; Turyn 76.

These two MSS were assigned by Turyn to the recension of Thomas
Magister and were studied in detail from that point of view by Miss
Bryson in a doctoral dissertation for the University of Illinois (1953).

I have collated them fully and have formed the opinion that, so far
as their texts are concerned, there is no difference in principle
between them and many or most of the other MSS in Dawe's list.
There has been some (not much more than is usual) emendation in
the dialogue, none (I believe) in the lyrics. The texts are typically
eclectic. Each has a few novel features which are unlikely to be the
products of accident or conjecture. They satisfy my criterion for
inclusion among the sources for the text,—that, as some of their
readings (however few) may represent a source unknown to us, all
their variants must be taken into account (though it usually proves
a waste of time so to take them). I must add that my own experience
confirms Dawe's suggestion that there never was an edition of the
text by Thomas Magister, only a commentary.

(a) The codex Lc.

Lc has three readings any or all of which may be unique preserva-
tions of truth:

PV 152 θ᾽ Ἀιδου Lc: τ᾽ Ἀιδου rell. There was no apparent reason
for the change of τ᾽ Ἀι- to θ᾽ Ἀι-, and no other scribe made it.
Turnebus read θ᾽ Ἀιδου by conjecture, but not all editors followed
him; even Schütz preferred the tradition.

ScT 686 μή τΐ σε Lc: μή τίς σε rell. The possibility of emendation
in dochmiacs is too remote; Triclinius found nothing amiss.
Accident cannot be ruled out, but neither can the possibility that
Lc got this true reading from a source unknown to us.

ScT 834 καρδίαν Lc^{sscr}: καρδία Lc rell. The suprascript καρδίαν
is not likely to be conjectural. What was good enough for Schütz was
good enough for anyone before him. Lc has this reading by collation
with a source unknown to us.

Pe 550 μὲν Lc: γὰρ NdFTr, μὲν γὰρ rell. The superfluous γὰρ may
have dropped out of Lc by chance (see Dawe 144 f.).

Lc is one of few virtuous MSS in a number of places, e.g. *PV* 99
πῆι LcYaTr, ποῖ Ya^{2sscr} rell.; 414 θνατοὶ LcM^{pc}ITr, θνητοὶ
Tr^{sscr} rell.; 518 ἐκφύγοι γε LcMQK, ἐκφύγοιτο, ἐκφύγη γε (or τε)
rell.; 520 οὐκέτ᾽ ἂν LcLhQKF (in ras.), οὐκ ἂν οὖν or οὐκ ἂν fere
rell. (οὐκ ἂν ἐκφύγοιτο G); 969 φῦναι LcLhΔF, φυῆναι Y, φῆναι
rell.; *ScT* 466 προσαμβάσεις LcHaLh^{ac}, πρὸς ἀμβάσεις Lh^2 rell.;
700 ὅταν LcM^{ac}LhF$^{\gamma\rho}$Tr, οὗ τ᾽ ἂν M^{2pc} rell.; 727 κλήρους Lc

ΔLhFP^{sscr} and perhaps M^{ac}, κλήροις rell. (-ρον Tr); 821 δυσπότμως LcYaC^{sscr}, -μους Lc^{sscr} rell.; *Pe* 431 μηδάμ' LcHaQKP^{γρ}, μηδ' ἂν rell.; 1056 πέρθε LcKGFTr, ὕπερθε(ν) rell.

Lc's numerous individual features show nothing else but errors or erroneous conjectures *metri gratia*, e.g. *PV* 873 λύσει γε τοῖον (see Turyn 77 on the reason for this), *ScT* 704 τί γοῦν. I attach no importance to the unique readings ταὐτό γ' ἐλθὼν in *PV* 845, δαμέντα in *PV* 861, ἀληθῶς in *ScT* 886, ἀντημείψατο (sscr. -μείβετο) in *ScT* 1049. κοσμήσεις in *ScT* 1046 (γρ. τιμήσεις) is a unique variant.

(b) The codex Lh.

Lh has only one reading which is likely to be a unique preservation of the truth:

Pe 208 πτεροῖν Lh, -οῖς rell.; cf. cod. O's ὤμοιν in *PV* 350 (Dawe 124). It is in the highest degree improbable that the dual was imported by conjecture. (In *PV* 867, where γνώμαιν was substituted for γνώμην, the reason for the change is obvious and the dual was suggested by the following δυοῖν; see Dawe 68).

In *ScT* 857 Lh has the correct reading ἄστολον suprascribed; no other ms has this reading in the text at all, but it was current in the scholia (Lh, K, and F, at least; no doubt others).

In *PV* 569 Lh has δολερὸν, elsewhere only known as a variant in FPΔ; both δόλιος and δολερός are familiar to late prose-writers, but δολερός may seem likelier in Aeschylus if you ask *utra in alteram abitura*.

Lh has the truth in the company of few mss in a number of places: *PV* 156 ὡς μήτε LhNcTr, ὡς μήποτε rell.; 476 μου LhMOI, μοι Lh^{sscr} I^{sscr} rell.; 479 οὔτε Lh only *in linea* (variant in QPB), οὐδὲ rell.; 520 οὐκέτ' ἂν LhLcQKF (*in ras.*), οὐκ ἂν οὖν or οὐκ ἂν rell.; 895 ἐν om. LLh (these two presumably accidentally) Tr; 945 ἐφημέροις (*sine* τὸν) LhYaHaΔ (τὸν add. Lh^{2sscr}); 969 φῦναι LhLcFΔ, φυῆναι Ya, φῆναι rell.; *ScT* 466 προσαμβάσεις (as one word) Lh^{ac}LcHa (πρὸς ἀμβ. Lh^{pc}); 686 μέμονας LhMIO^{ac}F, μέμηνας Lh^{sscr} M^{2sscr} O^{pc} F^{sscr} rell. (ἐκμέμον- Tr); 700 ὅταν LhM^{ac}LcF^{γρ}Tr, οὖ τ' ἂν M^{2pc} rell.; 727 κλήρους LhLcΔFP^{sscr} and perhaps M^{ac}, κλήροις rell. (-ρον Tr); *Pe* 195 διασπαράσσει LhIYa, -άττει rell.; 588 προπίτνοντες LhFTr, προσπ- rell.; 685 πρευμενὴς LhHaMQKP^{sscr}, -νεῖς Q^{sscr} K^{sscr} rell.; 864 ὅσσας LhMAKTr, ὅσας rell.

At *ScT* 532 Lh, A, and F are the only mss which have *in linea* the reading δορός attested by P. Oxy. 2179 and as a variant in many other mss (Lh, like F, has δορός, γρ. διός).

Lh's numerous other individual features show nothing else of much interest except the spelling ηὑρόμην in *PV* 267 (presumably inherited from an unknown source; εὑρ- is the standard spelling, and is never corrected to ηὑρ-). The reading τοῦ σοῦ δὲ in *PV* 1026 recurs in GP^{γρ}. No other ms has καὶ πρῶτα in *Pe* 412; *PV* 1086 πάντως Lh (and Y^{sscr}).

I should add that both Lh and Lc have τήνδε τὴν νόσον in *PV* 384. If this is the truth, as Dawe believes (and I am inclined to agree with him), it is a truth which has survived in very few mss: *in linea*, only LcLhHaTr (also G^{sscr} P^{γρ}).

There are some strong points of resemblance between (a) Lc and Lh; (b) LcLh and QK; (c) LcLh and Tr. But there are also many equally strong points of difference, and it soon becomes obvious that we are dealing (as usual) with eclectic texts which are constantly changing their allegiances. I give a few examples out of long lists:

(a) Lc and Lh. Both have the incorporated scholion πόνος οὔφ' ἡμῖν ἐξημμένος (elsewhere Ya only) in *ScT* 994; both have πάντων Θέμι αἰθὴρ (elsewhere F only) in *PV* 1092. At *PV* 1002 both have the incorporated gloss ἔννοια (before μήποθ'; elsewhere YaΔ and a number of later mss). But the discords are numerous: e.g. *PV* 389 θακοῦντι Lc, κρατοῦντι Lh; 435 πικρὸν Lc, οἰκτρὸν Lh; 505 πάντα Lc, ταῦτα Lh; 676 Κερχνείας Lc, Κεγχρείας Lh; *ScT* 321 ὧδ' Lc, τήνδ' Lh; 473 πέπεμπτ' οὐ Lc, πέμπετ' οὐ Lh; 549 τοῖσδ' Lc, δείν' Lh; *Pe* 449 ἁλὸς Lc, ἀκτῆς Lh; etc.

(b) LcLh and QK. These four mss stand together and alone in a few places; together and almost alone in a considerable number (e.g. *PV* 520 οὐκέτ' ἂν QKLcLhF). But a long list of sharp discords is quickly compiled, and it is apparent that Lc and Lh range widely outside the sources of Q and K: *PV* 186 τραχύς LcLh, θρασύς QK; 296 ποτ' ἐρεῖς LcLh, ποτέ φῃς QK; 384 τήνδε τὴν νόσον LcLh, τῆιδε τῆι νόσωι QK; 419 τόπον LcLh, πόρον QK; 449 βίον LcLh, χρόνον QK; 477 πόρους LcLh, δόλους QK; 525 βίας LcLh, δύας QK; etc. etc.

(c) LcLh and Tr. Triclinius' numerous corrections *metri gratia* are not found in LcLh, except a few coincidences in the dialogue.

It is therefore probable that in the very few places where Lc or Lh stands alone (or almost alone) in a true reading in anapaests or lyrics together with Tr, Lc or Lh has the reading as an inheritance from an earlier and otherwise unknown source. Even when Triclinius claims an emendation as his own, the truth may have been extant in a ms unknown to or unnoticed by him. Comparison of LcLh and Tr in the first hundred lines of *Pe* will suffice to show the degree of discord:

Pe 5 Δαρείου υἱὸς *in linea* LcLh, sscr. Tr; 21 Ἄμιστρις LcLh, -τρης Tr; Ἀρταφέρνης LcLh, -φρένης Tr; 32 Σοσθάνης Lh, Σωσθ- LcTr; 35 Αἰγυπτιογενὴς LcLh, Αἰγυπτογενὴς Tr; 40 ἀνάριθμον Lh, -μοι LcTr; 42 Μιτρογαθὴς Lh, Μητ- LcTr; 44 βασιλῆες δίοπτοι LcLh, βασιλεὺς διέπει Tr; 61 οὓς περὶ LcLh, οὕσπερ Tr; 67 χώραν Lh, -ρον Tr, χθόνα Lc; 77 ὀχυροῖσι Lh, ἐχ- LcTr; 80 ἰσόθεος LcLh, ἰσσό- Tr; 82 φοινίου LcLh, φον- Tr; 84 ἀσσύριον LcLh, σύριον Tr; 91 ἀπρόσιτος Lh, ἀπρόσοιστος LcTr; 94 θνατὸς LcLh, θνητ- Lc^sscr Tr; 96 εὐπετέος LcLh, -έως Tr; 100 θνητὸν Lh, θνατ- LcTr; 107 πόλεων τ' LcLh, καὶ πόλεων Tr; 109 θαλάσσης LcLh, -ας Tr.

In the dialogue Lc and Lh are very often on the same side as Tr, but differences both major and minor are quite abundant: e.g. *PV* 30 πέρα δίκης LcLh, δίκης πέρα Tr; 111 πέφηνε LcLh, πέφυκε Tr; 257 ἄθλου LcLh, -ων Tr; 386 δοκήσει LcLh, δοκεῖ σοι Tr; 520 οὐκέτ' ἂν LcLh, οὐκ ἂν οὖν Tr; 525 βίας LcLh, δύας Tr; 637 τἀποκλαῦσαι LcLh, κἀποκλαῦσαι Tr; 838 παλιμπλάγκτοισι Lc, πολυπλάκτοισι LhTr; 907 αὐθάδη φρονῶν LcLh, αὐθάδης φρενῶν Tr; *ScT* 549 δεῖν'...κραίνοι Lh, τοῖσδ'...κράνοι LcTr; *Pe* 157 εὐνάτειρα LcLh, ευνήτ- Tr; etc. etc.

IV. The codices W and D.

W = Vat. gr. 1332, saec. xiv; Turyn 35, 62.

D = Ambros. G. 56 sup., saec. xiv; Turyn 36, 62.

See Dawe 37–42. I have collated these mss and have little of interest to add to Dawe's selection of readings from them. They are typically eclectic "*veteres*".

PV 405 ἐνδείκνυσι(ν) D, the true reading, elsewhere only TrP^γρ and perhaps O^ac; *Pe* 932 πατρώαι D, elsewhere only Tr; *PV* 191 ἀρθμὸν W, (ἀρ θμὸν thus, but no trace of writing or erasure in the gap, and with gloss ἁρμονίαν), a true reading elsewhere *in linea* only XV; *PV* 223 τιμαῖς (for ποιναῖς) D as well as W, else-where only Pʸᵖ; *PV* 490 εὐώνυμοι DWˢˢᶜʳ, also F; 729 στενοπόρου DW, also OPˢˢᶜʳ, a reading to be seriously considered; 950 ἕκαστ᾽ ἔκφραζε D, also VP (see Dawe 52: "The substitution of compound verbs for simple, especially compounds in ἐκ-, is part of the stock-in-trade of the ordinary Byzantine philologist"); in *Pe* 260 W has an unique variant, ὡς πάντ᾽ ἐκεῖνά γ᾽ ἐστὶ, and in *Pe* 648 another, χθονὸς Wˢˢᶜʳ. In *Pe* 607 D has the curious reading ἄνις εὐτυχημάτων, hitherto attested only in Pʸᵖ (see Dawe 81 f.).

Cambridge, 3 March 1970

THE DAUGHTER OF OEDIPUS

ELIZABETH BRYSON BONGIE

It may be fairly claimed that few playwrights have conveyed with such an economy of means as much as Sophocles in the prologue of the *Antigone*. In the space of ninety-nine lines he outlines the background of events, states his themes, indicates his line of development, initiates the movement of the plot, and firmly establishes before our eyes the characteristics of the protagonist.

Even the first line strikes us with its weight of connotation: ὦ κοινὸν αὐτάδελφον Ἰσμήνης κάρα. Here Sophocles has managed to identify the two characters on stage and also, by means of Antigone's unusual, untranslatable[1] form of address to her sister, he introduces the kinship theme that will be so important to an understanding of Antigone's character and of the play itself. Lines 2 and 3 relate Zeus and, by extension, divine influence to the past disasters of the House of Oedipus and look ahead to the certainty of disasters still to come for the two surviving members of the family. These lines serve the additional function of setting the time of the play after the death of Eteocles and Polyneices. The dual in νῷν ζώσαιν (3) emphasizes the closeness of the ties that Antigone feels unite her and her sister. At the beginning of the play Antigone treats Ismene as her associate in every way; she speaks as if there were two daughters of Oedipus, although later she will cease to do this.

In lines 4–6 the quality and character of the evils that have befallen the family of Oedipus are described with a series of adjectives telling both of the intensity of the evils themselves and of Antigone's reaction to them. She finds this protracted experience of evil personally bitter and painful (ἀλγεινόν), she sees it as proof of the ἄτη that plagues the family, and she sees it from the more external or objective

---

[1] Bernard M. W. Knox, *The Heroic Temper: Studies in Sophoclean Tragedy* (Berkeley and Los Angeles 1964), 79.

point of view as degrading (αἰσχρόν) and as a visible sign of dishonour (ἄτιμον). Antigone's use of the last two words suggests at once that she thinks in terms of what we may call the heroic value-system. These evils are emphatically described as belonging both to Antigone herself and to Ismene (τῶν σῶν τε κἀμῶν).

Once Sophocles has identified the characters, reminded the audience of the background, given the time of the play, and revealed something of Antigone's general outlook, he proceeds to the specific dramatic situation, the recent decree of Creon to the citizens of Thebes. Antigone's reference to Creon as στρατηγόν (8) cannot fail to catch the eye of the reader as it must have caught the ear of a fifth-century audience. Creon's rôle in the Theban legend was not primarily that of a "general in the field"[2] and nowhere else in the play is his military character mentioned; he is referred to variously as ἄναξ, τύραννος, βασιλεύς and, by his servants, as δεσπότης. It seems likely that here Sophocles employs στρατηγός in conjunction with πανδήμῳ πόλει κήρυγμα in an intentionally anachronistic way. At this early stage in the play, before the audience becomes too involved with the setting of monarchy and the atmosphere of legend, these expressions occurring together would surely remind the Athenians of their own office of στρατηγός.[3] But why should Sophocles choose to arouse this association? Certainly not because he wished to suggest that Creon be identified with the best-known στρατηγός of his own

[2] Ivan M. Linforth, "Antigone and Creon," *University of California Publications in Classical Philology* (Berkeley and Los Angeles 1961), 184. S. M. Adams, "The *Antigone* of Sophocles," *Phoenix* 9 (1955), 49, also comments on the significance of στρατηγός in this line. Like Linforth he feels that the word is used in a military sense; however, he suggests the implication that the decree had been proclaimed by Creon on the field where his authority was absolute. "As general he had the right to expect absolute obedience; how will he act now that his position is that of a civil ruler?" This reasoning can also lead to the interpretation that Creon is issuing the decree *after* the battle, just as if he still had the authority of a military commander, to the πάνδημος πόλις, a body over which he does not have legitimate authority. Understanding στρατηγός in this latter sense would produce a strong contrast between πανδήμῳ πόλει and κήρυγμα...τὸν στρατηγόν. Whether a general did in fact have this absolute authority as a military commander is quite another question.

[3] Knox 83; Victor Ehrenberg, *Sophocles and Pericles* (Oxford 1954), 105 ff. Ehrenberg rejects the idea that στρατηγός could express contempt since it is a word that "in a moral sense is entirely neutral" (106); in a moral sense, perhaps, but in the sense of a temporary and elected official such a connotation still seems possible. The significance of any word used only once in a play should not, of course, be overemphasized.

day, namely, Pericles! One possible explanation is that he wished to take advantage of the connotation of the word as a fifth-century political term. Just as "president" would bring to our minds ideas not necessarily of a well-defined political term but rather of an official elected for a specific length of time, so στρατηγός to an Athenian could well carry the connotation of an official both elected and temporary. Coming from the mouth of Antigone, who is so conscious of being the grand-daughter, daughter, and sister of kings, the reference to Creon as στρατηγός might well convey strong tones of contempt, as if she were saying something like, "By what right does this 'temporary official' make pronouncements affecting the royal and ancient family of Oedipus?" On the other hand, Sophocles might have intended no such thing and might simply be using terms familiar to his audience.

In lines 9–10, however, the case is quite different. The significant words here, φίλους and ἐχθρῶν, do occur again and again throughout the play and are key words in the fullest sense.[4] Whether one translates line 10 as "Woes proper to enemies are being directed against our family" or as "Woes are being directed against our family by enemies" does not affect the impact of the expression.[5]

[4] Knox (80 f.) discusses the meanings of φίλος and ἐχθρός as they are used in this play; he points out that φίλος in the mouth of Antigone always refers to "kin", whereas in the mouth of someone else it may have its extended, more general meaning of "friend." Unfortunately, we have no one word in English that conveys exactly the meaning and connotation of φίλος in the sense in which Antigone uses it to denote someone related by blood. There are two common translations and both are misleading (as anyone who has had to teach the *Antigone* in translation well knows). To render φίλος as "beloved" or "loved one" can lead to the extreme interpretation that Antigone's feeling for, if not her actual relationship with, Polyneices was incestuous and to the explanation of the play in terms of sexual abnormality. (E.g., Walter Agard, "*Antigone* 904–20," *Cl. Philol.* 32 [1937], 264: "It is obviously more than religious duty that impels her to bury his body. She loves him passionately . . . ." To support this statement Agard refers to such lines as 81 where Antigone speaks of Polyneices as φιλτάτῳ.) The idea of "love" in English is much too broad to represent what Antigone means by φίλος, and although it conveys the idea of the affection that may or may not accompany a family-relationship, it contains no hint of the actual blood-relationship itself. The second translation, on the other hand, that of "friend", actually excludes the idea of a blood-relationship as it is currently used in English, as our common phrase "family and friends" illustrates. It is necessary, then, if we are to translate the *Antigone* accurately into English, to use what are at times awkward and prosaic expressions to convey the special sense of kinship contained in Antigone's φίλος.

[5] Either translation is acceptable and probably the ancient Greek found the line as ambiguous as we do. Jebb in his note on line 10 gives "evils belonging to (proper for) our

Πρὸς τοὺς φίλους at the beginning of the line is set against τῶν ἐχθρῶν κακά at the end and the force of the contrast could not be missed: "family" and "foe."

It is obvious that Sophocles has exerted all his powers to pack these first ten lines of his prologue with information pertinent to his subsequent treatment of the legend itself. It has been insufficiently taken into account, however, that these lines are delivered by Antigone herself. Since they are spoken by her, we must realize that the expository material presented here is not all we should be considering when we read this passage; besides gaining such information we are witnessing as well the establishment of Antigone's character and are being given clues to her attitudes and motivations. As close to the opening as possible Sophocles is showing us how important considerations of family are to Antigone; her family becomes an exclusive unit opposed to outsiders; we note her extravagant term of address to Ismene, her use of the old-fashioned dual, and her opposition of φίλος and ἐχθρός. Her haughtiness and arrogance are suggested by the curtness of her references to the στρατηγός and his κήρυγμα. And perhaps the combination of these two aspects of her character with her employment of the traditional value-terms αἰσχρός and ἄτιμος prepares us for her conservative political and religious positions (see Knox 75 ff.). Certainly her immediate identification of Zeus as the source of her family's evils and her unequivocal description of those evils as a legacy from Oedipus reveal without question that she accepts the primitive belief of an inherited curse inflicted on a family by a supernatural force. But much more important than the simple fact that she believes in this old doctrine is her knowledge that she herself belongs to such a family.

---

enemies," and Knox (81) follows him. The ancient scholiast specifies the second interpretation, however, and Linforth (184) agrees with him. The impact of the line remains intact either way, as I have said, but it should be noted that the meaning is affected, and rather significantly. The second interpretation of the line, which makes τῶν ἐχθρῶν express the source of the evils or the agent, gives a straightforward meaning to the statement that Antigone is making. The first, however, has far greater implications. If Antigone is in fact describing refusal of burial to Polyneices as an evil that is appropriate for foes, then quite a different light is cast upon her position with regard to Creon's decree and the "unwritten laws." In other words, her sentiments about burial refer only to the burial of kin, not to burial in general. This interpretation of the line is more in accord with my own view of Antigone's character and attitudes.

The implications of Antigone's belief as they relate to the interpretation of her character have never been sufficiently appreciated
or adequately developed by critics of the play. Antigone's reference
to the evils inherited from Oedipus that are being brought to pass by
Zeus for herself and Ismene as the sole survivors of the cursed
family accomplishes a great deal more than the identification of the
two people on the stage and the establishment of an aura of foreboding; it gives the first clear indications of Antigone's own image of
herself. She tells the audience not just that she is the daughter of
Oedipus and that her family is one that Zeus has afflicted with many
misfortunes; she is saying that she and Ismene, daughters of Oedipus
as they are, are destined for misfortune and disaster as part of the
divine plan of Zeus. She and Ismene, in short, are doomed inevitably to suffer in one way or another.

Antigone begins, then, with an image of herself as a doomed
person. In this she is unlike the heroes of other extant plays of
Sophocles, for she is not searching to find her fate.[6] Every word she
utters in the play, every action she takes, must be understood in
relationship to her conviction that she is cursed to some sort of
misfortune. The exact details of this misfortune are not known to her,
but she is convinced that she cannot escape unhappiness and
disaster, because she has been born the daughter of Oedipus. This
is an unusual situation not only for a Sophoclean hero; it is uncommon
in Greek tragedy in general. The spectators are frequently enough
aware of the fate ordained for a character and are able, therefore,
to appreciate the irony of watching the hero discover what they
already know and of seeing how he reacts when he discovers his true
situation. This is not the case with Antigone; the audience know
that she is doomed to some misfortune the minute she announces
her identity, but so does she, and no one in the play does more to
shape that doom than does Antigone herself. The other characters
in the play may also believe in the power of a family curse as do
Ismene and the Chorus, but they do not presume to know how that
curse will affect the living members of the family. Or, like Creon
and Haemon, they do not think in terms of a curse at all, but in
terms of the practical situation they see before them.

[6] Some might say that *Oedipus at Colonus* is also an exception.

An appreciation of the fact that the *Antigone* begins at a later stage than do such tragedies as the *Oedipus*, that it begins with its heroine already aware of her true situation and conscious of her destined rôle in the plan of the gods, and that only the question of how she will react to her fate is left unanswered, invites comparison with the *Seven Against Thebes* of Aeschylus in which the hero also knows his ultimate fate and his actions are decided in terms of his knowledge. In both plays the protagonists have evaluated their situations accurately in terms of the rôles they must play in destiny and they base their decisions and actions on their acceptance of their fate. Of Eteocles and Antigone, more than of any other characters in Greek tragedy, it may be said that in the end their fate was determined by their characters, rather than their characters by their fate.[7] Although Eteocles and Antigone both start with a knowledge of their fate, the moment of decision for Eteocles is delayed very effectively until the play is more than half over. Only then does he realize that Polyneices will attack the seventh gate and only then does he decide that the right moment has come to fulfil his destiny. Antigone's moment of decision, on the other hand, has arrived before the play has even begun. At the opening she is already convinced that she has been given an opportunity to fulfil her destiny on terms acceptable to her, and she is determined to do so. The heroine, then, from the outset accepts the fact that she is doomed and she has decided not to postpone what she knows is inevitable; if we recognize this, then many of the so-called problems of the play disappear.

Before we examine the play itself in greater detail, we must digress in order to define what Antigone's conception of an "acceptable disaster" might be. I mentioned earlier that such terms as αἰσχρός and ἄτιμος suggest immediately that Antigone believes in the traditional aristocratic values of the Greeks. Her language throughout the play and her attitudes corroborate this initial impression. What were these values? What had a Greek aristocrat to be in order to be adjudged ἀγαθός, that is, a man who had achieved ἀρετή?[8]

---

[7] Heracleitus, fragment 119. But cf. C. M. Bowra, *Landmarks in Greek Literature* (Cleveland and New York 1966), 123.

[8] Much has been written in recent years on this subject both by historians and analysts of Greek thought such as Werner Jaeger (especially in *Paideia: the Ideals of Greek Culture*,[2]

In the first place, the man who was truly ἀγαθός had to be born of parents who were suitably ἀγαθοί themselves; his father in particular must himself have shown the qualities of a hero.[9] In the second place, he must have wealth and social position such that he is able to live the life appropriate to a hero. In time of war he must be a warrior of courage, daring, and skill; in time of peace he was expected to show the same qualities by protecting his dependents and suppliants and by demonstrating physical prowess at the athletic competitions. But at any time, in war or peace, he had to be successful in what he undertook and the means by which he achieved this success were not nearly so important as the success itself. To be victorious or successful was καλόν; to be defeated or to fail was αἰσχρόν. With victory or success the ancient hero achieved what he valued more than anything else, honour and fame, the respect and admiration of other men; if he failed, he became what he scorned and despised more than anything else, a man without honour (ἄτιμος), and he revealed himself as base and unworthy (κακός). Such, in short, would be the general ethical system guiding Antigone.

If it has not always been recognized that Antigone is the direct spiritual descendant of Achilles, Ajax, and the rest of the Homeric heroes, it is no surprise. Homeric heroes, in addition to possessing the traditional heroic virtues, shared one other attribute—they were all men. A woman in Homeric times might also possess ἀρετή, but Penelope's ἀρετή was by no means identical with that of her husband. And so in fifth-century Athens it is doubtful whether the majority expected a woman to direct her efforts to the acquisition of honour,

---

tr. Gilbert Highet [New York 1945]) and A. W. H. Adkins, *Merit and Responsibility* (Oxford 1960) and by literary critics such as Cedric Whitman, *Sophocles: a Study of Heroic Humanism* (Cambridge 1951), and Bernard M. W. Knox, *op. cit.* For an excellent summary of heroic values as they appear in the plays of Sophocles, however, D. Butaye, "L'Idéal de l'*aretè* dans les tragédies de Sophocle," *Les Études Classiques*, 32 (1964), 337–55 is particularly useful.

[9] *Philoctetes* is the play of Sophocles that stresses this aspect of a hero, namely, that the propensity for achieving ἀρετή is innate and inherited. Neoptolemus' noble nature is repeatedly attributed to the fact that he is Achilles' son: ἀλλ' εὐγενὴς γὰρ ἡ φύσις κἀξ εὐγενῶν (874). But even more telling is Philoctetes' refusal to accept the possibility that a rogue like Odysseus could ever have been sired by a respectable nobleman like Laertes. Although Neoptolemus calls Odysseus the son of Laertes specifically (87), Philoctetes refers to him as the son of Sisyphus (417, 625, and see especially 384: πρὸς τοῦ κακίστου κἀκ κακῶν Ὀδυσσέως).

glory, and status. Quite to the contrary, most Athenians probably agreed with Pericles[10] when he said that a woman's ἀρετή consisted in not being talked about. Sophocles could write about that sort of woman, too, as he does in the *Women of Trachis*, where he presents a Deianeira as lovely, as faithful, as devoted to her domestic rôle as Penelope ever was—and as self-abasing and submissive as any respectable Athenian could have desired. On the other hand, he could also show us women who are every bit as αὐθάδης, ὠμός, and αὐτόνομος as Ajax and Oedipus and who are capable of the greatest courage and daring in their pursuit of personal honour and recognition from their society. In the *Electra* and the *Antigone* he shows two women who refuse to be content with a second-class feminine ἀρετή; both accept only the physical limitations of their sex and regard honour and fame as the proper goals not just of men but of human kind.

The means by which Electra must fulfil her rôle as a heroic character, that is, the murder of her mother, were distasteful enough even in the fifth century to make of her a basically unsympathetic figure, although she is not really different from the usual Greek hero in her complete lack of concern for what is normally regarded as justice in her pursuit of revenge and the restoration of her family-honour. Antigone, however, similar though she is in outlook, purpose, and character to Electra, is a more compelling and appealing heroine. This is true not because her motives are any different from Electra's, but because the action she undertakes in order to reach her ends is a much more attractive one; in Antigone's case her own honour and external right coincide.[11] It is interesting also to compare Medea with Antigone and Electra from this point of view. Like both of them she adheres to the standards of masculine ἀρετή; unlike both of them, however, her degradation and dishonour are due not to general human causes, but specifically to causes arising from her sex and her political situation as an outsider in the community in which she lives. These three heroines start from the same point, the desire to seek revenge from their enemies and to

---

[10] As reported in Thucydides II 45.2.

[11] Butaye 345: "La force de sa position réside en ceci qu' honneur et droit coïncident et, chaque fois qu'elle en trouvera l'occasion, elle n'hésitera pas à montrer qu'elle a la δίκη pour elle."

restore their honour, but they end in very different positions. Antigone's efforts to restore her own honour and that of her family lead her to uphold the primacy of the "unwritten laws" of the gods against the powers of civil authority, and hence she becomes a symbol of the individual conscience in conflict with the authority of the state. But whether or not one agrees with the political and religious implications of her stand, one can still sympathize with a woman who wants to bury her brother. The result, then, of Antigone's resolve to live heroically is, if not right, at least admirable, and Creon, defender of the state, seems to have chosen an unfortunate issue on which to make a stand. As for Electra, her determination to murder her mother is as justifiable in terms of the ancient heroic code as Antigone's resolve to bury her brother. And yet Electra's act can arouse only horror and revulsion and the suspicion that a woman who can follow her principles so far is unbalanced. The results of Medea's commitment to the honour code are even more horrifying; the murder of her children is the logical conclusion to her search for revenge and the restoration of her honour, but it is an act so extreme that it calls into question any code that could lead to it. By showing the horrors that could be perpetrated in its name, so to speak, Euripides questioned the validity of the entire heroic value-system. Interestingly enough, not even Euripides could imagine a mortal woman quite so relentless in the defence of her own honour as to kill her children and so he makes this monster of heroism a witch.

Let us return now to the question of the kind of disaster that would meet Antigone's requirements. First, it would have to be one that was worthy of a member of a distinguished family and that would in no way reflect to the disadvantage of the family name. Secondly, it must represent a striking assertion of Antigone's will, an active reaching out for her fate that could not be interpreted as a passive submission to her circumstances. Thirdly, it must bring with it the admiration of other men and a renown that would give her a kind of immortality as a worthy member of a noble family. By burying her brother as ancient custom demanded, although in defiance of the authority of the state, Antigone could meet all the conditions of a suitable disaster. There might be no way in which she could avoid the evil destiny that threatened her as a member of a doomed family, but she could choose the form of her disaster, meet her destiny of her own free will, and in this way give clear proof of her heroic nature.

Assuming the conceptual framework outlined so far, let us see how the play develops.

When Antigone summons Ismene to a meeting in the predawn, she is acting on the premise that there are two daughters of Oedipus, each of whom is equally cursed. She, as I contend, has already decided not to wait passively to be overwhelmed by disaster, but is determined to meet it on her own terms by precipitating it. What she does not know is whether Ismene will grasp the possibilities of the situation as she sees them. Her first words remind her sister of their common heritage of disaster as the descendants of Oedipus (2–6); only then does she proceed to the matter of Creon's decree. But Ismene has not yet heard of the decree; the latest news that has reached her is that their brothers have slain each other. She does not know, she says, whether it is her good fortune or her misfortune (ἀτωμένη 17) that has increased since the death of her brothers. In Ismene's eyes the situation as it stands with two brothers dead, both stained by kindred murder and one a traitor to his country, is in itself a great disaster. She has already suffered much shame and grief; she does not know, of course, whether she will be forced to suffer even more, but she can hope that the misfortunes have been sufficient to satisfy the demands of the divine force that is punishing her family. She has accepted the evils in the past as part of her destiny and she expects to accept the new evil brought on her by Creon's decree in the same passive way. That Creon has forbidden the burial of her brother, that she must witness the insult to her family's honour that lack of burial entails is for her a dreadful punishment, but one that she must endure and count as yet another sign of the continuing displeasure of the gods with the House of Oedipus. She cannot understand why Antigone wants to run the risk of bringing more trouble and disgrace down on them; she fails to see how any act of theirs could improve the situation. In Ismene's reactions to Antigone's suggestion that they bury Polyneices, there is no reference whatever to any religious obligation. Antigone herself does not mention such a justification until after Ismene has stated her cogent reasons for not joining her in the act of burial;

only when Ismene has formally rationalized her refusal (49–68) does Antigone respond with a suggestion of the priority of religious considerations (75–77). In her first long speech (21–38) she is concerned not with religious duty but with family honour. Creon has deemed one brother worthy of a public funeral; Eteocles, then, will be ἔντιμος in the judgement of the dead below (25). Creon will not allow burial for Polyneices, however, τὸν ἀθλίως θανόντα...νέκυν (26); he will deprive him of the last public tributes of the people[12] as well as of a position of respect among the dead to which his rank and origin entitle him.

It is significant that in this speech Antigone, with what is generally conceded to be irony, calls Creon ἀγαθόν (31). If Creon were truly ἀγαθός, he could not disgrace his own sister's son in this way and he could not fail to realize that such an action called for retribution from the surviving members of the family, for in dishonouring Polyneices Creon shames the whole family, including Antigone and Ismene. The reaction of the two sisters to this disgrace will soon show their true natures, in Antigone's opinion, as either noble and worthy of their descent (εὐγενής, 38) or as base, cowardly, and unlike the natures of their ancestors (ἐσθλῶν κακή, 38). The rest of the play revolves around Antigone's attempt to show herself a true daughter of Oedipus with a nature in the fullest sense εὐγενής.

Ismene's reply is much more forceful and relevant than is generally recognized. She understands well that Antigone has in mind a demonstration of ἀρετή and she answers her in the same terms. She begins by reminding Antigone of the large number of degradations that their family has already suffered and asks her to consider (59–60) how by far the greatest degradation of all would be their deaths as outlaws who had transgressed the solemn decree of their ruler. Disobedience to Creon's decree will not restore the family-honour or reflect credit on the sisters themselves; rather it will

---

[12] It is the lack of public funeral rites that concerns Antigone. Obviously Polyneices would not be ἄκλαυτος literally since no decree could be effective against the private grief of his sisters. But private grief was of little value in Antigone's view. Only the public recognition of the loss of Polyneices could satisfy her understanding of honour. Similarly when she refers to herself as dying ἄκλαυτος (876), she is not discounting the loyalty of such supporters as Haemon and the townspeople who she feels agree with her; but private grief cannot be a substitute for public recognition and mourning. Of this public ritual there can be none for her since she is dying outside the law.

brand them as criminals. Ismene believes that one cannot win honour by an act that is essentially dishonourable. Disobedience to the law and to the will of one's rulers is dishonourable; thus Antigone is proposing to bring even more dishonour on a family that already has had more than its fair share.

In the second place, Ismene feels that Antigone is striving after a form of ἀρετή that is inappropriate for a woman and here she is on solid ground indeed.[13] What Antigone intends to do might perhaps be justifiable in terms of masculine ἀρετή, but it is not so in terms of feminine ἀρετή. No one finds fault with Penelope for sitting in her bedchamber spinning and weaving and weeping for twenty years; no one expected her to devise any bold scheme for dispatching the suitors, for it was not her rôle to take action of this sort. Her husband and her son, when he reached maturity, were the ones on whom this duty fell. In Ismene's eyes Antigone is proposing to exceed her feminine rôle. She says nothing in this speech (49–68) of the primacy of state laws over those of religion; her arguments are couched entirely in terms of her idea of the family-curse and her belief that feminine ἀρετή quite properly yields to superior strength and force: ἀρχόμεσθ' ἐκ κρεισσόνων (63) and ὡς βιάζομαι τάδε, τοῖς ἐν τέλει βεβῶσι πείσομαι (66–67). Her concluding remark is entirely in keeping with this view of a woman's place: τὸ γὰρ περισσὰ πράσσειν οὐκ ἔχει νοῦν οὐδένα (67–68). "To act beyond one's proper limits makes no sense."

But Antigone's response is also in heroic language and reflects heroic values: ἀλλ' ἴσθ' ὁποῖά σοι δοκεῖ (71). "Be what you think best," that is, εὐγενής or κακή. Antigone knows what she "thinks best," she understands her own nature, and she intends to show the world what she is by burying her brother in defiance of Creon's decree because καλόν μοι τοῦτο ποιούσῃ θανεῖν (72). "For me to die in this act is noble." Καλόν is the highest term of approbation (Butaye 338) she could have used and is the opposite of αἰσχρόν, the term she used earlier (5) to describe the misfortunes that have befallen her family.

---

[13] It is astonishing that normally perceptive critics can write about the "womanliness" of Antigone's action in burying her brother; e.g. Linforth (251): "Her heroic action is of a kind that would be more readily undertaken by a woman than by a man." Certainly Ismene and Creon did not take this point of view; and neither did Teucer in the *Ajax*. See also Knox, 78 f.

It must be noted that Antigone does *not* say that it is noble for her to bury her brother, and yet the play is commonly interpreted as if she has said that. From the very beginning she concentrates on the manner of her own death, and the act of burial is secondary to this as it is only a means to an end. In any case, the decision to bury her brother carried with it the possibility of death and she would be foolish to try to ignore this fact. But, on the other hand, there is also the possibility that she could bury her brother and not be caught. She never considers this second possibility at all; she fully intends to die and sees herself as lying in the bosom of her family ὅσια πανουργήσασ' (74). Now, only at this point, does she begin to rationalize her decision in terms of religious custom and belief and to identify her own will with that of the gods. Let Ismene show dishonour to what the gods honour, if she thinks it best (76–77). Ismene immediately protests that she intends no dishonour; she is merely recognizing the limitations of her own nature, her powerlessness to act in defiance of the citizens: βίᾳ πολιτῶν δρᾶν ἔφυν ἀμήχανος (79). Antigone is not swayed by Ismene's reasoning, nor is she moved at all by her sister's concern for her (82). She replies only: μὴ 'μοῦ προτάρβει· τὸν σὸν ἐξόρθου πότμον (83). "Don't waste your fears on me; straighten out your own fate." [14] We must conclude that Antigone has already "straightened out" hers.

In the next exchange between the sisters Ismene speaks as if Antigone's prime object is to bury her brother and as if she plans to escape detection and punishment if possible. But nothing is further from Antigone's mind. The burial of her brother would accomplish little in her view if it were not at the same time known that she was the one who had done it. All must know that she, Antigone, has the courage, daring, and strength of purpose to carry out this act. She must be detected, she must be punished by death, she must win fame and renown by her deed. If she really placed the highest value on the opinion of "those whom it is most necessary to please" (89), there would be no good reason for proclaiming her intentions or her actions to the general public. But the fact is that pleasing the dead and the gods of the dead is Antigone's secondary

[14] It is not possible to judge the extent to which Sophocles' use of πότμος was intended to arouse the common association of θάνατος, but it is likely that Antigone here is represented as thinking of Ismene's ultimate destiny.

concern; to prove her own worth and right to be called a daughter of Oedipus and thereby to win fame and renown is her main goal.

Ismene again reminds Antigone that she is overstepping the limits of her own nature as a woman when she says: ἀρχὴν δὲ θηρᾶν οὐ πρέπει τἀμήχανα (92). "It is not right to search out at all what is beyond one's powers." But Antigone has anticipated this argument by saying that she will stop when her powers fail her (91), as if somehow the mere fact that she has the necessary resources of spirit indicates that it is right for her to carry out her deed. She is not exceeding her own limitations but rather she is being true to herself by fulfilling her own nature.

Her harsh words and her brusque dismissal of Ismene reveal Antigone's basic self-centredness and render highly questionable the judgement of those who see her as the incarnation of selfless love.[15] Antigone actually disowns Ismene as a member of the family when she says: εἰ ταῦτα λέξεις, ἐχθαρῇ μὲν ἐξ ἐμοῦ, ἐχθρὰ δὲ τῷ θανόντι προσκείσῃ δίκῃ (93–94). Her sense of values is such that she does not regard Polyneices' treasonable actions sufficient reason to damn him as an ἐχθρός and she will affirm somewhat grandiloquently later on: οὔτοι συνέχθειν, ἀλλὰ συμφιλεῖν ἔφυν (523). In contrast, however, Ismene's refusal to accept Antigone's position is enough to banish her from the family as unworthy and to damn her in her sister's eyes as an ἐχθρά. Thus Antigone makes clear in her treatment of Ismene that all her fine talk about obeying the "unwritten laws" of kinship and burial is no more than a rationalization of the more compelling personal motives that arise out of her sense of degradation and her desire to restore honour to herself and her family. It is not a desire to obey the gods or to bury her brother that drives Antigone to defy Creon but rather her concern with her own fate and her own reputation; nothing worse could happen to her than to die an ignoble death: πείσομαι γὰρ οὐ τοσοῦτον οὐδὲν ὥστε μὴ οὐ καλῶς θανεῖν (96–97). Ismene, on the other hand, refuses to reject Antigone regardless of how ἄνους she is, but assures her that, no matter what she does, she remains a member of the family in the eyes of her relatives: τοῖς φίλοις δ' ὀρθῶς φίλη (99). To Ismene, Antigone will always be φίλη, not ἐχθρά. It is quite incorrect to accuse Ismene of timidity and

[15] E.g. Albin Lesky, *Greek Tragedy*, tr. H. A. Frankfort (London, New York 1967), 107; Knox 116.

cowardice;[16] to do so is to imply that Antigone's evaluation of the situation is the only possible one, and it is doubtful indeed that Sophocles meant to imply any such thing. If one grants Ismene's premises that it is not honourable to die in a criminal act and that it is not natural for women to oppose those in authority over them, then she is more than justified in refusing to help Antigone bury Polyneices. That fear of death is not her motive in refusing to help becomes clear later when she is willing to share Antigone's punishment. In this first part of the play she steadfastly upholds the traditional view of feminine ἀρετή and represents what the Greeks admired in a woman; she is submissive when she should be, courageous when it is proper to be so, and completely loyal to her sister in the face of extreme provocation.

In the character of Ismene Sophocles has portrayed the good woman as defined by the conventional standards of his time; in the character of Creon, whom he introduces in the next scene, he shows us at first the good citizen, one who places the welfare of the community above personal good and who has replaced the narrow loyalties of the family with the wider ones of the state.[17] As Creon's character is developed, however, we learn that he is hardly less egocentric than Antigone, for he promotes the good of the community only as long as that good coincides with his own will.

Creon sees Eteocles as a member in good standing of the citizen body, deserving of all the honour due to a military hero; Polyneices he sees as a traitor who has attacked his ancestral land and its gods (199), a bad member of the citizen body. By his actions Polyneices has disqualified himself as a citizen;[18] once a φίλος of Thebes and her people, he has become an ἐχθρός, and can legitimately be treated as such. It was a time-honoured "commandment" of the heroic ethical code "to do good to one's φίλοι and evil to one's ἐχθροί." There is no reason, moreover, for Creon to feel that his decree might offend the gods, for the gods of Thebes must surely regard as an ἐχθρός a man who had undertaken to destroy their shrines with fire.

---

[16] E.g. C. M. Bowra, *Sophoclean Tragedy* (Oxford 1944), 80.

[17] Knox (76 ff.) has an interesting account of the political implications of the conflict between Antigone and Creon.

[18] It was on this theory that Athenian law forbade the burial of traitors within the boundaries of Attica and denied customary burial rites to criminals.

Just as he views Polyneices as having forfeited the honours and rights of a citizen, so Creon expects Antigone and Ismene to regard their brother as having forfeited the rights of kinship. Creon does not intend to act against either the claims of the gods or those of the family; he regards Polyneices as beyond the protective pale of both religion and kinship. His position, like that of Ismene, is a defensible one and, initially at least, even sympathetic.

When Creon finally prevails upon the Guard to tell him what has happened, the Guard says: "Someone has just now gone off after burying the corpse and sprinkling thirsty dust on the flesh and performing the rites that are required" (245–47). These lines are extremely important to our study of Antigone's character because they state clearly that the ritual burial has been completed. We are thus left with the old question: why did Antigone return to bury her brother a second time? Of the many and varied answers that have been proffered one of the most common is that the first burial was incomplete.[19] And yet there is nothing in the Guard's account to suggest that he regards the ritual burial as incomplete, and indeed he says even that the burial looked like the act of someone avoiding a curse (256).[20] If Antigone's purpose is merely to fulfil her religious obligations to her dead brother and to enable him to take his place of honour among the dead (so Knox 92), then she has accomplished her object with the first burial.

---

[19] Jebb posed the problem and offered this solution in his note to line 429. Among more recent critics to accept this explanation is Linforth (200). Holger Friis Johansen, "Sophocles 1939–1959," *Lustrum* 7 (1962), 186, discusses some of "the more readable contributions" to the subject with the comment: "With quite an incredible enthusiasm several scholars still discuss the uninteresting question of the double burial." Why this problem should be any less interesting than scores of others that have fascinated scholars is not at all clear.

[20] λεπτὴ δ' ἄγος φεύγοντος ὣς ἐπῆν κόνις (256): this line also counts against the unlikely but striking proposal of S. M. Adams (above, note 2) 52, that the gods had performed this first burial. But it should not be overlooked that Sophocles does seem to surround the burial deliberately with a supernatural aura and thus makes the Chorus' suggestion that the burial might be an act of divine intervention (278–79) not entirely unexpected. There is no sign of human hand and the body is undisturbed by animals. This line also renders invalid the theory of E. J. Messemer, "The Double Burial of Polyneices," *Class. Journ.* 37 (1942), 515–26, that the first burial was a complete covering of the body sufficient to serve as protection against desecration by animals. Such a burial would have required more than the λεπτὴ κόνις mentioned in this line and would certainly have left tool marks (249–52).

The reason for the second burial must lie elsewhere. Bowra's suggestion (93) that by uncovering the body the guards "undid" the whole burial process and made a repetition of the ritual necessary seems attractively simple, but it raises the question whether a burial could be "undone" in this way and corroboration from other sources is essential. It is reasonable, after all, to assume that a ritual burial is of use to a deceased person only through some effect that it has on his afterlife; it can be of no service whatever to his physical remains and the only function it could have in the world of the living is to assuage the feelings of the survivors. Bowra, then, is suggesting that Polyneices' soul, regularized, so to speak, by the first burial, was in some way returned to its previous state of dishonour when the dust was swept away. It does not seem likely. No explanation of the second burial that relies on some mechanical or physical aspect of the burial procedure can be satisfactory because it must depend on some detail or fact that is not mentioned in the text. It is quite clear that, in the Guard's opinion, and he is our only first-hand witness, the first burial satisfied the requirements for a ritual burial. We conclude that Polyneices' soul had found its haven.

It is not the burial procedure to which we must look for an explanation of the second burial but the mind of Antigone. The woman Sophocles portrays for us can have had only one real reason for returning to her brother's body and performing the burial rites a second time. She does this because she has not been caught the first time and because it is apparent that neither the guards nor Creon has any suspicion of the identity of the criminal. It is never part of Antigone's plan that she should not be caught, found guilty of violating the decree, and sentenced to death. When it looks as if she may actually escape detection, she returns immediately to the scene of the crime and repeats step by step[21] what she has done before. She insists on being caught and later she insists on being put to death.[22]

---

[21] The pouring of libations in 431 has no exact parallel in the first burial. In the second account, however, the Guard is describing what he saw Antigone do, whereas in the first he is describing only the results of what she has done; the results of the pouring of libations would not be particularly noticeable. In any case, his expression κἀφαγιστεύσας ἃ χρή (247) must include the libations.

[22] A number of critics feel that Sophocles' only or main purpose in having the two burials is a structural one. H. D. F. Kitto, *Form and Meaning in Drama* (London 1956),

The Chorus observed earlier οὐκ ἔστιν οὕτω μῶρος ὃς θανεῖν ἐρᾷ (220). "No one is so foolish as to want to die." Well, possibly Antigone does not *want* to die more than anyone else, but she has none the less *decided* to die. Her earlier statements to Ismene (72, 96–97) clearly indicate that she regards dying in this cause as noble and that more than anything else she wants to die nobly. In the next scene with Creon Antigone follows these feelings through to their logical conclusion, showing that she is reaching out for death on her own terms and that she will not be thwarted from her purpose.

The first view we have of Antigone after her capture reveals a young lady somewhat more subdued than the fierce and aggressive sister of Ismene; Creon addresses her thus: σὲ δή, σὲ τὴν νεύουσαν ἐς πέδον κάρα (441). Her first answers to Creon's questions are brief until he gives her the key words τούσδ' ὑπερβαίνειν νόμους (449) to which she responds with her famous argument of the "unwritten laws," ἄγραπτα κἀσφαλῆ θεῶν νόμιμα (454–55). This line of reasoning is one that has been scarcely more than hinted at in the earlier scene with Ismene; there Antigone's preoccupation is with her family, their misfortunes and degradations, and religious considerations are given no prominence at all.

That these religious considerations were not quite so compelling for the ancient Greek as they seem in this speech of Antigone is fairly clear from the fact that she is the only person who talks at all about them. The danger of failing to fulfil a law of the gods never occurs to Ismene; Creon is convinced that he is aiding and abetting the divine punishment of an enemy of the gods of Thebes. Even the Chorus, consisting of old men who are acknowledged conservatives (164–69), are uneasy at Creon's decree only in a rather superstitious way. And yet, although little stress is laid in the play on this argument, it is a striking rationalization which has caught the attention and interest of many and which has assumed undue importance in the interpretation of the play as a whole and of Antigone's character.

152: "Why did Sophocles want her to go twice? The answer, naturally, is to be found in the effect which it produces." D. W. Lucas, *The Greek Tragic Poets*[2] (London 1959), 143: "No doubt what he actually had in mind was that the play would be more effective if the burial were discovered before the identity of the burier, and the stage shows that his device is brilliantly successful." No one can deny that the final effect is striking, but it is unlikely, in my opinion, that Sophocles would divorce structural considerations so completely from plot and characterization.

Without a doubt Antigone believes what she is saying about the primacy of religious law—once she thinks of it!—but this argument is not, I am certain, one of her strongest reasons for defying Creon's decree. Face to face with Creon, however, she needs a less personal justification for what she has done and his reference to νόμοι inspires her appeal to a higher law than his civil law. But she returns quickly to her deeper and more cogent motivations: θανουμένη γὰρ ἐξῄδη, τί δ᾽οὔ; κεἰ μὴ σὺ προυκήρυξας (460–61). "I knew that I was destined to die; and how not? even if you had not proclaimed your decree." Every man knows, of course, that he is destined to die at some time or other, and translators and editors have generally—indeed, exclusively, to my knowledge—taken this statement of Antigone's in its universal sense. It is much more striking, however, when it is understood less as an undeniable description of man's mortality than as an expression of Antigone's own sense of impending doom. This interpretation becomes even more likely when one looks at the lines immediately following, which refer without any doubt only to her own particular circumstances as a member of a cursed family. If lines 460–61 might well have been spoken by any mortal creature, lines 461–66 most certainly apply to no one except Antigone herself: "If I die before my time, I declare that gain. For how could anyone who lives as I do in the midst of many evils not consider death a gain? And so, as far as I am concerned, to meet this end brings a grief not worth thinking about." A life that is difficult enough to start with because of the number and nature of the misfortunes that have afflicted her family becomes altogether intolerable for her, with a brother's body exposed and disgraced for all the citizens of Thebes to see. To allow this dishonouring of her family, of her brother, and of herself to continue would be an agony more excruciating for her to endure than the penalty of death that she now faces.

The remark of the Chorus after this speech is significant; they do not comment at all on the nobility or the justice of her act or of her argument.[23] They note only the resemblance between her spirit and that of Oedipus (471–72); her spirit, like his, is untamed (ὠμός) nor does she know how to yield (εἴκειν) to evil circumstances.[24] The

---

[23] Linforth (204) remarks on this point but deduces nothing from it.

[24] On the significance of the terms used by the Chorus with respect to the heroic ideal, see Knox 23, 65 (ὠμός): 15 ff. (εἴκειν).

Chorus is beginning to see Antigone as she sees herself and as she wants others to see her, as the heroic daughter of a heroic father. Once they have recognized her basic character, they know what to expect and henceforth they offer her no sympathy or advice, only their respect and their painfully honest appraisal of her character. They do not necessarily approve of the choice she has made, but they understand what she is and why she has started down the path to death, and they know that she will not turn back— or even glance back. In their next lyric (Stasimon II, 582–625), they sing of inherited misfortune and the curse of the House of Oedipus and Labdacus.[25]

Creon, however, has failed to recognize what the Chorus has seen and, instead of the courage, audacity, and wilfulness of the heroic character, he sees only intransigence and insolence on the part of one who should properly be submissive, since she is subordinate to those around her and since she is a woman. Like Ismene, Creon is struck by the masculine character of Antigone's act. Had there been male kin still surviving to perform burial rites for Polyneices, perhaps Creon might have expected some such action; as it is, he expected trouble only from political opponents and is quite taken off guard by the defiance of Antigone, his own niece. How can he, a man, fight honourably against a woman? He cannot, and yet he also cannot allow her to defy him and mock him (483),[26] or he will himself lose face. He is not entirely unaware of what to him are Antigone's pretensions, as he reveals when he says: "I hate it when someone caught in base deeds then wishes to glorify (to make $\kappa\alpha\lambda\acute{o}\nu$) what he has done" (495–96).

But Antigone is not interested in arguing fine points with Creon any longer, since she is anxious that her death come soon, before the glory she has acquired in burying her brother can be marred in any way either by a failure of will on her part or by some unforeseen development arising from the curse. She is confident that she has won genuine $\kappa\lambda\acute{e}os$ (502) and she insists that her deed is recognized

---

[25] Lucas 143: "But Sophocles nowhere, in this or any other play, lays stress on the familiar doctrine of the inherited curse." This assertion seems to express wishful thinking on the part of a modern critic who perhaps would like to think Sophocles too sophisticated for such a primitive belief.

[26] Nothing could be more insulting in terms of Greek values than mockery from one's enemies since it symbolized a loss of respect; see Knox 30 f.

and applauded by her fellow citizens, if only they dared say so. As long as she feels that she has won this public recognition she is triumphant; later, when she feels that she is, in Creon's words, μούνη τῶνδε Καδμείων(508), she becomes less sure of herself.

In this later part of her scene with Creon she does not revert to her "unwritten laws" as justification, but speaks in terms of her obligations to her family and, in particular, to siblings (513). Creon objects that Polyneices cannot be regarded as a member of the family any more than he can be regarded as a citizen of Thebes. By attacking Thebes he ceased to be a citizen; by attacking Eteocles he ceased to be a brother and became the ἐχθρός of the family as he was the ἐχθρός of the state. Antigone is quite unable to refute Creon's argument here since she has already demonstrated that she herself believes it is possible to forfeit one's membership in a family and to be disowned (93-94). And so she begs the question by saying that all this may be true for the living but that perhaps values are not the same for the dead and funeral observances are owed to all (519).[27] But when Creon points out that this view involves paying honour to base and noble alike, he is attacking her in her own value-system and, since she cannot answer him satisfactorily, she deflects his challenge by not answering at all and by posing another question, in order to avoid the issue altogether. But Creon insists that enmity and friendship do not cease at death (522), and it is this assertion that elicits from Antigone her famous, and ambiguous,[28] οὔτοι συνέχθειν, ἀλλὰ συμφιλεῖν ἔφυν (523). "I was not born a member of their factions, but of their family." Lesky is disturbed that the idea of attachment in this line has been restricted to Polyneices and denied to humanity in general.[29] But in her next exchange with

[27] Reading τούτους.

[28] Knox (82) understands this line as "I was born not to join in their political hatred for each other but in their love for each other as blood brothers." The objection could be made that "love" is too affective a word in English to describe the relationship in question. Although Knox at this point explains the full sense of this line, for some reason he reverts (on 116) to the more traditional and distressingly misleading "I was not born to join in hatred but in love." He further asserts that Antigone's "deepest motive" for her action was love. Here he seems to contradict all the evidence he has so carefully and effectively compiled to support a heroic interpretation of Antigone's character and to join all those critics who see Antigone as some sort of embodiment of womanliness and womanly affection.

[29] Lesky 107: "It throws a curious light on recent cultural history that scholars have tried very hard to limit the significance of this saying to Polyneices and to deny it the

Ismene (commencing at 536) Antigone shows clearly how small a rôle "love" in any sense, either of personal affection or of involvement with her fellow man, plays in her character. Feelings for the grief and distracted state of her sister move her little, if at all, but the thought that Ismene might actually share in her honour and win the same reward for which Antigone strives, recognition and glory, through a failure of will rather than by an assertion of will, infuriates her. That her sense of justice should be outraged is understandable, but it ought not to be denied in any case that her treatment of Ismene is as harsh and self-centred as was Ajax' treatment of the gentle Tecmessa. The deed is her own and no "love" is present to urge her to share the prize she has won. λόγοις δ'ἐγὼ φιλοῦσαν οὐ στέργω φίλην (543). "I have no fondness for a relative who is a relative only in words." The natural opposition that one anticipates with λόγοις, the one that comes first to mind, is ἔργοις: a relative in name but not in deed. In this context, however, Antigone cannot really intend to oppose words with deeds since, regardless of her earlier refusal to join in burying Polyneices, Ismene now shows clearly that she is as willing as Antigone to die for what she values. Her loyalty and fidelity, her affection, she can offer to her sister and she does so, although she still does not approve of what Antigone has done (556). As far as her deeds are concerned, Ismene shows that she is a true φίλη by rejecting as worthless a life without her sister. What Antigone is implying here, it seems, is that Ismene is related to her in name, but not in character or in spirit; for she, Antigone, is εὐγενής and Ismene is, by Antigone's standards, κακή and no fit member of the family of Oedipus. Κρέοντ' ἐρώτα· τοῦδε γὰρ σὺ κηδεμών (549). Creon is Ismene's true kin, says Antigone. There is little evidence here of that "love" for the individual members of her family that Knox sees (107) as the source of Antigone's strength and conviction. She rejects Ismene just as emphatically as Creon thought she ought to reject Polyneices. Ismene pleads with Antigone not to dishonour her (544–45), an appeal that Antigone would be sure to

---

wider human application which we consider so typically Sophoclean." See also his *A History of Greek Literature*, tr. James Willis and Cornelis de Heer (London 1966), 282: "No effort has been spared by scholars to strip these words, the basic expression of western humanism, of their full and true meaning, and to exclude from them a notion of love which Sophocles has been thought incapable of entertaining."

appreciate, and yet Antigone displays no feeling, no respect, no compassion for Ismene's plight, only a sort of jealous possessiveness about her own claim to distinction. The most she will grant her sister is that she feels grieved to mock her (551) and that she does not resent Ismene's survival (553). When Ismene asks, almost incredulously, if she is not to share Antigone's lot, she reveals how closely intertwined she believes their fates to be, that she never believed in the possibility of escape from her fate as a member of Oedipus' family. But Antigone will not allow her to share her fate: σὺ μὲν γὰρ εἵλου ζῆν, ἐγὼ δὲ κατθανεῖν (555). "You chose to live, but I chose to die." Here again Antigone reveals that death is the end she foresees and desires from the moment of her decision to bury her brother. The chance failure of the guards to apprehend her the first time and the fact that no one had any suspicions of the identity of the guilty person forced her to return for the second burial. ἡ δ' ἐμὴ ψυχὴ πάλαι τέθνηκεν (559–60). "My life was over long ago," she goes on to say, showing how completely committed she is to her own death. That she was a dead woman from the moment she was born into a cursed family is perhaps what she means here, or, more probably, that she was a dead woman from the moment of her decision to accept the full implications of her destiny as a member of a cursed family by burying Polyneices. For her there never was any other possibility except death. There is a certain irony in Creon's remark at this juncture, for he attributes to Antigone a folly dating from the day of her birth (562) and that is exactly the way in which Antigone sees the situation, although what he terms folly or lack of sense when he calls her ἄνους she sees rather as an innate capacity for ἀρετή.

Antigone leaves the stage now to make way for a scene between Haemon and Creon. The functions that this scene serves are undeniable. Once we have seen Creon react with such unnecessary cruelty toward his remarkably loyal and faithful son, we are prepared to accept his ultimate disaster as not so totally unmerited as we might have thought on the basis of his actions up to this point. Furthermore he reveals clearly in his exchanges with Haemon that he is not simply a well-intentioned head of state who just happened to become involved in an awkward and difficult situation. On the contrary, he has within him all the characteristics of a tyrant and, far from being the devoted servant of the state as he represented himself in the earlier part of the play, he is interested primarily in his own personal power.[30] It follows, then, that Antigone's act offends him not so much because of its effect on the state as because it is an affront to his authority and has piqued his pride both as a ruler and as a man. He reveals also in this scene a crassness that has already been strongly suggested in his exchange with the Guard. He was very quick, we recall, to accuse the Guard, without any evidence whatever, of lying and treachery and to jump to the conclusion that he had accepted a bribe from Creon's political opponents. Later, he will be just as quick to accuse the respected Teiresias of the same venality. He does not accuse Haemon of acting through motives of profit, but he suggests another motive of an equally base character, namely, lust. He has already indicated (569) how little esteem he has for relationships between men and women; Ismene's suggestion that the accord that exists between Haemon and Antigone is rare and not easily replaceable draws only a coarse rejoinder from him. Now again (648) he warns Haemon not to be misled by lust, as if that were the only feeling that might bind Haemon to Antigone. Political ambition, love of money, physical lust—these are the things that now appear to have the greatest meaning for Creon; he does not understand people who act on higher principles and hence he fails to understand the people with whom he has to deal, all of whom are singularly high-minded and idealistic in their approach to life.

While this scene gives us a fuller comprehension of Creon's character, it contributes as well to a more detailed portrait of Antigone, and we are able to glimpse a side of her that she does not reveal during her appearances on stage. Ismene's devotion to her sister tells us more about herself than it does about Antigone, but Haemon's loyalty to her gives intimations of a warmer, more sympathetic sort of person than the fierce champion of honour, kinship, and divine rights whom we have listened to so far. Haemon reminds the audience that Antigone is after all a young girl who is about to die a hideous death. This impression of her heightens the

---

[30] The Chorus never does accept Creon's magnanimous description of himself as a man who desires only the good of the state (162–210). After he has made his impressive statement, they remark rather cynically that in any case he can do what he likes about both the living and the dead (211–14).

effect of her next appearance as she makes her way to the rocky chamber where she is sentenced to a slow and agonizing death; the physical presence on the stage of Haemon, her betrothed, adds immeasurably to the pathos of Antigone's situation and makes her laments seem more heartfelt and less ritualistic. But the most important function of Haemon is to link the destinies of Creon and Antigone. If it were not for Haemon, Antigone's death might cause political troubles for Creon, but it would not cause him personal grief. Antigone's death, however, causes the death of Haemon, which in turn causes that of Eurydice; thus, just as Creon makes Antigone suffer through her family, so she brings punishment on him through his.

Although Haemon is important for the revelation of Creon's character and the dramatic structure of the play, he is none the less irrelevant to Antigone herself[31] once she decides to abandon any pretense that she is an ordinary mortal and to fulfil her destiny as the daughter of a cursed father. Her decision isolates her from Ismene, her closest living kin, it cuts her off from the state by making her an outlaw, and it must inevitably separate her from Haemon and the normal concerns of a woman's life. In the end Antigone must walk alone to the death she has chosen for herself; Sophocles, by keeping her away from Haemon and by representing the Chorus as rather disapproving and unsympathetic, is careful to ensure that she does that.

Remote is perhaps the best word for the attitude of the Chorus toward Antigone and her deed. In the Kommos they supply the responses to her laments, but they refrain from offering sympathy or comfort. They seem to stand back, commenting on what they see and hear, but remaining essentially uninvolved. She for her part sings laments that are largely conventional, although the audience's memory of Haemon doubtlessly mitigates the formal character of what she says. The Chorus for their part remind her not to lapse too deeply into self-pity since by her death she is achieving fame and praise, κλεινὴ καὶ ἔπαινον ἔχουσ᾽ (817), and is avoiding an undistin-

---

[31] At least in Sophocles' conception of Antigone's character Haemon is irrelevant. Euripides, with a different attitude towards fate and a different dramatic purpose, evidently did have Haemon rescue and marry Antigone (Antigone, Hypotheses I and II).

guished death through disease or violence. They remind her that she
has the unique opportunity of choosing the time and manner of her
own death (821–22). But as if she has not heard them she continues
her lament until they reply to her allusion to Niobe. Her sentimental
and self-pitying comparison of her own fate to that of Niobe (832–33)
moves the Chorus to remind her that, although her mortality in fact
makes the comparison invalid, it is still greatly to her credit to have
experienced in life and death a fate that resembles that of the godlike
(834–38). Their reluctance to praise her without qualification causes
Antigone to accuse them of mocking her (839) and of insulting her
(841); in a fit of pique she turns away from them and addresses
herself to the city of Thebes with its sacred fount and grove. The
reaction of the Chorus to this gesture is only to comment that she
did a deed of great daring and is now reaping the consequences, as a
result of some blight inherited from her father (853–56). The mention
of her ill-fated family elicits from Antigone an account of the sufferings of individual members of the family, ending, significantly
enough, in a reference to herself. Again the Chorus offers her only
an objective appraisal of what they have seen; religious reverence
has its place, but one must not offend those in power. She has, they
say, brought on her own destruction by her self-willed passion or
obsession (αὐτόγνωτος ὀργά 875). Antigone's last stanza in the
Kommos shows that she feels completely abandoned as she ap-
proaches death.

Instead of a triumphant victory over her enemies Antigone finds
that what seemed so right and logical to her does not seem so to
others. As the "last" of her race (λοισθία 895) she goes down to her
death κάκιστα δὴ μακρῷ, echoing Ismene's ὅσῳ κάκιστ' ὀλούμεθ' (59).
And a wretched death it is that awaits her, for she is cheated of the
quick and spectacular death by stoning that she had expected and
is condemned instead to die a slow, miserable, degrading death by
entombment in a cave where her brave spirit will not be visible to
anyone, or, worse still, where she may lose her courage. Yet still
the thought of her family below waiting to welcome her gives her
some comfort.

As she thinks about what has happened and realizes that she is
indeed perishing most miserably of all her family, as Ismene has
foreseen, her mind perhaps returns to that earlier discussion with her

sister. For, in a much-disputed passage (904–20),[32] it seems to be of Ismene's βίᾳ πολιτῶν δρᾶν ἔφυν ἀμήχανος (79) that she is thinking. At least she finally admits that she is not completely without respect for the laws of the state and that, in fact, she would not have acted βίᾳ πολιτῶν (907) except in the single instance of a brother. Neither husband (who is not normally, in the strictest interpretation, kin at all) nor child (who is only half-kin, so to speak) could exert as strong a claim on the ties of kinship as a brother who is ὅμαιμος ἐκ μιᾶς τε καὶ ταὐτοῦ πατρός (513). Perhaps the nearness of a brother's relationship, his stronger claims on the bonds of kinship, and Antigone's admission that the laws of the state are a serious consideration sum up all Sophocles intended to convey by his adaptation of the well-known and striking story from Herodotus.

Even if one disregards as spurious this last passage, however, the impression is strong in this final speech of Antigone that she feels cheated in some way, that the results she had expected have failed to materialize. Why, when she is on the way to the death she planned for so energetically, does she feel so deserted by the gods? Is she merely wallowing in self-pity or uttering conventional laments without much thought of their appropriateness? She cannot expect to escape from death, nor at any point in the play does she act as if she wants to. What, then, is it that she hopes for? Perhaps a more enthusiastic reception for her deed, more open acknowledgement and admiration, or perhaps some obvious punishment visited upon the heads of her enemies, the very thing that does happen after her death. To be denied these satisfactions is the last test of Antigone's heroic character. She goes to her death without knowing that she will be vindicated and that her deed has been approved by the gods.

Nor is it with any expression of "womanly tenderness and affection" or of "humanistic love" that she leaves the stage, but rather with a curse on her lips in the finest tradition of the true Greek hero: μὴ πλείω κακὰ πάθοιεν ἢ καὶ δρῶσιν ἐκδίκως ἐμέ (927–28). "Let them suffer no greater evils than they inflict unjustly on me." The Chorus remark only on her unbroken spirit (929–30) as she goes off crying out to her fellow Thebans that she dies "alone, the last of the royal line" (941) and that at the hands of such men as Creon

---

[32] Few critics are easy about these lines; e.g. Whitman 92. We have no choice but to accept them as genuine, however, on the grounds of the available evidence.

she is suffering an undeserved and horrible death in return for an act of piety. As the Chorus has said, the same storms of the soul still possess Antigone despite her feeling of abandonment by men and gods. Just as at the beginning she made it clear that she would not wait to see what misfortunes fate had in store for her as a doomed daughter of Oedipus, so now she will not wait for death to come to her. Rather than submit to a form of death she considers ignominious, she takes the initiative once more and commits suicide as a final and unmistakable assertion of her strength of will (αὐτόγνωτος ὀργά, 875) and independence (αὐτόνομος, 821).

Antigone's act of suicide is the only possible resolution of the plot that is consistent with the characterization Sophocles has conceived for her. Everything that happens to Antigone in the course of the play happens because she forces it to happen consciously, deliberately, and autonomously. She chose to assume an active rôle in life and to display the heroic character that she considered fitting for the worthy daughter of a noble sire, although perhaps one should say the worthy offspring of a noble sire for, unlike Ismene and Creon, Antigone attached no gender to nobility. Creon's decision not to have Antigone stoned to death, in fact, plays right into her hands and allows her to control her destiny to an even greater degree than she had at first anticipated. Stoning would have been a passive death inflicted on her by others, whereas entombment allows Antigone to die by her own hand, by an exercise of her own will, completely isolated and unsupported by fellow human beings or, as she believes, by the gods. She has enough courage in the end to finish the journey she began in search of honour for herself and for her family as an extension of herself, even though she is no longer so certain of the favourable reaction of the people of Thebes and of the gods as she had been at the beginning.

But if Antigone goes to her death totally isolated, abandoned by men and gods, without the sign of justification and recognition she craves, the audience are not left long in doubt about how she and her action should be judged. The sign she wanted comes quickly. First Teiresias announces that Creon is wrong to deny burial to Polyneices, he is wrong to bury Antigone alive; Creon is forced to yield. Even then, although he tries to correct his errors, he is overwhelmed with personal disaster in the deaths of his son and wife.

Yet the ending should not be considered Creon's disaster so much as Antigone's vindication. From start to finish the play is hers and it is her character that Sophocles presents for our consideration by comparing her concept of ἀρετή with that of Ismene, by contrasting her singleness of purpose with Creon's progressive degeneration, by revealing her ultimate self-sufficiency in the face of opposition and rejection. Creon has to derive his wisdom from his experiences and he has to learn his place in the scheme of things through an enforced revaluation of his own nature and its limitations. Antigone is wise from the beginning, for she understands her nature and its requirements, and she accepts her rôle in the destiny assigned her family by the gods. She knows that she is born to misfortune and disaster as a member of a doomed family; she might try to escape or postpone her fate, but, like a true hero, she decides to choose the moment and the manner of her doom and to show herself a worthy daughter of Oedipus not in name only but in character as well.

Vancouver, 7 July 1970

COMMENTS ON SOME PASSAGES
OF SOPHOCLES' *ELECTRA* (871–1057)

J. C. KAMERBEEK

I.

General observations on the second scene between Electra and Chrysothemis.

Chrysothemis had been sent to Agamemnon's grave and returns in a state of joyous excitement; she is certain that Orestes and vengeance are close at hand. The irony of the situation lies in the fact that she is perfectly right and Electra wrong; that she seems to move in a world of vain illusion while Electra is facing the—apparently—grim reality, and that she is soon convinced of her deplorable—as it then seems to her—error or delusion.

The scene may be divided into two parts, each to be subdivided into three sections:

a 1 Chrysothemis' arrival and introductory dialogue with Electra 871–91
  2 Her report of her visit to the grave 892–919
  3 The ensuing dialogue, in which Chrysothemis is disabused 920–37
b 1 Dialogue leading up to Electra's *rhêsis* by which she will try to persuade her sister to take part in the revenge 938–46
  2 Electra's exhortation and Chrysothemis' refusal 947–1016
  3 Altercation between the two, soon taking the form of stichomythia 1017–57.

The effects contrived by this scene may be summed up as follows. The spectator identifying himself, up to a point, with the protagonist cannot help taking pity on her distress and admiring her for her desperate resolve to take the revenge upon herself; this admiration will be mingled with a sense of fear and horror. The contrast between the two sisters stands out in full relief: the contrast between the heroine sticking to her absolute norm and going to any lengths in order to attain her aim, if need be at the cost of death, and the other girl whose sentiments are honourable enough but whose normal love for life and fear of death prevent her from taking part in Electra's design. The heroine, after the preceding utmost despair, is shown to have overcome even that; she remains unflinching when she sees that she will have to achieve her terrible purpose alone.

But at the same time the spectator will know that the real situation is quite the reverse of what Electra thinks, and so the tension in his mind will be the counterpart, as it were, of that experienced by the spectator of the *Oedipus Tyrannus*. One might distinguish between dramatic irony in the *Electra* and tragic irony in the *Oedipus* as the dominant factors in the respective plays by which the tension is caused in the spectator's mind, divided as it is between his knowledge of the truth and his (partial) identification with the protagonist. The really "tragic" element in this tragedy, however, consists in this, that Electra, unaware of the real situation, is represented as living up to her high norm at the cost of becoming a murderess, the murderess of her mother. This above all is conveyed to the spectator by the highly dramatic confrontation of the two sisters in this scene, and apart from being a piece of very effective drama, the scene is essential to a correct understanding of the meaning of the play as a whole and to the evaluation of Electra's fundamentally tragic character.

2.

888 θάλπῃ τῷδ' ἀνηκέστῳ πυρί: ἀνιάτῳ ἐλπίδι Σ.

Cf. *Ai.* 478 ὅστις κεναῖσιν ἐλπίσιν θερμαίνεται, but perhaps also *Ant.* 615 sqq. ἁ γὰρ δὴ πολύπλαγκτος ἐλ- / πὶς πολλοῖς μὲν ὄνασις ἀνδρῶν, / πολλοῖς δ' ἀπάτα κουφονόων ἐρώτων· / εἰδότι δ' οὐδὲν ἔρπει, πρὶν πυρὶ θερμῷ πόδα τις προσαύσῃ. The danger, inherent in ἐλπίς and symbolized by πῦρ, would seem to stand for ἐλπίς itself. But since πῦρ is also used for 'fever' it cannot be denied that the metaphor may be simply medical. For θάλπῃ we may compare *Trach.* 1082 ἔθαλψεν ἄτης σπασμός. In either case ἀνηκέστῳ may be taken to mean (strictly passive) "incurable" or "pernicious"; cf. *Ai.* 52 τῆς ἀνηκέστου χαρᾶς. It is not to be forgotten that Electra has said ἀλλ' ἦ μέμηνας (879), that ἐλπίς can be called μαινομένη (Hdt. VIII 77, oracle), and that πῦρ can be a subject of μαίνεσθαι (Hom. *Il.* XV 606).

3.

898　ἐγχρίμπτῃ vel ἐνχρίμπτει.

Between ἐγχρίμπτῃ (ἐνχρίπτῃ L) and ἐγχρίμπτει (ἐγχρίπτει G) the choice is difficult. The indicative would express a fear "that something is now going on" (Goodwin, *Gk. Moods & Tenses* § 369, cf. *Ant.* 1254); I do not see why (cf. Jebb) "in fear lest someone be close by" would suit better than "(to see) whether someone is not close by." In defence of the indicative one may even argue that by looking around Chrysothemis can only ascertain whether or not somebody is in the neighbourhood, not whether anybody *will* turn up. If one prefers the subjunctive, one has to concede that one does so for the sole (and in this case weak) reason that our best manuscript has it. Pearson's preference of ἐγχρίμπτει is quite understandable.

4.

941　οὐκ ἔσθ᾽ ὅ γ᾽ εἶπον.

Since γ᾽ is not only in A and L^{sl} but also in R, the case for its authenticity is fairly strong. If this is the correct reading, γ᾽ belongs to εἶπον rather than to ὅ: the propensity of enclitics for creeping up to near the beginning of a clause or sentence is a well-known fact, established by Wackernagel. So the comparative rareness of γε with relatives (see Denniston, *Gk. Particles*[2] p. 123 [5]) cannot be used as an argument against the reading. The meaning is not intrinsically inferior to that yielded by ἐς τόδ(ε), found by Campbell in Ambros. G. 56 sup. = Turyn's W, conjectured by Haupt and adopted by many editors ("with this purpose in mind", *LSJ* s.v. εἰς V 2). If ἐς τόδ(ε) represents the correct reading, L's reading ἔσθ᾽ ὅδ᾽(ε) possibly derives from ἐστι ὅδε < ἐς τόδε. If ἔσθ᾽ ὅ γ᾽ is correct, ἔσθ᾽ ὅδ᾽ is a simple mistake and ἐς τόδε a conjecture. The second possibility seems easier to account for.

5.

957　Αἴγισθον· οὐδὲν γάρ σε δεῖ κρύπτειν μ᾽ ἔτι.

Αἴγισθον: its position and the occurrence of the name itself (she could have done without naming the hateful tyrant) lend to her words a sinister force. It is a matter of speculation and of dramatic interpretation whether we should regard Αἴγισθον as Electra's reaction to Chrysothemis' shrinking back at μὴ κατοκνήσεις κτανεῖν.

Οὐδὲν γὰρ...ἔτι refers to Electra's resolve, implied in the preceding words, to take the matter of revenge into her own hands, not of course to the naming of Aegisthus (though a certain amount of ambiguity is involved). In point of fact she does keep secret from her sister the other half of her purpose, viz. to kill Clytaemestra as well. That such are her intentions (according to the poet) is rendered probable by the ambiguous τοῖσιν ἐχθροῖς (979) and still more by the words of the Chorus διδύμαν ἑλοῦσ' Ἐρινύν (1080). And generally speaking, the killing of the one involves the killing of the other and Electra would act out of character if indeed she planned the death of Aegisthus while sparing Clytaemestra. She is using guile in order to induce Chrysothemis to help her.

The wording of 957 takes its full meaning if we bear in mind that had she avowed her full intentions καὶ μητέρ' would take the place of Αἴγισθον; as it is, Αἴγισθον, though sinister in itself, comes, in combination with the rest of the line, as a deceptive reassurance, as a means not to deter Chrysothemis from the attempt. How could Jebb aver: "Sophocles avoids everything that could qualify our sympathy with Electra; while it suits the different aims of Euripides to make her plan the matricide"? If that were true, he would not have had her cry: παῖσον, εἰ σθένεις, διπλῆν at the moment of the murder. On this important issue I agree entirely with H. Friis Johansen, "Die Elektra des Sophocles," Class. et Med. 25 (1964), 21–22, whose concluding words on this problem are quite convincing: "So hat uns der Dichter auf Elektras Rolle während der Ermordung ihrer Mutter vorbereitet."

6.

968–69 ἐκ πατρὸς κάτω / θανόντος.

Κάτω goes with πατρός, cf. Ant. 197, where κάτω seems to belong to νεκροῖς rather than to ἔρχεται. This is better than to connect κάτω with θανόντος; but θανόντος is not the same as τεθνεῶτος. The words do not mean: "from our dead father in Hades" but "from our father in Hades, ⟨our father⟩ who died (= was murdered)." Only thus are the tense as well as the position of θανόντος accounted for.

7.

979–80   ὦ τοῖσιν ἐχθροῖς...προυστήτην φόνου.

"Who dealt with their enemies as champions of the murder." In my opinion φόνου refers to Agamemnon's unavenged blood (cf. 955) *on behalf of which* they would enter the lists against the enemies. Thus προίστασθαί τινί τινος amounts to τιμωρεῖσθαί τινά τινος. It is improbable that προστῆναι here has its proper meaning 'to place oneself at the head of' (Jebb and others) for they are not to be supposed to have followers.

8.

986–88   ἀλλ', ὦ φίλη, πείσθητι, συμπόνει πατρί,
          σύγκαμν' ἀδελφῷ, παῦσον ἐκ κακῶν ἐμέ,
          παῦσον δὲ σαυτήν,...

The two pairs of anaphora lend urgency to her exhortation. Συμ- and συγ- i.e. "with me"; πατρί and ἀδελφῷ are *dativi commodi*. Thus *i.a.* Kaibel and Bruhn; the alternative interpretation, viz. "work with thy sire, share the burden of thy brother" (Jebb and others), is less likely in my opinion. The starting-point of her *rhêsis* is revenge for Agamemnon (951–52) and her appeal to Chrysothemis to help her, Electra (ξὺν τῇδ' ἀδελφῇ 956), in taking this revenge. Συμπονεῖν and συγκάμνειν are to be regarded as synonyms. For συμπονεῖν in a comparable context cf. *Ant.* 41 εἰ ξυμπονήσεις καὶ ξυνεργάσῃ σκόπει (∼ 43 εἰ τὸν νεκρὸν ξὺν τῇδε κουφιεῖς χερί). Cf. also *Ai.* 1378 καὶ τὸν θανόντα τόνδε συνθάπτειν θέλω, / καὶ ξυμπονεῖν καὶ μηδὲν ἐλλείπειν ὅσων / χρὴ τοῖς ἀρίστοις ἀνδράσιν πονεῖν βροτούς. For συγκάμνειν cf. *Ai.* 988.

9.

1005–6   λύει γὰρ ἡμᾶς οὐδὲν οὐδ' ἐπωφελεῖ
          βάξιν καλὴν λαβόντε δυσκλεῶς θανεῖν.

Λύειν = λυσιτελεῖν commonly takes the dative, cf. (e.g.) Eur. *Med.* 566 (no instances in Soph.; as to τέλη λύει *O.T.* 317, cf. my note *ad loc.*; μόχθων τῶν ἐφεστώτων ἐμοὶ λύσιν τελεῖσθαι [*Trach.* 1171] is quite another matter). So it is understandable that the scholia *a.h.l.* already hesitate between two interpretations: οὐ λυσιτελεῖ γὰρ ἡμῖν, φησίν, οὐκ ἀπαλλάσσει τῶν κακῶν. ἀντὶ οὐδὲν ἡμᾶς ἐκλύσεται (hence λύσει Erfurdt), and that modern interpreters are divided accordingly (some of them accept Elmsley's ἡμῖν). The border-line between the notions 'release one ⟨from trouble⟩' and "avail," "profit" is elusive; if it is true that λύειν has come to mean "avail," "profit," tantamount to ὠφελεῖν, it is also true that ὠφελεῖν normally takes the accusative, although the dative is possible. Comparable to our line is Eur. *Sthen.* prol. 35 sqq. (H. v. Arnim, *Suppl. Eur.* p. 45) οὐ γάρ με λύει τοῖσδ' ἐφήμενον δόμοις / κακορροθεῖσθαι μὴ θέλοντ' εἶναι κακόν, / οὐδ' αὖ κατειπεῖν καὶ γυναικὶ προσβαλεῖν / κηλῖδα Προίτου καὶ διασπάσαι δόμον. I do not believe that, as at Xen. *An.* III 4, 36 λύειν and at Hipp. *Fract.* I 2 λυσιτελεῖν (*LSJ* s.v., I 2), λύει here is construed with an acc. c. inf. *sensu stricto* as its subject as we read in *LSJ* s.v. λύω, V 2 "*it is* not *expedient that* we should die (οὐδ' ἐπωφελεῖ being parenthetic)"; 1007–1008 are against this interpretation. Possibly the normal construction of (ἐπ)ωφελεῖν has facilitated the accusative with λύει. I do not see the necessity of taking οὐδ' ἐπωφελεῖ as a parenthesis nor of attributing to λύειν the precise and exclusive meaning of "setting free," although this original meaning is also perceptible.

10.

1026 XP. εἰκὸς γὰρ ἐγχειροῦντα καὶ πράσσειν κακῶς.

The statement being general (ἐγχειροῦντα), Jebb's interpretation, viz. "(I will not act with thee), for it is likely that one who makes the attempt should e'en (καὶ) fare ill" (similarly Campbell), is unlikely. It is better to supply (from πράσσειν κακῶς) κακά, κακοῖς or even κακῶς to ἐγχειροῦντα and to take καὶ as meaning "also," cf. frg. 962 P. εἰ δεῖν' ἔδρασας, δεινὰ καὶ παθεῖν σε δεῖ. I cannot agree with Jebb's remark "had the poet meant this, he might rather have written πάσχειν κακά." If κακῶς is to be supplied to ἐγχειροῦντα, it would no more imply an ethical evaluation than it has with πράσσειν; it would amount to "*perperam*" as in Aesch. *Pers.* 454 κακῶς τὸ μέλλον ἱστορῶν or to κακῶς βουλευόμενον (cf. *Trach.* 589). Thus Mazon: "Toute entreprise mal conçue risque de se terminer mal." In Chrysothemis' eyes the venture is 'bad' because it is bound to meet with failure. Pindar's γνώμη *Nem.* 4, 31 ἐπεὶ ῥέζοντά τι καὶ παθεῖν ἔοικεν (quoted by the scholiast) involves a rule of wider application than Chrysothemis' words; so does Soph. frg. 229 P. τὸν δρῶντα γάρ τι καὶ παθεῖν ὀφείλεται.

Of course if we refrain from supplying κακῶς or the like to ἐγχειροῦντα and reject all the same Jebb's interpretation on the ground of the general character of the sentence (note that he translates: *the* attempt, not *an* attempt), Chrysothemis is presented as rejecting any endeavour whatsoever because it might turn out badly: this is not impossible but would seem less relevant in the context.

II.

1028   ἀνέξομαι κλύουσα χὤταν εὖ λέγῃς.

What she means is, broadly speaking, made clear by 1056–57: ὅταν γὰρ ἐν κακοῖς | ἤδη βεβήκῃς, τἄμ' ἐπαινέσεις ἔπη. But the implications of ἀνέξομαι are not clear. The words presuppose something like: ⟨ὡς νῦν ὅτε κακῶς με λέγεις κλύουσα ἀνέχομαι, οὕτως. . . .⟩ I do not believe that Bruhn is right in assuming that ἀνέξομαι implies the sorrow with which she will at some time listen to Electra's admission of her error, nor can I entirely understand Jebb's remark, viz. "The point of ἀνέξομαι is that it will be a trial of patience—not less than that of being reproached with δειλία—to hear Electra's acknowledgments and regrets when her rash attempt has failed." I should rather think that Campbell's interpretation is the correct one: "I will listen with the same equanimity when you shall praise me," i.e. "As I am indifferent to your censure, so I will be to your commendation, when you have learned the truth." As Kaibel says, there is no noble-mindedness in these words; on the contrary they are the scornful utterance of one who congratulates herself that events will put her in the right, and Mazon's translation (his insertion of ⟨μ'⟩ before εὖ is not strictly necessary) is strikingly correct: "J'accepterai sans plus d'émoi tes compliments un autre jour."

12.

1042   ἀλλ' ἔστιν ἔνθα χἠ δίκη βλάβην φέρει.

Indubitably Chrysothemis is referring to the risks involved in Electra's stubborn stand with Δίκη. But in my view a tragic irony is intended. For Electra's stand with Δίκη, involving as it does the murder of Clytaemestra, will bring her βλάβη at a deeper, more tragic level than Chrysothemis means to convey.

Santpoort, 6 August 1970

SUL RAPPORTO FRA I CODICI L e P NEL TESTO DEGLI *ERACLIDI* DI EURIPIDE

ANTONIO GARZYA

La questione se il Laur. gr. XXXII 2 (=L), *ca.* 1315, e il Vat. Pal. gr. 287 (+ Laur. Conv. soppr. 172 che ne comprende una parte, per un'arbitraria suddivisione in due del manoscritto originario intervenuta prima del 1420), *ca.* 1320–25 (=P),[1] sieno da considerar *gemelli*, o figlio il secondo del primo, e se per tutto il testo di Euripide o per solo parte dello stesso, è stata a lungo dibattuta a partir da quasi ormai un secolo. Non sarà qui necessario rifarne la storia, giacché anche a tale còmpito s'è egregiamente sobbarcato il dottissimo euripideista al quale il presente studio è dedicato.[2] Ci limiteremo a ricordare i resultati ai quali egli è pervenuto e quelli dei dotti che si sono occupati dopo di lui del problema.

Occorrerà premettere che L reca numerosi additamenti, rifacimenti, emendamenti, rasure e, in piú, una certa quantità di annotazioni metriche, per lo piú marginali, nonché rarissime note di carattere scoliastico. Codesto materiale non è della stessa mano che ha copiato il testo se non in un numero assai limitato di casi; di norma risale a altra mano. A sua volta, codesta mano non ha aspetto unitario e costante, ma si differenzia, piú o meno nettamente, dall'un luogo all'altro. *Prima facie* si è portati a credere alla presenza di piú mani correttrici; l'osservazione piú attenta può mostrare che trattasi della stessa mano in fasi diverse. Nel passato sono state impiegate al riguardo due differenti sigle: L² o Lᶜ a indicare un primo stadio

---

[1] Per le date cfr. Turyn (= A. Turyn, *The Byzantine Manuscript Tradition of the Tragedies of Euripides*, Urbana 1957 [Illinois Studies in Language and Literature, Vol. 43]), pp. 224 s., 269; Turyn, *Codices* (= A. Turyn, *Codices Graeci Vaticani saeculis XIII et XIV scripti annorumque notis instructi*, Città del Vaticano 1964), pp. 127 s., congiuntamente con Tuilier (= A. Tuilier, *Recherches critiques sur la tradition du texte d'Euripide*, Parigi 1968 [Études et Commentaires, 68]), pp. 188 e n. 1, 192 e n.3.

[2] Cfr. Turyn, pp. 264–69.

dell'operosità correttrice, *l* a indicare uno stadio piú recente, ritenuto posteriore di circa un secolo alla copia del testo.[3] Quanto a P, a parte il fatto, che in questo momento non interessa, che anche questo codice reca un certo numero di correzioni posteriori alla copia, la sua posizione nei confronti delle correzioni di L non è unitaria: alcune di esse ricorrono nel suo testo altre no. In genere gli editori hanno adoprato la sigla *l* appunto per quelle che n o n vi ricorrono. È chiaro che nella discussione sui rapporti fra L e P la varia presenza, o influenza, di codeste correzioni abbia avuto e abbia un posto preminente.

Il Turyn, dopo le lunghe e spesso cavillose discussioni pro (Wilamowitz [nell' *Einleitung* del 1889, non negli *Analecta Euripidea* del 1875], Radermacher, Murray, ecc.) e contro (Wecklein, Vitelli, editori delle "Belles Lettres", ecc.) l'indipendenza di P da L, riprese il problema su nuova base, ossia su base storica, giacché il suo punto di partenza fu l'identificazione di *l* con Demetrio Triclinio ($=L^t$) e la conseguente retrodatazione non solo della mano già indicata con *l* ma anche, sulla base, ovviamente, di argomenti congiunti, di P, spostato dal sec. XIV[ex] ad "as early as c.1340 A.D."[4] La serrata argomentazione del dotto non si può qui riassumere nel particolare. Sarà sufficiente richiamarne le conclusioni con le stesse lucide parole dell'autore (p. 278 s.): "The conclusion from the facts quoted above is inescapable. If P agrees closely with L in countless common errors; if L and P have singly and individually several faults of their own; if P did not know the interpolations of Triclinius symbolized before by *l* and now by us as L^t; if P has some elements which were omitted by L^1 though they were often supplemented by L^t; if P has some elements which were omitted by L and even were not supplemented by L^t; if P has some readings that are correct while the corresponding readings of L are corrupt; if those correct elements in P corresponding to corrupt or missing elements of L look authentic and cannot be presumed to be invented by P; if then L and P agree closely but have singly their own faults not

---

[3] Cfr., p.es., gli apparati del Murray o degli editori dell'*Euripide* delle "Belles Lettres".

[4] Turyn, p. 269; per tutta la questione delle relazioni L/P cfr. pp. 264–88; v. anche 288 ss. (a proposito di Q = Lond. Harl. 5743, *ca.* 1475, un negletto testimone della famiglia di LP); 298 ss. (a proposito della triade bizantina *Ecuba Oreste Fenicie* in LP).

repeated in the other manuscript, *then L and P must be presumed to stem from one common source*, and the fallacy of the Vitelli-Wecklein theory should be committed to complete oblivion."

Le conclusioni del Turyn riguardavano sia i drammi della così detta 'serie alfabetica', non commentata (*Elena, Elettra, Eraclidi, Eracle, Supplici, Ifigenia in Aulide, Ifigenia in Tauride, Ione, Ciclope*), sia quelli della 'selezione' commentata, ivi compresa la triade bizantina (*Ecuba, Oreste, Fenicie; Ippolito, Medea, Alcesti, Andromaca, Reso*). Rimanevano escluse le *Baccanti* e le *Troadi* che sono tràdite, la prima in parte la seconda completamente, nel solo P. Fra i due gruppi vi è una certa differenza quanto al grado di correttezza della copia di L rispetto a P e, in particolare, le divergenze fra L e P sono sensibili nella triade. Ma anche di codesti fatti il Turyn diè convincente spiegazione, che peraltro non è qui il caso di ripetere.[5] La postulazione di un unico antigrafo comune veniva anzi rinforzata dall'argomentazione riguardante le interpolazioni nella triade. La presenza di Eustazio di Tessalonica nelle vicende della prima formazione della famiglia LP(Q), già intuita per altre vie e in altro senso da precedenti dotti,[6] veniva ora a esser felicemente riproposta su rinnovate basi storiche: "... we can consider as demonstrated the existence of the common source of LP early in the fourteenth century in Thessalonica,[7] for most probably there it was copied by the two scribes of L, one of whom was Nicolaus Triclinius [*sc.* per il blocco *Reso, Ione, Ifigenia in Tauride, Ifigenia in Aulide*], and subsequently inspected by Demetrius Triclinius during his revision of L" (p. 304); "... at least a part of the immediate source of LP must have survived somewhere until *ca.* 1475 A.D. when a part of Q was transcribed from it" (p. 305).

Queste, succintamente, le conclusioni del Turyn su L e P e sul loro rapporto di gemellaggio. Esse gittavano luce singolare congiuntamente sulla *Textüberlieferung* e sulla *Textgeschichte* e trovaron súbito

---

[5] Cfr. pp. 287 s., 301.

[6] Cfr. G. Zuntz, *The Political Plays of Euripides* (Manchester 1963²), pp. 147 ss.; v. già H. W. Miller, "Euripides and Eustathius," in *Am. Journ. Phil.* 61 (1940), pp. 422–28.

[7] Eustazio passò da C.poli a Tessalonica nel 1175 (cfr. H.-G. Beck, *Kirche und theologische Literatur im byzantinischen Reich*, Monaco/B 1959 [Byzantinisches Handbuch II T. 1. Bd.], p. 635) e dové allora portar seco il manoscritto euripideo che sarà stato alla base della famiglia LP(Q).

larghi[8] anche se, com'è ovvio, non del tutto unanimi[9] consensi.

La questione fu poi ripresa *ex novo* con dovizia di documentazione e con agguerrita dialettica, a distanza di otto anni dalla pubblicazione del libro del Turyn, da G. Zuntz.[10] Le sue conclusioni si posson cosí sintetizzare: P è copia diretta di L nel *Reso* e nei nove drammi della 'serie alfabetica'; è indipendente da L negli altri sette (oltre al *Reso*) drammi della scelta commentata e, naturalmente, nelle *Troadi* e nelle *Baccanti*. Riprendendo alcune ipotesi dei citati Lloyd-Jones e Mason,[11] lo Zuntz sostiene che nei dieci (9 + *Reso*) drammi P copiò L dopo la prima delle tre fasi di correzioni che egli crede di distinguere in quest'ultimo e che tutte attribuisce a Demetrio Triclinio. La distinzione di codeste tre fasi, o almeno della prima contro le altre due, è quindi, nella ricostruzione del dotto, criterio di giudizio non esclusivo[12] ma, indubbiamente, fondamentale. Occorreva che la distinzione fosse netta e inequivoca e in tal senso lo Zuntz si adopra con ammirevole industria. Se sempre in modo convincente, si vedrà innanzi.

È da dir súbito che gl'interventi di mano diversa in L sono dei

[8] Cfr., fra altri, le recensioni di H. Hunger, in *Byz. Zeitschr.* 51 (1958), pp. 382–88; J. Irigoin, in *Rev. phil.* 22 (1958), pp. 320–23; J. C. Kamerbeek, in *Mnemosyne* s. 4 v. 12 (1959), pp. 353–56; A. Pertusi, in *Dioniso* 20 (1957), pp. 106–18.

[9] Riserve espressero in particolare H. Lloyd-Jones, in *Gnomon* 30 (1958), pp. 505–10 e P. G. Mason, in *Journ. Hell. Stud.* 82 (1962), pp. 162–64. Fra altro, nel mentre si accettava la teoria del Turyn a proposito della identificazione di *l*, si rilevava che Triclinio (=L^t), conforme a un suo costume, ben attestato, p.es., nel Rom. Angel. gr. 14 (=T), avrebbe potuto eseguire a piú riprese distanziate nel tempo la sua opera di διορθωτής su L e che ciò potrebbe spiegare la disuguale presenza di L^t in P confermando l'ipotesi della discendenza diretta del secondo dal primo senza doverli fare risalire entrambi a un capostipite comune.

[10] Cfr. G. Zuntz, *An Inquiry into the Transmission of the Plays of Euripides*, (Cambridge 1965 [nel séguito = Zuntz]), capp. I-II (soprattutto pp. 13 ss., 38 ss.) e *passim*.

[11] Ma, *mutatis mutandis*, cfr. già H. Grégoire–L. Parmentier, *Euripide*, III (Parigi 1924) pp. I-III.

[12] Il ricorso ad argomenti anche di ordine interpretativo e storico-critico è frequente nel discorso dello Zuntz, ma nessuno di essi, date le premesse, può sovrastare l'argomento primo, ch'è paleografico. Interviene a un momento a sostegno della teoria del dotto anche un elemento del tutto esterno e fortuito (cfr. pp. 13–15): una pagliuzza, presso che invisibile, depostasi per secoli in L f. 106^v prima della parola στερεῖς del v. 95 dell'*Elena* e distaccatasi in presenza del dotto stesso nel giugno 1960, la quale, poiché in corrispondenza P reca un erroneo segno d'interpunzione, gli sembra una prova inoppugnabile che P abbia copiato L. Ma, a parte il fatto che nessuno dei tre apografi noti di L riproduce il segno, il valore decisamente probativo dell'episodio è stato opportunamente messo in dubbio da J. Irigoin, in *Journ. Hell. Stud.* 87 (1967), p. 144; cfr. anche Tuilier, p. 200, 4.

piú varî: si va dalla scrittura di intiere *hypotheseis* nello spazio lasciato vuoto dallo scriba originario alla rasura di una lettera o di parte di lettera; dal rifacimento di una desinenza all'apposizione di un'annotazione metrica piú o meno estesa; dall'aggiunta di un -*v* efelcistico a quella di tutta una parola, o in rasura o sopra la linea; ecc. (Già in partenza occorrerebbe pertanto rendersi conto del fatto che a una distinzione troppo sottile dell'origine e dello scaglionamento cronologico di t u t t e le operazioni diortotiche in L non si potrà giunger mai.) Il *ductus* di Triclinio, è noto, assunse tratti diversi nel tempo,[13] ma ciò non pertanto gli si possono attribuire tutti *grosso modo* gl'interventi in L che non sieno dello scriba. Ma resta il problema di distinguerne i varî momenti. Unico elemento discriminante al riguardo, a parte i casi, disperati, di rasura, poteva essere il colore degl'inchiostri usati, o meglio l'aspetto cromatico da essi assunto nello stato attuale.[14] Già da tempo si era notato, per esempio, che alcuni additamenti in L eran decisamente neri, altri di tinta meno marcata. Ma lo Zuntz è andato molto piú avanti. Egli ha cercato con ogni mezzo[15] di giungere a una classificazione rigorosa delle variazioni nella coloritura della mano di Triclinio fin nelle sue sfumature piú sfuggenti. Una volta fissato un certo numero di stadî cromatici (tre principali, ma spesso con suddivisioni interne), ha cercato di individuare, per saggi ovviamente, le lezioni risalienti all'uno o all'altro di essi e quindi ha tratto la conseguenza che, essendo presenti in P solo quelle del primo stadio, la copia di questo su L sia stata eseguita prima degli altri due. Buona parte del suo libro è occupata dalla paziente analisi mirante alla costruzione del grande mosaico. Alla fine si esclama con sollievo: *tout se tient!* Ma il pericolo che una sola tessella sia fuori posto e che tutto crolli rimane.

Occorre dare atto allo Zuntz di essersi reso conto súbito della

[13] Cfr. Tuilier, p. 190, 7, il quale giunge anche a supporre che fin parti del testo di L possano esser di Triclinio giovane; sulla mano tricliniana in generale v. Turyn, p. 23, 32; R. Aubreton, *Démétrius Triclinius et les récensions médiévales de Sophocle*, (Parigi 1949); W. J. W. Koster, *Autour d'un manuscrit d'Aristophane écrit par Démétrius Triclinius. Études paléographiques et critiques sur les éditions d'Aristophane de l'époque byzantine tardive* (Groninga 1957).

[14] Non si dimentichi che L, contrariamente al membranaceo P, è in carta occidentale, elemento di sensibile influenza sull'assorbimento e il fissaggio dell'inchiostro.

[15] Si legga, p.es., il capitolo "A Note on Inks," pp. 57–62, nel quale riferisce anche di esperimenti di laboratorio condotti nel Dipartimento di Chimica della sua Università per spiegare alcuni fenomeni di evoluzione cromatica visibili in L.

perigliosità della sua intrapresa. E sono certamente istruttive le sue perplessità, anche se poi cangiate in certezza. Citiamo a caso: "...here indeed the distinction between ink colours becomes increasingly precarious, as a dark shade of 'brown' may, in places, become indistinguishable from a lighter kind of 'black'..." (p. 22); "here again P agrees with L* and this fact must here serve to show that this alteration is due to a later effort—for the colour of the ink which Triclinius used is here so dark that it could with *equal right* [il corsivo è nostro] be described as 'dark brown' or 'light black'..." (p. 24); "...the 'black' alterations in L, and these only, would be part of the original text in P. This in fact proves to be generally true, though in examination of details many puzzles arise..." (p. 38); "...it has been seen...how far from rigid the definition of these colours is..." (p. 57). Ben conscio dei pericoli cui si espone, lo Zuntz, che è studioso di statura tale che non gli si può certo muovere accusa di sprovvedutezza metodica, cerca di prevenirli: "We have been led to assert...that basically *black* ink may appear, in places, *dark brown*; while characteristically *brown* ink would appear *dark brown* in many places (and even *near-black* in some) and show, at the same time, very often a *red* hue. Finally that shade that we described as essentially *grey* or *pale* tends to appear, in places, more *brownish* but may show in others a *greenish* shade [i corsivi sono nostri]. Can so ambiguous a criterion be trusted to afford reliable indications?—There are no doubt passages where it would be wrong, and indeed impossible, to base inferences upon this criterion alone; in fact, it has always to be used (as we have done) in combination with other pointers. Thus used, it proves sometimes vague but often highly significant..." (p. 57). Il dotto, in altri termini, riconosce che il criterio dei colori è in sé ambiguo epperò irrilevante: può—a suo dire—non esserlo, se accoppiato ad altri elementi di giudizio. Di codesti elementi egli fa tenace ricerca in tutta la trattazione e qua e là ne esibisce, in particolare a proposito delle annotazioni e degl'interventi tricliniani nelle parti liriche. Ma, è qui il punto a nostro avviso fondamentale, trattasi sempre di elementi a c c e s s o r î, che intervengono solo d o p o che la valutazione del colore della lezione in questione è stata fatta. E se la valutazione è giusta, possono avere il peso che hanno tutti gli argomenti di rincalzo; se è falsa, non hanno nessun peso. In breve, un esempio: a meglio confermare il rapporto L $\rangle$ P può valere ogni argomento che si aggiunga alla constatazione, secondo Zuntz, basilare che sia presente nel secondo una correzione decisamente nera del primo; ma ciò a condizione che su quel 'nero' non vi sia ombra di dubbio: ché se dubbio ci sia, tutto l'edifizio crolla; e lo stesso accade, viceversa, quando si tratti di un 'bruno', piú o meno definito, che ritorna in P mentre non dovrebbe. (Il che, come si vedrà, accade.)

Le riserve presenti sono già state sollevate dal Tuilier il quale, sulle orme dell'Irigoin, è ritornato alla teoria del gemellaggio LP e la cui argomentazione non occorre qui ripetere, ma presupporre.[16] Nostro scopo non è di riprendere *in toto* la questione, ma di tenerci all'oggetto indicato dal titolo.[17] È ovvio che occorreva muovere da un inquadramento preliminare dell'insieme e che, d'altra parte, le osservazioni che seguiranno a proposito del dramma che qui c'interessa potranno di per sé comportare applicazioni piú vaste; ma nessuna deduzione *ex silentio* è nelle nostre intenzioni, convinti come siamo che la questione dei rapporti fra L e P vada affrontata caso per caso, solo dall'analisi dei singoli problemi potendosi giungere a qualche certezza.[18]

* * *

Cominciamo dalla disamina della questione paleografico-cromatica.[19]

[16] Cfr. Tuilier, pp. 196–209; J. Irigoin, in *Rev. phil.* e *Journ. Hell. Stud.* citt.

[17] L'avvio all'indagine ci è venuto dal fatto che abbiamo in preparazione l'edizione di alcuni drammi euripidei, fra cui gli *Eraclidi*, per la Bibliotheca Teubneriana. Cfr. anche *Boll. Comit. Ed. naz. class. gr. e lat.* 16 (1968), pp. 77–81.

[18] La necessità che la dimostrazione dello stato dei rapporti fra L e P vada eseguita dramma per dramma fu già affermata da G. Vitelli, *ap.* H. van Herwerden, *Euripidis Helena* (Leida 1895), p. VII; cfr. anche A. Mancini, in *Riv. fil. cl.* 2 (1896), pp. 401 s., 485 s., *Riv. st. ant. e sc. affini* 4 (1899), p. 15; A. Olivieri, in *Riv. fil. cl.* 2 (1896), p. 484; al.

[19] Come si doveva, abbiamo proceduto a ricollazionare per intero, su riproduzioni e sugli originali, i due codici. All'occasione si rivelano utili i dati offerti dai tre apografi diretti di L, che anche abbiamo ricollazionati: il Laur. gr. XXXI 1, *ca.* 1470, copiato per Francesco Filelfo (cfr. A. Pertusi, in *Italia Med. e Umanistica*, 3 [1960], p. 114) dal θύτης "Αγγελος (= Fl); il Par. gr. 2887, s. XV^ex o XVI^1 (cfr. Turyn, p. 370), di mano di Aristobulo Apostolidis (= E); il Par. gr. 2817, *ante* 1504 (cfr. R. Kannicht, *Euripides. Helena*, I [Heidelberg 1969], p. 110), appartenuto al Ridolfi (= Mr). Per L e P esistono le mirabili, e tuttavia per la questione delle varie fasi della mano di Triclinio nel primo relativamente utili, riproduzioni fototipiche *in folio* curate da J. A. Spranger: *Euripidis quae inveniuntur in codice Laurentiano Pl. XXXII 2* (Firenze 1920), e *Euripidis quae in codicibus Palatino gr. inter Vaticanos 282 et Laurentiano Conv. soppr. 172 (olim Abbatiae Florentinae 2664) inveniuntur phototypice expressa*, I-II (Firenze 1939–46).

Lo Zuntz (pp. 83–87) riconosce negli *Eraclidi* tre fasi successive dell'operosità di Demetrio Triclinio, che designa rispettivamente con Tr¹ Tr² Tr³ (laddove con L* indica la lezione primaria del codice).

Tr¹ è riconosciuto come decisamente nero ('markedly black'), ma non sempre: a volte sfumerebbe in un bruno molto scuro ('shading ...into a very dark brown'); Tr² come grigio ('grey'); Tr³ come bruno scuro ('dark brown'), talvolta con sfumatura rosso vivo ('red glow'). Se a riguardo di Tr² le cose sembran disposte in modo univoco, lo stesso non può certo dirsi per Tr¹ e Tr³. Lo stesso Zuntz indirettamente riconosce che fra i due bruni la distinzione è quanto mai sottile (il secondo soltanto 'hardly ever as dark as Tr¹ at its lightest'), se non impossibile. Ma alla tesi della dipendenza di P da L è indispensabile che in P ritorni solo Tr¹ e mai Tr² o Tr³: si può in teoria evitare il pericolo che in ognuno dei tanti 'dark brown' si finisca col riconoscere o Tr¹ o Tr³ solo a seconda che il fatto s'accordi o no con la tesi? Temiamo proprio di no. E la tesi essa stessa sembra così compromessa in partenza.[20]

Ma veniamo ai fatti particolari.

—Gl'interventi di Triclinio in L, di qualsiasi specie, con inchiostro conservatosi propriamente nero sono nel complesso una minoranza. Per la loro individuazione c'è più di un punto di riferimento inequivoco: la sottoscrizione τέλος τοῦ κύκλωπος (f. 89) al dramma che precede, l'*hypothesis* e l'*inscriptio* degli *Eraclidi*, il numero d'ordine *ΙΓ´* in margine, le *dramatis personae*, l'indicazione del primo interlocutore, ἰόλ(αος), la sottoscrizione εὐριπίδου ἡρακλεῖδαι f. 96ᵛ. Noi impiegheremo per tutti gli additamenti in nero la sigla L¹, L sarà la mano dello scriba.[21]

---

[20] L'apriorismo paleografico fu, in altro senso, uno dei punti deboli anche della teoria Wecklein–Vitelli, come a più riprese ebbe a rilevare il Turyn, pp. 264 ss. (*praesert.* 268, 272, 271, 274: "Of course, Wecklein had the tendency to attribute vaguely some of the above corrections in L not to *l* [Lᵗ = Triclinius], but to a different corrector. He used the term 'postmodum additum in L' on additions in *El.* 132, *Ion* 345, *Ion* 813, *Ion* 847, for obviously he was anxious not to upset his derivation theory by attributing these corrections [as he should have done] to his corrector *l* (= our Lᵗ) whom he considered later than P ...").

[21] L'inchiostro relativo si presenta color bruno piuttosto pallido. Alcuni minuti ritocchi o additamenti sopra linea o in margine risalgono allo scriba L, o per ripensamento *inter scribendum* o perché identico egli ha riprodotto l'aspetto della sua fonte. Cfr. rispettiva-

L¹ corrisponde a Tr¹ di Zuntz; le sue innovazioni (quelle or ora citate e molte altre) sono spesso comuni a P, ma non lo sono con la generale regolarità che si richiederebbe, e che il dotto ammette, per provare che P derivi da L dopo la prima revisione tricliniana. Ecco gli esempî: 90 τοῦ L¹: ποῦ LP²²; 673 τὰ ante σφάγια add. L¹ om. LP (exh. FlEMr); 713 μελήσει L¹: μελήση LP; 855 λυγαίῳ νέφει L¹: λυγαίῳ ἔφη P (P¹, mano posteriore, reca λυγαίῳ νέφει, ma la cosa qui non ha interesse: di norma in quest'articolo non faremo mai riferimento a P¹) λυγαίῳ νέφει L²³; 858 ἡβητὸν L¹: ἥβη τὴν LP.²⁴ Per cautela, forse eccessiva, non richiamiamo qui casi pei quali sulla correzione, o sul suo colore nero, vi possa essere qualche, pur minima, incertezza, come,

---

mente, p.es., 187 μὕκηναίους (sic) da μὕκηναίους e 285 ἐνθένδ̇' ⁶ᵉ 789 ἐλευθερῶσαι ᶜᶻ ⁻ᶯ e 859 αἴρεῖ (γρ. i.m.) per αἴρει L. Questi ultimi tre casi sono degni di attenzione. La lezione di 285 (ove a torto l'apparato del Murray parla di L² per la parte sopra la linea) è stata rettamente intesa (ἐνθένδε δ') da FlEMr ma non appare in P, che reca ἐνθένδ̇': evidentemente la fonte di L e P (che chiamiamo λ) esibiva un δε assai piccolo o al margine o sopra la linea, sí che a prima vista esso poteva anche non esser notato, come appunto accadde allo scriba di P e, ma solo per un momento, ché poi si riprese, a quello di L. Anche in 789 erra il Murray nell'attribuire la parte s.l. a L², gli apografi riproducono il corretto ἠλευθερῶσθαι (FlE) o la *lectio duplex* (Mr), P ha ἐλευθερῶσαι: L ha riprodotto λ piú accuratamente di P. In 859 L reca ancora *lectio duplex*, i tre apografi riproducono solo la *lectio potior*, P solo la *deterior*, quella che si trovava appunto in λᵗ (contro λᵐ). Su questa base si può già affermare che λ fosse corredato di lezioni duplici e che L si mostra tendenzialmente piú attento di P nel riprodurle. Sul che cfr. peraltro Turyn, p. 278.

²² L¹ trasformò π in τ riempiendo a nero il vuoto fra le due aste verticali della lettera non senza che una certa forma della lettera primitiva rimanesse visibile. Degli apografi Fl e E riproducono correttamente τ, ma Mr ha π, sí che teoricamente relativo è il valore del caso presente ai nostri fini.

²³ È questo un altro caso nel quale, a parte il fatto che in P non c'è traccia del chiarissimo ι nero sottoscritto a -ω in L da L¹, la divergenza fra L e P si spiega con lo stato della lezione in λ: ivi doveva leggersi qualcosa come o λυγαίωνέφει o λυγαίων ἔφει, un' incertezza nella divisione delle parole probabilmente antica, della quale è rimasta traccia lieve in L (che in effetti scrive il ν- piuttosto vicino a -ω che a -έ-, onde L¹, che pure di ι non usa sottoscriverne, ha inteso il bisogno di chiarire la divisione esatta trasformando -ω in -ῳ), meno lieve in P, che si è preoccupato di dare un senso alla *vox nihili* ἔφει cangiandola nella copia in ἔφη. Degli apografi di L, due (EMr) hanno bene inteso l'intervento di L¹ e hanno scritto la lezione esatta, Fl non lo ha notato e ha riprodotto fedelmente λυγαίων ἔφει.

²⁴ Su questo significativo caso, notato dallo Zuntz, p. 87, ma stranamente risolto con l'attribuzione, assolutamente impossibile, della correzione non a Tr¹ ma a Tr³, richiama opportunamente l'attenzione Tuilier, p. 197: "La main correctrice de Triclinius (o factum ex η) est noire, comme le reconnaît G. Zuntz ["practically black"], et celui-ci a tort d'affirmer que cette couleur provient ici de la surcharge sur l'écriture primitive ["because it is written over the original writing"] et ne peut être originale."

p. es., 372 κακόφρον L¹ (Fl): κακόφρων L(EMrᶜ)P; 568 κοσμῆσαι
L¹(FlEMr): κοσμεῖσθαι LᵖʳᵒᵇP²⁵; ecc.²⁶

—La massa degli interventi su L di colore diverso dal nero presenta
anche negli *Eraclidi* una notevole varietà cromatica. Assai frequente
ricorre il bruno, non molto dissimile in genere da quello del testo, ma
con gradazioni varie d'intensità, dal pallido (qualcosa come il terra di
Siena chiara) allo scuro (terra di Siena bruciata). Talora il bruno ha
tendenza al nero e ciò accade spesso, ma non esclusivamente, quando
una lettera è stata rifatta.²⁷ In alcuni casi il bruno ha sfumatura
rossastra, come di cinabro sbiadito o di 'rosso inglese' (tipico, p.es., a
f.89ᵛ nelle parole καὶ ἰαμβικά κτλ. della nota metrica a vv. 75 ss.);
in altri piú che di bruno si potrà parlare di grigio.²⁸ Si potrebbero

---

²⁵ È da metter senz' altro da parte 5 αὐτῷ L(FlEMr): αὐτῷ L¹ ᵖʳᵒᵇ P. Negli apparati
critici correnti si attribuisce αὐ- in L a mano correttrice, ma in realtà lo spirito aspro
è senz' altro di prima mano. Nel suo tratto superiore invero è visibile come una macchio-
lina nera, di incerta origine: ma se si tratti di correzione, sarà da intender che L¹ abbia
voluto semmai cangiare lo spirito da aspro in dolce.

²⁶ Per casi significativi di assenza di L¹ in P negli altri drammi alfabetici cfr., *contra*
Zuntz, Tuilier, p. 197 s.

²⁷ Spesso si tratta soltanto di una iniziale rifatta piú grande, ad apertura di parte
lirica o a inizio di unità corale interna (cfr. p.es. ἔα 73, οὕτινα 608, γᾶ 748, δεινὸν 759),
all' ingresso di nuovo personaggio (ἐπείπερ 120) o a sottolineare l'attribuzione di una
battuta a interlocutore diverso da quello della linea (o delle linee) precedente (σοφῶς 558);
talora semplicemente per indicare un nome proprio (Παλληνίδος 849, Ἀλκμήνην 585)
tal altra per motivo che sfugge (καλῶς 726, μάντεις 819). Codesto genere di richiami
tricliniani non ha rilevanza testuale, giacché non comportano innovazioni nella lezione
(qualche dubbio, tutt'al piú, può rimanere quando il rifacimento dell'iniziale è eseguito in
modo tale da non lasciar piú intravedere la lettera originaria, com'è, p.es., il caso di μὴ
500 ch'è stato rifatto dopo rasura). Illustra soltanto un aspetto dell'operosità di Triclinio
(per quel che riguarda le parti liriche vi richiamò l'attenzione già il Turyn, p. 249).

²⁸ Ovviamente, non è il caso di pensare all'impiego di altrettanti tipi d'inchiostro
quante sono le riscontrabili variazioni cromatiche. Oltre alle variazioni quantitative
dell'uno o l'altro ingrediente intervenuto nella preparazione dell'inchiostro base, che
sarà stato sempre nero (e per le quali cfr. Zuntz, pp. 57 ss.), possono aver influito sull'-
aspetto attuale della scrittura il rendimento del calamo, piú o meno scorrevole, lo stato
della carta, piú o meno liscia, accidenti varî e imprevedibili. L'alone rossastro (il "red
glow" di Zuntz) che circonda talora il bruno coincide spesso manifestamente o con
scrittura *in rasura* (p.es. a *El.* 633, per cui cfr. Tuilier, p. 197) o con l'impiego di un calamo
'grattante' (cfr., p.es., λαός *Heracl.* 87, riscritto sull'originario λαός di L già corretto da
L¹ in λεώς; εὐγενίας su εὐγενείας 626; νεῶν su ναῶν 780; ἐπίσημα con -α rifatto sopra
-ατα 906; αἰεί su ἀεί 909). La tinta che designiamo come grigia ("grey" "greyish"
Zuntz; qualcosa come il "nero di seppia" dei pittori) è praticamente qualcosa fra il nero
e il bruno, sbiadito per probabile aggiunta di acqua in un calamaio prossimo all'esaurimento
mento (ricorre generalmente, oltre che in *marginalia* metrici del tipo ἰαμβικοί f. 89ᵛ, in
ritocchi di poco conto: rifacimenti d'iniziali—6, 12, 26, ecc., singole lettere—39, 42,
103, 203, 204, ecc., -ν efelcistici—128, 295, 296, 347, ecc.—e simili).

additare anche sfumature minori, piú o meno occasionali. Ma quel che a nostro avviso s'impone è la rinuncia, per evitare estrapolazioni antimetodiche, a ogni rigidità, peraltro infruttuosa, in questo campo. Indicheremo pertanto tutte le aggiunte non dichiaratamente nere in L mediante la sigla L², includendovi cosí e Tr² e Tr³ di Zuntz.²⁹

In ogni caso L²(=Tr² o Tr³) indica secondo Zuntz stadî di revisione di L cronologicamente posteriori a L¹: P sarebbe stato trascritto da L dopo la fase L¹ e prima delle fasi successive: nessuna traccia di L² dovrebbe pertanto esser presente in P, ed è quello appunto che il dotto asserisce. Ma, pur essendo generalmente vero che L² non concorda con P, non mancano esempî in senso contrario, che compromettono anch'essi decisamente, come, pel verso loro, quelli rilevati poc'anzi a proposito di L¹ x L, la tesi della discendenza di P da L. Ne citiamo alcuni:—115 Chori notam om. L exh. L²(bruno scuro)P (delev. P¹); 159 πεπανθῆς L²(bruno)P¹ (erra il Murray in app.: π- è originale, solo -ν- è stato ricalcato da P¹, forse su un -ρ-): ἐπανθῆς L; 201 νομίζεται L²(bruno)P: κομίζεται L; 220 ἀπαιτοῦσιν L²(bruno scuro)P: ἀπαιτοῦσι L; 455 τέκν' L²(bruno scuro, in rasura; anche lo Zuntz, p. 84, attribuisce l'apostrofo a Tr³)P: τέκνα o τέκνον L; 564 Iolai notam om. L exh. L²(bruno scuro)P; 877 θύσετ' L²(bruno scuro, non 'nero', come vuole Zuntz, p. 87)P: θύσετε L³⁰—39 δυοῖν L²(grigio; a proposito di numerosi casi simili, anche negli altri drammi—solo in *Heracl.* 653 pare che δυοῖν, e non δυεῖν, sia originario di L—, lo Zuntz, p. 164,2, nota genericamente che "all these instances were sooner or later corrected by Tr.")P: δυεῖν L; 103 ἀπολείπειν σ' L²(grigio)P: ἀπολείπει γ' (an τ'?)L; 171 ὡπλισμένοι L²(grigio)P: ὁ- Lᵖʳᵒᵇ; 347 κακίοισιν L²(grigio)P(-ῑ): κακίοισι L; 386 εἰσιν Elmsl.] ἔστιν L²(grigio un po' meno debole del solito)P: ἔστι L; 393 ἐφῆκέ L²(grigio)P: ἔφηκέ L; 505 ἄλλοισιν L²(grigio un po' meno debole del solito)P: ἄλλοισι L; 727 ὀξύην L²(grigio; in rasura larg. spatio) P: ὀξείην Lᵖʳᵒᵇ; 819 ἐπειδὴ L²(grigio) P: -δὲ Lᵖʳᵒᵇ; 927 εἴη L²(grigio)P: εἴην Lᵖʳᵒᵇ; 928 δέσποιν' ὁ- L²(grigio, anche l'ὁ-)P: δέσποινα ὁ- L; 992 κἄγνων L²(grigio, un po' meno debole del solito)P: καὶ ἔγνων L.³¹

---

²⁹ Di tale avviso è anche il Tuilier, p. 190, 3; cfr. Kannicht, *o.c.*, I p. 132.

³⁰ Tralasciamo qualche caso che si presti a dubbio, come p.es.: 163 ἀργείοις L² *seu* Lᶜ (propriamente ἀργε⁺ος [*sic*], in cui il punto è bruno, ma potrebbe anch'essere di prima mano, lo scriba avendo tralasciato di eraser completamente la dieresi) P: ἀργείοις L; 358 μεγάλαισιν L² (bruno il compendio finale soprascritto) P: μεγάλαις Lʳᵃˢ (con -ς grigio) μεγάλαισιν Lᵖʳᵒᵇ (rimane quindi la possibilità teorica che P abbia attinto non da λ, ma da L).

³¹ Vi sono infine diversi casi nei quali in L sono state praticate delle rasure che è impossibile attribuire a L¹ (Tr¹) o L² (Tr²Tr³). La cosa è indifferente nel caso si

A conclusione di questa parte diremo che si può ritener per dimostrato che nessuna rilevanza positiva può aver l'argomento paleografico ai fini della teoria della dipendenza di P da L. (Semmai, ne avrà una negativa.) A parte la difficoltà in sé della classificazione e della collocazione cronologica di t u t t i gl'interventi tricliniani in L ff. 89–96ᵛ (= *Eraclidi*), rimane il fatto che essi, pur quando sieno cromaticamente inequivoci (e solo su casi del genere ci siamo soffermati), ricorrono cosí irregolarmente in P che nessuna deduzione è permessa sulla presunta priorità della copia di questo rispetto ad alcuni di quelli.[32]

* * *

La teoria che L e P sieno *gemelli* riceve evidentemente sicura conferma da quanto si è esposto. Ma giova addurre gli altri argomenti vecchi e nuovi che militano in suo favore.

Degli errori comuni (taluno risaliente alla maiuscola, come 602 δύεται LP λύεται Milton, 769 εἶτ' LP ἐκ γ' Kirchhoff) è appena il caso di dire, per la loro ricerca essendo sufficiente aprire una qualsiasi edizione del dramma fornita di apparato critico nel quale figuri anche P. Né occorre addurre esempî di "Trennfehler" di P contro L, essendo noto che il primo erra contro il secondo in gran numero di casi, né mai essendo stata sostenuta, neanche teoricamente, la possibilità di P > L. "Trennfehler" di L contro P, viceversa, son rari, ché evidentemente— ma altro si dirà *infra*—L ha riprodotto assai fedelmente la sua fonte,[33] ma non del tutto assenti:

---

assuma λ > LP; ovviamente non lo è, dal punto di vista metodico, nel caso di L > P, giacché non è lecito stabilire se le rasure sono intervenute prima o dopo la presunta copia di P da L. Esempî: 117 καὶ ante μάλιστ' LᵃʳᵃˢP; 138 ὁμαρτῇ Lᵖʳᵃˢ ἁμαρτῇ LP(l'o- è stato ottenuto mediante il semplice grattaggio dei tratti superflui dell' α-); 195 οἷαπερ Lᵖʳᵃˢ -ά- LP; 252 κυρήσει L (dopo la rasura di una lettera) κυρήσειε P; 590 προὔθανον L πρού- Lᵖʳᵃˢ P; 716 θάρσος LP ma in L sembra scritto in rasura.—Non abbiamo menzionato prima il caso di 42 ὑπηγκαλισμένη Lᶜ (forse da ἀπ-? tale è la lezione di E) P, poiché non si può affermare con sicurezza, ma solo con grande verisimiglianza, che ὑ- sia dovuto a L² (grigio).

[32] Bene al riguardo, e anche a proposito degli altri drammi, Tuilier, pp. 199,2,4; 201 s.

[33] La cosa non ha in sé nulla d'inverisimile, né è giustificato lo scetticismo aprioristico di P. Maas, *Textkritik* (Lipsia 1957³), p. 18: "...L könnte ja beim Abschreiben aus einer gemeinsamen Vorlage nur eben jene wenigen Fehler [*sc.* quelli che cita poco prima: *Iph. T.* 1006, 1141ab, 632] begangen haben. Aber erstens ist das bei einem so umfangreichen Text sehr unwahrscheinlich..."

—494 κἀμοὶ P: κἀμοὶ δὲ L *contra metrum*. L ha commesso, per "suggestion régressive" [34] (il verso termina per λέγει δέ πως), un errore metrico che, una volta penetrato nel testo, non era facile da scoprire per copisti medievali o umanistici: ritorna infatti regolarmente in FlEMr ed è da escluder che lo scriba di P lo abbia rimosso per congettura.[35]

—526 τινὶ P(Mr): τίνι L(FlE).

—672 ὥπλισται P(E): ὥπλισται L(Fl[ŏ-]Mr).

Tre casi son pochi e gli ultimi due hanno manifestamente scarso valore,[36] ma non bisogna dimenticare che occorre aggiungervi tutti gli altri nei quali P reca la lezione poziore contro il gemello L, a n c h e s e i n a c c o r d o c o n L¹ o L². L'operosità di Triclinio su L si è infatti esplicata in parte mediante divinazione, e questo soprattutto nelle parti liriche, in parte per (ri)collazione dell'originale. Né è da escludere, vista la ormai dimostrata quasi contemporaneità dei due manoscritti e la loro provenienza da uno stesso *scriptorium*, che alcuni degli errori della copia L sieno stati rettificati, nelle prime fasi della revisione, proprio su P.[37]

A confermare l'indipendenza di P da L non sarebbe forse neppure il caso di richiamare errori del primo che non sono assolutamente giustificabili con l'aspetto della lezione relativa in L, se appunto non si fosse addotto, dal Wecklein in poi,[38] come argomento fondamentale a pro della dipendenza quello di errori di P originati da peculiarità paleografiche di L. Codesto argomento, astrazion fatta della sua opinabilità in gran parte dei dettagli, viene svalutato in partenza dal fatto, generalmente riconosciuto, che l'antigrafo di L (e di P) aveva un *ductus* simile a quello dell'apografo.[39] Un solo

[34] Cfr. B. A. van Groningen, *Traité d'histoire et de critique des textes grecs* (Amsterdam 1963, Verhandel. der konink. Nederlandse Ak. van Wetensch. Afd. Letterkunde: N.R. 70, 2), p. 94.

[35] Lo stesso Zuntz, p. 84, n. 1, riconosce che P dà abitualmente "scant evidence" di "right instinct," ma emette súbito dopo l'ipotesi che δὲ¹ sia dovuto non a L* ma a Tr³. L'attenta autopsia del codice mi porta a escludere ogni dubbio sull'originarietà di δὲ.

[36] Esempî di P unico verace in altri drammi alfabetici e nel *Reso* v. in Tuilier, p. 202 s. (cfr. Turyn, p. 267, 277).

[37] Cfr. Tuilier, p. 202.

[38] Cfr. Zuntz, pp. 2 ss., ma già Turyn, pp. 267 s.

[39] Oltre a Turyn, p. 268, cfr. Zuntz, pp. 125, n.: "an ancestor written in the style of L" (a proposito delle *Troadi*); 181: "it is therefore plausible that the model of L was written in the same style as L itself" (e adduce vasta esemplificazione, anche nelle pagine seguenti); 109: "...in which case L is shown, once more, to have been copied from a manuscript written in the same style as L itself" (a proposito di *El.* 633); ecc.

esempio varrà a chiarimento. Lo scriba di L ha un cosí tipico modo di effettuare il legamento $\epsilon\xi$ che questo può essere scambiato per $\epsilon\lambda$; ugualmente si prestano a fraintendimenti alcuni suoi $\delta\epsilon$. In *El.* 633, in luogo del corretto δούλων restaurato, per collazione di λ, in L da L² (Tr³ per Zuntz) P esibisce, cosí come indubbiamente faceva L prima del restauro, in rasura, tricliniano, l'impossibile λέξων. È chiaro che tanto L quanto P (mentre di solito a legger male è solo P) sono stati indotti nello stesso errore di lettura dalla grafia di λ (cosí si spiega fors'anche *Heracl.* 237 ξένους LP λόγους Kirchhoff). Lo Zuntz interpreta qui rettamente l'evidenza (cfr. l. cit. alla n. 39). Non si vede allora come lo stesso dotto, di fronte a casi del tutto analoghi, quali p.es. *Suppl.* 64 δεξιπύρους L δελιπύρους P, possa sostenere che P d e b b a derivare de L e non da λ![40]

Ma ecco alcuni casi nei quali la lezione di P negli *Eraclidi* non può, come si diceva, assolutamente risalire a errore di lettura di L, la relativa grafia di questo essendo chiarissima e regolarmente confermata dagli apografi (evitiamo di proposito errori nei quali abbia potuto giocare manifestamente uno dei motivi abituali di ordine meccanico o di pronuncia o d'interpretazione di compendio desinenziale: v. p.es. a 724; 45, 205, 249, 305, 473, 551, 582, 588, 736, 848; 77, 395, 500, 597, 801, 1037): 11 δεόμενος L(e, come in tutti gli esempî che seguono, FlEMr): δεχόμενος P; 282 ἤβην L: ὕβριν P[41]; 338 λάθη L: λάβη P; 433 ἔτερψας L: ἔτρεψας P; 472 βουλήν L: βολήν P; 499 γ' L: δ' P (et E); 581 τ' L: δ' P; 724 μὲν L: δὲ P; 781 ἀνεμόεντι L: ἀνεμόνεντι P; 836 ἐπαλλαχθεὶς L: ἀπαλλαχθεὶς P; 918 *(δισσοὺς)* παῖδας L: παῖδα P; 985 λέξονθ' Mr] λέγοντ' P: λέξοντες L.

Questi esempî invece suffragano per vie diverse quanto s'è sopra osservato sull'influenza di λ su L da una parte e su P dall'altra: —498 κἀχόμεσθα Elmsl.] κεὐχόμεσθα LP: l'errore si spiega col fatto che in λ α ed ευ dovevano essere scritti in maniera da potersi confondere,

[40] *Ibid.* p.2. Quanto mai contorto è lo sforzo di spiegare in *Suppl.* 171 ἔξωροι P dalla forma del verace δεῦρο in L: P avrebbe dovuto non solo vedere un εξωρο nel δεῦρο, sul che si potrebbe ancora esser d'accordo, ma altresí uno ι nel puntino che a questo segue e spirito e accento nel...vuoto! Mentre ch'è molto piú semplice ammettere che l'errore di P si spieghi con la singolarità della scrittura di λ, della quale è rimasta traccia anche in L, appunto in quell'ingiustificato segno d'interpunzione. A meno che un'altra spiegazione non sia possibile: che cioè in λ occorressero le due lezioni e che L abbia scelto quella delle due, la verace, che peraltro ritorna nel margine di P come γρ.

[41] P si trova piú volte in difficoltà nei nessi con ρ (449 ἐχθοῦ per ἐχθροῦ, 512 ἐχρῶν per ἐχθρῶν, 692 δᾶν per δρᾶν): λ dev'esser certamente il responsabile, L seppe invece non lasciarsi ingannare.

come peraltro notoriamente accade a scribi di diverse epoche (in
Iph. T. 438 occorre il caso uguale e contrario: ἄξεινον LᵃᶜP per εὔξεινον);
se lo Zuntz avesse preso in considerazione questo luogo, avrebbe
probabilmente impostato in altro modo la lunga discussione (p. 3) su
El. 730, ecc.

—573 ὑστάτοις Blomfield] ὕστατον L (con i tre apografi, come sempre, salvo indicazione contraria) ὕστατος P: il compendio non chiaro
in λ è stato letto diversamente dai due discendenti.[42]

—778 s. λάθει L recte λεύθει Pᵖʳᵒᵇ: anche qui, come a 498, lo
scambio α/ευ, se c'è, risale a λ; L ha scritto la parola cosí stranamente
che non il solo α vi è di difficile lettura, come appare dagli apografi,
nessuno dei quali ha saputo decifrare: Fl verbum om. spatio relicto,
Mr κεύθει, E λήθει;

—805 τί Heath] ἐπὶ L ἐπεὶ P.

—899 s. τελεσσιδώτειρ' Aldina] τελεσιδώτειρ' Lᶜ τελευσιδώτειρ' P: in λ
era d'incerto tratto il nesso -εσ-, tanto da poter sembrare anche -ευ-:
tale infatti apparve a P e a L in un primo momento, ma poi questo
inter scribendum si riprese e cangiò -υ- in -σ-, del che è rimasta traccia
negli apografi, due dei quali (MrE) hanno τελεσι-, uno (Fl) τελευ-.

—915 χροΐζει L recte χροΐους P: che la strana deformazione di P
risalga a λ (a parte il fatto che L è chiarissimo, e regolarmente riprodotto
dai tre apografi) è confermato dal caso analogo di *Cycl.* 498: ὑπαγκα-
λίζων L recte ὑπαγκαλίους P (errato l'apparato del Murray in entrambi
i luoghi).

La divergenza di P da L(FlMrE) si spiega infine con la presenza di
lectio duplex in λ[43] nei casi seguenti:

—27 συμπράσσω L συμπάσχω P

—597 ἐκπρέπουσ' L ἐ̋κπρέπουσ' P.

Ai quali sono verisimilmente da aggiungere due fatti piuttosto di
natura esterna, ma non per questo insignificanti:

—Nell'*hypothesis* degli *Eraclidi* aggiunta in L, come s'è detto, da L¹, e
nelle *dramatis personae* che seguono, i nomi proprî sono irregolarmente
sovrastati dal caratteristico tratto orizzontale (nella prima lo ha solo
κοπρέως, fra le seconde tutte eccetto χορός e μακαρία παρθένος); lo
stesso accade in P (con la differenza che ha il segno χορός e non lo ha
εὐρυσθεύς). Il divario fra i due codici, lungi dal provare che P deriva
da L, come sembra a Zuntz (p. 4), risale certamente a λ, nel quale i

---

[42] In genere L è piú accurato di P nella copia e questo spiega come gli errori in
compendio finale sieno molto piú frequenti nel secondo.

[43] Sul che cfr. anche *supra*, n. 21.

segni in questione dovevano essere o piú o meno leggibili nei varî luoghi.

—L e P, cartaceo il primo membranaceo il secondo, sono scritti entrambi su due colonne, ma mentre nel primo, alquanto piú recente e destinato manifestamente all'uso di uno studioso, si è adottato il sistema, piú pratico e moderno (che ritorna in Fl, l'unico dei tre apografi scritto su due colonne), di far seguire i versi uno per ogni colonna da sinistra a destra, in P, copiato, sí, un po' dopo L ma con le caratteristiche di un libro di lusso, ricorre il sistema delle colonne da leggere ciascuna per proprio conto e dall'alto in basso, che paleograficamente è piú antico e che indubbiamente risale a λ.[44]

* * *

Se, come crediamo si evinca da quanto precede, L e P sono *gemelli*, la conseguenza, a parte il rilievo che la cosa assume nella storia del testo, è che P deve ritornare a esser presente negli apparati critici. Esso rappresenta la tradizione confluita in λ allo stesso titolo di L, col vantaggio di non essere stato, come quest'ultimo, sfigurato in piú parti. Anche le modifiche subíte da L a opera di Triclinio debbono essere registrate in apparato. Di esse alcune sono di manifesta origine divinatoria, soprattutto, se non esclusivamente, nelle parti liriche[45]; altre provengono invece da collazione e restaurano la tradizione là dove L aveva mal riprodotto λ, il che trova di regola utile conferma in P; altre infine lasciano incerti sulla loro natura, ma, appunto per la loro problematicità, occorre che sieno ugualmente documentate in apparato.[46]

Napoli, 1 luglio 1970

---

[44] L'importante osservazione è in Tuilier, p. 202,2; ma cfr. anche Irigoin, in *Rev. phil.* cit. p. 321.

[45] Bene al riguardo Zuntz, pp. 193 ss.

[46] A tale criterio s'ispira il nostro apparato teubneriano degli *Eraclidi*. Indagini analoghe alla presente saranno pubblicate prossimamente per l'*Andromaca* e l'*Alcesti*, drammi dei quali anche prepariamo l'edizione.

DIONISO, FRA *BACCANTI* E *RANE*

RAFFAELE CANTARELLA

In un recente articolo[1] Jean Carrière ha proposto—per la prima
volta, che io sappia[2]—un preciso se pur non esauriente confronto
fra le due opere: confronto che, pur nella sua evidenza non soltanto
cronologica,[3] era finora sfuggito agli studiosi, forse anche a causa

[1] "Sur le message des Bacchantes," *L'Ant. Cl.* 35 (1966), 118–39.

[2] Alcune utili osservazioni in proposito, ma ancora in parte legate al concetto tradi-
zionale della diversità fra commedia e tragedia, in C. P. Segal, "The Character of
Dionysus and the Unity of the Frogs," *Harv. Stud. Cl. Phil.* 65 (1961), 207–17, 227–30 =
D. J. Littlefield (ed.), *Twentieth century interpretations of the Frogs* (Englewood Cliffs, N.J.
1968), 45–57 (in particolare 54–57: A. conobbe le *Ba.*); un rapidissimo cenno in R. P.
Winnington-Ingram, *Euripides and Dionysus* (Cambridge 1948, rist. 1969), 168.

[3] Le *Rane* furono rappresentate nell'a. 405: al Leneo, come afferma esplicitamente
Argum. I (Coulon, Cantarella); alle Dionisie dello stesso anno ebbe luogo la ripetizione
(unica a noi nota nel sec. V) della commedia, a causa della tristemente attuale parabasi:
cfr. W. Schmid, *Gesch. gr. Lit.* IV, 211 sg.; R. Cantarella, *Aristophanis Comoediae.* I.
Prolegomena (Milano 1949), § 295 b. È difficile pensare (con van Leeuwen, Körte,
Murray: per i quali cfr. Schmid, *op. cit.* 212, 2; anche C. F. Russo, *Storia delle Rane di
Ar.* [Padova 1961], 93, *Ar. autore di teatro* [Firenze 1968], 317) a una replica "pochi
giorni dopo" (cioè due al massimo, dal 10 al 12 Gamelione: cfr. L. Deubner, *Attische
Feste* (Berlin 1932, rist. 1956), 123 sgg.: non ho sotto mano la 2ª ed. 1966 riv. da B.
Doer), che avrebbe sconvolto il ristretto, fisso e non modificabile *ex abrupto* calendario
della festa; e che, per la sua eccezionalità, avrebbe lasciato—riteniamo—precisa traccia
nella tradizione. Le *Baccanti*, composte in Macedonia, furono messe in scena ad Atene
(insieme con *Ifigenia in Aulide* e *Alcmeone*) da Euripide jr., figlio del poeta, dopo la morte
di lui, alle Dionisie (ἐν ἄστει: Σ Aristoph. *Ran.* 67, sull'autorità delle aristoteliche
Didascalie, frg. 627 Rose) dell'a. 406: cfr. Carrière, *art. cit.* 122, 20; G. Murray, *Eur.
fabulae*, III² (Oxonii 1949), dopo la prosopografia di *Ba.*, *I.A.*; mentre il Webster,
The tragedies of Euripides (London 1967), 257, ritiene probabili le Dionisie dell'a. 405. Ma
se pensiamo che le *Baccanti*, per essere rappresentate nel marzo 405, avevano avuto
bisogno della necessaria preparazione scenica, è ben possibile che Aristofane, componendo
le *Rane* nella seconda metà del 406 (cfr. Cantarella, *op. cit.*, V [1964], 22,5), abbia avuto
conoscenza delle *Baccanti* (e delle altre due tragedie in allestimento). E nulla vieta di
credere che il manoscritto delle *Baccanti* fosse giunto e diffuso in Atene anche prima
dell'allestimento scenico, cioè subito dopo la morte del poeta, di cui la notizia giunse in
Atene (poco) prima del proagone (8 di Elafebolione: cfr. A. Pickard-Cambridge
[J. Gould, D. M. Lewis], *The dramatic festivals of Athens²* [Oxford 1968], 64, 67) delle

del preconcetto tradizionale di incomunicabilità fra tragedia e commedia. In questa direzione si muove appunto la presente ricerca, nel proposito—o nella speranza—di approfondire l'interessante tema, anche per alcune considerazioni, che se ne possono trarre, utili ad illustrare i due drammi, ciascuno in se stesso ed entrambi nella vita ateniese degli ultimi anni del secolo V.

I luoghi addotti dal Carrière[4] a dimostrare un riferimento, parodico o comunque allusivo, delle *Rane* alle *Baccanti*, sono i seguenti; che qui ripetiamo (in ordine; e all'occorrenza discutiamo) anche per offrirne un quadro completo:

1) *Ra.* 66 sq.

> *ΔI.*   τοιουτοσὶ τοίνυν με δαρδάπτει πόθος
> Εὐριπίδου.
>
> *HP.*   καὶ ταῦτα τοῦ τεθνηκότος;

Osserva giustamente il Carrière che la implicita allusione ad Euripide jr. è dovuta appunto alla messa in scena dei tre drammi paterni, che gli diede notorietà, come è confermato da Σ Aristoph. *Ran.* 67.[5]

2) *Ra.* 100 χρόνου πόδα è, fra altri, un esempio del παρακεκινδυνευμένον dello stile euripideo che tanto piaceva a Dioniso; il *flosculus* euripideo è ripreso tal quale, caricaturalmente, dal servo Xantia a v. 311. Ed Euripide, proprio in *Ba.* 888 aveva detto κρυπτεύουσι δὲ ποικίλως δαρὸν χρόνου πόδα.[6]

Dionisie del 406 (cfr. Schmid, *op. cit.* III, 328). Che anzi Euripide jr. doveva aver presentato i manoscritti (dopo aver completato la *Ifigenia* rimasta incompiuta per la morte del padre) all'arconte eponimo, per "chiedere il coro"; ciò che avveniva (pare: cfr. A. Müller, *Lehrbuch der griech. Bühnenaltertumer* [Freiburg i.B. 1886], 331, 5; Pickard—Cambridge, *op. cit.* 75,2: le fonti riguardano i coreghi del ditirambo, ma è probabile che altrettanto avvenisse per la tragedia) il mese dopo le Dionisie dell'anno precedente: quindi nel febbraio del 406, subito dopo la morte del padre. Cade dunque, già per questo, la difficoltà cronologica, come confermeranno anche altri indizi: e appare confermato che Aristofane, mentre componeva le *Rane*, conosceva le *Baccanti*.

[4] *Art. cit.*, 121 sg. (cfr. anche 131, 134–39).

[5] E da *Vita Eur.* 2,14 Schwarz, che si riferisce allo stesso avvenimento (ἐδίδαξε τοῦ πατρὸς ἔνια δράματα) e che deriva, probabilmente, dalla stessa fonte. Si osservi che sono, queste due, le uniche menzioni di Euripide jr. E si tenga presente che—con tutta probabilità se non con certezza—Euripide jr. assisteva alla rappresentazione delle *Rane*: come forse può essere confermato da v. 1476, dove si contrappone implicitamente e scherzosamente all'Euripide morto l'Euripide vivo e presente.

[6] Già in frg. 42 (dal '*Alessandro* dell'a. 415) aveva detto καὶ χρόνου προὔβαινε πούς ma qui, nelle *Rane*, sembra evidente, anche nella ripetizione, la ripresa letterale dell' espressione delle *Baccanti*.

3) *Ra.* 345. *XO. γόνυ πάλλεται γερόντων*, nella celebrazione della notturna festa bacchica. E anche Cadmo e Tiresia (vecchi entrambi, e cieco quest'ultimo!) bramano slanciarsi a danza, invasi dal dio: cfr. *Ba.* 184–86: *KA. ποῖ δεῖ χορεύειν, ποῖ καθιστάναι πόδα / καὶ κρᾶτα σεῖσαι πολιόν; ἐξηγοῦ σύ μοι / γέρων γέροντι, Τειρεσία.*[7]

4) *Ra.* 372–74. *XO. χώρει νυν πᾶς ἀνδρείως / ἐς τοὺς εὐανθεῖς κόλπους / λειμώ- νων: Ba.* 865 sq. *ὡς νεβρὸς χλοεραῖς ἐμπαί- / ζουσα λείμακος ἡδοναῖς; I.A.* 1296 sq. *λειμών τ' ἄνθεσι θάλλων / χλωροῖς.*[8]

5) *Ra.* 402 sq.

   XO. *καὶ δεῖξον ὡς ἄνευ πόνου*
      πολλὴν ὁδὸν περαίνεις.

Ba. 194. *TEI.* *ὁ θεὸς ἀμοχθὶ κεῖσε νῷν ἡγήσεται.*

E cfr. *Ba.* 614

   ΔI. *αὐτὸς ἐξέσωσ' ἐμαυτὸν ῥαδίως ἄνευ πόνου.*

6) *Ra.* 477 *διασπάσονται Γοργόνες: Ba.* 338 sq. *σκύλακες... διεσπάσαντο.*

7) *Ra.* 628–30 *ΔI.*   *ἀγορεύω τινὶ*
      ἐμὲ μὴ βασανίζειν ἀθάνατον ὄντ'· εἰ δὲ μή,
      αὐτὸς σεαυτὸν αἰτιῶ.

Cfr. *Ba.* 516 sq. *ΔI. ἀτάρ τοι τῶνδ' ἄποιν' ὑβρισμάτων μέτεισι Διόνυσός σ', κτλ.*

8) *Ra.* 631

  ΔI. ἀθάνατος εἶναί φημι Διόνυσος Διός, che il Carrière considera una "transposition plaisante" di *Ba.* 507, dove Penteo esibisce pomposamente la propria discendenza da Echione: *Πενθεύς, Ἀγαύης παῖς, πατρὸς δ' Ἐχίονος*. Ma Aristofane, qui, trascurando la madre, afferma piuttosto la paternità divina di Dioniso, da Zeus. Ed è precisamente quanto afferma, con ripetuta e significativa insistenza, il Dioniso delle *Ba.*, per il quale, ai vv. 1, 27, 84 s., 366, 417, 466, 725, 859 citati da W. Schmid, *op. cit.* III 681, 6, si possono aggiungere vv. 242 s., 286 ss., 522–24, 550, 581, 603, 1341 s., 1349. Lo Schmid sostiene che la cronologia vieta di considerare *Ra.* 631 come allusione ai luoghi delle *Ba.* Ma, a parte quanto abbiamo osservato circa la possibilità—la certezza; anche per noi—della priorità delle *Ba.*, sta a conferma dell'allusione il verso *Ra.* 22

   ἐγὼ μὲν ὢν Διόνυσος υἱὸς Σταμνίου,

---

[7] Cfr. anche v. 193 (*KA.*) *γέρων γέροντα παιδαγωγήσω σ' ἐγώ;* 204 (*TEI.*) *ἐρεῖ τις ὡς τὸ γῆρας οὐκ αἰσχύνομαι / μέλλων χορεύειν;* 206 *οὐ γὰρ διήρηχ' ὁ θεός, οὔτε τὸν νέον / εἰ χρὴ χορεύειν οὔτε τὸν γεραίτερον.*

[8] Carrière, *art. cit.* 121,14: "Connaître l'*Iphigénie à Aulis*, c'était connaître les *Bacchantes*, les deux pièces ayant été représentées ensemble."

di cui si intende appieno il valore comico soltanto se lo si considera una precisa parodia[9] (posta quasi al principio del dramma, anch'essa) proprio dell'inizio delle *Ba.* 1 s.:

> Ἥκω Διὸς παῖς τήνδε Θηβαίων χθόνα
> Διόνυσος, κτλ.

9) *Ra.* 838 ΕΥ. ἔχοντ᾽ ἀχάλινον ἀκρατὲς ἀπύλωτον στόμα, κτλ.[10] è Eschilo, naturalmente. Senza dubbio, questo luogo si avvicina piuttosto a frg. 492,4 per la presenza del medesimo verbo: mentre, dunque, sembra chiaro che Aristofane si è ricordato della *Melanippe Saggia*,[11] non si può escludere che abbia avuto presente anche il luogo delle *Ba.*

10) *Ra.* 1309–12

> ΑΙΣ. ἀλκυόνες, αἳ παρ᾽ ἀενάοις θαλάσσης
> κύμασι στωμύλλετε,
> τέγγουσαι νοτίοις πτερῶν
> ῥανίσι χρόα δροσιζόμεναι· κτλ.

Questi versi costituiscono un grosso e complicato problema. Σ[v] 1310 afferma ἔστι δὲ τὸ προεγκείμενον (scil. κόμμα) ἐξ Ἰφιγενείας τῆς ἐν

---

[9] Come conferma Σ ad l.: δέον εἰπεῖν υἱὸς Διός, Σταμνίου εἶπε παρ᾽ ὑπόνοιαν. Σ *Plut.* 525, fraintendendo questo luogo, al quale si riferisce, farnetica di uno Zeus Στάμνιος: cfr. F. V. Fritzsche, *Aristophanis Ranae* (Turici 1845), *Comm.* p. 11. È interessante osservare che nei luoghi sopra indicati, molto spesso (v. 1, 27, 242, 466, 550, 859) la paternità di Zeus viene messa efficacemente in rilievo con l'evidente allusione etimologica Διόνυσος / Διός: su cui cfr. H. Frisk, *Griech. etymol. Wörterb.* (Heidelberg 1960 sqq.), p. 396. L'insistito richiamo alla paternità di Zeus non è gratuito, ma costituisce un mezzo (e non l'unico nella tragedia: particolarmente significativi i v. 200–203 di Tiresia "dionisiaco" che si appella alle πάτριοι παραδοχαί che nessun *logos* sofistico, di Protagora, potrà abbattere: vedi la nota ad l. di H. Grégoire, *Euripide*, tome VI, 2 (Paris 1961), il quale però generalizza e sopravvaluta il luogo per dimostrare la "conversione" di Euripide; E. R. Dodds, *Euripides Bacchae*[2] (Oxford 1960), *ad loc.* p. 94 trova "surprising" questo linguaggio, in quanto Dioniso è un dio *nuovo*) per inserire il culto di Dioniso nella sfera olimpia, cioè dei culti tradizionali, e leciti, della polis. È interessante osservare che invece, a v. 631, Aristofane riprende il motivo della paternità tradizionale, con la stessa evidente intenzione etimologica.: ἀθάνατος εἶναί φημι Διόνυσος Διός.

[10] Manca in Carrière *art. cit.*; e negli elenchi di A. C. Schlesinger "Indications of Parody in A.," *Trans. Am. Philol. Ass.* 67 (1936), 296–314 dello stesso, l'art. "Identification of Parodies in A.," *Am. J. Phil.* 58 (1937), riguarda soltanto *Av. Thesm. Lys.*; P. Rau, *Paratragodia* (Zetemata 45, München 1967) 215: ma a p. 203 si rimanda a p. 124, dove, a riscontro di A., si cita prima *Ba.* 386 e poi frg. 492,4. È registrato in C. Prato, *E. nella critica di A.*[2] (Galatina 1955), p. 121, il quale rimanda a Eur. frg. 495 (scil. 492,4 ἀχάλιν᾽ ἔχουσι στόματα) e anche a *Ba.* 386 ἀχαλίνων στομάτων τὸ τέλος δυστυχία. Cfr. anche (ma in senso proprio, le cavalle di Diomede) *Herc. F.* 382 ἀχάλιν᾽ ἐθόαζον.

[11] Cfr. Schmid, *op. cit.* III 672,8. La *Melanippe Saggia* fu composta prima del 412.

Αὐλίδι.[12] Ma poiché essi non si leggono nella tragedia (o almeno nella redazione di essa a noi pervenuta),[13] sono state escogitate varie soluzioni per risolvere l'aporia:

a) i versi apparterrebbero a una *I.A.*, ma non a quella a noi pervenuta, che sarebbe di Euripide jr., bensì alla omonima, e perduta, tragedia di Euripide. È una strana idea, in verità, dovuta nientemeno che a A. Boeckh[14] e seguita da alcuni dotti,[15] ma oggi del tutto abbandonata;

b) i versi non sono una citazione testuale, ma si ispirano a *I.T.* (onde lo spiegabile errore di Σᵛ) 1089 sgg.

> ὄρνις, ἃ παρὰ πετρίνας
> πόντου δειράδας, ἀλκυών, κτλ.

La spiegazione, che rimonta a St. Bergler,[16] ed ha avuto largo seguito,[17] non è sostenibile poiché—come è stato osservato[18]—anche questi versi, per costituire una efficace parodia, devono essere, come molte altre del brano, di citazione testuale, e non una parafrasi "à la manière de."

[12] J. Tzetzes, *Comm. in Aristophanem*, fasc. III ed. W. J. W. Koster, (Amsterdam 1962), 1070 B: ἔστι δὲ τὸ προκείμενον ἐξ Ἰφιγενείας τῆς ἐν Αὐλίδι.

[13] La tragedia, rimasta incompiuta per la morte del poeta, fu certamente completata (ma non sappiamo in qual modo) dal figlio per poterla presentare all'arconte e poi mettere in scena: cfr. Schmid, *op. cit.* III 631 e sopra, nota 3, in fine.

[14] *De tragoediae graecae principibus* (Heidelberg 1808), 218 sg.

[15] T. M. Mitchell, *The Frogs of A.* (London 1839), p. 308 ad v. 1260 (cita "Eichstadt and Boeckh"); F. V. Fritzsche, *op. cit.* 399 (cfr. *Aristophanis Thesmophoriazusae* [Leipzig 1838] 457), "A. Boeckhio auctore" e aggiunge che nella perduta tragedia la menzione delle alcioni poteva essere ben opportuna, ad invocare la tranquillità del mare mentre la flotta era trattenuta in Aulide dai venti contrari. Ma è doveroso qui ricordare che il commentario del Fritzsche alle *Rane* è ancora oggi il migliore e il maggiore. F. H. M. Blaydes, *Aristophanis comoediae. Pars VIII. Ranae* (Halis Saxonum 1889), 465 riferisce ampiamente l'opinione di Boeckh-Fritzsche e di Bergler-Brunck, ma in fine propende per l'*Issipile*. Th. Kock, *Ausgewählte Komoedien des A. erklärt*, III. *Die Frösche*⁴ (Berlin 1898), 199 sembra aderire al Fritzsche (ma senza citare il Boeckh). Così, pur con la riserva "wenn dem Scholiasten zu trauen ist," L. Radermacher, *Aristophanes' Frösche* (Wien 1921²; 1954 ed. W. Kraus, rist. Graz 1967), 322; P. Rau, *op. cit.* 129, ricorda la tesi (Boeckh-) Fritzsche-Kock-Radermacher, ma senza pronunziarsi, come aveva fatto il Prato, *op. cit.* 122. Anche B. B. Rogers, *The Frogs of A.*² (London 1919), 200 ricorda il Boeckh, ma senza aderirvi.

[16] *Aristophanis comoediae undecim, graece et latine* etc. (Lugd. Bat. 1760).

[17] R. F. Ph. Brunck, *Aristophanis comoediae*, I (Oxford 1810), 238; Ph. Invernizi-C. D. Beck, *Aristophanis comoediae. Commentarii*, vol. III (Lipsiae 1811), 306 sq. (riproduce Bergler e Brunck); I. Bekker, *Aristophanis Ranae* etc. (London 1829), 259 (riproduce Bergler, Beck, Brunck); B. Tiersch, *Aristophanis comoediae*. Tom. VI, Pars I. (Lipsiae 1830), 253; W. Dindorf, *Aristophanis comoediae*, III (Oxford 1835); Fr. Dübner, *Scholia graeca in A.* (Parisiis 1842), 536 A; I. van Leeuwen J. F., *Aristophanis Ranae* (Leidae 1896), 193; W. B. Stanford, *Aristophanes. The Frogs* (London 1958, 1963²), 183; W. J. W. Koster, *op. cit.* (cfr. sopra nota 12), 1170 ("ita iam Bergler: veri simillime").

[18] Cfr. Blaydes, *op. cit.* ibid.

c) È di W. H. Van de Sande Bakhuyzen[19] l'ipotesi che si tratti di un mero errore grafico di Σ, che avrebbe scritto ἐξ Ἰφιγ. invece di ἐξ Ὑψιπ. (come era nella sua fonte), alla quale perciò apparterrebbero i versi. Nonostante che abbia avuto anch'essa largo seguito, questa ipotesi non è sostenibile: α) nella fonte di Σ il titolo era scritto in unciale onde, anche se in abbreviazione,[20] ΥΨΙΠ difficilmente poteva dare origine all'errata trascrizione ΙΦΙΓ, che molto ne differisce;

β) rimane da spiegare perché soltanto in questo caso Σ avrebbe errato, mentre in altri vicini luoghi (Σ Ran. 1211, 1320, 1328) ha scritto correttamente Ὑψιπύλη. Quindi l'argomento spesso addotto, della frequenza di parodie dell'Ipsipile nelle Rane (anzi soltanto nelle Rane),[21] finisce col diventare negativo.

γ) L'errore grafico—per chi voglia ancora ammetterlo—potrebbe spiegare lo scambio, ma non l'aggiunta τῆς ἐν Αὐλίδι: che, naturalmente Σ, dopo avere sbagliato, avrebbe aggiunto suo Marte.

Gli editori della Ipsipile, infatti, sono stati in genere più cauti.[22] E anche noi, per concludere, riteniamo che i versi siano una citazione testuale dall'Ifigenia in Aulide[23]: che essi non siano nel testo attuale della tragedia, deriva dalle vicende che essa ha subito.

11) Ra. 1396   ΔI. πειθὼ δὲ κοῦφόν ἐστι καὶ νοῦν οὐκ ἔχον.

Ba. 270 sq.   TEI. θράσει δὲ δυνατὸς καὶ λέγειν οἷός τ' ἀνὴρ
                         κακὸς πολίτης γίγνεται νοῦν οὐκ ἔχων.

12) Ra. 1400. EY. βέβληκ' Ἀχιλλεὺς δύο κύβω καὶ τέτταρα.[24]

Anche questo verso costituisce un difficile rebus. Ma anzitutto, sia esso pronunziato da Euripide o da Dioniso (la tradizione è incerta), è sicuro

[19] De parodia in comoediis Aristophanis (Utrecht 1877), 167 sq.

[20] Il Blaydes, op. cit. 466, dà altri esempi di simili, ma non tutti convincenti, scambi grafici.

[21] Vedi Schlesinger, art. cit. p. 312 nota 11; Prato, op. cit. p. 122; Rau, op. cit. 216.

[22] Il Nauck TGF² p. 639 pur ritenendo probabile l'ipotesi dell'Ipsipile, assegna i versi al frg. 856 "incertarum fabularum"; H. von Arnim, Supplementum Euripideum (Bonn 1913), pubblica solo i frammenti di tradizione diretta (tranne frg. 752 N²); G. Italie, Euripidis Hypsipyla (Berlin 1923), 57 accetta l'ipotesi del Van de Sande Bakhuyzen e comprende frg. 856 N² fra quelli dell'Ipsipile; U. Scatena, Studio sulla Ipsipile euripidea (Roma 1934), non fa menzione di detto frammento; G. W. Bond, Euripides Hypsipyle (Oxford 1963, rist. 1969), pur ritenendo verisimile (p. 140) l'ipotesi del Van de Sande Bakhuyzen, colloca il frammento fra i "dubia" (p. 52); dubita dell'Ipsipile H. J. Mette, "Euripides. Die Bruchstücke," Lustrum 12 (1967), p. 260, 1080?? P. Pucci infine, Aristofane ed Euripide: ricerche metriche e stilistiche (Atti Accad. Naz. Lincei, Memorie S. VIII, Vol. X, 5, Roma 1961), 389, si limita a osservare che i versi derivano "senza dubbio...da un dramma euripideo perduto."

[23] Cfr. sopra, nota 8.

[24] Il verso non è preso in esame dal Carrière.

che appartiene ad Euripide (nonostante alcuni dubbi, per cui vedi qui innanzi). Dalle varie fonti compendiate in Σ apprendiamo:

a) Euripide:

1) *Telefo* (ma da un episodio di *Telefo* I che il poeta avrebbe soppresso in *Telefo* II, perché messo in ridicolo dai comici: cfr. Eustath. p. 1084,2; 1397,19; Zenob. II 85)[25];

2) *Filottete*

3) *Ifigenia in Aulide.*

b) Eschilo, *Mirmidoni*

c) invenzione scherzosa di Aristofane,[26] secondo Aristarco il quale φησὶν ἀδεσπότως τοῦτο φέρεσθαι. Σ aggiunge che il verso era noto ad Eupoli (frg. 342 inc. fab. K. ἀποφθαρεὶς δὲ δύο κύβω καὶ τέτταρα).

Da quanto sopra si può concludere soltanto, ripetiamo, che il verso è di Euripide[27]: la ipotesi più probabile sembra il *Telefo*; come potrebbe confermare il verso di Eupoli, che difficilmente avrebbe potuto riferirsi alla *I.A.*[28]

13) Il Carrière,[29] pur approvando l'opinione di Éd. Delebecque[30] secondo il quale nel Dioniso delle *Ba.* sarebbero elementi allusivi alla ambigua personalità di Alcibiade,[31] non ritiene[32] che possa trarsi frutto,

---

[25] Di questo *Telefo* II (non segnalato da alcun'altra fonte) non fanno parola i moderni: per es. Schmid, *op. cit.* III 352 sq.; E. W. Handley-F. Rea, *The Telephus of Eur.*, Bull. Inst. Cl. Stud., U. London, Suppl. No. 5, 1957; T. B. L. Webster, *The tragedies of Eur.* (London 1967), 43 sg.

[26] A questa opinione si associa lo Schlesinger, *art. cit.* 307.

[27] Frg. 888 N² inc. fab.: cfr. Phot., *Lex.* p. 602, 11; *Lex. Sud.* s. τρὶς ἕξ.

[28] L'ultima data sicura è il 412 (*Demi*), dopo la quale manca ogni altra notizia: Schmid, *op. cit.* IV 112,14; 113. L'allusione a *I.A.* sarebbe a v. 195 sqq. (Protesilao e Palamede giocano ai dadi). Ma è più probabile che, tanto in Euripide quanto in Eupoli, si tratti di espressioni indipendenti, prese quasi proverbialmente (insieme con altre simili: cfr. Blaydes, *op. cit.* 482) dal gioco dei dadi: da intendere quindi in senso "metaforico" (Rau, *op. cit.* 121,12: il quale però attribuisce a torto al Fritzsche [*op. cit.* 425] l'opinione che il verso non sia euripideo). Il Radermacher, *op. cit.* 333, pensa a una tragedia euripidea già perduta per i grammatici alessandrini.

[29] *Art. cit.* 131 sgg.

[30] *Eur. et la guerre du Péloponnèse* (Paris 1951), 396–99.

[31] In verità il Delebecque, *op. cit.*, *ibid.*, trova elementi allusivi ad Alcibiade, più ancora che in Dioniso e in Cadmo, in Penteo (per il quale, a proposito della metafora del leone, il Delebecque cita *Ba.* 990, 1018 sq., 1173, 1196, 1215, 1278). Cosa poco credibile per il fatto che il Penteo-leone è vittima di Dioniso: anche se, col Delebecque, si interpreti la morte di Penteo-leone non come una ovviamente impossibile allusione a quella di Alcibiade, ma come una specie di morte politica e simbolica del personaggio, "un adieu du poète (Euripide) à celui dont il déplore l'échec, la fuite, la retraite en un pays barbare" (398).

[32] Adducendo anche l'osservazione di J. Hatzfeld, *Alcibiade* (Paris 1951), 331,1, che *Ra.* 1431a è tutt'altro che sicuro. Questo argomento però non è valido perché la tradizione

a confermarli, dalla metafora del leone impiegata da entrambi i poeti (*Ra.* 1431 sq., *Ba.* 1215). E quale che sia il giudizio sul parallelo Dioniso-Alcibiade, a noi sembra in verità poco probabile che Aristofane, impiegando la metafora Alcibiade-leone, abbia voluto, in tal modo, alludere al Dioniso (-Alcibiade)-leone delle *Ba.*

A questi luoghi possiamo aggiungere:

14) *Ra.* 354 XO. εὐφημεῖν χρή ~ *Ba.* 69 sq. XO. στόμα τ᾽ εὔφημον ἅπας ἐξοσιούσθω: proprio l'incontro nella formola rituale è significativo.

15) *Ra.* 399 sq.   XO. Ἴακχε πολυτίμητε, μέλος ἑορτῆς
                        ἥδιστον εὑρών, κτλ.

    Ba. 140   XO. ὁ δ᾽ ἔξαρχος βρόμιος,³³ εὐοῖ.

16) *Ra.* 404 = 410, 416. XO. Ἴακχε φιλοχορευτά.

Sarebbe lungo citare tutti i luoghi delle *Ba.* in cui Dioniso è φιλοχορευτής: ricordiamo v. 21, 63, 114, 132, 184, 195, 205, 207, etc. etc.

17) *Ra.* 477. AIA. Γοργόνες Τειθράσιαι ~ *Ba.* 990. XO. Γοργόνων Λιβυσσᾶν γένος.³⁴

L'allusione (rinforzata dal verbo: cfr. sopra, no. 6) è—direi—evidente; e chiaramente nonché irriverentemente parodistica, in quanto sono proprio le Gorgoni a provocare la solita... effusione di paura in Dioniso. Le terribili Gorgoni libiche qui diventano "Titrasie," cioè di casa, alla buona³⁵; e per giunta ridicolizzate col richiamo a quei "fichi titrasi,"

---

manoscritta è incerta, e quindi vario il giudizio degli editori e critici: l'espunzione di 1431b rimonta al Brunck seguito da Invernizi, Bekker, Bergk, Kock, Meineke, Van de Sande Bakhuyzen, Blaydes, Van Leeuwen, Hall-Geldart, Radermacher; anche per H. J. Mette, *Die Fragmente der Tragödien des Aischylos* (Berlin 1959), ad frg. 608 [nulla nell'*Anhang* in *Lustrum* 13 (1968): ma cfr. Rau, *op. cit.* 123,17] il 1431a (scil. b) è uno "Zusatzvers"; ma Coulon e Stanford espungono invece 1431a; mentre Fritzsche e von Velsen conservano entrambi i versi (attribuendo 1431a ad Eschilo, 1431b a Dioniso, 1432 a Eschilo), e così ho fatto io stesso nella mia edizione (*Aristophanis comoediae* V [Milano 1964]), ma attribuendo 1431b ad Euripide, secondo suggerisce Σᵛ ᴬˡᵈ 1432. Comunque, quale che dei due versi si espunga, la metafora Alcibiade-leone rimane.

³³ Su questo e altri singolari aspetti del Dioniso nelle *Baccanti*, vedi il mio articolo "Precedenti della teoria aristotelica sulle origini della tragedia," in corso di pubblicazione in *Scritti in onore di V. De Falco* (Napoli 1971).

³⁴ Cfr. Eur. frg. 383 N² (= *Ra.* 470–477); Mette, *Euripides* cit. 125; Schlesinger, *art. cit.* 304; Prato, *op. cit.* 121; Rau, *op. cit.* 115 sg. Sulle Gorgoni, cfr. Preller-Robert, *Griech. Mythol.* I⁴ (Berlin 1894), 191–93; M. P. Nilsson, *Gesch. d. griech. Rel.* I² (München 1955; non ho sotto mano l'ed.³ 1967), 225–28.

³⁵ Σ 477 ἀπὸ δήμου τῆς Ἀττικῆς πονηροῦ. οὐκ εἰκῇ δὲ τοῦτο εἶπεν, ἀλλ᾽ ἐοίκασι τὸν δῆμον τοῦτον διαβάλλειν ὡς κακοπράγμονα. Il demo, della tribù Egeide, prendeva nome dall'eroe Tithras figlio di Pandione. L'altra spiegazione di Σ 477 di derivare "Titrasie" da

famosi per la loro dolcezza e certamente ben noti ad ogni spettatore ateniese.[36]

18) *Ra.* 966. *EY. σαρκασμοπιτνοκάμπται* potrebbe contenere una scherzosa allusione al Dioniso che in *Ba.* 1068 sq. *κλῶν' ὄρειον...χεροῖν ἄγων / ἔκαμπτεν ἐς γῆν.* [37]

Ricordiamo infine alcuni temi che, pur non comportando riscontri testuali, ricorrono con varia frequenza in entrambe le opere.

19) Dioniso-toro. *Ra.* 357 *Κρατίνου τοῦ ταυροφάγου γλώττης Βακχεῖ':* cioè Cratino identificato con lo stesso dio della ispirazione drammatica: come conferma *Σ* ad loc., il quale cita Soph. frg. 607 N² *Διονύσου τοῦ Ταυροφάγου;* Taurofago era lo stesso Dioniso in quanto, secondo una frequente ambivalenza, vittima e simbolo del dio-toro,[38] quale appare già dal famoso canto delle donne Elee (*PMG* frg. 871/25 Page). Non occorre ricordare che il Dioniso delle *Ba.*, invocato anche come serpente e leone (v. 1017 sq.) è anzitutto toro: cfr. v. 100, 618, 743, 920–22, 1017, 1159, 1185 e E. R. Dodds, *Euripides Bacchae²* (Oxford 1960), XVIII–XX.

20) È frequente nelle *Ra.*, particolarmente verso la fine, cioè alla decisione della scelta fra i due poeti da parte di Dioniso, il motivo della *σωτηρία τῆς πόλεως*[39]: e il dio salva la città riportandovi Eschilo e lasciando Euripide nell'Ade. Ma è interessante osservare, ad indicare l'importanza che il motivo ha per il poeta, il fatto che esso appare esplicitamente già nella parodos, con l'invocazione alla *Σώτειρα...ἣ τὴν χώραν / σώζειν φήσ' ἐς τὰς ὥρας* (379 sqq.), rinforzata subito dopo dalla

---

Τίθρασος, luogo o fiume di Libia (anche in *Lex. Sud.* s. *Τιθράσιαι Γοργόνες, Τίθρασος*) di cui manca qualsiasi altra menzione, è l'evidente ma significativo autoschediasma di uno che ricordava le Gorgoni libiche di Euripide. Il Blaydes, *op. cit.* 297, annota "fortasse pro tragico *Γοργόνες Λιβυστικαί* positum."

[36] Theopomp. frg. 11 (I p. 736 K.).

[37] Cfr. Schmid, *op. cit.* III 676,6; il quale, pur dubbiosamente, avanza l'ipotesi che il *πιτυοκάμπτης* di Cratin. frg. 296 K.E. (= frg. 138 Meineke II 217) sia Dioniso. Se il frammento, come congettura il Meineke (il quale già richiama *Ba.* 1064 sq. *λαβὼν γὰρ ἐλάτης οὐράνιον ἄκρον κλάδον / κατῆγεν, ἦγεν, ἦγεν ἐς μέλαν πέδον*), appartiene alla *Πυτίνη* dell'a. 423), si verrebbe a istituire un rapporto sommamente interessante Cratino-Euripide-Aristofane.

[38] Preller-Robert, *op. cit.* I⁴ 713; su Dioniso-toro (e gli altri aspetti animaleschi del dio), vedi H. Jeanmaire, *Dionysos* (Paris 1951), 249 sgg.; K. Kerényi, *Der frühe Dionysos* (Oslo 1961), 24 (di origine cretese, connesso col culto minoico del toro), 31.

[39] Cfr. Schmid, *op. cit.* IV p. 353 e n. 2, il quale cita *Ra.* 1419 sqq., 1427, 1433, 1436, 1458, 1487 sqq., 1501; e vedi anche v. 1448, 1530, innanzi, nota 49. Ma è superfluo ricordare che questo della *σωτηρία πόλεως* nei suoi vari aspetti è veramente il pensiero dominante di Aristofane, in tutta la sua opera.

preghiera a Demetra, patrona del coro degli iniziati (v. 388): σῷζε τὸν
σαυτῆς χορόν.

Anche nelle *Ba.* la polis dev'essere salvata: ma qui, invece, proprio
contro il dio che, ispirando nelle donne la sua nuova νόσος (v. 353 sg.), le
travolge nelle folli orge montane a disertare i talami e i focolari (v. 217):
distruggendo cioè la polis, creazione degli uomini.[40] Ed è soltanto un
feroce sarcasmo che proprio Dioniso si offra σωτήριος (v. 806, 965) a
Penteo, in quella sinistra scena della vestizione e del delirio, per condurlo,
umiliata e vacillante [41] vittima di un ingeneroso inganno, verso lo σπαραγμός rituale.[42]

Connesso con Dioniso è, in entrambe le opere, il motivo della meta-
morfosi e del travestimento. Oltre il dio-animale (toro: vedi sopra, no. 19;
ma anche serpente e leone), abbiamo nelle *Ba.* il dio-uomo, messo in ceppi
in una oscura stalla, e infine il dio vero, nella terribile e insieme benefica
maestà della sua potenza (v. 859–61 *ΔI.*)

> γνώσεται δὲ τὸν Διὸς
> Διόνυσον, ὃς πέφυκεν ἐν τέλει θεός,
> δεινότατος, ἀνθρώποισι δ'ἠπιώτατος.

E il travestimento femminile, a cui il dio induce Penteo, è appunto
l'aspetto esteriore della presa di possesso, da parte del dio, di Penteo
invano riluttante e già preda della follia dionisiaca.[43] Nelle *Ra.*, Dioniso
fin dal principio appare sulla scena in un composito buffo travestimento:
la lunga veste femminile color giallo-zafferano, con i coturni; e, sopra,
la pelle di leone caratteristica di Eracle, con la clava (v. 46 sg.) [44]; onde

---

[40] Cfr. *Ba.* 216 (*ΠΕ.*) νεοχμὰ τήνδ' ἀνὰ πτόλιν κακά e v. 360 sq., 1295, 1368–70.
Onde—dall'altra parte—chi, come Penteo, si oppone a Dioniso, non soltanto è θεομάχος,
ma (v. 270 sq.) stolto e κακὸς πολίτης γίγνεται νοῦν οὐκ ἔχων (cfr. la frase ironica di
Dioniso, v. 963, e sopra, no. 11): perciò Penteo è stato paragonato al Creonte dell'
Antigone (Schmid, *op. cit.* III 679). Cfr. anche Winnington-Ingram, *op. cit.* 96 sg., 158.

[41] Per la precisione clinica nella descrizione del menadismo e della follia di Penteo,
vedi in particolare S. Musitelli, "Riflessi di teorie mediche nelle Baccanti di Euripide,"
Dioniso 42 (1968 [1969]), 93–114.

[42] Per lo σπαραγμός (e relativa ὠμοφαγία) e in generale per la natura della religione
dionisiaca, vedi le sostanziose pagine del Dodds, *op. cit.* XI–XX (e il commento ai
luoghi relativi), nonché, dello stesso,"Maenadism in the Bacchae," *Harv. Theol. Rev.*
33 (1940), 155 (rist., con alcune correzioni e aggiunte, come Appendice I, al vol. *The
Greeks and the Irrational*, Berkeley 1951, trad. it. Firenze 1959).

[43] Sul cosiddetto elemento comico di questa scena, lo Schmid, *op. cit.* III 676,2, osserva
giustamente che essa è tenuta invece sul filo di una tragica ironia; e conserva altresì un
elemento rituale, per cui cfr. il commento del Dodds a v. 854 sq. Sul travestimento, cfr.
Carrière, *art. cit.* 120,8.

[44] Questo travestimento allude (con l'indumento femminile: lo stesso col quale il
dio appare nella epifania finale delle *Ba.*, cfr. Carrière, *art. cit.* 132, 71) e insieme mette

suscita l'inestinguibile riso di Eracle (v. 42 sg.), al quale va a chiedere consiglio per il viaggio agl'inferi. E come se questo non bastasse, scambia vestito col servo Xantia, ogni volta che c'è da evitare una situazione pericolosa. A suo modo, anche la commedia ricordava così il caratteristico metamorfismo del dio: che, in forma realistica e visibile, quasi allegorizzava (e spiegava) la trasformazione dall'iniziale Dioniso φιλευριπίδης nel Dioniso fileschileo della conclusione.

Ma più ancora di questi particolari, pur interessanti e significativi, importa il fatto della costante presenza scenica, dal principio alla fine in entrambe le opere, di Dioniso come protagonista.[45]

* * *

Siamo così di fronte a un complesso di fatti, di vario peso e di varia importanza, ma concorrenti tutti a permetterci di affermare, in piena sicurezza, che quando Aristofane componeva le *Rane*, conosceva certamente le *Baccanti*, alle quali alludeva con molti e molteplici riferimenti. Si pone così il problema del significato di questo presenza di Dioniso sulla scena, tragica e comica, di Atene negli anni 406–405; e delle conseguenze che ne derivano nella valutazione del rapporto Euripide-Aristofane. Presenza che se poi fosse del tutto casuale, cioè non deliberata e intenzionale da parte di Aristofane, sarebbe forse ancora più indicativa: ma che, anche collocata nel quadro del dimostrato incontro, non cessa perciò di essere un fatto importante e significativo; anche se Dioniso, sulla scena tragica e comica del sec. V, non era una novità.[46]

---

in rilievo (per contrasto col valore di Eracle) la viltà spesso dimostrata dal dio nella commedia: Dioniso δειλός, del resto, non era nuovo in commedia, come attesta Σ Aristoph. *Pax* 740 che richiama il precedente di Eupoli (così Schmid, *op. cit.* IV 134,10) o piuttosto di Cratino frg. 308 K.; o forse di entrambi, ricordati nominatamente dallo scoliasta.

[45] Presenza la quale, nelle *Ra.*, assicura perfettamente la "unità" dell'opera: cfr. C. P. Segal, *art. cit.* (sopra, n. 1). Ma sia detto di passaggio che questa dell' "unità" è una insussistente e caratteristica preoccupazione di filologi razionalisti ma digiuni dei principi elementari di estetica, che spesso si perdono in discussioni inutili (valga per tutta la "querelle" sulla unità dell'*Aiace*).

[46] Per i precedenti di Dioniso tragico, vedi la cit. edizione del Dodds, XXVIII–XXXIII. Ai quali si possono utilmente aggiungere i seguenti precedenti comici (limitati alla ἀρχαία), i quali comunque confermano il valore di tale presenza: Magnes, *Dioniso*; Ecfantide, *Dioniso* (?: cfr. Meineke I p. 37); Cratino, *Dionisalessandro*; Cratete, *Dioniso*; Aristomene, *Dioniso ἀσκητής*; Lisippo, *Baccanti*; Eupoli, *Tassiarchi*; Amipsia, Ἀποκοτταβίζοντες; Platone, Ζεὺς κακούμενος, Ξάντριαι; Polizelo, *La nascita di Dioniso*; Diocle, *Baccanti*;

L'argomento delle *Ba.* (un episodio della "storia sacra" di
Dioniso la quale celebrava l'irresistibile marcia trionfale del dio
in Grecia e mostrava la crudele punizione dei θεομάχοι invano
oppostisi, come Licurgo, Megapente, le Pretidi: qui Penteo, re di
Tebe, patria della madre del dio) fu naturalmente una scelta
autonoma dell'uomo Euripide, nella quale l'intima aspirazione etica
e religiosa della travagliata anima trovò una perfetta espressione
drammaturgica e poetica: sulla quale scelta, una volta avvenuta per
cause del tutto soggettive, poterono anche influire alcuni elementi di
un culto menadico-estatico particolarmente vivo in quella Macedonia
dove, sul finire della vita del poeta,[47] l'opera fu composta; ma in
vista della rappresentazione ad Atene, cioè destinata appunto al
pubblico ateniese.[48] E non è da pensare che il poeta, pur lontano e
deliberatamente esule, si fosse straniato dalla sua città, alla cui vita
spirituale aveva così intensamente partecipato e della quale era
stato egli stesso una delle espressioni più significative e originali.
E molte erano in Atene le cause che turbavano la vita della polis e
gli animi dei cittadini: la lunga e rovinosa guerra, l'esiziale epidemia
e la morte di Pericle, il disastro di Sicilia, l'incapacità della dirigenza
politica e la demagogia sempre più radicale, la corruzione e
l'incompetenza, le defezioni degli alleati, la vana aspirazione di
molti alla pace nella sensazione della fine oramai imminente.[49]

Aristofane (?), ⟨*Dioniso?*⟩ *naufrago* (cfr. *Aristophanis comoediae. Prolegomena*, § 265,
13 bis, p. 154). Sul Dioniso comico in generale cfr. C. Pascal, *Dioniso* (Catania 1911),
25–67. Nel dramma satiresco, bastava il coro ad assicurare l'elemento dionisiaco, anche
senza la presenza scenica del dio; comunque, abbiamo: Pratina, *Satiri palestriti*; Eschilo,
Polifrasmon, Timocle, *Licurgo*; Eschilo, *Theoroi e Nutrici* ⟨di Dioniso⟩; Cheremone,
Dioniso; Sofocle, Διονυσίσκος. Non occorre ricordare che, secondo la nota tradizione,
i σάτυροι scenici rappresentavano la restaurazione dell'elemento dionisiaco scomparso
dalla tragedia.

[47] Naturalmente, Euripide non poteva sapere che sarebbe morto poco dopo: è quindi
fuori luogo ogni speculazione (di sapore piuttosto cristianeggiante), su una religiosa
meditazione nell'approssimarsi della morte. Ma rimane il fatto che l'esperienza delle
Ba. si colloca nel tratto discendente, se non terminale, della vita del poeta; che già da
molto tempo, del resto, aveva mostrato interesse all'aspetto estatico-iniziatico della
religione e al "demoniaco" della passione d'amore (nei *Cretesi*, per cui cfr. R. Cantarella,
Euripide. I Cretesi (Milano 1964), 66–69; 127 sgg.; la tragedia è dell'a. 433 circa, cfr. *op.
cit.* 107).

[48] Come ricorda opportunamente Winnington-Ingram, *op. cit.* 151,1; cfr. Dodds,
op. cit. XL, 1.

[49] Onde, nelle *Ra.*, il motivo della σωτηρία τῆς πόλεως (cfr. sopra, no. 20); v. 361
XO. τῆς πόλεως χειμαζομένης, v. 704 *XO.* τὴν πόλιν καὶ ταῦτ' ἔχοντες κυμάτων ἐν ἀγκάλαις.

Queste e molte altre cause negli ultimi anni si erano venute aggravando nella psicosi della guerra e dell'assedio, e molte manifestazioni denunziavano il turbamento generale nel decadimento politico, religioso e morale:[50] il favore incontrato dai culti orgiastici stranieri di recente introdotti in città (Sabazio, Adone, Magna Mater, Bendis, Attis, Cotyttò); la mutilazione delle erme e la sacrilega parodia dei misteri; i processi di empietà (Aspasia, Anassagora, Diagora: fra poco il processo e la condanna di Socrate), le feroci repressioni contro gli alleati insorti e la paura,[51] il tristo processo contro i comandanti vittoriosi alle Arginuse. E, con la morte di Euripide e di Sofocle a pochi mesi di distanza, la fine della tragedia: anzi della poesia drammatica, poiché le *Rane* segnano appunto la fine della grande commedia ateniese.

Che cosa vuol dire questa ventata dionisiaca, che, pur con le ovvie amplificazioni poetiche,[52] squassava le anime (femminili, in particolare) in un turbine di follia, travolgendole incoscienti ed ebbre nel felice stato di natura di un paradiso perduto; in un mondo lontano e immemore di ogni vincolo familiare e sociale, antico come l'orda primitiva; nella incolpevole crudeltà di sanguinosi riti ferini? Che cosa vuol dire, nell'anima del poeta e nella vita ateniese della fine del secolo?

Ovviamente, non è questo il luogo non solo di affrontare ma

[50] Si ricordi il mirabile capitolo (II 53) nel quale Tucidide descrive i disastrosi guasti, nella morale, prodotti dalla moria.

[51] Vedi la interessante notazione di Xenoph. *Hell.* II 2,3: "Quella notte (dopo che la Paralo ebbe recato in Atene la notizia della disfatta di Egospotamo: Boedromione a. 405) nessuno dormì, non soltanto perché piangevano i morti, ma ancor più essi piangevano se stessi, pensando di dover soffrire quel che essi avevano fatto ai Meli, coloni degli Ateniesi, quando l'avevano presa dopo l'assedio; e a quelli di Istica, di Scione, di Torone, di Egina, e a molti altri Greci."

[52] Il Dodds, *op. cit.* XXII (XIX,[1] 1944) rileva opportunamente che, all'epoca delle *Ba.*, il menadismo in Atene aveva oramai perduto, o quasi del tutto attenuato, il carattere orgiastico (con i relativi riti: ὀρειβασία etc.); e Winnington-Ingram, *op. cit.* 151, osserva che l'estasi era scomparsa dal culto ateniese di Dioniso e che le donne ateniesi, nei riti, non portavano tirsi ma canestri. Entrambi però mettono in rilievo l'incremento, dovuto alle condizioni psicologiche, di culti orgiastici non soltanto stranieri e della superstizione; e, pur senza sopravvalutarlo, il significato della composizione in Macedonia. E già lo Jeanmaire, *op. cit.* 163-67, pur parlando di un "renouveau dionysiaque à Athènes au Vᵉ siècle" (documentabile anche coi risultati di una interessante ricerca archeologica della Lawler sulla frequenza e sugli aspetti delle rappresentazioni figurate delle menadi nella ceramica attica), prospettava la possibilità che, in Atene, Dioniso avesse lasciato "atrofizzare" (166) i caratteri orgiastici ed estatici della sua personalità.

nemmeno di toccare appena l'annosa e complessa questione del significato delle *Ba.* e del valore del suo "messaggio": su cui riteniamo di poter mantenere l'interpretazione che, pur succintamente, ne abbiamo dato in altra sede.[53] Ma, comunque le *Ba.* vadano interpretate, rimane significativa, nella vita ateniese della fine del secolo, la presenza di elementi e di fatti contrastanti, quando non inconciliabili—si direbbe—nella medesima realtà. Ed è chiaro altresì che, sul clima illuministico-razionalistico del periodo anassagoreo-pericleo dominante nei primi decenni della seconda metà, viene prevalendo verso la fine del secolo—soprattutto per effetto della guerra e nella consapevolezza della sconfitta—uno stato d'animo irrazionale e quasi miracolistico (la città ridotta a sperare salvezza da Alcibiade, ovvero dal governo delle donne!), in cui vigoreggiano smisurate ambizioni, amare delusioni, oscure superstizioni. Tutte queste contraddizioni, operanti nella vita della polis, si riflettono senza dubbio nell'anima del poeta, già tanto travagliata da propri interiori dissidi, e lasciano traccia nelle sue opere ultime.[54] Onde, come il loro dio, le *Baccanti* hanno molti e contraddittori aspetti.

* * *

Quale fu, dunque, l'aspetto che in esse vide, o volle vedere, Aristofane, per quanto ce ne possono dire le *Rane*?[55] La cosa può

[53] *La letteratura greca classica*[2] (Firenze-Milano 1967), 308–310. Fra le cose più recenti e più equilibrate, vedi (oltre gli autori già citati in queste note): H. Diller, "Die Bakchen u. ihre Stellung im Spätwerk des E." *Akad. Wiss. u. Lit. Mainz, Abhandl.* 1955, Nr. 5 p. 453–71 = *Euripides*, hrsgg. von E.-R Schwinge (Darmstadt 1968), 469–92; Th. G. Rosenmeyer, "Tragedy and religion: the Bacchae," in *The mask of tragedy* (Univ. of Texas Press 1963) = E. Segal, *Euripides. A collection of critical essays* (Englewood Cliffs, N.J. 1968), 150–70 (lievemente abbreviato); A. Lesky, *Die tragische Dichtung der Hellenen*[2] (Göttingen 1964), 199 sg. (con bibl.); T. B. L. Webster, *The Tragedies of E.* (London 1967), 268–77.

[54] Alla base del dramma regale e familiare della *I.A.* c'è un fatto di superstizione religiosa (cfr. v. 520 sq., 746–48).

[55] Anche qui, naturalmente, non è il caso di una interpretazione totale delle *Rane*: che, per sommi capi, abbiamo dato in *op. cit.* V (1964), 13–23 = *Aristofane. Le commedie*, trad. e presentate da R. Cantarella (Milano 1970), 563–76. Fra le cose recenti più notevoli, oltre la raccolta di saggi (nota 1) citata e gli autori ricordati in queste note: H.-J. Newiger, *Metapher u. Allegorie. Studien zu A.* (Zetemata 16, München 1957); C. F. Russo, *I due teatri di A.* (Firenze 1958); Th. Gelzer, *Der epirrhematische Agon bei A.* (Zetemata 23, München 1960); O. Seel, *A. oder Versuch über Komödie* (Stuttgart 1960); C. F. Russo,

riuscire interessante come la testimonianza della più antica (contemporanea) valutazione polemica delle *Ba.*, e quindi per l'atteggiamento di Aristofane verso Euripide negli ultimi anni.

L'opinione del Carrière in proposito si può riassumere nelle parole con le quali si chiude il citato articolo (p. 138 sg.): "Les *Bacchantes*, pièce faussement religieuse et pièce à thèse, pour ne pas dire pièce à clé, chargeaient durement Dionysos. Le bonhomme Dionysos des *Grenouilles*, non plus que bien d'autres bonshommes d'Athènes, ne s'en était clairement avisé. Aristophane, lui, l'avait vu, et nous l'a fait entendre à mots couverts."[56] Euripide, dunque, sarebbe rimasto ateo fino all'ultimo e, con le *Ba.*, avrebbe messo gli Ateniesi in guardia contro l'Irrazionale (Dioniso) in agguato che minacciava la civile e illuminata Atene. E Aristofane, secondo questa interpretazione, sarebbe stato il primo degli "anticonversionisti", senza farsi ingannare dalla falsa pietà di Euripide, che egli anzi, pur copertamente, denunziava ai suoi concittadini.

Senza entrare nel dibattuto "enigma" della concezione religiosa delle *Ba.*, fra "palinodisti" e "anticonversionisti",[57] quel che è difficile spiegare nella pur acuta interpretazione del Carrière è il perché della "falsa" pietà di Euripide, della tragedia "falsamente" religiosa. Per quale motivo Euripide avrebbe nascosto sotto una apparenza di pietà la rappresentazione di una religiosità pericolosa per la polis, fino a rendere del tutto ambigua (come dimostra la storia della sua interpretazione) tale rappresentazione? Non certo la paura di una accusa ateniese di ἀσέβεια che, comunque, non avrebbe raggiunto l'esule in Macedonia: e l'empietà dell'opera non

---

Storia delle Rane di A. (Padova 1961); Id. *A. autore di teatro* (Firenze 1962); E. Fraenkel, *Beobachtungen zu A.* (Roma 1962); A. Pickard-Cambridge, T. B. L. Webster, *Dithyramb, tragedy and comedy*[2] (Oxford 1962); C. M. I. Sicking, *A. Ranae* (Assen 1962); W. Kassies, *A.' traditionalisme* (Amsterdam 1963); P. Händel, *Formen u. Darstellungsweisen in der aristophanischen Komödie* (Heidelberg 1963); C. H. Whitman, *A. and the Comic Hero* (Cambridge Mass. 1964); K. D. Kock, *Kritische Idee u. komisches Thema* (Bremen 1965); G. Wills, "Why are the Frogs in the Frogs?" *Hermes* 97 (1969), 306–317.

[56] Cfr. anche p. 124, 135–37 (il Dioniso di E. è la *mania* sempre rinascente, l'Irrazionale in agguato a distruggere, con i suoi assalti, i progressi dello spirito critico e delle società civili in via d'emancipazione); p. 138, n. 98 (il Carrière fa propria l'opinione del Dalmeyda che le *Ba.* hanno "un'apparenza di pietà").

[57] Per la quale ci riferiamo a quanto ne abbiamo scritto altrove: vedi sopra, nota 53, in principio.

sarebbe sfuggita—pensiamo—all'arconte che concesse il coro ad
Euripide jr. E se il Dioniso delle *Ba.* con i suoi crudeli riti e con la sua
vendetta vile e spietata insieme, il Dioniso-mania insomma,
costituiva un pericolo per la polis (Penteo), il poeta, con questa
denunzia, intendeva (o tentava almeno) di provvedere alla difesa
della città: e non si vede perché, in tal caso, egli avrebbe nascosto
la sua intenzione sotto tante e così contraddittorie ambiguità. In
realtà poi, come è stato osservato da varie parti,[58] sulla fine del V
secolo il culto di Dioniso in Atene aveva lasciato "atrofizzare" i
suoi aspetti più crudi e oramai repellenti: e sembra difficile, pertanto,
che esso costituisse per la polis quel pericolo che Euripide avrebbe—
così copertamente—denunziato.

A nostro avviso, Euripide non volle fare opera di propaganda, né
pro né contro Dioniso: e le *Ba.* non sono un dramma a tesi, in alcun
senso. La scelta della materia mosse anzitutto da un impulso del suo
spirito, da un bisogno della sua anima: e caratteristicamente
euripidea è la maniera di trattarla *in utramque partem.* Non perché
egli volesse proporre—agli Ateniesi del suo tempo ed ai filologi in
avvenire—un enigma: ma soprattutto perché il duplice aspetto del
dio (beatifico ai seguaci, spietato agli avversari [v. 861]: secondo una
tradizione che rimontava ben lontano e che nasceva dalla natura
stessa del dio) gli dava il modo di costruire uno splendido dramma
intorno a una figura divina ambiguamente fascinosa. Si potrebbe
dire—sotto la specie del paradosso—che il poeta veniva così a
rivelare il vero significato di questa figura divina:[59] in un momento nel
quale egli stesso—e i suoi concittadini, per le molte ragioni note—ne

[58] Vedi sopra, nota 52.

[59] Della *Licurgia* di Polyfrasmon nulla sappiamo, tranne la data (a. 476: insieme con
la tetralogia tebana di Eschilo). La perdita della *Licurgia* di Eschilo (non databile: cfr.
H.-J. Mette, *Die Fragmente der Tragödien des Aischylos* [Berlin 1959], 257) ci priva purtroppo
di un prezioso termine di confronto, perché molti elementi delle *Ba.* euripidee apparivano
già in essa (ancor meno sappiamo di una seconda [?] tetralogia dionisiaca, per cui cfr.
Mette, *op. cit.* 132 sgg.; delle *Baccanti* rimane solo frg. 52 M. di due versi): sembra però
che si trattasse piuttosto della contrapposizione fra il culto dionisiaco e l'apollineo
(forse con conciliazione, nel santuario di Delfi: cfr. Aesch. frg. 86 M., nel quale Apollo
è κισσεύς, βακχειόμαντις). A proposito del quale frammento eschileo è interessante
osservare che poi anche Euripide frg. 477 N² nel *Licimnio* (prima del 414?: Schmid,
Gesch. gr. Lit. III (1940), 462; fra le primissime opere, circa 455, secondo Webster,
op. cit. 32) identificherà Dionisò con Apollo, come attesta esplicitamente Macrob. *Sat.*
I 18, 6, che cita entrambi i frammenti (cfr. Mette, *Der verlorene Aischylos* (Berlin 1963),
139, 2). E nessuno, pensiamo, vorrà vedervi già una "conversione" del poeta.

sentivano particolarmente il fascino. Le *Ba.* dunque sono un dramma necessariamente ambiguo: in quanto tale è l'intima essenza del dio, e così—con intuito poeticamente esatto—il poeta la rappresentò.[60]

Se così stanno le cose, se Euripide cioè non solo non volle comporre, ma non compose una tragedia falsamente religiosa, perché mai Aristofane l'avrebbe ritenuta tale? Ed egli soltanto si sarebbe accorto di quello che era sfuggito non solo ai "bonshommes" ateniesi, ma allo stesso interessato, al "bonhomme Dionysos des *Grenouilles*"? E perché mai—soprattutto—in questo solo caso si sarebbe servito di "mots couverts", nel denunziare la "falsa" religiosità di Euripide, quell'Aristofane che tante volte, tanto apertamente e senza esclusione di colpi anche mancini, aveva accusato Euripide?

Poco infine convince anche il motivo politico che avrebbe indotto Aristofane alla cautela verso Alcibiade.[61] Dal famoso luogo di *Ra.* 1420–34 si rileva una cosa sola sicura: che il richiamo di Alcibiade si imponeva come il primo ($\pi\rho\hat{\omega}\tau\sigma\nu$: v. 1422) mezzo per la salvezza della città, e che egli aveva fautori e avversari egualmente decisi nella città; la quale tuttavia—in maggioranza, sembrerebbe— finiva col considerarlo un male necessario e inevitabile.[62] Seguono, alla precisa domanda di Dioniso, le opinioni dei due poeti: di aspra e recisa condanna, quella di Euripide;[63] impersonalmente gnomica e quasi conciliativa, quella di Eschilo.[64] Ma poiché Dioniso non sa decidere (v. 1433 $\delta\upsilon\sigma\kappa\rho\acute{\iota}\tau\omega\varsigma\ \gamma'\ \check{\epsilon}\chi\omega$) e se n'esce con un ambiguo gioco di parole (v. 1434 $\sigma\sigma\varphi\hat{\omega}\varsigma/\sigma\alpha\varphi\hat{\omega}\varsigma$), pur sembrando

---

[60] La sopra (nota 9) osservata insistenza sulla paternità di Zeus è significativa della tendenza ad inserire Dioniso fra i culti cittadini tradizionali.

[61] Secondo Carrière, *art. cit.* 139, 2: "Sa comédie prônait le retour d'Alcibiade. Il est donc possible qu'il n'ait pas voulu, par des allusions trop précises ou des rappels trop directs, trop visibles, réveiller chez les gens avertis le souvenir d'une pièce (le *Ba.*) qui peignait trop bien ce personnage sous les traits d'un cruel $\delta\alpha\acute{\iota}\mu\omega\nu$."

[62] È il significato del v. 1425 $\pi\sigma\theta\epsilon\hat{\iota}\ \mu\acute{\epsilon}\nu$ (scil. $\dot{A}\lambda\kappa\iota\beta\iota\acute{\alpha}\delta\eta\nu$), $\dot{\epsilon}\chi\theta\alpha\acute{\iota}\rho\epsilon\iota\ \delta\acute{\epsilon},\ \beta\sigma\acute{\upsilon}\lambda\epsilon\tau\alpha\iota\ \delta'\ \check{\epsilon}\chi\epsilon\iota\nu$, parodia di Jone frg. 44 N².

[63] Col vibrato $\mu\iota\sigma\hat{\omega}$ iniziale (v. 1427), per cui cfr. Schmid, *Gesch. gr. Lit.* IV, 353, 4.

[64] Sul testo di v. 1431–31a–32, vedi sopra, nota 32. In realtà, ci si attenderebbe il contrario: dunque, un estremo riguardo, da parte di Eschilo, verso il nobilissimo rampollo in cui confluivano Eupatridi e Alcmeonidi, verso il pupillo di Pericle? Ricorda che Agariste, poco prima della nascita di Pericle, aveva sognato di partorire un leone (Herodot. VI 131, Plut. *Per.* 3); e poco dopo (v. 1463–65) Eschilo fa proprio il noto consiglio di Pericle sulla condotta della guerra (per cui cfr. Thuc. I 143, II 23 e soprattutto II 55 sq.).

approvare piuttosto il consiglio di Eschilo,[65] l'opinione di Aristofane riguardo al richiamo di Alcibiade rimane deliberatamente incerta: vanificando così, in sostanza e non senza ironia, il quesito che egli stesso aveva posto come il più importante e il più urgente. Non sembrerebbe quindi—per concludere—che le *Ra.* esprimano (e tanto meno vogliano "prôner") una opinione chiaramente favorevole al richiamo di Alcibiade.[66]

* * *

Quale rimane, dunque, il senso—e il valore—di questo deliberato incontro di Aristofane con Euripide in Dioniso?

Il Dioniso delle *Ba.*—quale che sia stata l'intenzione o il risultato del poeta nel descriverne la figura—è, senza possibilità di dubbio, il dio dell'ebbrezza, dell'estasi e della follia; il dio dell'irrazionale, dei prodigi e dei miracoli; il dio che largisce beatitudini agli iniziati ma distrugge spietatamente gli empî; il dio che sovverte non pur la polis[67] ma le stesse leggi di natura: e per introdurre il proprio culto egli si serve soprattutto delle donne, sulle quali agisce con fascino irresistibile, riducendole in soggezione assoluta. Di tutto questo, il Dioniso delle *Ra.* è la perfetta e caricaturale antitesi: spaccone e vigliacco, donnaiuolo e pederasta, avaro e senza dignità, spergiuro e ghiottone; un pover'uomo insomma.[68] Onde si potrebbe dire—

---

[65] Per una equilibrata interpretazione di questo luogo, vedi Hatzfeld, *op. cit.* 329 sgg.

[66] Al quale, come uomo politico, sarebbe questa la prima allusione di A. (cfr. Schmid *Gesch. gr. Lit.* IV, 197, 7), poiché gli attacchi ad Alcibiade dai Ταγηνισταί (fra 415-400: cfr. P. Geissler, *Chronologie der altatt. Komödie* (= Philol. Untersuch. 30, Berlin 1925) 48, 83; poco prima o poco dopo il 406, secondo A. Meineke, *Frg. Com. Gr.* II 1 (1839), 1146) e del Τριφάλης (del 410: Geissler, *op. cit.* 59 sg., 83) avrebbero toccato soltanto l'uomo privato e i suoi costumi (sessuali): Schmid, *Gesch. gr. Lit.* IV, 425, 1; 438, 2. Cosa che in verità sembra poco credibile anche in generale, chi consideri il carattere globale dell' ὀνομαστὶ κωμῳδεῖν, e tenga conto dell'importanza politica dell'uomo, particolarmente dopo il 415. Comunque, nel Τριφάλης, che precede di pochi anni le *Ra.*, Alcibiade, sotto l'osceno trasparente (cfr. frg. 553, 554, 555) soprannome, era così pesantemente attaccato (per i suoi costumi, frg. 544; e non mancavano allusioni politiche: frg. 550, 551; particolarmente significativo frg. 549 per cui cfr. Σ *Ra.* 541) che sembra difficile vedere, nelle *Ra.* del 405, un sia pur coperto invito al suo richiamo.

[67] Anche se, come abbiamo osservato (sopra, note 9 e 60), il poeta, con l'insistere sulla paternità di Zeus, sembra volerne "costituzionalizzare" il culto.

[68] È questa la tesi di C. Pascal, *Dioniso. Religione e parodia religiosa in A.* (Catania 1911, il quale però si ferma a questo aspetto negativo), su cui vedi É. Lapalus, "Le Dionysus et l'Héraclès des Grenouilles," *Rev. ét. grecques* 47 (1934), 1-20 (trad. e lievemente abbreviato senza note nella raccolta del Littlefield sopra, nota 2, citata).

rovesciando piuttosto paradossalmente la conclusione del Carrière—
che Aristofane, poco dopo lo splendidamente ambiguo Dioniso
delle *Ba.*, ha voluto qui raffigurare il dio nella sua miseria, quasi a
mettere in guardia gli Ateniesi da un culto fascinoso e pericoloso,
mostrandone la faccia negativa per neutralizzare gli effetti del culto
orgiastico, estatico e maniaco. Per Aristofane, dunque, le *Ba.*
sarebbero state una tragedia veramente e pericolosamente religiosa.

Ma il Dioniso della *Ra.* è, in sostanza e soprattutto, il dio della
tragedia, cioè della ispirazione poetica: condizione reale e tradizionale
in Atene, almeno da quando—lasciando da parte la questione delle
origini—i concorsi drammatici e ditirambici erano stati inseriti da
Pisistrato nel rituale dionisiaco. Ed è in quanto dio della tragedia
che egli provvede alla salvezza della città in pericolo, scendendo
all'Ade per riportare alla luce il diletto Euripide...e risuscitando
invece Eschilo. Ma anche nel Dioniso delle *Ba.* c'è—sia pure in
molto minor grado—qualche cosa del Dioniso "tragico", nello
spirito—si potrebbe dire "nietzschiano"—della danza, della
musica e del canto.[69] Ed è qui forse che avviene l'incontro—non
l'unico[70]—fra Aristofane ed Euripide, di là dall'intenzione parodica,
che pur esiste, visibile soprattutto nei particolari ma che è piuttosto,
si direbbe, contingente e occasionale. La rappresentazione di
Dioniso, del resto, non è più irriverente di quelle che lo stesso poeta
ha fatto di Ermes, Poseidon, Eracle, Prometeo. Ma soltanto Dioniso,
pur in questa dimensione comica, adempie qui ad una funzione
essenziale, e, come dio del teatro, con la propria decisione provvede
alla salvezza della polis.[71]

[69] Vedi sopra, nota 33.

[70] Vedi il breve accenno che ho fatto in proposito in "Aristoph. 'Plut.' 422-425 e
le riprese eschilee," in *Rendic. Accad. Naz. Lincei*, S. VIII, vol. 20, fasc. 7-12 (1965),
379 e n. 72; "L'ultimo A.," in *Dioniso* 40 (1966), 35-42 (cfr. p. 39-41).

[71] Non è però accettabile la posizione del Lapalus, *art. cit.*, il quale, pur giustamente
affermando che Dioniso è qui introdotto come dio del teatro, conclude (Littlefield, p. 29)
che "*egli realmente è stato scelto da A. come eroe dell'opera perché il poeta, nell'evocare la memoria
della iniziazione mistica di Dioniso, poteva mettere in caricatura alcuni aspetti dei misteri eleusini.*"
A parte il fatto che nelle *Ra.*, a nostro avviso, non esiste alcuna caricatura (nemmeno
lontanamente allusiva o irriverente) dei misteri eleusini (i quali anzi, con il coro degli
iniziati, hanno nell'economia drammatica e nel clima religioso dell'opera una funzione
molto importante sulla quale non è qui il caso di soffermarsi), osta soprattutto la considerazione che non si poteva mettere in caricatura i misteri eleusini senza mettere in
caricatura lo stesso Dioniso-Iacco che da lungo tempo formava, con le dee di Eleusi,
una triade cultuale, anche se non si possa identificarla nel famoso gruppo d'avorio di

Il complesso Dioniso delle *Ra.*, dunque, è, nella prima parte, un uomo e per giunta di qualità morali molto scadenti; ma è pur sempre, e soprattutto nella seconda parte, un dio: il dio del teatro; che, per un Ateniese del V secolo, val quanto dire il dio della poesia della ispirazione poetica. Ed è qui che—oltre gli aspetti esteriori della divinità nelle due opere—Aristofane simbolicamente si incontra con Euripide. Finita la grande tragedia, il poeta comico ne assume l'eredità, anche "politica", sotto il segno dell'unico Dioniso: in quel dramma, nel quale Aristofane identificava l'essenza e il fastigio della civiltà ateniese.

Così, il disperato strazio di Agave e il gracidare dei batraci nella palude Acherusia compongono, insieme, il trionfale epicedio sul grande dramma attico del V secolo.

Milano, 27 febbraio 1970

Micene, per cui cfr. G. E. Mylonas, *Eleusis and the Eleusinian Mysteries* (Princeton 1961), 51 sg.; L. Palmer, *Mycenaeans and Minoans*[2] (London 1965), 135 sg., frg. 13; p. 92 e frg. XIII della traduz., *Minoici e Micenei* (Torino 1970). Sebbene tuttora incerta e discussa, una qualche parte, nei misteri, Dioniso l'aveva: cfr. M. Ventris–J. Chadwick, *Documents in Mycenaean Greek* (Cambridge 1957), 127, 242; C. Gallavotti, "Demetra micenea," *Parola Pass.* fasc. 55 (1957), 242–49; T. B. L. Webster, *From Mycenae to Homer* (London 1958) 43 sg., 118; Mylonas, *op. cit.* 238, 276–78; L. Deubner, *Attische Feste* (Berlin 1932 rist. 1956), 73; 83,2; Nilsson, *op. cit.* 599. Demetra, inoltre, era la dea di cui Eschilo, contro le nuove e particolari divinità euripidee, si professa devoto (*Ra.* 886 sq.: donde però non si può e non si deve dedurre, come troppo spesso si ripete, che Eschilo era iniziato ai misteri): il poeta cui Dioniso-Aristofane decreta la vittoria.

DE DUABUS RECENSIONIBUS BYZANTINIS ARISTOPHANIS

W. J. W. KOSTER

I

Quamquam in Aristophanis traditione byzantina enucleanda illo firmo auxilio destituti sumus, quod propter indefessos labores Turynii nobis in tragicis praesto est, tamen propriis viribus pedetemptim progredientes percipimus, quam frequenter et quam varia ratione in comici quoque dramatibus tractandis grammatici et scribae, qui saepe eodem nomine appellari possunt, Medii Aevi saeculis id egerint, ut, quae in exemplaribus prioribus legebant, suo iure et iudicio mutantes renovarent. Hoc, sicut in tragoediis, praesertim in eis dramatibus accidisse, quae adhuc lectitabantur, non est quod miremur; itaque trias byzantina *Plutum, Nubes, Ranas* amplectens et dyas *Pluti* et *Nubium* postremo selecta[1] primo loco variationi obnoxia erant; quae etiam magis ad commentarium quam ad textum pertinet.

Quam utilis illius investigatio sit ad recensiones separatas cognoscendas, idem Turyn saepius monuit,[2] ut neque eum neque alios huius materiae peritos gravaturos esse opiner, si in eis, quae sequuntur, me praesertim commentario, cui prolegomena adnumero,

---

[1] Sicut in dramatibus tragicorum, de quibus Turyn egit (ultimo loco *The Byzantine Manuscript Tradition of the Tragedies of Euripides* [Urbana 1957], p. 212 sq.), etiam in comici tradendis altera parte saeculi XV dyas (*Plutus* et *Nubes*) multis sufficere visa est. Huius generis maxime conspicua editio quaedam est novo commentario in praecedentibus nitenti munita, quae in magno numero codicum magna cum varietate traditur. De hac editione, cuius commentarium nomine *Scholiorum leidensium* ex eo codice qui eum uberrimum continet (Leid. B.P.G. 61c) sumpto designavi, iam obiter scripsi in *Mnemosyne*, S. IV Vol. XVII[2] (1964), p. 157, n. 1; Vol. XIX[4] (1966), p. 395; Vol. XX[2] (1967), 166 sq.; fusius de ea agam in editione scholiorum recentiorum in *Nubes*, quae mox prodibit.

[2] E.g. op. cit. p. 18: "the road to the identification of separate Byzantine recensions will lead through an analysis of the scholia."

contineam. Ex magno numero editionum separatarum earumque recensionum diversarum sive ab ipsis editoribus sive ab aliis originem ducentium duo exempla ultimi generis selegi, ex quibus alterum ad recensiones mixtas (sc. ubi editiones discrepantes coniunguntur, quibus recensionis auctor aut nihil aut pauca suo Marte intermiscet), alterum ad recensiones contaminatas (sc. quarum auctor larga manu et licenter componit, addit, omittit, mutat, quae sibi utilia videntur) illustrandas mihi aptum visum est.

II

Prioris exempli notitia plenior denuo Turynio accepta referenda est; is enim codicis **Vaticani Gr. 38** saec. XIV paginam in splendida illa imaginum phototypice confectarum codicum vaticanorum sylloga iterandam curavit,[3] ex qua quaedam de hoc triadis Aristophanis exemplari discimus, quae ad eius recensionem cognoscendam alicuius momenti sunt.[4] Praeterea hic codex primus inter aristophaneos

---

[3] *Codices graeci vaticani saeculis XIII et XIV scripti annorumque notis instructi* (in Civitate Vaticana 1964), Tab. 99, quae continet *Ran.* 680–701 cum scholiis et glossis.

[4] E.g. hic codex v. 684 in textu (l. 3 a fast.) et in lemmate (l. 15 a fast.) genuinam lectionem ἀηδόνιον falsae priori ἀηδόνειον adiungit, sicut Triclinius in editione priore, quam Par. Suppl. 463 continet, licet apud eum in textu solo, nam codices thomanotricliniani lemmatibus plerumque carent Vaticano 38 ea constanter adhibente; praeterea Vat. 38 in textu errans ἀηδόνιον priorem lectionem fecit ει super -ι- exarato (recte ιον super -ειον Triclinius). Illud ἀηδόνειον lectio Thomae Magistri erat in utraque editione (sic Cant. 1 = Cantabrigiensis Nn. 3, 15.1, prioris editionis codex, et F [Par. 2820], qui inter codices alterius est). In altera denique tricliniana, ex cuius codicibus praeter optimum, sed castigatum (v. infra) Vat. 1294 etiam M9 (Ambr. L 41 sup.) adhibui, textus rectam lectionem ἀηδόνιον solam exhibet adscripto διὰ τὸ μέτρον γράφεται ι τὸ νι et scholium ad h.v., quod ex codicibus editionis thomanae alterius T (Marcianus sive Venetus 472) et Cr (Cremonensis 171, antea 12229) sub n. 683 edidit C. O. Zuretti, *Scolii al Pluto ed alle Rane* (Torino 1890), p. 139, falso l. 3 scripto περὶ ἑαυτῆς pro περὶ ἑαυτοῦ et iniuria l. 4 καὶ inter [ ] posito, retractatum est. In tricliniana altera prima sententia evasit ἐπειδὴ ἡ ἀηδών, ὡς ὁ μῦθος φησί (enclisi, ut saepe, neglecta cuncti codd.), τὸν ἑαυτῆς υἱὸν Ἴτυν θρηνεῖ, καὶ τοῦτον ἐπίκλαυτον ᾄδειν λέγει, ἐπειδὴ κτλ. (fuerat ἡ γὰρ ἀηδών…θρηνεῖ· λέγει δὲ καὶ…ᾄδειν, ἐπειδὴ κτλ.). Tunc in fine inter ψῆφοι ἴσαι ἐγένοντο et τὴν δίκην ἀπέφευγε (l. 16 sq. a calce in Vat. 38) inserta est haec observatio: ἃς ἐν τῷ κάδ(δ)ῳ (-δδ- in Vat. 1294) καθίεσαν οἱ κριταί. Singulorum codicum errores, velut in Vat. 38 δεινότερον pro δεινότατα (l. 21 a fast.) et μέλαινες (l. 17 a calce), aliasque discrepantias minoris momenti omittens hoc tantum addo: scribam Vaticani 1294, ut solet, in commentario sermonem arbitratu suo ad normam severioris usus scribendi emendavisse (ὅτέ τις ἐκρίνετο pro ὅτάν τις ἐκρίνετο Vat. 38 (l. 19 sq. a calce) ceterique (enclisis in paroxytono, ut saepe); εἰ μὲν…ἐγένοντο pro ἂν μεν…ἐγένοντο Vat. 38 (l. 18–16 a calce) ceterique).—In v. 689 Thomas, ut Vat. 38 (l. 8 a fast.), παλαίσμασιν per glossam ἀγωνίσμασιν interpretatus est, cui

huius saeculi et praecedentium, quantum sciam, nota anni, quo scriba laborem ad finem perduxit (1322), insignitur. Licet in aliis poëtis, quos tradit, nempe in Hesiodo et in Theocrito (in hoc siglo T indicari solet), saepius adhibitus sit, tamen in Aristophane delituit; quod magna ex parte eo factum esse videtur, quod inter codices aristophaneos ante catalogum, quem Mercati et Franchi de' Cavalieri composuerunt, publici iuris factum[5] parum notus, quin etiam falso indicatus erat.[6] Ea huius codicis, quantum ad Aristophanem attinet, obscurata notitia non solum propter eius aetatem exacte definitam, sed etiam eo dolenda est, quod recensionem singularis indolis, quam unicam esse credo, continet, neque dubium est, quin investigationibus celeberrimis Zacheri, quibus traditionis scholiorum in Aristophanem cognitioni fundamentum iecit,[7] magno usui fuisset, si eius codicis, sicut prioris editionis Triclinii (Par. Suppl. 463) ei aeque ignotae, rationem habere potuisset. Cum etiam editio prior Thomae Magistri in Cant. 1 (= Cantabrigiensis Nn. 3, 15.1) partim servata[8] eum latuerit, quamquam iam Dobree nonnulla ex eius scholiis et subscriptionem claris verbis originem thomanam indicantem publici iuris fecerat,[9] factum est, ut Zacheri expositio parum accurata evaserit; idem pertinet ad eorum studia, qui post Zacherum de scholiis aristophaneis agentes recentiora respexerunt.

tamen Triclinius iam in priore editione ex scholio vetere adiunxit ἤγουν δράματι, ἐν ᾧ περὶ παλαισμάτων διεξῆλθεν (cf. 688, p. 295b l. 15–17 Dübner).—Iam ex hoc conspectu apparet, quod copiosiore argumentatione ostendam, auctorem recensionis Vaticani 38 editione thomana pro fundamento usum triclinianam priorem adhibuisse, sed triclinianam alteram ignoravisse.

[5] Cf. *Codices Vaticani Graeci*, I (1923), p. 34.

[6] In tabula codicum aristophaneorum, quam composuit J. W. White (*Classical Philology* I, [1906], p. 9–20), Vat. 38 repraesentatur p. 17 duorum codicum siglis falsis numeris designatorum, sc. 35 et 37; prior ex his f. 253 sqq. *Ranas*, alter f. 192 sqq. *Plutum* et *Nubes* continere dicitur; et 38 f. 192 sqq. *Plutum*, f. 219 sqq. *Nubes*, f. 253 sqq. *Ranas* continet.

[7] K. Zacher, *Die Handschriften und Classen der Aristophanesscholien* (XVI. Supplb. der Jahrbücher für Classische Philologie, Leipzig 1888).

[8] Cant. 1 ex duabus partibus constat; altera (inde a *Nub.* 500) editionem Thomae priorem ex nullo alio codice mihi notam tradit; prior additamentum recentius est.

[9] *Ricardi Porsoni notae in Aristophanem, quibus Plutum comoediam partim ex eiusdem recensione partim e manuscriptis emendatam et variis lectionibus instructam praemisit, et collationum appendicem adiecit* P. P. Dobree (Cantabrigiae MDCCCXX). Subscriptio codicis iam a Dobreeo siglo Cant. 1 designati legitur p. IX; eam repetivit Turyn, op. in n. 1 cit., p. 45, n. 77. Scholia, quae Dobree sparsim iuxta varias lectiones textus edidit in Appendice p. (1) sqq., velut ad *Nub.* 1330 (hodie 1327), ex eo fonte in scholiorum editiones pervenerunt.

Sicut in n. 4 supra in exemplo ex *Ranis* petito iam apparuit, recensio in Vat. 38 tradita nititur in editione Thomae, et quidem in priore,[10] quae tamen inde a versu 500 *Nubium* tantum conferri potest (v. n. 8 supra), sed cum priore Triclinii collata est; at eius auctor Triclinii alteram non adhibuit, quam a. 1322 nondum extitisse ex temporum ratione in universum apparet[11] et eo probatur, quod auctor recensionis Vaticani 38 editionem priorem Triclinii nondum ad finem perductam ante oculos habuisse videtur. Ex variis vario tempore introductis additamentis, lituris, correctionibus, quae in illo codice autographo[12] conspiciuntur, quaedam in Vat. 38 ignorantur, id quod in additamentis saepe eo accidere potuit, quod huius recensionis auctor talia, quamquam in editione Triclinii iam adfuerunt, minus apta iudicavit vel aliam ob causam (fortasse etiam mera neglegentia) praetermisit. Attamen in lituris et correctionibus, in quibus, quae antea exarata erant, plerumque vix vel omnino non distinguuntur, veri simile est, ubi auctor recensionis Vaticani 38 nondum deleta vel correcta habet, ea tunc temporis a Triclinio nondum deleta vel correcta esse; quamquam prior causa ne hic quidem plane excluditur, si eadem iam in editione priore Thomae extabant, ut ponere possimus illum auctorem talia ex hoc fonte habere Triclinii mutationibus repudiatis vel neglectis. Hoc argumentum adhiberi potest in primo ex speciminibus ex *Nubibus* petitis, quibus rationem inter recensionem Vaticani 38 et Thomam Tricliniumque intercedentem fusius illustrabo.

Inter scholia thomana-tricliniana, quae mox ex editione mea plene cognosci posse spero, memorabile est ad v. 638, cuius auctor

---

[10] Alterius editionis Thomae, quae priori Triclinii subest, congruentiae pauca et parvi momenti vestigia discernuntur, velut νῦν constanter perispomenon (e.g. *Nub.* 731 codices illius editionis Thomae et Vat. 38 νῦν habent, sed Cant. 1 (Thomas[1]) et Par. Suppl. 463 (Triclinius[1]) νυν). Enclisis huius voculae sensu leviore usurpatae una ex proprietatibus est, in quibus Triclinius[1] cum Thoma[1] facit, non cum Thoma[2]; cf. dissertationem meam "De priore recensione thomana Aristophanis," *Mnemosyne* S. IV, Vol. XVII[4] (1964), p. 358 sq.

[11] Editionem Aristophanis Triclinii alteram annis inter eius editiones Hesiodi et Pindari (1320–32) adscripsit R. Aubreton, *Démétrius Triclinius et les recensions médiévales de Sophocle* (Paris 1949), p. 23.

[12] Etiam comoediarum textum, non solum commentarium Triclinius sua manu scripsit pace Turynii (op. in n. 1 cit., n. 35 ad p. 23) aliorumque virorum doctorum. Quamquam pluribus de hac quaestione disserere huius loci non est, tamen obiter lectorem delegare liceat ad n. 23 et n. 39.

metri et rhythmi studium apud antiquos cultum suis temporibus neglectum iacere queritur et utile esse ad poëtarum textum emendandum monet. Eum Triclinium, huius studii apud seros Byzantinos instauratorem, esse putaveris, sed illud scholium iam in Cant. 1 traditur, ut a Thoma originem ducat. Inter alia statuit, cum Deus mundum metro et rhythmo sapienter composuerit—quae observatio rursus pietate Thomae, cuius nomen inter monachos Theodulus fuerit, digna est—poëtas eundem modum imitatos verba sua metro et rhythmo ordinavisse:

τὸν αὐτὸν δὴ τρόπον καὶ ποιηταὶ μιμούμενοι μέτρῳ καὶ ῥυθμῷ τὸν αὐτῶν (sic) λόγον ἐρύθμισαν (sic).

Haec Triclinius in priore editione ad verbum iteravit, nisi quod una vox inter ποιηταὶ et μέτρῳ deleta est, quam, licet vix ulla vestigia vocis deletae discernantur, spatio congruente illud μιμούμενοι fuisse pro certo statuere possumus, in quo Triclinius nescioqua de causa offendit. In altera editione idem scholium recepit nulla voce interposita ποιηταὶ μέτρῳ κτλ. repetens; ceterum nonnulla mutavit (i.a. sermone castigato τὸν αὐτῶν ἐρρύθμισαν λόγον scripsit). At in Vat. 38 scholium, quale in Cant. 1 legitur, extat voce μιμούμενοι non deleta. Quamquam ponere licet eius recensionis auctorem codice Par. Suppl. 463 usum esse hac voce in eo nondum deleta, tamen fieri potest, ut eam, quamvis a Triclinio eiecta esset, retinere maluerit.[13]

Est tamen, ubi ad alteram explicationem confugere nequeamus. In textu v. 945 iuxta lectionem genuinam ἀναγρύξῃ[14] extat rarior ἀναγρύζῃ, quae codicum veterum RV est (in R mutilata, sed desinentia certa). Prior in paene omnibus recentioribus traditur, ex qua classe altera hucusque ex uno Bodleyano saec. XV tantum innotuit.[15]

---

[13] Auctorem recensionis Vaticani 38 per neglegentiam correctionis Triclinii rationem non habuisse credi vix potest, cum in Par. Suppl. 463 macula grandior ex lineis transversis confluentibus facta, quae vocem deletam obtegit, neminem effugere possit.—In editione altera Thomae hoc scholium deest.

[14] ἀναγρύξῃ i.a. scripserunt Blaydes, Van Leeuwen, Starkie, Coulon, ἀναγρύζῃ Rogers; novissimus editor Dover in textu habet ἀναγρύζῃ, sed in commentario statuit ἀναγρύξῃ fortasse rectum esse.—Ut solitum, ι subscriptum in codicibus plerumque omissum tacite addo.

[15] Hic Bodleyanus codex est, quem Dorvillianum vocare solent (X.1.3.13 = O4 ap. White, op. in n. 6 supra cit.), ex quo lectio ἀναγρύζῃ affertur in notis Porsoni apud Dobreeum, op. in n. 9 supra cit. p. 36, ubi versus numerus est 942; Blaydes eius codicis mentionem facit.

Prior etiam thomana est cum in altera tum in priore editione
(Cant. 1), sed Triclinius in priore scripsit ἀναγρύζῃ,[16] quod tamen
ξ ex ζ facto (sc. in media hasta verticali, ut dicunt, puncto crassiore
in formam ellipseos posito) correxit; in alterius editionis codicibus
ἀναγρύξῃ statim scriptum legitur. Hoc loco auctor recensionis Vaticani 38 exemplo suo primario, nempe editioni priori Thomae,
obsecutus non est, sed ἀναγρύζῃ, quod Triclinius primo scripsit,
praetulit, quam verbi formam sine ulla correctione in Vat. 38
legimus. Itaque fieri non potest, quin auctor eius recensionis hic
codicem Triclinii nondum correctum ante oculos habuerit.

Tertium specimen alicuius pretii est, ut grammatici nostri haud
ingeniosi labores in Triclinii verbis suo commentario aptandis
positos cognoscamus. Extat scholium Tzetzae, in quo de numero
syllabarum παπα in voce v. 390 ventris Strepsiadae tonantis sonitum
imitantium, qui varie traditur, sermo est (sch. 387a in *Scholia in
Aristophanem* IV 2 [ed. D. Holwerda, Groningen 1960]). Huius
scholii partem alteram τὸ ἐν...δίχα (p. 475, 12–476, 4), cuius ultima
verba ἄμετρος ὁ στίχος γὰρ τῶν ἑπτὰ δίχα trimetrum iambicum efficiunt, Triclinius ipsis verbis citavit in editione priore tantum; alibi
in scholiis thomano-triclinianis sinceris nullum vestigium scholii
Tzetzae invenitur. At in Vat. 38 excerptum receptum est, ita
quidem, ut auctor versui Tzetzae mutato duo a se ipso confectos
pro verbis pedestri sermone apud Tzetzam praecedentibus praemi-
serit; eum hoc scholium ex exemplari ipsius editionis Tzetzae
cognovisse veri simile non est, quippe quam eum adhibuisse nusquam
appareat. Ecce scholium Vaticani 38:

> μὴ πέντε, μὴ τέσσαρα, μὴ τούτων ἄνω
> παπα δοκῶν ἔμμετρον εὑρεῖν τὸν στίχον,
> ὡς ἄμετρος πέφυκε τῶν ἑπτὰ δίχα.[17]

---

[16] Triclinius lectionem ἀναγρύζῃ ex Veneto sumere poterat, quem cognovisse ex
compluribus indiciis apparet, e.g. ex Veneti lectione singulari ἡμῶν pro αὐτῶν *Plut.* 162,
quae in Par. Suppl. 463 varia lectio (γρ. ἡμῶν) super αὐτῶν est (cf. liber meus *Autour
d'un manuscrit d'Aristophane écrit par Démétrius Triclinius* [Groningen, Djakarta 1957],
p. 162). Alia indicia invenies infra in n. 21 et in n. 42.

[17] Et Tzetzes et auctor recensionis Vaticani 38 Byzantinorum doctrinam de α, ι, υ,
quippe quae δίχρονα essent, brevibus pro longis adhibendis in his versibus secuti sunt.
Praeterea Tzetzes in trimetris iambicis, quos ἀτέχνους vocabat (cf. eius *Iambi technici de
comoedia* = Prolegomena Xc Dübner, VIII Kaibel *CGF*, v. 1), spondeos etiam locis
paribus admisit (γὰρ τῶν in eius trimetro in textu citato); tales trimetri in eius *Versus*

Operae pretium est inquirere, quomodo curarum metricarum Triclinii, iam eius prioris editionis ornamenti principalis, ab auctor recensionis Vaticani 38 ratio habita sit. Quamquam eas non plane neglexit, tamen more aequalium suorum illam partem textus interpretandi pro minime necessario habuisse videtur; artis enim metricae antiquae studium, ut iam ex scholio 638 apparuit, eis temporibus neglegebatur, ut carmina insolitis metris composita legentes horum explicationem in textu interpretando non requirerent.

Grammaticus noster novam viam a Triclinio apertam cunctanter ingressus pauca ex scholiis metricis in Par. Suppl. 463 adscriptis commentario suo inseruit eaque ex solo genere conciso, quo summatim cuiusdam partis dramatis metra indicantur, et ne haec quidem plene recepta, ut e.g. ex duobus Triclinii (ad v. 476: ἀναπαιστικοὶ τετράμετροι καταληκτικοὶ β', et ad v. 478: ἰαμβικοὶ τρίμετοι λβ', ὧν τελευταῖος "χώρει...θύραν" [v. 509]) unum fecerit, dum scholio ad v. 476 adiungere satis habet ἰαμβικοὶ λβ'. Ampliora autem scholia metrica, quibus loci ex versibus lyricis constantes ita explicantur, ut singula cola enumerentur eorumque indoles indicetur, praetermisit, velut ad v. 510.

Eo loco, ubi parabaseos commation incipit, Triclinius huius cantici analysi metricae nonnulla de parabasi deque eius partibus praemisit, quarum numerum sex esse perhibet (sc. parabasi *Nubium*, quippe quae tertia parte, πνῖγος vel μακρόν dicta, careat, aptum);[18] idem statuit in multo ampliore scholio ad hunc v. in editione altera, quamquam in huius scholii ultima parte Hephaestionem citans numerum partium parabaseos plenae (septem) affert.[19] Ex scholio

---

de differentia poëtarum = Prolegomena Xb Dübner, VII Kaibel occurrunt (e.g. in v. 144 (145) verborum Διόνυσον γράφοντες syllabae -σον γρά- quartum pedem efficiunt); hanc licentiam auctor recensionis Vaticani 38 versum Tzetzae reficiens evitavit.—In huius excerpto γράφε subaudiendum, quod in scholio Tzetzae legitur (*Scholia in Aristophanem* IV 2, p. 476 sq.); in eius v. 1 ἄνω idem valet, quod "etiam pauciora"; Tzetzes se in uno ex duobus codicibus, qui ei praesto erant, quinquies, in altero ter illud παπα invenisse testatur.

[18] Attamen Triclinio nomina cunctarum partium parabaseos, etiam tertiae, nota erant. Hanc difficultatem ita solvit, ut nomini alterius partis (παράβασις proprie ita dictae) adiunxerit tertiae (καὶ μακρὸν ἢ πνῖγος), quibus nominibus in editione altera addidit alterum nomen alterius partis ἀνάπαιστος (pro ἀνάπαιστοι, Ar. *Ach.* 627 e.a.; singulari numero etiam Sch. Heph. A, p. 161, 12 Consbruch).

[19] Scholium alterius editionis Triclinii ad v. 510 editum est a Zachero, op. cit. p. 632 sq.; locus Hephaestionis in hac sola citatus extat in Περὶ σημείων, p. 75,19 sqq. Consbruch.

editionis prioris auctor recensionis Vaticani 38 priorem partem tantum recepit (omissa sententia initiali τοῦτο κομμάτιον τοῦ χοροῦ ὀνομάζεται); alteram, in qua commatii cola singula describuntur (τὸ α΄ "ἀλλ'... ἀνδρείας" χοριαμβικὸν δίμετρον ὑπερκατάληκτον, etc.) omisit.

Igitur ex duabus causis, cur accidere potuerit, ut quaedam ex editione priore Triclinii in commentario Vaticani 38 desint, quas supra (p. 314) commemoravi, prior (sc. eius recensionis auctorem sive consulto sive per incuriam talia praetermisisse) certo in scholia metrica cadit. Alteram (talia nondum in codice Par. Suppl. 463 addita vel mutata esse eo tempore, quo grammaticus noster hoc codice usus est) eis locis aptam esse opinor, quibus Triclinius editionem priorem retractans auxit, qui loci atramento pallidiore et litterarum forma discernuntur; ea ratione praecipue addita sunt, quae Triclinius ex scholiis veteribus excerpsit.[20] Iam supra in n. 2 in huiusmodi additamentum scholii ad *Ran.* 689 incidimus; ex *Nubibus* e.g. affero sch. ad v. 584 (inter lineas super ἡ σελήνη δ᾽ ἐξέλιπε), quod in editione priore Thomae (Cant. 1) sic legitur: ἤγουν ἔκλειψις τῆς σελήνης τότε ἐγένετο; Triclinius autem scripsit in editione priore (Par. Suppl. 463), sicut iam Thomas in altera: ἤγ. τότε σελήνης ἔκλ. ἐγ. eademque extant in Vat. 38 (non plura). Eis verbis in Par. Suppl. 463 atramento pallidiore haec adiunguntur: ἐπὶ Στρατοκλέους Βοηδρομιῶνι μηνὶ δευτέρου [ἔτους] (haec vox margine resecto excidit), quae ex scholio vetere sumpta sunt.[21] Vides auctorem recensionis Vaticani 38 Triclinium secutum esse, quocum τότε σελήνης scripsit textu scholii editionis prioris Thomae repudiato, sed antequam Triclinius scholium suum auxit.[22] Huiusmodi omissiones tam constanter occurrunt, ut illius auctoris incuriae tribui non possint.

---

[20] Cf. librum meum iam citatum (n. 16) *Autour d'un manuscrit* p. 20–22.

[21] δευτέρου est pro προτέρου; in scholio vetere in V extat τῷ β΄ ἔτει. In altera editione Triclinius ipsum scholium vetus (cf. p. 109b, 34–36 Dübner) in margine apposuit leviter mutatum et in fine addito mensis nomine latino (ἤτοι Νοεμβρίῳ μηνί); nunc recte scripsit τῷ προτέρῳ ἔτει.

[22] Dixerit aliquis ex eis exemplis, quibus ad rationem inter recensionem Vaticani 38, Thomam[1], Triclinium[1] intercedentem demonstrandam usus sum, sequi, ut necesse non sit in ea comparatione Thomam[1] ullas partes agere, cum cuncta ad solum Triclinium[1] referre liceat, si concedamus fieri posse, ut eius editio nondum aucta vel correcta exemplo fuerit. Attamen in complures locos haec explicatio non quadrat, velut in v. 1106, ubi supra textus verba δὴ λέγειν in Cant. 1 (= Thomas[1]) duae variae lectiones superscribuntur (γρ. "σοὶ" ἢ "τὸ"), ex quibus in Vat. 38 prior sola superscipta est (γρ. "σοὶ") textu, ut in Cant. 1, non mutato, sed Triclinius textum corrigens pro δὴ deleto

Capiti Vaticano 38 destinato finem faciam parvulam annotationem commemorando, quae codicem Par. Suppl. 463 exemplo fuisse luce clarius prodit quaeque nos iterum ad rem metricam ducit.

Triclinius editionem priorem compositurus exemplar alterius editionis Thomae descripsit, in quo textus comoediae, ut in aliis codicibus huius classis et etiam alibi, recte divisus non erat, ut singulae lineae exaratae identidem ab iustis versibus abhorrerent; praeterea Triclinio in colis lyricis definiendis singulorum ambitus, qui saepe non congruebat cum ambitu linearum exemplaris thomani, designandus erat. Ut textum descriptum secundum suum iudicium retractaret, varias rationes adhibuit: aut verba, quae ex altera in alteram lineam transponenda erant, altero loco delevit, altero addidit,[23] aut, si duae lineae coniungendae erant, lineolam (−) in fine prioris et in initio alterius apposuit, aut super initium versus vel coli, quae determinare volebat, compendium vocis ἀρχή et super eorum finem vocis τέλος scripsit; praeterea in colis lyricis distinguendis super eorum initium coli numerum (numero in scholio analysi praemisso respondentem) et ad eius finem crucem (+) et duo puncta (sive : sive ..) ponere solebat.[24]

Talia editoris textum emendantis adiumenta ab eo, qui hanc editionem in textus sui recensione adhibet, iterari non expectamus, neque erat cur auctor recensionis Vaticani 38 in codice Triclinii tractando eorum rationem redderet. Nihilo tamen minus semel

---

scripsit σοι (enclitice) nulla varia lectione addita. Haec varietas eam tantum explicationem admittit auctorem recensionis Vaticani 38 et Triclinium diversa ratione utriusque exemplo usos esse.—In editione altera Thomae varia lectio altera (τό), quamvis invito metro, unica lectio facta est; Triclinius[2] lectionem in editione priore p.c. scriptam σοι recepit.

[23] Scriptura verborum a Triclinio textum primum scriptum retractanti additorum a scriptura huius textus distingui non potest, quod unum ex variis argumentis est, quibus opinio eorum refutatur, qui varietatis scripturae Triclinii etiam ex additamentis scholiorum supra commemoratis apparentis rationem non habentes negant textum codicis Par. Suppl. 463 ab eo scriptum esse. Si quis obiciet fieri posse, ut Triclinius data opera id egerit, ut, quae textum retractans adscripserit, similia evaderent eis, quae scripta iam erant, reputato eum alibi tali similitudini non studuisse. In Euripidis codice notissimo L, cuius textus sine dubio ab alio scriptus est, Triclinius scripturam verborum, quae hunc textum retractans addidit, non mutavit, ut clare a textus primum scripti distet (v. e.g. imaginem paginae huius codicis ap. Zuntzium, *An inquiry into the transmission of the plays of Euripides* [Cambridge 1965], Pl. VI).

[24] Plura de his Triclinii curis in libro meo iam saepius allato *Autour d'un manuscrit*, p. 11–13.

(v. 935/6) illa compendia vocum ἀρχή et τέλος superscripsit eisdem locis, ubi Triclinius idem colon distinxerat, qui tamen hic numero coli et signis (— et + : vel + ..) contentus fuerat.[25]

III

Inter recensiones thomano-triclinianas contaminatas vetustissima, quantum sciam, et certe maxime conspicua ea editio est, quacum recensiones codicum **Vaticani Chisiani Gr. R. IV. 20** et **Parisini Gr. 2821** cohaerent. Prior codex antea latitans primum in editione commentariorum Tzetzae in Aristophanem adhibitus est (*Scholia in Aristophanem* IV 1–3; eius descriptioni fasc. 1, p. LXIX–LXXIV, nonnulla addentur in editione scholiorum recentiorum in *Nubes*), alter iam diu notus erat sive nomine Regii a Dübnero et a me adhibito (concise Reg) sive siglo Q (ita Studemund eumque secutus Zacher, op. cit. p. 627) designatus. Editio, quae utriusque codicis recensioni subest, non iam servata est; eam ca. mediam partem saec. XIV compositam esse veri simillimum est; eius auctor commentario thomano-tricliniano liberius in suum usum converso addidit multa ex Tzetzae, complura ex Eustathii, quaedam ex Moschopuli annotationibus ad Aristophanem, etiam pauca frustula

---

[25] *Nub.* 935–38 lineae textus a Triclinio ex exemplari thomano descriptae hae sunt:

> ἀλλ' ἐπίδειξαι σύ τε τοὺς προτέρους
> ἅττ' ἐδίδασκες, σύ τε τὴν καινὴν παίδευσιν,
> ὅπως ἂν ἀκούσας σφῷν ἀντιλεγόντοιν
> κρίνας φοιτᾷ.

Omissis glossis explicativis accedunt duae variae lectiones eodem modo in Par. Suppl. 463 et in Vat. 38 superscriptae: ⟨ἐπίδειξ⟩ον super‚ἐπίδειξαι et ⟨σφῶ⟩ιν super σφῷν (σφῶν codd., ι subscriptum, ut saepe, omittentes); etiam ipsius textus verba in utroque eadem sunt errore in Vat. 38 (v. infra) excepto.

Cola, quae Triclinius in hac editione distinxit (monom. + dim. + monom. + dim. + dim.), in textu descripto ita indicata sunt (duplici puncto iacenti etiam per : reddito): 1) num. νζ super ἀλλ'; + : post ἐπίδειξαι ; 2) num. νη super σύ τε;—post προτέρους et ante ἅττ'; + : post ἐδίδασκες; 3) num. νθ super σύ; + : post καινὴν; 4) num. ξ super πα(ίδευσιν); — post παίδευσιν et ante ὅπως; + : post σφῶν; 5) num. ξα super ἀντ(ιλεγόντοιν); + : post φοιτᾷ (lineolae hic desunt).

Auctor recensionis Vaticani 38 colometriam Triclinii suam fecit et ita reddidit: 1) una linea ἀλλ'...ἐδίδασκες = col. 1 et 2 Triclinii, distincta per ἀρχή super σύ τε et τέλος super (ἐδίδ)ασκες; 2) una linea σύ τε...σφῶν = col. 3 et 4 Triclinii, distincta per spatium vacuum inter καινὴν et παίδευσιν ; 3) una linea ἀντιλέγοιν (sic) ...φοιτᾷ.

In editione altera Triclinius numerum monometrorum multum minuens in toto systemate 889–948 tria tantum distinxit, sc. v. 916, 923, 927, ubi etiam plerique editores hodierni monometra agnoscunt (sed v. 916 dimeter est ap. Blaydesium et Leeuwenium).

scholiorum veterum, et insuper paraphrasin continuam in commentario thomano-tricliniano et in Tzetzae nitentem.[26] Huius
editionis imaginem sinceriorem Chisianus praebet, quamvis iunior
sit (saec. XV ineuntis);[27] contra vetustior (Reg teste signo pellucido
post mediam partem saec. XIV scriptus est[28]) recensionem ex
editione illa magna cum libertate refectam continet.

De Chisiano eiusque scriba, qui ex gente indocta est exemplar non
sine erroribus, sed pro viribus cum fide reddenti, amplius hic non
agam; maiore animi intentione dignus est, qui recensionis Regii
auctor fuit. In editione illa contaminata tractanda hominem acuti
audacisque ingenii et novandi studiosum se praebuit; inter paucos
fuit, qui eis temporibus suo Marte rei metricae operam dare ausi
sunt, ut iam eam ob causam imaginem Triclinii in animum revocet.[29]

Itaque mirandum non est Zacherum primum fusius de hoc codice
agentem[30] putavisse auctorem eius commentarii Triclinium esse
eumque hunc composuisse ante alterum, quem ego quoque alterius
editionis fuisse iudico. At priore editione genuina Triclinii in Par.
Suppl. 463 detecta haec opinio, cui etiam alii, velut Holzinger,
assensi sunt,[31] non iam valet. In libro meo iam citato *Autour d'un
manuscrit* multis argumentis, primo loco in comparatione editionum
Thomae Tricliniique et recensionis Regii positis, ostendi huic inter
illas locum non esse, cum nunc cum vetustiore, nunc cum recentiore
ex eis consentiat, ut necessario a grammatico quodam post Triclinium

---

[26] Cf. iam nunc quae scripsi "De Eustathio, Tzetza, Moschopulo, Planude Aristophanis commentatoribus," *Mnemosyne* S. IV Vol. VII[2] (1954), p. 138–43 et p. 152;
Autour d'un manuscrit p. 61 e.a.; *Scholia in Aristophanem* l. in text. cit.; plura exponam in
editione scholiorum recentiorum in *Nubes*. Easdem partes in commentario Regii iam
distinxit Zacher (op. cit. p. 627 sq., 640, 641 sq.) exceptis eustathianis, quas non agnovit.

[27] Cf. *Scholia in Aristophanem* IV 1 p. LXX sq.

[28] Foliorum Regii signa pellucida congruere cum Briquetii n° 3230 anni 1367 primus
ostendit K. Holzinger in: *Mélanges offerts à M. Émile Chatelain*, (Paris 1910), p. 217 (p. 14
exemplaris seorsim impressi).

[29] Attamen solus praeter Triclinium rei metricae interpres in Aristophane eis temporibus
non fuit; in codice Cremonensi 171 (antea 12229) saec. XIV vel XV in. annotatio
metrica ad magnas partes triadis byzantinae extat, cuius Zuretti mentionem iam fecit
op. in n. 4 cit. *Scolii*, p. 18, 75, 87. Haec tamen annotatio, quae hominis in re metrica
rudis est, a scholiis metricis Vaticani (1294), i.e. Triclinii, longe distat, quibuscum
Zuretti eam comparavit (p. 87).

[30] Zacher, op. cit. p. 644.

[31] K. Holzinger, "Kritische Bemerkungen zu den spätbyzantinischen Aristophanesscholien," in ΧΑΡΙΣΤΗΡΙΑ *Alois Rzach dargebracht* (Prag 1930), p. 59 sqq., de scholiis
metricis solis agens.

scribenti composita sit, qui ex libidine variis editionibus thomano-triclinianis usus est. Accedit, quod ex correctionibus in Reg factis, ex quibus nonnullas infra afferam, concludere possumus eius recensionis auctorem, sicut in Par. Suppl. 463 editionis triclinianae prioris, eundem esse ac scribam codicis, ex quo eam cognoscimus, ut eo ipso, quod Regius minime tribus decenniis post alteram editionem triclinianam scriptus sit,[32] Triclinius auctor excludatur.

De hac quaestione pluribus h.l. non acturus me duobus speciminibus continebo, ut rationem inter recensionem Regii et editiones Thomae Tricliniique intercendentem illustrem. Prius est scholium iam supra (p. 314) tractatum, cuius ultimam partem Dübner ex Regio publici iuris fecit (*Adnotatio* p. 436b).[33] Ad editionem priorem Thomae nos delegat vox μιμούμενοι in Reg, ut in Vat. 38, servata (de codice prioris editionis Triclinii Par. Suppl. 463 nondum correcto hic cogitare vix possumus). Rursus ad editionem alteram Triclinii referimur, cum videmus verba priorum editionum τὸν αὐτῶν λόγον ἐρύθμισαν a Triclinio in editione posteriore demum emendatius scripta (τὸν αὐτῶν ἐρρύθμισαν λόγον) eodem modo emendata in Reg extare vi pronominis reflexivi etiam clarius expressa, licet ordine verborum editionum praecedentium servato (τὸν ἑαυτῶν λόγον ἐρρύθμισαν). Idem studium textum scholii thomano-tricliniani magis perspicuum reddendi deprehendimus in ultima parte, quam Dübner edidit; pro verbis Regii πολλὰ τῶν ποιητικῶν στίχων cunctae editiones thomano-triclinianae habebant πολλὰ τῶν τοῖς ποιηταῖς ῥηθέντων; praeterea ordo verborum ultimorum editionum thomano-triclinianarum διορθοῦν ἔχοι τις τῷ χρόνῳ παραφθαρέντα in Reg funditus mutatus hic est: παρ. / τ. χρ. / δι. ἔχ. τις.[34]

Alterum exemplum ex *Ranis* selegi, ubi v. 1276 versus Aeschyli *Ag.* 104 κύριός εἰμι θροεῖν ὅδιον κράτος κτλ. citatur. Iuxta ὅδιον in textu Aristophanis iam antiquitus ὅσιον tradebatur, quam lectionem scholium vetus (corruptum; αἴσιον pro ὅσιον habet) Asclepiadi cuidam in scholiis ad *Ranas* saepius allato tribuit. In Ravennate utraque lectio conflata ὃς δῖον legitur; in plerosque codices (etiam V) illud

---

[32] Cf. de utriusque aetate p. 314 cum n. 11 et p. 321 cum n. 28.

[33] In textu Dübneri l. 2 post μανθάνειν omissum est ζητεῖν.

[34] Puto auctorem recensionis Regii id egisse, ut ordinem verborum insolentem evitaret, id quod etiam ad ordinem verborum λόγον ἐρρύθμισαν inversioni in altera editione Triclinii obviae praelatum pertinet.

ὅσιον receptum est; non tamen in omnibus ceteris, ut ex apparatu plurimarum editionum colligimus, nam ὅδιον ex Cant. 2, qui unus ex codicibus editionem alteram Triclinii tradentibus est, iam notavit Dobree.[35] In apparatu copiosissimo, licet non semper fide digno, quo Blaydes editionem suam ditavit, duo alii codices adduntur, sc. Laurentianus Conv. Soppr. 140 (olim Abb. Flor. 2779) inter codices scholiorum aristophaneorum notissimus et vulgo siglo Θ designatus, et Laurentianus 31, 35 saec. XV–XVI secundum White,[36] in quo ex correctione legitur (Ω ap. Blaydes, quod siglum White retinuit).[37] Haec genuinae lectionis restitutio Triclinio accepta referenda est, qui eam ex codicibus *Agamemnonis* Aeschyli, cuius editor erat,[38] cognoscere poterat. In editionis prioris codice Par. Suppl. 463 ὅδιον statim sine correctionis vestigiis scriptum est,[39] et in editionis alterius codicibus, quos contuli (sunt Vaticanus 1294, Bodleyanus Holkhamicus 88, Cant. 2 = Cantabrigiensis Nn. 3, 15.2, supra commemoratus, Laurentianus 31, 22 + Vaticanus 61, M9 = Ambrosianus L 41 sup.) eadem vox legitur.[40] Attamen in Reg

---

[35] V. op. in n. 9 cit. *Porsoni notae*, p. (69).

[36] Op. in n. 6 cit., p. 15.

[37] Lectionem ὅδιον frustra quaeres inter codicum Aristophanis lectiones e.g. apud Leeuwenium, Coulonium, Radermacherum, Stanfordium in editionibus *Ranarum*; in *Agamemnonis* editione Fränkelii decipimur annotatione "ὅσιον rell." (sc. praeter R). Rogers tamen illos codices in textu commemoratos notavit (ex Blaydesii editione, ut puto) errore tamen in codicum siglis commisso. Pro Θ siglo F[5], pro Ω siglo F[3] usus est; et legimus apud eum lectionem ex correctione natam in F[5] extare. Ecce exemplum erroris, qualem editores in siglis ex littera, cui numerus adscribitur, constantibus saepius committunt (cf. A. Severyns, *Texte et apparat* [Bruxelles 1962], p. 309 sq.).

[38] Cf. Turyn, *The Manuscript Tradition of the Tragedies of Aeschylus* (New York 1943, iterum Hildesheim 1967), p. 100 sqq.

[39] A Triclinio ipso, ut opinor, eam lectionem ex Aeschylo memoria tenenti, non a quovis scriba. Num putandum est Triclinium librarii manum oculis sequentem, postquam huc perventum esset, iussisse ὅδιον scribere, non ὅσιον (quod etiam codices editionis Thomae alterius habent, velut Venetus 472 et Cremonensis 171 a Zurettio adhibiti [cf. n. 4] et F = Par. 2820, cuius generis codex in Par. Suppl. 463 descriptus erat)?

[40] Sextus codex, quem in editione scholiorum Triclinii[2] ad *Nubes* adhibui, sc. Vindobonensis 163, priorem tantum *Ranarum* partem (v. 1–675) servavit.—Codicem Θ re vera ὅδιον habere, ut Blaydes annotavit, vidi. Quamvis hic codex eodem saec. XIV scriptus sit, quo Triclinius editiones suas composuit, in universum veri similius est lectionem ὅδιον in Θ ex Triclinio, cui textum *Agamemnonis* bene notum esse iam animadverti, sumptam quam a quovis scriba inventam esse. Praeterea in Θ nonnulla scholia tricliniana adiecta sunt, et quidem editionis alterius; e.g. scholii Triclinii ad *Nub.* 46 a Dindorfio et hunc secuto Dübnero ex Θ editi (p. 83a, 6–8 Db) pars altera (δὶς... εἰρωνευόμενος) in altera demum editione addita est. Haec scholia exarata sunt

ὅσιον expuncto σ et superscripto δ correctum est multis annis, postquam lectio ὅδιον a Triclinio restituta erat, quem auctori recensionis Regii exemplo fuisse patet.

Alia correctio huius auctoris, quae memoratu digna est, occurrit in uno ex Prolegomenis de Comoedia iam in codicibus scholia vetera continentibus traditis, sc. V ap. Dübnerum, ubi differentiae Veteris et Novae Comoediae enumerantur et explicantur. Hanc tractatiunculam ille auctor inseruit suae isagogae in comoediam, quam ex variis fontibus constituit cuique titulum ἐκ ποίας αἰτίας συνέστη ἡ κωμῳδία imposuit. Saeculo sequenti haec Regii isagoga prior pars facta est opusculi, quod primus Cramer inter anecdota parisina edidit[41] quodque nomine *Anonymus Crameri* designabo; numero IXa insignitum est inter Prolegomena de Comoedia editionis Dübneri, ubi pars ex Regio sumpta desinit l. 112 (εἰς Ξανθίαν) et huius partis locus ex Proleg. V originem ducens legitur l. 67–93 (cf. Proleg. V usque ad ult. l. 26 Db).

In Proleg. V quinque differentiae utriusque generis comoediae tractantur: 1) secundum tempus, 2) secundum dialectum, 3) secundum materiam, 4) secundum metrum, 5) secundum constructionem, ita, ut post uniuscuiusque differentiae mentionem factam explicatio sequatur. Ex harum explicationibus tertia (sc. differentiae secundum materiam) una cum differentiae insequentis mentione excidit, ut tertiae differentiae mentio (ὕλη δὲ) excipiatur

---

a manu discrepanti ab utraque coaeva, quae textum et scholia vetera scripsit, quamquam mihi non multo recentior videtur; etiam ex verbis Zacheri hunc codicem describentis (op. cit. p. 548) non apparet eum scholia adiecta, postquam textus et scholia vetera scripta sunt, pro additamentis multo post adiunctis habuisse. Quod ad scripturam utriusque manus primae attinet, Dover eam nimis antiquam iudicavisse mihi videtur ("early XIV" in eius editione *Nubium*, p. CVII); equidem eam ex imaginibus aestimans ultimis decenniis prioris partis huius saeculi (ca. 1330–1350) tribuerim. Opinioni meae assentitur D. Holwerda, qui codicem ipsum inspexit et eius chartam signis pellucidis ("watermarks") carentem illam aetatem admittere iudicat. Itaque iam propter rationem chronologicam Triclinius editionem priorem componens ante a. 1322, quo scriba Vaticani 38 ea usus finem labori scribendi imposuit, me iudice lectionem ὅδιον a Θ mutuatus non est.—ὅδιον denique etiam in recensionem mixtam Vaticani 38 receptum est (statim scriptum, ut in Par. Suppl. 463); contra Thomas¹ (Cant. 1), ut Thomas² (v. n. 39), ὅσιον scripsit. Etiam in editione contaminata, ex qua Chisianus et Regius originem ducunt, ὅσιον legebatur, quod non solum in Regio a.c., sed etiam in Chisiano non correctum extat.

41 *Anecdota graeca e codd. manuscriptis Bibliothecae Regiae Parisiensis*, ed. J. A. Cramer (Oxonii 1839–41), p. 3–18.

explicatione quartae (καθὸ ἡ μὲν νέα... στρέφεται περὶ τὸ ἰαμβικόν κτλ.; cf. l. 8 sqq. Db). In hoc loco, ubi Dindorf eumque secutus Dübner iure lacunam indicaverunt, iam auctor recensionis Regii offendit, qui tamen de lacuna non cogitans verba tradita corrupta esse putavit. Itaque textum, qui sensum quendam materiae tractatae aptum praeberet, restituere conatus in differentiarum enumeratione, quae in initio Proleg. V extat (l. 3 Db), μέτρῳ primum scriptum correxit in μέτρου et interpunctionem inter hanc vocem et praecedentem ὕλη erasit, ut ex quinque differentiis quattuor relinqueret, sicut etiam quattuor explicationes in eius exemplo erant. Nunc explicatio differentiae ὕλη non requiritur et explicatio differentiae secundum metrum, quae in Proleg. V post mentionem differentiae ὕλη legitur, ad vocum coniunctionem ὕλη μέτρου pertinet. Hanc coniecturam viri acuti ingenii esse negari non potest, quamvis eius temeritas, quam etiam alibi deprehendimus, eluceat.

Coniecturam ὕλη μέτρου Anonymus Crameri recepit. Haec lectio unum ex argumentis suppeditat, quibus probatur hoc opusculum, quanquam eius altera pars fere congruit cum magnis partibus Prolegomenorum Tzetzae in Aristophanem, tamen a Tzetza scriptum non esse, cui auctori Kaibel illud assignavit (P a + P b, *CGF* p. 17 sqq.; sequuntur genuina Prolegomena Tzetzae M a + M b). Immo Anonymus Crameri alteram partem opusculi ex Tzetzae Prolegomenis mutuatus est, sicut priorem ex Regii isagoga.

Sunt etiam coniecturae, quas auctor recensionis Regii non in codice iam exarato, sed textum praeparans fecerit, ut in codice statim scriptae inveniantur. Huius generis in alio ex Prolegomenis occurrit, sc. in ea Aristophanis *Vita*, quam Dübner sub numero XII habet quaeque multis codicibus traditur, quamvis l.c. ex solo V adiectis lectionibus Regii edita sit. In eius *Vitae* fine (l. 40 sq. Db) versus Aristophanis ex hoc loco solo noti citantur (frg. 588 K. et Edm.)

τὴν γυναῖκα δὲ
αἰσχύνομαι τώ τ' οὐ φρονοῦντε παιδίω,

quorum ultima verba praesertim ante φρονοῦντε variis modis corrupta sunt (τὼ τοῦ V, τώ τε omissa negatione G, etc.). Triclinius, qui hanc *Vitam* inter prioris editionis prolegomena recepit, ea verba funditus mutavit. Dualem reiciens -ω pro -ῳ esse opinatus est; insuper participii formam homericam praetulit coniunctionum verborum, qualis est ἐὺ φρονέων (A 73 e.a.), memor, nisi fallor. Itaque ultima verba illius fragmenti apud Triclinium sunt τῷ τ' οὐ φρονέοντι παιδίῳ.

Triclinius in hac *Vita* exemplo fuit Chisiano iam commemorato, cuius prolegomena cuncta ex editione priore Triclinii sumpta sunt, et Regio,[42] ita tamen, ut utriusque more scriba Chisiani ipsa verba exempli repetere satis habuerit, sed auctor recensionis Regii ea cum quadam licentia tractaverit. Hoc tamen loco scriba Chisiani, licet formam homericam retinuerit, a Triclinio descivit:[43] genuinam lectionem (omissa forma homerica participii) restituit scribens τώ τ' οὐ φρονέοντε παιδίω desinentia participii correcta (-ε ex -ι). At auctor recensionis Regii, quamquam et ipse formam homericam recepit, totum locum ad suum arbitrium plane retractavit: τούτου φρονέοντε παιδίω καταλιπών (hac voce ex παῖδας καταλιπὼν δύο [l. 38 Db] repetita), quasi Aristophanem uxoris puderet, quod istos stultos pueros reliquisset. Qualis erat audaciae in rebus prosodicis et grammaticis, crasin verborum τούτω οὐ admittere gravatus non est.

Huius audaciae nonnulla exempla addam. Crasin eiusdem notae introduxit in suum Argumentum *Nubium* (X ap. Dübnerum), quod eadem ratione, qua isagogam suam in comoediam (cf. supra) ex variis antiquioribus Argumentis *Nubium* conflavit. Quae l. 41–43 Db ex Argumento Thomae Magistri (VIII, l. 2–4 Db) verbis mutatis interpolata sunt in medium Argumentum II Db,[44] incipiunt a τοῦθ' ἕνεκεν, i.e. τούτου ἕνεκεν (falso τοῦθ' ἕνεκεν Dübner).

Synizeseos specimina adhuc insolentiora in analysi metrica Regii inveniuntur, ex quibus duo citavi in libro meo *Autour d'un manuscrit*, p. 48, n. 1 et p. 51, n. 1: syllabarum -ά- et -γη- in εὐάγητον (*Nub.* 277), et -λος- et ἐ- in πρόβολος ἐμός (*Nub.* 1161).[45] Quod ad grammaticam

---

[42] Inter testimonia huius Chisiani et Regii originis insigne est, quod in versu *Ach.* 378 in *Vita* l. 22 Db allato Triclinii περσικὴν κωμῳδίαν pro πέρυσι κωμῳδίαν in utroque extat; illud περσικὴν coniectura Triclinii est ex falsa lectione Veneti περσικωμῳδίαν facta.

[43] Hic locus documento est, ne arbitremur eos codices, quos pro apographis habere solemus, necessario ubicunque eadem habere, quae in exemplo extant: et G ("copy of 474" [sc. V] White, op. in n. 6 cit. p. 19) et Chisianus (in prolegomenis ex Par. Suppl. 463 descriptus) eundem locum aliter reddiderunt (τώ τε pro τὼ τοῦ G, τώ τ' pro τῶτ' Chisianus).

[44] Arg. II Db Argumento Regii inde a p. 78b, 33 Db (inc. ἄλλοι δέ φασιν) usque ad p. 79a, 10 Db (des. προγόνων) insertum est. In parte ex Argumento Thomae originem ducenti fontis mutatio verbis ὡς λόγος (l. 43 Db) designatur. Simili ratione in Regii isagoga in comoediam supra tractata (IXa Db, prior pars), alius fons (sc. Proleg. V) verbis καὶ πάλιν καθ' ἑτέραν διαίρεσιν (l. 67 Db) inducitur.

[45] Textum scholii metrici Regii ad *Nub.* 275 sqq., in quo synizesis τῆς α καὶ τῆς γη εἰς μακράν docetur, edidi op. in text. cit. p. 106.

attinet, lectorem delegare satis habeo ad duo exempla rarissimae formae dualis medii 1. pers. plur. in -μεθον op. cit. p. 168 allata, quae auctori recensionis Regii debentur:[46] φευξούμεθον (ον super rasuram, nempe α deleto, ut suspicari licet) et διαμαχούμεθον (Plut. 447 sq.).

Sicut de Vaticano 38 disserens, disputationi ad Regium pertinenti finem impositurus de metrorum tractatione pauca addam. Quamquam auctor eius recensionis praesertim propter operam rei metricae navatam innotuit, cuius admodum peritum se praebet, tamen eam materiam non semper felici manu attigit. Hoc primo loco pertinet ad illud novum, quod a Triclinii usu et praecepto in exordio isagogae editionis alterius (Proleg. XVII, l. 1–2 Db) claris verbis proclamato discedens cola dactylica non secundum monopodiam, sed secundum dipodiam scandere constituit. Ipse tamen hanc scandendi rationem non constanter adhibuit, sed identidem ad Triclinii relapsus est et nominibus colorum ex quodam numero pedum et semipede constantium (πενθημιμερές, ἐφθημιμερές), nunc in scansione secundum monopodiam, nunc in scansione secundum dipodiam usus est, cui apta non sunt. Ita e.g. hanc adhibens Nub. 465 ἆρά...ἐγώ ($\_ \cup \cup / \_ \cup \cup / \_$) vocavit δακτυλικὸν μονόμετρον ὑπερκατάληκτον et πενθημιμερές, sed eadem cola dactylica Nub. 1158 et 1159 οἷος...τρέφεται / τοῖσδ'...παῖς scansione secundum monopodiam dimensus est (πενθημιμερῆ ἐκ δύο δακτύλων καὶ συλλαβῆς).[47]

Est tamen, ubi auctor recensionis Regii Triclinium correxerit, velut in analysi illius perlongi systematis Iustae et Iniustae Rationis altercantium, quod iam attigi de Vaticano 38 agens (p. 319 cum n. 25). In Regio huius systematis colometria et analysis in universum eaedem sunt ac in Triclinii editione priore, quamquam et in textu et in scholio metrico quaedam discrepant; i.a. huius recensionis auctor brevitati studens in scholio singula cola enumeravit omisso uniuscuiusque textu, quem Triclinius lemmatis vice coli numero addebat. Maioris momenti est, quod utriusque analysis nonnullis locis differt. I.a. Triclinius in tanta anapaestorum pedumque pro

---

[46] Prius ex editione Iuntina II et ex annotatione Petri Victorii in exemplari editionis Aldinae innotuit, ubi sine dubio ex Regio (vel ex codice ex eo descripto) sumptum est. Etiam complura scholia Regii ex his fontibus edita sunt, e.g. ad Nub. 678, p. 133b, 5–7 Db.

[47] Cf. Holzinger op. in n. 31 cit., p. 60–65, ubi colorum dactylicorum Nubium scansiones Regii iuxta Vaticani (1294, i.e. editionis alterius Triclinii) typis redditae sunt.

eis substitutorum frequentia in aliquot colis anapaestum inesse scripsit, ubi pro eo alter pes trisyllabus, sc. dactylus, extat; his locis auctor recensionis Regii recte dactylum distinxit.[48]

Attamen hic auctor errorem a Triclinio commissum ipse non plane evitavit:[49] postquam col. ϛ′ (v. 893b λόγος. ἥττων γ᾽ ὤν) recte ἐξ ἀναπαίστου καὶ σπονδείου constare dixit, ad col. ζ′ (v. 894a ἀλλά σε νικῶ) nihil annotavit praeter ὅμοιον. Triclinius autem ad col. ζ′ recte μονόμετρον ἐκ δακτύλου καὶ σπονδείου scripsit. Alterius generis errorem grammatici nostri deprehendimus in col. ι′ (v. 896 γνώμας καινὰς ἐξευρίσκων), ubi in utriusque textu contra metrum legitur ἐφευρίσκων. At Triclinius in textu ἐξ super ἐφ- scripsit et in scholio recte hoc colon δίμετρον ἐκ δ′ σπονδείων esse statuit (praetermissa tamen correctione lemmatis: in scholio in versu analysi praemissa remansit ἐφευρίσκων). Contra auctor recensionis Regii correctione Triclinii neglecta eius textum non correctum recepit huiusque textus analysin in scholio dedit: ἐκ β′ σπονδείων, ἰάμβου καὶ σπονδείου.

Spero ex eis, quae in hac dissertatione exposui, perspici posse varietatem traditionis byzantinae Aristophanis magna ex parte non a scribarum fluctuanti libidine et incuria, sed ab editorum ratione et iudicio suam quamque recensionem constituentium pendere. Insuper ex investigationibus huc pertinentibus eum quoque fructum percipimus, ut praecursorum nostrorum labores ex propinquo cognoscamus. Quod studioso animo philologiae operam dantes parum caverunt, ne in errorem inciderent, hoc eo facilius condonamus, quo magis nobis ipsi conscii sumus ne nobis quidem contingere, ut nunquam fallamur.

Groningae Batavorum,
21 decembris 1969

---

[48] Ecce prima cola, ubi Triclinius in editione priore anapaestum loco dactyli induxit, sed auctor recensionis Regii dactylum:

col. ια′ (v. 897a ταῦτα γὰρ ἀνθεῖ): μονόμετρον ἐξ ἀναπαίστου καὶ σπονδείου Triclinius, ἐκ δακτύλου καὶ σπονδείου auctor rec. Reg;

col. ιβ′ (v. 897b + 898 διὰ τουτουσὶ τοὺς ἀνοήτους): δίμετρον ἐξ ἀναπαίστου, σπονδείου, ἀναπαίστου καὶ σπονδείου Triclinius, ἐξ ἀναπαίστου, σπονδείου, δακτύλου καὶ σπονδείου auctor rec. Reg.

[49] Haec pedum trisyllaborum rhythmi oppositi permutatio apud grammaticos rem metricam pro illius aetatis scientia callentes eo explicatur, quod syllabarum quantitas, qua pedes distinguuntur, tunc temporis auribus non iam percipiebatur.

ZENO OF ELEA IN PLATO'S
PARMENIDES

KURT VON FRITZ

In a paper read at the joint meeting of the American Philological
Association and the American Society for Ancient Philosophy at
San Francisco in December 1969,[1] Friedrich Solmsen has taken
issue with Plato's report on Zeno of Elea's relations to Parmenides
and on the meaning of the arguments which he is there supposed
to have used in support of the doctrine of his master. After having
reminded his audience that "Plato's attitude to earlier thinkers is
that of a productive philosopher who finds in his precursors whatever
suits his own thought, not at all that of a philological and historical
interpreter," Solmsen first points out that even Plato's account of
Parmenides' doctrine is, as he says, "out of focus." For according to
Plato, Parmenides said ἕν τὸ πᾶν, while, as the preserved verbatim
fragments of his poem clearly show, his main doctrine was "there
is nothing but the ὄν." From this, it is true, the conclusion may be
drawn that inasmuch as all is ὄν, all is one; and this consequence, as
Solmsen himself points out, appears to have been drawn by
Parmenides *expressis verbis*, since he called the ἐόν both ἕν[2] and
μουνογενές.[3] But this is not, as in Plato's report, his *main* doctrine. In
this respect then Plato's report appears to be "out of focus."

The objection to Plato's report on Zeno's relation to Parmenides

---

[1] A revised version is to appear in *Phronesis*. Quotations below are made from a
mimeographed draft which was circulated before the meeting.

[4 Sept. 1973] See now *Phronesis* 16 (1971), 116 ff. Though the wording of the
argument has been somewhat changed, the contention that Zeno committed a "logical
gaffe" has remained essentially the same in the new version. A refutation, however, on
about the same lines as in the present paper, has been offered by William A. Abrahem in
an article with the title "The Nature of Zeno's Argument Against Plurality in DK 29 B1"
in *Phronesis* 17 (1972), 40–52. Apart from this I cannot find that anything said in the
present article has been anticipated by someone else in the meantime.

[2] Parmenides Frg. B 8,6 Diels/Kranz.

[3] *Ibidem* B 8,4.

and the nature of his arguments is much more fundamental. According to this report[4] Zeno wrote his book in order to come to the support of Parmenides' doctrine that everything is one. Parmenides, Plato says, had been ridiculed by men who pointed out that many strange things followed if the assumption was made that all is one. Thus Zeno wrote his treatise in order to show that even stranger conclusions followed if one assumed that there are many things. From this it appears to follow that all of Zeno's arguments were exclusively designed to refute the existence of many things (πολλά). This is confirmed by Plato *expressis verbis* again and again. A report of Simplicius,[5] which contains a good many more or less verbatim quotations from Zeno's works, repeats what Plato in the *Parmenides* says about Zeno's relation to Parmenides. But a little later, polemicizing against Alexander of Aphrodisias, he says that the latter had derived from Eudemos of Rhodes the opinion that Zeno denied the existence of the ἕν (ὡς ἀφαιροῦντος τὸ ἕν). Eudemos is also quoted as having said that there was a tradition according to which Zeno had said: if someone could tell him what the One was, then he could also tell what the ὄντα are. This can hardly mean anything else but that he could tell what the many things are. Thus Zeno's denial of the existence of the πολλά, according to Eudemos, was based on a preceding denial of the existence of the ἕν. Eudemos of Rhodes is generally considered a very good and reliable historian of philosophy and science. What is more, his statement appears to be confirmed by Simplicius' own report of Zeno's arguments. For he says that Zeno was puzzled about the One (περὶ τοῦ ἑνὸς ἀποροῦντα), and in his following exposition shows that, according to Zeno, what has size is always divisible, hence has parts, hence is not really one, so that the One dwindles to nothingness. In the end, it is true, Simplicius affirms that Zeno did not argue in this way in order to deny the existence of the One, but in order to show the difficulties arising from the assumption of the existence of many things. Yet in the arguments leading up to the latter part of this argument, the One has also disappeared, in perfect agreement with the statements made by Alexander of Aphrodisias on the authority of Eudemos of Rhodes.

So far then, it seems to me, Solmsen is perfectly right, and what he

[4] Plato, *Parmenides* 128 a–d.
[5] Zeno, Frg. 29 A 23 Diels/Kranz = Simpl. in Arist. *Phys.* 134.

has pointed out is certainly of considerable importance for a correct understanding of Zeno's thought, and for Plato's attitude towards Zeno's philosophy. But I cannot follow Solmsen further, when, in agreement with a paper published earlier by Gregory Vlastos, he says that Zeno "committed a logical gaffe," when he assumed that by infinitely continued division one finally ends with particles "of no size." It is true that Simplicius' somewhat confused wording can easily suggest such a logical error. But if one looks at the text a little more closely one sees clearly that Zeno committed no such logical gaffe, but that his reasoning is perfectly sound. Far from assuming that by infinitely continued division one finally ends up with particles "of no size" his argument is based on the very opposite assumption: however far the division may have proceeded, what remains still always has size, hence is further divisible, hence has parts, hence is not really one. Hence in order to be really One, i.e. indivisible—and this conclusion, if one starts from Zeno's primary assumptions, is perfectly sound—it must be without size. It is from this point that Zeno's further argument proceeded. What has no size does not make the thing to which it is added bigger, nor a thing from which it is subtracted, smaller. But if it has no such effect, it is (we might add, in the realm of size and quantity) zero or nothing. Furthermore (we may again say, in the realm of size and quantity) what is composed of zero quantities remains zero, i.e. has no size (ὥστε μηδὲν ἔχειν μέγεθος). I cannot see that anything is wrong with this argument.

However, even granting this, one can still contend that Zeno committed a "logical gaffe" in the second part of his argument. For here he speaks in fact of an infinite number of parts which would make the size of the object composed of them grow beyond measure; and what he says here appears to be at variance with one of the most elementary applications of the mathematical theory of convergent series, namely that the sum of the infinite series $\frac{1}{2} + \frac{1}{4} + \frac{1}{8} + \frac{1}{16} + \frac{1}{32}\ldots = 1$. But this mathematical formula is a convenient mathematical symbol for the fact that infinitely continued bisection of a unit naturally cannot exceed the unit, and that the difference between the sum of the particles and the whole can be made smaller than any given magnitude and so becomes negligible, which makes this sum or other sums of convergent series mathematically manageable.

But it does *not* make it possible for the￢human mind actually to
build up such a sum, starting from the other end, that is, starting
from a *limes*, which is just a word for something that the human
mind cannot actually envisage. It is exactly this peculiarity of the
structure of the human mind—a structure that reveals itself again
in modern set theory when it is assumed that an infinite set of extensionless points can have multidimensional extension and in the fact
that the ℭ set demonstrably cannot be identified with any one of the
Alefs in Cantor's infinite series of Alefs in spite of the fact that in
Cantor's theory this series contains all possible infinite cardinal
numbers that can be assigned to infinite sets—it is this peculiarity of
the human mind with which Zeno is concerned in all his so-called
paradoxes. It seems to me that it is from this fact that any further
analysis of Plato's report on Zeno's doctrine has to proceed.

Plato's report presents a number of other historical and philological
problems in addition to the one that Solmsen pointed out quite
correctly. Perhaps the most important one appears right at the
beginning of the report, when Socrates asks Zeno[6] to repeat the first
argument of his treatise, namely that if there are many things, they
are both like (ὅμοια) and unlike (ἀνόμοια), which is impossible. No
such demonstration, at least on the face of it, is found anywhere in
the preserved fragments of Zeno's work. Yet it is the very starting-
point of Socrates' objections to Zeno's argument, namely that it
would be indeed surprising if likeness itself could be proved identical
with unlikeness, but that there is nothing strange or contradictory in
the assumption that the same thing can—in different respects—
partake both in likeness and in unlikeness. Is this just another
instance of Plato's habit of attributing to his predecessors anything
he wants to if it can serve him to make his point? In this case the
charge would be much more serious than in the case pointed out by
Solmsen, where it is merely the interpretation of Zeno's argument
that is in question. Yet it is perhaps not too difficult to find, even in
the report of Simplicius, the point where the ὅμοιον and ἀνόμοιον could
come in. This is at the very end of his exposition where he says that
Zeno had previously demonstrated that the One has no size and that
he had proved this on the basis of the assumption that each of the
many things is the same with itself and therefore one. If this argument

---

[6] Plato, *Parmenides* 127 d/e.

is to make sense within the given context, it must have run approx-
imately as follows. A multitude (πολλά), in order to be a real multitude, must consist of units. Such a unit must be identical with itself
and therefore one. But a thing that has size is divisible, hence has
parts, hence is not a real unit. If on the other hand, you do take a
thing that has size as a unit, it will be at the same time like itself
(namely a unit) and unlike itself (namely a multitude: πολλά).

It is not difficult to see why Plato was extremely pleased with an
argument of this kind. For it tended to prove that the One could not
be found among the things that have size, i.e. not in the world of
spatial extension, in fact, not in the world of things in space and
time. This is obviously also the reason why Plato could with good conscience make Pythodoros say[7] that he expected Parmenides and Zeno
to be angry or upset over Socrates' attempt to refute their doctrines,
but that to his surprise they turned out to admire Socrates for his
sagacity and that they merely questioned him further in order to
find out whether he was really aware of all the implications of what
he had said. It shows furthermore why Plato could with good
conscience assert that Zeno, in spite of the fact that in a way he
appeared to destroy the One along with the πολλά by reducing it to
(spatial) nothingness, did not mean to combat Parmenides' theory
of the One—insofar as such a theory was implied in his theory of
being—but rather tried to give it indirect support. For in Plato's
view the reduction of the One to spatial nothingness did not mean its
destruction at all, but, on the contrary, its elevation to a higher
mode of being.

It is then interesting and helpful for the interpretation of Plato's
Parmenides to look at the way the Eleatics and Eleatic philosophy are
used and referred to in dialogs immediately preceding and following
the *Parmenides*. In the *Theaetetus* Socrates says[8] that when he met
Parmenides at a time when he, Socrates, was still very young, he
appeared to him awe-inspiring (αἰδοῖός τε δεινός τε) and it seemed
to him that he had an altogether genuine depth (βάθος τι ἔχειν
παντάπασι γενναῖον: eine ganz adlige Tiefe, as Kurt Riezler translated
the words). Obviously this points forward to the role played by
Parmenides in the dialog named after him. In the somewhat later

[7] *Ibidem* 130 a.
[8] Plato, *Theaetetus* 183 e.

dialogs *Sophistes* and *Politicus* Socrates, who up to the *Theaetetus* had been the main interlocutor in all of Plato's dialogs, is replaced in this role by an Eleatic stranger. What does this mean? That in the earlier dialogs it is always Socrates who asks the questions, who poses the problems, and assumes the leadership in the discussion obviously means that, though what Socrates says in these dialogs moves farther and farther away from what the historical Socrates had said, Plato considered his whole philosophy up to that point as a natural expansion of Socratic thought. And in fact, though what is left of the works of other disciples of Socrates leaves not the slightest doubt that Socrates had no theory of ideas in the Platonic sense, a part of the remainders of the works of these same disciples of Socrates clearly indicates that Socrates did ask the question what the good in itself or the just in itself was: that notion of the good or the just or the καλόν, by which we orient ourselves when we say that a certain thing is good or that a certain action is right or just. It was then quite possible for Plato to feel that such questions naturally presuppose the existence of what Plato later came to call the idea of the good or of the just or of the beautiful, and that this again in its consequences inevitably led to a theory of ideas in its more fully elaborated form, in which it is presented in the *Phaedo*, in the *Meno*, and in the *Republic*. On this basis it is understandable; but it is also characteristic of the way in which Plato dealt with his predecessors, that up to that point he in a way presented the content of his own thought as the product of the thinking of his master Socrates.

But when, in the course of the further development of the theory of ideas, problems turned up which could be only very remotely connected with Socrates' own philosophizing, like the problem of an existence of the ideas outside space and time or the question of the meaning of "being" and "not-being," Plato was in need of another father of this part of his thought, who could be used to present it to his readers in the form of a dialog with questions and answers. He found this father or these fathers in the Eleatic philosophers Parmenides and Zeno of Elea and in Eleatic philosophy in general. In the dialog which deals most specifically with the Eleatic problem of being and not-being, the Eleatic philosopher directs the discussion altogether. That this is also the case in the *Statesman*, which on the whole does not deal with Eleatic questions, is obviously due to the fact that the three dialogs, the *Sophist*, the *Statesman*, and the *Philosopher*, which latter was never written or not completed, were meant to form a coherent sequence and that in the last of these planned dialogs the problem of being and of truth would naturally again have played a very important part.

The problem arising from the fact that it is impossible to equate precisely Parmenides' philosophy as it is expressed in his poem with Plato's own philosophy is solved in the *Sophist* by making the Eleatic stranger at one turn of the discussion say[9] that, in defending themselves (and Parmenides: ἀμυνομένοις ἡμῖν) against the counterarguments of the sophist it becomes necessary for them to subject the thesis of "father" Parmenides itself to an examination (βασανίζειν) and to assert forcefully (βιάζεσθαι) that in a way the μὴ ὄντα may have a kind of existence and in a way that which is may not be. In having the Eleatic stranger make this admission it becomes possible for Plato to deviate to some extent from the doctrine of Parmenides as expressed in the latter's poem and yet to make it appear that of all philosophers previous to Plato, Parmenides had had the deepest insight into the nature of true being or true reality and that Plato's own philosophy was the true unfolding and deployment of the insight that had been germinating in a still not quite perfect form in Parmenides' philosophy.

Looking backward from this upon Plato's earlier dialog *Parmenides*, it is then perhaps not too difficult to see that in this dialog Plato has used a somewhat different device that enabled him to represent his theory of ideas as the natural development or as the unfolding of the real, if somewhat hidden, meaning of the doctrines of the early Eleatic philosophers Parmenides and Zeno, this time without criticizing their doctrines explicitly in any way. He achieved this by making the two Eleatics test his own theory of ideas in the person of the young Socrates, especially in regard to the space-and-timelessness of the ideas, by raising against him the objections that had been raised by various opponents of the theory of ideas up to the time when the dialog was written. Since in the dialog these objections are supposed to be raised not in order to refute the theory of ideas as such, but in order to test Socrates' awareness of its implications, the question of how far Parmenides and/or Zeno would have approved

[9] Plato, *Sophistes* 241 d.

of the theory of ideas in its Platonic form is entirely left open. In this way the confrontation we find in the *Sophist* is avoided.

The concentration on the problem of the space-and-timelessness of the ideas is especially clear in the beginning of the test, when Parmenides tests the meaning of the term "participate" (μετέχειν), which is first used by Socrates to describe the relation between the things in space and time and the ideas. Parmenides first asks[10] whether Socrates believes that the ideas have an existence independent of and separate from (χωρίς) the things which participate in them, and furthermore[11] whether Socrates assumes ideas of all kinds of things, not only of man for instance, but also of water, of fire, of hair, and even of dirt; and when Socrates hesitates to assume the existence of ideas of such lowly things as hair or dirt, Parmenides answers: this is because you are still very young. This latter exchange of opinions is on the face of it not directly connected with the question of the space-and-timelessness of the ideas, but it is, as a later part of the discussion shows, not quite without relation to it either. For the moment, at any rate, Parmenides returns to the main question of the meaning of "participation" when applied to the relation of individual things to the ideas. Parmenides asks Socrates whether he thinks that the whole idea is present in the thing which participates in it or whether "participating" (in agreement with the literal meaning of the word) means that it has only a part in common with it.[12] Socrates answers that he cannot see any reason why the whole idea should not be present in each one of the things that participate in it. Parmenides objects that one and the same thing could not very well be in many separate things at the same time (ἅμα). When Socrates counters: "but cannot the same day be at the same time in different places?" Parmenides in his reply replaces the day by the daylight which is spread out over an area—like a tent, as he says—and of which only one part is above every single part of the area over which it spreads. This is obviously a crucial passage, though in accordance with the nature of the dialog, the purpose of which is to state the problems and not to give their final solution, it is passed over lightly. For the word ἡμέρα used by Socrates, though it can mean "daylight"

[10] Plato, *Parmenides* 130 b.
[11] *Ibidem* 130 c.
[12] *Ibidem* 131 a ff.

when it is contrasted with νύξ, in the expression μία ἡμέρα: *one day*, clearly does not mean daylight, but the day as a determination of time. In this sense, however, we may say that there is the very same day at least at all places on the same degree of longitude, and that there is not one part of that day at a place farther north and another part of the same day at a place farther south. As a pure time-determination the day like any other pure time-determination is free from spatiality, though, since our time-determinations are derived from the revolutions of the earth around its center and around the sun, which are revolutions in space, they are still to some extent bound up with space, which makes it somewhat difficult to grasp the full impact of Socrates' first objections; not to speak of modern theories concerning the relations between time and space which could not play any role in Plato's arguments. But the expression "one day" used by Socrates is so clearly a reference to time and not to daylight, that there can be hardly any doubt that Plato wanted to give a hint, to the effect that there is no difficulty in the assumption that what is neither in space nor in time should be in a way fully present in things separated in space and time. Yet Plato does not further insist on this solution of the problem at this point of the dialog, but contents himself with having hinted at it, because he wishes to take up other arguments that had been set forth against his theory of ideas and which are more closely connected with the explanation of the ideas as paradigms of which the individual things in space and time are considered as copies.

The stage for these problems has been set in the passage preceding the passage dealing with the exact meaning of the term μετέχειν. The question asked there by Parmenides and his stricture on Socrates' answer concern a very crucial aspect of Plato's theory of ideas. In regard to ideas of such lowly things as hair or dirt, one may assume that the idea contains nothing but what is common to all individuals or individual occurrences of the thing in question, i.e. it may be considered as pure abstraction, even if the assumption is made that this abstraction exists not only in our heads but must have a correlate somewhere in a real world outside ourselves. The famous τρίτος ἄνθρωπος argument which is discussed in the *Parmenides* can then hardly be applied, since there appears to be no reason why looking upon what is common to all individuals should not be sufficient to let us recognize them as belonging to the same genus. But the ideas of higher forms, i.e. for instance of living beings of all kinds, are supposed (or at least were at some time in the course of the development of Plato's theory of ideas supposed) to contain in some way more than what is common to all individuals "participating" in the idea, inasmuch as the individual is but an *imperfect* copy of the idea. It is here that the τρίτος ἄνθρωπος appears to attain a certain validity, since it can then be asked, what holds the individual and the idea together, if all of them, including the idea, contain something that is not common to all of them; unless, of course, it can be shown on the basis of the space-and-timelessness of the ideas, that such an idea, i.e. an idea containing more than the individuals, can yet in a way be fully present in each of the individuals so that a man looking with his νοῦς at its imperfect copy through this copy can nevertheless see the perfect idea. This obviously appears to have been Plato's solution of the problem. The two problems of the space-and-timelessness of the ideas and of the perfection of the ideas were then clearly closely connected with each other in Plato's mind. For this reason they are interlaced with each other in the discussion, which would be rather inexplicable on any other assumption.

It is, however, most interesting, that Aristotle, while rejecting Plato's assumption of a transcendent existence of the ideas (the famous χωρισμός), in his teleology retained just that feature of Plato's theory of ideas which in the *Parmenides* is discussed in connection with Aristotle's τρίτος ἄνθρωπος argument. For in Aristotle's teleology the development of a pine seed is not only directed towards the τέλος of a pine tree, pure and simple, but also essentially towards the form of a perfect pine tree, though this latter end is never fully attained. This aspect of Aristotle's teleology which is closely—and positively—related to an aspect of Plato's theory of ideas, in fact plays an extremely important role in the whole of Aristotle's philosophy, especially in his ethics.

This last part of our analysis has seemingly led us rather far away from our problem concerning Plato's handling of Zeno's philosophy in his dialog *Parmenides*. It was, however, necessary to touch upon these things, since only in this way does it become possible to show, how in this dialog various problems are deliberately interlaced with one another and that Plato in this dialog has no intention to present a solution of any of them but merely to give hints as to the direction in which a solution might be looked for. That Plato intended to take these problems up again and to attempt a positive solution, as far as this is possible with the help of the imperfect means of communication at our disposal,[13] is clearly shown by the *Sophist*, where the problem of different types of reality is taken up in all seriousness.[14] The problems of the space-and-timelessness of the ideas and of the "perfection" of the ideas were probably to be taken up again in the *Philosopher*, which was never written or never completed and never published.

To sum up then, the analysis so far has fully confirmed Solmsen's claim that it was not Plato's aim to present a historically accurate description of Parmenides' and Zeno's philosophies and of their relation to one another, but that he used both of them for his own purposes. But Plato's way of handling these things has perhaps been cleared up somewhat further, and this in turn may help to determine to some extent how much historical truth may be contained in his report nevertheless. As Solmsen has correctly pointed out, Parmenides' fundamental concern was different from Plato's. He was concerned with being as being, and what he wanted to prove was that it is impossible for anything that exists to become nothing since the nothing simply does not exist. The logical complement to this is that no thing can arise out of nothing, since the nothing does not exist. The conclusion then is that there can be no real coming to be or passing away, but that what is, is eternal or in a way exempt from time. Yet since this doctrine runs counter to apparent experience and to the common belief based on this experience, Parmenides had to admit the existence of a world of δόξα, of appearance or belief, in which things do come into being or pass away or at least appear to do so. To some extent in the *Theaetetus*,[15] but most thoroughly in the *Sophist*[16] Plato deals with the problem, how false appearance or false opinion is possible, and comes to the conclusion that it is necessary to distinguish between different modes of being. Though he says that it is necessary to modify "father" Parmenides'

[13] Concerning the imperfection of man's means of communication with respect to insight into ideas, cf. Plato, *Epist. VII*, 242 ff.

[14] Plato, *Sophistes* 241 d ff.

[15] Plato, *Theaetetus* 187 d ff.

[16] Plato, *Sophistes* 236 e ff.

doctrine in this respect, he shows at the same time that in his opinion
it was the consequence of Parmenides' thought to assume the
existence of two different realms of being, one in which coming to be
and passing away is possible and does occur, and another one, the
realm of ideas, in which this is not the case, because it is not temporal
but extratemporal, hence exempt from change which is a change in
time.

Zeno had pointed out the paradoxes to which an analysis of a time
or space continuum leads because of the inclination of our mind to
divide a continuum by means of extensionless points and its inability
to build up a continuum out of extensionless points.[17] In Plato's
view this, and especially Zeno's proof that a real One can have no
spatial extension, in its natural consequences likewise leads to the
assumption of a world outside space and time, in which the real
One finds its place. There is no indication in the ancient tradition
outside Plato to show that either Parmenides or Zeno drew the
conclusions that Plato considered the inevitable logical consequences
of their thought, and Plato himself clearly indicates that such was
not the case.

But how does this affect the problem of Zeno's actual relation to
Parmenides' philosophy? It is hardly possible that the whole ancient
tradition concerning the close relation between Parmenides and
Zeno is entirely due to Plato's construction, since Plato's *Parmenides*
was written at least a century after Zeno is supposed to have written
his treatise, and since an interest in a history of philosophy and
science unprejudiced by the tenets of any particular school began
only a generation or two after the time of the dialog in the school of
Aristotle. All of Zeno's paradoxes deal with problems of the continuum. But his most famous paradoxes deal with motion and change.
Motion and change belong to Parmenides' world of δόξα. The objections to Parmenides' philosophy came from the apparent evidence
provided by what Parmenides called the world of δόξα. Is it then not
quite possible that in a way Zeno did try to come to the help of

---

[17] For a more detailed analysis of Zeno's arguments see my article on Zenon of Elea
in the *RE*. For a more general discussion of the meaning and purpose of Plato's dialog
Parmenides and its position within the series of Plato's late dialogs cf. my review of G.
Calogero, *Studi sull' Eleatismo* in *Gnomon* 14 (1938), 106–108, reprinted as appendix to
the German translation of Calogero's work by the Wissenschaftliche Buchgesellschaft
(Darmstadt 1970), 318–20.

Parmenides by showing that an analysis of the world of δόξα led to no less strange paradoxes than an analysis of Parmenides' "real" world of undiluted being, though he did not do it exactly in the way attributed to him by Plato in order to make him serve Plato's philosophical purposes?

Berkeley (Calif.), 12 March 1970

CALLIMACHUS AND THE EPIC

J. K. NEWMAN

Hellenistic Greek poetry has a double importance. Not only is much of it of great intrinsic value, but its influence on the classical period of Latin poetry lends it significance for the whole European tradition. Nowhere is the question of the nature of this influence more pressing than in relation to epic, simply because the Roman exponent of epic, Virgil, is so fundamental to the entire history of poetry after him.

When we ask about the debt of Augustan Latin poets in general to their Hellenistic predecessors, and in particular to the techniques established by the Alexandrians, scholars seem to give oddly divided answers. Sometimes we are told [1] that of course the Roman Augustan poets accepted Alexandrian methods, and that all they did was apply these methods to different ends. But on the other side one reads Professor Brooks Otis on Virgil, Professor Brink on Horace, and above all Professor Konrat Ziegler on the Hellenistic epic, and to them it seems not in the least evident that the greatest of the Alexandrians, Callimachus, can have had much to say to those poets who were most specifically Augustan. Professor Otis, for example, denies that Callimachus can have been at the back of Virgil's narrative style; [2] Professor Brink thinks that Horace had moral ideals which were alien to Callimachus; [3] Professor Ziegler that the Callimacheans were successful propagandists who monopolized the critical stage while true poets continued their activities behind the scenes. [4]

There is a point of difference here which is still worth investigating.

---

[1] E.g. by A. Traina, *Latinitas* 17, 2 (April 1969), 153–54.

[2] *Virgil, a Study in Civilized Poetry* (Oxford 1964), 39–40.

[3] *Horace on Poetry* (Cambridge University Press 1963), 161. Contrast H. Herter in *RE* Suppl. part V col. 451, though even he curiously confines Callimachus's moral earnestness largely to his epigrams. But do the *Iamboi* make no moral appeal?

[4] *Das hellenistische Epos*[2] (Leipzig 1966), 12.

At the outset we ought perhaps to recall just what it is that most non-specialists are likely to have picked up about Callimachus's attitude to large-scale poetry. On that attitude a lot depends. If Callimachus rejected a big book as a big nuisance, to quote the famous phrase,[5] then Virgil assumes an extraordinary position in the poetry of his time, since it is clear that contemporary poets, even, in spite of Professor Brink, Horace, did not share the powerful anti-Callimachean feeling which the writing of an epic would imply.[6]

The conventional picture of Callimachus then[7] begins with the idea that he turned away, in the changed circumstances of Egyptian Alexandria, from the grand genres which had pleased Ionia or Athens. He was a scholar and librarian, and so liked to show off his erudition in his verses. So far did he take his dislike for the accepted tradition of Greek literature that he even quarrelled bitterly with his own pupil Apollonius when the latter had the temerity after all to write an epic. He favoured only small-scale composition. He influenced Roman elegy and the less interesting poems of Catullus. He wrote one or two moving epigrams, but the rest of his work is best left to the experts. If we belong to an older school of literary taste we may be inclined to look with suspicion anyway on the whole phenomenon of "Alexandrianism" and to believe that the sooner poets move away from that kind of thing the better and healthier their works are likely to be.

All this misses the essential truth about Callimachus, and for that truth we have to look carefully at the Preface to the *Aetia*, written by the poet at the end of his life in answer to his critics, the Telchines.[8] The Telchines accused Callimachus of not writing ἐν ἄεισμα διηνεκές. We have to note this. Callimachus is not laying down

---

[5] Frg. 465 Pf. But Wilamowitz (*Die hellenistische Dichtung* [Berlin 1924], I, 212) and Pfeiffer (*ad loc.*) warn against using this remark as a clue to Callimachus's literary attitudes.

[6] On Horace as Callimachean see the pioneering article by F. Wehrli, *Museum Helveticum* 1, 2 (1944), 69 f.: W. Wimmel, *Kallimachos in Rom* (Wiesbaden 1960), 43 f., 148, 187 f., 266, 282 f.: my *Augustus and the New Poetry* (Brussels 1967), 270 f.

[7] E.g. as found in F. Susemihl, *Geschichte der griechischen Literatur in der Alexandrinerzeit* (Leipzig 1891), I, 347 f. Though this picture ignores amongst other things Callimachus's admiration for Ion of Chios, a practitioner of the grand genres, as explained in the diegesis to *Iambos* 13, it is still traceable in the portrait of the leg-pulling poet of K. J. McKay's *Erysichthon* (Leiden 1962, 61 f.) and the unsympathetic sketch given by Otis on p. 5–6 of *Ovid as an Epic Poet* (Cambridge University Press 1966).

[8] Frg. 1,1 f., along with the Florentine scholia printed by Pfeiffer.

a positive programme of qualifications which must be observed by the budding poet. He is quoting what is said about him by men whom he abuses a few lines later on (frg. 1, 7 f.) for their insensitivity, just as at the beginning of the whole piece we were told that these same men had never been friends of the Muse. Apparently Callimachus then went on to show that long poems were not necessarily superior to short ones:[9] when he returns directly to his critics again, we find him declaring that in any case the criterion of good poetry is art, and not length at all (lines 17–18).

A fair reading of this Preface thus suggests that it is wrong to make Callimachus the enemy *tout court* of the ἓν ἄεισμα διηνεκές. Such crudeness fails to do justice to the subtlety of his position. At the same time, one would not wish to deny that for him attention to art meant in his circumstances that there simply was no time for the traditional genres of the drama and the epic, or at least not as those genres had been traditionally treated, since there is some indication in the epigrams that the poet had dabbled in the writing of drama,[10] and in the *Hecale* he had certainly thrown out some hints about the way in which the epic might be brought up to date.[11] But when we look at the list of the names of the Telchines given by the Florentine Scholiast (lines 3 f.) and find among them Posidippus and

[9] Schol. Flor. lines 12 f.: cf. schol. Lond. ad vv. 11–12: H. J. M. Milne, *Cl. Rev.* 43 (1929), 214. A. Lesky, *Geschichte der griechischen Literatur*[2] (Bern and Munich 1963), 762, gives details of the continuing controversy about these lines, but surely an interpretation which made Callimachus compare the short poems of Mimnermus and Philetas with the long poems of someone else would rob his case of its cogency, since he would still have failed to define his attitude to the long poems of his own chosen examples.

[10] E.g. nos. 7, 8, 60 Pf. A. Giannini, "Callimaco e la tragedia," *Dioniso* 37 (1963), 48 f., takes a disappointingly negative view of his theme. G. Capovilla, *Callimaco* (Rome 1967), I, 385–87, summarizes recent scholarship but does not make the point that the puzzling interest shown by Horace's *Ars Poetica* in satyr-play could well go back to Callimachean circles (cf. Porphyrion's comment on *A.P.* 95 f.). T. B. L. Webster notes in *Miscellanea di Studi Rostagni* (Turin 1963), 531 f. Alexandrian interest in the satyr-play, and in *Hellenistic Poetry and Art* (London 1962), 107, suggests that Callimachus actually ends *ep.* 43 Pf. with a reminiscence of the *Dyscolus* (303). It is easy to see how satyr-play as the primitive stage of tragedy (*Poetics* 1449 a 19 f.), yet with obvious affinities with comedy, could have attracted a poet concerned with renewal.

[11] The discussion must not of course be prejudiced from the outset by the notion that the *Hecale* is "only an epyllion." W. Allen's essential contribution here (*Trans. Am. Phil. Ass.* 71 [1940], 6 f.) has still not been properly evaluated by scholars (e.g. not by A. Colonna, *La letteratura greca* [Turin 1962], 554). The *Hecale* was an epic—this was the claim made by Callimachus which the Telchines found so galling. Cf. frg. 530 Pf. where Callimachus is ἐποποιός.

Asclepiades, how can we possibly maintain that Callimachus was the advocate of the short poem and nothing more? How could Posidippus, for example, have regarded it as a grave offence in Callimachus that he had not written anything on the large scale, when there seems not the slightest evidence that Posidippus ever wrote anything large-scale either?[12] Again, if we put side by side what we have from Callimachus and from Asclepiades, is it not clear that of the two it was Callimachus who had at least come as near to the long poem as Alexandrian conditions permitted, with the four books of *Aetia* if with nothing else? Without wishing to labour a point I have made elsewhere[13] I believe that only one explanation fits the facts of the "Battle of the Books": what the Telchines had against Callimachus was not that he wrote on the small scale, which was a perfectly proper choice for a Greek poet to make, but that he exaggerated small-scale techniques beyond what in their opinion was their proper sphere. For the short epigram or lyric τὸ κάτισχνον[14] was all very well: but to take this "thin" style and apply it to poems which, though larger, were not yet as large as literary tradition sanctioned, and then to turn round and imply that this was the way ahead for poetry in the changed circumstances of the Hellenistic age, was a little bit more than conservatives could swallow. This was why a theorist like Praxiphanes moved in to deliver to Callimachus what he no doubt believed to be a well-earned rebuke.

How had Callimachus implied that his was the way ahead for modern poetry? Partly of course by the very act of writing work like the *Aetia* or the *Hymns*, which were clearly meant to press his characteristic methods far beyond the epigram, and we are expressly told by a scholiast[15] that the *Hecale* was written as a reply to those

---

[12] The nature of the *Aethiopia* or *Asopia* is obscure: cf. Susemihl, *op. cit.*, 2, 532, note 68.

[13] *Augustus and the New Poetry*, 324 f.

[14] Schol. Flor. lines 8–9. The discussion by E. Reitzenstein in the *Festschrift Richard Reitzenstein* (Leipzig and Berlin 1931), 25 f., remains absolutely basic to the understanding of Alexandrian literary doctrine both in Greek and Latin. It explains, for example, why Quintilian is not "reluctantly" (D. A. Campbell, *Greek Lyric Poetry* [London and New York 1967], 381) praising Simonides when he calls him *tenuis* (X, 1, 64; on *alioquin* here see the introduction to W. Peterson's ed. of this book [Oxford 1891], p. li) and why *sermo proprius* does not mean simply "choice of words" but "choice of common words; ὀνόματα κύρια."

[15] On *Hymn* 2, 106. Wilamowitz's out-of-hand rejection of this scholium (*op. cit.*, II, 87) is far too cavalier. In *Über die Hekale des Kallimachos* (Göttingen 1893), 744, he had been more inclined to compromise.

who accused him of not being able to compose anything on the large scale. But we can also perhaps detect some traces of the point at issue in the use by the poet of the word μέγα in his epigram about Creophylus:[16] "I am the labour of the Samian who once welcomed the divine bard in his house, and I celebrate the sufferings of Eurytus and fair Iole, and I am called a work of Homer: dear Zeus, this is Creophylus's definition of μέγα." That is, Creophylus, and those of Callimachus's contemporaries who still thought like him, believed that the way to attain the μέγεθος demanded by serious poetry was simply to reiterate the clichés of the epic style, of which we may take ξανθὴ Ἰόλεια to be an instance.[17] Now when Praxiphanes intervened against the views of Callimachus, he did it to some extent indirectly, by attacking the *Phaenomena* of Aratus, and thus provoking Callimachus into writing the Πρὸς Πραξιφάνην, in which Aratus was defended as "a learned and excellent poet" (frg. 460 Pf.). It is possible that in making this attack on didactic poetry Praxiphanes was influenced by his reading of the opening of the *Poetics*, where Aristotle appears to throw some doubt on the status of Empedocles as a poet in the true sense precisely because of the unpoetic subject-matter of his work.[18] But it was also in the *Poetics* that Aristotle had introduced his theory of μέγεθος, which at one moment seems to mean physical length and then again grandeur of content.[19] Can we just detect here the outline of the debate which raged later in Alexandria?

[16] No. 6 Pf. The two interpretations discussed by E. Eichgrün on p. 69 of his dissertation *Kallimachos und Apollonios Rhodios* (Berlin 1961), do not take us very far.

[17] Contrast Apollonius's use of epithets: H. Fränkel, *Noten zu den Argonautika des Apollonios* (Munich 1968), 636, under 1. 42.

[18] It is impossible to understand the credulity with which some scholars have greeted the assertion that after Aristotle's death the *Poetics*, along with his other "esoteric" works, was not known until the first century B.C. (Cf. *Oxford Classical Dictionary*[1], under "Aristotle, (6)"). G. F. Else in *Aristotle's Poetics, the Argument* (Harvard University Press 1957), 337, has actually extended this period to the fourth century A.D. Strabo says in fact that the Peripatetics retained "a few" of Aristotle's manuscripts (XIII 54, 609), not that they were all lost. From frg. 3–7 we see that Callimachus may have drawn on the Παρίων πολιτεία (cf. schol. Flor. 36–37, p. 13 in Pfeiffer) and frg. 407 shows his interest in the Peripatetic tradition of research. Some account of Aristotle's views on poetry must have been known in Alexandria: whether it coincided exactly with our modern text of the *Poetics* does not seem all that important, especially in view of Pfeiffer's cautionary remarks in his *Ausgewählte Schriften* (Munich 1960), 156. Fortunately in the *RE* articles on "Apellikon," "Aristoteles," and "Peripatos," the story told by Strabo and Plutarch (*Sulla*, 26, 1) is treated with due reserve.

[19] Cf. D. W. Lucas's note on 1449 a 19.

In that later debate on the one side would have stood the "orthodox" Aristotelians, rejecting Aratus because he wrote ultimately in the same sort of manner as Empedocles, criticizing Callimachus because he used ὀνόματα κύρια as well as γλῶτται,[20] but above all because he avoided μέγεθος in the crude spatial sense of that word. On the other side Callimachus would have patiently tried to point out that Aristotle does not condemn didactic poetry merely because he raises a technical difficulty about the poverty of Greek stylistic vocabulary; that it was perfectly possible to write good poetry while eschewing the excesses of the dithyrambic manner,[21] and that there was enough ambiguity about Aristotle's treatment of μέγεθος to suggest that it could not simply be equated with physical length, so that one might raise claims to grandeur in some sense even if one did not write "many thousands" of verses. This it is which later enables Leonidas of Tarentum to salute Aratus as καμὼν ἔργον μέγα.[22] Clearly in the traditional and spatial sense Aratus had not written a large work. In Callimachus's sense he had, and καμών hints that this is the sense which matters.

When Callimachus turns back to the Telchines with abuse of their jealousy (lines 17 f.), he says that the proper criterion for a poem is not a Persian chain, but art. What unfaithfulness to his thought then is shown by those interpreters who make him crudely the advocate of the short poem when his whole point is that length does not matter! The only reason why poems written in the Callimachean

[20] Cf. *Poetics* 1457 b 3. This would presumably be the point of saying that the style of Callimachus's poems was κάτισχνον, since Demetrius (assigned to the Alexandrian period by G. M. A. Grube ["A Greek Critic" *Phoenix* Suppl. Vol. 4, 1961], p. 56. G. P. Goold, *Trans. Am. Phil. Ass.* 92 [1961], 189, note 49, while rejecting Grube's dating, nevertheless accepts as a possibility that Demetrius's origin and even literary training may have been Alexandrian.) *De Eloc.* 190–91, notes the use of λέξις κυρία and avoidance of ὀνόματα διπλᾶ as marks of the ἰσχνός style. For the former in Callimachus see E. Cahen, *Callimaque et son oeuvre poétique* (Paris 1929), 491 f. The most amusing instance is perhaps in *ep.* 28,4 Pf., where in the act of rejecting the popular taste the poet uses a prosaic verb, σικχαίνω, on which see F. Bredau, *De Callimacho verborum inventore*, (diss. Bratislava 1892), 67. For the latter see Pfeiffer on frg. 773. Thus the diminution in the use of compound adjectives in the Augustan poets (Norden on *Aen.* VI 141) is not expressive of a new classicism but of a stricter adherence to Callimachean principles, like so much else in Augustan poetry.

[21] Cf. frg. 604: Wilamowitz, *Hell. Dichtung* I, 168.

[22] *A.P.* IX 25: Gow and Page, *Hellenistic Epigrams* (Cambridge University Press 1965), no. CI.

manner are likely to be short is that with new standards of technique there simply is no time to compose at length. But that does not preclude the possibility that one day a super-human genius might emerge who was capable of reconciling length in the accepted sense and art. Meanwhile the obvious need was for poets at Alexandria to explore what could be done with the new artistic standards, under which the dead wood, the trite, the mechanical repetition of formulas had to be replaced by freshness of vocabulary and ideas and made fit to be read by a highly intelligent and easily bored audience. From these experiments the traditional grand genres could not be excluded. We should dearly like to know what Callimachus made of the dramatic challenge. Only his epigrams now give us rueful hints of his experiences there. Of his attempt to revive the epic however, the *Hecale*, more important traces remain. They show that the poet possibly chose a myth from a prose source, Philochorus, but felt himself free to modify that source. One of these modifications came at the very beginning, where the young Theseus was made to leave his father's palace under cover of darkness and without his father's knowledge, thus becoming the sort of backdoor hero who finds his apotheosis in Aeneas.[23] No sooner had his adventure begun than he was inconvenienced by an event which finds particular sympathy in a modern breast, a heavy cloudburst, which forced him to take refuge in the hut of a lady whom the Victorians would have classified as a decayed gentlewoman, Hecale (frg. 238 f.). The invention seems commonplace, because we ourselves have become used to dramatically helpful thunderstorms.[24] But was it not a discovery which had to be remade in at least one art-form, the Western? Mr. George Stevens's *Shane* of 1952 is the first such film I remember in which the weather was made a factor in the traditional *topos* of such films, the gun duel. The action of capturing the Marathonian bull was subordinated to the long scene in which Theseus swapped reminiscences with Hecale. There were other digressions, whose connection with the story is now far from clear.

One shock which the unwary reader received from the *Hecale*, quite apart from the treatment of the story, was the use of language.

[23] Cf. *Aen.* II 752, with Servius's comment.

[24] E.g. *Aen.* IV 160 f. J. Henry, *Aeneidea* II (Dublin 1878), 643 f., finds this passage based on Apollonius IV 1130 f., where precisely the storm is missing. Closer to Callimachus's spirit is Ariosto, *Orlando Furioso* XXXII, 71 f.

Pfeiffer comments on frg. 233 that "Callimachus follows tragic and comic diction everywhere." The strangeness of this combination is apparent. We might perhaps accept *tragic*: that would merely indicate once again that the poet had read his *Poetics* with more care than Praxiphanes and noted the lessons which Aristotle declared (*Poetics* 1462 a 5 f.) the modern epic writer could learn with advantage from the stage. But *comic* diction? Once again we must turn to the *Aeneid* for the supreme development of this technique. How often, for example, in R. G. Austin's commentaries do we note the parallels he draws with the colloquial language of Latin comedy. Thus from Book II of the *Aeneid* alone one can cite the opening word, *conticuere*. "The verb occurs in Plautus," says Austin, "and Virgil introduced it to epic." *Remeare* at line 95 is another Plautine word. *Arrectis auribus* is another colloquialism at 303. With Hecuba's *huc concede* at 523 we find an idiom of familiar speech used in a scene which lacks nothing in dignity and pathos, and yet Austin notes that it occurs nowhere else in high poetry. How interesting that Callimachus's ἴσχε τέκος, μὴ πῖθι should have borne such fruitful progeny![25]

The basic problem which the attempt to revivify the epic style faced was—what attitude should the modern epic writer take towards Homer and Homer's stories? Callimachus was intelligent enough to realise that repudiation of mechanical imitation of Homer, as found in the ποίημα κυκλικόν, could not be replaced merely by studious avoidance of the Homeric model altogether, and indeed such iconoclasm would have been foreign to the devoted cataloguer of the Alexandrian Library. What he did was to sanction another technique which finds supreme development in Virgil, and that is to

---

[25] Capovilla's attempt to play down the importance of this expression (*op. cit.* 181) does not do justice to the complexity of the material cited by Pfeiffer. In any discussion of Virgil's vocabulary we must give his contemporary Agrippa's remark due prominence, that he was the inventor of a bad style drawn from *communia verba* (*Vit. Don.* p. 10 in I. Brummer's ed., Leipzig, 1912). The failure to understand the germ of truth in Agrippa's remark is seen however in this same *Life* p. 14; contrast Macrobius V 5 f., where the *Aeneid* is still recognized as showing mastery of all styles, and Servius on *Aen.* IV ad init. *paene comicus stilus est.* It continued to mar Renaissance poetic theory, though in view of the criticisms levelled at Tasso (C. P. Brand, *Torquato Tasso* [Cambridge University Press 1965], 121 f.) not perhaps poetic practice. I. M. Tronsky, *Istoriya antichnoy literatury* (Leningrad 1951), 396, states quite rightly: "Very great effects are obtained by (Virgil's) discovery of the expressive possibilities of everyday words and formulas used in artistic conjunction."

take for granted that the educated reader will immediately think of a Homeric scene if supplied with hints of language, and will then be able to note the contrast between the original and its modern adaptation. One must ascribe some sort of technique of this kind to the Alexandrians, rather than take it as springing from Virgil, if only because of the evidence of Catullus 64, where the departure of the *Thessala pubes*, for example, after admiring Peleus's wedding presents is described with the help of a simile which Homer uses of the Greek advance to war.[26] It is tempting to interpret this echo device as simply an ironical reversal of the values of the older epic. But when we remember that the baby to be born from the marriage of Peleus and Thetis was Achilles, can we be quite sure that Catullus does not intend a double effect? Certainly, the departure of the guests is a welcome change from war: but that war is still to come one day all the same.[27] In the *Hecale* it is clear that the scene in the hut between the fresh young hero and the old woman was intended to recall that between Odysseus and Eumaeus in the second half of the *Odyssey* (cf. Pfeiffer on frg. 239). This in itself was piquant enough. It told the reader, by a method that later became typical of Virgil,[28] that Theseus was to be just as successful in conquering the bull as Odysseus was in conquering the suitors. But we may see more parallels with Virgil than this. Not only Odysseus visited Eumaeus's hut, but also Telemachus. Thus the character of Theseus in Callimachus became a blend of two Homeric heroes, as Dido, for example, is a blend of Calypso and Circe (and of course of Apollonius's Hypsipyle and Medea). Moreover, like Virgil, Callimachus seems to have aimed to break up his Homeric material. Thus *after* the capture of the bull by Theseus, the curious conversation between the two crows, of which frg. 260 contains a section, uses at lines 62 f. a phrase reminiscent of a passage in the *Odyssey* where Odysseus and Eumaeus have been conversing, along with another in which Odysseus's ship is wrecked just before he is cast up on the island of

[26] Catullus 64, 269; *Iliad* IV 422 f.; cf. Aesch. *Agam.* 1180 f.

[27] Cf. Bacchylides 5, 169 f.; the end of J.-M. de Hérédia's sonnet on Antony and Cleopatra; Millais's picture of the boy Christ in the carpenter's shop at Nazareth; the superimposed shots in George Stevens's *A Place in the Sun*. This motley collection of examples is intended as a reminder of what is often forgotten, that there is never anything wrong with the potential of the European tradition, only with the energy of its exponents.

[28] G. N. Knauer, *Die Aeneis und Homer* (Göttingen 1965), 158.

Ogygia.[29] The first phrase must confirm the symbolism of the earlier part of the narrative, that Theseus was to be just as successful with the bull as Odysseus with his adversaries. Does the second point forward to the clouding of Theseus's victory by the discovery of Hecale's death? Perhaps we are wrong to read too much into the passage, and of course it would be surprising if Callimachus had anticipated Virgil's use of Homeric reminiscence in all its complex irony. In a question which depends so much on knowledge of contexts, the fragmentary nature of our knowledge of the *Hecale* makes definite assertion dangerous. There is one passage elsewhere in Callimachus which certainly seems to anticipate Virgil: in the *Hymn to Demeter* we read that after the luckless Erysichthon had rejected the goddess's plea to spare her sacred trees "she was angered beyond telling and put on her goddess shape. Her steps touched the earth, but her head reached to Olympus." Here the poet has adapted Homer's picture of Strife from the *Iliad*, just as Virgil uses the same picture for *Fama* in bk. IV of the *Aeneid*.[30] In both cases the description signposts what is to happen later in the story.

We can say then that Callimachus was not regarded as useless to the epic writer by Virgil. The obvious question is: was he useless to Apollonius, who after all stood nearer to the teachings of the master? The answer must now be no. Pfeiffer's comment on frg. 7, p. 17, admits of no doubt. "It is now agreed that Apollonius followed hard upon Callimachus's footsteps." The interesting point is that Pfeiffer says this about the treatment of the Argonaut saga in the *Aetia*. Even Callimachus's elegiacs then could hold lessons for the epic writer. If we look at frg. 12 of the *Aetia* we find a curious light shed on the nature of Apollonius's imitation. Here Callimachus described the fate of the Colchians who pursued Jason. One party, not being able to secure Medea's surrender, settled in the island of the Phaeacians sooner than return home, but eventually were expelled from there. Apollonius tells the same story in bk. IV, and includes

[29] o 493 plus μ 407. See Pfeiffer's note. F. Leo, *Geschichte der römischen Literatur* (Berlin 1913), 110, sees evidence of this echo technique in New Comedy. When Virgil uses forms like *direxti* or hypermetric -*que* in epic, recalling Terentian idioms (cf. Dziatzko–Kauer on *Adelphoe* 217, 561), we must ask what stylistic principle is at work. It can only be that of the κάτισχνον detected in Callimachus by the Telchines.

[30] Call. *hy. Dem.* 58; *Iliad* IV 443; *Aen.* IV 173 f.

a line similar to Callimachus's remark that "these things were to be fulfilled in this way long after." His line resembles Callimachus's in sense, but repeats from Callimachus no single word.[31] It looks so far as if we have a clear case of borrowing with attempt at re-phrasing such as we find so often in Callimachus's own adaptations of Homer.[32] But why then does Apollonius use Callimachus's exact line, which he was so careful to vary in bk. IV, word for word in another context, describing the death of the sons of Boreas at the hands of Heracles in bk. I?[33] The same technique occurs again. On frg. 43, 70 f., Pfeiffer notes that "As often, Apollonius transfers Callimachus's words to another topic." When we examine frg. 18 we find that Apollonius has twice utilised a passage from the first book of the *Aetia*, splitting the material offered by Callimachus between his first and last books.[34] In the last instance we can deduce an obvious reason, since the connection of the two passages provides a good example of ring-composition, a device to which there is other evidence that Apollonius was attentive.[35] We can only guess at the motives behind the other changes. The sons of Boreas were to be killed by Heracles as they returned from the funeral of Pelias, who died as the result of a trick played by Medea. We can say then perhaps that already in his first book Apollonius reminded his audience that the Argonauts' quest was to be successful, and yet that this very success was to be tainted with the ambiguity inherent in the character of Medea as both maiden and witch.[36]

There are other things which Apollonius and Callimachus have in common. They both have an interest in *aetia*.[37] Comparison of the hints which Pfeiffer throws off about the euphony of the *Hecale*[38] and one's own impression of how much we miss of Apollonius by

[31] *Aetia* 12, 6; *Arg.* IV 1216. H. Herter, *Bursians Jahresbericht*, vol. 285, 235, seems to give tempered assent to Callimachus's priority in time here, which, following Pfeiffer, I assume for the *Aetia* and the *Hecale* as a whole over the *Argonautica* as we have it.

[32] E.g. frg. 260, v. 55; Pfeiffer on frg. 312.

[33] *Arg.* I 1309. ἤμελλε here stands out all the more in Apollonius as he does not use this doubly augmented form elsewhere (H. Fränkel, *op. cit.* 151, note 346). Callimachus has it three other times.

[34] *Arg.* I 411–24; IV 1701 f.

[35] E.g. I 2, and IV 1002; I 608 and IV 1759; I 774 f. and IV 167 f.

[36] An aspect already hinted at by Pindar, *Pyth.* 4, 250; cf. ἀθανάτου στόματος 11.

[37] E.g. *Arg.* I 956, 1019, 1075; Fränkel's index, 1, 39.

[38] E.g. p. 278–79 on frg. 303; p. 361 on frg. 483.

not hearing his poem read[39] suggest that they both took seriously
the need to renew language.[40] One notes in both authors a slower
pace of narrative than in Virgil.[41] Apollonius believes in brevity
however. His exordium is cut down to four lines, while the *Hecale*
looks as if it dispensed with a conventional appeal to the Muses
altogether.[42] Apollonius's catalogue of heroes in his first book is
seventy lines shorter than the Catalogue of Ships in Homer. We are
not told how the heroes came to know about the projected expedition,
nor even the name of the town where they assembled.[43] In line 6 of
this first book we even have a τέην which needs a reference to the
Aetia to explain its point (cf. Pfeiffer on frg. 18, 9). Like Callimachus,
Apollonius is pious towards the gods.[44] He plays down the heroic and
horrific.[45] Antimachus had said that Heracles was left behind by the
Argonauts because he was too heavy for the ship. Apollonius hints

[39] E.g. the passage through the Clashing Rocks, II 549 f., seems peculiarly rich in
sound effects.

[40] They both wanted to make words sing again, and this is why Cicero's *cantores* in
cantores Euphorionis (*Tusc. Disp.* III 19) and Horace's *cantare* in *Sat.* I 10, 19, have more
in them than has commonly been realized. Cf. my article in *Latinitas* 13, 2 (April 1965),
99 f. When the author of *A.P.* XI 130, attacks the mechanical αὐτὰρ ἔπειτα of the cyclic
poets no doubt the chief ground of complaint is the failure of these poets to organize
their narrative. But it is interesting that this actual phrase should only occur seven times
in Apollonius, while there are passages of 50 and 100 lines or more where even αὐτάρ is
absent. By contrast the fragment of the *Bassarica* of Dionysius printed by Page in *Greek
Literary Papyri* (Loeb Classical Library), 538 f., shows 6 uses of αὐτάρ in 46 lines, including
one αὐτὰρ ἔπειτα if the supplement at 43 is correct.

[41] Of course Virgil often conducts his narrative with such peculiar rapidity, most
notably in bk. IV, that it is hardly fair to compare Apollonius and Callimachus with him.
It is striking though that when Virgil wants to create an impression of particular speed
in bk. VI he borrows Apollonius's technique of adherence to a strict time schedule: cf.
Fränkel's index 1, 32; Norden on *Aeneid* VI 893 f.

[42] If frg. 230 is genuinely the opening line of the poem, Callimachus certainly broke
with the Homeric tradition in not mentioning the Muse in it. Moreover the whole tone
of this line suggests a "downbeat" exordium which would leave no scope for a prayerful
appeal. It would be instructive if one could show that Lucan (so criticized by Petronius,
Sat. 118) and Claudian (*De Bello Gothico* 598) had this ancestor in mind. The contrast
with the role of the Muses in the first two books of the *Aetia* would also be striking.

[43] Fränkel has an excellent note here, *op. cit.*, 24 f.

[44] Cf. Fränkel *op. cit.* on I 1152; also p. 539, note 172. Callimachus sums up his attitude
in *Hymn* 2, 25 f. Cf. K. Kuiper, *Studia Callimachea*, 2 (Leyden 1898), 117 f.

[45] Although Fränkel feels that by contrast with the brevity of the main narrative the
subordinate action is very carefully explained by Apollonius, the particular example
which he cites (*op. cit.* p. 29–30) does not justify this sharp distinction when one remembers
that the Λήμνια ἔργα were proverbial for their horror (Herod. VI 138; Aesch. *Choeph.* 631).
Yet how little of this do we hear from Apollonius!

at this aspect of the story,[46] but the tale of Hylas romanticises the reason for the leaving-behind far beyond it. By contrast Posidippus, one of the Telchines, followed Antimachus. Apollonius contradicts Antimachus again in bk. II, about the genealogy of Phineus.[47] On bk. III we are told by Mooney that the long passage in *oratio obliqua* at 579 f. is un-Homeric and prosaic. One can only think of one authority who might have defended the poet, and that is Callimachus, who also believed in refreshing the old clichés with a modern admixture, as we saw in Virgil's use of comic vocabulary.[48] Again in the third book there is extraordinary displacement of the expected proportions of the action. Most of the narrative is taken up with psychology, and there is much dramatic irony: the actual yoking and ploughing with the bulls is crammed into the last 150 lines. This recalls the technique of, for example, Callimachus's fifth hymn, where there are 14 lines on the bath of Pallas and Teiresias's blinding, followed by 11 lines of reaction from Chariclo and 34 of reaction by Athena, a proportion of about 3 to 1 in favour of *pathos*. In many places in the poem we see that Apollonius has taken to heart Callimachus's line αὐτὸς ἐπιφράσσαιτο, τάμοι δ' ἄπο μῆκος ἀοιδῇ.[49]

A major reassessment in English of Apollonius's achievement is clearly overdue. In particular the sources of his vocabulary need examining, and his use of the simile as an articulating device to give unity to his narrative.[50] For example, at II 70, Amycus is compared to a wave threatening a ship in the very book in which the Argonauts are to pass through the Symplegades. Obviously the poet is signposting his meaning here, just as Callimachus and Virgil do. At III

---

[46] Cf. Wendel's ed. of the Apollonius scholia, p. 116, and *Arg.* I 533.

[47] Cf. Mooney on II 178; at II 237, Phineus is Agenor's son.

[48] Cf. the use of *oratio recta* and *oratio obliqua* in the Acontius and Cydippe fragment of the *Aetia* (no. 75; the *oratio obliqua* starts at line 56). At II 662, Mooney notes πλαδάω as a prosaic word. There is a useful further list in G. Boesch, *De Apollonii Rhodii Elocutione* (diss. Göttingen 1908), 42 f.

[49] Frg. 57, 1. Cf. Fränkel's index, s.v. *Kurzsprache*.

[50] The available studies of Apollonius's language, noted by Herter, *op. cit.* 314 f., seem to concentrate on its relationship to Homer, which H. Erbse suggests (*Hermes* 81 [1953], 163 f.) was rather less scientific than had previously been imagined. Fränkel too observes that Apollonius by no means confines himself to traditional epic vocabulary (*op. cit.*, 105, note 205). J. F. Carspecken (*Yale Cl. Stud.* 13 [1952], 59 f.) mars some excellent remarks with the statement on p. 74 that there are no repeated similes in Apollonius. On the contrary, a study of the cross-references in the imagery of these similes seems basic to any appreciation of the poet's art.

276 f., the simile of the gadfly echoes I 1265 f. and II 88 f. Later, on III 287, Mooney notes that the flame comparison recurs at I 544, and IV 173. Above all it becomes relevant in this context to ask what Apollonius would have understood by Callimachus's reference to the ἓν ἄεισμα διηνεκές. Certainly he is not in favour of a διηνεκές style. At I 649, II 391, III 401, we find that to do things διηνεκέως is bad, while at IV 1247, it is the adjective used for the landscape in which the Argonauts are stranded. Much has been made of the word ἕν, and we have even been told (by K. O. Brink, *Cl. Q.* 40 [1946], 18) that Callimachus rejected the imitation of Homeric poetry for the very quality for which Aristotle admired it, viz. its inherent unity. But this line of reasoning is surely perverse. First of all, it is ambiguously phrased. Aristotle did not admire imitation of Homeric poetry because of its unity. In one part of his *Poetics* (c. 23, 5) he contrasts the actual poems of Homer with their imitations because Homer shows superior unity, while at the very end of his work (1462 a 18 f.) he says that in any case tragedy has a superior unity. This rather suggests that any modern epic along Aristotelian lines would have to learn from tragedy, and it seems clear that as a matter of fact the Peripatetics did not approve of the cyclic epic.[51] Moreover we can have some glimpse into what Callimachus meant by ἓν ἄεισμα if we look at Horace and the ode (I 7, 5–7) in which he declares *Sunt quibus unum opus est intactae Palladis urbem | Carmine perpetuo celebrare et | Undique decerptam fronti praeponere olivam.* So orthodox an editor as Heinze refers us here to Callimachus. But what Horace took Callimachus as meaning then was certainly not that the authors of the kind of poetry he is rejecting showed unity in any good sense. *Unum opus* is rather poetry that is monotonous, that lacks variety. So in rejecting ἓν ἄεισμα Callimachus was not rejecting anything which could be considered good. If he thought that unity in Aristotle's sense had no place in poetry, how do we account for his preoccupation with ring-composition?[52]

If Callimachus was not against the epic in principle, but simply on the grounds that its nature needed rethinking, what becomes of the story of his quarrel with Apollonius? This is such an accepted part

---

[51] The Peripatetic tradition is reflected in the unfavourable verdict of Duris on Antimachus: B. Wyss, *Antimachi Colophonii Reliquiae* (Berlin 1936), Testimonia, 1.

[52] For example at *Aetia* frg. 2, 1 and 112, 5–6.

of conventional literary history[53] that it comes as rather a shock when one first opens Wilamowitz's *Hellenistische Dichtung* and discovers that so great a scholar asserts firstly that Apollonius would not have retired right outside the jurisdiction of the Ptolemies merely because of some literary upset, and secondly that the safest thing to do with Callimachus and Apollonius is to set them side by side as examples of the same literary art. Yet the more one looks at the problem, the more Wilamowitz seems to be right. The *Argonautica* is an Alexandrian poem through and through: if anything, it is Callimachus who has the more intellectually vigorous style. The evidence for the quarrel marshalled by Pfeiffer (on frg. 382) is certainly too meagre to justify the conclusion that if Apollonius was attacked by Callimachus he was attacked on literary grounds. Clearly Callimachus did not say who his adversary was at all. We know from Euphorion's Ἀραὶ ἤ Ποτηριοκλέπτης that curse-poems took the fancy of Alexandrian poets. Housman argued that Ovid's imitation of the *Ibis* was simply a *jeu d'esprit* and was not directed against anyone in particular.[54] We find in the fourth *Iambus* that Callimachus identifies himself with the peaceful olive against the prickly laurel, as indeed in the very first *Iambus* of all he had professed to have robbed Hipponax's metre of its personal spite (cf. *Ia.* I 3–4, IV 45 f.). Why should not then the *Ibis* also have been written as a literary exercise? The evidence for a quarrel between the two poets looks so untrustworthy—for example, we find Mooney actually introducing it into the *Life* of Apollonius given in some of the manuscripts[55]—that no purpose is served by treating this quarrel as the orthodox viewpoint. The two poets may have fallen out: so have many artists. But these incidents are often not very relevant to art.[56]

[53] Sanctioned even by A. Lesky, *op. cit.*, 781. Contrast Wilamowitz, *op. cit.*, 1, 209–10.

[54] *Journal of Philology* 35 (1920), 316: "Who was (Ovid's) Ibis? Nobody." Cf. F. Wehrli, "Apollonios von Rhodos und Kallimachos," *Hermes* 69 (1941), 18; H. Fränkel, *Ovid, a poet between two worlds* (Berkeley 1956), 151 f.

[55] In the Preface to his 1912 edition, p. 2, note 1.

[56] E. Eichgrün, *op. cit.*, 176–77, shows the extremes to which the defenders of the "orthodox" viewpoint have now been driven. He admits that the *Argonautica* was not written in defiance of Callimachus, and argues that the aggression in the quarrel came from Apollonius, annoyed by Callimachus's cool reception of certain parts (but only certain parts) of his poem, and egged on by third parties. A. Hurst seems to hit the nail on the head when he says: "Il semble de plus en plus que s'il devait y avoir eu dispute entre les deux poètes, ce ne serait sans doute pas pour une question littéraire" (*Apollonios de Rhodes* [Institut suisse de Rome 1967], 170).

One of the points which may have united the Telchines in their attacks on Callimachus was their admiration for Antimachus, the fourth-century author of both a *Thebaid* and an elegiac poem, the *Lyde*. Asclepiades and Posidippus had both joined in praise of the latter, while Callimachus had disparaged it (cf. Pfeiffer on Call. frg. 398). Quintilian gives a most interesting judgment: "In Antimachus on the contrary (the contrast is being drawn with Hesiod) we have to praise force, weight, and a style very far from commonplace. But though nearly all scholars agree that he should be placed second, he is deficient in feeling, charm, arrangement of matter, and in art generally, thus making it clear how different a second may be from a good second" (*Inst. Or.* X 1, 53). When we hear a poet being criticised for lack of art, we are surely not very far away from the language of the *Aetia-preface* (line 17). May we perhaps detect in Quintilian's other remarks then some echo of what Callimachus had against Antimachus? He accuses him of lacking feeling—*pathos*: it was the emphasis on the psychological background of which we find so much in the *Bath of Pallas* or bk. III of the *Argonautica*. He complains that he does not show *iucunditas*. Antipater's defence of the *Lyde* suggests that this meant attention to euphony.[57] Again, this attention distinguished Callimachus and Apollonius. A third objection is Antimachus's failure to arrange his material successfully. If this criticism too is Callimachean, how well it tallies with the inference that the ἕν of the notorious ἓν ἄεισμα διηνεκές did not mean a rejection of unity, since unity surely is a facet of arrangement. Once again we have to look in Callimachus, unless he fell victim to his own criticism, for the arrangement which he missed in Antimachus. One aspect of this would be ring-composition. Another would be the use of ordered reference to predecessors, notably Homer, to supply a unity of tone and feeling not only in individual passages but across different books or sections. Both these Callimachean concerns are shared by Apollonius.[58] When finally we are told that Antimachus lacks art, we have some clue to what is

[57] *A.P.* VII 409. Cf. Gow and Page on line 3 of this epigram (*op. cit.*, vol. 2, 87) and on Callimachus's τορόν (*ibid.* 217). If however τορόν in Callimachus refers to "clarity," it is interesting that σαφήνεια is noted by Demetrius (*Eloc.* 203) as a virtue of the ἰσχνός style.

[58] The use of Homeric references to provide an ironical contrast with individual passages looks like a device of Greek lyric (A. E. Harvey, *Cl. Quart.* n.s. 7 [1957], 213). Capovilla (*op. cit.*, 111) suggests that it may have been developed by Antimachus. The

meant by examining Callimachus's own surviving criticisms of the
Lyde, that it was παχὺ γράμμα καὶ οὐ τορόν (frg. 398). *Παχύ* echoes
the πάχιστον of the *Aetia-preface* (line 23), and corresponds to the
pingue of Latin Alexandrian doctrine, as we find it, for example, in
the *Eclogues*, the *Satires*, or the *Appendix Vergiliana*.[59] Its implication
appears to be that its victim is devoid of all intellectual and artistic
nimbleness and grace. Once again we find that even Antimachus's
admirers in the ancient world were forced to admit that he did reveal
a certain αὐστηρὰ ἁρμονία.[60] Perhaps another mark of the *pingue* was
verbosity. This is at the back of Plutarch's allusion to Antimachus
(*de Garr.* 21), and in its turn it indicates that Callimachus did not
separate ἕν from διηνεκές in his phrase ἓν ἄεισμα διηνεκές. He was not
describing poetry with two separate qualities, unity and continuity:
he was describing poetry with only one characteristic, that it was
boring and went on too long.

In so far then as the acceptance or rejection of Antimachus made
a man one of the Telchines, Apollonius looks as if he was on
Callimachus's side. But perhaps the quarrel over Antimachus is
something else which scholars, in the absence of other evidence,
have blown up out of all proportion. Thus if we examine other
epigrams of Posidippus, a striking point is his emphasis on sobriety.[61]
One epigram he actually writes in praise of water-drinkers (Gow and
Page no. 7). But certainly in later literary jargon, the water-drinkers
were the Callimacheans.[62] Again, Asclepiades can praise Erinna for
writing a small, highly-finished book of poems, better than many
others—exactly the argument employed by Callimachus in the
Aetia-preface in his appreciation of Mimnermus and Philetas.[63]
Asclepiades perhaps also admired Hesiod, as did the author of the
Aetia.[64] In one puzzling epigram he quotes directly from

---

large-scale use of the *Odyssey* as the background to the *Hecale* was perhaps new. On
ring-composition in Apollonius cf. *supra*, note 35, and of course his whole poem presupposes knowledge of Homeric technique and language.

[59] *Ecl.* 6, 3 f.; *Sat.* II 6, 14 f.; *Catal.* 9, 64.

[60] Dion. Hal. *Comp.* 22; cf. *De Imitatione*, II, p. 19, in H. Usener's ed. (Bonn 1889).

[61] Cf. nos. 7 and 9 in Gow and Page, *op. cit.* The tantalizing fragment which they print
as no. 24 shows how much evidence is missing.

[62] Wimmel, *op. cit.*, 225.

[63] Asclepiades no. 28 in Gow and Page; *Aet.-pref.* 11 f.

[64] Cf. Gow and Page, no. 45. The ascription however is doubtful.

Callimachus.[65] It could be withering irony: but it could equally be a witty adaptation such as Callimachus himself might have appreciated.[66] Posidippus too shares a phrase with Callimachus.[67] As the phrase in question when it occurs in the *Aetia* is intended to have some self-depreciatory effect in the first place, it is hard to see how Posidippus could have been poking fun at it: and, of course, it is always possible that Callimachus was the borrower.

If Apollonius was a Callimachean and mediated to Virgil a new kind of approach to the epic, the *Argonautica* acquires vastly increased importance in the whole European tradition. Even if he was not, enough hints about how modern epic needed to be written could be deduced from Callimachus's *Hecale* to provide at least the outline of a programme alternative to the cyclic epic. There are even some hints that such a programme was actually put into practice by Alexandrian poets. Ziegler himself (*op. cit.*, p. 20) has to note that in the case of some of the epic poems and authors he cites the length of treatment is uncertain. If we examine such evidence as there is about Nicaenetus, we find that a *Catalogue of Women* and an epic, the *Lyrcus*, is attributed to him, and the latter is quoted by Parthenius for the stories of Byblis and Lyrcus.[68] But Nicaenetus's epigrams show acquaintance with Apollonius and perhaps Callimachus, while one is apparently modelled on Asclepiades.[69] Then there is Pancrates, noted by Athenaeus in a list of epic writers of *halieutica*.[70] Phaedimus wrote a *Heracleia*, possibly in elegiacs.[71] Even Posidippus was the author of an *Aethiopia* or *Asopia*, and he is reported to have altered the reading of one of his lines in the *Soros* to correspond with

---

[65] Gow and Page no. 35, line 4.

[66] If they were such bitter enemies, it is odd that Theocritus should have been able to praise Asclepiades in *Idyll* 7, 39 f., while enunciating at 45 f. an essentially Callimachean position. R. Petroll's scepticism about the force of these lines (*Die Äusserungen Theokrits über seine Person und seine Dichtung* [diss. Hamburg 1965], 54–55) seems misplaced. M. Treu, "Selbstzeugnisse alexandrinischer Dichter," *Miscellanea Rostagni*, 273 f., rightly warns of the difficulty in interpreting these Alexandrian quarrels. Cf. also G. Lawall, *Theocritus' Coan Pastorals* (Center for Hellenic Studies, Washington 1967), 82–83.

[67] Cf. Gow and Page, Posidippus, no. 16, line 8; Call. frg. 75, line 77.

[68] Gow and Page, vol. 2, p. 417.

[69] Gow and Page, no. 2. Epigram 5, attacking water-drinkers, is of doubtful ascription.

[70] Gow and Page, vol. 2, p. 444.

[71] *Ibid.* p. 453.

Zenodotus's recension of Homer.[72] One of his extant epigrams
certainly shows the study of Homer's vocabulary.[73] Rhianus, who is
noted as the author of at least four epics in what looks like the cyclic
manner, was also responsible for a *Heracleia* in only four books and
certainly there is some Callimachean flavour about his epigrams.[74]
Possibly then even a cyclic poet thought there was something worth
learning from the opposing school.

In any case, the whole point of Callimachus's attention to Hesiod
was that Hesiod provided a model for an epic which, while respectful
of Homer, should not simply be the uncritical repetition of his
mannerisms.[75] In this age of the anti-hero, the rediscovery by
scholars of the complexity represented by this double tradition
within epic is a pressing need if their authors are to speak with any
kind of conviction, or indeed to speak at all, to the contemporary
world.[76]

Champaign, 26 May 1970

[72] *Ibid.* p. 483–84. For Zenodotus and Callimachus see Pfeiffer on frg. 12, 6, and in
History of Classical Scholarship (Oxford 1968), 139–40.

[73] Gow and Page, no. 13, 3.

[74] Cf. Gow and Page, vol. 2, p. 503.

[75] Cf. E. Reitzenstein, *op. cit.*, 41 f.

[76] In other words, we have to abandon the puritanism which makes us believe that
imperfect motives cannot sponsor great actions and that great poets, both ancient and
modern, have not seen this truth before us.

A CYNIC HOMEROMASTIX*

JOHN TH. KAKRIDIS

I

The second part of the Cynic papyrus of Geneva (Pap. Genev. inv. 271),[1] belonging to the second century A.D., contains (col. IX ff.) the 7th pseudo-Heraclitean letter (*Epistol. Gr.* 283 ff. Herch.). Except for some small variation in the wording, a practice not uncommon in this popular literature, the papyrus presents the usual text completed by a new and extensive supplement at the end (col. XII 31 ff.).

The philosopher's letter is addressed to his friend Hermodorus and accuses the Ephesians of preparing to pass an ostensibly general law according to which ὁ μὴ γελῶν καὶ πάντα μισανθρωπῶν must leave the city before sunset (IX 2 ff.). Since, however, οὐδείς ἐστιν ὁ μὴ γελῶν...ἢ Ἡράκλειτος (21 f.), it is evident that the legislators' sole target is Heraclitus: ὥστ' ἐμὲ ἐλαύνουσιν (23).[2] Thus the philosopher's inability to laugh constitutes the leitmotiv of the entire epistle: IX 25 δ[ιὰ τί ἀεὶ ἀγελαστῶ;]—37 f. ['Ἡράκλειτον |...ἀγέλαστον]—X 12 [ὅτι οὐδέπ]οτε γ[ελῶ]—25 f. [ταῦτα γ]ελάσω...;—49 ff. ἢ τοὺς [ἀλη- | θινοὺς πολέ]μους...γελ[ά- | σω...;]—XI 39 f. [ἢ δι' ἐκεῖ] νο παύσε- | τέ [με κατηφείας;]—54 f. [ταῦ- | τα ἀγελαστῶ]—XII 18 [δύνα]μαι γελᾶν..;—XIV 13 f. πληρωθῆτέ ποτε ἀδικίας, ἵνα | κ[αὶ ἐγ]ὼ γέλωτος.[3]— 14 f. ἢ γελάσω ποιη- | τάς;

* I should like to thank Mrs. Helen Kay, New York, and Miss Brigitte Zaiss, Freiburg, Germany, for their most valuable help in supplying me with a number of books and periodicals not available in Greece. Also Miss Dorean Magazian, Athens, for her translation of my paper into English.

[1] Published by Victor Martin, *Mus. Helvet.* 16 (1959), 77 ff. See also P. Photiades, *ibid.* 116 ff.; John Th. Kakridis, *ibid.* 17 (1960), 34 ff., *Parola Pass.* 16 (1961), 383 ff., Ἑλληνικὰ 21 (1968), 154 ff.; G. Ch. Hansen, *Klio* 43/45 (1965), 351 ff.

[2] ὥστε μ[ε ἐλαύνουσιν]: Hercher, Martin.

[3] κ[αὶ ἐγ]ὼ (ironice): sodales seminarii thessalonicensis.—Post γέλωτος periodus nova incipit; ἵνα | κ[ρατ]ῶ γέλωτος, ἢ γελάσω ποιη- | τάς: Martin.

In this paper I propose to examine the heretofore unknown polemic against Homer, Hesiod, and Archilochus (XIV 14 ff.). That the real Heraclitus was strongly opposed to these poets was already known (cf. 22 A 22, B 40, 42, 57 D.-K.). It is unfortunate that we cannot have a clear picture of the Cynic's accusations against Hesiod and Archilochus since in the relevant text (XV 5 ff.; see below) only a few letters from the beginning of each line are preserved.

2

THE TEXT

XIV 14   Ἢ γελάσω ποιη- / τάς; Μισῶ μὲν οὖν αὐτούς, Ὁμή- / ρους καὶ Ἡσιόδους καὶ Ἀρχιλόχους. / Ὅμηρος κελεύει λέγειν τὴν / [θ]εὸν

20   αὐτῶι μῆνιν Ἀχιλλέως, / ὡς δὴ τοῦτο μέλον θεοῖς, πάθη / [ἀ]νθρώ- [π]εια ᾄδειν· οὐκ ἠιδέσθη / παρθένου δεόμενος ὑπὲρ παλ- / λακίδος· ἐμὴ ἂν ἠιδέσθη σοφία, / κρίσσων Ὁμήρου. Φιλογύνης ἦν, / καὶ ἃ

25   ἔπασχεν ἄλλους ἔπλασσε, / κόσμωι ποιημάτων ἥρωας ἀ- / κοσμῶν· Αἴαντα διὰ γυναῖκα / ἀπέκτεινε, Ἀγαμέμ<ν>ονα διὰ τὴν / [αὐτ]ὴν

30   ἀπέκτεινε Κασσάνδραν / ἐν οἴκωι, τοὺς ἐν Ἰθάκηι νέους / διὰ Πηνελόπην, τοὺς ἐν Ἰλίωι / [δ]ιὰ Ἑλένην· αἰεὶ διὰ γυναῖκας / [τ]ὴν Ἑλλάδα ὑβρίζει, καὶ θαυμά- / [ζ]εται ἁμαρτάνων. Ἰλιὰς

35   αὐτῶι / [καὶ Ὀδύσ]σεια, τὰ μεγάλα ἔ[ρ]γα, δύο / [γυ]ναικ[ῶν] ἐστιν [π]άθη, τῆς / [μ]ὲν ἁρπασθείσης, τῆς δὲ βου- / [λο]μένης· ἡ μὲν ἁρπασθεῖσα / + [ ]δ[ ]ξεδεινηρωος + , ἡ δ', εἰ μὴ ἐ- / [βούλε]-

40   το, ἅπασαν δεκαετίαν ἤρ- / [μοσ]το; Ταχὺ παύεται ὁ μὴ βουλό- / μ[εν]ος· ἡ διατριβὴ μεῖγμά ἐστι / κ[ρίσ]εως. Ὅσην δ[ε]καετίαν Ὀ- / δυ[σ]σεὺς ἐν Ἰλίωι ἐπολέμησε, / ἴσον που χρόνον ἐν Ὀδυσ-

45   σείαι / με[τ]ὰ γυναικῶν θηλυπαθεῖ: / πα[ρ]ὰ Καλυψοῖ ἑπταετίαν, παρὰ / Κίρ[κ]ηι ἐνιαυτόν· εἶτα κόρωι / Πη[ν]ελόπη[ς] ἐπεθύμει·

50   Ἀρήτη / ἦν [δή]που σωφρονεστέρα· ἐπεὶ / κα[ὶ π]αρ' ἐκείνηι ἂν ἔμεινεν. / Οὐδ[ὲ]ν εὑρίσκω Ὀδυσσέα τὸν σο- / φὸν [π]οιοῦντα, εἰ μὴ ἐσθίοντα / ἢ γυ[ν]αικοπαθοῦντα· ὅσα δὲ / πλανᾶται, οὐ ποιεῖ,

55   ἀλλὰ πάσχει· / ἄξιος τῆς κακουργίας μᾶλλον / δὴ Ὁμήρου ψυχή·

XV 1   αὕτη γὰρ καὶ / Ὀδυσ[σε]ὺς ὁ γόης καὶ Ἀγαμέμνων / ὁ δημ[οβόρος βασιλεὺς καὶ Ἑλένη] φίλαν[δρος ταὐτόν ἐστιν.]

Col. XIV 14 sq. interpunctionem restitui   18–37 suppl. Martin   38 ἔ]δ[ο]ξε δεῖν ἥρωος Martin vix recte   38 sqq. supplevi et interpunxi; εἰ μὴ ἐ[πήρχε]το, ἅπ. δεκ. ἥρ[μοσ]το. Martin   41–57 suppl. Martin

Col. XV 1 sq. δημ[οβόρος Martin; cett. supplevi e.g.

ἐκειν[

τα επο[

5   μεισῶ [μὲν οὖν καὶ ʽΗσίοδον κα]- / κολογ[οῦντα θεοὺς]

Col. XV   5 sqq. supplevi exempli gratia.

COMMENTARY

XIV 14 f. ʽΗ γελάσω ποιητάς; The meaning is clear: "Or should I laugh for joy at the things poets write about?"[4] The difficulty lies in the syntax, because the person or the thing that causes laughter (well-intentioned or insulting) is indicated in ancient Greek by a prepositional phrase (ἐπί τινι, εἴς τινα) or an instrumental dative. Γελᾶν followed by an object accusative means *deridere aliquem*,[5] a meaning which does not fit the context at all. This peculiar syntax is however confirmed in X 49 ff. (ἢ τοὺς [ἀλη- / θινοὺς πολέ]μους ὑμῶν γελ[ά- / σω;]) so that all we have to do is recognize it and include it in our dictionaries.[6]

15. Μισῶ μὲν οὖν αὐτούς: "No, I hate them!" For the adversative use of μὲν οὖν following a question, see J. D. Denniston, *The Greek Particles*[2] (1966), 475.

21. παρθένου refers to the Muse (cf. 17 f. τὴν [θ]εόν). The expression is deliberately chosen to contrast with παλλακίδος (21 f.). Παλλακίς indicates Briseis; that the author might be referring to Chryseis or even to Helen is less probable.

25 f. κόσμωι...ἀ- / κοσμῶν: Oxymoron. Cf. IX 3 f. νόμον ἀνομώ[τ]ατον, XI 3 f. διὰ μου[σικῆς εἰς] / ἄμουσα πάθη παροξυν[όμενοι]. Cf. also IV 4 [ἵνα <μὴ ἀ>τιμάσω τιμῶντα σο]φίαν,[7] XIII 35 δικ[αιοσ]ύνην δοκεῖ τὸν ἄδικον.

33 ff. τὰ μεγάλα ἔ[ρ]γα: Ironically. I believe that μεγάλα refers to the significance rather than to the length of the poems.—We should supply βουλομένης zeugmatically after ἁρπασθείσης with ἁρμόζεσθαι (or something similar).—All efforts to reconstruct the phrase which refers to Helen (38) proved to be in vain. Martin suggests [ἔ]δ[ο]ξε δεῖν ἥρωος, "semble avoir recherché un héros," which does not make any sense. Nor do his supplements always seem to accord with the traces of the papyrus.—ʽΗ δ', εἰ μὴ ἐ[βούλε]το...: Here the Cynic is imitating

---

[4] Always bearing in mind the Ephesians' accusation, Pseudo-Heraclitus uses the word γελᾶν almost as a synonym of χαίρειν. Cf. X 11 ff.: [θ]αυμάζ[ετε / ὅτι οὐδέπ]οτε γ[ελῶ, ἐγὼ δὲ / τοὺς γελῶν]τας (scil. θαυμάζω), ὅτ[ι ἀδικοῦντες / χαίρουσι, σ]κυθρ[ωπάζειν δέον].

[5] See Kühner–Gerth 1, 367 n. 13 and 439 f.

[6] In X 25 ff. [ταῦτα] is a direct object to π[οιοῦντας]; [γ]ελάσω is intransitive. In XI 54 f. [ταῦ- / τα ἀγελαστῶ] the verb is also intransitive, so that we have no problem with ταῦτα.

[7] Dandames' answer to Alexander's request (III 23 f.): [καὶ] μή με ἀτιμ[άσῃς· ἐγὼ γὰρ / εὐεργε]τοῦμαι σ[οφίαν τιμῶν].—[ἵνα τιμάσω τιμῶντα σο]φίαν: Martin.

Herodotus I 4, speaking of the women who had been abducted in mythical times: δῆλα γὰρ δὴ ὅτι, εἰ μὴ αὐταὶ ἐβούλοντο, οὐκ ἂν ἡρπάζοντο. For the omission of ἂν (if it is not a haplography: δεκαετίαν ἂν), see Kühner-Gerth 1, 215 f. The substitution of a rhetorical question for the apodosis of the conditional sentence (οὐκ ἂν ἥρμοστο) seems to have favored this omission.—That Penelope allowed the suitors to attend her for ten whole years is an exaggeration. (Cf. Odyssey β 89 ff.). The *malignitas* of the Cynic is also manifested further on when he accuses Odysseus that during his ten years of wandering the only thing he distinguished himself in was the conquest of women.

45. θηλυπαθεῖν is taken up by its synonym γυναικοπαθεῖν (53) to wind up the chapter on Odysseus' eroticism. Θηλυπαθεῖν was hitherto known only from Philodemus (*Herc.* 312, 4),[8] and γυναικοπαθεῖν only from Athenaeus (12, 523 c), both in the sense of *muliebria pati*. Our author uses both verbs in the sense of *mulierum desiderio affici*.

49. σωφρονεστέρα: Odysseus was a γόης (57) who seduced women;[9] he was unsuccessful only with Arete because she happened to have more control over her passions than Calypso and Circe. I don't believe Martin is right when he thinks that the comparison is between Arete and Odysseus ("plus sage que lui").

55 f. ἄξιος...Ὁμήρου ψυχή: *constructio ad sententiam*. Cf. Hom. *Od.* λ 90 f. ἦλθε δ' ἐπὶ ψυχὴ Θηβαίου Τειρεσίαο / χρύσεον σκῆπτρον ἔχων. Martin considers ἄξιος as an adjective having two endings and refers to Nonnus, *Dion.* VIII 314.

57 f. The unexpected mention of δημ[οβόρος] Agamemnon [10] suggests that at the end of his exposition the author meant to broaden the basis of his polemic. Whether the list was to go on (e.g. [καὶ Ἑλένη] / φίλαγ-[δρος...]) we don't know.—Instead of ταὐτόν ἐστιν one might supply ψυχὴ μία or something similar.

XV 5 ff. From the introductory phrase (XIV 15 f.) μισῶ μὲν οὖν αὐτούς, Ὁμή-/ρους καὶ Ἡσιόδους καὶ Ἀρχιλόχους it becomes evident, I think, that the Cynic has not confined his criticism to Homer. We therefore must first discover the points at which the Cynic turns his polemic from Homer to Hesiod and from Hesiod to Archilochus. By having the epic poet shoulder all his heroes' faults (XIV 55 ff.), we may feel certain that

---

[8] I have not been able to check this reference (made by *LSJ*).

[9] Taken in its entirety the phrase indicates that the characterization of the hero as a γόης refers to his eroticism. Perhaps the Cynic is remembering the passage of the Odyssey (λ 334 = ν 2) which describes how the hero exerted his charm on the Phaeacians just by talking to them (κηληθμῷ δ' ἔσχοντο), and thus seeks to explain the harmful influence of Odysseus' eloquence on women.

[10] δημ[οβόρος]: Martin. Cf. *Il.* A 231.

the chapter on Homer had closed in an absolutely satisfactory manner. Thus μεισῶ (XV 5) which repeats μισῶ of XIV 15 [11] must be the point of transition to Hesiod. (Cf. 5 f. [κα]- / κολογ[οῦντα θεούς], 9 θεῶν, 13 θεογ[ονι-.) It is more difficult to identify the exact point in the text where Archilochus' turn came. I suspect that it is at line 18: Θαυμά[ζω δὲ καὶ Ἀρχίλοχον] / λοιδορ[οῦντα. . .]. The Cynic does not seem to have much to say about these two poets, at least if we are to judge from line 36 (ὦ Συβαρ[εῖται]) where he renews his attack on the Ephesians in order to condemn them for their dissolute way of life.[12] In any case, whatever the author has to say against Hesiod and Archilochus seems to belong to the traditional accusations brought against these poets: κακολογεῖν τοὺς θεοὺς as regards Hesiod and λοιδορεῖν as regards Archilochus. When dealing with Homer, however, he sought to battle him not only more thoroughly but, as we shall see below, with new weapons which he himself devised.

3

The list of Homer's crimes is quite long. At the beginning (17 ff.) the poet is accused of asking the Muse to tell him about Achilles' anger, as if the gods could care about the passions of men; he is also blamed for not hesitating to entreat a virgin goddess on behalf of a concubine; ἐμὴ ἂν ᾐδέσθη σοφία, / κρίσσων Ὁμήρου (22 f.).[13] In thus contrasting the wisdom of the philosopher to the wisdom of other men, the Cynic seems to be following a traditional theme. Cf. Xenophanes 21 B 2, 11 f. D.-K.: ῥώμης γὰρ ἀμείνων / ἀνδρῶν ἠδ' ἵππων ἡμετέρη σοφίη. Shame (αἰδώς) is also a favorite theme of the Cynics.[14]

Further down (51 ff.) the author accuses Homer of presenting Odysseus as having done nothing else during his ten years' wandering except to eat and run after women. We shall discuss the hero's θηλυπάθεια below. As regards his gluttony, it is evident that the Cynic is remembering the hero's repeated references to the needs of the

[11] Such ἀναφορά, a characteristic of the cynic style in general, is used quite frequently by our author: XII 3 ff. ἁρπάζεται. . .ἁρπάζεται, XIII 9 ff. λέγει τις ὑμῖν. . .λέγει τις ὑμῖν, XIV 8 ff. ξίφη ἐπὶ πατέρας, ξίφη ἐπὶ μητέρας, ξίφη ἐπὶ τέκνα, etc.

[12] Max Treu, RE Suppl. XI 149, 40 ff., assumes that the author was talking about Archilochus all through to the end of col. XV. I find this improbable since the iambic poet could hardly be accused of having led the life of a Sybarite (cf. line 36 and 44). Also νομοθ[ετ- (29) and ζημιω[- (34) seem rather to apply to the Ephesians.

[13] About Homer's wisdom, see Heraclit. 22 B 56 D.-K., Isocr. 13,2, Plato Alcib. II 147 c, Xenoph. Conv. 4, 6, Alcidamas (Aristot. Rhet. 2, 1398 B 10 ff.), Aeschin. 1, 142, Themist. 6, 77 d, Plut. Cons. ad Apoll. 104 D and De vita et poësi Homeri, 151 (7, 423 Bern.), etc.

[14] Cf. Diog. Laert. 6, 9 and 65. See Helm, RE XXIII 14, 14 ff., s.v. Kynismus.

belly (η 216 ff., o 344 f., ρ 286 ff., 473 f., σ 53 f. Cf. *T* 225 ff.),
something which has bothered others also, both ancient and modern
critics;[15] he may also be remembering the hero's opinion on what he
believed to be κάλλιστον (ι 5 ff.), which provoked the reaction of
Plato.[16] In any case, the Cynic does not seem to be giving too much
importance to this weakness of Odysseus since the allusion is made
only incidentally in the concluding phrase of the chapter on his
amorousness (51 ff.): οὐδ[ὲ]ν εὑρίσκω Ὀδυσσέα τὸν σο- / φὸν [π]οιοῦντα,
εἰ μὴ ἐσθίοντα / ἢ γυ[ν]αικοπαθοῦντα.

Apart from these elements—the poet's irreverence to the gods and
Odysseus' gluttony—the remaining items in the accusation are seen
as a consequence of the poet's own love for women (23 ff.): φιλογύνης
ἦν, / καὶ ἃ ἔπασχεν ἄλλους ἔπλασσε / κόσμωι ποιημάτων ἥρωας ἀ- / κοσμῶν.
He had presented a number of men—Aias, Agamemnon, Penelope's
suitors, the warriors at Ilium—all of whom had died for the sake of a
woman: αἰεὶ διὰ γυναῖκας / [τ]ὴν Ἑλλάδα ὑβρίζει, καὶ θαυμά- / [ζ]εται
ἁμαρτάνων (31 ff.). His two great works, the Iliad and the Odyssey,
deal with the passions of two women, one of whom let herself be
seduced and the other let herself be desired by many men for several
years. Then comes the turn of Odysseus; except for his wanderings,
which were in fact a series of accidents (53 f. ὅσα δὲ / πλανᾶται, οὐ ποιεῖ
ἀλλὰ πάσχει), he did nothing of his own free will but live with various
women: seven years with Calypso, one with Circe; εἶτα κόρωι /
Πη[ν]ελόπη[ς] ἐπεθύμει (48 f.). By κόρωι the author is no doubt
alluding to ε 153 (οὐκέτι ἥνδανε νύμφη). But had Arete not shown more
restraint, κα[ὶ π]αρ' ἐκείνηι ἂν ἔμεινεν. The meaning of this phrase
clearly is: had the Queen of the Phaeacians responded to Odysseus'
desires, she would have helped him overcome the boredom experienced in his long relationship with Calypso and it would not have
been necessary—or not yet—for him to return to his lawful wife.—
There is no allusion to the hero's encounter with Nausicaa. In his
eagerness to discredit Odysseus as much as possible, the Cynic
chose to present him as the likely lover of a married woman had
she been prepared to offer herself to him.

---

[15] Athen. X 412 c ff.: τὸν Ὀδυσσέα δὲ Ὅμηρος πολυφάγον καὶ λαίμαργον παραδίδωσιν—P.
Von der Mühll, *RE* Suppl. VII 715, 65 ff.; 739, 58 ff.; 744, 49 ff.; *Kritisches Hypomnema
zur Ilias* (1952), 286.

[16] Plato *Republ.* III 390 A. Cf. Athen. XII 513 AB.

4

The Cynic was not the first to challenge Homer. As we know, the polemic against him begins with the Ionian philosophers and continues through the centuries down into the Christian era. It is not our intention to present a history of Homeromastigy.[17] What interests us here is the topics of criticism that were made on various occasions. Was the Cynic following known patterns or was he able to enrich his critique with new arguments about the poet's faults?

The polemic, in its purest form, is directed against the poet himself. Above all, the philosophers accuse him of irreverence to the gods: Pythagoras (Hieron. the Rhodian frg. 42 Wehrli = Diog. Laert. VIII 21), Xenophanes (21 B 11; 12 D.-K.), Heraclitus certainly (22 B 42 D.-K.), Plato, especially in his *Republic*,[18] and Epicurus (fr. 228, 229 Usener).[19]

Only a few years ago we learned that Stesichorus in his first *Palinode* (frg. 193 Page) had attacked Homer for presenting Helen coming into Ilium.[20] Plato too criticized him for letting his heroes behave in an undignified manner.[21] Pindar's accusation against the ἀδυεπὴς Ὅμηρος (*Nem.* 7, 20 ff.) centers on the fact that the poet was so partial to Odysseus that he glorified him beyond his deserts. The same criticism is taken up by Philostratus;[22] he presents Protesilaus characterizing Odysseus as an Ὁμήρου παίγνιον, among other things, because the poet shows a number of goddesses falling in love with the hero who, however, had reached ὠμὸν γῆρας.[23]

---

[17] See J. Geffcken, *Ilb. Neue Jahrb.* 29 (1912), 593 ff.; St. Weinstock, *Philologus* 82 (1926), 121 ff.; H. V. Apfel, *Trans. Am. Philol. Ass.* 69 (1938), 245 ff.—See also W. B. Stanford, *The Ulysses Theme*² (1968) passim, F. Buffière, *Les mythes d'Homère et la pensée grecque* (1956), passim, and A. J Podlecki, *Phoenix* 23 (1969), 114 ff.

[18] Plato *Republ.* 363A–364D, 377B–394A, 599B–608B. Cf. Eurip. *Herc. F.* 1346, Isocr. 11, 38 f., Zoilus (*Frg. Gr. Hist.* 71 F 18), Dio Chrys. 11, 17 ff., etc., Philostr. *Her.* 301, 20 Kayser.

[19] Cf. A. Lesky, *Sb. Heidelb. Ak.*, Phil.-Hist. Kl. 1961, 4, 20.

[20] For the still unsolved problem of the two Palinodes see now M. Treu, *RE* Suppl. XI, 1254 f., and Podlecki, *op. cit.*, 121.—On the contrary, Philostratus (*Her.* 300, 5) believes that Homer ἐχαρίσατο τῇ Ἑλένῃ.

[21] Plato *Republ.* III 388A–391C. Cf. also I 334AB.

[22] Philostr. *Her.* 292, 16; cf. also 318, 22 ff.—Homer was unfair to Sthenelus and partial to Diomedes (*ibid.* 304, 20 ff.).

[23] Philostr. *Her.* 302, 5 ff. Cf. 313, 6 ff.

Homer is described by Dio Chrysostomus as ἀνδρειότατος ἀνθρώπων πρὸς τὸ ψεῦδος.[24] Dio also finds that Homer tends to glorify his compatriots to a degree they do not really deserve; that is why he πολλῆς ἀπορίας μεστός ἐστι καὶ πᾶσι φανερὸς ὅτι ψεύδεται.[25] In any event, one should not blame him, if, being a Greek, he tried to serve his countrymen with every means possible.[26]

It is quite a different thing when criticism, altering its target, aims at the characters of the Homeric poems. In this case heroic tradition is considered as presenting historical facts rather than poetic inventions, and the actions of its characters constitute the material upon which the critic will exercise control. Whether by this procedure the poet is relieved of all responsibility is not a question that can be answered by a mere Yes or No; because one cannot but suspect that the critic who passes judgment on the behavior of Homeric characters is at the same time implicitly condemning the poet himself who, even if he has not invented all his heroes' reprehensible actions, has nevertheless made a point of including them in his work.

In addition, the restless Greek spirit began to question the value of the Trojan expedition as a whole: Had it really been worth-while that so much blood had been shed for a woman who had run away? And who was responsible for all this catastrophe? It seems that the most significant moral problem that bothered the conscience of archaic and classical Greeks alike was whether the Trojan war was at all justified as far as the Greeks were concerned. We can detect an echo of this preoccupation in Homer himself. The well-known words exchanged among the Trojan elders upon sighting Helen on the tower of Ilium (Γ 146 ff.) seem to be an answer to the doubts which had in the meantime beset either the poet himself or his audience. Concurrently, the poet shows Achilles pointing in his

[24] Dio Chrys. 11, 23. Cf. Apollodorus the Erythraean (Frg. Gr. Hist. 422 1: ...Homerum mendacia scripturum); Luc. Philops. 2; Jupp. trag. 39 f.—For the ψευδογράφος Homer in the Sibylline Books (3, 419 ff.) and the polemic launched by the Orphics, see Geffcken, op. cit. 595 ff.

[25] Dio Chrys. 11, 86.

[26] Dio Chrys. 11, 147.—Similarly, one should not look for a hint of reproach in the ancient Scholia on the Iliad when the poet's sympathetic feelings towards the Greeks and his antipathy towards the Trojans are often emphasized. That Homer should be a φιλέλλην is perfectly natural. For the problems of Homer's philhellenism see my paper in Wiener Studien 69 (1956), 26 ff.

wrath to the absurdity of a war which had rallied all the forces of
Greece for what was essentially a private matter (*A* 152 ff.).[27] As
another effort to justify the Panhellenic expedition we might instance
the Hesiodic myth (frg. 204, 78 ff. Merkelbach–West) in which the
general participation of the Greek heroes was interpreted as an
inevitable moral obligation. Aeschylus in the *Agamemnon* finds no
reason to justify the war: All of the main characters involved are
guilty.[28] Euripides launches an even stronger polemic: Apart from
the two Laconian leaders of the expedition, whom the Athenian
patriot finds pleasure in humiliating, the war in the *Trojan Women*
is presented as a series of unjustified killings, rapes, enslavement, and
acts of arson, with calamity hitting both victors and vanquished
indiscriminately.[29] According to Herodotus (I, 1 ff.) it seems that
the question had become a matter of international law. Thus, the
Persian λόγιοι explained to the historian that since the accounts
between the barbarians and the Greeks had been settled—the
barbarians having abducted two Greek women and the Greeks two
barbarians—it was silly of the Greeks to have destroyed Troy for
Helen who, after all, had she not been willing, would not have
let herself be stolen.[30]

With respect to the attacks against the various characters that
played a significant part in the myth of the Trojan War, most of the
arrows are of course directed against Paris and Helen, especially
Helen. To enumerate all the charges brought against Helen would
require quite a few pages, for we would have to start with Eumaeus'
curse in the Odyssey (ξ 68 f.: ὡς ὤφελλ' Ἑλένης ἀπὸ φῦλον ὀλέσθαι /
πρόχνυ, ἐπεὶ πολλῶν ἀνδρῶν ὑπὸ γούνατ' ἔλυσε) and end with the exclamation of Alexander the Great (*Der byzantinische Alexanderroman*,
Cod. Vindob. Theol. Gr. 244, ed. Mitsakis, p. 59): ὦ πόσοι ἀνδρειωμένοι,
ὑψηλότατοι καὶ ἐκλαμπρότατοι ἀπελάτες ἔπεσαν διὰ μίαν γυναῖκα μαγαρισμένη.[31] In addition to being accused of having been unfaithful to her

---

[27] Cf. also *I* 337 ff.

[28] Aesch. *Agamemn.* 218 ff., 799 ff.—60 ff., 362 ff., 399 ff.—403 ff., 437 ff., 681 ff., 738 ff.,
1455 ff.—699 ff.—527. Cf. 338 ff.

[29] Cf. A. Lesky, *Geschichte der griechischen Literatur*² (1963), 419 f.

[30] See K. Reinhardt, *Von Werken und Formen* (1948), 190 ff. (except that Reinhardt
omits the rape of Europa), D. Maronitis, Εἰσαγωγὴ στὸν Ἡρόδοτο (1964), 43 f.

[31] μαγαρισμένη = soiled, filthy. In other versions of the Novel the word has been replaced
by μιαρά.

husband, of having abandoned her daughter and her country and of having been the cause of the war, she is found guilty of fickleness, vanity, shamelessness, hypocrisy, heartlessness, etc.[32]

Among the heroes of the Odyssey, Penelope has stood out as the classical symbol of conjugal fidelity. We shall not concern ourselves with the later unpalatable myths, according to which Penelope was murdered by Odysseus for her illicit liaison with Amphinomos (Apollod. *Epit.* 7, 38), or that she gave birth to Pan after having had affairs with all of her suitors (Douris, *Frg. Gr. Hist.* 76 F 21, etc.). What interests us here is Homer and his creations: did the poet in the Odyssey unintentionally leave the heroine exposed to certain accusations?

According to an epigram of Palladas (*Pal. Anth.* IX 166) Homer showed that all women are κακαὶ and σφαλεραί, since like Helen by her adultery so Penelope by her virtue was the cause of the death of several men.—Dicaearchus' criticism (frg. 92 Wehrli) is even closer to the Cynic's polemic against the wife of Odysseus; for Dicaearchus accuses her of vanity from the very first moment that she appears before the suitors (α 328 ff.):

οὐδαμῶς εὔτακτον εἶναί φησι τὴν Πηνελόπην, πρῶτα μὲν ὅτι πρὸς μεθύοντας αὕτη παραγίνεται νεανίσκους, ἔπειτα τῷ κρηδέμνῳ τὰ κάλλιστα μέρη τοῦ προσώπου καλύψασα τοὺς ὀφθαλμοὺς μόνους ἀπολέλοιπε θεωρεῖσθαι· περίεργος γὰρ ἡ τοιαύτη σχηματοποιία καὶ προσποίητος, ἥ τε παράστασις τῶν θεραπαινίδων ἑκάτερθεν εἰς τὸ κατ' ἐξοχὴν φαίνεσθαι καλὴν οὐκ ἀνεπιτήδευτον δείκνυσι.

Lycophron's characterization of Penelope (*Alex.* 771 f.: βασσάρα σεμνῶς κασωρεύουσα) also seems to refer to her alleged vanity.[33]

With respect to Odysseus, it was quite natural that his legendary craft and wisdom should have been distorted by his critics and interpreted as perfidy and falsehood. They remember that he is the grandson of Autolycus, and accuse him of avarice (on account of his fear that the Phaeacians might have stolen his treasure, ν 215 f.), of

---

[32] Gorgias' Ἑλένης ἐγκώμιον is quite clearly an apology (cf. Isocr. 10, 14 f.) which enables us to know what public opinion thought of the heroine at that time. Isocrates' sophistic Ἑλένη (10) is a real enkomion; the author praises Helen emphasizing her beauty (κάλλους..., ὃ σεμνότατον καὶ τιμιώτατον καὶ θειότατον τῶν ὄντων ἐστίν) and the fact that she was the cause of the Greeks' victory over the barbarians (§§ 54, 68).

[33] See C. von Holzinger, *Lycophrons Alexandra* (1895), 283.

the murder of Palamedes, of cruelty to the defeated Trojans, etc.[34] Our Cynic, however, did not wish to emphasize these particular aspects of Odysseus' character.

What is of importance to us is the fact that when the Cynics began to look for mythical prototypes, their thoughts turned not only to Heracles, the Cynics's saint *par excellence*, and to Thersites[35] but also to Odysseus—both because he had disguised himself as a beggar[36] and because he embodied some of the virtues dear to the Cynics: self-sufficiency, endurance of the hardships of life and of the insults showered upon him while unknown, etc.[37] In his well-known pair of speeches *Aias-Odysseus* Antisthenes had endowed the king of Ithaca with cynic characteristics.[38]

Reaction to this attitude had to come sooner or later; until recently an echo of it could be found only in the 19th letter of Pseudo-Crates (*Epistol. Gr.* 211 f. Hercher):

Μὴ λέγε τὸν Ὀδυσσέα πατέρα τῆς κυνικῆς, τὸν πάντων μαλακώτατον ἑταίρων καὶ τὴν ἡδονὴν ὑπὲρ πάντα πρεσβεύοντα, ὅτι ποτὲ τὰ τοῦ κυνὸς ἐνεδύσατο· οὐ γὰρ ἡ στολὴ ποιεῖ κύνα, ἀλλ' ὁ κύων στολήν· ὅπερ οὐκ ἦν Ὀδυσσεύς, ἡττώμενος μὲν ἀεὶ ὕπνου, ἡττώμενος δὲ ἐδωδῆς, ἐπαινῶν δὲ τὸν ἡδὺν βίον, πράττων δὲ οὐδὲν οὐδέποτε ἄνευ θεοῦ καὶ τύχης, αἰτῶν δὲ πάντας καὶ τοὺς ταπεινούς, λαμβάνων δ' ὁπόσ' ἄν τις χαρίσαιτο. Λέγε δὲ Διογένη...

Pseudo-Crates' testimony, whose importance had been emphasized by Ed. Norden many years ago,[39] is now corroborated by the pseudo-Heraclitean letter; it echoes even more strongly the reaction of the later followers of the School to the audacity of their predecessors in

---

[34] See E. Wüst, *RE* 17, 1913, 66 ff., s.v. Odysseus.—According to Plutarch (*De aud. poet.* 27E), Odysseus was also accused of being φύσει ὑπνώδης, which explains why he was found asleep while the Phaeacian sailors were bringing him ashore in Ithaca.

[35] On Heracles see R. Höistad, *Cynic Hero and Cynic King* (1948), 33 ff.—Thersites as κυνικὸς δημηγόρος: Luc. *Demon.* 61.

[36] To get into Ilium as a spy (δ 244 ff.) and to avoid early identification upon arriving in Ithaca (ν 397 ff.).

[37] See Stanford, *op. cit.* 98; Buffière, *op. cit.* 372 ff.—I was not able to use D. Dudley's *A History of Cynicism. From Diogenes to the 6th century A.D.* (London 1937).

[38] L. Radermacher, *Artium Scriptores*, 122 ff. For the cynic element in the Antisthenian Odysseus see Höistad, *op. cit.* 94 ff.; Apfel, *op. cit.* 247; Stanford, *op. cit.* 96 ff.

[39] Ed. Norden, *Jahrb. f. Klass. Phil.*, Suppl. 19 (1892), 394 f. Norden finds traces of the cynics' criticism of Odysseus in Epictetus (3, 24, 12 ff.) too. Cf. J. Geffcken, *Kynika und Verwandtes* (1909), 23.

representing Odysseus as a Cynic. For there is no doubt that here
too the intensity of the attack was dictated by a desire to contest
the theory of a cynic Odysseus. Similarly, I believe that the ironical
phrase of our Cynic (51 f.) : οὐδ[ὲ]ν εὑρίσκω 'Οδυσσέα τὸν σο- / φὸν
[π]οιοῦντα..., refers to the public opinion on Odysseus' wisdom[40]
but even more so to the judgment of Antisthenes who defended
him as σοφός (frg. 10 Radermacher, *Art. Script.*) :

λύων οὖν ὁ Ἀντισθένης φησί· τί οὖν; ἀρά γε πονηρὸς ὁ 'Οδυσσεύς, ὅτι πολύτροπος
ἐρρέθη, καὶ μή, διότι σοφός, οὕτως αὐτὸν προσείρηκε;...Εἰ δὲ οἱ σοφοὶ καὶ
<ἀνθρώποις συνεῖναι> ἀγαθοί εἰσι, διὰ τοῦτό φησι τὸν 'Οδυσσέα "Ομηρος σοφὸν
ὄντα πολύτροπον εἶναι...[41]

Ἄξιος τῆς κακουργίας μᾶλλον / δὴ 'Ομήρου ψυχή (55 f.). It is worth
noting that κακουργία is attributed to Homer himself since the characters are his very own creatures. (Cf. 24 ff., 31 ff.) We now know that
pre-Homeric tradition supplied Homer with, among other things, the
special character of the gods, their weaknesses and their interference
in human affairs, as well as with the causes and the general outline
of the Trojan War; yet the Cynic, whether wilfully or not, ignored
the fact—and so did Plato[42] and, implicitly, all those who put the
blame on Homer alone.

5

This review of the charges brought by earlier criticism against
Homer will, I believe, indicate the extent of the originality of the
Cynic's polemic. The well-known accusation that the poet was
disrespectful of the gods is now based on new facts (17 ff.). And if
we except Helen—whose role in the myth did not leave much room
for transmuting the basic charges of infidelity that accompanied her
reputation throughout antiquity,[43] Penelope's passion for men and

[40] Cf. Plato, *Republ.* III 390 A: ἄνδρα τὸν σοφώτατον. For characterizations of the hero as
wise by other philosophical schools, see Buffière, *op. cit.* 374 ff.

[41] See Stanford, *op. cit.* 98 f.; Buffière, *op. cit.* 367 f.; Apfel (*op. cit.* 247) gives a different
interpretation of this difficult passage. Whatever its meaning, however, it is certain that
Antisthenes acknowledged the hero's wisdom.

[42] Plato, *Republ.* II 377 D: οὗτοι (i.e. Hesiod and Homer) γάρ που μύθους τοῖς ἀνθρώποις
ψευδεῖς συντιθέντες ἐλεγόν τε καὶ λέγουσι.

[43] Although we do not know what the Cynic was accusing her of in XIV 37 f. (See
above p. 363.)

Odysseus' passion for women are certainly original accusations.[44] An equally novel theory is that the cause for all the amorous adventures of the Homeric heroes was the poet's own weakness for women which led him to insult Greece διὰ γυναῖκας.

Certainly, the Cynic was very unfair to Homer; we must allow, however, that he had studied him thoroughly; it was this that enabled him to enrich his polemic with new material. The Geneva papyrus has revealed to us a hitherto unknown chapter in the centuries-old history of Homeromastigy.

Thessaloniki, 2 June 1970

---

[44] My American editor kindly reminds me of the letter Odysseus gives to Lucian, without the knowledge of Penelope, to carry to Calypso; there he confesses his regret at having left her, and his hope of coming back to her (Luc. *Vera Hist.* II 29 and 35). Given that Odysseus is now living in the Island of the Blest, so that the cause of his regret could not be the loss of the immortality which Calypso had offered him, I am inclined to believe that Lucian hints at Odysseus' weakness for other women: Πηνελόπης κόρῳ αὖθις Καλυψοῦς ἐπεθύμει. Even if the letter is invented by Lucian, as I believe, his device probably presupposes a knowledge of our Cynic's accusations against the Homeric hero. The influence of Cynic doctrine upon the sophist is well known.

FIFTY HIPPOLYTEAN EMENDATIONS:
ELENCHOS, BOOK VI

MIROSLAV MARCOVICH

(1) p. 134.17 We[1] Ὅσα μὲν οὖν ἐδόκει τοῖς ἀπὸ τοῦ ὄφεως τὰς ἀρχὰς παρειληφόσι (sc. Ophitis) καὶ κατὰ τελείωσιν (Bunsen, agn. omn.: μείωσιν P) τῶν χρόνων εἰς φανερὸν τὰς δόξας ἑκουσίως προενεγκαμένοις, ἐν τῆι πρὸ ταύτης βίβλωι οὔσηι πέμπτηι τοῦ ἐλέγχου τῶν αἱρέσεων ἐξεθέμην. νυνὶ δὲ καὶ τῶν ἀκολούθων τὰς γνώμας οὐ σιωπήσω...καὶ τὰ τούτων ἀπόρρητα ὄργια, ἃ δικαίως ὄργια κλητέον· οὐ γὰρ μακρὰν ἀπέχουσιν ὀργῆς τοιαῦτα τετολμηκότες, ἵνα καὶ τῆι ἐτυμολογίαι χρήσωμαι.

Read: (*a*) κατὰ ‹ση›μείωσιν τῶν χρόνων εἰς φανερὸν τὰς δόξας ‹αὐτῶν› ἑκουσίως and cf. *Apocal.* 12:3 καὶ ὤφθη ἄλλο σημεῖον ἐν τῶι οὐρανῶι, καὶ ἰδοὺ δράκων. (*b*) οὐ γὰρ μακρὰν ἀπέχουσι ‹θεοῦ› ὀργῆς and cf. *Rom.* 1:18 et al.

SIMON MAGUS

(2) p. 135.31 ...κατέκαυσαν τὸν Ἄψεθον. Οὕτως ἡγητέον Σίμωνα τὸν μάγον ἀπεικάζοντας τῶι Λίβυϊ † τάχιον, ἀνθρώπωι γενομένωι οὕτως θεῶι.

Read: Οὕτως ἡγητέον ‹τοὺς› Σίμωνα τὸν μάγον ἀπεικάζοντας τῶι Λίβυϊ τάχιον ‹τούτου τοῦ› ἀνθρώπου γενόμενον [οὕτως a dittography] θεόν. For the construction (ἡγητέον) cf. Kühner - Gerth, *Satzlehre*, I 448.

(3) p. 137.27–138.3: A heavy corruption.

[1] Abbreviations:
  P = Parisinus Suppl. Gr. 464 s. XIV.
  H = Hippolytus.
  Mi = *Origenis Philosophumena sive Omnium haeresium refutatio*, e cod. Parisino nunc primum edidit Emmanuel Miller (Oxonii 1851).
  Go = *S. Hippolyti episcopi et martyris Refutationis omnium haeresium librorum decem quae supersunt*. Recensuerunt, Latine verterunt, notas adiecerunt Lud. Duncker et F. G. Schneidewin, professores Gottingenses (Gottingae 1859).
  Cr = *Philosophumena sive Haeresium omnium confutatio*, opus Origeni adscriptum, e cod. Par. productum recensuit, Latine vertit, notis variorum suisque instruxit, prolegomenis et indicibus auxit Patricius Cruice (Parisiis 1860).
  We = *Hippolytus Werke, dritter Band: Refutatio omnium haeresium*, herausgegeben von Paul Wendland (Die griech. christl. Schriftsteller der ersten drei Jahrhunderte, 26, Leipzig 1916).

We:

Τοιούτου δὲ ὄντος, ὡς δι' ὀλίγων εἰπεῖν, κατὰ τὸν Σίμωνα τοῦ πυρὸς καὶ πάντων τῶν ὄντων ὁρατῶν καὶ ἀοράτων, ὧν αὐτὸς ἐνήχων καὶ <ἀν>-ήχων, ἀριθμητῶν καὶ <ἀν>αρίθμων ἐν τῆι Ἀποφάσει τῆι μεγάληι καλεῖ, τελείων νοερῶν, οὕτως ὡς ἕκαστον τῶν ἀπειράκις ἀπείρως ἐπινοηθῆναι δυναμένων καὶ λαλεῖν καὶ διανοεῖσθαι καὶ ἐνεργεῖν, οὕτως ὥς φησιν Ἐμπεδοκλῆς· (Emped. fr. 109 D.-K.).

Read:

Τοιούτου δὲ ὄντος, ὡς δι' ὀλίγων εἰπεῖν, κατὰ τὸν Σίμωνα τοῦ πυρός, καὶ πάντων τῶν <μερῶν αὐτοῦ,> ὄντων ὁρατῶν καὶ ἀοράτων, ἐνήχων καὶ <ἀν>ήχων, ἀριθμητῶν καὶ <ἀν>αρίθμων, <φρόνησιν ἐχόντων> (ὧν αὐτὸς ἐν τῆι Ἀποφάσει τῆι μεγάληι καλεῖ τελείων νοερῶν), [οὕτως ὡς a dittography Cr] *ἕκαστον τῶν ἀπειρά(κι)ς ἀπείρων <μερῶν ἐπιδέχεται> ἐπινοηθῆναι <ὡς> δυνάμενον καὶ λαλεῖν καὶ διανοεῖσθαι καὶ ἐνεργεῖν, οὕτως ὥς, φησίν* (sc. Simon), *Ἐμπεδοκλῆς <λέγει>·*

Cf. p. 273.7 *πάντα δέ, φησί* (sc. Simon), *νενόμισται τὰ μέρη τοῦ πυρός, ὁρατὰ καὶ ἀόρατα, φρόνησιν ἔχειν.* p. 138.7 *πάντα γάρ, φησίν, ἐνόμιζε* (sc. Empedocles) *τὰ μέρη τοῦ π(υ)ρός, τὰ <ὁρατὰ καὶ τὰ> ἀόρατα, "φρόνησιν ἔχειν καὶ νώματος αἶσαν"* (Emped. fr. 110.10 = H p. 215.12).

(4) p. 138.21 . . . *καὶ ἀπόλλυται οὕτως ὡς ἡ δύναμις ἡ γραμματικὴ <ἢ* ci. We> *ἡ γεωμετρικὴ ἐν ἀνθρώπου ψυχῆι· προσλαβοῦσα γὰρ ἡ δύναμις τέχνην φῶς τῶν γινομένων γίνεται, μὴ προσλαβοῦσα δὲ ἀτεχνία καὶ σκότος καὶ* . . .

Read: *τεχν<ίτ>ην* and cf. p. 273.20 *καὶ ἀπόλλυται οὕτως ὡς ἡ δύναμις ἡ γραμματικὴ <ἢ* add.> *ἡ γεωμετρικὴ <ἐν> ἀνθρώπου ψυχῆι ὑπάρξασα, μὴ προσλαβοῦσα τεχνίτην τὸν διδάξοντα.*

p. 139.12 *Μωσέως οὖν εἰρηκότος· "ἐξ ἡμέραις* (P: *ἡμέραι* ci. We) *ἐν αἷς ὁ θεὸς ἐποίησε τὸν οὐρανὸν καὶ τὴν γῆν, καὶ τῆι ἑβδόμηι κατέπαυσεν ἀπὸ πάντων τῶν ἔργων αὐτοῦ"* (*Gen.* 2:2 et *Exod.* 20:11), *τὸν εἰρημένον τρόπον μετοικονομήσας ὁ Σίμων ἑαυτὸν θεοποιεῖ. ὅταν οὖν λέγωσιν, ὅτι εἰσὶ τρεῖς ἡμέραι πρὸ ἡλίου καὶ σελήνης γεγενημέναι* (cf. *Gen.* 1:5–13; H p. 121.11), *αἰνίσσονται νοῦν καὶ ἐπίνοιαν, τουτέστιν οὐρανὸν καὶ γῆν, καὶ τὴν ἑβδόμην δύναμιν τὴν ἀπέραντον.*

Read: *"<ἐν> ἐξ ἡμέραις ἐν αἷς ὁ θεὸς. . .καὶ τὴν γῆν. καὶ <τῆι ἡμέραι> τῆι ἑβδόμηι κατέπαυσεν"* (=LXX). . . *ὅταν <γὰρ> οὖν <αἱ γραφαὶ> λέγωσιν ὅτι εἰσὶ. . .αἰνίσσονται, <φησί* sc. Simon>, *Νοῦν καὶ Ἐπίνοιαν*. . . The reference to OT as *αἱ γραφαί*: pp. 89.8; 140.9.

(5) p. 140.18 *ἐπειδὰν δέ, φησίν, ἀπὸ τοῦ Ἐδὲμ χορίου ἐκπορευόμενος ὁ ὀμφαλὸς ἐμφυῆι τῶι γενομένωι κατὰ τὸ ἐπιγάστριον, ὃ κοινῶς πάντες προσαγορεύουσιν ὀμφαλόν* ⁎ ⁎ ⁎ *αἱ δὲ δύο φλέβες, δι' ὧν ῥεῖ καὶ φέρεται ἀπὸ τοῦ Ἐδὲμ τοῦ χορίου τὸ αἷμα, κατὰ τὰς καλουμένας πύλας τοῦ ἥπατος, αἵτινες τὸ γεννώμενον*

τρέφουσιν· αἱ ἀρτηρίαι, ἃς ἔφημεν ὀχετοὺς εἶναι πνεύματος, ἑκατέρωθεν περιλαβοῦσαι τὴν κύστιν κατὰ τὸ πλατὺ ὀστοῦν, πρὸς τὴν μεγάλην συνάπτουσιν ἀρτηρίαν, τὴν κατὰ ῥάχιν καλουμένην ἀορτήν, καὶ οὕτως διὰ τῶν παραθύρων ἐπὶ τὴν καρδίαν ὀδεῦσαν τὸ πνεῦμα κίνησιν ἐργάζεται τῶν ἐμβρύων.

Read: ἐπειδὰν...ἀπὸ τοῦ Ἐδὲμ ‹τοῦ› χορίου ἐκπορευόμενος ὁ ὀμφαλὸς ἐμφυῆι τῶι γεν(νω)μένωι (= P) κατὰ τὸ ἐπιγάστριον (ὃ κοινῶς...ὀμφαλόν), αἱ δὲ δύο φλέβες...(sc. ἐμφύωσι) κατὰ τὰς καλουμένας πύλας τοῦ ἥπατος (αἵτινες τὸ γεννώμενον τρέφουσιν), αἱ δὲ (= P) ‹δύο› ἀρτηρίαι (ἃς ἔφημεν... ὀστοῦν) πρὸς τὴν μεγάλην συνάπτωσιν ἀρτηρίαν (τὴν κατὰ ῥάχιν καλουμένην ἀορτήν), [καὶ] οὕτως ‹τὸ› διὰ τῶν παραθύρων...ὀδεῦσαν [τὸ] πνεῦμα κίνησιν ἐργάζεται τῶι ἐμβρύωι. Cf. Galen. De usu partium XV 5 (IV p. 231 Kühn; II pp. 351 f. Helmreich).

(6) p. 141.22 καὶ ὅτι ταῦθ᾽ οὕτως ἔχει, κοινῆι πάντων ἐστὶν ἀκοῦσαι κατὰ τοὺς ποιητὰς λεγόντων· (Odyss. 10. 304–06). ἀρκεῖ, φησί, ‹τὸ› λεχθὲν ὑπὸ τῶν ἐθνῶν πρὸς ἐπίγνωσιν τῶν ὅλων τοῖς ἔχουσιν ἀκοὰς (τῆς ἀκ)οῆς· τούτου γάρ, φησίν, ὁ γευσάμενος τοῦ καρποῦ ὑπὸ τῆς Κίρκης οὐκ ἀπεθηριώθη μόνος, ἀλλὰ καὶ τοὺς ἤδη τεθηριωμένους...εἰς τὸν πρῶτον ἐκεῖνον...ἀνεκαλέσατο χαρακτῆρα.

Read: κοινῆι πάντων ‹τῶν ἐθνῶν, φησίν,› ἔστιν ἀκοῦσαι...τοῖς ἔχουσιν ἀκο(ὰς) (ὑ)πακοῆς (= P Mi)...τοῦ καρποῦ ‹οὐ μόνον› ὑπὸ τῆς Κίρκης οὐκ...μόνος, ἀλλὰ καὶ...

(7) p. 142.9 Ἀριθμοὶ τὸ τέταρτον τῶν βιβλίων· γεῦσιν λέγει, ὅπου λόγος ἐνεργεῖ· διὰ γὰρ τοῦ λαλεῖν πάντα ἀριθμοῦ τάξει καλεῖται. Δευτερονόμιον δέ, φησίν, ἐστὶ πρὸς τὴν ἁφὴν τοῦ πεπλασμένου παιδίου ἐπιγεγραμμένον. ὥσπερ γὰρ ἡ ἁφὴ τὰ ὑπὸ τῶν ἄλλων αἰσθήσεων ὁραθέντα θιγοῦσα ἀνακεφαλαιοῦται καὶ βεβαιοῖ, σκληρὸν ἢ θερμὸν ἢ γλίσχρον δοκιμάσασα, οὕτως τὸ πέμπτον βιβλίον τοῦ νόμου ἀνακεφαλαίωσίς ἐστι τῶν πρὸ αὐτοῦ γραφέντων τεσσάρων.

Read: Ἀριθμοὶ ‹δὲ› τὸ τέταρτον...γεύσιν, ‹φησί,› λέγει, ὅπο(υ) ‹ὁ› λόγος ἐνεργεῖ· διὰ γὰρ τὸ λαλεῖν πάντα ‹τῆι τῶν› ἀριθμῶν (i.e. in rhythm: LSJ, s.v., VIII) τάξει ‹οὕτως› κ(α)λεῖται. Δευτερονόμιον δὲ ‹τὸ πέμπτον βιβλίον, ὅπερ,› φησίν, ἐστὶ πρὸς...γεγραμμένον (= P)·...σκληρὸν ἢ γλίσχρον, ἢ θερμὸν ‹ἢ ψυχρὸν Mi Cr› δοκιμάσασα...

(8) p. 142.26 Ἔστιν οὖν κατὰ τὸν Σίμωνα τὸ μακάριον καὶ ἄφθαρτον ἐκεῖνο (cf. Epicur. Sent. 1; ep. Menoec. 123) ἐν παντὶ κεκρυμμένον δυνάμει, οὐκ ἐνεργείαι, ὅπερ ἐστὶν ὁ ἑστώς, στάς, στησόμενος· ἑστὼς ἄνω ἐν τῆι ἀγεννήτωι δυνάμει, στὰς κάτω ἐν τῆι ῥοῆι τῶν ὑδάτων (cf. Gen. 1:2) ἐν εἰκόνι (cf. Gen. 9:6; Ps. 38:7) γεννηθείς, στησόμενος ἄνω παρὰ τὴν μακαρίαν ἀπέραντον δύναμιν, ἐὰν ἐξεικονισθῆι. τρεῖς γάρ, φησίν, εἰσὶν ἑστῶτες, καὶ ἄνευ τοῦ τρεῖς εἶναι ἑστῶτας αἰῶνας οὐ κοσμεῖται ὁ γεννητὸς (Go: ἀγέννητος P) ὁ κατ᾽ αὐτοὺς ἐπὶ τοῦ ὕδατος φερόμενος, ὁ καθ᾽ ὁμοίωσιν (cf. Gen. 1:26) ἀναπεπλασμένος

τέλειος ἐπου(ράνιος), κατ' οὐδεμίαν ἐπίνοιαν ἐνδεέστερος τῆς ἀγεννήτου δυνάμεως γενόμενος. τοῦτ' ἔστιν ὃ λέγουσιν· ἐγὼ καὶ σὺ ἕν, πρὸ ἐμοῦ σύ, τὸ μετὰ σὲ ἐγώ. αὕτη, φησίν, ἐστὶ δύναμις μία, διῃρημένη ἄνω κάτω, αὐτὴν γεννῶσα, αὐτὴν αὔξουσα, αὐτὴν ζητοῦσα, αὐτὴν εὑρίσκουσα, αὐτῆς μήτηρ οὖσα, αὐτῆς πατήρ, αὐτῆς ἀδελφή, αὐτῆς σύζυγος, αὐτῆς θυγάτηρ, αὐτῆς υἱός, μήτηρ, πατήρ, ἕν, οὖσα ῥίζα τῶν ὅλων.

Read: ...ἐν παντὶ ⟨ἀνθρώπωι⟩ κεκρυμμένον δυνάμει...στὰς κάτω ἐπὶ τῆς ῥοῆς τῶν ὑδάτων...τρεῖς γάρ, φησίν, εἰσὶν ἑστῶτες ⟨αἰῶνες⟩, καὶ ἄνευ τοῦ τρεῖς εἶναι ἑστῶτας αἰῶνας οὐ κοσμεῖ ὁ γεννητός...τέλειος ἐπουρά(ν)ιος, ⟨ὁ⟩ κατ' οὐδεμίαν ἐπίνοιαν...(γε)ν⟨ν⟩ώμενος. τοῦτ' ἔστιν, ⟨φησίν,⟩ ὃ λέγουσιν· ἐγὼ καὶ σὺ ἕν· ⟨τὸ⟩ πρὸ ἐμοῦ σύ, τὸ μετὰ σὲ ἐγώ. αὕτη, φησίν, ἐστὶ⟨ν⟩ ⟨ἡ⟩ δύναμις μία, διῃρημένη ⟨δ'⟩ ἄνω κάτω...αὐτῆς υἱός, [μήτηρ, πατήρ,] ἓν οὖσα· ῥίζα τῶν ὅλων.

Cf. p. 142.16 πάντα οὖν, φησί, τὰ ἀγέννητά ἐστιν ἐν ἡμῖν δυνάμει, οὐκ ἐνεργείαι...; p. 139.23 "καὶ πνεῦμα θεοῦ ἐπεφέρετο ἐπάνω τοῦ ὕδατος" (Gen. 1:2), τουτέστι, φησί, τὸ πνεῦμα τὸ πάντα ἔχον ἐν ἑαυτῶι, εἰκὼν ⟨ὂν add.⟩ τῆς ἀπεράντου δυνάμεως. περὶ ἧς ὁ Σίμων λέγει· "εἰκὼν ἐξ ἀφθάρτου μορφῆς, κοσμοῦσα μόνη πάντα." αὕτη γὰρ ἡ δύναμις, ἡ ἐπιφερομένη ἐπάνω τοῦ ὕδατος, ἐξ ἀφθάρτου, φησί, γεγεν⟨ν⟩ημένη μορφῆς, κοσμεῖ μόνη πάντα.

(9) p. 143.21 στρέφεται γὰρ τὸ αἷμα εἰς σπέρμα καὶ γάλα, καὶ γίνεται ἡ δύναμις αὕτη μήτηρ καὶ πατήρ, πατὴρ τῶν γινομένων καὶ αὔξησις τῶν τρεφομένων, ἀπροσδεής, αὐτάρκης. φυλάσσεται δέ, φησί, τὸ ξύλον τῆς ζωῆς διὰ τῆς στρεφομένης φλογίνης ῥομφαίας (cf. Gen. 3:24), ὡς εἰρήκαμεν, ἡ δύναμις ἡ ἑβδόμη ἡ ἐξ αὐτῆς, ἡ πάντας ἔχουσα, ἡ ἐν ταῖς ἓξ κατακειμένη δυνάμεσιν.

Read: ...εἰς σπέρμα καὶ γάλα, καὶ γίνεται ἡ δύναμις αὕτη πατὴρ καὶ μήτηρ, σπορὰ (P: perperam παρὰ Mi, πατὴρ Go cett.) τῶν γινομένων καὶ αὔξησις τῶν τρεφομένων...ὡς εἰρήκαμεν, ⟨ἥτις ἐστὶν⟩ ἡ δύναμις ἡ ἑ(βδ)όμη, ἡ ἐξ αὐτῆς ⟨πάντα γεννῶσα = p. 144.15⟩, ἡ πάντα (Cr) ἔχουσα...

(10) p. 144.1 ...ἀρξάμενος ὡς ἀπὸ σπινθῆρος ἐλαχίστου παντελῶς μεγαλυνθήσεται καὶ αὐξήσει καὶ ἔσται δύναμις ἀπέραντος, ἀπαράλλακτος, ⟨ἴση καὶ ὁμοία Go conl. pp. 138.17; 142.21⟩ αἰῶνι ἀπαραλλάκτωι μηκέτι γινομένωι εἰς τὸν ἀπέραντον αἰῶνα.

Read: ...καὶ ἔσται δύναμις ἀπέραντος ⟨καὶ⟩ ἀπαράλ⟨λ⟩ακτος, ⟨καὶ τὸ μέγα ἔσται⟩ εἰς τὸν ἀπέραντον αἰῶνα [αἰῶνι] ⟨καὶ⟩ ἀπαράλ⟨λ⟩ακτον, ⟨τὸν⟩ μηκέτι γινόμενον. Cf. p. 140.4 ...ὡς γέγραπται ἐν τῆι Ἀποφάσει, τὸ μικρὸν μέγα γενήσεται, τὸ δὲ μέγα ἔσται εἰς τὸν ἄπειρον αἰῶνα καὶ ἀπαράλ⟨λ⟩ακτον, τὸ⟨ν⟩ (Hilgenfeld: τὸ P) μηκέτι γινόμενον.

(11) p. 144.5 Γέγονεν οὖν ὁμολογουμένως κατὰ τοῦτον τὸν λόγον τοῖς ἀνοήτοις Σίμων θεός, ὥσπερ ὁ Λίβυς ἐκεῖνος ὁ καὶ Ἄψεθος, γεννητὸς μὲν καὶ

παθητός, ὅταν ἦι ἐν δυνάμει, ἀπαθὴς δὲ ἐκ γεννητοῦ, ὅταν ἐξεικονισθῆι καὶ γενόμενος τέλειος ἐξέλθηι τῶν δυνάμεων τῶν πρώτων δύο, τουτέστιν οὐρανοῦ καὶ γῆς.

Read: ...ὁ Λίβυς ἐκεῖνος [ὁ καὶ] Ἄψεθος· γεννητὸς μὲν καὶ παθητός, ὅταν ἦι ἐν ⟨τῆι⟩ δυνάμει, ἀπαθὴς δὲ καὶ ⟨ἀ⟩γέννητος, ὅταν...

p. 145.2 ἔστιν οὖν οὕτως καὶ τὸ φανὲν ἀπ' αὐτῶν· ἐν ὂν δύο εὑρίσκεται, ἀρσενόθηλυς ἔχων τὴν θήλειαν ἐν ἑαυτῶι. οὕτως ἐστὶ νοῦς ἐν ἐπινοίαι...

Read: ...εὑρίσκεται· ἀρσενόθηλυς ⟨δύναμις ὄν, = p. 144.19⟩ ἔχει τὴν θήλειαν ἐν ἑαυτῶι. οὕτως ἐστὶ ⟨καὶ⟩ Νοῦς ἐν Ἐπινοίαι...

(12) p. 146.1 ...μετενσωματουμένην ⟨δὲ⟩ (sc. Helenam) ὑπὸ τῶν ἀγγέλων καὶ τῶν κάτω ἐξουσιῶν, οἳ καὶ τὸν κόσμον, φησίν, ἐποίησαν, ὕστερον ἐπὶ τέγους ἐν Τύρωι τῆς Φοινίκης πόλει στῆναι, ἧι ("wo Simon sie fand" We: ἦν P) κατελθὼν εὗρεν. ἐπὶ γὰρ τὴν ταύτης πρώτην ζήτησιν ἔφη παραγεγονέναι, ὅπως ῥύσηται αὐτὴν τῶν δεσμῶν· ἣν λυτρωσάμενος ἅμα ἑαυτῶι περιῆγε...

Read: ...μετενσωματουμένην ⟨δ' αὐτὴν καὶ ἀεὶ ἐνυβριζομένην⟩ ὑπὸ τῶν ἀγγέλων...στῆναι. ἦν κατελθὼν εὗρεν· ἐπὶ γὰρ τὴν τα(ύ)τ(η)s πρώτης ζήτησιν ἔφη παραγεγονέναι... Cf. Iren. Adv. haer. I 23.2 et semper contumeliam sustinentem (sc. Helenam); I 23.3 quapropter et ipsum venisse, uti eam assumeret primam et liberaret eam a vinculis. H pp. 89.8; 223.9; 247.14.

p. 148.1 Οἱ οὖν τούτου μαθηταὶ μαγείας ἐπιτελοῦσι καὶ ἐπαοιδὰς (Go cett.: ἐπαοιδαῖς P) φίλτρα τε καὶ ἀγώγιμα καὶ τοὺς λεγομένους ὀνειροπόμπους δαίμονας ἐπιπέμπουσι πρὸς τὸ ταράσσειν οὓς βούλονται· ἀλλὰ καὶ παρέδρους τοὺς λεγομένους ἀσκοῦσιν...

Read: καὶ ἐπαοιδαῖς ⟨χρῶνται,⟩ φίλτρα τε...ἀλλὰ καὶ τοὺς λεγομένους παρέδρους ἀσκοῦσιν. Cf. Iren. I 23.3 magias autem perficiunt...exorcismis et incantationibus utuntur. amatoria quoque et agogima et qui dicuntur paredri et oniropompi...apud eos studiose exercentur.

VALENTINUS

(13) p. 150.2 παρὰ τῆς δυάδος δὲ πάλιν, ὡς ὁ Πυθαγόρας λέγει, ἡ τριὰς καὶ οἱ ἐφεξῆς ἀριθμοὶ μέχρι τῶν δέκα. τοῦτον γὰρ οἶδε μόνον τέλειον ἀριθμὸν Πυθαγόρας τὸν δέκα· τὸν γὰρ ἕνδεκα καὶ δώδεκα προσθήκην καὶ ἐπαναποδισμὸν τῆς δεκάδος, οὐκ ἄλλου τινὸς ἀριθμοῦ γέννησιν [τὸ προστιθέμενον secl. ut gloss. We].

Read: ...ὡς ὁ Πυθαγόρας λέγει, ⟨γίνεται⟩ ἡ τριὰς...ἀριθμὸν ⟨ὁ⟩ Πυθαγόρας, τὸν δέκα· τὸν γὰρ ἕνδεκα...οὐκ ἄλλου τινὸς ἀριθμοῦ γένεσιν (= p. 75.22: γέννεσιν P) ⟨εἶναι⟩ [τὸ προστιθέμενον].

p. 150.23 Δύο οὖν κατὰ τὸν Πυθαγόραν εἰσὶ κόσμοι, εἷς μὲν νοητός, ὃς ἔχει τὴν μονάδα ἀρχήν, εἷς δὲ αἰσθητός· τούτου δέ ἐστι τετρακτὺς ἔχουσα ἰῶτα, τὴν "μίαν κεραίαν" (Mt. 5:18; Lk. 16:17), ἀριθμὸν τέλειον·

Read: τούτου δέ ἐστι‹ν ἀρχὴ ἡ› τετρακτύς, ἔχουσα ἰῶτα...The tetrad containing the decad (Δ = I):

$$\begin{matrix} & \cdot & \cdot & \\ & \cdot & \cdot & \cdot \\ \cdot & \cdot & \cdot & \cdot \end{matrix}$$

(14) p. 151.11 οὐδ' αὖ πάλιν τῶι λόγωι εἰς γνῶσιν τῶν αἰσθητῶν οὐχ οἷόν τε ἐλθεῖν τινος, ἀλλὰ δεῖ ὅτι λευκόν ἐστιν ἰδεῖν, καὶ γεύσασθαι ὅτι γλυκύ, καὶ ὅτι ὠιδικὸν ἢ ἀπωιδικὸν (Go cett.: δίκαιον ἢ ἄδικον P) ἀκούσαντας εἰδέναι·

Read: ...ἀλλὰ δεῖ ‹ἡμᾶς› ὅτι ‹τι› λευκόν ἐστιν ἰδεῖν, καὶ γεύσασθαι ὅτι ‹τι› γλυ(κ)ύ, καὶ ὅτι ‹τι› ὠιδικὸν ἢ δύσηχον ἀκούσαντας εἰδέναι. Cf. p. 151.9 οὐδέν, φησί, τῶν νοητῶν γνωστὸν ἡμῖν δύναται γενέσθαι δι' αἰσθήσεως.

p. 151.28 = Empedoclis fr. 16 D.-K = H p. 211.23:

ἦ γὰρ καὶ πάρος ἦν καὶ ἔσσεται, οὐδέ ποτ', οἴω,
τούτων ἀμφοτέρων κενεώσεται ἄσπετος αἰών.

ἦ ci. Mi: ἦν P: εἰ H: ἦι Nauck   ἦν καὶ P H: ἦν ‹τε› καὶ Go: ἦν ὡς Nauck: ἔσκε, καὶ Diels   ἔσται οὐδέπω τοίω P H, corr. Mi   κενεώσεται Roeper: καινὸς ἔσται P: κενώσεται H   ἄσπετος Mi: ἄσβεστος P H

Read: ἦι γάρ καὶ πάρος ἦν, καί ‹γ'› ἔσ‹σε›ται and cf. Emped. frr. 108.1; 128.4.

(15) p. 152.8 καὶ ἔστι τῆς γενέσεως τῶν γινομένων πάντων κατ' αὐτοὺς δημιουργὸς τὸ νεῖκος· ἡ δ' αὖ φιλία ἐπιτροπεύουσα καὶ προνοουμένη τοῦ παντὸς ἵνα μένηι καὶ εἰς τὸ ἓν ‹τὰ› διηιρημένα καὶ τοῦ παντὸς ἀπεσπασμένα συνάγουσα καὶ ἐξάγουσα τοῦ βίου, συνάπτει (Go: συνάγει P) καὶ προστίθησι τῶι παντί, ἵνα μένηι καὶ ἔσται (We: ἔστιν P) ἕν. οὐ παύσεται οὖν οὔτε τὸ νεῖκος τὸν κόσμον διαιροῦν οὔτε ἡ φιλία τὰ διηιρημένα τῶι κόσμωι προσνέμουσα. ‹τοι›αύτη τίς ἐστιν, ὡς ἔοικε, κατὰ Πυθαγόραν ἡ τοῦ κόσμου διανομή.

Read: ...τῆς γενέσεως τῶν γενομένων (cf. p. 211.17–20)...καὶ προνοουμένη τοῦ παντός, [ἵνα μένηι καὶ εἰς τὸ (i.e. ἔσται) ἕν] ‹τὰ› διηιρημένα... συνάγουσα καὶ ‹τὰ ὑπὸ τοῦ νείκους γενόμενα› ἐξάγουσα τοῦ βίου, προσάγει καὶ προστίθησι τῶι παντί, ἵνα μένηι καὶ ἔσται ἕν...ἡ τοῦ κόσμου διαμονή. Cf. p. 212.2 ὅταν μὲν οὖν ἀποθάνηι τὰ ὑπὸ τοῦ νείκους γενόμενα (scr.: γινόμενα P), παραλαμβάνουσα αὐτὰ ἡ φιλία προσάγει καὶ προστίθησι καὶ προσοικειοῖ τῶι παντί, ἵνα μένηι τὸ πᾶν ἕν...; p. 151.26 τοιγαροῦν καὶ περὶ τῆς διαμονῆς τοῦ κόσμου ἀποφαίνονται τοιοῦτόν τινα τρόπον οἱ Πυθαγορικοί.

(16) p. 152.15 λέγει δὲ Πυθαγόρας εἶναι ἀπορραγάδας τοῦ ἡλίου τοὺς ἀστέρας... Read: ἀπορρωγάδας.

p. 152.19 ὅθεν ὁ Πλάτων ἐρωτηθεὶς ὑπό τινος· τί ἐστι φιλοσοφία; ἔφη· χωρισμὸς ψυχῆς ἀπὸ σώματος, Πυθαγόρου (Roeper: Πυθαγόρας οὖν P) καὶ τούτου (We: τούτων P) τῶν λόγων γενόμενος μαθητής, ἐν οἷς λέγει καὶ δι᾽ αἰνιγμάτων [καὶ τοιούτων λόγων secl. Cr.]·

Read: τί ἐστι‹ν ἡ› φιλοσοφία...Πυθαγόρου καὶ ‹ἐν› τούτωι τῶν λόγων γενόμενος μαθητής, ‹καὶ› ἐν οἷς λέγει [καὶ Cr] δι᾽ αἰνιγμάτων·

(17) p. 153.19 διδάσκει οὖν ὁ Πυθαγόρας τοὺς μαθητὰς λέγων· "τὸν στρωματόδεσμον δῆσον," ἐπεὶ οἱ ὁδοιπορεῖν μέλλοντες εἰς δέρμα δεσμοῦσι τὰ ἱμάτια αὐτῶν πρὸς ἑτοιμασίαν τῆς ὁδοῦ, οὕτως ἑτοίμους εἶναι θέλων (We: θέλειν P) τοὺς μαθητάς...

Read: ἐπεὶ ‹ὡς› οἱ ὁδοιπορεῖν μέλλοντες... τὰ ἱμάτια αὐτῶν..., οὕτως ἑτοίμους εἶναι θέλει (Mi) τοὺς μαθ(η)τά(ς)...

p. 154.8 "ἀπὸ ὅλου ἄρτου μὴ ἀπόδακνε"· τὰ ὑπάρχοντά σου μὴ μειοῦ, ἀλλὰ ἀπὸ τῆς προσόδου ζῆθι, φύλασσε δὲ τὴν οὐσίαν ὡς ἄρτον ὁλόκληρον.

Read: ἀπὸ ὁλ‹οκλήρ›ου ἄρτου μὴ ἀπόδακνε. Cf. Suda, s.v. Ἀναξίμανδρος· ἀπὸ ὁλοκλήρου ἄρτου μὴ ἐσθίειν.

(18) p. 154.14 δημιουργὸν δὲ εἶναι τῶν γενομένων (Go: λεγομένων P) πάντων φησίν ὁ Πυθαγόρειος λόγος τὸν μέγαν γεωμέτρην καὶ ἀριθμητὴν ἥλιον καὶ ἐστηρίχθαι τοῦτον ἐν ὅλωι τῶι κόσμωι, καθάπερ ἐν τοῖς σώμασι ψυχήν, ὥς φησιν ὁ Πλάτων. πῦρ γάρ ἐστιν ἥλιος ‹ὡς Roeper› ψυχή, σῶμα δὲ γῆ (Roeper: σελήνη P).

Read: ...τὸν...ἥλιον, καὶ ἐστηρίχθαι τοῦτον ‹μέσον› ἐν ὅλωι τῶι κόσμωι, καθάπερ ἐν τῶι σώματι ‹τὴν› ψυχήν...πῦρ γάρ ἐστιν ‹ὁ› ἥλιος, ‹ὡς καὶ ἡ› ψυχή, σῶμα δὲ ἡ γῆ. Cf. Cleanthes, SVF I frr. 499–500 (ἥλιος = τὸ ἡγεμονικὸν τοῦ κόσμου); Chrysippus, SVF II fr. 879; Tertull. De anima 15.4 (Waszink[2] pp. 219 f.; 225 f.); Procl. In remp. II p. 220. 14 Kroll (τὸ ἡλιακὸν πῦρ κραδίης τόπωι ἐστήριξεν); Hisdosus Scholasticus, ad Chalcid. in Tim., cod. Par. Lat. 8624 f. 17ᵛ vv. 18 ff.: alii autem dicunt quod mundi medietas est sol, quem cor totius mundi esse volunt: quemadmodum enim, inquiunt, anima hominis sedem et domicilium in corde habet..., ita vitalis calor a sole procedens omnibus quae vivunt vitam subministrat.

(19) p. 155.8 πάλιν τῶν δώδεκα μοιρῶν ἑκάστην διαιρεῖ (sc. ὁ ἥλιος) εἰς μοίρας τριάκοντα, αἵτινές εἰσιν ἡμέραι μηνός. πάλιν αὖ[των] τῶν τριάκοντα μοιρῶν ἑκάστην μοῖραν διαιρεῖ εἰς λεπτὰ ἑξήκοντα καὶ τῶν λεπτῶν λεπτὰ καὶ ἔτι λεπτότερα. καὶ τοῦτο ἀεὶ ποιῶν καὶ μὴ παυόμενος, ἀλλ᾽ ἀθροίζων ἐκ τούτων ‹τῶν Go› μοιρῶν τῶν διηιρημένων καὶ ποιῶν ἐνιαυτόν (cf. Plato, Rep. 516 b 10; Plut. qu. Plat. 1007 d), καὶ αὖθις ἀναλύων καὶ διαιρῶν τὸ συγκείμενον τὸν μέγαν ἐνιαυτὸν (Roeper cett.: ἀθάνατον P) ἀπεργάζεται κόσμου (Roeper cett.: κόσμον P).

Read: ...διαιρεῖ εἰς λεπτὰ ἑξήκοντα, καὶ τῶν λεπτῶν ‹ἕκαστον εἰς› λεπτὰ [καὶ] ἔτι λεπτότερα (i.e. δεύτερα λεπτά, minutae secundae). καὶ τοῦτο ἀεὶ ποιῶν [καὶ] μὴ παυόμενος...τὸν μέγαν ‹καὶ› ἀθάνατον ἀπεργάζεται κόσμον.

Cf. p. 155.2 ἀριθμεῖ δέ, φησί, καὶ γεωμετρεῖ τὸν κόσμον ὁ ἥλιος τοιοῦτόν τινα τρόπ(ο)ν.

(20) p. 156.2 οἱ δὲ ἀδύνατον νομίζοντες δύνασθαι ἐξ ἄρρενος μόνου γένεσιν ὅλως τῶν γεγενημένων γενέσθαι τινός, καὶ τῶι Πατρὶ τῶν ὅλων, ἵνα γένηται πατήρ, Σιγὴν ἐξ ἀνάγκης συναριθμοῦσι τὴν σύζυγον. ἀλλὰ περὶ μὲν Σιγῆς, πότερόν ποτε σύζυγός ἐστιν ἢ οὐκ ἔστιν, αὐτοὶ (Mi: αὐτοῖς P) πρὸς ἑαυτοὺς τοῦτον ἐχέτωσαν τὸν ἀγῶνα. τὰ δὲ νῦν αὐτοὶ (Mi: αὐτοῖς P) ἡμεῖς φυλάττοντες τὴν Πυθαγόρειον ἀρχήν, μίαν οὖσαν (Go: οὐσίαν P) καὶ ἄζυγον ἄθηλυ‹ν›, ἀπροσδεῆ, μνημονεύσαντες ὅσ᾽ (Cr: ὡς P) ἐκεῖνοι διδάσκουσι ἐροῦμεν· † τε ὅλως, φησί, γεν‹ν›ητὸν οὐδέν, Πατὴρ δὲ ἦν μόνος ἀγέννητος...

Read: οἱ δὲ ἀδύνατον νομίζοντες εἶναι (cf. H p. 273.27 οἱ δὲ ἀδυνάτως ‹νομίζοντες add.› ἔχειν γεννᾶν ἄνευ θηλείας)...[τὴν] σύζυγον...τὰ δὲ νῦν [αὐτοῖς] ἡμεῖς φυλάττοντες τὴν Πυθαγόρειον ἀρχήν, μίαν οὐσίαν (i.e. Monad, cf. p. 150.27) καὶ ἄζυγον, ἄθηλυ‹ν›, ἀπροσδεῆ,...ἐροῦμεν. Ἦν (Go: ἐρουμένην P) ‹μέν› γε ὅλως, φησί, γεν‹ν›ητὸν οὐδέν, Πατὴρ δὲ ἦν μόνος, ἀγέννητος... (Cf. Denniston, Gr. Part.² 160).

(21) p. 156.11 ἀλλὰ ἦν μόνος, ἠρεμῶν, ὡς λέγουσι, καὶ ἀναπαυόμενος αὐτὸς ἐν ἑαυτῶι μόνος. Read: αὐτὸς ἐν ἑαυτῶι, μονάς and cf. p. 155.22 καὶ γὰρ τούτοις ἐστὶν ἀρχὴ τῶν πάντων μονὰς ἀγέννητος...καλεῖται δὲ ὑπ᾽ αὐτῶν ἡ προειρημένη μονὰς Πατήρ.

p. 156.15 προέβαλεν οὖν καὶ ἐγέν‹ν›ησεν αὐτὸς (Mi cett.: αὐτὴν P) ὁ Πατήρ, ὥσπερ ἦν μόνος, Νοῦν καὶ Ἀλήθειαν, τουτέστι δυάδα... Read: ἐγέν‹ν›ησεν ‹ἐν› ἀρχῆι ὁ Πατήρ, ὅσπερ (ci. We) ἦν μονάς...δυάδα... (Cf. the epithet of Bythus: Προαρχή, Iren. I 1.1.)

p. 156.26 ἔδει γὰρ τέλειον ὄντα τὸν Πατέρα ἀριθμῶι δοξάζεσθαι τελείωι· τέλειος δέ ἐστιν ὁ δέκα, ὅτι πρῶτος τῶν κατὰ πλῆθος γινομένων οὗτός ἐστι τέλειος. τελειότερος δὲ ὁ Πατήρ, ὅτι ἀγέννητος ὢν μόνος διὰ πρώτης τῆς μιᾶς συζυγίας τοῦ Νοῦ καὶ τῆς Ἀληθείας πάσας τὰς τῶν γενομένων προβαλεῖν εὐπόρησε ῥίζας.

Read: ...τέλειος δέ ἐστιν ὁ δέκα, ὅτι πρῶτος τῶν κατὰ πλῆθος γενομένων (= P) ‹αἰώνων› οὗτός ἐστι τέλειος. τελειότερος δὲ ὁ Πατήρ, ὅτι ἀγέννητος ὢν μονάς, διὰ τῆς πρώτης ‹καὶ› μιᾶς συζυγίας κτλ. Cf. v. 23 ηὐχαρίστησαν τῶι Πατρὶ τῶν (ὅλω)ν καὶ προσφέρουσιν αὐτῶι τέλειον ἀριθμόν, αἰῶνας δέκα.

(22) p. 158.4 ...ἀγνοοῦσα (sc. Sophia) ὅτι ὁ μὲν ἀγέννητος, ὑπάρχων ἀρχὴ τῶν ὅλων καὶ ῥίζα καὶ βάθος καὶ βυθός, δυνατῶς ἔχει γεννῆσαι μόνος, γεν‹ν›ητὴ δὲ οὖσα ἡ Σοφία καὶ μετὰ πλείονας γενομένη, τὴν τοῦ ἀγεννήτου δύναμιν οὐ δύναται ἔχειν.

Read: ἀγνοοῦσα ὅτι ὁ μὲν ‹Πατήρ,› ἀγέννητος ὑπάρχων ‹καὶ› ἀρχὴ τῶν ὅλων ‹ὢν› καὶ ῥίζα...

p. 158.15 Γενομένης οὖν ἐντὸς πληρώματος ἀγνοίας κατὰ τὴν Σοφίαν καὶ ἀμορφίας κατὰ τὸ γέν‹ν›ημα τῆς Σοφίας, θόρυβος ἐγένετο ἐν τῶι πληρώματι· ‹ἐφοβοῦντο γὰρ add. Mi› οἱ αἰῶνες οἰόμενοι (Bunsen: οἱ γενόμενοι P), ὅτι παραπλησίως ἄμορφα καὶ ἀτελῆ γενήσεται τῶν αἰώνων τὰ γεννήματα καὶ φθορά τις καταλήψεται οὐκ εἰς μακράν ποτε τοὺς αἰῶνας.

Read: θόρυβος ‹καὶ φόβος› ἐγένετο ἐν τῶι πληρώματι [οἱ αἰῶνες οἱ γενόμενοι secl. ut gloss. Go] ὅτι...οὐκ εἰς μακρὰν πάντας τοὺς αἰῶνας. Cf. Iren. I 2.4. ἐκ τῆς ἀγνοίας καὶ τῆς λύπης καὶ τοῦ φόβου καὶ τῆς ἐκπλήξεως.

(23) p. 159.3 ...εὐθέως τὸ ἔκτρωμα τὸ ἄμορφον τοῦτο τῆς Σοφίας, μονογενὲς καὶ δίχα συζύγου γεγεν‹ν›ημένον, ἀποχωρίζει (sc. ὁ Χριστὸς) τῶν ὅλων αἰώνων, ἵνα μὴ βλέποντες αὐτὸ ταράσσωνται διὰ τὴν ἀμορφίαν οἱ τέλειοι αἰῶνες. Read: ἀποχωρίζει τῶν ἄλλων αἰώνων and cf. v. 25 μετὰ τῶν ἄλλων αἰώνων δοξάζων τὸν Πατέρα.

p. 159.12 καλεῖται δὲ Ὅρος μὲν οὗτος, ὅτι ἀφορίζει ἀπὸ τοῦ πληρώματος ἔξω τὸ ὑστέρημα, Μετοχεύς δέ, ὅτι μετέχει καὶ τοῦ ὑστερήματος, Σταυρὸς δέ, ὅτι πέπηγεν ἀκλινῶς καὶ ἀμετακινήτως (Roeper: ἀμετανοήτως P: ἀμεταβλήτως ci. Go), ὡς μὴ δύνασθαι μηδὲν τοῦ ὑστερήματος καταγενέσθαι (Go: καὶ γενέσθαι P) ἐγγὺς τῶν ἐντὸς πληρώματος αἰώνων. Read: ἀμετανοήτως P ('assuredly; unwaveringly') and cf. G. W. H. Lampe, *Patristic Greek Lexicon*, s.v.

p. 159.20 ἐπειδὴ δὲ μεμόρφωτο ἡ Σοφία ἔξω καὶ οὐχ οἷόν τε ἦν [ἴσον del. Cr = Ἰησοῦν] τὸν Χριστὸν καὶ τὸ ἅγιον ‹Πνεῦμα Mi› ἐκ τοῦ Νοὸς προβεβλημένα καὶ τῆς Ἀληθείας ἔξω τοῦ πληρώματος μένειν, ἀνέδραμεν ἀπὸ τῆς μεμορφωμένης ὁ Χριστὸς καὶ τὸ ἅγιον Πνεῦμα πρὸς τὸν Νοῦν καὶ τὴν Ἀλήθειαν, ἐντὸς τοῦ ὅρου ‹ἢ Mi› μετὰ τῶν ἄλλων αἰώνων δοξάζων τὸν Πατέρα. Read: ...ἡ Σοφία ‹ἡ Mi› ἔξω, καὶ οὐχ οἷόν τε ἦν ‹κατ'› ἴσον ('equally') τὸν Χριστὸν καὶ τὸ ἅγιον ‹Πνεῦμα, τὸ› ἐκ τοῦ Νοὸς προβεβλημένον καὶ τῆς Ἀληθείας ἔξω τοῦ πληρώματος μένειν..., τὴν Ἀλήθειαν, ‹ἵν' Mi› ἐντὸς τοῦ Ὅρου ἦι (Mi)...

(24) p. 161.2 ὁ δημιουργὸς ἀπὸ τοῦ φόβου· τοῦτ' ἔστιν ὃ λέγει, φησίν, ἡ γραφή· "ἀρχὴ σοφίας φόβος κυρίου" (Ps. 110:10; Prov. 1:7; 9:10). αὕτη γὰρ ἀρχὴ τῶν τῆς Σοφίας παθῶν· ἐφοβήθη γάρ, εἶτα ἐλυπήθη, εἶτα ἠπόρησε, καὶ οὕτως ἐπὶ δέησιν καὶ ἱκετείαν κατέφυγεν. ἔστι δὲ πυρώδης, φησίν, ἡ ψυχικὴ οὐσία, καλεῖται δὲ καὶ τόπος ‹μεσότητος› (Go conl. Iren. I 5.3; I 6.4; Epiphan. Panar. 31.6.5: ‹ὑπερουράνιος› τόπος Cr conl. Iren. I 5.4) ὑπ' αὐτῶν καὶ ἑβδομὰς καὶ "παλαιὸς τῶν ἡμερῶν" (Dan. 7:9; 13; 22)· καὶ ὅσα τοιαῦτα λέγουσι περὶ τούτου, ταῦτα εἶναι τοῦ ψυχικοῦ, ὅν φησιν εἶναι τοῦ κόσμου δημιουργόν.

Read: ‹Ἀρχὴν δὲ ἔχουσιν ἡ ψυχὴ καὶ› ὁ δημιουργὸς ἀπὸ τοῦ φόβου...αὕτη γάρ ‹ἐστιν ἡ› ἀρχὴ τῶν τῆς Σοφίας παθῶν...καλεῖται δὲ καὶ Τόπος (i.e. Δημιουργός: cf. Clem. Exc. ex Theod. 34. 1–2; 37; 38.1 et 3; 39; 59.2) ὑπ' αὐτῶν, καὶ Ἑβδομάς...καὶ ὅσα τοιαῦτα ⟨αἱ γραφαὶ cf. no. 4⟩ λέγουσι περὶ τοῦ θεοῦ (Bunsen: τούτου P), ταῦτα ⟨θέλει = p. 161.11⟩ εἶναι τοῦ ψ⟨υχ⟩ικοῦ, ὅν φησιν εἶναι τοῦ κόσμου δημιουργόν.

(25) p. 162.1

<table>
<tr><td>We:</td><td>Read:</td></tr>
</table>

We:

Ὥσπερ οὖν τῆς ψυχικῆς οὐσίας ἡ πρώτη καὶ μεγίστη δύναμις γέγονεν * * * εἰκὼν διάβολος, ὁ ἄρχων τοῦ κόσμου τούτου· τῆς δὲ τῶν δαιμόνων οὐσίας, ἥτις ἐστὶν ἐκ τῆς ἀπορίας, ὁ Βεελζεβούλ * * * ἡ Σοφία ἄνωθεν ἀπὸ τῆς ὀγδοάδος ἐνεργοῦσα ἕως τῆς ἑβδομάδος.

Read:

Ὥσπερ οὖν τῆς ψυχικῆς οὐσίας ἡ πρώτη καὶ μεγίστη δύναμις γέγονεν ⟨ὁ δημιουργός, ἡ⟩ εἰκὼν ⟨τοῦ Πατρός, οὕτως τῆς ὑλικῆς οὐσίας ὁ⟩ διάβολος, "ὁ ἄρχων τοῦ κόσμου τούτου" (Jn. 12:31; 14:30; 16:11), τῆς δὲ τῶν δαιμόνων οὐσίας [ἥτις ἐστὶν ἐκ τῆς ἀπορίας seclusi ut glossema, cf. p. 160.29] ὁ Βεελζεβούλ, ⟨"ὁ ἄρχων τῶν δαιμόνων" (Mt. 12:24; Lk. 11:15). ἔστι δ'⟩ ἡ Σοφία ἄνωθεν ἀπὸ τῆς ὀγδοάδος ἐνεργοῦσα ἕως τῆς ἑβδομάδος.

Cf. Clem. *Strom.* IV 90.2; *Exc. ex Theod.* 47. 2–3; H p. 162.12 καλεῖται δὲ ἡ μὲν Σοφία πνεῦμα, ὁ δὲ δημιουργὸς ψυχή, ὁ διάβολος δὲ "ὁ ἄρχων τοῦ κόσμου", Βεελζεβούλ ⟨δὲ Roeper⟩ "ὁ ⟨ἄρχων addidi ex NT⟩ τῶν δαιμόνων".

p. 162.18 ὡς γὰρ οἱ Πυθαγορικοὶ διεῖλον εἰς δώδεκα καὶ τριάκοντα καὶ ἑξήκοντα, καὶ λεπτὰ λεπτῶν εἰσιν ἐκείνοις, ⟨ὡς Go⟩ δεδήλωται, οὕτως οὗτοι (sc. Valentiniani) τὰ ἐντὸς πληρώματος ὑποδιαιροῦσιν. Read: διεῖλον ⟨τὸν κόσμον⟩ εἰς ⟨μοίρας⟩ δώδεκα and cf. p. 155.4 διῄρηκε δ' αὐτὸν (sc. τὸν κόσμον)...εἰς μοίρας δώδεκα.

(26) p. 163.5 προέβαλε καὶ ὁ δημιουργὸς ψυχάς· αὕτη γὰρ οὐσία ψυχῶν· οὗτός ἐστι κατ' αὐτοὺς Ἀβραὰμ καὶ ταῦτα τοῦ Ἀβραὰμ τὰ τέκνα (Jn. 8:39). Read: προέβαλε ⟨δὲ Cr⟩ καὶ ὁ δημιουργὸς ψυχάς· [αὕτη γὰρ οὐσία ψυχῶν seclusi ut glossema: cf. no. 25] οὗτός ἐστι...Ἀβρα⟨ά⟩μ, καὶ ταῦτα⟨ς⟩...τὰ τέκνα. Cf. Iren. I 5.2 et 5; Clem. *Exc. ex Theod.* 50–51.

p. 163.9 "καὶ ἔπλασεν ὁ θεὸς τὸν ἄνθρωπον, χοῦν ἀπὸ τῆς γῆς λαβών, καὶ ἐνεφύσησεν εἰς τὸ πρόσωπον αὐτοῦ πνοὴν ζωῆς· καὶ ἐγένετο ὁ ἄνθρωπος εἰς ψυχὴν ζῶσαν" (Gen. 2:7). οὗτός ἐστι κατ' αὐτοὺς ὁ ἔσω ἄνθρωπος, ὁ ψυχικός, ἐν τῶι σώματι κατοικῶν τῶι ὑλικῶι, ὅ ἐστιν ὑλικός, φθαρτός, τέλειος ἐκ τῆς διαβολικῆς οὐσίας πεπλασμένος. ἔστι δὲ οὗτος ὁ ὑλικὸς ἄνθρωπος οἱονεὶ κατ' αὐτοὺς πανδοχεῖον ἢ κατοικητήριον ποτὲ μὲν ψυχῆς μόνης, ποτὲ δὲ...

Read: οὗτός ἐστι κατ' αὐτοὺς "ὁ ἔσω ἄνθρωπος" (Rom. 7:22; Eph. 3:16; 2 Cor. 4:16; H p. 87.20 et 22; Clem. *Exc. ex Theod.* 51.1; Iren. I 5.5; Zosim. ap. R. Reitzenstein, *Poimandres* p. 104; Plato *Rep.* 589 A 7; Plotin.

V 1.10; Philo *De congressu* 97; *De plantat.* 42 et al.), ὁ ψυχικός, ἐν τῶι σώματι κατοικῶν τῶι χοϊκῶι, ὅ ἐστιν ⟨ἄνθρωπος⟩ ὑλικός, φθαρτός, τελείως (Mi) ἐκ τῆς διαβολικῆς οὐσίας πεπλασμένος. ἔστι δὲ οὗτος ὁ ὑλικὸς ἄνθρωπος κατ᾽ αὐτοὺς οἱονεὶ πανδοχεῖον...and cf. v. 18 κατοικοῦντες ἐν (σώμ)ατι χοϊκῶι μετὰ ψυχῆς...

(27) p. 164.13 ὅτε οὖν τέλος ἔλαβεν ἡ κτίσις καὶ ἔδει λοιπὸν γενέσθαι "τὴν ἀποκάλυψιν τῶν υἱῶν τοῦ θεοῦ" (*Rom.* 8:19), τουτέστι τοῦ δημιουργοῦ, τὴν ἐγκεκαλυμμένην, ἥν, φησίν, ἐγκεκάλυπτο ὁ ψυχικὸς ἄνθρωπος, καὶ εἶχε "κάλυμμα ἐπὶ τὴν καρδίαν" (2 *Cor.* 3:15)· ὁπότε οὖν ἔδει ἀρθῆναι τὸ κάλυμμα καὶ ὀφθῆναι ταῦτα τὰ μυστήρια, γεγένηται ὁ Ἰησοῦς διὰ Μαρίας τῆς παρθένου...

Read: ὅτε οὖν...ἔδει λοιπὸν γενέσθαι "τὴν ἀποκάλυψιν τῶν υἱῶν τοῦ θεοῦ" (τουτέστι τοῦ δημιουργοῦ) ⟨καὶ ἀνακαλύψαι (cf. 2 *Cor.* 3:14 et 18) τὴν πνευματικὴν οὐσίαν (cf. p. 165.1; Iren. I 1.4; 5.1; 5.6; 6.1)⟩, τὴν ἐγκεκαλυμμένην...καὶ εἶχε "κάλυμ⟨μ⟩α ἐπὶ τὴν καρδίαν ⟨αὐτοῦ = NT⟩",— ὁπότε οὖν...

p. 165.10 τοῦτό ἐστι, φησί, τὸ εἰρημένον· "ὁ ἐγείρας Χριστὸν ἐκ νεκρῶν ζωοποιήσει καὶ τὰ θνητὰ σώματα ὑμῶν" (*Rom.* 8:11; cf. Clem. *Exc.* 3), ἤτοι (Go: καὶ τὰ P) ψυχικά. ὁ χοῦς γὰρ "ὑπὸ κατάραν" (cf. *Gal.* 3:10) ἐλήλυθε· "γῆ γάρ," φησίν, "εἶ, καὶ εἰς γῆν ἀπελεύσηι" (*Gen.* 3:19).

Read: "...καὶ τὰ θνητὰ σώματα ὑμῶν", ⟨τουτέστι⟩ [καὶ] τὰ ψυχικά, ⟨οὐ καὶ τὰ χοϊκά⟩. ὁ χοῦς γὰρ "ὑπὸ κατάραν" ἐλήλυθε·

(28) p. 165.18 Ταῦτα οὖν ἐκεῖνοι ζητείτωσαν κατ᾽ αὐτοὺς καὶ εἴ τινι ἄλλωι γένηται φίλον ζητεῖν. ἀλλ᾽ ἐπιλέγει (Mi: ἐπεὶ λέγει P: ἔτι λέγει Bunsen)· ὡς διώρθωτο μὲν τὰ κατὰ τοὺς αἰῶνας ἔσω σφάλματα, διώρθωτο δὲ καὶ κατὰ τὴν ὀγδοάδα, τὴν ἔξω Σοφίαν, διώρθωτο δὲ κατὰ τὴν ἑβομάδα...

Read: ...καὶ ἐάν τινι ἄλλωι γένηται φίλον ζητεῖν. ἀλλ᾽ ἔτι λέγουσι· διώρθωτο μὲν ⟨οὖν⟩ τὰ κατὰ τοὺς αἰῶνας ἔσω σφάλματα, διώρθωτο δὲ καὶ ⟨τὰ Cr⟩ κατὰ τὴν ὀγδοάδα (⟨τουτέστι⟩ τὴν ἔξω Σοφίαν), διώρθωτο δὲ καὶ ⟨τὰ Cr⟩ κατὰ τὴν ἑβδομάδα... Cf. p. 162.14 ταῦτά ἐστιν ἃ λέγουσιν· ἔτι ⟨δὲ⟩ πρὸς τούτοις...

p. 165.26 τοῦτ᾽ ἔστιν, ὡς φησιν, ὃ λέγει πρὸς Μωϋσῆν· "ἐγὼ ὁ θεὸς Ἀβραὰμ καὶ ὁ θεὸς Ἰσαὰκ καὶ ὁ θεὸς Ἰακώβ, καὶ τὸ ὄνομα θεοῦ (Go: μου P: τοῦ θεοῦ H p. 203.13) οὐκ ἀπήγγειλα αὐτοῖς" (*Exod.* 6:3)...

Read: τοῦτ᾽ ἔστιν, [ὡς] φησιν, ὃ ⟨ὁ θεὸς⟩ λέγει πρὸς Μωϋσῆν...καὶ τὸ ὄνομά μου (P = LXX) οὐκ...

(29) p. 166.5 τούτου χάριν ἐγεννήθη Ἰησοῦς ὁ σωτὴρ διὰ τῆς Μαρίας, ἵνα διορθώσηται ⟨τὰ⟩ ἐνθάδε, ὥσπερ ὁ Χριστός, ὁ ἄνωθεν ἐπιπροβληθεὶς ὑπὸ τοῦ Νοὸς καὶ τῆς Ἀληθείας, διορθώσατο τὰ πάθη τῆς ἔξω Σοφίας, τουτέστι τοῦ ἐκτρώματος· καὶ πάλιν ὁ διὰ Μαρίας γεγεν⟨ν⟩ημένος ὁ Σωτὴρ ἦλθε διορθώσασθαι τὰ πάθη τῆς ψυχῆς.

Read: ... ⟨τὰ⟩ ἐνθάδε· ὥσπερ ⟨γὰρ⟩ ὁ Χριστός, ὁ ἄνωθεν ... διωρθώσατο τὰ πάθη τῆς ἔξω Σοφίας (τουτέστι τοῦ ἐκτρώματος), ⟨οὕτως⟩ πάλιν καὶ ὁ διὰ Μαρίας γεγεν⟨ν⟩ημένος ⟨Χριστὸς⟩ ὁ σωτὴρ ἦλθε ...

(30) p. 167.6 "διὰ τοῦτο ἐγὼ περὶ τούτων γέγρ(α)φ(α) (οὐ)δέν, οὐδὲ ἔστι Πλάτωνος σύγγραμμα οὐδὲν οὐδὲ ἔσται πώποτε, τὰ δὲ νῦν λεγόμενα Σωκράτους ἐστὶ καλοῦ καὶ νέου γεγονότος" (Ps. Plat. ep. 2 p.313 c). τούτοις περιτυχὼν Οὐαλεντῖνος ὑπεστήσατο τὸν πάντων βασιλέα, ὃν ἔφη Πλάτων, οὕτως (Hilgenfeld: οὗτος P)· Πατέρα καὶ βυθὸν καὶ [πᾶ] Σιγὴν (Bernays et Roeper: πᾶσι γῆν P: πλάστην R. Scott: προαρχὴν ci. Go conl. Iren. I 1.1 τέλειον Αἰῶνα προόντα· τοῦτον δὲ καὶ Προαρχὴν καὶ Προπάτορα καὶ Βυθὸν καλοῦσιν: πηγὴν Hilgenfeld) τῶν ὅλων αἰώνων. δεύτερον πέρι τὰ δεύτερα τοῦ Πλάτωνος εἰρηκότος, τὰ δεύτερα Οὐαλεντῖνος τοὺς ἐντὸς Ὅρου [τὸν Ὅρον secl. Roeper] ὑπέθετο πάντας αἰῶνας, καὶ τρίτον πέρι τὰ τρίτα τὴν ἔξω τοῦ Ὅρου καὶ τοῦ πληρώματος διαταγὴν συνέθηκε πᾶσαν.

Read: ... γέγρ(α)φ(α) (οὐ)δὲν ⟨πώποτε = Plato⟩, οὐδὲ ἔστι ... οὐδὲ ἔσται [πώποτε], τὰ δὲ νῦν ... ὑπεστήσατο τὸν πάντων βασιλέα, ὃν ἔφη ⟨ὁ⟩ Πλάτων οὕτως, Πατέρα καὶ Βυθὸν καὶ † πᾶσι γῆν † (gravius corruptum: an πα⟨ρασκευα⟩στὴν? cf. Io. Chrysost. Hom. 23.3 In Hebr. 12, p. 215 A Gaume: ὧν γὰρ ἑτοιμαστὴς καὶ παρασκευαστὴς ὁ θεὸς ἀγαθῶν, ποῖα εἰκὸς εἶναι ταῦτα;) τῶν ὅλων αἰώνων ... καὶ τρίτον πέρι τὰ τρίτα ⟨τοῦ Πλάτωνος εἰρηκότος, τὰ τρίτα⟩ τὴν ἔξω τοῦ Ὅρου ...

(31) p. 167.17 = T. Wolbergs, pp. 5 et 24:[2]

Θέρος (P: ⟨αἰ⟩θέρος male Go cett.)

Πάντα κρεμάμενα πνεύματι βλέπω,
πάντα δ' ὀχούμενα πνεύματι νοῶ·
σάρκα μὲν ἐκ ψυχῆς κρεμαμένην,
ψυχὴν δ' ἀέρος ἐξεχομένην (Bunsen: ἐξειχουμένην P),
5 ἀέρα δ' ἐξ αἴθρης κρεμάμενον,
ἐκ δὲ βυθοῦ καρποὺς φερομένους,
ἐκ μήτρας δὲ βρέφος φερόμενον.

οὕτως ταῦτα νοῶν· σάρξ ἐστιν ἡ ὕλη κατ' αὐτούς, ἥτις κρέμαται ἐκ τῆς ψυχῆς τοῦ δημιουργοῦ. ψυχὴ δὲ ἀέρος ἐξοχεῖται, τουτέστιν ὁ δημιουργὸς τοῦ πνεύματος ⟨τοῦ We⟩ ἔξω πληρώματος. ἀὴρ δὲ αἴθρης ἐξέχεται, τουτέστιν ἡ ἔξω Σοφία τῆς (Go: τοῦ P) ἐντὸς Ὅρου καὶ παντὸς πληρώματος. ἐκ δὲ βυθοῦ καρποὶ φέρονται, ἡ ἐκ τοῦ πατρὸς πᾶσα προβολὴ τῶν αἰώνων γενομένη.

Read: ... ἥτις κρέμαται ἐκ τῆς ψυχῆς, ⟨τουτέστι⟩ τοῦ δημιουργοῦ· ψυχὴ δὲ ἀέρος ἐξέχεται (cf. v. 20 et p. 168.2), τουτέστιν ὁ δημιουργός, τοῦ Πνεύματος ⟨τοῦ⟩ ἔξω πληρώματος· ἀὴρ δὲ αἴθρης ἐξέχεται, τουτέστιν ἡ ἔξω Σοφία, τοῦ

[2] Griechische religiöse Gedichte der ersten nachchristlichen Jahrhunderte. Band 1: Psalmen und Hymnen der Gnosis und des frühen Christentums, herausgegeben und erläutert von Thielko Wolbergs (Beiträge zur klass. Philologie, 40, Meisenheim am Glan 1971).

ἐντὸς Ὅρου καὶ παντὸς πληρώματος ‹Πνεύματος›. ἐκ δὲ βυθοῦ καρποὶ φέρονται, ‹τουτέστιν› ἡ ἐκ τοῦ Πατρὸς...

SECUNDUS

(32) p. 168.12 ἦν ἡ πρώτη ἀρχὴ ἀνεννόητος, ἄρρητός τε καὶ ἀνωνόμαστος, ἣν Μονότητα καλεῖ· ταύτηι δὲ συνυπάρχειν δύναμιν, ἣν ὀνομάζει Ἑνό(τητ)α. αὕτη ἡ Ἑνότης ἥ τε Μονότης προήκαντο μὴ προέμεναι ἀρχὴν ἐπὶ πάντων νοητήν, ἀγέν‹ν›ητόν τε καὶ ἀόρατον, ἣν Μονάδα καλεῖ. ταύτηι τῆι δυνάμει συνυπάρχει δύναμις ὁμοούσιος αὐτῆι, ἣν καὶ αὐτὴν ὀνομάζει τὸ Ἕν.

Read: ...ταύτηι δὲ (σ)υ(νυπ)άρχειν δύναμιν, ἣν ‹καὶ αὐτὴν = Iren. I 11.2; Epiphan. Panar. 32. 5.4; Tertull. Adv. Val. 37› ὀνομάζει Ἑνό(τ)η(τ)α. αὕτη ἡ Ἑνότης ἥ τε Μονότης, ‹τὸ Ἕν οὖσαι = Ir.; Ep.; Tert.›, προήκαντο... ἣν Μονάδα καλεῖ. ταύτηι τῆι Μονάδι (= Ir.; Ep.; huic Tert.) συνυπάρχει δύναμις...

MARCUS

(33) p. 170.11 Ἄλλος δέ τις διδάσκαλος αὐτῶν Μάρκος, μαγικῆς ἔμπειρος,... Read: Μάρκος ‹τοὔνομα,› μαγικῆς and cf. Iren. I 13.1 Marcus est autem illi nomen.

p. 171.5 φάρμακον γάρ τι τοιαύτην δυνάμενον χρόαν παρασχεῖν λαθραίως ἐνιῶν τῶι κεράσματι, ἐπὶ πολὺ φλυαρῶν ἀνέμενεν, ὅπως τῆς ὑγρότητος μεταλαβὸν λυθῆι καὶ ἀναμιγὲν ἐπιχρώσηι τὸ πόμα. τὰ δὲ δυνάμενα τοῦτο παρασχεῖν φάρμακα ἐν τῆι κατὰ μάγων βίβλωι προείπομεν ἐκθέμενοι... Read: ὅπως ‹τὸ φάρμακον› τῆς ὑγρότητος μεταλαβὸν λυθῆι...

p. 171.12 Ὅς καὶ ποτήριον μικρότερον (Go: παρ' ἑτέρου P: ποθ' ἕτερον Diels) κιρνῶν ἐδίδου γυναικὶ εὐχαριστεῖν, αὐτὸς παρεστὼς καὶ ἕτερον κρατῶν ἐκείνου μεῖζον κενόν, καὶ εὐχαριστησάσης τῆς ἀπατωμένης δεξάμενος ἐπέχει εἰς τὸ μεῖζον, καὶ πολλάκις ἀντεπιχέων ἕτερον εἰς ἕτερον ἐπέλεγεν οὕτως· Read: Ὅς καὶ ποτήριον πάλιν ἕτερον (cf. Iren. I 13.2 πάλιν δὲ γυναιξὶν ἐπιδοὺς ἐκπώματα κεκραμένα) κιρνῶν... αὐτὸς παρεστώς· καὶ ἕτερον ‹ποτήριον = Ir› κρατῶν, ἐκείνου μεῖζον, κενόν, καὶ...δεξάμενος ‹τὸ μικρότερον (cf. Iren. ἀπὸ τοῦ μικροτέρου τοῦ ὑπὸ τῆς γυναικὸς ηὐχαριστημένου; H p. 171.20),› ἐπέχει εἰς τὸ μεῖζον...

(34) p. 172.2 ...ἐξεθέμεθα δείξαντες πλεῖστα φάρμακα δυνάμενα αὔξησιν παρασχεῖν ἐπιμιγέντα οὕτως ὑγραῖς οὐσίαις, μάλιστα οἴνωι κεκερασμένωι, ὧν ἕν τι φάρμακον ἐν τῶι κενῶι ποτηρίωι κρύβδην ἔ(μπρ)οσ(θεν) χρίσ(ας), ὡς μηδὲν ἔχον δείξας, ἐπιχέων ἐκ τοῦ (σύνεγγ)υς (We: μικροτέρου Go: ἑτέρου Mi Cr) καὶ ἐπαναχέων, ἀναλυομένου τοῦ φαρμάκου ὑπὸ τῆς τοῦ ὑγροῦ μίξεως, ὄντος φυσώδους, πλεονασμὸς τοῦ κεράσματος ἐγίνετο, καὶ ἐπὶ τοσοῦτον ηὔξανεν, ἐς ὅσον ἐπαναχυνόμενον ἐκινεῖτο, τοιαύτης οὔσης τῆς τοῦ φαρμάκου φύσεως.

Read: ...μάλιστα ‹δ'› οἴνωι κεκερασμένωι. ὧν ἐν‹ί› τι‹ς› φαρμάκωι [ἐν] τὸ κενὸν ποτήριον κρύβδην ἔμ(π)ροσ(θεν) (π)α(ρα)χρίσ(ας) (= P),...

ἐπιχέων ἐκ το(ῦ) (πλήρ)ους (scripsi: . . . . . ους P) καὶ ἐπαναχέων, ἀναλυομένου τοῦ φαρμάκου ὑπὸ τῆς τῶι ὑγρῶι μίξεως. . . καὶ ἐπὶ τοσοῦτον ηὔξανεν, ἐς ὅσον <τὸ ποτήριον> ἐπαναχυνόμενον ἐκινεῖτο. . .

(35) p. 172.24 . . . ἀφέσεως· καὶ διὰ τοῦ τοιούτου πανουργήματος συνέχειν δοκοῦσι τοὺς ἀκροατάς, οὓς ἐπὰν νομίσωσι δεδοκιμάσθαι καὶ δύνασθαι φυλάσσειν αὐτοῖς τὰ πιστά, τότε ἐπὶ τοῦτο ἄγουσι, μηδὲ τούτωι μόνωι ἀρκούμενοι, ἀλλὰ καὶ ἕτερόν τι ἐπαγγελλόμενοι πρὸς τὸ συγκρατεῖν αὐτοὺς τῆι ἐλπίδι, ὅπως ἀχώριστοι ὦσι. λέγουσι γάρ τι φωνῆι ἀρρήτωι, ἐπιτιθέντες χεῖρα τῶι τὴν ἀπολύτρωσιν λαβόντι, ὃ φάσκουσιν ἐξειπεῖν εὐκόλως μὴ δύνασθαι, εἰ μή τις εἴη ὑπερδόκιμος, ἢ ὅτε τελευτᾶι πρὸς τὸ οὖς ἐλθὼν λέγει ὁ ἐπίσκοπος.

Read: . . . ἀφέσεως. <οἳ> καὶ διὰ τοῦ τοιούτου. . . ἀκροατάς· οὓς ἐπὰν <οὖν> νομίσωσι. . . τότε ἐπὶ <τὸ πρῶτον> λουτρὸν ἄγουσι. . . ἀλλὰ καὶ ἕτερον [τι] ἐπαγγελ<λ>όμενοι. . . λέγουσι γοῦν τι φωνῆι ἀρρήτωι. . . ἢ ὅτε τελευτῶν<τι> πρὸς τὸ οὖς ἐλθὼν λέγει ὁ ἐπίσκοπος. Cf. p. 172.21 οἷς [καὶ] μετὰ τὸ <πρῶτον ci. We> βάπτισμα <καὶ> ἕτερον ἐπαγγέλλονται, ὃ καλοῦσιν ἀπολύτρωσιν; p. 173.17 ἃ καὶ ἐν τῶι πρώτωι λουτρῶι παραδιδόασιν, <οὕτως add.> τὸ τοιοῦτο καλοῦντες, καὶ ἐν τῶι δευτέρωι, ὃ ἀπολύτρωσιν καλοῦσιν.

(36) p. 174.2 ὅτε τὸ πρῶτον ὁ Πατὴρ † αὐτοῦ ὁ ἀνεννόητος καὶ ἀνούσιος, ὁ μήτε ἄρρεν μήτε θῆλυ, ἠθέλησεν αὐτοῦ τὸ ἄρρητον ῥητὸν γενέσθαι. . . Read: ὁ Πατήρ, <οὗ πατὴρ οὐδεὶς ἦν, = cuius pater nemo est: Iren. I. 14.1 ff.> [αὐτοῦ] ὁ ἀνεν<ν>όητος. . . ἠθέλησεν αὐτοῦ τὸ ἄρρητον. . .

p. 174.13 ἕκαστον δὲ τῶν στοιχείων ἴδια γράμματα καὶ ἴδιον χαρακτῆρα καὶ ἰδίαν ἐκφώνησιν καὶ σχήματα καὶ εἰκόνας ἔχειν, καὶ μηθὲν αὐτῶν εἶναι, ὃ τὴν ἐκείνου καθορᾶι μορφήν, οὗπερ αὐτὸ στοιχεῖόν ἐστι, οὐδὲ (Mi: ἐστί, τόνου δὲ P) μὴν τὴν τοῦ πλησίον αὐτοῦ ἕκαστον ἐκφώνησιν γινώσκειν, ἀλλ᾽ ὃ αὐτὸς ἐκφωνεῖ (Go ex Epiph. 34. 4.5 = Iren. 1.1.: ἄλλο μὴ δὲ ἐκφωνεῖν P), ὡς τὸ πᾶν ἐκφωνοῦντα τὸ ὅλον (Mi ex Ep. Ir.: ὅτι το P) ἡγεῖσθαι ὀνομάζειν αὐτόν· ἕκαστον γὰρ αὐτῶν μέρος ὄντα τοῦ ὅλου τὸν ἴδιον ἦχον ὡς τὸ πᾶν ὀνομάζειν. . .

Read: . . . οὗπερ αὐτὸ στοιχεῖόν ἐστι<ν· ἀλλ᾽ οὐδὲ γινώσκειν αὐ>τόν, οὐδὲ μὴν (= Epiph.; sed nec cognoscere eum, sed ne quidem: Ir.) . . . γινώσκειν, ἀλλ᾽ ὃ [μὴ δὲ] <αὐτὸς (=Ep., Ir.)> ἐκφωνεῖ, ὡς τὸ πᾶν ἐκφωνοῦντα (= Ep.) [ὅτι] τὸ <ὅλον> ἡγεῖσθαι ὀνομάζειν [αὐτόν om. Ep.]. ἕκαστον γὰρ αὐτῶν, μέρος ὂν (= Ep.) τοῦ ὅλου, τὸν. . .

(37) p. 175.24 . . . καὶ μὴν πάλιν τὰ ἕτερα δι᾽ ἄλλων ὀνομάζεσθαι γραμμάτων, καὶ τὰ ἄλλα δι᾽ ἄλλων, ὥστε εἰς ἄπειρον ἐκπίπτειν τὸ πλῆθος, ἰδίαι (Mi: διὰ P) τῶν γραμμάτων γραφέντων (Mi: γραφέντος P). Read: τὸ πλῆθος [διὰ] τῶν γραμμάτων [γραφέντος om. Ir. Ep. 34. 4.12].

p. 177.14 (πάλιν ἡ Τετρακτὺς) παρελθοῦσα εἰς τὸ μέσον φησίν· οὕτως εὐήθη ἡγήσω (R. Scott, agn. Go Cr We: ἡ πηθνηγήσω P) τὸν λόγον τοῦτον, <ὃν Mi> ἀπὸ στομάτων τῆς Ἀληθείας ἤκουσας; Read: π(άλι)ν ἡ Τετρακτὺς. . .

φησίν· ὡς [ἡ] <ἀ>πίθανον (cf. pp. 38.20; 76.11) ἡγήσω τὸν λόγον [τοῦτον] <ὃν> ἀπὸ στομάτων...Cf. Epiph. 34. 6.3 φησίν· ὡς εὐκαταφρόνητον ἡγήσω τὸν λόγον, ὃν ἀπὸ στομάτων τῆς Ἀληθείας ἤκουσας. Ir.: *Tamquam contemptibile putasti esse verbum, quod ab ore Veritatis audisti.*

(38) p. 178.14 ...ἐπὶ διωρθώσει τῶν πραχθέντων, ἵνα ἡ τῶν πληρωμάτων ἑνότης ἐν τῶι ἀγαθῶι οὖσα καρποφορῆι μίαν ἐν πᾶσι τὴν ἐκ πάντων δύναμιν. καὶ οὕτως ὁ τῶν ἑπτὰ τὴν τῶν ὀκτὼ ἐκομίσατο δύναμιν, καὶ ἐγένοντο οἱ τρεῖς τόποι ὅμοιοι τοῖς ἀριθμοῖς, ὀγδοάδες ὄντες· οἵτινες τρὶς ἐφ' ἑαυτοὺς ἐλθόντες τὸν τῶν εἰκοσιτεσσάρων ἀνέδειξαν ἀριθμόν.

Read: ...ἵνα ἡ τῶν πληρωμάτων ἑνότης, ἐπὶ τῶι <ἴσωι> ἀριθμῶι οὖσα, καρποφορῆι and cf. Epiph. 34. 6.10 ἵνα ἡ τῶν πληρωμάτων ἑνότης ἰσότητα ἔχουσα καρποφορῆι; Iren.: *ut pleromatum unitas aequalitatem habens fructificet...* Οἱ τρεῖς τόποι: 9 ἄφωνα (β γ δ; κ π τ; θ φ χ) + 8 ἡμίφωνα (ζ ξ ψ λ μ ν ρ σ) + 7 φωνήεντα (α ε η ι ο υ ω) = 24 (cf., e.g., Dionys. Thrac. *Art. gramm.* 6, pp. 9 ss. Uhlig). The aeon who descends from the Ennead to the Heptad is Σωτήρ.

(39) p. 179.20 τὸν μέντοι ἐπίσημον ἐπὶ τοῦ παρόντος, φησί, τὸν ἐπὶ τοῦ ἐπισήμου μορφωθέντα νόησον, τὸν ὥσπερ μερισθέντα καὶ ἔξω μείναντα... Read: τὸν μέντοι ἐπίσημον <τοῦτον ἀριθμὸν = Ir.; Epiph. 34. 7.5> ἐπὶ τοῦ παρόντος φησὶ τὸν ἀπὸ (*ab* Ir.: ἐπὶ P Ep.) τοῦ ἐπισήμου μορφωθέντα νοῆσαι (i.q. *significare*, cf. p. 183.6 σημαίνοντα: *intelligi* Ir.: νόησον P Ep.), τὸν ὥσπερ μερισθέντα <ἢ διχοτομηθέντα = Ir. Ep.> καὶ ἔξω μείναντα.

p. 180.5 κέχρηται μὲν οὖν καὶ οὗτος τῶιδε <τῶι> ἔργωι, ὡς αὐθαιρέτως ὑπ' αὐτοῦ γενομένωι, τὰ δὲ διακονεῖ, μιμήματα ὄντα τῶν ἀμιμήτων, τῆς ἐνθυμήσεως τῆς μητρός. Read: ...καὶ <αὐτὸς = Ir., Ep.> οὗτος τῶιδε <τῶι> ἔργωι...τὰ <δὲ ἄλλα = Ir.> διακονεῖ, μιμήματα ὄντα τῶν ἀμιμήτων, τὴν ἐνθύμησιν (= Ir., Ep.) τῆς μητρός.

(40) p. 180.18 καθὼς οὖν <αἱ> ἑπτά, φησί, δυνάμεις δοξάζουσι τὸν Λόγον, οὕτω καὶ ἡ ψυχὴ ἐν τοῖς βρέφεσι κλαίουσα. Read: κλαίουσα <καὶ θρηνοῦσα δοξάζει αὐτόν>. Cf. Epiph. 34. 7.9 οὕτως καὶ ἡ ψυχὴ ἐν τοῖς βρέφεσι κλαίουσα καὶ θρηνοῦσα, <κατὰ τὸν Holl> Μάρκον, δοξάζει αὐτόν. *sic et anima in infantibus plorans et plangens <secundum> Marcum glorificat eum.* Iren.

p. 181.1 ἐπὰν δὲ ἐν πόνοις γένηται ἡ ψυχή, [ὡς Mi] ἐπιβοᾶι οὐδὲν ἕτερον ἢ τὸ ω ἐφ' ὧι ἀνιᾶται, ὅπως γνωρίσασα ἡ ἄνω ψυχὴ τὸ συγγενὲς αὐτῆς, βοηθὸν αὐτῆι καταπέμψηι. Read: ἢ τὸ ω, ἐφ' ὧι ἀνίεται... Cf. Epiph. 34. 7.10 καὶ διὰ τοῦτο ἔν τε πόνοις καὶ ταλαιπωρίαις <ἡ add.> ψυχὴ γενομένη, εἰς διυλισμὸν αὐτῆς (scr.: αὐτῆς V M) ἐπιφωνεῖ τὸ ω ὡς (scr.: εἰς V M) σημεῖον ἀνέσεως (scripsi: αἰνέσεως V M, *in signum laudationis* Iren.: ἀνιάσεως Grabe), ἵνα γνωρίσασα ἡ ἄνω ψυχὴ κτλ.

(41) p. 181.8 καὶ πάλιν αἱ δύο καὶ τέσσαρες εἰς τὸ αὐτὸ συντεθεῖσαι τὸν τῶν ἓξ ἐφανέρωσαν ἀριθμόν, οὗτοι δὲ οἱ ἓξ τετραπλασιασθέντες τὰς εἰκοσιτέσσαρας.

Read: τὰς εἰκοσιτέσσαρας ⟨ἀπεκύησαν μορφάς = Epiph. 34. 8.4; *viginti quattuor generaverunt figuras* Iren.⟩.

p. 181.13 τὰ ⟨δὲ We⟩ μετὰ σιωπῆς καὶ μετὰ πίστεως ὀνομαζόμενα παρ' αὐτῶι ἐστι ταῦτα· Ἄρρητος καὶ Σιγή, Πατὴρ καὶ Ἀλήθεια. Read: τὰ ⟨δὲ ἄλλα, τὰ μετὰ σεμνότητος καὶ⟩ μετὰ τιμῆς καὶ μετὰ πίστεως ὀνομαζόμενα and cf. Iren.: *alia vero, quae cum gravitate et honore et fide nominantur apud eum sunt haec.* Epiph. τὰ δὲ † σεμνὰ V M † καὶ μετὰ πίστεως ὀνομαζόμενα...

(42) p. 181.19

We:

καὶ τὸ τοῦ Σωτῆρος ῥητὸν ὄνομα ⟨τουτέστι τὸν Ἰησοῦν Go⟩ γραμμάτων ὑπάρχειν ἕξ, τὸ δ' ἄρρητον αὐτοῦ ἐπ' ἀριθμῶι τῶν κατὰ ἓν γραμμάτων [τουτέστι τὸν Ἰησοῦν Go] στοιχείων ἐστὶν εἰκοσιτεσσάρων, υἱὸς δὲ Χρειστὸς δώδεκα, τὸ δὲ ἐν τῶι Χριστῶι ἄρρητον γραμμάτων τριάκοντα καὶ αὐτὸ τοῖς ἐν αὐτῶι γράμμασι κατὰ ἓν ⟨τῶν Go⟩ στοιχείων ἀριθμουμένων (Go: στοιχεῖον ἀριθμούμενον P), τὸ γὰρ Χρειστός ἐστι στοιχείων ὀκτώ. τὸ μὲν γὰρ χεῖ (Mi: χρι P) τριῶν, τὸ δὲ ρ̄ δύο, καὶ τὸ εἶ δύο, καὶ ῑ τεσσάρων, τὸ σ̄ πέντε, καὶ τὸ τ̄ τριῶν, τὸ δὲ οὗ δύο, καὶ τὸ † ν̄ τριῶν. οὕτως τὸ ἐν τῶι Χριστῶι ἄρρητον φάσκουσι στοιχείων τριάκοντα.

Read:

καὶ τὸ τοῦ Σωτῆρος ⟨δὲ = Iren.; Epiph. 34. 8.8⟩ ῥητὸν ὄνομα ⟨'Ιησοῦς = Ir., Ep.⟩ γραμμάτων ὑπάρχειν ἕξ, τὸ δὲ ⟨ἄρ⟩ρητον αὐτοῦ (⟨τὸ⟩ ἐπ' ἀριθμῶι τῶν κατὰ ἓν ⟨στοιχεῖον⟩ γραμμάτων) [τουτέστι τὸν Ἰησοῦν Go] στοιχείων ἐστὶν εἰκοσιτεσσάρων· υἱὸς καὶ (= Ir.) Χρ⟨ε⟩ιστὸς ⟨γραμμάτων = Ir., Ep.⟩ δώδεκα, τὸ δὲ ἐν τῶι Χριστῶι ἄρ(ρ)ητον (sc. ὄνομα) γρ(αμ-μ)άτων τριάκοντα (καὶ αὐτὸ ⟨ἐπὶ⟩ τοῖς ἐν αὐτῶι γράμμασι κατὰ ἓν στοιχεῖον ἀριθμουμένοις· τὸ γὰρ Χρ⟨ε⟩-ιστός ἐστι στοιχείων ὀκτώ· τὸ μὲν γὰρ χεῖ τριῶν, τὸ δὲ ρ̑⟨ῶ⟩ δύο, καὶ τὸ εἶ δύο, καὶ ⟨τὸ⟩ ἰ⟨ῶτα⟩ τεσσάρων, τὸ ⟨δὲ⟩ σ⟨ῖγμα⟩ πέντε, καὶ τὸ τ⟨αῦ⟩ τριῶν, τὸ δὲ οὗ δύο, καὶ τὸ ⟨σὰ⟩ν (Mi) τριῶν * * * οὕτως τὸ ἐν τῶι Χριστῶι ἄρρητον ⟨ὄνομα⟩ φάσκουσι στοιχείων ⟨εἶναι⟩ τριάκοντα).

It stood in the lacuna, e.g.: ⟨ἃ συντεθέντα τὸν τῶν εἰκοσιτεσσάρων στοιχείων ἐποίησεν ἀριθμόν· τούτωι δὲ προστιθέασι τὸ ἐπίσημον αὐτοῦ ὄνομα,⟩ τουτέστι τὸν Ἰησοῦν (= p. 182.2), ⟨ὅπερ ἐστὶ στοιχείων ἕξ.⟩ Cf. Iren. I 15.2 (I, pp. 148 f. Harvey) = Epiph. 34. 9.8–9 πρὶν μὲν οὖν, φησί, τούτου τοῦ ὀνόματος τὸ ἐπίσημον φανῆναι, τουτέστι τὸν Ἰησοῦν [τὸν υἱόν seclusi], ἐν ἀγνοίαι πολλῆι ὑπῆρχον οἱ ἄνθρωποι καὶ πλάνηι· ὅτε δὲ ἐφανερώθη τὸ ἑξαγράμματον ὄνομα, ὃ σάρκα περιεβάλετο...ἔχον ἐν ἑαυτῶι αὐτὰ τὰ ἓξ καὶ τὰ εἰκοσιτέσσαρα, τότε γνόντες...

(43) p. 182.11 ἀπὸ γὰρ τῆς μητρὸς τῶν ὅλων, τῆς πρώτης τετράδος, ἐν θυγατρὸς τρόπωι προῆλθεν ἡ δευτέρα τετράς, καὶ ἐγένετο ὀγδοάς... Read: ἐν θυγατρὸς τόπωι (*in filiae locum* Iren.: τρόπωι P Ep.).

p. 182.19 τὸ γὰρ Ἰησοῦς ὄνομα κατὰ τὸν ἐν τοῖς γράμμασιν ἀριθμόν ἐστιν ὀκτακόσια ὀγδοηκονταοκτώ. καὶ τὸν ἀλφάβητον δὲ τὸν Ἑλληνικὸν ἔχειν μονάδας ὀκτὼ ‹καὶ δεκάδας ὀκτὼ Mi› καὶ ἑκατοντάδας ὀκτώ... καὶ διὰ τοῦτο ἄλφα ‹καὶ ὦ Go› ὀνομάζεσθαι αὐτόν, τὴν ἐκ πάντων γένεσιν σημαίνοντα. Read: ὀγδοηκονταοκτώ. ‹διὸ = Ir., Ep.› καὶ... καὶ διὰ τοῦτο... τὴν ἐκ πάντων ‹αὐτοῦ = eius Ir.: om. P Ep.› γένεσιν σημαίνοντα.

(44) p. 183.11 οὕτως ὁ κατ' οἰκονομίαν διὰ τῆς Μαρίας γενεσιουργεῖται παρ' αὐτῶι ἄνθρωπος. ἐλθόντος δὲ αὐτοῦ εἰς τὸ ὕδωρ, κατελθεῖν εἰς αὐτὸν ὡς περιστερὰν τὸν ἀναβαίνοντα ἄνω καὶ πληρώσαντα τὸν δωδέκατον ἀριθμόν, ἐν ὧι ὑπάρχει τὸ σπέρμα τούτων τῶν συγκατασπαρέντων αὐτῶι καὶ συγκαταβάντων καὶ συναναβάντων. ταύτην δὲ τὴν δύναμιν τὴν καταβᾶσαν εἰς αὐτὸν ‹σπέρμα Go ex Ir., Ep.› φησὶν εἶναι τοῦ πληρώματος, ἔχον ἐν ἑαυτῶι καὶ τὸν Πατέρα καὶ τὸν Υἱόν...

Read: οὕτως ‹τε = Ir., Ep.› ὁ... ἄνθρωπος, ‹ὃν ὁ Πατὴρ τῶν ὅλων διελθόντα διὰ μήτρας ἐξελέξατο διὰ Λόγου εἰς ἐπίγνωσιν αὐτοῦ = Iren. I 15.2; Epiph. 34. 10.3›. ἐλθόντος δὲ αὐτοῦ εἰς τὸ ὕδωρ, κατελθεῖν εἰς αὐτὸν ὡς περιστερὰν τὸν ἀναδραμόντα (P = Ir. = Ep.) ἄνω... ἐν ὧι ὑπῆρχε (inerat Ir.: ὑπάρχει P Ep.) τὸ σπέρμα τούτων τῶν συσπαρέντων (= Ep.) αὐτῶι... ταύτην δὲ τὴν δύναμιν τὴν καταβᾶσαν [εἰς αὐτὸν om. Ir., Ep.] ‹σπέρμα› φησὶν εἶναι τοῦ Πατρός (= Ir., Ep.)...

(45) p. 183.19 καὶ τοῦτο εἶναι τὸ πνεῦμα τὸ ἐν αὐτῶι φωνῆσαν (Mi cett.: ἔφασαν P) διὰ τοῦ στόματος τοῦ υἱοῦ, τὸ ὁμολογῆσαν ἑαυτὸ Υἱὸν ἀνθρώπου καὶ φανερῶσαν τὸν Πατέρα...

Read: ... τὸ πνεῦμα τὸ [ἐν αὐτῶι om. Ir., Ep.] λαλῆσαν (= Ep.) διὰ τοῦ στόματος τοῦ Ἰησοῦ (= Ir., Ep.)...

p. 184.3 ‹καὶ Go› καθεῖλε μὲν τὸν θάνατον, φασίν, ὁ ἐκ ‹τῆς Go› οἰκονομίας Σωτήρ, ἐγνώρισε δὲ τὸν Πατέρα Χριστὸν Ἰησοῦν.

Read: ... τὸν θάνατον, φησίν (= Ir., Ep.), ὁ ἐκ ‹τῆς› οἰκονομίας σωτὴρ ‹Ἰησοῦς = Ir.: om. P Ep.›, ἐγνώρισε δὲ τὸν Πατέρα Χριστὸν [Ἰησοῦν om. Ir., Ep., del. Go].

(46) p. 184.11 Ταῦτα μὲν οὖν πρόδηλα εἶναι πᾶσιν ἐλπίζω τοῖς ὑγιαίνοντα νοῦν κεκτημένοις ὄντα ἄκυρα καὶ μακρὰν τῆς κατὰ θεοσέβειαν γνώσεως, ὄντα μέρη ἀστρολογικῆς ἐφευρέσεως καὶ ἀριθμητικῆς Πυθαγορείου... Read: καὶ μακρὰν τῆς κατὰ θεοσέβειαν γνώσεως ‹ἀπεμφαίνοντα,› ὄντα μέρη...

p. 185.5 ... καὶ διὰ τοῦτο, περὶ τὸν δωδέκατον ἀριθμὸν τοῦ σφάλματος γενομένου, τὸ πρόβατον ἀποσκιρτῆσαν πεπλανῆσθαι (cf. Lk. 15:4–7; Mt. 18: 12–14), ὁμοίως δὲ καὶ ἐκ τῆς δεκάδος. καὶ ἐπὶ τούτων τὴν δραχμὴν λέγουσιν, ἣν ἀπολέσασα γυνή, ἅψασα λύχνον ἐζήτει (cf. Lk. 15:8–10), τήν τε ἐπὶ ἑνὶ προβάτωι ἀπώλειαν καὶ τὴν τῶν ἐνενήκοντα ἐννέα συντιθέντες ἑαυτοῖς (Go:

ἑαυτοὺς P) ἀριθμοὺς μυθεύουσιν, ὡς τῶν ἔνδεκα ἐπισυμπλεκομένων τοῖς ἐννέα
ποιεῖν τὸν τῶν ἐνενήκοντα ἐννέα ἀριθμόν...

Read: ...πεπλανῆσθαι, ‹ἐπειδὴ τὴν ἀποστασίαν ἀπὸ δωδεκάδος φάσκουσι
γεγενῆσθαι = Iren. I 16.1; Epiph. 34. 12.4›. ὁμοίως δὲ καὶ ἐπὶ τῆς δεκάδος·
καὶ ἐπὶ τούτων... ἐζήτει. τὴν δὲ ἐπὶ ἑνὶ προβάτωι ἀπώλειαν καὶ τὴν ‹ἐπὶ μιᾶς
δραχμῆς› συντιθέντες, ‹τὸν› τῶν ἐνενήκοντα ἐννέα ἑαυτοῖς ἀριθμὸν μυθεύουσιν... I.e. (12 − 1) × (10 − 1) = 99. Cf. Ep. 34. 12.6 οὕτως οὖν καὶ τοὺς
ἀριθμοὺς τοὺς καταλειφθέντας (ἐπὶ μὲν τῆς δραχμῆς τοὺς ἐννέα, ἐπὶ δὲ τοῦ
προβάτου τοὺς ἔνδεκα) ἐπιπλεκομένους ἀλλήλοις τὸν τῶν ἐνενήκοντα ἐννέα
τίκτειν ἀριθμόν, ἐπεὶ ἐννάκις τὰ ἔνδεκα ἐνενήκοντα ἐννέα γίνεται = Ir.

(47) p. 185.16

We:

ἀρξάμενος γάρ τις ἀπὸ τοῦ ἄλφα
ἕως τοῦ ἦτα, τὸν ἀριθμὸν τῶν στοιχείων, ὑπεξαιρούμενος τὸν ἐπίσημον,
εὑρήσει ‹τὸν Go τῶν Mi› τριάκοντα
ἀριθμόν. ἐπεὶ οὖν ἐκ τῶν τριῶν
δυνάμεων ἥνωται ὁ τῶν τριάκοντα
ἀριθμός, ‹τρὶς Mi› αὐτὸς γενόμενος
τὰ ἐνενήκοντα ἐποίησε· τρὶς γὰρ
τριάκοντα ἐνενήκοντα. οὕτως ἡ ὀγδοὰς
τὸν τῶν ἐνενήκοντα ἐννέα ἀπεκύησεν
ἀριθμὸν ἐκ πρώτης ὀγδοάδος καὶ
δεκάδος καὶ δωδεκάδος, ἧς ποτὲ μὲν
εἰς ὁλόκληρον συνάγοντες τὸν ἀριθμὸν
ποιοῦσι τριακοντάδα, ποτὲ δὲ τὸν
δωδέκατον ὑφαιροῦντες ψηφίζουσιν
ἔνδεκα· ὁμοίως καὶ τὸν δέκατον ποιοῦ-
σιν ἐννέα· ταῦτα δὲ ἐπισυμπλέκοντες
καὶ δεκαπλασιάσαντες ἀριθμὸν ἐπιτελοῦσι τῶν ἐνενήκοντα ἐννέα.

Read:

ἀρξάμενος γάρ τις ἀπὸ τοῦ ἄλφα
‹καὶ τελευτῶν = Ir., Ep. 34. 12.8›
εἰς τὸ ἦτα ‹κατὰ = per Ir.› τὸν
ἀριθμὸν τῶν στοιχείων, ὑπεξαιρούμενος
‹δὲ = Ir., Ep.› τὸ ἐπίσημον ‹καὶ
ἐπισυντιθεὶς τὴν ἐπαύξησιν τῶν γραμμάτων, = Ir., Ep.› εὑρήσει ‹τὸν τῶν›
τριάκοντα ἀριθμόν· ‹καὶ ἐντεῦθεν
ἀποδεικνύουσι τὴν ὀγδοάδα μητέρα
τῶν τριάκοντα αἰώνων = Ir., Ep.›.
ἐπεὶ οὖν ἐκ τῶν τριῶν δυνάμεων ἥνωται
ὁ τῶν τριάκοντα ἀριθμός, ‹τρὶς› αὐτὸς
γενόμενος τὰ ἐνενήκοντα ἐποίησε (τρὶς
γὰρ τριάκοντα ἐνενήκοντα). ‹καὶ αὐτὴ
δὲ ἡ τριὰς ἐφ᾽ ἑαυτὴν συντεθεῖσα ἐννέα
ἐγέννησεν Cr ex Ir., Ep.›. οὕτως ἡ
ὀγδοὰς τὸν τῶν ἐνενήκοντα ἐννέα
ἀπεκύησεν ἀριθμόν. (‹τουτέστιν› ἐκ
‹τῆς› πρώτης ὀγδοάδος καὶ ‹ἐκ›
δωδεκά(δ)ος καὶ δεκάδος· ἧς ποτὲ μὲν
ὡς ὁλοκλήρου συνάγοντες τὸν ἀριθμὸν
ποιοῦσι τριακοντάδα· ποτὲ δὲ ‹δωδεκάδος› τὸν δωδέκατον ὑφαιροῦντες
ψηφίζουσι(ν) ἔνδεκα, καὶ ὁμοίως ‹δεκάδος ὑφαιροῦντες› τὸν δέκατον ψηφίζουσιν ἐννέα, ταῦτα δὲ ἐπισυμπλέκοντες
[καὶ δεκαπλασιάσαντες] ‹τὸν› ἀριθμὸν ἐπιτελοῦσι τῶν ἐνενήκοντα ἐννέα).

(48) p. 187.3

We:

...μεταδιώκειν δὲ τὸ ἕν, ὃ προστεθὲν τοῖς ἐνενηκονταεννέα εἰς τὴν δεξιὰν αὐτοῦ‹ς› χεῖρα μετέ‹στησε. Κατε›σκευάσθαι (Go: μετὰ σκευάσθαι P) ‹δὲ Go› διὰ τῆς μητρὸς λέγουσι πρῶτον μὲν τὰ τέσσαρα στοιχεῖα, ἃ φησιν, πῦρ, ὕδωρ, γῆν, ἀέρα, εἰκόνα προβεβλῆσθαι τῆς ἄνω τετράδος·

Read:

...εἰς τὴν δεξιὰν αὐτοῦ‹ς› χεῖρα μετέ‹στησεν. Αὐτὴν δὲ τὴν κτίσιν κατ᾽ εἰκόνα τῶν ἀοράτων ὑπὸ τοῦ δημιουργοῦ, ὡς ἀγνοοῦντος αὐτοῦ, κατε›σκευάσθαι διὰ τῆς Μητρὸς ‹οὕτως› λέγουσι· πρῶτον μὲν τὰ τέσσαρα στοιχεῖα [ἅ] φασιν (πῦρ, ὕ(δ)ωρ, γῆν, ἀέρα) εἰκόνα προβεβλῆσθαι τῆς ἄνω τετράδος...

Cf. Iren. I 17.1 = Epiph. 34. 14.1 Βούλομαι δέ σοι καὶ ὡς αὐτὴν τὴν κτίσιν κατ᾽ εἰκόνα τῶν ἀοράτων ὑπὸ τοῦ Δημιουργοῦ, ὡς ἀγνοοῦντος αὐτοῦ, κατεσκευάσθαι διὰ τῆς Μητρὸς λέγουσιν διηγήσασθαι. πρῶτον μὲν τὰ τέσσαρα στοιχεῖά φασιν, πῦρ ὕδωρ γῆν ἀέρα, εἰκόνα προβεβλῆσθαι τῆς ἄνω πρώτης (om. Ir.) τετράδος...

p. 187.12 καὶ ταῦτα δέκα ὄντα τὸν ἀριθμὸν εἰκόνας λέγουσιν εἶναι τῆς ἀοράτου δεκάδος, τῆς ἀπὸ Λόγου καὶ Ζωῆς· Read: τῆς ἀπὸ Λόγου καὶ Ζωῆς ‹προελθούσης = Ir., Ep.›.

(49) p. 187.16 καὶ ἐπεὶ ἀντ‹επ›εζεύχθη, φησί, τῆι τῶν ὅλων [ἀνα]φορᾶι, ὠκυτάτηι ὑπαρχούσηι, ὁ ὕπερθεν οὐρανὸς... Read: φασί (Cr ex Ir.)...ὁ ὑπερ‹τε›θεὶς ο(ὐ)ρανὸς...(quod superpositum est caelum Ir.).

p. 188.2 τὴν σελήνην τε πάλιν, τὸν οὐρανὸν ἐκπεριερχομένην (Go: ἐκπεριεχομένην P) ἐν τριάκοντα ἡμέραις, διὰ τῶν ἡμερῶν τὸν ἀριθμὸν τῶν αἰώνων ἐκτυποῦν (Go, significare Ir.: ἐκτυποῦσαν P)· καὶ τὸν ἥλιον δέ, ἐν δώδεκα μησὶν ἐκπεριερχόμενον (Cr: ἐνπεριεχόμενον P) καὶ τερματίζοντα τὴν κυκλικὴν αὐτοῦ ἀποκατάστασιν, τὴν δωδεκάδα φανεροῦν· καὶ αὐτὰς δὲ τὰς ἡμέρας, δώδεκα ὡρῶν τὸ μέτρον ἐχούσας, τύπον τῆς κενῆς δωδεκάδος εἶναι·

Read: τὴν σελήνην...τὸν ‹ἑαυτῆς = Ir., Ep.› οὐρανὸν ἐμπεριε‹ρ›χομένην (: ἐμπεριεχομένην Ep.) ἐν τριάκοντα ἡμέραις...τὸν ἀριθμὸν τῶν ‹τριάκοντα = Ir., Ep.› αἰώνων ἐκτυποῦν. καὶ τὸν ἥλιον δὲ...ἐμπεριε‹ρ›χόμενον...ἀποκατάστασιν, ‹διὰ τῶν δώδεκα μηνῶν = Ir., Ep.› τὴν δωδεκάδα φανεροῦν. καὶ αὐτὰς δὲ τὰς ἡμέρας...τύπον τῆς φαεινῆς (= Ep.: non apparentis Ir.) δωδεκάδος εἶναι.

(50) p. 189.4 Ταῦτα μὲν οὖν οἱ ἀπὸ τῆς Οὐαλεντίνου σχολῆς περί τε τῆς κτίσεως καὶ περὶ τοῦ παντὸς λέγουσιν, ἑκάστοτε καινότερα (Bunsen: κενώτερα P) ἐπιγεννῶντες, καὶ τοῦτο καρποφορίαν νομίζουσιν, εἴ τις μεῖζον ὁμοίως ἐφευρὼν τερατουργεῖν δόξει.

Read: ...ἑκάστοτε καινότερόν ‹τι› ἐπιγεννῶντες· καὶ τοῦτο...εἴ τις μεῖζον ‹ψεῦσμα› ὁμοίως ἐφευρὼν τερατ(ουρ)γ(εῖν) δόξει. Cf. Iren. I 18.1 = Epiph. 34. 15.1 Καὶ περὶ μὲν τῆς κτίσεως τοιαῦτα λέγοντες, καθ᾽ ἑκάστην ἡμέραν ἐπιγεννᾶι ἕκαστος αὐτῶν, καθὼς δύναται, καινότερόν ‹τι› (Dindorf: aliquid novi Ir.). τέλειος γὰρ οὐδεὶς ὁ μὴ μεγάλα ψεύσματα παρ' αὐτοῖς καρποφορήσας.

p. 189.11 ...ἤδη τοῦ μακαρίου πρεσβυτέρου Εἰρηναίου δεινῶς καὶ πεπονη-μένως [ὡς] τὰ δόγματα αὐτῶν διελέγξαντος, παρ' οὗ καὶ αὐτῶν ἐφευρήματα ‹παρειλήφαμεν Go› ἐπιδεικνύντες αὐτοὺς Πυθαγορείου φιλοσοφίας καὶ ἀστρολόγων (π)εριε(ργ)ίας ταῦτα σφετερισαμένους ἐγκαλεῖν Χριστῶι ὡς ταῦτα παραδεδωκότι (Bunsen: παραδεδωκέναι P).

Read ...παρ' οὗ καὶ ‹ἡμεῖς ego τὰ Cr› αὐτῶν ἐφευρήματα ‹μεταλαβόντες ἐξεθέμεθα,› ἐπιδεικνύντες αὐτοὺς ‹ἐκ τῆς Cr› Πυθαγορείου φιλοσοφίας... ἐγκαλεῖν Χριστῶι [ὡς Go] ταῦτα παραδεδωκέναι.[3]

Urbana, 10 October 1970

[3] For more textual criticism on Hippolytus' *Elenchos* cf. M. Marcovich, "Textkritisches I zu Hippolyt Refutatio B. III–X," *Rhein. Mus.* 107 (1964), 139–58 and 305–15; "Note on Hippolytus' *Refutatio*," *Journ. Theol. Stud.* (Oxford), N.S. 15 (1964), 69–74; "Textual Criticism on Hippolytus' *Refutatio*," *JTS* 19 (1968), 83–92; "Displacement in Hippolytus' *Elenchos*," in *Philomathes: Studies...in Memory of Philip Merlan* (The Hague 1971), 240–44; "One Hundred Hippolytean Emendations," in *Festschrift Luitpold Wallach* (Stuttgart; now in press); "Eighty Fresh Hippolytean Emendations," *Živa Antika (Antiquité Vivante)* 21 (1971), 635–58 = *Festschrift Mihail Petruševski*; "The Text of Hippolytus' *Elenchos*, Book X," in *Festschrift Marcel Richard* (Texte u. Untersuchungen, Berlin; now in press).

UN FRAGMENT INÉDIT DE S. HIPPOLYTE
SUR GENÈSE IV 23

MARCEL RICHARD

Le problème des commentaires de S. Hippolyte sur la Genèse est assez compliqué.[1] Certains faits sont cependant assurés. Cet auteur a commenté toute la Genèse. Il a écrit un commentaire sur l'hexaméron. Il a commenté séparément plusieurs passages de la Genèse, certainement les ch. xxvii et xlix dans son traité sur les bénédictions d'Isaac, de Jacob et de Moïse,[2] peut-être d'autres dans des ouvrages perdus.

La liste des écrits d'Hippolyte donnée par Eusèbe au ch. vi 22 de son Histoire ecclésiastique commence par deux traités sur le livre de la Genèse, Εἰς τὴν ἑξαήμερον, Εἰς τὰ μετὰ τὴν ἑξαήμερον. Les historiens de l'ancienne littérature chrétienne admettent que le premier commentait le ch. i, le second, les ch. ii–iii. Achelis partage entre eux les six fragments intéressant *Gen.* i–iii conservés par les chaînes sur la Genèse (I–II, IV–VI) et les florilèges Damascéniens (III, IV).[3] Il attribue au premier les fragments I–II (*Gen.* i 5, 7), au second les fragments III–VI (*Gen.* ii 7, ii 8 sqq., iii 7, iii 21).[4] O. Bardenhewer nomme le second "Bericht über das Paradies und den Sündenfall (*Gen.* 2–3)."[5] Il faut noter que le fragment III est intitulé ἐκ τῆς εἰς τὴν γένεσιν πραγματείας.

Au ch. 61 du *De uiris inlustribus*, S. Jérôme commence sa liste des

---

[1] Les seules notices valables sur ce sujet restent celle de H. Achelis, *Hippolytstudien* (Texte u. Untersuchungen, 16, 4; Leipzig 1897), 94–110, et celle d'O. Bardenhewer, *Gesch. d. Altkirchl. Lit.*, t. II, 2e éd. (Fribourg en Br. 1914), 378–580. La meilleure édition des fragments d'Hippolyte sur la Genèse est celle d'Achelis, *Hippolytus Werke*, t. I,2 (*Griech. christl. Schriftsteller*, 1; Leipzig 1897), 51–81; 87–97.

[2] La meilleure édition de cet ouvrage est celle de M. Brière, L. Mariès et B. Mercier (Patrologia Orientalis, t. 27, 1–2; Paris 1957).

[3] Achelis, éd. cit., 51–53; K. Holl, *Fragmente Vornicänischer Kirchenväter aus den Sacra Parallela* (Texte u. Untersuchungen, 20,2; Leipzig 1899), 143 sq.

[4] *Hippolytstudien*, 108.

[5] *Op. cit.*, 578.

écrits de S. Hippolyte par les commentaires *in hexemeron, in exodum, in canticum canticorum, in genesim*.... Comme il a manifestement utilisé la notice d'Eusèbe, *H.E.* VI 22, pour rédiger la sienne, on admet communément qu'il a traduit *Εἰς τὰ μετὰ τὴν ἑξαήμερον* par *in exodum*.[6] J'ai peine à croire qu'il ait commis une erreur aussi grossière. Il semble plutôt qu'il ait volontairement brouillé l'ordre de la liste d'Eusèbe pour déguiser son emprunt.

Si Achelis et Bardenhewer ont raison, le traité *Εἰς τὰ μετὰ τὴν ἑξαήμερον* cité par Eusèbe et le commentaire *in genesim* cité par Jérôme sont deux ouvrages différents. Mais une sérieuse difficulté s'oppose à la conjecture proposée par les deux éminents savants. Hippolyte, en effet, pouvait difficilement séparer les deux récits de la création de l'homme, *Gen.* I 26–27, prophétique et eschatologique selon lui, et *Gen.* II 7, création réelle du premier Adam.[7] Qu'il ait inclu cette création réelle dans l'oeuvre des six jours est d'ailleurs prouvé par son exégèse des mesures de la statue de Nabuchodonosor: "Par la largeur de six coudées il a indiqué l'hexaméron. C'est en effet le sixième jour que l'homme modelé avec de la poussière (*Gen.* II 7) est apparu."[8] Il est bien évident qu'il ne pouvait pas séparer la création d'Ève de celle d'Adam et ceci conduit jusqu'à la fin du ch. II.

Mais si le traité sur l'hexaméron commentait le ch. II, il devait à peu près nécessairement commenter aussi le ch. III. Ces deux chapitres sont, en effet, intimement liés. D'autre part, un commentaire du seul ch. III, si important qu'il soit, pourrait difficilement justifier le titre *Εἰς τὰ μετὰ τὴν ἑξαήμερον*, qui est d'ailleurs équivoque. Pourquoi, en effet, ne signifierait-il pas tout le reste du livre de la Genèse? Nous avons tout lieu de croire que les six fragments d'Hippolyte cités par les chaînes (*Gen.* I 5... III 21) proviennent d'un seul ouvrage, le commentaire sur l'hexaméron. Quant au titre discuté, n'est ce pas la façon la plus simple d'exprimer qu'un commentaire sur le livre de la Genèse exclut le récit de la création?

---

[6] Achelis, *Hippolytstudien*, 108; Bardenhewer, *op. cit.*, 581. Contrairement à l'opinion de Bardenhewer, je crois qu'Hippolyte a commenté au moins des parties importantes de l'Exode.

[7] Voir mes remarques, *Dict. de Spiritualité*, t. 7, col. 550. J'aurais dû noter que la phrase *κατ᾿ εἰκόνα θεοῦ ἐποίησεν αὐτὸν* de la Chronique d'Hippolyte § 22 est certainement une addition postérieure, d'ailleurs à peu près inévitable.

[8] *In Dan.* II 27, 8.

Quoi qu'il en soit, le commentaire sur la Genèse, cité à plusieurs reprises par S. Jérôme[9] et utilisé par une chaîne arabe sur le Pentateuque,[10] s'étendait certainement, peut-être avec des coupures, du ch. IV à la fin du livre. Les chaînes grecques sur la Genèse qui nous sont parvenues ne citent aucun extrait de cet ouvrage. Il faut, en effet, écarter les fragments d'un opuscule sur les bénédictions de Jacob (ch. XLIX),[11] qui ne sont, dans l'hypothèse la plus favorable, qu'un remaniement très libre du texte original d'Hippolyte. J'ai donc été fort surpris en remarquant au fol. 128[r] du cod. Athènes, Bibl. nat. 2492 (XIIe s.), précédemment Serrès, Prodrome Γ 28, un commentaire de *Gen.* IV 23 attribué à cet auteur.[12] Ce curieux manuscrit, de caractère encyclopédique, contient une collection de textes spirituels, exégétiques, historiques assez désordonnée, mais d'un grand intérêt. Aux fol. 124[r]–128[r] il donne vingt textes sur *Gen.* IX 25, 26, XI 3, 17, 13–14, XV 1, 2, 9, XVII 14; *Exod.* XX 25, XXV–XXVI; *Num.* XII 10, XIV 22; II *Sam.* VI 1 sqq.; II *Reg.* II 14; *Gen.* IV 23, IX 27. La plupart de ces textes proviennent de la chaîne du type III sur l'Octateuque et sont donc connus depuis longtemps. Les exceptions les plus notables sont le premier texte, sur la malédiction de Cham et sa descendance jusqu'à la tour de Babel, apparemment inédit, et les deux scolies sur *Gen.* IV 23 (fol. 127[v]–128[r]) que voici:[13]

Καὶ ἄλλως[1]· Ἀνήρ τις τῶν πατροαδελφῶν ἐξ Ἀδὰμ τοῦ Λάμεχ νεανίσκος[2] γονεῖς αὐτοῦ ἦν καταδυναστεύων καὶ ἐν θυμῷ δεινῶς διαπληκτιζόμενος· διεκδικῆσαι δὲ θέλων Λάμεχ τὸν ἴδιον καθάπερ Μωϋσῆς τὸν ὁμόφυλον Ἰσραηλίτην[3]—τὸ γὰρ φονεῦσαι τὸν Αἰγύπτιον καὶ χῶσαι αὐτὸν ἐν τῇ
5 ἄμμῳ[4] τῆς Ἐρυθρᾶς διαβάσεως [128[r]] τεκμήριον ἦν καθ' ὃ[5] ἔμελλον οἱ Αἰγύπτιοι δι' αὐτοῦ δυνάμει κυρίου ἐν τῇ Ἐρυθρᾷ πνιγμῷ ὑδάτων κατακεχῶσθαι[6]—τείνας οὖν τὸ τόξον εἰς ἀναίρεσιν τοῦ ἐναντίου, τοὺς δύο[7] ἄμφω καὶ ἀκόντως[8] ἀπέκτεινεν.

Ὁ δὲ[9] ἀρχιερεὺς μάρτυς Ἱππόλυτος[10] τοῦτο μᾶλλον σαφέστερον διηγεῖται
10 ὡς ὅτι ὁ Λάμεχ ἀσθενεῖς ἔχων τοὺς ὀφθαλμοὺς ἀμυδρῶς πως ἦν ἐ<μ>βλέπων

---

[9] Voir Achelis, *Hippolytstudien*, 109 sq.; *Hipp. Werke* I,2, p. 54 (frg. VII).

[10] *Hipp. Werke* I,2, 87–97. Cf. *Hippolytstudien*, 113–120.

[11] *Hipp. Werke* I,2, 55–71.

[12] Ce texte m'a été signalé par mon collègue le R. P. J. Paramelle.

[13] J'ai corrigé tacitement les fautes d'accents, d'esprits et 56 mots entachés d'un ou plusieurs iotacismes, dont certains très curieux. Il est assez rare de voir l'article τῇ écrit τεῖ et νεανίσκον écrit ναιἀνήσκον.

τοῦ δὲ Κάϊν δεινῶς τὸ στένειν καὶ τρέμειν[11]—δικαίᾳ ἀποφάσει θεοῦ κατάκρι-
τος—ἔχοντος, τουτέστιν φόβο(ν) καὶ δειλίαν, ἐν ἀσθενείᾳ σὺν τρόμῳ πολλῷ
ἀπὸ κεφαλῆς μέχρι ποδῶν συνεχομένου καὶ δίχα χειραγωγοῦντος μὴ ἰσ-
χύοντος ἐκ τόπου εἰς τόπον διελθεῖν, τὸ μάλιστα καὶ πρὸς ἑβδόμην γενεὰν[12]
15 ἐγγόνων αὐτοῦ—ἀδύνατος καὶ γηράλγητος—καταντήσαντος καὶ οὕτως τὰς
ζ' γενεὰς τὴν τῆς ἀδελφοκτονίας διηγουμένου ποινήν. Ἔτυχεν κατ' οἰκονομίαν μετὰ ταῦτα τὸν μὲ<ν> Λάμεχ, τὸν αὐτοῦ ἀπόγονον, ἐν τόπῳ εἶναι
δασέῳ[13] σύνεγγυς τῆς αὐτῶν παροικίας, δι' ἐκείνης δὲ καὶ τὸν Κάϊν διέρχεσθαι.[14] Τοῦ δὲ Λάμεχ εὐστοχωτάτου ὄντος ἐν τόξου βολαῖς καὶ δόξαν-
20 τος[15] θήραν ἀλόγου εἶναι τὸ διερχόμενον διὰ τὸν κρότον, τοῦ τρόμου λή-
θῃ κρατηθεὶς κατ' οἰκονομίαν τῆς ποινῆς τοῦ προπάτορος, καὶ τείνας τὸ[16]
τόξον ἐν δυνάμει, ἐν μιᾷ βολῇ ἄμφω τοὺς δύο ἀπέκτεινεν, τόν τε χειραγω-
γούμενον Κάϊν καὶ τὸν χειραγωγοῦντα νεανίσκον.

[1] Καὶ ἄλλως post Ἀνήρ τις cod.   [2] νεανίσκον cod.   [3] ιηλήλίτην cod.   [4] Cf. *Exod.* 2,
11–12   [5] καθὸν cod.   [6] Cf. *Exod.* 15, 27–28   [7] δύο: καὶ ἀλλά Γ in marg. + cod.
[8] ἄκοντας cod.   [9] Ὁ δὲ : ἀρχ in marg. + cod.   [10] Εἰπόλοιτος cod.   [11] Cf. *Gen.* 4, 14
[12] γεννὰς cod.   [13] δασαίω cod., fortasse leg. δασεῖ   [14] διέρχεσθαι scripsi: διέρχεσθεν
cod.   [15] δῶξαντας cod.   [16] τῶ cod.

La déclaration de Lamech à ses deux femmes:

> ὅτι ἄνδρα ἀπέκτεινα εἰς τραῦμα ἐμοί,
> καὶ νεανίσκον εἰς μώλωπα ἐμοί,

a beaucoup intrigué les exégètes anciens, tant juifs que chrétiens, et a
naturellement excité leur imagination, d'où un certain nombre
d'interprétations différentes. Une enquête, un peu superficielle, je
l'avoue, ne m'a pas permis de découvrir d'autres témoins de la
solution proposée par le premier fragment. Celui-ci est surtout
précieux pour son introduction καὶ ἄλλως, qui assure que la source
d'où proviennent ces textes proposait au moins trois explications
de *Gen.* IV 23. Cette source pourrait être soit une chaîne sur la
Genèse différente de celles qui nous sont parvenues, soit une
Chronique perdue, soit, enfin, un recueil de questions et réponses
sur l'Ancien Testament. Le fragment sur *Gen.* IX 25 pourrait provenir
de la même source[14] et peut-être aussi le fragment de S. Jean

[14] Ce texte expose comment la malédiction de Cham par Noé, Ἐπικατάρατος Χαναάν·
παῖς οἰκέτης ἔσται τοῖς ἀδελφοῖς αὐτοῦ, ne s'est réalisée qu'à la 19e génération, quand Josué
a réduit en servitude les Gabaonites (*Jos.* IX 3–27). En effet, les premiers descendants
de Cham, loin d'être soumis aux descendants de Sem et de Japhet, ont fondé le premier
royaume. Nemrod (Νεβρὼδ), son petit-fils, fut le premier tyran, fondateur de Babylone
responsable de l'entreprise de la tour de Babel. Suivent quelques notes sur l'étymologie
des noms de Sem et de Phalek, la localisation de Senaar en Perse et l'oubli du site du
paradis terrestre après le déluge, expl. ἕως ἂν ἔλθῃ ὁ ἀνοίγων τὴν ὁδὸν τοῦ παραδείσου.

Chrysostome (non nommé)[15] sur *Gen.* ix 27 qui clôt la petite chaîne du manuscrit.

Le second fragment n'est pas une citation littérale du commentaire d'Hippolyte. Celui-ci n'était pas un écrivain de première catégorie, mais il avait un style simple et de bonne qualité. Il n'aurait jamais accouplé une phrase avec un verbe au mode personnel et une longue période au génitif absolu ornée de deux incises au nominatif. J'ai respecté celles-ci, n'ayant pu décider s'il s'agissait de restes de la rédaction originale ou de gloses insérées. Cette réserve faite, il semble que ce fragment donne tout de même assez exactement l'essentiel du commentaire d'Hippolyte. L'exégèse qu'il propose est nettement apparentée à la légende juive sur le meurtre de Caïn par Lamech rapportée par L. Ginzberg,[16] mais en diffère sur plusieurs points. D'après cette légende, au moment de l'accident, Lamech était complètement aveugle et ne pouvait plus aller chasser sans être accompagné par son jeune fils. D'autre part, le signe (cf. *Gen.* iv 15) attribué par Dieu à Caïn était une paire de cornes. Un jour donc, le jeune garçon, apercevant des cornes au dessus des buissons, crut voir une bête fauve et les signala à Lamech. Celui-ci lança sa flèche et tua Caïn. En découvrant son erreur il voulut joindre les mains en signe de désespoir et, en faisant ce geste, il tua involontairement son fils.

Dans l'exégèse d'Hippolyte comme dans cette légende, Caïn est tué accidentellement par Lamech au cours d'une partie de chasse. Les deux récits expliquent cet accident, d'une part, par l'état des yeux de Lamech, d'autre part, par le comportement de Caïn. Mais les différences commencent ici. Dans la légende Lamech était aveugle; chez Hippolyte il a très mauvaise vue. Dans la légende Caïn portait des cornes; chez Hippolyte il est affligé d'un tremblement nerveux (cf. *Gen.* iv 14). Et nous arrivons à la principale différence, qui explique les précédentes: le jeune homme, chez Hippolyte, n'est plus le fils de Lamech, mais le guide de Caïn. Il semble que l'exégète romain ait trouvé la légende juive trop cruelle et qu'il ait cherché à l'humaniser autant que possible.

---

[15] *In Genesim hom.* 29 (*PG* 52, 271, lin. 13–3 ab imo).

[16] *The Legends of the Jews* by Louis Ginzberg translated from the German Manuscript by Henrietta Szold, t. I (2e éd., Philadelphia 1961), pp. 116 sq. Voir aussi t. V, *Notes to Volumes I and II from the Creation to the Exodus* (Philadelphia 1955), p. 146, note 44.

Le principal intérêt de ce fragment est de montrer qu'Hippolyte a utilisé des légendes juives pour son commentaire sur les premiers chapitres de la Genèse, mais qu'il s'en est servi très librement. On constate la même chose en comparant avec ces légendes ce que l'on peut glaner dans les oeuvres de cet auteur sur la tour de Babel et les attitudes opposées d'Eber et de Nemrod à l'égard de cette entreprise.[17]

La découverte du texte complet des commentaires d'Hippolyte sur l'hexaméron et le reste du livre de la Genèse est sans doute un rêve irréalisable. Mais nous pouvons espérer accroître la collection de fragments de ces ouvrages rassemblée par Achelis. Le fragment du manuscrit d'Athènes nous rappelle qu'il y a encore dans les bibliothèques un grand nombre de florilèges et de recueils de mélanges byzantins qui n'ont pas encore été sérieusement analysés. D'autres découvertes sont donc possibles. Toutefois je ne crois pas que l'éditeur d'Hippolyte puisse attendre grand chose d'une enquête dans ces compilations. Les chaînes exégétiques grecques sur la Genèse ont été étudiées de très près avec les maigres résultats que l'on sait.[18] Peut-être un examen attentif des Chroniques byzantines donnerait-il quelques résultats.[19]

Il y a beaucoup plus à attendre de recherches dans les littératures du moyen orient. Notamment, il est à souhaiter qu'un arabisant reprenne l'étude de la chaîne jacobite sur le Pentateuque,[20] dont les citations attribuées à S. Hippolyte intriguent depuis le XVIIIe siècle les historiens de l'ancienne littérature chrétienne.[21] L'édition la plus complète de ces citations est celle d'Achelis, qui donne, dans la version allemande de Fr. Schultess, 27 fragments dont 13 sur la

[17] Selon Hippolyte, Nemrod chassait pour fournir du gibier aux constructeurs de la tour (*Chron.* § 54. *In Cant.* II 13). Eber, au contraire, a refusé toute compromission avec cette entreprise (*In Cant.* II 12). Son nom est devenu le patronyme des Hébreux (*Refut.* X 30, 4. Cf. *Chron.* § 172).

[18] R. Devreesse, *Les anciens commentateurs de l'Octateuque et des Rois* (Studi e Testi, 101; Cité du Vatican 1959), pp. 25 sq., n'ajoute rien à l'édition d'Achelis.

[19] À titre d'exemple je citerai un texte sur la tour de Babel que l'on trouve sous diverses formes dans certains manuscrits interpolés de Georges Hamartolos (*PG* 97, 76 A 7–B 11; *PG* 110, 93 C 6–96 A 13) et probablement ailleurs. Nous retrouvons dans ce texte toutes les thèses d'Hippolyte sur Eber, sur Nemrod et aussi sur les 72 nations. Sur ce dernier point, voir les remarques de Mlle M.-J. Rondeau dans la *Revue de l'histoire des religions*, t. 171 (1967), 4–11.

[20] Voir G. Graf, *Geschichte der christlichen arabischen Literatur*, t. II (Studi e Testi, 133; Cité du Vatican 1947), 284–89.

[21] Voir Achelis, *Hippolytstudien*, 116 sq.

Genèse.[22] O. Bardenhewer est sans doute le premier à avoir remarqué que certains de ces fragments portaient nettement la marque d'Hippolyte.[23] Il faut aller plus loin. Je laisse de côté les fragments I et II, qui ne pourront être jugés qu'après une étude des sources de la chaîne.[24] Mais je ne vois aucune raison de récuser le témoignage de cette chaîne pour les fragments III–XIII. La commentaire d'Hippolyte sur la Genèse comprenait certainement des passages historiques empruntés surtout à la Bible, mais aussi à des sources juives, et des interprétations typologiques. La typologie Hippolytienne se reconnaît nettement dans les fragments IV, V, et surtout X–XIII, dont l'authenticité est indiscutable.[25] Je n'ai découvert aucune raison de refuser au même auteur le commentaire sur les 40 jours du déluge du fragment III. Les fragments VI–IX sont purement historiques, mais ne contiennent rien qu'il n'ait pu écrire. Il semble donc qu'au moins pour la Genèse on ait sous-estimé l'intérêt de cette chaîne.

Paris, 8 août 1970

---

[22] *Hipp. Werke*, t. I,2, 87–119.

[23] *Des hl. Hippolytus von Rom Kommentar zum Buche Daniel* (Freiburg i. Br. 1877), 30–34.

[24] Achelis n'a retenu que les premières lignes de ces deux fragments, sans doute avec raison. Il s'agit dans les deux cas d'emprunts à des sources juives.

[25] Il s'agit de Thamar (*Gen.* 38, 11–30). On trouve dans ces fragments, non seulement la typologie habituelle d'Hippolyte, mais son intérêt pour la lignée des ancêtres du Christ. Voir sur ce sujet mes remarques, *Dict. de Spiritualité*, t. 7, col. 564. Hippolyte rangeait Thamar parmi les saints de l'Ancien Testament qui ont désiré ardemment le parfum répandu par le Père, c'est-à-dire le Verbe (*In Cant.* II 18).

ROMANUS MELODUS AND THE GREEK TRAGEDIANS*

NICHOLAS B. TOMADAKES

This short paper is presented in honor of the distinguished palaeographer, student of the manuscript tradition of the foremost Greek poets, and Hellenist, Professor Alexander Turyn. Although not primarily a classicist, I have published similar studies on modern Greek poets such as Dionysios Solomos, Andreas Kalbos and John Billaras in which I have shown the extent of their classical learning. Nor is this the first time that I have attempted to connect the sixth-century Byzantine poet Romanus with the Greek tragedians. Commonly Romanus has been considered either as a Greco-Syrian or even of Jewish origin. However, the diction and style of his poems convince us that he was not only Greek-educated but that Greek was also his mother tongue and that he knew it intimately. With this paper, I hope not only to establish that Romanus knew the tragic poets of the past but also to show the way to a field of study which can fruitfully be explored by classical scholars.[1]

* This paper, originally presented in Modern Greek, has been translated with the author's permission by Professor Mark Naoumides.—Ed.

[1] All references are made to the following two editions of Romanus Melodus:

(a) *Hymnoi* = ʽΡωμανοῦ τοῦ Μελῳδοῦ ῞Υμνοι vols. I–IV (and supplement of vol. IV), Athens 1952–64. Reference is made first to the number of the poem and the lines and then to volume and page.

(b) *Cantica* = *Sancti Romani Melodi Cantica. Cantica Genuina.* Edited by †Paul Maas and C. A. Trypanis, Oxford 1963. Reference is made to the poem, stanza, and page.

(c) *Dubia* = *Sancti Romani Melodi Cantica. Cantica Dubia.* Edited by †Paul Maas and C. A. Trypanis, Berlin 1970. I do not agree that all poems included in this volume are dubious. Reference as in *Cantica*.

Of little use were the studies on the language of Romanus by Professor K. Mitsakis, viz. *The Language of Romanos the Melodist,* München 1967, pp. XX + 217 (cf. review by J. Grosdidier de Matons in *Byz. Zeitschr.* 62 [1969], 359–62), and "The Vocabulary of Romanos the Melodist," *Glotta* 43 (1965), 171–97 (where many words not previously listed in the extant lexica are included). For my views on Romanus' diction cf. my book ʽΗ Βυζαντινὴ ʽΥμνογραφία καὶ Ποίησις, Athens 1965 (esp. pp. 108–109). Several words

I

As has been pointed out elsewhere the extent of Romanus' debt to Euripides can be seen in the following passage from the "Hymn to Abraham's Sacrifice" (*Hymnoi* No. 3. 222–42, vol. I. 54–55), where the poet puts in Sarah's mouth (a mute character in *Genesis*) the following words:

Ἀκμάσας γενήσῃ μου στήριγμα γήρους, ὦ σπλάγχνον ἐμόν,
τὰ σὰ δὲ τέκνα βακτηρία πολιᾶς.
Κατίδω σῆς ὀσφύος ἔκγονα καὶ οὕτω θνήξομαι,
σὺ δὲ κόρας τὰς ἐμὰς ἀποκλείσεις.
Σὺ σὺν τοῖς τέκνοις κόλποις προπέμψεις με τῶν πατέρων μου.
Σὺ κλίνῃς μου πρῶτος πορευόμενος κλαύσεις.
Ἐγὼ δὲ θνῆσιν οὐδαμῶς μὴ θρηνήσω,
ὀλετῆρα σὸν πατέρα ἀκούσασα,
ὅτι μόνος ἀγαθὸς ὁ σωτὴρ τῶν ψυχῶν ἡμῶν.

These lines recall the well-known passage from Euripides, *Medea* 1029–39:

Ἄλλως ἄρ' ὑμᾶς, ὦ τέκν', ἐξεθρεψάμην,
1030 ἄλλως δ' ἐμόχθουν καὶ κατεξάνθην πόνοις
στερρὰς ἐνεγκοῦσ' ἐν τόκοις ἀλγηδόνας,
ἦ μήν ποθ' ἡ δύστηνος εἶχον ἐλπίδας
πολλὰς ἐν ὑμῖν γηροβοσκήσειν τ' ἐμὲ
καὶ κατθανοῦσαν χερσὶν εὖ περιστελεῖν,
1035 ζηλωτὸν ἀνθρώποισιν· νῦν δ' ὄλωλε δὴ
γλυκεῖα φροντίς· σφῶν γὰρ ἐστερημένη
λυπρὸν διάξω βίοτον ἀλγεινόν τ' ἐμοί.
ὑμεῖς δὲ μητέρ' οὐκέτ' ὄμμασιν φίλοις
ὄψεσθ', ἐς ἄλλο σχῆμ' ἀποστάντες βίου.

Romanus' portrait of Sarah appears here more humane than Euripides' portrait of Medea, in that unlike Medea Sarah is not a murderess, being herself not responsible for the approaching doom of her son Isaac, the sacrifice decreed by God. She had hoped to see her son reach manhood, beget children who would support her in her old age. She had expected her son to close her eyes when she would die and to follow her funeral procession. Nor does she want to

---

originating from the Greek tragedians and Aristophanes and recurring in Romanus' poems have been pointed out by the editors of the Athenian edition; cf. especially M. Naoumides, *Hymnoi* III, pp. 225–26.

mourn for the death of her child (since it is more natural for the parents to die before their children), especially when Isaac's father himself is to become his slayer.

Medea's predicament is similar. She also labored to raise her children, to see them grow hoping that one day they will care for her in her old age and that when the time of her death comes they will give her a proper burial, as people like to do for their beloved. After their death, however, she will be left alone and the children will never see their mother again, since they will have exchanged their life for death.

In the same Hymn of Romanus Sarah asks Abraham:

Σπορεὺς αὐτοῦ πέλεις / καὶ σφαγεὺς τούτου μέλλεις;

Then turning to Isaac who is not aware that he is about to be sacrificed, she says:

Πορεύου οὖν τέκνον / καὶ γίνου Θεῷ θῦμα
σὺν τῷ σῷ γενέτῃ / φονευτῇ δέ σου μᾶλλον.
πιστεύω δὲ γονεὺς / σφαγεὺς οὐ γίνεται.

(lines 298–303, vol. I, 56)

I believe that there is here a distant echo from Euripides' *Hercules Furens*, whose main character is also an involuntary slayer of his children (maddened by Lyssa).

1367 ὦ τέκν', ὁ φύσας καὶ τεκὼν ὑμᾶς πατὴρ
ἀπώλεσ', οὐδ' ὤνασθε τῶν ἐμῶν καλῶν...
1374 οἴμοι δάμαρτος καὶ τέκνων, οἴμοι δ' ἐμοῦ,
ὡς ἀθλίως πέπραγα κἀποζεύγνυμαι
τέκνων γυναικός τ'.

In the case of Heracles his wife is dead, whereas in the "Sacrifice" there is fear that Sarah might commit suicide. Nevertheless Abraham, whose sense of duty is stronger than paternal affection, is completely aware that besides losing his child he will be constantly confronted with Sarah's hatred, who already sees him as a murderer, slayer, and destroyer. The φύσας καὶ τεκὼν καὶ ἀπολέσας becomes σπορεὺς καὶ σφαγεύς.

II

We can, however, demonstrate Romanus' first-hand knowledge of Euripides' tragedies *Medea* and *Hercules Furens* by following another path.

It is commonly believed that Romanus wrote in his contemporary koinê. He certainly was not an Atticist. However the diction of his hymns is not confined to the koinê known to us through the Old and New Testaments or the papyri, but it betrays a deep and unusual familiarity with the classical authors. I list here a number of passages where we find words common not only to the tragedians but also to Homer, Pindar, Bacchylides and other Greek poets and prose writers:

ἀθανής, ὁ adj.: ἀθανῆ καὶ θνητόν σε γινώσκοντες. Hymnoi 1.426 (III, 106). Cf. id. ἀμερής, ὁ adj.

αἴγλη, ἡ subst.: Ὑπὲρ τὴν τοῦ ἡλίου φαίνει ἀκτῖνα / ἡ τοῦ ἐνθέου τούτου ἄδυτος αἴγλη. Dubia 63, γ′ (p. 27).

αἰθήρ, ὁ subst.: Αἰθήρ, ἐξευτρεπίσθητι τῷ διὰ σοῦ ὁδεύοντι· ἀνοίχθητε, οὐρανοί. Cantica 32, ι′ (p. 255).

ἀμειδής, ὁ adj.: Νύκτα ἠφάνισε τὴν ἀμειδῆ / καὶ ἔδειξε μεσημβρίαν τὸ πᾶν. κατηύγασε τὴν οἰκουμένην τὸ ἀνέσπερον φῶς, Ἰησοῦς ὁ σωτὴρ ἡμῶν. Cantica 6, ις′(p. 47). Νὺξ ἀμειδὴς ἡ φύσις ἡ ἐμὴ καὶ πῶς ἐξ αὐτῆς λάμψει ὁ ἥλιος. Cantica 37, ια′ (p. 293).

γαῖα, ἡ subst. (for γῆ, ἡ): Οὐκ οὐρανὸς οὔτε γαῖα οὐδ' ὅλος τούτῳ ὁ κόσμος / συγκρίνεται τῷ σπεύσαντι ῥύσασθαί με / τοῦ βορβόρου τῶν ἔργων μου. Cantica 10, ι′ (p. 77).

θάλαμος, ὁ subst.: Ἐγὼ μὲν ἐν θαλάμῳ σὺ δ' ἐν ξύλῳ (= σταυρῷ). Hymnoi 21. 204 (II, 170). —Καὶ εἰς τὸν θάλαμον εἰσῆλθε τοῦ Φαρισαίου. Cantica 10, ιβ′ (p. 77).—Θαλάμῳ γαμικῷ ἐπέστη...καὶ θόρυβος παρῆν οὐ μικρὸς τῷ θαλάμῳ.... Cantica 7, β′ (p. 49).

θεόσδοτος, ὁ adj. (for θεόδοτος): ὡς ἀριστεύσας ἀνδρικῶς τὰ θεόσδοτα δῶρα. Dubia 66, η′ (p. 50).

*θεοστυγίας, ὁ adj.: υἱὸν ἰατρὸν ἔχων θεοστυγίαν (= θεοστύγητος. Cf. Aeschylus, Choeph. 635).

Cf. also θεοστυγής, ὁ adj.: Τοῦτον συνέχοντες οἱ θεοστυγεῖς / εἰς τὸ συνέδριον αὐτῶν τὸ πικρόν. Hymnoi 32. 49–50 (III, 163). Καταλάλους, θεοστυγεῖς, ὑβριστάς. Ep. Rom. 9. 30.

λάϊνος, ὁ adj. (= λίθινος): σπονδὰς προσάγαγε / τῇ τοῦ βασιλέως εἰκόνι τῇ λαΐνῃ (= τῷ ἀνδριάντι τοῦ βασιλέως). Dubia 65, ις′ (p. 44). This adjective in Euripides, HF 979, 1038, 1096, 1332, refers to ὀρθοστάτας, κίονας οἴκων, τύκισμα, ἐξογκώματα.

μέλεος, ὁ adj. (= δυστυχής): δι' ἔργων τοιαῦτα ἔδρασέ μοι τῷ μελέῳ. Hymnoi 30. 238 (III, 90). Very common in the tragedians.

νέκυς, ὁ (for νεκρός, ὁ) adj.: θάψαντες ἄφετε τὸν νέκυν. Cantica 24, ζ′ (p. 183).

ὀμβροτόκος, ὁ adj.: Τὸν τὰς νεφέλας ἡνιοχοῦντα καὶ ὀμβροτόκους αὐτὰς ποιοῦντα. Cantica 32, ια′ (p. 225).

ραψῳδία, ἡ subst.: Ῥαψῳδίας μὲν λόγους. Dubia 61, ια′ (p. 13).—Ῥαψῳδίαις πολυπλόκοις ἀντεβόλουν τῷ ἄνακτι οἱ ἱερεῖς τῆς αἰσχύνης. Dubia 69, κϛ′ (p. 69).

τόλμα, ἡ subst.: κατίδω τὴν τόλμαν τῶν τιμώντων τὸν Μωσῆν. Hymnoi 46. 77 (cf. Λεξιλόγιον, IV, 549).

ὑδατόρρυτος, ὁ adj.: Ὁ τῷ φθέγματί σου στήσας τὰ ὑδατόρρυτα νέφη (= the clouds that produce rain). Cantica 45, Προοίμιον (p. 367).

φάος, τό subst.: τυφλὸν ἐκ γενετῆς τοῦ Χριστοῦ δόντος φάος. Hymnoi 32. 68 (III, 164).

φλόγεος, ὁ adj.: Φλόγεον ὀστοῦν (sc. τοῦ ἀναστάντος Χριστοῦ!). Hymnoi 31. 11 (III, 130).

χάος, τό subst.: Ἔκστηθι φρίττων, οὐρανέ! / Δῦνον εἰς χάος, ὦ γῆ! Hymnoi 22. 12–13 (II, 185).

The words listed above (and many others similar to these) cannot always be attributed to the direct influence of ancient authors but some at least may have become known to Romanus via the New Testament where words such as ἄρουρα, αὐγή, βροτός, γαῖα, γλυκερός, δείλαιος, δώρημα, ἐλεεινός, λιπαρός, λίττεσθαι, ὁμόφρων, πολιός, στεναγμός, τάλας, τρομεῖν, occur with varying frequency.

Let me now cite a dozen-odd passages where we find words that were well-known terms of ancient dramatic production but which subsequently changed meaning:

ἄγγελος, -οι, ὁ, οἱ subst. Referring now to angels. From it the adjective ἀγγελικός: Αἱ ἀγγελικαὶ προπορεύεσθε δυνάμεις. Dubia, App. I (p. 164).

βωμός, ὁ subst. Cf. infra, τύμβος.

Cf. εὗρον καὶ βωμὸν ἐν ᾧ ἐπεγέγραπτο· Ἀγνώστῳ Θεῷ. Act. Ap. 17. 23.

δρᾶμα, τό subst.: Πρὶν λογίσωμαι γὰρ ποιῆσαι τὸ δρᾶμα, / σὺ ὑπῆρχες συμβιβάζων με πρὸς αὐτό. Hymnoi 41. 164–165 (IV, 203).—Τῆς γὰρ βουλῆς μου δράματα ὑπάρχουσι. Hymnoi 44. 96 (cf. St. Kourouses, IV, 546).—Λέγε μοι τί ἐστι τοῦτο τὸ δρᾶμα. Hymnoi 25. 173 (II, 277).

δραματούργημα, τό subst.: Νῦν ἐγνώρισα τὸ δραματούργημα / νῦν ὑμῖν ἐκκαλύπτω τὸν κλέψαντα. Cantica 12, ιδ′ (p. 91).

θέατρον, τό (= θέαμα) subst.: Πανήγυρις ἵσταται, κἀγὼ οὐκ ἐργάζομαι... πρὸ τοῦ λυθῇ τὸ θέατρον, δώρησαι τὴν ἐπιστροφήν.... Cantica 56, ιγ′ (p. 486).—Τῶν εἰδώλων ἔλυσε τὸ θέατρον, ὡς διδάσκει τὸ σύγγραμμα. Dubia 69, ιη′ (p. 67).—Οὔτε ὤφθη ἐν θεάτρῳ (sc. St. Panteleemon). Dubia 69, ε′ (p. 64).

Cf. ὥρμησάν τε ὁμοθυμαδὸν εἰς τὸ θέατρον. *Act. Ap.* 19. 29. Cf. also *ib.* 19. 31...ὅτι θέατρον ἐγενήθημεν τῷ κόσμῳ καὶ ἀγγέλοις καὶ ἀνθρώποις. 1. *Ep. Cor.* 4. 9.

θίασος, ὁ subst. (= ὁ ὅμιλος) : Τῶν κεκλημένων πᾶς λοιπὸν ὁ θίασος ὡς ἐδείπνει. *Cantica* 49, ι' (p. 425).

κατορχοῦμαι verb: ἀνεφύησαν καὶ γυναῖκες προφητεύουσαι / ἐμοῦ κατορχούμεναι (= ἐμὲ ἐμπαίζουσαι). *Hymnoi* 29. 167–68 (III, 30–31).

κωμῳδῶ verb: ὅταν τὴν πτῶσιν αὐτῶν (sc. τῶν δαιμόνων) κωμῳδοῦμεν γηθόμενοι. *Cantica* 11, β' (p. 81).

σκηνή, ἡ subst.: ἐν ταῖς τῶν ἁγίων σκηναῖς. *Cantica* 55, ιθ' (p. 479) ; κατοικῆσαι ἐν ταῖς τῶν ἁγίων σκηναῖς. *ib.* κε' (p. 481).

Cf. Εἰς τὰς αἰωνίους σκηνάς. *Luke* 16. 9; and in many other passages in reference to the tabernacle.

τραγῳδία, ἡ subst.: (description of the wedding at Cana) Ἤχθετο ὁ νυμφίος καὶ οἱ οἰνοχοοῦντες ἐψιθύριζον ἄπαυστα, / καὶ μία ἦν αὐτοῖς τραγῳδία πενίας (sc. ἐκ τῆς ἐξαντλήσεως τοῦ οἴνου), / καὶ θόρυβος παρῆν οὐ μικρὸς τῷ θαλάμῳ. *Cantica* 7, ε' (p. 51). Ὦ συμφορὰ ἀδιήγητος, ὦ τραγῳδία ἀνέκφραστος. *Cantica* 11, ς' (p. 82).

τραγῳδῶ verb: ὄντως πενθεῖ ὁ διάβολος, ὅταν δαιμόνων τὸν θρίαμβον / ἐν ἐκκλησίαις τραγῳδῶμεν! (= διηγούμεθα, ἀποκλαίωμεν). *Cantica* 11, β' (p. 81).

τύμβος, ὁ subst.: βλέπω τύμβον / τὸν βωμόν. *Hymnoi* 3. 377–78 (I, 59).

χορός, ὁ subst.: Ὕμνον ὁ χορὸς τῶν ἀγγέλων ἀναμέλπει. *Dubia* App. I, ιγ' (p. 167).

Cf. *ib.* I, κε', p. 170: Οἱ χοροὶ τῶν ἀσωμάτων (sc. ἀγγέλων). Χορὸς (-οὶ) ἀγγέλων ἢ ἀγγελικὴ χορεία.

Cf. Ἤκουσεν συμφωνίας καὶ χορῶν. *Luke* 15. 25.

From these passages we see that the terms δρᾶμα, τραγῳδία, θέατρον, θίασος, σκηνή, τραγῳδῶ, κωμῳδῶ were preserved, even though the ἄγγελοι are no longer "earthly" but φαεινοί and πύρινοι as the angel of the Annunciation (*Hymnoi*, No. 14.55, 72, vol. I, 312), δραματούργημα indicates action in general, σκηναί are the heavenly abodes of the saints, and the χορός consists of angels.

The influence of the tragedians on Romanus will become more evident from the following words which I have excerpted from his works and which are more likely to have come directly from the Greek tragedians than indirectly from the works of Gregory of Nazianzus, Nonnus of Panopolis, or any other of the Christian poets who were in turn influenced by the diction of dramatic and epic poetry. Concerning these words we may assume either that Romanus took them directly from the tragedians with the meaning which they had in these passages (this would be the case with the adjectives δύσμορος, εὐκάματος, τεκνοκτόνος), or that he changed their meaning (cf. ὀμματόω), or that he coined a new word (e.g. κρεοκοπία) on the model of similar forms found in the tragedians (i.e. the verb κρεοκοπῶ).

There is of course another possibility, which also exists in all similar cases, namely that these words were used either extensively or to a limited extent by authors later than the tragedians, who for us are lost but who were known to Romanus. However, we must confine our discussion to what is known.

The words mentioned above are the following:

ἀποσυλέω verb (not ἀποσυλάω: ὑφ' ὅτου σκῆπτρον τιμάς τ' ἀποσυλᾶται. Aeschylus, Pr. 171): (ὁ ἐχθρός, sc. ὁ διάβολος) κατὰ μέρος τῶν θείων ἀποσυλεῖ σε, / δεικνύων σοι ἐνύπνια καὶ δι'αὐτῶν πτοῶν σε. Hymnoi 23. 228–29 (II, 219) = Cantica 53, κα' (p. 461).
Cf. ὅς μ' ἐξέωσε κἀπεσύλησεν πάτρας. Sophocles, OC 1330... τοῖον ὅμηρόν μ' ἀποσυλήσας / "Αιδη θάνατος παρέδωκεν. Euripides, Alc. 870–71.

δύσμορος, ὁ adj.: 'Υμεῖς, δύσμοροι, φθόνῳ κεκράτησθε· ὅθεν ἐμὲ σωθῆναι οὐ βούλεσθε. Εἰς τὴν αἱμόρρουν. Cantica 12, θ' (p. 90).
Cf. Ὦ σκῆπτρα φωτός, δυσμόρου γε δύσμορα. Sophocles, OC 1109.

ἐγκύμων, ὁ adj.: Εὐθὺς δὲ νεφέλαι, τῇ προστάξει τοῦ ποιήσαντος / ἐγκύμονες ὑδάτων τὸν ἀέρα ἐπενήξαντο. Εἰς προφήτην Ἡλίαν. Cantica 45, κθ' (p. 378).
Cf. ἐγκύμον' ἵππον τευχέων ξυναρμόσας / πύργων ἔπεμψεν ἐντὸς ὀλέθριον βρέτας (= δούρειον ἵππον!). Euripides, Tr. 11.

ἐκτυφλόω verb: Πόλος (= οὐρανὸς) ἐκτυφλοῦται, / οὐκ ἀνοίγει ὀφθαλμὸν ἕως ἂν εἴπω. Hymnoi 21. 219, 220 (II, 171).
Cf. Πολλοὶ δ' ἀνῆθον, ἐκτυφλωθέντες σκότῳ / λαμπτῆρες ἐν δόμοισι δεσποίνης χάριν. Aeschylus, Choeph. 536–537.

εὐκάματος, ὁ adj.: διὸ μνησθέντες πρότερον τῆς εὐκαμάτου συλλογῆς τῶν ἁγίων ἁπάντων. Εἰς τὸν Ἅγιον Γεώργιον. Dubia 66, α' (p. 46).
Cf. κάματόν τ' εὐκάματον. Euripides, Ba. 66.
The word also occurs in Paulus Silentiarius, Ἔκφρασις Ἁγίας Σοφίας 452, 496 (cf. Migne, PG 86, 2137 A, 2138 B).

κατάγελως, ὁ adj.: Μὴ αὐτομολήσῃς πρὸς τὰ πρότερα / καὶ γένῃ κατάγελως τοῦ νῦν σε φοβουμένου. Hymnoi 23. 163–64 (II, 217).
Cf. τί δῆτ' ἐμαυτῆς καταγέλωτ' ἔχω τάδε; Aeschylus, Agam. 1264.
The word is also found in Demosthenes 56, 43: ὥσπερ ἐπὶ καταγέλωτι ἀντιδικοῦντες εἰσεληλύθατε.

*κρεοκοπία, ἡ subst. (= ἡ ἐν τῇ χειρουργίᾳ κοπὴ τῶν σαρκῶν): Ἱπποκράτη, εἰπὲ καί, Γαληνέ, διασάφησον / καὶ ὑμεῖς ὅσοι σὺν τούτοις μύσται / οἱ τὴν κρεοκοπίαν εἰδότες ἄκρως. Εἰς τὸν Θεολόγον. Hymnoi 4, Παράρτημα p. 144 (= Dubia 60, η′, p. 4).

Cf. παίουσι, κρεοκοποῦσι δυστήνων μέλη, / ἕως ἁπάντων ἐξαπέφθειραν βίον. Aeschylus, Pers. 462–63.—Κρεοκοπεῖν μέλη ξένων. Euripides, Cyc. 359.

The verb is also used by Palladius (4th cent.) in his Life of John Chrysostom (Migne, PG 47, 67).

The adjective κρεοκόπος, ὁ is also found in Dionysius of Halicarnassus.

μαραίνομαι verb: Τρανὸς εἶ, λαμπρὸς εἶ καὶ ζηλωτὸς ὤν, Ἀδάμ, / τοῦ σὲ μισοῦντος ἐκτήκεις βάσκανον ὄμμα· / ὁρῶν σε γὰρ ὁ τύραννος μαραίνεται καὶ κράζει· / τίς ἐστιν ὃν βλέπω, οὐκ ἐπίσταμαι. Hymnoi 23. 40–42 (II, 211). Μαρᾶναι τὸ ἄνθος μου, τὸ ἄνθος τῆς χάριτος, ἐγὼ οὐκ ἀνέχομαι. Cantica 43, ιβ′ (p. 343).

Cf. Πῶς ἔτλης τοιαῦτα σὰς / ὄψεις μαρᾶναι; Sophocles, OT 1327–1328.— Βρίζει γὰρ αἷμα καὶ μαραίνεται (= ἀποξηραίνεται, ἐξαφανίζεται) χερός. Aeschylus, Eum. 280; and elsewhere. Οὕτως ὁ πλούσιος ἐν ταῖς πορείαις αὐτοῦ μαρανθήσεται. Ep. Jac. I. 11.

ὀμματόω verb: Πηρὸν πάλιν λόγῳ ὀμματώσας, ἀγαθέ, / ἀπαθὴς μεμένηκας. Hymnoi 21. 108–109 (II, 163).

Cf. ξυνῆκας· ὠμμάτωσα γὰρ σαφέστερον (= I opened your eyes so that you may understand) Aeschylus, Supp. 467; οὗτοι φρέν' ἂν κλέψειεν ὠμματωμένην. Aeschylus, Choeph. 854. The word was known to Basil of Seleucia (Migne, PG 85, 288 C, 305 B).

τεκνοκτόνος, ὁ adj.: Μὴ γένωμαι ὁ ξένος τοῦ θανάτου ταύτης πρόξενος, / μηδὲ τῇ ξενοδόχῳ τεκνοκτόνος λογισθήσομαι. Cantica 45, ις′ (p. 373).

Cf. Ὀφθησόμεσθα, καὶ τεκνοκτόνον μύσος / ἐς ὄμμαθ' ἥξει φιλτάτῳ ξένων ἐμῶν. Euripides, HF 1155–56.

The word also occurs in Clement of Alexandria, Strom. 8, 9 (= Migne, PG 9, 595 A).

τύραννον, τό subst. (sc. ἡ τυραννίς): Τῆς ἔχθρας ἐλύθη τὸ τύραννον (= τοῦ ἐχθροῦ, sc. διαβόλου, ἐλύθη ἡ τυραννίς), / τῆς Εὔας ἐπαύθη τὸ δάκρυον. Hymnoi 22. 6–7 (II, 184).

τύραννος, ὁ adj.: τυραννικός· τυραννικὸν δῶμα = παλάτιον.

Cf. Πλούτει τε γὰρ κατ' οἶκον, εἰ βούλει, μέγα / καὶ ζῇ τύραννον σχῆμ' ἔχων, ...Sophocles, Ant. 1168–1169.—Εἴποι τις ἂν τὸ πραχθέν, ἢ μάτην ὄχλον / στέγει τύραννον δῶμα προσπόλων ἐμῶν; Euripides, Hipp. 843.

ὑπασπίζω verb: Τὸν τοπάρχην σὺν τοῖς ὑπασπίζουσι. Dubia 66, κδ′ (p. 52). Cf. Φημὶ γάρ ποτε / σύμπλους γενέσθαι τῶνδ' ὑπασπίζων πατρί ...Euripides, Heracl. 215–16.

φονεύτρια, ἡ subst.: Καὶ φατρίαν φθάσας φονεύτριαν. *Hymnoi* 22. 226 (II, 244). Cf. schol. on Euripides, *Or.* 260, *Hymnoi* 2. 384. The word also in Clement of Alexandria (Migne, *PG* 69, 737 D) and subsequently in Gregory of Pisidia.

If one must draw a general conclusion from this study, it cannot be other than the following. Romanus, who was familiar with the works of John Chrysostom, Basil of Seleucia, and many others of the Greek Church Fathers who had preceded him, and who was influenced by the Syrian Ephraim much less than was assumed towards the end of the nineteenth and the beginning of the twentieth century, who furthermore depended basically on the Greek text of the Septuagint and the New Testament and partially on the Apocrypha and the earlier liturgical texts—this Romanus was not, as he was thought to be, so ignorant of classical Greek literature. His diction is the best proof of this. And if for supposedly metrical considerations his language is distorted by some editors, especially insofar as the accents and the syntax are concerned (in spite of the unanimous testimony of the manuscript tradition), nevertheless, his diction and vocabulary are true witnesses to his familiarity with classical Greek. Romanus, however, deliberately avoided the higher, more learned style, because he followed a tradition already formed by the need to make the liturgical texts comprehensible to the masses, a tradition which called for the composition of liturgical texts in meters based on the accent rather than the prosody of the words, and in simpler and more straightforward language.

Athens, 25 June 1970

ON SOME MSS OF THE ATHOUS RECENSION OF THE GREEK PAROEMIOGRAPHERS

WINFRIED BÜHLER

I

When E. Miller, in 1868, published the text of four collections of Greek proverbs from a fourteenth century manuscript which he had found in a monastery on Mt. Athos and brought to Paris,[1] he opened a new chapter in the investigation of the Greek paroemiographers. Most of the Athous proverbs, it is true, were already known from the "vulgar" tradition of Zenobius, Diogenianus, and others; but the new find, apart from furnishing better readings and a number of valuable quotations, made it possible to clear up essential points in the history of paroemiographical tradition. Whereas all collections of Greek proverbs known before the discovery of the Athous, with one notable exception, are arranged in a more or less strict alphabetical order, the first three Athous collections, headed by the title ⟨Ζηνο⟩βίου ἐπιτομὴ τῶν Ταρραίου καὶ Διδύμου παροιμιῶν, display a nonalphabetical arrangement. As alphabetization, in this kind of literature, is always open to the suspicion of later origin,[2] the conclusion was obvious that the Athous has preserved the original form of the work or at least represents an earlier stage of its transmission. The conclusion was confirmed by the statement in the Suda article on Zenobius that his epitome consisted of three books.[3] Unlike the Athous, the alphabetical collection of Zenobius preserved in a twelfth century Parisinus shows no trace of this division. Thus the label "genuinus" which was soon attached to the Athous Zenobius

[1] M. E. Miller, *Mélanges de littérature grecque* (Paris 1868; repr. Amsterdam 1965), 341 ff. The Athous is now in the Bibliothèque Nationale (suppl. 1164).

[2] On alphabetization see now Lloyd W. Daly, *Contributions to a History of Alphabetization in Antiquity and the Middle Ages* (Collection Latomus, 90; Brussels 1967).

[3] Z 73 Adl.

is legitimate despite the comparatively late origin of the manuscript and the peculiar alterations its text has suffered.

Fifteen years after the publication of the *Mélanges*, O. Crusius, enlarging Miller's conclusions by a penetrating analysis of the whole tradition, outlined the first critical text history of the Greek paroemiographers.[4] He stated that in late antiquity there was a Corpus of five collections of proverbs, three of them being the three books of Zenobius, the fourth the so-called proverbs of Plutarch, different from those known under this title,[5] and finally the fifth— identical with the fourth of the Athous—an anonymous compilation intended for use in schools and already arranged alphabetically. All existing collections of proverbs go back ultimately to this Corpus. But whereas the "vulgar" tradition, i.e. Zenobius, Diogenianus, the Bodleian recension,[6] not to speak of the Byzantine compilers, depends on a redaction in which the single collections of the Corpus were put together and brought into an alphabetical arrrangement, the Athous, though mutilated, shortened, etc., still reflects the original form of the Corpus with its constituent parts separated from each other. With this general outline, Crusius had laid down the firm basis for a new critical edition of the Greek paroemiographers which he planned and for which nobody was better qualified than he. But despite several preliminary publications—among them an edition of the proverbs of Plutarch[7] followed by a commentary[8]— he died before carrying out his main project,[9] and since then no

---

[4] O. Crusius, *Analecta critica ad paroemiographos Graecos* (Leipzig 1883; repr. in *Corpus paroemiographorum Graecorum* [Leutsch–Schneidewin], *Supplementum* [Hildesheim 1961], part II).

[5] See *Corpus paroemiographorum Graecorum*, ed. E. L. v. Leutsch and F. G. Schneidewin, vol. 1 (Göttingen 1839; repr. Hildesheim 1958), 321 ff. and below, note 20.

[6] Edited by Th. Gaisford, *Paroemiographi Graeci* (Oxford 1836), 1 ff.

[7] *Plutarchi de proverbiis Alexandrinorum libellus ineditus*, rec. et praefatus est O. Crusius (Universitätsprogramm Tübingen 1887; repr. in *Corpus...Supplementum* [see note 4], part III a).

[8] *Ad Plutarchi de proverbiis Alexandrinorum libellum commentarius*, scripsit O. Crusius (Universitätsprogramm Tübingen 1895; repr. in *Corpus...Supplementum*, part III b).

[9] Important work in the field of MSS investigation of the vulgar tradition had been done in the eighties and nineties by L. Cohn, the rich results of which were published in two papers: *Zu den Paroemiographen, Mitteilungen aus Handschriften* (Breslau 1887 = Breslauer Philologische Abhandlungen 2, 2, repr. in the *Supplementum* [above, note 4], part I), and "Zur Ueberlieferung des alphabetischen Corpus," in O. Crusius and L. Cohn, *Zur handschriftlichen Ueberlieferung, Kritik und Quellenkunde der Paroemiographen*

serious attempt at a new edition of the Greek paroemiographers seems to have been made.[10]

Given the prime importance of the Athous for the transmission of the paroemiographers, it is obvious that the first step towards a new critical edition of the whole Corpus must be a reconstruction of that redaction of late antiquity on which the Athous depends. We do not even dispose of a reliable text of the Athous, for Miller contented himself with publishing a collation which was made upon the text of the vulgar tradition and which, in more than one point, lacks exactness.[11] What is more important is that the Athous is no longer the only known manuscript to reflect that early stage which served as a basis for all later tradition. In the decades following the publication of the Athous, no less than seven other manuscripts emerged from the darkness of libraries, all of them belonging to the same "Athous recension."[12] Although most of them are but scanty excerpts, they still furnish many a better reading and, above all, help to cover a big gap in the Athous due to the loss of a whole quaternion. It was owing to one of them, the Laurentianus 80,13 (which was discovered first), that Crusius was able to state that the archetype of the Athous contained not four, but five collections. The inconvenience of the scattered publications of these texts is only partly alleviated by the Supplement to the *Corpus paroemiographorum Graecorum* of Leutsch–Schneidewin (see above, note 4) in which the original publications of the four most important witnesses are gathered together. For an accurate knowledge of the transmitted wording and a conclusive appreciation of the mutual relationship of the texts it is still indispensable to refer to the manuscripts, since several of the transcriptions are either inexact or incomplete, or both. In preparing a critical edition of the "Athous recension" I have collated afresh the manuscripts of all eight witnesses (using

---

(Philologus, Suppl.-Bd. 6, 1891), 224 ff. (repr. in the *Supplementum*, part IV). Cohn was to collaborate with Crusius in the new edition of the whole Corpus, but after the turn of the century no progress was made. Cohn died in 1915, Crusius in 1918.

[10] R. Strömberg, *Greek Proverbs* (Göteborgs K. Vetenskaps- och Vitterhets-Samhälles Handlingar, Sjätte Följden. Ser. A. Bd. 4. N:o 8; Göteborg 1954) is a collection of proverbs not listed by the ancient paroemiographers.

[11] A revision of Miller's collation, correcting most of his errors, was given by L. Cohn, *Jahrbücher für classische Philologie*, 32 (1886), 840–42 (not reprinted in the *Supplementum*).

[12] A list is to be found in K. Rupprecht's article "Paroimiographoi," in the *RE*, XVIII 4 (1949), 1748. For a more detailed description, see the next section.

photocopies). The present paper is concerned with the relationship between the Athous and two other witnesses of the "Athous recension." I hope to be able to correct the current opinion in one point and to decide another left open by Crusius.

II

The cornerstone of my paper is the following description of all the manuscripts of the "Athous recension," since it must furnish essential data for the subsequent conclusions. Special attention is called to the extent of epitomization and to the gaps that occur. Particularly the latter are of prime importance for the classification. The principle of the arrangement of the list is the date of first publication.

1 (**M**). Athous, now Paris. suppl. Graec. 1164, 14th cent. Paper; 48 ff. Among other texts [13] ff. 30^r–40^v four collections of proverbs (see below); ff. 41^r–48^v excerpts from seven lexicographical works, parts of which occur also in other MSS of the Athous group (I f. 41^r four articles from the *Lexicon rhetoricum Cantabrigiense*,[14] here attributed to Claudius Casilo; II f. 41^r–43^r a Plato lexicon, [wrongly] attributed to Didymus; III f. 43^r–44^r Zenodorus, π. συνηθείας [15]; IV f. 44^r–46^r Suetonius, π. βλασφημιῶν [16]; V f. 46^r Aristophanes Byz., π. τῶν ὑποπτευομένων μὴ εἰρῆσθαι τοῖς παλαιοῖς; VI f. 46^r–47^v id., ὀνόματα ἡλικιῶν; VII f. 48^{rv} Suetonius, π. παιδιῶν [beginning missing] [17]).

More detailed description of ff. 30^r–40^v. F. 30^r *inscriptio* B (rubr.) ἰου ἐπιτομὴ τῶν Ταρραίου καὶ Διδύμου παροιμιῶν. (1) ff. 30^r–33^r first collection (Ath. I). An index of 89 numbered lemmata is followed by the complete text (numbers agreeing with the index). First proverb: Καδμεία νίκη; last proverb: Ἑρμώνιος χάρις. (2) ff. 33^v–38^r second collection (Ath. II). F. 33^v index of 108 numbered lemmata. Rest of f. 33^v empty. After two completely empty leaves of a more recent date (ff. 34 and 35), the text of the collection begins on f. 36^r with the 15th proverb (φρουρεῖν ἢ πλουτεῖν, first line), ending regularly on f. 38^v. First proverb

---

[13] See Bibliothèque Nationale, Département des manuscrits, *Catalogue des manuscrits grecs, 3ème partie: le supplément grec*, t. III (n°s 901–1371) par Ch. Astruc et M.-L. Concasty (Paris 1960), 328 ff.

[14] Last edition by A. Nauck on pages following the *Lexicon Vindobonense* (Petersburg 1867; repr. Hildesheim 1965), 329 ff.

[15] A fuller version of the beginning of this work is preserved in Marc. 386, 13th cent., and has been edited by Ch. Th. Michaelis, *De Plutarchi codice man. Marciano* (Programm Charlottenschule, Berlin 1886), 25 f.

[16] See now the edition by J. Taillardat, *Suétone Περὶ βλασφημιῶν. Περὶ παιδιῶν* (Paris 1967), 48 ff.

[17] See preceding note (text of π. παιδιῶν on p. 64 ff.).

(according to the index): τὸν Κολοφῶνα ἐπέθηκεν; last proverb: τὸ παρὰ δρῦν σκότος. (3) f. 38ʳᵛ third collection (Ath. III). An index of 175 numbered proverbs is followed by the text of the first 17 proverbs, breaking off at the bottom of f. 38ᵛ in the middle of the explanation of no. 17 (last words ἀποκριναμένη δὲ πρὸς αὐτοὺς ἡ Ἀντιάνειρα ἡγεμὼν τῶν Ἀμαζόνων εἶπεν). The rest of the text is missing. First proverb: ἀμουσότερος Λειβηθρίων; last proverb (according to the index): ὁ ἐν Τεμέσῃ ἥρως. (4) ff. 39ʳ–40ᵛ fourth collection (Ath. V). Bigger line distance, different script but same hand. The beginning is apparently missing (first words ὥς φασιν Ἄτλας ὑποδεξάμενος...). The whole consists of three parts, the limits of which are not marked: (a) ff. 39ʳ–40ʳ collection of proverbs, arranged alphabetically by the first two letters. The main proverbs are mostly followed by parallel proverbs. The first letter of the main proverb is written with red ink. First main proverb preserved on f. 39ʳ (line 11): αἰγιαλῷ λαλεῖς; last proverb: ἀνὴρ δὲ φεύγων οὐ μένει λύρας κτύπον. (b) f. 40ʳᵛ 7 proverbs, not arranged alphabetically. First proverb: τάχ' εἰσόμεθα μάντεων ὑπέρτερον; last proverb: μήπω μέγ' εἴπῃς πρὶν τελευτήσαντ' ἴδῃς. (c) f. 40ᵛ mixed collection of λέξεις and proverbs, arranged alphabetically after the first two letters. First lemma: Ἀδράστεια; last lemma: βουκολήσεις. The explanation of the last lemma ends in the middle of the last line of f. 40ᵛ, the rest of which is filled out with crosses.

The MS was found by E. Miller shortly before 1865 on Mt. Athos in an unknown monastery "near Karyes." The text was edited (partly in the form of a collation) by Miller in 1868.[18]

2 (**L**). Laurent. 80, 13, 14th cent. Parchment; 189 ff.[19] Ff. 174ʳ–189ʳ 5 collections of proverbs interrupted by excerpts from lexicographical works. (1) ff. 174ʳ–76ᵛ collection of 131 proverbs with marginal numeration (L I = Ath. III). No title. First proverb: οἴκοι τὰ Μιλήσια; last proverb: ὁ ἐν Τεμέσῃ ἥρως. F. 176ᵛ subscriptio Πλουτάρχου παροιμίαι, αἷς Ἀλεξανδρεῖς ἐχρῶντο[20]; rest of page empty. This collection was first edited by J. Gronovius at the beginning of the 18th century and is also published in Leutsch–Schneidewin's Corpus, v. 1, 321 ff.[21] (2) f. 177ʳᵛ collection of 31 proverbs with marginal numeration (L II = Ath. IV).

---

[18] See above, note 1. For corrections of Miller's text see above, note 11.

[19] See A. M. Bandini, Catalogus codicum Graecorum bibliothecae Laurentianae, t. III (Florence 1770; repr. Leipzig 1961), 202 ff. Since Bandini, the numeration has been slightly changed. I refer to the new numeration.

[20] Crusius, Analecta (see above, note 4), 14 f., has shown that these words were originally the title of the following collection.

[21] Results of a new collation of L were published by F. Schöll, "Zu den sogenannten Proverbia Alexandrina des Pseudo-Plutarch (cod. Laur. pl. 80, 13)," in Festschrift zur Begrüssung der...36. Philologen-Versammlung (Freiburg i. Br. and Tübingen 1882), 37 ff.

No title. First proverb: οἶδα Σίμωνα καὶ Σίμων ἐμέ; last proverb: † τρωικὰ† παρεισφέροντες.[22] First edited by H. Jungblut, Rhein. Mus. 38 (1883), 402 ff. (reprinted in Supplementum [see above, note 4], part VI). Critical edition and commentary by Crusius 1887 and 1895 (see above, nos. 7 and 8). (3) ff. 178ʳ–81ʳ different λέξεις (ff. 178ʳ–79ᵛ excerpts from the works of Zenodorus, Suetonius π. βλασφημιῶν, Aristoph. Byz., ὀνόματα ἡλικιῶν, Suetonius π. παιδιῶν, and—last—Ps.-Didymus, λέξεις Πλάτωνος mentioned above p. 413 in the description of M, in a very abridged form; ff. 179ᵛ–81ʳ glosses from Plutarch, Xenophon and Theodoretus[23] which do not occur in other witnesses of the Athous group with the exception of Lond. Brit. Mus. Add. 5110 [see below, no. 7]). (4) ff. 182ʳ–89ʳ (last quaternion of the manuscript[24]) 3 other collections of proverbs, headed by the common title παροιμίαι. (a) ff. 182ʳ–84ʳ collection of 83 proverbs with marginal numeration[25] (L III = Ath. V). First proverb: Ἄβρωνος βιοῖ βίον; last proverb: βουκολήσεις.[26] L has preserved the beginning of Ath. V which is missing in M (see above, p. 414): αἰγιαλῷ λαλεῖς is in L III the 35th proverb, the preceding lines in M (f. 39ʳ) coinciding with L III 34. (b) ff. 184ᵛ–86ᵛ collection of 71 proverbs preceded by an index (L IV = Ath. I). First proverb: Καδμεία νίκη; last proverb: Ἑρμώνιος χάρις. (c) ff. 187ʳ–89ʳ collection of 71 proverbs preceded by an index (L V = Ath. II). First proverb: φρουρεῖν ἢ πλουτεῖν (= first proverb of M II, but 15th of Ath. II); last proverb: τὸ παρὰ δρῦν σκότος. Apparently, the beginning of Ath. II was missing in L's archetype as well as in that of M. (d) f. 189ʳ Index of L III with a reference to f. 182ʳ. A collation of the text of (a)–(c) was published by Jungblut, loc. cit. 405–20.

L's strange arrangement (Ath. III, IV, excerpta grammatica [ff. 174ʳ–181ʳ] / Ath. V, I, II [ff. 182ʳ–89ʳ]) is probably due to an exchange of the two last quaternions.[27] For the classification of the mss of the "Athous

---

[22] This is in reality not a proverb in its own right though counted as such by L and Vind. philol. 185 (see below, no. 3), but is part of the explanation of the preceding proverb (see Crusius, edition ad loc.).

[23] See A. Fresenius, De λέξεων Aristophanearum et Suetonianarum excerptis Byzantinis (Aquis Mattiacis 1875), 9 note 4.

[24] "Blatt 180 bis 187 [182–89 of the new numeration] sind...als besonderer Fascikel der Handschrift angeheftet" (Jungblut, loc. cit. 402). See also below.

[25] The last number of the marginal numeration is 79, some proverbs having been skipped in the numeration.

[26] As a matter of fact, after βουκολήσεις the rest of f. 184ʳ is occupied by 3 other proverbs beginning with ακ through βα which the excerptor had previously omitted and then added, seeing some space left at the end.

[27] See O. Crusius, "Die griechischen Parömiographen," in Verhandlungen der 37. Versammlung deutscher Philologen und Schulmänner in Dessau 1884 (Leipzig 1885), 218, and

recension" it should be remembered that whereas L shares with M the loss of M II, it has, unlike M, preserved the entire text of Ath. III, Ath. IV, and the beginning of Ath. V.[28]

3 (**V**). Vindobon. philos. et philol. 185, 2nd half of 15th cent. Paper; 78 ff.[29] Contains part of the Athous tradition interrupted by the text of Zenobius vulgatus. (1) ff. 2ʳ–5ᵛ collection of 131 proverbs. No title. First proverb: οἴκοι τὰ Μιλήσια; last proverb: ὁ ἐν Τεμέσῃ ἥρως. Subscriptio: Πλουτάρχου παροιμίαι αἷς Ἀλεξανδρεῖς ἐχρῶντο. Identical with L I (= Ath. III). Two hands. (2) f. 6ʳ and 5ᵛ (last lines) [30] collection of 31 proverbs. First proverb: οἶδα Σίμωνα καὶ Σίμων ἐμέ; last proverb: †τρωικὰ† παρεισφέροντες. Identical with L II (= Ath. IV). Smaller writing. (3) After the collection of Zenobius vulgatus (ff. 7ʳ–65ʳ) ff. 66ʳ–67ᵛ (same writing as f. 6ʳ) lexicographical excerpts, identical with that in L f. 178ʳ–79ᵛ, see above p. 415. The intrusion of the text of Zenobius vulgatus into the Athous tradition is a special feature of V and certainly of late date.[31] Attention to V was first drawn by Crusius in 1884 (see above, note 27). Crusius made use of V in his edition of the Plutarch collection.[32] Of the first collection of V, no collation has so far been published. The coincidence in the extent of the excerpts proves that V is either a twin or a copy of L.[33]

4 (**L²**). Laurent. 58, 24. 128 ff.[34]: ff. 7–78 parchment, end of 12th cent.; ff. 1–6 and 79–128 (with which we are concerned) paper, 13th cent. Miscellaneous content. (1) ff. 113ʳ–14ᵛ collection of 111 proverbs. Title παροιμίαι. First proverb: Καδμεία νίκη; last proverb: τὸ Δίωνος γρῦ. Excerpts from Ath. I–IV (limits of the collections not marked), mostly lemmata without explanation. (a) 37 proverbs, from Ath. I. Last proverb:

---

particularly L. Cohn, "Ein Londoner Exemplar der L-Klasse," *Philol.*, Suppl.-Bd. 6 (1891; see above, note 9), 223. For a different view, see Jungblut, *loc. cit.* 402.

[28] More precisely, L's archetype, not L; for L is but an excerpt of the Athous tradition.

[29] See H. Hunger, *Katalog der griechischen Handschriften der Österreichischen National-bibliothek*, 1 (Museion, Veröffentlichungen der Österreichischen Nationalbibliothek, N.F., 4, 1; Vienna 1961), 294.

[30] Hunger (see the preceding note) has failed to recognize that the collection begins on f. 6ʳ, the end being added on f. 5ᵛ.

[31] The collection of Zenobius vulgatus occupies exactly 6 quinternions (see Hunger, *loc. cit.*) and originally had its own numeration (cf. Crusius, "Die griechischen Parömio-graphen" [above, note 27], 219). Hence Crusius' assumption (*loc. cit.*) that this part was taken from another manuscript. However, Hunger (*loc. cit.*) asserts that f. 2 was written by the same hand as ff. 7–65.

[32] See above, note 7.

[33] Crusius, in the preface of his edition, p. xi f., argues in favour of the first alternative, referring to better readings of V.

[34] See L. Cohn, "Die Sprichwörter des cod. Laur. LVIII 24," in *Zu den Paroemiographen* (see above, note 9), 3; and Bandini, *Catalogus*... (see note 19), t. II, 1768, 464 ff.

μανία δ' οὐ πᾶσιν ὁμοία. (b) 17 proverbs, from Ath. II. First proverb: τὸν Κολοφῶνα ἐπέθηκεν (=M II 1 [index, lost in the text of M]); last proverb: τὸ παρὰ δρῦν σκότος. (c) 39 proverbs, from Ath. III. First proverb: ἀμουσότερος Λειβηθρίων; last proverb: Ἀμαλθείας κέρας (= M III 169 [index, lost in the text of M]). (d) 18 proverbs, from Ath. IV. First proverb: ὑπερβερετία (= L II 3). (2) ff. 114ᵛ–17ᵛ 3 other alphabetical collections of proverbs, not belonging in the Athous tradition.

The text of L² was published in 1887 by L. Cohn, *Die Sprichwörter des cod. Laur. LVIII 24*, (see note 34), 27 ff. In view of the small number and extent of its excerpts, L² is of little practical use. But the archetype from which the excerpts of L² were made was even more complete than that of L in that it contained not only Ath. IV and the entire text of Ath. III, but also the beginning of Ath. II, lost in L and M.

5 (**P**). Palatinus 129, end of 14th cent. Paper; 141 ff. Miscellaneous content.[35] ff. 118ᵛ and 120ʳᵛ 3 series of proverbs, of which the first (f. 118ᵛ) is headed by the title παροιμίαι τῶν ἔξω σοφῶν, the second (f. 120ʳᵛ) by the title παροιμίαι καὶ αὖται; the third, written on the margins of f. 120ʳ and f. 118ᵛ, bears no title. Published by M. Treu, "Griechische Sprichwörter," *Philol.* 47 (1889), 193–201, and analyzed by O. Crusius, *ibid.* 202 ff. The external division into 3 groups is superficial, since the beginning of series 2 continues the text of the second part of series 1; on the other hand, series 1 and 2 comprehend at least 3 different sections. I give here a survey of the sections as revealed by Crusius, referring for further details to the above-mentioned article by Treu and Crusius. (1) Alphabetical series of 17 proverbs. (2) f. 118ᵛ *infra* and f. 120ʳ *supra*: nonalphabetical series of 22 proverbs belonging to the "Athous recension." The first 20 proverbs are excerpts from Ath. I. First proverb: τὸ Δωδωνεῖον χαλκεῖον (= M I 2); last proverb: λύκος πτερωτὰ ζητεῖ (= M I 87). The two remaining proverbs belong to Ath. II. No. 21: Καύνειος ἔρως (=M II 8 [index, text in M lost]); no. 22: Ταντάλου τάλαντα (=M II 66). (3) Alphabetical series of 24 proverbs. (4) New series of 7 proverbs, partly alphabetical, perhaps a supplement to (3). (5) Alphabetical series of 22 proverbs, written on the margins.

Out of these 5 series, only the second belongs properly to the "Athous recension."[36] The number of excerpted proverbs is still considerably smaller than in L² (22 against 111), but the explanations of P are longer.

---

[35] See H. Stevenson, *Codices manuscripti Palatini Graeci Bibliothecae Vaticanae* (Bibliotheca Apostolica Vaticana codicibus manuscriptis recensita; Rome 1885), 61 f.

[36] Crusius, *loc. cit.* 203, has pointed out that there are also some "Athous proverbs" in (3). But since the redactor of this group has mixed them up with proverbs of the vulgar tradition, arranging the whole alphabetically, the third series is excluded from the present investigation. See also below, p. 423.

P shares with L² the privilege of depending on an archetype which disposed of a complete text of Ath. II.

6 (**E**, formerly A). Ambros. E. 64, end of 14th cent. Paper; 264 ff. Miscellaneous content.[37] ff. 142ᵛ–148ʳ proverbs followed by ⟨Aristophanes'⟩ ὀνόματα ἡλικιῶν. (I) ff. 142ᵛ–46ᵛ Collection of 139[38] proverbs. Title: παροιμίαι. First proverb: Καδμεία νίκη; last proverb: βοῦς ἐν αὐλίᾳ κάθη.[39] The collection consists of excerpts from 4 books of the "Athous recension": Ath. I, II, III, and V. The book divisions are not marked in E. (1) ff. 142ᵛ–43ᵛ (last line) 55 proverbs, from Ath. I. First proverb (see above) = M I 1; last proverb: Ἑρμώνιος χάρις (= M I 89). (2) ff. 144ʳ (first line)—145ʳ (lower third) 48 proverbs, from Ath. II. First proverb: Κρὴς τὴν θάλασσαν (=M II 17 and third in the text of M II); last proverb: τὸ Αἰσώπειον αἷμα (=M II 107). (3) ff. 145ʳ (lower third)—145ᵛ (lower third) 20 proverbs, from Ath. III. First proverb: ἀμουσότερος Λειβηθρίων (=M III 1); last proverb: ἡ φιλο-χρηματία Σπάρταν ἕλοι, ἄλλο δὲ οὐδέν (=M III 71 [index, text lost in M]). Of the first 17 proverbs of Ath. III preserved in M, E has excerpted the following ones: nos. 1–3, 10, 12, and 15. The explanation of no. 15 is immediately (same line) followed by no. 18 (first of the proverbs not preserved in M). Of this part, E has excerpted the following nos.: 18–21, 26, 27, 30, 36, 58, 60, 62, 64, 66, and 71. The excerpts from Ath. III stop at no. 71 although Ath. III comprehends altogether 175 proverbs. Note also the absence of excerpts from nos. 37–57. (4) ff. 145ᵛ (lower third)–46ᵛ (third last line[40]) 36 proverbs, from Ath. V. First proverb (beginning in the same line in which the last proverb of Ath. III ends; different pen, but same hand): αἰγιαλῷ λαλεῖς (identical with the first main proverb of Ath. V preserved in M); last proverb (see above) identical with the last but one proverb of M IV. (II) ff. 147ʳ–48ᵛ Aristophanes of Byz., ὀνόματα ἡλικιῶν, identical with part VI of the lexicographical excerpts of M (see above, p. 413). In 1891, O. Crusius published a collation of the proverb part of E based on a transcription by M. Treu.[41] E shares with M and L the loss of the beginning

---

[37] For a more detailed description, see O. Crusius, "Ein neuer Parallel-Codex zum Miller'schen Athous," in O. Crusius and L. Cohn, *Zur handschriftlichen Ueberlieferung...* (above, note 9), 205 f. and Aem. Martini and D. Bassi, *Catalogus codicum Graecorum Bibliothecae Ambrosianae*, t. 1 (Milan 1906), 319 ff.

[38] According to the numeration of Crusius (see the preceding note), 176; but Crusius counts also the parallel proverbs of part 4 as single items.

[39] The two last lines of f. 146ᵛ are filled out with the proverb χαλεπὸν χορίου κύνα γεύειν, written in a different manner and not belonging to the "Athous recension."

[40] See the preceding note.

[41] See note 37.

of Ath. II, and with M the loss of the second half of Ath. III, of the whole of Ath. IV, and of the beginning of Ath. V. On the other hand, it has preserved more proverbs of the first half of Ath. III than M. The problem raised by this almost complete coincidence of M and E will be dealt with later (see sections IV and VI).

7 (**Lo**). Lond. Brit. Mus. Addit. 5110, beginning of 15th cent. Paper; 212 ff.[42] Written by two hands. The part written by the second hand (f. 85^r–191^v) contains Xenophon's *Opuscula* and, at the end, 5 collections of proverbs followed by lexicographical excerpts (ff. 179^r–191^v). L. Cohn, who first drew attention to the proverb part of Lo,[43] noticed that the content of the part of Lo written by the second hand coincides with that of the original stock of L.[44] However, the arrangement of the proverbs and the lexicographical excerpts of Lo differs from that of L:

(1) ff. 179^r–181^r Lo I [45]   = L III = Ath. V
(2) ff. 181^v–184^r Lo II   = L IV = Ath. I
(3) ff. 184^r–185^v Lo III   = L V = Ath. II
(4) ff. 185^v–187^v Lo IV [46] = L I   = Ath. III
(5) ff. 187^v–188^v Lo V   = L II = Ath. IV
(6) ff. 188^v–191^r [47] lexicographical excerpts = L ff. 178^r–181^v.

Given the identity of content, there can be no doubt that Lo is either a twin or a copy of L. The first alternative seems at first sight more likely since the arrangement of Lo is, with the exception of the first collection, that of the archetype of the "Athous recension." But Cohn ascribed the greater deviation of L to an exchange of leaves (see above, p. 415) and, observing further that there are no better readings in Lo but, on the contrary, peculiar faults, stated that Lo depends on L. Cohn's view was tacitly rejected by K. Rupprecht who, in his stemma of the "Athous recension" (see below, p. 424), assigns Lo a place independent of L. No collation of the proverb part of Lo has so far been published.

8 (**A**, formerly Θ). Athen. 1083, 16th cent. Paper; 203 ff.[48] From the

---

[42] See L. Cohn, "Ein Londoner Exemplar der L-Klasse," in *Zur handschriftlichen Ueberlieferung* etc. (above, note 9), 221–23 and M. Richard, *Inventaire des manuscrits grecs du British Museum* (Publications de l'Institut de Recherche et d'Histoire des Textes, 3; Paris 1952), 3.

[43] See the preceding note.

[44] The first leaves of L were added later; see Cohn, *loc. cit.*

[45] *Inscriptio* ἀριμίαι, i.e. παροιμίαι.

[46] New *inscriptio* ἔτεραι παροιμίαι.

[47] F. 191^{rv} is occupied by ἔτεραι λέξεις not to be found in L.

[48] See J. and A. Sakkelion, Κατάλογος τῶν χειρογάφων τῆς Ἐθνικῆς Βιβλιοθήκης τῆς Ἑλλάδος (Athens 1892), 194; further C. Fredrich (with supplements by G. Wentzel), "Anecdota aus einer athenischen Handschrift," *Nachr. d. K. Ges. d. Wissensch. zu Göttingen*, Philol.-hist. Kl., 1896, 309 and 336 f.; finally, S. Kugéas, "Der cod. Atheniensis 1083

Thessalian monastery of Dusiku. The manuscript became famous when, in 1896, C. Fredrich published from it part of the *Lexicon* of Photius.[49] It contains also, among other texts, on ff. 132ʳ–76ᵛ four collections of proverbs and lexicographical excerpts belonging to the "Athous recension." Though Crusius was sent a collation of the proverbs by Fredrich as early as 1896, it was S. Kugéas who, in 1910, first published the surplus of A against M and a collation of the rest.[50] In order to abridge the following description, it ought to be said beforehand that A is closely related to M. F. 132ʳ (first line) *inscriptio*: βίου[51] ἐπιτομὴ τῶν Ταρραίου καὶ Διδύμου παροιμιῶν. (1) ff. 132ʳ–142ᵛ index and text of Ath. I (completely identical with M I). (2) ff. 142ᵛ–153ʳ index and text of Ath. II. The index occupies ff. 142ᵛ–143ᵛ (second line); rest of this page and the two following pages empty. The text starts f. 146ʳ (first line). First proverb of the text: ῑε φρουρεῖν ἢ πλουτεῖν (=M II 15, also the first proverb preserved in the text part of M II). The text of A ends regularly with no. 108 as in M. (3) ff. 153ʳ–158ʳ index and part of the text of Ath. III. After the index (which, like that of M, comprehends 175 nos.) first proverb: ἀμουσότερος Λειβηθρίων (=M III 1). Last proverb: ἁ φιλοχρηματία Σπάρταν ἕλοι, ἄλλο δὲ οὐδέν (=M III 71 [index, lost in the text of M] and also the last proverb of Ath. III preserved in E). While on the whole A, like M, is comprehensive, i.e. presents the text of all proverbs listed in the index,[52] there is one exception: nos. 38–57 are missing from the text, the numeration running on as if nothing was left out.[53] This omission is presumably due to a loss in the model of A.[54] A has preserved 34 more proverbs from Ath. III than M, of which 14 are also to be found in E.[55] (4) ff. 159ʳ–162ᵛ proverbs from Ath. V. The third collection ends on f. 158ʳ last line. F. 158ᵛ is empty. The fourth collection starts on f. 159ʳ first line. No title. First proverb: αἰγιαλῷ λαλεῖς; last proverb: βουκολήσεις. Apart from the rest of the explanation of the proverb preceding αἰγιαλῷ λαλεῖς preserved in M at the top of f. 39ʳ (see above, p. 414), A IV is completely identical with

---

und die Textgeschichte der Paroemiographen," in O. Crusius, "Paroemiographica," *Sitz.-Ber. d. Bayer. Akad. d. Wissensch.*, Philos.-philol. u. hist. Kl., 1910, 4 (reprinted in the *Supplementum* [see above, note 4]), 5 ff., 25 and 34.

[49] See the preceding note.

[50] See note 48.

[51] According to Kugéas, *loc. cit.* 6 note 2, a later hand has added Ζηνο; but I cannot detect any trace of this in my photo. Anyway, the B of Βίου was written with red ink.

[52] This holds good of all collections of A and also of the lexicographical excerpts.

[53] No. 58 (index) bears in the text number 38, and so on.

[54] Neither are there excerpts of nos. 38–57 in E; see above, p. 418.

[55] See above, p. 418.

M IV. (5) ff. 162ᵛ–176ᵛ 7 lexicographical excerpts, completely identical with those of M ff. 41ʳ–48ᵛ.

The "Athous texts" of A coincide in extent, arrangement and presentation completely with that of M with the exception of the surplus in the third and the lack of some lines in the fourth collection. Relying on this surplus and some better readings of A, Kugéas, followed by Rupprecht,[56] stated that A is independent of M. This statement will be subjected to a revision (see sections IV and V).

These are the direct witnesses of the "Athous recension" so far known.[57] For the sake of completeness, two indirect witnesses should be added to the list:

(a) Συναγωγὴ τῶν Ταρραίου καὶ Διδύμου καὶ τῶν παρὰ Σούδᾳ καὶ ἄλλοις διαφόροις παροιμιῶν συντεθεισῶν κατὰ στοιχεῖον. First published in the Aldina of Aesop (1505), from an unknown manuscript.[58] Two other manuscripts are: Scorial. Σ — I — 20 (15th cent.) a collation of which was published by Ch. Graux, Revue de Philologie n.s. 2 (1878), 219 ff.,[59] and Hierosol. bibl. Patr. 273, ff. 22ʳ–91ᵛ (18th cent.).[60] The collection contains some 1200 proverbs which, as the title indicates, were compiled from various sources, one of them being the epitome of Zenobius; the compiler disposed of a copy similar to L which included all 5 collections of the "Athous recension."[61]

(b) The *Adagia* of Erasmus. Erasmus, too, used a collection of proverbs similar to L, one which was, it seems, ascribed as a whole to Plutarch.[62] The manuscript is lost.

---

[56] See below, p. 424.

[57] Since 1910, no other manuscript of the "Athous group" has been found. Not much is to be hoped from a systematic consultation of the printed catalogues of Greek manuscripts since such excerpts are often overlooked (see the remark by Crusius, *Philol.* 47 [1889], 205). We rely on the vigilance of those who look up manuscripts for other purposes.

[58] See Crusius, *Analecta* (above, note 4), 32 ff.

[59] Graux did not know that the text of the Scorialensis was already published in the Aldina of Aesop. It was Crusius who discovered the identity (first in *Rhein. Mus.* 38 [1883], 307).

[60] See A. Papadopulos-Kerameus, Ἱεροσολυμιτικὴ βιβλιοθήκη, I (Petersburg, 1891), 329. The manuscript has not hitherto been referred to in this connection.

Two more can now (15 Sept. 1973) be added: (iii) cod. Leovardiensis 36, 16th cent., pp. 359–445; (iv) Monac. 579ᵃ, 16th cent., ff. 28ᵛ–39ʳ (excerpts, see *Herm.* 100 [1972], 540).

[61] See H. Jungblut, *Rhein. Mus.* 38 (1883; above, p. 415), 396; and Crusius, *loc. cit.* (note 58).

[62] See Crusius, *Analecta* (above, note 4), 5 ff.; *Verhandlungen...Dessau* (above, note 27), 218; and the preface to his edition of the "Plutarch" proverbs (above, note 7), vii.

CORPUS OF PROVERBS OF LATE ANTIQUITY   **LEXICOGRAPHICAL EXCERPTS**

	I	II	III	IV	V	I Casilo	II Didym.	III Zenod.	IV Suet. π. βλ.	V Ar. B. π. τ. ὑποπτ.	VI Ar. B. ὀν. ἡλ.	VII Suet. π. παιδ.
M	×	× (1–14 missing)	× (18–175 missing)	—	× (beginning missing)	×	×	×	×	×	×	×
L	×	× (1–14 missing)	×	×	×	—	×	×	×	—	×	×
V	—	—	×	×	—	—	×	×	×	—	×	×
L²	×	× (1, 3, 20, etc.)	×	×	—	—	—	—	—	—	—	—
P	×	× (8, 66)	—	—	—	—	—	—	—	—	—	—
E	×	× (1–14 missing)	× (excerpts from 1–35, 58–71)	—	× (beginning missing)	—	—	—	—	—	×	—
Lo	×	× (1–14 missing)	×	×	×	—	×	×	×	—	×	×
A	×	× (1–14 missing)	× (1–36, 58–71, rest missing)	—	× (beginning missing)	×	×	×	×	×	×	×

The indirect tradition may be helpful for the constitution of the text. But since the proverbs of the "Athous recension" are there mixed up with proverbs from other sources and the original arrangement is destroyed, this group is excluded from the following considerations.

III

A table will recapitulate the extent to which the "Athous texts" (including the lexicographical excerpts) are preserved in each of the eight direct witnesses of the "Athous recension." In order not to complicate the survey no account has been taken of whether a manuscript is an excerpt or has preserved the whole text. For the classification of the manuscripts this does not matter (see immediately below).

We may now proceed to a classification of the 8 MSS. First, no extant manuscript has preserved the complete text of the "Athous recension." Therefore a lost archetype is to be postulated. Next, considering the extant manuscripts which are all, in one way or another, incomplete, we have to distinguish between deliberate selection and mechanical mutilation. Only M and A have the character of a true copy; all the others are excerpts (with a varying degree of selection). But this is no reliable criterion. For it may happen that a copy was made of a mutilated model and, on the other hand, an excerpt was made from a complete model. What really matters, therefore, are the gaps. The two decisive passages are the beginning of Ath. II and the big gap between Ath. III and V. As for the former, there are only two manuscripts which have preserved proverbs from Ath. II 1–14: L² and P.[63] Therefore the two manuscripts in which the original number of proverbs was most reduced are closer to the archetype than all the others. The other point of divergence is the gap between Ath. III and V. Since, of the remaining 6 manuscripts, L, V, and Lo show no sign of this gap, they form the next group. Finally E and A, having preserved more proverbs from the beginning of Ath. III than M, seem to depend on a less mutilated model than M. The stemma which results from this classification is the following (I reproduce the one

---

[63] Ath. II is completely absent from V. But V is in the other parts so close to L (see above, p. 416) that both manuscripts must belong together.

published by K. Rupprecht in the *RE*, XVIII 4 [1949], 1747–48[64]:

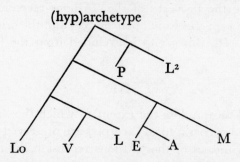

(hyp)archetype

The general classification into three groups (P L², Lo V L, and E A M) is, I think, fairly well established. What deserves further discussion is the relationship of the single witnesses within these groups. For instance, the position given to Lo by Rupprecht seems to be wrong since, as has been pointed out before,[65] this manuscript is very likely a copy of L.[66] But I want to leave the two first groups aside and concentrate the further discussion on the relationship between E, A, and M. In Rupprecht's stemma—which reflects the current opinion—the most famous manuscript of the "Athous recension," M, occupies the last place. It is, I think, time to rehabilitate the Athous a little.

IV

There were mainly two arguments that induced Kugéas to state that A is independent of M:[67] the surplus proverbs in the third collection and some seemingly better readings. As for the latter, it should be remembered that Kugéas relied for M on Miller's not always trustworthy collation.[68] We shall see later that a careful reexamination of M will considerably reduce the number of

[64] I have adopted my own sigla for Ambros. (E [A in Rupprecht]) and Athen. (A [Θ in Rupprecht]) and left out the indirect witnesses Aldina and Scorialensis. A different stemma was established by Kugéas in his article mentioned above (note 48), p. 34. It was rightly objected to by Rupprecht, *loc. cit.* 1748, 31.

[65] See above, p. 419.

[66] Rupprecht does not give any reasons for his stemma. He promised to do so later (*loc. cit.* 1748, 30) but, as far as I know, he has not fulfilled his promise. As for Lo, I suppose Rupprecht was impressed by the fact that Lo is free from the disturbance of the arrangement found in L (for this, see above, p. 415).

[67] See above, p. 421.

[68] See above, p. 412.

discrepancies. But the other argument—which is also valid for E—seems, at first sight, cogent. Since E and A obviously depend on a hyparchetype which contained the proverbs 1–37 and 58–71 of Ath. III, whereas M III breaks off in the middle of no. 17, M cannot be the model of E and A—at least not in its present condition. However, there is another piece of evidence which runs directly counter to that conclusion. Already Crusius, when dealing with the relationship between E and M, had pointed to the fact that E (we may now also add A) begins Ath. V with the first rubricated proverb preserved in M after the big gap[69] and that this gap was caused by a loss of leaves (probably a whole quaternion) proper to M. It would be a strange coincidence if both M and the common model of E and A had independently suffered a mechanical loss ending exactly at the same spot. Crusius grasped the point when he wrote:[70] "Das [i.e., the fact that E starts Ath. V with the first complete proverb preserved in M] würde sich denn doch am ersten durch die Annahme erklären, dass das Archetypon des Ambr. hier ähnlich verstümmelt war, wie der Athous; ja, es liesse sich vermuthen—und die oben S. 216 f. angeführten Kleinigkeiten [some better readings of E] fielen nicht dagegen in die Wage—, dass der Athous selbst[71] in etwas vollständigerer Form, insbesondere ohne die Blattverluste im 3. Buche,[71] oder ein echter Bruder von ihm dies Archetypon gewesen ist." But he did not dare to draw the necessary conclusion, and Kugéas, confronted with the same problem in regard to A, decided in favour of the independence of A (and E), alleging, besides better readings in A, also a discrepancy between A and M in the lexicographical excerpts, which, in reality, does not exist.[72]

I want to take up the problem where it was left by Crusius. My aim is to prove that E and A are copies of M, supposing that at

[69] See O. Crusius, "Ein neuer Parallel-Codex zum Miller'schen Athous" (above, note 37), 218.

[70] Loc. cit. (see the preceding note).

[71] The interspacing is Crusius'.

[72] The excerpts of Suetonius' π. παιδιῶν begin in A f. 175ᵛ in the middle of the page (new line, the preceding excerpts finishing at the end of the line before). Kugéas knew from Fresenius, op. cit. (see above, note 23), p. 50, that the transition from Aristophanes' ὀνόματα ἡλικιῶν to the treatise of Suetonius is not marked in L either. On the other hand, he believed, following Miller's rather vague indications, that in M the mutilation at the beginning of the Suetonius excerpts, and with it the transition from one text to the other,

the moment the copies were made M still contained one leaf more of Ath. III than it does now.[73] I have but one argument but this I consider to be decisive: the above-mentioned coincidence of the beginning of Ath. V in M, E, and A[74] after the big gap due to mechanical damage of M. In my view, this outweighs everything that has been brought forward in favour of an independence of E and A in regard to M. In order to defend my case, I shall now discuss some—allegedly or really—better readings of E and A. If my thesis is right, the latter must be taken as conjectures—unless there was contamination from another source. I begin with A.

V

First, it ought to be emphasized that A is, among the 7 representatives of the "Athous recension" besides M, the only one to contain, with the exception of some lines of Ath. V (for which see note 74), all "Athous texts" of M including the indexes of Ath. I–III. In other words: A has all the appearance of a copy of M or of a true twin. Furthermore, both manuscripts originate from Northern Greece; M was written in the fourteenth century, A in the sixteenth

---

is externally visible. The fact is that in M Aristophanes' ὀνόματα ἡλικιῶν end with the last line of f. 47ᵛ and Suetonius' π. παιδιῶν begins on the first line of f. 48ʳ (no title). Miller, op. cit. (see above, note 1), p. 395, thought of a loss of some leaves, but Fresenius, op. cit. 49 f., objected to this hypothesis. However this may be, A's presentation is quite compatible with the idea that it is a copy of M. As for the first letter of the first word of the Suetonius text, omitted in A (by fault of the rubricator, as Kugéas believed), it is missing in M as well (both manuscripts have υβους instead of κύβους).

[73] Assuming that the proverbs nos. 38–57 were already missing in the archetype of E and A, the proverbs exceeding those of M amount to 34. This is about the number to fill out two pages: the average of proverbs per page in M I is 15, in M II, 22. A parallel to the case supposed here is offered by the transmission of the text of Pseudo-Longinus: there the codex unicus (Par. 2036) has suffered the loss of a considerable number of leaves, but the text of some of them is preserved in the copies (see, e.g. Du sublime, texte établi et traduit par H. Lebègue [Paris 1952], Introd. xiii ff.). It cannot be ruled out altogether that E and A changed the model in the third collection after reaching the gap in M. But even that supposed model could not have gone further than Ath. III 71—a rather unlikely assumption.

[74] Kugéas (loc. cit. [above, note 48], 27), stressing the fact that A has omitted the first lines of Ath. V preserved in M, advanced the opinion that these were already missing in A's model. But what is more natural for a copyist than to start, after a gap in the model, with the first self-supporting sentence, that is in our case, with the first rubricated proverb?

century. But there is more evidence to support my view. I have found some readings in A which I seriously suspect to be mis-readings of letters or signs of M. For illustration I would need photographical reproductions. Forced to description, I pick out only a few instances.

1. Ath. III 172 (only lemma preserved in the indexes of M and A): instead of M's ἀφύας πῦρ [75] A offers a senseless ἀφύας πύρων. The (rather long) circumflex upon πῦρ in M seems to have been taken by the scribe of A as an abbreviation of the ending ων.

2. Ath. III 99 Τιθωνοῦ γῆρας M (ind.): Τίθωνου γῆρας A (ind.). A's strange accent is perhaps a misinterpretation of the stroke on the ι of Τιθωνοῦ in M which in reality belongs to the numeral ϙθ'.

3. Ath. I 47 μητρυιᾶς M: μητρηᾶς A. In M the υι is written by a ligature which looks very similar to η.

4. Ath. I 67 γνψώσαντες M: γνψάσαντες A. In M the ώ is written by a ligature which looks very similar to the ligature ά.

5. Ath. I 16 ἐκ φαυλοτέρας διαίτης M: ἐκ φαυλοτέροις διαίτης A. The bend-shaped abbreviation for ας in M was probably taken by the scribe of A as the (similar-looking) abbreviation for οις.

6. Ath. V βάμμα Κυζικηνόν p. 383 Miller: δειλίαν M: γειλίαν A. The δ in M is unusually small and, in consequence, its loop is not clearly marked, so it could easily be misread as γ.

7. Ath. V ἄλλο γένος κώπης p. 379 Miller: τὰς Γηρυονείους βοῦς M: τὰς νηρυονείους βοῦς A. M's γ which is in ligature with η looks like ν.

Taken together these instances, (and there are more), are unlikely to be due to mere chance. The natural conclusion would be that A is a direct copy of M. This raises a certain difficulty to be discussed later (see below, section VII).

I come now to the better readings of A. In the list drawn up by Kugéas, loc. cit.[76] 26, we must first cancel a number of instances in which, contrary to what Kugéas asserts,[77] there is in fact no discrepancy between A and M; e.g., I 62 (ξβ') ἐσήμανε γὰρ αὐτῷ ὅτι

[75] Whether this or rather ἀφύα πῦρ (Schneidewin ad Zen. vulg. 2, 32) or perhaps ἀφύα ἐς πῦρ (Diog. 2, 41) is the right reading, is another question. What matters is that πύρων is out of the question and that ἀφύας πῦρ is to be regarded as the transmitted wording of the "Athous recension."

[76] See above, note 48.

[77] For the reason of Kugéas being mistaken, see above p. 412.

M⁷⁸ A; I 70 (οʹ) εἰς κρίσιν M⁷⁹ A; II 105 (ρεʹ) ἐπὶ τῶν... διαιρουμένων πραγμάτων M⁸⁰ A.⁸¹

A second category to be dropped includes instances in which A does diverge from M, but—*pace* Kugéas—to the wrong reading. Thus in I 63... ὅθεν παροιμιασθῆναι τὴν ἀγαθὴν ἡμῶν ἡμέραν λεγόντων ἐκ τῆς φαρέτρας ὑπάρχειν (M), I see no sense in A's ὑπάρχον (all we need is a comma after παροιμιασθῆναι).⁸² There are in Kugéas' list two instances in which A, unlike M, has a particle when, at the end of the explanation, the author who used the proverb is mentioned: I 47 (μζʹ)... μέμνηται αὐτῆς ἐν Ἐφεσίῳ (frg. 176 K.-Th.) Μένανδρος M: μέμνηται οὖν ἐν Ἐφ. M. A and I 66 (ξϛʹ)... μέμνηται ταύτης καὶ Πίνδαρος (*Nem.* 7, 105) M: μέμνηται δὲ ταύτης κ. Π. A. In both cases, the absence of the particle is unobjectionable (in the first instance, οὖν which has supplanted the indispensable αὐτῆς is clearly wrong; in I 66, δέ is not impossible,⁸³ but there are far more instances with asyndeton⁸⁴). In II 22 (κβʹ)... ὅθεν ἐπὶ τῶν ἐργώδεις τὰς διατριβὰς ποιουμένων εἰρῆσθαι τὴν παροιμίαν (M), A's insertion of καί after ὅθεν is hardly an improvement.⁸⁵ Another insertion, that of ὦ between Ἀστυδάμας and γύναι (II 83 [πγʹ]), is an obvious interpolation. When in I 30 (λʹ) A offers the wrong reading Κάροι whereas M has Καρ[..] with the two last letters *in rasura* it is not M's quality but A's knowledge of Greek which is at stake. Of all the instances listed by Kugéas, there is only one which raises some doubt:⁸⁶ I 21 (καʹ) M reads ὅταν οὖν θαυμαστόν

⁷⁸ Miller, by mistake, has omitted αὐτῷ (not corrected by Cohn [see above, note 11]).

⁷⁹ Zenob. vulg. 5, 39 has ἐπὶ κρίσιν. Miller p. 357 does not mention that M here diverges from Zenob. vulg., nor was Miller's oversight corrected by Cohn.

⁸⁰ Πράγματα Zenob. vulg. 2, 83. M's divergence from Zenob. vulg. was mentioned neither by Miller nor by Cohn.

⁸¹ Ἔχονται (M I 79 [οθʹ], see Miller p. 358) and μοιχομένης (M II 16 [ιϛʹ], see Miller p. 360) are probably not misreadings by Miller, but simple misprints.

⁸² See Zenob. vulg. 6, 13 (where, by the way, the reading εἶναι instead of ὑπάρχειν confirms the infinitive).

⁸³ Cf. Zenob. vulg. 6, 34.

⁸⁴ See, e.g., Zenob. vulg. 6, 7; 6, 19; 6, 24; 6, 25; 6, 27; 5, 9; 5, 93; etc.

⁸⁵ An exact parallel without καί is Zen. vulg. 3, 86.

⁸⁶ I leave aside II 65 (ξεʹ) where, I think, M has κερδῶν (not κερδῶ) like A; but I abstain from a definitive judgment until inspection of the manuscript. In I 89 (πθʹ) M offers the right reading ἐκστήσονται τῆς χώρας αὐτοῖς (not αὐτοῦ [Miller, not corrected by Cohn]). A's αὐτούς is clearly wrong.

Addendum 1973: after inspection of M, I can confirm that it has (II 65) κερδῶν.

τι πραχθῇ οὐχ ὑπὸ μόνου τινός, εἰώθαμεν ἐπιλέγειν αὐτῷ 'οὐκ ἄνευ γε Θησέως', whereas A offers λέγειν instead of ἐπιλέγειν. Not that ἐπιλέγειν is to be rejected,[87] but λέγειν is also offered by Zenob. vulg. (5, 33). Were there more instances of coincidence in wrong readings between A and Zenob. vulg., a closer relationship would be worth considering; as it is a single case, I am inclined to take it as mere chance.

Finally, there are some better readings in A (not received by Kugéas in his census of the more remarkable instances) of which I give here a list:[88]

I 29 (κθ') ἐδολοφονήθη A: ἐδολοφωνήθη M
I 70 (ο') ἀκολουθοῦντος A: ἀκολοθοῦντος M
? II 34 (λδ') Κροτωνιατῶν A: Κρωτωνιατῶν M[89]
II 76 (ος') θριᾶσθαι A: θηριᾶσθαι M
III 50 (ν') ind. Φρυνίχου A: Φρουνίχου M
V Ἄμβρις μαίνεται (p. 380 Miller). βροτὸν A: βρωτὸν M
V ib. ἀποσπασθέντα A: ἀποσπαθέντα M
? V τάχ' εἰσόμεθα κτλ. (p. 380 M.). μάντις A: μάντης M[90]
V οὐ πάνυ κτλ. (p. 381 M.). ὑπισχνούμενος A: ὑπισχούμενος M
V βατταρίζειν (p. 383 M.). ἰσχνοφώνου A: ἰσχοφώνου M

Everybody, I think, will agree that, with the exception of II 76, these instances may be considered as very easy, not to say automatic corrections any scribe could make. As for II 76, the correct reading θριᾶσθαι, which is indeed remarkable considering the rarity of the word, was in all probability suggested by the context which reads Φιλόχωρός (Frg. gr. Hist. 328 F 195 J.) φησιν ὅτι νύμφαι κατεῖχον τὸν Παρνασσὸν τροφοὶ Ἀπόλλωνος, ἀφ' ὧν αἵ τε μαντικαὶ ψῆφοι θρίαι καλοῦνται καὶ τὸ μαντεύεσθαι θηριᾶσθαι.

On the other hand, it must be emphasized that the wrong, and often stupidly wrong, readings of A amount to several hundreds. It was their very stupidity which made it impossible for Kugéas to

---

[87] For ἐπιλέγειν (ἐπιφωνεῖν is more usual) see I 66 (ξς').

[88] I neglect trifles like accents and breathings as well as two instances where the first letter of ἐπί, omitted by the rubricator of M, was supplied by A.

[89] The shape of the first ω on my photo is such that a later correction to ο cannot be ruled out. The correct writing of the word occurs twice in the next proverb but one (II 36 [λς']).
Addendum 1973: the original ο in M is corrected to ω: so cancel this instance altogether.

[90] To judge from my photo, the η may have been corrected later to ι; but I am not sure.
Addendum 1973: there is no correction in M.

believe that a scribe capable of writing down the sheerest nonsense
could at the same time, occasionally, improve his model. But, leaving
psychology apart, our experience with copies teaches us that such
things do happen. To come to a conclusion, the arguments in favour
of the dependence of A on M are much stronger than those few
better readings which are easily explained as simple corrections.

VI

The case of E is more complicated because there the number of
divergences is greater and the quality of better readings is higher.
On the other hand, once my thesis is accepted—as I think it must
be—that A is a copy of M, it is *a priori* likely that E too, A's twin
in the third collection, depends on M.

Crusius, *Ein neuer Parallel-Codex*[91] 216 f., adduced 8 instances[92] in
which E seems to offer better readings than M. Three of them have
to be cancelled,[93] but there are many more to be added instead. The
following list, which includes also the ὀνόματα ἡλικιῶν, comprehends
all readings of E which may have some claim to be better than those
of M. In order to widen the view for a better judgment, I add also
the readings of A, those of the other manuscripts of the "Athous
recension" (as far as they are extant), and, where it is of interest,
those of Zenobius vulgatus.

1. I 3 *(γ')* lemma τὰ πάντα ὀκτώ E: πάντα ὀκτώ MA Zenob. vulg. 5, 78.
At the end of the explanation (missing in E) the proverb is repeated with
the article (MA; without the article Zenob. vulg.).

2. I 4 *(δ')* Ἄρραβας E: Ἀρραβίους MA (Ἀραβίους Zenob. vulg. 2, 39). The
lemma (which immediately precedes) is Ἀρράβιος αὐλητής.

3. I 5 *(ε')* lemma οὐδὲ Ἡρακλῆς ELL²[94] Zenob. vulg. 5, 49[95]: οὐδὲ ὁ
Ἡρακλῆς MAP.

4. I 11 *(ια')* lemma Ὕλαν κραυγάζεις EA(tab., text.)M(tab.)L Zenob.
vulg. 6, 21[96]: τὸν Ὕλαν (τὸν extra lineam, rubrum) κραυγάζεις M(text.)
L².

---

[91] See above, note 37.

[92] I am not here concerned with E's readings in the third collection, where M is
missing (discussed by Crusius on p. 217 f.).

[93] In nos. 41 and 101 (Crusius' numeration of E), M offers the same reading as Ė
(41 αὐτῷ, 101 πραγμάτων). In no. 78, συχνῶς (E) is a wrong reading for συνεχῶς (MA).

[94] L² reads οὐδ' Ἡρακλῆς.

[95] The lemma reads in Zenobius vulgatus οὐδὲ Ἡρακλῆς πρὸς δύο, whereas the "Athous
recension" offers πρὸς δύο οὐδὲ (ὁ) Ἡρακλῆς.

[96] Zenob. vulg. reads κραυγάζειν.

5. I 12 *(ιβ')* text. οὐδὲν ἱερὸν εἶ E: εἶ om. MA Zenob. vulg. 5, 47. Lemma οὐδὲν ἱερὸν εἶ MAE (εἶ om. L²).

6. I 20 *(κ')* lemma καθευδ( )⁹⁷ E (καθεύδει PL): καθεύδεις MAL² Diog. 4, 40.

7. ib. Ὕπνος EL: ὁ Ὕπνος MAP Diog. 4, 40.

8. I 57 *(νζ')* παλλάδιον E: παλλάδων MA. Shortly afterwards in the same explanation, the correct form παλλαδίου occurs in M.

9. I 62 *(ξβ')* lemma Δήλια καὶ Πύθια E: Πύθια καὶ Δήλια MAL Zenob. vulg. 6, 15. In the explanation, the lemma recurs in E's arrangement καὶ Δήλια καὶ Πύθια (MAE).

10. I 67 *(ξζ')* πέτεσθαι EL Zenob. vulg. 3, 87: πετᾶσθαι MA.

11. I 68 *(ξη')* Σαρδόνι EL(fort. corr. ex. -η L): Σαρδόνη (i.e. -η) MA.

12. I 69 *(ξθ')* ἐκβαλόμενος E: ἐκλαβόμενος MA. The right reading is ἐκβαλλόμενος (Zenob. vulg. 6, 28).

13. I 80 *(π')* λαγωοὶ E: λαγοὶ MA. Two lines before, λαγωούς occurs (MAE).

14. II 27 *(κζ')* οὔθ' ὕεται EL: οὐ θύεται MA.

15. II 33 *(λγ')* συνέπεισεν (recte) E Zenob. vulg. 3, 91: συνέπεσεν MAL.

16. II 36 *(λϛ')* Ἀφάνας EL: Ἀφάννας MA Zenob. vulg. 3, 92.

17. II 40 *(μ')* πρασιῶν E^corr. (πρασεῶν E^a.corr.): πράσεων MA.

18. II 62 *(ξβ')* οἱ Κίλικες E: Κίλικες MA.

19. II 70 *(ο')* τέτακται E: τέταται M^corr. (τέτταται M^a.corr. A).

20. II 72 *(οβ')* ρνζ ἔτη E: ρν ἔτη ζ MA.

21. II 90 *(Ϟ')* κεράμεια E Zenob. vulg. 1, 49: κεράμια MA.

22. III 2 *(β')* τρυφὴν E^corr.: τροφὴν MAE^a.corr. Τρυφὴν occurs later on in the same explanation.

23. V *(ἄμ')* ἔπος (p. 379 Miller). ἰχθύδιον E^corr. (ut coniecerat Nauck⁹⁸): λυκίδιον MAE^a.corr.

24. V ib. (p. 380 M.) ἦ (i.e. ἦ) ἐπεγέγραπτο E: ἡ ἐπεγέγραπτο MA.

25. V ἀνὴρ δὲ φεύγων (p. 380 M.). ἡδέος E^corr.: ἡδέως MAE^a.corr.

26. V τάχ' εἰσόμεθα (p. 380 M.). μάντις EA⁹⁹: μάντης M (a. corr. ?)⁹⁹

27. V οὐ πάνυ κτλ. (p. 381 M.). ὑπισχνούμενος EA¹⁰⁰: ὑπισχούμενος M.¹⁰⁰

28. ὀνόματα ἡλικιῶν p. 428 Miller. ἀντίπαιδα E: ἀντίπεδα MA. Immediately before, βούπεδα (instead of -παιδα) MAE, but the section is headed by παῖς.

29. ὀν. ἡλ. p. 432 M. σύννυμφοι E: σύνυμφοι MA.

---

⁹⁷ One of the many abbreviations of E, rather to be resolved as καθεύδει than καθεύδεις.

⁹⁸ *Bulletin de l'Académie Impériale des Sciences de Sᵗ-Petersbourg*, 13 [1869], 379.

⁹⁹ See above, p. 430.

¹⁰⁰ See above, p. 430.

30. ὀν. ἠλ. p. 432 M. συγγενὴς EA: συγενὴς M.

31. ὀν. ἠλ. p. 432 M. τιθηνὸς E: τηθινὸς MA. Shortly afterwards, the wrong reading τηθινοί is exhibited by MAE.

This rather impressive list comprehends very different classes of "better readings." Many of them seem to be simple corrections not above the average intelligence of a copyist. In three cases, such corrections were made after the text was copied (nos. 17, 22, and 25).[101] Of these, no. 22 is characteristic of E's procedure: E had first copied the wrong reading τροφήν; but then, coming across, within the same explanation, the right reading τρυφήν, he corrected the first entry. This, I think, also holds good of no. 8 (παλλάδιον), no. 13, and some other instances to be discussed in a moment. In other instances, nothing but a moderate knowledge of Greek was needed (nos. 10, 14, 19, 20, 21, 26, 27, 29, 30). I am inclined to rank with this category also some corrections of wrong spellings due to iotacism (nos. 11 [Σαρδόνι], 28 [ἀντίπαιδα], and 31 [τιθηνός], see also no. 21); of course, E was not always observant (in no. 28, he did not correct the preceding βούπεδα, in no. 31 he copied shortly afterwards the wrong τηθινοί). The insertion of οἱ before Κίλικες in no. 18 looks like a normalization (the article is equally absent in L's excerpt[102]). This may also be said of the form Ἄρ[ρ]αβας (instead of Ἀραβίους) in no. 2, for οἱ Ἀράβιοι (to be found in Herodotus, Xenophon, etc.) is the older denomination.[103] However, I cannot suppress the suspicion that Ἀραβίους in MA (and also in Zenob. vulg. 2, 39) was influenced by the lemma Ἀράβιος αὐλητής. In this case, E has either preserved a better tradition or innovated. The fact that Zenobius vulgatus, too, has Ἀραβίους is rather an argument against the first alternative.

I have no doubt that the scribe of E was quite an intelligent man. Thus in no. 15, he has restored from the context the right reading συνέπεισεν (the wrong reading συνέπεσεν is also to be found in L). In no. 9, where there is a divergence between lemma (Πύθια καὶ Δήλια, unanimous tradition, including prov. Bodl. 894 Gaisf., except

---

[101] For no. 23, see below, p. 433. As far as I can judge from my photos, the corrections are written by the same hand (see also Treu with Crusius, "Ein neuer Parallel-Codex" [above, note 37], 209; "am Rand, wohl von derselben Hand").

[102] The explanation of L reads Κίλικες λῃστείαις χρώμενοι ἐπ᾽ ὠμότητι διεβάλλοντο.

[103] See W. Pape and G. Benseler, Wörterbuch der griechischen Eigennamen (3rd ed., Braunschweig 1911), s.v. Ἀράβιος.

E) and the form of the oracle given in the explanation ($\Delta\dot\eta\lambda\iota\alpha$ καὶ
$\Pi\dot\nu\theta\iota\alpha$), E has obviously *suo Marte* assimilated the lemma to the form
found in the explanation. Whether or not he was right in so doing
is another question. What matters is that the form of the lemma
presented by E cannot be regarded as the transmitted wording.
There are two other instances of the same kind. In no. 1, the lemma
in MA, as well as in Zenob. vulg. 5, 78, prov. Bodl. 774 Gaisf. and
Pollux 9, 100, reads πάντα ὀκτώ; but when the proverb is repeated at
the end of the explanation, MA (not Zenobius vulgatus!) add the
article. Now E, though suppressing the last part of the explanation,
must have read it before writing down his excerpt. Therefore, if we
find the article in E's lemma, we should not let it deceive us. The
reverse case, assimilation to the lemma of the form of a proverb
occurring in the explanation, has happened in no. 5.

A man capable of critical thinking may also make good conjectures
like ἰχθύδιον in no. 23 (though, here, the influence of a better tradition
cannot be ruled out altogether, especially since the right reading was
added *supra lineam*) or ᾗ in no. 24 (paleographically very easy, but
requiring a certain degree of intelligence). Another case, no. 4,
admits of several different explanations. Like A, L, and Zenob.
vulg. 6, 21, E has omitted the article τὸν before "Υλαν. As the article
stands in M outside the line and is written with red ink, it could
easily be overlooked (as indeed it was by the scribe of A). I incline to
this explanation. But what of the absence of the article in L and
Zenobius vulgatus? Did E, by any chance, dispose of a better
tradition? Or did the scribe—a third explanation—suppress the
article because he knew the proverb without it? We shall come back
to this general alternative.

Of the instances not yet discussed, there is one that seems, at first
sight, incompatible with the thesis that E depends on M. In no. 12,
the correct reading is ἐκβαλλόμενος; in E, we find ἐκβαλόμενος with one
λ which does not make sense (the passive being required), but is still
more nearly right than the reading ἐκλαβόμενος found in MA. The
natural conclusion would be that there was a progressive deteriora-
tion from ἐκβαλλόμενος (archetype) through ἐκβαλόμενος (E) to ἐκλαβόμενος (MA). If there were more instances of this kind, my thesis
would necessarily break down. But such a unique case is not in my
view sufficient proof that the stemma should be inverted. Supposing

E started from ἐκλαβόμενος, his ἐκβαλόμενος is either an attempted conjecture or an unconscious second alteration, only by chance reaching midway to the truth.

Finally, there are four items left. In two cases (nos. 3 and 7), they concern the omission of an article, in one case (no. 6), the ending of a verb (second or third person), and in the last case (no. 16), the spelling of a proper name. In all cases, it is rather difficult to say what is the right reading, since the other witnesses of the "Athous recension" and the vulgar tradition are divided as well. For instance the spelling Ἀφάναι (with one ν) is to be found not only in E, but also in L and prov. Bodl. 439 Gaisf. (cf. also the Latin *Apinae*), while the spelling with νν is found in MA, Zenob. vulg. 3, 92 and Steph. Byz. (*s.v.*). In two other cases (nos. 3 and 6), the variants occur in the lemma, where a certain fluctuation is, on the whole, not unusual. But I want to call attention to one point. In all four cases—and also in some others, as appears from my list—E shares its readings with L. Does this force us to conclude that there was some kind of connection between the two manuscripts? A common hyparchetype is out of the question because of the different extent of the collections excerpted. But some secondary influence from L to E should at least be considered. If I am rather sceptical about this, it is because, first, the variants concern but trifles and could, I think, have arisen independently; moreover, I hope to have shown that the scribe of E was an intelligent man who certainly enjoyed some education. He may, therefore, occasionally have followed not his model but his instinct or his general knowledge in the field of proverbs.

To sum up, the coincidence between E and A in the extent of their excerpts from the third collection leaves no doubt that both manuscripts belong closely together. The fact that, in almost all instances of divergence between E and M, A stands with M confirms the conclusion reached in section V that A is a copy of M. But then, E too must be a copy of M since it cannot be separated from A. For the explanation of E's better readings, we have to take into account not only the intelligence of the scribe but also the fact that E is an excerpt. The idea that an excerptor tried to improve the text he excerpts by collating another manuscript (here L or some cognate) seems rather strange to me. My conclusion is therefore that all better readings of E are either conscious corrections or accidental improvements. E's case is indeed of general interest in that we can learn from it the kinds of emendation of which an intelligent scribe is capable.

VII

There is still one point to be touched on. If E and A both depend on M, the question arises whether they are direct copies or depend on a common intermediary. I feel unable, for the time being, to give a definitive answer to this question, but I want to call attention to three striking coincidences between E and A against M which seem to favour the thesis of an intermediate copy:

II 95 (Ϟε´) τοῦ Μεγαρέως βασιλέως θυγατέρα M: βασιλέως om. EA. The right reading is τοῦ Μεγαρέων βασιλέως θυγατέρα (Zenob. vulg. 5, 8).

II 83 (πγ´) γράψας οὖν αὐτὸς ἐπίγραμμα ὁ Ἀστυδάμας M: γράψας οὖν ἐπί-γραμμα αὐτὸς ὁ Ἀστυδάμας E, γράψας οὖν αὐτὸς, (signum vocabuli omissi et additi in margine: ἐπίγραμμα) ὁ (supra lineam) Ἀστυδάμας A. It seems as if E and A go back to a common model in which ἐπίγραμμα was written above the line.

V ἄκρον λάβε κτλ. (p. 377 Miller). συμβαλόντες (recte) M: συμβαλλόντες E (priore λ postea deleto) A (supra λλ altero solo λ scripto).

These instances are, I admit, hardly a sufficient basis for a decision, but the assumption of an independent origin seems to me rather unsatisfactory. On the other hand, the observation (communicated above, p. 427) that some wrong readings of A look like misreadings of M could be regarded as an argument against the thesis of an intermediary, though it is not altogether incompatible with it (supposing the writing of the intermediary was very similar to that of M).

However this may be, it does not, I think affect the main conclusion of this paper: that A and E are copies of M and may be neglected in a critical edition of the "Athous recension" except in the third collection where they have preserved a number of proverbs now lost in the Athous.

Hamburg, 29 June 1970

THE SHORTER VERSION OF PSEUDO-ZONARAS, *LEXICON*

MARK NAOUMIDES

Of all extant lexica the one falsely attributed by its first and sole editor[1] to John Zonaras has received the least attention. R. Reitzenstein bypassed it in his brilliant study of the Greek etymologica,[2] because an edition by L. Cohn, an expert in Greek lexicography, was imminent. Cohn's edition, however, never materialized. There is scanty reference to the lexicon in subsequent studies on Greek lexicography.[3] H. Sell has succinctly outlined the current state of the problem: "Über die Überlieferung wissen wir nichts Genaues."[4] The present study (an outgrowth of my investigation into the MSS of St. Cyril's Lexicon) attempts to advance our knowledge of the textual tradition of Pseudo-Zonaras' Lexicon by concentrating on one significant problem, the tradition of the shorter version.[5] This ran parallel to the fuller version but was independent of it and, as will be shown, must have preceded it.

[1] J. A. H. Tittmann, *Iohannis Zonarae Lexicon ex tribus codicibus manuscriptis*, 2 vols. (Leipzig 1808; repr. 1967).

[2] R. Reitzenstein, *Geschichte der griechischen Etymologika: Ein Beitrag zur Geschichte der Philologie in Alexandria und Byzanz* (Leipzig 1897). Brief discussion of this lexicon on pp. 279–82.

[3] Cf. L. Cohn, "Griechische Lexikographie" in K. Brugmann, *Griechische Grammatik*[4] (Handbuch der klassischen Altertumsw. 2. Band, 1. Abt.; München 1913), 704–705; K. Rupprecht, *Apostolis, Eudem und Suidas* (Philologus, Supplementband XV, Heft 1; Leipzig 1922), 99–101; cf. A. Adler's review in *Göttingische gelehrte Anzeigen*, 185 (1923), 135; [J.] Tolkiehn, art. "Lexikographie" in the *RE*, vol. 12 (1925), 2475; A. Adler, art. "Suidas," *RE*, ser. 2, vol. 4 (1931), 714–15. See also below, note 131.

[4] H. Sell, *Das Etymologicum Symeonis* (α–ἀίω) (Beiträge zur Klassischen Philologie, Heft 25; Meisenheim am Glan 1968), p. xx, note 1.

[5] The existence of two versions was first noticed by Tittmann (cf. pp. xx–xxi), although he identified the shorter version with the text of Augustanus (= Monac. gr. 510) and considered it as an epitome of the fuller version. This view was attacked by G. Bernhardy, *Suidae Lexicon*, vol. I (Halle-Brunswick 1853), p. xxxii. Bernhardy thought that the shorter version was earlier and that it was free from interpolation from the *Suda Lexicon*. A. Adler, "Suidas" (above, note 3), rightly identified the shorter version with that of

This shorter version has come down to us in a goodly number of MSS, many of them dating from the XIII and XIV centuries, a period so superbly elucidated by Professor Turyn's profound studies. Before discussing the relationships of the MSS, I offer a brief description of them.[6]

The Manuscripts of the Shorter Version

A = Paris, Bibl. Nat., grec 2655 (Omont III, 19). Paper (Oriental), 237 × 165 mm., 198 fols., XIII s. Written, possibly in Sicily,[7] by Ἰωακεὶμ ἁμαρτωλός (cf. fol. 198ᵛ). Contents: 1ʳ–190ʳ, Λεξικὸν τοῦ ἁγίου Κυρίλλου Ἀλεξανδρείας (= Ps.-Zonaras interpolated); 190ʳ–end, minor lexica of the type usually found in the MSS of St. Cyril's lexicon.[8] Bibliography: Drachmann 15–18; Latte l; P. Burguière, "Cyrilliana: Observations sur deux manuscrits parisiens du Lexique de Cyrille," *Rev. Ét. Anc.* 63 (1961), 345–61 and 64 (1962), 95–108; one page of this MS was reproduced in my study "The Fragments of Greek Lexicography in the Papyri," *Classical Studies Presented to B. E. Perry* (Illinois Studies in Language and Literature, vol 58; Urbana 1969), plate iii.

Aa = Athens, 'Εθν. Βιβλ. No. 1082 (Sakkelion 193–94). Paper (Western, with watermarks resembling Briquet 428, 2478, 3404, 3409). 22 × 15 cm., 167 fols., XV/XVI s. Contents: 1ʳ–117ᵛ, Λεξικὸν τοῦ ἐν ἁγίοις πατρὸς ἡμῶν Κυρίλλου Ἀλεξανδρείας (= Ps.-Zonaras)[9]; 117ᵛ–end, minor lexica as above. Bibliography: Drachmann 17 (note 1); Latte l.

---

cod. Vat. gr. 11 (our J) and stipulated that it is probably older than the fuller version, because it is found in MSS older than those of the fuller version, notably the Vatican MS On the actual date of J, see below.

[6] The standard catalogue descriptions of the MSS have been referred to briefly by the author's name except for the most recent ones. For a full title see M. Richard, *Répertoire des bibliothèques et des catalogues de manuscrits grecs*[2] (Publications de l'Institut de Recherche et d'Histoire des Textes, I; Paris 1958); and *Supplément I (1958–1963)*, Paris 1964. Other abbreviations used in this article besides Tittmann (cf. note 1): Cramer *AP* = J. A. Cramer, *Anecdota Graeca e codicibus manuscriptis bibliothecae regiae Parisiensis*, 4 vols. (Oxford 1839–41); Drachmann = A. B. Drachmann, *Die Überlieferung des Cyrillglossars* (Det Kgl. Danske Videnskabernes Selskab. Hist.-filol. Meddelelser XXI, 5; Copenhagen 1936); Latte = K. Latte, *Hesychii Alexandrini Lexicon*, 2 vols. (Copenhagen 1963–66); Vogel–Gardthausen = M. Vogel and V. Gardthausen, *Die griechischen Schreiber des Mittelalters und der Renaissance* (Zentralblatt für Bibliothekswesen, Beiheft xxxiii; Leipzig 1909).

[7] On account of an Arabic note in fol. 35ʳ; cf. P. Burguière (below), p. 347.

[8] On these lexica, cf. Drachmann, 53–58.

[9] The ω-section, which was missing from the exemplar, was copied from another MS, according to a statement written by the copyist himself in fol. 116ᵛ.

Ab = Bucharest, Acad. Române, gr. 608 (Litzica 300–301). Paper, 27 × 21 cm., 178 fols., XVI/XVII s. Contents: 1ʳ–115ʳ Ps.-Zonaras with the beginning missing: 115ᵛ–19ᵛ, minor lexica; 120ʳ–78ᵛ, canons (hymns) with interpretation.

Am = Meteora, *M. Μεταμορφώσεως*, No. 498 (N. Bees, *Τὰ χειρόγραφα τῶν Μετεώρων*, vol. I [Athens 1967], 502–503). Paper. 213 × 156 mm., 153 fols.[10] Written probably A.D. 1511[11]. Contents: 1ʳ–79ᵛ, *Λεξικὸν τοῦ ἁγίου Κυρίλου* (sic) *Ἀλεξανδρείας* (= Ps.-Zonaras); 80ʳ–87ᵛ, minor lexica; 88ʳ–end, varia.

Ap = Patmos, *M. Ἰωάννου τοῦ Θεολόγου*, No. 320 (Sakkelion 156). Paper, 170 × 127 mm., iii + 588 pages.[12] XV s.[13] written at least in part by *Δανιὴλ τάχα καὶ ἱερομόναχος* (cf. p. 459).[14] Contents: pp. 1*–124*, *Ἐρωτήματα* (= Grammar), incomplete; 1–410, *Λεξικὸν τῶν ἁγίων Κυρίλλου καὶ Ἀθανασίου Ἀλεξανδρείας* (= Ps.-Zonaras); 410–425, minor lexica; 425-end, varia.

Av = Vienna, Oesterr. Nationalbibl., suppl. graec. 147 (Hunger 92). Paper, 215 × 140 mm., ii + 116 fols., c. A.D. 1400. Contents: 1ʳ–109ᵛ, *Λεξικὸν τῶν ἁγίων Κυρίλλου καὶ Ἀθανασίου Ἀλεξανδρείας* (= Ps. Zonaras); 110ʳ-end, minor lexica.

B = Berlin, Deutsche Staatsbibl., gr. 181 (formerly Phillipps 1584; cf. Studemund - Cohn I, 79). Paper, 328 × 240 mm., 171 fols. Copied in Venice between 1539–1542 by order of Cardinal G. Pelicier, ambassador of the French king Francis I (cf. Omont, *op. cit.* [below, note 16], p. 46). Contents: 1ʳ–160ᵛ, Ps.-Zonaras[15]; 161ʳ–171ʳ, Nicetas Heracleensis, *Rhythmi*; 171ʳᵛ, etymologia alphabeti. A trilingual note in fol. 160ᵛ (cf. also fol. 171ᵛ) states that the MS was "read" by Claude Naulot du Val etc., A.D.

---

[10] Two leaves of the original MS are now missing, one between fols. 83–84 and another between 87–88.

[11] The year ͵αφια' (= A.D. 1511) is given as an example of how to calculate the moon cycles in 153ʳ.

[12] Numbered 1–124 and again 1–465. Three numbers (348, 383, 384) have been skipped and two pages (between 127–128) have been left unnumbered. One folio of the original is missing between pp. 78–79. Pages 432–47, forming a complete quire and written by another hand, are inserts. The first part (pp. 1–124) is incomplete and may also come from another MS.

[13] Pp. 455–59 contain Easter Tables of the years ͵ϛϡξϛ' (= A.D. 1458) to ζ' (= A.D. 1492).

[14] Daniel's signature written in a monocondylion can be seen on p. 459 (after the Easter Tables) preceded by the familiar exclamation δόξα σοι ὁ Θ(εὸ)ς ἡμῶν.

[15] The title (*Λεξικὸν Ἑλληνικόν*) is written by Naulot; cf. below.

1573.[16] Other owners before Phillipps: Clermont College, G. Meermann.

C = Sinai, M. Ἁγ. Αἰκατερίνης, Gr. 1204 (Gardthausen 249). Paper, 218 × 160 mm., 322 fols., XV/XVI s. Contents: 1ʳ–297ᵛ, Ps.-Zonaras (title: 'Ἐκλογὴ τῶν λέξεων ἐκ τῶν ἔξωθεν φιλοσόφων καὶ τῶν καθ' ἡμᾶς διδασκάλων); 297ᵛ–316ʳ, Nicetas Heracleensis, Rhythmi; 316ʳ–end, various notes, some of them referring to local events in the island of Cyprus. The last note was written διὰ χειρός...Χαρίτ(ου?) ἁμαρτωλοῦ καὶ τάχα ἱερέως τοῦ Νικηφόρου on May 28, A.D. 1507.

D = Paris, Bibl. Nat., grec 2617 (Omont III, 14). Paper (Oriental), 246 × 175 mm., 186 fols., XIV s. Written in a hand similar to that of 'Ρωμανὸς ἁμαρτωλὸς ἀναγνώστης χαρτοφύλαξ τῆς Λαμείας (?).[17] Contents: 1ʳ–68ʳ, St. Cyril's lexicon falsely attributed to St. Athanasius; 68ᵛ–82ʳ, minor lexica; 83ʳ–177ᵛ, Ps.-Zonaras (title: 'Ἐκλογῆ λέξεων ἐκ τῶν ἔξωθεν φιλοσόφων καὶ τῶν καθ' ἡμᾶς διδασκάλων); 177ᵛ–183ʳ, Nicetas Heracleensis, Rhythmi; 183ᵛ, 186ʳ, later notes. Bibliography: Cramer, AP IV, 201–215; M. Schmidt, Hesychii Alexandrini Lexicon, vol. IV. 2 (Jena 1864), xlvii–xlix; H. Omont, Missions archéologiques françaises en Orient aux XVIIᵉ et XVIIIᵉ siècles (Collection de documents inédits sur l'histoire de France, vol. 84; Paris 1902), 964; Drachmann 20.

E = Modena, Bibl. Estense, α.S.5.7 (Puntoni 463–465, No. 124). Paper 26 × 18 cm.[18] 175 fols. XIV s. Contents: 1ʳ–23ᵛ and 162ʳ–end, varia; 24ʳ–160ᵛ, Ps.-Zonaras, with beginning and end missing.

F = Paris, Bibl. Nat., Coisl. gr. 392 (Devreesse 371). Paper, 167 × 117 mm., iii(1ᵃ–3ᵃ) + 323 fols., XIV/XV s. Contents: Ps.-Zonaras with the beginning and end missing. Bibliography: Tittmann xxxix. Specimens of glosses from this lexicon have been given by B. de Montfaucon, Bibliotheca Coisliniana olim Segueriana (Paris 1715), 599–601.

G = Philadelphia, The Library Company of Phil., MS. No. 2 (cf. de Ricci II, 2103). Vellum, 19 × 13 cm., 144 fols., XIV s. Contents:

---

[16] On Naulot, an heir to G. Pelicier's library, and his habit of inscribing his MSS with similar notes, cf. H. Omont, "Catalogue des manuscrits grecs de Guillaume Pelicier," Bibliothèque de l'École des Chartes, 46 (1885), 51–52; W. Studemund and L. Cohn, Codices ex Bibliotheca Meermanniana Phillippici Graeci nunc Berolinenses (Die Handschriften-Verzeichnisse der Königlichen Bibliothek zu Berlin, Bd. XI: Verzeichniss der griechischen Handschriften; Abt. I; Berlin 1890), pp. ii–iii. Vogel–Gardthausen 454 erroneously list Naulot as a scribe of MSS.

[17] See now [Febr. 1974] my article "Εὔμμεικτα Παλαιογραφικά" in Epet. Het. Byzant. Spoudôn 39–40 (1972–73), 380–83.

[18] For the dimensions, hands and dates of the various parts, cf. Puntoni p. 465.

1ʳ–144ᵛ, Ps.-Zonaras, with the beginning missing; etymol. alphabeti, beg. 144ᵛ (the rest is lost).

H = Copenhagen, Kong. Bibliotek, Add. 280 (Krarup II, 183). Paper, 158 × 115 mm., 253 fols. (numbered by page from 1–456). Written on November 22, A.D. 1295 διὰ χειρός...τοῦ ταπεινοῦ μοναχοῦ Νικοδήμου probably in the monastery of Patmos (cf. note on p. 456). Contents: Ps.-Zonaras. The title "Ερανος λέξεων seems to be by a later hand. On the inside of the front cover there is the ex-libris of J. Chr. Kall.[19] In a fly leaf there is a note stating that the ms belonged to Th. Bartholin.[20] The ms formed part of the University Library before 1938. Bibliography: Tittmann xl–xli.

I = Athos, M. Ἰβήρων 991 (formerly 76; cf. Lambros II, 7–8, No. 4196). Vellum, 221 fols.,[21] XIII s. Contents: 1ʳ–179ʳ, Ps.-Zonaras with the beginning missing; 79ᵛ, etymol. alphabeti; 180ʳ–end, varia. Bibliography: Drachmann 21.

J = Vatican, Bibl. Apost. Vaticana, gr. 11 (Mercati - Franchi de' Cavalieri I, 7). Vellum, 230 × 175 mm., i + 107 fols., XIII s.[22] Contents: 1ʳ–104ᵛ, Ps.-Zonaras (title: "Ερανος λέξεων ἐκ τῶν ἔξωθεν φιλοσόφων καὶ τῶν καθ' ἡμᾶς διδασκάλων); 104ᵛ–105ʳ, etymol. alphabeti; 105ʳ–106ʳ, various excerpts and later notes. Bibliography: cf. P. Canart – V. Peri, Sussidi bibliografici per i manoscritti Greci della Biblioteca Vaticana (Studi e Testi, 261; Città del Vaticano 1970), 354–55 (with some errors).

K = Paris, Bibl. Nat., gr. 2663 (Omont III, 22). Paper, 183 × 120 mm., 168 fols., XIV s. Contents: 1ʳ–168ʳ, Ps.-Zonaras (title: Στέφανος λέξεων ἐκ τῶν ἔξωθεν φιλοσόφων καὶ τῶν καθ' ἡμᾶς διδασκάλων); 168ʳᵛ etymol. alphabeti. Bibliography: H. Omont, Catalogues des manuscrits grecs de Fontainebleau sous François Iᵉʳ et Henri II (Paris 1889), p. 115 (No. 341).

---

[19] "κτῆμα / 10. Christiani Kallii / hebr. Lingu. P. P. O. / Hafn. c|ɔ|ɔccxlii." On [J.] Christ. Kall (1714–75) cf. Biographie Universelle², XXI, 409–10 and Dansk Biografisk Leksikon, vol. 12 (1937), 314–15. Codex Haun. Add. 442 contains a list of "codices Joh. Chr. Kallii"; cf. Krarup II, 3.

[20] This is in all probability the famous Danish Professor of Medicine Thomas Bartholin (died A.D. 1680), on whom cf. Biographie Universelle² III, 194, Dansk Biografisk Leksikon, vol. 2 (1933), 205–14. Another Greek ms of the same library to pass from Bartholin to Kall is mentioned by Krarup in II, 172–73.

[21] The first two quires and three leaves of the third quire of the original ms are missing. Also missing are one leaf between fols. 67–68 and at least one whole quire after fol. 179.

[22] Mercati–Franchi de' Cavalieri date the ms in the XII s. The date is also accepted by A. Adler (above, note 3), 714 and G. Moravcsik, Byzantinoturcica, vol. I (Berlin 1958), p. 346. This seems to be impossible, however, in the light of Tittmann's observation (p. lxxii) about the entry ἤλεκτρον (cf. below, 486).

L = Florence, Bibl. Laurenziana, S. Marco 301 (Rostagno - Festa 178). Paper (Western), 226 × 155 mm., 316 fols., XIV s. Contents: 1ʳ–310ᵛ, Ps.-Zonaras (title: "Ἔρανος λέξεων ἐκ τῶν ἅπαξ ἁπασῶν βίβλων συναθροισθήσα ἐκ τῶν ἔξωθεν φιλοσόφων καὶ καθ' ἡμᾶς διδασκάλων); 310ᵛ–312ᵛ, etymol. alphabeti. The margins bear copious Latin notes and Greek-Latin glosses. Bibliography: Drachmann 19.

M = Vienna, Oesterr. Nationalbibl., phil. gr. 77 (Hunger 191–192). Paper (Briquet 5992, 11953), 295 (–298) × 212 (–215) mm., i + 54 fols., XIV s. Contents: 1ʳ–53ᵛ, Ps.-Zonaras (title: "Ἔρανος λέξεων ἐκ τῶν απαξ ἁπασῶν βίβλων συναθροισθῆσα ἐκ τῶν ἔξωθεν φιλοσόφων καὶ καθ' ἡμᾶς διδασκάλων; 53ᵛ–54ʳ, etymol. alphabeti; 54ʳᵛ, theological excerpts. Former owners: Ἰωάννης ὁ Τουρκόπουλος (cf. fol. 54ᵛ) and J. Sambucus (1531–1584) who purchased it in Rome.[23] Bibliography: H. Gerstinger (cf. note 23).

P = Paris, Bibl. Nation., gr. 2665 (Omont III, 22). Paper, 210 × 135 mm., iii + 210 fols.[24] XIV s. Contents: 1ʳ–20ᵛ, minor lexica; 21ʳ–171ʳ, Ps.-Zonaras with the original beginning missing; 172ʳ–end, varia. Bibliography: H. Omont, *Catalogues des manuscrits* (above, under K), p. 115 (No. 339).

Pb = Oxford, Bodleian Libr., Barocc. gr. 95 (Coxe I, 160–163). Paper, 218 × 146 mm., 311 fols., XV s. Contents: 1ʳ–210ʳ, Λεξικὸν τοῦ ἁγίου Κυρίλλου Ἀλεξανδρείας συντεθὲν παρὰ τοῦ κυροῦ Ἀντωνίου τοῦ φιλοσόφου (= Ps.-Zonaras interpolated); 210ʳ–223ʳ, minor lexica; 223ʳ–end, *Physiologus*, et al. Bibliography: Cramer, *AP* IV, 197–201; M. Schmidt, *Hesychii Alexandrini Lexicon*, IV, 2, pp. xlix-l; F. Sbordone, *Physiologus* (Milan 1936), xv.

Pc = Rome, Bibl. Casanatense, 1202 (Bancalari 186). Paper, 193 × 143 mm., i + 143 fols., XV s. Contents: Ps-.Zonaras without beginning and end.[25] On the fly leaf 1ʳ: *ex codicibus Johannis Angeli ducis ab Altaemps.*[26] Bibliography: Drachmann 21.

---

[23] Cf. H. Gerstinger, "Johannes Sambucus als Handschriftensammler," *Festschrift der Nationalbibliothek in Wien* (Wien 1926), p. 331, 367.

[24] Fols. 1–27, written in a fifteenth-century hand and containing the minor lexica and the beginning of Ps.-Zonaras, were added later. The first two quires and the first leaf of the third quire of the original ms are missing as is also one leaf between fols. 119–20 containing the ξ-section. The order of the leaves in the latter part of the lexicon is disturbed and should be restored as follows: 143, 151–58, 144–50, 167, 160–66, 159, 168–71.

[25] The order of the folios has been restored and the volume rebound in the "laboratorio restauro di libro" in Grottaferratta in 1960.

[26] On Giovanni Angelo d'Altaemps († 1620), cf. Carlo Frati, *Dizionario bio-bibliografico dei bibliotecari e bibliofili italiani* (Biblioteca di bibliografia Italiana, xiii; Firenze, 1933), 16–17; *Dizionario biografico dei Italiani*, vol. II (Roma 1960), 550–51.

Pe = Escorial, y-III-8 (Andrés II, 226–227). Paper (Briquet 3370, 3976, 5958, 11959), 215 × 137 mm., iv + 158 fols., XV s. Contents: Λεξικὸν τοῦ ἁγίου Κυρίλλου Ἀλεξανδρείας συντεθὲν παρὰ τοῦ κυροῦ Ἀντωνίου τοῦ φιλοσόφου. "Ερανος λέξεων (= Ps.-Zonaras interpolated).

Po = Oxford, Bodleian Libr., Auct. F.4.14 (formerly Misc. 113; cf. Coxe I, 684–686). Paper, 220 × 164 mm., 307 fols. XVI s. Contents similar to Pb. Bibliography: F. Sbordone, *Physiologus* (Milan 1936), xv.

Pv = Venice, Bibl. Marciana, Append. X.25 (= colloc. 1413; formerly Nanianus 303; cf. Mingarelli 506–508). Paper, 219 × 145 mm., 381 fols., XVI s. Contents: 3ʳ–194ᵛ, Ps.-Zonaras with the beginning missing; 195ʳ–227ʳ, lexica minora; 227ʳ–232ᵛ, varia; 233ʳ–266ᵛ, St. Cyril's lexicon (α- επ only); 269ʳ–end, theological excerpts. The MS was, until the beginning of the XVIII s., the property of the monastery τῶν Στροφάδων in Zante (cf. fols. 1ʳ, 2ʳ, 3ʳ etc.). Bibliography: Drachmann 20.

Q = Patmos, M. Ἰωάννου τοῦ Θεολόγου, 32 (Sakkelion 17). Vellum (palimpsest), 145 × 125 mm., 204 fols.,[27] XIII s. Contents: 1ʳ–201ʳ, Ps.-Zonaras with the beginning missing; 201ᵛ–end, troparia.

R = Rome, Bibl. Angelica, gr. 20 (Franchi de' Cavalieri - Muccio, 50). Paper, 127 × 115 mm., v + 199 fols.[28] XIV s. Contents: Ps.-Zonaras with the original beginning and end missing. The MS in all probability once belonged to Cardinal Guido Ascanio Sforza (1518–1564) and was subsequently passed on to Cardinal Domenico Passionei before entering the Angelica; cf. A. Piccolomini, *Studi Italiani di Filologia Classica*, 6 (1898), 175.

S = Paris, Bibl. Nat., suppl. grec 462 (Omont III, 265). Paper (Western), 210 × 142 mm., 147 fols. Written A.D. 1312/13 διὰ χειρός...τοῦ ἁμαρτωλοῦ Ἰωάννου καὶ τάχα ἱερέως (cf. fol. 147ʳ).[29] Contents: 1ʳ–142ᵛ, Ps.-Zonaras with the beginning missing;

[27] Thirty more paper leaves (numbered separately 1–30), written by a later hand and containing Manuel Moschopulus, *Schedae*, at the beginning of the lexicon, have been added before the vellum leaves.

[28] There are also four blank, unnumbered folios between fols. 2–3 and five more at the end. The first leaf of the original MS and an undetermined number of leaves from the end are missing. A sixteenth-century hand has substituted the missing beginning and end (fols. 1ʳ–2ʳ, 198ʳ–199ʳ) from another MS.

[29] Probably in Italy according to J. Irigoin, "Les filigranes de Fabriano (noms de papetiers) dans les manuscrits grecs du debut du XIVᵉ siècle," *Scriptorium* 12 (1958), 49.

142ᵛ–145ʳ, minor lexica; 145ʳ–146ᵛ, poems with alphabetical acrostic attributed to St. Gregory of Nazianzus; 147ʳᵛ list of Jewish kings and prophets. The MS was acquired in Greece by Minoides Mynas during his first mission to the Orient in 1842.[30] Bibliography: H. Omont, *Fac-similés des manuscrits grecs datés de la Bibliothèque Nationale du IXᵉ au XIVᵉ siècle* (Paris 1891), 20; Vogel - Gardthausen, 208; J. Irigoin, "Les premiers manuscrits grecs écrits sur papier et le problème du bombycin," *Scriptorium* 4 (1950), 204; *id., op. cit.* (above, note 29), 45–49.

T = Milan, Bibl. Ambrosiana, F34 sup. (Martini - Bassi, No. 335). Paper, 215 × 143 mm., i + 210 fols. Written A.D. 1462/3 *(ὑπὸ) εὐτελοῦς Φιλοθέου μοναχοῦ* (cf. fol. 209ᵛ).[31] Contents: 1ʳ–127ᵛ, Ps.-Zonaras with the beginning missing; 129ʳ–209ᵛ, varia lexico-graphica; 210ʳ, prayer. Bibliography: Vogel - Gardthausen 420; Drachmann 19; Latte l.

U = Uppsala, Universitetsbibl., gr. 17 (Graux - Martin, 336). Paper (Oriental), 171 × 128 (–133) mm., 190 fols. Written c. 1300 in the style "practiced in Constantinople among Byzantine erudites at the turn of the XIII s."[32] Contents: 1ʳ–187ᵛ, Ps.-Zonaras with the beginning missing: 187ʳ–188ʳ, minor lexica; 188ʳ–190ᵛ, alphabetical poems attributed to St. Gregory of Nazianzus; 190ᵛ, list of cities. Bibliography: C. E. Aurivillius, *De glossariis Graecis manuscriptis in Bibliotheca Reg. Acad. Upsaliensis asservatis disquisitio* (Uppsala 1821–1822), pp. 18–21.

V = Vienna, Oesterr. Nationalbibl., phil. gr. 322 (Hunger 418–419) Paper (Oriental), 170 × 115 (–125) mm., i + 290 fols. First half of XIV s. Contents: 4ʳ–206ᵛ, Ps.-Zonaras [title: Συναγωγὴ λέξεων συλλεγεῖσα ἐκ διαφόρων βιβλίων τῆς παλαιᾶς τε φημ(ὶ) γρα(φ)ῆς καὶ τῆς νέας καὶ αὐτῆς δ(ή)π(ου) τῆς θύραθ(εν)]; 1ʳ–3ʳ, 207ʳ–end, various small treatises. Purchased in Constantinople by Augerius de Busbecke (cf. fol. 3ᵛ).[33] Bibliography: Tittmann xxxii–xxxiii.

---

[30] Cf. H. Omont, "Minoide Mynas et ses missions en Orient," Académie des Inscriptions et Belles Lettres: *Mémoires de l'Institut National de France*, vol. 40 (1916), 337–419 (esp. p. 376).

[31] Two hands can be distinguished, one copying fols. 1ʳ–127ᵛ, i.e. the section containing Ps.-Zonaras, the other copying the rest. The subscription resembles the first hand. The verses preceding the subscription (cf. Martini–Bassi 388, with some errors) were clearly taken from the subscription of a Tetraevangelon.

[32] Cf. A. Turyn, *Codices Graeci Vaticani saeculis XIII et XIV scripti annorumque notis instructi* (Codices e Vaticanis selecti, vol. xxviii; Vatican City 1964), p. 96.

[33] On the MSS acquired by Busbecke in Constantinople, cf. J. Bick, "Wanderungen griechischer Handschriften," *Wiener Studien* 34 (1912), 143–54 (no mention of this MS). For

W = Paris, Bibl. Nat., grec 2669 (Omont III, 23). Paper. 212 × 145 mm., iv + 326 fols.[34] Copied from an old codex which belonged to Nicholas Maurokordatos, Prince of Wallachia, in the XVIII s.[35] Contents: 2ʳ–200ᵛ, Ps.-Zonaras with a different beginning from that of the other MSS; 200ᵛ–end, varia lexicographica et grammatica. Bibliography: Cramer, *AP* IV, 82–162; K. Nickau, *Ammonius de adfinium vocabulorum differentia* (Leipzig 1966), xii.

X = Paris, Bibl. Nat., gr. 1123 (Omont I, 224). Paper, 221 × 145 mm., 330 fols., XV s. Contents: 3ʳ–187ᵛ, varia theologica; 188ʳ–330ʳ, Ps.-Zonaras (title: Ἔρανος λέξεων). This MS, which formerly belonged to the monastery of the Transfiguration at Meteora, was brought to France by the priest Athanasius Rhetor in the middle of the XVII s.; cf. H. Omont, *op. cit.* (above, footnote 35), 855, 857.

Y = Paris, Bibl. Nat., gr. 2597 (Omont III, 11). Paper, 215 × 146 mm., 226 fols., XV s.[36] Contents: 1ʳ–5ʳ, grammatical excerpt; 5ʳ–6ᵛ, Latin notes; 7ʳ–225ᵛ, Ps.-Zonaras (title: Λεξικὸν σὺν Θ(ε)ῷ ἁγίῳ) with the end missing (about one leaf). The MS according to a note in fol. 226ᵛ once belonged to the monastery τῆς ἁγίας Ἀναστασίας τῆς Φαρμακολυτρίας τῆς ἐν τῶ μεγάλω βουνῶ κειμέν(ης). It was acquired somewhere in the East by the French manuscript-hunters in the eighteenth century; cf. H. Omont, *op. cit.* (above, footnote 35), 1118.

Z = Bologna, Bibl. Univers., 3560 (Olivieri, 430–431). Paper, 235 × 157 mm., 236 fols.,[37] XIV s.[38] Contents: Ps.-Zonaras (only part of the title, Λεξι[κόν], has been preserved). Bibliography: T. W. Allen, "Notes on Greek MSS. in Italian Libraries," *Cl. Rev.* 3 (1889), 252.

---

his biography cf. *Biographie Universelle*², vol. VI, 219–21; *Allgemeine Deutsche Biographie*, vol. III (Leipzig 1876 = Berlin 1967), 633; Ch. Th. Forster and F. H. B. Daniell, *The Life and Letters of Ogier Ghiselin de Busbecq*, vol. I (London 1881), 1–72.

[34] The folios are numbered 1–123, 114ᵃ–123ʲ, 124–70, 170ᵇⁱˢ, 171–315.

[35] Cf. Cramer, *AP* IV, 82; Cramer dates it in the XV s., Omont in the XVII. The MS however must have been copied after Maurokordatos' death in 1730. For attempts by Sevin and others to obtain Maurokordatos' MSS, or at least copies of them, during the Prince's life and after his death, cf. H. Omont, *Missions archéologiques françaises en Orient aux XVIIᵉ et XVIIIᵉ siècles* (Collection de documents inédits sur l'histoire de France, vol. 84; Paris 1902), 459 sqq., 669 sqq.

[36] Before 1426; cf. note recording the death of the priest Λέων Εὐγενικός (fol. 3ᵛ) and dated February 27, A.M. 6935.

[37] One leaf is missing between fols. 218–19 (i.e., the first of quire κ̄η̄) and two more between fols. 224–25 (i.e. the last of quire κ̄η̄ and the first of κ̄θ̄).

[38] Before A.D. 1360; cf. marginal note in fol. 8ʳ and 65ʳ.

Γ = Athos, M. 'Iβήρων, 348 (formerly 77, cf. Lambros II, 8–9, No. 4197). Paper, 225 fols.,[39] XV s. Contents: 1ʳ–223ʳ, Ps.-Zonaras with the beginning missing; 223ʳᵛ, etymologia alphabeti with the end missing.

Δ = Athos, M. Διονυσίου, 712 (Euth. Dionysiates, 255). Paper, 197 × 145 mm., 225 fols.,[40] XVI s. Contents: 1ʳ–205ᵛ, Ps.-Zonaras with the beginning missing; 207ʳ–214ᵛ, Christmas iambic canon; 215ʳ–225ᵛ, anonymous lexicon. A note in fol. 205ᵛ states that the book was bought from a certain (monk) Sisoes at the monastery of Vatopedi by hieromonk Clement, possibly the same as the hegoumenos of the monastery of Dionysios and scribe of codex Dionys. 465 (formerly 224; cf. Lambros I, 368–373, No. 3758).

Λ = Athos, M. Μεγίστης Λαύρας, I 85 (Spyr. Lavriotes - Eustratiades, p. 193, No. 1169). Paper, 222 × 152 mm., 214 fols., XIV s.[41] Contents: 1ʳ–212ᵛ, Ps.-Zonaras (title: Συναγωγὴ λέξεων συλλεγεῖσα ἐκ διαφόρων βιβλίων τῆς παλαιᾶς τε φημὶ Γραφῆς καὶ τῆς νέας καὶ αὐτῆς δήπου τῆς θύραθεν); 213ʳ–end, Περὶ ἐτυμολογίας. A note written over the headpiece in fol. 1ʳ states that this ms was one of the books τῶν κατηχουμένων τῆς λαύρας τοῦ ὁσί(ου) κ(αὶ) θεοφ(ό)ρου π(ατ)ρ(ὸ)s ἡμῶν [Ἀθανασίου].[42]

Π = Paris, Bibl. Nat., Coisl. gr. 393 (Devreesse, 371–372). Vellum (palimpsest), 198 × 140 mm., 215 fols.,[43] XIII s. Contents: Ps.-Zonaras with the beginning and end missing. Bibliography: Tittmann xxxix.

Σ = Munich, Bayer. Staatsbibl., gr. 308 (Hardt III, 245–250). Vellum, 172 × 126 mm., vi + 251 fols.,[44] XIII s. Possibly written by 'Ιγνάτιος ἱερομόναχος, whose signature appears in the lower margin of fol. 117ʳ. Contents: 1ʳ–129ʳ, Ps.-Zonaras (title: "Ερανος λέξεων ἐκ τῶν ἀπαξαπασῶν βίων (sic) ἐκσυναθροισθείς); 219ʳ–220ᵛ, etymologia alphabeti; 220ᵛ–248ᵛ, varia. In fol. 247ʳ an eschatological prophesy expected to be fulfilled in the years ͵ϛωέ (= 1296/7) and ͵ϛ϶π' (1471/2). Bibliography: Tittmann xxx–xxxi.

---

[39] Numbers 143, 167 have been used twice in the numbering of the folios.

[40] One leaf is missing from the beginning of the first quire.

[41] Fols. 193–200 are written by a sixteenth-century hand.

[42] A similar note is found in cod. K71 of the same monastery (cf. Spyridon Lavriotes and S. Eustratiades, p. 229, No. 1358). Cf. also cod. Vindob. iur. gr. 12 (mentioned by J. Bick, *Wiener Studien* 34 [1912], 150).

[43] One leaf is missing between fols. 55 and 56, the last of quire ζ.

[44] Of these 236 folios, numbered 1–234 and including fols. 53ᵃ and 66ᵃ, are from the original ms. Fols. 235–249 (paper) were written by a later hand.

Φ = Florence, Bibl. Laurenz., plut. 59.38 (Bandini II, 569–571). Paper, 210 × 144 mm., 461 fols., XV s. Contents: 3ʳ–195ᵛ, Eudemus, Lexicon; 197ʳ–405ʳ, Ps.-Zonaras (title: *Συναγωγὴ λέξεων συλλεγεῖσα ἐκ διαφόρων βιβλίων τῆς παλαιάς τέ φημὶ γραφῆς καὶ τῆς νέας καὶ αὐτῆς δήπου τῆς θύραθεν*); 405ᵛ–409ᵛ, Ἑρμηνεία περὶ ἀντιστοίχων; 410ʳ–428ᵛ, iambic canons; 428ᵛ–440ᵛ, minor lexica; 441ʳ–end excerpt from *de mensuris et ponderibus* and ὅροι. Bibliography: A. Kopp, *Beiträge zur griechischen Excerpten-Litteratur* (Berlin 1887), 61.

Ψ = Athos, M. Βατοπεδίου, 416 (Eustratiades - Arcadios 81). Paper, 250 × 170 mm., 237 fols.[45] XIV s. Contents: 1ʳ–232ᵛ, Ps.-Zonaras (title: *Συναγωγὴ λέξεων συλλεγεῖσα [ἐκ διαφόρων] βιβλίων τῆς παλαιᾶς τε φημὶ [γραφῆς καὶ] τῆς νέας καὶ αὐτῆς δήπου τῆς [θύραθεν]*);[46] 233ᵛ–236ʳ, Psellus, Περὶ ὅρου πίστεως.

Ω = Rome, Collegio Greco, Greek MS. No. 3 (Lambros 8–11). Paper (Oriental), 163 × 120 mm., iv + 228 fols., XIV s. The codex consists of three different parts each written by a different hand. Part ii contains the following: 23ʳ–120ʳ, Ps.-Zonaras with some gaps [47] (title: *Συναγωγὴ λέξεων ἔκ τε τῶν ἔξω ποιητῶν καὶ τῶν καθημας ποιητῶν τὲ καὶ διδασκάλων*); 120ʳ, lexicon vocum hebraicarum; 120ʳ–121ʳ, etymologia alphabeti; 122ʳ–175ᵛ, St. John Chrysostom, *Letters*, and other short Patristic texts.

To the above, the following MSS should be added of which I have no microfilm and which do not appear in the critical apparatus:

Cairo, Library of the Greek Patriachate of Alexandria, No. 123 (cf. Moschonas 112; Charitakes 148–155). A.D. 1575. The lexicon extends from 205ʳ to 343ʳ and begins with the admonition characteristic of the **pi** family *(Δεῖ εἰδέναι τὸν λέξιν τινὰ ζητοῦντα κλπ.)* [48]

Dresden, Sächsische Landesbibl. Da. 39 (Schnorr von Carolsfeld 293). This is an eighteenth-century copy of Mosquensis (cf. below) made by Chr. F. Matthaei. Excerpts from this MS are given by M. Schmidt, *Hesychius*, vol. IV, 1, pp. 352–360.

---

[45] Number 65 has been used twice.

[46] Towards the end the MS departs from the text of Ps.-Zonaras and follows St. Cyril's lexicon, the recension designated by Drachmann as **g**. Note also that in fol. 83ʳ in the middle of the βα-section the scribe for some reason thought his task finished and wrote: κἀνταῦθα δόξαν τῶ Θ(ε)ῶ προσοιστέον. Some troparia and definitions in alphabetical order follow (−84ʳ). Fols. 84ᵛ–85ᵛ are left blank. The text resumes with fol. 86ʳ.

[47] There is one leaf missing between fols. 102–103, two between 108–109 (with most of the ῥ-, the entire σ-, and part of the τ-section) and one between fols. 115–16.

[48] On this admonition which also occurs in Hesychius, cf. Drachmann 17–18; Latte xiii.

Another Dresden MS, Da 38, [49] may also be included here on Tittmann's testimony (p. xxii–xxvi) that its text resembled that of Coisl. gr. 392 (F).

Leiden, Univers. Biblioth., Voss. Misc. 7 (de Meyier 238–241). XVII s. It contains (among other things) a description and excerpts from cod. Barocc. gr. 95 (= Pb).

Leningrad, Bibl. Akad. Nauk, No. 187 of the former Russian Archaeol. Institute in Constantinople. XVI s. The text of a page reproduced by E. E. Granström in *Vizant. Vrem.* 8 (1956), Pl. 1 (opp. p. 198), resembles that of the shorter version.

Milan, Bibl. Ambros., B81 sup. (Martini–Bassi, No. 108). XV/XVI s. To judge from a sample taken from the beginning of the volume, it contains an abbreviated text of the shorter version.

Moscow, cod. Typ. Synod. f21 (cf. Matthaei, 272–73; now in the Moscow Historical Museum). XV s. The end of the lexicon (sections φ–ω) has been published by Chr. F. Matthaei, *Glossaria Graeca minora* (Moscow 1775) and seems to agree with the text of the **p1** family. References to this MS are found in Tittmann xxxvi; M. Schmidt, *Hesychii Alexandrini Lexicon*, vol. IV.2, xliv–xlv; Drachmann p. 15, n. 1: Latte l.

Oxford, Bodleian Library, MS Cherry 11 (Madan, III, 72); stated to be a copy of Barocc. 95 (= Pb) made in England in the XVII s.

Paris, Bibl. Nat., gr. 2641 and 2642 (Omont III, 17). Both are copies of MSS belonging to the Prince Maurokordatos of Wallachia, obtained through the agency of Draco Suczo (= Δράκος Σούτζος), "agent du prince de Valachie," c. 1738 and sent to Paris by the French ambassador at Constantinople marquis de Villeneuve; cf. H. Omont, *op. cit.* (above, footnote 35), 683 (n. 1), 684 (n. 3), 685.

Also suppl. gr. 1238 (Astruc–Concasty, 433–434), fols. 119^r–126^v, contains a fragment of a lexicon which, according to Astruc, agrees so far as it goes (from αγ- to αφ-) with Coisl. gr. 393 (= Π), and possibly also suppl. gr. 1255 (five folios from a XIII s. MS described as containing an abbreviated form of Zonaras, Lexicon).

Rome, Bibl. Angelica, gr. 6 (Franchi de' Cavalieri–Muccio, 36). This MS contains a conflation of the shorter version of Ps.-Zonaras with the **g**-recension of St. Cyril's Lexicon.

Vienna, Oesterr. Nationalbibl., phil. gr. 233 (Hunger 342). XV s. This MS also contains (fols. 9^r–191^r) a mixed text combining a version similar to **p4** with some other unknown source.

---

[49] In a reply (dated February 21, 1969) to a request for a microfilm the head of the manuscript collection of the library informed me that the MS "ist völlig kriegszerstört und nicht mehr lesbar."

To the shorter version apparently belonged the lost MS of the monastery τοῦ Σουμελᾶ in Trabzon, to judge from the meager specimens published by A. Papadopoulos-Kerameus in his description of the MS. (p. 304),

Affiliations of the Manuscripts

A together with Aa, Ab, Am, Ap, and Av form an easily-recognizable family (**p1**).[50] A is clearly the oldest and best representative of the family, indeed it seems to be the ancestor of all the other MSS. It is only rarely that one of the latter records a better reading; cf. ξ5: κομεῖσθαι A vs. κοσμεῖσθαι Aa, Ab,[51] which is almost certainly due to emendation.

The **p1** family is clearly interpolated especially in the beginning.[52] In the sections studied here interpolation appears in the form of a few additional glosses (cf. θ56, 71, ξ79) or expanded explanations (cf. ξ44; cf. also θ22, ξ48). The other features of the family include omissions of glosses (θ3, 10–14, 18, 26, 30, 44, 51; ξ10, 21) or of parts thereof (cf. θ21, 29, 35, 40, 42, 43, 49, 50; ξ18, 35), as well as peculiar readings without parallels in any other family or independent MS.[53]

The other MSS contain a very abbreviated text. Aa has 22 regular **p**-entries (plus a number of additional ones) in the θα-section out of a total of 52, and 42 in the ξ-section out of a total of 69. The others have even fewer entries. Am, the shortest of all, has 13 entries in the θα- and 21 in the ξ- section.

Ap and Av are especially close: cf. θ9, 16; ξ17, 22, 34, 36, 38, 40.[54] Moreover, some of the marginalia of Av[55] reappear in Ap either as independent glosses[56] or in the form of additions to the

---

[50] Cf. especially the characteristic introductory note Δεῖ εἰδέναι κλπ. on which cf. note 48 above.

[51] For the superior readings of Ap in θ29, 40 and ξ20, see below, p. 449.

[52] Cf. P. Burguière, op. cit. (above, under A), and the title of the lexicon. Burguière maintains that A's text is essentially St. Cyril interpolated with glosses from Ps.-Zonaras. This is true only for the beginning of the lexicon. From letter *theta* on the opposite seems to be the case.

[53] Cf. θ34 (ἀνδρία), 35 (καὶ πᾶν vs. ἢ πᾶν), 45 (θακέουσι), 49 (ὡς Ἰώσηπος); ξ33 (ὄνομα κύριον), 45 (om. ἤ); ξ30 is split into two glosses, whereas ξ42 has been attached to ξ41, as if a part of the latter's explanation.

[54] The order and number of glosses with the exception of the additional matter listed by Ap is with few exceptions the same.

[55] These originate from different sources one of which was clearly a **p**-MS.

[56] In the θα-section these glosses appear in two batches, one between θ25–27 and the other at the end of the entire section.

explanation of the original entries.[57] Since these were added in the margins of Av by more than one hand, it becomes evident that Ap was derived from Av. All the superior readings of Ap are found in glosses originating from these additions (cf. θ29, 40, and ξ20).

Am is closely related to Av; cf. especially θ9 (which both split into two separate glosses), 17, ξ8, 15, 34, 69. Each MS has separative errors of its own, but Am is generally inferior to Av especially in the total number of glosses.[58] Both MSS descend from a common parent. Finally Ab shows a few common errors with Am, Ap, Av (cf. ξ15, 34, 69). It also agrees with them in listing θ52 before θ50. The **p1** family stemma appears therefore as follows:

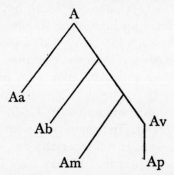

The second and clearly the oldest family (**p2**) is also the most numerous, consisting of twelve MSS: B, C, D, E, F, G, H, I, J, K, L, and M. Their common origin is established beyond any doubt by the error of haplography which has combined θ42 and 43 into one hybrid gloss.[59] Other common readings are $\tau\iota\theta\hat{\omega}$ (θ3),[60] $\dot{\alpha}\pi o\theta\alpha\nu\hat{\omega}\nu$ (θ11),[61] omission of $\theta\dot{\alpha}\lambda\lambda os$ (after $\kappa\dot{\alpha}\lambda\lambda os$)[62] in θ35 and the spelling $\tau\alpha\rho\dot{\alpha}\tau\tau\epsilon\iota$ in θ39.[63] In the ξ-section with the exception of L, M (cf. below) the MSS of this family agree in omitting ξ31, 32, 33;[64] in

[57] Cf. especially ξ22, 55, 58, 68.

[58] Thus all Am glosses are found in Av but Am omits a number of Av glosses in the ξ-section.

[59] The same error is found also in **p3**, which seems to be an offshoot of the present family (cf. below).

[60] $\tau\dot{\iota}\theta\hat{\omega}$ in M.

[61] Also in Pc, V, Σ, Φ, Ψ. B, a thoroughly erratic MS, reads $\dot{\alpha}\pi o\theta\dot{\alpha}\nu\omega\nu$.

[62] Also omitted by **p4**, V, W, Z, Ω.

[63] Also in Pc, Z. K has $\tau\alpha\rho\dot{\alpha}\tau\tau\eta$.

[64] ξ31, 32 are also omitted by **p3** and by some MSS of the **p1** family, while ξ33 is attested only by **p6**, A, L, M, Y, Γ, Σ, Φ, Ψ, Ω.

reading σχέσεων in ξ8; and in omitting the ἀντὶ τοῦ in the explanation of ξ60. The variable treatment of the lemma of θ2 and the explanation of ξ52 suggest that the archetype had supralinear readings such as those found in G and I.

Within the family there are two apparently distinct groups characterized by common errors. A striking feature of the first group (**p21**) is the listing of the ξε-glosses before those beginning with ξα-(cf. G, H, I, J, K). To this group L and M belong but only in the θα-section. Of the MSS that comprise this group, K stands quite apart from the rest and must have either branched out early or been emended. The closeness of the other MSS is shown by such readings as Χαρχη-δονίους (θ17), τὸ θάλλων (θ35), βοτάνη [65] (ξ22), ἰχθῦς (ξ29), etc.

H, J, L, and M form an interesting sub-group; cf. θ2 (θωακοι accented variously by each MS), 16 (τὰ εἰς πυρίδας), 48 (omission of the explanation), 50 (θαμαί). In the ξ-section, however, L and M have completely broken their affiliation with **p2** and show greater affinity with branch **b** (cf. below). Their common exemplar has clearly followed two different sources.[66] Of the two MSS H and J, the latter seems superior. Its separative errors (θ1, ξ35, 39) are trifling as against those of H (cf. especially θ20, 35, 36, ξ53). Moreover, there is slight evidence that H may have been copied from J. In ξ58 J has squeezed in the explanation by erasing part of the lemma and using the margins—clearly an afterthought. The explanation is missing from **p22** as well as from I and K. It is clear that we have here an omission that may go back to **p2**. J as well as G probably corrected the omission[67] and H copied it from J.

The second group (**p22**) consists of five MSS (B, C, D, E and F). Common readings unattested outside of the group: διάθεσις for

---

[65] I reads βατάνη. The reading βοτάνη is found also in B, C, and was apparently the original reading of Pb.

[66] A typical example of a MS with split allegiance is cod. Messan. S. Salv. 167 (XIII s.) which in its first half follows St. Cyril's **n** recension while in its latter half it follows cod. Haun. 1968 (Drachmann's *h*), a member of the **g** recension. On this MS cf. Drachmann 14–15, Latte xlviii and my article "New Fragments of Ancient Greek Poetry," *Gr. Rom. Byz. Stud.* 9 (1968), 267–268. Actually the two parts written by two different hands come from two different volumes accidentally bound together, since the first part breaks at the end of a quire and the second begins with another quire. A copy, however, of such a MS would not supply any clue as to where the break occurred.

[67] The supplement is an easy one (ξυνιέναι : συνιέναι) and could have occurred independently.

διάχυσις (θ24), θαλατοπορῆσαι (θ38), omission of τῶν ποντικῶν (ξ34), addition of δίφθογγον[68] (ξ49), ξυμβαίην : συμβαίην (ξ57).[69] This group shares a number of peculiar readings with I (cf. θ12, ξ20, 21, 22, 30, 41), which thus appears to stand between the two groups. This can only be explained if **p22** was not a group which sprang independently from **p2** but was derived from an immediate ancestor of I. The correct alphabetical order in the ξ-section may be due to correction. There are indeed no other errors attested in **p21** which could not have been corrected easily by **p22**.

Within the **p22** group there is a distinct sub-group consisting of D, E, and F (cf. especially ξ7, 39, 46, 47, 48),[70] and furthermore of E and F. The agreement of the last two goes so far that the question of direct relationship arises. F is not only somewhat younger but it is generally inferior to E. It also follows E even where the latter seems to be corrected (cf. especially θ17, 24, 48). It must therefore have been copied from E. B and C, although both late, were derived independently from an ancestor of D, E, F.[71]

The relationship of the **p2** mss can be illustrated in the stemma below (the relative position of G, K, I, **p22**, insofar as our evidence goes appears correct, but may be slightly modified with the study of larger portions).

Closely related to **p2** (cf. especially θ2,[72] 42, ξ60) is the **p3** family which consists of six mss: P, Pb, Pc, Pe, Po, and Pv.[73] It is a closely-knit family with clear signs of interpolation from a ms of the so-called **g**-recension of St. Cyril's *Lexicon*;[74] cf. especially additional glosses θ57, ξ86, 87, 88, and 102,[75] and increments in glosses θ1, 22, and

---

[68] This reading also in **p3**. For the relationship of **p3**, **p22**, cf. below.

[69] Cf. also ὁ ὑπό (θ7); also θ17 (Χαρκηδονίους), θ24 (θαλπτωρή), ξ52 (addition of ἢ ὁ κοντός cf. below), ξ65 (ξυνίασιν/ξυνίασις), which may descend from **p22** although they are not attested in all the mss.

[70] Cf. also ξ22 where all other **p2** mss read βοτάνη (βατάνη I) as against βοτάνης of D, E, F, which must be due to correction.

[71] The reading θάωκοι (θ2) indeed suggests that B may have been copied (with many errors to be sure) from the archetype of the entire group.

[72] The reading θάκοι καὶ θῶκοι clearly originated from the reading θ ᾷ′κοι (cf. app. criticus).

[73] The ξ-section of P is missing (cf. description above).

[74] On the **g**-recension cf. Drachmann 11 sqq., Latte xlvii.

[75] All the additional glosses of this family, with the exception of θ62, ξ80 and the false glosses ξ72, 84, 105 (originating probably from supralinear variant readings), are found also in **g**. Note also that all but one (ξ102) of the additional glosses beginning with ξυ- are

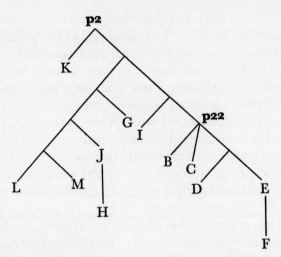

§62.⁷⁶ The other extraneous material may come from another source,⁷⁷ or may be due to error and trivial elaboration.⁷⁸

Among the characteristic features of this family are omissions of entries (θ35, §31–33), or individual words (cf. θ9, 11, 26, 44; §12), different word order within the entries (cf. θ4, 12, 31) and plain blunders or spelling errors (cf. θ14, 16, 33, 40, 49; §10, 36, 49,⁷⁹ 54, 65). Occasional superior readings (cf., e.g., §46) are clearly due to the influence of outside sources, such as the Cyrillean **g** recension.

The exact relationship of **p3** with **p2** is somewhat problematic. In some rather trivial instances (θ3, 11, 17, 39) it shows a superior text as compared to the entire **p2** family. There are three cases, however, in which it clearly agrees with **p22** against all other **p2** MSS (cf. θ7, §48 [D, E, F], 49; cf. also §59). In view of the reading $\xi\,\acute{\omega}\,\nu$ (or $\xi\,\hat{\omega}\,\nu$) $\kappa\alpha\grave{\iota}\,\xi\,\hat{\omega}\,\theta\,\epsilon\,\nu$ (in the lemma of §69) which apparently has

---

listed as a group (in violation of the principle followed in the arrangement of the Lexicon) between genuine glosses §67 and 68.

⁷⁶ Cf. also §17, 58, 68.

⁷⁷ Cf. add. gloss. §81 and additions in genuine glosses §2, 43, 56.

⁷⁸ Thus add. gloss. §72 is probably a *falsa lectio* for $\xi\,\alpha\,\nu\,\theta\,\iota\,\kappa\,o\,\mu\,o\,s$ (§3); and $\xi\,\acute{\omega}\,\nu$ (§105) preceding $\xi\,\hat{\omega}\,\theta\,\epsilon\,\nu$ points to the reading $\xi\,\acute{\upsilon}\,\nu\,\theta\,\epsilon\,\nu$ of §69 (cf. app. crit.). On the other hand the addition of $\acute{\eta}\,\sigma\upsilon\nu\omega\mu\sigma\sigma\acute{\iota}\alpha$ in §48 and $\kappa\sigma\iota\nu\acute{\alpha}$ in §51 are trivialities inserted by the scribe of the archetype or his exemplar. The addition in §48 is found independently also in **p1**.

⁷⁹ The reading $\xi\,\upsilon\,\xi\,\epsilon\,\acute{\iota}\,\alpha$ is actually found only in Pb, Pc, Pe. There is no doubt, however, that in Po, Pv this entry has been corrected.

originated in a supralinear reading ($\xi v \overset{\omega}{\nu} \theta \epsilon \nu$ [80]), the agreement with **p22** may well be accidental. Note also that in two of the three cases the **p22**, **p3** readings have independent parallels in completely unrelated groups of MSS.

A close examination of the MSS reveals that P must be the archetype of the family. For not only do the readings of P invariably occur in most or all the other MSS,[81] but there is evidence that at least some of them did actually originate in P. Thus the omission of the connective $\kappa \alpha \acute{\iota}$ in $\theta 26$ and 44 is clearly due to negligence on the part of P's rubricator as is shown both by the space left by the scribe in the place of $\kappa \alpha \acute{\iota}$ and by $\theta 2$ where in a similar situation the conjunction $\kappa \alpha \acute{\iota}$ is written with red ink. The same rubricator is responsible for the variant $\theta \acute{\alpha} \kappa \mu \alpha \hat{\iota} o s$ in $\theta 4$.[82] Moreover, $\theta 7$ and 8, which are missing from all the other **p3** MSS are listed in P after $\theta 17$ but cancelled by the original scribe (probably because they disturb the alphabetical order) before the rubricator took over, since the customary red initials of the lemmata are missing. Finally all **p3** MSS list $\theta 62$ which was added in the margin of P before entry $\theta 27$.[83]

Of the other members of this family Po is clearly an apograph of Pb[84] with a number of blunders of its own and a few minor improvements; cf. $\theta 42$ ($\acute{\epsilon} \pi \iota \theta \upsilon \mu \hat{\omega} \nu$ vs. $\acute{\epsilon} \pi \iota \theta \upsilon \mu \acute{\omega} \nu$), $\xi 49$ ($\xi \upsilon \lambda \epsilon \acute{\iota} \alpha$ vs. $\xi \upsilon \xi \epsilon \acute{\iota} \alpha$). Both the script and the tendency to misplace the accent betray a non-Greek scribe.[85]

Pv is very close to Pe as is shown by a number of characteristic errors that it shares with it; cf. $\theta 11$ ($\grave{\alpha} \pi \grave{o} \theta \alpha \acute{\iota} \omega \nu$), 17 ($K \alpha \rho \chi \eta \delta o \nu \acute{\iota} o \upsilon s$),

---

[80] $\nu \nu$ was usually joined in a ligature consisting of three loops. Thus $\xi \omega \nu$ as well as $\xi \alpha \nu$ are possible variations of $\xi \upsilon \nu$ due to a misunderstanding of the ligature.

[81] There are only two minor errors in accentuation in the $\theta \alpha$-section without parallels in any other MS of this family: $\pi \acute{\alpha} \sigma \eta s$ ($\theta 10$) and $\grave{\alpha} \nu \delta \rho \epsilon \hat{\iota} \omega s$ ($\theta 51$).

[82] Only Pc omits the unwarranted θ, but even there the space left before the word as well as the position of the breathing show that the scribe read $\theta \acute{\alpha} \kappa \mu \alpha \hat{\iota} o s$ (with the θ written in red ink) in his exemplar, and that the rubricator whether deliberately or not left the space unfilled.

[83] I am deeply indebted to Mr. Charles Astruc of the Bibliothèque Nationale for examining the MS on my behalf and answering questions on the origin of the cancellation and the marginal addition which could not be determined from the microfilm.

[84] Cf., e.g. $\xi 49$ where Po's $\acute{\epsilon} \xi \upsilon \lambda \acute{\iota} \alpha$ is clearly a misunderstanding of the script of Pb. In $\xi 8$ Pb's dittography $\acute{o} \ \acute{o} \ \pi \acute{\alpha} \sigma \eta s$ has been changed to $\acute{o} \ \acute{o} \pi \acute{\alpha} \sigma \eta s$ in Po. Note also that in some cases (e.g., $\sigma \chi \acute{\epsilon} \sigma \epsilon \omega \nu$, $\kappa \alpha \tau \alpha \gamma \acute{\omega} \gamma \iota o \nu$ in $\xi 8$, 11) the scribe has crossed out the ending and inserted the corresponding tachygraphic sign in order to imitate his model.

[85] Cf. $\pi \acute{\alpha} \nu \tau o s$ ($\theta 9$), $\kappa \acute{\alpha} \rho \pi \omega \nu$ ($\theta 20$), $\chi \acute{\alpha} \rho \alpha$ ($\theta 24$), $\pi \acute{\upsilon} \kappa \nu \alpha$ ($\theta 28$) etc.

19 (θαλαῖος), 21 (ὀνομούσης),[86] 22 (ξύλα for ξύλον), 49 (ἀλπίδι), ξ20 (γενόμενος), 23 (ἄλειπτον) etc. Each MS has separative errors of its own.[87] However, Pv in some cases has superior readings as against all **p3** MSS, sometimes even of the archetype; cf. especially θ14 (ἀπαλός vs. ἀπαλός), 17 (βόρειον vs. βόριον), and ξ49 (ξυλεία vs. ξυξεία). It is therefore a corrected MS. Thus it is not clear whether Pv reflects the readings of a common exemplar whenever its text is superior to Pe or has corrected its exemplar which in this case may well be Pe itself.[88]

Pe shows signs of affinity with Pb as against Pc; cf. θ3 (om. θᾶκος), 19 (θαλο***-θαλαῖος for θαλάμιος), ξ8 (σχέσεων), 23 (ἀλειπτόν-ἄλειπτον), 36 (add ὁ ἐξεσμένος before τόπος), 40 (ὁ κυνός), 65 (ξυνία-σον). Also in the title of the lexicon (cf. above). Pe is usually inferior to Pb, whereas the latter has few and insignificant separative errors.[89] Some of Pe's superior readings (cf. ξ48: ξυνόμοσις in Pe vs. ξυνόμωσις in Pb, Pc) may be due to emendation based on the text itself, while θαλαῖος for θαλο*** seems to be an unsuccessful correction. However, Pe seems to be independent of Pb in at least one significant point: θαλέθοντες: θάλλοντες vs. θαλέθονες: θάλλονες[90] (θ48).

The stemma of the **p3** family thus appears as follows:

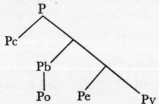

Q, R, S, T, and U form another family (**p4**) with very distinct features. These include omission of glosses (θ3, 8, 9–14; ξ10, 21, 33), occasional additions (cf. θ44, ξ48), a predilection for shorter entries (cf. θ35, 36, 43, 49, 50; ξ18, 23, 35), and other changes within the explanations (cf. θ24, 35; ξ4, 34, 53).[91]

[86] Clearly from a misunderstanding of the abbreviation ὀν° μούσης.

[87] Cf. especially θ 17, 29, 47, and ξ34, 64 for Pv and θ3, ξ3, 22, 28 for Pe.

[88] There is slight evidence in support of this view from the fact that the dittography θάτερον: ἑκατέρου, θάτερον: ἑκάτερος in Pv corresponds to change of page in Pe.

[89] θ2 (κάθεδροι), 23 (κώπαι), 42 (ἐπιθυμών), ξ8 (ὁ ὁ πάσης).

[90] Clearly on account of a false abbreviation in P.

[91] Other special readings: θ6 (omission of τούς), 16 (θαλοί), ξ23 (τὸ λούεσθαι), 37 (κνισμονή), 48 (συνόμοσις).

Within the family there are two easily-recognized branches: Q, R, and S, U. The special bond that exists between Q and R is well illustrated in the following unique readings: θαλαμίδιον (θ23), κακῶ (θ46), ὑποδέχομαι καὶ συναθροίζω (ξ16), ξύννενος (ξ42). Of the two R is by far the fuller and better.[92] The pair S, U has also some pronounced features such as interpolated matter from an outside source in the form of additional glosses[93] and additions within the entries (cf. θ22, ξ35), omission of some entries (θ26, ξ54, 55, 56), as well as a number of plain blunders (cf. θ2, 35, 39; ξ8, 19, 28, 34, 38, 58, 68). In θ41 συχνάζει has been changed to πυκνάζει. A closer examination shows that S is in reality a copy of U. For not only has S faithfully adopted all the readings of U including one marginal addition,[94] but it has clearly misread U in a number of cases. Thus the reading χθράσος in θ29 is but a misunderstanding of the writing of U where a circumflex from the line below touches the lower part of the letter θ of θράσος and could be read by a careless scribe as χθ. In ξ77 S reads πρωῖος vs. πρῶιος (i.e. π(ατ)ρώϊος) in U, and in ξ76 it reads ξενοπόγους from a misunderstanding of the monocondylion-type writing of U.

T besides a good many blunders of its own shares a number of readings and errors with both groups. Thus it agrees with Q, R in θ7 (om. ὁ), 23 (ἐναύνουσαι), ξ8 (σχέσεων), 48 (ξυνωσία);[95] and with S, U in ξ16 (ὑποδέχομαι vs. ὑποδέχομαι καὶ συναθροίζω),[96] 42 (ξύνενος vs. ξύννενος). The agreement with S, U in ξ16 is, I believe, decisive for the position of T in the stemma. Agreement in error between T and Q, R must reflect the reading of the family archetype, whereas the corresponding superior readings in S, U must be due to emendation which may or may not have been influenced by the source of the additional glosses.[97]

---

[92] Besides other errors (cf. θ1, 51, ξ20, 25, etc.), Q shows extensive omissions in θ17, 25, 35, 42; ξ34, 35, 49, 62.

[93] These as a rule appear betweeen sections in clusters of two or more.

[94] Cf. θ22; the addition, however, is by the first hand.

[95] Cf. also θ23 (θαλάμιον vs. θαλαμίδιον).

[96] Since all three mss also omit ξ17, it seems that we have here a typical case of omission due to haplography.

[97] All these glosses with one exception (ξ77) have parallels in one family of the v-recension of St. Cyril's Lexicon, which I call v3, and in particular in the following two mss: Vossianus gr. Q 63 and Monacensis gr. 230; cf. also (with some omissions) Monacensis gr. 298 and Laurentianus plut. 5.20. Some of these glosses seem to have replaced

The family stemma can be drawn as follows:

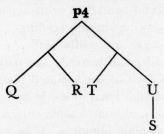

Closely connected with **p4** is X, as is shown by unique agreements in θ6, ξ23, and the second (regular) entry θεόληπτος, where they agree in supplanting συσχεθείς with συλληφθείς. Agreement (but not unique) can also be seen in θ16, 35, 36, 49, 50, ξ18, 35, 37, 47, 52, and 69, and in the omission of glosses θ3, 8, ξ10, 21, 33. The agreement is quite consistent, apart from the peculiarities of **p4** noted above and the frequent but minor errors of X. Consequently they must have originated from a common exemplar.

Four MSS (V, W, Y, Z) form the **p5** family. This family has been inflated with interpolations which resemble the fuller version. None of the MSS of this family, however, appears to be complete in so far as the number and the extent of the entries of the archetype are concerned. Thus W, Y, Z omit θ36, which in V appears misplaced (i.e. before θ29), while V, W, Z omit ξ33; Y, Z also omit θ3, 12, 13, 14; and V, W omit ξ24; finally individual MSS omit a number of genuine glosses.[98] It is therefore understandable that there should be no complete agreement in the listing of the additamenta. For reasons that will become evident in the course of discussion, I consider that all additions even when appearing in only one MS of this family, especially if they have parallels in the fuller version, go back to the family archetype.

This archetype listed five additional independent glosses in the θα-[99]

---

genuine **p**-glosses; cf. θ55 with θ26. Note also that θ27 is out of place in the midst of a batch of additional glosses, whereas θ1 is listed twice, in the original position and among the additamenta.

[98] W omits ξ18, Y omits θ9, 10, 11 and ξ20; and Z omits θ7, 8, 40, 45, 48 and ξ52, 56.

[99] θ59, 61, 70, 75b, 76. To these the etymology of the letter *theta* should be added which appears at the beginning of the θ-section in V, W, while in the fuller version it occurs among the θη-glosses. Of these θ70 has been conflated with θ11 by W. Y lists no other additional gloss in the θα-section except θ70. Z omits add. gl. θ61.

and another five in the ξ-section.[100] All but one (ξ95) have parallels in the fuller version and the majority of them appear there as independent glosses. However, θ59, 70, and ξ94 appear conflated with related entries (θ9, 21, and ξ40), and ξ82 is much more extensive in the fuller version than in **p5**.

The special relationship that exists between this family and the published version is carried also within the entries either in the form of additions to the explanations (cf. θ13, 14,[101] 33, ξ56,[102] 62, 65,[103] 67,[104]) or in the form of common readings (cf. θ25, 35, 38, ξ30); cf. also the correct reading $\xi \upsilon \sigma \tau \iota \delta \alpha$ in ξ47. The significance of these similarities for the origin of the versions will be assessed later.

Apart from the readings common to this family and to the fuller version, the four MSS have a small number of common variants the most important of which is $\dot{o}$ $\varphi \iota \lambda o s$ $\xi \acute{\epsilon} v o s$ (ξ9).[105]

Within the family the four MSS are grouped differently in each section examined. Thus in the $\theta \alpha$-section V and W stand consistently together as against Y, Z,[106] whereas in the ξ-section W is close to Z in at least one important respect, the order of glosses ξ1–5.[107] V on the other hand is close to Y in listing additional gloss ξ95 which the other two omit. However, W agrees here again with V in omitting ξ24 and in changing $\sigma \upsilon \nu o \upsilon \sigma \iota \alpha$ to $o \dot{\upsilon} \sigma \iota \alpha$ (ξ45). Since the position of ξ1–5 after the $\xi \epsilon$-section has parallels outside of this family, (cf. **p21** above) the correct order may be due to independent correction and may not reflect the reading of the archetype. If this is true, one can dismiss the possibility of close relationship between V and Y in the ξ-section and connect V to W as in the $\theta \alpha$-section.

---

[100] ξ80, 82, 83, 94, 95. Of these ξ83 has been conflated with ξ22 by Z, while ξ94 is conflated with ξ40 in Y and is absent from Z; ξ95 is absent from both W and Z.

[101] The additions in both θ13 and 14 are listed only in V, W; Y, Z omit the two glosses altogether.

[102] Z omits the entire gloss.

[103] The addition is absent in Y and quite shortened in V.

[104] There are only traces of the addition in Y. In V only the first line. Note that the addition in θ6 found in V, W has no parallel in the fuller version.

[105] Cf. also $\tau \alpha \nu \alpha o \acute{o} s$ (θ11), $\theta \epsilon \rho \mu \acute{\alpha} \nu \alpha \iota$ (θ37), and $\theta \overset{\alpha}{\alpha}' \kappa o \iota$ in θ2 (W has $\theta \hat{\omega} \kappa o \iota$, Y $\theta \acute{\alpha} \kappa o \iota$)

[106] Common V, W readings: the etymology of *theta* in the title, the conflation of θ2 with θ3, the addition in θ6 and the splitting of θ50 into two glosses; also $\kappa o \iota \tau \hat{\omega} v$ in θ26. Y, Z agree in a negative way by omitting glosses θ3, 12, 13, 14 and part of θ50.

[107] The two MSS also have preserved alone the additions in ξ65, 67 in their entirety.

This will be consistent not only with the reading οὐσία (cf. above) but also with such readings as κομεῖσθαι (ξ5), Ξήϊνος (ξ21), and ξυνίασιν (ξ65). As for the relationship of Y, Z, there are no compelling reasons besides common omissions of glosses (which may well be accidental in view of the fact that both these MSS also omit other glosses individually) to support a theory of a common examplar.

Quite closely connected with **p5** is Ω; cf. θ2,[108] 25, ξ 47, and especially ξ67 where it agrees closely with Y.[109] It also shares two additional glosses with **p5** (ξ80 and 82) but shows no traces of the other additional material. On the whole its text is marred by numerous errors in spelling and by arbitrary and unnecessary changes (some completely ridiculous; cf. θ22, 41, 45, etc.) in the explanations usually in the form of addition of τό, ἤ, καί etc. This may explain away the only seemingly important difference in θ35 (cf. below, note 111).

Three MSS (Δ, Λ, Π) form the sixth family (**p6**). Their common (and exclusive) readings are more frequent in the θα- than in the ξ-section, and consist of additions or omissions of words within the explanations (cf. θ14, 44, 49; ξ30, 53), substitution of words (θ11, ξ61), or plain corruption of the text (θ19).

Δ and Λ display a further degree of closeness (cf. θ15, 25, 51; ξ41)[110] and must either have come from the same source, or Δ have been copied from Λ. Lack of photographs for verification of some finer points prevents me from elaborating on this point.

Akin to this group, especially in the ξ-section, is Φ. It is a MS full of errors, omissions of some glosses (θ18, 19, ξ19, 69) as well as a small number of additional glosses clearly from the fuller version. Its special relationship with **p6** is shown in θ49 (θαλπομόνους). In four more instances it agrees closely with Δ and Λ only (ξ4, 22, ξ30 = καὶ Ξιφῖνος, ξ34 = τὸν πόντον σου); see also below.

---

108 θωάκοι comes clearly from a misunderstanding of the reading found (among other MSS) also in V, Z.

109 Further agreement with Y in minor points, mostly in spelling errors: Μούσης (θ21), ξενοδοχεῖον (ξ14a), ἤτοι (ξ34) γαμετῆ (ξ46), and ξυλίφιον (ξ54). On the other hand Ω agrees in error with V, W in θ26 (κοιτῶν) and ξ65 (ξυνίασιν). But all these may well be accidental.

110 Cf. also ξ30, 34 and the use of the plural form ἀρσενικά in the titles.

Two more MSS, Γ and Σ which are close to **p6** (cf. especially $\theta 49$ and $\xi 69$), appear to be consistently close so as to form a group of their own. The agreement covers many minor points besides those that they share with **p6**, Φ (cf. $\theta 15$, 17, 26, 35, 42, $\xi 18$, 23, 35, 47, 49, 51, 61). On the whole Σ, the older of the two, is superior to Γ. Besides it seems as if Γ has been influenced by the supralinear readings of Σ in $\theta 2$, $\xi 52$. It is quite possible therefore, that Γ was copied from Σ (or from a descendant of that MS), although lack of photographs of the Athos MS prevents me again from a final judgment on this matter.

Of the remaining MSS Ψ shows no special affiliation with any particular family or group of MSS, but agrees with **p2**, **p3**, **p5** and Ω whenever their readings converge. Conversely L and M in the ξ-section agree consistently with a large group of MSS which includes **p1**, **p4**, **p6** and the related MSS (Γ, Σ, Φ, and X). These two super-groups represent a split in the **p** recension which seems to be an old one, since in both branches there are several thirteenth-century MSS. The following chart illustrates the variants of the two sub-archetypes of the recension:

a (**p2**, **p3**, **p5**, Ψ, Ω)	b (**p1**, **p4**, **p6**, X, Γ, Σ, Φ)
$\theta 35.$ $\beta\lambda\acute{\alpha}\sigma\tau\eta\mu\alpha$[111]	$\tau\grave{o}$ $\beta\lambda\acute{\alpha}\sigma\tau\eta\mu\alpha$
$\xi 18.$ add $\xi\epsilon\nu\acute{o}\omega$[112]	omit $\xi\epsilon\nu\acute{o}\omega$
$\xi 26.$ $\xi\acute{\iota}\rho\iota s$	$\xi\acute{\iota}\rho\upsilon s$
$\xi 35.$ add $o\mathring{v}\tau\omega$ $\Phi\acute{\iota}\lambda\omega\nu$	omit $o\mathring{v}\tau\omega$ $\Phi\acute{\iota}\lambda\omega\nu$
$\xi 47.$ $\xi\upsilon\sigma\tau\acute{\iota}\sigma\tau\alpha$[113]	$\xi\upsilon\sigma\acute{\iota}\sigma\tau\alpha$
$\xi 49.$ $\xi\upsilon\lambda\epsilon\acute{\iota}\alpha$	$\xi\acute{\upsilon}\lambda\epsilon\iota\alpha$[114]
$\xi 69.$ $\xi\mathring{\omega}\theta\epsilon\nu$	$\xi\acute{\upsilon}\nu\theta\epsilon\nu$

The **b**-MSS also agree in omitting gloss $\theta 8$ in the $\theta\alpha$-section.

---

[111] **p3** omits the gloss altogether, while **p1** omits the first part of the explanation. Ω agrees with the **b**- MSS here. Since however, it is the habit of its scribe to insert the article even when it is completely unwarranted by the context (cf. $\theta 18$, 37, 39, etc.), the agreement is completely fortuitous.

[112] Ω omits $\xi 18$.

[113] Note however that **p5** and Ω have restored the correct form $\xi\upsilon\sigma\tau\acute{\iota}\delta\alpha$ probably through emendation.

[114] T has $\xi\upsilon\lambda\epsilon\acute{\iota}\alpha$ but this is an easy correction.

The final stemma of the shorter version appears as follows:

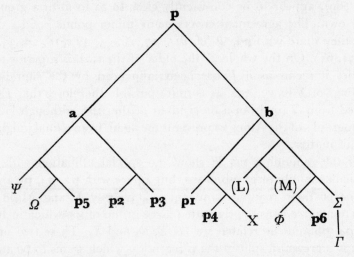

The common origin of **p2, p3** is established beyond any doubt, and so is that of **p5**, *Ω*. That *Ψ* is close to the latter is shown by *θ*35 (*ἡ παῖς* and the development of the latter part of the entry into a separate gloss). **a** probably read *Χαρκηδονίους* in *θ*17, an anagrammatism for *Καρχηδονίους* which has survived in *Ω* and **p22**; **p3, p5**, and *K* have restored the original form probably through emendation. *Ψ* on the other hand together with **p21** show assimilation of *κ* to *χ*. In *θ*25 I cannot explain the reading *μέρος* for *κέρας* found in **p3, p5** (but not in **p2**) except as a coincidence. (For the use of the word *μέρος* cf. *θ*17.)

The common origin of **p4**, *X* has already been discussed. They furthermore agree with **p1** in omitting gloss *ξ*21, the quotation of *θ*35 as well as part of *θ*36 and in reading *σπυρίδια* in *θ*16. The kinship of **p6** with (*Γ*), *Σ*, *Φ* has also been demonstrated in the reading *θαλπομένους* for *ὑποθαλπομένους* (*θ*49). The precise position of L, M in the *ξ*-section is not certain.

In a small number of instances the stemma as reconstructed above does not account for readings which appear in isolated groups not directly related; cf. *θ*7 (*ὁ ὑπὸ Θεοῦ*), *ξ*8 (*σχέσεων*), *ξ*12 (omission of *δέ*), *ξ*21 (*Ξ ἥϊνος*), *ξ*48 (addition of *συνωμοσία*). In all these cases the agreement is probably coincidental, especially since in most of them the MSS within a family disagree.

The Text

To illustrate and document the preceding discussion I offer here two sample sections (*Stichproben*) taken from about the middle of the lexicon. The order of the genuine glosses is that of the presumed archetype. Variations in the order of the lemmata are recorded immediately below the text (ORD.). The additional glosses (θ53–76, ξ70–105) are listed in alphabetical order and are accompanied by the *sigla* of the MSS or families in which they occur. The list of PARALLELS (at the end of each section) is as extensive and complete as possible. The order in which they are listed is determined first by the degree of their closeness to our text and subsequently by their relative dates.[115] The critical apparatus (APP.) contains a complete list of all variants and errors to serve both as a reference to the discussion of manuscript affiliations and as a check of my conclusions by the reader.[116] It is not, strictly speaking, critical in that it makes no distinction between true variants and trivia. In a truly critical edition it will be reduced considerably.

---

[115] The abbreviations are similar to those used by K. Latte in his edition of Hesychius, vol. I, pp. lii–liv, with the following additions and/or changes: *AG* = *Anecdota Graeca* ed. L. Bachmann et al.; Ammon. = Ammonius ed. K. Nickau (Leipzig 1966); *EG* for E. Gud.; *Et. Sym.* for the unpublished *Etymologicum Symeonis*; Hes. for Hesychius; Ps.-Herod. for Herodianus, *Partitiones*, ed. by J. Fr. Boissonade (London 1819 = Amsterdam 1963); Lagarde = Paul de Lagarde, *Onomastica sacra* (Göttingen 1887 = Hildesheim 1966); *Lex. Patm.* = Lexicon Patmiacum, ed. by J. Sakkelion in *Bull. Corr. Hellén.* 1 (1877), 1–16, 137–155; Orion = *Orionis Thebani Etymologicum*, ed. F. G. Sturz (Leipzig 1820); Pollux = Pollux, *Onomasticon*, ed. E. Bethe (1900–1936); Th. Mag. = Thomas Magister, *Ecloga vocum Atticarum*, ed. Fr. Ritschl (Halle 1832); Tim. = Timaeus, *Lexicon vocum Platonicarum*, ed. D. Ruhnken (Leiden 1789). Note also that the Lexicon Bachmannianum is indicated as Σ, that various families of St. Cyril's Lexicon (as indicated by Drachmann) are given in parenthesis after the siglum K, and that the abbreviation schol. followed by a simple reference to Homeric passages indicates the so-called scholia D or Didymi.

[116] The conventions adopted here in designating marginal supralinear or pen corrections and readings (A^{ac}, A^{pc}, A^m, etc.) are similar to those used by Professor Turyn in his *editio maior* of Pindar.

Ἀρχὴ τοῦ θ στοιχείου
Τὸ θ μετὰ τοῦ ᾱ
ἀρσενικόν

1   θαλαμηπόλος : ὁ περὶ τὸν θάλαμον ἀναστρεφόμενος
2   θᾶκοι : καθέδραι, θρόνοι
3   θᾶκος ὁ καὶ θῶκος : παρὰ τὸ θῶ τὸ τίθω γέγονε θᾶκος καὶ θῶκος
4   θαλερός : ἀκμαῖος, ἰσχυρός, νέος
5   θαυμάλωψ : ὁ ἡμίφλεκτος
6   θαιρούς : τοὺς στροφεῖς τῆς θύρας

ORD. 1 bis hab. S, U (alt. post 55)
APP. Titulus: ἀρχὴ (ἀρχῆ P, Pc) τοῦ θῖτα (θήτα Pe) στοιχείου (τὸ στοιχεῖον Pe) P, Pc, Pe
  ἀρχὴ τοῦ θῆτα στοιχείου. ἀρσενικόν Pv
  ἀρχὴ τοῦ θ στοιχείου. τὸ θ μετὰ τοῦ ᾱ A, Ab, Av
  ἀρχὴ τοῦ θ στοιχείου (στοιχείου Ap) μετὰ τοῦ ᾱ Aa, Ap
  ἀρχὴ τοῦ θ στοιχείου μετὰ τοῦ ᾱ. ἀρσενικόν Φ
  ἀρχὴ τοῦ (τῆς L, M) θ. τὸ θ μετὰ τοῦ ᾱ L, M, Ω
  ἀρχὴ (ἀρχῆ T, Π) τοῦ (τὸ C, E) θ μετὰ τοῦ ᾱ (τῆς ἄλφας Π) C, E, T, Π
  ἀρχὴ τοῦ (τὸ B) θ μετὰ τοῦ ᾱ. ἀρσενικόν B, D
  τὸ θ μετὰ τοῦ ᾱ (ἄλφα G, I, S, Ψ) F, G, I, J, K, Q, R, S, U, Y, Z, Ψ
  τὸ θ (ᾱ X) μετὰ τοῦ ᾱ. ἀρσενικόν (ἀρσενικά Γ, Λ) X, Γ, Δ, Λ, Σ
  ἀρσενικόν. τὸ θ μετὰ τοῦ ᾱ H
  θ μετὸ ᾱ Am
  θήτα τὸ στοιχεῖον Ρο
  θήτα τὸ στοιχεῖον. ἀρσενικόν Pb
  θήτα τὸ στοιχεῖον παρὰ τὸ τὴν θέσιν τοῦ παντὸς μιμεῖσθαι ἤτοι τοῦ οὐρανοῦ
    τὸ κυκλοτερὸν καὶ τὸν διὰ μέσου ἄξονα τῇ κατὰ τὸ μέσον μακρᾷ ἔχει V, W
1. θαθαλαμηπόλος J, θαλαμιπόλος S, U (gloss. alt.)   τὸν om. S, τὸ Φ, τὴν (pro
  τόν) T   θάλαἂμον C, τὴν θάλασσαν (pro τὸν θάλαμον) Q   ἀναστρεφόμαινος B
  καὶ φυλάττων add. p3
2. Gloss. om. Ψ   θᾶκοι Δ, Λ: θᾱ̂κοι I, V, Z, Π, Σ, θ[[.̂.]]κοι G, θῶκοι C, E,
  F, K, Q, R, T, W, θώκοι D, θῶκαι S, U, θωάκοι J, θωακοι H, θωάκοι L,
  Φ, θωάκοι Γ, Ω, θωακοί M, θάωκοι B, θάκοι καὶ θῶκοι p3, θάκοι cett.
  καθαῖδραι Ap, κάθεδροι Pb, Ρο, καθέδρα Aa   θρόνοι om. Aa, Ap, θρῶνοι Γ, θρόνοι
  ante καθέδραι X   παρὰ τὸ θῶ τὸ τιθῶ κλπ. (= gloss. θ3) add. V, W
3. Gloss. om. p1, p4, X, Y, Z, Ψ   θᾶκος p6, K: θάκος cett. θώκος L   παρὰ–
  θῶκος om. Φ   περὶ pro παρὰ Pe   τιθῶ (τίθῶ M) p2; cf. V, W (gloss. θ2)   γέγονε–
  θῶκος om. Ω   γίνεται pro γέγονε Π   θᾶκος B, C: om. Pb, Pe, Ρο, Pv, θάκος cett.
  καὶ θώκος V   θᾶκος καὶ θᾶκος W
4. Gloss. om. Ab, Am, Ap, Av   θαλαῖρός Γ, θαλαιρός Y, θαλεροί B   θάκμαῖος
  p3 (exc. Pc), ἀκμαῖος Ω, ἀκμαίως T   ἰσχυρός, νέος om. Aa, ἰσχυρῶς Ap   νέος om.
  Ap, νεός T   νέος ante ἰσχυρός p3
5. Gloss. om. Aa, Am, Ap, Av   θαυμαλώψ A, Ab, θαμάλωψ L, Z, Π, θᾱ̈μάλωψ
  M   explic. om. S   ἡμήφλεκτος M
6. Gloss. om. Aa, Ab, Am, Ap, Av   θαῖρους D, θερούς M   τούς om. p4, X Ψ,
  τοῦς L   στροφεὶς Q, X, Y, Φ, στροφοὺς p3, τροφεῖς Γ   τῆς [[πορ]] θύρας W   ἀπὸ
  τοῦ (τὸ W) δι᾽ αὐτῶν θεῖν τὰς θύρας add. V, W

7 θεόληπτος : ὑπὸ Θεοῦ συσχεθείς

8 θεοσέπτωρ : ὁ θεοσεβής

9 θάνατος : στοιχείων διάζευξις ἢ βίου λύσις, φροντίδων ἀπαλλαγή, ἄδηλος πορεία, τέλος παντὸς ζώου

10 θάνατος Χριστοῦ ἐστι νέκρωσις τῶν σαρκικῶν παθῶν καὶ πάσης δαιμονικῆς ἐνεργείας, φανέρωσις ἀρίστη

11 θάνατος δὲ παρὰ τὸ τείνω τάνατος καὶ θάνατος, ὁ τείνων τὸ σῶμα· ἢ ὅτι τάνασός ἐστιν, ὁ ἐπὶ πάντας ἑαυτὸν διατείνων· ἢ παρὰ τὴν ἄτην, ὃ σημαίνει τὴν βλάβην, γέγονεν ἄνατος καὶ θάνατος, ὁ ἄνευ τῆς ἄτης μένων ἀποθανών· ἢ ἀπὸ τοῦ θεῖν ἄνω τὰς ψυχάς

12 θάλαμος : θάλπαμός τις ὢν παρὰ τὸ θάλπειν

13 θαυμάλωπες : οἱ ἡμίφλεκτοι ἄνθρακες

ORD. 7 tum inter θα- cum inter θε- glossas exhib. **p2, p4, p6,** P (post 17 posteaque deletam), V, W, X, Y, *Γ, Σ, Φ, Ψ*; semel post 50 Ab, Am, Av; post 52 *Ω*, post 71 A, post alt. part. gloss. 9 Ap; Aa, Z omnino carent; ceteri inter θε- gloss. hab.
8 inter θα- et θε- glossas exhib. **p2,** P (cum 7 post 17 similiterque deletam), V, W, Y, *Ψ*; post 52 (cum 7) **p4,** *Ω*; Aa, Am omnino carent; cett. inter θε- gloss.
9–11 post 17 **p3**

APP. 7.[117] ⟨θ⟩εόληπτος P, θεόλυπτος F, W^ac, *Ω*, θαόληπτος X   ὁ ante ὑπὸ add. **p22, p6,** P, S, U   ἀπὸ pro ὑπὸ Av   συσχεθεῖς Am, Ap, Av, L, T, *Ω*, συσχεθεί B
8.[117] ⟨θ⟩εοσέπτωρ P, θεοστέπτωρ *Ψ*   ὁ om. V   θεοσε θ^β ής B, θεόσεβῆς M
9. Gloss. om. **p4,** Y   στοιχείων Am, L, Pv, *Ω*, στοιχεῖον Ap, Av   διάψευξις Z   ἢ βίου λύσις om. Ap   ἢ om. **p3**   βō^ι Φ   φρωντίδων M, ἢ φροντίδων Am   ἀπαλλαγῆ B, M, *Ω*   θάνατος : ἄδηλος πορεία κλπ. sep. Am, Ap, Av   ἄδηλος–ζώου om. Aa   ἄδειλος Am   πορεῖα Am, L, *Φ*   πάντος Ro   ζώου I, *Λ*, ζῶου L, *Φ, Ω*
10. Gloss. om. **p1, p4,** Y   θάνατ(ως) *Ω*   ἐστι om. Z, ἐστιν **p3,** B, I, X, *Γ, Φ*^ac   νέκρωσις bis F   τῶν om. *Π*   πάσης D, L, P, πᾶσις *Φ*   δεμονικῆς *Ω*   ἀρίστη om. *Ω,* ἀρήστη M^ac   γίνεται δὲ παρὰ τὸ τείνω κλπ. (i.e. gloss. θ11) post ἀρίστη add. Z
11. Gloss. om. **p1, p4,** Y, *Ω*   τὸ (ante τείνω) om. *Φ*   τάνασος pro τάνατος Pc, τάνακτος L, M, τάνος F   ὁ τείνω τῶ σῶμα *Φ*   σῶμα M   ἢ (ante ὅτι) om. **p3,** supra lin. add. *Ψ*   τανασός H, I, J, M, V, W, Z *Σ, Φ,* τανοσός L, τάνασοι B, τάνατός F, E   ἐστι C, E, G, H, I, J, L, M, V, W, *Λ, Π, Φ*^ac, ἐστί B   πάντας *Φ*   ἑαυτὸν B, C, M, Ro, Pv, ἑαυτῶν X ἑαυτῆ D   διατείνω *Φ,* διάτει⁀ B, ἀνατείνων *Γ*   ἢ B   ἄτην Pv, ἄττην X   γέγονε Ro, γέγωνεν *Γ, Π*   τῆς (ante ἄτης) om. D   ἄτης Pv   ἀποθανῶν **p2** (exc. B, L), Pc, V, *Σ, Φ, Ψ,* ἀποθάνων B, ἀπὸ θαίων Pe, Pv   ζῶν pro ἀποθανῶν **p6**   θῆν *Ψ,* θῖν Z, ἄνωθεῖν X   χωρισμὸς ψυχῆς ἀπὸ σώματος pro ὁ ἄνευ τῆς ἄτης–ψυχάς W
12. Gloss. om. **p1, p4,** Y, Z   θεάλαμος **p3**   θάλπαμος om. M, θάλπατος K, θάλπομός E, F, θάλπομος I, θαλπομός B, C, D, θάλπωμος Ro^ac   καλεῖται post θάλπαμος add. *Ω*   τί σῶν *Ω*   ὢν M, ὥν X   διὰ pro παρὰ *Π*   παρὰ τὸ θάλπειν ante θάλπαμος **p3**
13. Gloss om. **p1** (exc. Ap), **p4,** Y, Z, in marg. hab. Av   θαυμάλωπες B, θαμάλωπες Ap, θαλαμάλωπες X   ἡμίφλεκτοί B, ἡμίφλεκτοι V, W, X, *Φ,* ἡμήφλεκτοι *Ω*   θάμψαι (θάψαι V, W) γὰρ τὸ καῦσαι add. Av, V, W

[117] Only those MSS are accounted for here which list θ7, 8 in the θα-section whether in the middle or at the end of the section.

14 θαλερός : ὁ ἁπαλός· τὰ γὰρ θάλλοντα φύλλα ἁπαλά
15 θαρραλέος : ἀνδρεῖος
16 θαλλοί : τὰ εἰς τὰς σπυρίδας ἐπιτήδεια
17 θαρσεῖς : τοὺς Καρχηδονίους λέγει τοὺς πρὸς τὸ βόρειον μέρος κειμένους
18 θαρσέων : ἀνδρείων
19 θαλάμιος : ὁ πρὸς τῇ πρώρᾳ καθήμενος

θηλυκόν

20 θαλυσίαι : αἱ τῶν καρπῶν ἀπαρχαί
21 θάλεια : εὐωχία, πανήγυρις καὶ ὄνομα Μούσης
22 θάμνος : φυτὸν πολύκλαδον ἀπὸ ῥίζης
23 θαλαμίδιοι κῶπαι : αἱ ἠρέμα ἐλαύνουσαι

ORD. 15 post 16 A, Ab   16 ante 9 Am   17 post 25 Am   19 post 21 Aa

APP. 14. Gloss. om. **p1**, **p4**, Y, Z   ἁπαλός B, F, H, I, J, L, M, P, Pc, Pe, Po, V, X, *Γ*, *Δ*, *Λ*,
Φ, *Ψ*, *Ω*, ἁπαλός W   καὶ θαλερὸν δάκρυ post ἁπαλός add. V, W   τὰ γὰρ–ἁπαλά
om. *Ω*, τῶν γὰρ θαλλόντων τὰ φύλλα ἁπαλά *Π*   βάλλοντα pro θάλλοντα B   ἁπαλά
p3 (exc. Pb), L, M, W, *Γ*, *Λ*, *Φ*, ἁπαλλά B   εἰσι add. **p6**
15. θαρραλλέος *Δ*, *Λ*, θαραλλέος A, Aa, Am, Ap, Av, *Π*, *Σ*, *Φ*, θαραλέος B, T,
θαραλλαῖος Ab, θαραλλίος *Γ*   ἀνδρείος Aa, Y ὁ ἀνδρείος *Ω*   σπουδαῖος add. Ab
                                                                                                      λ
16. Gloss. om. Aa   θαλλοῖ Y, *Φ*, θάλλοι Av, Ro, θάλοι Ap, θαλοί (θαλοιτά T)
p4   τὰς pro τὰ **p3**, *Φ*   τὰς om. H, J, L, M   σπυρεῖδας *Ω*, πυρίδας H, J, L, M
τὰ (om. X) σπυρίδια (σπηρίδια Am, Ap, Av) **p1**, **p4**, X   ἐπιτήδια *Γ*, ἐπιτήδεια T,
ἐπιτήδεια Ap, Av, *Π*
17. Gloss. om. Aa   θαρσείς S   τοὺς D, R   Καρχηδονίους Pe, Pv, Καρχιδονίους W,
Χαρκηδονίους C, D, E^ac, *Ω*, Χαρχηδονίους **p21**, *Γ*, *Π*, *Σ*, *Ψ*, Χαλκηδονίους E^sl, F Χαρκη-
φονίους B^ac   λέγει–κειμένους om. Am, Q   τούς–κειμένους om. Ap, Av   τούς om. H, J,
L, M τὰς pro τοὺς B   βόριον **p3** (exc. Pv), C, S, T, βόριον *Γ*   μερὸς *Φ*, μέρους B
κειμένου Pv
18. Gloss. om. **p1**, *Φ*   θαρσαίον *Ω*   ἀνδρείων L, M, ἀνδρίων T, τὸ ἀνδρεῖον *Ω*
19. Gloss. om. Ab, Am, Ap, Av, *Φ*   θαλάμενος **p6**, θαλαῖος Pe, Pv, ˙θαλο ***
Pb, Po πρώρα Aa, H, L, T, W^ac, *Γ*, πρόρα Pc, S, τὴν πρώραν *Ψ*, *Ω*
20. Gloss. om. Aa, Ab, Am, Av   θαλύσιαι B, C, E, F, S, W^ac, θαλασίαι H   αἱ B
Ω, οἱ (pro αἱ) Ap   ἀπαρχαί T   κάρπων Ro
21. Gloss. om. Ab, Am, Ap, Av, Z   θάλια **p3** (exc. Po), Aa, V, θαλία Ro   εὐωχεία
X, Y, εὐοχ[[ε΄]]α W, ἡ εὐωχία *Ω*   πανήγυρις–Μούσης om. Aa   καὶ πανήγυρις *Ω*
καὶ ὄνομα Μούσης om. A, T   καὶ ονομούσης Pe, Pv   ὄνομα M, *Ω*   Μούσης L, Y,
Φ, *Ω*
22. Gloss. om. Ab, Am, Av   θάμενος L   τὸ φυτόν τε καὶ πολλύκλαδον *Ω*   πολλύκλαδον X, πλύκλαδον Aa, πολλυκλάδια T, πολύκαρπον Ap   ἀπὸ ῥίζης om. Aa, Ap   βάτος
add. A, ἢ ξύλον (ξύλα Pe, Pv) ἀκανθῶδες (ἀκανθώδες Pc). λέγεται δὲ καὶ ὁ βάτος add.
p3, λέγεται δὲ καὶ βάτος add. S, U^m
23. Gloss. om. Aa, Ab, Am, Ap, Av, X   θαλαμήδιοι E, θαλαμίδιον Q, R, θαλάμιον T   θαλαμήδι, οἱ κῶπαι F   κώπαι Pb, Ro, οἱ κώπαι *Ω*   αἱ T, *Φ*, αἵ *Ω*
ἠρέμα A, C, F, G, H, I, J, K, L, M, Pc, Pe, Po, Q, R, V, Y, Z, *Γ*, *Π*, *Σ*, *Ψ*, ἠρεύμα Pv
ἐναύνουσαι Q, R, T, καὶ ἐλαύνουσαι *Ω*

24 θαλπωρή : τέρψις, χαρά, διάχυσις
25 θαιμάν : ἡ ἀνατολή· τινὲς δὲ τὸ νότιον κέρας φασί
26 θαλάμη καὶ θάλαμος : οἶκος ἢ κοιτών

οὐδέτερον

27 θάμβος : ἔκπληξις, θόρυβος
28 θαμινά : πυκνά, συνεχῆ
29 θάρσος, ἡ εὐτολμία· θράσος δὲ ἡ ἀλόγιστος αὐθάδεια
30 θάτερον θατέρου : ἔτερον ἐτέρου
31 θάτερον : τῶν δύο τὸ ἔτερον
32 θαλπνότερον : λαμπρότερον, θερμότερον
33 θαλυκρόν : διάπυρον
34 θάρρος : ἀνδρεία

ORD. 27 bis hab. Φ (alt. gloss. post 72), post 1 alt. S, U

APP. 24. Gloss. om. Ab, Am, Av   θαλπωρῆ Pc, Ω, θαρπωρή Φ, θαλπτωρή B, C, D
ἡ τέρψις Ω, τέρψις post χαρά p4   χαρά om. Aa, χαρᾶ Y, χάρα Ro   διάχυσις om. Ap,
καὶ διάχυσις Ω   διάθεσις (διάθεσης B) pro διάχυσις p22, θάλψις Aa
25. θαιμᾶν p1, B, C, D, I, L, M, V, Π, Ψ, Ω, θαιμανή X   ἀνατολή D, M, Y, Ω
ἐστίν post ἀνατ. add. Ω   τινὲς–φασί om. Aa, Ap, Av, Q   τινᾶις W   καί ante
τὸ νότιον add. Δ, Λ   νώτιον Ω, νότειον Ab   μέρος pro κέρας p3, p5, Ab Ω   φασίν
p3, A, F, S, Y   λέγουσιν εἶναι ἀλλ' οὐχ' οὕτως pro φασί Ab
26. Gloss. om. p1, S, U   θάλαμη Π   καί om. p3   οἶκος Ω, οἴκος Y, ὁ οἶκος Π
ἢ R, ἢ I   οἰκητῶν pro ἢ κοιτών Pc   κοιτῶν H, J, M, V, W, X, Γ, Σ, Φ, Ψ, Ω,
κοιτῶ T
27. θαύμβος Aa   ἔκπληξις ἐστὶν καὶ θόρυβος Ω   θόρυβος om. Aa, θόριβος Am, ἢ
θόρυβος Γ
28. Gloss. om. Ab, Am, Ap, Av   θαμινᾶ Ab, X   πυκνᾶ Y, πύκνα Ro, πικνά Aa, B,
Π, ταπικνά Ω   συνεχῆ Aa, Pe, Pv, X, Φ, Ψ, συνεχεῖ Pc, συνέχη B, καὶ συνεχῆ Ω
29. Gloss. om. Aa, Ab, Am, Av   θάρσος ἡ εὐτολμία om. Ap   ἡ εὐτολμία θράσος om.
Pv   ἡ om. Z   καὶ τὸ εὔτολμον παράστημα τῆς ψυχῆς (cf. gloss. θ36) post εὐτολμία
add. Z θράσος–αὐθάδεια om. p1, Ω   <θ>ράσος Pe, θράσος L, θρασός Ap,
θάρσος H, T, χθράσος S   θρῆνος pro θράσος Φ   δὲ om. Ap   ἀλόγιστος I
αὐθάδια T, Γ, αὐθ'άδια Φ   τοὐναντίον pro ἡ ἀλόγ. αὐθ. Z
30. Gloss. om. p1   θάτερον [[θάτερον]] θατέρου R   θάτερον om. T   ἔτερον B, Ro,
Pv, T, W, ἢ ἔτερον Ω   ἐτέρου Ro, T, W, τοῦ ἐτέρου Ω   τὸ ἔτερον τῶν δύο (τῶν δύο
ἔτ. L; cf. gloss. θ31) pro ἔτερον ἐτέρου L, Pc   ἢ (om. M) τῶν δύο τὸ ἔτερον (ἔτερον
M) add. M, Z
31. θάτερον : ἑκάτεροο̈ P, θάτερον : ἑκάτερος (ἐκ. Ro) Pb, Pe, Ro, Pv   τῶν δύο cum
lemm. D   ἔτερον Am, Ap, B, Ro, T, Ω   τὸ ἔτερον (ἔτερον Pv) ante τῶν δύο p3
32. Gloss. om. Aa, Ab, Am, Ap, Av   lemma in marg. hab. J, θαλπότερον Ω, θαλπότερον C, θαλπνότερον M, θαλπνότερο̅ς B   λαμπρότερον Γ, τὸ λαμπρότερον
Ω, λαινπρότερον C, λαμπρότερως B   θερμότερον om. Ω, θερμότερος B
33. Gloss. om. Aa, Ab, Am, Ap, Av, Ω   θαλυρόν Ω   διάπειρον p3, Γ, διάπειρον T
καὶ τὸ θαλυκρὸν (θαλικρον Y) κεῖνο κατημβλύνθη κέντρον add. p5
34. Gloss. om. Ab, Am, Ap, Av, Ω   θάρος T, Γac   ἀνδρεῖα D, ἀνδρία A, Aa, ἀνδρεῖαν Γ

35 θάλλος: βλάστημα· "ἦν δὲ ὁ παῖς ἐρώτων χαρίτων ἀμβρόσιόν τι
κάλλος" (cf. Anthol. Pal. 6. 292. 3-4). καὶ ὁ τῆς ἐλαίας κλάδος ἢ πᾶν τὸ
θάλλον

36 θάρσος, τὸ εὔλογον παράστημα τῆς ψυχῆς· θράσος δὲ τοὐναντίον

ῥῆμα

37 θάλψαι: θερμᾶναι, συντηρῆσαι

38 θαλαττοπορῆσαι: διὰ θαλάσσης πλεῦσαι

39 θαλαττοκοπεῖς: ματαιολογεῖς, ταράττῃ, θορυβῇ

40 θαλφθῇ: ἐξαπατηθῇ ἢ θερμανθῇ

41 θαμίζει: συχνάζει, συνεχῶς ἔρχεται

42 θανατῶν: ὁ ἐπιθυμῶν θανάτου· λέγεται δὲ καὶ ὁ ἀποκταίνων

ORD. 35 post 36 X   36 ante 29 V

APP. 35. Gloss. om. p3, Aa, Ab, Am, Ap, Av   θάλος Z, θάλλες Γ, θάλλος cett.: leg.
θαλλός βλάστημα–κάλλος καὶ om. A   τὸ βλάστημα p4, p6, X, Γ, Σ, Φ, Ω   ἦν–πᾶν τὸ
θάλλον om. Q, X, ἦν–κάλλος om. p4   ἦν γὰρ Ἐρώτων καὶ Χαρίτων ἡ παῖς ἀμβρόσιόν τι
θάλος Anthol., Suda   ἦν Γ, ἦν Ω, ἦν Μ   ὁ παῖς p2, p6, Γ, Σ, Φ: ἡ παῖς (παίς Ω) p5, Ψ,
Ω ἐρώτων Φ   καὶ χαρίτων p5, χαριτῶν Ω, χάριν Γ   ἀμβρόσιον Η, καὶ ἀμβρόσιον Ω, ὁ
ἀμβρόσιως Β   ἔχουσα post κάλλος add. Ω   θάλλος: καὶ (om. Φ) ὁ τῆς ἐλ. κλάδος
κλπ. sep. p6, Υ, Γ, Σ, Φ, Ψ   καὶ ὁ τῆς ἐλαίας–θάλλον om. Z, Ω   ἐλέας Μ
καρπὸς pro κλάδος p4   ἤ–θάλλον om. T   ἢ Ψ   ἢ τὸ πᾶν S, U, καὶ πᾶν A   πᾶν
Μ, Υ   θᾶλλον Φ, Ψ, θάλλων G, H, I, J, L, M, Π
36. Gloss. om. Aa, W, Y, Z, Ω   παράστιμα Ab   τῆς om. T   θράσος δὲ τοὐναντίον
om. p1, p4, X   θρᾶσος L, Ro, θάρσος Η   τοὐναντίον L, Pb, Po, Pv, Γ, Φ, Ψ,
τοὐναντίου Η, I, J, τὸναντίων Μ
37. Gloss. om. Ab, Am, Ap, Av   θάλψαι Ω   θερμᾶναι p1, p4, p5, p6, C, D, E, F, G,
H, I, J, K, Pc, Γ, Σ, Φ, Ψ, θερμαῖναι Ro, τὸ θερμᾶναι Ω   συντηρῆσαι om. Aa, συντηρῆσαι
B, καὶ συντηρῆσαι Ω
38. Gloss. om. Aa   θαλ⟦λ⟧ατοπορῆσαι Ro, θαλαττοπ ορῆσαι T, θαλατοπορῆσαι C, D, E, F, θαλ^λ ατοπορῆσαι B, θαλατ^τ οπορῆσαι Av   τὸ διὰ τῆς θαλάσσης
Ω, διαλάσσης Γ   θαλάττης W, Y, Z, Ψ, θάσσης I   πλεῦσαι B, Ω
39. Gloss. om. Aa, Ab, Am, Av   θαλαττοκοπῆς Y, Φ, θαττοκοπεῖς Π ματαιολογῆς
Y, τὸ ματαιολογεῖς Ω   ταράττῃ, θορυβῇ om. Ap,   ταράττει p2 (exc. K), Pc, Z,
ταράττ^π ει W, καὶ ταράττει Ω, ταράττεις Π, ταράττῃς U, ταράτης S, τὰκράττῃ Y, θράττῃ T
θορυβεῖ L, M, Z, καὶ θορυβεῖ Ω, θορυβεῖς Π, θορυβῇς Γ, φοβῇ S, U
40. Gloss. om. Aa, Ab, Am, Av, Z   θαλφθὴ Ψ, θαλφθῆ δὲ Pc   ἐξαπατηθῇ ἢ om. A
ἐξαπατηθή Ψ, ἐξαπατηθεῖ (ἐξαπατήθει Ro) p3, ἐξαφατηθῆ U^{ac}, ἐξατηθῆ C, τὸ ἐξαπατηθῆ
Ω   ἢ Ω   θερμανθῇ X, θερμανθεῖ (θερμαθεῖ Pc, Pv^{ac}), p3, θερμανθῆναι Μ
41. Gloss. om. Aa, Ab, Am, Ap, Av   θαμήζει Μ, θαμάζει Pv   συχνάζει om. T, Z,
συναχάζει Pc, τὸ συχνάζει Ω, συχνάζει Q, πυκνάζει S, U, πυκνά X   συχνάζει post
συνεχῶς Γ   συνεχώς B, M, καὶ συνεχός Ω   ἔρχεται Φ
42. Gloss. om. Aa, Ab, Am, Ap, Av, Z (cf. gloss. θ44)   ὁ B   ἐπιθυμῶν Pb, ἐπιθυμῶ B
λέγεται δὲ καὶ ὁ ἀποκτ. om. Q   λέγεται δὲ om. A   ἀποκτένων A, R^{ac}, V, W, X, Y,
Δ, Λ, Ψ, ἀποκταίνον Ω, ἀπαταίνων Φ   λέγεται καὶ τὸ κατηγορῶ (κατηγῶρῶ C,
κὰτηγορεῖν Μ) ὃ (ὁ Ro, ὃ Μ) καὶ (καὶ om. p3) μετὰ γενικῆς (γυναικῆς Μ) συντάσσεται
(cf. gloss. θ43), pro λέγεται–ἀποκταίνων p2, p3

43 θαυμάζω: ἐπαινῶ· λέγεται καὶ τὸ κατηγορῶ, ὃ καὶ μετὰ γενικῆς
συντάσσεται

44 θανατᾶν καὶ θανατιᾶν

45 θακεύουσι: κάθηνται

46 θακῶ: κάθημαι

47 θαάσσων: ἐγκαθεζόμενος

48 θαλέθοντες: θάλλοντες

49 θαλπόμενοι: ἐξαπατώμενοι· "τοὺς δὲ ὑποθαλπομένους ἐλπίδι," Ἰώσηπος (cf. BJ 4. 221)

ἐπίρρημα

50 θαμά: συνεχῶς, πυκνῶς· παρὰ τὸ ἅμα θαμά, πλεονασμῷ τοῦ θ

51 θαρραλέως: ἀνδρείως, εὐθαρσῶς

52 θᾶττον: συντόμως, ταχέως

ORD. 50 post 52 Ab, Am, Av
APP. 43. Gloss. om. Ab, Am, Ap, Av, p2, p3 (cf. gloss. θ42) θαυθάζω V τὸ ἐπαινῶ Ω
λέγεται–συντάσσεται om. Aa κατηγορῶ pro λέγεται–συντάσσεται A δὲ post
λέγεται add. X, Y κατοιγορῶ X ὅ–συντάσσεται om. p4, Ω γεννικῆς Γ
συντάσεται Φ
44. Gloss. om. p1, Ψ, Ω θανατᾶν L, M, X, Y, θανατῶν T καὶ om. p3 θανατιάν
M, X, Y τὸ ἐπιθυμεῖν θανάτου add. p4, τὸ κεκρατεῖσθαι ὑπὸ τοῦ θανάτου add p6
ὁ ἐπιθυμῶν θανάτου. λέγεται δὲ καὶ ὁ ἀποκτένων (cf. gloss. θ42) add. Z
45. Gloss. om. Aa, Ab, Am, Ap, Av, Z, Ψ θακεύουσιν Pc, Ω, θαλκεύουσι Ψ,
θακέουσι A, θακεῦγσι X καθήνται C, τὸ κάθηνται Ω, κάθηται L, M, V
46. Gloss. om. Ab, Am, Ap, Av θάκω B, Po, κακῶ Q, R τὸ κάθημαι Ω
47. Gloss. om. Ab, Am, Ap, Av θαάσων C, Eᵃᶜ, θαάσσω Pc, ἄσσων B ἐνκαθεζό-
μενος Po, ἐγˣκαθεζόμαινος B, ἐκκαθεζόμενος Pc, ἐγκαθεζόμενον Pv, τὸ ἐγκαθεζόμενος Ω
48. Gloss. om. Ab, Am, Ap, Av, Z θαλλέθοντες K, θαλέθοντες P, Pb, Po, θαλέ[[.]]-
οντες E, θαλέοντες F, θαλεύοντες X explic. om. H, J, L, M, T, θάλοντες
S, τὸ θάλλοντες Ω, θάλλονες P, Pb, Po, ψάλλοντες Aa
49. Gloss. om. Am, Ap, Av θαλπώμενοι p3, Φ, θαλπόμαινος B ἐξαπατόμενοι
Ab, X, Ψ, ἐξαπατόμενοι T, τὸ ἐξαπατόμενοι Ω, ἐξαπτόμενοι D, ξἀπατώμαινοι B τούς–
Ἰώσηπος om. p4, X, Ω τούς–ἐλπίδι om. p1 ὑποθαλπομαίνους B, ὑποθαλπομένουο
Pv, ἐπιθαλπομένους W, θαλπομένους p6, Γ, Σ, Josephus, θαλπομόνους Φ, ὑπομενούσας
(ὑπομένουσας M) pro ὑποθ. L, M ἀλπίδι Pe, Pv Ἰώσηπος om. Φ, Ἰώσηππος Pe,
Po, Y, Ἰώσιπος C, ὡς Ἰώσηπα A, Ab, ὡσιότητος Aa οὕτως add. p6
50. Gloss. om. Ω θαμᾶ Q, R, S, U, X, Y, θάμα Po, θαμαί H, J, L, M, θαύμα Aa
συνεχῶς H, M, συνεχός Am πυκνῶς om. Ap πικνῶς Q, Φ πυκνῶς ante συνεχῶς
p1 (exc. Ap) παρὰ τό–τοῦ θ om. p1, p4, Y ἅμα M, Po, Pv, X, ἅμα D θαμᾶ
D, Ψ πλεον. τοῦ θ om. Z πλέον (πλέων M) pro πλεονασμῷ L, M, Γ, καὶ πλεο-
(νασμῷ) Π θαμά add. Π θαμά: συνεχῶς πυκνῶς post θαμά: παρὰ τὸ ἅμα–τοῦ
θ V, W
51. Gloss. om. p1 θαρραλαίως X, θαρραλλέως Δ, Λ, θαραλλέως Φ, θαραλέως
T ἀνδρείως, εὐθαρσῶς bis V ἀνδρείως P, ἀνδρίως T, ἀνδρεῖος M, Φ, τὸ ἀνδρεῖος
Ω εὐθάρσως X, εὐθαρσός Q, εὔθαρσος B, καὶ εὐθαρσῶς Ω
52. θάττον D, F, L, M, Q, R, T, X, Y, Γ, Φ, Ψ, θάττων Aa, Ω συντόμος T, τὸ
συντόμως Ω ταχέως om. Aa, καὶ ταχέως Ω

53　θαιρός : ἡ στρόφιγγα τῆς θύρας Ap, Av^m

54a　θάκων : θρόνων, καθεδρῶν **p3**

54b　θάκων καὶ θώκων : θρόνων, καθεδρῶν S, U

55　θάλαμος : ὁ κοιτὼν καὶ ὁ οἶκος S, U

56　θάλαμος : παστάς, κοιτών **p1**

57　θαλάμους : οἴκους ἐνδοτέρους **p3**

58　θάλασσα : παρὰ τὸν σάλον σάλασσα καὶ θάλασσα, παρὰ τὸ ᾆσσον ἤτοι
　　　ἐγγὺς εἶναι τοῦ θανάτου. καὶ ἄλλως· παρὰ τὸ εἰληφέναι τὴν ὀνομασίαν
　　　ἐκ τοῦ θ̄ᾱ τοῦ σημαίνοντος τὸ τρέχω καὶ τοῦ λ̄ᾱ τὸ ἁλμυρόν, ἤγουν τὸ
　　　ἅλα, ἐκ τοῦ ἀσσάτου τινάσσασθαι (leg. ⟨καὶ⟩ ἐκ τοῦ ᾱσ̄σ̄ᾱ τοῦ τινάσ-
　　　σεσθαι) τουτέστιν θέον ἅλα τινασσόμενον. συναφθέντων οὖν αὐτῶν κατὰ
　　　τὰ ἰδιώματα ἐκλήθη θάλασσα S, U

59　θάλεια : παρὰ τὸ θάλλειν τοὺς εὐωχουμένους V, W, Z

60　θαλερὸν πνεῦμα : θερμὸν ὡς ἀπὸ ἡλίου Ap, Av^m καὶ νεώτατον Av^m

61　θάλλω : τὸ αὔξω, παρὰ τὸ θῶ τὸ τρέφω V, W

62　θάμαρ : εὐλογίαι **p3**, (P^m)

63　θαμειός : συχνός Ψ

64　θάμνος : κλάδος καὶ ἡ ῥίζα τῶν δένδρων S, U^m

65　θάμψαι : τὸ καῦσαι Ap (vid. θ13 app. crit.)

66　θάνατός ἐστιν αἰώνιος ὕπνος, διάλυσις σώματος, νοσούντων εὐχή,
　　　ταλαιπωρούντων ἐπιθυμία, πνεύματος ἀποστάτης, πλουσίων φόβος,
　　　πενήτων ἐπιθυμία, ἀνάλυσις μελῶν, ὕπνου πατήρ S, U

67　θάνατος : ἀπὸ τοῦ θεῖν ἄνω τὰς ψυχάς (cf. θ11) S, U

68　ἐρώτησις: Τί θάνατος; ἀπόκρισις: θάνατός ἐστιν χωρισμὸς ψυχῆς καὶ
　　　σώματος, βίου λύσις, φροντίδων ἀπαλλαγή, ἄδηλος πορεία, τέλος
　　　παντὸς ζώου (cf. θ9) S, U

69　θάνατος : παρὰ τὸ τάνατος· τείνει γὰρ τὸ σῶμα τῇ ψύξει. ἢ τάναρός ἐστι
　　　καὶ ἐπὶ πάντα διατείνων (cf. θ11) S, U

70　θάνατος : χωρισμὸς ψυχῆς ἀπὸ σώματος V, Y, Z (cf. W, s.v. θ11)

ORD. 53 post 39 Ap　　54a post 1 **p3**　　54 b post 27 S, U　　55 post 19, S, U
56 post 2 Am, Ap, Av; post 4 Aa, post 5 Ab, post 6 A　　57 post 12 **p3**
58 post 69 S, U　　59 post 20 Z, post 21 V, W　　60 post 20 Ap　　61 post 76 V, W
62 post 26 **p3**　　63 post 19 (additam ab alia manu) Ψ　　64 post 22 S, U
65 post 13 Ap　　66–69 post 49 S, U　　70 post 6 Z, post 8 Y, post 11 V
APP. 53. στρόφυγγα Ap
54a. θακῶν codd.
54b. καθέδρων codd.
55. κοιτῶν codd.
56. κοιτῶν Am, ἢ κοιτῶν Aa　　γάμου συνάλλαγμα add. Ab
57. οἶκους Pb
58. ἄσσον codd.　　ἁλμυρόν S　　τουτέστι S
59. θάλλεια W

71 θάνοιεν : ἀποθάνοιεν A

72 θαρσεῖς : οἱ ἀνδρεῖοι Φ

73 θάσια : τὰ ἀμύγδαλα, ἀπὸ τοῦ θᾶσσον καρπεύειν· πρώϊμα γὰρ ὑπὲρ τῶν
λοιπῶν δένδρων S, U

74 θάτερον : ἑκατέρου Pv

75a θαῦμα : τὸ ὑπὲρ φύσιν διὰ Θεοῦ τελούμενον Φ

75b θαῦμα : τὸ ὑπὲρ φύσιν διὰ Θεοῦ τελούμενον· παρὰ τὸ θαυμάζω θαύμασμα
καὶ κατὰ συγκοπὴν καὶ ἀποβολὴν τοῦ σ θαῦμα. οἱ δὲ παρὰ τὸ θεῶ,
θεῶμαι, θαῦμα V, W, Z

76 θαυμάζετε : ταράττεσθε, θορυβεῖσθε, ὡς καὶ ἐν τῷ Εὐαγγελίῳ· "ἓν
ἔργον ἐποίησα καὶ πάντες θαυμάζετε" (Ιο. 7: 21) V, W, Z

ORD. 71 post 52 A   72 post 52 Φ   73 post 58 S, U   74 post 30 Pv
75a post 27 alt. Φ   75b post 26 V, W, post 31 Z
76 post 35 W, post 36 V, post 46 Z
Glossas 39, 53, 22, 24, 4, 40, 50, 20, 60 inter 25, 27; gloss. 13, 65, 29, 9 (alt. part.) post
52 exhib. Ap

APP. 73. ἀμίγδαλα codd.
75b. ἀποβολῇ Z   οἱ δέ–θαῦμα om. W   θαῦμα om. Z
76. θορυβεῖσθαι–θαυμάζετε om. V   θορυβεῖσθαι W^ac

PARALLELS

1 = K(v, g); cf. Ap. Soph., schol. η' 8, K(a), Hes., Σ, Ph., Su., EM 441.22, EG
253.17-19, An. Ox. II, 376.9-10, K(n, P), Hes.
2 cf. Σ (θρ. καθ.) = Ph., Su.; K(P) = Hes.; –καθέδραι: Bk. 263.26; θρόνοι = K(n); cf.
also θ54
3 cf. EM 441.11, Et. Sym.
4 cf. schol. Δ' 474 = sch. κ' 457 = K(a, g); K(n); Ph. = Su.; EM 441.34
5 = Su.; cf. also θ13
6 = Σ, Ph., Su.; cf. K(n), EG 253.12; Et. Sym. = EM 444.4; Poll. I, 76, Hes.
7 = Su.
8 = K(a, g, n, v), Hes., Σ, Ph., Su.
11 cf. Et. Sym., EM 442.30 (cf. Orion 72.1)
12 = EG 253.27, Et Sym.; cf. EM 441.18
13 = EG 254.17, EM 443.50, Et. Sym.
15 cf. EM 443.5 (θαρσαλέος)
16 cf. Geoponica 10.6, 2 (ed. Beckh)
17 –τοὺς καρχηδονίους; cf. Su., Lagarde 262.59
19 cf. schol. Arist. Ran. 1074 = Su. (s.v. θαλαμακεῖς); cf. Hes., (s.v. θαλάμιαι
κῶπαι), EM 441.24 (s.v. θαλαμίδιοι κῶπαι)
20 = K(a, g, v, P), Hes., EG 255.35; cf. Ap. Soph., K(n), schol. AB ad Γ' 534
21 –πανήγυρις = K(a, g), Hes.; ὄνομα Μούσης = K(v3), Su., EG 255.39; cf. Hes.
22 cf. schol. Λ' 56, K(a), Hes.
23 = Ph., Su., EM 441.23; cf. Hes.
24 cf. K(a, g, n, v), EG 255.34, Ap. Soph., Hes.
25 –ἀνατολή: cf. EG 253.22, Ps.-Herod., Hes. (s.v. θεμάν); τὸ νότιον κέρας: cf. K(a,g, v)
Lagarde 192.72, 260.1

26 = Su.; θάλαμος–κοιτών = K(**a, g, v**), Σ, Ph.; cf. *EG* 253.17 = *EM* 441.21

27 = K(**g, v**); ἔκπληξις = K(**a, n**), schol. Γ' 342, Δ' 79, Hes.

28 = K(P); πυκνά = K(**a, g, v**, s), Erot., Hes., Moer., Th. Mag.

29 –ἡ εὐτολμία: cf. K(**n**); θράσος–αὐθάδεια: cf. *EG* 255.30; cf. also θ36

30 = K(**a, g, v**, P)

31 cf. K(**g**, P) (τὸ ἔτ. τῶν δύο)

32 = Su.; cf. schol. Pind. *O.* I, 8

33 = Su.

34 cf. schol. *E'* 2 (θάρσος), Hes. (θάρσος), *EG* 225.25 (θάρσος)

35 –βλάστημα = schol. *X'* 87, K(**a, g, n**); ἦν γὰρ–κάλλος: cf. Su. (s.v. θαλέεσσι); θάλλος καὶ ὁ τῆς ἐλαίας–θάλλον: cf. Σ = Ph., Su.; K(**a, g, v**) = Hes.; Tim., *EM* 441.48 (s.v. θάλλω)

36 = schol. *E'* 2, Su.; cf. *EG* 255.29, Ammon. No. 233, schol. Apoll. Rh. II, 75–78c

37 cf. K(**a, g, n, v**: συντ. θερμ.)

38 cf. K(**a, g**: πλ. διὰ θαλ.) = Hes.; cf. K(**v**) = *EG* 255.36

39 = Su.; –ματαιολογεῖς = Hes., Ph.; cf. Phryn. *Praep. soph.*, Th. Mag.; ταράττῃ, θορυβῇ: cf. schol. Aristoph. *Eq.* 830

40 –ἐξαπατηθῇ = Su.

41 cf. K(**g, v**), Hes., *EG* 255.42; συχνάζει: cf. schol. Plat. *Resp.* 328C; συνεχῶς ἔρχεται: cf. sch. ε' 88, K(**a, n**)

42 cf. K(**g, v**), Σ, Ph., Su.; –θανάτου: cf. K(**a**), Hes., schol. Plat. *Phaed.* 64B, *EM* 422.51

43 cf. Σ = Ph., Su.; Ammon. No. 233 = *EG* 256.5; *EM* 443.45

44 = Su., Lex. Vindob. 102.17 Nauck; cf. *EG* 255.4

45 cf. K(**a, n**, P), Hes. (θακεύουσι)

47 cf. *EM* 441.6 (ex *EGen.*; cf. Wendel, *Schol. Apoll. Rh.*, p. 202); K(**a, g**, s), Hes. (s.v. θάσσων)

48 = sch. *Ψ'* 32, ζ' 63, K(**a, g, n**), Hes., Su.

49 = Su.

50 = *EM* 442.18; –συνεχῶς = K(**g, v**), Σ, Ph., Su.; παρὰ–τοῦ θ = Orion 72.23, *An. Ox.* I, 199.20, *EG* 254.15

51 = K(**v**), *EG* 255.43; cf. K(**g**), Hes. (εὐθ. ἀνδρ.)

52 ταχέως = K(**g**, P, s), Hes.

53 cf. Ps.-Herod., *EG* 253.10, *EM* 446. 31, Eust. 914.33; cf. also θ6

54a = K(**a, g, v**); cf. also θ2

54b = K(**v3**)

55 = K(**v3**), *EG* 253.17, *EM* 441.21; cf. also θ26

56 = K(s)

57 = K(**g**)

58 = K(**v3**); –θανάτου = *EG* 253.45; cf. *EM* 441.26, *Et. Sym.*; παρὰ τὸ εἰλ.–ἐκλήθη θάλ. = *EG* 253.40

59 = *EM* 441.56; –θάλλειν: cf. schol. A ad *I'* 143, Ph., Su.

60 –ἡλίου = Gal. *Lex. Hip.*

61 = *Et. Sym.*; cf. Orion 73.14, *An. Ox.* I, 198.12, *EG* 254.10

63 = Ps.-Herod.; *An. Ox.* I, 199.25, *EG* 254.30

64 = K(**v3**)

65 cf. *EM* 443.50, Hes. (s.v. θάψαι)

66 = K(**v3**), cf. Secundus, *Quaest.* no. 20 (Perry)

67 = K(**v3**); cf. θ11

68 = K(**v3**); cf. θ9

69 = K(**v3**); cf. θ11
70 cf. θ67
71 = K(**a, g, v**), Hes.
72 cf. θ18
73 = K(**v3**), *EG* 255.50, cf. *EM* 443.11 = *Et. Sym.*
74 cf. θ30
75a = K(**v3**), *EG* 255.44
75b παρὰ τὸ θαυμάζω κλπ. cf. Orion 74.23, *EG* 256.28, *EM* 443.39

Ἀρχὴ τοῦ ξ στοιχείου
Τὸ ξ μετὰ τοῦ ᾱ
ἀρσενικόν

1   ξανθός : πυρροειδής
2   Ξάνθος : ποταμὸς καὶ ἵππος
3   ξανθίκομος : ὁ ξανθόθριξ

ῥῆμα

4   ξαίνω : τύπτω ἢ διαλύω
5   ξανθίζεσθαι : τὰς τρίχας κοσμεῖσθαι

τὸ ξ μετὰ τοῦ ε̄
ἀρσενικόν

6   ξεινοδόκος : ὁ ξενοδόχος
7   ξεῖνος : ὁ ἀπὸ ξένης φίλος
8   ξένος : ὁ πάσης ἰδίων καὶ ἀλλοτρίων σχέσεως φυγάς

ORD. 1–5 post 18 hab. G, H, I, J, K, Z, post 17 W   8 bis habet Am

APP. Titulus: ἀρχὴ τοῦ ξ (ξῖ Pb, Pe) στοιχείου Av, Pb, Pe, Po, Pv
        ἀρχὴ τοῦ ξ στοιχείου. τὸ ξ μετὰ τοῦ ᾱ A, Ab
        ἀρχὴ τοῦ ξ (ξ̄η̄ V) στοιχείου (στοιχείου Ap) μετὰ τοῦ ᾱ Ap, V
        ἀρχὴ τοῦ ξ. τὸ ξ μετὰ τοῦ ᾱ Ω
        ἀρχὴ τοῦ (τὸ E, F)ξ μετὰ τοῦ ᾱ (ἄλφα E, F, M, τῆς ἄλφας Π) Aa, C, E, F, L,
            M, Q, T, Π
        τὸ ξ μετὰ τοῦ ᾱ. ἀρσενικον B, D, Φ
        τὸ ξ μετὰ τοῦ ᾱ. ἀρσενικόν (ἀρσενικά Δ, Λ) X, Γ, Δ, Λ
        τὸ ξ μετὰ τοῦ ᾱ (ἄλφα Ψ) P, R, S, U, Y, Σ, Ψ
        τὸ ξ μετᾶν ᾱ Am
        ἀρχὴ τοῦ ξ στοιχείου μετὰ τοῦ ε̄ W
        τὸ ξ μετὰ τοῦ ε̄ G, H, I, J, K, Z
        + ξῖ τοῦ στοιχείου ἀρχὴ Pc

1. πυρροειδής Am, X, πυροειδής E, K, Z, πυ͛οειδής T, πυρρωειδής Π, πυρωειδής F, πυρρο-
    ειδῶς Y, ὁ πυρροειδής Ω   εὐμετάβολος add. Ab
2. Gloss. om. Aa   ὄνομα κύριον ἢ ante ποταμός add. p3   ποταμόν T   ἵππος Γ
3. ξανθήκομος Uac   ἐξανθόθριξ pro ὁ ξανθ. Pe, ξανθύθριξ Ψ, ξανθήθριξ W   ξάνθακος
    add. Pc (cf. gloss. ξ72)
4. ‹ξ›αίνω Pe, ξαίξω Y   τὸ τύπτω Δ, Λ, Φ   ἢ om. Z   διαλύω Ap, Av   τὸ
    διαλύω καὶ μαστίζω pro τύπτ. ἢ διαλ. p4   ἢ νεωτερίζω add. Ab
5. Gloss. om. Am, Ap, Av   ‹ξ›ανθίζεσθαι Z   τᾶς T   κοσμείσθαι L, κομείσθαι
    A, S, V, W, X, κῦσμείσθαι B
6. Gloss. om. Am   ξενοδόξος Pvac   ὁ ἀναδεχόμενος τοὺς πένητας add. Ab
7. Gloss. om. Am   ξείνος A, Aa, Ap, Av, L, Q, T, Y, Φ, Ω, ξένος Ab   ξένοις
    D, E, F, Ω   ἐρχόμενος ante φίλος add. Ab
8. ὁ om. S, bis hab. Pb   πάσης Ap, M, R, Φ, ὁπάσης Po   ἰδίων om. S, U, ἰδείων Ψ
    καὶ ἀλλοτρίων σχέσεως om. Am, Ap, Av, ἀλλοτριῶν Ω   σχέσεων p2, Pb, Pe, Po, Pv,
    Q, R, T, Λac   φύγας M   καὶ ἀποδρασμούς add. Ab

9 ξένιος Ζεύς: ὁ φιλόξενος
10 Ξένετος: κύριον

θηλυκόν

11 ξενία: καταγώγιον, κατάλυμα
12 ξεστὴ δὲ ἡ ἐξεσμένη

οὐδέτερον

13 ξεστόν: ὡμαλισμένον
14 ξεινήϊον: ξένιον
14a ξενοδοχεῖον

ῥῆμα

15 ξεναγεῖται: ὑποδέχεται
16 ξεναγίζω: τὸ τοὺς ξένους συναθροίζω
17 ξεναγῶ: ξένον ὑποδέχομαι
18 ξενιτεύω: ξενόω, ξενῶ, ξενίζω

τὸ ξ μετὰ τοῦ η
ἀρσενικόν

19 ξηνός: ὁ κορμός

ORD. 19–24 post 36 L

APP. 9. Gloss. om. Aa, Am, X, Ω ‹ξ›ένιος Pe Ζεῦς Ap, Av, D, L, Φ, Ψ, Ζές (?)
T ὁ φίλος ξένος **p5** ὁ ἀποδεκτικός add. Ab
10. Gloss. om. **p1, p4**, X Ξέννωνος ante Ξένετος add. **p5** Ξένοτος Pc, Ξίνοτος
Pb, Pe, Po, Pv, Ξετός Ω κύρια **p5**, κυρίως L, M
11. Gloss. om. Aa, Am ‹ξ›ενία Ω, ξένια Pv κατάλημα W
12. Gloss. om. Aa, Ab, Am, Ap, Av, Ω ξεστῆ L, ξεἰστή M δὲ om. **p3**, A, F, Z,
Ψ ἡ om. H, J, ἡ T ἐξεσμαίνη B
13. Gloss. om. Aa, Ab, Am, Ap, Av ὡμαλισμένον Y, Ψ, ὁμαλισμένον Pc, Pe, X, Zac,
ὁμαλισμένον Pb, Po, ομαλισμαίνον Pv, ὤμαλισμαίνον B, ὡμαλόν Φ
14. Gloss. om. Aa, Ab, Am, Ap, Av ξεινητῖον B, ξείνηῖον Γ, Π, ξενῆῖον L, M, T,
Δ, Λ ξένιον om. B, ξένον H, J, Ω, τὸ ξένιον Π
14a. Gloss. cum ξ14 confund. codd. exc. Pb, Pc ξενοδοχείον B, L, Y, Ω ὁ ὑπο-
δεχόμενος τόπος τοὺς ξένους add. Π
15. ξεναγωγεῖται L, M, ξεξαναγεῖται Φ ἀποδέχεται Ab, Am, Ap, Av
κυβερνᾷ, δίδει add. Ab
16. Gloss. om. Aa, Ab, Am, Ap, Av τοὺς om. X, τοὺς L, M συναθρίζω Ω, συνανα-
θροίζω X, συναθροίζων Y ὑποδέχομαι pro συναθροίζω S, T, U, ὑποδ. καὶ συναθρ. Q, R
17. Gloss. om. S, T, U ξεναγωγῶ D, ξεναστῶ Π, ξενή C ξενοδοχῶ ante
ξένον ὑποδ. add. **p3** ἀποδέχομαι Ap, Av ὑποδέχε[[ῆ]]αι H
18. Gloss. om. Am, Ap, Av, W, Ω ξενόω–ξενίζω separ. **p3**, om. Z ξενόω om. **p1, p4,
p6**, L, M, X, Γ, Σ, Φ, ξενῶ bis pro ξενόω, ξενῶ C ξενίζω B, ξελίζω Y
19. Gloss. om. Aa, Ab, Am, Av, Φ ξήνος Ρο, ξηρός T, Ψ κορμένος, Ρο κοσμός
S, U

20 ξηρὸς ἱδρώς : ὁ μὴ ὑπὸ λουτρῶν ἀλλ' ὑπὸ γυμνασίων καὶ πόνων γινόμενος

21 Ξήϊος : κύριον

οὐδέτερον

22 ξηρίον : φυτὸν ἤ εἶδος βοτάνης ἰατρικόν

ῥῆμα

23 ξηραλοιφεῖν καὶ ξηραλοιφῆσαι : τὸ ἄνευ τοῦ λούεσθαι ἀλείφεσθαι·
μήποτε δὲ καὶ τὸ ὑπὸ τῶν ἀλειπτῶν λεγόμενον ξηροτρίβεσθαι οὕτως
ἐλέγετο

24 ξηραίνω : ψυχραίνω

τὸ ξ μετὰ τοῦ ι
ἀρσενικόν

25 ξιφήρης : ὁ κατέχων ξίφος
26 ξίρις : φυτόν
27 ξιφήν : ὁ φέρων ξίφος

ORD. 20 post 22 Ap   25 post 27 Ap

APP. *20.* Gloss. om. Aa, Am, Av, Y   ξξηρός Pc, ξηροῖς Ω   ἱδρώς om. Ab, ἱδρώς
Ψ, ἱδρῶς Pc, Q, S, U, Vᵃᶜ, Φ, ἱδρῶς Β, Ω, ὑδρώς Α, Σ, ὑδρῶς L, Μ,, ηδρῶς W
ὁ ἱδρώς (in expl.) T, Z, Δ, Λ, ὁ ἱδρῶς Ap, ὁ ἱδρός Π   μὴ om. Pc   λυτρῶν Β, C,
D, E, F, I, λουτρόν Q, λοᵒτροῦ T   ῡγυμνασίων Pc, γυμνασίως Β   γινόμενος post
λουτρῶν transp. Λ, Π   γενόμενος Pe, Pv, Ω, γινόμενον W, γιόμαινος Β, δινόμενος T
21. Gloss. om. **p1, p4,** Pe, Pv, X   Ξήϊνος **p22,** I, V, W, Π
22. Gloss. om. Am.   ξηρύον Ap, Av, Uᵃᶜ, ξηρίων C, D, E, F, I, Pe, Π, ξηρίω Β
τὸ φυτόν Π   ἤ–ἰατρικόν om. Aa, Av   ἤ om. Δ, Λ, Φ, ἤ Ω   βοτάνη Β, C, G, H, J,
βοτάνη Pb, βοᵗᵛ′ Pc, βατάνη I   ἰατρικόν S, Γ, Ω, ἰατρικῆς Β παρὰ τὸ ξῶ ῥῆμα κλπ. (cf.
gloss. ξ83) add. Z   εἶδος βοτάνης καὶ φυτόν pro φυτόν–ἰατρικόν Ap ξηρίον καὶ
ξηλοιραφῆσαι : τὸ ἄνευ τὸ λούεσθαι ἀλείφεσθαι (i.e. cum gloss. sequente conf.) T
23. Gloss. om. Aa, Ab, Am, Ap, Av, Ω   <ξ>ηραλοιφεῖν S, U, ξξηραλοιφεῖν Pc,
ξηραλόφειν C, ξηραλοιφαγεῖν Φ, ξυραλοιφεῖν Β, ξηραληφεῖον X   τοῦ
ἄνευ L, Μ   τὸ λούεσθαι (λούεσθαι Q) **p4** (exc. T, sed cf. gloss. praeced.), X   λούεσθαι Μ   ἀλείφεσθαι Pe, Γ, Π, Σ   μήποτε–ἐλέγετο om. **p4**   καὶ ἐπὶ 〚τὸ ἐπὶ〛 τὸ
ὑπὸ W   τὸ om. V, Γ   τῶν om. Ro   ἀλειπτῶν Π, ἀλειπτόν Pb, Ro, ἄλειπτον Pe, Pv,
ἀλειπιῶν L   λεγόμαινον Β   οὕτως Β, Ro   ἀντὶ τοῦ ξηραίνω ψυχραίνω (cf. gloss.
sequentem) Z
24. Gloss. om. V, W (Z cf. gloss. praeced.)   τὸ ψυχραίνω Ap, Ω   ὑγρεύω, λογιοῦμαι
add. Ab
25. Gloss. om. Ab, Am, Av   ξιφήρις Ap, R, S, Y, <ξ>ιφήρις Ψ, ξιφίρις V,
ξηφήρης Pc, Pe, ξιξήρις Q, ἰφήρης T   ξίφο Β, τὸ ξίφος L, Μ
26. Gloss. om. Aa, Ab, Am, Ap, Av   ξίρυς **p6,** A, L, Μ, Q, R, S, U, X, Γ, Σ, Φ,
ξιρύς Ro, ξύρυς T, ξίρης Β, ξιρῆς Ω
27. Gloss. om. Aa, Am, L, Μ   ξιφῆν Y   ὁ φέρων T, ὁ φέρον Av, ἡ φέρον Ap   ξύφος
Pe   καὶ ξιφηφόρος ὁμοίως (i.e. gloss. sequentem) add. **p6**   καὶ ξιφηφόρος add. Z
ὁ αὐτὸς καὶ ξιφηφόρος add. Ψ   καὶ μαχόμενος add. Aa

28 ξιφηφόρος : ὁμοίως
29 ξιφίας : ἰχθύς
30 Ξιφιλῖνος, Ξιφῖνος : ὀνόματα κύρια

τὸ ξ μετὰ τοῦ ō
ἀρσενικόν

31 ξουθός : ὁ ξανθός
32 Ξόϊς καὶ Ξοῖσδος : ποταμοί
33 Ξούϊς : κύριον

θηλυκόν

34 ξουφηρία : ἡ μυωξία, ἤτοι τῶν ποντικῶν ὁ φωλεός. ἢ τὴν πολυτέλειαν.
ἐκ τῆς ἐπιστολῆς τοῦ ἁγίου Γρηγορίου τοῦ Θεολόγου· "ἐγὼ δέ σου
τὸν Πόντον θαυμάσομαι καὶ τὴν ποντικὴν ξουφηρίαν" (epist. iv. 3
Gallay)

ORD. 29 post 24 Ap   31 post 35 Ab

APP. *28.* Gloss. om. Aa, Am, Ap, Av, Ω   ξ ῗ φηφόρος G, ξ〚ῆ〛 φηφόρος I, ξιφυφόρος
Pe, ξιφιφόρος W, ξιφοφόρος S, U, ξιφιφορῶ X   ὁμοίως B, Po, ὅμοιον Y
στρατιώτης καὶ δυνατὸς ἐν ῥώμῃ pro ὁμοίως Ab
29. Gloss. om. Am.   ξιφίσας καὶ ξιφίας Ap, ξιφία Po   ἰχθῦς p1, p6, G, H, I,
J, Pv, Rᶜ, S, U, V, W, Z, Σ, Ψ, ἰχθύς Ω, ἰχθύες Iᵃᶜ   θαλάττιος μέγας add. Ab
30. Gloss. om. Aa, Ab, Am, Ap, Av, Ω   Ξιφιλῖνος p3, Q, T, Wᵃᶜ, Y, X, Φ   καὶ ante
Ξιφῖνος add. p3, Γ, Δ, Λ, Φ   Ξιφῖνος om. D, K, W, Ξιφίνος B, Pb, Pe, Po, Pv,
Y, Φ, Ξυφῖνος X, Ξυφῖνός T   explic. om. p5   κύρια om. p6   ὄνομα κύριον
B, D, E, F, I, K, Φ, κύριον ὄνομα C   Ξιφιλῖνος ὄνομα κύριον· Ξιφῖνος ὁμοίως A
31. Gloss. om. p2 (exc. L, M), p3, Am, Ap, Av   ὁ om. Φ   ὁ ὡραιότατος, ὁ λαμπρός
add. Ab
32. Gloss. om. p2 (exc. L, M), p3, Aa, Ab, Am, Ap, Av   Ξόοις Q, Γ, Ξοῖς T, Ξοίης
X   Ξίσδος Ω, Ξοῖσδας W, Ξάνδος X
33. Gloss. om. p2 (exc. L, M), p3, p4, Aa, Ab, Am, Ap, Av, V, W, X, Z   Ξούις L,
Mᵃᶜ, Y, Ω   ὄνομα κύριον A
34. ξουφυρία Ab, ξουφουρία Ap, Av   ἡ B, ὁ Av   μυοξία p3, Π, μυωξί Aa, μυρεψία
Wᵃᶜ   ἤτοι om. Ap, ante ἡ μυωξία transp. S, U   ἤτοι Am, Y, Ω   τῶν ποντικῶν
om. p22   ποτικῶν W   ὁ Ap, B, Π, Ω, ω Q   φωλαιός Wᵃᶜ, φολεός L, X, Φ, φωλέος
Av, I, φελεός M, Ω   ἢ τήν-ξουφηρίαν om. Am, Ap, Av, Q   ἢ τὴν πολυτ. om. Aa
ἢ om. Φ, ἤ I, ἤτοι pro ἢ R, S, T, U   πολυτελείαν Tᵃᶜ, X, Ω, πολυτελειαν C, πολυτελίαν
Y   ἐκ σῆς Pc   ἐπιστολῆς T, Σ, ἐπιστηλῆς W, ἐπιστός Aa   τοῦ ἁγίου om. D   τοῦ
om. K   ἁγίου B, Po, Pv   ἐγὼ L, T, ὡδέ Φ   σου bis habet Pc, post πόντον
transp. Δ, Λ, Φ   πόντος B, τόπον T, τῶν ποτικῶν pro τὸν πόντον W   θαυμάσωμαι
Rᵃᶜ, Ω, θαυμάσωμεν Pc   τ(ὸν) ποντικ(ὸν) Po   ποντηκὴν Ω, ποτικὴν Y   γράφει
πρὸς τὸν μέγαν βασίλειον post θαυμάσομαι add. Ab   καὶ τὰ ἐν αὐτοῖς post ξουφηρίαν
add. Ab

οὐδέτερον

35   ξόανον : ἄγαλμα, εἴδωλον· παρὰ τὸ ξέω, ξέανον καὶ ξόανον. οὕτω Φίλων
       τὸ ξ μετὰ τοῦ ῡ
       ἀρσενικόν

36   ξυστός : τόπος ἀνειμένος ἀθλητῇ
37   ξυσμός : ἡ κνησμονή
38   ξύμμαχοι : σύμμαχοι
39   ξύλοχος : ὁ σύνδενδρος τόπος
40   ξυνός : ὁ κοινός
41   ξυνωμότης
42   ξύνευνος καὶ ξυνευνέτης
43   ξυρός : τὸ ξυράφιον ἢ τὸ ἠκονημένον ξίφος
       θηλυκόν
44   ξυνωρίς : ἡ δυάς
45   ξυνουσία : ἡ συνουσία

ORD. 35 post 36 Aa, Am   42 post 52 Am

APP. **35.** εἴδωλον Am, εἴδωλον J, εἴδολον Aa, εἴδῶλον T   τὸ εἴδωλον καὶ ἄγαλμα Ω   ὁ ἐξεσμένος
λίθος ἢ ὁ ἐλεφάντινος. βρέτας δὲ τὸ τοῦ ἀνθρώπου ὅμοιον. ξόανον παρὰ τὸ ξέω κλπ.
post εἴδωλον add. S, U   παρά–ξόανον om. Aa, Am, Ap, Av, Q   ξένω pro ξέω B,
ὀξέω T   ξάανον pro ξέανον Ω   ξούανον L, Γ, ξοῦανον M   ξόανον καὶ ξέανον Ψᵃᶜ
οὕτω Φίλων om. **p1**, **p4**, **p6**, L, M, X, Z, Γ, Σ, Φ   οὕτω Pv καὶ ὁμοίωμα add. Ab

36. Gloss. om. Aa, Am   ξυστος Ω   τόπως T   ὁ ἐξεσμένος ante τόπος add. Pb, Pe,
Po, Pv   ἀνημένος **p3** ἀνυμένος Ap, Av, ἀνειμαίνος B   ἀθλητῇ Pc, Γ, Ψ, ἀθλητῆσ
Tᶜ, ἀθλητῶν Avᵖᶜ, ἀθητῇ Po

37. Gloss. om. Aa, Ab, Am, Ap, Av   ξύσμος Ro   κνησμονή Dᵃᶜ, L, Pc, Σ, Φ, κνισμονή
(κνη-Rᶜ) **p4**, κνισμονή X, κνυσμονή Y, ξυσμονή Re, Pv, ξνησμονή Wᵃᶜ

38. Gloss. om. Am   ξύμαχοι Ap, Av, B   σύμμαχοι om. S, U, σύμμαᾶχοι Pc, σύμαχοι
B, οἱ σύμμαχοι Π, Ω, ξύμμαχοι Aa δεινοποιηταὶ ἐν ἀγάπη add. Ab

39. Gloss. om. Aa, Ab, Am, Ap, Av   ὁ Ro   σύνδεδρος J, Δ, Σ, Φ   τόπος om. D, E, F

40. Gloss. om. Am   ξηνός T   ὀκεινός Av, ἐκεινός Ap   κυνός Pb, Pe, Pv, κύνος Ro
κοινὸς οἶμμαι ὅτι συνός, ὁ συνὼν τινί. παρὰ τὸ συνιέναι τινί (cf. gloss. ξ94) add. Y
ὁ διοδεύων μετ᾿ αὐτῶν add. Ab   ξυνής ἡωμότης (i.e. cum gloss. sequ. conf.) Φ

41. Gloss. om. Aa, Ab, Am, Ap, Av, Ω   ξυνομότης **p6**, B, C, D, E, F, I, T, Y,
ξυνϙμότης W, ξενωμότης X   συνομότης add. Δ, Λ, ξύνευνος (σύνευνος A) καὶ
ξυνευνέτης (cf. gloss. ξ42) add. A, Pe, Pv

42. Gloss. om. Aa, Ab, Am, Ap, Av, Ω   ξύνενος S, T, U, Π, ξύνεννος L, M, Σ,
ξύνεῠος Φ, ξύννενος Q, R, Γ   καὶ om. Pc   ξυνενέτης T, ξυνεῠἔτης
Φ, ξυννυνέτης L, M, ξυνέτης D

43. ξηρός M, ξυρώς T, ξυνός Am   ἢ–ξίφος om. Aa, Am, Ap, Av   ἢ om. Φ, ἢ
Ω, ἤτοι pro ἢ Z, καὶ pro ἢ T   ἠκονημένον I, ἠκονημαίνοον B, ἠκονιμένον F, ἀκονημένον
Ω, ἠκονησμένον Γ, ἠκομένον M   ξίφος Π, ξίφον B   ῡ add. **p3**

44. <ξ>υνωρίς T, ξύνωρις Ro, ξυναρρίς Aa   ἡ om. X   δυάς M, Q, διάς Ap,
Wᵃᵒ   τῶν ἵππων add. **p1**

45. Gloss. om. Am   ξυνοσία Π   ἡ om. **p1**   <σ>υνουσία Φ, οὐσία V, W   φιλία,
ἀγάπη add. Ab

46 ξυνάορος : ἡ γαμετή

47 ξυστίδα : λεπτὸν ὕφασμα

48 ξυνωμοσία· ξυνόμοσις δέ μικρόν

49 ξυλεία : ἡ τῶν ξύλων σωρεία· ἀξυλία δὲ ἰῶτα
οὐδέτερον

50 ξυνήϊα : κοινὰ πράγματα

51 ξυνῳδά : ὅμοια

52 ξυστόν : τὸ κοντόν

53 ξύνθημα : σύνθημα

54 ξυλήφιον : τὸ μικρόν ξυλάριον

55 ξυνόν : τὸ κοινόν

56 ξύλον· παρὰ τὸ ξύω

ORD. 50 post 51 Ab

APP. *46.* Gloss. om. Ab, Am, Ap, Av   ξυνάορος **p3**: ξυνούαρος D, E, F, ξυνόαρος
ceteri ἡ om. Y, ἡ Po   γαμετῆ D^ac, H, J, L, M, Q, Y, Ω
47. Gloss. om. Ab, Am, Ap, Av   ξυστίδα W, Y, Z, Ω: ξυστήδα V, ξυστίστα **p3**,
B, C, G, H, I, J, Ψ, ξυσίστα (ξυσίτα Q) **p4**, **p6**, A, Aa, L, M, X, Γ, Σ, Φ,
ξυστία D, E, F, ξυστίστα καὶ ξυστίς K
48. Gloss. om. Ab, Am, Ap, Av, Ω   ξυνομοσία B, I, ξυνῶμοσία C, ξυνωσία Q,
R, T   συνωμοσία post ξυνωμοσία add. **p1**, ἡ συννωμοσία, μέγα add. **p3**, μέγα
add. **p4**, D, E, F   ξυνόμοσις δὲ μικρόν om. Aa, Pe, Pv   ξυνόμωσις Pb, Pc,
Po, Y, Φ^ac, ξυνόσιμος X, συνόμοσις **p4**
49. Gloss. om. Ab, Am, Ap, Av, Ω   ξύλεια **p1**, **p4**, **p6**, L, M, Δ, Σ, Φ, ξύλεία B,
ξυξεία Pb, Pc, Pe   σωρία **p1**, Λ, Σ, Φ, σωρεῖα D, σωρεία X, σωρέα L, M   δίφθογγον
post σωρεία add. **p22**, **p3** ἀξυλία δὲ ἰῶτα om. Aa, Q   [[ἀ]]ξυλία L, ἀξιλία
Pe, Pv, R^ac, Y, Ψ, ἀξολία B, ἐξυλία Ro   ἰῶτα B   πράγματα pro ἡ τῶν ξ.–
ἰῶτα (i.e. conf. cum ξ50) T
50. Gloss. om. Am, T (sed cf. gloss. praec.) ξυνῆ͜α Av, ξυνία Ap, κοινᾶ Y, κοίνα Ro
ἀγαπητικά add. Ab
51. ξυνωδᾶ Y, X, Γ, Π, Σ, Φ, ξυνοδά Ap, Av, C   ὅμοια Aa, Ro, Pv, ὅμια T, ὅμεια Am,
ὅμοιον Y, Ω   κοινά add. **p3**, αὐτόμοια add. Ab
52. Gloss. om. Aa, Ab, Am, Ap, Av, Z   ξύστον **p4**, **p6**, A, H, J, L, M, X, Γ, Σ, Φ,
ξυστον G   explic. om. W   τὸ om. Aa   κόντιον Ω   τὸ κοντόν I, V, Σ, ὁ̇τὸ
κοντός G, ὁ τὸ κοντός H, J, ὁ κοντός **p4**, **p6**, K, L, M, X, Γ, Φ   ἢ (om. B) ὁ κοντός
add. B, C, D, E
53. Gloss. om. Ab, Am, Ap, Av   <ξ>ύνθημα Pe, ξύνθησμα T   explic. om. H
σύνθεμα Φ, τὸ σύνθημα **p6**, Ω, σύστημα pro σύνθημα **p4**
54. Gloss. om. Aa, Ab, Am, Ap, Av, S, U   ξυλύφιον L, M, ξυλίφιον Y, Ω,
ξυλούφιον **p3**   ξλάριον B, ξύλον Π
55. Gloss. om. S, U   <ξ>υνόν Pe, ξύνον Ro   τὸ om. Ω   κοίνον Ro, κυνόν Σ   τὸ
ξύλον ante τὸ κοινόν add. Ap, Av^m   ξύλον, παρὰ τὸ ξύω (i.e. ξ56) add. C, D, E, F, τὸ
μέσον ἡμῶν διοριστικόν add. Ab
56. Gloss. om. Aa, Ab, Am, Ap, Av, S, U, Z, Ω   ξύλο B   τὸ om. Pc   ξέω Q, R, T
τὸ ἐπιτήδειον πρὸς τὸ ξύεσθαι add. **p3**   οὐδεμία γὰρ ὕλη πρὸς ξύσιν (ξῆσιν Y) ἐπιτηδειο-
τέρα ξύλου add. V, W, Y

ῥῆμα

57 ξυμβαίη : συμβαίη
58 ξυνιέναι : συνιέναι
59 ξυνών : συνυπάρχων
60 ξύνες : ἀντὶ τοῦ σύνες
61 ξυμπονῆσαι : συνάρασθαι, συμβοηθῆσαι
62 ξύει : γράφει · ὅθεν καὶ ξύσματα, τὰ γράμματα
63 ξύμβλητον : συνέτυχον
64 ξύνιον : ἤκουον
65 ξυνίασι : συνέρχονται
66 ξυνιεις : νοεῖς ἢ ἐνενόεις
67 ξυνέηκε : συνῆκε

ORD. 61 post 63 Am   66 bis hab. Av

APP. 57. Gloss. om. Am ξυμβαίην C, D, E, F, ξυμβαίει Aaᵃᶜ, ξήμβαίη Y, ξυμβαίοι Q, ξυμβαίνη X συμβαίην **p22** διῆλθεν, ἐμαχέσατο add. Ab
58. ξυνιένε T explic. om. B, C, D, E, F, I, K, U, in marg. add. J, S² (= συνιαίναι) ἀντὶ τοῦ συνιέναι Ap νοῆσαι add. **p3** διὰ τοῦτο ἦλθεν add. Ab
59. Gloss. om. Am, Ap, Av ξυνῶν **p3** C, D, E, F, L, M, Q, T, W, Y, Φ. Ω, ξυνόν X συμπάρχων Ρο συνυπαρχόντων ἢ συνυπάρχων D μελετῶν, λέγων add. Ab
60. ἀντὶ τοῦ om. **p2** (exc. L, M), **p3**, Avᵃᶜ, ἀντὶ τῆς T ἄκουσον add. **p3**, διανόησον add. Ab
61. Gloss. om. Ab, Am, Ap, Av ξυμπονῆσαι Cᶜ, T ἀντὶ τοῦ συμπονῆσαι ante συνάρασθαι add. W συναράσθαι T, συναρᾶσθαι Q, S, U, συνάρεσθαι M, συνάρα B συμβοηθῆσαι om. Aa, συμβοηθῆσαι T, συνβοηθῆσαι **p2** (etiam L, M), **p3**, A Z, Γ, Σ, Φ, βοηθῆσαι **p6**
62. Gloss. om. Ω γράφῃ M παρ' Ὁμήρῳ ('Ομήρῳ Ρο) post γράφει add. **p3**, ὡς καὶ παρ' Ὁμήρῳ add. **p5** ὅθεν–γράμματα om. Aa, Am, Ap, Av, Q ὅθεν M, Ρο Ψ καὶ om. W
63. Gloss. om. Ab, Am, Ap, Av ξύμβητον Rv, ξυμβλυτόν T συνέτειχον Aa
64. Gloss. om. Ψ ξυνίον Pe, ξυνίονι Rv, ξύνηον Av, ξύνοον Qᵃᶜ ἤκουον Am, B, M, ἤκουον Aa, ἄκουον Ap, Av ἔλαβον add. Ab
65. Gloss. om. Aa, Ab, Am, Ap, Av, Ψ ξυνίασιν B, D, V, W, Φ, Ω ξυνίασις Cᶜ, E, F, ξυνίασον Pb, Pe, Ρο, Rv, ξυνιᾶσι M, ξυνιᾶς L, ξυνίας Rc ἵημι ὁ σημαίνει τὸ ἀπολύω add. V, ἵημι ὁ σημαίνει τὸ ἀπολύω. τὸ τρίτον τῶν πληθυντικῶν ἱεῖσι (ἱείσι W) καὶ ἰωνικῶς ἱέασι. καὶ κατὰ κρᾶσιν (κράσιν codd.) ἵασι. καὶ ἐν συνθέσει add. W, Z
66. ξυνιεῖς T, Π, ξυνίοις X, ξυνιεις ceteri ἢ ἐνενόεις om. Ap ἤ Am, Ω ἐνενόεις D, ἐνηνοεῖς Ρο, ἐνόεις Av (gloss. prior), Z ἢ ἔλεγες add. Ab
67. Gloss. om. Ab, Am, Ap, Av <ξ>υνέηκε Pe, ξυνέηκεν L, T, X, Ω, ξυνέηκες Φ, ξυνέοικε D συνῆκε L, W, συνῆκεν A, Aa, Rv, X, Δ, Λ, συνῆκεν T, συνέβαλεν pro συνῆκε Y, Ω συνέβαλεν. ἵημι, ἥσω, ὁ παρακείμενος ἧκα, τὸ ÿ ἧκε, add. V ἵημι (ἵημι Z), ἥσω (ἥσω Z), ὁ παρακείμενος ἧκα, τὸ τρίτον ἧκε καὶ πλεονασμῷ τοῦ ε̄ ἔηκε (ἔηκεν Z) καὶ ἐν συνθέσει ξυνέηκε add. W, Z

ἐπίρρημα

68 ξυνεχῶς: συνεχῶς

τὸ ξ μετὰ τοῦ ῶ
ἐπίρρημα

69 ξῶθεν καὶ ἔξωθεν

70 ξαίνω: νήθω, σωρεύω **p3**
71 ξαίνω: τὸ τύπτω Φ
72 ξάνθακος Pb, Pe, Po, Pv (cf. s.v. ξ3)
73 ξεῖνον: φίλον **p3**
74 ξεναγός: ὁ τοὺς ξένους τῶν ὁδηγῶν ξενοδοχῶν **p3**
75 ξενηκούσθησαν: ἔστι ξένον, ⟨ὃ⟩ σημαίνει τὸν θαυμαστόν, καὶ τὸ
   ἀκούω καὶ ἐκ τούτου κατὰ σύνθεσιν γέγονεν S, U
76 ξενολόγος: ξένους συλλέγων S, U
77 ξένος: σημαίνει γ̄· τὸν φίλον, ὡς τὸ "ἦ ῥά νύ μοι ξεῖνος πατρώιός ἐσσι
   παλαιός" (Ζ′ 215). καὶ τὸ ἐν τῇ συνηθείᾳ λεγόμενον, "ξεῖνε τίς εἶ;
   πόθεν εἰλήλουθας;" (ι′ 273?). τάσσεται δὲ καὶ ἐπὶ θαύματος, ὡς τὸ
   "ξένον καὶ παράδοξον" (Cosmas Maiuma, Canon Chr. Natal. 177
   [Christ - Paranicas, p. 168]) S, U
78 ξενοσύνη: ξένη φιλία **p3**
79 ξενών: κατάλυμα A, Aa
80 ξενών: τὸ νοσοκομεῖον **p5**, Ω
81 Ξενοφῶν: κύριον **p3**
82 ξέστης: εἶδος μέτρου **p5**, Ω

ORD. 70 post 5 **p3**   71 post 5 Φ   72 post 3 Pb, Pe, Po, Pv   73 post 13 **p3**
74 post 81 **p3**   75 post 18 S, U   76 post 77 S, U   77 post 24 S, U
78 post 11 **p3**   79 post 9 A, post 8 Aa   80 post 10 **p5**, Ω   81 post 10 **p3**
82 post 80 **p5**, Ω

APP. 68. ξ̈εινεχῶς M   explic. om. S, U   συνεχώς Ψ, συννεχῶς Am   καὶ συνεχῶς Ω,
ἀντὶ τοῦ συνεχῶς Ap   διὰ παντός add. **p3**, ἐπιδρομικῶς add. Ab
69. Gloss. om. Ap, Pe, Pv, Φ, Ω   ξξῶθεν Pc, ξώθεν **p2** (exc. L, M), Ψ, ξύνθεν **p4**,
A, Aa, L, M, Δ, Λ, ξῦνθεν X, ξάνθεν vel ξαύθεν Γ, Π, Σ, ξύνοθεν Av, ξύνωθεν
Ab, Am, ξών καὶ ξῶθεν Pb, Po   καὶ om. **p1**, **p3**, **p6**   ἔδιδεν add. Ab
70. σορεύω Pc, σορρεύω cett.
73. ⟨ξ⟩εῖνον Pe
74. ⟨ξ⟩εναγός Pe   ὁδηγῶν Po
76. ξενολόγους U, ξενοπόγους (?) S
77. ἦ ῥά codd.   πρώιος S   ἐστί pro ἐσσι codd.   ἐν τῶ συν. codd.
78. ξενωσύνη codd.
80. ξενῶν Υ, Ω   νοσοκομείον Ω
82. ἦδος Ω

83   ξηρόν : παρὰ τὸ ξῶ ῥῆμα ἀπὸ μεταφορᾶς τῆς ὕλης τῶν ξύλων· εἴ τι
     γὰρ ἔξυσται, ξηρὸν γίνεται. καὶ κατὰ τροπὴν τοῦ η εἰς ε ξερόν. οὕτω
     Φίλων V, W, Y (vid. ξ22, app. crit.)

84   ξυλάρια Pb, Po

85   ξυλιζομένη {ξυλεύω} : ξύλα συλλέγουσα **p3**

86   ξυμβαίνει : ὁ νυμφών ἢ συμπορεύεται **p3**

87   ξυμπονῆσαι : συμπονῆσαι, συνάρασθαι (cf. ξ61) **p3**

88   ξυναίρεται : συναίρεται, συνάπτεται **p3**

89   ξυνάρασθαι : συναρμόσασθαι, συγκαταθέσθαι S, U

90   ξυναρμόσας : συναρμόσας, συνάψας **p3**

91   ξύνθακος : συγκάθεδρος **p3**, Aa^m

92   ξυνθήματος : συνθήματος. ἔστι δὲ σημεῖον ἢ πρόσφθεγμα διδόμενον
     ἐπὶ γνωρισμῷ τῶν οἰκείων ἐν πολέμῳ ἢ ἑτέρᾳ τινὶ ἐπιβουλῇ **p3**, S, U

93   ξυνοδόκος : ξενοδόχος Aa^m

94   ξυνός : κοινός. οἶμαι ὅτι συνός, ὁ συνών τινι· ἢ ξύνιος παρὰ τὸ συνιέναι
     τινί· ἢ παρὰ τὴν ξὺν πρόθεσιν V, W (cf. ξ40)

95   ξυνοχῇσιν ὁδοῦ (Ψ′ 330) V, Y

96   ξυνῳδά : συνῳδά **p3**

97   ξυνών : συνών **p3**

98   ξυνωρίδα : ἅρμα ἐκ δύο ἵππων συνεζευγμένων S, U

99   ξυνωρίδα : ζυγήν. κυρίως δὲ ἐπὶ τῶν ἡμιόνων· ὀρεὺς γάρ ὁ ἡμίονος S, U

100   ξυνωρίς ἐπὶ δυσί, ζεῦγος ἐπὶ πλειόνων S, U

101   ξυνωρίς : συζυγία. κυρίως δὲ ἐπὶ τῶν ἡμιόνων· ‹ὀ›ρεὺς γάρ ἐστιν ὁ
     ἡμίονος Aa^m

102   ξύσματα : γράμματα· ὅθεν καὶ ξύω τὸ γράφω **p3**

ORD.   83 post 22 V,W,Y   84 post 54 Pb, Po   85 post 67 **p3**   86 post 91 **p3**
87 post 103 **p3**   88 post 90 **p3**   89 post 67 S, U   90 post 86 **p3**
91 post 96 **p3**, post 101 Aa^m   92 post 87 **p3**, post 53 S, U   93 post 91 Aa^m
94 post 43 V, W   95 post 49 V, Y   96 post 92 **p3**   97 post 88 **p3**
98 post 100 S, U   99 post 49 S, U   100 post 98 S, U   101 post 103 Aa^m
102 post 56 **p3**

APP. *83.* μεταφοράς Y
85. ξυλιζομένη om. Pe, Pv   ξυλεύω om. Pc
86. νυμφῶν Pc, Po   leg. συμφωνεῖ vel ὁμοφωνεῖ
90. συναρμόσας om. Pc
91. συνκάθεδρος Pb, Pc, Po
92. ὁ πρὸς φθέγμα **p3**   οἰκείων Pv, οἰκίων Pb, Pe   ἢ Pc   ἕτερα Pb, Pe, ἔτερα Po,
    Pv   ἐπιβουλῇ Pb, Pc, Pe, S, ἐπίβουλ(η?) Pv, ἐπιβολή Po
94. ἢ παρὰ τὴν ξῢν πρόθεσιν om. W
96. ξυνῳδᾶ : συνῳδᾶ Pe
97. ξυνῶν codd.   συνῶν Pb, Pe, Po, Pv, σύνων Pc
102. ὅθεν Po

103 ξυστίδας: περιβόλαια **p3**, Aa^m

104 ξύστρα: χλανίς Pb, Pc, Po

105 ξῶν Pc (cf. ξ69)

ORD. 103 post 97 **p3**, post 50 Aa^m   104 post 49 **p3**   105 ante 69 Pc

APP. *103.* ⟨ξ⟩υστίδας Pe
104. πλανίς codd.

PARALLELS

1 cf. K(**a, g, n, v**: ξανθήν) = Σ, Ph., Su., *EG* 413.39; Hes. (ξανθή)

2 cf. Hes. (s.v. ξανθόν); –ποταμός: cf. *EG* 413.33, *EM* 610.19, Su.; schol. *B′* 877, *Z′* 4

4 –τύπτω: cf. *Lex. Patm.* p. 146 (ξαίνειν) = Su.; διαλύω: Ps.-Herod, Su., Th. Mag.

5 cf. K(**a, g, v**), Hes., Bk. 284.9, Σ, Ph., Su.

6 = K(**g**), Ap. Soph.; cf. schol. *Γ′* 354, K(**n**: ξεινοδόκον, **v**: ξυνοδόκος, **a**, **g**: ξυνοθόκος), Σ (ξυνοδόκης), Ph. (ξυνοθόκος), Su. (ξυνοδόκος), Hes. (ξυνοθόκος)

7 = Hes ; cf. K(**a, g, n, v**: ξεῖνοι) = Σ, Ph., Su.

9 cf. Σ, Su., Ps.-Herod.

10 = Su.

11 cf. Hes.; K(**g, v**: ξενίαν) = Σ, Ph., Su.

12 cf. Hes. (ξεστήν), schol. *α′* 138 (ξεστήν)

13 = K(**a, g, v**), Σ, Ph., Su.; cf. Hes. (ξεστός)

14 = schol. *Λ′* 20; cf. K(**v** = ξύνειον, **g** = ξυνήϊον, **n** = ξύνιον)

16 cf. Su. (ξεναλίζω)

19 = Su., *EG* 415.33

20 = Ph., Su., *EM* 612.30

22 cf. Su., Ps.-Herod.; cf. K(**n**) s.v. ξίρις

23 cf. Harp., Ph., Su.; –ἀλείφεσθαι = Ph., Su.; cf. Hes., Bk. 284.13

24 cf. Su.

25 cf. K(**g**) = Σ, Ph., Su.; Hes. (ξιφήρεις)

26 cf. K(**n**), Hes. (ξειρίς), *An. Ox.* II, 242.10, *Et. Sym.*, Su., *EG* 415.42, Phot. (ξείρης)

27 = Su.

28 cf. Ph., Su. (ξιφηφορία)

29 = Ps.-Herod., Hes.; cf. K(**a**)

31 = K(**a, g, v**), Σ, Ph.

32 cf. St. Byz. (Ξόϊς), Georg. Choerob., *Schol. in Theod. Alex. Canones I*, 196,12 Hilgard

33 cf. Theodos. Alex. *Canones* ed. Hilgard, II, 405.1

35 –εἴδωλον = K(**a, g, n, v**), Σ, Ph., Su.; cf. Hes. (ξόανα), Ps.-Herod.; παρά–ξόανον =
EG 415.55, *Et. Sym.*; cf. Orion, 112.9, *EM* 611.12

36 cf. K(**a, g, v**), Hes., Σ, Ph., Su., Bk. 284.19 (s.v. ξυστόν), *EM* 612.25

37 cf. K(**a, g, n, v**, s), Hes.

38 = K(**a, g, n, v**), Hes.

39 = K(**a**), Hes.; cf. K(s), *EM* 611.22, Ph. (ξυλοῦχος), Su., Ps.-Herod.; K(**g, n**:
ξύλοχον), schol. *E′* 162

40 = *EG* 416.57, *EM* 611.29, K(s); cf. K(**a, g, n**: ξυνόν) = Hes., Su., Ps.-Herod.;
cf. also θ55

41 cf. Su.

42 cf. Su. (ξυνευνέτης), K(s)

43 –ξυράφιον = Λεξικὸν τῆς Γραμμ. (Bachmann, *AG* I, 436.3), Λεξικὸν σχεδογραφ. 583
(Boissonade, *AG* IV, 395)

44 = Ps.-Herod.; cf. *An. Ox.* II, 395.14, *EG* 417.1, *EM* 611.33
45 = K(**a, g, n, v**, P, s); cf. Hes.
46 = K(**n**, s); cf. K(**a, g, v** = ξυνάορον) = Σ, Ph., Su.; Hes. (ξυνάορον)
47 = K(**a, g, n, v**), Hes., Σ, Ph., Su.; cf. K(P = ξυστίς)
49 –σωρεία: cf. Ps.-Herod., Su.
50 = K(**a, g, n, v**), *EG* 416.30; cf. Hes., Σ, Ph., Su., *EM* 612.10
51 cf. K(**a, g, v**, s), Hes.; cf. also ξ96
52 cf. K(**a, g, n**), Σ, Ph.
53 Ph.; cf. K(**a, g, v**: ξυνθήματος) = Hes., *EG* 416.42
54 cf. *An. Ox.* II, 242.29 = *EM* 611.23, *Et. Sym.*; Th. Mag.
55 = Ps.-Herod.; cf. K(**a, g, v**, P), Hes., Su.; cf. also ξ40
56 = *EM* 611.19, *Et. Sym.*
57 = K(**g**)
58 = K(**g, v**, P); cf. Hes.
59 cf. K(**a, g, n, v**), Hes.
60 cf. schol. *B'* 26, K(**a, g, v**), Hes., Su., Ph., *EM* 611.52
61 –συνάρασθαι = K(**a, g**, P); cf. K(**g**)
62 = K(**v**); cf. K(**g**), Hes., Ph., Su.
63 = schol. *Ξ'* 27, *Ω'* 709
64 = Hes., Su.; cf. K(**a, n**), *EM* 612.5
65 = Su.
66 –νοεῖς: cf. schol. Arist. *Plut.* 45 (οὐ ξυνίης), schol. θ'241 (ξυνίει)
67 Apio 96.9; cf. *EM* 317.53 (s.v. ἔηκεν); cf. K(**a**)
68 = K(**a, g, v**), Hes.
69 cf. K(**a, g, n, v**, P, s), Hes.
70 = K(**g, v**), Σ, Ph., Su.; cf. Hes. (ξαίνει
71 = Ps.-Zon. (fuller version); cf. *Lex. Patm.* (ξαίνειν), Su. (ξαίνειν e schol. Aristoph. *Eq.* 369)
73 = K(**g, n, v**); cf. Ps.-Herod.
74 cf. K(**g. v**: ξεναγῶν), Hes. (ξεναγῶν)
75 = K(**v3**), *EG* 414.29
76 = Hes.; cf. K(**a, n**), Σ, Ph., Su., sch. Luc. 94.17 Rabe
77 = *EM* 610.36; cf. *EG* 415.1, *Et. Sym.*
78 cf. K(**g, v**: ξενοσύνην)
79 = K(**a, n**, P), Hes.
82 cf. Orion 112.11, *EG* 414.40, *EM* 610.54, *Et. Sym.*
83 cf. Orion 111.14, *EG* 415.17, *EM* 611.3, *Et. Sym.*
85 = K(**a, g, n, v**); cf. Hes. (ξυλιζομένην)
86 = K(**g**)
87 = K(**g**), cf. also ξ61
88 cf. K(**a, g**), Hes., Σ, Ph., Su.
89 = K(**v3**), *EG* 416.11, *EM* 611.37, αἰμωδεῖν *Etym.* 627.22 Sturz; cf. *Et. Sym.*
90 = K(**g, v**); –συναρμόσας = K(**a, n**, P); συνάψας: Hes.
91 = K(**a, g, v**, s), Hes., *EG* 416.45
92 = K(**g, v**), Hes., *EG* 416.42
93 = K(**v**), Su.; cf. K(**a, g**), Ph., Hes.
94 = *EM* 611.29; cf. *EG* 416.57
96 = K(**a, g, v**, s), Hes.; cf. also ξ51
97 = K(**a, g, n, v**, P), Hes.; cf. also ξ59

98 = K(**g**, **v**); cf. K(**a**, **n**: ξυνωρίς) = Hes., Σ, Ph., Su.
99 = K(**a**, **g**, **v**), Hes., *EG* 416.55
100 = K(**v3**), *EG* 418.1
101 cf. ξ99
102 –γράμματα = K(**g**); ξύω τὸ γράφω: cf. *Λεξικὸν σχεδουρ.* 581 (Boissonade *AG* IV, 395);
cf. also ξ62
103 = K(**g**, **v**); cf. Σ = Ph., Su., Hes.
104 cf. K(**g**, **v**)

Relationship of the Two Versions

A comparison of the two versions shows that the shorter is not an abridgment of the fuller or printed version; on the contrary there are good reasons to believe that the latter is an expansion and further development of the former. The main argument in support of this thesis is the tendency of the "Bearbeiter" of the extended version to conflate similar entries; thus θ2 and 3 in **p** correspond to Tittm. 1 (θᾶκος); θ4 and 14 = Tittm. 6 (θαλερός); θ12 and 26 = Tittm. 3 (θάλαμος); θ17 and 18 = Tittm. 9 (θαρσεῖς); θ45 and 46 = Tittm. 33 (θακεύουσιν); θ42 and 44 = Tittm. 42 (θανατῶν); ξ12 and 13 = Tittm. 17 (ξεστή); ξ15 and 17 = Tittm. 21 (ξεναγεῖται); ξ25 and 28 = Tittm. 33 (ξιφήρης καὶ ξιφηφόρος); ξ36 and 52 = Tittm. 48 (ξυστός). Although it is conceivable that a scribe could break a composite gloss into a number of smaller units, the opposite process is much better attested.[118] Besides I cannot see how the entry θᾶκοι in **p** (θ2) with the lemma in the plural could have originated from θᾶκος (= Tittm. 1), or the gloss ξεστόν (ξ13) would have come from ξεστή (= Tittm. 17). Furthermore, some of the component parts of the composite glosses of the printed version come from distinctly different sources. Thus θ2 comes probably from the *Suda Lexicon*, whereas θ3 is an etymological gloss; similarly θ12, another etymological gloss, has been combined with another Suda gloss (θ26), etc.

Further evidence for the priority of the shorter version is provided by the alphabetical arrangement. The arrangement of the printed version seems indeed slightly improved over that of the shorter version. Thus θ7, 8 have been removed from the θα-section, θάκος precedes θαλαμηπόλος, θάμνος is among the masculine nouns, θαάσσων appears at the head of the verbs, etc. Finally the reading

[118] Cf. my article (above, page 437), pp. 194–195.

θαλπότερον of the fuller version vs. θαλπνότερον and the change of θαιρούς to θαιροί furnish additional evidence in favor of the seniority of the shorter version.

For the same reason the special closeness which was observed earlier between the fuller version and the **p5** family, seen in the light of this discussion, points to a dependence of the former on the latter. The absorption of additional glosses θ59, 70 by Tittmann entries 15 and 7 respectively bears heavily on this point, and so does the appearance of the quotation θαλερόν δάκρυ in the composite entry Tittm. 6. Furthermore the addition Ξέννων before Ξέννωνος Ξένετος in **p5** is but an attempt by the redactor of the fuller version to improve on what seemed to be an awkward combination of a genitive noun with a nominative. Suda ξ38 (Ξενίωνος : ὄνομα κύριον), the apparent source of the addition Ξέννωνος in **p5**, helps to determine the steps which led from ξ10 to Tittm. 11, with a good degree of probability.

A study of the parallels confirms in the main the commonly-held view that the glosses originate from three distinct sources: a version of St. Cyril's Lexicon, *Suda*, and an etymologicum.[119] The Cyrillean glosses usually occur at the beginning of each group or section of the Lexicon and are followed by those originating from the *Suda*. They cannot be traced back to any particular family or recension with certainty, but as a rule they agree closely with one or more of the recensions **a, g, v** and more particularly with **g, v**.[120] In a number of cases the **p** entry has undergone some changes which affect either the form of the lemma or the word order and/or the size of the explanation.[121] Similar changes occur also in glosses originating in the *Suda Lexicon* (cf. θ2, 35, 40, 43; ξ9, 10, 22, 24, 49). This together with the fact that some of the **p** glosses have parallels in both St. Cyril and the *Suda* (to say nothing of other lexica) greatly complicates the

---

[119] Cf. above, note 3. Bernhardy (above, note 5) actually suggested that only the fuller version had come under the influence of the *Suda Lexicon*, whereas Rupprecht (above, note 3) attributed all these glosses to Eudemus.

[120] Cf. especially θ1, 20, 27, 30, 48, 51; ξ38, 39, 45, 50, 57, 58, 68, 69.

[121] Cf. θαλερός : ἀκμαῖος, ἰσχυρός, νέος (θ4) vs. θαλερόν : ἀκμαῖον, νέον (**a, g**; cf. also **v**. Σ, Ph., Su. have θαλεροί : δίυγροι, νέοι, ἀκμαῖοι ἢ ταχεῖς); θαλπωρή : τέρψις, χαρά, διάχυσις (θ24) vs. θαλπωρή : χαρά, διάχυσις, θάλψις (**a, g, v**); θάτερον : τῶν δύο τὸ ἕτερον (θ31) vs. θάτερον : ἑκάτερον, τὸ ἕτερον τῶν δύο (**g, P**); θαμίζει : συχνάζει, συνεχῶς ἔρχεται (θ41) vs. θαμίζεις : συνεχῶς ἔρχῃ συχνάζεις (**g**; cf. also **a, n, v**, Hes., etc.).

problem of assigning a particular gloss to a definite source. Nevertheless the evidence is strong enough to show that the influence of the *Suda
Lexicon* extends beyond the K-section,[122] against Adler's assertion.[123]

The tendency to effect changes and (to a lesser degree) to combine
related entries[124] makes it difficult to determine the exact source of
the etymological glosses. On the whole, however, there are several
close parallels between **p** and the unpublished Symeon's Etymologicum.[125] It is doubtful, however, that Symeon was the sole
source of all etymological glosses as is commonly believed.[126] The
omission by Symeon of θ50 and of the reference in ξ35 on the one
hand, together with slight but not always negligible changes in the
parallel glosses, show that the dependence of our version on Symeon
is far from conclusive. Since there is no evidence of Symeon's dates
(the only *terminus ante quem* resting on the assumption that he must
have preceded our Lexicon) and since Symeon's MSS are a bit later
than ours, some caution is necessary. There were certainly many
more versions of the etymological dictionaries than those preserved.

Besides glosses traceable to the above three sources there are some
that must have come from elsewhere. Thus θ9, 10 come from a
lexicon of definitions such as the one found in Vat. gr. 868 from fol.
171ʳ on; θ17, 25 are Biblical; θ29 (like its correspondent θ36) and
possibly also ξ66 are *differentiae*; ξ49, 50 are of grammatical-
orthographic[127] nature whereas ξ21, 30, 32, and 33 are proper
names.[128] There are besides some glosses which are completely
unparalleled and/or unattested in ancient writers: cf. θ18, ξ3, 16,

---

[122] Cf. especially ξ10, 24, 27, 65 which have unique parallels in the *Suda*.

[123] Cf. *Suidae Lexicon*, ed. A. Adler (Lexicographi Graeci, vol. I), part I (Leipzig 1928),
p. xv.

[124] Combined entries: θ21, 25, 35; ξ4, 35, 43, 49, 61, 66.

[125] Cf. θ3, 11, 12, 13, ξ35, 54, 56. Note however that in all these cases (except θ11)
there are close parallels also in *EM* and/or *EG*.

[126] Cf. especially R. Reitzenstein, *op. cit.* (above. note 2), 279 sqq.; L. Cohn (above,
note 3), 704; Tolkiehn (above, note 3), 2475; Sell (above, note 4), xx. Reitzenstein,
however, modified his earlier more extreme view in Pauly-Wissowa, *RE* vol. 6 (1907),
817 (art. "Etymologika").

[127] The arrangement of the entire lexicon also betrays the influence of grammatical
classification similar to the one found in the so-called *Lexicon Ambrosianum* (= cod.
Ambros. B12 sup); cf. also cod. Atheniensis 1065, Laur. 59.16, Patm. 322, Zavord. 95.

[128] These together with the former were probably excerpted from a work similar to
Choeroboscus, *Scholia in Theodosii Alexandrini canones*, or the *Epimerismi* falsely attributed
to Herodianus.

34; or unattested in the meaning attributed to them: cf. ξ15, 17, 18, 22 (the first meaning), 43 (the second meaning). Of special interest are ξ34 with the quotation from the letters of St. Gregory of Nazianzus[129] and θ16 which echoes the entry περὶ θαλλῶν of the *Geoponica*.

Two basic questions can now be examined under a different light: that of the authorship and that of the date of the dictionary. Nowhere is there a reference to John Zonaras. Ascription to Antonius Monachus is found only in the late MSS Pb, Pe and may be reasonably attributed to all **p3** MSS. Since it occurs in some MSS of the fuller version much earlier,[130] the **p3** MSS may have borrowed it from the fuller version. Whether, however, Antonius had anything to do with the fuller version is still an open question which may be settled with a study of the MSS of that version.

Concerning the date of composition, I believe Tittmann's observation about the entry ἤλεκτρον (pp. lxxii–lxxiii) to be valid and, since the form ἦν appears even in the earlier MSS of both versions, a date after 1204 should be assigned. A *terminus ante quem* is provided by cod. Vat. gr. 10 (a MS of the fuller version) dated A.D. 1253. The quick proliferation of the new dictionary is shown both by the fact that there are in existence thirteen MSS of the fuller and seven (A, H, I, J, Q, Π, Σ) of the shorter version written in the XIII century; and by the establishment of the two versions as well as the basic families in that century. Within the XIII and the XIV centuries it ranked first in popularity with St. Cyril's Lexicon. The degree of its success can no longer be overlooked by the student of intellectual history of this important period.[131]

Urbana, 10 November 1970

---

[129] It is a testimony to the accuracy of our lexicon as against the exaggerated criticisms of modern scholars that it has here preserved the right reading which was restored in the text only in the last edition of Gregory's letters by Paul Gallay (Berlin 1969).

[130] The earliest occurrence, to the best of my knowledge, is in cod. Ottob. gr. 252 (A.D. 1291/1292); cf. A. Turyn, *op. cit.* (above, note 32), pp. 81–82, plate 48.

[131] Addendum, Sept. 1973. This study was completed before K. Alpers' extensive article "Zonarae Lexicon" appeared in Pauly-Wissowa, *RE* 2. Reihe, 19. Halbband (Munich 1972), and it has not been possible to revise it so as to take into account Alpers' discussion of the sources. It may be noted, however, that the main thesis of the present study, which establishes the seniority of the shorter over the fuller version, puts the whole question of the sources and the authorship under a different light.

APPENDIX

Checklist of MSS of the Fuller Version

Athens, cod. Lambros 19 (XVI s.)

Athos, M. Βατοπεδίου 514 (XVI s.)

    M. Διονυσίου 465 (olim 224 = A.D. 1558)

    M. Μεγίστης Λαύρας I 42 (XVIII s.), K71 (XIV s.)

    M. Παντελεήμονος 824 (XVII s.)

Bern, Burgesbibl. 288 (XIII/XIV s.)

Bologna, 3559 (A.D. 1290/1)

Cambridge, Kk. v. 25 (XV s.)

Dresden, Da 37 (now in Kharkov, USSR = XIV s.)

Edinburgh, 226 (XV/XVI s.)

Escorial, Ψ-III-16 (A.D. 1256)

Florence, Laur. plut. 5.7 (A.D. 1473/4), 9.27 (XIV s.), conv. soppr. 146 (XIV s.)

Lawrence, Univ. of Kansas Library, MS. 20 (XV s.)

London, Brit. Mus., Harl. 5572 (XIII s.)

Milan, M80 sup. (XIV s.)

Modena, Bibl. Est., α W.5.5 (XV s.)

Munich, gr. 263 (XIII s.), 510 (XIV s.)

Paris, gr. 1142 (XIV s.), 2408 (XIII s.), 2619 (XIV s.), 2620 (XV s.), 2633 (XIII s.), 2634 (XV s.), 2637 (XV s.), 2639–2640 (XVI s.),[132] 2664 (XIV s.), 2667 (XV s.), 2668 (XVIII s.)

  Coisl. gr. 178 (XV s.), 346 (XIII s.)

  Suppl. gr. 461 (XV s.), 662 (XIV s.)

Sinai, gr. 1202 (XIV s.), 1203 (XIV/XV s.), 1205 (XIV s.), 1369 (XVI s.), 2072 (XIV s.)

Uppsala 16 (XIV s.)

Vatican, gr. 9 (XIII s.), 10 (A.D. 1253), 868 (XIII/XIV s.), 872 (XIV s.), 873 (XIV s.), 875 (XIV s.), 876 (XIV s.)

  Ottob. gr. 252 (A.D. 1291/2)

  Palat. gr. 46 (XIII s.)

  Urbin. gr. 158 (XIII s.)

Venice, gr. 140 (XIV s.), 492 (XV s.)

  Append. X.2 (XIII/XIV s.), X.19 (XIV s.), X.23 (XV s.)

Vienna, phil. gr. 32 (XVI s.), 122 (XIII s.), 154 (XIV s.), 178 (A.D. 1429/30), suppl. graec. 173 (formerly Nikolsburg I. 133) XV s.

The lost MS 38 of the monastery τοῦ Μεγάλου Σπηλαίου (XIV s.) also belonged to the fuller version as appears from the specimen given by Bees.

---

[132] Cod. 2640 contains the first and 2639 the second part of the Lexicon.

Fragments of the Fuller Version

Athos, M. Διονυσίου 539 (olim 355) fols. 226ʳ–29ʳ only (XV s.)

Leiden, B.P.L. 484 (XVIII s.), Periz. Q 59 (XVIII s.), Voss. Misc. 1 (XVII s.). All contain the same excerpts from the fuller version.

Paris, gr. 902 (XIV s., contains only entries beginning with *alpha*), 2551 (XV/XVI s.) entries from ἀϊδῶς to ἀρίζηλος.

The exact affiliation of the following mss is not known to me, but they must belong to one or the other version as their titles and/or beginnings suggest: Cairo, Patriarch. of Alexandria 71; Dresden Da 41 (XVI s.); Istanbul, Serail No. 4 (A.D. 1464), Μετόχιον Παναγίου Τάφου 43 (XV s.); Leningrad, Gosud. Publ. Bibl., No. 256 (cf. E. E. Granström, *Vizant. Vrem.*, N.S. 8, 1856, 197); cf. also Berlin, Phillipps 1611 (XVI s.), Paris, grec 2643 (XIV s.?), Utrecht, Univ. Bibl., No. 10 (XVII s.), all containing fragments of the lexicon.

EINE FRÜHBYZANTINISCHE WACHSTAFEL DER WIENER PAPYRUSSAMMLUNG (ÖSTERREICHISCHE NATIONALBIBLIOTHEK GWT 2)

HERBERT HUNGER

Das bisher ungelesene Objekt befindet sich seit dem Ende des 19. Jahrhunderts in Wien. Der anläßlich der ersten großen Papyrus-Ausstellung in Wien 1894 publizierte "Führer durch die Ausstellung" der von Erzherzog Rainer erworbenen Papyri verzeichnet unter Nr. 50 (S. 11): "Griechische Wachstafel des V.-VI. Jahrhunderts n.Chr. mit einem Dictat oder Brouillon einer Bittschrift. (K. Wessely.) Wachstafel. Breite 14,8: Höhe 9,1 cm."

Der Gräzist und Papyrologe Karl Wessely, ein hervorragender Kenner der griechischen Paläographie, muß damals nur einen flüchtigen Blick auf die Tafel geworfen haben. Wahrscheinlich las er das zu Beginn der zweiten Zeile stehende Wort ἱκετηρίαν und ließ sich dadurch zu der obenstehenden, falschen Angabe verleiten. Tatsächlich enthält die Tafel einen Gebetstext, der zwar in paläographischer Hinsicht nur mäßige Schwierigkeiten bietet, der sachlichen und sprachlichen Erklärung jedoch einige Nüsse zu knacken gibt.

Die Schrift (vergl. Taf. I) zeigt die Merkmale des griechischen Kanzleistils der späten Kaiserzeit, unter dessen Einfluß sich die ehemalige Zweizeilenschrift (Majuskel) seit dem 4. Jahrhundert allmählich in eine Vierzeilenschrift (Minuskel) verwandelte. Der Vergleich mit datierten Papyrusurkunden gestattet es uns, die Schrift der Wachstafel mit ziemlicher Sicherheit in die zweite Hälfte des 5. Jahrhunderts zu setzen. Bei dem Vergleich einzelner Buchstabenformen ist freilich zu bedenken, daß manches abweichende Detail durch den unterschiedlichen Beschreibstoff und das Schreibgerät (stilus) bedingt sein kann. Im ganzen ist die Hand keineswegs als elegant oder auch nur ausgeglichen, jedoch auch nicht als ungeübt zu bezeichnen.

Text

ο θεοσ εκ τησ αρχιασ μειζων
ικετηριαν αναχειν αυτοισ [. .]υποισ των
ολων περιγιων οικουντων ανωθεν
την επαρχειαν γηητων περιγιων εν
5   ταυτι διαγοντων νυνε[. .]ιτων επι
ιαξεν υπερ πραξιαι[.] σισμουσ τουτουσ
υπομηγαι περατα [.]υν διαυβαινων
και κατεπεμφθη περι τοπων θειον και
προσκυνουμεν σε χε πισμα προσ τουσ

'Ο Θεὸς ἐκ τῆς ἀρχίας μείζων,
ἱκετηρίαν ἀναχεῖν αὐτοῖς κτύποις τῶν
ὅλον περίγειον οἰκούντων ἄνωθεν,
τὴν ἐπαρχίαν γηῖτων περίγειον ἐν-
5   ταυθὶ διαγόντων Νινεουιτῶν ἐπ-
ίαξεν, ὑπὲρ πραξίαις σεισμοὺς τούτους
ὑπομεῖναι. πέρατα οὖν διαβαίνων
. . . .
καὶ κατεπέμφθη περὶ τόπον θεῖον καὶ
. . . .
προσκυνοῦμέν σε, Χριστέ, πεῖσμα πρὸς τοὺς

Übersetzung

Gott, der von Anbeginn die Macht hat, mit bloßem Donner von oben die Gebete der Bewohner des ganzen Erdkreises auszulösen, hat die Provinz der hier als Eingeborene lebenden Niniviter gezwungen, für ihre Missetaten diese Erdbeben auf sich zu nehmen. Auf dem Wege über die Grenzen (des Erdkreises?)...und Schwefel wurde auf die Gegend herabgeschleudert und...wir beten Dich an, Christus, unser Schutz gegen die ...

* * *

Die Schlußzeile zeigt, daß es sich um ein Gebet gegen drohende Erdbeben handelt. Mit den letzten Worten des unvollständigen Satzes war der Platz der Wachstafel ursprünglich noch nicht verbraucht. Im jetzigen Zustand ist die Tafel allerdings ein

Fragment, an dessen unterem Rand man die Spuren von Oberlängen einiger Buchstaben der nächsten, nicht mehr lesbaren Zeile erkennt.

Der Beschreibstoff deutet darauf hin, daß es sich um einen Entwurf oder einen nach Diktat geschriebenen Text handelt. Die itazistischen Verschreibungen und sonstigen Verstöße gegen die Orthographie überschreiten nicht das Maß von Fehlern, wie wir sie von Leuten mäßiger Schulbildung in allen Jahrhunderten der byzantinischen Zeit kennen. Auffälliger sind verschiedene sprachliche, morphologische und syntaktische, Eigenwilligkeiten, die daran denken lassen, daß der Schreiber das Griechische nicht als Muttersprache, sondern nur in einem gewissen Umfang in der Schule erlernt hatte.

(1) Das ἐκ τῆς ἀρχίας in Zeile 1 muß dem Sinn nach einem ἐξ ἀρχῆς (von Anfang an) entsprechen. Nun gibt es bekanntlich die verschiedensten Komposita wie ἀναρχία, ἱππαρχία, κωμαρχία, μοναρχία, τοπαρχία, συναρχία u.a., aber nur das nomen simplex ἀρχή. Ἀρχία = principatus zitiert Ph. J. Kukules aus dem *Corpus Gloss. Lat.* III 510,34 in *Byz. Zeitschr.* 20 (1911), 417 (freundlicher Hinweis von E. Kriaras).

(2) μείζων (Z. 1) scheint an Stelle von δυνατός zu stehen, von dem ein Infinitiv (ἀναχεῖν) abhängig gedacht werden kann.

(3) Z. 6 ὑπὲρ πραξίαις: πράξεις wird im NT zumeist abwertend in Sinne von "böse Taten", "Praktiken" gebraucht (vgl. Kittel–Friedrich, *Theolog. Wörterbuch zum NT*, VI 644). Eine ähnliche Bedeutung ist auch hier erforderlich. Wiederum scheint ein Metaplasmus wie bei ἀρχία vorzuliegen, da zwar ἀπραξία, δικαιοπραξία, ἱεροπραξία, κοινοπραξία, ματαιοπραξία, πρωτοπραξία u.a. bekannt sind, das nomen simplex selbst jedoch fehlt. Der falsch verwendete Dativ ὑπὲρ πραξίαις erklärt sich allerdings leicht aus dem allmählichen Schwinden dieses Casus und der wachsenden Unsicherheit in seiner Anwendung. Gerade bei unserem Schreiber werden wir uns darüber nicht wundern dürfen.

Der Anakoluth nach Z. 7 (διαβαίνων καὶ κατεπέμφθη) macht den Ausfall einer Zeile bzw. mehrerer Worte sehr wahrscheinlich. Dasselbe scheint für den abrupten Übergang zwischen vorletzter und letzter Zeile des Textes zu gelten.

Die Erwähnung der Nineviter, aber auch andere Vokabel und Wendungen, erinnern an die Septuaginta. Wir haben es mit einem

Gebetstext zu tun: Zunächst wird Gottes Macht geschildert, die sich in atmosphärischen und seismischen Erscheinungen drohend äußert und böse Menschen für ihre Missetaten straft. Was dieser Text und manche spätere, im byzantinischen Euchologion überlieferte, analoge Texte ausdrücken wollen, ist in dem einen Satz des Propheten Jeremias programmatisch vorgebildet (*Jer.* 23, 19): ἰδοὺ σεισμὸς παρὰ Κυρίου καὶ ὀργὴ ἐκπορεύεται εἰς συσσεισμόν, συστρεφομένη ἐπὶ τοὺς ἀσεβεῖς ἥξει. Die Not lehrt die Menschen beten. Das seltene ἀναχεῖν (Z. 2 = lockern, lösen) findet sich etwa bei Philon, *Leg. alleg.* III 87: ἡ χαρὰ οὐ παροῦσα μόνον, ἀλλὰ καὶ ἐλπιζομένη ἀναχεῖ τε καὶ εὐφραίνει τὴν ψυχήν. Alle Menschen reagieren auf diese drohenden Zeichen von oben (ἄνωθεν), auf der ganzen Welt—περίγειον in dieser Bedeutung: Joh. Jerus., *Vita Joh. Damasc.* (*PG* 94), 432 A, 453 A.

Nun heißt es, daß Gott speziell die Provinz der Niniviter geschlagen habe; sie werden als γηῖτων περίγειον ἐνταυθὶ διαγόντων charakterisiert. Γηίτης wird bei Stephanos von Byzanz s.v. γῆ mit ὁ αὐτόχθων glossiert; es sollen also die Niniviter als eingeborene Bewohner dieses Landes bezeichnet werden; ἐνταῦθα διάγειν bedeutete "hier seinen Wohnsitz haben."[1] Die Niniviter mußten für ihre Schandtaten Erdbeben über sich ergehen lassen (σεισμοὺς τούτους ὑπομεῖναι). Aus dem Propheten Jonas wissen wir allerdings, daß der Herr den Ninivitern wegen ihrer Missetaten den Untergang androhte, sich dann aber angesichts der Bußfertigkeit des ganzen Volkes ihrer erbarmte. Mit den in unserem Text genanntenErdbeben kann also keine Vernichtung der Niniviter gemeint sein; an sich konnte höchstens von einer Bedrohung der Niniviter gesprochen werden. So formuliert ein Sticheron im Rahmen eines byzantinischen Gebetes gegen Erdbeben, das ebenfalls auf die Niniviter als abschreckendes Beispiel hinweist: Νινευΐται τοῖς παραπτώμασι τὴν διὰ σεισμοῦ ἀπειλὴν κατάχωσιν ἤκουον.[2] Der Gedanke, daß Gott derartige Naturkatastrophen wie Erdbeben wegen der sündigen Menschen schicke, kehrt in diesen Gebeten oft wieder, z.B.: ἐκτρίψαι σεισμῷ πάντας ἡμᾶς διὰ πληθὺν ἁμαρτιῶν ἐπαπειλοῦντα δεινῶς[3] oder: οἴδαμεν, ὅτι διὰ τὰς πολλὰς ἡμῶν ἁμαρτίας συνέσεισας τὴν γῆν καὶ συνετάραξας

---

[1] Beispiele für das 6.–7. Jh. bei Preisigke, *Wörterbuch der griechischen Papyrusurkunden*, s.v.

[2] Εὐχολόγιον τὸ μέγα (Rom 1873), S. 414,6 f. (= *Euchologion*).

[3] *Euchologion*, S. 412,11 f.

αὐτήν[4] und τοῦτο τῶν πονηρῶν καὶ ἀκαθάρτων ἡμῶν πράξεων τὸ κατάλ-
ληλον ἀποτέλεσμα.[5]

Das grammatisch isolierte πέρατα οὖν διαβαίνων[6] scheint Gott als
Subjekt zu verlangen. Zu vergleichen ist *Is.* 34, 5, wo es vom Schwert
Gottes heißt: ἰδοὺ ἐπὶ τὴν Ἰδουμαίαν καταβήσεται καὶ ἐπὶ τὸν λαὸν τῆς
ἀπωλείας μετὰ κρίσεως. In den Septuaginta findet sich πέρατα zumeist
mit τῆς γῆς verbunden; es kommt aber auch allein vor, *Ps.* 64, 9:
καὶ φοβηθήσονται οἱ κατοικοῦντες τὰ πέρατα ἀπὸ τῶν σημείων σου.

Bekannt ist der Schwefel- und Feuerregen, der über Sodom und
Gomorra niederging.[7] Wie in unserem Text heißt es an mehreren
Stellen des *AT*, daß es Schwefel regnete. *Ezech.* 38, 22: καὶ πῦρ καὶ
θεῖον βρέξω ἐπ' αὐτόν; *Is.* 34, 9: καὶ ἡ γῆ αὐτῆς εἰς θεῖον (scil. στραφή-
σεται); *Ps.* 10, 6: ἐπιβρέξει ἐπὶ ἁμαρτωλοὺς παγίδας, πῦρ καὶ θεῖον. Die
Verbindung "Feuer und Schwefel" findet sich auch an mehreren
Stellen der Apokalypse des Johannes.[8]

Nach dem Ende der vorletzten (lesbaren) Zeile ist scheinbar noch
irgendein ergänzender Satzteil über die Folgen dieses Schwefel-
regens zu erwarten; vielleicht hat es ursprünglich θεῖον καὶ ⟨πῦρ⟩
geheißen. Jedenfalls fehlt auch irgendeine Konjunktion, die das
προσκυνοῦμεν an das Vorhergehende anschließen würde. Wie eine
solche Verbindung aussehen kann, möge wiederum ein Beispiel aus
dem Euchologion zeigen: νῦν ἔγνωμεν, Κύριε, ὡς ἐλέησας ἡμᾶς καὶ
οὐδαμῶς συνέχωσας ὑπὸ τὴν γῆν συμπτώματι χαλεπῷ πολλὰ πλημμελή-
σαντας· εὐχαρίστως διό σε προσκυνοῦμεν, Χριστέ.[9] Hier handelt es sich
allerdings um das Dankgebet nach glücklich überstandenem Erdbeben. In unserem Text scheint eher die Bitte um Abwehr des
Verderbens gefolgt zu sein. Darauf deutet m.E. die Verwendung des
seltenen Wortes πεῖσμα (= Haltetau, im übertragenen Sinn: Rück-
halt, Zuflucht) für Christus hin. Mehrfach gebraucht das Wort
Philon.[10]

---

[4] *Euchologion*, S. 415,20 f.

[5] *Euchologion*, S. 417,11 f.

[6] Die Wachstafel schreibt διαυβαίνων mit abundierendem Ypsilon vor Beta: St. G.
Kapsomenakis, *Voruntersuchungen zu einer Grammatik der Papyri der nachchristlichen Zeit*
(München 1938), S. 9 ff.

[7] *Gen.* 19, 24; *3 Makk.* 2, 5.

[8] *Apok.* 9, 17 f.; 14, 10; 19, 20; 20, 10; 21, 8.

[9] *Euchologion*, S. 411, 4.—2. Z. von unten.

[10] Vgl. den Index von J. Leisegang in der Ausgabe von Cohn–Wendland.

Trotz Verstümmelung und sprachlicher Mängel zeigt der Text dieser Wachstafel, daß man bereits zu Zeiten Kaiser Zenons bei drohendem Erdbeben in ähnlichen Gedanken und Wendungen zu Gott betete wie ein Jahrtausend später und noch heute in den tradierten Gebetsformeln der orthodoxen Kirche.

Dem verehrten Jubilar und Freund aber sei diese bescheidene Edition gewidmet im Hinblick auf die unschätzbaren Dienste, die er der griechischen Paläographie mit seinem monumentalen Band der datierten Codices der Bibliotheca Vaticana aus dem 13. und 14. Jahrhundert erwiesen hat.

Wien, 21. März 1970

A BYZANTINE (1011) METRICAL INSCRIPTION

ANDRÉ GUILLOU

From the small corpus of Byzantine inscriptions of South Italy and Sicily which I am preparing, I extract here a text whose commentary requires expansion to a degree not permitted by the limitations of an ordinary edition.

The Text

The text is cut on the face of a block of Lecce stone which was found in 1932, mutilated, in one of the walls of the basilica of St. Nicholas of Bari. The block was removed and first displayed in the small lapidary museum installed in the "Portico dei Pellegrini," opposite the church of St. Nicholas; it is now in the museum in the gallery of St. Nicholas', where I examined it on several occasions, most recently in May 1969. Its present dimensions are: height, 68.5 cm.; width, 31 cm.; maximum thickness, 5 cm., of which 1.08 cm. now form the thickness of the inscribed panel. The block, originally much longer and at least one third wider, was cut along all its sides and its back to the shape of a truncated pyramid, in order to be used in the construction of the basilica, probably before the end of the eleventh century. Incised horizontal grooves mark the divisions between the lines of writing. The height of the letters is from 3 to 3.05 cm., the depth of the grooves is about 2 mm., and the overall space between the lines is 1 cm. The bottom line is very much obliterated at its end by the erosion of the stone.[1]

Bibliography.—The text, accompanied by an Italian translation and a photograph, has been published twice before this; first by F. Babudri,

[1] See photograph, Plate II. It was taken by my young colleague Jean-René Gaborit in 1966, at a time when he was a member of the École Française of Rome. For my present transcription I owe much to the suggestions of Professors C. Mango, M. Manoussakas, N. B. Tomadakis, and I. Dujčev, whom I warmly thank, also Mrs. Fanny Bonajuto, who translated the French text of this paper.

"L'iscrizione inedita bizantina barese del secolo IX e le costruzioni dell' imperatore Basilio I," in *Archivio storico pugliese*, 14 (1961), 58–89 (including a long commentary), and pl. I; the author (hereafter B), owing to an incorrect reading, took it to be a dedicatory inscription of the founder of the Macedonian dynasty (867–86), a conclusion which a mere glance at the palaeography rules out; Errica Follieri criticized this edition in the bibliographical notes of the *Byzantinische Zeitschrift*, 55 (1962), 427, and proposed the reading Μεσαρδονίτης in line 2. The second publisher was F. Schettini, *La basilica di San Nicola di Bari* (Bari 1967), 47 and fig. 52 (inset plate), who based his edition on the transcriptions of G. Ferrari and F. Babudri. Neither Babudri nor Schettini (hereafter S) noticed that a considerable part of the text was cut off along the right-hand side and that each line originally constituted a verse.

1 ΚΟΠΩι ΤΕ ΠΟΛΛΩι Κ| ΦΡΟΝΗΣΕ[
ΒΑΣΙΛΕΙΟΣ ΚΡΑΤΙΣΤΟΣ ΜΕΣ[
ΠΡΟΥΧΩΝ ΑΡΙΣΤΟΣ ΕΞ ΑΝΑΚΤ[
ΗΓΕΙΡΕΝ ΑΣΤΥ ΠΑΝΣΟΦΩι Τ[
5 ΠΛΙΝΘΩι ΠΕΤΡΩΔΕΙ ΤΟ̃ΤΟ ΠΡΟΣΚΑ[
]ΛΛΗΝ ΚΙΒΩΤΟΝ ΤΕΥΞΑΣ Ω[
]ΠΥΛΟΝ ΑΥΤΟ ΚΡΗΠΙΔΩΣ[
] ΤΩΝ ΑΠΛΗΚΤΩΝ ΕΚΛΥΤΡΩ[
] ΔΟΞΑΝ ΕΙΣ ΚΑΥΧΗΜΑ ΤΩΝ Α[
10]ΩΝ ΔΕ ΘΕΙΟΝ ΑΓΛΑΟΥ ΔΗΜΗ[
]ΘΩ ΔΟΜΗΣΑΣ ΕΙΛΙΚΡΙΝΕΙ ΤΩ [
]ΩΣΕΝ ΑΥΤΟΝ ΩΣ ΔΙΚΗΝ ΦΡΥΚ[
]ΕΙΝ ΠΡΟΔΗΛΩΣ ΠΑΝΣΘΕΝΕΙ Α[
]ΚΟ̃ΣΙ ΠΑΣΙ ΔΕΥΡΟ Τ Α̣Φ̣ΙΚΝΟ̃Μ[
15]Υ̣ΤΟΣ Η ΤΟ̃ ΣΤ....Ε̣.Ε̣Ν[

I transcribe and supplement as follows:

1 Κόπωι τε πολλῶι κ(αὶ) φρονήσε[ι μεγάλη]
Βασίλειος κράτιστος Μεσ[αρδονίτης]
Προύχων ἄριστος ἐξ ἀνάκτ[ων τὸ γένος]
Ἤγειρεν ἄστυ πανσόφωι τ[εχνουργίᾳ]
5 Πλίνθωι πετρώδει τ(οῦ)το προσκα[ινουργήσας]
[Ἄ]λλην κιβωτὸν τεύξας ὠ[χυρωμένην],
[Πρό]πυλον αὐτὸ κρηπιδώσ[ας ἐκ βάθρων]
[Εἰς] τῶν ἀπλήκτων ἐκλύτρω[σιν τῶν φόβων]
[Εἰς] δόξαν, εἰς καύχημα τῶν ἀ[νακτόρων].

10 [Νε]ὼν δὲ θεῖον ἀγλαοῦ Δημη[τρίου]
[Λί]θω δομήσας εἰλικρινεῖ τ[ῷ πόθῳ]
["Υψ]ωσεν αὐτὸν ὡς, δίκην φρυκ[τωρίας],
[Λάμ]πειν προδήλως πανσθενεῖ ἀ[γλαΐᾳ]
[Οἰ]κ(οῦ)σι πᾶσι δεῦρο τ᾽ ἀφικν(ου)μ[ένοις]
15 [.]ντος ἡ τ(οῦ) στ....ε. εν[ ]

2. Μεσαρδονίτης Follieri: μέ(γιστος) ο(κηπ) B, μέ(γιστο)s S   3. προὔχων: τροὔχων
B, S   4. τεχνουργίᾳ: τέχνη B, S   5. πετρώδει: πετρώδε[ι] B   προσκαινουργήσας:
πρὸς κ[αὶ] α- B, S   6. ἄλλην: λλην B, S   ὠχυρωμένην: ω[s] (προ) B, S   7.
πρόπυλον: πυλον B, S   αὐτὸ κρηπιδώσας ἐκ βάθρων: αὐτοκρηπίδως B, S   8. ἐκλύτρωσιν:
ἐκλυτρῶ[ν] B, S   9. ἀνακτόρων: Ἀ(γί)- B, S   10. νεὼν: ων B, S   Δημητρίου:
Δημη(τρί)- B, S   11. λίθω δομήσας: ο[υ] ὠδομήσας B, S   τῷ πόθῳ: τῶ [νῶ] (ὤρθ)-
B, τῶι [νῶ] S   12. ὕψωσεν: ωσεν B   φρυκτωρίας: φρουρ- B, S   13. λάμπειν:
ειν B, S   14. οἰκοῦσι πᾶσι: οἰκοῦσ[ι] πᾶσ[ι] B   τ᾽ ἀφικνουμένοις: τοῖς ἱκνουμένοις B,
S   15. Ultima linea deest B, S

I propose the following translation: "At the cost of much labor and with great wisdom the most powerful Basileios Mesardonites, highest of the notables, of imperial blood, has erected the *asty* with consummate technique, renovating it with bricks as hard as stones, fashioning (thus) another fortified Ark; he has also built the vestibule, in order to deliver the troops of the camp from their anxieties, and for the glory and the pride of the Palace. Moreover, out of sincere piety, he has erected the holy church of the glorious Demetrios, built of stone, to shine brightly, like a beacon, in its omnipotent glory for all who live here and those who will come to live here...."

Commentary

This will concern the form and composition, the contents, and the date of this important historical text.

1. *The Form.* The one line whose reading is assured—the tenth—reveals that the inscription was composed of dodecasyllabic verses. This metrical form is known to occur in dedicatory inscriptions of military buildings.[2] We know that this verse with iambic rhythm, which replaced the old trimeter, had been given definite form by

[2] See, for example, the inscription dating from the time of Basil II which was on the Anastasius wall at Constantinople and was edited epigraphically, but without a photograph, by C. Schuchhardt, "Anastasius-Mauer bei Constantinopel und die Dobrudscha-Wälle," *Jahrbuch des Archäologischen Instituts*, 16 (1901), 114; its edition by E. Dirimtekin, "Le mura di Anastasio I," *Palladio* 5 (1955), 85, is not epigraphical and does not mention the previous, and apparently better, edition.

Georges Pisides in the seventh century.[3] The author of our text has followed its essential rules concerning the foot (iambic throughout), the caesura, and the accentuation of the word preceding it. If one disregards the last verse (for its reading is incomplete), one finds that the caesura is either hepthemimeral (vss. 2, 5, 6, 9, 14) or penthemimeral (vss. 1, 3, 4, 7, 8, 10, 11, 12, 13); the oxytone at the caesura is avoided (except vss. 1, 7 and 12), the paroxytone being used in its place, and three times (vss. 2, 3, 9) even the proparoxytone —which is remarkable. The rule of accenting the penultimate syllable has governed my supplements.

The wording conforms to the current language, not especially poetic and not averse to using technical terms such as πλίνθος, πετρώδης, ἄπληκτον. A somewhat archaizing taste is shown only by the adscript iotas. I have not detected a single orthographic mistake caused by vowel isochrony, a fact which is quite remarkable for this period.

Thus, from the point of view of form, the inscription must be considered to be of very good quality; this observation raises a question as to both the place where the text may have been composed and the author.

The composition is entirely clear: (a) preamble, which includes the titles of the personage here celebrated (vss. 1–3); (b) statement concerning the erection of military buildings (vss. 4–9) and of a religious building (vss. 10–15).

2. *The Contents*

vss. 2–3   Βασίλειος κράτιστος Μεσαρδονίτης
Προὔχων ἄριστος ἐξ ἀνάκτων τὸ γένος.

Let me first point out that the reading of the word Μεσ[αρδονίτης], the name of a known catepanus, is, because of the meter, incontrovertible. The adjective κράτιστος would indicate an imperial figure,[4] and the expression ἐξ ἀνάκτων leaves no room for doubt: Basileios Mesardonites was of imperial blood.[5] This fact, which so far has escaped attention,

---

[3] See P. Maas, "Die byzantinische Zwölfsilber," *Byz. Zeitschr.* 12 (1903), 278–323; Fr. Dölger, *Die byzantinische Dichtung in der Reinsprache* (Handbuch der griechischen und lateinischen Philologie; Berlin 1948), 39–40.

[4] See Fr. Dölger, "Die Entwicklung der byzantinischen Kaisertitulatur und die Datierung von Kaiserdarstellungen in der byzantinischen Kleinkunst," in *Byzantinische Diplomatik* (Ettal 1956), 138.

[5] *Ibidem*, 138, 143.

requires some explanation. A passage—until now misunderstood—
in the Latin annals of Lupus Protospatarius allows us to perceive the
solution of the problem posed by these verses. In these annals we read
under the year 1017: Obiit in Butruntio Marsedonici catepanus et,
in mense Novembrio, interfectus est Leo, frater, Argyro.[6] The
meaning of the last words of this sentence is not immediately
obvious. By omitting the punctuation between *frater* and *Argyro*,
the modern editor understands that Leo is the brother of Argyro;
this interpretation would not be precluded by the morphology
followed by the author of the text, who never declines the name
Argyro.[7] If so, who are the Leo and the Argyro mentioned here—
both being first names? The examination of several chronological
notices in Lupus has convinced me that the author has made use of
similar notices in Greek; thus, for example, he writes under 1059:
Isaki o Comni factus est imperator, a straightforward transcription
of Ἰσαάκιος ὁ Κομμηνὸς βασιλεὺς ἐγένετο; and under 1067: Mortuus
est Constantinus o Ducos imperator, a transcription of Ἀπέθανε
Κωνσταντῖνος βασιλεὺς ὁ Δούκας.[8] Lupus may well have had at his
disposal a Greek notice ending as follows: Καὶ ἐν μηνὶ Νοεμβρίῳ
ἐφονεύθη Λέων ἀδελφὸς αὐτοῦ ὁ Ἀργυρός, which would give the transcription this meaning: "And, in the month of November, his
brother, Leo Argyros, was slain."

Mesardonites' (*Marsedonici*) brother Leo being an Argyros, the
catepanus Basileios must himself a member of that same great
Byzantine family which, according to our inscription, was directly
connected with the throne. This latter statement is true on two
counts: First, the family of the Argyroi allied itself with that of the
Lekapenoi through the marriage of Romanos Argyros and Agathe,
daughter of the Emperor Romanos Lekapenos, who was crowned
in 920.[9] On the other hand, the marriage in April 919 of Constantine

[6] Ed. G. H. Pertz, in *Mon. Germ. Hist., Scriptores,* vol. V (Hannover 1844), 57. I have
corrected the punctuation of this sentence, in order to make it intelligible.

[7] *Ibidem,* 58 f.

[8] *Ibidem,* 59.

[9] C. Du Cange, *Historia byzantina duplici commentario illustrata* (Paris 1680), 154;
Theophanes Cont., Χρονογραφία, ed. Im. Bekker (Bonn 1838), 399: Ῥωμανὸν δὲ τὸν υἱὸν
Λέοντος, ὡς ἔφθην εἰπών, τοῦ Ἀργυροῦ Ῥωμανὸς ὁ βασιλεὺς γαμβρὸν ἐποιήσατο ... δοὺς αὐτῷ
τὴν θυγατέρα αὐτοῦ Ἀγάθην. The date is provided by George Kedrenos, Σύνοψις ἱστοριῶν, ed.
Im. Bekker, vol. II (Bonn 1839), 297. See also Fig. 1, below.

VII, grandson of Basil I, with Helena, another daughter of Romanos
Lekapenos, made Romanos Argyros the brother-in-law of the direct
descendant of the Macedonian dynasty, which was again to seize
power from the Lekapenoi in 944.[10]

The Argyroi family enters history, if we are to believe George
Kedrenos' chronicle,[11] with Leo Argyros, who became famous for
his battles against the Paulicians (about 855) and the Arabs.[12]
This same Leo rebuilt the monastery of Hagia Elizabeth at
Charsianon,[13] where he was later buried. He had a son, Eustathios
Argyros, future drongarios of the Vigils, who, under Andronikos
Doux, defeated the Arab armies at Germanicea toward the end of the
year 904, subsequently governed the theme of Charsianon as
strategos, was dismissed for unknown reasons by Leo VI and sent
home to Charsianon, but died on his way there, having been
poisoned by one of his men; his body was transported by two of his
sons, the Manglabites Pothos and Leo, to the family church of
Hagia Elizabeth at Charsianon.[14] A third son of Eustathios, Romanos
Argyros, had not been present at the translation of his father's
remains, but he is known to have fought (ἐστρατήγει) with his brother
Leo (ὁ ἀδελφὸς αὐτοῦ)[15] under the domesticus of the Scholai Leo
Phokas in the bloody battle of Acheloos, which ended with the
definitive victory of the Bulgar army, in August 917.[16] This Romanos

---

[10] See S. Runciman, *The Emperor Romanus Lecapenus and his Reign* (Cambridge 1929),
pp. 60, 232 f. See also Fig. 2, below.

[11] Vol. II, 270: ὃς καὶ τὸ τῶν Ἀργυρῶν ἐπίθετον ἐπληρώσατο πρῶτος; cf. Theophanes
Cont., 374.

[12] George Kedrenos, *loc. cit.* See D. I. Polemis, *The Doukai. A Contribution to Byzantine
Prosopography* (London 1968), 16.

[13] George Kedrenos, vol. II, 269. Charsianon was the center of a kleisourarchia (end
of the seventh century), and later of a theme (about 873) situated between the theme
Armeniakon, those of the Boukellarioi and of Cappadocia, and the Arab frontier; cf.
De Thematibus, ed. A. Pertusi = Studi e Testi 160 (Vatican City 1952), 123–24; *De
administrando imperio*, vol. II; *Commentary*, by R. J. H. Jenkins (London 1962), 188.

[14] Ὁ δὲ βασιλεὺς...εἰς τὸν οἶκον αὐτοῦ ἀπέστειλεν εἰς τὸ Χαρσιανόν, Theophanes Cont.,
374.

[15] See R. Guilland, "Contribution a l'histoire administrative de l'empire byzantin.
Le drongairė et le grand drongaire de la Veille," *Byz. Zeitschr.*, 43 (1950), 347–48,
with references to sources.

[16] Theophanes Cont., 389; George Kedrenos, vol. II, 285. Runciman, *op. cit.*, 55,
understands the passage of Theophanes Cont. Ῥωμανὸς δὲ ὁ Ἀργυρὸς ἐστρατήγει (not ἐστρα-
τήγησε, as he writes) καὶ Λέων ὁ ἀδελφὸς αὐτοῦ καὶ Βάρδας ὁ Φωκᾶς, οἷς συνῆν μὲν καὶ ὁ Μελίας
μετὰ τῶν Ἀρμενίων καὶ οἱ ἄλλοι πάντες στρατηγοὶ τῶν θεμάτων, to mean that Romanos Argyros

Argyros must be the one who married Agathe, daughter of the Emperor Romanos Lekapenos, in 920.[17] We know that Pothos and Leo (who meanwhile had been made patricius), managed to escape from the Bulgars at the disaster of Pegae in 922, for which Pothos, who was domesticus of the Scholai, may himself have been to blame.[18] Leo had been turmarchus of Larissa in the theme of Sebastea, adjoining that of Charsianon where—as we have mentioned—the properties of the family were situated; subsequently, during the reign of Constantine Porphyrogenitos, he became magistros and domesticus of the Scholai.[19] Pothos, at the time of Romanos Lekapenos' fall in 944, was patricius and domesticus of the Exkoubitoi, and later was put in charge of an important expedition against the Hungars, whom he completely defeated.[20] Of the following generation of the Argyroi—the fourth—only Marianos is known. Marianos Argyros, called Apambas (a former monk), after a checkered career begun at the time of the Emperor Romanos Lekapenos' eviction by Constantine VII in 944, ends as domesticus of the Scholai of the West under Nicephorus II Phokas; he was patricius Leo Argyros' son and, therefore, nephew of Romanos Argyros and Agathe Lekapena. He is the first of the Argyroi to have

---

was strategos of the theme Anatolikon. I do not see a reason for this interpretation, especially since the text of Symeon Logothetes ends at Ἀρμενίων (see Symeon Logothetes, Χρονογραφία, ed. Im. Bekker [Bonn 1838], 724).

[17] See Runciman, op. cit., 54 f.

[18] Theophanes Cont., 399; Runciman, op. cit., 64. There is, however, a problem, ignored by Runciman (loc. cit.) who refers to one source only, Theophanes Cont.; this is the reason why R. Guilland ("Le Domestique des Scholes," in Recherches sur les institutions byzantines, I [Berliner byzantinische Arbeiten, 35; Berlin 1967], 442, who, in turn, does not refer to the Theophanes Cont. text) marries Agathe to Leo, relying on the corresponding passage of George Kedrenos (vol. II, 297): ἠγάγετο δὲ τούτῳ τῷ ἔτει καὶ γαμβρὸν ἐπὶ τῇ αὐτοῦ θυγατρὶ Ἀγάθῃ Ῥωμανὸς ὁ βασιλεὺς Λέοντα τὸν τοῦ Ἀργυροῦ. Symeon Logothetes, who in this part of his work copies Theophanes Cont., is silent; so are the later chronicles. Since the version of Theophanes Cont. was written at a date closer to the events which it recounts, and since the sources mentioning Leo and his son Marianos (see below) say nothing of their connection with the Lekapenoi, I think that we should hold to the passage of Theophanes Cont.

[19] Symeon Logothetes, 732–33; Theophanes Cont., 400–402; George Kedrenos, vol. II, 300.

[20] De administrando imperio, 2nd ed. by Gy. Moravcsik and R. J. H. Jenkins, Dumbarton Oaks Texts, I = Corpus Fontium Historiae Byzantinae, I (Washington, D.C., 1967), chap. 50, lines 149, 151, p. 240; Runciman, op. cit., 87 f., 135.

held a post in Italy.[21] We do not know the names of Marianos' cousins, the offspring of Romanos and Agathe and the only children of imperial blood in this generation. One of them—possibly the only one—had a daughter, Maria Argyropoula, whom Basil II, in order to gain influence at Venice, was to give in marriage to John, son of Doge Pietro Orseolo (II); thus the Venetian chronicler John Diaconus is justified in writing that Maria was of imperial origin (*imperiale editam stirpe*)[22] and that her son, whose name is Basil, was nephew (in a broad sense) of Basil II.[23] Maria's brothers were Basileios Argyros (Mesardonites) and Leo. Of the latter, all we know is that he was slain in South Italy in 1017,[24] but no evidence survives of his having held any official position there.

Since until now the fact that Basileios Mesardonites was an Argyros has not been recognized,[25] his career could not be told in full. The sources, however, allow us to reconstruct it as follows:

[21] Symeon Logothetes, 756; Theophanes Cont., 463. Marianos' career was traced by R. Guilland, "Les patrices byzantins sous le règne de Constantin VII Porphyrogenète (913–59)," in *Studi bizantini e neoellenici*, 9 = *Silloge bizantina in onore di S. G. Mercati* (1957), 190–92. He was strategos of Calabria and Longobardia from 955 on, but relinquished this post to go to the Bulgar frontier before Romanos II's death (15 March 963): see Vera von Falkenhausen, *Untersuchungen über die byzantinische Herrschaft in Süditalien vom 9. bis ins 11. Jahrhundert* (Schriften zur Geistesgeschichte des östlichen Europa, 1; Wiesbaden 1967), 81; the author, however, is wrong in making Leo Argyros, Marianos' father, the son-in-law of Romanos I, since the text of Kedrenos, vol. II, 323, only says: τὸν μοναχὸν Μαριάνον τὸν υἱὸν Λέοντος τοῦ Ἀργυροῦ ὑπὸ τοῦ βασιλέως Ῥωμανοῦ λίαν καὶ τιμώμενον καὶ πιστευόμενον.

[22] G. Monticolo, *Chronache veneziane antichissime*, I (Istituto storico italiano, Fonti per la storia d'Italia; Roma 1890), 168: τότε καὶ τῷ ἄρχοντι Βενετίας γυναῖκα νόμιμον ἔδωκεν ὁ βασιλεὺς τὴν θυγατέρα τοῦ Ἀργυροῦ ἀδελφὴν δὲ Ῥωμανοῦ τοῦ μετὰ ταῦτα βασιλεύσαντος, τὸ ἔθνος οὕτως ὑποποιούμενος (George Kedrenos, vol. II, 452). Petrus Damianus (†1072) was shocked that she would require her servants to prepare for her baths of dew water, that she would not use her fingers to eat her food but would have it cut in small pieces which she would then take to her lips with some kind of gold forks ending with three prongs (*fusciculae*) or two (*bidentes*), and finally that she would sleep on a perfumed bed (*Patr. Lat.*, vol. 145, col. 744).

[23] Monticolo, *op. cit.*, 169: Ob avunculi sui imperatoris nomen imposuit. Maria Argyropoula and her husband died of the plague in 1007 (*ibid.*, 170). On the meaning of the words θεῖος and ἀνεψιός, see St. Binon, "À propos d'un prostagma d'Andronic III Paléologue," *Byz. Zeitschr.* 38 (1938), 146–55.

[24] Lupus Protospatarius, ed. Pertz, 57.

[25] In spite of the mention in J. Gay, *L'Italie méridionale et l'empire byzantin* (Bibliothèque des Écoles françaises d'Athènes et de Rome, 190; Paris 1904), 410; the author only points out the (apparent) discrepancy of the sources on this matter. See recently Vera von Falkenhausen, *op. cit.*, 86.

having first been strategos of the theme of Samos, he was later sent by Basil II to Italy, with the title of protospatharios and the functions of catepanus, to end the uprising headed by Meles;[26] he entered Bari in 1010;[27] at the beginning of 1017 he was succeeded in his post of catepanus by the protospatharios Kontoleon Tornikios (an Armenian), strategos of Cephalonia—who, on Basileios' arrival, had assisted him against the rebellious populace[28] and was to return to Bari in 1017[29]—to go to Asprakarnia (Vaspurakan) as governor of this new theme in the territory of ancient Media, with the title of patricius in 1021.[30] In this connection one text presents some difficulty. As I have mentioned before, Lupus Protospatarius writes of Basileios under the year 1017, *obiit in Butruntio* (on the coast of Epiros). Since there is no reason to doubt George Kedrenos' information, and since throughout the Middle Ages Butrinton was an active seaport facing the island of Corfu, I propose to correct *obiit* (although this reading is confirmed by the manuscript tradition)[31] to *abiit*; thus Basileios Argyros may be allowed to continue his career. The correction is a minor one and is justified by the fact that Lupus Protospatarius makes the same mistake a little further on in his text, when he says that *Argyro Barensis* died (*obiit*) in Constantinople in 1034, although he also reports that the same person laid siege to Bari in 1040.[32] The use of the ablative case, rather than the accusative following the preposition of movement *in*, is no objection; Lupus is often negligent in this respect.[33] If indeed the annalist availed himself of a Greek notice, we may think of a misreading of ἀπέθανε (*obiit*) for ἀπῆλθε (*abiit*).

George Kedrenos[34] gives us, perhaps, the name of the most

---

[26] George Kedrenos, vol. II, 456–57.

[27] Lupus Protospatarius, 57; Anonymous of Bari, ed. L. A. Muratori, *Rerum Italicarum Scriptores, vol.* V (Milan 1724), 148.

[28] George Kedrenos, vol. II, 456.

[29] Lupus Protospatarius, 57; Anonymous of Bari, 148.

[30] George Kedrenos, vol. II, 464, and N. Adontz, "Les Taronites en Arménie et à Byzance," in *Études arméno-byzantines* (Lisbon 1965), 253.

[31] So I am told by Miss Vera von Falkenhausen, whom I wish to thank here; on Butrintum, see the *RE*, s.v. "Buthroton."

[32] Lupus Protospatarius, 58. I see no reason for postulating, because of the *obiit* of the annalist, the existence of two different Argyroi of Bari, as does Vera von Falkenhausen, *op. cit.*, 93.

[33] Pp. 52 (ann. 875), 57 (ann. 1023, 1024), 58 (ann. 1038, 1041), etc.

[34] Vol. II, 489.

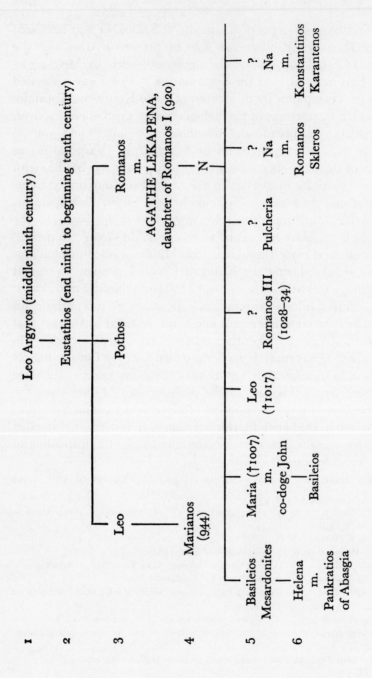

Fig. 1. ARGYROI FAMILY (ninth to eleventh cent.)

1   Leo Argyros (middle ninth century)

2   Eustathios (end ninth to beginning tenth century)

3   Leo   Pothos   Romanos
                                             m.
                                 AGATHE LEKAPENA,
                            daughter of Romanos I (920)

4   Marianos
     (944)   N

5   Basileios   Maria (†1007)   Leo   ?   ?   ?   ?
     Mesardonites   m.   (†1017)   Romanos III   Pulcheria   Na   Na
            co-doge John   (1028–34)   m.   m.

6   Helena   Basileios   Romanos   Konstantinos
     m.   Skleros   Karantenos
     Pankratios
     of Abasgia

famous among Basileios Argyros' brothers when he recounts that, probably in 1029, after the death of George, king of Abasgia, his widow sent an embassy to Constantinople to obtain a renewal of the peace treaty and also to find a suitable wife for her son Pankratios; and that the Emperor sent to her Helena, daughter of his brother Basileios.[35] A glance at the genealogical tree as illustrated here (Fig. 1), permits us to advance the hypothesis that this brother of the Emperor Romanos III Argyros (1028–34) was indeed our Basileios Mesardonites who had a daughter Helena. If our hypothesis—based only on the identity of names and contemporaneity of persons—is correct, we must add the known sisters of Romanos III to the fifth generation of Argyroi, where we have listed the grandsons of Romanos Argyros and Agathe Lekapena. Two of them we cannot identify by name, but we know that one was the wife of Romanos Skleros,[36] blinded by Constantine VII and later made magistros by Romanos III, his brother-in-law; and the other was the wife of the patricius Konstantinos Karantenos;[37] a third sister was named Pulcheria.[38] The sources provide the name of yet another member of the Argyros family, who must have belonged to this same fifth generation, though evidence that he belonged to the imperial branch of the Lekapenoi is not available; this member is Pothos, protospatharios and catepanus of Italy, the third member of the family, counting from the mid-tenth century, to be sent to Italy as a high government official. Having first held a post at Antioch,[39] he was put in command of Byzantine Italy, where he remained from July 1021 to March (?) 1032, being the last of the Argyroi with an official post in the West.[40]

The assassination of Romanos III Argyros seems to have marked the end of this family in public life, at least for a time. Since the beginning of the tenth century they had been closest by blood ties to the reigning Macedonian dynasty (Fig. 2).[41] Henceforth, until

[35] Τὴν θυγατέρα τοῦ ἀδελφοῦ αὐτοῦ βασιλείου, ibid., 489.

[36] Ibid. 487.

[37] Ibid. 488.

[38] John Zonaras, Χρονικόν, ed. Th. Büttner-Wobst, vol. III (Bonn 1897), 583.

[39] George Kedrenos, vol. II, 490.

[40] For references, see Vera von Falkenhausen, op. cit., 88.

[41] Argyros, son of Meles of Bari, dux of Italy in the second half of the eleventh century, does not belong to the family. Argyros as first name is known in South Italy, especially

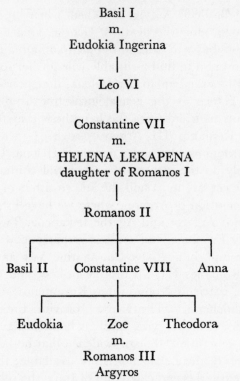

Basil I
m.
Eudokia Ingerina

Leo VI

Constantine VII
m.
HELENA LEKAPENA
daughter of Romanos I

Romanos II

Basil II   Constantine VIII   Anna

Eudokia   Zoe   Theodora
m.
Romanos III
Argyros

Fig. 2. MACEDONIAN DYNASTY

the beginning of the fourteenth century,[42] no more is said about any Argyros in the Greek chronicles.

It cannot be ruled out, however, that either the catepanus Pothos

---

at Bari and Taranto, at least since the end of the tenth century (Fr. Trinchera, *Syllabus graecarum membranarum* [Naples 1865], no. 11, p. 10: Argyros of Bari, turmarchus in December 999; A. Guillou and W. Holtzmann, "Zwei Katepansurkunden aus Tricarico," *Quellen und Forschungen* 41 [1961], 18: the same Argyros of Bari, magistros in 1001; Trinchera, *op. cit., Index*, s.v.; *Codice diplomatico barese*, vol. IV [Bari 1900], *Index*, s.v., vol. V [Bari 1902], *Index*, s.v., etc.: for later Argiri). Argyros is a grecized form of the Roman *nomen* and *cognomen* Argyrus (see Forcellini, *Lexicon*, s.v.). The blood ties between Argyroi–Lekapenoi and the "Macedonians" explain, I believe, why in 1028 Constantine VIII, when doctors advised him shortly before his death to make plans for his succession, first thought of a Dalassenos, the patricius Constantine (also an Armenian, see N. Adontz, "Notes arméno-byzantines," *Byzantion* 10 [1935], 183), a member of another great family, but finally gave his preference to an Argyros, Romanos (III); to this end he forced him to divorce his wife and marry his, the Emperor's, sister Zoe, so that he could ascend the throne with her; see Theophanes Cont., 400–402.

42 See Du Cange, *op. cit.*, 156.

or a lesser known Argyros left descendants in Italy. In this respect there exist in the archives two documents which require interpretation. (1) In August 1059 Pope Nicholas II confirms to the monastery of the Saviour and the Virgin at Bari its statute and properties; as of equal importance as the rule established by its foundress, he mentions *nec non et Argyroi* (sic) *concessionem*—probably a concession (of properties or rights) made by the Argyros family (?);[43] (2) In July 1093 a certain Brunellus, filius f. Nikolay spatarii kandidati, qui dicitur de Argyro de civitate de Bari, exchanges some property in the city.[44] Unless these two archival documents simply refer, as does happen in other instances, to persons whose first name (not unknown in South Italy) was Argyrus—a rather unlikely explanation, because of the unusual formulas employed—we may have here an indication that the Argyroi had left both descendants and properties in Italy. Such an inference is entirely plausible if one recalls the presence in Italy of Basileios Mesardonites' brother, Leo Argyros, as mentioned above.

The history of the Argyroi shows clearly that the foremost positions in Byzantine administration were assigned to members of great families—which were far from numerous. Moreover, it also shows that some of the rules most often reaffirmed by legislators could be broken whenever the interest of the state was concerned. In the early years of the tenth century Eustathios Argyros is assigned to administer the theme of Charsianon where all the land properties of his family, which had originated in this region, were located; this, despite the fact that Leo VI in one of his Novels had reaffirmed that the strategoi should be forbidden to either build or acquire anything whatsoever in the provinces under their administration.[45] We also said above that the same family had probably taken a tangible interest in the lands of Byzantine Italy, of which several of its members had been imperial administrators.

The alliance of the Macedonians and Lekapenoi, both of Armenian origin, with the family of the Argyroi may be explained by their

---

[43] *Codice diplomatico barese*, vol. I (Bari 1897), no. 24, p. 41.

[44] *Ibid.*, no. 35, p. 66.

[45] Ed. P. Noailles and A. Dain (Paris 1964), no. 84, 285; see J. and P. Zepos, *Jus graeco-romanum*, vol. IV (Athens 1931), 34 (*Peira*); vol. V (Athens 1931), 96, 104 (*Synopsis Basilicorum*).

being neighboring landowners. We have seen that the real properties of the Argyroi were situated in the Charsianon region—perhaps identifiable with Musalim Qal'e on the easternmost border of Cappadocia, west of Sebasteia, and south of Sebastopolis,[46] a region probably inhabited mainly by Armenians. However, the name Argyros is not Armenian.

In the West the catepanus Basileios Argyros is known exclusively as Basileios Messardonites; he signs his only surviving original document, dated August 1016, as $Βασίλειος\ πρωτοσπαθάριος\ καὶ\ κατεπάνω$ 'Ιταλίας ὁ Μεσαρδονίτης.[47] He appears with the same name in an act, of March 1032, of the catepanus of Italy Pothos Argyros, a relative of his: ἐπὶ τοῦ Μεσαρδονίτου.[48] No other name, in more or less distorted form, is given him in the surviving Latin translations of official Greek documents now vanished, or in the Latin chronicles.[49] What is the origin of this name? Having failed either to discover anywhere a site called Mesardonia from which Basileios might have drawn his origins, or to find a Latin, Greek, Armenian, or Georgian word which might have become a kind of surname for him, I was induced to examine the Persian sources.[50] Old Persian has a word, 'rdatam,[51] which may well have given origin to the name Mesardonites; like ἄργυρος, it means "silver". One may perhaps see in Ἀργυρός the Greek translation of some Persian word, whose transcription in Greek produced Μεσαρδονίτης.

However, why should the catepanus of Italy have been known in the West under the name Mesardonites only, and in the East under that of Argyros? Possibly because in Longobardia (where

---

[46] E. Honigmann, *Die Ostgrenze des byzantinischen Reiches von 363 bis 1071* (Byzance et les Arabes, 3; Brussels 1935), 50; *idem*, "Charsianon Kastron," *Byzantion* 10 (1935), 129–59; against this identification, see P. Wittek, "Von der byzantinischen zur türkischen Toponymie: III. Mušalim Qal'esi," *Byzantion* 10 (1935), 60–64.

[47] *Codice diplomatico barese*, vol. I, no. 16, p. 17.

[48] *Ibid.* no. 23, p. 25.

[49] For the bibliography, see Vera von Falkenhausen, *op. cit.*, 86, 175–76; however, from the list of Basileios Messardonites' acts one must delete no. 39a which is instead to be attributed to Basileios Boioannes (see A. Guillou and W. Holtzmann, *art. cit., Quellen und Forschungen* 41, p. 27).

[50] This suggestion was made by my colleague J. Ghanem, to whom I here express my thanks. One could also suppose, at the cost of a metathesis, that Mesardonites means "originating from the Persian province of Māzandarān" (south-east of the Caspian province).

[51] E. Herzfeld, *Altpersische Inschriften* (Berlin 1938), 283–84.

family names were as yet unknown) Argyros was the first name of some well-known person and one wished to avoid confusion.[52]

Moreover, Basileios could either have been a Mesardonites on the side of his maternal ascendants,[53] or have been adopted by the Argyros family.[54]

vs. 4: ἄστυ. The Anonymous of Bari, writing about the works carried out in the capital of the catepanate by Basileios Mesardonites, says: Laboravit castello domnico.[55] *Castellum domnicum*, therefore, may be considered as translating the word ἄστυ of the inscription: it is the πραιτώριον or βασιλικὸν πραιτώριον,[56] an attested equivalent of the Latin *curtis imperialis*,[57] or *curtis domnica*.[58] Although ἄστυ in the chronicles, hagiographical texts, or archival documents has no other meaning than "city" generally, the language of the tenth century, and possibly also of the eleventh century, still defined the sense of the word πραιτώριον by opposing it to πόλις. Constantine Porphyrogenitos, in writing on the region which under Byzantine rule became the theme of Anatolikon, states that there the ὕπαρχοι πραιτωρίων are πρίγκιπες (*principes*) responsible for the food supply of the imperial armies, the organization of their camps, and the maintenance of the access roads,[59] whereas the ὕπαρχοι πόλεων are not military chiefs but administrative officials (σκρινιάριοι).[60] The same author defines the πραιτώριον as a city (πόλις) residence of the strategos of a theme[61] who, as we know, is responsible for military and civilian administration.

[52] See above, note 41.

[53] A well-known instance of the same kind is that of Irene Doukaina, eldest daughter of Nikephoros Bryennios and Anna Comnena, and granddaughter of Irene Doukaina (see Polemis, *op. cit.* [above, note 12], 114). This example was suggested to me by Miss Vera von Falkenhausen, whom I again wish to thank here.

[54] On the adoption ritual, see S. A. Papadopulos, "Essai d'interprétation du thème iconographique de la paternité dans l'art byzantin," *Cahiers archéologiques* 18 (1968), 121–36.

[55] P. 148 (1011).

[56] Fr. Trinchera, *op. cit.*, no. 25, p. 29 (1031–32).

[57] *Codice diplomatico barese*, vol. IV, no. 21, p. 45 (1032).

[58] Anonymous of Bari, p. 51 (1047); *in curte que olim pretorium publicum fuerat*, found in an act of 1089 (*Codice diplomatico barese*, vol. I, no. 34, p. 64), *in predicta curte que fuit domnica*, again in 1089 (*Codice diplomatico barese*, vol. V, no. 13, p. 25), *juxta ipsa curte de lu catepano*, in 1086 (*Codice diplomatico barese*, vol. V, no. 6, p. 13), *in curte pretorii publici*, in 1100 (*Codice diplomatico barese*, vol. V, no. 32, p. 55).

[59] *De Thematibus*, ed. Pertusi, chapt. 16, p. 82.

[60] *Ibidem*.

[61] Ὁ δὲ στρατηγὸς τοῦ θέματος αὐτὴν ἔλαχε Σμύρναν τὴν πόλιν πραιτώριον (*ibidem*).

However, since in a will of 1041 we read that the oratory of St. Sophia was situated in the fortified city (κάστρον) of Bari, within the *praitorion* (ἔνδων τοῦ πρετορίου) (*sic*)[62] we must see in the term ἄστυ both a broader sense, such as was used by Constantine Porphyrogenitos,[63] and a narrower sense, such as we find in our inscription.[64] A military, judicial,[65] and fiscal[66] center, residence of the catepanus, the ἄστυ-πραιτώριον of Bari included the catepanus' living-quarters, offices, barracks for the guards or possibly for the

[62] Gertrude Robinson, *History and Cartulary of the Greek Monastery of St. Elias and St. Anastasius of Carbone*, II: *Cartulary* (Orientalia Christiana, XV, 2; Rome 1929), 140. This is confirmed by the Greek version of the translation of St. Nicholas' relics, Τὸ βασιλικὸν πραιτώριον τοῦ κάστρου (Λόγος εἰς τὴν ἀνακομιδὴν τοῦ λειψάνου τοῦ ὁσίου πατρὸς ἡμῶν καὶ θαυματουργου Νικολάου), ed. G. Anrich, *Hagios Nikolaos. Der heilige Nikolaos in der griechischen Kirche. Texte und Untersuchungen*, I (Leipzig–Berlin 1913), 445.

[63] Also in speaking of Naples, of which he says: Νεάπολις ἦν ἀρχαῖον πραιτώριον τῶν κατερχομένων πατρικίων, *De administrando imperio*, ed. Moravcsik and Jenkins, chap. 27, line 58, p. 116.

[64] This is also the sense that should be attributed to the two *praitoria* of Constantinople, whose role, as compared to those of the provinces, was certainly limited by the presence of the imperial administration; their role, however, could not be confined, as R. Janin seems to imply (*Constantinople byzantine*, 2nd ed.; Archives de l'Orient, 4 [Paris 1964], 165), to that of prisons, for, at the beginning of the eighth century, Maslama ibn Abd-al-Malik was allowed to have a mosque built in it, ἐκτίσθη τὸ τῶν Σαρακηνῶν μασγίδιον ἐν τῷ βασιλικῷ πραιτωρίῳ, *De administrando imperio*, ed. Moravcsik and Jenkins, chap. 21, 114, p. 92; cf. vol. II, *Commentary*, p. 78, in which Jenkins refers erroneously to Janin, who makes no mention of this text.

[65] The protomandator ἐπὶ τῶν βασιλικῶν ἁρμαμέντων, Basileios, in 1031–32, before returning to Constantinople sells a *kalybion* at Bari and stipulates that anyone contravening the clauses of the act should have to pay 30 *nomismata* to the new owner and 30 *nomismata* λόγῳ δὲ τοῦ βασιλικοῦ πραιτωρίου (Fr. Trinchera, *op. cit.*, no. 25, p. 29); *in pretorio domnico* is found in certain Latin donations which were made not at Bari, but at Terlizzi (1044) and Giovinazzo (1054) (*Codice diplomatico barese*, vol. III [Bari 1899], no. 6, p. 13; no. 7, p. 15); *in ipso pretorio domnico*, is found in a verdict of the judge of Giovinazzo, Amentelo, in about the mid-eleventh century (*Codice diplomatico barese*, vol. III, no. 2, p. 6) with a variety of penalties. In all these examples the catepanus' court of justice is always meant. Later, in Norman times, the sense of court of justice is preserved in Greek for local courts: καθεζωμένου μου κἄμου Ἰωάννου Φαράκλη κατεπάνω Νοῶν (Noha, in Western Lucania) ἐν τῷ συνήθει πρετωρίῳ τῆς προριθείσης χώρας (Fr. Trinchera, *op. cit.* no. 184, p. 241, in 1175). Here it is the *curia quae dicitur catepani* of the Latin version of the translation of St. Nicholas' relics (F. Nitti di Vito, "La traslazione delle reliquie di San Nicola," *Japigia* 8 [1937], 366).

[66] To the references given in the preceding note, add Fr. Trinchera, *op. cit.*, no. 65, p. 83 (1098), ζημιούσθω εἰς τὸ πρετόρι νομίσματα λς', the equivalent of the well-known formula, ζ. εἰς τὸ βασιλικὸν σακκέλιον, appearing in many penal clauses: see, for instance, A. Guillou, *Saint-Nicolas de Donnoso* (Corpus des actes grecs d'Italie du Sud et de Sicile, I; Vatican City 1967), no. 2, lines 23–24, p. 32 (1036); no. 4, lines 36–37 (1060–61), etc.

city's garrison,[67] undoubtedly a prison, churches or chapels (St. Basilios,[68] St. Sophia,[69] St. Eustratios,[70] St. Demetrius);[71] moreover farming land lay within its precinct, as well as outside it.[72]

Is it possible to identify the site of the *praitorion* in the *kastron* of Bari? In October 1100, Judge Nicholas Melipezzis recognizes the rights of St. Nicholas' church to some properties formerly belonging to a certain Rigellus, who had died intestate. According to the Judge's verdict, this Rigellus was *defensus ecclesiae sancti Basilii, que olim fuit in curte pretorii puplici, ubi nunc est prephata ecclesia beati Nicolai.*[73] The *praitorion*, then, was on the same site—not far from the harbor— where St. Nicholas' basilica was erected in the second half of the eleventh century and stands to this day. A text relating the translation of St. Nicholas' relics from Myra in Lycia, in the year 1087, states that both the church of St. Eustratios, where the sailors had deposited their precious load, as well as the other religious buildings of the *praitorion*, were later levelled (ἀνεσκάφη) (or excavated), to make room for the new monument,[74] which in its main parts was probably finished within two years,[75] but was consecrated only in June 1197.[76] Therefore we must suppose that, with the possible exception of the church of St. Eustratios, whose condition at the time still permitted the sheltering of St. Nicholas' relics, the other churches—of St.

---

[67] The barracks could not house large numbers of troops; this, anyway, is how I interpret the passage which says that during the summer of 1046 the catepanus Iohannes Raphael spent one day there (*in curte domnica*) with his Varangian guards and then had to depart (Anonymous of Bari, 151).

[68] *Codice diplomatico barese*, vol. V, no. 32, p. 55.

[69] Gertrude Robinson, *op. cit.*, vol. II, p. 140.

[70] *Codice diplomatico barese*, vol. IV, no. 21, pp. 43, 45; F. Nitti di Vito, *art. cit.*, p. 349; Λόγος..., ed. G. Anrich, p. 447, who adds μετὰ καὶ τῶν ἐντυγχανόντων τῷ πραιτωρίῳ ἑτέρων ἁγίων ναῶν.

[71] See the remarks in the following note.

[72] In August 1075, Maurelianus, patricius and catepanus (on the meaning of the term in the Norman period, see L.-R. Ménager, *Les actes latins de S. Maria di Messina* [1103–1250], Istituto siciliano di studi bizantini e neoellenici. Testi e monumenti: Testi, 9 [Palermo 1963], 34–39), viscount-lige, in a donation to Bisantius Struzzo mentions: Omnibus terraneis quibus sunt sub castello...totis terraneis quantos continet castellum ipsum usque badit in ecclesia Sancti Nicolai super porta vetere (*Codice diplomatico barese*, vol. V, no. 1, p. 3).

[73] *Codice diplomatico barese*, vol. V, no. 32, p. 55.

[74] Λόγος..., ed. Anrich, 447.

[75] Schettini, *op. cit.*, 17–19.

[76] See the dedicatory inscription in Schettini, *op. cit.*, p. 84, note 65.

Sophia, St. Basilius, and St. Demetrius—must have been in a very
poor state of repair in the year 1087. This, incidentally, is an
interesting piece of information on the duration of Byzantine
buildings, in this province at least: only about three quarters of a
century. We must point out here that there is no document mentioning a pre-existing "palace" of the catepanus, which also would have
been destroyed along with the various religious buildings in order to
make room for the construction of St. Nicholas'. Heterogeneous
portions in the new basilica (the piers in the apse, the towers at the
sides of the entrance, and the exterior arcades) have led some
scholars to imagine[77] and even to draw plans of[78] the presumed
"palace". To me all this seems to have no basis whatsoever, for the
praitorion, as we have learned from the sources mentioned above, could
have been nothing but a "rustic-urban" complex, as were others like
it, situated within the *kastron*,[79] though, admittedly, more imposing,
fortified, and relatively more sumptuous than the rest of them.[80]

vs. 7: Πρόπυλον, vestibule, with the meaning (*mutatis mutandis*) of
the Chalke of the Great Palace at Constantinople.[81] Ἐκ βάθρων: one
might also consider βεβαῖον.

vs. 8: ἄπληκτον, equivalent of φοσσᾶτον according to the summary of
the *Taktika*, attributed to Leo the Wise,[82] may mean either "camp"
or "army."[83] Here it refers to the troops encamped in Bari.

vs. 10: νεών, a well-attested form,[84] which would avoid an ortho-

---

[77] F. Jacobs, *Die Kathedrale S. Maria Icona Vetere in Foggia. Studien zur Architektur und
Plastik des 11–13. Jh. in Süditalien* (Hamburg 1968), 218–20.

[78] Schettini, *op. cit.*, figs. 36 and 37, which would represent a unique type of Byzantine
palace of the eleventh century.

[79] The *curtis Eustasio de Trifilio*, the *curtis Gidii* (*Codice diplomatico barese*, vol. V, no. 1,
pp. 3 and 4), etc.; I believe it is possible to differentiate it from others on the map of
Bari in the seventeenth century: see Ada Amati, *Bari, Richerche di geografia urbana* (Centro
di studi per la geografia antropica. Memorie di geografia antropica, II; Rome 1948),
inset fig. 7.

[80] See the city maps published by Ida Baldassare, *Bari antica* (Istituto nazionale d'archeologia e storia dell'arte. Studi di archeologia e d'arte in Terra di Bari, 1; Molfetta
1966), fig. 1 and pl. 1, 2.

[81] See C. Mango, *The Brazen House* (Arkaeol. Kunsthist. Medd. Dan. Vid. Selsk., 4,
no. 4; Copenhagen 1959), 30 f.

[82] XI, *PG* 107, col. 792.

[83] E. A. Sophocles, *Greek Lexicon*, s.v. φοσσᾶτον.

[84] For instance, in a similar dedicatory poem, in Mango, *op. cit.*, 68, and C. Mango
and E. J. W. Hawkins, in *Dumbarton Oaks Papers*, 18 (1964), 365.

graphic mistake, ναών for ναόν. Δημη[τρίου], one of the most popular Byzantine military saints.

vs. 11: λίθῳ, rather than πλίνθῳ, which would be too long for the lacuna.

vs. 13: λάμπειν; the second upright stroke of a letter which cannot be other than a π suggests this reading, which makes good sense.

Thus, our inscription attributes to the catepanus Basileios Mesardonites the renovation in brick of the *praitorion* of Bari (by this we must understand the renovation of its walls),[85] the construction of a vestibule and of a church of St. Demetrius, in stone—all three structures being undoubtedly part of the *praitorion* itself.

3. *The Date.* The inscription is dated by the notice in the Anonymous of Bari, previously mentioned. It is of the year 1011, indiction 9; more precisely, before the beginning of indiction 10, i.e. before September 1, 1011. Since we know that Basileios Mesardonites arrived in Bari in March 1010,[86] we must suppose that he immediately gave orders for the construction he wished to carry out; which would mean that this part of the *kastron* was then in a poor state of repair. However, it is possible that he only ordered completion of a building program already initiated by his predecessors. In either case, I would suppose that Mesardonites, being a person of imperial descent and possessor of considerable financial means, also gave some thought to a suitable embellishment of his official residence. This would explain the quality, exceptional for the catepanate, of the document I have here examined.

Dumbarton Oaks (Washington),
9 May, 1970

---

[85] Similarly, in one of the towers of the Nicaea (Iznik) walls, an inscription attributes to the Emperors Leo and Constantine the restoration of the city (πόλις) of Nicaea— obviously, of the walls; see A. M. Schneider, *Die Stadtmauer von Iznik (Nicaea)* (Istanbuler Forschungen, 9; Berlin 1938), p. 49, no. 29 and pl. 50, bottom.

[86] Lupus Protospatarius, 77; Anonymous of Bari, 148.

THE AGE OF SOME EARLY GREEK
CLASSICAL MANUSCRIPTS

AUBREY DILLER

It was the mode in the last century to attribute early manuscripts of the Greek classics to the eleventh century. This is noticeable in Wattenbach and Velsen's *Exempla* and Omont's *Inventaire Sommaire*. T. W. Allen in 1894 stated the doctrine explicitly: "This period, the years about 1000 A.D., has given us the greatest quantity of important MSS of the classics. ... The MSS that decide the text of the majority of Greek authors will be found to date from about the year 1000 A.D." He gives a list of some twenty worthy codices that come under this statement.[1] When A. Jacob in 1910 proposed to put one of these back in the tenth century,[2] Gardthausen protested that this would upset our notions of the age of many, especially classical, manuscripts.[3] Allen supported his statement with a dated MS, Paris. suppl. gr. 469A *an.* 986, which he regarded as a forerunner of the group he listed. In 1936, in a review of the first fascicle of the Lakes' facsimiles, he returned to the subject with a little less assurance and on the basis of codex Patm. 138 *an.* 988 (Lakes' I cod. 18 pl. 37) attributed his group of classical MSS to A.D. 950–1000. This was a move in the right direction, but not far enough. Since 1894 much has been learned about the development of the Byzantine minuscule script and about Byzantine bookdom in general, with the result that the upset Gardthausen deprecated has taken place. Many instances could be cited, but perhaps few as spectacular as the case of a ninth-century MS of Aristotle attributed to the twelfth.[4]

---

[1] T. W. Allen in *Journal of Philol.* 22 (1894), 157–60; *Journal of Hell. Stud.* 56 (1936), 116.

[2] A. Jacob, "La minuscule grecque penchée et l'âge du Parisinus grec 1741," *Mélanges offerts à M. Émile Chatelain* (1910), 52–56.

[3] V. Gardthausen, *Griechische Palaeographie*, II (1913), 210 f.

[4] H. J. Drossaart Lulofs in *Mnemosyne*, 3rd ser. 13 (1947), 290–301.

The reason for this change is of course the broader array of dated and datable MSS made available for study by photography. We are still much in the dark for the ninth century, for the greater part of which only three dated minuscule MSS are known—two Studite codices, of 835 and 880,[5] and one codex of 862 now in the Meteora and still little known.[6] Beginning with the Bodleian Euclid of 888 the series becomes denser. Probably due to this situation there is a certain resistance to attributing undated MSS to the ninth century, but it is unreasonable. The blank in that century makes it more rather than less likely that a MS of an early type unmatched in the tenth century belongs to the ninth. The Paris Plato group is a case in point, some members of which persist in being attributed to the tenth century.[7]

We are not well provided with specific criteria for determining the age of undated MSS of these centuries. Some supposed criteria have proved to be unreliable. The form of ruling, the position of the writing on the line, the leaning of the writing, are of little help. Writing above the line is not always early. Leaning minuscule occurs already *c. an.* 900,[8] but probably the earlier minuscule was always erect or even backhand. The earliest minuscule is pure, but the intrusion of majuscule forms began soon, and strictly pure minuscule is found rarely if ever after 900.[9] The forms of single letters and ligatures and breathings were ever subject to innovation, and such novelties may be useful indicators of age when their origin is fairly certain. It is not easy, however, to determine their origin. The absence of a particular form before a certain time is hard to ascertain

[5] Leningrad. gr. 219 and Mosq. gr. 117; see L. Th. Lefort and J. Cochez, *Palaeographisch Album van gedagteekende grieksche minuskelhandschriften uit de IXe en X^e eeuw* (1932), pl. 4 and 5; K. Lake and S. Lake, *Dated Greek minuscule manuscripts to the year 1200* (ten fascicles and index, 1934–45), VI codd. 234 and 214.

[6] Meteora, Metamorph. 591; see N. A. Bees in *Revue des ét. gr.* 26 (1913), 53–74; idem, *Les manuscrits des Météores* (Athens 1967), pp. 621–25, pl. 68–69; K. Weitzmann, *Die byz. Buchmalerei des IX. und X. Jahrh.* (1935), p. 39, Abb. 270–73.

[7] A. Diller, "The scholia on Strabo," *Traditio* 10 (1954), 29–50, esp. 31 f.; J. Irigoin, "L'Aristote de Vienne," *Jahrb. der österr. byz. Gesellsch.* 6 (1957), 5–10.

[8] Urbinas gr. 35 *c. an.* 900 (Lefort 13, Lake IX cod. 333 pl. 606–608), Mosq. gr. 231 *an.* 932 (Lefort 25, Lake VI cod. 217 pl. 379–81, 384), also Lake I cod. 1 pl. 1–2, cod. 2 pl. 4–5, V cod. 204 pl. 352.

[9] E. Follieri, "La reintroduzione di lettere semionciali nei più antichi manoscritti greci in minuscola," *Bull. dell'arch. paleogr. ital.* 3rd ser. 1 (1962), 15–36.

and at best is only an argument *ex silentio*.[10] It is also possible to compare entire scripts with dated or datable specimens and seek for identifications or close resemblances. Such comparison should be done with all circumspection and attention to details, lest there be anything that contradicts the contemporaneity. Moreover, it must be admitted that two specimens of the same script may differ tens of years in age, and still more two merely similar scripts. Nevertheless a good match is the best argument available for the age of an undated MS.

The palaeography of the Greek classics in the early tenth century is represented by the codices written for Arethas of Caesarea, beginning with the Bodleian Euclid of 888 and ending with cod. Mosq. gr. 231 *an.* 932. With a view to defining a later stage I have chosen as a basis the four codices written by the scribe Ephraim Monachus,[11] two of which are dated (*an.* 948 and *an.* 954), and examined them for innovations—details of script not found before but fairly common later. Probably several others could be cited, but I will give the following as the result of my examination.

1. Majuscule β. This was one of the last majuscules to penetrate the minuscule. It occurs rarely already in cod. Mosq. gr. 231 *an.* 932.
2. Ligature of $\epsilon\pi$ with a high apex. This form of ϵ occurs in $\epsilon\xi$ in earliest minuscule and later in the famous "ace of spades" ($\epsilon\rho$) characteristic of South-Italian Greek scripts, but $\epsilon\pi$ is new.
3. Open θ in one stroke, especially in $\sigma\theta$.
4. Ligature of $\lambda o\gamma$ and $\lambda o\iota$, the o in the form of a low knot continuous with the preceding and the following letter.
5. ρ and φ joining the following letter in a large low loop. Previously ρ and φ did not join at all.
6. High τ and high majuscule γ.

[10] A. Jacob (54 n. 5) thought crossed double majuscule lambda began in the middle of the 10th cent., but it is already common in cod. Mosq. 231 *an.* 932 and can be found still earlier (Lefort 23, Lake IX pl. 609).

[11] K. and S. Lake, "The scribe Ephraim," *Journal of Bibl. Lit.* 62 (1943), 263–68; A. Diller, "Notes on Greek codices of the tenth century," *Trans. Am. Philol. Assoc.* 78 (1947), 184–88; J. Irigoin, "Le scriptorium d'Ephrem," *Scriptorium* 13 (1959), 181–95. The four codices are Vatic. gr. 124 (Polybius), Marc. gr. 201 (Aristotle *an.* 954), Vatop. 949 (Four Gospels *an.* 948), Laura B 64 (Acts and Epistles). My examination rested chiefly on the Polybius, which is probably the earliest and of which I have several specimens and a microfilm. See below, plate III.

7. Majuscule (open) ω in the large form (Follieri pp. 35 f.). Small open ω occurs rarely already in cod. Mosq. gr. 231 *an.* 932 (cf. *β supra*).

8. Signatures of quires in the lower inner corner of the first and the last page. This is unusual, but I cannot say whether or not it occurs in earlier codices.

9. A small plain cross in the upper margin of the first page of each quire.

Most of these symptoms are by no means constant in Ephraim's work, and some of them are not even common there. I do not suppose they were original with him. Except as noted I have not found them in earlier scripts. I can only hope they will not be found there in frequencies that invalidate them as criteria of age, as indicators of the middle of the tenth century or later time. Many contemporary and later MSS have no trace of them, especially liturgical, monastic, or provincial products, conservative and aloof from the classical tradition. Here is a list of some early dated followers with the numbers of the symptoms found in them.

Turon. 980, Historical excerpts of Constantine Porphyrogennetus (d. 959), not dated, but probably the original fair copy. *Scriptorium* 13 (1959), pl. 17. Symptoms 3, 4, 5.

Paris. gr. 668 *an.* 954, Chrysostom, written by Joannes presbyter (Vogel and Gardthausen, *Die Schreiber* [1909], p. 204). Lefort 33, Lake IV 139 pl. 236. The two specimens are not by the same hand. Symptoms 2, 3, 5.

Athous Dionysii 70 *an.* 955, Chrysostom, written by Nicephorus notarius for Basil patricius (Lecapenus) (Vogel 341). Lake III 87 pl. 154 f. Symptoms 5, 8.

Kosinitza 32, now Princeton, Garrett 14, *an.* 955, Chrysostom, written by the same for the same as the preceding. I have not seen any specimen. See C. U. Faye and W. H. Bond, *Supplement to the Census* (1962), p. 311.

Ambros. F 12 sup. *an.* 960/1, Psalter with comm. Lefort 36, Lake III 124 pl. 210. Symptoms 3, 4, 5, 6.

Vatic. Ross. gr. 5, formerly in Vienna, *an.* 961, Chrysostom, written by Basil calligraphus monachus for Basil (Lecapenus) (Vogel 56). Lefort 35. Symptoms 1, 3, 5, 6, 7.

Patmos 136 *an.* 962, Chrysostom, written by Hilarion abbot of Calamon in Palestine for Paul abbot of St. Sabbas (Vogel 163). Lake I 16 pl. 35, 44. Symptoms 1, 2, 3, 4, 5, 6, 7, 8.

Paris. gr. 497 *an.* 966 (not 970), Basil and Chrysostom, written by Nicetas protospatharius (Vogel 336). Lefort 39, 84, Lake IV 140 pl. 239 f. Symptoms 1, 2, 3, 5, 8 (in subscr. 1, 2, 6, 7).

Ambros. B 106 sup. *an.* 966/7, Psalter with comm. Lefort 40, Lake III 125 pl. 211. Symptoms 1, 2, 3, 5, 6, 7, 8.

Marc. gr. 53 *an.* 968, Basil of Caesarea, written by Athanasius monachus (Vogel 10). Wattenbach–Velsen 6, Lefort 41, Lake II 45 pl. 82, 83, 85 (pl. 82 is by a different hand, much earlier). Symptoms 1, 2, 5, 6, 8, 9.

Paris. gr. 724 *an.* 974, Chrysostom, written by Stephanus monachus of the monastery of Studius (Vogel 404). Lefort 45, Lake IV 141 pl. 241, 244. Symptoms 2, 3, 8.

Laur. 9, 22 *an.* 974, Chrysostom, written by Basil clericus (Vogel 56). Lefort 86. Symptoms 3, 5, 6.

Kosinitza 16, part now Bruxell. II. 2404. 1, *an.* 976, Chrysostom, written by Basil presbyter, the same as the preceding. Lefort 87, M. Wittek, *Album de paléographie grecque* (1967), pl. 17. Symptoms 1, 2, 3, 5, 6.

Mosq. gr. 140 *an.* 975, Gregory of Nazianz, written by Nicolaus monachus and presbyter (Vogel 348). Lefort 46, Lake VI 218 pl. 383. Symptoms 2, 3, 4, 5, 6.

Mosq. gr. 125 *an.* 976/7, Basil and Chrysostom, fol. 236–313 written by Nicolaus (Vogel 364). Lefort 49, Lake VI 219 pl. 385–87. Symptoms 1, 5, 6, 8.

Bodl. Laud gr. 75 *an.* 976 or 977, Chrysostom. Lefort 47, Lake II 55 pl. 100–102. Symptoms 1, 3, 4, 5.

We see that Ephraim's symptoms spread rapidly in the third quarter of the century. Their absence, in mss of similar type, and their presence probably divide about the year 950. Returning now from this digression to those undated classical mss of problematical age, let us examine some of them in the light of modern knowledge of tenth-century Greek palaeography.

Paris. 92. gr. 1741, Rhetorica (Aristotle, Dionysius Halic., Demetrius Phaler., *et al.*), a composite codex of parts written by several different but certainly contemporary hands.[12] Most of them are leaning, but fol. 200–45 are in an erect hand. This was the codex A. Jacob wished to relocate in the middle of the tenth century on the basis of the leaning scripts. Gardthausen, while rejecting the relocation, pointed out that Jacob's account of leaning scripts was defective,

---

[12] H. Rabe in *Rhein. Museum* 67 (1912), 337–43. H. Omont, *La Poétique d'Aristote* (1891, facs. of fol. 184–99); *idem, Fac-similés des plus anciens mss. grecs* (1892), pl. 37,1 (fol. 143ʳ); *Palaeogr. Soc.* II 47 (fol. [*ca* 173]); W. Rhys Roberts ed., *Demetrius on Style* (1902), pp. 64 (fol. 226ʳ), 208 (fol. 245ᵛ).

omitting the strong example in cod. Mosq. gr. 231 *an.* 932. Actually there are several earlier examples going as far back as 900 (see note 8 *supra*). H. Rabe independently relocated the codex in the time of Constantine Porphyrogennetus (d. 959).[13]

The erect script of fol. 200–45 is similar to that of Arethas' scribe Baanes, who wrote Paris. gr. 451 *an.* 913/4 (Apologetica) and Harley 5694 (Lucian, undated).[14] Also similar is Vatic. gr. 90, Lucian complete, corrected by Alexander bishop of Nicaea (early tenth century).[15] These three MSS share many novelties and peculiarities. They have a like admixture of majuscule letters, avoiding majuscule β, δ, η, μ, and ω; ξ and ζ are always majuscule, even in εξ. A striking feature is the large lunar σ before the vowels α, ω, ο, and υ.[16] Another is the broken ε, in which the upper and lower parts of the large minuscule letter fall apart and the upper tends to enlarge and the lower to diminish and even vanish. Majuscule λλ is not crossed, but minuscule λλ is sometimes in ligature. The erect hand of Paris. 1741 shares most of these features.

The leaning script of Paris. 1741 also shares the features of the Baanes and the Lucian MSS, but differs from them in the small-leaning feature, which is not exemplified in early dated MSS. Allen's comparison in this feature with Paris. suppl. gr. 469A *an.* 986 and Patmos 138 *an.* 988 is not convincing. These two scripts look earlier than they are, but still have signs of lateness in the use of tachygraphy, the plain (unhooked) pendants, and open θ (σθ). Both seem to me rather enervate. Except in the small-leaning feature Paris. 1741 is not much like them. Its hooked pendants are characteristic of the ninth and early tenth century. The admixture of majuscule is less than in the erect script. Majuscule λλ is not yet quite crossed. The ligature εξ is avoided. I do not see any palpable distinction in age between Paris. gr. 1741 and the MSS of Baanes and Alexander, and I conclude that it belongs to the first half or even the first third of the tenth century.

[13] H. Rabe quoted in Usener and Radermacher edd., *Dionysii Halic. opuscula* II (Teubner 1929), p. I n. 2.

[14] Lefort 17, 18; Lake II cod. 65 pl. 117, IV cod. 136 pl. 230 f.

[15] P. Franchi de' Cavalieri and J. Lietzmann, *Specimina codd. graec. Vatic.* (1910, 1929), pl. 10.

[16] This feature is seen rarely in Paris. gr. 1470 *an.* 890 (Lefort 7, Lake IV codd. 134–35 pl. 226–29).

Anthologia Palatina, in Heidelberg with 48 leaves (pp. 615–710) in Paris. suppl. gr. 384.[17] Uncertainty and error seem to reign still over the age of this famous codex. When it was still in the Vatican Library Giuseppe Spalletti edited the Anacreontica from it (1781) and made a complete transcript to serve as the basis of the edition of the Anthology by Fr. Jacobs (1798–1814). These two were the first to express themselves on the age of the codex. Unfortunately their publications are not accessible to me just now, and I know them only from references. They seem to have pointed out both lines of external evidence bearing on the age and wavered between them. The first line is the contents of the Anthology, including pieces from every century down to the early tenth, where they stop suddenly. The other line is the scholion by the hand J on *A. Pal.* I 10, 28 f. The text regards the pious works of Juliana Anicia, in particular the church of St. Polyeuctus, which she rebuilt. The scholiast says: μενουσιν ἄριστε πάντα μέχρι τῆς σημερον ετεσι πεντακοσίοις και εξηκοντα. The last two words are erased. Since Juliana Anicia died *an.* 526/7, this scholion would refer to the eleventh century, either late or early (with or without the 60 years).

Opinions on the palaeography of the codex have been unusually elastic. V. Rose made the amazing statement that it could be of the tenth, eleventh, or twelfth century.[18] Preisendanz at first, ignoring the scholion, attributed the codex to the tenth century, but later yielded to the scholion and put it in the eleventh.[19] Recently Waltz and Beckby give it as the common opinion that it is *c.* 980. I do not know how this date was obtained. A. S. F. Gow, apparently overlooking Preisendanz' appendix, gives the tenth century as the common opinion.[20]

The fact is the palaeography contradicts that scholion. The codex cannot be of the eleventh century. The scholion must be erroneous. I think the error is confirmed elsewhere. The *Patria*

---

[17] *Anthologia Palatina. Codex Palatinus et Codex Parisinus phototypice editi.* Praefatus est Carolus Preisendanz (two parts, 1911); Wattenbach – Velsen 36 (pp. 452–53); Omont, *Fac-similés des plus anciens mss. grecs* (1892), 33 (pp. 616, 669).

[18] V. Rose ed., *Anacreontis Teii quae vocantur συμποσιακὰ ἡμιαμβεῖα* (Teubner 1876), p. XI.

[19] Preisendanz pp. XVI and CXLVIII f. (appendicula).

[20] P. Waltz ed., *Anthologie grecque* I (1928), p. XL n. 3; H. Beckby ed., *Anthologia graeca* I (1957), p. 81 n. 1; A. S. F. Gow, *The Greek Anthology, sources and ascriptions* (1958), p. 10.

Constantinopoleos (PsCodinus) say quite wrongly that the Juliana who built St. Polyeuctus was a daughter of Valentinian (I, d. 375) and sister-in-law of Theodosius the Great (d. 395).[21] If we assume our scholion attaches to this tradition, it could refer to the early tenth century and thus fall in line with the evidence of the contents and the palaeography of the codex.

The Palatine codex has a complicated structure, consisting of two earlier blocks A and B joined together and supplemented by a later scribe J. Block B (pp. 453–642), which seems to be the oldest, is mostly in an erect hand, but a few pages in the middle (518–24, 21) and a large part at the end (622–42) are in leaning hands.[22] The main hand belongs to the type of Baanes and the Lucians. Broken ε is rare; λλ is not crossed; ζ has both forms, but ξ is always majuscule, even in εξ, as in Paris. 1741. I was surprised to find some symptoms of Ephraim (open θ 469,5, λογ 531,9), but they are very rare. The leaning hand in the middle, which must be simultaneous, has later features—much more admixture of majuscule letters (all except β, η, μ, and ω), crossed λλ, ξ in both forms, even in εξ, but ζ only majuscule. This MS (pp. 453–621) is probably later than Baanes (*an.* 913/4) and earlier than Ephraim (*an.* 948).

The scripts of A (pp. 51–61, 64–422) and J (1–50 *et al.*) are much alike, sometimes scarcely distinguishable—small, leaning, mixed, minuscule. A has all the letters in both forms, even β and μ; J avoids majuscule α, β, η, and μ. A has majuscule λλ uncrossed, J, crossed. These hands are of the type T. W. Allen lumped together at the end of the tenth century. The absence or great rarity of Ephraim's symptoms seems to me to tell against such a late age. For comparison cod. Mosq. 231 *an.* 932 is equally or even more eligible than the two late codices Allen adduced.

The latest authors of pieces in the Palatine Anthology are Arethas and his contemporaries, including Constantine Cephalas. The codex itself, as Gow remarks, appears to be not much later. The scribes A and J may well have remembered these men personally, and the scribe B would be even closer.

---

[21] Th. Preger ed., *Scriptores originum Constantinopolitanarum* II (Teubner 1907), p. 237; R. Janin, *Les églises et les monastères (de Constantinople)* (1953), 419.

[22] The scribe of pp. 622–42 is not the same as 518 ff. He has fewer majuscules, different ζ and ξ, avoids broken ε and the ligature εξ.

Laur. 32,9. This also famous codex was written in four parts, viz. fol. 1–118 Sophocles, fol. 119–126 and 127–189 Aeschylus, fol. 190–264 Apollonius Rhodius, all with ample marginal scholia in semi-majuscule.[23] There is some disagreement on the number and identification and age of the hands. In the common view[24] all are the same except the third (fol. 127–89), and that one is contemporary, as are the scholia. On the basis of the specimens at hand I judge the three large parts to be all different.

The fourth part (fol. 216^r) has the least impurities in its minuscule. The only majuscule letters are κ and ξ and rarely lunar $o\varsigma$ at the end of a line. Broken ϵ is avoided. There are few ligatures, minuscule $\lambda\lambda$ is the only later one I see. This is a purer minuscule even than Baanes'.

In contrast the first part has majuscule α (at the ends of lines), $\gamma, \epsilon, \eta, \lambda, \nu, \xi$ (rarely minuscule), π, ω, and rarely lunar $o\varsigma$ at the end of a line. Broken ϵ is frequent and degenerate. There are several late ligatures—$\gamma\alpha, \gamma\omega$, majuscule $\lambda\lambda$, etc.

The third part (fol. 149^v) is intermediate as regards impurities: majuscule $\zeta, \kappa, \lambda, \xi$, broken ϵ. It has a peculiar $\epsilon\iota$ and a ligature $\alpha\nu$ unknown to the others. This hand is the least calligraphic of the three.

I do not think these differences signify difference in age. The parts are bound together by similarity of format and signatures of quaternions, and the scripts themselves have a general resemblance. The parts were doubtless all produced together, as in Paris. gr. 1741.

The whole codex is usually attributed to the early eleventh century or *c. an.* 1000. The only comparisons with dated MSS I know of are those offered by Allen (see *supra*), which seem irrelevant in this case. For the age I would stress the absence of all of Ephraim's symptoms in all the parts. I think the codex must be attributed to the middle of the tenth century.

Ravennas 429 (*olim* 137, A, 4), Aristophanes.[25] Immanuel

---

[23] See the bibliography in A. Turyn, *The Manuscript Tradition of the Tragedies of Aeschylus* (1943), 17 f. I have used the facsimiles in Wattenbach, *Scripturae graecae specimina* (1883), pl. 25 (fol. 41^v), Wattenbach–Velsen 34, 35 (fol. 117^r, 216^r), *Pal. Soc.* I 83 (fol. 149^v).

[24] N. Wecklein ed., *Aeschyli fabulae cum lectionibus et scholiis codicis Medicei...ab Hieronymo Vitelli denuo collatis* (1885), p. XIV; T. W. Allen in *Journal of Philol.* 22 (1894), 166.

[25] *Aristophanis comoediae undecim cum scholiis. Codex Ravennas phototypice editus.* Praefatus est J. van Leeuwen (1904); Wattenbach, *Specimina* (1883), 26 (fol. 131^r); *Pal. Soc.* II 105, 106; B. A. van Groningen, *Short Manual of Greek Palaeography* (1955), pl. VI (fol. 34^r).

Bekker discovered the close resemblance between this MS and Laur. 32,9. In fact the Aristophanes and the Sophocles are by the same hand. Consequently both codices have been and still must be given the same age.

Laur. 59,9, Demosthenes (P).[26] Bekker identified the hands in this codex (fol. 19–182) and the Ravennas of Aristophanes, but Vitelli rightly rejected the identification, at least as regards the text-hands (the script of the scholia is very like that in Laur. 32,9 [and Rav. 429]). The Demosthenes is more calligraphic, closer to Baanes, and has different majuscule letters (δ, ζ often, γ, η, λ seldom or never). Ephraim's symptoms are again quite lacking. The two MSS are probably of about the same age, mid tenth century.

Paris. gr. 2935, Demosthenes (Y). These two Demosthenes codices are cognate in text and scholia, and Vitelli saw great similarity, but short of identity, in the scholia. Recently N. G. Wilson[27] has identified the main hand of Paris. 2935 (fol. 27–301) with Vatic. gr. 1 (Plato), attributed to the early tenth century.[28] Fol. 1–8 are in a different hand, which he finds very like the hand (*sic*) of Sophocles and Apollonius in Laur. 32,9. The two MSS P and Y of Demosthenes are commonly attributed to the tenth/eleventh century, certainly too late.

Palat. gr. 252 in Heidelberg, Thucydides (E).[29] This MS is old angular minuscule; γ and χ in particular are primitive, also α before τ or π; ε is not broken. Only λ and ξ are majuscule, λλ is not crossed. There are few newer ligatures (εγ εχ αγ). The MS is of the ninth/tenth century, not eleventh, as commonly stated. It is apparently the earliest of the mediaeval MSS of Thucydides.

Marc. gr. 454 (colloc. 822), the leading MS (A) of the Iliad.[30] This codex has always been attributed rightly to the tenth century, but

---

[26] G. Vitelli and C. Paoli, *Collezione fiorentina di facsimili paleografici* (1884–97), greco XII; *Pal. Soc.* II 88, 89.

[27] N. G. Wilson in *Class. Quart.* 54 (1960), 200–202.

[28] Franchi pl. 9; T. W. Allen in *Class. Quart.* 22 (1928), 75.

[29] Wattenbach – Velsen 37, *New Pal. Soc.* I 26.

[30] *Homeri Ilias cum scholiis. Codex Venetus A phototypice editus.* Praefatus est Dominicus Comparetti (1901); W. Dindorf ed., *Scholia graeca in Homeri Iliadem* I (1875) with photographic facsimiles of fol. 48ʳ and 132ᵛ; Wattenbach–Velsen 32, 33 (fol. 15ᵛ, 34ʳ); van Groningen, *Manual* (1955), pl. V (fol. 253ʳ); R. Merkelbach and H. van Thiel, *Griechisches Leseheft* (1965), pp. 93–96 (fol. 6ʳᵛ, 4ʳᵛ).

lately some mistaken identifications have been made. The scholia, in small minuscule, and the prolegomena (Proclus) seem still to be by the same hand as the text, which is in large minuscule. It has some symptoms of Ephraim—open θ, continuous ρ, high τ. The θ is frequent in Proclus and the scholia, but rare in the text; the τ I find only in the scholia. I do not think the MS can be as early as Arethas, as Severyns wishes to believe.[31] Nor is the hand very similar to Ephraim, as Hemmerdinger avers,[32] though it is probably contemporary.

Laur. 32,24, the earliest mediaeval MS of the Odyssey (G).[33] Wattenbach–Velsen attribute it to the eleventh century, Molhuysen to the tenth, Allen to the tenth/eleventh, van Leeuwen to the end of the tenth. The MS is a rough thicket of Ephraimisms, surely later than codex A of the Iliad, but I do not see anything in it that postpones it to the eleventh century.

There are quite a few other cases of undated classical MSS wrongly attributed to the eleventh instead of the tenth century, but I hope the ones I have discussed are sufficient to show the need of revision in this field. Once the revision is made it will appear that the peak of production of these codices was *c. an.* 950 instead of 1000, in the reign of Constantine Porphyrogennetus instead of Basil Bulgaroctonus. The least that can be said for this is that Constantine is well known for his interest in scholarship and Basil is not. At any rate, editors of the Greek classics will be well advised not to repeat obsolete attributions without examination and confirmation.

Bloomington, 12 August 1970

---

[31] A. Severyns, "Aréthas et le Venetus d'Homère," *Bull. Acad. Roy. Belg.* (*Classe des Lettres*) 1951, pp. 283–306; *idem, Recherches sur la Chrestomathie de Proclos,* III (Bibl. de la Faculté de Philos. et Lettres de l'Univ. de Liège 132 [1953]), 245–52.

[32] B. Hemmerdinger in *Revue des ét. gr.* 69 (1956), 433 f., *Journal of Theol. Stud.* n.s. 11 (1960), 354, *Byz. Zeitschr.* 56 (1963), 24.

[33] Wattenbach–Velsen 38; P. C. Molhuysen, *De tribus Homeri Odysseae codicibus antiquissimis* (1896); T. W. Allen in *Papers of the British School in Rome,* 5 (1910), 6, 50; J. van Leeuwen ed., *Homeri carmina* I (1912), p. LVII.

UN FRAGMENT DE MANUSCRIT GREC
(EXTRAITS DE MARC-AURÈLE ET D'ÉLIEN) CONSERVÉ À LA BIBLIOTHÈQUE MAZARINE DANS LA COLLECTION FAUGÈRE

CHARLES ASTRUC

Le fragment grec du XIVe siècle que nous présentons ici constitue, avec plusieurs pièces annexes datant du siècle dernier, la liasse n° 5 du manuscrit 4556 de la Bibliothèque Mazarine. Le manuscrit est l'un des trente volumes (portant aujourd'hui les cotes 4529 à 4558) qui furent légués à cette bibliothèque parisienne par Prosper Faugère. Né en 1810, mort en 1887, Faugère avait été fonctionnaire au ministère de l'Instruction publique puis au ministère des Affaires étrangères,[1] et s'était fait connaître par ses travaux sur Pascal: on lui doit notamment la première édition critique des *Pensées*.[2]

La collection Faugère a été décrite par Paul Marais, au tome XLV du Catalogue général des manuscrits des bibliothèques françaises, dans le "Deuxième Supplément" consacré à la Mazarine;[3] elle y est définie par la formule que voici: "Matériaux de diverses éditions des oeuvres de Pascal, publiées par P. Faugère (1844–86); imprimés et manuscrits."[4] D'après la même description,[5] le recueil

---

[1] Sur Armand-Prosper Faugère, voir pour l'essentiel la notice rédigée par E. Regnard, dans la *Nouvelle Biographie générale*...[Didot–Hoefer], t. 17 (Paris 1873), col. 167–68. Faugère était chef du secrétariat au ministère de l'Instruction publique en 1839. Il démissionna en mars 1840, et entra au ministère des Affaires étrangères dans le courant de la même année.

[2] *Pensées, fragments et lettres de Blaise Pascal, publiés pour la première fois conformément aux manuscrits originaux en grande partie inédits*, par M. Prosper Faugère...(Paris 1844, 2 vol. in 8°).

[3] *Catalogue général des Manuscrits des Bibliothèques publiques de France...Tome XLV. Paris (Arsenal, Mazarine, Sainte-Geneviève). Besançon. Aix-en-Provence*...(Paris 1915), pp. 35–43.

[4] *Catalogue* cité, 35.

[5] *Ibid.*, 42.

coté 4556 se présente comme un carton renfermant cinq liasses: les trois premières (journaux manuscrits, dossiers, notes variées, opuscule imprimé) ont trait à Port-Royal, à Asson de Saint-Gilles, au chevalier de Méré; la quatrième est un exemplaire imprimé d'un travail en allemand sur les *Pensées* de Pascal, qu'accompagne une traduction (manuscrite) en français; enfin, la cinquième et dernière liasse aurait pour contenu, nous dit le Catalogue, des "Pièces diverses, sans importance, ayant servi à P. Faugère pour ses études sur Pascal." En vérité, on peut affirmer que P. Marais n'a pas ouvert la liasse n° 5, car s'il avait procédé à un examen moins superficiel des éléments placés au fond du carton à décrire, il aurait été forcé de constater qu'ils n'ont aucun rapport direct avec les études pascaliennes de Faugère. La cinquième liasse contient avant tout un fragment grec du XIVe siècle, rapporté d'Orient par Minoïde Mynas,[6] à quoi s'ajoutent quelques documents modernes, dont les plus importants sont des autographes du même Mynas et concernent principalement ce fragment découvert par lui. La présence de l'ensemble dans le recueil s'explique par le fait que Faugère ne s'intéressait pas seulement aux *Pensées* de Pascal, mais aussi à celles de Marc-Aurèle. On verra plus loin qu'il avait demandé à Mynas, quand celui-ci était parti pour sa première mission, de lui trouver, si possible, en Orient un manuscrit des *Pensées* du grand stoïcien. Désir bien difficile à exaucer: on sait comme est pauvre la tradition manuscrite de Marc-Aurèle, en ce qui concerne les témoins complets du texte. Cependant, l'astucieux voyageur ne devait pas revenir entièrement bredouille à cet égard, puisque le fragment qu'il rapporta pour en faire don à Prosper Faugère contient surtout, entremêlés de passages tirés d'Élien, une quarantaine de brefs extraits des *Pensées* de l'empereur philosophe.

Le contenu réel de la liasse n° 5 aurait pu, dans les conditions que nous venons d'expliquer, rester inconnu de façon irrémédiable. Le

---

[6] Sur Minoïde Mynas, voyageur grec qui effectua en Proche-Orient trois missions de recherche de manuscrits grecs pour le compte du gouvernement français, voir essentiellement l'étude bien documentée d'H. Omont, "Minoïde Mynas et ses missions en Orient (1840–1855)," in *Mémoires de l'Académie des Inscriptions et Belles-Lettres*, t. XL (Paris 1916), pp. 337–419. Prosper Faugère, du fait des fonctions de secrétaire qu'il avait exercées, en 1839–40, auprès du ministre de l'Instruction publique, fut très utile à Mynas durant le temps de ses missions: de là, le ton amical de leurs relations, attesté par nombre de lettres de Mynas à Faugère.

mérite d'avoir remarqué, en 1962, son caractère aberrant par rapport au contexte pascalien de la collection revient à Mademoiselle Marie-Thérèse d'Alverny, alors Conservateur à la Bibliothèque nationale, qui avait été chargée d'organiser une exposition à l'occasion du troisième centenaire de la mort de Pascal.[7] Elle signala le fait à Monsieur Jacques Renoult, Conservateur en chef, à cette époque, de la Bibliothèque Mazarine, et c'est ainsi que la liasse nous fut confiée pour identification de ses divers éléments. Le présent article reprend et développe considérablement la notice descriptive que nous avons remise à M. Renoult, vers la fin de juillet 1963, en lui restituant les documents.[8]

1. Description du fragment grec

Le fragment se compose de quinze feuillets de papier oriental, qui mesurent chacun 245 × 168 mm. Les ff. 14^v et 15^{rv} sont entièrement vides d'écriture, le texte s'achevant dans la partie supérieure du f. 14^r : il est donc possible que les quinze feuillets représentent la fin du manuscrit auquel ils ont été arrachés.[9] Dans l'état actuel du fragment, sept feuillets (ff. 1 à 4, 11, 12, 14) se trouvent détachés; au contraire, les huit autres forment, comme à l'origine, quatre *bifolia* demeurés intacts (ff. 5/10, 6/9, 7/8, 13/15); le feuillet attenant au f. 14 a été coupé (sans doute à date ancienne) au ras de la ficelle, qui est conservée; enfin, on peut conjecturer la disparition d'un feuillet à la suite du f. 15^v. Aucune marque de cahier n'apparaissant aujourd'hui, l'appartenance des feuillets subsistants à des fascicules distincts ne peut être retrouvée avec une entière certitude; la répartition la plus plausible nous semble être la suivante: ff. 1–3^v = trois derniers feuillets d'un quaternion; ff. 4–11^v = un quaternion complet (trois de ses *bifolia* sur quatre étant encore dans leur état originel); ff. 12–15^v = quatre feuillets d'un ternion (peut-être le dernier cahier du codex primitif), dans lequel ont disparu le quatrième et le sixième élément (soit un feuillet après 14^v, et un autre après 15^v).

---

[7] Cf. le catalogue: *Blaise Pascal, 1623–1662* (Paris, Bibliothèque nationale, 1962). On y peut voir que les recueils de la collection Faugère avaient été mis à contribution plus de vingt fois pour cette exposition.

[8] Cette notice, dont la rédaction fut achevée le 27 juillet 1963, est demeurée inédite.

[9] L'absence de foliotage original et de signatures de cahiers nous prive d'indices qui auraient pu permettre des conclusions plus catégoriques.

Le papier du manuscrit, avons-nous dit, est un papier oriental: on peut s'en convaincre en observant un faisceau de caractéristiques (absence de filigrane; vergeures assez fines, obliques par rapport aux bords du feuillet; pontuseaux à peu près indiscernables) qui correspondent à plusieurs des critères, définis par Jean Irigoin, grâce auxquels on distingue assez facilement le "bombycin", papier d'origine arabe, du papier de fabrication italienne.[10] Rappelons que, d'après les résultats obtenus par le même savant, le papier oriental fut employé de 1050 à 1380 environ.

L'encre qui a servi pour le texte est une encre bistre, dont la forte teneur en sels minéraux a exercé une action corrosive sur le papier, qui a pris une coloration rougeâtre. Pour la rubrication, on a utilisé une encre de nuance carmin, qui n'a pas conservé son éclat premier: dans la plupart des feuillets, la couleur a passé, tirant aujourd'hui sur le bistre-jaune. Les éléments traités par le rubricateur sont le titre du f. 1ᵛ, les initiales, les gloses interlinéaires et les signes de renvoi aux scholies marginales.

L'ensemble des feuillets subsistants offre, quant à l'écriture, une apparence homogène. Pourtant, il faut probablement distinguer deux mains contemporaines: chacune a écrit une minuscule du XIVᵉ siècle, fine et régulière; toutefois, la première écriture (ff. 1–7), légèrement inclinée vers la droite, est un peu plus nette que la seconde—tracée à peu près verticalement—qui occupe, sauf erreur, toute la fin à partir du f. 7, ligne 19 du texte, et ligne 25 des scholies. Notons que scholies et gloses sont écrites dans un module très petit, et qu'elles présentent de nombreuses abréviations, alors que celles-ci sont rares dans le texte principal.

À l'époque où Mynas découvrit le fragment, c'est-à-dire en 1842 (v. *infra*), l'état de conservation des feuillets était déjà fort médiocre comme leur "inventeur" lui-même le déclare dans une lettre envoyée du Mont Athos à Faugère, le 25 février 1842, et figurant parmi les pièces annexes: "...c'est dommage que le papier soit cassant à cause de la vetustité [*sic*], et en voulant le plier, il se casse. J'ai le cousu [*sic*] dans un carton,[11] et il ne nous sera pas difficile de faire rapporter les morceaux à leur place." Effectivement, tous les

---

[10] Cf. J. Irigoin, "Les premiers manuscrits grecs écrits sur papier et le problème du bombycin," in *Scriptorium* IV (1950), 194–204 (v. notamment p. 196).

[11] Ce "carton" n'a pas été conservé.

feuillets, à l'exception du f. 15, ont été endommagés par des pliures
et des cassures;[12] les manques qui, en conséquence, affectent le
texte sont surtout sensibles dans les ff. 9 à 13.

Les ff. 1, 2, 3, 4 (dans la marge inférieure), et le f. 14 (en son
milieu) portent l'estampille de la Bibliothèque Mazarine, où le
fragment grec, avec les pièces annexes dont la description est donnée
plus loin, entra en même temps que tous les autres papiers légués par
Prosper Faugère.

Tel qu'il nous est parvenu, le fragment contient deux éléments—
(f. 1^{rv}) extraits de l'*Anthologie Palatine*, puis (ff. 1^{v}—14) extraits de
Marc-Aurèle et d'Élien—qui voisinent de façon identique ou
analogue dans d'autres recueils de miscellanées. Citons, à titre
d'exemples, deux manuscrits de la Bibliothèque nationale (tous deux
du XIVe siècle), le Parisinus Coisl. gr. 341, ff. 317^{v} à 355^{v},[13] et le
Parisinus Suppl. gr. 1164, f. 14^{v} à f. 22, ligne 1, et ff. 3^{v}–4.[14] On
notera que, dans le fragment de la Mazarine, la mutilation du début
a fait disparaître la majeure partie des extraits de l'*Anthologie
Palatine*.

Nous donnons, ci-après, une description détaillée des deux
éléments qui viennent d'être définis.

I (f. 1^{rv}). Fin d'une série d'Épigrammes extraites de l'Anthologie
Palatine, avec gloses interlinéaires et scholies marginales. Il ne
subsiste que cinq pièces, et la première est aujourd'hui amputée de
ses quatre premiers vers; soit: *Anth. Pal.* X, 56, vers 5–14 (le copiste,
comme ceux des deux témoins cités plus haut, ayant omis les quatre
vers qui suivent le v. 14 dans les éditions); X, 68; X, 99; IX, 442;
X, 35 (*inc. Μὴ πταίων*, comme dans l'Anthologie planudéenne, au
lieu de *Εὖ πράττων*: v. l'apparat de l'édition procurée par H. Beckby,
Anthologia graeca, Buch IX–XI [Munich 1958], p. 492).

Ces cinq épigrammes, offrant les mêmes particularités textuelles,
constituent également la fin de la série dans l'un des Parisini cités, le
Coisl. 341, où elles occupent les ff. 331–332; elles y sont immédiatement suivies, comme dans notre fragment, de l'arrangement

---

[12] Selon le souhait que M. Renoult avait exprimé à ce propos, chacun des feuillets a
été restauré et placé sous mousseline, en 1962, par les soins d'une ouvrière spécialisée
de la Bibliothèque nationale.

[13] Cf. R. Devreesse, *Le Fonds Coislin* (Paris 1945), p. 326.

[14] Voir la notice de M.-L. Concasty, in Ch. Astruc et M.-L. Concasty, *Le Supplément
grec. Tome III. N°s 901–1371* (Paris 1960), p. 329.

d'extraits de Marc-Aurèle et d'Élien décrit ci-dessous. La même séquence se retrouve dans le second manuscrit déjà mentionné, le Suppl. gr. 1164, au f. 11ʳᵛ, mais là, elle ne figure pas en fin de série: vingt-sept autres épigrammes lui font suite, et la séparent des extraits de Marc-Aurèle et d'Élien.[15]

II (ff. 1ᵛ–14). Sous le titre (à l'encre rouge) Μάρκου Ἀντωνίνου ἐκ τῶν καθ' αὑτόν, Extraits des Pensées de Marc-Aurèle (39 morceaux) entremêlés de fragments tirés de l'Historia animalium d'Élien (24 morceaux).

Cette curieuse compilation était connue jusqu'à présent par dix-sept témoins (tous du XIVᵉ ou du XVᵉ siècle), qui ont été classés et étudiés par H. Schenkl dans la préface de son *editio maior* de Marc-Aurèle.[16] Neuf ans avant Schenkl, E. L. De Stefani avait analysé le même ensemble, en le désignant du nom d' "Excerpta Laurentiana," dans une étude générale sur les manuscrits contenant des extraits de l'*Historia animalium* d'Élien.[17] Comme le premier nommé de ces savants en a fait la remarque, le but poursuivi par le compilateur de cet amalgame nous demeure obscur,[18] et il est impossible d'attribuer le travail à un auteur déterminé, en dépit des efforts déployés autrefois par un éditeur de Marc-Aurèle pour en faire endosser la paternité à Maxime Planude.[19]

Notre fragment—dix-huitième témoin, donc, du singulier arrangement de morceaux de Marc-Aurèle et d'Élien—présente les soixante-trois extraits, accompagnés, comme les épigrammes qui précèdent,

---

[15] Cf. la description citée à la note précédente.

[16] *Marci Antonini imperatoris in semet ipsum libri XII.* Recognovit Henricus Schenkl. *Editio maior* (Leipzig 1913), pp. xv–xvi; liste des manuscrits (avec leurs sigles) aux pp. xxxiii–xxxiv, et tableau de leur contenu à la p. xxxv.

[17] E. L. De Stefani, "Gli excerpta della 'Historia Animalium' di Eliano," in *Studi italiani di filologia classica*, XII (1904), 145–80: il est traité des "Excerpta Laurentiana" aux pp. 150–53; quatre morceaux d'Élien (I 1, 2, 3, 4) sont édités aux pp. 173–75 d'après cinq manuscrits où figure notre compilation.—Il faut signaler que R. Hercher ne fait aucune allusion, dans ses éditions d'Élien (Paris 1858; Leipzig 1864–66), aux extraits dont nous nous occupons.

[18] Schenkl, éd. citée, p. xv.

[19] Schenkl, *ibid.*, pp. xv–xvi. L'auteur réfuté par Schenkl est J. Stich, qui avait proposé l'attribution à Planude dans les pp. x–xii de la préface de son édition de Marc-Aurèle (*D. imperatoris Marci Antonini Commentariorum quos sibi ipsi scripsit libri XII.* Recensuit Ioannes Stich, Leipzig 1882); dans cette édition, une quinzaine de manuscrits contenant nos extraits sont énumérés aux pp. viii–ix, et un tableau de leur contenu occupe la p. xiii.

de gloses interlinéaires et de scholies marginales, exactement dans le même ordre que la majorité des autres manuscrits; cet ordre, qu'on trouve indiqué (parmi d'autres) dans le tableau de l'édition Schenkl,[20] et, plus clairement, dans la liste dressée par De Stefani,[21] est le suivant:[22] *Ant.* VII 22 (*inc.* Ἴδιον ἀνθρώπου φιλεῖν καὶ τοὺς πταίοντας); *Ael.* I 22 (*inc.* Βαβυλωνίους τε καὶ Χαλδαίους σοφούς); *Ant.* VII 18; *Ael.* I 25, 28; *Ant.* VII 7, IV 49 (§§ 2–5);[23] *Ael.* V 22, II 29, I 17, 34, 3, 52, 49; *Ant.* V 8; *Ael.* IV 25; *Ant.* V 18, 26; *Ael.* IV 50, 49; *Ant.* VI 13 (§§ 1–4), 31; *Ael.* IV 57, 60; *Ant.* VI 39 et 40 (copiés d'un seul tenant); *Ael.* I 1; *Ant.* VII 53, 62, 63; *Ael.* I 2; *Ant.* VII 66, 70, 71, VIII 15, 17 (§ 2); *Ael.* I 4; *Ant.* VIII 34, 48, 54; *Ael.* I 7 et 8 (d'un seul tenant), 13; *Ant.* VIII 57, 56; *Ael.* I 9, 10; *Ant.* IX 1 (§§ 1–9); *Ael.* I 11; *Ant.* IX 40, XI 19; *Ael.* I 16 (*des.* καὶ ἐκεῖνος πάλιν νήχεται); *Ant.* IX 42, X 28, 29, 32, 34, 35, XI 34 et 35 (d'un seul tenant), XII 2, XI 9, 21, XII 4 (§ 1), 14 et 15 (d'un seul tenant), 34 (*des.* ὅμως τούτου κατεφρόνησαν).

Des deux manuscrits parisiens que nous avons déjà rapprochés du fragment de la Mazarine, l'un, le Coisl. 341 (auquel Schenkl a affecté le sigle p 6), offre lui aussi les extraits dans l'ordre que nous venons d'indiquer: ils occupent les ff. 332^v–355^v, mais la série s'interrompt brusquement dans le soixantième morceau, cette partie du manuscrit étant mutilée de la fin.[24] Quant au Suppl. gr. 1164 (p 5 dans l'édition Schenkl), il avait été copié sur un exemplaire brouillé: du f. 14^v, ligne 19, au f. 22, ligne 1, figurent, présentés comme un tout qu'encadrent respectivement des extraits de l'*Anthologie Palatine* et le *Manuel* d'Épictète, les soixante premiers extraits de notre liste; d'autre part, les trois derniers morceaux ont été copiés plus haut, entre la fin des *Imagines* de Philostrate et le début des extraits de l'*Anthologie*, soit du f. 3^v, ligne 13, au f. 4, ligne 14.[25]

[20] Éd. citée, p. xxxv.

[21] Article cité, pp. 152–53.

[22] Dans notre énumération, comme chez De Stefani, les extraits de Marc-Aurèle sont introduits par l'abréviation *Ant*(onini), et ceux d'Élien par *Ael*(iani).

[23] Les subdivisions de chapitres de Marc-Aurèle sont citées ici d'après le découpage institué par Schenkl dans son édition, système qu'ont repris ultérieurement les autres éditeurs (ainsi, par exemple, Trannoy: *Marc-Aurèle, Pensées*. Texte établi et traduit par A. I. Trannoy..., Paris 1925).

[24] Cf. Devreesse, catalogue cité, p. 326.

[25] Cf. Astruc–Concasty, catalogue cité, p. 329, où il faut, à la ligne 17, corriger "21^v" en "22, ligne 1."

L'omission de divers paragraphes dans cinq extraits de Marc-Aurèle n'est pas une anomalie propre à notre fragment: les mêmes paragraphes des morceaux numérotés 7, 21, 35, 46 et 61 dans la liste de De Stefani ont été laissés de côté par le scribe du Suppl. gr. 1164; il en était de même dans le Coisl. 341, mais sa mutilation ne nous permet de constater le fait que pour les quatre premiers des extraits concernés.

Notons enfin que, comme dans les deux Parisini cités, la première scholie marginale commente ainsi le premier mot du premier extrait de Marc-Aurèle (VII 22): Ἴδιον λέγει, οὐχ ὅπερ ἔχουσιν οἱ ἄν(θρωπ)οι, ἀλλ' ὃ δεῖ ἔχειν αὐτούς.

2. Description des pièces annexes

La cinquième liasse du manuscrit 4556 de la Bibliothèque Mazarine contient encore, à côté du fragment grec du XIVe siècle, un certain nombre de documents modernes, dont trois sont de la main de l'"inventeur" dudit fragment, Minoïde Mynas. Nous décrivons ci-dessous, de façon détaillée, l'ensemble de ces pièces annexes, qui sont toutes du XIXe siècle; toutes (à deux exceptions près) sont écrites sur papier blanc.

I. Un double feuillet (de 205 × 157 mm.), à l'intérieur duquel a été inséré un feuillet simple d'autre provenance (mesurant 208 × 135 mm.).

Aux pp. 1–2 du feuillet double, Minoïde Mynas a copié la petite dissertation de Philostrate sur le style épistolaire, introduite, en guise de titre, par les mots Φιλόστρατος Ἀσπασίῳ (éd. C. L. Kayser, *Flavii Philostrati opera*..., t. II [Leipzig 1871], p. 257, ligne 27— p. 258, ligne 28; l'opuscule avait été édité antérieurement comme une lettre de Philostrate à Aspasios par G. Olearius, *Philostratorum quae supersunt omnia*... [Leipzig 1709], t. II, pp. 916–17; rappelons que ce Philostrate [i.e. Philostratus, Nerviani filius] doit être distingué de Flavius Philostratus).[26] Le texte copié par Mynas diffère de celui des éditions citées, notamment par l'omission de la phrase ἐν οἶς—τοῖς γράμμασι (éd. Kayser, p. 258, lignes 3–5; cf. éd. Olearius, p. 916, lignes 6–8). Il diverge aussi en plusieurs endroits—ce qui est plus surprenant—du texte qu'offrent les pp. 103–104 du Parisinus Suppl.

---

[26] Cf. Olearius, *tom. cit.*, p. 914 et p. 916, n. 1; voir aussi F. Solmsen, *RE* 39. Halbband (Stuttgart 1941), col. 134.

gr. 1256, célèbre manuscrit (*codex unicus* pour la *Gymnastique* de Philostrate) qui, comme on sait, fut aussi rapporté d'Orient par Mynas lui-même.[27] On croirait volontiers que, pour la présente copie, Mynas avait pris ce précieux témoin comme modèle, mais il n'est pas certain que ce fut le cas; en effet, le Suppl. gr. 1256 n'a pas la suscription que donne la copie, et il offre sept variantes de détail dans le texte par rapport à celle-ci (comme elle, en revanche, il omet la phrase ἐν οἷς—τοῖς γράμμασι); à supposer donc que ces divergences ne proviennent pas simplement d'un manque d'acribie dont le personnage a donné bien d'autres exemples, nous ignorons de quel exemplaire Minoïde Mynas s'est servi en cette occasion.

En haut de la p. 3 du même feuillet double, une main française a inscrit (en latin) la référence à l'édition Olearius. Le reste de la p. 3 et la p. 4 sont vides d'écriture.

Au recto du feuillet inséré dans le *bifolium* dont il vient d'être question, une main distincte de la précédente et de celle de Mynas a écrit une traduction en français de l'opuscule de Philostrate, faite, selon toute vraisemblance, à partir du texte copié par Mynas. À la fin, référence (en latin) à l'édition Olearius.

Le verso de ce feuillet est resté blanc.

II. Un feuillet, écrit recto-verso, mesurant 275 × 210 mm.

Lettre autographe[28] de Minoïde Mynas ⟨à Prosper Faugère⟩, envoyée du "mont Athos ce 25 fevrier 1842," et signée "M. Ménas voyageur français" (*inc.* "mon cher Monsieur, je viens enfin de decouvrir quelque chose relativement à votre commission; mais mon Manuscrit, ou le vôtre, differe des tables déjà imprimées; le titre en est Μαρκου Αντωνίνου ἐκ τῶν καθ᾽ ἑαυτὸν [*sic*]"—*des.* "à dieu mon cher Monsieur et soyez toujours ce que vous étiez pour moi. De votre ami et serviteur" etc.).

Comme on le voit, c'est par cette lettre que Mynas annonce à Faugère la découverte du fragment de manuscrit grec qui constitue aujourd'hui le principal article de notre liasse. Il donne l'*incipit* du texte et celui des scholies, puis il décrit sommairement le fragment

---

[27] Voir la description de M.-L. Concasty, dans le catalogue cité, pp. 495–96 (compléter la notice, p. 495, quant aux pp. 103–104 du manuscrit, où se lit la petite dissertation sur le style épistolaire).

[28] Dans les citations que nous faisons, ici et par la suite, des documents sortis de la plume de Mynas, nous respectons (sans multiplier les *sic*) leurs anomalies orthographiques.

("24 pages in 4° ecriture déliée"), en insistant sur sa fragilité.[29] Ensuite, après avoir stigmatisé au passage la nonchalance des moines, la mauvaise nourriture et le manque de chauffage, ainsi que la façon scandaleuse dont les livres sont traités dans les couvents ("des volumes jétés dans des caves, pleins de poussières et en moitié pouris; les feuilles collées par l'humidité et les ordures des animaux"), il justifie la prolongation de son séjour au Mont Athos par l'espoir de "quelque decouverte plus importante." Puis il charge son correspondant de communiquer à "monsieur le Ministre"[30] une petite liste de manuscrits par lui découverts (liste qu'a publiée H. Omont[31] d'après le brouillon conservé à la Bibliothèque nationale).[32] Mynas poursuit en réclamant des nouvelles de Faugère, et fournit lui-même quelques informations fraîches concernant le personnel diplomatique français à Constantinople. Il demande à son ami de proposer au Cabinet des Médailles deux pièces de cuivre (dont il fait, au bas de la p. 1, des croquis grossiers), et de rechercher si Strabon "est imprimé en complet, savoir en 17 livre." Enfin, il espère que, sur les instances de Faugère, le ministre de l'Instruction publique "a bien voulu seconder la personne qui garde [son] domicile pour le payement des termes...," et il conclut en priant encore son correspondant de lui écrire.

Le brouillon de cette lettre est conservé aux ff. 195–96 du Parisinus Suppl. gr. 1251, important recueil contenant le journal et la correspondance de Mynas pour les années 1840–43, soit pendant sa première mission en Orient.[33] Ce brouillon comporte un certain nombre de divergences de détail, l'auteur ayant modifié ensuite la rédaction de plusieurs phrases et ayant omis dans le texte définitif

[29] Voir les deux phrases de la lettre que nous avons reproduites plus haut, dans la description du fragment grec.

[30] Il s'agit de Villemain, qui fut ministre de l'Instruction publique de 1839 à 1844, avec une interruption de mars à fin octobre 1840 (Faugère avait été son secrétaire au ministère jusqu'en février 1840, et avait démissionné le 1er mars, lors de la chute du cabinet). Mynas déclare aussi avoir adressé directement au ministre, dans sa dernière lettre du mois de janvier, "une liste des ouvrages inedits."

[31] Omont, *Minoïde Mynas et ses missions...* (*supra*, n. 6), 369–70. La liste du mois de janvier (v. note précédente) ne semble pas avoir été retrouvée, non plus que la lettre: Omont n'en fait pas état.

[32] Parisinus Suppl. gr. 1251, f. 195ᵛ.

[33] Voir notre description du recueil dans Astruc–Concasty, catalogue cité, 464–84 (sur le brouillon de la lettre du 25 février 1842, v. p. 474).

l'alinéa du f. 196; au f. 195ᵛ se lit l'équivalent de la petite liste qui accompagnait la lettre, mais dont l'original ne figure plus dans la liasse de la Mazarine, ayant été certainement remis par Faugère au ministre, comme l'expéditeur l'avait demandé.

Conformément à l'usage constant de Mynas, la lettre, adressée à un correspondant occidental, est datée selon le style récent, alors que, lorsqu'il écrit à des Grecs, il suit l'ancien style, ou, plus souvent, juxtapose les deux datations.[34]

III. Dix feuillets (de 210 × 160 puis 170 mm.), paginés au crayon par nous (il sont formés de cinq *bifolia* placés à la suite les uns des autres, à cela près que le deuxième englobe les trois derniers; Mynas avait paginé à l'encre les pp. 2 à 5; puis, de nouveau, les pp. 8 à 15, notées par lui 2–9).

Relation autographe, non signée, de ⟨Minoïde Mynas à Prosper Faugère⟩, traitant de la provenance de l' "abrégé" de Marc-Aurèle et d'Élien, puis faisant quelques remarques paléographiques sur le manuscrit, et prétendant enfin découvrir l'auteur de cet abrégé. Le texte présente un bon nombre de ratures et de corrections, généralement de faible étendue, les unes de la main de Mynas, les autres de la main qui figure également à la p. 3 du *bifolium* décrit dans la première section.

Le document ne porte aucune date, et fut manifestement composé en plusieurs fois: une reprise est marquée en haut de la p. 7 par le mot "suite," venant après un blanc important à la p. 6; une autre peut être décelée par l'existence d'un autre blanc à la p. 10, et par le fait que l'encre change à la p. 11 pour rester la même jusqu'à la fin (encre noire, alors que les pages précédentes sont dans une encre bistre). Bien qu'elle soit rédigée—tout au moins quant aux premières pages—à la manière d'une lettre (elle commence par "mon cher monsieur"), la relation ne fut sans doute pas envoyée à Faugère par la poste, mais donnée de la main à la main, ce qui explique qu'elle ne soit ni signée, ni datée. Elle est nécessairement postérieure à l'automne 1843, époque du retour de Minoïde Mynas à Paris,[35] car, à la p. 4, l'auteur fait allusion aux manuscrits qu'il a envoyés et à ceux qu'il a rapportés "en 1844 [corrigé, de première main, en: 1843]."

[34] Cf. *ibid.*, p. 464.
[35] Cf. Omont, *op. cit.*, p. 347.

Ce texte se subdivise comme suit:

ᵃ (pp. 1–6). Exposé (fallacieux, ainsi qu'on le verra plus loin) des circonstances de la découverte du manuscrit de Marc-Aurèle (*inc.* "mon cher monsieur, vous êtes curieux peut-être de savoir d'où vient le manuscrit qui contient l'abrégé de Marc Aurèle parsemé de quelques fragment d'Histoire d'animaux, extrait, ce me semble, de Eudemus [*sic*]"). Nous en extrayons, ci-dessous, l'essentiel.

Mynas évoque (p. 1) "la dernière revolution grecque de 1820," qui "fut la cause de grandes destructions en hommes et en man⟨u⟩-scrits precieux qui servaient aux turcs pour faire des cartouches."[36] Eurent à souffrir notamment "les bibliothèques des princes grecs à Constantinople," confisquées par les autorités turques, et "trans-portées pêle mêle dans une tour du vieux palait." Description (p. 2) des conditions déplorables (humidité, "ordure" des pigeons) qui régnaient dans cette tour du Sérail, où les livres des princes phanariotes restèrent entreposés "pendant quatre ans." Au bout des quatre ans, "l'autorité locale" obligea le patriarche grec à "faire l'acquision de ces volumes." Le patriarche dut, pour cela, débourser 100000 piastres (p. 3). On transporta les livres "dans un magasin en pierre situé près de la barrière du quartier qu'on appelle Phanari," magasin contenant aussi "les archives de l'église grecque," et surmonté d'un appartement où se réunissaient "quelques membres du synode pour délibérer sur les depenses de l'eglise." Tout cela fut expliqué à Mynas, arrivé à Constantinople "au commencement du mois de septembre 1840,"[37] par un archevêque, membre du Synode, et lui fut confirmé par d'autres prélats. Les malheurs des temps firent qu'on avait négligé ces volumes, "et on ne savait pas ce qu'ils étaient devenus" (p. 4). Un incendie détruisit (vers 1835) les archives de l'église "et une grande parties de ces volumes." Mynas ajoute: "et quand j'y entrai je ne vit que quelques volumes imprimés, des pères d'église." L'événement, dit-il, lui suggéra "une double idée." D'abord, prospecter systématiquement "avec la permission du patriarche" les armoires "des églises de Constantinople et des alentours," et s'adresser "presque à tous les curés et moines, ainsi qu'aux libraires du Galata"; c'est de là que provient "la plus grande partie des ouvrages" envoyés ou rapportés par Mynas en

[36] Mynas avait d'abord écrit "cartons," mot qu'il a corrigé lui-même.
[37] Selon Omont, *op. cit.*, p. 342, c'est le 12 octobre que Mynas arriva à Constantinople.

1843. Secondement, "pouvoir entrer dans la tour" du Sérail où les livres grecs avaient d'abord été entreposés, car "les turcs insouciants auraient pu negligé quelque volumes dans quelques coin ou planché"; Mynas dit y avoir réussi grâce à son ami Zagouras,[38] et affirme (p. 5) y être resté quarante-huit heures, "sans calculer le danger" auquel il s'exposait. C'est, selon lui, dans "un enfoncement" du mur de cette tour qu'il a trouvé: quatre cahiers en parchemin, "où l'on traite du droit canonique"; le discours de Galien "sur l'empsycose"; le traité de Philostrate "sur la Gymnastique"; l'abrégé de Marc-Aurèle (Mynas précise ici: "l'abregé...que j'eux l'honneur de vous apporter, à la place des œuvres complet[39] de ce savant empereur que vous m'avez demandés, et que je n'ai pas pu trouvés"). Mynas ajoute: "vous voyez par là pourquoi ces manuscrits sont en mauvais état," surtout celui de Philostrate (p. 6), "qui est tout à fait perdu, réduit en poussière; sans la précausion que j'ai prise d'en prendre avec peine une copie, ce traité aurait été à jamais perdu."[40] Enfin, il conclut par les mots: "telle est mon cher monsieur l'histoire de ce manuscrit, abregé de celui du Marc Aurèle."

b (pp. 7–8). Remarques paléographiques incohérentes sur le manuscrit "trouvé dans la Tour de Byzance" (p. 7). Mynas le date "du 13e siècle, ou entre le 13me et le 14me," à cause de "la forme de l'orthographe" et de l'emploi de l'iota souscrit; il a été écrit "par une main érudite," et les scholies marginales décèlent "un copiste bien versé dans les lettres grecques" (p. 8). Ici, l'auteur, qui disait "nous" depuis le début de la page 7, change de personne et fait parler Faugère à sa place ("le voyageur qui m'a envoyé ce

---

[38] Un certain nombre de copies de lettres de Mynas à Jean Zagouras, et quatre lettres originales de Zagouras à Mynas sont conservées dans le Suppl. gr. 1251 (cf. notice citée, pp. 466 ss.). Voir aussi Omont, *op. cit.*, p. 343.

[39] Après ce mot, l'auteur avait d'abord écrit "que," mot qu'il a ensuite biffé lui-même.

[40] Assertions tout à fait mensongères; Mynas, en effet, décrit sa trouvaille ("deux cahiers que j'ai sauvés de la pourriture") dans son Rapport sur sa première mission (paru dans le *Moniteur universel* du 5 janvier 1844, et reproduit par Omont, *op. cit.*, p. 390); cependant, mécontent du gouvernement français, il gardera et cachera le manuscrit de Philostrate (qui sera retrouvé, bien après sa mort, chez le fils d'un de ses créanciers), et, à la place, il déposera au ministère de l'Instruction publique la copie dont il parle dans sa relation à Faugère. Le manuscrit lui-même n'entrera à la Bibliothèque nationale qu'en 1898, et constitue aujourd'hui les pp. 43–104 du Parisinus Suppl. gr. 1256 (le début du recueil étant occupé par la copie de Mynas). Cf. catalogue cité, p. 496.

manus⟨crit⟩ pense...''), pour présenter une tentative d'attribution à un copiste déterminé, attribution qui repose sur des déductions aussi gratuites qu'absurdes: Mynas, donc, pense qu'il est de la main de Manuel Moschopoulos, "le père du fils qui portait le même nom: le 1ʳ vivait au commencement du 13 siècle''; il "etablit son assertion sur d'autres manus⟨crits⟩ faits de la main de Moshopulus, le fameux grammairiens qui a tant ecrit sur la langue greque..."

ᶜ (pp. 8–16). Essai, encore plus extravagant, d'identification de l'"abréviateur" des *Pensées* de Marc-Aurèle. Quel est-il, se demande Mynas, "et dans quel but a-t-il fait cet abregé ?" (p. 8). Réponse à la seconde question (p. 9): "le but de ce travail est tout à fait dans l'interet de la morale," et de la morale "de pratique"; c'est pourquoi l'"abréviateur" a voulu faire oeuvre de vulgarisateur. Sur le chapitre de la morale, Mynas devient lyrique ("l'humanité sans morale est un vaisseau sans pilot," *etc.*), ce qui ne manque pas de sel, venant d'un personnage comme lui, habitué à user du mensonge au mieux de ses intérêts. Néanmoins, en cette occasion, étant plus proche que les occidentaux modernes de la mentalité du compilateur byzantin à qui l'on doit ce mélange, bizarre à nos yeux, de Marc-Aurèle et d'Élien, Mynas a, pour justifier l'entreprise, quelques lignes somme toute assez plausibles, eu égard à la psychologie probable de l'"abréviateur" et de son public: "pour donner plus de force aux maximes de Marc Aurèle, l'abréviateur a jugé à propos d'intercaler les moeurs de quelques animaux, qui tout guidés qu'ils sont par l'instinct, ne laisse pas de montrer à l'homme une conduite qui dénote chez eux quelque chose de plus d'un instinct...." Mynas n'a pas reconnu Élien dans les extraits d'histoire naturelle, quoiqu'il ait trouvé (p. 10) une formule ("les animaux moralisés pour ainsi dire") qui s'adapte fort bien à l'*Historia animalium* du sophiste de Préneste, énorme compilation d'anecdotes zoologiques à intentions moralisantes. Il croit que l'abréviateur a puisé dans Ctésias, dans Eudème, dans Eudoxe...Il passe ensuite à la première question: "tachons maintenant de decouvrir l'auteur de cet abregé." À partir de là, tout se gâte, et le texte défie presque l'analyse. On a d'abord (p. 11) un développement sur l'empereur Constantin Porphyrogénète, qui "avait une passion singulière pour faire des abregés des auteurs de grand mérite." Cependant, Constantin VII (traité en passant de "disciple de Photius") est écarté, par "la comparaison de ses abregés avec celui dont nous parlon."[41] Et aussitôt Mynas lâche cette énormité que les cinq dernières pages vont s'employer à démontrer: il s'agit d'un travail de "Marc Aurèle lui même." Tout sert de preuve: le titre, la conformité du texte à celui des *Pensées* (p. 12), et même "l'histoire des animaux intercalée opportunément"... Suit (pp. 12–13) une longue exégèse des deux premiers extraits (*Ant.* VII 22 et *Ael.* I 22), avec, pour conclusion, ces assertions décidées: "nous n'examinons pas ici l'opportunité de cet exemple que l'empereur tire des animaux: nous soutenons seulement que Marc Aurèle est l'auteur de cet abregé." À la page 14, Mynas revient au but poursuivi par l'auteur de l'"abrégé", et reprend ses déductions touchant une intention de vulgarisation dans l'intérêt de la morale, en la faisant endosser maintenant à Marc-Aurèle en personne: "il fit donc un extrait des idées de son ouvrage, les plus simples pour instruire le peuple, et y ajouta des exemples pris dans l'histoire des animaux, comme Ésope avait placé des affabulations à la suite de ses fables." Enivré de certitude, notre homme ajoute: "il est donc évident et clair comme le jour que ce travail n'est pas un ouvrage d'un autre qui que ce soit que de Marc Aurèle le modèle des Rois et le vrai père de son peuple, qui cherchait à le rendre heureux par la pratique des vertus morales." À la suite, "pour prouver surabondamment" son assertion, Mynas reprend l'exégèse des extraits, et commente (pp. 14–16) les numéros 3 à 5 de la compilation (*Ant.* VII 18 et *Ael.* I 25, 28). Aristote, Diodore de Sicile, Ctésias sont cités, à propos de la génération spontanée et du sexe de l'hyène, sujets des deux petits chapitres d'Élien. Après avoir reproduit un assez long passage d'Aristote sur l'anatomie de l'hyène, Mynas tourne court de façon plutôt cocasse, et la relation s'achève (p. 16) par cette phrase que nous transcrivons intégralement: "nous n'insistons pas à justifier Marc Aurèle d'avoir été induit dans l'erreur par des idées reçues de son temps sur cette transformation, nous voulons dire que dans le désire de prouver surabondamment le changement naturel des êtres, il a cité cet exemple, et que l'auteur de cet abrégé ne peut être que celui des pensées de cet empereur." Il est bien évident que Mynas, n'ayant pas identifié les extraits d'Élien, né, comme on sait, aux alentours de l'an 175 de notre ère,

---

[41] Mynas avait d'abord écrit: "que nous publions," ce qui prouve qu'un projet d'édition du fragment avait germé temporairement dans son esprit.

n'éprouvait aucune gêne à les faire utiliser par Marc-Aurèle, mort lui-même en 180!

Les pages 17 à 20 sont restées vides d'écriture.

IV. Un double feuillet de papier bleuâtre (de 242 × 188 mm.), paginé au crayon par nous.

(pp. 1–3) Lettre autographe signée de Éd. Grasset, consul de France à Salonique, adressée de Paris, le 24 janvier 1850, à un destinataire non précisé[42] (*inc.* "Monsieur, vous m'avez fait l'honneur de me demander des informations sur M^r. Minas"—*des.* "l'expression de mes sentiments les plus distingués et les plus dévoués. Éd. Grasset, Consul de France à Salonique. Paris, 24 Janvier 1850"). L'auteur de la lettre assure que Mynas est d'une bonne famille de Vodéna (Macédoine); qu'un de ses oncles a été archevêque de Serrès, ville où Mynas lui-même a été professeur de littérature grecque; qu'il a rempli des missions littéraires, couronnées de succès, en Macédoine; enfin, qu'il pourrait "rendre de nouveaux services aux lettres" en effectuant des recherches au Mont Athos ou dans les couvents des Météores.

La page 4 est vide d'écriture.

V. Un double feuillet (de 198 × 161 mm.).

Ce *bifolium* ne porte d'écriture qu'en haut du premier recto, soit: "Του βασιλεος Κωνσταντινου, περι ξοῶν [*sic*] (ouvrage abrégé sur les animaux—1er livre apporté par M. Mynas).[43] P^r. voir s'il y aurait des fragmens d'Eudemus."

La main est celle qu'on a déjà recontrée dans les sections I et III.

VI. Un feuillet double (mesurant 203 × 159 mm.), à l'intérieur duquel a été inséré un *bifolium* plus petit (136 × 105 mm.) de papier bleu.

Le plus grand *bifolium* contient, de la même main que ci-dessus: (p. 1) copie de la page de titre de l'édition des *Philosophoumena* d'Origène par Emmanuel Miller (Oxford 1851); (pp. 3–4) copie du début de la préface de Miller (éd. citée, pp. v–vi), puis (p. 4) d'un autre extrait de cette préface (*ibid.*, p. vi): ces extraits donnent la description du manuscrit utilisé par Miller, à savoir Parisinus Suppl. gr. 464.

---

[42] Il s'agit certainement de Faugère, qui dut s'employer alors à obtenir pour la troisième fois l'envoi de Mynas en mission; cette troisième mission durera de mai 1850 à novembre 1855 (cf. Omont, *op. cit.*, p. 339).

[43] Il s'agit de l'actuel Parisinus Suppl. gr. 495 (cf. Omont, *op. cit.*, p. 393).

La page 2 est vide d'écriture.

Le petit feuillet double inséré dans le précédent ne porte d'écriture (toujours de la même main) que dans la première moitié du premier recto: ce sont quelques notes, formules prises comme exemples pour dresser un apparat critique.

3. Recherche de la provenance exacte du fragment grec

Au début de sa monographie consacrée à Mynas, H. Omont observait que ce voyageur "serait bien oublié aujourd'hui, s'il n'avait eu la bonne fortune de découvrir au Mont Athos les manuscrits qui nous ont conservé les Fables de Babrius et le traité de la Gymnastique de Philostrate";[44] achevant de présenter le bilan de l'activité du personnage, le même auteur évoquait en conclusion "l'important ensemble des deux cents manuscrits grecs rapportés par Minoïde Mynas de ses missions en Grèce, en Macédoine, au Mont Athos, à Constantinople et à Trébizonde, dans la première moitié du XIXe siècle."[45] Certes, le bilan est impressionnant, et l'on doit admettre, à considérer seulement le résultat final, que Mynas s'est remarquablement acquitté des missions dont on l'avait chargé. Il n'est pas douteux que sa persévérance, son flair, et une connaissance assez bien informée de la littérature grecque de toutes les époques lui ont permis de réussir dans ses entreprises à un degré rarement égalé par les autres prospecteurs qui, depuis la Renaissance, ont pratiqué la même chasse aux manuscrits grecs pour le compte de l'Occident. Cependant, comme c'est souvent le cas, hélas, chez ces aventuriers d'un genre spécial, la ténacité et le savoir-faire avaient pour contrepartie, dans la personnalité de Mynas, un manque à peu près total d'honnêteté intellectuelle. La chose est bien connue, et jette une ombre regrettable sur les résultats obtenus par cet homme déconcertant, dont l'esprit, d'autre part, comme on l'aura constaté plus haut,[46] à côté d'une certaine forme d'érudition qu'il faut bien lui reconnaître, hébergeait des ignorances ahurissantes et pouvait sécréter imperturbablement les raisonnements les plus incohérents et les assertions les plus folles.

Les lacunes du caractère de Mynas n'avaient évidemment pas échappé à ses contemporains, et la méfiance des milieux savants,

[44] Omont, *op. cit.*, p. 337.
[45] Id., *ibid.* p. 352.
[46] Cf. notre analyse du long exposé adressé par lui à Faugère.

d'abord intéressés par ses découvertes, avait été bientôt alertée par
le brouillard de réticences et d'affirmations contradictoires qu'il
déployait autour de la provenance et du sort des manuscrits les plus
précieux rapportés dans ses bagages, manuscrits que souvent il
parvint à dissimuler à tout le monde, montrant seulement les copies
qu'il en avait tirées lui-même. Bornons-nous à rappeler le mystère
dont il entoura ses deux trouvailles les plus spectaculaires, celles
mêmes que citait Omont dans la phrase reproduite ci-dessus, à
savoir le manuscrit des *Fables* de Babrios, et celui de la *Gymnastique* de
Philostrate. En ce qui concerne le Babrios, A. Dain a consacré toute
une étude [47] à démêler le vrai du faux dans la version des faits que
Mynas avait voulu imposer. L'auteur de cet article n'y a pas réussi
sur toute la ligne : comment exactement le voyageur s'était procuré
le manuscrit de Lavra, et dans quelles conditions, après l'avoir
longtemps caché, il parvint à le vendre au British Museum en
août 1857, c'est ce que nous ignorons encore. [48] Du moins Dain a-t-il
pu convaincre Mynas de mensonge sur un point précis : le manuscrit
entra en la possession de notre personnage dès son sejour de 1842 au
couvent de Lavra, et non, comme il le prétendait, au début de 1845
à Constantinople, où les autorités du couvent le lui auraient envoyé. [49]
Quant au manuscrit de Philostrate, nous avons déjà dû, plus haut,
rectifier les déclarations mensongères de Mynas touchant sa ruine : [50]
contrairement à ce qu'il racontait à Faugère, ce manuscrit n'était
pas "tout à fait perdu, réduit en poussière," puisque la Bibliothèque
nationale le conserve sous la cote "Suppl. gr. 1256". Mais il faut
surtout lire l'"Avis au lecteur" de Ch. Daremberg, dans son édition
de la *Gymnastique* de Philostrate, [51] pour prendre la mesure de
l'impudence de Mynas à ce propos : malgré d'innombrables
démarches, Daremberg, chargé officiellement par le ministre de faire

[47] A. Dain, "Sur deux recueils de Babrios trouvés par Minoïde Mynas," in *Bulletin de l'Association Guillaume Budé* (1960, 1 [mars]), pp. 113–21.

[48] Cf. Dain, article cité, pp. 116–19. Rappelons que cet important manuscrit porte, au British Museum, la cote "Additional 22087."

[49] Id., *ibid.*, p. 117.

[50] Voir *supra*, n. 40.

[51] *Philostrate. Traité sur la gymnastique.* Texte grec accompagné d'une traduction en regard et de notes par Ch. Daremberg (Paris 1858), pp. vii–xxiii.—Sur Charles-Victor Daremberg, savant médicin qui fut nommé en 1849 Bibliothécaire à la Bibliothèque Mazarine, voir la notice anonyme de la *Nouvelle Biographie générale*...[Didot–Hoefer], t. 13 (Paris 1866), col. 108–10.

cette édition, ne put jamais voir le manuscrit, et dut se contenter de la copie de Mynas, qu'il put améliorer un peu... en la comparant avec l'édition que celui-ci publia quelques mois avant lui, et où les leçons authentiques du manuscrit dissimulé se reflètent plus fidèlement que dans la copie déposée au ministère. Des pages à bon droit indignées de Daremberg, retenons quelques phrases sur la provenance du Philostrate: "Personne n'a jamais pu savoir exactement d'où provenait le manuscrit. M. Mynas a dit tantôt qu'il l'avait découvert au mont Athos, et tantôt ailleurs.—Quel sphinx donnera le mot de l'énigme?"[52] Tantôt ailleurs...: la version définitive choisie par Mynas, et officialisée en quelque sorte par les vers qu'il inscrivit de sa main sur le f. I du Parisinus Suppl. gr. 1256, indique la fameuse tour du Sérail de Constantinople où—nous l'avons vu dans les pages écrites pour Faugère—il se serait introduit clandestinement. J. Jüthner, qui, plus heureux que Daremberg, put enfin éditer la *Gymnastique*[53] d'après le manuscrit que son "inventeur" avait si longtemps caché, prend au sérieux la version de Mynas, et pense[54] que celui-ci a dû réaliser l'exploit dont il se vante (pénétrer dans la tour du Sérail) lors du séjour qu'il fit à Constantinople vers la fin de sa première mission, entre le 7 avril et le 27 juillet 1843.[55] Quant à nous, rapprochant le cas du fragment de la Mazarine de celui du Babrios de Lavra, et de celui du Philostrate dont Mynas avait dit aussi pendant un temps (comme nous le rappelle Daremberg) qu'il l'avait trouvé à l'Athos, nous avons l'impression que, par trois fois, les choses se sont déroulées à peu près de la même manière: découverte et prise de possession (mieux vaut ne pas savoir comment) du manuscrit pendant le séjour à Lavra, en 1842; après coup, élaboration d'un scénario qui, affectant à l'action une date sensiblement postérieure, en transporte le lieu à Constantinople (où le couvent, selon Mynas, envoie le Babrios, et où, d'autre part, lui-même aurait audacieusement déniché, dans une tour du Sérail, le Philostrate

[52] *Ibid.*, p. xii, n. 1.

[53] *Philostratos über Gymnastik*, von Julius Jüthner (Leipzig–Berlin 1909).

[54] Jüthner, éd. citée, p. 77.

[55] Dans un travail antérieur, "Der Gymnastikos des Philostratos," paru dans les *Sitzungsberichte* de Vienne, phil.-hist. Kl., CXLV (1902), p. 15, Jüthner cite plusieurs lettres à Faugère montrant que, malgré ses efforts, Mynas n'avait jamais obtenu la permission officielle d'entrer dans la tour. L'auteur ajoute qu'il dut y réussir secrètement entre les deux dates mentionnées.

et le Marc-Aurèle). Ce changement de temps et de lieu avait l'avantage de brouiller les pistes et d'éviter par là-même des questions gênantes; et puis aussi, l'évocation de Byzance et de l'ancien palais de ses empereurs faisait rejaillir un peu de la gloire de jadis sur les manuscrits prétendument trouvés dans un site si prestigieux.

Même si l'on estime que Jüthner peut avoir raison à propos du manuscrit de Philostrate, c'est notre interprétation qui s'impose dans le cas du fragment de la Mazarine, pour lequel on dispose de repères chronologiques plus précis. Dans trois lettres à Faugère de l'année 1841 (dont les brouillons ou copies sont conservés dans le Parisinus Suppl. gr. 1251),[56] Mynas, alors à l'Athos, faisait allusion, chaque fois vers la fin de la missive, à la "commission" dont son correspondant l'avait chargé, à savoir de découvrir en Orient un manuscrit de Marc-Aurèle; le 12 juillet: "Je n'ai pas oublié votre commission"; le 18 septembre: "Je n'ai pas encore trouvé votre Marcus"; le 7 décembre (lettre envoyée du couvent athonite d'Esphigménou): "Mais je suis faché de n'avoir pas encore trouver vos tablettes, mais je n'ai pas encore parcouru tous les couvents." Effectivement, en décembre 1841, Mynas n'était pas encore allé, notamment, à Lavra, le plus riche en manuscrits des couvents de la sainte montagne. Selon l'emploi du temps de notre voyageur, tel que l'a reconstitué Omont d'après ses papiers et sa correspondance,[57] c'est précisément en partant d'Esphigménou que Mynas, au début de janvier 1842, gagna directement Lavra. Omont a reproduit là-dessus un témoignage capital de l'intéressé, sous la forme d'une page d'un carnet de voyage[58] (où Mynas n'avait aucun intérêt à maquiller les faits). Citons à notre tour le début de ce petit texte: "Les moines de Lavra sont les plus fiers et les plus impolis. J'ai été obligé de rester dans leur couvent depuis le 12 janvier 1842 jusqu'au 13 avril..." (suivent des doléances sur les retards qu'on a mis à lui ouvrir les bibliothèques de l'établissement, et sur l'incommodité des installations). Dans le même carnet, aucune notation contradictoire ne figure, qui laisserait ouverte la possibilité d'un voyage à Constantinople venant interrompre ce séjour de trois mois dans le grand couvent athonite. L'ex-

[56] Suppl. gr. 1251, ff. 79–80^v, 121 et 127^{rv} (cf. Astruc–Concasty, catalogue cité, pp. 468, 470 et 471).

[57] Omont, *op. cit.*, pp. 345–46.

[58] Parisinus Suppl. gr. 733, f. 37 (cf. Omont, *op. cit.*, p. 346, n. 1).

amen de la correspondance pour cette période[59] impose la même conclusion: du 12 janvier au 13 avril 1842, Mynas n'a pas quitté Lavra. Or, le 25 février, il écrit à Faugère la lettre dont l'original aujourd'hui retrouvé est conservé à la Bibliothèque Mazarine.[60] Dès les premiers mots, il annonce la trouvaille: "je viens enfin de decouvrir quelque chose relativement à votre commission..." C'est donc bien à Lavra, en février 1842 (et peu de temps avant le 25 de ce mois) que le fragment de Marc-Aurèle et d'Élien a été trouvé, et non pas "dans la Tour de Byzance," selon la version ultérieure qu'imaginera Mynas,[61] version dont Faugère ne semble pas avoir remarqué qu'elle était incompatible avec celle de la lettre du 25 février 1842, bien qu'il ait gardé les deux documents dans le même dossier, à côté du fragment grec au sujet duquel ils avaient été écrits.

Dans les lettres postérieures adressées à Prosper Faugère, Mynas reviendra plus d'une fois sur le manuscrit de Marc-Aurèle. Le 7 mars 1842, il promet que, s'il trouve "quelqu'autre marc-aurèle qui aurai de la difference" par rapport à celui qu'annonçait la lettre du 25 février, il ne le manquera pas.[62] Le 27 octobre de la même année (il est alors à Vatopédi), il répond à des reproches de Faugère, impatient de recevoir le fameux fragment, en disant que s'il ne l'a pas envoyé, c'est à cause de son extrême fragilité.[63] De Constantinople, le 27 mai 1843, il écrit: "je vous l'apporterai moi-même."[64] Enfin, vers la fin de la lettre du 4 août 1843 (envoyée de Malte): "vous me donnerait raison de ce que je n'ai pas voulu vous l'envoyer."[65] Arrivé à Marseille au début de septembre 1843,[66] il est bloqué là plus d'une semaine par le manque d'argent.[67] C'est peu de temps après, dès son retour à Paris, que Mynas dut remettre le fragment grec à son destinataire, qui l'avait si longtemps attendu.

[59] Voir le catalogue cité, pp. 473–75.

[60] C'est la deuxième des pièces annexes analysées plus haut (le brouillon, rappelons-le, occupe les pp. 195–96 du Suppl. gr. 1251).

[61] Voir les pp. 4 et suivantes de la troisième de nos pièces annexes.

[62] Copie dans le Suppl. gr. 1251, f. 199.

[63] Voir le début de la lettre dans la copie, manuscrit cité, f. 333ʳᵛ (cf. notre catalogue, p. 479).

[64] Cf. *Suppl. gr.* 1251, f. 359ᵛ (corriger la date dans notre catalogue, p. 482, où l'on a imprimé "17 mai" au lieu de "27 mai").

[65] Voir le même manuscrit, ff. 377–78 (cf. catalogue cité, p. 483).

[66] Cf. Omont, *op. cit.*, p. 347.

[67] Voir les deux dernières lettres copiées dans le Suppl. gr. 1251 (en date du 8 et du 9 septembre 1843), f. 385 et ff. 385–86 (cf. notre catalogue, p. 483).

En guise de conclusion, qu'il nous soit permis de dire que la liasse n° 5 du manuscrit 4556 de la Bibliothèque Mazarine n'est pas seulement intéressante par le fragment grec qu'elle a conservé. Il est certes appréciable avant tout de disposer d'un nouveau témoin de la curieuse compilation médiévale où de hautes pensées de Marc-Aurèle ont été interpolées à l'aide d'anecdotes sorties de la plume moins sublime du sophiste Élien. Mais d'autre part, l'analyse des documents modernes accompagnant ce fragment s'est révélée plus fructueuse que l'on n'aurait pu l'escompter. Elle nous a aidé à déterminer le lieu d'où provenait en réalité le manuscrit grec, et nous a amené à verser un nouvel exemple au dossier de l'étonnant comportement de son "inventeur", le maître trompeur que fut Minoïde Mynas. Nous avons surpris celui-ci sur le vif, en quelque sorte, dans son entreprise de maquillage des circonstances réelles de ses trouvailles au Mont Athos, et nous pensons, quant à nous, que la leçon vaut tout autant pour le célèbre manuscrit de Philostrate, qui aura très probablement été découvert, lui aussi, sur la montagne sainte, et non dans une tour de l'ancien Palais impérial de Byzance.

Paris, 30 juin 1970

NOTES SUR QUELQUES MANUSCRITS GRECS DES BIBLIOTHÈQUES DE POLOGNE

PAUL CANART

En septembre 1968, au cours d'un voyage en Pologne, j'ai eu l'occasion de travailler quelques jours à la Bibliothèque Nationale de Varsovie, ainsi qu'à la Bibliothèque Czartoryski et à la Bibliothèque Universitaire Jagellonne à Cracovie. J'ai pris, sur les manuscrits grecs de ces établissements, un certain nombre de notes, destinées à compléter les indications parfois sommaires des catalogues.[1] C'est pour moi un plaisir que de les dédier, en hommage de reconnaissance et d'amitié, à un savant qui fait le plus grand honneur à son pays natal. Je saisis aussi l'occasion de remercier publiquement la direction des bibliothèques susdites et mes amis polonais: ils se sont ingéniés, avec la courtoisie et l'hospitalité qui leur est propre, à faciliter mon travail de toutes manières.

Qu'il me soit permis encore, en guise de préliminaire, d'insister sur les limites de cette contribution. J'ai déjà dit qu'il s'agissait de notes. Prises le plus soigneusement possible, mais assez vite, elles n'ont aucune prétention à épuiser le sujet. De retour à la Bibliothèque Vaticane, je me suis efforcé de compléter ma documentation, surtout bibliographique; mais je n'ai pu, faute d'avoir revu les manuscrits, contrôler certains points douteux ni résoudre des

---

[1] Pour ceux-ci, on se reportera aux indications de M. Richard, *Répertoire des bibliothèques et des catalogues de manuscrits grecs* (Publications de l'Institut de Recherche et d'Histoire des Textes, 1; Paris 1958²), sous Pologne (p. 17, n° 83), Varsovie (p. 232) et Cracovie (p. 82, avec renvoi au n° 53, p. 10). Dans le courant de cet article, je citerai en abrégé les deux travaux suivants:

Aland = K. Aland, *Die Handschriftenbestände der polnischen Bibliotheken* (Deutsche Akad. der Wiss. zu Berlin. Schriften der Sektion für Altertumswissenschaft, 7; Berlin 1956).

Gollob = E. Gollob, "Verzeichnis der griechischen Handschriften in Österreich ausserhalb Wiens," *Sitzungsberichte der Kais. Akad. der Wiss. in Wien, Philos.-hist. Kl.* 146, 7 (Wien 1903).

problèmes qui sont apparus seulement au moment de la rédaction; dans tous les cas, j'ai tâché de préciser les lacunes ou les incertitudes de mon information. Je suis ainsi en mesure de présenter la description complète, suivant les règles de la Bibliothèque Vaticane,[2] de trois manuscrits de la Bibliothèque Nationale de Varsovie; pour un autre manuscrit de Varsovie et huit de Cracovie, je ne fournis que des indications partielles.

VARSOVIE: BIBLIOTHÈQUE NATIONALE

BOZ Cim. 58.[3] Saec. XVI, chart., mm. 280 × 194, ff. 310.

1 (ff. 1–139^v) **Olympiodori** commentarius in Platonis Phaedonem (ed. W. Norvin [Bibl. Teubner., Lipsiae 1913]; quem auctorem hic codex latuit).

2 (ff. 139^v–178^v) ⟨Eiusdem*⟩ (revera **Damascii**) commentarius in Platonis Philebum (ed. L. G. Westerink, *Damascius, Lectures on the Philebus* [Amsterdam 1959]; qui codicem hunc non citat).—Ff. 179–181 vacua.

3 (ff. 181^v–310^v) **Olympiodori** commentarius in Platonis Gorgiam (ed. W. Norvin [Bibl. Teubner., Lipsiae 1936]), des. mut. in πράξει 46, 4 (cod. με΄!): ὅτι μοχθηρὸς ἔχει βίος ἀνθρώπων γενέσθαι, additis verbis "reclamantibus" ὃς τιμᾶ (Norvin, p. 218, 29–30). [1973: nuper denuo ed. L. G. Westerink (Bibl. Teubner., Lipsiae 1970), quem hic codex latuit; des. = Westerink, p. 238, 18.]

MATIÈRE—Les derniers ff., abîmés, ont été restaurés.

COMPOSITION—31 quinions, signés par le copiste au moyen de réclames verticales inscrites dans le prolongement de l'extrémité interne de la surface écrite.

FILIGRANES—1° Ancre dont la tige est formée d'un trait simple, inscrite dans un cercle sommé d'une étoile à 6 rais, avec contremarque ⋉ (pas de parallèle chez Briquet); 2° id., avec contremarque ∃B ou ⵑE (manque chez Briquet; cf. p. ex. les Vat. gr. 1770 **2** et 1783 II); 3° id., avec contremarque A·A (manque chez Briquet); 4° tête de bœuf d'où s'élève une tige terminée en croix, avec contremarque HS (manque chez Briquet). ·

DIMENSIONS—Surface écrite: mm. 171 × 100/101, lignes 25.

ÉCRITURE—Copié par Camille Zanetti, alias Camille le Vénitien

---

[2] Pour la dernière partie de la description, d'ordre plus technique, j'ai préféré utiliser la langue vulgaire. Dans les notes partielles, j'ai conservé le latin pour les noms d'auteur et les titres d'œuvres.

[3] Aland, 21–22.

(d'après l'écriture; ce copiste est à identifier avec celui que j'ai
baptisé scribe *C*: P. Canart, "Les manuscrits copiés par Emmanuel
Provataris...," dans *Mélanges Eugène Tisserant*, VI [Studi e Testi,
236, Città del Vaticano 1964], 203-204).

ORNEMENTATION—Aux ff. 1 et 181 : ligne ondulée rouge, ornée de
petits arcs de cercle. Titres (en minuscule) et lettres initiales rouges.
Au f. 178ᵛ, la fin du texte est disposée en triangle.

POSSESSEURS—F. 1 : diverses notes de possession (que je n'ai pas
recopiées), dont une barrée.

RELIURE—Velours rouge avec fermoirs aux armes des Zamoyski.

BOZ Cim. 156.[4] Ann. 1569 (ff. 1–131; v. f. 131) et saec. XVI post
med. (reliqua), chart., mm. 222 × 160, ff. III. 160.

   1 (ff. 1–131) S t e p h a n i t e s et I c h n e l a t e s (ed. V. Puntoni, Στεφανί-
της καὶ Ἰχνηλάτης [Pubblicazioni della Società Asiatica Ital., 2, Firenze
1889] 3–316; de codice, qui ad recensionem B et familiam θ pertinet,
v. L.-O. Sjöberg, *Stephanites und Ichnelates. Überlieferungsgeschichte und Text*
[Acta Univ. Upsal., Studia Graeca Upsal., 2, Stockholm-Göteborg-
Uppsala 1962], 43–44, 49).—Ff. 131ᵛ–132ᵛ vacua.

   2 Hagiographica et exegetica nonnulla. ¹(ff. 133–49) Commentarius de
i m a g i n e D e i p a r a e τῆς Πορταϊτίσσης (*BHG* i.e. *Bibliotheca Hagiographica Graeca* [Bruxellis 1957³], 1070); ²(ff. 149ᵛ–150) περὶ ποῦ ἐπεκάθισεν ὁ
Χριστός (cf. Mt. 21, 1–9), inc. Ὁ Χριστὸς ἐπεκάθισεν ὦ πατέρες καὶ ἀδελφοὶ·
οὐκ εἰς ἡμίονον, ὅπερ ἐστι τὸ ἰδιωτικῶς λεγόμενον μουλάριον, des. καὶ εἰς τὸν
πῶλον αὐτῆς· ἐν αὐτῷ γὰρ τινές φασι τῶν ἐξηγητῶν; ³(f. 150) περὶ τοῦ Χριστοῦ
διαλεγομένου πρὸς τὸν Ἰούδα, οἷον· τὸ ἑταῖρε ἐφ᾽ ᾧ πάρει (Mt. 26, 50), inc.
Ἐπὶ ποίω φησὶ σκοπῶ, παρεγένου ὦ φίλε, des. οὐ γὰρ ἦλθες ἵνα φιλήσης, ἀλλ᾽
ἵνα προδώσης;—ff. 150ᵛ–151 vacua; ⁴(ff. 152–160) sub tit. ἑτέρα διήγησις
περὶ τοῦ πλανηθέντος ἐκείνου παιδὸς etc., n a r r a t i o (e vita et miraculis s.
B a s i l i i C a e s a r i e n s i s excerpta) de iuvene qui Christum per scriptum
negaverat (*BHG* 253), addita subscriptione τέλος καὶ τῷ θεῷ χάρις· ἀμήν.
—F. 160ᵛ vacuum.

MAT.—Le f. 1 est un peu taché par l'humidité.

COMP.—Trois parties, dont aucune ne présente de signatures. I
(ff. 1–131) 3 + 4 ff. (7), 15 quat. (127), 1 bin. restauré (131). II (ff.
132–51) 2 quat. (147), 1 bin. restauré. III (ff. 152–60) 1 tern. (157),
2 + 1 ff. (160).

  ⁴ Aland, 23.

FILIGR.—I. 1° (ff. 1 + 6) Tête de bœuf sommée d'une croix (la croix est du type Briquet 14.474 ou 14.511); 2° (ff. 59 + 60) étoile à 6 rais dans un losange aux côtés incurvés inscrit dans un cercle (parallèles possibles: Briquet 6097: Lucques 1566–67; Lichačev 4224: Rome 1567, et 4231: Rome 1571; Zonghi 1729–31: Fabriano 1572–74). II. (ff. 135 + 136) Ancre dont la tige est formée d'un trait simple, inscrite dans un cercle sommé d'une étoile à 4 rais (seul filigrane de type semblable chez Briquet: 571, mais avec contre-marque; de toute façon, le type appartient à la deuxième moitié du XVIᵉ s.). III. (ff. 159 + 160) Ancre dont la tige est formée d'un trait double, inscrite dans un cercle sommé d'une étoile à 6 rais, avec, semble-t-il, (visible seulement au f. 154) la contremarque PS (manque chez Briquet).

DIM.—Surface écrite: I: mm. 150 × 90, lignes 27. II: mm. 155/6 × 90, lignes 22. III: mm. 155 × 90, lignes 22.

ÉCRIT.—Trois copistes différents (à moins que III soit identique à I, ce qui n'est pas impossible). I (ff. 1–131) Encre brun foncé à noir, écriture penchée à droite; souscription (f. 131) τέλος τοῦ φυσιολόγου / ἐν ἔτει, ,ζοῆ μηνὶ δεκεμβρίω καⁿ (cf. Sjöberg, p. 44). II (ff. 133–50) Encre gris-noir, écriture droite peu élégante. III (ff. 152–60) Encre gris-noir, écriture très proche de celle de I.

ORN.—I: Bandeaux à dessins géométriques de facture assez grossière, tracés à l'encre rouge et noir; f. 1: croix et invocation I̅C̅ X̅C̅ N̅K̅ au-dessus du bandeau; initiales ornées rouges, parfois recouvertes d'une couche d'un noir vernissé ou rehaussées d'un peu d'or; lemmes et titres en rouge. II et III: titres et initiales en rouge.

ANNOT.—Un morceau d'un f. de garde ancien (f. I) a été collé avant les ff. de garde récents; au recto: *Liber* / *Physiologicus*; au verso: **nᵒ 1072**, et une brève description du contenu (d'une main du XVIIᵉ s. ?).—Deux ff. de garde plus récents; sur le recto du second (f. II) la description du contenu a été répétée (d'une main du XIXᵉ s. ?).

POSS.—F. 1 (en marge): *Ex libris Alberti Bozęcki*.

BIBL.—Sjöberg, op. et loc. cit.

REL.—Récente (XIXᵉ s. ?): ais de carton recouverts d'un papier marbré à fond grisâtre.

BOZ Cim. 157.[5] Saec. XIV (pp. 41–44 saec. XV), chart., mm. 218 × 145, pp. 466 (+ 319a, 320a; pp. 461–66 haud numeratae).

1 Varia iuridica, chronologica, dogmatica, ascetica. ¹(pp. 1–6) Βαθ-μολόγιον γενεαλογίας, inc. ὁ πατήρ μου ἐγέννησεν ἐμέ· και ιδου μία γέννησις, ἵνα βαθμὸν ἀπετέλεσαν, des. δύο δεύτεροι ἐξάδελφοι, ἔκτος βαθμὸς· μίαν γυναικα κεκώλευται; ²(pp. 6–8) ⟨chronologica varia de Pasqua, indictione, dominica τῆς ἀπόκρεω etc.⟩, inc. Γίνωσκε ὅτι τὸ μία δύο τὸ πρῶτον, ὁ κύκλος σελήνης ἐστί; ³(pp. 8–11) florilegium dogmaticum de Christi incarnatione, ῥήματα δογματικὰ αγίων πατέρων περὶ τῆς ἐνσάρκου οἰκονομίας τοῦ κυριου και θεου καὶ σωτηρος ἡμῶν Ιησοῦ Χριστοῦ cod. Auctores citantur Gregorius ⟨Nazianzenus⟩, Cyrillus ⟨Alexandrinus⟩, Gregorius Nyssenus, Amphilochius; alia excerpta sunt anonyma; ⁴(pp. 12–14) sub tit. διδασκαλία, incerti homilia quaedam, inc. ἕως ἤδη ἡμέρα ἐστὶ καὶ ζῶμεν καὶ βλέπομεν ταύτην, λαβωμεν κατὰ νοῦν τὴν κρίσιν τὴν μέλλουσαν, des. ἵνα τῶν ἐπικειμένων κακῶν ἐλευθερωθῶμεν· ἵνα τῶν παρόντων καὶ μελλόντων ἀγαθῶν ἐπιτύχωμεν, χάριτι τοῦ ἀληθινοῦ θεοῦ καὶ σωτηρος ἡμῶν Ιησοῦ Χριστοῦ ᾧ πρέπει δόξα εἰς τους αιωνας; ⁵(pp. 15–16) ⟨de divortio⟩, inc. τὸ ἔννομον συνοικέσιον λύεται, ἐὰν πορνεύσῃ ἡ γυνὴ, des. ταυτα δὲ καὶ ἐπὶ τοῦ ἀνδρὸς και ἐπὶ τῆς γυναικὸς κελεύομεν πράττεσθαι μετὰ φόβου θεοῦ; ⁶(pp. 16–18) sub tit. ετερ...τῶν βαθμῶν, de gradibus parentelae (agitur verisimiliter de opella quam descripsit N. G. Svoronos, *La Synopsis Major des Basiliques et ses appendices* [Bibliothèque Byzantine. Études, 4, Paris 1964], 55, ubi editiones citantur; cf. Évelyne Patlagean, "Une représentation byzantine de la parenté," in *L'Homme. Revue française d'anthropologie*, 6 [1966], 76). Inc. Συγγένεια, ὄνομα ἐστὶ γενικὸν διαιρεῖται δὲ εἰς τάξεις τρεῖς, des. καὶ καθ' ἑξῆς ἔκτου καὶ ἑβδόμου καὶ ὀγδόου; ⁷(pp. 18–20) ⟨varia canonica de matrimonio⟩, inc. ὁ δεξάμενος ἐκ τοῦ ἁγίου βαπτίσματος παίδα θηλυ ὕστερον λάβη ταύτην εἰς τὸν υἱόν αὐτοῦ, ἵνα χωρίζωνται, des. ταυτα φυλάξει, ταγμα τῶν διακόνων· ὑποδιακόνων τε πληθὺς ὡς δέον; ⁸(pp. 21–30) sub tit. rubro qui legi non potest (uno tantum verbo constat), ⟨oratio de 318 Patribus Nicaenis⟩, inc. σήμερον ἡ τοῦ Χριστοῦ ἐκκλησια μνήμην ἑορτάζει τῶν ἁγίων θεοφόρων πατέρων τῶν τριακοσίων δέκα καὶ ὀκτὼ, des. εἰς αὐτὴν τὴν χαρὰν τοῦ κυρίου ἡμῶν εἰσελθεῖν ἀξιωθέντες· καὶ τῶν ἀκηράτων ἀγαθῶν ἀπολαύοντες· ὧν γένοιτο πάντας ἡμᾶς ἐπιτυχεῖν, ἐν Χριστῷ Ιησοῦ τῶ κυριω ἡμῶν· ᾧ ἡ δόξα εἰς τους αἰωνας τῶν αἰώνων ἀμήν (deest in *BHG*). Ad calcem additae sunt manu recentiore paragraphi duae ⟨de re canonica⟩; ⁹(pp. 33–31) e s. **Basilii Magni** epistula ⟨260⟩ ad Optimum εἰς τὰ κατὰ Κάιν ἑπτὰ ἐκδικούμενα (*PG* 32, 957 B 6 Ἐκδικούμενα - 961 C 5 καὶ ὀνειδισμόν); ¹⁰(pp. 34–37) s. **Ephraem Syri** περὶ μετανοίας, inc. Ἡ ἀποταγὴ ἣν ἐπὶ τοῦ ἁγίου βαπτίσματος ποιούμεθα,

---

⁵ Aland, 23.

des. ἢ κατακρινοῦσιν ἡμᾶς, ἢ δικαιοῦσι ἐν τῇ ὥρα ἐκείνῃ (est prima pars responsionis de abrenunciatione: S. Ephraem Syri opera omnia ed. J. Assemani, III [Romae 1746], 215 B–216 D; v. D. Hemmerdinger-Iliadou, art. "Éphrem" in Dictionnaire de Spiritualité, IV [Paris 1959], col. 807 sub num. 5, 8°, et col. 815 sub num. 10; cf. A. Ehrhard, Überlieferung und Bestand der hagiogr. und homil. Literatur der griech. Kirche [Texte und Untersuch., 50–52, Leipzig 1937–1943], I, 552, II, 243; cf. etiam codd. Vat. gr. 468 f. 278ᵛ et Ambros. C 92 sup. [= gr. 192] f. 166); ¹¹(p. 37) ⟨eiusdem⟩ περὶ ἀρετῆς (nempe de virtute cap. 1: Assemani I, 217 C–D; cf. Dict. de Spirit. supra cit., col. 811 sub num. 9, 8°); ¹²(pp. 37–39) eiusdem ⟨de beatitudinibus et infelicitatibus⟩, inc. Οὐαὶ τὸ λέγοντι ὅτι τὸ παρὸν χρήσομαι τῇ σαρκὶ, καὶ ἐν γήρα μετανοήσω (altera scil. pars: Assemani II, 335 A 1–2 ad finem paginae; cf. Dict. de Spirit., col. 808 sub num. 7, 6°).—P. 40 vacua.

2 Additamenta manu posteriore iniecta in ff. ante Synopsin vacuis relictis. ¹(pp. 41–42) **Georgii Scholarii** libellus die 1 nov. 1452 portae domus suae affixus, Γενναδίου ποίημα τὸ προσηλωθὲν παρὰ τῇ θυρα τοῦ κελίου αὐτοῦ τῇ πρώτῃ τοῦ νοευβρίου τοῦ ͵ςϠλξβ ἔτους ἰνδικτιωνος β cod. (L. Petit— X. A. Sidéridès—M. Jugie, Œuvres complètes de Gennade Scholarios, III [Paris 1930], 165, 27–166, 19), suffixo (p. 42) ⟨commentariolo de rebus a se gestis adversus latinismum eodem die⟩ (ibid., 165,16–26); ²sequuntur textus breves tres, quorum prima et ultima verba tantum exscripsi (an hi quoque Georgio Scholario tribuendi sunt?): ᵃ(pp. 42–43) inc. Μέγα τὸ ὄνομα σου Χριστε βασιλεῦς (sic) · μεγάλη σου ἡ πίστις δικαία καὶ ἀληθινὴ ἡ κρίσις σου, des. τάλανες δὲ, οἱ σκανδαλισθησόμενοι καὶ μικροψυχήσοντες, ᵇ(p. 43) inc. Καὶ ἐξαρεῖτε τὸν πονηρὸν ἐξ υμῶν αὐτόν, des. μηδεὶς τοίνυν φαῦλον ἐχέτω φίλον, ᶜ(pp. 43–44) inc. Ἐπείπερ ἐπεκράτησε φίλους φιλεῖν οἱ φίλοι ιδοὺ σοι σχέσιν δείκνειμι, des. καὶ κύριος ἀξιόσει, με σὺν σοι συνευφρανθῆναι.

3 ⟨Synopsis minor Basilicorum⟩ (ed. C. E. Zachariae a Lingenthal, Jus Graeco-Romanum, II [Lipsiae 1856], 9–264; quam editionem denuo typis expresserunt J. et P. Zepos, Jus Graeco-Romanum, VI [Athenis 1931], 327–547): (pp. 45–89) tabula capitum (a Lingenthal omissa);—(pp. 89–460) textus.—Pp. 461–466 vacua, praeter notulas de quibus v. infra.

Mat.—Des taches d'humidité; quelques trous de vers; le coin inf. ext. des ff. rongé. Les premiers ff. ont été restaurés au moyen de papier.

Comp.—Ff. ajoutés en tête du ms. primitif (pp. 1–40): 1 tern. + 1 f. restauré (14), 1 quat. (30), 3 + 2 ff. restaurés (40); les cahiers sont signés α'-γ' (de première main, semble-t-il) au milieu de la marge inf. de la dernière page, et une fois de la première (p. 31); pour le premier cahier, la signature est inscrite et sur la p. 13 et sur la p. 14. Corps du ms. (pp. 41–466): 26 quat. (454; attention aux

p. 319a et 320a), 1 tern.; les cahiers ont d'abord été signés de première main, dans la marge inf. de la première et de la dernière page, plutôt vers l'extérieur du feuillet (mais parfois au milieu); plusieurs signatures ont été coupées en même temps que les marges: les premières qui subsistent sont celles du cahier γ' (pp. 73–88); un peu plus tard, la main qui a signé les cahiers en tête a continué la numérotation des cahiers de δ' à λ'.

Filigr.—Feuillets préliminaires: 1° (pp. 5/6 + 7/8) roue (ou croix inscrite dans un cercle; seul ex. du type chez Mošin-Traljić 6913: Split 1358); 2° (pp. 19/20 + 25/26) lettre T (papier à grosses vergeures); 3° (pp. 35/36 + 37/38) armoiries: écu parti chapé (cf. Mošin-Traljić 513–15: plutôt la première moitié du XIVe s.). Corps du ms.: 4° (pp. 45/46 + 51/52) lettre B à traits simples; 5° (pp. 121/22 + 135/36) fruit: poire accompagnée de deux feuilles (ces deux filigranes alternent; je ne puis fournir de parallèle, ne les ayant pas dessinés).

Dim.—Surface écrite: ff. préliminaires: mm. 140/50 × 95, lignes 19–21; corps du ms.: mm. 153 × 90/93, lignes 28.

Écrit.—Le corps du ms. (pp. 45–460) a été copié par un seul scribe; les pp. 1–39 ajoutées en tête sont l'œuvre d'un autre copiste du XIVe s. (sauf 9 lignes de supplément à la p. 30, d'une main plus récente); les pp. 41–44 sont un remplissage du XVe s.

Orn.—Ff. préliminaires: titre et initiales du premier texte en rouge passé. Corps du ms.: p. 45, petit bandeau d'entrelacs noirs et rouges; les titres principaux manquent (l'espace a été laissé vide); encre du texte: brun ocre à verdâtre.

Annot.—P. 461: un monocondyle (que je n'ai pas déchiffré).—P. 463, d'une écriture extrêmement grossière: + ετουτο το βεβληο υπαρχη της | αγηας μητροπολης και οπο το ξε | νοση υνε αφορεσμενος (j'ai omis les accents et les esprits mis sur à peu près toutes les voyelles).—P. 465–66 (retourner le ms.): d'une main du XIVe s., 9 lignes de comptes avec des noms et des chiffres.—P. 466: d'une main du XIVe s., une série de remèdes: le premier περὶ οφθαλμῶν καυσωδ. (λιθάργυρον καὶ ἔλαιον συν ὄξει τρίψεις, ἄλιφε αὐτοὺς καὶ ἰᾶται), le dernier περὶ τοῦ γνῶναι τὸ τικτόμενον.

Poss.—P. 1 (marge inf.): une note de possession barrée à l'encre.

Rel.—De technique byzantine (je n'ai pas vu les plats, dissimulés par une couverture moderne).

BOZ Cim. 142.[6]

Pour ce ms. et les suivants, mes notes ne sont ni assez précises ni assez complètes pour présenter une description en règle. Je me contente de quelques remarques sur le contenu et les particularités externes.

CONTENU

À propos du Commentaire sur la Métaphysique du pseudo-Hérennius. C'est sur cette partie du ms. que R. Foerster s'est étendu dans son article du *Rheinisches Museum* de 1900, 444–448. K. Praechter a indiqué la bibliographie postérieure dans son article du *RE* et dans *Die Philosophie des Altertums* (Fr. Ueberwegs Grundriss der Geschichte der Philosophie, I, Berlin, 1926 [12]), p. 188*; depuis, j'ai relevé deux titres: K. D. Geôrgoulès, "Αὐγουστῖνος καὶ Ψευδοερέννιος," dans Πλάτων, 1 (1949), p. 36–78 (sur les sources du pseudo-Hérennius); J. Irigoin, "Un manuscrit grec du cardinal de Richelieu," dans *Scriptorium*, 10 (1956), 98–100, qui complète l'article de Ch. Astruc, "Les manuscrits grecs de Richelieu," dans *Scriptorium*, 6 (1952), 3–17; je reviendrai plus bas sur ces deux articles.

Du point de vue de l'histoire du texte, la contribution décisive est une note de G. Pasquali, "Parerga. III. La così detta Metafisica di Erennio e Andrea Darmario," dans *Xenia Romana* (Roma-Milano 1907), 23–27. D'après lui, il est très probable que toutes les copies du pseudo-Hérennius remontent à un exemplaire difficilement lisible (ou abîmé par endroits?) qui appartenait à Jean-Vincent Pinelli, le fameux érudit de Padoue. Celui-ci en fit exécuter une copie par Camille de Venise (alias Camille Zanetti): c'est l'actuel Ambrosianus R 117 sup. (gr. 724), ff. 3–47ᵛ; à la fin, on lit la note suivante, transcrite dans le catalogue de Martini et Bassi: "camillo copista di q(uest)o libro ha fatto dei punticini nel mezzo ∴ doue non intendeua la scrittura dell'originale." Il serait intéressant de soumettre à vérification la théorie de Pasquali: les filigranes, l'identification des copistes, la collation du texte permettraient de reconstituer l'histoire de la diffusion de l'opuscule à partir du modèle de Camille Zanetti et, probablement, de faire justice pour de bon du reproche fait à Darmarios d'être le responsable de la falsification. La liste des manuscrits du pseudo-Hérennius fournie par A. Wartelle, *Inventaire des manuscrits grecs d'Aristote et de ses commentateurs* (Coll. d'Études anciennes..., Paris 1963), est loin d'être complète. D. Harlfinger et J. Wiesner (*Scriptorium*,

---

[6] Brève mention chez Aland, 22. Traitement détaillé, mais partiel, chez R. Foerster, "Zur Handschriftenkunde und Geschichte der Philologie. VI. Handschriften der Zamoyski'schen Bibliothek. Simon Simonides und Herennios' Metaphysik," dans *Rheinisches Museum für Philologie*, 55 (1900), 435–459.

18 [1964], 238–257) y ont ajouté le Monacensis gr. 401, le Taurinensis gr. 45 (Pasini), la Barberinianus gr. 188 (= II 9). Mais l'article de Foerster cité plus haut, s'il ignorait le Vaticanus gr. 2598, était encore plus complet, puisqu'il signalait en outre (440–441) les Oxonienses Bodleiani D'Orville 103 et 104 (nos 16.981 et 16.982 du *Summary Catalogue of Western Manuscripts*), le Barberin. gr. 258 (= II 79; cité fautivement ZZ. 79 par Foerster) et l'Ottobonianus gr. 124, copie du XVIIe siècle destinée à substituer, dans la bibliothèque Altemps, le Vaticanus gr. 1442, un des manuscrits achetés par le pape Paul V pour la Bibliothèque Vaticane.[7] Enfin, Ch. Astruc, dans l'article mentionné plus haut, a signalé que le cardinal de Richelieu possédait une copie du pseudo-Hérennius. Celle-ci, si elle n'a pas péri, n'a pu encore être identifiée; J. Irigoin (art. cité) écarte en effet l'hypothèse qu'il s'agirait du Vossianus gr. F. 14; il resterait à vérifier si aucune des copies existantes ne pourrait être le manuscrit de Richelieu (je ne vois guère comme possibilité qu'un des deux manuscrits D'Orville).

PARTICULARITÉS EXTERNES

Comp.—Les cahiers sont signés au moyen de réclames verticales inscrites dans le prolongement de l'extrémité interne de la surface écrite. Ce sont en général des sénions, mais, au début et à la fin, on rencontre des cahiers de 14, 16 et 18 feuillets.

Dim.—Surface écrite: mm. 174/196 × 98/99, lignes 19/21.

Écrit.—Le style rappelle celui d'Ange Vergèce, mais je connais plusieurs scribes contemporains qui vérifient cette condition. Une analyse plus détaillée permettrait probablement d'identifier le copiste. De toute façon, le manuscrit date de la seconde moitié du XVIe siècle.

Filigr.—1o Tête de bœuf d'où s'élève une tige se terminant en trèfle, et contremarque ZC (cf. Briquet 14.775: Bergame 1583; var. sim.: Bergame 1589); 2o soleil avec contremarque ZZ (cf. Briquet 13.960: Reggio d'Emilie 1594–97; var. sim.: ibid., 1599).

Orn.—Bandeaux non encadrés constitués de rinceaux qui se recourbent vers le haut ou le bas. Titres en minuscules rouges. Initiales principales: onciales rouges ornées de rinceaux. Fins de textes disposées en triangle.

[7] Voir, dans G. Mercati, *Codici latini Pico Grimani Pio* ... (Studi e Testi, 75, Città del Vaticano 1938), le chapitre intitulé "I codici Altempsiani acquistati da Paolo V" (106–43); le Vaticanus gr. 1442 est brièvement décrit 118–19; c'est ce manuscrit, et non l'Ottobonianus gr. 124, qui est l'ancien Sirletianus gr. philos. 9.

CRACOVIE: BIBLIOTHÈQUE CZARTORYSKI

Cod. 2852.[8]

BIBLIOGRAPHIE

Voir sur le ms.: C. Van de Vorst et H. Delehaye, *Catalogus codicum hagiographicorum graecorum Germaniae Belgii Angliae* (Subsidia hagiographica 13, Bruxellis 1913), 91 (datent le ms. du XIIIe– XIVe siècle, sur la foi de C. Ranoschek); A. Ehrhard, *Überlieferung und Bestand der hagiograph. und homilet. Literatur der griech. Kirche*, III (Texte und Untersuchungen, 52, Leipzig 1943), 847 (n'a pas vu lui-même le ms.).

CONTENU

1. La deuxième pièce chrysostomienne (ff. 43–50ᵛ; pp. 85–100).

Cette homélie sur l'Ascension (inc. Φέρε καὶ σήμερον ἀπὸ τῆς εὐαγγελικῆς ἱστορίας, ἣν ἐπιτόμως διεδράμομεν) est-elle attestée ailleurs? Elle ne figure pas parmi les pièces recensées dans les volumes déjà parus des *Codices Chrysostomici Graeci* (Documents, Études et Répertoires publiés par l'Institut de Recherche et d'Histoire des Textes).

2. Les feuillets palimpsestes (ff. 49–52; pp. 97–103).

Je n'ai malheureusement pu déterminer si l'écriture sous-jacente était une onciale grecque ou du slave, ce qui, pour la provenance du manuscrit, est d'importance. D'après la disposition du texte (divisé en tropaires, dirait-on), il s'agit peut-être d'un manuscrit liturgique.

CARACTÉRISTIQUES EXTERNES

MAT.—Parchemin de médiocre qualité: v. f. 37 (pp. 73–74): trou; f. 43ᵛ (p. 86): laissé vide d'écriture (le scribe a noté: ζήτει εἰς τὸ ἕτερον πάγιν).

COMP.—6 quat. (ff. 1–48, pp. 1–96), 1 bin. (ff. 49–52, pp. 97–103). Les cahiers sont signés dans le coin inf. int. de la dernière page, mais pas de première main; les signatures, qui ont disparu du premier et du dernier cahier, sont difficilement identifiables: je n'ai pu déterminer s'il s'agissait de chiffres grecs ou arabes.—Deux feuillets non numérotés arrachés d'un ms. latin palimpseste ont été ajoutés comme garde, l'un au début, l'autre à la fin.

DIM.—Réglure: Lake I 2c (les lignes horizontales débordent parfois irrégulièrement dans la marge externe). Surface écrite: mm. 119 × 69/72, lignes 28.

---

[8] Gollob, 27–28. Très brève mention d'Aland, 32.

Écrit.—Encre brune, petite écriture (26 à 30 lettres à la ligne) assez régulière, avec pas mal d'abréviations. Le ductus n'est pas typiquement italo-grec. Je la date du XIIe ou du XIIe–XIIIe siècle (contre Gollob: XVe, et Ranoschek: XIIIe–XIVe).

Ornat.—F. 1 (p. 1): lignes constituées de traits interrompus rehaussées de vermillon; au-dessus, un nœud et deux croix, à côté, deux astérisques, tous rehaussés de la même couleur. Ff. 29[v], 30, 43 (pp. 58, 59, 85): au-dessus des titres, traits interrompus rehaussés de vermillon. Les titres sont écrits en petite onciale, de l'encre du texte. Les grandes initiales (p. ex. f. 30 = p. 59) sont rehaussées de vermillon; les autres, à l'encre du texte, sont parfois enduites de jaune, parfois rehaussées de vermillon. Les lemmes sont souvent recouverts d'un trait de couleur jaune. Ce type d'ornementation autorise l'hypothèse d'une origine italo-grecque, mais l'écriture n'est pas typique. Evidemment, si l'écriture sous-jacente des feuillets palimpsestes était slave, la supposition perdrait beaucoup de sa vraisemblance. De toute façon, il doit s'agir d'un produit d'origine provinciale.

Annot.—Dans les marges du premier texte, notes grecques et latines d'une main occidentale.

Rel.—Moderne, en plein cuir marron.

Cod. 2853.[9]

Bibliographie

Sur le texte de Plutarque, v. l'édition de la Bibliotheca Teubneriana: *Plutarchi Moralia*, t. II, edd. W. Nachstädt—W. Sieveking—J. B. Titchener (Lipsiae 1935), p. XIII n. 1: le ms. est une copie de O[1 + 2], c'est-à-dire de l'Ambrosianus M 82 sup. (= gr. 528), sur lequel v. le t. I de l'édition, p. XX, et le catalogue de Martini et Bassi.

Possesseur

Gollob a omis de signaler que le manuscrit, une copie sur parchemin de luxe de la Renaissance, porte au f. 7 (du côté interne) un bandeau vertical orné et, dans la marge inf., des armoiries, qui permettent d'identifier le propriétaire. L'écu est écartelé: au 1 et au 4, les armes d'Aragon, au 3 et au 4, un lion d'azur sur fond or. Ce sont les armes de la famille napolitaine des Acquaviva d'Aragona.

[9] Gollob, 28–29. Très brève mention d'Aland, 32.

Dès lors, il est facile de reconnaître celui pour qui la copie fut
exécutée. C'est Andrea Matteo Acquaviva d'Aragona (1458–1529),
à la fois homme de guerre et humaniste.[10] Il se constitua une belle
bibliothèque, où figuraient nombre de manuscrits enluminés grecs
et latins.[11] De plus, c'était un spécialiste de Plutarque, dont il
traduisit et commenta le *De virtute morali*.[12] L'écu dessiné sur le
manuscrit de Cracovie se présente tout à fait, au point de vue de la
forme et de la disposition des éléments, comme celui de l'Aristote de
Vienne, Vindobonensis phil. gr. 2 (Hermann, pl. V). De Marinis
fait observer que la bibliothèque d'Andrea Matteo fut rapidement
dispersée après sa mort. Une note inscrite sur un feuillet de garde
non numéroté, en tête du manuscrit de Cracovie,[13] nous apprend
qu'il appartint, vers le milieu du XVIe siècle, à un autre membre de
la noblesse napolitaine, Ferrante Monsorio:[14] *Dionora Monsoria è
nata* [*allo* barré] *lo sabato à notte ad hore sette* | *sonate delli 24 d'Agosto
1561 à nap(o)li in casa della contessa di* | *Nicot(er)a à seggio di Nido.—* |
Fer(ran)te monsorio. Je ne sais comment, dans la suite, il passa aux
princes Czartoryski.

J'ai noté que le manuscrit de Cracovie était copié d'une main
occidentale peu élégante du XVe–XVIe siècle; il y aurait lieu de la
comparer avec les écritures reproduites par Hermann (pl. V–XII)
et avec celle du Vaticanus lat. 10.655, de même type.

[10] Voir sur lui la notice (anonyme) du *Dizionario biografico degli Italiani*, I (Roma
1960), 185–87.

[11] Voir H. J. Hermann, "Miniaturhandschriften aus der Bibliothek des Herzogs
Andrea Matteo III. Acquaviva," dans *Jahrbuch der kunsthistorischen Sammlungen des aller-
höchsten Kaiserhauses*, 19 (1898), 147–216, qui étudie 14 manuscrits conservés à Vienne
et à Naples. T. De Marinis en a retrouvé 10 autres, qu'il a signalés dans son étude "Un
manoscritto di Tolomeo fatto per Andrea Matteo Acquaviva e Isabella Piccolomini,"
Nozze D. Bodmer ed A. Stahel (Verona 1956), p. 4.

[12] L'ouvrage a été publié à Naples en 1526, chez l'imprimeur Antonio Frezza da
Corinaldo. L'exemplaire de la Bibliothèque Vaticane (Stamp. Barberini J. V. 92)
porte le titre suivant: *Plutarchi de Virtute morali libellus Graecus. Eiusdem libelli translatio per
Illustriss. Andream Matth. Aquivivum Hadrianorum Ducem. Commentarium ipsius Ducis in eiusdem
libelli translationem in libros quatuor divisum.* De Marinis a signalé deux manuscrits du
Vatican qui contiennent l'œuvre: l'Urbinas lat. 1380 n'a que le commentaire, précédé
d'une préface adressée à Troiano Caracciolo; le Vaticanus lat. 10.655 présente le texte
grec, la traduction latine et le commentaire, avec une préface dédiée à Troiano Caracciolo
et son fils Giovanni.

[13] Négligée, elle aussi, par Gollob.

[14] Sur la famille Monsorio ou Monsolino, voir B. Candida Gonzaga, *Memorie delle
famiglie nobili delle province meridionali d'Italia*, t. VI (Napoli 1882), 116–18.

D'après les derniers éditeurs des *Moralia* de Plutarque, le Cracoviensis est une copie de l'Ambrosianus M 82 sup., manuscrit qui, dans la deuxième moitié du XVIe siècle, appartint à Pinelli.[15] Vers le début du XVe, il était entre les mains d'un Chypriote.[16] Il a dû être transféré en Italie dans le courant du XVe siècle, ce qui permit à Acquaviva d'en faire tirer une copie pour sa bibliothèque.

CRACOVIE: BIBLIOTHÈQUE UNIVERSITAIRE JAGELLONNE

Cod. 156 (XI Gollob).[17]

DATE—Copie du XVIIe siècle, d'une main occidentale.

CONTENU—(pp. 11–12 = f. 7rv) S. Ephraem Syri exhortatio 44 (*S. Ephraem Syri opera omnia*, ed. J. Assemani, II [Romae 1743], 164–65; cf. Hemmerdinger-Iliadou supra cit., col. 812, num. 9, 13°).

Cod. 620 (IV Gollob).

DATE—Manuscrit sur papier oriental, donc certainement antérieur au XVe siècle, où le place Gollob. Paléographiquement, il pourrait remonter jusqu'au début du XIVe siècle, mais la monodie sur la mort de l'empereur Michel IX (voir plus bas) fournit un *terminus post quem*: 1320. Je ne descendrais pas plus bas que le milieu du siècle.

BIBLIOGRAPHIE—Le ms. a été inclus par A. Pertusi dans sa liste des témoins du *De consolatione* de Boèce, traduit en grec par Maxime Planude: v. A. Pertusi, "La fortuna di Boezio a Bisanzio," dans Παγκάρπεια. *Mélanges Henri Grégoire*, III (= *Annuaire de l'Institut de Philologie et d'Histoire Orientales et Slaves*, t. 11, 1951), 308.

CONTENU

Le f. 59rv contient un poème en vers politiques, dont Gollob a transcrit les premières lignes. Je l'ai recopié entièrement et compte le publier ailleurs. C'est une monodie en l'honneur d'un empereur byzantin défunt. Le contenu, qui fait allusion aux Catalans, montre qu'il s'agit de Michel IX; le poème parle également, sans les nommer explicitement, de son père Andronic II et de son fils Andronic III.

---

[15] Voir le catalogue de Martini et Bassi, II, 640.

[16] Ibid., 639.

[17] Je renvoie entre parenthèses aux numéros du catalogue de Gollob, 18–27, ou aux pages d'Aland.

Cod. 932 (Aland, 29–30).

Écriture sous-jacente—Il s'agit d'un beau petit manuscrit liturgique, datable du XIe siècle, à mon avis. Surface écrite: mm. 117 × 91/92, lignes 24; écriture élégante. L'ornementation, sobre, est constituée par des lignes de traits interrompus; titres en petite onciale; certaines initiales sont recouvertes d'un trait jaune (à noter que l'écriture supérieure est slave). Le texte est assez lisible; il s'agit d'un triode.

Cod. 2363 (VI Gollob).

CONTENU

1 (pp. 2–37) Iohannis Morezeni oratio in festum s. Titi.—Il s'agit d'un sermon en grec vulgaire, avec la traduction latine en regard; inc. Ἐὰν ἴσος καὶ εἶναι δίκαιον οἱ φίλοι οἱ εὐεργετηθέντες, ἀπὸ τοὺς φίλους τος (sic) νὰ χέρουνται εἰς τὴν χαρὰν τῶν ἠγαπιμένων τος, des. καὶ τὴν παροῦσαν ὥραν νὰ μᾶς δώσει τὴν πεποθημενην μας καὶ ὠφέλημον εὐλογίαν. L'auteur, le prêtre crétois Jean Morézènos (Μορεζῆνος, Μορζῆνος), qui a vécu durant la deuxième moitié du XVIe siècle, est connu comme auteur de sermons et de poésies religieuses, et comme possesseur de manuscrits.[18]

2 (pp. 836–845 [et non 855: faute d'impression du catalogue]). Ce sont des schémas astronomiques, en grec et en latin, du XVIIe siècle. Ils ne semblent pas présenter d'intérêt.

Cod. 2526 (VII Gollob).

DATE ET FILIGRANES

Le manuscrit est écrit d'une main assez peu élégante (un moine? A. P. Kouzès a donné une reproduction en blanc sur noir de trois pages du manuscrit dans l' Ἐπετηρὶς Ἑταιρείας Βυζαντινῶν Σπουδῶν, 10 [1933], 372–74, fig. 2–4), sur du papier vénitien à contremarque; j'ai relevé p. ex. le filigrane suivant: ancre dont la tige est formée d'un trait simple, inscrite dans un cercle sommé d'une étoile à 6 rais, avec contremarque HS; le type ne se retrouve pas tel quel dans Briquet, mais il rentre dans le groupe 551–71, qui s'échelonne de 1556 à 1601; on peut donc dater le ms. de la deuxième moitié du XVIe siècle. Gollob a signalé le filigrane (p. 148 n° 26 et p. 154

---

[18] Voir maintenant (1973) l'étude d'Elenē D. Kakoulidē, " Ὁ Ἰωάννης Μορεζῆνος καὶ τὸ ἔργο του," dans Κρητικὰ Χρονικά, 22 (1970), 7–78, 389–506. Le sermon du Cracoviensis y est édité p. 466–471.

n° 2) et l'a reproduit (fig. 2 de la planche 6), mais sans la contre-marque; cela ne l'a pas empêché de dater la copie du XVe siècle.

CONTENU

1. Meletii monachi de natura hominis.—Gollob ne signale pas explicite-ment les éditions, bien qu'il ait dû connaître, par les *Opuscula* de Ritschl, celle de J. A. Cramer (*Anecdota Graeca Oxon.*, III [Oxonii 1836], 1–157). H. Diels (*Die Handschriften der antiken Ärzte*, II [Abh. der kön. Preuss. Akad. der Wiss. Philos.-hist. Kl., 1906, 1], p. 63, qui cite le ms. de Cracovie), et G. Helmreich (*Handschriftliche Studien zu Meletius* [Abh. comme plus haut, 1918, 6]) paraissent ignorer l'édition de la *Patrologie* de Migne (t. 64, col. 1076–1309), qui fournit en plus la collation du Parisinus gr. 2299 et un fragment inédit sur les quatre éléments. Dans ses *Opuscula philologica* (I, Lipsiae 1866, p. 696), Fr. Ritschl, après avoir noté que le cod. Bodleianus Roe 15 "des. ut apparet...p. 142, 13 [Crameri]," ajoute: "Cracoviensis (K), desinens ibidem. 5) Monacensis (*M*), exitu eodem." Mais le ms. de Cracovie, à en juger par le catalogue (je n'ai pas vérifié moi-même, faute de m'être rendu compte à temps du problème), se termine par les mots καὶ ἔξωθεν ἐμπλάσας ἐπιτίθει, que je n'ai pas retrouvés dans les éditions. D'autre part, le ms. de Munich, comme l'indique le catalogue de Hardt et le confirme l'étude de Helm-reich, finit à la p. 157 de Cramer, et non à la p. 142, 13. Il faudrait donc, pour résoudre la question, revoir le manuscrit lui-même.

2. Theophili de urinis.—Après Ideler, ce traité a été publié par A. P. Kouzès dans un ouvrage qui m'est resté inaccessible et que je connais seulement par la mention de Kouzès lui-même (dans l' ᾿Επετηρίς citée plus haut, 375): Βυζαντινῶν ἰατρῶν τὰ εὑρισκόμενα fasc. 11, p. 1–16.

3. Petosiridis epistula ad Nechepsum.—Cette pièce a été signalée par H. Diels, *Die Handschriften*, II, p. 82, et par W. Kroll dans le *Catalogus codicum astrologorum graecorum*, t. VI. *Codices Vindobonenses* (Bruxelles 1903), p. 57. Tous deux renvoient à l'édition d'E. Riess, "Nechepsonis et Petosiridis fragmenta magica," dans *Philologus*, Supplementband VI (Göttingen 1892), 384–385, 53. Je compte donner ailleurs une petite note sur les différentes recensions de ce système d'onomatomancie arithmétique, d'un intérêt intrinsèque médiocre, mais qui a connu une large diffusion. Sur le fond, A. Bouché-Leclercq a dit l'essentiel dans le chapitre sur la médicine astrologique de *L'Astrologie grecque* (Paris 1899), 537–540.

4. Iohannis Prisdyanorum episcopi de urinis.—Édité par A. P. Kouzès, "Τὸ «περὶ οὔρων» ἔργον τοῦ ᾿Ιωάννου ἐπισκόπου Πρισδριανῶν", dans ᾿Επετηρὶς ῾Εταιρείας Βυζαντινῶν Σπουδῶν, 10 (1933), 362–382 (le texte aux p. 364–371). Comme le note Kouzès, qui a étudié sur photos le ms. de Cracovie,

le texte de celui-ci est amputé du dernier paragraphe de l'opuscule et finit
à p. 371, 6. Le ms. a été cité par Diels, *Handschriften*, II, p. 55.

5. Il s'agit des deux opuscules médicaux en forme de canon liturgique
composés par Nicéphore Blemmyde, et sur lesquels on peut voir A. P.
Kousis,[19] "Les œuvres médicales de Nicéphore Blémmydès selon les
manuscrits existants," dans les Πρακτικὰ τῆς Ἀκαδημίας Ἀθηνῶν, 19
(1944; publié en 1948), 56–75. Le premier sur les urines (Kousis, 60–63),
le second sur le sang (Kousis, 59–60). Il est curieux que Diels, *Handschriften*, ne mentionne pas Blemmyde, alors que ses canons médicaux ne
sont pas rares dans les manuscrits.

Cod. 2528 (Aland, 29).

Caractéristiques externes

Manuscrit du XVIe siècle, de 45 ff. Filigrane (p. ex. ff. 3 + 6):
croissant (je n'ai pas relevé la forme exacte). Encre très noire.

CONTENU

1 (ff. 1–33v) ⟨S. Iohannis Chrysostomi contra eos qui subintroductas
habent virgines⟩ (*PG* 47, 495–514; *Saint Jean Chrysostome, Les cohabitations
suspectes*, ed. J. Dumortier [Nouvelle coll. de textes et documents...,
Paris 1955], 44–94; ce dernier n'a pas connu le ms. de Cracovie[20]), sans
doxologie à la fin.

2 (ff. 34–45v) ⟨Eiusdem quod regulares feminae viris cohabitare non
debeant⟩ (*PG* 47, 513–532; ed. Dumortier, op. cit., 95–137). Inc. normal,
des. οὕτως ἅπαντα πράττειν, ὡς προσῆκε τὰς τοιούτων ἐχούσας νυμφίον, ᾧ ἡ
δόξα etc. (c'est le des. du *De non iterando coniugio*: *PG* 48, 609–620).
Comme me l'a signalé très aimablement le P. Carter, la même anomalie
se présente dans l'Ottobonianus gr. 76 (ff. 19–25), du XVIe siècle
également; et, d'après mes calculs, le contenu des 12 ff. du Cracoviensis
correspond bien à celui des 6 ff. de l'Ottobonianus. Or, si l'on examine ce
dernier, on constate qu'au f. 22v (ligne 6) il passe sans crier gare des mots
διασώσαντα καὶ πρὸς du *Quod regulares* (*PG* 47, 518, ligne 22; Dumortier,
p. 104, 56) à πλείονος ἀνάγκης ὑποστήσεται du *De non iterando* (*PG* 48,
616, ligne 16 *ab imo*). La phrase qui en résulte n'offrant pas de sens
satisfaisant, il est clair que nous avons affaire à une conflation accidentelle:
le modèle (immédiat?) de l'Ottob. gr. 76, mutilé, avait perdu la fin du

---

[19] Le même que plus haut; je respecte ici la transcription de son nom telle qu'elle
se présente dans les Πρακτικά.

[20] Cf. R. E. Carter, "The Future of Chrysostom Studies," dans *Studia Patristica*, X
(Texte und Untersuchungen ..., 107; Berlin 1970), qui cite le manuscrit de Cracovie à
la p. 15.

Quod regulares et le début du *De non iterando*. Grâce à l'introduction de Dumortier, il n'est pas difficile de l'identifier; c'est le Marcianus gr. 111, qui présente la mutilation requise (v. Dumortier, 27–28; celui-ci cite l'Ottob. "pour mémoire," sans l'avoir examiné: v. p. 34). Selon toute probabilité, le manuscrit de Cracovie dérive, lui aussi, de celui de Venise.[21]

Cité du Vatican,
15 juin 1970

[21] À cause de la mutilation, l'Ottobonianus et le Cracoviensis ont échappé aux derniers éditeurs du *De non iterando*: B. Grillet et G. H. Ettlinger, *Jean Chrysostome, À une jeune veuve. Sur le mariage unique* (Sources chrétiennes, 138; Paris 1968). Mais cela n'a pas d'importance au point de vue de la constitution du texte, puisque le modèle des deux manuscrits est conservé. En dernière minute, le P. Carter me signale un autre manuscrit qui présente la même conflation: c'est l'Ottobonianus gr. 271, ff. 29–39 (copie du XVIe siècle, de la main de Jean Mauromatès); le passage d'une œuvre à l'autre est au f. 34^v, ligne 6 *ab imo*; cette copie a échappé aux éditeurs modernes.

MUSUROS-HANDSCHRIFTEN

MARTIN SICHERL

Der verehrte Jubilar, dem diese Festgabe gewidmet ist, hat durch seine umfassenden Untersuchungen zur Überlieferung Pindars und der Tragiker auch die Kodikologie, "das jüngste Kind der klassischen Philologie,"[1] und unsere Kenntnis der Geschichte der Philologie mächtig gefördert. Es ist deshalb nicht verwunderlich, daß wir in seinen Arbeiten in der Grenzzone zwischen handschriftlicher Überlieferung und drucktechnischer Verbreitung der Texte wiederholt dem Namen eines Mannes begegnen, der der wichtigste Mitarbeiter des Aldus Manutius bei der Herausgabe der griechischen Autoren gewesen ist: Markos Musuros aus Kreta (ca. 1470–1517), Professor des Griechischen an der Universität Padua (1503–1509), später in Venedig (1512–16) und schließlich an dem von Leo X. in Rom errichteten Griechischen Kolleg (1516–17),[2] den Wilamowitz[3] "wohl als das bedeutendste emendatorische Talent" bezeichnete, "welches das griechische Volk bisher hervorgebracht hat," und der

[1] H. Hunger, *Gnomon* 30 (1958), 285. [Korrekturzusatz 1973. Sternchen (*) hierunter verweisen auf das Postkriptum, S. 600 ff. Mit *Johannes Cuno* wird auf mein Buch über diesen Nürnberger Humanisten (in Vorbereitung) verwiesen. Nur mit Verfassernamen werden zitiert: Chr. G. Jöcher, *Allgemeines Gelehrten-Lexikon* (Leipzig 1750–51), und E. A. Cicogna, *Delle inscrizioni veneziane* (6 Bde., Venezia 1824–53). Korrekturzusätze stehen in eckigen Klammern.]

[2] R. Menge, "De Marci Musuri Cretensis vita studiis ingenio narratio," in *Hesychii Alexandrini Lexicon*, post Ioannem Albertum rec. M. Schmidt, 5 (Halis Saxonum 1868), 1–88; A. Firmin-Didot, *Alde Manuce et l'hellénisme à Venise* (Paris 1875), passim (vgl. Register); É. Legrand, *Bibliographie hellénique des XVᵉ et XVIᵉ siècles*, 1 (Paris 1885, Nachdruck Paris 1962), CVIII–CXXIV; F. Foffano, "Marco Musuro professore di greco a Padova ed a Venezia," *Nuovo Archivio Veneto*, 3,2 (1892), 453–74 und zuletzt D. J. Geanakoplos, *Greek Scholars in Venice. Studies in the Dissemination of Greek Learning from Byzantium to Western Europe* (Cambridge, Mass. 1962), 111–66; M. E. Cosenza, *Biographical and Bibliographical Dictionary of the Italian Humanists and of the World of Classical Scholarship in Italy, 1300–1800* (Boston, Mass. 1962), 3, 2399–2404; 5, 1225 f.

[3] U. v. Wilamowitz-Moellendorff, *Einleitung in die griechische Tragödie* (Berlin 1907), 220 = *Euripides Herakles*, 1 (4. unv. Abdruck, Darmstadt 1959), 221, vgl. Geanakoplos 165, 288.

durch seine Schüler wie kaum ein anderer für die Ausbreitung des griechischen Humanismus bis in die Länder jenseits der Alpen gewirkt hat. Bei meinen Arbeiten über die Vorlagen der Aldinen, mit denen die vorliegende Studie aufs engste zusammenhängt, waren die Bücher Alexander Turyns über weite Strecken meine Begleiter. So mögen diese Seiten, die sich mit den Handschriften aus der Feder oder dem Besitz des Musuros oder mit solchen, die wenigstens durch seine Hände gegangen sind, beschäftigen, eine Gegengabe für alles sein, was ich ihnen verdanke.

Im Jahre 1937 hat Artur Biedl[4] aus den Angaben von Vogel–Gardthausen[5] und Omont[6] eine Liste von Handschriften aufgestellt, die zeitweilig in der Hand des Musuros gewesen seien: Vat. gr. 1336; Vat. Pal. gr. 261, 287; Paris. gr. 2799, 2810, 2840, 2858, 2915, 2947; Mut. gr. 101, 127; Holkh. gr. 280. Aus dieser Liste hat er Paris. gr. 2858 als von Christoph Auer geschrieben ausgeschieden, dafür aber acht neue Handschriften hinzugefügt: Pal. gr. 275; Vat. gr. 41; Mut. gr. 143, 185; Vind. hist. gr. 33; Paris. gr. 2887; Ambros. gr. 12 und 60. Die Hälfte davon, nämlich Mut. gr. 101, 127, 143 und Paris. gr. 2799, 2810, 2840, 2887, 2915 und 2947; Holkh. 280 konnte ich in den Jahren 1968 und 1969 an Ort und Stelle prüfen. Ein Teil ist seit 1937 in der kodikologischen Literatur behandelt worden.

Den Vat. gr. 1336 mit Xenophons Hypomnemata, den Briefen der Sokratiker und des Isokrates, mit Dion Chrysostomos und den Prolegomena zu Aristeides hatte P. de Nolhac[7] auf Grund des Vergleiches mit Paris. 2799 "malgré le silence d'Orsini [seines früheren Besitzers] à cet égard et quelques différences assez sensibles entre les diverses parties de la copie" dem Musuros zugeschrieben. Aber schon G. Mercati[8] sah offenbar nur das Exlibris Μουσούρου καὶ τῶν χρωμένων

---

[4] *Byz. Zeitschr.* 37 (1937), 36–38.

[5] M. Vogel und V. Gardthausen, *Die griechischen Schreiber des Mittelalters und der Renaissance* (Zentralbl. f. Bibliothekswesen, Beih. 33, Leipzig 1909; Nachdruck Hildesheim 1966), 290 f.

[6] H. Omont, *Bibliothèque de l'École des Chartes*, 47 (1886), 291. Vgl. auch Legrand 1, CXXIV, 4.

[7] *La bibliothèque de Fulvio Orsini* (Paris 1887), 150 f. (Bibliothèque de l'École des Hautes Études, sciences philol. et hist. 74). Danach Vogel–Gardthausen 290 und J. Sykutris, *Philol. Wochenschr.* 48 (1928), 1292. Vgl. Geanakoplos 115, 19.

[8] *Codici latini Pico Grimani Pio e di altra biblioteca ignota del secolo XVI esistenti nell' Ottoboniana* etc. (Città del Vaticano 1938), 72 (Studi e Testi 75). Vgl. *Dio Chrysostomus* ed. I. de Arnim, 1 (Lipsiae 1892), S. XII.

und den lateinischen Index, denen das Datum *Florentiae 1493* beige-
schrieben ist, als autograph an. Die Identität der Schrift hat De
Marco [8a] bestätigt, aber inzwischen wurde Ianos Laskaris als Schreiber
des Parisinus erkannt. Nach Gallavotti und Turyn [9] ist der erste Teil
(die Memorabilien Xenophons) des Vat. gr. 1336 von Ianos Laskaris
geschrieben. P. Canart [10] hat nach eingehender Prüfung Musuros als
Schreiber ausgeschlossen und hält für ff. 1–70^v Ianos Laskaris für
wahrscheinlich und für den Rest des Codex für möglich.* Dazu würde
auch der Vermerk ἐν Φλωρεντία am Ende des Dion Chrysostomos
passen, da Laskaris in Florenz tätig war. Das Datum *Florentiae 1493*
deutet darauf hin, daß Musuros den Codex als Schüler des Laskaris
erworben hat, bevor er sich nach Venedig begab.[10a]

Der Pindarcodex Vat. gr. 41 (erstes Viertel des 14. Jh.),[11] der die
Olympischen und Pythischen Oden mit Scholien, die Batrachomyo-
machia 1–31 und Dionysios Periegetes 308–35 enthält, trägt auf dem
Verso des ersten Vorsatzblattes das Exlibris des Musuros: Μουσούρου
κτέαρ ἦν εὖτε τάδ᾽ ἐγράφετο. Die Handschrift hatte keinen Einfluß auf
die Editio Aldina von 1513;[12] es ist deshalb auch nicht wahrscheinlich, daß diese von Musuros besorgt wurde. Aldus würde es nicht
versäumt haben, dies zu vermerken, wie es sein Grundsatz war.[13] Man
kann auch nicht mit Irigoin (S. 401) auf die Aldinen des Sophokles und
des Euripides verweisen, um sicher zu sein, daß Musuros den Text der
Aldina wenigstens revidiert hat. Denn keine der beiden Ausgaben
geht, wie ich an anderem Orte zeigen werde,[14] auf Musuros zurück.

[8a] V. De Marco, "Gli scolii all'Edipo a Colono di Sofocle e la loro tradizione manoscritta," *Rendiconti Accad. di Archeol., Lettere e Belle Arti di Napoli*, n.s. 26, 1951 (Napoli 1952), 10.

[9] C. Gallavotti, "Planudea II," *Bollettino per la preparazione dell' Edizione Nazionale
dei classici greci e latini*, n.s. 8 (Roma 1960), 23, A. 12; vgl. Ch. G. Patrinelis, "Ἕλληνες
κωδικογράφοι τῶν χρόνων τῆς ἀναγεννήσεως," Ἐπετηρὶς τοῦ Μεσαιωνικοῦ Ἀρχείου 8/9,
1958/59 (Athen 1961), 93 f., 98.

[10] *Scriptorium* 17 (1963), 78 f.

[10a] Vgl. Geanakoplos 115. Musuros wäre demnach über die Orientreise des Laskaris
hinaus in Florenz geblieben.

[11] G. Mercati und P. Franchi de' Cavalieri, *Codices Vaticani Graeci*, 1 (Romae 1923),
37; A. Turyn, *De codicibus Pindaricis* (Cracoviae 1932), 36 f. (Archiwum Filologiczne, 11);
J. Irigoin, *Histoire du texte de Pindare* (Paris 1952), 176 ff. (Études et commentaires, 13).

[12] Irigoin 399 ff.; anders Turyn 36, 1; vgl. auch Geanakoplos 146, A. 133; 264, A. 44.

[13] Vgl. die Praefatio der Appendix der Statius-Ausgabe (1502) und Menge (oben
A. 2) 29, 33.

[14] "Die Editio princeps Aldina des Euripides und Ihre Vorlagen" (in Vorbereitung);
vgl. schon Menge, 29 f.

I. Österreichische Nationalbibliothek, GWT 2

(*see page* 489)

II. Inscription, Church of St. Nicholas, Bari

(*see page* 495)

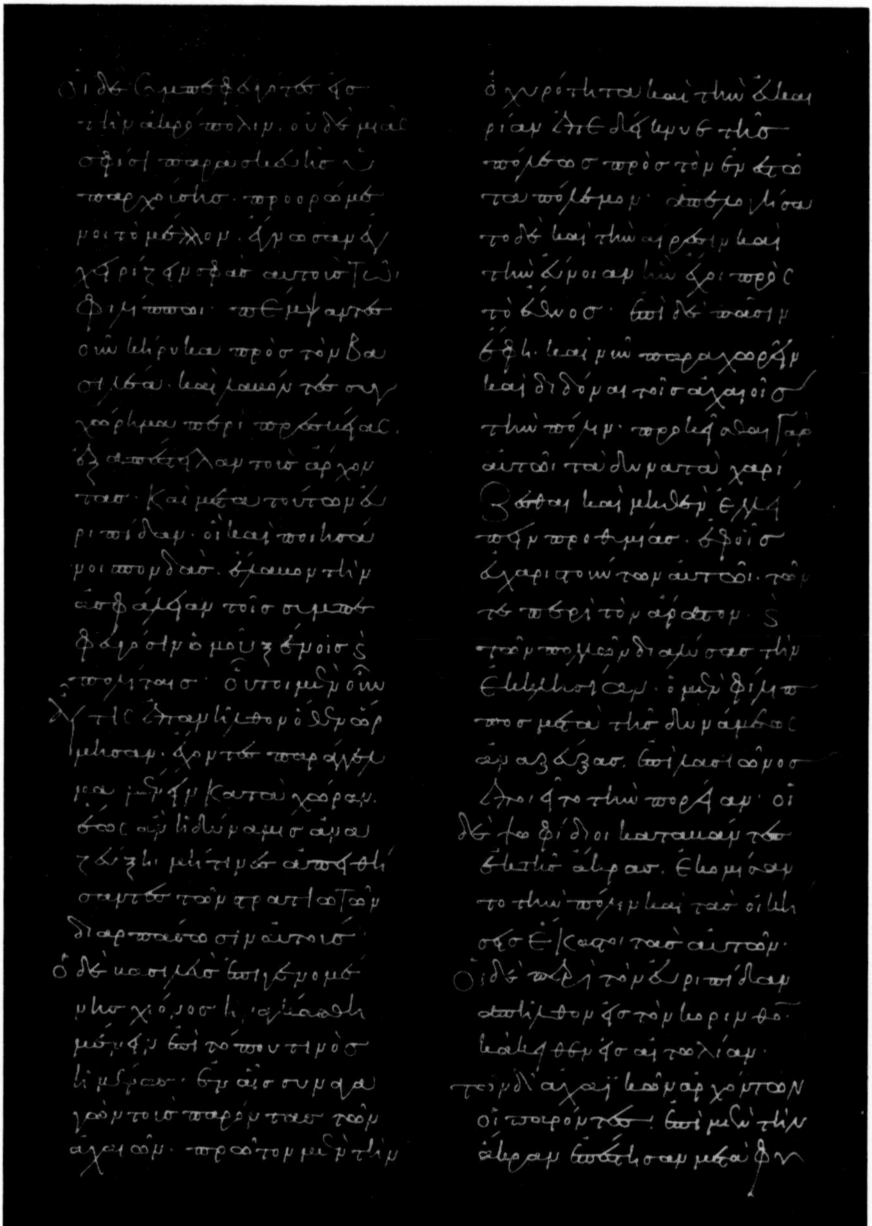

III. Codex Vatic. gr. 124 fol. 224^{v} (Polybius IV 72)
(*see page* 516)

a. Marc. gr. IV 26, fol. II^v
(*vgl. S. 585*)

b. Marc. gr. IX 5, fol. I^v
(*S. 590*)

c. Marc. gr. IV 29, fol. I^v
(*S. 601*)

IV. Drei Widmungen von der Hand des Markos Musuros
(*vgl. S. 602*)

ΙΩΑΝΝΟΥ ΣΤΟΒΑΙΟΥ ΕΚΛΟΓΩΝ ΑΠΟ
ΦΘΕΓΜΑΤΩΝ ΥΠΟΘΗΚΩΝ ΠΕΡΙ ΦΡΟ
ΝΗΣΕΩΣ ΛΟΓΟΣ Α· ΟΥ ΑΡΧΗ

VI. Marc. gr. IV 29, fol. 1ʳ (see page 605)

VII. Marc. gr. VII 9, fol. 143ʳ (*see page 602*)

Der berühmte Pal. gr. 287 (14. Jh.) war zwar im Besitze des Musuros, bildete aber nicht, wie immer wieder behauptet wird, die Vorlage der Euripides-Aldina von 1503. Sein Bearbeiter ist Musuros ebenfalls nicht gewesen.[14a] Die fragliche manus correctrix ist nicht die seine und der Schluß der Iphigenie in Aulis und der Anfang der pseudoeuripideischen Danae ist ebensowenig von ihm geschrieben.[15] Nur die Gedichte f. 2^v und 237^v und die Subskription unter letzterem, *X^o Iulii M.D.XI. Venetiis Musuri*[16] sind von seiner Hand. Bereits Wünsch hat darauf hingewiesen, daß die jambischen Trimeter in dem Diogenes-Laertios-Codex Pal. gr. 261, f. a^v, in denen die Besitzerschaft spielerisch zwischen Musuros, Κάρλος, den Freunden, der Tyche, und den χρώμενοι variiert wird,[17] von der gleichen Hand sind, und ebenso die drei Distichen im Pal. gr. 275, f. 8^v, die Κάρλος als Besitzer feiern.[18] Letzterer enthält Werke des Libanios und Michael Apostolis und ist laut Subskription f. 176^v von diesem selbst geschrieben: μιχαῆλος ἀποστόλης βυζάντιος μετὰ τὴν τῆς αὐτοῦ πατρίδος ἅλωσιν πενίᾳ συζῶν καὶ τόδε τὸ βιβλίον ἐξέγραψεν.[19]

[14a] Dazu ebenfalls in der A. 14 genannten Studie.

[15] So R. Wünsch, "Der pseudoeuripideische Anfang der Danae," *Rhein. Mus.* 51 (1896), 146; widerlegt von A. Turyn, *The Byzantine Manuscript Tradition of the Tragedies of Euripides* (Urbana 1957), 259, A. 244 (Illinois Studies in Language and Literature, 43). Schon Mercati a.O. hat offensichtlich nur die gleich zu erwähnenden Gedichte dem Musuros zugeschrieben.

[16] H. Stevenson, *Codices manuscripti Palatini Graeci Bibliothecae Vaticanae* (Romae 1885), 161 f.; *Euripidis Tragoediae* ex rec. A. Kirchhoffii, 1 (Berolini 1855), IX; Legrand CXIII f.; Wünsch 141–45; das Gedicht von f. 237^v teilweise faksimiliert bei Mercati, Tafel VI 2. Vgl. auch Turyn 259, A. 243, und *The Manuscript Tradition of the Tragedies of Aeschylus* (New York 1943; Nachdruck Hildesheim 1967), 69 f. (Polish Institute Series, 2); P. G. Mason, "The Manuscript Tradition of Euripides' Troades," *Class. Quart.* 43 (1950), 63 f. Daß in dem Gedicht Pal. gr. 287, f. 237^v entgegen den Angaben Kirchhoffs und Menges (S. 50) die letzten beiden Verse von der gleichen Hand sind wie die übrigen, zeigt das Facsimile bei Mercati mit aller Deutlichkeit. Ob *Musuri*, das mit hellerer Tinte in eigener Zeile steht, von derselben Hand ist, läßt Wünsch 141, A. 1 Ende (S. 142) offen.

[17] Stevenson 143; Wünsch 144. Der erste Trimeter ist nach Wünsch von einer anderen Hand, was ziemlich unwahrscheinlich ist. De Marco, "Gli scolii" 10, A. 1, sagt davon nichts. Ich habe den Codex nicht gesehen. [Vgl. auch G. Donzelli, "Per un'edizione di Diogene Laerzio: I codici VUDGS," *Boll. del Com. per la prepar. del' Edizione Nazionale dei classici greci e lat.*, N.S. 8 (Roma 1960), 105. E. Martini, *Analecta Laertiana 1*, Leipziger Studien z. class. Philol. 19 (1899), 93, der die Verse zitiert, meint, sie seien *diversis manibus* geschrieben.]

[18] Stevenson 150; Wünsch 144.

[19] Danach ist P. Canart, *Scriptorium* 17 (1963), 73, zu berichtigen.

Der Paris. gr. 2799 (um 1500), der Scholien zu Sophokles ohne Text enthält,[20] ist nicht, wie Omont und de Nolhac meinen, von Musuros geschrieben, sondern nach dem Urteil Turyns von Ianos Laskaris,* den auf ff. 21^r–22^v ein zweiter Schreiber, Aristobulos Apostolides, der Sohn des Michael Apostolis, ablöste. Er war in Musuros' Besitz, wie dessen eigenhändige Eintragungen auf f. A^r Μουσούρου καὶ τῶν χρωμένων und f. E^v Μουσούρου κτέαρ ἦν· εὖτε τάδ' ἐγράφετο lehren. Musuros verglich den Codex mit seiner Vorlage, Laur. 32,9, und ergänzte auf den Rändern einige Scholien und Glossen, die der Schreiber ausgelassen hatte.[21] Turyn vermutet, daß das Interesse des Musuros an den Sophokles-Scholien mit seiner Ausgabe des Sophokles bei Aldus Manutius (1502) zusammenhängt; aber Musuros ist als dessen Editor nicht erwiesen.[22] Herausgegeben wurden die Scholien erstmalig von Ianos Laskaris (Rom 1518), nach Turyn nach dem Codex L (Laur. 32,9).[23] Da aber Paris. gr. 2799 eine Abschrift von L ist und im Besitze des Laskaris war, könnte man vermuten, daß er und nicht der Laurentianus die Quelle des Druckes gewesen ist. Er zeigt aber ebensowenig wie dieser Spuren der Benutzung in der Druckerei.

Paris. gr. 2810,[24] der auf ff. 1–99^v Euripides Hekabe und Orestes mit alten Scholien enthält, trägt f. 100^v, am Ende seines ersten Teiles, der von zwei Händen des späten 15. Jh. geschrieben ist,[25] die Notiz: ἐκ τῆς μουσούρου δωρεᾶς, M.D.XII. XV Novemb.[26] Der zweite Teil der Handschrift, ff. 101^r–10^v (Herodiani excerptum de nominum prosodia) trägt am Ende, f. 110^v, die Subskription: *Absoluta diligenti lucubratione Venetiis, II Sextilis MDVIIII, quo ex*

---

[20] H. Omont, *Inventaire sommaire des manuscrits grecs de la Bibliothèque Nationale*, 3 (Paris 1888), 42; De Marco, "Gli scolii" 9 ff.; *Scholia in Sophoclis Oedipum Coloneum* rec. V. De Marco (Romae 1952), V, VI f.; A. Turyn, "The Manuscripts of Sophocles," *Traditio* 2 (1944), 30 f.; *Studies in the Manuscript Tradition of the Tragedies of Sophocles* (Urbana 1952), 184 f.; *Euripides* 228 mit A. 209.

[21] Bei rascher Durchsicht des Codex ist mir die Schrift des Musuros nicht aufgefallen.

[22] Vgl. oben S. 566.

[23] A. Turyn, "The Sophocles Recension of Manuel Moschopulos," *TAPhA* 80 (1949), 96.

[24] Omont, *Inventaire sommaire* 3, 43; Turyn, *Euripides* 353; vgl. Biedl (oben A. 4) 37, A. 3 von S. 36.

[25] Omont bezieht unrichtig die Datierung 1509 am Ende des zweiten Teils (Herodian), f. 110^v, auf den ganzen Codex.

[26] Legrand 1, CXXIV, 4; Vogel-Gardthausen 290, 4.

Patavio Concessimus fugiendi Gallicos, Germanicos Pontificiosque Tumultus gratia.[27] Der dritte Teil (112–22), von einem weiteren Kopisten geschrieben, enthält nach Omont: Anonymi opusculum de verborum conjugationibus. Das Herodian-Exzerpt (vielleicht auch das opusculum anonymi) gehörte offenbar einem Schüler des Musuros, der es durcharbeitete und mit Marginalnoten versah, nachdem die Universität Padua im Sommer 1509 infolge des Anrückens der Armeen der Liga von Cambrai ihre Pforten geschlossen hatte. Dieser Schüler, wer immer es sei, dürfte 1512 den Euripides-Text von Musuros zum Geschenk erhalten haben,[28] als dieser seine Lehrtätigkeit in Venedig wieder aufgenommen hatte.[29]

Der Paris. gr. 2947 (chart., 15. Jh.) mit drei Reden des Aischines, geschrieben von Michael Apostolis um 1465–70, trägt auf dem Verso des letzten Vorsatzblattes vorn den eigenhändigen Besitzvermerk des Musuros: μουσούρου κτῆμα. μᾶλλον καὶ τῶν χρωμένων.

Alle übrigen Parisini sind aus der Liste der Musuros-Handschriften zu streichen. Paris. gr. 2840 (Lycophronis Cassandra), der nach Omont[30] von Musuros kopiert ist, stammt wie 2799 von der Hand des Ianos Laskaris.* In dem von Aristobulos Apostolides geschriebenen Euripides-Codex Paris. gr. 2887[31] ist der auf dem Verso des letzten unnumerierten Folium zweimal geschriebene Vers Eurip. Cycl. 1 nicht von der Hand des Musuros,[32] sondern nach Turyn der des Ianos Laskaris, aus dessen Besitz die Handschrift auf Kardinal Ridolfi als Geschenk überging, was ein Distichon auf dem unteren Rand von f. 1ʳ bezeugt: Σοὶ τόδε θεῖε ʿΡίδολφ᾽ οὐκ εὐτελὲς εἴγε ποθεινὸν | ἀντ᾽ εὐεργεσίας Λάσκαρις ἀντίδοσιν. Paris. gr. 2915 (Eustathios Makrembolites' Hysmine und Hysminias, Briefe des hl. Johannes Chrysostomos)[33] enthält f. 102ᵛ das Distichon: Μάρκος ἐγὼ τάδε πάντα κελαινοτάτοιο ῥεέθρου | τὸν κάλαμον πλήσας γράψα φίλ᾽ (leg. μάλ᾽) ὀτραλέως und darunter von anderer Hand, vermutlich der des Bibliothekars des

---

[27] H. Omont, "Les mss grecs datés des XVᵉ et XVIᵉ siècles de la Bibliothèque Nationale et des autres bibliothèques de France," *Revue des bibl.* 2 (1892), 147, 20.

[28] Die Identität der Eintragungen f. 100ᵛ und f. 110ᵛ ist allerdings problematisch.

[29] Dazu Geanakoplos 142 f.

[30] *Inventaire sommaire* 3, 48.

[31] Omont 3, 55; Turyn, *Euripides* 370 f.

[32] So Wünsch 145, 1; danach Biedl a.O.

[33] Omont 3, 58.

Königs, Jean Boivin (1663–1726),[34] den Vermerk *Huius distichi auctor Marcus Musurus, non tamen scripsit totum codicem, sed folia tantum octo, ultima, quae videntur avulsa esse ab integro aliquo volumine.*[35] Aber weder die letzten acht Blätter noch das Distichon sind von der Hand des Musuros noch sonst etwas auf f. 102ᵛ, soweit es überhaupt leserlich ist.*

Im Mutin. gr. 101 (Aristoteles-Kommentare des Josephus Rhakendytes)[36] ist die Eintragung f. 97ᵛ *ἰω(άννης) ὁ Γρηγορο͞π(ουλος)* von der Hand des Johannes Gregoropulos, des Mitarbeiters des Aldus Manutius[37] und Freundes des Musuros. Die Hand des letzteren konnte ich nicht entdecken; jedenfalls ist die Subskription f. 175ᵛ nicht von ihm. Es muß offen bleiben, ob er Musuros gehört hat. Im Aristophanes-Codex Mut. gr. 127,[38] den Musuros für die Editio princeps des Aristophanes (1498) beigezogen hat,[39] ist der Besitzvermerk auf f. Iʳ *De miser Marco Musuro* autograph, ebenso derjenige von Mut. gr. 143 (Triodium)[40] f. 3ᵛ *Μουσούρου καὶ τῶν χρωμένων.* Der Mut. gr. 185 (Diodor I–V 84, 1),[41] von Michael Apostolis auf Kreta geschrieben (f. 215ᵛ *μιχαῆλος ἀποστόλης βυζάντιος μετὰ τὴν ἄλωσιν τῆς αὐτοῦ π(ατ)ρίδος πενία συζῶν, καὶ τήνδε τὴν βίβλον μισθῶ ἐν Κρήτῃ ἐξέγραψεν*), hat auf dem Vorsatzblatt vorn den gleichen autographen Vermerk wie Vat. gr. 41 und Paris. gr. 2799: *μουσούρου κτέαρ ἦν εὖτε τάδ᾽ ἐγράφετο.*

Der Vindob. hist. gr. 33 (Thukydides) ist um 1500 geschrieben, gehörte nach dem Exlibris f. VIʳ *μουσουρος κρης* dem Markos

---

³⁴ Omont 4 (1898), XI mit Facsimile Taf. VIII.

³⁵ Vgl. Wünsch 146, 1. Biedl 36, 3 auf S. 37 nimmt diese Notiz für bare Münze und hält auch mit Wünsch das Distichon für autograph, offenbar ohne den Codex selbst eingesehen zu haben, Vogel–Gardthausen 290 dagegen nur das Distichon. Vgl. auch Patrinelis (oben, A. 9) 98.

³⁶ V. Puntoni, "Indice dei codici greci della Biblioteca Estense di Modena," *Stud. ital.* 4 (1896), 450 = Ch. Samberger, *Catalogi codicum graecorum qui in minoribus bibliothecis Italicis asservantur,* 1 (Lipsiae 1965), 366.

³⁷ Firmin-Didot 455 f. und Index; Legrand 2, 263 ff.; Geanakoplos 109 und Index. Facsimile seiner Hand bei Legrand 2, 266 = M. I. Manusakas, Ἡ ἀλληλογραφία τῶν Γρηγοροπούλων χρονολογουμένη (1493–1501), Ἐπετηρὶς τοῦ Μεσαιωνικοῦ Ἀρχείου 5/6, 1955/56, 206.

³⁸ Puntoni 466 f. = Samberger 382 f.

³⁹ M. Sicherl, "Die Vorlagen der Editio princeps des Aristophanes" (in Vorbereitung).

⁴⁰ Puntoni 474 f. = Samberger 390 f.

⁴¹ Puntoni 497 f. = Samberger 413 f.

Musuros.[42] Ambros. gr. 12 (A 64 sup., olim T 307),[43] eine Pergament-handschrift des 13. Jh. mit der Aristotelischen Physik und der Paraphrasis des Themistios auf den Rändern, trägt f. 160ᵛ *litteris paene evanidis* den Vermerk μάρκου μουσούρου. Auf diesen Codex dürfte sich ein Brief des Musuros an den *Graecus monachus Lucas* beziehen, von dem uns eine Abschrift im Selest. 102, f. 249ʳ erhalten ist. Darin bittet er den Adressaten, ihm τὴν θεμιστίου παράφρασιν εἰς τὸ περὶ ἀρχῶν καὶ κινήσεων τοῦ φ(ιλοσόφ)ου zurückzusenden, also Themistios' Para-phrase zur Aristotelischen Physik.[43a] Das erste der drei Distichen des Musuros im Pal. gr. 275 steht auch im Ambros. gr. 60 (A 164 sup.)[44] auf der Innenseite des Vorderdeckels mit dem Vermerk μαρκου μ, was schon Martini und Bassi zweifelnd auf Musuros bezogen haben; ihnen waren die Verse des Palatinus offenbar entgangen. Die beiden Verse stehen darunter noch zweimal *alia lectione*. Der Codex enthält den Kommentar des Proklos zum ersten Buch der Elementa Euklids.

Die Zuschreibung des Holkh. gr. 280 an Musuros beruht auf einem Lesefehler; auf f. 23ᵛ ist nicht *Marcus Musurus* zu lesen, sondern *Marcus Morsinus*, wie ich im April 1968 selbst feststellen konnte. Musuros wird deshalb von R. Barbour[45] nicht als Vorbesitzer erwähnt. Daß der Urb. gr. 24 nicht von der Hand des Musuros sein kann, hatte bereits Biedl festgestellt. Nach Mercati[46] ist er von Johannes Skutariotes geschrieben.

Biedl erwähnt nicht den von Antonios Eparchos König Franz I. von Frankreich (1534–47) εἰς εὐχαριστίας σημεῖον dargebrachten und unter diesem gebundenen Paris. gr. 1774, einen Miszellancodex, in dem die gleiche Hand, von der in unserem Codex der Index auf f. Mᵛ und die oben ausgeschriebene Notiz im Paris. gr. 2915, f. 102ᵛ

---

[42] Vgl. H. Gerstinger, "Johannes Sambucus als Handschriftensammler," *Festschrift der Nationalbibliothek in Wien* (Wien 1926), 328, 379. H. Hunger, *Katalog der griechischen Handschriften der Österreichischen Nationalbibliothek*, 1 (Wien 1961), 35 (= Museion N.F. 4, 1, 1).

[43] Ae. Martini und D. Bassi, *Catalogus codicum Graecorum Bibliothecae Ambrosianae*, 1 (Mediolani 1906), 13 f.

[43a] Zum Titel der Aristotelischen Physik vgl. E. Zeller, *Die Philosophie der Griechen*, 2, 2⁴ (Leipzig 1921; Nachdr. Hildesheim 1963), 85, 1.

[44] Martini–Bassi 1, 74 f.

[45] "The Library at Holkham Hall," *The Bodleian Library Record*, 6 (1960), 606, Nr. 76.

[46] Mercati 72, 3.

stammt, also wohl Jean Boivin, auf dem Recto des ersten freien Vorsatzblattes (A) notierte: *Manu Constantii. Ant. Epar. | Musuri | Eparchi*, ebenso am oberen Rand des f. 1ʳ, wo κέβητος πίναξ θηβαίου beginnt, *An manu Musuri* (durchgestrichen, dahinter *J. Lascaris*).[47] Der Schreiber verrät selbst seine Unsicherheit; in der Tat ist der Pinax des Kebes nicht von Musuros geschrieben, und auch sonst habe ich dessen Hand nicht entdeckt. Nach Dain ist der Schreiber des Kebes Ianos Laskaris.[48]

Kurz nach dem Erscheinen von Biedls Abhandlung identifizierte G. Mercati die Hand des Musuros in den griechischen Exlibris des Alberto Pio von Carpi und den lateinischen Inhaltsangaben in dessen griechischen Handschriften.[49] Diese Notizen in zahlreichen Codices der Biblioteca Estense in Modena, aber auch anderwärts,[50] stammen aus der Zeit, als Musuros zum Hofstaat des Fürsten gehörte, das ist aus den Jahren 1499 und 1500 und darüber hinaus, wahrscheinlich bis zum Antritt seiner Professur in Padua (1503).

Darüber hinaus konnte er in Musuros den Schreiber des Vat. lat. 3067 erkennen, in einer lateinischen Übersetzung von Johannes Philoponos' Kommentar zu Aristoteles De generatione et corruptione aus dem Jahre 1505. Da es sich hier um das Konzept der Übersetzung handelt, war damit gleichzeitig Musuros als Übersetzer ermittelt.[51] E. Cranz[52] hat im Vat. lat. 4564 Musuros' Übersetzung von Alexander Aphrodisiensis in Topica gefunden; Teile dieser Handschrift können nach seiner Ansicht autograph sein.

Im Ambros. gr. 881 (= C 195 inf.), einer der Vorlagen des Demetrios Dukas für die Edition von Plutarchs Moralia bei Aldus

---

[47] C. C. Mueller, *De arte critica Cebetis Tabulae adhibenda* (Virceburgi 1877), 14 f.

[48] A. Dain, *Les manuscrits d'Onésandros* (Paris 1930), 71; vgl. Patrinelis 93. Nach Omont 2, 140 ist der Codex teilweise von Ianos Laskaris geschrieben. Keine Äußerung bei M. R. Dilts, "The manuscript tradition of Aelianus' *Varia Historia* and Heraclides' *Politiae*," *Trans. Am. Philol. Assn.* 96 (1965), 62. Die Schrift finde ich nicht identisch mit der des Paris. gr. 2799 (oben S. 568), eher mit der des Paris. gr. 2887 (Aristobulos Apostolides, s. oben S. 569).

[49] a.O. 62, 71 f., 203–20. Vgl. Geanakoplos 126 mit A. 63.

[50] a.O. 60 f. und das Facsimile von Vat. gr. 1314, f. 1ᵛ auf Taf. VI 3. Vgl. Turyn, *Euripides* 201 und 38, A. 57.

[51] a.O. 24, 57, 3; 74 und Tafel VI 1.

[52] "Alexander Aphrodisiensis," in *Catalogus translationum et commentariorum: Mediaeval and Renaissance Latin Translations and Commentaries*, annotated lists and guides ed. P. O. Kristeller, 1 (Washington 1960), 101.

1509,[53] hat Markos Musuros Ausgelassenes ergänzt, darunter drei längere Textpartien auf ff. 283ᵛ und 325ᵛ. Aus einer bisher nicht ermittelten Plutarch-Handschrift entnahm Musuros die Zitate, die in der Aristophanes-Aldina zu Nub. 447, 1189, Eq. 1016 in den Scholien stehen.[54] Ebenfalls bisher nicht identifiziert ist ein Codex seines Lehrers Musuros, aus dem der deutsche Dominikaner Johannes Cuno den Brief 38 des hl. Basileios (*PG* 32, 325–40) übersetzte. Auch einen Codex mit den Briefen Gregors von Nazianz hat Musuros besessen. Cuno hat sich daraus Abschriften gemacht.[55]

Auf einen autographen Brief im Vat. lat. 4105, f. 111 hat Mercati (S. 72) hingewiesen. Zehn griechische Originalbriefe befanden sich in einer Sammlung, die durch Johannes Cuno an Beatus Rhenanus gelangten, häufig den Besitzer wechselten und heute einer unbekannten Privatsammlung angehören. Die meisten wurden von Firmin–Didot und Legrand ediert, von einem davon ist ein lithographisches Facsimile dem Paris. suppl. gr. 924 beigegeben.[56] Dem Codex Arundel 550 im Britishen Museum ist ein gefalteter Zettel (ff. 75/84) eingeheftet, der, von der Hand des Musuros geschrieben, die Verse Sophokles Aias 646 f. enthält.[57] Die Druckvorlagen der von Musuros besorgten Ausgaben[58] sind

---

[53] M. Treu, *Zur Geschichte der Überlieferung von Plutarchs Moralia*, 3, 119 (Programm des Kgl. Friedrichs-Gymnasiums zu Breslau 1884, 15–30).

[54] K. Ziegler, *Die Überlieferung der vergleichenden Lebensbeschreibungen Plutarchs* (Leipzig 1907), 138.

[55] Sicherl, *Johannes Cuno.* [Inzwischen konnte ich nachweisen, daß es sich um einen einzigen Codex handelt, höchstwahrscheinlich Mut. gr. 229.]

[56] Sicherl a.O. Facsimiles haben publiziert A. A. Renouard, *Annales de l'imprimerie des Alde*³ (Paris 1834), nach S. 520 (= Paris. suppl. gr. 924, f. 44; vgl. Ch. Astruc und M.-L. Concasty, Bibliothèque Nationale, *Catalogue des manuscrits grecs*, 3: *Le supplément grec*, 3, Nos. 901–1371 [Paris 1960], 24); Firmin-Didot nach S. 500; Legrand 2, 321. Nicht autograph ist der Brief des Musuros im Ambros. gr. 843 (= C 6 inf.) ff. 1–3, den Chr. G. Patrinelis vor einiger Zeit ediert hat: Μάρκου Μουσούρου ἀνέκδοτος ἐπιστολή, Ὁ Βιβλιόφιλος (Athen), 6, 1962–63, 3–7 (vgl. *Scriptorium* 18 [1964], 322 f.). Für Auskunft danke ich dem Präfekten der Ambrosiana.

[57] Sicherl, *Johannes Cuno.* Ob es sich bei dem Gedicht des Markos Musuros auf dem Bifolium Modena, Archivio di Stato, Letterat. scritti greci Bᵃ 1, pars II.14 (E. Mioni, "I frammenti di manoscritti greci dell' Archivio di Stato di Modena," *Rassegna degli Archivi di Stato*, 21 [1921], 224 = Samberger 470; vgl. P. Canart, *Scriptorium* 17 [1963], 66) um ein Autograph handelt, habe ich nicht geprüft. Nach Mioni ist das Bifolium, das nur auf der ersten Seite beschrieben ist, "ut videtur, ab auctore ipso descriptum." [Das Stück ist autograph, wie die Photokopie zeigt, die ich am 18.9.73 erhielt.]

[58] Dazu Menge 14 f., 33 f.

nun zu einem beträchtlichen Teil wenigstens in Fragmenten festgestellt. Es sind der Selest. 347 (= K 1105e) und der Mut. gr. 127 für Aristophanes (1498); Paris. suppl. gr. 924, ff. 33–39 und wahrscheinlich Paris. suppl. gr. 212, ff. 163–85 für die Epistulae Graecae (1499),[59] der Marc. 622 für Hesychios (1514),[60] der Ricc. 29 für Pausanias (1516).[61] Vom Marc. gr. 622 abgesehen, den Musuros emendiert und für den Druck hergerichtet hat, ist in keinem dieser Codices die Hand des Musuros mit Sicherheit festzustellen.

Der Platonausgabe (1513)[62] hat Musuros eine Probe seines dichterischen Könnens beigegeben, ein griechisches Poem.[63] Die Vorlage des Platon-Textes, den Musuros *accurate recognovit cum antiquis conferens exemplaribus*, ist nicht gefunden.[64] Für den Kommentar des Alexander von Aphrodisias zu den Topica des Aristoteles (1513),[65] den Musuros *cum antiquis conferens exemplaribus accuratissime recognovit*, wird von M. Wallies[66] festgestellt, daß die Aldina meistens mit Paris. gr. 1874 zusammengehe. Der Codex zeigt weder Spuren von Musuros noch solche der Druckerei. Bei Athenaios (1514),[67] dessen Bücher Musuros *sic accurate recensuit collatos et cum multis*

[59] Astruc–Concasty a. O.

[60] *Hesychii Alexandrini Lexicon* rec. M. Schmidt, 4 (Halle 1862; Nachdruck Amsterdam 1965), XXVII–XXXI; *Hesychii Alexandrini Lexicon* rec. K. Latte, 1 (Hauniae 1953), XXIV–XXXIII. Zur Aldina vgl. Renouard, 66; S. F. W. Hoffmann, *Bibliographisches Lexicon der gesammten Literatur d. Griechen*, 2 (Leipzig 1839; Nachdruck Amsterdam 1961), 261; B. Botfield, *Praefationes et epistolae editionibus principibus auctorum veterum praepositae* (Cantabrigiae 1861), 304 f.; Legrand 1, 122–24; vgl. Firmin-Didot 377–79; Geanakoplos 154 f.

[61] A. Diller, "The Manuscripts of Pausanias," *Trans. Am. Philol. Assn.* 88 (1957), 181. Zur Ausgabe Renouard 76; Hoffmann 3, 48; Botfield 311 ff.; Menge 34, 68–71; Legrand 1, 143–50; vgl. Geanakoplos 158.

[62] Renouard 62; Hoffmann 3, 117 f.; Botfield 286 ff.; Legrand 1, 100 ff.; vgl. Firmin-Didot 342–54; Geanakoplos 149 f.

[63] Legrand 1, 106–12; Botfield 290–96; Firmin-Didot 491–98 (vgl. 351 ff.); mit der lateinischen Übersetzung des Zenobio Acciaioli, Menge 76–87. Vgl. Geanakoplos 150 ff. Eine Wort-für-Wort-Übersetzung, also nicht die Acciaiolis (Menge 50), findet sich handschriftlich im Laur. 35, 36, ff. 37–[30].

[64] Keine der bisher als solche bezeichneten Handschriften weist Spuren der Benützung in der Druckerei (Umbruchvermerke) auf.

[65] Renouard 62; Hoffmann 1, 115; Legrand 1, 99 f.; vgl. Firmin-Didot 367–70; Geanakoplos 154.

[66] *Commentaria in Aristotelem Graeca*, II 2 (Berlin 1891), XIII.

[67] Renouard 67; Hoffmann 1, 394 f.; Botfield 301 ff.; Legrand 1, 121 f.; vgl. Firmin-Didot 379–83; Geanakoplos 155.

exemplaribus et cum epitome, ut infinitis paene in locis eos emendaverit carminaque, quae veluti prosa in aliis legebantur, in sua loca restituerit, ist die Druckvorlage, ein Abkömmling des Marc. gr. 447 (= A) aus dem 15. Jh., verloren.[68] Für die 16 Reden des Gregorios Nazianzenos (1516),[69] die Musuros für den Druck *ex multis exemerat* und mit einer lateinischen Vorrede versah, deren Text er auch wohl rezensiert hat, ist die Druckvorlage noch nicht identifiziert.[70]

Wir wissen außerdem von einem Exemplar des Theokrit, das Musuros nach einem ἀρχαιότατον βιβλίον korrigiert und ergänzt hatte, das dem Παῦλος ὁ Βουκεφάλας (Bucarus, Capivacius: Paolo Capodivacca, gestorben 1553) von Padua gehörte und vermutlich beim Brand von dessen Villa unterging. Das von Musuros auch konjektural emendierte Exemplar erwarb Filippo Pandulfini in Venedig, als er die Vorlesungen des Musuros besuchte, und schickte es später an Eufrosino Bonini, der es seiner Ausgabe des Theokrit bei Giunta (Florenz 1516) zugrundelegte.[71] Für die Iuntina der Halieutika des Oppian (1515) hat Musuros das Exemplar des Bernardus Iunta mit Hilfe dreier Exemplare korrigiert; ebensoviele hat der Drucker selbst noch herangezogen.[72] Um welche Handschriften es sich im

---

[68] Vgl. G. Kaibel, *Athenaei Naucratitae Dipnosophistarum libri XV*, 1 (Lipsiae 1887), XIII (danach Wentzel, *RE* 2, 2 [1896], 2027); A. M. Desrousseaux und Ch. Astruc, *Athénée de Naucratis, Les Deipnosophistes I et II*, texte établi et traduit (Paris 1956), XLIII f.; M. Imhof, in *Geschichte der Textüberlieferung*, 1 (Zürich 1961), 303; G. Turturro, *Ateneo, I Deipnosofisti*, testo riv. con note e trad. ital. (Bari 1961), VII und besonders J. Irigoin, "L'édition princeps d'Athénée et ses sources," *Rev. ét. gr.* 80 (1967), 418–24.

[69] Renouard 75; Hoffmann 2, 174; Menge 64–68; Legrand 1, 136–43; Geanakoplos 157.

[70] A. Misier, "L'origine de l'édition de Bâle de Saint Grégoire de Nazianze," *Rev. de phil.* 27 (1903), 131 f.

[71] Legrand 1, CXVIII und 124 ff.; *Theocritus* ed. Gow (Cambridge 1950), 1, XLV, XLVII f.; A. Tovar, *Anales de Filol. clás.* 4 (1949), 15; Geanakoplos 144, A. 126; 156; C. Gallavotti ("Revisioni sul testo degli epigrammi di Teocrito," *Riv. filol. class.* n.s. 18 [1940], 241 ff.; *Theocritus quique feruntur Bucolici Graeci*[2] [Romae 1955], 315 ff.) glaubt, daß das *antiquissimum exemplar Patavinum* der Ambros. gr. 886 (= C 222 inf., saec. XIII/ XIV) sei und daß Musuros jedenfalls auch den Paris. gr. 2726, eine aus anderen Quellen ergänzte Abschrift des Ambrosianus, und eine zweite aus dem Ambrosianus genommene Abschrift gehabt habe; daraus sei jenes Exemplar entstanden, das er bei seinen Vorlesungen in Padua benützte. [Vgl. auch R. J. Smutny, "The Text History of the Epigrams of Theocritus," *U. Calif. Publ. Class. Philol.* 15, 2 (1955), 51 ff.]

[72] F. Fajen, *Überlieferungsgeschichtliche Untersuchungen zu den Halieutika des Oppian* (Meisenheim am Glan 1969), 22 (Beiträge z. klass. Philologie, 32). Die Ausgabe bei Renouard, Anhang XXXIX; Hoffmann 3, 11; Botfield 311; Legrand 1, 126 ff.; vgl. Geanakoplos 156.

einzelnen gehandelt hat, ist schwer auszumachen. F. Fajen glaubte mehrere davon bestimmen zu können: Salmant. M 31, Vindob. phil. gr. 135, Pal. gr. 40, ferner Matrit. 4642 oder Prag. bibl. univ. VIII. H. 36, sowie Marc. gr. 480 oder / und Laur. 86, 21, letzteres mit Vorbehalt. Diesen Identifizierungen wird man wenigstens in einigen Fällen schon wegen des heutigen Aufbewahrungsortes mit Reserve gegenüberstehen. Jedenfalls bedürften die fraglichen Handschriften einer eingehenden kodikologischen Untersuchung.

Daß Musuros an der Edition des Rhetores Graeci (1508–1509) beteiligt war, wie Schück[73] und neuerdings Geanakoplos (S. 140) behaupten, hat schon Menge (S. 31) mit guten Gründen widerlegt. Man kann hinzufügen, daß das griechische Vorwort des Dukas an Musuros im ersten Bande ein Mitwirken des Musuros geradezu ausschließt. Darin erwähnt er nur Aldus, seinen und des Musuros Freund, als Helfer.[74] Wenn Aldus in der Vorrede zum zweiten Bande sagt: *non solum profuisti semper et prodes assidue huic nostrae durae provinciae*,[75] so bedeutet das nichts anderes als wenn er in seiner Vorrede an Ianos Laskaris im 1. Bande sagt: *Cuius rei sum vel ipse testis a te in hac mea dura, curarumque et laborum plena provincia vel consilio vel re semper adiutus.* Desgleichen gibt es keine Anhaltspunkte dafür, daß Musuros für die Edition des Musaios[76] verantwortlich war. Dasselbe gilt, wie bereits oben S. 566 erwähnt, für Sophokles und Euripides. Die Ausgabe des Etymologicum Magnum bei Zacharias Kallierges (1499) wurde nicht von ihm besorgt.[77]

Während also wenigstens ein lateinischer Codex ganz und ein zweiter vielleicht teilweise von Musuros geschrieben sind, wobei es sich in beiden Fällen freilich nicht um Kopien, sondern um eigene Übersetzungen handelt, ist bisher keine Kopie eines griechischen Autors aufgetaucht. Und doch wissen wir, daß er in seiner Jugend

---

[73] J. Schück, *Aldus Manutius und seine Zeitgenossen in Italien und Deutschland* (Berlin 1862), 44.

[74] Legrand 87.

[75] Botfield 277; Legrand 88.

[76] Vgl. Menge 18 f. [K. H. Kost, *Musaios Hero und Leander*. Einleitung, Text, Übersetzung und Kommentar (Bonn 1971), 59 (Abh. z. Kunst-, Musik- und Literaturwiss. 88).]

[77] Dazu Menge 16–18; Geanakoplos 124 f.; vgl. auch R. Reitzenstein, *Geschichte der griechischen Etymologica* (Leipzig 1897), 220 f.; *RE* 6, 1 (1907), 815. Musuros nennen Legrand 1, S. CXI, Schmid–Stählin 2⁶, 2, 1082 und neuerdings auch H. Erbse, *Lexikon d. Alten Welt* (Zürich–Stuttgart 1965), 904. Die Vorlage ist verloren.

sich in Florenz auch als Kopist betätigt hat. Das geht aus einem Brief hervor, den er am 21. Juli 1499 aus Ferrara an seinen Freund Zacharias Kallierges in Venedig schrieb.[78] Diesem teilt er darin mit, daß ihm sogleich nach seiner Ankunft in Ferrara der Magister [Nicolaus] Leonicenus seine Galen-Handschriften gezeigt habe, von denen ein Teil von Musuros selbst in seinen jungen Jahren in Florenz geschrieben waren, ein anderer von Alexander Euemeros, also Alessandro Bondini,[79] dem Venediger Arzt und Mitarbeiter des Aldus Manutius bei der großen Aristoteles-Ausgabe (1495–98), zu der Leonicenus seine Werke des Aristoteles zur Verfügung stellte.[80] Der gelehrte Greis (Leonicenus) habe sie alle emendiert (διώρθωται) und war bereit, sie für den Druck zum Selbstkostenpreis abzugeben. Aus der Edition wurde freilich nichts. Die Opera Galeni kamen erst 1525 in der Officina Aldina heraus, und unter den Druckvorlagen sind bisher keine Handschriften des Musuros oder Leonicenus festgestellt worden.

Ziehen wir nun aus dem Gesicherten die Bilanz, so waren folgende Handschriften in Musuros' Besitz: Vat. gr. 41 und 1336; Pal. gr. 261, 275 und 287; Paris. gr. 2799, 2810 und 2947; Mut. gr. 127, 143, 185; Vindob. hist. gr. 33; Ambros. gr. 12 und 60. Die darin enthaltenen Autoren sind, geordnet nach literarischen Genera, die Dichter Aischylos (Pal. gr. 287), Sophokles (Pal. gr. 287) mit Scholien (Paris. gr. 2799), Euripides (Pal. gr. 287, Paris. gr. 2810), Aristophanes (Mut. gr. 127), Pindar (Vat. gr. 41), Theokrit; die Historiker Thukydides (Vindob. hist. gr. 33), Diodor (Mut. gr. 185); die Philosophen Xenophon (Vat. gr. 1336), Aristoteles' Physik mit dem Kommentar des Themistios (Ambros. gr. 12), Lukian (Pal. gr. 261), Diogenes Laertios (Pal. gr. 261), Proklos (Ambros. gr. 60); die Redner Aischines (Paris. gr. 2947), Dion Chrysostomos (Vat. gr. 1336), Aristeides (Vat. gr. 1336), Libanios (Pal. gr. 275); Briefliteratur (Sokratiker und Isokrates Vat. gr. 1336, Libanios Pal. gr. 275, Basileios, Gregor von Nazianz); byzantinische und liturgische Texte (Michael Apostolis Pal. gr. 275, Triodion Mut. gr. 143). Schreiber

---

[78] Firmin-Didot 516 f.; Legrand 2, 212; vgl. Legrand 1, CIX; Geanakoplos 123.

[79] Der Name Bondinis wird entweder zu Agathemeros (so Aldus im Vorwort des 1. Bandes der Aristoteles-Ausgabe und er selbst ebenda; vgl. auch Firmin-Didot 89) oder Euemeros (Firmin-Didot 67, 1) gräzisiert. Zu ihm vgl. auch Firmin-Didot 148 f., 415, 446 f.

[80] Vorwort zum 2. Band der Aristoteles-Ausgabe (1947), Botfield 199.

waren Michael Apostolis (Pal. gr. 275, Paris. gr. 2947, Mut. gr. 185), sein Sohn Aristobulos Apostolides = Aristobulos (Arsenios) Apostolis (Paris. gr. 2799, ff. 21^r–22^v) und Ianos Laskaris (Vat. gr. 1336, Paris. gr. 2799, 2840),* erstere kretische Landsleute des Musuros. Den ersten hatte Musuros vielleicht noch in seiner Jugend in Kreta kennengelernt,[81] der zweite war in der Heimat sein Lehrer gewesen,[82] mit dem dritten, seinem Lehrer in Florenz, verband ihn zeitlebens eine enge Freundschaft.[83]

Wir wissen, daß Musuros über einen Teil der genannten Autoren Vorlesungen an der Universität Padua gehalten hat,[84] und wir können annehmen, daß er auch entsprechende Handschriften dafür benützte, wenn auch schon von einigen gedruckte Ausgaben vorlagen. Das gilt für Aristophanes, Euripides, Pindar, Theokrit und wohl auch für Aristoteles. Anderseits ist bei mehreren Autoren, über die er nachweislich oder wahrscheinlich gelesen hat, bisher keine Musuros-Handschrift identifiziert worden, so bei Homer, Sophokles,[84a] der Griechischen Anthologie, Lukian, Philostrat und vielleicht auch noch anderen Schriften des Aristoteles als der Physik. Man kann annehmen, daß er sich hiefür der damals bereits vorliegenden gedruckten Ausgaben bediente. Vielleicht sind aber auch Vorsatzblätter von Handschriften dieser Autoren mit seinem Exlibris verlorengegangen.

Die Bibliothek des Musuros wurde nach seinem Tode zerstreut. Zwei Codices (Paris. gr. 2799 und 2947) finden wir später im Besitze seines Freundes Ianos Laskaris (ca. 1444—7.12.1534),[85] mit dem Musuros in seinem letzten Lebensjahre am Griechischen Kolleg in Rom zusammengearbeitet hatte. Beide tragen das Sigel *Λ*^{σ}*(= Λάσκαρις)* und die entsprechenden Signaturen seiner Bibliothek *N XXXVIIII de la 8^a und N° 37 Ca. X^{ma}* von der Hand seines

[81] Zum Todesjahr des Michael Apostolis vgl. Geanakoplos 107.

[82] Geanakoplos 111 f., 161. Das Verhältnis zu ihm war offenbar nicht herzlich und später durch Rivalität getrübt, vgl. Geanakoplos 177.

[83] B. Knös, *Un ambassadeur de l'hellénisme: Janus Lascaris et la tradition greco-byzantine dans l'humanisme français* (Upsala–Paris 1945), 18 f., 27, 150 ff.; Geanakoplos 114 f., 131, 147, 158 f., 161 f.

[84] Sicherl, *Johannes Cuno.*

[84a] Wohl enthält der Pal. gr. 287 fünf Tragödien, aber es fehlen gerade zwei der byzantinischen Trias, die wohl allein in Betracht kommt, Aias und Oidipus Tyrannos.

[85] G. Mercati, *Rhein. Mus.* 65 (1910), 318 = *Opere minori,* 3 (Città del Vaticano 1937), 185 (Studi e Testi, 78).

Sekretärs Matthaios Devaris. Sie sind an den entsprechenden Stellen des von Devaris nach Laskaris' Tode aufgestellten Inventars seiner Bibliothek aufgeführt.[86] (Von einem dritten, Paris. gr. 2810, vermutet Turyn,[87] daß Musuros ihn Laskaris geschenkt haben könnte, weil er später dem Kardinal Ridolfi gehörte.) Mit einer großen Zahl von Laskaris-Handschriften gingen sie in die Sammlung des Mediceer-Kardinals Ridolfi (1501–50) ein. Auf dessen Bibliothek beziehen sich die Zusätze *duodecime* und *undecime*, von der Hand des Nikolaos Sophianos. Matthaios Devaris, der nach Laskaris' Tode Bibliothekar der Kardinals wurde, hat mit Nikolaos Sophianos auch den Katalog von dessen Sammlung redigiert.[88] Mit Caterina de' Medici (1519–89), der Gemahlin Heinrichs II. von Frankreich (1547–59), kam die Sammlung Ridolfis nach Paris und fand nach deren Tod ihren Platz in der Bibliothèque du Roi.[89]

Die meisten Handschriften des Musuros finden wir im 16. Jh. in Venedig. Der Pal. gr. 287 ist nach den eigenhändigen Versen des Musuros auf f. 2^v und f. 237^v Eigentum eines gewissen Κάρλος gewesen, dem nach ähnlichen Eintragungen auch Pal. gr. 275 und als Mitbesitzer Pal. gr. 261 gehört haben.[90] Dieser Κάρλος war jedenfalls ein Freund, vielleicht ein Lieblingsschüler des Musuros, dessen Bücher auch von seinen Freunden mitbenutzt wurden. Nach der Subskription des Musuros im Pal. gr. 287, f. 237^v unter dem Gedicht *X Julii M.D.XI. Venetiis Musuri* scheint es so, daß der Codex aus dem Besitz des Κάρλος auf Musuros übergegangen ist.

[86] P. de Nolhac, "Inventaire des manuscrits grecs de Jean Lascaris," *Mélanges d'archéologie et d'histoire*, 6 (1886), 259, Nr. 98; 258, Nr. 89. Vgl. De Marco, "Gli scolii" 11, A. 3; Turyn, *Sophocles* 185.

[87] *Euripides* 353.

[88] Vgl. G. Mercati, "Indici di manoscritti del cardinale Niccolò Ridolfi," *Mélanges d'archéol. et d'hist.* 30 (1910), 51–55 = *Opere minori*, 3, 126–29; H. Omont, "Un premier catalogue des manuscrits grecs du cardinal Ridolfi," *Bibl. de l'École des Chartes*, 49 (1888), 309 ff. (dazu Ch. Astruc und M. L. Concasty, *Supplément grec*, 3 (Paris 1960), 228, Nr. 1097); B. de Montfaucon, *Bibliotheca bibliothecarum manuscriptorum nova* (Paris 1739), 2, 766–78. Vgl. auch Turyn, *Euripides* 88, 140, 142, 146, 147, 220, 371, 372. Zu den Signaturen vgl. die Facsimile bei Omont, *Inventaire sommaire* 1, S. XV und *Fac-similés* (unten A. 109), Taf. 40.

[89] M. Sicherl, *Die Handschriften, Ausgaben und Übersetzungen von Iamblichos De mysteriis* (Berlin 1957), 143 (Texte u. Unters. z. Gesch. d. altchristl. Lit. 62), wo zur Literatur zu ergänzen ist: R. Ridolfi, "La biblioteca del card. N. Ridolfi (1501–1550)," *La Bibliofilia*, 31 (1929), 173–93; ders. *Enciclopedia Cattolica*, 10 (1953), 890–92.

[90] Vgl. oben S. 567.

Dieser Κάρλος ist nach einer probablen Vermutung G. Mercatis der spätere venezianische Diplomat Carlo Cappello (+ 1546),[91] dem Musuros später bei seinem Weggang von Venedig nach Rom u.a. zwei Codices Bessarions, die er gekauft hatte (Apsyrto et la Defensione di Platone) anvertraute.[92] Einer von den Palatini (275) gehörte nachher einem Georgios Balsamas, der wohl mit dem anderwärts bekannten Georgios Balsamos identisch ist, dem Korrespondenten des Georgios Korinthios und Vertrauten des Kardinals Salviati (1490–1553), eines Neffen Papst Leos X. und vielleicht Schülers des Griechischen Kollegs in Rom. Die Pal. gr. 261, 275 und 287 gehören zu den mit *cyp.* signierten Handschriften der Palatina und wurden nach der einleuchtenden Erklärung P. Lehmanns dem Ulrich Fugger von dem Cyprioten Hieronymus Tragodistes aus Venedig geliefert.[93] Mit der Sammlung Fuggers kamen sie von Augsburg nach Heidelberg (1567) und später (1623) in die Vaticana.

Von den beiden Ambrosiani war der eine (12) im Besitze des Erzbischofs von Philadelphia, Gabriel Severos (1541–1616), einer der hervorstechendsten Persönlichkeiten der griechischen Kolonie in Venedig, die ihr hohes Amt in der lydischen Diözese nie angetreten hat.[94] Von diesem wurde er 1603 von Federico Borromeo gekauft.[95] Der andere (60) kommt mit der Sammlung des Gian-Vincenzo Pinelli aus Padua (1535–1601) auf abenteuerlichem Wege nach Mailand und geht 1609 in die Ambrosiana ein.[96]

Die Mutinenses gr. 101, 143, 185 und vielleicht auch 127 kommen aus der Sammlung des Fürsten Alberto Pio von Carpi (†1531), dessen Lehrer und Bibliothekar Musuros einst gewesen war. Von ihm erbte sie sein Neffe, Kardinal Rodolfo Pio di Carpi (†1564). Neun Jahre nach dessen Tode (1573) erwarb seine griechischen

[91] J. Chr. Adelung, *Fortsetzung und Ergänzungen zu Chr. G. Jöchers allgemeinem Gelehrten-Lexicon*, 2 (Leipzig 1787; Nachdr. Hildesheim 1960), 93.

[92] Mercati, *Codici latini Pico Grimani Pio* (oben A. 8), 72, 2; danach Geanakoplos 159.

[93] K. Christ, "Zur Geschichte der griechischen Handschriften der Palatina," *Zentralbl. f. Bibliothekswesen*, 36 (1919), 54, 66; P. Lehmann, *Eine Geschichte der alten Fuggerbibliotheken*, 1 (Tübingen 1956), 112–14, 135 (Schwäb. Forschungsgem. bei d. Komm. f. Bayer. Landesgesch. 4, 3, Studien z. Fuggergesch. 12); 2 (Tübingen 1960), 79, 86, 88, 93, 96, 102.

[94] Legrand 2, 144–51.

[95] Martini–Bassi XIII.

[96] Literatur bei Sicherl, *Die Handschriften...von De myst.* (vgl. A. 89), 147, 1.

Handschriften Herzog Alfonso II. d'Este von Ferrara (1559–97), von wo sie die Este nach dem Verlust von Ferrara an den Kirchenstaat (1598) in ihre neue Residenz Modena überführten.[97] Auch der Faszikel mit dem Gedicht des Musuros im Archivio di Stato in Modena[98] kommt aller Wahrscheinlichkeit nach wenigstens zum Teil aus der Bibliothek des Kardinals Rodolfo Pio und Alfonsos II. Der Mut. gr. 127, welcher in den Verzeichnissen Albertos und Rodolfos nicht eindeutig zu identifizieren ist, trägt mehrere Exlibris, die auf Venedig weisen: *Andronico Manolesso, Alvise barbaro, fran(cisci) barbari veneti patricii.*

Der oben erwähnte Georgios Korinthios,[99] der Neffe des Aristobulos Apostolis, ist seinerseits mit dem Sammler Fulvio Orsini (1529–1600), der den Musuros-Codex Vat. gr. 1336 besaß, sehr befreundet. Mit Orsinis Sammlung kam diese Handschrift 1602 in den Vatikan.[100] Der Vindobonensis schließlich hatte sich nach Süditalien verirrt. In Otranto kaufte ihn im Jahre 1563 Johannes Sambucus von einem Cosmas um 6 Dukaten (f. 1r). Unter dem Bibliothekar Hugo Blotius (1575–1608) gelangte er in die Wiener Hofbibliothek.[101]

Der Codex unicus des Hesych, Marc. gr. 622, den Musuros für die Edition bearbeitet hat, ist nicht sein Eigentum gewesen. Jacobus Bardellone, *nobilitatis Mantuanae decus, graece et latine doctissimus, mathematicarumque disciplinarum longe peritissimus,*[102] hatte ihn dem Aldus Manutius für den Druck zur Verfügung gestellt.[103] Der Codex war später im Besitze des Venediger Patriziers Giovanni Battista Recanati. Dessen Testament zufolge ging er mit 46 weiteren griechischen Handschriften 1734 in die Marciana ein.[104]

---

[97] Mercati 39 f. 243 f. D. Fava, *La biblioteca Estense nel suo sviluppo storico* (Modena 1925), 150 ff., 165 ff.

[98] Oben A. 57, Mioni 217 = Samberger 463.

[99] Zu diesem vgl. Legrand 1, CLI, 2; Biedl 37; Turyn, *Sophocles* (1952) 173. Zu seinen Handschriften Vogel–Gardthausen 78; M. Wittek, *Scriptorium* 7 (1953), 288. Einen Katalog seiner Handschriften bereitet David E. Pingree (Chicago) vor.

[100] P. de Nolhac, *La bibliothèque de Fulvio Orsini* (Paris 1887; Bibl. de l'École des Hautes Études, sc. philol. et hist. 74).

[101] H. Gerstinger, "Johannes Sambucus" (oben A. 42), 328, 379; Hunger 35.

[102] Cosenza 1, 422; 5, 200a (unter "Bardulo").

[103] Vorrede des Aldus, Renouard 66; Botfield 304; Firmin-Didot 378; Legrand 1, 123.

[104] *Bibliothecae Divi Marci Venetiarum codices graeci manuscripti* rec. E. Mioni, 2: Codices qui in sextam, septimam atque octavam classem includuntur (Roma 1960), IV. Im

Noch bevor ich die kritische Sichtung der Reste der Bibliothek des Markos Musuros und seines handschriftlichen Nachlasses in Angriff nahm, entdeckte ich im Juli 1968 in der Marciana in Venedig eine homogene Gruppe von etwa zwanzig Handschriften, die durch seine Hände gegangen sind; nicht zuletzt durch diese Entdeckung wurde diese Untersuchung angeregt. Die erwähnten Handschriften tragen auf der Innenseite des Vorderdeckels oder einem Vorsatzblatt griechische Widmungen, die von der Hand des Musuros stammen. Ein minutiöser Vergleich mit den Facsimile bei Mercati schließt alle Zweifel aus. Die Beschreibung der Schrift des Musuros in ihrem allgemeinen Charakter und ihren Besonderheiten durch Mercati (72) trifft auch hier vollkommen zu: *spontaneità, sicurezza e leggerezza della mano, la tendenza a fare ritte e spesso leggermente inclinate all'indietro le lettere e a terminare in uncino di forma particolare le aste scendenti sotto le linee, e nella scrittura greca la forma delle legature e segnatamente del s finale, che è falcato, con l'appendice di un semicerchietto al basso.* Dieses letzte Detail ist ein besonderes individuelles Kennzeichen seiner Schrift, dem ich sonst nirgends begegnet bin. Später, bei der Verarbeitung meines Materials, stellte ich fest, daß die Hand des Musuros in der Widmung des Euripides-Codex Marc. gr. IX 10 bereits von Alexander Turyn erkannt worden war.[105]

Auf die ersten dieser Handschriften bin ich im Zuge meiner Forschungen nach den Vorlagen der Aldinen mehr zufällig gestoßen. Da die Widmungen für die Beziehungen des Musuros zu den Patriziern von Venedig und offenbar für seinen Schülerkreis wichtig schienen, bin ich ihnen weiter nachgegangen. Durch den Katalog der Classes VI–VIII von Mioni ließen sich alle darin enthaltenen Codices rasch feststellen. Es zeigte sich, daß sie fast alle von dem Schreiber Kaisar Strategos[106] hergestellt sind und alle aus dem Kloster SS. Giovanni e Paolo kommen. Ich habe daraufhin alle von Kaisar Strategos geschriebenen Handschriften nach dem maschinenschriftlichen Index der Classes I–V von Mioni im Handschriftensaal der Marciana angesehen und meine Enquête

---

Catalogus Codicum mss. quorum amplius CC a Joanne Baptista Recanato Patricio Veneto Publicae Venetiarum Bibliothecae Testamento relicti (Marc. lat. XIII 77) ist unser Codex als Nr. IX zweimal beschrieben, auf f. 4ʳ und f. 6ᵛ.

[105] *Euripides* 275 f.

[106] Vogel–Gardthausen 224 f.; Patrinelis 110; P. Canart, *Scriptorium* 17 (1963), 81 f.

aufgrund des Katalogs von Berardelli ergänzt.[107] Die Sichtung der Beschreibungen weiterer Kaisar-Strategos-Codices in anderen Bibliotheken brachte keine neuen Ergebnisse. Von der nun folgenden Liste* habe ich die Nummern 1–12 selbst in der Hand gehabt. Die Angaben zu den übrigen habe ich der Literatur, besonders dem Katalog Berardellis, entnommen; Ergänzungen lieferte mir freundlicherweise die Marciana,[108] wofür ihr hier mein Dank ausgesprochen sei.

1) Marc. gr. IV 8 (coll. 1152) = SS. Iohannis et Pauli 7; Berardelli S. 178. Membr. 295 × 205 mm., ff. 292. Enthält Ἀλεξάνδρου Ἀφροδισιέως ἀποσημειώσεις εἰς τοὺς σοφιστικοὺς ἐλέγχους in zwei Exemplaren, ff. 1–134 und ff. 159–295, dazwischen, ff. 135–57, dieselbe Paraphrase wie im Paris. gr. 1917, ff. 538ᵛ–50ʳ, vgl. M. Wallies, Comm. in Aristot. Graeca, II 3 (Berolini 1898), XIII. Nach Berardelli und Mioni von Kaisar Strategos geschrieben. Es sind zwei Hände zu unterscheiden. Die erste, ff. 1–157ᵛ, ist sehr ähnlich, vielleicht identisch mit der des Aristobulos Apostolides bei Omont[109]; Unterschiede sind in der Form des τ festzustellen.* Die zweite, ff. 159–295ʳ, beginnt mit neuer Lagenzählung. Im ersten Teil sind die Titel in Majuskeln, rot; für die fehlenden Initialen ist Raum freigelassen. Im zweiten sind die Titel in Minuskeln; kleine rote Initialen. Auf der Innenseite des Vorderdeckels von der Hand des Musuros: Τῶ θεοῖς καὶ ἀνθρώπις (sic) πεφιλημένῳ κυρίῳ Λαυρεντίῳ πριουλλίῳ τῶν φιλομούσων εὐπατριδῶν.

Um welchen Lorenzo Priuli es sich handelt, ist nicht auszumachen. Marino Sanuto erwähnt in den Jahren 1503 bis 1524 nicht weniger als vier Träger dieses Namens, von denen zwei eine bedeutende Rolle gespielt haben. Der eine davon ist der Sohn des Pietro procuratore; er war Capo dei Dieci, Cassiere dei Dieci, Consiglier ducale, Provveditore sopra il recupero del danaro, Savio agli

---

[107] [D. M. Berardelli], "Codicum omnium graecorum, arabicorum, aliarum linguarum orientalium, qui in Bibliotheca SS. Ioannis et Pauli Venetiarum asservantur, catalogus," in *Nuovo raccolto d'opuscoli scientifici e filologici*, 20 (Venezia 1779), 161–240. Auf Berardelli beruhen die Angaben bei Vogel–Gardthausen 225.

[108] Brief vom 6. Mai 1969. Es handelt sich in erster Linie um den Wortlaut der Zueignungen in Marc. gr. IX 5, IX 12, XI 13 und XI 14 mit dem Vermerk: Tali dediche sembrano della stessa mano che ha scritto la dedica nel verso del foglio di guardia del cod. gr. IV 8 (= 1152), come pure della stessa mano è forse la dedica del cod. gr. IX 8 (= 1039).

[109] H. Omont, *Fac-similés de manuscrits grecs des XVᵉ et XVIᵉ siècles d'après les originaux de la Bibliothèque Nationale* (Paris 1887), Taf. 5.

ordini[110] und starb am 16. September 1518 (Diarii 26, S. 54). Der andere ist der Sohn des Alvise, des Sohnes des Nicolò; er war Camerlengo di commun (22, 576: September 1516), Oratore (Gesandter) in England (33, 507: November 1522), Oratore a la Cesarea et Catholica Maesta (35, 73: Oktober 1523). Außerdem werden erwähnt Lorenzo, Sohn des Girolamo, des Sohnes des Lorenzo (32, 128: November und Dezember 1521) und Lorenzo, Sohn des Sier Francesco (22, 170 f.: April 1516).

2) Marc. gr. IV 10 (coll. 833) = SS. Iohannis et Pauli 9; Berardelli S. 179. Membr. in fol., ff. 141. Enthält ff. 1–87ᵛ Alexander Aphrodisiensis, Quaestiones naturales et ethicae, ff. 88ʳ–111ʳ De fato,[111] ff. 111ᵛ–41ʳ Galeni Definitiones medicae (ὅροι ἰατρικοί), sehr sauber, mit breiten Rändern geschrieben, nach Berardelli und Mioni von Kaisar Strategos. Titel rot, am Anfang fehlt jeweils die Initiale. Auf f. Iᵛ von der Hand des Musuros: Τῷ εὐφυεῖ καὶ ἐλευθέρου τετυχηκότι ἀγωγῆς νεανίσκω ἀντωνίω τῷ τοῦ μεγαλοπρεποῦς ἱππέως ἀλοεισίου μοκαινίκου τῶν τῆς γερουσίας εὐπατριδῶν.[112]

Über diesen Sohn des Alvise Mocenigo, *illustre per la gloria militare durante la guerra di Cambray*, 1501 zum *Savio agli ordini eletto*, 1502/3 Gesandter bei Kaiser Maximilian I., der ihn 1504 zum Ritter schlug,[113] berichtet Marino Sanuto,[114] daß er als Schüler des Raphael Regius, *lector publico conduto a stipendio di la signoria nostra*, im Alter von 17 Jahren am 22. November 1514 in der Kirche S. Moixe vor einem illustren Publikum eine Rede *De laudibus eloquentiae* hielt. Später Senator und seit 1523 durch 35 Jahre Procurator, starb er 1540 oder 1541 und wurde in der Kirche S. Lucia begraben.[115] Die Ausgabe des Joannes Jovianus Pontanus bei den Nachfolgern des Aldus (1518) ist ihm gewidmet. Francesco d'Asola sagt in der Praefatio, daß er Pontanus sehr geschätzt und ein Bild von ihm in seiner Bibliothek gehabt habe.[116] Sein Vater Alvise, den Blume als

---

[110] Vgl. Sanuto, *Diarii* (unten A. 114), Register der Bände 5–26.

[111] Druckvorlage der Ausgaben Trincavellis von 1536 und 1534.

[112] Nach I. Bruns, der *Suppl. Aristot.* 2, 2 (1892), XX diese Widmung ausschreibt, ist der Codex aus dem 16. bis 17. Jh. (!).

[113] Cicogna 2, 154–56 und passim. Vgl. auch Cosenza 3 (1962), 2329.

[114] *I diarii di Marino Sanuto (1496–1533)*, ed. R. Fulin, F. Stefani, N. Barozzi, G. Berchet, M. Allegri (Venezia 1879–1903), 19, 184.

[115] Cicogna 2, 153.

[116] Renouard 85.

Büchersammler erwähnt,[117] hatte Aldus Manutius den wertvollen Plinius-Codex aus Paris mitgebracht, nach dem die Aldina 1508 gedruckt wurde.[118]

3) Marc. gr. IV 26 (coll. 1442) = SS. Iohannis et Pauli 33, Berardelli S. 194 f. Membr. 330 × 218 mm., ff. 332. Enthält Sextus Empiricus (vollständig).[119] Die ff. 1–76 sind sauber mit breiten Rändern geschrieben von Kaisar Strategos (f. 76ᵛ θ(εο)ῦ τὸ δῶρον. ἠδὲ καίσαρος πόνος τοῦ στρατηγοῦ). Die ff. 77–331ᵛ schrieb eine zweite Hand, wie es scheint, die der des Vindob. philos. gr. 264[120] ähnlich, aber wohl nicht mit ihr identisch ist.* Raum für Titel und Initialen ausgespart, aber roter Titel in Minuskeln von erster Hand über freiem Raum f. 24ᵛ. Auf dem Verso des zweiten Vorsatzblattes von der Hand des Musuros: Τῶ μεγαλοπρεπεῖ νεανία κυρίω ἰωάννη κορνηλίω τῶ γεωργίου μὲν τοῦ ἐπιφανοῦς υἱῶ τῆς δὲ κυπρίων βασιλίσσης αἰκατερίνης ἀδελφιδῶ (Plate IV a).

Danach ist der Adressat der Sohn des Giorgio Cornaro und Neffe von dessen Schwester Caterina Cornaro, der Königin von Cypern, die die Insel gegen die Herrschaft von Asolo an die Republik Venedig abtrat. In Asolo residierte sie von 1489–1509 und machte dort ihren Hof zu einem Mittelpunkt der Poesie und Literatur. Unter der Bedrohung der kaiserlichen Truppen floh sie nach Venedig, wo sie 1510 starb.[121]

4) Marc. gr. V 4 (coll. 544) = SS. Iohannis et Pauli 41; Berardelli S. 197 f. Membr. 385 × 275 mm., ff. 310. Enthält zahlreiche Schriften Galens. Ganz von der Hand des Kaisar Strategos geschrieben (f. 310ʳ θ(εο)ῦ τὸ δῶρον, ἠδὲ καίσαρος πόνος).[122] Breite Ränder; für die fehlenden Titel und Initialen ist breiter Raum ausgespart. Auf der Innenseite des Vorderdeckels auf angeklebtem Blatt von der Hand des Musuros: Τῶ πανσόφω καὶ παντοίαις ἀρεταῖς κατηγλαισμένω περιπατητικῶ κυρίω γασπάριδι τῶ καταρηνῶ τοῦ εὐπατριδῶν τάγματος θεοειδεῖ νεανία.

---

[117] *Iter Italicum* 1, 241; vgl. Vogel–Gardthausen 473.

[118] Vgl. Firmin-Didot 305 ff.; Pasquali, *Storia della tradizione e critica del testo* (1952), 58. Ein Fragment des Parisinus glaubten E. A. Lowe und E. K. Rand im Besitz von J. P. Morgan gefunden zu haben, vgl. die Literatur dazu bei M. Schanz und C. Hosius, *Geschichte der römischen Literatur*, 2⁴ (München 1934), 672 (Hdb. d. Alt. 8, 2, 4).

[119] H. Mutschmann, *Rhein. Mus.* N.F. 64 (1909), 246.

[120] Sicherl, *Die Handschriften...von Iamblichos De mysteriis*, 38.

[121] *Enc. Ital.* 4 (1949), 961; zu Georgio Cornaro ebd. 11 (1949), 418. Vgl. Cicogna (Register); H. Kretschmayr, *Geschichte von Venedig*, 2 (1930; Neudruck Aalen 1964), 389–92, 426; Cosenza 2 (1962), 1100.

[122] Vgl. E. Wenkebach, *CMG* V 10, 3 (1951), X.

Der Adressat ist offenbar der spätere Kardinal Gasparo Contarini (1483–1542)[123] aus der alten und weitverzweigten venezianischen Adelsfamilie der Contarini, der seit 1501 in Padua Philosophie und Naturwissenschaften studierte.

5) Marc. gr. V 5 (col. 1053) = SS. Iohannis et Pauli 40; Berardelli S. 197. Membr. 410 × 270 mm., ff. 443, ll. 39. Der Codex enthält 27 Schriften Galens und wird häufig in der Überlieferungsgeschichte Galenscher Schriften genannt.[124] Daß er von Kaisar Strategos geschrieben ist, hat nach Berardelli zuerst Helmreich gesehen, durch Vergleich mit dem subskribierten Marc. V 4.[125] Auf der Innenseite des Vorderdeckels auf dem aufgeklebten Blatt die Widmung des Musuros: Tῷ εὐφυεῖ λόγῳ τε καὶ ἤθει κεκοσμημένῳ νεανίᾳ κυρίῳ ἀντωνίῳ τῷ βροκάρδῳ τοῦ ἐξόχου ἀρχιατροῦ ἀγαπητῳ καὶ μονογενεῖ.

In dem Adressaten erkennt Wenkebach[126] den Antonio Brocardo eines Bildes Giorgiones.[127] Über diesen Sohn des Marino Brocardo[128] sind wir recht gut informiert. Er lebte in der ersten Hälfte des 16. Jh. und studierte in Padua Jura. Als junger Literat und Dichter geriet er in einen Literaturstreit mit dem Humanisten und Dichter Pietro Bembo (1470–1547, Kardinal seit 1539), der hohe Wogen schlug und ihm so zu Herzen ging, daß er starb.[129] Cicogna (3,

[123] Cicogna 2, 226–41, 71 ff. und passim; *Enc. Ital.* 11 (1949), 228 mit Lit.; *Lex f. Theol. u. Kirche* 3² (1959), 49 f.; G. de Leva, *Della vita e delle opere del Card. Gasparo Contarini* (Padua 1863); Cosenza 2, 1082–84.

[124] H. Diels, *Die handschriftliche Überlieferung des Galenschen Commentars zum Prorrheticum des Hippokrates* (Abh. Preuß. Akad. 1912), 21 ff.; *CMG* IX 2 (1915), XI, 1; E. Wenkebach *Beiträge zur Textgeschichte der Epidemienkommentare Galens*, 1 (Abh. Preuß. Akad. 1927, phil.-hist. Kl. 4; Berlin 1928), 61; *CMG* V 10, 1 (1934), XIV ff.; V 10, 2, 1 (1936), XI u. ö. Bei Diels 21 und Wenkebach 61 ist die Zueignung ausgeschrieben.

[125] *CMG* V 9, 1, S. XXXIII; vgl. auch Wenkebach, *CMG* V 10, 1 (1934), XV; V 10, 2, 1, XI; V 10, 3 (1951), X.

[126] *Beiträge* 61 f.; *CMG* V 10, 1 (1934), XV, 3; vgl. Diels, *CMG* V 9, 2, XI, 1.

[127] L. Justi, *Giorgione* (1908), 1, 171 f.; 2, Taf. 31.

[128] Jöcher 1, 1390: *Medicus aus Venedig, lebte in dem 13. seculo, und schrieb de lue venerea.* Die Angabe seiner Zeit wird von Adelung 1, 2276 korrigiert: *Marini Broccardi im Jöcher, der aber nicht, wie es dortselbst heißt, im 13. Jahrhundert, sondern in der ersten Hälfte des 16.-ten und noch 1536 lebte.* Er wird bei A. Cicogna, *Saggio di bibliografia veneziana* (Venezia 1847), 732 neben Vettor Trincavello und anderen Ärzten genannt.

[129] G. Tiraboschi, *Storia della letteratura italiana* (Modena 1787–94; Neuausgabe Milano 1833), 7, 1650; G. M. Mazzuchelli, *Gli scrittori d'Italia* (Brescia 1753–63), 2, 4, 17, 2117; Adelung 1, 2276; D. Vitaliani, *Antonio Broccardo, una vittima del bembismo* (Longo 1902); C. Miani, *Una contesa letteraria del Cinquecento, Bembo e Broccardo* (Sassari 1904); P. Molmenti, *Venice. Its Individual Growth from the Earliest Beginnings to the Fall of the Republic*, transl. by H. F. Brown, 2, 1 (1907), 231–33; *Enc. Ital.* 7 (1930), 906; vgl. Cicogna 4, 218 (Sonetti in morte del Brocardo).

210) nennt ihn unter den Schülern Tryphons und führt (3, 216) einen *Petrarca d'antichissima stampa* an, der Marginalnoten von Antonio Brocardo gehabt habe mit dessen Notiz, daß ihm dieses Buch von Tryphon erklärt worden sei.

6) Marc. gr. VII 6 (coll. 1096) = SS. Iohannis et Pauli 49; Berardelli S. 201 f.; Mioni 23. Membr. 315 × 219 mm., ff. 177, ll. 30. Enthält Dionysios v. Halikarnass, Antiquitates Romanae I-V. Geschrieben von Kaisar Strategos (f. 177ᵛ Θ(εο)ῦ τὸ δῶρον, ἠδὲ καίσαρος πόνος τοῦ στρατηγοῦ). Der Titel ist für den Rubricator ausgespart. Auf f. Iᵛ von der Hand des Musuros, nicht, wie Mioni sagt, *ipsa manu librarii: Τῷ πολυμαθεῖ εὐπατρίδη εὐμουσίας τε ὀνομαστῷ καὶ φιλοσοφίας τροφίμῳ κυρίῳ βερτουτίῳ τῷ σουπερ—αντίῳ.

Da die Widmung von Musuros ist, kann der Adressat nicht, wie Mioni, der die Hand des Musuros nicht erkannte, meint, jener Bertuccio Soranzo sein,[130] der in Venedig im Jahre 1480 starb, als Musuros gerade zehn Jahre alt war. Es wird vielmehr der von Marino Sanuto seit 1513 häufig erwähnte Sohn des Girolamo Soranzo sein, der im September dieses Jahres zum Savio agli ordini gewählt wurde und in der Folge verschiedene Ämter der Republik bekleidet hat.[131]

7) Marc. gr. VII 7 (coll. 1078) = SS. Iohannis et Pauli 31; Berardelli S. 194; Mioni 23 f. Membr. 313 × 212 mm., ff. 189, ll. 30. Enthält Diodor I-V. Geschrieben von Kaisar Strategos (f. 188 θεοῦ τὸ δῶρον, ἠδὲ καίσαρος πόνος). Für Titel und Initialen ist Raum ausgespart. Breite Ränder. Auf der Innenseite des Vorderdeckels auf dem aufgeklebten Blatt von der Hand des Musuros: πρῶτον τῷ ἐπιεικεῖ πεπαιδευμένῳ εὐπατρίδη κυρίῳ Ἱερωνύμῳ Ζήνῳ. Zeno erhielt noch einen zweiten Codex (Marc. gr. XI 13, unten Nr. 18), daher πρῶτον.

Der Adressat ist nach Mioni *Hieronymus Zeno, Simonis filius, procurator Venetae Reipublicae a. 1530*,[132] begraben vor dem Altar des heiligen Aloysius in der Kirche SS. Giovanni e Paolo mit der Inschrift: *Hieronymus Zeno D. Marci procurator et haered. MDLI.*[133] Ein

---

[130] Cicogna 2, 1837, 284 f.
[131] Sanuto, *Diarii* 17, 81. Im übrigen vgl. die Register der Bände 17, 21, 27, 28, 31, 32, 33, 35, 36, 42. Zum Geschlecht der Soranzo vgl. *Enc. Ital.* 32 (1949), 154 mit Literatur; Cicogna passim.
[132] G. Cappellari, Il Campidoglio Veneto, Marc. It. VII 18 (coll. 8307), IV, f. 218ᵛ.
[133] Mus. Correr. Ms. Cicogna 2011, Inscrizioni della chiesa di SS. Giovanni e Paolo, Nr. 270.

anderer Girolamo Zeno, Sohn des Baccalario (gestorben 1507) und der Marina (verehelicht 1483), setzte zu seinen Lebzeiten im Jahre 1534 seiner verstorbenen Mutter das Grabmal in S. Zaccaria. Er wurde im Mai 1516 *officiale alla Ternaria nuova* (*cioè à dazii sull' olio, legna e grassina*) und 1522 wurde er zum *Savio* gewählt.[134]

8) Marc. gr. VII 8 (coll. 1097) = SS. Iohannis et Pauli 32, Berardelli S. 194; Mioni 24. Membr. 313 × 212 mm., ff. 414, ll. 30. Er enthält Diodor Buch XI–XX, geschrieben von Kaisar Strategos (f. 414 + καῖσαρ στρατηγὸς λακεδαιμόνιος ἐν φλωρεντία ἐξέγραψεν). Auch hier fehlen wieder die Titel bei breiten Rändern, wie der Codex denn dem vorangehenden (VII 7), mit dem er zusammengehört, sehr ähnlich ist. Auch dieser Codex trug eine ähnliche Widmung wie die vorangehenden, sicher ebenfalls von der Hand des Musuros, sie ist aber mit dem alten Einband zugrunde gegangen. J. Morelli hat den griechischen Text bewahrt: τῶ ἐν ἀρχαίων υἱοῖς γενναίω καὶ φιλοκάλω κυρίω ἰωάννη τῶ Ἀβράμη.[135]

9) Marc. gr. VII 9 (coll. 1098) = SS. Iohannis et Pauli 19, Berardelli S. 186; Mioni 24 f. Membr.[136] 303 × 212 mm., ff. 621, ll. 30. Der Codex enthält ff. 1–140 Arrian, Alexandri Anabasis und De bello Indico, für die er als Vorlage der Editio princeps von Trincavelli 1535 diente,[137] ff. 142ʳ–258ᵛ Polyainos' Strategemata. In beiden Teilen[138] ist er von Kaisar Strategos geschrieben (f. 140 + θεοῦ τὸ δῶρον, ἠδὲ καίσαρος ὁ πόνος). Von der Hand des Musuros, nicht der des Librarius, wie Mioni behauptet, findet sich auf der Innenseite des Vorderdeckels die Widmung: τῶ νουνεχεῖ καὶ ἐλλογίμω ἀνδρὶ κυρίω ἀντωνίω τῶ μαρσυλλίω.

Der Adressat, dem die Ausgabe des Aulus Gellius von Egnatius in der Aldusdruckerei 1515 gewidmet ist,[139] war um die Mitte des 16. Jh. *Cancellier ducale*.[140]

10) Marc. gr. VIII 6 (coll. 1101) = SS. Iohannis et Pauli 4; Berardelli S. 176 f.; Mioni 128 ff. Membr. 310 × 217 mm., ff. 140, ll. 30. Der Codex,

---

[134] Cicogna 2, 130 f. nach Sanuto.

[135] Cod. Marc. Riserv. Morelli 92. Berardelli übersetzt *Joanni Abramae Atheniensi*. Danach dürfte in der griechischen Wiedergabe durch Morelli ein Lesefehler statt ἐν ἀθηναίων υἱοῖς vorliegen.

[136] Nicht chart., wie Mioni sagt. Kein Wunder, daß er keine Wasserzeichen finden konnte.

[137] Näheres dazu in einer Studie über die Vorlagen der Ausgaben Victor Trincavellis, die ich vorbereite. Hier auch zu Marc. gr. IV 10 (vgl. oben).

[138] So Mioni; zwei verschiedene Schreiber, aber aus derselben Werkstatt nach A. Dain, *La Collection Florentine des tacticiens grecs* (Paris 1940), 51.*

[139] Renouard 73; Firmin-Didot 406.

[140] Cicogna 4, 588; vgl. auch 593. Nach Dain a.O. kommt seine Familie aus Bologna (ohne Verweise).

seit Jernstedt [141] als Druckvorlage der Aldina der Rhetorum Graecorum
Orationes (1513) angesehen, enthält die Reden des Andokides, Isaios,
Deinarchos, Antiphon, Lykurgos, Gorgias, Lesbonax und Herodes.
Nach Mioni ist er von Kaisar Strategos geschrieben,* aber die Schrift ist
anders als in Marc. VII 6 und bei Omont Taf. 7; sie ist nach Vergleich
mit Omont Taf. 5 die des Aristobulos Apostolides (= Arsenios von
Monembasia). Dazu paßt, daß Marc. VIII 6 aus Laur. 4,11 (= B)
stammt [142]; Aristobulos kopierte in Florenz. [143] Auch hier breite Ränder
und Raum für die Initialen ausgespart, aber Titel rot in Majuskeln.
F. I^v von der Hand des Musuros: τοῖν καὶ παλαιᾶ γένους εὐδοξία καὶ περὶ
ἄμφω τὼ λόγω προκοπῇ διαφερόντοιν ἐφήβοιν παύλω καὶ λαδίσλεω πουρλιλιῶν
κομήτοιν. [144]

Die beiden Adressaten sind Sprößlinge der venezianischen
Patrizierfamilie der Priuli oder Prioli, der auch der oben S. 583
erwähnte Lorenzo Priuli entstammt. In den *Diarii* des Marino
Sanuto Bde. 5–43 und 58, die mir allein greifbar waren, kommt
Ladislao nicht vor, und Paolo ist, da er νεανίας ist, mit keinem der
dort Genannten mit einiger Wahrscheinlichkeit zu identifizieren.

11) Marc. gr. VIII 7 (coll. 1069) = SS. Iohannis et Pauli 14; Berardelli
S. 182–184; Mioni 130 ff. Membr. 324 × 226 mm., ff. 300, ll. 19–26
(ff. 10–23) et 36 (ff. 24–300). Der Codex enthält die Reden des Ailios
Aristeides. Er stammt nach Berardelli etwa aus dem 10. Jh., nach Mioni
aus dem 12. Jh., ist aber vorn (ff. 1-6) und hinten (294–299) im 15. Jh.
ergänzt, nach Berardelli und Mioni von Kaisar Strategos. Nach meinem
Urteil kann das jedoch nicht stimmen; seine Schrift ist ganz verschieden,
außerdem sind die Ergänzungen vorn und hinten nicht von derselben
Hand. F. I Widmung von der Hand des Musuros, nicht des Strategos,
wie Mioni meint: οὐρβανοῦ τοῦ εὐλαβεστάτου ἱερομονάχου τῆς ἁγίας
φραγγιστῶν θρησκείας καὶ τοῖς πάλαι περὶ τὴν γραμματικὴν εὐδοκιμήσασι
ἐφαμίλλου χερσὶ δέδοται.

Der Adressat ist der bekannte Franziskaner Fra Urbano Bolzanio

---

[141] *Antiphontis orationes* ed. V. Jernstedt (Petropoli 1880), XIV ff. Jernstedt hat allerdings
auch die Möglichkeit erwogen, dass die Vorlage der Aldina eine sehr genaue Abschrift
des Marcianus gewesen sein könne—zu Recht, denn dieser zeigt keine Spuren einer
Benutzung in der Druckerei.

[142] H. Erbse in *Geschichte der Textüberlieferung der antiken und mittelalterlichen Literatur*, I
(Zürich 1961), 226 f. mit Lit. Nach Jernstedt S. XVI, A. 8, wäre er allerdings nicht direkt,
sondern über ein Zwischenglied aus dem Laurentianus geflossen.

[143] Geanakoplos 170 f.

[144] Vgl. V. Jernstedt, *Opuscula* (Petersburg 1907), 45; vgl. Vogel–Gardthausen 225.

von Belluno (1443–1524),[145] einer der besten Hellenisten seiner Zeit, Schüler des Konstantinos Laskaris in Messina, Lehrer Giovannis de' Medici, des späteren Papstes Leo X., in Florenz, nach 1490 in Venedig Lehrer des Griechischen, Mitarbeiter des Aldus und Musuros bei der Edition griechischer Texte, Verfasser der ersten griechischen Grammatik in lateinischer Sprache, die 1497 bei Aldus erschien. Seine Bücher hinterließ er dem Kloster Sancti Nicolai in Venedig, in dem er starb.

12) Marc. gr. VIII 10 (coll. 1349) = SS. Iohannis et Pauli 50; Berardelli S. 202 f.; Mioni 135 ff. Membr. 298 × 212 mm., ff. 366, ll. 31. Der Codex enthält Dionysios von Halikarnaß Ars rhetorica, Demetrios De elocutione, Apsines, Minukianos, Ailios Aristeides, den Rhetor Menandros, Sopatros und Kyros. Er ist z.T. von Kaisar Strategos geschrieben (f. 365ᵛ θεοῦ τὸ δῶρον, ἥδὲ [sic] καίσαρος πόνος). Die Titel rot, in großer Schrift; einige sind für den Rubricator ausgespart. Breite Ränder. F. II von der Hand des Musuros, nicht des Schreibers, wie Mioni sagt: τῶ αἰδεσιμωτάτω καὶ ἐκλαμπροτάτω ἐπισκόπω καινετέων κυρίω μαρίνω γριμάνω τῶ ἀντωνίου μὲν ἐγγόνω τοῦ πάνυ ἀδελφιδῶ δὲ δομηνίκου τοῦ θεοφιλοῦς καὶ πανσόφου καρδηνάλεως.[146]

Marino Grimani (gestorben 1546), der Neffe des Kardinals Domenico Grimani (1461–1523) und dessen Nachfolger als Patriarch von Aquileia (1517–29 und 1535–45), erhielt diesen Codex zwischen dem 16.8.1508 und 1517, als er Bischof von Ceneda war.[147]

13) Marc. gr. IX 5 (coll. 1336) = SS. Iohannis et Pauli 52, Berardelli S. 204. Membr. in fol., ff. 236. Der Codex enthält nach Berardelli Scholia in Homeri Iliadem und ist von Kaisar Strategos geschrieben, trägt aber nach Mitteilung der Bibliothek keine Subskription.* Auf der Rückseite des Vorsatzblattes vorn die Widmung: Τοῖς εὐφυέσι καὶ πεπαιδευμένοις μουσῶν

---

[145] Tiraboschi, Nuova ed. 7, 1091 ee; Renouard 12; Firmin-Didot passim, bes. 95 u. 445 f.; *Enc. Ital.* 7, 1930, 358, mit Lit.; Cosenza 4 (1962), 3541 f.; Geanakoplos passim (Index S. 340).

[146] Mionis Transkription leidet an Lesefehlern (μετὰ statt μὲν, θεοφιλοῦ statt θεοφιλοῦς), außerdem läßt er den Codex dem Marino und Domenico Grimani gewidmet sein.

[147] Mercati, *Pico Grimani Pio* passim (s. Register); Cicogna (s. Register); Jöcher 2 (1750), 1184 f.; Cosenza 2, 1684; G. van Gulik und C. Eubel, *Hierarchia catholica medii et recentioris aevi sive Summorum Pontificum, S. R. E. Cardinalium, ecclesiarum antistitum series*², 3 (Monasterii 1923), 114, 162; P. B. Gams, *Series episcoporum Ecclesiae Catholicae*² (Leipzig 1931), 774, 784; Mercati 7, A. 1, erinnert daran, daß er im Testament verfügte, daß seine Handschriften, die er den Benediktinern von S. Giorgio Maggiore in Venedig vermacht hatte, in letzter Instanz an die Dominikaner von SS. Giovanni e Paolo übergeben werden sollten, wenn seine Bestimmungen nicht eingehalten würden.

ἔρνεσι ἰωάννη ἀνδρέα ἱερωνύμω περίνω ἀδελφοῖς ὁμοψύχοις πατρὸς δὲ Θαδαίου Κονταρηνοῦ τῶν γερουσίας εὐπατριδῶν (Plate IV b).

In den *Diarii* Sanutos wird mehrfach ein *sier Zuan Andrea Contarini di sier Tadio qu(ondam) sier Nicolò* erwähnt,[147a] der mit dem einen der drei Brüder identisch sein könnte. Wenn dies stimmt, so ist der zweite, Girolamo, in den Bänden 5–43 nicht identifizierbar. Ein Girolamo, Sohn des Taddeo, wird zwar häufig genannt, aber sein Vater ist im Gegensatz zu dem des Zuan Andrea bereits im Jahre 1515 tot und sein Großvater hieß nicht Nicolò, sondern Andrea. Daß er der in der Widmung genannte Girolamo sei, ist deshalb unwahrscheinlich, weil er bereits im Jahre 1515 Savio agli ordini ist (21, 1, 143), während die Adressaten des Codex IX 5 offenbar selbst noch nicht zu solchen Würden aufgestiegen waren. Der dritte, Perino, wird überhaupt nicht erwähnt.

14) Marc. gr. IX 8 (coll. 1039) = SS. Iohannis et Pauli 69; Berardelli S. 216. Membr. 235 × 160 mm., ff. 306.[148] Enthält Pindars Olympia und Pythia (ff. 1–89ʳ) und Scholien dazu (ff. 91ʳ–305ʳ). Geschrieben von Kaisar Strategos (f. 305ʳ θεοῦ τὸ δῶρον· ἠδὲ καίσαρος πόνος). Auf der Innenseite des Vorderdeckels die Zueignung: μάρκω μουσούρω τῶ κρητὶ δημοσίω καθηγητῆ. Berardelli gibt hier ausnahmsweise keine lateinische Übersetzung. Es ist kein Zweifel möglich, daß auch hier der Eintrag von Musuros selbst ist.

15) Marc. gr. IX 10 (coll. 1160) = SS. Iohannis et Pauli 37; Berardelli S. 196. Membr. 310 × 220, ff. 272, ll. 20.[149] Der Codex enthält Euripides, Hekabe, Orestes, Phoenissen, Hippolytos, Medea, Alkestis, Andromache, alle mit Hypothesis. Geschrieben ist er nach A. Turyn von Ianos Laskaris.* Auf dem Verso des Vorsatzblattes vor dem f. 1ʳ die Widmung: τῶ εὐγενεῖ μουσῶν τε τροφίμω καὶ χαρίτων, ἰακώβω τῶ σιμαιθοκόλω.

Der Adressat ist gewiß jener Jacopo Semitecolo, der seit 1517 von Sanuto häufig in verschiedenen öffentlichen Ämtern erwähnt wird. Als Capo dei Quaranta *fe' lezer un' altra parte, che si stampi i libri greci per cadauno, nè se li possi far grazia, aziò quelli hanno tal gratie non li tengano in gran precio* (23, 593: Februar 1517). Bald darauf *fo*

[147a] 19, 466: Februar 1515; 23, 196: November 1516; 32, 502: Februar 1522; 34, 159: Mai 1523.

[148] Zur Beschreibung vgl. Turyn, *De codicibus Pindaricis* (oben A. 11), 49; Irigoin, *Histoire du texte de Pindare*, 378–79.

[149] Beschreibung nach Turyn, *Euripides* 375 f.

pubblichà in Rialto una termination fata per la Signoria, autor Sier Jacomo Semitecolo cao di XL, amator di doctrina e di lettere greche: *come hessendo compita la gratia fu concessa a Aldo stampador, tutti possano stampar in greco e portar libri grechi in questa terra senza pena alcuna a venderli* (23, 604: Februar 1517).[150]

16) Marc. gr. X 1 (coll. 1374) = SS. Iohannis et Pauli 11; Berardelli S. 180 f. Membr. 223 × 152, ff. 266.[151] Er enthält ff. 1–118ᵛ die vier Bücher des Apollonios Dyskolos Περὶ συντάξεως, ff. 119ʳ–216ʳ eine Anthologie verschiedener Texte Περὶ τῶν ἐμμέτρων λόγων, und ff. 217ʳ–66ʳ die Progymnasmata des Ailios Theon. Nach Berardelli ist der Codex von Kaisar Strategos geschrieben. Italo Lana bestreitet jedoch nach Vergleich mit dem subskribierten Laur. 81,3, daß eine der im Codex auftretenden Hände die des genannten Schreibers sei. Das ist zweifellos richtig, kann aber das Urteil Berardellis nicht entkräften, da der Laurentianus entweder von einem anderen Schreiber gleichen Namens ist oder die Subskription seiner Vorlage reproduziert.* Da die Subskription lautet: θεοῦ τὸ δῶρον καὶ καίσαρος πόνος στρατηγοῦ τάχα καὶ ἀναγνώστου κρητός, scheint eher das erstere der Fall zu sein. Jedenfalls ist die Schrift völlig verschieden von jener der subskribierten Marciani.[152] Auf der Innenseite des Vorderdeckels steht die Widmung: τῶ μεγαλοπρεπεῖ καὶ τοὺς τρόπους εἰλικρινεῖ κυρίω ἀλοεισίω πέμπω· λογίω τε καὶ πεπαιδευμένω.

Einen Alvise (Luigi) Bembo erwähnt Cicogna 2, 254 f.; er bekleidete von 1509 an verschiedene Stellungen in der Verwaltung Venedigs. 1510 wurde er nach Padua *als provveditore del fieno di quel territorio* geschickt. Auch mit militärischen Aufträgen wurde er betraut. Im Jahre 1513/14 hatte er die Aufsicht über die Ausbesserung und Befestigung der Mauern von Padua. Ob er identisch ist mit jenem Alvise Bembo, von dem Cappellari berichtet,[153] kann ich nicht feststellen. Es ist aber wahrscheinlich, da auch dieser um die gleiche Zeit militärische und zivile Aufträge hatte.

17) Marc. gr. XI 12 (coll. 1084) = SS. Iohannis et Pauli 47; Berardelli S. 201. Membr. in fol., ff. 327. Er enthält die Geoponica und ist laut

---

[150] Vgl. Cicogna 3, 143, der als Jahr 1516 nennt.

[151] Beschreibung nach I. Lana, *I Progimnasmi di Elio Teone*, 1: *La storia del testo* (Torino 1959), 44 ff.

[152] Zwei verschiedene Träger des gleichen Namens Kaisar Strategos, einen Lakedaimonier und einen Kreter, unterscheidet J. M. Moore, *The manuscript Tradition of Polybius* (Cambridge 1965), 12 f.

[153] G. A. Cappellari Vivaro, Campidoglio Veneto, Cod. Marc. VII 15 (coll. 8304), vol. 1, ff. 139ᵛ–40ʳ, nach Lana 47; vgl. auch Cicogna 5, 240.

Subskription von Kaisar Strategos geschrieben.* Auf der Rückseite des Vorsatzblattes vorn steht die griechische Widmung: Τῷ εὐλαβεστάτῳ καὶ λογιωτάτῳ ἐν ἱερεῦσι κυρίῳ Ἀλεξάνδρῳ τῷ βεργομεῖ ἀνδρὶ χρηστῷ καὶ ἐπιεικεῖ.

18) Marc. gr. XI 13 (coll. 1009) = SS. Iohannis et Pauli 64; Berardelli S. 214. Membr. in fol., ff. 192. Er enthält Dionysii Periegetae orbis descriptio, Epiktets Encheiridion cum expositione Simplicii und ist laut Subskription geschrieben von Kaisar Strategos. Auf der Rückseite des Vorsatzblattes vorne trägt er eine griechische Widmung: Τῷ ἐπιεικεῖ καὶ πεπαιδευμένῳ εὐπατρίδῃ κυρίῳ Ἱερωνύμῳ Ζήνῳ, also die gleiche wie VII 7.

19) Marc. gr. XI 14 (coll. 1233) = SS. Iohannis et Pauli 38; Berardelli S. 196 f. Membr. in 4, ff. 236. Er enthält Eustathios, Herodian, Dionysios von Halikarnaß und ist nach Berardelli von Kaisar Strategos in Florenz geschrieben, trägt aber nach Mitteilung der Bibliothek keine Subskription. Die Widmung steht auf dem angeklebten Blatt an der Innenseite des Vorderdeckels: τῷ μεγαλοπρεπεῖ καὶ τοὺς τρόπους εἰλικρινεῖ κυρίῳ Ἀλοεισίῳ πέμπῳ λογίῳ τε καὶ πεπαιδευμένῳ, also die gleiche wie X 1. Beide Codices sind sich auch darin ähnlich, daß sie grammatisch-rhetorische Traktate beinhalten.

Die stattliche Liste von 19 oft dicken Codices, die wahrscheinlich noch nicht einmal alle umfaßt, die einst eine solche Widmung des Musuros enthielten, gibt manche Fragen auf. Betrachten wir zuerst den Kreis der Adressaten. Es sind fast ausschließlich Angehörige venezianischer Adelsfamilien, an die sich der Venezianer Antonio Brocardo und der aus dem Venezianischen gebürtige und in Venedig wirkende Fra Urbano anschließt. Als Nichtvenezianer sind nur Ioannes Abrames aus Athen, wenn Berardelli richtig gelesen hat, und der Adressat von XI 12, ein Bergamener Priester Alexander, anzusehen. Auffällig ist ferner, daß sich unter den Adressaten eine größere Zahl solcher befindet, die als junge Männer bezeichnet oder durch Angabe des Vaters als solche erkennbar werden: Antonio Mocenigo, Sohn des Senators Alvise Mocenigo (IV 10), Giovanni Cornelio, Sohn des Giorgio Cornaro und Neffe der Königin Katharina von Cypern (IV 26), Gasparo Contarini (V 4), Antonio Brocardo, Sohn des Protomedicus Marino Brocardo (V 5), Paolo und Ladislao Priuli (VIII 6), die Söhne des Taddeo Contarini (IX 5).

Die beiden jungen Priuli werden ausdrücklich mit Lob für die Fortschritte in beiden Sprachen, also Griechisch und Lateinisch, bedacht (VIII 6). Das legt die Vermutung nahe, daß es sich bei den Adressaten um Studenten des Musuros in Padua oder Venedig handelt, zumal sich Musuros in der Selbstzueignung des Codex IX 8 als δημόσιος καθηγητής, professor publicus, bezeichnet. Es ist bekannt, daß die Söhne des venezianischen Adels bei Musuros studierten.[154] Zu diesem Kreis junger Männer gehört auch der spätere Kardinal Gasparo Contarini (V 4), der 1483 geboren ist und seit 1501 in Padua seinen Studien oblag,[155] und gewiß auch Bertuccio Soranzo, dessen εὐμουσία gerühmt und der als φιλοσοφίας τρόφιμος, Zögling der Philosophie, bezeichnet wird (VII 6), was auf einen Studenten sehr gut paßt. In ähnlicher Weise wird Jacopo Semitecolo (IX 10) μουσῶν τε τρόφιμος καὶ χαρίτων genannt. Von diesem berichtet Sanuto (25, 165, 170, 173, 191), daß er im Dezember 1517 sein Amt als Savio agli ordini niederlegte, um nach Padua studieren zu gehen. Man wird diesen Schritt vielleicht nicht zu Unrecht mit dem Weggang des Musuros aus Venedig (1516) und seinem Tode, durch den alle Hoffnung auf Rückkehr geschwunden war, in Verbindung bringen. Auch die Zueignung an den Priester Alexander von Bergamo, obwohl er bereits als λογιώτατος = eruditissimus bezeichnet wird (XI 12), legt die Vermutung nahe, daß er Schüler des Musuros gewesen ist, ebenso die an den Athener Ioannes Abrames (VII 8).

Manche der gewidmeten Handschriften lassen sich gut mit den Interessen, vielleicht mit den Studienfächern, der Empfänger in Verbindung bringen, so die Widmung des Galen (V 5) an den Sohn des Arztes Marino Brocardo und des Galen (V 4) an Gasparo Contarini, den Studenten der Naturwissenschaften; auch die Widmungen zweier Handschriften mit grammatisch-rhetorischen Traktaten (X 1 und XI 14) an Alvise Bembo und zweier weiterer mit Diodor und Dionysios Periegetes (VII 7 und XI 13) an Hieronymus Zeno wird damit zusammenhängen, vermutlich auch die Widmung philosophischer Traktate an die jungen Patrizier Antonio Mocenigo und Giovanni Cornelio Cornaro (IV 10 und 26), vielleicht auch die an Lorenzo Priuli (IV 8); wenn letzterer der

---

[154] Morelli, *Memorie per servire alla storia dell' Università di Padova* (Cod. Univ. Padovano 1675), 3, 623; vgl. G. Marangoni, "Lazzaro Bonamico e lo studio Padovano," *Nuovo Archivio Veneto*, n.s. 1 (1901), 126; Geanakoplos 159, A. 160; [Menge 63; Legrand 1, 132. Zu Marino Grimani als Schüler des Musuros vgl. Mercati 74; Geanakoplos 145.]

[155] Marangoni a.O.; Geanakoplos 135 f.

Doge ist, muß er zur Zeit des Musuros ein junger Mann gewesen sein.

Nicht alle Adressaten freilich waren junge Männer. Der Franziskaner Fra Urbano Bolzanio (VIII 7) war zu jener Zeit schon 60 Jahre alt und selbst Lehrer des Griechischen in Venedig und Kollege des Musuros auch als Mitarbeiter des Aldus und Mitglied der Neacademia; er wird denn auch ob seiner Verdienste um die Grammatik gerühmt. Marino Grimani (VIII 10) war bereits Bischof, aber jung. Andere wie Lorenzo Priuli (IV 8), Hieronymus Zeno (VII 7), Ioannes Abrames (VII 8), und Antonio Marsyllio (VII 9) werden nur als κύριος bezeichnet. Trotzdem können auch sie noch seine Schüler gewesen sein.[156] Ähnliches gilt für Jacopo Semitecolo, der 1517 bereits Savio agli ordini war. Dass zu Musuros' Füßen nicht nur junge Männer saßen, ist bekannt; es sei nur an Erasmus' Bericht erinnert, daß der betagte Raphael Regius die Vorlesungen seines gefeierten Kollegen eifrig besuchte.[157]

Einen zeitlichen Anhaltspunkt erhalten wir durch die Zueignung von VIII 10 an Marino Grimani als Bischof von Ceneda: 1508–17. Nimmt man hinzu, daß sich Musuros in IX 8 als *professor publicus*, nicht *ordinarius* bezeichnet, möchte man die Zueignungen eher auf seine Zeit in Venedig (1512–16) als in Padua (1503–1509) beziehen. Dazu stimmt vorzüglich, daß Antonio Mocenigo im Jahre 1509, als Musuros' Lehrtätigkeit in Padua schon zu Ende ging, erst zwölf Jahre alt war, also dort kaum sein Schüler gewesen sein kann, während auf die Zeit in Venedig (seit 1512) die Bezeichnung νεανίσκος durchaus passt. Man wird aber die Lieferung so vieler umfangreicher Handschriften eines einzigen Kopisten nicht auf einen zu engen Zeitraum zusammendrängen dürfen. Die gleichlautenden Widmungen (in X 1 und XI 14 einerseits, in VII 7 und XI 13 anderseits) wird man sich allerdings gleichzeitig geschrieben denken.

Die Quelle für die Handschriftenkäufe des Musuros ist in Florenz zu suchen. Nach Berardelli zeigen alle genannten Codices außer IX 10 die Hand des Kalligraphen Kaisar Strategos; nur in zwei Fällen (IV 8, VIII 6) finde ich diese Zuweisung nicht bestätigt.* Nicht selten hat er subskribiert, meistens in Form eines jambischen

---

[156] Vgl. die Verbindung von νεανίας und κύριος in V 5 (Antonio Brocardo). Marino Grimani als Schüler des Musuros: Cosenza 5, 1226 und oben, A. 154.

[157] *Opus epistolarum Des. Erasmi* ed. P. S. Allen, 5, 244: vgl. Geanakoplos 135, 144.

Trimeters: θεοῦ τὸ δῶρον ἠδὲ καίσαρος πόνος. Dieser Grieche hat unter Lorenzo de' Medici (1469–92) und auch noch später in Florenz gewirkt. Einer unserer Codices, Diodor XI–XX (VII 8), hat auch die entsprechende Ortsangabe: καῖσαρ στρατηγὸς λακεδαιμόνιος ἐν φλωρεντίᾳ ἐξέγραψεν.[158] Ein weiterer mit dem Geschichtswerk des Polybios (VII 4) trägt eine ähnliche Subskription: καῖσαρ στρατηγὸς λακεδαιμόνιος ἐξέγραψεν ἐν φλωρεντίᾳ.[159] Ebenso ist XI 14 von ihm in Florenz geschrieben. Darüber hinaus läßt sich in mehreren Fällen zeigen, daß die Vorlage Kaisars in Florenz lag. So stimmt der Diodor I–V in VII 7 mit dem Laur. 70, 16 sowohl im Text als auch in äußeren Dingen überein.[160] Der Polyaen in VII 9 ist aus Laur. 56, 1 geflossen.[161] Auch mehrere Galen-Texte in V 4 sind eng mit Laur. 74, 3 verwandt.[162] Während aber Westenberger[163] leugnet, daß er aus ihm abgeschrieben ist, spricht nach J. Kollesch[164] bei den in Marc. gr. V 4 und Laur. 74, 3 gemeinsam überlieferten Schriften nichts dagegen, daß der erstere aus dem letzteren stammt. Für *De odoratu* ist dieses Verhältnis durch Zeilenüberspringungen gesichert.

Bei einigen anderen Handschriften ist der Standort der Vorlage zur Zeit, als sie kopiert wurde, nicht festzustellen; auch hier wird es sehr wahrscheinlich Florenz gewesen sein. Der Pindar-Codex IX 8 ist nach Turyn 49 und Irigoin 376 f. direkt aus Paris. gr. 2403 abgeschrieben. Dieser wurde in der zweiten Hälfte des 16. Jh. von

[158] Seine Vorlage war Laur. 70, 12: G. Schneider, *Wochenschr. f. class. Philol.* 8 (1891), 677; Diodorus ed. F. Vogel, 3 (Lipsiae 1893), XIX; ed. C. Th. Fischer, 4, (Lipsiae 1896), XVII.

[159] Moore a.O.; die Vorlage von Marc. VII 4 war Lond. Mus. Brit. Add. MS. 11728, der um 1437 noch in der Abbatia Florentina (Badia) war, ebd. 24.

[160] Vgl. G. Schneider, "De aliquot libris Diodori Siculi manu scriptis," *Jahresber. Kgl. Joachimsthalsches Gymn.* (Berlin 1884), 18. Schneider gibt auch eine kurze Beschreibung von VII 7 und VII 8 unter Anführung der Widmung von VII 7 und der Subskriptionen; vgl. auch ed. F. Vogel (Lipsiae 1964; ed. ster.), XV.

[161] Ed. Woelfflin–Melber (1887), XV; Dain (oben A. 138), 48 f. [Vgl. jetzt F. Schindler, *Die Überlieferung der Strategemata des Polyainos*, Sitz.-Ber. Österr. Akad. d. Wiss., phil.-hist. Kl. 284, 1 (1973), 108 ff., 120. Der Text ist, wie im Postkriptum gezeigt wird, von Markos Ioannu geschrieben.]

[162] Vgl. Helmreich, *Galeni scripta minora*, 3 (Lipsiae 1893), V (Thrasybulos); Wenkebach, *CMG* V 10, 3, X mit Bezug auf I. Müller, *Scripta min.* 2 (Lipsiae 1891), IV; Westenberger *CMG* V 9, 1, XLI. Nach G. Helmreich, ed. *Galeni de temperamentis liber I* (Progr. Augsburg 1897), 5 f. steht er zwischen Laur. 75, 5 und Marc. 275 und ist mit diesem und Paris. gr. 2267 aus demselben Archetypus abgeschrieben.

[163] a.O.

[164] *CMG* Suppl. V, S. 15 ff.

Hurault de Boistaillé (†1572) wahrscheinlich in Venedig einem Griechen abgekauft.[165] Marc. gr. V 5 ist in mehreren seiner Traktate aus dem Reg. gr. 175 geflossen.[166] Wo sich dieser in der fraglichen Zeit befand, kann ich nicht feststellen.

Auch andere Kopien des Kaisar Strategos wurden in Florenz ausgeführt, so der Harpokration im Genav. mg. 43, ff. 54–158 mit der Subskription: καῖσαρ στρατηγὸς λακεδαιμόνιος μισθῷ ἐξέγραψε ἐν φλωρεντία.[167] Dasselbe gilt für Marc. gr. VII 10 (Appian), der f. 297 die Subskription trägt: καῖσαρ στρατηγὸς λακεδαιμόνιος ἐξέγραψεν. Er ist aus dem Codex Rehdigeranus 14 der Universitätsbibliothek von Breslau geflossen mit Ausnahme der Bücher III–V, die aus Laur. 70, 33 stammen. Diese beiden Exemplare scheinen nach Mervin R. Dilts in der Bibliothek von San Marco in Florenz gewesen und von Nikolaus V. für die Übersetzung durch P. C. Decembrio ausgeliehen worden zu sein.[168] Die Praeparatio Evangelica des Euseb im Paris. gr. 466* ist nach Mras aus Laur. 6, 9 abgeschrieben,[169] der Horapollo im Paris. gr. 2992 aus Laur. 69, 27.[170] Der Galen-Codex Laur. 74, 8 mit der Subskription des Kaisar Strategos (θεοῦ τὸ δῶρον ἠδὲ καίσαρος πόνος τοῦ στρατηγοῦ) und mit dem Wappen der Medici geschmückt,[171] ist sicher ebenfalls in Florenz entstanden.[172] Der Galen-Codex Paris. gr. 2159, geschrieben 1492, kommt aus dem Besitz des Mediceers Ridolfi.[173]

---

[165] Irigoin 264, 1.

[166] A. Minor, *De Galeni libris περὶ δυσπνοίας* (Diss. Marburg 1911), 9 f.; H. Diels, *Abh. Preuß. Akad.* 1912, 13 und *CMG* V 9, 2, XI (Komm. zum Prorrheticum); Heeg, *CMG* V 9, 2, XXI (Prognosticum).

[167] *Procopii De aedificiis libri VI* ed. J. Haury (Lipsiae 1964, VII).

[168] Briefliche Mitteilung vom 2.1.1969. Möglicherweise trug auch dieser Codex eine Widmung des Musuros, die wie bei VII 8 verlorengegangen ist. Allerdings könnte Berardelli sie dann nicht mehr gesehen haben. [Vgl. jetzt M. R. Dilts, *Rev. d'hist. des textes* (1971), 54 ff.]

[169] *Eusebius Werke*, 8: *Die Praeparatio Evangelica*, 1 (Berlin 1954), XLI (Die Griechischen Christlichen Schriftsteller der ersten Jahrhunderte, 43, 1).

[170] *Hori Apollonis Hieroglyphica* ed. F. Sbordone (Napoli 1940), LIII und LIX. Nach Sbordone sind Paris. 2992 und Marc. 391 zwar über ein Zwischenglied aus dem Laurentianus geflossen; sein Material schließt jedoch nicht aus, daß Marc. 391 aus dem Parisinus stammt.

[171] A. M. Bandini, *Catalogus codicum mss. Bibl. Mediceae Laurentianae*, 3 (Florentiae 1770; Nachdruck Lipsiae 1961), 93 f.

[172] Nach Heeg, *CMG* V 9, 2, XXII ist er aus Paris. gr. 2266 abgeschrieben.

[173] Der Hippokrates-Codex Paris. gr. 2141, für den für eine Reihe von Schriften der Paris. 2144 als Vorlage nachgewiesen wurde, wird von A. Rivier, *Recherches sur la tradition du traité hippocratique "De morbo sacro"* (Bern 1962), 134, 1, dem Kaisar Strategos mit

Die Verbindung des Musuros mit Kaisar Strategos wird aus der
Zeit datieren, da ersterer sich in Florenz aufhielt, das damals, unter
Lorenzo de' Medici, Mittelpunkt des Humanismus war, wo sich
viele byzantinische und westliche Gelehrte einfanden. Musuros mag
gegen 1486 nach Florenz gekommen und bis 1493 geblieben sein.
In diesen entscheidenden Jahren seiner geistigen Entwicklung (er
mag 16–23 Jahre alt gewesen sein) war er Schüler von Ianos
Laskaris[174] und stand zu Ficino in Beziehung.[175] Daß er den
griechischen Schreiber, der für die Medici arbeitete, nicht gekannt
habe, ist undenkbar. Vielleicht, so könnte man vermuten, hat er
schon damals alle jene Handschriften für sich erworben, um sie
später an seine Schüler und Freunde weiterzugeben. Dazu würde
gut passen, daß von den fraglichen Handschriften eine oder
zwei (VIII 6 und vielleicht IV 8) von Aristobulos Apostolides
geschrieben sind, der sich gleichzeitig mit Musuros in den 90er
Jahren in Florenz aufhielt[176] und dort sehr wahrscheinlich VIII 6
herstellte.*

Eine solche Annahme ist aber wenig wahrscheinlich. Alle be-
schriebenen Handschriften fallen durch ihre sumptuose Ausstattung
auf. Sie sind von wenigen Ausnahmen (IX 8, X 1 und XI 14)[177]
abgesehen, Foliobände, zwei davon (V 4 und V 5) von einem
übergroßen Format. Ausnahmslos sind sie in Pergament, mit dem
nicht sparsam umgegangen worden ist; bei den meisten springen die
breiten Ränder in die Augen. Sie sind fast alle von einem bekannten
Kalligraphen ausgeführt und sollten mit großen Initialen, Or-
namenten und Titeln illuminiert werden. Freilich ist diese Arbeit
oft nicht ausgeführt worden oder nicht ganz zum Ziele gekommen.
Musuros war zwar nicht wie viele seiner Landsleute als Flüchtling
nach dem Westen gekommen, sondern um sich zu bilden. Er

Recht abgesprochen; Paris. 2141 und Paris. 2144 kamen beide aus Konstantinopel
nach Florenz, Rivier 113, 124, 5.

[174] J. E. Sandys, *A History of Classical Scholarship*, 2 (Nachdruck New York 1964), 79;
Legrand I, CVIII; Knös 18 f., 27; Geanakoplos 113–15.

[175] H. Alline, *Histoire du texte de Platon* (Paris 1915), 302 (Bibliothèque de l'École des
Hautes Études, 218).

[176] Vgl. Geanakoplos 112, 170.

[177] Diese sind in Quartformat; der erste ist Musuros selbst zugeeignet, die anderen
beiden Alvise Bembo.

entstammte vermutlich einer Kaufmannsfamilie[178] und mußte sich
gewiß nicht wie viele seiner Landsleute als Schreiber seinen Unterhalt
verdienen. Es ist aber sehr unwahrscheinlich, daß ein Student sich so
viele teuere Pergamentbände angeschafft haben würde, zumal er
selbst während seiner Studienzeit in Florenz das Kopieren von
Handschriften nicht ganz verschmähte.[179]

Auch später hat ihm sein Gelehrtendasein schwerlich erlaubt, sich
aufwendige Pergamentbände, die zudem noch illuminiert werden
sollten, anzuschaffen. Bei einem Verleger wie Aldus Manutius
waren keine Reichtümer zu holen.[180] Beim Fürsten Alberto Pio von
Carpi lebte er zwar in behaglichen Verhältnissen, aber kaum im
Überfluß.[181] Als Professor in Padua und später in Venedig bezog er
ein auskömmliches, aber sicher nicht fürstliches Gehalt.[182] Es nimmt
deshalb nicht wunder, daß seine Bibliothek sich aus anspruchsloseren
Bänden zusammensetzte. Nur zwei Pergamentcodices sind darunter
(Pal. gr. 287, Ambros. gr. 12), der eine davon mäßigen Umfangs
und in Quartformat. Man wird also annehmen, daß die fraglichen
Codices von den Empfängern, vielfach wohlhabenden venezianischen
Patriziern, über Musuros für ihre studierenden Söhne bestellt
wurden, die nicht unbedingt auch Schüler des Musuros selbst
gewesen sein müssen und sie gewiß nicht alle im Zusammenhang mit
dessen Vorlesungen benötigten. Dafür spricht auch der Inhalt dieser
Bände, der sich von dem der Bücher des Musuros erheblich unter-
scheidet. Die Dichter, dort mit an erster Stelle, treten hier zurück.
Zieht man den bezeichnenderweise für Musuros selbst bestimmten
Pindar (IX 8) ab, so bleiben nur zwei Euripides-Tragödien (IX 10)
und Homerscholien (IX 5). Dagegen nehmen Grammatik (X 1,
XI 14), Rhetorik (VIII 10, X 1, XI 14) und Fachwissenschaften
(Medizin IV 10, V 4, V 5; Landwirtschaft XI 12; Geographie
XI 13), die in der Bibliothek des Musuros überhaupt fehlen, einen
breiten Raum ein, während sich die philosophische Literatur (IV 8,
IV 10, IV 26, XI 13), die Historiker (VII 6, VII 7, VII 8, VII 9)
und die Redner (VIII 6, VIII 7) eher die Waage halten. Auch
das Fehlen aller Exlibris von Musuros, vielleicht auch die noch in

---

[178] Geanakoplos 112 f.
[179] Vgl. oben S. 577.
[180] Geanakoplos 261.
[181] Mercati, *Codici Pico Grimani Pio*, 73; Geanakoplos 125–27.
[182] Vgl. Geanakoplos 133, A. 89; 144.

verschiedenen Handschriften erhaltenen Preisangaben[183] und die Bestimmung je zweier Codices für dieselben Empfänger unterstützen unsere Hypothese.

Dies setzt natürlich voraus, daß Kaisar Strategos noch zwischen 1508 und 1517 tätig war. Das ist aber keineswegs ausgeschlossen, da die einzige von ihm datierte Handschrift (Paris. gr. 2159) aus dem Jahre 1492 stammt.[184] Er mag nach dem Tode seines Brotherrn Lorenzo (†8.4.1492) in Florenz für andere Auftraggeber weitergearbeitet haben.

Die Bibliothek des Dominikanerklosters SS. Giovanni e Paolo geht auf die Sammeltätigkeit von Gioacchino Torriano und Girolamo Vielmi zurück, worüber Berardelli nach Tomasini[185] berichtet: *Maximam horum codicum* [scil. SS. Iohannis et Pauli] *cum Latinorum tum Graecorum partem, eorum maxime, quorum rariora exstant exemplaria, aut elegantiori forma venustantur, ab Joachimo Turriano Veneto* [ca. 1416–1500][186] *eiusdem Coenobii alumno, ... summa cura magnisque impensis collectam fuisse, sicut ex authenticis documentis in Coenobii eiusdem Tabulario servatis edocemur. Plures etiam Dominum Hieronymum Vielmium, eiusdem et ipsum Coenobii alumnum, Episcopum prius Argolicensem, deinde Aemoniensem vel donasse vel legasse, Thomasinus idem loco supra laudato arbitratur.* Letzterer starb im Jahre 1582 zu Venedig im 63. Lebensjahre.[187] Aus Gründen der Chronologie könnten unsere Handschriften nur durch ihn aufgebracht worden sein. In die Marciana gingen die Handschriften von SS. Giovanni e Paolo im Jahre 1789 ein.[188]

Münster, 7. Juli 1970

POSTSKRIPTUM

Die vorstehende Arbeit lag der Redaktion der *Serta Turyniana* seit mehr als einem Jahre vor, als im August 1971 ein Aufsatz von E. Mioni, "La biblioteca greca di Marco Musuro," im *Archivio Veneto*, Serie V, vol. XCIII (1971) erschien, der mir vom Verfasser freundlicherweise zuge-

---

[183] In V 4 steht auf dem äußersten unteren Rand der Innenseite des Vorderdeckels *Libras ἑπτά*, in V 5 an derselben Stelle *Lire* (?) *septem*.

[184] Vogel–Gardthausen 264.

[185] J. P. Tomasini, *Bibliothecae Venetae Manuscriptae publicae et privatae* (Utini 1650).

[186] Jöcher 4 (1751), 1368. [I. Quetif–J. Echard, *Scriptores Ordinis Praedicatorum*, 1 Paris 1719), 869 f.]

[187] Jöcher ebd. 1588 f. [Quetif-Echard, 2 (1721), 264 f.]

[188] J. Valentinelli, *Bibliotheca manuscripta ad S. Marci Venetiarum, Commentarium* (Venetiis 1868), S. 96–101 (vgl. Lana 44 f.); Mioni S. IV.

sandt wurde. Auch in dieser Arbeit stehen die Widmungen des Musuros in den Codices der Appendix Marciana im Mittelpunkt, deren Urheber Mioni in seinem Katalog der Classes VI–VIII noch mit Kaisar Strategos identifiziert hatte.* Mionis Arbeit dürfte jedoch meinen Beitrag nicht überflüssig machen, zumal die Publikationsorgane beider Arbeiten sich an verschiedenes Publikum wenden und unterschiedliche Verbreitung finden werden. Die Redaktion der Festschrift hat mir freundlicherweise die Möglichkeit gegeben, zu dem Aufsatz Mionis Stellung zu nehmen und dabei einige Probleme, die er aufwirft, weiter zu verfolgen. Dafür sei ihr mein besonderer Dank ausgesprochen. Zu danken habe ich auch Herrn Dr. Dieter Harlfinger/Berlin, der die Freundlichkeit hatte, nach dem Erscheinen von Mionis Arbeit eine größere Anzahl von Handschriften in der Marciana für mich zu prüfen; seine Ergebnisse teilte er mir mit Brief vom 31.10.1971 mit, auf den ich im folgenden öfter verweisen werde. Nach Fertigstellung dieses Postskriptes erhielt ich von ihm noch eine Reihe von Photokopien, die einige meiner unten dargelegten Ansichten bestätigen und für sie weiteres Material liefern. Schließlich danke ich der Biblioteca Marciana für Mikrofilme, die ich im Januar 1971 bestellt, aber erst im Januar 1972 erhalten habe.

Obwohl meine Möglichkeiten, Handschriften mit Widmungen des Musuros in den noch nicht katalogisierten Teilen der Appendix Marciana festzustellen, beschränkt waren (oben S. 582 f.), ist mir nur eine einzige entgangen, der nicht von Kaisar Strategos geschriebene Marc. gr. IV 29 mit der Widmung an den segretario ducale Nicolao Sagundino den Jüngeren (†1551): *Τῷ κοσμίῳ καὶ φιλοκάλῳ νεανίᾳ κυρίῳ νικολάῳ σαγουνδινῷ γραμματεῖ τῆς ἐκλαμπροτάτης ἐνετῶν γερουσίας υἱιδεῖ τε καὶ ὁμωνύμῳ τοῦ πάνυ σαγουνδινοῦ ἀνδρὸς ἕλληνος καὶ κρατίστου γνῶναί τε τὰ δέοντα καὶ ἑρμηνεῦσαι αὐτά.* Da die Widmung in den Jahren 1511 bis 1514 erfolgt sein dürfte, wird dadurch mein Zeitansatz für die übrigen (oben S. 595) bestätigt (Plate IV c).

Nachdem Mioni bekannt geworden war, daß die Widmungen alle von der Hand des Markos Musuros sind,[1] war die im Katalog in drei Fällen (VII 6, VII 9, VIII 10) vollzogene Gleichsetzung mit dem Schreiber des Codex nicht aufrechtzuerhalten; denn dieser hatte sich als

---

* Die von Mioni S. 5 erwähnte Communication auf dem XIII. Byzantinischen Kongreß in Oxford (September 1966) scheint nicht gedruckt zu sein; ich hatte davon keine Kenntnis.

[1] Zu den Adressaten gibt über meine Angaben hinaus Mioni zusätzliche Informationen bei IV 8, IV 26, VII 6, VII 8, VII 9, VIII 7, IX 5, IX 10, X 1. Interessant ist auch die Hypothese, S. 19 ff., daß Handschriften trotz ihrer Widmungen nicht in die Hände der Adressaten übergegangen, sondern als Lehr- und Lernmittel in der Bibliothek und Schule des Musuros verblieben und so auch nach seinem Tode zusammengeblieben seien.

Kaisar Strategos subskribiert. Kaisar Strategos hatte Mioni auch die Widmung in VIII 7 zugeschrieben, der nach seiner Ansicht vorn und hinten von diesem Schreiber ergänzt worden war. Daß letzteres nicht stimmen konnte, habe ich bereits oben (S. 589) bemerkt. Inzwischen hat Mioni 16 selbst richtig gestellt, daß die erste Lage (ff. 1–6) von einem unbekannten Schreiber und die letzte (ff. 294ᵛ–99ᵛ) von Johannes Rhosos geschrieben ist, was mir D. Harlfinger bestätigte.

Dafür setzt Mioni nun (S. 12) den Schreiber von VII 9, ff. 142–258ᵛ (vgl. Plate VII), IX 10 und XI 12, ff. 1–150ᵛ mit dem der Widmungen gleich, also mit Markos Musuros. Diesem weist er auch zwei Codices ohne Widmungen ganz oder teilweise zu, Marc. gr. IX 6 und XI 22, ff. 98–Ende. Zum Beweis gibt er auf Tav. II ein Facsimile aus IX 10, das man mit dem Facsimile dreier Widmungen auf Tav. I vergleichen kann. Der Vergleich fällt aber nicht zugunsten Mionis 'aus. Der Ductus des Schreibers von IX 10 zeigt gegenüber den Widmungen bei einer gewissen Ähnlichkeit unverkennbare Unterschiede im Gesamtcharakter wie in den einzelnen Buchstabenformen. Vor allem fehlt in IX 10 das hervorstechendste Charakteristikum der Schrift des Musuros, das schon Mercati (oben S. 582) aufgefallen war und auch Mioni selbst S. 11 an erster Stelle nennt: die Form des Schluß-Sigma mit dem unverwechselbaren Schlußstrich, wie sie das Facsimile bei Mercati aus Pal. gr. 287 und die Widmungen (Tav. I bei Mioni und unten Plate IV) zeigen. Dieses Schluß-Sigma erweist, von allem anderen abgesehen, auch den Brief des Musuros, von dem eine Lithographie im Paris. suppl. gr. 924 enthalten ist (oben S. 573), eindeutig als Autograph, so sehr der Gesamteindruck der Schrift sich auf den ersten Blick von der der Widmungen einschließlich Pal. gr. 287 zu unterscheiden scheint. Die Ähnlichkeit springt allerdings bei einem Vergleich der lateinischen Adresse des Briefes mit dem lateinischen Facsimile bei Mercati in die Augen. Ähnliches gilt auch für den Brief des Musuros, von dem Firmin-Didot ein Facsimile gibt (oben S. 573, A. 56). Die Schrift dieses Briefes steht der der Widmungen näher als die im Parisinus, zeigt andererseits aber auch zu dieser eine klare Affinität; insbesondere findet sich auch hier wieder das charakteristische Schluß-Sigma. Daß beide Briefe autograph sind, kann auch deshalb nicht zweifelhaft sein, weil sie einer größeren Sammlung von Originalbriefen an den gleichen Adressaten, Musuros' Freund Johannes Gregoropulos, angehören.[2] Die Differenzen in der Schrift erklären sich aus dem zeitlichen Abstand der um 1500 geschriebenen Briefe von den Widmungen von etwa 15 Jahren und aus dem mehr zur Kurrentschrift als zur Kalli-

---

[2] A. Oleroff, "L'humaniste dominicain Jean Conon et le crétois Jean Gregoropulos," *Scriptorium* 4 (1950), 104–107. Näheres dazu in meinem Buche *Johannes Cuno*.

graphie neigenden Ductus besonders des erstgenannten Briefes.[3] Wer allerdings die Schrift der Widmungen mit der des Kaisar Strategos gleichzusetzen vermag, hat gewiß noch weniger Schwierigkeit, sie auch in Marc. IX 10 wiederzuerkennen.

Es scheint Mioni entgangen zu sein, daß Turyn[4] die Hand des Marc. gr. IX 10 als die des Ianos Laskaris bezeichnet hat, wenigstens erwähnt er davon nichts. Indes, diese Identifizierung kann nicht aufrecht erhalten werden, wenn man sie mit den Schriftproben des Laskaris bei de Nolhac, Omont und Follieri[5] vergleicht, wohl aber springt ihre Identität mit der des Laur. 57,52 (Plate V) in die Augen. Dieser Laurentianus trägt die Subskription: Τούσδε λόγους λυσίου φλωρεντίδι γράψ᾽ ἐνὶ γαίη μάρκος ἰωάννου κρὴς τὸ γένος τελέθων.

Wie Laur. 57,52 und Burn. 96, ff. 1–297 vom selben Schreiber in Florenz geschrieben sind, so gewiß auch Marc. gr. IX 10. Seine Vorlage, Paris. gr. 2713, gehörte Ianos Laskaris, der sich etwa von 1472 bis 1495 in Florenz aufhielt,[6] was zur Entstehungszeit des Marcianus gut paßt. In diesem Kreter Markos glaubte Mioni Markos Musuros erkennen zu können, und deshalb zählt er auch Laur. 57,52 und den vom gleichen Schreiber subskribierten Burn. 96 zu den Kopien des Musuros (S. 11 f). Aber die Übereinstimmung der Schrift mit Marc. gr. IX 10 einerseits und die Unterschiede zur Schrift des Musuros (auch hier gibt es nicht sein charakteristisches Schluß-Sigma) andererseits lassen eine solche Identifizierung nicht zu. Die Differenz zu den Briefen des Musuros wiegt hier noch schwerer als bei Marc. gr. IX 10, da die beiden Laurentiani in

---

[3] Von der zeitlichen Variationsbreite einer Schrift können die Beispiele des Emmanuel Protovaris und des Johannes Mauromates eine Vorstellung geben, vgl. P. Canart, "Les manuscrits copiés par Emmanuel Protovaris (1540–70 environ), essai d'étude codicologique," in *Mélanges Eugène Tisserant*, 6 (Studi e Testi, 236; Città del Vaticano 1964), 193 ff. und Tafeln 1–6. Die Tafel 14 bei Canart (vgl. dazu S. 209 f.) und die Abb. 2 bei O. Kresten, *Röm. Hist. Mitt.* 12 (1970) bei S. 193 sind mit denen von Ch. Graux und A. Martin, *Fac-similés de manuscrits grecs d'Espagne* (Paris 1891), Taf. 59; K. A. de Meyier, *Scriptorium* 18 (1964), pl. 31a und bei D. Harlfinger, *Die Textgeschichte der pseudo-aristotelischen Schrift περὶ ἀτόμων γραμμῶν. Ein kodikologisch-kulturgeschichtlicher Beitrag zur Klärung der Überlieferungsverhältnisse im Corpus Aristotelicum* (Amsterdam 1971), Taf. 15 zu vergleichen.

[4] *Euripides* S. 375 und Plate XXIV.

[5] P. de Nolhac, *La bibliothèque de Fulvio Orsini* (oben Anm. 100), Taf. VI; Omont, *Fac-similés XVe et XVIe siècle* (oben Anm. 109), Taf. 44 Marginalien; H. Follieri, *Codices graeci Bibliothecae Vaticanae selecti temporum locorumque ordine digesti commentariis et transcriptionibus instructi* (Exempla scripturarum 4, Bibliotheca Vaticana 1969), Taf. 65. Durch die Freundlichkeit Herrn Dr. Harlfingers konnte ich auch Photokopien von Paris. gr. 1038 (Marginalien), 2038 (Marginalien), 2131 und 3054 zum Vergleich heranziehen; vgl. dazu Harlfinger, *Textgeschichte* 414 (1038), Lobel, *The Greek mss. of Aristotle's Poetics* (Oxford 1933), 4 (2038), Vogel–Gardthausen 157 (2131, 3054).

[6] Legrand 1 (1885), S. CXXXI ff.; vgl. oben S. 566 und 598.

Florenz geschrieben sind, und, wenn sie von Musuros wären, in den Jahren 1486–93 entstanden sein müßten (oben S. 598). Die Schrift des Laur. 57,52 ist aber keinesfalls mit der der Briefe, die ihm zeitlich viel näher stehen als die Widmungen, zu vereinbaren. Auch ist nirgends überliefert, daß der Vater des Musuros Johannes geheißen habe, und der ungemein häufige Name Markos rechtfertigt für sich gewiß noch keine Gleichsetzung mit Musuros, auch wenn beide von Kreta stammten.

Wie mir durch ein Facsimile in der noch ungedruckten Textgeschichte des Cornutus Περὶ θεῶν von Peter Krafft bekanntgeworden ist, stammt auch Laur. 56,20 von der Hand des Schreibers des Laur. 57,52, also des Markos Ioannu aus Kreta, und die Hand des Laur. 56,20 ist nach Krafft identisch mit der des oben (S. 565 f.) erwähnten Vat. gr. 1336.[6a] Dazu paßt, daß Vat. 1336 unter dem Text des Dion Chrysostomos die Subskription ἐν φλωρεντία trägt.[7] Wie bereits oben erwähnt, wollte de Nolhac auf Grund eines Vergleiches mit Paris. gr. 2799, den Omont dem Musuros zugewiesen hat, im Schreiber des Vaticanus Musuros erkennen,[8] aber Canart hat diese Hypothese mit Rechte zurückgewiesen, weil die Schrift trotz der Ähnlichkeit des Stils nicht das für Musuros charakteristische Schluß-Sigma habe, dafür aber Ianos Laskaris in Betracht gezogen, ohne sich mit Sicherheit entscheiden zu können.[9] Andererseits hat Turyn den Paris. gr. 2799 ebenso dem Ianos Laskaris zugesprochen wie Marc. gr. IX 10 (oben S. 568). Es dürfte nun klar sein, daß der Paris. gr. 2799 ebenso von der Hand des Markos Ioannu ist wie Vat. gr. 1336 und Marc. gr. IX 10. Dann ist aber auch der Schreiber von Paris. gr. 2840 (oben S. 569) wegen seiner Identität mit Paris. gr. 2799 derselbe Markos.[9a] Aus den Marciani, deren Schrift mit IX 10 nach Mioni identisch ist (s. oben S. 602), ist allerdings, wie mir Harlfinger mitgeteilt hat, IX 6 auszuscheiden; von ihm wird gleich noch die Rede sein. Dagegen weist Harlfinger auf die Identität der Schrift von Laur.

[6a] Bestätigt durch eine Mikrofilm-Schriftprobe f. 1ʳ, die mir die Biblioteca Vaticana übersandte. [P. Canart stimmte mit Brief vom 26. Februar 1972 zu, mit der Einschränkung, daß nur der erste Teil *mit Sicherheit* von der Hand des Laur. 57,52 sei.]

[7] Nolhac a.O. 150.

[8] Mit falscher Begründung übernommen von R. R. Bolgar, *The Classical Heritage and its Beneficiaries* (Cambridge 1963), 471, 494 ("marked as copied by Musurus"!). Der Besitzvermerk des Musuros auch in *Isocratis Opera omnia* rec. E. Drerup 1 (Lipsiae 1906), XVII; W. W. Baker, "Some of the less known manuscripts of Xenophon's Memorabilia," *Trans. Am. Philol. Assn.* 43 (1912), 167.

[9] Die Ansicht Canarts ist von Patrinelis 98 und Mioni 12, A. 23 falsch wiedergegeben. Falsch ist auch Mionis Angabe, daß der Mut. gr. 101 (s. oben S. 570) von Johannes Gregoropulos geschrieben ist.

[9a] Diese Folgerungen werden vollkommen bestätigt durch Photokopien aus Paris. gr. 2799 und 2840, die mir Herr Dr. Harlfinger übersandte.

57,52 und Burn. 96 mit Marc. VII 9, ff. 142–258ᵛ, Laur. 60,10 und der Restaurierung von Vat. gr. 2215 hin.[10] Damit hat dieser Kreter Markos, von dem Vogel-Gardthausen nur zwei Codices verzeichnen, stark an Profil gewonnen. Wir können ihm nicht weniger als 13 Handschriften zuweisen: drei Laurentiani (56,20; 57,52; 60,10), vier Marciani (VII 9, ff. 142–258ᵛ, IX 10, XI 12, ff. 1–150ᵛ, XI 22, ff. 98–Ende), zwei Parisini (2799, 2840), zwei Vaticani (1336, 2215) und einen Burneianus (96, ff. 1–297). Weitere werden wahrscheinlich folgen. Vermutlich gehört auch Paris. gr. 2915 (oben S. 569 f.) hierher.[11]

Der von Berardelli dem Kaisar Strategos, von Mioni dagegen dem Musuros zugeschriebene Marc. gr. IX 6 ist weder von dem einen noch von dem anderen noch auch, wie bereits erwähnt, von Markos Ioannu geschrieben, sondern von einem anonymen Schreiber, von dem erstmals E. Lobel[12] eine Gruppe von sechs Handschriften ausgewiesen, R. Pfeiffer[13] eine, ich zwei weitere[14] erkannt und D. Harlfinger[15] zahlreiche weitere entdeckt hat. Harlfinger hat ihm, da er bis zur Stunde in der Anonymität verharrt, vom Ort seiner Tätigkeit den Namen Librarius Florentinus gegeben. Er arbeitete in der zweiten Hälfte des 15., wohl auch noch im Anfang des 16. Jh.[16] Von ihm stammen, von Mioni nicht wie IX 6 für Musuros reklamiert, auch drei weitere Marciani mit Widmungen des Musuros (IV 26, ff. 77–331ᵛ, IV 29 [Plate VI], und IX 5).[17] Auch sie kommen also gewiß wie die Kopien des Kaisar Strategos und des Markos Ioannu aus Florenz, auch wenn sie nicht entsprechende Subskriptionen

---

[10] *Textgeschichte* 412; Brief vom 31.10.71.

[11] Einer Prüfung bedarf danach auch der von Turyn, *Euripides* 365, teilweise Ianos Laskaris zugeschriebene Laur. 91,6; ebenso die Angaben von D. C. C. Young, "A codicological inventory of Theognis manuscripts," *Scriptorium* 7 (1953), 3–36, der nicht weniger als 18 Theognis-Handschriften (zu denen noch der Vindob. phil. gr. 321, ff. 86–140 und der Epistolographencodex Vindob. phil. 318 käme, vgl. H. Hunger, *Katalog d. griechischen Handschriften der Österr. Nationalbibliothek*, 1 [Wien 1961], 408, 426) dem Ianos Laskaris zuschreibt (Patrinelis 92 f.), was teilweise schon durch P. Canart, *Scriptorium* 17 (1963), 78 f. (vgl. auch J. Irigoin, *Lustrum* 7 [1962], 71) geschehen ist.

[12] *Greek Manuscripts of Aristotle's Poetics*, 53.

[13] *Callimachus* 2 (Oxford 1963), LXIV.

[14] *Class. Phil.* 58 (1963), 179 f.

[15] *Textgeschichte* 417; vgl. 222 ff. und Taf. 7.

[16] Vgl. auch meine in Vorbereitung befindliche Studie "Der Codex Grimanianus graecus 11 und seine Nachkommenschaft."

[17] Identifikation durch Harlfinger (brieflich 31.10.71), bestätigt durch Mikrofilm aus Marc. IV 29 und IX 5. Ich selbst hatte oben S. 585 diese Identifikation bei IV 26, ff. 77–332ᵛ noch nicht gewagt. [Der oben S. 597 nach Vogel-Gardthausen 224 unter Kaiser Strategos erwähnte, in Florenz geschriebene Paris. gr. 466 ist, da ihn Montfaucon und Melot dem Schreiber von Paris. gr. 1394 zuweisen, sicher vom Librarius Florentinus.]

tragen und ihre Vorlagen verloren zu sein scheinen oder nicht bestimmt werden können.

Auch der vierte Schreiber, der uns in den Handschriften mit einer Widmung des Musuros begegnet, Aristobulos Apostolides, arbeitete in Florenz. Er traf hier im Herbst 1492 ein, hielt sich bis 1494 auf und kopierte griechische Handschriften.[18] Musuros muß er vor dessen Abgang nach Venedig noch dort angetroffen haben, da dieser noch 1493 in Florenz nachgewiesen ist.[19] Schon oben hatte ich gezeigt, daß Marc. gr. VIII 6, den nunmehr auch Mioni dem Aristobulos Apostolides zuweist, in Florenz entstanden ist. Er ist nicht der einzige Codex von seiner Hand, den Musuros mit einer Widmung versehen hat. Ich habe oben S. 583 die ff. 1–157[v] des Marc. IV 8 noch mit Zurückhaltung ihm zugewiesen; Mioni und Harlfinger tun es nun mit Bestimmtheit.[20] Den Marc. gr. X 1 hatte Berardelli Kaisar Strategos gegeben, aber er ist nach Harlfinger von zwei Schreibern angefertigt, ff. 1–118 (Apollonios Dyskolos u.a.) von Aristobulos Apostolides und ff. 119–266 (Theon) von einem Anonymus, dessen Ductus entfernt dem des Kaisar Strategos ähnlich sei, also nicht mit ihm identisch, wie Berardelli behauptet.[21] Der Text des Apollonios Dyskolos ist nach Uhlig[22] eine Kopie von Paris. gr. 2549, Theon ist eine Kopie von Paris. gr. 2918.[23] Wenigstens letzterer gehörte dem Ianos Laskaris, und beide kommen aus der Bibliothek des Mediceer-Kardinals Ridolfi, des Neffen Leos X. (Giovanni de' Medici). Auch die Euripides-Codices Paris. gr. 2887 und 2888 der gleichen Herkunft (oben S. 569) sind aus einer Florentiner Handschrift, Laur. 32,2, kopiert, die Sophokles-

---

[18] Geanakoplos 170 f., 185. Ein Facsimile seiner Hand jetzt auch bei Follieri Taf. 66. Apostolides ist etwa gleichaltrig mit Musuros, geb. 1468/69 (Geanakoplos 168).

[19] Geanakoplos 115–21 mit Berufung auf das Datum im Vat. gr. 1336, oben S. 566.

[20] Die ff. 159–295 wurden von Harlfinger, *Textgeschichte* 410, auf Grund einer Schriftprobe in Mikrofilm mit einer Kautel dem Demetrios Chalkondyles zugewiesen, nach Autopsie im September 1971 dem Kaisar Strategos (brieflich 31.10.71).

[21] Die Subskription des von I. Lana zum Vergleich angezogenen Laur. 81, 3 (oben S. 592) ist ähnlich wie die der Marciani, aber ihnen gegenüber erweitert: θεοῦ τὸ δῶρον καὶ καίσαρ(ος) πόνος τοῦ στρατηγοῦ τάχα καὶ ἀναγνώστου κρητός. Daß der hier verdorbene Trimeter der Subskriptionen des Kaisar Strategos in den Marciani nicht dessen ausschließliches Eigentum, sondern überhaupt beliebt war, zeigen Subskriptionen wie die des Marc. II 66, f. 138˙ (E. Mioni, *Bibliothecae D. Marci Venetiarum codices graeci manuscripti*, 1: Codices in classes a prima usque ad quintam inclusi 1: Classes I–II, codd. 1–120 [Roma 1967], 187) θεοῦ τὸ δῶρον καὶ νικηφόρου πόνος, Marc. II 94, f. 9 (Mioni 284) θεοῦ τὸ δῶρον καὶ πολλῶν ἀνδρῶν πόνος, Paris. gr. 2944, f. 247[r] θεοῦ τὸ δῶρον καὶ ἰω(άνν)ου [d.i. Johannes Skutariotes] κῶπος (sic). [Den ersten Teil des Codex weist nunmehr auch Mioni (S. 18 und 23, A. 52) dem Aristobulos Apostolides zu.]

[22] *Apollonii Dyscoli quae supersunt* recc. R. Schneider — G. Uhlig, 2 (Grammatici Graeci 2, 2; Lipsiae 1910), XLI.

[23] Lana 53 ff., 104; vgl. M. Sicherl, *Gnomon* 33 (1961), 270.

Scholien des Vindob. phil. gr. 253 aus Laur. 32,9.[24] Die Wasserzeichen des letzteren (Hunger 363) passen bestens zu der Zeit von Apostolides' Aufenthalt in Florenz. Schließlich ist darauf hinzuweisen, daß Aristobulos Apostolides den Librarius des Paris. gr. 2840, als den wir nun den Florentiner Schreiber Markos Ioannu identifiziert haben, für drei Seiten abgelöst hat (s. oben S. 568). Das deutet freilich darauf hin, daß diese Kopien schon früher, als oben (S. 600) bei Kaisar Strategos angenommen wurde, entstanden sind.

Aus Mionis Liste von Musuros-Handschriften (S. 11 f.) ist schließlich auch noch die letzte auszuscheiden, der Brief im Ambros. gr. 843 (C 6 inf.), so daß von ihr überhaupt nichts mehr übrig bleibt. Die frühere Auskunft der Ambrosiana, er scheine nicht autograph zu sein, hat sich nunmehr durch den Mikrofilm bestätigt. Aus dem Datum des Briefes (1507) läßt sich nicht mit Mioni (S. 12, A. 22) schließen, daß die Blätter des Ambrosianus nicht im ausgehenden 16. Jh. beschrieben wurden, wie Martini–Bassi angeben!

Es ist durchaus möglich, daß Handschriften von den gleichen Schreibern wie die mit Widmungen versehenen und gleicher Provenienz wie diese (SS. Giovanni e Paolo) ebenfalls Musuros gehört haben. Insbesondere möchte man dies annehmen bei den Kaisar-Strategos-Handschriften Marc. gr. IV 1, VII 4, VII 10 und XI 3, ff. 1–337 (Mioni 23, 25), bei den Apostolides-Handschriften Marc. gr. IV 9, IV 12, VIII 1 (Mioni 27) sowie Marc. gr. IX 6, den wir ganz dem Librarius Florentinus, und IX 22, den wir zum Teil dem Markos Ioannu zuweisen konnten. Aber hier wie bei allen übrigen, die Mioni S. 23 ff. miteinbezieht, bleibt alles im Bereich der Vermutung.

Zu den signierten Handschriften aus dem Besitz des Musuros zählt Mioni S. 25 auch den Vindob. phil. gr. 185 mit dem Monogramm eines Besitzers: Nel monogramma si legge Μάρκος Μουσοῦρος, il codice reca la data scritta dal Musuro: *1497 die nono februarii, venetiis.* Beides ist nicht bewiesen. Das Monogramm, in dem unter einem M die Buchstaben MSR in Ligatur erscheinen, ist uns als Monogramm des Musuros nicht bekannt; er schreibt seinen Namen immer aus. Und die Schrift des Datums ist nicht ohne weiteres mit der des Musuros gleichzusetzen. Daß Musuros den von Francesco Vitali geschriebenen Vindob. phil. gr. 167 besessen habe (Mioni 25), ist durch nichts bewiesen; der Codex zeigt keine Spur von Musuros.[25] Damit weist auch Mionis Liste der versprengten Handschriften, die nachweislich im Besitze des Musuros waren (S. 24 f.), gegenüber der meinigen kein Plus auf.

[24] Turyn, *Sophocles* 68.
[25] Für die Besorgung von Photokopien der beiden Vindobonenses danke ich der Österreichischen Nationalbibliothek.

Dagegen kann ich heute zu den oben (S. 573) genannten Autographen des Musuros ein weiteres hinzufügen, das sich durch die Übereinstimmung mit dem Ductus der Widmungen einschließlich des charakteristischen Schluß-Sigmas als solches unzweifelhat erweist. Es ist die untere Hälfte eines geklebten Blattes in der Autografoteca Campori in der Biblioteca Estense in Modena, auf das mich Ende Juli 1970 P. O. Kristeller bei einer Begegnung in London wegen seiner Beziehung zu Johannes Cuno, einem Schüler des Musuros, aufmerksam machte. Es gibt die Grabinschrift des Sardanapal aus Athenaios 8, 336 (= Anth. Graeca 16, 27, ed. H. Beckby IV², S. 318) in parodierender Form wieder unter dem Titel: ἀθήναιος φησι τὸ εἰς σαρδανάπαλον ἐπίγραμμα χρύσιππον οὑτωσὶ παρῳδῆσαι.

10. Februar 1972

INDEX AUCTORUM

NOTE: Our index hopes to include the names of all authors—ancient, mediaeval, and modern—whose work is mentioned or discussed in the text or footnotes. We extend the term "authors" to include editors, commentators, compilers, informants, and even (in the case of classical but not modern writers) translators—any name with which a student of classical literature or the history of classical scholarship might be concerned. But we do not include scribes or mere owners of manuscripts, unless they are also known as authors or editors themselves.

Names of Greek authors, however they are spelled in the text, are here Latinized in accordance with the practice of *LSJ*, with abbreviated indication of place or profession when it is necessary to distinguish a less well-known bearer of a common name; again the list of authors in *LSJ* has been our guide. This applies to Byzantine and Italian Greek scholars as late as the sixteenth century. Modern names are here spelled as in the text, disregarding minor inconsistencies (as with modern Greek names); and for these persons initials only (not full given names) have been supplied, usually as indicated in the footnotes but sometimes, we confess, at a guess, especially in the case of contributors to a critical apparatus. The British Museum *Catalogue of Printed Books* has been helpful here.

That part of a modern editor's name which may appear in an abbreviated reference is here set in round brackets.

A few entries are not of authors but of books or kinds of documents, e.g. *Euchologion*, tabula cerea byzantina. This happens when discussion or mention in the text was made without specifying an author; also in the case of collections such as *Testamentum Vetus* where it seemed unnecessary to index individual books or to distinguish the person to whom an epigram is attributed in the *Anthologia Palatina*. When a work is commonly but falsely ascribed to an author, his name is set within quotation-marks; thus we have references to "Anacreon" as well as to Anacreon, and to *Suda* ("Suidas"). But some works of doubtful authorship are indexed under the name of the author with whom they are usually associated, e.g. the *Scutum* under Hesiodus (but the Homeric Hymns under "Homerus"); and scholia are recorded under the name of the author they comment on.

These were our hopes for an *index auctorum*. In actuality (March 1974) it was made in limited time by a person of no infallible nature, and it is bound to contain errors both of commission and of omission, for which I apologize. J.L.H.